THE WHEEL
OF TIME
COMPANION

THE WHEEL OF TIME®

BY ROBERT JORDAN

The Eye of the World

The Great Hunt

The Dragon Reborn

The Shadow Rising

The Fires of Heaven

Lord of Chaos

A Crown of Swords

The Path of Daggers

Winter's Heart

Crossroads of Twilight

Knife of Dreams

**BY ROBERT JORDAN
AND BRANDON SANDERSON**

The Gathering Storm

Towers of Midnight

A Memory of Light

THE WHEEL
OF TIME
COMPANION

The People, Places, and History of the Bestselling Series

ROBERT JORDAN
· HARRIET McDOUGAL ·
· ALAN ROMANCZUK · MARIA SIMONS ·

A Tom Doherty Associates Book
New York

THE WHEEL OF TIME COMPANION

Copyright © 2015 by Bandersnatch Group, Inc.

All rights reserved.

A Tor Book
Published by Tom Doherty Associates, LLC
175 Fifth Avenue
New York, NY 10010

www.tor-forge.com

Tor® is a registered trademark of Tom Doherty Associates, LLC.

The Library of Congress Cataloging-in-Publication Data is available upon request.

ISBN 978-0-7653-1461-1 (hardcover)
ISBN 978-1-4668-8123-5 (e-book)

Our books may be purchased in bulk for promotional, educational, or business use.
Please contact your local bookseller or the Macmillan Corporate and Premium Sales
Department at (800) 221-7945, extension 5442, or by e-mail at
MacmillanSpecialMarkets@macmillan.com.

First Edition: November 2015

Printed in the United States of America

0 9 8 7 6 5 4 3 2 1

ILLUSTRATION CREDITS

This book is dedicated to all the readers who love The Wheel of Time.

INTRODUCTION

When I began editing *The Eye of the World*, I started a list of proper nouns, keeping them in a file known as "Raw Glossary." It is a thing copy editors do—and I had been one, many and many a year ago, in a kingdom by the sea called Manhattan—with the idea that it is useful to have a canonical list of the spellings in a series. This "Raw Glossary" expanded through—oh I don't know—about the first seven books; I then turned its care and maintenance over to Maria Simons, and the stalwart Alan Romanczuk.

This is not an extension, or an update, to the earlier reference called *The World of Robert Jordan's The Wheel of Time*. Instead, this is an alphabetized adjunct that will allow the reader to check on characters, locations, herbs, kinship structures and many other things that appear in the series.

Now I, Harriet, join Maria and Alan in the comforting, cozy, editorial "we."

We hope that this Companion will be useful for those reading or rereading the series, or those just wishing to refresh themselves about some aspect of the series. To those new to The Wheel of Time, though, we offer the following warning: there are SPOILERS in here! In fact, this volume might be called The Big Book of Spoilers because there are so many of them. Tread lightly, novices.

We in no way claim that each entry exhausts its subject. We had no desire to do so, mainly for practical considerations—the book's size would be prohibitive. If you want detail beyond this Companion, we refer you to various impressive online efforts, such as Encyclopaedia-WoT.org and TarValon.net.

We also don't claim that this book is without errors. Our entries draw as much as possible from Robert Jordan's abundant notes, in order to show the reader what the writer wished to note for his own reference. One can infer that what Robert Jordan noted were points that were particularly important for him in the manuscripts; in some cases this was true. On the other hand, you can see that there are backstories on and descriptions of the various quirks and motivations of many characters, things that never made it into the books, but that informed the writer and helped him bring the characters to life.

Some entries were pulled directly from Robert Jordan's notes with little alteration, to give you the flavor of his writing for his own personal use. As you will see, his phrases could be amusing at times.

While we hope that the reader will find a lot that is new and interesting here, we make certain disclaimers about the material. In some instances, the descriptions may vary from what is in the books. Writers constantly change their minds about characters, events and places in their creations, and adjustments often fail to be made in background notes. We have tried to correct all discrepancies of this sort, but sometimes let the more interesting ones stand, to show a change from the writer's original intention compared with what finally arrived on the printed page. Or, the error remained because of our own oversight.

If this seems like a sneaky way to avoid taking responsibility for any errors found here, well, maybe it is; that's for you to decide.

We at Bandersnatch Group wish to thank past, present and future fans of the Wheel of Time series for your devoted interest. You are the ones who have kept and who will continue to keep alive the world created by Robert Jordan. He said many times that he wished these books to be read for decades to come, and to be as relevant to future generations as they are to readers today. He sincerely loved his fans, and was always just a little humbled by the positive worldwide reception of his books. Thank you for staying through the whole set, all the way to Shayol Ghul.

Speaking of endings, we also wish to thank the talented writer Brandon Sanderson, who accepted the daunting challenge of seeing the Wheel of Time series to completion after Robert Jordan's untimely death.

And most of all, thanks to Tom Doherty, publisher of The Wheel of Time, who stuck his neck out on this series many years ago, and never flagged in his support and belief. Without him and Brandon Sanderson, you would not be reading these lines today.

Onward.

ROBERT JORDAN

HARRIET MCDOUGAL

ALAN ROMANCZUK

MARIA SIMONS

THE WHEEL OF TIME
OF TIME
COMPANION

A

a'Balaman, Rhys. *See* Rhys a'Balaman

a'Conn, Paitr do Fearna. *See* Paitr do Fearna a'Conn

a'Cowel, Nisain. *See* Nisain a'Cowel

a'dam. A *ter'angreal* used to control a channeler. Traditionally it was composed of a bracelet and a necklace connected by a silvery chain and was used to control female channelers. A modified *a'dam* without the chain was shown to work as well, and a device to control male channelers was discovered that was made of two bracelets and a necklace. The channeler being controlled wore the necklace, and the person wearing the bracelet had to be someone who could at least be taught to channel. The *a'dam* would fit itself to anyone who tried it on. The first *a'dam* was created by Deain, an Aes Sedai, to help Luthair Paendrag control the channelers he had found in Seanchan; it was then used on her. The *a'dam* created a link between the two women, a circle of two, with the woman wearing the bracelet always leading the circle. She could control the other woman's flow of *saidar* completely, in addition to feeling her emotions and physical reactions and being able to influence or change them, or combine her own abilities with those of the other woman to channel a single, combined set of flows herself. This was known to Deain, of course, and to others after her, but that knowledge was eventually lost. After many years, the *a'dam* was used merely to control the *damane* and make her channel to command.

There were differences between the link entered by Aes Sedai and the link created by an *a'dam*. One was that while a circle of one man and one woman was possible, a man who could channel would be in intense pain and usually killed by wearing the bracelet. No experimentation was done regarding a woman wearing the bracelet and a man the necklace, but it might well have done the same thing. Even touching the *a'dam* while it was worn by a woman who could channel was painful for a man who could channel, and also for the woman. In a normal link, a woman who only had the potential to learn to channel could not be brought into it, but the *a'dam* could control those women, too. In addition, whatever the woman wearing the bracelet experienced was also felt by the woman wearing the necklace as though it had happened to her, but at several times the intensity; this feedback did not occur from the woman leading a normal link.

One odd effect of the *a'dam* which might be called beneficial was that it was impossible to burn oneself out while wearing one. The *a'dam* acted as a governor or buffer so that the maximum amount of the Power which could be drawn was just short of that which would damage the wearer. This was probably incorporated into the original device to prevent any possibility that a captive might manage to deliberately burn herself out in an effort to stop herself being used. *See also* Seanchan, *damane, sul'dam,* Domination Band *and* sad bracelets

a'Lordeine, Donel do Morny. *See* Donel do Morny a'Lordeine

a'Macansa, Cian do Mehon. *See* Cian do Mehon a'Macansa

a'Naloy, Roedran Almaric do Arreloa. *See* Roedran

a'Roihan, Elaida do Avriny. *See* Elaida do Avriny a'Roihan

a'Roos, Segan do Avharin. *See* Segan do Avharin a'Roos

a'solma. A gown with slits at the sides to allow movement; leggings were worn underneath. Tuon wore such a garment while practicing hand combat forms.

a'yron. The Old Tongue word for "watchers."

Aan'allein. The Aiel name for al'Lan Mandragoran. It was the Old Tongue term for "One Man" or "Man Alone" or "Man Who Is an Entire People."

Abaldar Yulan. The fiery Seanchan Captain of the Air, commanding all the fliers and subordinate to Captain-General Galgan. A member of the low Blood, Yulan was short, with the nails of his little fingers painted green, and he wore a black wig, cut in the appropriate hairstyle for his station, to conceal his baldness. His skin was coal dark. He wept after Miraj was killed, partly for the death of a friend and partly because the Ever Victorious Army had been defeated. Yulan's *raken* were one of the points of contention between Galgan and Suroth. He proposed raiding the White Tower and worked to make it happen. Under Compulsion from Mesaana, he attempted to keep Tuon from sending forces to help Mat win the Last Battle; he was exposed by a viewing of Min's.

Abar. A Domani sword-swallower and fire-eater with Luca's show. His brother was Balat.

Abareim, Ellid. *See* Ellid Abareim

Abayan. A nation that rose after the Trolloc Wars. It occupied most of the western part of what came to be known as Arad Doman.

Abdel Omerna. A Child of the Light who was a Lord Captain, Anointed of the Light and a member of the Council of Anointed. Tall, with dark eyes set in a bold, strong-chinned face and waves of white at his temples, he was thought to be spymaster of the Children of the Light, but he was actually a patsy put in place by Pedron Niall to draw attention from Sebban Balwer, the true spymaster. Omerna was tricked into assassinating Pedron Niall and was killed by Eamon Valda.

Abell Cauthon. A farmer in Emond's Field. Born in 955 NE, he was known for his horse-trading abilities and proficiency with the quarterstaff and Two Rivers bow. He was the husband of Natti Cauthon and father of Matrim, Bodewhin and Eldrin. He and Tam al'Thor traveled to Tar Valon to try to find out what happened to their sons, but were told nothing. Abell managed to avoid being taken by the Whitecloaks, and helped rescue his wife and daughters, who were taken. He helped Perrin plan the defense of Emond's Field, and fought bravely in the Last Battle.

Abelle Pendar. A lord in Andor and the High Seat of House Pendar, a strong House with many retainers. His sigil was three six-pointed golden stars, one above and two below, on a field of seven vertical red-and-white stripes. Pendar had a hard angular face and graying hair. He supported Morgase when she gained the throne. Under Rahvin's influence, Morgase exiled him from Caemlyn. He was one of four nobles who met Rand, along with Dyelin, Ellorien and Luan, when Rand told them he wanted Elayne on the Andoran throne. After Elayne took Caemlyn, he stood for Trakand.

Abila. A somewhat large town in Amadicia located forty leagues south of Bethal. A wooden bridge over a stream led into the town, which had paved streets and stone marketplaces. There were several tall watchtowers and many four-story buildings with slate roofs, but it was not a walled town. Balwer told Perrin that he believed the Prophet had been there recently, and that Masema had torn down a number of inns and disreputable houses in the town. Perrin and his men, along with Aes Sedai, visited the Prophet and told him that they would accompany him to the Dragon Reborn, who had summoned him. Faile learned from her agents that the Prophet had met with the Seanchan, but before she could warn Perrin, she and her group were all captured by Sevanna and the Shaido Aiel, except Berelain, who escaped.

Ablar, Logain. *See* Logain Ablar

Abor'maseleine. An Ogier-built city in Aridhol, one of the Ten Nations after the Breaking.

Abors. An Asha'man who did not need to be Turned to follow Taim and work for the Shadow. He held a shield on Androl; Androl used his knowledge of Evin's madness to make Evin attack and kill Abors.

Abunai. A village where it was never cold on the Sea of L'Heye in Seanchan. It was the birthplace of Bethamin.

Academy of Cairhien. A center of learning and invention established in Lord Barthanes' palace in the city of Cairhien. Its headmistress was Idrien Tarsin. Rand established the school in case he did end up breaking the world, in the hope of saving something.

Academy of the Rose. A center of learning and invention in Caemlyn. Established by Rand, it was taken over by Elayne, who dedicated it in memory of her mother. She insisted on financing it; she wanted it to be Andor's, not Rand's.

Accan, Jurad. *See* Jurad Accan

Accepted, the. The level after novice that a student had to achieve before becoming Aes Sedai. Normally, a novice was recommended for testing by the Mistress of Novices. This recommendation had to be approved by the Amyrlin Seat, by a Sitter, or by three sisters. An approval by three sisters or one Sitter could be rejected by the Amyrlin, and she could only be overruled by the lesser consensus of the Hall. Even if the Mistress of Novices did not make such a recommendation, the testing could be ordered by the Amyrlin acting in conjunction with at least two Sitters, or by three Sitters, or by six sisters. A recommendation in

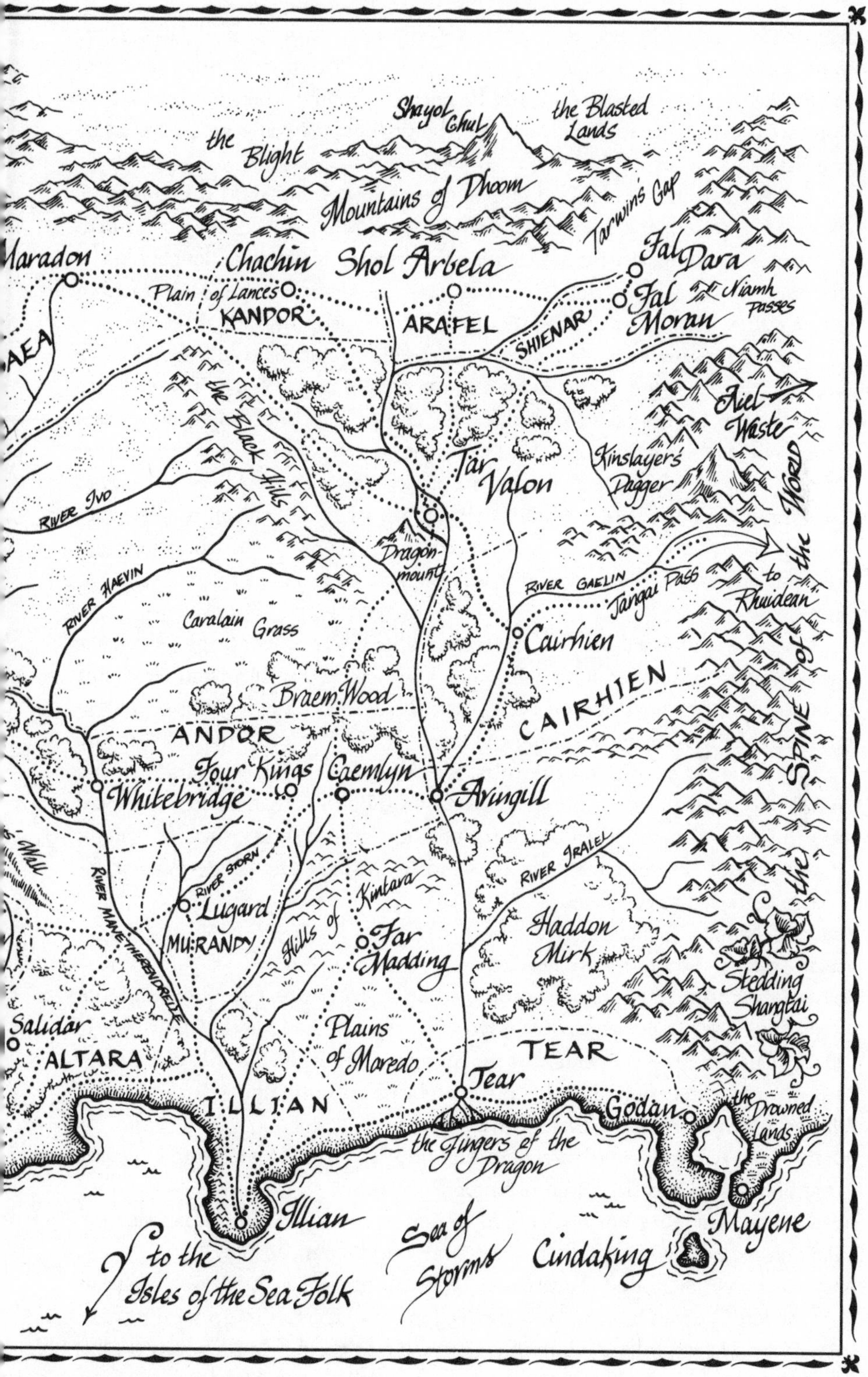

Shayol Ghul
the Blasted Lands
the Blight
Mountains of Dhoom
Tarwin's Gap
Chachin
Shol Arbela
Fal Dara
Fal Moran
Niamh Passes
Plain of Lances
KANDOR
ARAFEL
SHIENAR
the Black Hills
Aiel Waste
Kinslayer's Dagger
Tar Valon
RIVER IVO
Dragonmount
RIVER HAEVIN
RIVER GAELIN
Jangai Pass
to Rhuidean
Caralain Grass
Cairhien
CAIRHIEN
Braem Wood
ANDOR
Four Kings
Caemlyn
Whitebridge
Aringill
the Spine of the World
RIVER STORM
RIVER IRALELL
RIVER MANETHERENDRELLE
Lugard
MURANDY
Hills of Kintara
Far Madding
Haddon Mirk
Stedding Shangtai
Salidar
ALTARA
Plains of Maredo
TEAR
Tear
ILLIAN
Godan
the Drowned Lands
the Fingers of the Dragon
Illian
Mayene
Sea of Storms
Cindaking
to the Isles of the Sea Folk

this manner could be rejected by the Amyrlin or in various other ways. Thus, a recommendation by six sisters could be rejected by three Sitters, and a recommendation by three Sitters could be rejected if three others felt it unsafe or unwise. If the Amyrlin herself ordered the testing, she could be overruled by six Sitters.

The point to be emphasized here is that the Amyrlin could stop a woman from being tested, and there was rarely any possibility of her being overruled, but it was much harder for her to force the testing. There were dangers in the testing, but none in waiting, so it was easier to stop even the Amyrlin from forcing a test than it was to stop her from refusing approval for a test.

The test required a novice to pass through a *ter'angreal* composed of three arches of silvery metal; it was located in the bowels of the White Tower. Three chances were offered to walk through the arches. The offer might be refused twice, but if it was refused the third time, the woman was put out of the Tower. Many women refused the arches a time or two. Once the test began, it had to be completed by passing through each arch, to face one's fears of what was, what is and what will be. A woman who refused to complete her three journeys was put out of the Tower even if it was the first time she had a chance at the test.

Once she completed the test, she received her Great Serpent ring, which she wore on the third finger of her left hand. The Accepted wore a white dress just like that worn by novices except that there were seven narrow bands of color at the hem of the skirt, representing the seven Ajahs. A more formal dress would also have bands of color on the cuffs. An Accepted's room was larger than a novice's room, with more comforts. Less confined by rules than novices, Accepted were allowed to choose their own areas of study, within limits; they also taught novice classes. The average Accepted studied for ten years before passing the test to be raised to Aes Sedai.

Acedone, Rubinde. *See* Rubinde Acedone

acem. An herb used to relieve headache.

Ackley Farren. An Andoran man mentioned by a farmer who gave Rand and Mat a short ride on their way to Caemlyn. The farmer thought that the story of Darkfriends in Market Sheran was the funniest story he had heard since Ackley Farren got drunk enough to spend the night on an inn roof.

Adamad. One of Renald Fanwar's farmhands.

Adan al'Caar. A Two Rivers boy whom Mat Cauthon tried to trick into believing that ghost dogs had been seen in Emond's Field.

Adan, Heran. The governor of Baerlon, Andor. When the Whitecloaks came to Baerlon, he decreed that only ten at a time could enter the city.

Adan. A Jenn Aiel around the time of the Breaking. When Adan was five years old, he left Paaran Disen with his father Jonai and the rest of his family. Years later, he and Jonai met a group of Ogier who told them that there was trouble in the north. Jonai had a heart attack, and as he died, he told Adan to take the people south. Adan married Siedre, and they had five children: Rhea, Malind, Sorelle, Elwin and Jaren. All either died or were carried off by bandits; he was left with Malind's wife Saralin and her children Maigran and Lewin. After Lewin and his friends used violence to save Maigran and another girl, Colline, Adan disowned Lewin.

Adanza. A great city of the Age of Legends. It thrived with a vitality in its beauty matched only by the vitality of its people.

Adar. The fifth month of the year.

Adarra, Bili. *See* Bili Adarra

Adarra, Jaim. The captain of the *Snow Goose,* which took Moiraine, Lan, Perrin, Loial and Faile from Remen to Illian. He was short and slight.

Adden. The leader of the band of Darkfriends who kidnapped Egwene, Nynaeve and Elayne on behalf of three Myrddraal; he was killed by being pinned to the wall by an Aiel spear.

Adela. A lanky young woman with a pimply face who worked as a stablehand for Toke Fearnim in Jurador.

Adeleas Namelle. An Aes Sedai of the Brown Ajah and the rebel contingent, with a strength level of 23(11). Born in 735 NE, she went to the White Tower with her sister Vandene in 752 NE. After spending five years as a novice and five years as Accepted, she was raised to the shawl in 762 NE. She progressed in near lockstep with her sister; they were raised within a month of each other in both instances. She was 5'4½" tall, slender and graceful, with dark eyes and a straight back—a mirror image of her sister. She wore her nearly white hair gathered at the back of her neck.

Adeleas retired in 970 NE to Tifan's Well in Arafel with Vandene to write a history of the world since the Breaking, but events surrounding the Dragon Reborn caused them to become active again. While traveling to Caemlyn, she and her Black Ajah prisoner Ispan Shefar were murdered outside Cullen's Crossing by Careane Fransi, using the poison crimsonthorn.

Adelin. A Maiden of the Jindo sept of the Taardad Aiel. Little more than a hand shorter than Rand, she had yellow hair and a handsome but hard face with a scar on her sun-dark cheek. She went to the Stone of Tear and was one of those who taught Mat how to play Maiden's Kiss. Rand acquired the bracelet that he gave to Aviendha from her, and she was a member of Rand's honor guard at Alcair Dal. One of those guarding Rand's tent near the Jangai Pass when it was attacked, she ran off to join the fighting, leaving Rand vulnerable to a Draghkar. Afterward, she carried a doll to remind her that she was not a child.

Adelorna Bastine. A Saldaean Aes Sedai of the Green Ajah and the loyalist contingent, with a strength level of 16(4). Born in 796 NE, she went to the White Tower in 813 NE. After spending seven years as a novice and eleven years as Accepted, she was raised to the shawl in 831 NE. Adelorna made slimness appear stately despite her lack of height; she was no taller than Egwene but had a regal, commanding air and gave Egwene lessons. She was the Captain-General of the Green Ajah in the Tower. Adelorna was cited by Elaida, on Alviarin's order, for possession of an *angreal* removed from the storeroom without permission and was birched, when the normal punishment would have been a slap on the wrist. She and Josaine, who was caught in the same raid and received the same punishment, had presumably been turned in by Kiyoshi of the Gray Ajah, Farellien of the Yellow Ajah and Doraise of the Brown Ajah, the latter three being rewarded for their action. The Greens were fit to be tied, and relations became tense with the Gray, Yellow and Brown Ajahs. Adelorna plotted with other Ajah heads to manage the rebellion, sending moles to Salidar. The Seanchan collared her, but Egwene freed her. One of her three Warders was killed in the Seanchan attack on the White Tower; a second, Talric, was wounded; a third was unharmed.

Adim. Almen Bunt's thirteen-year-old nephew. He had golden hair.

Adine Canford. An Andoran Aes Sedai of the Blue Ajah and the rebel contingent, with a strength level of 34(22). Born in 905 NE, she went to the White Tower in 920 NE. After spending twelve years as a novice and eleven years as Accepted, she was raised to the shawl in 943 NE. She was a friend of Moiraine and Siuan after they were raised, and also a friend of Leane. In the White Tower she was the recipient of messages for Moiraine from Nieda Sidoro. Adine was sympathetic to Moiraine, and a friend, though she knew nothing of her and Siuan's schemes. In Moiraine's view, she was "not at all arrogant despite being Andoran."

Adine Lewin. A Two Rivers woman who was Flann's wife. She was at Jac al'Seen's farm when Perrin went there to persuade the farmers to go to the towns for safety. Adine was willing to believe ill of Perrin, and implied that he was not to be trusted.

Adley, Jonan. *See* Jonan Adley

Admar. A soldier of the Band of the Red Hand under Captain Mandevwin. He participated in the attack on the Seanchan.

Admer Nem. A stout farmer with lank hair in Kore Springs, Andor. He was married to Maigan. His barn burned when Logain, Siuan, Leane and Min were discovered there; Logain fought with him, knocking the lantern into the hay. The three women were caught and Nem prosecuted them; Logain escaped.

Admira, Master. A Tairen merchant whom Rand eavesdropped on in Far Madding at an inn called The Golden Wheel.

Adora. Perrin's granddaughter in a scenario created in the battle between Rand and the Dark One.

Adora Aybara. The young sister of Perrin Aybara. When she was sixteen years old, she, along with the rest of her family except Perrin, was murdered by Padan Fain, although the killing was thought to have been done by Trollocs.

Adria. A slim contortionist in Valan Luca's show. She worked with Mulaen and three others; they shared a virulently yellow wagon until Adria took up with up with Rumann, the sword-juggler. Her lips made Olver want to kiss them.

Adrielle. An Aes Sedai of the Gray Ajah and the loyalist contingent. She was tall and beautiful. She was part of the expedition to take the Black Tower; she was captured and bonded by Mezar Kurin. She vanished when Mezar was Turned.

Adrin. A Saldaean soldier. While guarding Lord Tellaen's manor, he was struck by a bubble of evil. He burned up from the inside with enough heat to set the manor alight.

Adrinne Bunt. Almen Bunt's dead wife.

Adsalan. A Warder to one of the ferrets sent to the White Tower. He was coopted by the Black Ajah hunters.

Aedelle Baryn. Andoran Lord Lir Baryn's sister. Her cook fed Arymilla, Naean and Elenia, among others, as they were preparing to take Caemlyn.

Aedmun Matherin. The High Seat of House Matherin in Andor and a supporter of Elayne.

Aedomon. An Ancient king of Safer who defeated a Manetheren army at Midean's Ford. Legend had that he let the Manetheren go instead of killing them all; Mat's memories revealed that he did let them go, and as soon as they were strung out, killed them. He was later killed by a young boy with a spear.

Aedwin Cole. A crewman for Bayle Domon on the *Spray*; he hailed from northern Altara or northern Murandy. At Falme, he started to cut the mooring cable with an axe during the uproar there while Domon was waiting for Egwene, Elayne, Nynaeve and Min. Domon grabbed him by the throat and stopped him.

Aeldene Stonebridge. An Aes Sedai of the Blue Ajah and the rebel contingent, with a strength level of 27(15). Born in an Andoran mining town in the Mountains of Mist, she was a wilder who went to the Tower at age twenty-four and lied about her age. The lie was not discovered until she had been a novice for five years. She spent ten years as a novice and nine years as Accepted and was raised to the shawl at age forty-three. She was the head of the Blue Ajah's eyes-and-ears network. When Aeldene joined with the rebels and took back the Blue network from Siuan, she was infuriated that Siuan had been using them, and even more infuriated that Siuan had revealed her position, especially to women not of the Blue. The reception she gave Siuan was more than rough; she could be heard shouting for a great distance. She was barely able to restrain herself from going for Siuan's throat.

Aeldra. A woman of Tanchico, never seen, who was called to by a man who had dreamed himself into *Tel'aran'rhiod*.

Aeldra Najaf. A Domani Aes Sedai of the Blue Ajah. Lean, with coppery skin and short white hair, she was a kindly woman in many ways. Aeldra succeeded Gitara Moroso as Keeper of the Chronicles for Tamra Ospenya. She was the sixth person to welcome Moiraine and Siuan to the Blue Ajah and claimed a pie from each; because the two were such bad cooks, she had to be Healed after eating their pies.

Aeldrine. The mother of Beonin Marinye. She was a merchant in Tanchico.

Aelfinn. A race of beings which possessed souls and were largely human in appearance but with snake-like characteristics. They were reputed to answer three questions truly. Whatever the question, their answers were always correct, if frequently given in forms that were not clear. Questions concerning the Shadow could be extremely dangerous. Their actual location, a parallel world, was unknown, but they could be visited by passing through a *ter'angreal*, once a possession of Mayene but in recent years held in the Stone of Tear. They could also be reached by entering the Tower of Ghenjei. The Aelfinn spoke a harsh dialect of the Old Tongue, mentioned treaties and agreements, and asked if those entering carried iron, instruments of music, or devices that could make fire. They have existed as long as the Wheel. *See also* Eelfinn

Aelgar. One of the Ten Nations formed after the Breaking of the World. Its capital was Ancohima; other cities included Condaris, Mainelle (later Tanchico) and Shar Honelle. The King was Remedan the Goldentongued. It had mines which were lost.

Aelgari. The people of Aelgar.

Aellinsar, Tel Janin. Sammael's name in the Age of Legends.

Aelmara. Romanda Cassin's longtime serving woman. She helped Romanda escape from some unpleasantness in Far Madding shortly after Romanda's retirement; Romanda trusted her very much.

Aeman Senhold. A nobleman who was the leader of the Amadician contingent at the Battle of the Shining Walls.

Aemin. A farrier in Perrin's camp in Ghealdan. He had graying hair, broad shoulders and thick arms, and seemed nearly as wide as he was tall, though since he was a Cairhienin, that was not very tall.

Aemlyn Carand. The plump High Seat of House Carand, a major House in Andor. Her sigil was three golden arrows, points upward, the center arrow slightly raised, on a field of red. Her husband was Lord Culhan; the two were nearly as powerful as Pelivar. She supported Morgase in her drive for the throne. Under Rahvin's influence, Morgase exiled her from Caemlyn. Aemlyn, Pelivar and Culhan were among the nobles who confronted the rebel Aes Sedai on the ice near the Murandy-Andor border. After Elayne took Caemlyn, Aemlyn stood for Trakand.

Aemon al Caar al Thorin. The last King of Manetheren. His wife was Eldrene, known as Ellisande, the Rose of the Sun. King Aemon and his men, after a forced march from victory at the Battle of Bekkar, known as the Field of Blood, held off overwhelming numbers of Trollocs and Shadowspawn for over ten days while awaiting promised reinforcements that never came. The King's battle cry, *"Carai an Ellisande!*, For the honor of the Rose of the Sun!,"* was said to echo over the land until Queen Eldrene could hear it from the city. Eventually Aemon and his armies were killed. It was said that Queen Eldrene's heart broke the moment Aemon died. An Aes Sedai, she reached out to the True Source to hunt down the victors and sent balefire to consume the Dreadlords, Myrddraal and Darkfriends where they stood. That effort required more Power than anyone could wield unaided, and she and the city of Manetheren died in flames.

Aeric Botteger. A man of the Two Rivers who appeared in Nynaeve's test for the shawl.

Aeron. A respected Wise One of the Black Water sept of the Nakai Aiel who could not channel. She had graying hair and sky-blue eyes. Her face was very tanned, just short of being leathery. Her apprentice was Estair. She was fairly easygoing for a Wise One; Egwene thought of her as a pleasant, smiling woman with never a cross word. She, along with Colinda and Edarra, was sent to the Royal Library in Cairhien because Nesune Bihara, a Brown who was part of the White Tower embassy to Rand, was seeking information there on the seals. Aeron convinced three Maidens to sneak into Lady Arilyn's palace to spy on the White Tower embassy, who were staying there; the Maidens were caught and beaten, and Aeron was chastised by the other Wise Ones. After Rand had been kidnapped and freed, Aeron felt the Aes Sedai captured at Dumai's Wells were too dangerous to keep alive. She was quite hard on Beldeine, among others.

Aerwin, Teven. The author of *The Dance of the Hawk and the Hummingbird*, a book that purported to set forth the proper conduct of men toward women and women toward men.

Aes Sedai. Old Tongue for "servant of all." It was a society of those who wielded the One Power, composed solely of women since the Breaking, when all men with the ability to channel went mad from the taint placed on *saidin* by the Dark One. The Aes Sedai divided themselves into seven groups, called Ajahs. Each Ajah had its own specialty: the Blue Ajah focused on causes; the Brown Ajah on scholarship; the Green Ajah on battle; the Gray Ajah on mediation; the Red Ajah on dealing with male channelers; the White Ajah on logic; and the Yellow Ajah on Healing. There was a secret eighth Ajah, whose existence was debated widely: the Black Ajah, who served the Shadow. The Aes Sedai were led by the Amyrlin Seat; the term was used both for the woman who led and for her throne. She was formally styled "The Watcher of the Seals, the Flame of Tar Valon, the Amyrlin Seat." The Amyrlin Seat was chosen by the Hall of the Tower. The Hall of the Tower acted as the legislature; it consisted of three representatives, called Sitters, from each Ajah.

To become an Aes Sedai, a young woman first served as a novice and was taught to safely use the One Power, carefully monitored. When she had attained enough skill, she was given the test to become Accepted, which required passing through a *ter'angreal*. If she passed that test, she received a Great Serpent ring and rose to the level of Accepted. An Accepted was allowed more independent study and also assisted in teaching novices. When she was judged ready, she was given the test to become Aes Sedai, which required passing through another *ter'angreal*. In that test, she had to perform one hundred set weaves, maintaining calm throughout, while various challenges were given her by Aes Sedai manipulating the *ter'angreal*. When she passed that test, she spent the night in meditation and the next morning chose her Ajah and swore the Three Oaths on the Oath Rod.

The social hierarchy of Aes Sedai was set by several factors, the first and most important of which was strength in the Power. If another woman was stronger than you, you were expected to let her speak first, to listen to her, to defer to some extent, depending on how far above you she stood. Even when two women were of the same apparent strength, one would surely be the stronger by some margin, but this could only be determined by the sort of contests that were strongly discouraged among novices and Accepted. After that factor came time spent as a novice and time as Accepted, with the one who spent less being the higher. A shorter time as Accepted outweighed a shorter time as novice by a factor of about two to one (i.e., if you were two years longer a novice but two years less Accepted, you came out ahead by a year, so to speak), but a shorter total time was better and would outweigh other considerations. This generally decided matters, but if there was a need to go further, the final step was age, taken reluctantly because of Aes Sedai customs against speaking about this. In this final step, the older woman was considered to stand higher.

The degree of deference depended in large part on how far there was between the two women. If the gap was very small, it amounted to little more than politeness. If the gap was larger, the lower of the two was expected to stand when the other entered, etc. If the gap was very wide, the lower of the two was expected to do as she was told by the higher; it wasn't put in terms of obedience, but if a woman sufficiently higher than you asked you to make tea, then you made tea for her. And you didn't fix a cup for yourself unless she invited you to one.

This social hierarchy had no weight with regard to appointments and official duties—usually, at least—and if a woman who was lower was appointed to a position of authority, even those who stood above her socially were expected to obey if they were in the line of command. It was true, however, that the social hierarchy invaded the official side to some extent. For example, even in official proceedings what was said by one of higher standing usually was given more weight than what was said by one of lower. *See also* Amyrlin, Hall of the Tower, novice, Accepted, Ajah *and* Three Oaths

Aes Sedai trial procedure. A court consisting of five Aes Sedai: three acting as judges, one acting as prosecutor sitting in the Seat of Rebuke, and one acting as defender sitting in the Seat of Pardon, all facing the accused.

Aesdaishar Palace. The royal palace of Kandor, located in Chachin.

Aesnan, Lorstrum. *See* Lorstrum Aesnan

Aethan Dor. Old Tongue for "Red Shields." It was the name given an Aiel warrior society which acted as police in addition to regular battle duties.

Aethelaine, Lady. The local lady of Jurador, a salt town in Altara. She swore the Oaths of Return to the Seanchan.

Afara. An Aes Sedai of the Green Ajah and the rebel contingent, with a strength level of 34(22). She was sent from Salidar to Tarabon with Guisin and Edesina to assess the situation there and was captured by the Seanchan. She remained in Tarabon as a *damane*.

Afrim Hansard. A loyal Guardsman of the Royal Guards in Caemlyn. He escorted Samwil Hark to meet with Elayne.

Agardo Saranche. The innkeeper of The Dragon in Tear. He was lean, balding, fair-complected and dark-eyed.

Age. The Wheel of Time is composed of seven Ages, each with its own distinct patterns; the cycle begins again once all seven Ages have been lived.

Age Lace. *See* Pattern of an Age

Age of Legends. The golden Age of peace and progress when Aes Sedai performed wonders now only dreamed of. The greatest feats of the Age of Legends required men and women working together with the One Power—a man and a woman working together were ten times as strong as they were apart. It was ended by the War of the Shadow and the Breaking of the World, over three thousand years before Rand al'Thor's birth.

Agelmar Jagad. The Lord of Fal Dara in Shienar, considered to be one of the five great captains of the time. His sign was three running red foxes. He was about six feet tall, muscular, with graying hair. He commanded the Shienaran forces against the Aiel at the Battle of the Shining Walls, and on the first day of that battle, he led the combined forces. Agelmar commanded the armies at Tarwin's Gap in the Last Battle. After it was discovered that he was the victim of Graendal's Compulsion, he was removed from command. His sister was Amalisa.

Aghan. A lancer with Bashere's army who accompanied Rand to meet the purported Daughter of the Nine Moons at Lady Deirdru's manor house outside King's Crossing. He searched the mansion after Semirhage was captured, and discovered a box of male and female *a'dam*.

Aginor. A Forsaken whose original name was Ishar Morrad Chuain. In the Age of Legends he was a noted biologist; after he went over to the Shadow, he created numerous Shadowspawn, including Trollocs, Draghkar, *gholam*, cafar and jumara. He claimed to have faced Lews Therin in the Hall of the Servants and to have matched the Lord of the Morning stroke for stroke. He had a strength level of ++2. He was trapped near the surface of the Bore; when he awoke in the Third Age, his face was parchment skin drawn too tight over a skull; it was a face of such age as to look beyond death already, with sunken eyes and withered ears. His scabrous scalp bore wispy tufts of brittle hair, his fingers were gnarled and his teeth were yellow. He and Balthamel attacked Rand and his party at the Eye of the World; Aginor drew on the pure *saidin* in the Eye, and grew younger and stronger, but not strong enough. Rand defeated and killed him. He was resurrected and given a new body that was male and not old, but not as young as he could wish, nor as good-looking. He was given the name Osan'gar, after the left-hand dagger in a form of dueling that had a brief popularity during the long run-up to the War of Power; the blades were poisoned and both duelists usually died. He slipped in among the Asha'man under the name Corlan Dashiva to be an assistant to Mazrim Taim, who thought he was only a high-ranking Darkfriend, which did not suit Osan'gar well. He wore both the Sword and the Dragon. His original purpose there was to keep a close eye on the gathering of men who could channel. *See also* Osan'gar *and* Corlan Dashiva

Agirin. A Maiden of the Spear of the Shelan sept of the Daryne Aiel who died at Dumai's Wells; Rand added her name to the list of women who died for him.

Agni Neres. The misogynistic, smuggling captain of the *Riverserpent* who gave passage to Nynaeve, Elayne and others to Salidar. He referred to them as "wenches." He was from Ebou Dar, and had a wife and a flock of children there. He was tall and bony, with a dour, narrow face and ears that stuck out from his head.

Agora, Haviar. *See* Haviar Agora

Ahan, Kenley. A young Two Rivers man who joined Perrin's band. He was killed in an ambush by Trollocs.

Ahan, Marisa. *See* Marisa Ahan

Ahan, Mistress. A woman of the Two Rivers; she was the mother of Kenley.

Ahelle, Meane sol. The Fourth Age composer of "Glory of the Dragon."

Ahf'frait. A Trolloc tribe. Its symbol was a whirlwind.

Ahmid, Toma dur. The developer of the Toman Calendar.

Ahzkan, Tumad. *See* Tumad Ahzkan

Aiden Shimura. A Sea Folk Aes Sedai of the Brown Ajah and the loyalist contingent. She worked in the Thirteenth Depository of the White Tower Library. Like all Sea Folk Aes Sedai, she was weak in the One Power. She lied about her age when she came to the White Tower. She was a shy, withdrawn woman with a very dark complexion, round figure, black hair and dark eyes. Aiden, Zemaille and Nyein shared rooms in the upper levels of the Library and spent most of their time either there or in the Thirteenth Depository. Alviarin passed Aiden and Zemaille in the Library when she returned from Tremalking.

Aiel. Old Tongue for "dedicated." They were the people of the Aiel Waste, descendants of pacifists who served the Aes Sedai during the Age of Legends. Fierce and hardy, they veiled their faces before they killed. Deadly warriors with weapons or bare hands, they would not touch a sword even on the point of death, or ride a horse unless pressed. Aiel called battle "the dance," and "the dance of the spears." They were divided into twelve clans: the Chareen, the Codarra, the Daryne, the Goshien, the Miagoma, the Nakai, the Reyn, the Shaarad, the Shaido, the Shiande, the Taardad and the Tomanelle. Each clan was divided into septs. They sometimes spoke of a thirteenth clan, the Clan That Is Not, the Jenn, who were the builders of Rhuidean. All believed that the Aiel once failed the Aes Sedai and were banished to the Aiel Waste for that sin, and that they would be destroyed if they ever failed the Aes Sedai again. *See also* Aiel warrior societies, Aiel Waste, bleakness, Da'shain, *gai'shain,* Jenn Aiel, Rhuidean *and* Tuatha'an

Aiel kinship. Aiel relationships of blood were expressed in complex ways which outsiders considered unwieldy, but which Aiel considered precise. A few examples must suffice to demonstrate, as an entire volume would be needed for a full explanation. Beyond this the complications grow and are thickened by such factors as the ability of close friends to adopt each other as first-brother or first-sister. When it is also considered that Aiel women who were very close friends sometimes married the same man, thus becoming sister-wives and married to each other as well as to him, the convolutions become even more apparent.

One was considered to be more closely related to one's mother than to one's father. First-brother and first-sister had the same mother, whether or not they had the same father. If two women were sister-wives, however, their children were considered first-brothers and first-sisters to each other.

Sister-mothers and sister-fathers were first-sisters and first-brothers of one's mother; thus, aunt and uncle through one's mother, and more closely related to one than aunts or uncles through one's father. The term was not used for one's mother's adopted first-sister who was also her sister-wife; she also was simply one's mother.

Brother-father and brother-mother were the first-brothers and first-sisters of one's father.

Second-brother and second-sister referred to the children of one's mother's first-sister or first-brother; thus, a cousin through one's mother. This term was also used for a child of one's father by a sequential marriage, as opposed to a child of a sister-wife.

A father-sister or father-brother was the child of one's father's first-brother; thus, a cousin through one's father. Father-sisters and father-brothers (aunts and uncles through one's father) were not considered as closely related as second-sisters or second-brothers, just as one was more closely related to one's mother than to one's father.

Greatfather or greatmother referred to the father or mother of one's own mother, while the parents of one's father were second greatfather or second greatmother.

An additional complication was that sister-wives were considered married to each other as well as to their husband; also, the ability of women to adopt one another as first-sisters added wrinkles.

Second-mother and second-father were mother-in-law and father-in-law equivalents.

A boy or man was expected to obey his mother before his father; a girl or woman was expected to obey her father before her mother. There were circumstances, however, when one's second-mother took precedence over one's mother, and when a second-father took precedence over one's father.

It was possible to adopt someone as a first-brother or first-sister by saying the proper words in front of the individuals' Wise Ones. This was most common among women, and nearly unheard of among men. There were occasionally cross-gender adoptions, but these were almost as rare as men adopting one another. Such an adoption brought in all of the familial relationships, duties, responsibilities, etc. For example, the sister-mother of one's first-sister was of course one's sister-mother.

As one was closer blood kin to one's mother than to one's father, the degree of relationship by rank was:

1) mother, first-brother, first-sister
2) father; greatmother and greatfather (maternal grandparents)
3) sister-mother, sister-father (maternal aunts and uncles)
4) second-brother, second-sister (maternal cousins)
5) second greatfather, second greatmother (paternal grandparents)
6) brother-father, brother-mother (paternal aunts and uncles)
7) father-sister, father-brother (paternal cousins)

Aiel law. Since most of Aiel life and activity was regulated by *ji'e'toh*, the Aiel did not have a great many laws. Most of these had to do with water, murder, theft or harming certain persons. While Aiel law was centered around and based on *ji'e'toh*, the two were not the same. It was possible to incur *toh* without breaking the law, though it was seldom possible to break the law without incurring *toh*. Generally, the more serious the offense under the law, the more serious the *toh*.

The few universal laws were a prohibition on murder, a prohibition on destroying or fouling water, a prohibition on theft (remembering that the fifth is not theft) and a prohibition on harming a Wise One, a pregnant woman, a child or a blacksmith.

These all-encompassing laws had been agreed to over the years by chiefs and Wise Ones. For a violation of one of these, a clan was expected either to hand over the accused for trial or to try the person and carry out punishment themselves. While there were cases of clans managing to avoid doing either, it was usually considered a matter of honor to do exactly that. It was also often considered a point of honor to give a harsher punishment than would have been handed out if the accused had been found guilty by those of the other clan.

Most Aiel trials consisted of the sept chief acting as judge with twelve men and twelve women, all chosen by lot, as a jury. An appeal could be made to the clan chief, who sat as judge with a jury of twelve Wise Ones. In either case, the jury decided guilt or innocence, and the judge decided the penalty.

In some cases a court of twelve Wise Ones could also sit, without a chief. Such a case was the instance of deciding whether to declare someone *da'tsang*, a despised one.

It was possible to be acquitted in the trial despite being guilty if one had managed to meet the *toh* incurred.

An Aiel considered it shaming to the extent of putting himself, or herself, outside humanity to fail to appear for a trial or to meet a sentence.

There was a death penalty and none other for: killing a Wise One, killing a pregnant woman, killing or sexually molesting a child and killing a blacksmith. Unlike any other homicide, there were no excuses for these, not even self-defense.

Murder was defined by circumstances; for example, there were times when stabbing a man in the back was not murder (in battle, say, or on a raid) and times when it was. The penalty for murder was usually death, but there were ways to meet the *toh* involved, although the killer would have to bring the closest survivors of the murdered person ("close" defined first as a surviving spouse or spouses, then the mother, then the father, etc.) to declare to the court that the accused had met *toh*. While the accused still set his own *toh*, this was the only time when, in effect, someone else could say whether one had met it sufficiently, though it was not stated in that way.

There was a death penalty for destroying a source of water. Fouling a source of water was a lesser crime, but not by much. Fouling water ranked with breaking oath or violating an agreed truce.

The Aiel death penalty was starkly simple. One was trussed like an animal for slaughter, the throat was slit and the corpse left for the vultures.

There were also strong penalties for harming a Wise One, a pregnant woman, a child or a blacksmith.

Some laws held only inside one clan, as well. They would certainly be enforced on anyone within clan lands, however.

The Aiel had no prisons nor any tradition of confinement for offenses. With the exception of the penalties for murder, destroying a water source, breaking oath, violating truce or fouling water, penalties were usually corporal punishment of some sort, being flogged or beaten publicly. There could be more than one beating, in more than one site. Someone who fouled a water source, for example, could well have expected to be beaten in every hold of the clan that owned the water source; and, if the fouler belonged to another clan, in every hold of the fouler's own clan as well.

Destroying water was considered so heinous that clans in blood feud had carried out sentence on someone who committed the crime on water owned by the other clan.

Since one was supposed to have set the worth of one's own honor, it was believed that one should meet the *toh* incurred by breaking a law entirely on one's own. As stated, meeting it to a degree that satisfied the jury resulted in acquittal. Attempting to meet it but failing, say, because there wasn't enough time before the trial, could have been considered mitigation, in proportion. Failing even to attempt to meet *toh* would certainly have resulted in a harsher sentence.

The Aiel had a very rigid tradition of prisoner treatment. There were *gai'shain*, there were hostages exchanged for various reasons, there were captured truce-violators, oathbreakers and water-foulers, and there were wetlanders taken in the Waste. (There was no provision for holding someone for trial or for execution of even a death sentence; you were expected to show up at the proper time and place, and failing to do so placed you on a par with vermin.) These were the only classifications they knew. Hostages were well treated unless there was a violation, and what was done then was determined under *ji'e'toh* by the violation. Any Aiel taken captive expected to be made *gai'shain* (except for truce-violators and oathbreakers, who were refused the white, and instead were put into black robes and expected a period of humiliation before being handed back to their own people under as humiliating circumstances as could be arranged). Wetlanders taken in the Waste fell into two classes: Treekillers (Cairhienin) who were taken to the tradeholds along the Cliffs of Dawn or the Great Rift and traded like animals; and other wetlanders who lacked the protection of being Tuatha'an or peddlers or gleemen. These unprotected wetlanders were usually killed out of hand, but sometimes given a chance to find their way back out, often naked and with a single waterskin.

Truce-violators and oathbreakers were allowed no garments but the black robes. They were worked, but generally at useless labor. If they were given useful labor, it was always under humiliating circumstances, such as nakedness. Beatings with a strap or switch were common, and they were directed almost like animals, a word of command, a gesture, a slap with a strap to get them started.

Examples of useless labor: Digging a deep hole, often with an implement as small as a spoon, then filling it in only to dig another and fill it, and so on. Being made to carry a heavy sack of rocks or sand around on one's back. Being made to run with a container of water; if you spilled any, the rest of the contents would be all the liquid you got that day, and you were forced to run to the point of collapsing. Running between two piles of dirt, scooping up a flat basket full at one place and emptying it at the other; when you had moved all of the dirt from one place to the other, you took it back. Pushing a rock ahead of you across the ground on your knees. Pulling a weighted sled across the ground for hours.

Examples of humiliation: The beating, of course, and the enforced public nudity. Carrying water to or serving *gai'shain*, as though you were *gai'shain* to *gai'shain*. Being made to kneel, to offer things with your wrists turned up, to lower your eyes when speaking to others or behave in other ways the Aiel considered submissive. Various forms of bondage—being caged, confined or bound—were considered *very* shaming.

Da'tsang (Old Tongue for "despised one," or "one who is despised") was the name given to criminals among the Aiel—criminals as opposed to simply being somehow on the wrong side of *ji'e'toh*, though a persistent violation of *ji'e'toh* or a refusal to meet an obvious *toh* might well have resulted in this designation. Generally it was for those who had committed rape, or broken truce or oath, or fouled water, or stolen (as the Aiel saw it, the fifth taken on a raid certainly did not count), or killed or sexually abused a child, a pregnant woman, a Wise One or a blacksmith. (Among the Aiel, ordinary murder was a thing for vengeance by family, sept, clan or society, depending on who did the killing and under what circumstances. The murderer was not *da'tsang*.)

In this, the Wise Ones acted as magistrates; only Wise Ones could name someone *da'tsang*. These criminals owed *toh* far beyond the ordinary. It was something not referred to once it was proclaimed; saying the word in the proclamation even, the speaker grimaced as if tasting something filthy. The black robe was the mark of *da'tsang*.

Da'tsang were severely limited in speech, since they were considered not quite human. They were not held to total silence, but were allowed to speak only in limited fashion. A few simple requests were allowed, and answers to questions, though few were asked. They were allowed to speak enough to understand the tasks they were given, not much more than that. If more than one *da'tsang* was present in a camp—a fairly rare circumstance, historically—they were kept apart and not allowed to communicate, so they could not lend one another support or plot escape.

The possessions of someone declared *da'tsang* were normally destroyed, including any jewelry, in the case of a woman. At least, those possessions they had with them. No one would want to use or own something taken from a *da'tsang*.

The Aiel had no tradition of how to deal with wetlander prisoners taken outside the Waste. The Shaido solved this by considering them as *gai'shain*, though with the difference that since they did not follow *ji'e'toh*, there was no need to release them after a year and a day. The other Aiel struggled with this problem.

Aiel methods of putting someone to the question centered around the Aiel view of life and the concepts of *ji'e'toh*. Shame was more biting than pain. They did use pain, but it was the shaming circumstances of it that were considered the real torture, not the actual amount of pain. Thus, they did not use pincers or hot irons or the like, as Whitecloak Questioners did. Enforced nudity was always a part, along with the useless labor, and beatings for failure to cooperate in your own humiliation. You could have been hung up by your ankles or wrists, switched or strapped; the Aiel could have used nettles or other stinging or burning plants, whole or ground to powder or made into oils and unguents applied to various parts of the body.

The key point was that you were shamed until you could bear the shame no more, and in truth, with Aiel, this worked faster than the Questioners' methods. Aiel often held out to death against wetlander methods of extracting information. The converse was not true, however. While wetlanders often began thinking that the Aiel methods were tame compared to "real" torture, the combination of pain, very much unrelenting if milder than hot irons, with shame (few wetlanders took enforced public nudity even as well as Aiel) and unceasing labor from waking to sleeping—all of that together usually broke a wetlander faster than it did an Aiel, though often not as fast as the hot irons would have worked.

The Aiel reaction to pain was also quite different from that of the wetlanders. While obviously there were times and places when pain had to be borne stoically, even to a degree that wetlanders would have considered impossible, the Aiel also held that flesh could only take so much. An Aielman under torture would see shame in the public nature of his mistreatment, in the fact of being mistreated against his will, but not in being made to cry out or weep. This was part of the reason why wetlanders who tried considered it impossible to break an Aielman with torture. Where the wetlander strained to fight the pain without relenting and was broken in part by the fact that he could not resist any further, the Aielman took it as a matter of course that he would eventually cry out or scream, and the fact that he did so did nothing to weaken his overall resolve. The fact that wetlanders didn't know about the importance of shame—wetlanders didn't go in for torture in ways that were truly, deeply shaming to Aiel; i.e., publicly, or before those the Aielman would not wish to see—aided in the Aiel's reputation as peculiar folk who could be made to howl, often sooner than a wetlander, but still refused to break.

Aiel War (976–978 NE). When King Laman of Cairhien cut down *Avendoraldera*, four clans of the Aiel crossed the Spine of the World. They looted and burned the capital city of Cairhien as well as many other cities and towns, and the conflict extended into Andor and Tear. By the conventional view, the Aiel were finally defeated at the Battle of the Shining Walls, before Tar Valon; in fact, Laman was killed in that battle, and having done what they came to do, the Aiel recrossed the Spine. *See also Avendoraldera,* Cairhien *and* Spine of the World

Aiel warrior societies. Aiel warriors were all members of one of twelve societies. These were Black Eyes (*Seia Doon*), Brothers of the Eagle (*Far Aldazar Din*), Dawn Runners (*Rahien Sorei*), Knife Hands (*Sovin Nai*), Maidens of the Spear (*Far Dareis Mai*), Mountain Dancers (*Hama N'dore*), Night Spears (*Cor Darei*), Red Shields (*Aethan Dor*), Stone Dogs (*Shae'en M'taal*), Thunder Walkers (*Sha'mad Conde*), True Bloods (*Tain Shari*) and Water Seekers (*Duadhe Mahdi'in*). Each had its own customs, and sometimes specific duties. For example, Red Shields acted as police, and Stone Dogs were often used as rear guards during retreats, while Maidens were often scouts. Aiel clans frequently raided and battled one another, but members of the same society would not fight each other if their clans did so. Thus there were always lines of contact between the clans, even during open warfare. *See also* Aiel

Aiel Waste. The harsh, rugged and all-but-waterless land between the Spine of the World and Shara. It was called the Three-fold Land by the Aiel. Traditionally, few outsiders entered; the Aiel considered themselves at war with all other peoples and did not welcome strangers. Only peddlers, gleemen and the Tuatha'an were allowed safe entry, although Aiel avoided all contact with the Tuatha'an, whom they called "the Lost Ones." *See also* Three-fold Land, the

Aiko. A serving woman in the Aesdaishar Palace in Chachin when Moiraine was searching for the Dragon Reborn. She assisted Moiraine on her arrival.

Aile Dashar. A Sea Folk island group in the Aryth Ocean, northwest of Arad Doman.

Aile Jafar. A Sea Folk island group in the Aryth Ocean, due west of Tarabon. Sailmistress Coine told Nynaeve that this was one of her destinations.

Aile Somera. A Sea Folk island group in the Aryth Ocean, due west of Toman Head. Sailmistress Coine told Nynaeve that this was one of her destinations. It was captured by the Seanchan.

Ailene Tolvina. The stern innkeeper of The Evening Star in Chachin. Moiraine hired two of her bodyguards for escort to a bank.

Ailhuin Guenna, Mother. A Wise Woman in Tear. Nynaeve, Egwene and Elayne stayed with her when they were seeking the Black Ajah; she introduced them to Juilin. When Thom was sick, Mat took him to her.

Ailil Riatin. A Cairhienin noblewoman. She was 5'6" tall, and slim and dignified, with big dark eyes, not young but quite pretty. She was Toram's younger sister, and it was whispered that she would do anything for Toram, although Verin told Cadsuane that Ailil disliked her brother intensely. Denharad was her Lance-Captain; Rand summoned them to fight in the campaign against the Seanchan, but she failed to convince Rand that her Lance-Captain should take to the field in her place. Ailil and Shalon became pillow friends, a fact that they wanted to hide. After the attack on Rand by the Asha'man, Rand found her with Shalon, tied them up and stuffed them under the bed. Verin learned of Ailil and Shalon's relationship and told Cadsuane; Cadsuane promised them silence in return for information. Ailil came to support Elayne openly for the Sun Throne.

Ailron Rovere Lukan. The King of Amadicia. He was not as handsome as rumor put him. Despite his grandiose title—Anointed by the Light, King and Defender of Amadicia, Guardian of the Southern Gate—the Children of the Light were the true rulers of Amadicia. He did have an army, and he fretted over the fact that the Whitecloaks had so much power. After the Seanchan invaded Amadicia, Ailron brought them to battle near the town of Jeramel, about a hundred miles east of Amador and a hundred miles west of Abila. The troops were killed or scattered and Ailron and his entire court were killed or captured and made *da'covale*. Since he had summoned the nobility of Amadicia to his court beforehand, the result was that, effectively, Amadicia had little or no nobility remaining. The battle was known as Ailron's Disaster.

Ailron's Disaster. Also known as the Battle of Jeramel, the battle in which the Seanchan defeated the Amadicians and the Children of the Light, leading to Ailron's death.

Ailys Candwin. An Emond's Field woman with a neat house.

Aine. The fourth month of the year.

Air. One of the Five Powers. *See* Five Powers, the

Aisha Raveneos. An Aes Sedai of the Gray Ajah with a strength level of 14(2). Born in 698 NE, she went to the White Tower in 714 NE. After spending seven years as a novice and six years as Accepted, she was raised to the shawl in 727 NE.

A plain-faced woman who wore lots of jewelry, she adhered to the strictest letter of the law. She was one of the sisters called in by Tamra Ospenya to carry out the secret search for the newborn Dragon Reborn. She and her Warder were killed in Murandy in the spring of 979 NE, reputedly by bandits, but in truth by the Black Ajah.

Aisling Noon. A Tuatha'an Aes Sedai of the Green Ajah and the loyalist contingent, with a strength level of 16(4). Born in 954 NE, she went to the White Tower in 970 NE. After five years as a novice and five years as Accepted, she was raised to the shawl in 980 NE. Aisling was born with the spark and (as was Tuatha'an custom), when it was discovered, the caravan headed to Tar Valon, where she was handed over to the White Tower. She was 5'6" tall and fierce-eyed; she was known to pepper her speech with Borderlander curses. She acted as advisor to King Easar of Shienar, but upon learning of the split in the White Tower, she vanished, leaving no message and no clue as to where she could be found. Eventually Aisling returned to the Tower and became a member of the expedition to the Black Tower, where she was captured and bonded by Arel Malevin. They were at Lord Algarin's manor when the Trollocs attacked and afterward incinerated Trolloc corpses.

Ajah. Societies among the Aes Sedai, seven in number and designated by colors: Blue, Red, White, Green, Brown, Yellow and Gray. All Aes Sedai except the Amyrlin Seat belonged to one. Each followed a specific philosophy of the use of the One Power and the purposes of the Aes Sedai. The Red Ajah bent its energies to finding men who could channel, and to gentling them. The Brown forsook the mundane world and dedicated itself to seeking knowledge, while the White, largely eschewing both the world and the value of worldly knowledge, devoted itself to questions of philosophy and truth. The Green Ajah (called the Battle Ajah during the Trolloc Wars) held itself ready for Tarmon Gai'don, the Yellow concentrated on the study of Healing, and Blue sisters involved themselves with causes and justice. The Gray were mediators, seeking harmony and consensus. A Black Ajah, dedicated to serving the Dark One, was long officially and vehemently denied. Until five hundred years after the founding of the White Tower, "ajah" was lowercase and meant a temporary association for a specific purpose; after the Trolloc Wars it became capitalized and assumed the above meaning.

Ajala, Dermid. A Tairen blacksmith who gave Perrin a hammer as payment for work done in his smithy. He had graying hair, blue eyes and thick arms and shoulders.

Ajalon Bridge. A bridge in Far Madding connecting the city to the mainland via the Caemlyn Gate.

Ajimbura. A Kaensada Hills tribesman who served Furyk Karede as manservant and scout for nearly twenty years. He was about 5'6" to 5'7" tall, and wiry, with blue eyes and white-streaked dark red hair worn in a thick braid that hung to his waist, to make a good trophy if he ever returned home and fell in one of the feuds between families or tribes. Ajimbura looked like a wizened rat, and his grin could be feral. He played a reed flute and carried a long knife. A hunch of the shoulders passed for a bow among his people, the Yngiot tribe of the Kaensada Hills. After more than three hundred years under the Empire, the Kaensada hill tribes still sometimes removed a man's hair, and his scalp, for a trophy. Karede had nearly killed him three times before he decided to employ him, and Ajimbura became extremely loyal to Karede, although Karede could never understand why. Ajimbura would eat anything except for lizards, which were forbidden to his tribe for some reason he would never make clear. He speared rats with a long knife in Karede's quarters at the inn and ate them out of sight. Ajimbura drank from an unwashed silver-mounted cup with a ram's-horn-patterned silver base; close inspection would reveal that it was made from the top of someone's skull. Ajimbura rode a lean chestnut with four white feet, which he thought was lucky. Before riding with Karede to meet Thom Merrilin, who Karede thought was leading Mat's group, he cut off his braid, which in his land would label him a coward; it was a measure of his devotion to Karede. He was eaten alive by rats on the battlefield during the Last Battle, overrun while trying to cull one out for his lunch from a huge swarm of the Dark One's attacking rodents.

Akarrin Comeris. An Aes Sedai of the Brown Ajah and the rebel contingent, with a strength level of 34(22). Born in 801 NE, she went to the White Tower in 816 NE. After eleven years as a novice and ten years as Accepted, she was raised to the shawl in 829 NE. She taught Moiraine and Siuan when they were novice and Accepted, and was known for having quick eyes. She was slender and nodded for emphasis with almost every other word. She could read residues, and was part of the expedition sent by the rebel Aes Sedai to investigate the site of the huge use of the One Power at Shadar Logoth.

Akashi, Lelaine. *See* Lelaine Akashi

Akein. The name of the Domani razor mare that Mat gave to Tuon; it is an Old Tongue word meaning "swallow."

Akima, Chin. The owner of a traveling circus who was beheaded by Masema in Samara for disobeying him.

Akir Mandragoran. The last crowned King of Malkier, and father to Lan Mandragoran. He was betrayed by his sister-in-law Breyan and Cowin Fairheart, a Great Lord of Malkier, and his nation was overrun with Trollocs. He and his wife, el'Leanna, had Lan brought to them in his cradle and gave him a sword and a locket and consecrated him as the next King of Malkier. They then sent him with twenty soldiers to Fal Moran. Al'Akir and el'Leanna were killed at Herot's Crossing, and Malkier was lost.

Akoure Vayet. An Amadician Aes Sedai of the Gray Ajah and the loyalist contingent, with a strength level of 24(12). She was 5'4" tall and stout, with brown eyes and dark hair. Akoure was a member of the expedition to take the Black Tower, and was captured and bonded by an Asha'man. She sent a report about it to the Gray Ajah in the Tower.

Akuum, River. A river flowing northwest from the Mountains of Mist and joining the River Dhagon just east of Bandar Eban in Arad Doman.

Al Chalidholara Malkier. Old Tongue for "for my sweet land Malkier." It was the oath Malkieri soldiers took during their first posting to the Border.

Al Ellisande! An Old Tongue expression: "For the Rose of the Sun!" Ellisande, the last queen of Manetheren, was known as the Rose of the Sun.

al'Akir Mandragoran. *See* Akir Mandragoran

al'Azar. A Two Rivers family name. *See* Kevrim *and* Milla al'Azar

al Ban, Thorin al Toren. A king of Manetheren, the father of Caar and grandfather of Aemon.

al'Caar. A Two Rivers family. *See* Adan, Jac, Jerilin, Nela, Paet, Tod *and* Wil al'Caar

Al'cair'rahienallen. The Ogier-built capital city of Almoren, one of the Ten Nations after the Breaking and the site of Cairhien. Its name was Old Tongue for "Hill of the Golden Dawn." *See also* Cairhien

Al'Dai. A Two Rivers family. *See* Bili, Hu, Lem, Willim *and* Rad al'Dai

al'Donel, Mistress. An Emond's Field woman who was concerned that the storks had not returned to Emond's Field. She also appeared in Nynaeve's test for the shawl.

Al'ghol. A Trolloc tribe whose symbol was the hooked axe.

al'Hune, Jer. A boy in the Two Rivers whom Mat saved from drowning.

al'Lan Mandragoran. *See* Lan Mandragoran

al'Landerin, Eleyan. An Aes Sedai of ancient times. A statue of her and her Warders was located on the southwestern side of Tar Valon.

al'Lora family. A hardworking family in the Two Rivers. *See* Had al'Lora

al'Meara, Nynaeve. *See* Nynaeve al'Meara

al'Moor, Master. A farmer in the Two Rivers; his scythe blade was broken by Perrin early in his blacksmith training.

al'San, Montem. A Two Rivers man in Perrin's army.

al'Seen family. A Two Rivers family, some of whom fought in Perrin's army at Malden.

al'Seen, Astelle. A Two Rivers woman. She was the oldest in her family, and poked Perrin with her cane when he visited Jac al'Seen's farm.

al'Seen. A Two Rivers family. *See* Ban, Elisa, Jac, Saml, Susa, Wil *and* Wit al'Seen

al'Taron, Dael. A young Two Rivers man who joined Perrin's band. He was killed in a Trolloc ambush.

al'Taron, Mistress. A Two Rivers woman who was Dael's mother.

al'Thone family. A Two Rivers family. *See* Azi, Dav *and* Widow al'Thone

al'Thor, Kari. *See* Kari al'Thor

al'Thor, Rand. *See* Rand al'Thor

al'Thor, Tam. *See* Tam al'Thor

al'Thor's Banner. A red banner bearing the ancient Aes Sedai symbol, so called by Mat's Band. It was also called the Banner of Light by Taim.

al'Van, Alwyn. The cobbler in Emond's Field.

al'Vere. An Emond's Field family. *See* Alene, Berowyn, Brandelwyn, Elisa, Egwene, Loise *and* Marin al'Vere

Ala. An Ogier who was the daughter of Soferra and the mother of Damelle, the last of whom wrote about the Ways.

Alaabar Harnesh. A Murandian Lord Captain of the Children of the Light. He was short and bald, and lost an ear fighting Dragonsworn. After hearing Galad's argument with Asunawa, Harnesh and other Lords Captain executed Asunawa and proclaimed Galad Lord Captain Commander of the Children of the Light. During the Last Battle, Golever chose him as one of the dozen best men to accompany Galad when Mat sent him to Hawal Ford.

Aladon, Turak. *See* Turak Aladon

Alaine Chuliandred. A Cairhienin noblewoman, wife of Doressin, who cornered Rand at Barthanes' party. Her head did not come to Rand's shoulder, but her array of curls reached his eyes. She was entitled to wear stripes on her dress reaching below her breasts. She later became afraid of Rand, but it didn't lessen her desire for him. Her House was one of those smaller Houses that met with Colavaere. Because of this, fearing that Rand would move against them for it, she and the rest of her House vigorously courted Caraline Damodred and Toram Riatin, but in what they thought was the strictest secrecy.

Alainia. A plump Amadician silversmith who was taken *gai'shain* by the Shaido. At Malden she swore to Faile.

Alalved. A chief of the Tomanelle Aiel after the Last Battle, seen in Aviendha's vision of the future in Rhuidean.

Alamindra Cutren. A member of the Domani Council of Merchants. She went into hiding, but Rhuarc found and held her. Rand ordered her returned to her palace when he left Arad Doman.

Alanna Mosvani. An Arafellin Aes Sedai of the Green Ajah and the rebel contingent, with a strength level of 17(5). Born in 951 NE, she went to the White Tower in 967 NE. After six years as a novice and six years as Accepted, she was raised to the shawl in 979 NE. She had three Warders: Owein, who was killed by the Whitecloaks in the Two Rivers; Ihvon; and Rand al'Thor, whom she bonded against his will. She was 5'4½" tall, and beautiful and slender, with long black hair and penetrating dark eyes. She was proud and fiery, with a mercurial temper and sense of humor; she could flash from one to the other. Alanna went with Siuan to Fal Dara. She assisted in Healing Mat of his connection to the Shadar Logoth dagger; she had some Healing ability, but not great. She went to the Two Rivers with Verin, hunting young women who could be taught to channel, and helped with the defense of the Two Rivers, then with Verin and those young women went to Caemlyn, where they met Rand. Alanna bonded Rand as a Warder, catching him by surprise and not asking his consent. Because this bonding against his will was akin to rape in the Aes Sedai view, she walked very small among those who knew. Most of those treated her fairly roughly, with little respect. In many ways, with many sisters, this negated her standing in the social hierarchy; even the lowest felt free to be rough on her, and because Alanna was Aes Sedai, with all the Aes Sedai beliefs, she found herself hard-pressed to fight back except occasionally. After bonding Rand, she began to work with the Salidar embassy under Merana, but was disapproving of the rebellion despite her strong dislike of Elaida. She followed after Rand when he went to Caemlyn and was forced to swear fealty to him after Dumai's Wells. She fell unconscious when Rand was bonded by Min, Elayne and Aviendha. Rand sent her off to pick up Rafela, Merana and others in Cairhien and proceed to Haddon Mirk in Tear to try talking the rebels there into an agreement. Upon receiving a letter from Verin, Alanna fled north. She was captured, injured and held at Shayol Ghul; Nynaeve healed her enough that she could release the bond before she was killed by Moridin.

alantin. Old Tongue for "Brother"; short for *tia avende alantin*, which is "Brother to the Trees" or "Treebrother."

Alar. The Eldest of the Elders of Stedding Tsofu. She was the mother of Iva and the grandmother of Erith. Alar could tell that Rand was *ta'veren*, which meant he was strong, since such Talents ran weakly in Ogier if at all.

Alarch. Son of Aviendha and Rand, seen in Aviendha's view of the future in Rhuidean. He had dark hair and was able to channel from a very young age.

Alarys. A Wise One of the Shaido Aiel (but not Jumai) with the ability to channel. She was about 5'8" tall with black hair, which was rare among the Aiel. She often ran her fingers through it, apparently absentmindedly, but it was her way to remind people that she had black hair instead of common yellow or red. She was one of Sevanna's inner circle of plotters. In Sevanna's opinion, she usually tried to ignore what she did not want to see. She took part in or at least was present at the murder of Desaine. Alarys was one of those who accompanied Sevanna to the Aes Sedai camp the day she saw Rand beaten. Alarys was at the meeting with "Caddar" and "Maisia" and was with Sevanna at Dumai's Wells. She helped question the Seanchan prisoner in Amadicia, while the Jumai were settled at a captured estate approximately ten days after their arrival. Alarys sided with Therava when Therava took some power from Sevanna.

Alcair Dal. In Old Tongue, *Al'Cair Dal*, the Golden Bowl. It was a round canyon in the Aiel Waste, three to four days from Cold Rocks Hold, that was the meeting place of Aiel clan chiefs.

Alcruna. A flyspeck village straddling a river in eastern Tarabon, near the northern border with the Almoth Plain. Pedron Niall sent some Children of the Light to Alcruna. It was pacified by Questioners, meaning that the people of the village were probably all killed by them.

Aldael Mountains. A mountain range in Seanchan.

Aldan, Captain. The officer in charge of recruitment for Bryne's army.

Aldazar. Furyk Karede's horse, a bay. The name was Old Tongue for "eagle."

Aldecain Damodred. Laman's brother and Moiraine's uncle. He was cruel and vicious and held Moiraine's father in contempt. He was killed at the end of the Aiel War, along with his brother Laman.

Aldeshar. A nation that rose after the Trolloc Wars and was taken by Artur Hawkwing.

Aldiaya. A noble House of Tear that included Nalesean.

Aldieb. Moiraine's mare that she rode when she went to the Two Rivers. The name was Old Tongue for "West Wind," the wind that brings the spring rains.

Aldin. An Amadician bookkeeper who was taken *gai'shain* by the Shaido. Aldin was tall and square-shouldered, which made him look more like a soldier than a bookkeeper. At Malden he swore to Faile and became enamored of Arrela, who had no interest in him. He gave up on her, and started pursuing Aravine.

Aldin Miheres. A mercenary commander working for Arymilla. He attacked Caemlyn and was killed by Birgitte with an arrow through the neck.

Aldorwin, Lacile. *See* Lacile Aldorwin

Aldragoran, Alida. The wife of Weilin Aldragoran; he thought that she would have loved to meet Nynaeve. *See also* Weilin Aldragoran

Aldred Gomaisen. A Cairhienin mercenary captain who took service with Elayne. He shaved and powdered the front of his head and wore stripes of color halfway down his chest though Elayne doubted he was entitled to do so. He turned traitor and took money from Arymilla to seize the Far Madding Gate and let her into the city. The attempt to gain control of the Far Madding Gate failed, and Elayne signed his death warrant, leading to his execution.

Aldrin Caldevwin. A captain in the Cairhienin army in charge of excavating the male Choedan Kal statue. Rand met him in Tremonsien, at The Nine Rings. He was a very minor noble with a single slash of red and one of yellow across his chest. The front of his head was shaved, though his black hair hung long in the back. His *con* had a single white star on a blue background. He was very suspicious of Rand and tried to trick him with a question about Gareth Bryne. He was loyal to Cairhien and adaptable. Once he learned that Rand was the Dragon Reborn, Caldevwin saw him as a necessary evil, both in his saving of Cairhien from the Shaido and for saving the world. He was surprised to learn that the Dragon Reborn was the same young man he had encountered in Tremonsien.

Aldwyn, Sybaine. *See* Sybaine Aldwyn

Aledrin Malenry. A Taraboner Aes Sedai of the White Ajah and the rebel contingent, with a strength level of 24(12). Born with the spark in 950 NE, she went to the White Tower in 964 NE. After nine years as a novice and six years as Accepted, she was raised to the shawl in 979 NE. Aledrin had no Warder. She was stout and despite her dark golden hair and chocolate-brown eyes, she didn't look all that pretty until she smiled, but then she looked quite beautiful. She stood between 5'4" and 5'5" tall, and sometimes wore her shoulder-length hair caught in a lacy white net. As Accepted, she was considered rather excitable. She was considered to have a prototypical White logic, but also a degree of practicality and worldliness that was for the most part foreign to Whites. These qualities might have weighed against her choice as a Sitter at any other time, but under the conditions in Salidar, they were considered useful. Despite her youth, she was elected Sitter in 999 NE. As the youngest after Kwamesa, she had certain responsibilities in the Hall, such as enjoining those reporting to the Hall. She was part of a group of rebel Aes Sedai that went to the Black Tower to bond Asha'man Warders in keeping with Rand's offer to let them bond forty-seven.

Aleis Barsalla. The stately First Counsel of Far Madding. She was 5'7" tall, with long black hair heavily winged with white, and an unlined face. Compassion and wisdom filled her large dark eyes, and it was command that she radiated, not simple authority. She had a mellifluous voice that was deep for a woman. Cadsuane had corrected a bad habit of Aleis' around the time of the Aiel War. After Nynaeve channeled in Far Madding and Rand was imprisoned, Cadsuane persuaded Aleis to let him go. Aleis was deposed shortly after that.

Aleis Romlin. An Aes Sedai of the Green Ajah who served as Amyrlin from 890 to 922 NE. Aleis was chosen after Cadsuane Melaidhrin fled the Tower rather than be chosen. Aleis was a weak Amyrlin. It was not that she did not have a strong personality; she just did not know her way in the politics of the Tower, a fact that may well have played its part in her selection. The secret records say that the Sitters realized their close call after Cadsuane fled—they had nearly lumbered themselves with another Sereille—and so went to the other extreme, choosing a woman who had no interest in running the White Tower and no ability in administration or consensus making. Aleis herself wanted only to be out in the world; the secret records say that she was watched closely and several times stopped from leaving Tar Valon—in effect, from sneaking out—and that, coupled with her knowledge that she was entirely unsuited for the position, forced her to cooperate, if somewhat sullenly, with being a puppet of the Hall and mouthing the words given her by the Hall.

Alene al'Vere. Egwene's second-eldest sister. She was born in 969 NE and allowed to braid her hair at sixteen, for she was considered very levelheaded. She was a bookworm, always reading about far-off lands. She never married, as some people suspected she might not. Alene accepted suitors, but she felt none were satisfactory for a husband. Some thought she'd run off to see the world. She wanted to be tested by Verin and Alanna, who refused because of her age, and put up enough of a fuss that Marin had to take a firm hand with her. It would possibly turn out that she could learn to channel, with a fair potential.

Alentaine, Teire. *See* Teire Alentaine

Aleria Elffin. An author of humorous tales.

Aleshin Talvaen. The leader of the Ghealdanin contingent at the Battle of the Shining Walls, and a Lord of the High Crown Council in Ghealdan. He was flogged by Masema for having expressed contempt for the word of the Lord Dragon.

Alesinde. The daughter of Ishara, and her successor to the throne of Andor. She reigned from FY 1020 to 1035.

Alesune Chulin. A woman who served as *shatayan* to King Easar of Shienar. She was the head housekeeper responsible for directing the servants in the operation of the estate, but she had further duties similar to a minister of state. Alesune was about 5'5" tall, and slim, pretty and fiery. She had determined eyes and thin white streaks in her long black hair. Alesune seemed born to her silks. Taking her at first glance could be a mistake; she was very sharp-witted, and anyone who thought her title as *shatayan* of the royal household meant her influence was restricted to ordering the maids and cooks and victualers was making a grave mistake.

Aleth nin Taerin alta Camora. The Breaking of the World, by an unknown author, cited in the epigraph at the beginning of *The Eye of the World.*

Aleth-Loriel. A place whose fall was a result of Mordeth's evil in Aridhol. It was the subject of a song in a gleeman's tale, "The Fall of Aleth-Loriel."

Alfara, Mistress. The innkeeper at The Bellon Ford Inn in Amadicia, where Elayne and Nynaeve stayed as Lady Morelin and Nana. She made Nynaeve take care of Elayne's needs instead of having her staff do it.

algai'd'siswai. Old Tongue for "the spear fighters" or "fighters of the spear." The name was given to those Aiel who carried the spear and regularly took part in battle, as opposed to those who followed crafts.

Algarin Pendaloan. A Tairen Lesser Lord of the Land, whose channeling brother Emarin was captured by Cadsuane. Rand and his group stayed at Algarin's manor house. He went to the Black Tower to be tested, and there took the name Emarin. Taim attempted to Turn him, but he resisted and went on to fight in the Last Battle.

algode. A plant fiber used by the Aiel.

Algoran. A noble House of Amadicia; Lady Marande was the sister of its High Seat.

Alguenya, River. A river situated east of Tar Valon flowing south to meet the River Gaelin just above Cairhien, then joining the River Erinin at Aringill.

Algwyn. The last man to sit on the Crystal Throne of Seanchan; he ruled over a thousand years before the Seanchan returned to the lands east of the Aryth Ocean. He was considered insane by some because he let his *Soe'feia* live and continue in her post after she slapped his face before the entire court.

Alhandrin Torelvin. A nobleman of a minor Cairhienin House and an officer in the Band of the Red Hand. He commanded the Third Banner of Horse.

Alhanra. A scout in the Children of the Light. Alhanra found Gawyn, badly injured, in the Last Battle, and led Galad to him.

Alharra, Furen. *See* Furen Alharra

Aliane Senican. An Aes Sedai of the White Ajah who served as Amyrlin from 332 to 355 NE. Aliane began as a strong Amyrlin, but her notions of running things according to logic—and her rages when others failed to see her logic—led by

339 NE to her becoming not so much a puppet of the Hall as ignored by them except when she had to be trotted out for ceremonies.

Alianelle Spring. A source of water and an oasis four days' ride from Dumai's Wells, between Cairhien and Tar Valon.

Alida Aldragoran. The wife of Weilin; he thought that she would have loved to meet Nynaeve.

Alievin, Doniella. *See* Doniella Alievin

Alight in the Snow. A book read by Graendal.

Aligning the Matrix. A Talent described by Moghedien as a way to make metals stronger.

Alijha. A young Jenn Aiel man who accompanied Lewin to rescue their sisters from bandits. They killed the bandits, and were disowned by their families.

Alin. A cavalry leader in Ituralde's army at Maradon.

Alin Seroku. A Kandori officer who commanded Lord Varan's guards at Canluum. Seroku had soldiered forty years along the Blight. Lan and Bukama met him while he was guarding the gate of Canluum; he warned them to keep the peace. He was bluff and graying with a white-scarred face.

Alind Dyfelle. A legendary Aes Sedai of the Gray Ajah. Merana thought her impressive, and felt that when Kiruna and Bera first saw Cadsuane, it must have struck them the same way seeing Alind would strike her.

Alindaer. A large bridge village just southwest of Tar Valon on the bank of the Alindrelle Erinin, on the road to Caemlyn. Alindaer was practically a town, with brick houses of two or even three stories roofed in blue tiles, and its own inns and shops and markets. It was burned at least three times during the Trolloc Wars, once during the War of the Second Dragon and twice during Hawkwing's siege of Tar Valon. Moiraine and Siuan gathered information there on women who had given birth near Dragonmount during the Aiel War.

Alindaer Gate. The most southerly bridge gate to the west out of Tar Valon; it led to the town of the same name.

Alindrelle Erinin. The southwestern split of the River Erinin that bifurcated at Tar Valon.

Alindrelle Gates. The southernmost gates of the White Tower.

Alis. A plump maid in the Tarasin Palace in Ebou Dar who Olver thought was sweet; she helped him move into his rooms.

Alise Tenjile. A Taraboner Kinswoman. Her strength level was 46(34), just below the minimum at which a woman would be allowed to test for Aes Sedai, and not strong enough for her to make a gateway of any size whatsoever. She was born in 819 NE, went to the White Tower in 835 NE. She was a novice for two and a half years. Parenia Demalle was Amyrlin at the time, and Sereille Bagand was Mistress of Novices. When met by Elayne and Nynaeve, she was a pleasant-appearing woman apparently in her middle years. There were light touches of gray in her dark brown hair. She was about 5'5" tall and of medium build, and carried herself with a straight back. Her face was unremarkable, mild usually, with a jaw that was perhaps a little long. Her smile could be warm and comforting or quite stern. People tended to do what she said without her raising her voice—even those who didn't know her. Alise ran the farm outside Ebou Dar until forced by the Seanchan to flee. Alise was not the oldest at the farm, but running it was her job, and that put her in charge of women who were older than she. She did not suffer fools gladly, and though she was not so acerbic about it as Nynaeve, she simply did not put up with foolishness, or with bending the rules, much less breaking them. The rules were what had kept the Kin safe all those years. For instance, when a noblewoman balked at being herded inside after the arrival of Nynaeve and her group, Nynaeve shouted at her, but Alise simply grabbed her by the scruff of the neck, hustled her inside despite voluble protests and did something in there to make her squawk like a huge goose that had been stepped on. Reanne considered Alise very intelligent, and also formidable, and she was indeed both. Alise felt that a chance to go back to the Tower was all very well for women like Reanne, who had some chance to become Aes Sedai, but she wondered about why she and the rest should. Alise was not so accepting of the Aes Sedai as the Knitting Circle and most other Kinswomen, in large part because she considered the offer of return mere trumpery in her case. In many ways, she behaved toward them exactly as she behaved toward any other woman—which is to say, she was rather dominant if not exactly dominating— and she rarely if ever allowed any degree of challenge or bitterness to show in it. While she didn't know how she could manage it, she quickly began coming around to the notion of somehow keeping the Kin going for women such as herself, who simply could not become Aes Sedai. When Elayne approached her with a plan to do just that, she readily agreed. Alise stayed with Elayne and the Kin when they went to Caemlyn, and presumably took part in the Last Battle.

Alivia. A *damane* from Seanchan who was captured by Rand's army. Though she looked in her forties, she had been *damane* for four hundred years, and was very strong in the Power: her strength level was 1(+12), the top level for women. Alivia had been collared at thirteen or fourteen. She had hawk-like blue eyes with fine lines at the corners, and golden yellow hair with a few threads of white. She was a handsome woman rather than beautiful, with a husky, throaty voice that men found appealing. She was 5'5" tall, of medium build and filled with intensity; she practically bristled with it. Many people found her intimidating, but Sharina had her measure, and became her friend. She was sent to Elayne in Caemlyn, and her collar was removed. She became very loyal to Rand, whom she considered as having given her her freedom. She appointed herself Rand's protector, told him about the Seanchan and how their military operated, and had a short way with those she considered Rand's enemies. Once she had come around to embracing her freedom, Alivia said that she wanted to kill all the *sul'dam*. Slowly. She insisted on going with Nynaeve and Lan when they accompanied Rand. She had no particular interest in being Aes Sedai, and would be surprised to learn that she had no choice, under the agreement that would be made between the Aes Sedai and the Kin. She was just about completely ignorant of men, and sexual matters. Min had a viewing showing that Alivia would help Rand die, and Min disliked her because of it. Alivia gathered supplies for Rand's final escape after the Last Battle, thus fulfilling Min's viewing.

Alix. A Warder who lost his Aes Sedai in the Last Battle and joined Galad to fight on and avenge her.

Alkaese, Zarya. *See* Zarya Alkaese

Alkindar. A tiny walled town on the west bank of the River Eldar in Altara. Alkindar was made up of tile-roofed stone buildings with half a dozen stone docks. A ferry ran from here to Coramen on the other side of the Eldar; it was an important crossing. The Seanchan had a camp outside the town. Luca's show took the ferry across the river from Alkindar to Coramen.

Alkohima, Tamore. A Domani seamstress in Tar Valon from whom Moiraine and Siuan ordered dresses.

All Summers. A prosperous neighborhood in the city of Tear which was stricken by a bubble of evil.

Alliandre Maritha Kigarin. The Queen of Ghealdan, Blessed of the Light, Defender of Garen's Wall and a dozen more titles. Her sign was the Wolfhound, a running dog with a crested ridge of black hair down its back. On her banner, the dog was dark golden except for the ridge of hair, on a red field. She was born in 972 NE. About 5'4" tall, she had dark hair almost to her waist. She was quite lovely despite a nose perhaps too long for beauty. She had an aloof air and bore herself with stately reserve and grace. Alliandre was somewhat under the Crown High Council's collective thumb, especially the highest-ranking noble. They removed her predecessors in one way or another, and put her on the throne. They stood aside for some time because she seemed to have handled the Prophet well, or at least kept his depredations to a minimum. She learned of the fall of Amador, the Seanchan's taking of Ebou Dar, and that Rand conquered Illian, all by spreading rumors and by reports from merchants, who learned by pigeon. Consequently, she swore allegiance to Perrin. She was captured by the Shaido and later freed by Perrin. Alliandre rode with her forces in the Last Battle.

Allin. A dark-haired Andorman, with a half-beard shaved at the sides, who served under Uno in the Last Battle.

Allorallen. An Ogier-built city in Jaramide, one of the Ten Nations after the Breaking. Bandar Eban later occupied the same site.

Allwine, Rulan. *See* Rulan Allwine

Almadar. A noble House of Arad Doman including King Alsalam and Ramsid.

Alman, Dumera. An Aes Sedai who lived at the time of the formation of the White Tower.

Almandaragal. High Lady Suroth's *lopar*.

Almen Bunt. An old Andoran farmer. He had a well-wrinkled, leathery face, half his teeth were missing, and his hands were gnarled, but his old man's voice was strong, as was his body. Bunt met Rand and Mat outside The Goose and

Crown and gave them a ride to Caemlyn. He traveled at night to avoid the merchants' dust. He went to Caemlyn, which he thought was the grandest city there was, to see Logain, but stayed to support Morgase. When Morgase was under Rahvin's influence, Bunt got into trouble for being a good Queen's man, and left Caemlyn and went to his sister's farm to help with her orchards after her husband died. He saw Rand when Rand came down from Dragonmount. Bunt went with other farmers to Merrilor and joined in the Last Battle.

Almindhra. The First Counselor of Tova, a nation that arose after the Trolloc Wars, located at the same site as Cairhien. Almindhra was one of three who sent armies into Shandalle against Artur Hawkwing in FY 943.

Almizar. A prosperous town in Amadicia, a hundred miles southwest of Amador. It was set in farm country with stone-walled pastures and thatch-roofed stone houses. Six tall watchtowers sat on its perimeter, but the town had no wall. The streets were paved with granite blocks, and lined with solid buildings of brick or stone, some gray, some black, many three or four stories high and most roofed in dark slate, the rest in thatch. Perrin and Tylee negotiated the acquisition of all the forkroot being cultivated here by the Seanchan. This was also where a Seanchan clerk died, filled with beetles; and where Perrin was almost assassinated by arrows.

Almoren. One of the Ten Nations. Its capital was Al'cair'rahienallen, later known as Cairhien; another city was Jennshain. Its king was Coerid Nosar at the signing of the Compact.

Almoren, Queen of. Her Right Hand, Jurith Dorine, wrote *Commentaries on the Prophecies of the Dragon*. Her rule included the year 742 AB in the Third Age.

Almoth. A nation that rose from the War of the Hundred Years. Its banner was blue for the sky above, black for the earth below, with the spreading Tree of Life to join them.

Almoth Plain. The former site of the nation of Almoth, lying between Tarabon and Arad Doman along the Aryth Ocean. Those two countries fought over it for over four hundred years.

Alms, Fellowship of. The beggars' guild in Ebou Dar.

Almurat Mor. A Seanchan Seeker for Truth, about 5'10" tall, with yellow hair and blue eyes. He was in his middle years and good-looking, if too slender for Egeanin's taste. As a Seeker, he had tattoos of a raven, a sign that he was property of the Imperial family, as were most Seekers for Truth and all of the Deathwatch Guards, and a tower, a sign that he was a Seeker, on each shoulder. His position was identified by a small, flat gold-bordered ivory plaque that he carried, engraved with a raven, the sign of the Imperial House, and behind it the Tower of Ravens, a symbol of Imperial justice. He was supposedly checking up on efforts to find and eliminate renegade *sul'dam*. He was suspicious of Egeanin. He thought that Tuon had been kidnapped in a White Tower operation led by Thom Merrilin. Mor believed in a complicated plot between Suroth and the White Tower involving Egeanin, among others. The disappearance of

Egeanin, Bethamin and two other *sul'dam*, along with two *damane* who were Aes Sedai, confirmed this in his mind, but he felt that moving too openly might endanger Tuon. Mor also believed there had been some corruption of the levels of Seekers above him. He shared his beliefs with Karede, who bought into the notion provisionally.

Alnora. A Jenn Aiel woman who lived during the Breaking. Her husband was Jonai, and she was mother to Adan and Willim.

Aloisia Nemosni. The oldest member of the Kin. She was nearly six hundred years old and her strength level was at least 17(5) or 18(6). She was working as an oil merchant in Tear when Elayne and Nynaeve learned of the Kin. Elayne wondered if she would fall over dead if made to take the Three Oaths.

Alpert Mull. An Andoran farmer living between Four Kings and Market Sheran. He was a stolid man with a square face and square hands, both worn and grooved from hard work and worry. He wanted someone to talk to, and gave Rand and Mat a ride as well as scarves.

Alqam. A city or region in Seanchan that had pale-eyed inhabitants. While battling Rand's army, Miraj thought about the named, honored regiments from different parts of Seanchan that were represented among his troops, including Alqam.

Alraed, Desandre. *See* Desandre Alraed

Alric. Siuan's Warder. He was killed the day she was deposed.

Alrom. An ancient scholar who wrote of Mesaana's schools in the War of Power.

Alruddin, Katerine. *See* Katerine Alruddin

Alsahhan, Sorelana. A scholar in the time of the Trolloc Wars who wrote about Darkhounds.

Alsalam Saeed Almadar. The King of Arad Doman, Lord of Almadar, High Seat of House Almadar. He was elected by the Council of Merchants, which could remove him with a three-quarter vote. His whereabouts became something of a mystery; he was kidnapped by Elaida, and the Shadow used his absence to its favor. Alsalam seemed to issue a stream of contradictory orders to Ituralde and others, but they in fact came from Graendal. He was found by Rand and rejoined Rodel Ituralde, but was killed in the Last Battle.

Alsbet Luhhan. The wife of Haral Luhhan, the blacksmith of Emond's Field. She was born in 955 NE. Alsbet was a big woman—not as large as her husband, but still as big as most men and almost as strong as her husband, and her temper was worse than his. It was a toss-up whether Alsbet or Daise Congar was the strongest woman in the Two Rivers. She had a round face and a gray braid. She and Haral had no children, but when Haral took on Perrin as an apprentice, he lived with them. Alsbet and Haral were arrested by Whitecloaks. At first it was only Haral the Whitecloaks wanted, but Alsbet made such a fuss, assaulting several Whitecloaks with a blunt instrument, that she was arrested as well. Perrin gathered a group of friends and freed them. She helped organize the defense of Emond's Field.

Alsera. A Wise One of the Salt Flat sept of the Nakai Aiel. She served as Bruan's Wise One at Shiagi Hold. Although she was not a dreamwalker, the dream-walkers spoke to her in the dream.

Alshinn, Ellaine Marise'idin. The translator of *The Karaethon Cycle: The Prophecies of the Dragon.*

Alstaing, Mistress. A Taraboner lacquerware merchant who played *Piri* in The White Ring in Maderin, the "hell" to which Mat and Thom brought Tuon and Selucia. Mat diced with the woman and the other gamblers with her, to his own benefit.

Altalin, Lady. A noblewoman of Amadicia who served as a lady-in-waiting to Morgase under the command of Pedron Niall. She had a plump face and made a bad pun about Galad. After Ailron's Disaster, she became a *da'covale*, likely in some menial capacity such as a chambermaid or kitchen helper.

Altara. A nation in the south. Little unified it except the name. The people of Altara thought of themselves as inhabitants of a town or village, or as this lord's or that lady's people, first, and only second if at all as Altaran. Few nobles paid taxes to the crown or offered more than lip service, if that. Its capital, Ebou Dar, rose on the ground that was once a city called Barashta, in the nation of Eharon, before and during the Trolloc Wars, though the major part of that city lay on land where the Rahad later stood. Altara's sigil was two golden leopards, one above the other: it was referred to as the Golden Leopards or simply the Leopards. Its banner was the Golden Leopards on a field checked four-by-four in red and blue; red was next to the staff on the topmost row.

The Trolloc Wars did not truly envelop Eharon until late, but not a stone remained in the present that could be linked to Barashta, the city having been destroyed by Trollocs. Altara was founded circa FY 1112 by Lord Maddin Todande, who claimed to be a descendant of the last Queen of Shiota and may actually have been so. Numerous earlier attempts to reestablish Shiota had failed, though one, early in the War of the Hundred Years, lasted for fifty years and three rulers. Maddin saw that the old nations were finished and made his claim to a new nation. His success was no doubt aided by the end of the war only five years after he was crowned. King Maddin and his first three successors were strong and respected rulers over a strong and increasingly wealthy land—at least, increasingly wealthy once the war finally ended. Approximately one hundred years after the war, however, Anarina Todande ascended to the throne, a capricious ruler at best and incompetent at worst. During her reign, Altara sank into the near anarchy which prevailed until the arrival of the Seanchan. In the space of twenty years, Anarina drained the national treasury and impoverished House Todande; she was deposed and murdered, and her House never recovered. No House after Todande held the throne of Altara for more than two generations until Beslan, the son of Tylin, became king, although he ruled only with the permission of the Seanchan.

The Seanchan occupation of the city was not easy at first, but it was relatively benevolent. The Seanchan, in effect, simply overlaid their system on top of the one that was already there. Seanchan soldiers were as subject to law as the people in the conquered territory. There was little interference with local custom; duels were not outlawed, but the Seanchan required that they be witnessed, and combatants were required to pay a fee. Street crime was cleared up, and corrupt magistrates were replaced; looting became minimal, though taxes had been imposed, and there were fines. Some holdings of corrupt officials and nobles involved with them were confiscated, and the owners themselves made property. Tylin, and then Beslan, reached an accommodation. The crown was retained and recognized by the Seanchan, with a pledge to uphold the Empress; in return, looting was stopped, and the present laws were left in effect, though Seanchan law held as well. Part of the taxes went to the crown, more than had been collected before, and the Seanchan recognized the crown as ruler over all of Altara, with nobles who refused acknowledgment and fealty (and by implication the Empress) held to be in rebellion and subject to confiscation and enslavement. This deal left the crown better off than before, with a chance to unify Altara.

Given the political situation in Altara, one could not say that there was any sort of national army. When an army was raised, it consisted of the levies of various nobles, who usually squabbled over the command and were known to take their soldiers away from the army because of such quarrels even in dire circumstances. Altara never had a standing force such as the Queen's Guards in Andor or the Defenders of the Stone in Tear. Any ruler who attempted to form such a group would have been pulled down immediately by the nobles, jealous of their own power.

Altara had even more regional differences in custom than most other lands. For example, the marriage knife was an Ebou Dari custom, not found more than fifty to a hundred miles from the city; dueling customs, on the other hand, were much more widespread. The marriage knife was one that Ebou Dari women wore on a necklace, hanging hilt-down; it was part of the marriage proposal and marriage ceremony, and was given to the woman with the words "To kill me if my heart proves untrue." It was sometimes used for just that. A woman in Ebou Dar who killed her husband was presumed to have had justification unless proven otherwise. This extended to other women who killed men, to a large extent. The knife was fairly small, but its four-inch blade could reach vital organs. The necklace alone was worn as a sign that a woman was betrothed. There was a system of colored stones on the hilt of the knife marking sons and daughters, living and dead: a white stone for each son and a red stone for each daughter. A red border around a son's stone or a red setting indicated that he died from a duel; a white border or white setting did the same for a daughter. A black setting showed that the child died from another cause. Women saw a red or white setting as a source of pride, whether the stones were pearls and firedrops or colored glass. Many Ebou Dari women removed the stones of their children past sixteen who refused a duel, and never acknowledged them again.

A widow used a white sheath on her marriage knife to signify that she had no intention of marrying again, a blue sheath meant a widow who was looking, or at least available, a green sheath indicated a married woman with a husband living, and a red sheath indicated a married woman who had forbidden her husband the house. Red and blue together meant divorced and willing to try again.

Ebou Dar was in many ways very matriarchal. In the vicinity of the city, it was women who asked men to marry; for a man to ask was considered incredibly pushy and overbold. Farther out in Altara, either men or women could ask, though in the north, close to Andor, the custom was for men to do the asking. In Altara, it was not at all uncommon for a woman to make arrangements as to who her husband would marry if she died. This custom was more common in the south than in the north, but it was done fairly far north by some.

Altarans as a whole were touchy about their honor. The region around Ebou Dar was where folk were the touchiest. While no more took part in dueling than anywhere else in Altara, both men and women around the city (especially commoners) had a custom of knife, and occasionally whip, duels, surrounded by elaborate custom, and while men rarely challenged women, women could and did challenge men. Elaborate rules and customs governed duels. Lower classes were prohibited from dueling with swords or on horseback. Duels among upper-class men were much more likely to involve swords, but they, too, often used daggers. Duels could be to the death, but most were to first blood. The victor in a mortal duel was required to pay a condolence call on the widow or widower if there was one. These visits could be sticky for a number of reasons, ranging from the bereaved's desire for revenge to a desire to be consoled in the age-old fashion. It was accepted as gospel that noblewomen did not fight duels, but it was widely known that they did; one was simply not supposed to acknowledge the fact. Women had their own customs and rituals for duels, and shrouded them in deepest secrecy.

Around Ebou Dar, certain crafts, trades and property rights belonged to men and certain others to women. Others were open. For example, wine and ale (though ale and beer were not popular among the locals) could be made and sold by either sex. And while only men could own ships, either sex could act as a broker for the cargoes. Women could own land, keep inns, weave cloth, sell fish or fowl to the public and butcher anything smaller than cows. Men could own or build ships or boats, keep alehouses and taverns that had no rooms to let, fish, weave rugs and butcher cows.

In and around Ebou Dar, death, daggers and the sea were considered female. Ships, swords and trade were considered male.

Altara produced fine lacquerwork and was famed for its lace. It also produced carpets and tapestries, although these were not considered of the best. There were many olive orchards in Altara, providing oil for lamps and cooking. They harvested salt from salt wells. From the waters around Altara came pearls, mother-of-pearl and fish. Shipping and shipbuilding were big business in Ebou

Dar, which was a major port, serving a considerable portion of what lay inland. They had a major portion of the trade coming out of Amadicia and Ghealdan, for example, and a good deal from Tarabon as well.

Altara Causeway. A wide, packed dirt road leading from Illian to roads reaching Altara and Murandy. It lay on the other side of the River Manetherendrelle and was reached by ferry.

Altaran Marches. The place where Dyelin's father died in a skirmish.

Altaran Noon. An expression referring to the pressure applied by Altarans that made the nation too hot to hold an occupying force of Whitecloaks.

Alteima. A High Lady of Tear who was the wife of Tedosian. She was tall and slender with large brown eyes and long black hair hanging halfway to her waist. She was High Lord Carleon's lover as well as High Lord Tedosian's wife, and when Tedosian arranged Carleon's death, she poisoned Tedosian. Tedosian was given into Estanda's care, however, and recovered. Alteima was given the task of seeing to the transfer of relief supplies to Cairhien by Rand, but she fled instead, knowing that not only would Tedosian try for revenge, but Estanda also hated her and would take any chance to bring her down. She fled to Andor, and became enthralled by Rahvin. She was one of seven women he kept as pets in addition to Morgase. She was in the Royal Palace when Rand took over and she fled, as did Rahvin's other pets. The death of Rahvin caused the effects of Compulsion to fade; she had the memory of things that happened, but no understanding of why. She was deathly afraid of returning to Tear and her estates, so she became a refugee and found work as a lady's maid.

Althyn Conly. A Two Rivers novice with the rebel Aes Sedai. She tried to convert two cups to *cuendillar* at the same time as Bode Cauthon and wound up with an unusable lump.

Aludra Nendenhald. An Illuminator and onetime Mistress of the chapter house in Cairhien. She was born in 959 NE. A pretty woman, slender and about 5'5" tall, she had large dark eyes and a small full mouth that seemed on the point of a pout, or a kiss. She usually wore her dark hair in a multitude of slim braids that went halfway down her back, but later, in Amadicia, she wore it loose because of feelings there about Taraboners. Her Taraboner accent was thick, and, by nature, she kept to herself. She lost her position at the Cairhien chapter house after events which led to riots, the burning of the granaries, the death of the King and civil war. One of the events was the burning of the chapter house when Rand and Loial sought refuge there from Trollocs and accidentally set off a display intended for Galldrian. Aludra fled, pursued by Tammuz and other men from the guild, and in a barn in Aringill was rescued from them by Mat, who was accompanied by Thom. As a reward, she gave Mat some fireworks, which he eventually used to blow an arrowslit in the Stone of Tear wide enough for him to enter. She was an experimenter, and one thing she worked on which she thought would make her fortune was what she sometimes called "strikers" and sometimes "firesticks," which were kept in holes drilled into a block of wood to keep them from rubbing against one another, which sometimes made them ignite. She joined Valan Luca's traveling show, where she encountered Thom once again, though she refused to acknowledge him. She also met Elayne and Nynaeve, though she knew them only by their traveling personae, as well as Juilin and Birgitte. With the circus, she was in Ebou Dar when the Seanchan invested the city. The Seanchan were not interested in fireworks, though— something that irritated Aludra no end—since the Sky Lights produced by trained *damane* were much more spectacular. She met Mat again there, and traveled with him when he left Luca's show. They developed the idea of "dragons" which fired shells that Aludra called dragons' eggs. The dragons were transported on wagons called dragon carts. They were used to great effect in the Last Battle.

Alvera Ramosanya. An Aes Sedai of the Yellow Ajah who served as Amyrlin from 549 to 578 NE. Alvera was a weak Amyrlin, though a woman with all the personal force and arrogance expected of her Ajah. The Hall, having gained another taste of power under her two predecessors, chose her because they calculated her personality and abilities closely and were not willing to let go. She continually attempted to establish her leadership, but failed miserably and died embittered, at a relatively young age for an Aes Sedai who died neither in a war nor an accident; she was only 248. There was some possibility that her death actually was by assassination caused by one of her attempts to assert authority going very badly wrong.

Alviarin Freidhen. An Amadician Aes Sedai of the White Ajah publicly and the Black Ajah in truth. She was a member of the loyalist contingent, with a strength level of 17(5). Born in 943 NE near the border with Tarabon, she went to the White Tower in 959 NE. After five years as a novice and five years as Accepted, she was raised to the shawl in 969 NE. She was 5'4" tall and slim with brown eyes, dark brown hair and slim hands. She was cool, calm and icy except when she meant to be sarcastic or cutting. Alviarin became a Darkfriend in 958 NE after murdering another girl. Darkfriends helped cover it up; the other girl was thought to have run away from home. In 959 NE she was asked to kill a young man who, she was told, had learned something about the Darkfriends and meant to turn them in. She seduced him and stabbed him at the base of the skull while they were in bed; she never lost her composure. She was watched by the Black Ajah from her first day in the Tower. Although no Black sister revealed herself, Alviarin was secretly contacted by the Black and tested a number of times as Accepted; she spied on Aes Sedai, never knowing whether the one she was spying on might be Black Ajah herself and so able to tell perfectly whether she reported correctly. In 968 NE she murdered another Accepted on Black orders, the only real friend she had during her time in the Tower. She was informed beforehand that the only reason for the killing was for her to prove that she would obey whatever orders were given her. She strangled the girl without hesitation. The Black Ajah covered it up, making it seem that the woman had run away. In 983 NE, she was handpicked by Ishamael to head the Black Ajah, replacing Jarna Malari, whom Ishamael killed for her part in the male channeler pogrom. She plotted with Elaida to depose Siuan Sanche, and was rewarded by being named Keeper of the Chronicles. When she learned of the disaster at Dumai's Wells, she used that knowledge to coerce Elaida into causing divisions in the Tower. She was sent away from the Tower by Mesaana, and during her absence, Elaida replaced her as Keeper and ordered punishment for her daily. The arrival of the rebels outside Tar Valon had dispelled her power over Elaida. She summoned Mesaana in panic; during their meeting, Shadar Haran came to punish Mesaana for not appearing at Shadar Logoth; he marked Alviarin as his and ordered her to find those who were searching for the Black Ajah. Alviarin was identified as a member of the Black Ajah in Verin's book, but she fled the Tower before she could be captured. She fought against Egwene in *Tel'aran'rhiod*, but escaped from that conflict as well. She bonded the Asha'man Nensen, and fought in the Last Battle. Alviarin, Nensen and others were lured by Androl into a *stedding* and captured by Ogier.

Alvistere. A Cairhienin novice in the White Tower. She was short and slim with big eyes and long dark hair. She had reached a strength where she could be tested for Accepted. She tripped Egwene in the dining hall after Egwene was demoted to novice by Elaida; she claimed that if Egwene turned her in, everyone would lie and say nothing had happened. She later came around to Egwene's side and admired her greatly.

Alvon. An Amadician woodcutter, a stocky man with a weathered face and a coarse, almost unintelligible accent, who was *gai'shain* in Sevanna's camp. He and his son Theril, famed for having escaped three times and getting farther each time before recapture, swore to Faile, and Theril procured Therava's binder for Faile.

Alwain, Doesine. *See* Doesine Alwain

Alwhin. A Seanchan *sul'dam* with blue eyes, sharp features, a tight, thin-lipped mouth and a permanent expression of anger. She became *so'jhin*, one of the hereditary upper servants of the Blood, and also a Voice of the Blood to the High Lady Suroth, because she knew too much concerning *sul'dam* and *damane* that Suroth needed to keep hidden, namely that *sul'dam* could be held by an *a'dam*. Afterward, the left side of her head was shaved, and the remnant of her light brown hair was worn in a braid. Her new position made her *da'covale*—a slave— but it was a position with more power and authority than her former place. She was poisoned by Liandrin to gain points, on the day that Suroth and Tylin left Ebou Dar on an inspection trip. Suroth was not pleased, as it brought the attention of the Seekers to her household.

Alwin Rael. A male servant in Lady Arilyn's house in Cairhien who liked to tickle maids' chins. The Aes Sedai embassy that Elaida had sent to Cairhien to escort Rand back to the White Tower were staying with Lady Arilyn. Egwene went to the palace and, detecting channeling inside, used Air and Fire to replicate Moiraine's eavesdropping trick on the inside, and thereby learned about Alwin's proclivities.

Alwyn al'Van. The cobbler in Emond's Field.

Alys. Moiraine's favorite alias.

Alysa. Almen Bunt's sister. She and her husband Graeger had two sons, Hahn and Adim. The family owned an apple orchard. One day Graeger vanished, and nothing but a gray tree was found. Almen went to her to help with the orchard.

Alyse. The name that Galina Casban used after being captured and taken to Perrin.

Amadaine. The seventh month of the year.

Amadicia. A nation in the southwest of the main continent. Its capital was Amador. The sigil of Amadicia was a red thistle leaf laid over a silver six-pointed star: the Thistle and Star. The banner was the Thistle and Star on a field horizontally striped blue and gold; three blue stripes and two yellow.

Although the determination of exact dates is difficult, the most reliable sources state that Amadicia was founded in approximately FY 1023 by Lord Santal Ramoth, a direct descendant of the last King of Kharendor. He began, in FY 1015, by attempting to reestablish Kharendor, but realizing that the people no longer saw Kharendor as a unifying symbol and that many of the resident nobles were from other lands, he deftly changed to the founding of a new nation and was crowned the first King of Amadicia. The Kings of Amadicia were quite powerful rulers, in the beginning, until a decline in the quality of Amadician kings coincided with a rise in the power of the Children of the Light. Eventually, no ruler of Amadicia made any major decisions without checking with the Lord Captain Commander of the Children.

Amadicia was the only land where being able to channel was a crime. Aes Sedai were outlawed, as was channeling, or even being trained in the White Tower. The law was enforced more by Whitecloaks than by the crown, but the crown did not abstain entirely.

The Guardians of the Gate were a permanent formation in the army of Amadicia, serving primarily as the personal bodyguard of the ruler. Perhaps because the Children of the Light were present in Amadicia in such strength, the Guardians were never allowed to enroll more than about a thousand men, and Amadicia's other standing forces, border guards and the like, never numbered more than three to four thousand men except in time of war.

Unlike the nobility in other nations, nobles were not allowed to keep standing forces of any size greater than a small bodyguard, and levies in wartime were raised by the ruler, not by nobles.

Amadicia's last king, Ailron, was killed fighting the Seanchan. Nearly all of the Amadician nobles were either killed or taken *da'covale* by the Seanchan, and all of the Guardians of the Gate were killed, were made *da'covale* or became fugitives after Ailron's Disaster.

Amadicia was known for weaving and dyeing, although its products were not considered as good as Taraboner work. Amador mined a little iron, mined silver and gold in the southern Mountains of Mist, and gems in the south, although some of this area was outside the actual boundaries of Amadicia.

Amador. The capital of Amadicia. It was home to the Seranda Palace and the Fortress of the Light.

Amaena. Leane's alias after she was stilled.

Amaetheon. A feast remembering the dead, not in a sad way, but joyously, celebrated everywhere except the Borderlands on the sixth day of Shaldine.

amahn'rukane, the hand of. A statue near the Jehannah Road that was never finished. It had the appearance of an enormous sword stabbing the earth.

Amalasan, Guaire. *See* Guaire Amalasan

Amaline Paendrag Tagora. The first wife of Artur Hawkwing. He loved her very much, wrote many poems to her and was devastated when she was poisoned and died.

Amalisa Jagad. A Lady of House Jagad in Shienar. Agelmar's sister, Amalisa was short and in her middle years when Rand visited Fal Dara. Liandrin managed to overawe her completely and frighten her with the suggestion that Agelmar might have been the target of Liandrin's—or worse, the Amyrlin's—wrath, and made her enlist the women of Fal Dara keep in an intensive search for Rand when they should have been making arrangements for the banquet for the Amyrlin.

Amar. The mother of Elora and the daughter of Coura, an Ogier. Elora wrote about Aes Sedai in the early days of Hawkwing's reign.

Amaresu. A female Hero of the Horn who carried the Sword of the Sun.

Amaryn. An Aiel woman, the greatdaughter of Sorilea and the greatmother of Taric, who Sorilea thought would be a good husband for Egwene. Amaryn was obviously a woman of some great age.

Amassa, Zemaille. *See* Zemaille Amassa

Amathera Aelfdene Casmir Lounault. A Taraboner woman. She was in born in 974 NE. She was about 5'5" tall and very pretty and slender, with a nice but somewhat small bosom. She had waist-length dark hair, big dark eyes and a pouty rosebud mouth. She became King Andric's lover, and with his support became Panarch. Held prisoner by the Black Ajah, she was freed by Elayne and Nynaeve. When captured by the Seanchan in the fall of Tanchico, she refused to swear the Oaths of Return and was made the property of High Lady Suroth. Given the name Thera, she was forced to dance scandalously clad in a troupe entertaining Suroth. Under those conditions, she lost her petulance and became timid. Rescued by Juilin Sandar in Ebou Dar, she afterward always stayed close to him, as if seeking his protection. She became his lover. *See also* Thera

Amayar. The land-dwelling inhabitants of the Sea Folk islands. Known to few people other than the Atha'an Miere, the Amayar were the craftsmen who made what was known as Sea Folk porcelain. Followers of the Water Way, which prized acceptance of what is rather than what might be wished for, they were very uncomfortable away from the land and only ventured onto the water in small boats for fishing, never leaving sight of land. Their way of life was exceptionally peaceful, and required little oversight from the governors appointed from among the Atha'an Miere. Since the Atha'an Miere governors had little desire to go far from the sea, the Amayar essentially ran their own villages according to their own rules and customs. The Amayar did have prophecies which spoke of "the end times" and "the end of Illusion." Some of these prophecies mentioned the huge hand holding a great crystal sphere which thrust out of a hill on Tremalking. If this sphere were to glow, certain things would happen, certain changes would occur, and certain things had to be done. The destruction of the sphere when Rand cleansed the Source signaled the end of Illusion, and as a result, the Amayar committed mass suicide.

Ambani, Lemai. *See* Lemai Ambani

Ambrey, Merana. *See* Merana Ambrey

Amel din Monaga Stone Anchor. The husband and Swordmaster of Zaida din Parede Blackwing. As Swordmaster, he merited a fringed red parasol of one tier. He wore five small, fat golden rings in each ear. When Zaida became Mistress of the Ships, he became Master of the Blades.

Amellia Arene. A Darkfriend woman in Amador, stern-faced and graying. She and her husband Jorin were rich merchants; their house was taken over by Liandrin and other Black Ajah members. Temaile damaged Jorin in punishment. After Liandrin revolted against Moghedien and was shielded, Moghedien turned her over to Amellia and her male cook Evon as a scullery maid. Amellia put her mind to making Liandrin's life miserable, not only by using her as a scullion in the kitchens and by having her perform as a personal maid, but by having her backside tanned and making sure she was otherwise mistreated on the slightest excuse or none at all. Part of this was making Liandrin the cook's bed-partner, since she so obviously despised him. Suroth might have rewarded them for handing over Liandrin, and she might have made use of them as Darkfriends.

Amenar Shumada. A member of the Seanchan Blood who attended Tuon's first audience in Ebou Dar.

Amerano, Saraline. An Aes Sedai who lived at the time of the formation of the White Tower.

Amhara Market. One of the three markets in Far Madding where foreigners were allowed to trade.

Amhara, Savion. One of the three most famous First Counsels in Far Madding history. A statue of her stood in Amhara Market in Far Madding, pointing to the Tear Gate.

Amico Nagoyin. An Arafellin Aes Sedai of the Yellow Ajah publicly, and of the Black Ajah in truth. She had a strength level of 27(15). Born in 967 NE, she went to the White Tower in 982 NE. After six years as a novice and four years as Accepted, she was raised to the shawl in 992 NE. Slender and pretty, with a long neck, pale skin and big dark eyes, she was a member of the group of thirteen Black Ajah who fled the Tower. She was captured in the Stone of Tear, stilled in the process, and was killed during the Trolloc attack on the Stone, murdered in her cell by Isam/Luc. Her tongue was nailed to the door and her throat slit.

Amira. A daughter of Artur Hawkwing and Amaline Paendrag Tagora. Her twin Modair was killed in battle in FY 959; she, her mother and two siblings were poisoned in FY 961.

Amira Moselle. A Taraboner Aes Sedai of the Red Ajah and the loyalist contingent, with a strength level of 27(15). Born in 823 NE, she went to the White Tower in 839 NE. After eleven years as a novice and nine years as Accepted, she was raised to the shawl in 859 NE. She was stocky and had a square face and brightly beaded braids long enough to flail. Sierin Vayu chose Amira as Mistress of Novices and she later became a Sitter in the Hall of the Tower; she stepped down at the time of Elaida's return to the Tower, allowing Elaida to take her seat and engineer the coup against Siuan. She was a member of the group of Aes Sedai sent by Elaida to kidnap Rand, and was killed in the battle at Dumai's Wells.

Amondrid Osiellin. A Cairhienin nobleman who supported Colavaere for the throne. Moon-faced, he was maybe fifteen to twenty years older than Rand. His wife was Belevaere. Rand summoned him to join his fight against the Seanchan, and he was put under Bashere's command. He was present when Elayne stripped Elenia, Arymilla and Naean of their titles and properties.

Amylia. An Aes Sedai of the Brown Ajah whom Zaida brought back with her from Caemlyn. She volunteered to help teach the Atha'an Miere, hoping to study them, but found that she had the lowly standing of a deckhand, and had to jump when Zaida said "frog."

Amyrlin Seat. The title of the leader of the Aes Sedai. A slightly less formal usage was simply "the Amyrlin." It was also the throne upon which the leader of the Aes Sedai sat. The Amyrlin was elected for life by the Hall of the Tower, the highest council of the Aes Sedai, which consisted of three representatives, called Sitters, from each of the seven Ajahs. The Amyrlin Seat had, theoretically at least, almost supreme authority among the Aes Sedai, and ranked socially as the equal of a king or queen. Other than death or resigning the Amyrlin Seat, the only way she could be removed was to be deposed by the Hall. Choosing an Amyrlin required the greater consensus. Although this could be done with a unanimous vote of eleven Sitters under the proper circumstances, tradition called for all Sitters to be present. Elaida was chosen by eleven only, though, and possibly this tradition had been violated before.

Deposing an Amyrlin also called for the greater consensus, but a truncated one so to speak, for it was specifically stated in the law that the Sitters for the Ajah from which she was raised might not be present when the vote was taken.

Just as the raising of Elaida by a Hall of only eleven Sitters was the basis for doubting her legitimacy, the removal, conviction and sentence to stilling of

Siuan by that same Hall of eleven was the basis for doubting the legitimacy of those actions.

Women were considered by the Hall for the position of Amyrlin Seat, often from a number of candidates. Most of these women were put forward by Sitters, alone or in coalition, but it was possible for any six sisters to propose a candidate. Oddly, the candidate herself did not have to agree and could not withdraw her name. The only way to withdraw, in effect, was to do as Cadsuane did and flee the White Tower.

Consideration of candidates was known to go on for a long time, and votes were seldom taken until a candidate's backers believed that the chances of victory were good. Any candidate could only be voted upon formally three times; if, after three votes, she had not gained the greater consensus, she was out of the running, though she could be proposed again if she was still living when the woman who was raised died.

Any candidate who had the backing of three Sitters, or any six other sisters, could in effect demand that a vote be taken. In truth, when a candidate was proposed by non-Sitters, this in itself constituted such a demand. This was a dangerous procedure, however; if she failed on the third vote, she and her proposers were almost always exiled to separate places for terms that could run from a few years to life, for such demands were considered disruptive and a source of contention.

Strangely, a woman did not actually have to be Aes Sedai in order to be raised Amyrlin. Perhaps because it seemed obvious that she must be, not one word in the laws describing the election or raising of an Amyrlin said that she had to be. On the other hand, the wording of a number of laws—"the Amyrlin as Aes Sedai," etc.—made it clear that the Amyrlin Seat was Aes Sedai.

On being raised Amyrlin, a woman left her old Ajah. The only vestige of it would be if she had a Warder, indicating she was not Red, or if she had more than one, indicating that she was Green. Otherwise, she was supposed to be "of all Ajahs and none." In fact, of course, Amyrlins always remained who they were before and retained many of the beliefs and goals of their old Ajahs; some of the better Amyrlins overcame this, and so did some of the worst. Some of the best behaved as if still of their old Ajah.

Supposedly the Amyrlin had absolute authority, and in fact she did—sort of. An Amyrlin's actual power depended in large part on her real support in the Hall of the Tower, and, among other things, on her own drive and personality. Although the facts were buried deeply in White Tower records, some Amyrlins were no better than puppets for the Hall, or for factions within the Hall.

While the Amyrlin Seat could declare the Tower at war by decree, few had ever done so, preferring to ask—in some cases, just short of demand, or even not short of demanding—that the Hall declare war. While the lesser consensus was much easier to achieve than the greater, the successful prosecution of a war required good, solid backing from and in the Hall of the Tower, something that generally had been easier to obtain in these cases when the Hall had been asked. Then, too, historically, the Hall had been slower and more reluctant to go to war than the Amyrlin—not always the case, but more often so—and an Amyrlin who declared war and then found out that the Hall did not back her was in a fine fix.

An Amyrlin was absolute ruler insofar as she could gain consensus in the Hall, whether the greater or the lesser. She could decree almost anything, and her decrees had the force of law, but many of those could be overturned by the greater consensus, or at least made into only so much hot air, and in most important things she needed the Hall's approval. The purse was a way the Hall could balk an Amyrlin, since if anything she decreed required money to be carried out, the Hall had to vote the funds to finance it. Some of the Amyrlins who were reduced to puppets fell to this. Appropriations needed only the lesser consensus, which still meant two of the three Sitters present.

The Hall could also overturn an Amyrlin's decree, not merely let it die through lack of action. This required the greater consensus, and it was inevitably a prelude to a power struggle. Some of these ended with the Amyrlin a puppet of the Hall. An Amyrlin had the authority to unchair any Sitter or all of them, but a wise Amyrlin did this extremely sparingly. An Ajah could choose the same Sitter again as a rebuke to the Amyrlin. An Amyrlin who unchaired the entire Hall and had the same women all chosen again, or even a significant number of them, very likely found that her real power as Amyrlin was at an end. An Amyrlin could decree any penance for any sister, including Sitters, short of stilling, right up to the most serious punishment of a public birching and/or exile. Some Amyrlins had used this to impose their will by fear, in effect, while others had had the decree backfire on them, causing the Ajahs to turn against her, and with them, of course, the Sitters.

Some Amyrlins were recorded who had taken public penances on themselves for rather vague reasons, according to the Chronicles. At least some of these women in fact were in a precarious position with respect to the Hall, and these penances were a way of regaining support. The Hall could not punish the Amyrlin, but if she took it on herself, it could appease the Sitters to a considerable degree.

Amyrlin, the. *See* Amyrlin Seat

Amys. A Wise One of the Nine Valleys sept of the Taardad Aiel. She was originally *Far Dareis Mai* and became the Wise One of Cold Rocks Hold. She was first-wife of Rhuarc, the clan chief of the Taardad, and Lian (Aviendha's sister-mother) was her sister-wife. Because she was a Wise One, her sister-wife was the roofmistress of Cold Rocks Hold; she could not hold both positions. Amys was the mother of some of Rhuarc's children; she was also sister-mother to Aviendha, since she had adopted Lian as her first-sister. She had sharp blue eyes and prematurely white hair; her hair had been a very light blond when she was

young, but turned white when she was in her early thirties. She was about 5'8"
tall. Amys could channel and was a dreamwalker. She taught Egwene about
Tel'aran'rhiod. Amys, along with Bair, Melaine, Sorilea and some others, either
knew that Aviendha saw herself inside the rings at Rhuidean fated to fall in
love with Rand, or else knew that the plan was to use Aviendha to tie Rand to
the Aiel by giving him an Aiel wife. Amys was among the ninety-three strongest Wise Ones who set out from Cairhien for Dumai's Wells to rescue Rand.
On the way there Amys challenged Sorilea's leadership and they worked out a
compromise. Sorilea retained the leadership, but Amys was often consulted.
She suffered the birth pangs during the adoption ceremony of Aviendha and
Elayne. She fought in the Last Battle near Shayol Ghul.

Anaiya Carel. An Aes Sedai of the Blue Ajah and the rebel contingent, with a
strength level of 15(3). Born in 868 NE, she went to the White Tower in 883
NE. After eight years as a novice and seven years as Accepted, she was raised
to the shawl in 898 NE. About 5'6" tall, with dark hair and a blunt face, she
was a plain-looking, motherly woman. Her smile was her only beauty. She had a
great fondness for ruffles. She was very astute politically, and a first-rate orga-
nizer. She was very good at Healing; she once Healed Moiraine after Lan rode a
horse to death, and nearly ran himself to death carrying Moiraine to her. She
accompanied Siuan to Fal Dara, and tested Egwene to try to determine if Egwene
was a Dreamer. She was also a part of the circle that Healed Mat of the connection to the Shadar Logoth dagger. After Siuan was deposed and stilled,
Anaiya went to Salidar, where she became part of the council that ruled there
until a Hall of the Tower was selected, and she helped to choose Egwene as
Amyrlin. She swore personal fealty to Egwene after Egwene learned that the
council had sent spies to the White Tower. Anaiya was a friend of Janya. Her
Warder was Setagana; both were murdered with the use of *saidin* by Aran'gar.

Anaiyella Narencelona. A High Lady of Tear and a Darkfriend. She was willowy
and darkly beautiful, but her frequent simpering lessened her beauty. Rand
summoned her to join his forces in the fight against the Seanchan; she was not
pleased to be on the field of battle. Her Master of the Horse was killed in the
fighting. Rand then took her to the Sun Palace of Cairhien and ordered her to
go with Darlin and Weiramon to Arad Doman. Without permission, she and
Weiramon traveled to Tear, angering Rand. After he returned from Dragonmount, Rand identified Anaiyella as a Darkfriend and exiled her.

Anan. A family in Ebou Dar. *See* Frielle, Jasfer, Marah, Ross *and* Setalle Anan

Ananda. An Aes Sedai of the Yellow Ajah. She was slim with long black hair.
Min saw an aura around her that indicated that she would die. She did so, in
the Tower fighting when Siuan was deposed.

Anangore. The ninth-largest city in Seanchan.

Anarina Todande. A former queen of Altara. Her family ruled for five generations,
the longest on record, but she was a capricious ruler at best and incompetent at

worst. Anarina drained the national treasury and impoverished House Todande; she was deposed and murdered, and her House never recovered. No House after Todande held the throne of Altara for more than two generations until Beslan became king after Tylin's death.

Anasai of Ryddingwood. A favorite poet of Moiraine.

Anath Dorje. Tuon's Truthspeaker, or *Soe'feia*; she was actually Semirhage in disguise. Slender, and tall even for a man or an Aiel, she dressed in unrelieved black and had a contemptuous air. Her charcoal-dark face, framed by wavy, short black hair, was beautiful but her large black eyes seemed to pierce like awls. *See also* Semirhage

Ancient and Honorable League of Nets. The guild of fishermen in Ebou Dar. A member wore a double earring in his left ear. Stones in the earring indicated how many ships he owned besides the one that he captained. There were no women in the league.

Ancient and Worshipful Guild of Stablemen. The guild for stablemen in Ebou Dar.

Ancarid. The place in Seanchan where Furyk Karede was born.

Ancohima. The Ogier-built capital city of Aelgar, one of the Ten Nations after the Breaking.

Andahar, River. A river in Tarabon flowing west-southwest into Tanchico Bay.

Andaya Forae. A Taraboner Aes Sedai of the Gray Ajah and the loyalist contingent, with a strength level of 24(12). Born in 901 NE, she went to the White Tower in 918 NE. After ten years as a novice and ten more as Accepted, she was raised to the shawl in 938 NE. She was 5'5" tall, with hazel eyes and light brown hair, no longer worn in Taraboner braids, that fell gleaming down her back. Elaida thought of her as neither particularly slim nor particularly short, but Andaya reminded her of a sparrow about to hop from limb to limb. Even her smile seemed sparrow-like to Elaida, perhaps because of the way she held her head. She was an unlikely-appearing negotiator, but in fact she was one of the best, with a well-earned reputation. Serancha Colvine, head of the Grays, ordered Andaya to serve on Elaida's advisory council when Elaida was first raised to the Amyrlin Seat, as both Serancha and Andaya doubted the legality of Siuan's removal and thought it best to keep an eye on Elaida. Andaya thought the world was hanging by a thread and that it was useless to waste precious time with idle speculation, "prattling about supposed logic" or "chattering over what every fool and novice knows." In 999 NE she was surprisingly chosen as Sitter for the Gray in the Tower to replace Varilin Zanaire.

Andaya Murasaka. An acrobat with Valan Luca's show. She was one of six purported sisters that Luca hired away from Sillia Cerano. She had blue eyes and almost white blond hair.

Ander Corl. A bootmaker in the town of Taien in the Jangai Pass. He, his wife and his brother-in-law survived the Shaido attack on their town.

Ander Tol. A skinny, toothless turnip farmer from the south of Cairhien who gave Rand and his companions a ride into Cairhien after the bubble of evil attacked the rebel Cairhienin camp and Fain slashed Rand with the dagger from Shadar Logoth.

Andere. A Malkieri who worked for a time as a Kandori soldier. When he greeted Lan and Bukama at the gates of Canluum, Bukama berated him for swearing to a Kandori lord. Years later, after hearing that Lan was riding across the Borderlands, Andere joined Lan on the Plain of Lances. He fought in Lan's army at Tarwin's Gap in the Last Battle.

Anderly, Sashalle. *See* Sashalle Anderly

Andhilin. A Maiden of the Red Salt Goshien. Her name appeared on Rand's list of women who died for him.

Andiama. A Tairen noble House. *See* Estean *and* Torean Nelondara Andiama

Andil. A woman who worked in the kitchen of the Sun Palace in Cairhien. She fussed over Karldin and Loial when they arrived there.

andilay. A root used medicinally to relieve fatigue, to clear the head and to treat sore muscles.

Andomeran, Rianna. *See* Rianna Andomeran

Andor. One of the largest and oldest nations of the land. Its capital was Caemlyn. The sigil of Andor was a rampant white lion: the White Lion. Its banner was a white lion rampant on a field of red. Its battle cry was "Forward the White Lion!"

Andor was founded circa FY 994 by Lady Ishara and Lord Souran Maravaile, then holding little more than the city of Caemlyn, with Ishara crowned as the first Queen of Andor, which was one of Hawkwing's provinces. She became queen rather than he king for the simple reason that she was native to the province, while he was from the Borderlands, most probably from Jaramide. In addition to facing opposition from those who wanted to reestablish the nation of Caembarin and those who wanted to seize the city for a reestablished nation of Esandara, they also confronted men and women who wanted to take all of Hawkwing's empire, and those who merely wanted to create a new nation of their own as well. Ishara followed a policy of slow assimilation, only gradually increasing her holdings and never moving on until she was sure that what she had taken was firmly in her grasp. Andor grew to stretch from the Mountains of Mist to the River Erinin. Its population was approximately ten million people. The Two Rivers lay within Andor, although Two Rivers folk ignored the fact.

Prior to the recruitment and changes made by Gaebril/Rahvin, the Queen's Guards were the only permanent formation of the Andoran army, providing not only a bodyguard for the Queen, but some policing in Caemlyn, border guards, and patrols to keep order in the countryside. They then numbered perhaps ten thousand men in total. The Queen's Guards seldom went farther west than Breen's Spring unless called for. Gaebril/Rahvin replaced most of the men in Caemlyn with his own recruits, increased the numbers of the Guards, and recruited another formation called the White Lions. Many men loyal to Morgase left the Guards, disliking the new men and her apparent willingness to let Gaebril shove them into the organization. Most men loyal to Morgase who remained in the Guards were sent out of the city, a good many into Cairhien, others west. With Gaebril's death, many of the men recruited by him deserted, and many others were purged later, leaving a much reduced number stationed in Caemlyn; many became mercenaries in Cairhien, supporting the claims of Toram Riatin.

The man in charge of training for the Queen's Guards bore the title of Master of the Sword. A high degree of skill with various weapons was considered a prerequisite for the job.

The uniform of the Queen's Guard included a red undercoat, gleaming mail and plate armor, a brilliant red cloak and a conical helmet with a barred faceguard. High-ranking officers wore knots of rank on their shoulder and golden lion-head spurs. The Captain-General had four golden knots on the shoulder, an ordinary captain had three, a lieutenant had two and an under-lieutenant had one. The Andoran salute was an arm across the chest. When Elayne arrived in Caemlyn to claim the throne, she discovered that the Guards, in Caemlyn at least, were a shell of a few good men and too many of Gaebril's shoulderthumpers and toughs. She appointed Birgitte, now Lady Birgitte Trahelion, as Captain-General of the Guards and set her to rebuild them, beginning with mercenaries and Hunters for the Horn, though these were temporary measures. They also created a new unit, the Queen's Bodyguard. It was composed of women, although it was led by a man for a brief period. The uniform was basically the same as the Queen's Guards: a red coat with a white collar and lapels, but with additions and changes. The white-collared crimson coats were silk, and altered to fit and hang better on women. There were also tight scarlet breeches with a white stripe up the outside of the leg, a bright red hat with a long white plume lying flat on the wide brim, and a wide red sash edged with snowy lace and with White Lions marching on it, worn slanted across the chest. Pale lace decorated the neck and cuffs, and snug black boots, waxed till they shone and turned down below the knee, completed the uniform.

In some parts of Andor, men wore flowers (or a flower) in their hair while courting. Unlike in most other lands, in Andor marriages between noble and commoners were not considered that unusual, although not that common, either. Royals had married commoners without comment inside Andor, at least, but that custom was looked upon as odd at best in other countries, even where the occasional noble had wed a commoner.

The royal succession in Andor was from mother to daughter. If there was no daughter, the noblewoman who could claim the most lines of descent from Ishara gained the throne. This succession was usually, but not always, peaceful.

Ishara sent her daughter to the White Tower in order to gain the Tower's acquiescence in, if not outright support for, her actions. Her successors followed, and by the end of the War of the Hundred Years both this and the succession in the female line had taken on the form of tradition. It was unclear precisely when these things became a matter of law, but they were so by the end of the war.

Naturally following the nature of the royal succession, titles also descended normally from mother to daughter, as did the largest part of property. Only when there was no daughter did a title descend to a son. A man who had thus inherited also left his main title and properties to his eldest daughter, though sons and other daughters could, of course, inherit smaller properties, and were nobility. Among the nobility, thus, most property and most land were in the hands of women.

Among commoners this rule did not hold. Inheritance was divided among sons and daughters, a daughter's share, or part of it, often going with her when she married. This part was her property, not her husband's, and it was her right to dispose of it as or leave it where she would, just as her husband could leave his property where he would. It was common in some areas for husbands to leave their property to their sons and wives to their daughters, though this was by no means a rule and was not followed in all circumstances.

Andor and Tear were major suppliers of grain and foodstuffs to Cairhien. Andor also was a major source of iron, and iron and steel products; these were considered the best available. Andor also produced bronze and copper. Gold, silver and copper were mined in the Mountains of Mist, though less of the gold and silver came from Andor than from other countries. Andor was considered to have the best bellfoundries, second possibly only to Arafel, and certainly the most numerous except for Arafel. Andor was a supplier of beef, mutton, wool, linen, woven goods and leather, although theirs was not generally considered as fine as Illianer leather. Two Rivers tabac was accounted the best to be found; it was known even in the Aiel Waste. Andor was considered to have good breeding stock for horses, though they were not generally considered as good as Tairen. Shortly before the Last Battle, alum of the first quality was discovered in Andor. Previously, Ghealdan was the only supplier of first-quality alum, while Tear and Arafel supplied a much inferior second-quality. With the arrival of refugees from elsewhere, glassmaking started to become a major industry, as did dyes and dyeing because of the alum.

The last four Queens of Andor before Elayne barely held on to the west of Andor. Since the mines in the Mountains of Mist were the most valuable western properties, the crown maintained as much authority as possible there, keeping some authority in Baerlon and the surrounding area—as a waypoint on the route out for ores and metals—and otherwise let the western lands pretty much go except on the map. This is why the Two Rivers folk had no real memory— in most cases, no memory at all—that they were part of Andor.

Andor, Royal Palace of. *See* Royal Palace of Andor

Andra. A name sometimes used by Lan while on the road.

Andric. The King of Tarabon at the time of the Seanchan invasion. He and Amathera were lovers. He wore a lion mask for anonymity when meeting with

Jaichim Carridin to ask for the Whitecloaks to take over the Panarch's Palace, so he could install Amathera as Panarch. He was killed defending Tarabon from the Seanchan.

Andril, Master. A man featured in a slightly bawdy song sung at The White Ring in Maderin.

Andris. Sammael's emissary to Rand who offered a truce and then died, sweating blood.

Andro. Meilyn Arganya's Warder. Lean and no taller than Meilyn, he appeared youthful and had an unblinking gaze.

Androl Genhald. A Taraboner Asha'man. Approximately thirty years old when he went to the Black Tower, he was clean-shaven and square with heavy eyebrows that drew down when he was thinking. He habitually clasped his hands behind his back and wore a signet ring on his left hand, like a nobleman. He had traveled widely in his life, visiting many remote places. He was part of Logain's faction and had a Talent for making gateways, although he was not very strong in the One Power. Logain had him and others encourage the men to try new ways of Healing. He reached the rank of Dedicated, but was demoted back to soldier by Taim. When it became impossible to make gateways at the Black Tower, Androl worked with Pevara to try to find a way out. They bonded each other, and were thereafter able to sense each other's thoughts as well as emotions. Taim planned to kill Androl and Turn Pevara, but Perrin removed Slayer's dreamspike just in time, enabling Androl to make a gateway and defeat Taim, his cronies and Myrddraal. Androl went on to fight in the Last Battle, steal the remaining seals on the Dark One's prison from Taim, and capture a number of Darkfriend channelers.

Andscale, Mistress. A banker in Caemlyn who made a loan to Elayne upon the discovery of first-quality alum on her estates in Danabar; she also lent money to Arymilla against her holdings.

Anemara. A plump Accepted of the loyalist contingent. She told Elaida of a woman seeking an audience; that woman was Beonin.

Anford, Mistress. One of Halwin Norry's most trusted clerks, a graying woman who worked for Birgitte in Caemlyn.

Anghar. A Seanchan soldier sent by Karede to Ebou Dar to report the Ever Victorious Army's retreat after battling Rand. He was a steady-eyed young man with a fast horse.

Anghara. An Amyrlin from the past. Isebele of Dal Calain had enough power to force Anghara to come to her.

Angharad Juerissen. An Aes Sedai of the Gray Ajah who was Sierin Vayu's Keeper of the Chronicles.

Angla. A novice with the Salidar Aes Sedai. Born in 973 NE, she went to the White Tower at the age of seventeen. She was part of the circle under Anaiya that formed to fight the bubble of evil in Salidar.

angreal. A very rare object which allowed anyone capable of channeling the One Power to handle a greater amount of the Power than would be safely possible unaided. They were remnants of the Age of Legends, and the means of their making was lost. Shortly before the Last Battle, Rand found a Seed, an item needed to create *angreal*, and gave it to Elayne.

Anhara, Ryn. A member of the Academy of Cairhien who trapped lightning in jars.

Anhill. *See* Clarine *and* Petra Anhill

Anjen. Leane's Warder, whom she bonded in 977 NE. He died in 984 NE.

Ankaer. A powerful Domani nobleman whom Ituralde courted to help with his plans against the Seanchan. After Lidrin was killed, Ankaer took over his command. He died in the fighting in Maradon.

Ankerin, House. An Andoran noble House; its High Seat was Lady Carlys.

Ankor Dail. A fortress in the Eastern Marches of Shienar, near the Spine of the World, which it guarded. Masema served three years there fighting Aiel. Ankor Dail was one of the armies that was going to join Agelmar at the battle at Tarwin's Gap while Rand went to see the Green Man. Ankor Dail was burned during the Last Battle to hinder the progress of the Trolloc armies.

Anla, the Wise Counselor. Someone of whom thousands of tales were told. Thom thought that she lived in an Age before the Age of Legends; it was thought by some that she was perhaps the sister of Elsbet, the Queen of All.

Anlee. An Aes Sedai of the Blue Ajah and a Sitter for the Blue at the time of the Aiel War. She was grave-faced and wore many rings and necklaces.

Annah. A messenger for Bryne in the Last Battle. She died when a *raken* was shot down and landed on her.

Annallin. A Cairhienin noble House. *See* Daricain *and* Dalthanes Annallin

Annariz, Fionnda. *See* Fionnda Annariz

Annharid Matoun. A Saldaean Aes Sedai of the Yellow Ajah and the rebel contingent, with a strength level of 17(5). Born in 894 NE, she went to the White Tower in 909 NE. After eight years as a novice and six years as Accepted, she was raised to the shawl in 923 NE. About 5'5" tall, with coppery skin, dark brown eyes that were not particularly large and black hair, she was just a tad on the stocky side—what might be called sturdy, though not heavy. A forceful woman, not particularly arrogant for a Yellow, but strong-willed and determined, she did not suffer fools gladly. She was one of the ferrets sent to the White Tower to try to undermine Elaida. Like all of the sisters chosen for the fifth column, Annharid was out of the White Tower when Siuan was deposed and the Tower broke, so there was no flight to arouse any suspicions toward her. Apparently, she simply returned in answer to Elaida's summons.

Annoura Larisen. A Taraboner Aes Sedai of the Gray Ajah, uncommitted to any faction. Her strength level was 33(21). Born in 838 NE, she went to the White Tower in 854 NE. After twelve years as a novice and ten years as Accepted, she was raised to the shawl in 876 NE. She served as advisor to Berelain, of whom she was quite fond, though this was kept secret because of Tear's attitude toward women who could channel.

Annoura was about 5'4" tall and stocky, with a beak of a nose and a wide mouth that could make a pleasant smile. Her hair was done in dozens of long, thin braids. When she was nervous, she rubbed her thumbs with her forefingers. She could be very self-effacing and could manage to fade into the background, staying so still that one forgot she was there. She could appear distracted by things that didn't seem important, but she never was, really. When Annoura Healed Perrin, she was afraid he would die even after she Healed him, which maybe reflected on her sense of her abilities. She was a good negotiator, but not considered one of the best.

She spent some time after the Aiel War as part of the Gray effort to keep the Grand Coalition going; after that she became Berelain's advisor. She stayed in Mayene when Berelain rode north to Cairhien because they were unsure of the reception that Rand would give an Aes Sedai he did not know. Berelain acted against her advice in going; she counseled caution. She was neutral regarding events in the Tower (i.e., she supported neither side; but that didn't mean she was neutral on the subject of rebellion per se), though not at all pleased that so many seemed to know about the divisions. Aes Sedai–like, she could be angry or upset with people just for knowing, but she also thought that both Elaida and the other side had mishandled it all badly—it should all have been kept secret, at whatever cost, for the good of the Tower. In Cairhien, she and Merana were taken off by Cadsuane for a consultation and questioning after Cadsuane first met and confronted Rand. She was unsettled by Cadsuane, though outwardly less so than Merana. She heard rumors that Moiraine had been killed. She didn't know of Rand's kidnapping until she arrived in Cairhien.

Basically, the Wise Ones looked on Annoura no differently than they had begun looking on all of the sisters, despite her connection to Berelain, whom some of them at least regarded with a degree of affection. At best, there was a sort of toleration of Annoura for Berelain's sake. Annoura did not like or understand the Wise Ones' view of Aes Sedai. She traveled with Berelain and Perrin to Ghealdan; she met secretly with Masema, which angered Berelain. In the Last Battle, she channeled too much getting Galad to safety and burned herself out.

Anointed of the Light. The title for a Lord Captain of the Children, a member of the Council of the Anointed, which commanded the Whitecloaks.

Anolle'sanna. An Ogier-built city in Aramaelle, one of the Ten Nations after the Breaking.

Ansaline Gardens. A superior establishment in the Age of Legends, where only the finest wines and dishes were served. There was also gambling at the *chinje* wheels, and there were immense sculptures by Cormalinde Masoon. The Gardens were in ruins by the third year of the War of Power.

Anselan. A Warder and hero during the Trolloc Wars; his Aes Sedai was Barashelle. Their story passed down through the ages as a romance, and Egwene read the story in *The Flame, The Blade and the Heart*. But Birgitte revealed the true story: Barashelle bonded a Warder while she was still Accepted; when she was found out, she was forced to pass the bond to another and remain Accepted three extra years, and then ordered to bond Anselan, a stubborn older man with a leathery face chosen for Barashelle by the Amyrlin.

Anshar. A major noble House of Andor. Its High Seat was Karind Anshar; its sign a red fox.

Antaeo, River. A river with headwaters in the Black Hills flowing southeast to join the River Erinin north of Tar Valon.

Antail. An Asha'man who was quiet and thin-haired, and skilled in Healing. He was with Ituralde in Maradon, and with Lan at the Last Battle. He toasted Deepe, a fellow Asha'man, who died in the battle at Maradon.

Anthelle Sharplyn. A stout Andoran noblewoman and High Seat of her minor House. She was loyal to Elayne.

Antol. The eldest son of Queen Ethenielle and Prince Brys and thus the heir to the throne of Kandor. Tall and born in 964 NE, Antol married a Kandori noblewoman. He was with the Borderlanders in the Last Battle, and advised that forces should concentrate on the Andoran battlefront, as Kandor had already fallen.

Anvaere Damodred. Moiraine's older sister, who cared for nothing but hawking and horses and had a terrible temper.

Anya. A serving woman in Aesdaishar Palace who served Lan when he visited. She had a square face and gray hair. Edeyn coopted her loyalties.

Aptarigine Cycle. A famous cycle of stories, which numbered in the hundreds, following the intrigues, loves and romances, both happy and doomed, that joined and divided two dozen noble families over fifty generations. The stories of the Aptarigine Cycle were usually told by bards, and few gleemen knew more than a handful of the stories.

Ara. A serving man at The Stag and Lion in Baerlon. He was a slight, dark-haired fellow who led Thom, Rand, Mat and Perrin to the bath chamber. He said that Rand had a funny accent, and asked if there was trouble downcountry. Mat started telling him about Trollocs before Thom, Rand and Perrin shut him up.

Arabah, Gueye. A young Seanchan officer under Tylee who told Perrin of additional Shaido approaching Malden.

Aracome. A High Lord of Tear who was slender and graying, with a long-smoldering temper and suspicious nature, and one of the most active plotters against Rand in the Stone. He disliked Aes Sedai and would have tried to screw up any Aes Sedai plan on general principles, though he wouldn't have thought of it as helping Rand. He was sent to Cairhien under Meilan; he, Torean and Meilan were at that time the three foremost High Lords there. He was worried about his previous association with Hearne and Simaan, who both went into open rebellion in the region of Haddon Mirk. He was in Illian with Rand during that campaign. Min saw him in a vision as dying violently in battle. Indeed, his death fighting the Seanchan was particularly bloody, causing Anaiyella to vomit violently. Flinn tried to Heal him, but in Bashere's opinion, he didn't want to live because the damage to his body was so great.

Arad. A person of significance from the days of Manetheren. After the battle with Trollocs which ended with Moiraine making a wall of fire, Egwene asked what Mat had been shouting, revealed to be Old Tongue. After translating, Moiraine said that the blood of Arad's line was still strong in the Two Rivers, and the old blood still sang.

Arad Doman. A nation in the west of the mainland. Its capital was Bandar Eban. Its sigil was a silver hand grasping a silver sword by the blade, point down: the Sword and Hand. Its banner was the Sword and Hand on a field of four green and three blue horizontal stripes. Its king, Alsalam, vanished mysteriously, and the country descended into chaos.

The nation was founded in approximately FY 1096 by forces led by Lord Jalaam Lazari, Lord Ahran Nawaz and Lady Bastine Almadar. Immediately after they took the city of Bandar Eban, which was already one of the major trading ports of the known world, they proclaimed the existence of a nation, taking the name of the province in Hawkwing's empire. The power and importance of merchants in the former nations of Abayan and Darmovan, and in Hawkwing's province of Arad Doman, led to Lazari, Nawaz and Almadar allying themselves to an informal council of the leading merchants, which in turn led, by the end of the War of the Hundred Years, to a very formal Council of Merchants. Shelaan Lazari, the second-eldest son of Jalaam, was the first to bear the title of King of Arad Doman, granted to him approximately FY 1116. Domani claimed descent from those who made the Tree of Life in the Age of Legends, but they did not claim to have ever possessed a sapling of the tree.

The King was elected for life by the Council of Merchants, composed of the heads of merchant guilds, who were mainly women. He legally had absolute authority, with the exception that he could be deposed by seventy-five percent vote of the Council. The King had to come from one of the noble Houses, called the Bloodborn, not from a merchant House. While the monarchy often passed down in one family, nothing required that; only the vote of the Council of Merchants carried weight.

Domani women were taught practically from the cradle the arts of flirtation, seduction and the snaring and befuddling of a man's senses and mind. Their reputation as femmes fatale was equaled only by that of Sea Folk women. They often promised far more than they delivered, however; at least, the outland men targeted by them frequently felt so.

Nevertheless, Domani men were hardly helpless in the face of their women, for they were taught the male versions of the same arts. Domani believed that women were better merchants and traders than men; it was for this reason that most Domani merchant houses were headed by women, and most Domani merchants were women. The men were more likely to handle accounts while the women did the actual trade and negotiation. Female Domani merchants were not above using the fabled Domani seductive wiles to aide their negotiations, at least on male merchants. Male Domani merchants also used seduction with female merchants from other countries, but they were not considered so dangerous as negotiators as Domani women.

Wearing an earring given by a member of the opposite sex was considered a sign or acknowledgment of being lovers.

Domani of a certain class, men and women, would receive their retainers in the baths. These servants, however, would be of the same gender. Receiving in the bath was considered a suitable time for handing out orders, while the master or mistress was relaxed.

The army of Arad Doman historically consisted of the personal levies of nobles and also levies raised by the guilds. There was never a permanent formation such as the Queen's Guards in Andor or the Defenders of the Stone in Tear, for the Council of Merchants did not want the King to be able to call on more than his own House could raise in case they decided to depose him. The guilds themselves did keep some troops permanently, in the guise of guards; these often numbered as many for a given guild as any House could call on, or even more. Arad Doman was unusual in that it had a standing navy, of sorts. Called the coast guards, it was maintained and controlled by the Council of Merchants, not by the King. It was a small force with only enough ships to ensure that shipping around the coast of Arad Doman was untroubled by pirates. It fell into disarray with the troubles in Arad Doman.

Arad Doman was renowned for its glasswork, especially fine bowls, and its carpetweaving. There was some manufacture of mirrors and looking glasses. Mutton, leather, iron, and iron and steel products were also produced. Most of the trade from Saldaea passed through the port of Bandar Eban.

Arafel. One of the Borderland nations, north of Tar Valon. Its capital was Shol Arbela. Its sigil was a red rose and a white rose: the Roses. Its banner bore three white roses on a field of red quartered with three red roses on a field of white; red is on the side away from the staff at the top, against the staff at the bottom. Paitar Nachiman was its king.

Saldaea, Kandor, Arafel, Shienar and Malkier all were provinces of Hawkwing's empire, with the borders between them very much as they were at the time of the Last Battle, though not stretching so far south in most cases. With the Blight to contend with, the governors of those provinces—Lord Rylen t'Boriden Rashad for Saldaea, Lord Jarel Soukovni for Kandor, Lady Mahira Svetanya for Arafel, Lady Merean Tihomar for Shienar and Lord Shevar Jamelle for Malkier—met soon after Hawkwing's death in FY 994 to reaffirm measures for cooperation against the Blight and to make agreements for mutual defense against attack from the south. Before the end of FY 995, when it became

clear that the rest of the empire was splintering, each of the governors took the title of King or Queen of his or her former province, now a nation. None of these nations would take part in any of the wider fighting of the War of the Hundred Years, except for defending themselves against attacks and punishing same, though individuals and groups did sometimes become involved, for political reasons or family connections or friendships.

Both men and women often wore their hair in braids—a braid over each ear, generally falling below the shoulders.

There was a similarity between the Borderland and Aiel views of shame: by and large, shame was worse than guilt, the worst thing there was, though this view of shame ameliorated as you moved west. Arafellin saw shame as less important than did Shienarans, Kandori less than Arafellin, Saldaeans less than Kandori. In all of the Borderlands, though, shame was given a much heavier weight than in lands to the south.

Arafellin would go to extremes to meet what they considered a debt of honor. In fact, in many ways, they were very close to Aiel in their beliefs, though without the formality of the Aiel *ji'e'toh* such as *gai'shain*.

As a general rule, Arafellin were extremely touchy. In duels, the choice of weapons went to the challenged. The choices were sometimes odd, such as two men on horseback with bows, or two men fighting in a darkened room. Women had been known to fight duels in Arafel, but this was considered improper by the women themselves. Even women who had fought duels would have denied that it had been done. Although women's duels rarely if ever involved swords, they did involve daggers, bows, lances and even whips.

It was forbidden to hide your face inside any village, town or city in the Borderlands, as a protection against Fades. In Arafel and Kandor, unlike Shienar or Saldaea, these laws came to be modified to allow women to wear veils, though the veils were to be of lace or else transparent, making it clear that they did have eyes. Lamps were required along every street in every village, town and city in the Borderlands, as a protection against Fades.

Arafel always had a king. The wife of the King was called the Queen, and was expected to rule in his place when he was on campaign. It was traditional in Arafel that certain matters were left in the hands and under the authority of the Queen at all times, even when the King was not campaigning.

Arafel had a fair number of gemstone mines producing gemstones other than diamonds, most notably firedrops; and less important mines of rubies, emeralds and sapphires, and a moderate number of gold and silver mines. Timber and furs were major exports.

Arafellin. A native of Arafel or a group of natives of Arafel.

Aram. A young Tuatha'an. He was the grandson of Raen and Ila, born in 978 NE. He was about 5'10", slender and very handsome. Aram was attracted to Egwene, and danced and laughed with her. His mood became darker after Trollocs attacked the Tinker camp in the Two Rivers and his mother was killed. He gave up the Way of the Leaf and had Tam teach him the use of the sword, becoming very good very quickly, enough to press Tam while practicing. After leaving the Two Rivers, he practiced the sword incessantly with anyone who would work with him. Aram and Elyas Machera knew each other but got on poorly; Elyas disapproved of Aram forsaking Tinker ways. Aram had a corrupted sense of hero worship for Perrin, the man who told him it was all right to defend himself, to pick up a sword. Aram also worshipped Faile—she was Perrin's wife, and thus the absolutely perfect woman. He was somewhat jealous of her entourage, and would not have minded at all if one of them had tried him with a sword, but he was ready to use the Prophet's methods to find her after she was kidnapped. Aram showed none of the nervousness or wariness toward the Asha'man that so many others did, but neither did he show any particular friendliness. He was an engine without a governor; growing up totally shunning violence, he had little sense of how much was acceptable. He was as willing to accept the Prophet's methods as he was Perrin's. Eventually Aram was corrupted by Masema and killed by Shaido while he was attempting to kill Perrin at Masema's urging.

Aramaelle. One of the Ten Nations after the Breaking. Its capital was Mafal Dadaranell (later Fal Dara); other cities were Rhahime Naille, Anolle'sanna and Cuebiyarsande. Mabriam en Shereed was its queen at the time of the signing of the Compact of the Ten Nations.

Aran son of Malan son of Senar. A respected Ogier author, born circa 50 AB, who wrote a manuscript claiming that Ishamael had been seen after the sealing of the Bore.

Aran'gar. The name given to Balthamel after he was resurrected and put into a woman's body; she assumed the name Halima Saranov. Her strength level was ++3. Although female, she still channeled *saidin*. Her body was slender and lush at the same time, of the sort that made men drool, with a swaying walk that made their tongues hang out. She was about 5'4" to 5'5" tall; her face was a perfect oval with large green eyes, framed by waves of black hair. She had a well-rounded bosom with a waist that was much smaller than her hips. Her hips were also well rounded, and her legs were long. Women often thought she looked like a woman dreamed by a particularly lascivious man. She seemed to have the same sort of look for men or women, challenging and smoky. Her smile was tempting, inviting, but Egwene, at least, thought this was just the shape of her mouth.

She was able to deduce certain things about the way people behaved in the present time with a greater ability than the other Forsaken. She also believed that her knowledge of primitive cultures qualified her uniquely to understand what the world had become, and to rule it. As when she was a man, she had a wildfire temper that she often could not control, and she often did not try to. Halima had relatively little skill in *Tel'aran'rhiod* compared to most of the other Forsaken. As Balthamel, he had been a lover of the ways of the flesh even more than Aginor, and delighted in various perversions and excesses. Of course, after "he" became "she," there were changes, although not as many as might have been expected. She found pleasure in pursuing men as she once did women, though usually for the purpose of causing trouble. She adapted to the female body and brain, and found sex with men quite pleasurable, though it wasn't common knowledge that she had gone farther than sometimes outrageous flirting. But she retained her love of women, too; she was completely bisexual. She had no desire for pets, but wanted any pretty woman or man she saw.

And she still wanted power, of course. While masquerading as Delana Mosvani's secretary, she had handwriting like a child's first attempts, awkward and ill-formed; she had had no time to learn any facility with the present script, and had little aptitude for it or desire to learn, either. She released Moghedien from the *a'dam* that was holding her prisoner in the camp, and told her she had been summoned to Shayol Ghul.

Halima was with the rebels to promote chaos and disorder, and to control/ guide/influence one of the major power centers, which any gathering of three hundred Aes Sedai had to be. She wanted to maintain the division in the White Tower, she wanted to increase tensions between the rebels and Rand, and she did not want any alliance, temporary or otherwise, between the rebel sisters and the Black Tower—at least, not unless it could be used in some way to worsen the break in the White Tower. Her claims regarding what her "friend" Cabriana Mecandes supposedly revealed to her about Elaida's plans for the rebels gained weight once Elaida's plans leaked out, since there was some congruence. She thought of claiming that Cabriana also had learned that Taim and Logain were Red Ajah setups, but this would have been looked at askance by Egwene, Siuan and Leane, who all knew that Logain, at least, had not been any such thing. At best, they would have thought that she was trying to pad her importance by claiming knowledge she didn't have, and their belief in other things she said would have decreased. She said that Cabriana Mecandes had proof that Elaida was Black Ajah, but few believed her, since she wisely backed off when they began wanting to know what the proof was. Even if she had said that Cabriana said it straight out, most of the rebels would be sure she had gotten it wrong somehow.

Halima became personal confidante to Egwene, and her head-rubs and massages were all that kept Egwene's headaches—caused by Halima—at bay. Halima killed Egwene's maids Meri and Selame because they were spies for Romanda and Lelaine; she didn't want spies watching Egwene because they might have seen or overheard something that would have endangered her own position and safety. Chesa survived simply because she wasn't a spy for anyone, just a maid. Halima followed Egwene to her meeting in *Tel'aran'rhiod* with Elayne and Nynaeve in the Grand Hall of the Royal Palace, and learned a lot by eavesdropping, but she used a door and shut it too hard, alerting them to someone else's presence.

When Narishma told a meeting of the Sitters the story of Eben's death, by *saidin* from a female Forsaken, Romanda connected the dots and ordered the arrest of Halima and Delana, but the two had already left from the Traveling grounds. The pair went to Graendal at Natrin's Barrow. Aran'gar was killed when Rand balefired Natrin's Barrow.

In the Old Tongue *aran'gar* (lowercase) was a right-hand dagger in a form of dueling that was popular during the time leading up to the War of Power; both daggers were poisoned, and both participants usually died. *See also* Balthamel

Arandaille, Balladare. An Aes Sedai of the Brown Ajah who served as a weak Amyrlin from 115 to 142 NE. The Kavarthen Wars occurred during her reign.

Arandi Square. A large square in the center of Bandar Eban.

Aranvor Naldwinn. The Captain-General of the Queen's Guard of Andor at the time of the Aiel War. He was chosen to lead on the third day of fighting in the Battle of the Shining Walls; he was killed on that day.

Arathelle Renshar. The High Seat of House Renshar, a very powerful Andoran House. Her sigil was three golden wolfhounds on a field of red. Arathelle was beautiful when young; later she had a lined face, streaks of gray in her hair and a stern gaze. Twice widowed, she supported Morgase when she gained the throne. Under Rahvin's influence, Morgase exiled her from Caemlyn. Aemlyn, Pelivar, Arathelle and Culhan were among the nobles who confronted the rebel Aes Sedai on the ice near the Murandy-Andor border. Arathelle supported Dyelin for the throne, but after Elayne took Caemlyn and Luan and Abelle stood for Elayne, Arathelle did as well.

Aravine Carnel. An Amadician woman who was a *gai'shain* in Sevanna's camp and the first in the camp to swear fealty to Faile. She was plump and plain, and her accents were cultured. She might have been a merchant of some note, or perhaps even a noble, before her capture; Faile thought the latter. She acquired more backbone as time went on and swore fealty to Faile because she was certain Faile would find a way to escape and wanted to be taken along. She was revealed to be a Darkfriend in the Last Battle when she turned Faile's party and the Horn of Valere over to the Shadow; Faile killed her.

Arawn. A noble House of Andor. Its High Seat was Naean Arawn; its sign the Triple Keys.

Arawn, Naean. *See* Naean Arawn

Archer, the. A constellation.

Archers, The. An inn being built in Emond's Field next to a smaller inn, presumably The Winespring Inn. Egwene and Elayne saw it while meeting in *Tel'aran'rhiod* the night before Egwene's army was to move on Tar Valon.

area, units of. 1) Land: 1 ribbon = 20 paces × 10 paces (200 square paces); 1 cord = 20 paces × 50 paces (1,000 square paces); 1 hide = 100 paces × 100 paces (10,000 square paces); 1 rope = 100 paces × 1,000 paces (100,000 square paces); 1 march = 1,000 paces × 1,000 paces (1/4 square mile). 2) Cloth: 1 pace = 1 pace and 1 hand × 1 pace and 1 hand

Arebis. An Aes Sedai of the loyalist contingent who helped to capture Leane at Southharbor. She had a Warder, who spotted Leane's boat before she was captured.

Ared Mosinel. Rahvin's name before he turned to the Shadow.

Areina Nermasiv. A Kandori woman. Born in 978 NE, she was 5'4" tall, with blue eyes and dark hair that she took to wearing in a braid. Areina went to Illian to fetch her younger brother Gwil home; she never found him, but somehow she had found herself taking the oath as a Hunter, setting out to see the world while not quite believing the Horn of Valere existed, half hoping that somewhere she would find young Gwil and take him home. She was not exactly reluctant to talk about all that, but put the best face on it, sometimes shading the truth. She was chased out of several villages, robbed once and beaten several times. She was free with her tongue. Even so, she had no intention of giving up or seeking sanctuary, or a peaceful village. The world was still out there, and Areina meant to wrestle it to the ground. She met Elayne, Nynaeve, Thom and Juilin on *Riverserpent* and went with them to join the rebel Aes Sedai, though she could not channel. She formed an alliance with Nicola, who bonded her as her Warder, illegal though that was. The pair of them attempted to blackmail Egwene with their knowledge of Elayne and Nynaeve's imposture as Aes Sedai while still only Accepted, but Egwene dissuaded them of that notion. Areina and Nicola together successfully—for a time—blackmailed Myrelle and Nisao over hiding Lan away from all the other sisters. Areina, sassy and insolent, admired power and warrior skills, and Birgitte became her role model, from whom she took archery lessons. She later tried to learn Lan's skills from him. She and Nicola ran away together, got into Tar Valon and betrayed the plan to block the harbors, though neither knew how it was to be done, just that it would be, in the night. Nicola died, and Areina's fate is unknown.

Arel Malevin. A Cairhienin blacksmith who became an Asha'man and bonded Aisling Noon of the Green Ajah. He was a wide man barely as tall as Logain's chest. Toveine saw him among those reporting to Logain, and he was present when Rand named the Asha'man and handed out the first pins. He and Aisling were with Rand at Algarin's manor when the Trollocs attacked; afterward, they worked together to incinerate Trolloc corpses. Malevin was with Logain during the Last Battle.

Aren Deshar. A former name of Far Madding.

Aren Mador. The capital city of Essenia, one of the Ten Nations after the Breaking; later it became Far Madding.

Arendor Haevin. The uncle and guardian of Catalyn Haevin of Andor.

Arene. *See* Amellia *and* Jorin Arene

Arent. An Ogier, the son of Halan and the father of Loial.

Arganda, Gerard. *See* Gerard Arganda

Arganya, Meilyn. *See* Meilyn Arganya

Argirin Darelos den Turamon. An Illianer nobleman who was a member of the Council of Nine.

Aridhol. The name of one of the Ten Nations and its capital. Other cities in the nation were Abor'maseleine and Cyrendemar'naille; its queen at the signing of the compact was Doreille Torghin. *See also* Shadar Logoth

Aried. An Ogier of the distant past; his son Jalanda wrote of Be'lal.

Arien. A one-inn village in Andor on the Caemlyn Road, between Whitebridge and Four Kings. This was the first place Rand and Mat performed at the local inn for their supper and bed, on their way to Caemlyn, following their escape from Shadar Logoth and the Trollocs.

Arienwin, Lyrelle. *See* Lyrelle Arienwin

Aril Corl. A woman who lived in Taien, Jangai Pass and survived the Shaido attack. Her husband was Ander; her brother, Tal Nethin.

Arilinde Branstrom. An Andoran noblewoman and High Seat of House Branstrom. She was loyal to Elayne and brought fifty armsmen to support her. She was normally so ebullient that one would have thought that her armsmen would turn the tide of battle by themselves.

Arilyn Dhulaine. A Cairhienin noblewoman who was part of the Gray Ajah's eyes-and-ears network. She was slightly above the middle rank of nobility, and thus would have worn stripes nearly to her waist. Her sigil was a pair of silver stars above red and green stripes. Thom performed for a party of hers the night after he met Rand in Cairhien. Her mansion in the city was used by Coiren and the embassy sent by Elaida; Rand and Min were held there for a time. After Coiren took over her city mansion, Arilyn reportedly went to join her husband on a country estate. Cadsuane and her entourage later took over Lady Arilyn's mansion, and possibly Lady Arilyn as well. Cadsuane did not like people trying to play too many sides, especially all at once. Arilyn's mansion was where Cadsuane kept the High Lord Darlin and the Lady Caraline as "guests" until Dobraine freed them on Rand's orders.

Arimon Darengil. Selande's brother, who was part of the Illian invasion army. He was a stocky young man who shaved the front of his head after the fashion of Cairhienin soldiers. He wore six stripes of color.

Arin. A gate guard in Baerlon. When Moiraine and her party started to leave, a Watchman agreed to let them out and called Arin and Dar to get out there and help him open the gate.

Arindrim. A wine-producing area. The Aes Sedai embassy that Elaida had sent to Cairhien to escort Rand back to the White Tower were staying with Lady Arilyn. Egwene went to the palace and, detecting channeling inside, used Air and Fire to replicate Moiraine's eavesdropping trick on the inside, and heard that a vintage from Arindrim was to be served to the Aes Sedai.

Arinelle, River. The river forming above Maradon and flowing south into the River Manetherendrelle below Whitebridge.

Aringill. A border town filled with refugees in Andor, on the west bank of the River Erinin, which held an army garrison, protecting Andor's eastern flank. Accommodations were expensive here. Across the river was the smaller Cairhienin town of Maerone. Aringill had long, tarred-timber docks, and was protected by high stone wingwalls. The main streets were paved with flat gray stones. The buildings were of every sort, wood and brick and stone all cheek by jowl, with roofs of tile, or slate, or thatch. A number of events took place here. When Elayne, Egwene and Nynaeve decided to go to Tear by boat, they thought that Elayne might be able to get a letter to her mother by giving it to someone in Aringill. Mat would get off a boat in Aringill and take the letter to Caemlyn. While in Aringill, Mat and Thom saved Aludra from being murdered. Comar told Rahvin, who wanted Elayne dead, that the vessel Elayne had been on had been found at Aringill, but that she had left it before reaching the town. After Caemlyn, Thom and Mat decided to go to Tear by boat from Aringill. Egwene had heard rumors that Andormen in Aringill had declared Dyelin queen. Dyelin proved how strong she was at Aringill by dispatching treasonous nobles. Elenia and Naean were held prisoner by Dyelin in Aringill, but were taken by Arymilla's troops five miles outside of town on the way to Caemlyn.

Arinvar. Sheriam's Cairhienin Warder. Slender and about 5'7" tall with gray at his temples, he was hard of face and moved like a stalking leopard.

Arjuna, Cieryl. *See* Cieryl Arjuna

Arlen Nalaam. A Saldaean Asha'man soldier, copper-skinned, with a thin mustache and a small pearl in his ear. Part of the attack on the Seanchan, he brought a captured *sul'dam* to Rand, and stared at Rand's saddle, not at Rand. He said that *saidin* felt strange, during battle with the Seanchan in the south. He frequently spoke in gibberish; it was his form of madness from the taint. He also told many far-fetched stories. When he, Androl and others were attempting to rescue Logain from Taim, the roof caved in and he was killed.

Arlene. Arymilla's maid. Her duties went beyond the usual. Slender and pretty, she jerked in shock when Arymilla ordered her to go with Nasin and prepare him spiced wine, since she knew very well that Nasin would tumble her as soon as they were alone, but she gave Nasin a tremulous smile and obeyed.

Armaghn, Dawlin. An Andoran man who was High Seat of a minor House; his sign was the Oak and Axe. He supported Naean.

Armahn, River. A river located in northern Murandy.

Arman, Chilares. *See* Chilares Arman

armcry. Aiel expression for raising an alarm.

Armies of the Night. The name given by Luthair Paendrag's armies to the defenders of Seanchan, composed of militant Aes Sedai and exotic creatures, which Luthair thought to be Shadowspawn.

Arms. The name Ituralde's troops called Trollocs with the features of bears.

Arnault, Laigin. *See* Laigin Arnault

Arnin. One of the two toughs with Falion and Ispan when they tortured the Kinswoman Callie in Ebou Dar. He was a Darkfriend with little brains, black hair, beady eyes and scars, and was very muscular. Arnin was the one who questioned Falion's order to make it look as if the Kinswoman was robbed. She channeled and threw him against the wall for that.

Arnon, Rahema. A grain merchant Perrin dealt with in So Habor, Altara. She was haggard and dirty with sunken eyes.

Arovni, Racelle. *See* Racelle Arovni

Arran Head. A promontory at the western end of Kabal Deep in southeastern Altara. Between Arran Head and the city of Illian lay a hundred leagues of open water, across the mouth of Kabal Deep. Rand speculated that the Seanchan needed two weeks to reach the border of Illian from Arran Head.

Arrata. A Seanchan soldier at Malden, under the command of Mishima. She assisted in putting forkroot into the aqueduct.

arrath. An herb applied to meat to add sweetness.

Arrays. A game wealthy women played with cards. Cards were placed in descending order in one of a set of patterns, but only certain suits could be played on others.

Arrel. *See* Edeyn ti Gemallen *and* Iselle Arrel

Arrela Shiego. A Tairen woman who was a member of *Cha Faile*. She wore her black hair cut as short as a Maiden's. Her eyes were dark, and she was fairly dark-complected. About 5'9" tall, Arrela did not have any feminine touches about her garments, neither in color or otherwise; they were quite masculine. She made it evident that she was not interested in kissing men, as she was gay. She was one of the fifteen or sixteen who followed Perrin and Faile from Cairhien to Ghealdan. Arrela was not so hot as Lacile concerning her own honor—not so hot as such things were accounted among them, anyway—but she was very concerned with Faile's. Faile considered that Camaille and Arrela had the quickest minds in the bunch, though Parelean and Selande were brighter. She, Parelean and Lacile learned of Masema's contacts with the Seanchan. She was captured by the Shaido along with Faile. She and Lacile had attempted escape, were recaptured, and were tied naked on a cart as punishment. Aldin wanted to marry her, but she was not interested. Marthea, a Maiden, protected Arrela during her captivity and was her lover. Arrela was with Faile's group that went to fetch the Horn of Valere from the White Tower, and, as a gateway opened to return them to the Field of Merrilor, they were sent instead to the Blight.

Arrow. Birgitte's lean gray horse. Arrow was also the name of Moiraine's bay mare, later replaced by Aldieb.

Arrows of Fire. A weave of Fire and Earth; it caused red filaments to flash from one's fingertips. The filaments heated blood and flesh beyond boiling, and killed many quickly.

Artein, Catlynde. An Aes Sedai Sitter who lived at the time of the formation of the White Tower.

Artham. A *ter'angreal* that prevented the Dark One from seeing its possessor; one in the shape of a dagger was found in Ebou Dar, identified by Aviendha and used by Rand when he approached Shayol Ghul.

Artur Hawkwing. A legendary king who united all lands west of the Spine of the World, and whose death touched off the War of the Hundred Years. His sign was a golden hawk in flight. Born Artur Paendrag Tanreall, he received this name for the swiftness with which he moved his armies. He was about 6'2" tall, and hook-nosed, with dark, deep-set eyes. He was *ta'veren*, the strongest until Rand. His great sword Justice was always with him. His voice was deep and carrying, a voice used to issuing commands. Hawkwing took on an advisor, Jalwin Moerad, who was Ishamael in actuality. Moerad, opportunistically taking advantage of the manipulative Bonwhin, the White Tower's Amyrlin at the time, turned Hawkwing against the Aes Sedai, which led him to engage in a twenty-year siege against them. Also on Moerad's advice, Hawkwing sent his son, Luthair Paendrag, with an army to Seanchan, and a daughter with an army to Shara, to consolidate his empire. He died cursing the Aes Sedai and mourning the loss of his son and daughter. Hawkwing led the Heroes of the Horn, both at Falme and in the Last Battle, after the Horn of Valere was blown.

Artur Paendrag Tanreall. *See* Artur Hawkwing

Arwin. A Youngling under Gawyn's command. He was a good ten years younger than Sevanna, but he expressed the wish to dance with her, not understanding what that meant to an Aiel. Gawyn, however, had some notion.

Aryman, Deane. *See* Deane Aryman

Arymilla Marne. High Seat of House Marne in Andor. Her sigil was four silver moons on a field of twilight blue. She was one of Gaebril's sycophants, pretty and plump with big brown eyes and old enough to be Rand's mother. She simpered and wore a gown that was low-cut by Andoran standards. Her eyes were always wide in feigned interest, and she was fool enough to think that Rand would be susceptible to her putting her hand on his arm while speaking to him. Arymilla fled after Rand reached an accommodation with Dyelin; Rand made no moves against her, but Dyelin was not so restrained. She had Elenia and Naean arrested. Arymilla declared for the Lion Throne, and Nasin allied his House with her, making her claim credible if only because of the relative strength behind it. Arymilla freed Elenia and Naean and made them sign documents supporting her in her quest for the Lion Throne. She laid siege to Caemlyn, but was defeated and captured by Elayne and her armies. Elayne stripped her of her titles and lands, although she planned to offer Arymilla other lands in Cairhien.

Aryth Ocean. The large body of water off the west coast of the main continent. *See* Eastern Sea *and* World Sea

Aryth yew. A tree that grew in Bandar Eban.

asa. A concubine in Seanchan. To become an *asa* to one higher in rank was considered by lower-class women—and to some extent by middle-class women—as a good way to advance socially. *Asa* often had power derived from the man who kept them: they were housed in luxury, their children were acknowledged (if not usually raised to the Blood) and advanced in rank, and they themselves were provided for in their older years. A man who set aside an *asa* without providing for her future and that of his children by her would be looked down on with disgust.

Asadine. In the Borderlands and Cairhien, a day of fasting observed ten days before Sunday, with no food taken between sunrise and sunset. The day after Asadine was considered an especially propitious time to wed in the Borderlands.

Asaheen, Sanaiye. A Domani Aes Sedai of the Green Ajah and the loyalist contingent. She was part of the group that kidnapped Rand, and escaped Dumai's Wells with Covarla Baldene.

Asan Sandair. A Cairhienin officer who met Rand, Hurin and Loial at their entrance to the city of Cairhien; he was in charge of the gate. He signed them in and told them to come back and report where they were staying. The front of his head was shaved, but he was already quite bald.

Asar Don. The site of an ancient battle in which Moghedien participated. When Moghedien revealed herself to Liandrin and the other Black Ajah, she brought up this and other battles to get across that they were not to think themselves her equal.

Asegora. A noble House of Tear. *See* Melanril Asegora

asha'man. Old Tongue for "guardian" or "defender," with a strong implication of a guardian of right and justice.

Asha'man. Men who could channel and who followed Rand. The term applied both to these men as a group and to the highest rank or degree among them. The Asha'man base of operations was a farm in Andor that became the Black Tower. A beginner at the Black Tower was termed a soldier; he wore a black coat with no decoration. The second rank was Dedicated; he wore a silver sword on the collar of his black coat. A full Asha'man wore the silver sword and a red-enameled gold dragon. Rand later raised some other men to Dedicated and/or Asha'man, but under Taim's leadership, with the exception of Logain, the only men who received both the Sword and the Dragon were those he recruited himself, all Darkfriends. Those men received special private training from Taim in things which he himself was taught by Dashiva/Osan'gar or by Demandred.

Taim did not like the Asha'man trying to learn things on their own; he wanted to limit the learning of all but his cronies. They still did learn on their own, though; most were curious men, with a touch of adventure in them, or they wouldn't have become Asha'man. There was some disturbance over the bond that the Asha'man used on their wives, but Taim eventually saw the potential of it, and realized that the men were going to bond with their wives whatever he did, short of killing them. Some of the students obeyed Taim's many strictures and limits on what they could learn or study or try to learn, because of the punishments for not obeying, and others because he was, after all, the M'Hael, and "the Voice of the Lord Dragon" as some took to calling him, but there were some who saw what the favored ones could do and copied the weaves in secret.

In their training, the Asha'man were pushed hard—forced, as Aes Sedai called it. A certain number were killed or burned out in the process. Where novices in the White Tower were prohibited from using the One Power to do chores, soldiers in training were required to do so. Men received no hot food until they could channel enough Fire to heat it up for themselves. The rules of the Asha'man were much more military-oriented than those of the Aes Sedai, in keeping with the view of Asha'man as soldiers in the war against the Shadow. It also helped Taim keep the sort of rigid control he needed. Running away from the Black Tower was considered desertion. The penalty for attempting it was flogging; the penalty for succeeding was death, once caught. Even attempting to run away in the face of the enemy carried a death penalty. So did refusing an order from a superior. The usual things were considered crimes among the Asha'man as elsewhere, but sometimes the penalties were harsher than elsewhere. The penalty for murder was death. The penalty for rape was death, unless the woman was willing to ask that you not be killed and to marry you; then you were merely flogged until you could not stand. The penalty for the first offense of stealing from a non-Asha'man was death and for stealing from another Asha'man was flogging; the penalty for the second offense was death. The penalty for arson was death.

ashandarei. Birgitte's name for Mat's spear. This weapon, derived from the Age of Legends, was a polearm with a haft of black wood about six feet long, and a head that was about two feet long and looked like the blade of a Japanese tanto. Given to Mat by the Eelfinn, it was inscribed with Old Tongue script reading "Thus is our treaty written; thus is agreement made. Thought is the arrow of time; memory never fades. What was asked is given; the price is paid." (*Ghiro feal dae'vin lormae; ghiro o'vin gemarisae. Nardes vasen'cierto ain; sind vyen loviyagae. Devoriska nolvae. Al ciyat dalae.*) Two ravens were engraved on the blade, and a metal raven was inlaid at either end of the script.

Ashelin. An Altaran novice in the White Tower. She was a plump, pretty girl with olive-colored skin. She brought Egwene her food in the novices' dining hall after Egwene had been captured by the loyalist Aes Sedai, and the tea contained honey.

Asher, Mistress. A merchant in Canluum who was also a wilder. She stayed at The Gates of Heaven; the Aes Sedai who were staying there were not interested in her because she was gray-haired, too old to be a novice.

Ashin. A superior servant of Barthanes in Cairhien. He wore the Tree and Crown large on the chest of his green coat and carried a staff. Ashin led Rand and his party into the manor, rapped his staff and introduced them.

Ashmanaille. An Aes Sedai of the Gray Ajah and the rebel contingent, with a strength level of 22(10). Born in 902 NE, she went to the White Tower in 918 NE.

After eleven years as a novice and ten years as Accepted, she was raised to the shawl in 939 NE. She was about 5'4" tall and so lanky that she appeared taller. She was part of a circle the night a bubble of evil struck Salidar. She had some ability for making *cuendillar*. She Traveled to Kandor to collect tribute, only to discover that Nesita, a loyalist, had beaten her to it. Ashmanaille was one of the sisters manning the Traveling grounds in the Last Battle when Min needed to Travel to give a message from Bryne to the Seanchan Empress to send them cavalry; she recognized Min as Elmindreda.

Ashraf, Sana. A man whom Mat fought at the falls of Pena in one of the memories received from the Eelfinn.

Asidim Faisar. A Whitecloak spy in Tanchico, sent there by Pedron Niall to sound out possibilities amid the chaos. It was his report sent through by Varadin that convinced Niall of the Seanchan threat, but Niall was killed before he could act on the information.

Asinbayar. The fourth-largest city in Seanchan. It was associated with Suroth, being mentioned in her title.

Asmodean. A Forsaken. His name in the Age of Legends was Joar Addam Nessosin. His strength level was ++3. He was born in the port of Shorelle. A musician and composer, he showed early promise, but failed to reach exalted heights. He claimed that he went over to the Shadow because of the lure of immortality; if he had an eternity to create music, he would achieve greatness. According to Lanfear, he stilled his own mother and gave her to the Myrddraal. When he awoke in the Third Age, he used the name Jasin Natael and accompanied a band of peddlers to the Waste. A dark-haired man with dark, deep-set eyes, seemingly in his middle years, Asmodean was taller than most, and likely attractive to women, but with an oddly apprehensive way of holding his head cocked as if trying to look at a conversant sideways. He talked with Rand, but Rand was not forthcoming with information or interest. Asmodean gave Couladin the marks of the *Car'a'carn*. When Rand was occupied at Alcair Dal, Asmodean Skimmed to Rhuidean. Rand followed him, and they fought over the access key to the Choedan Kal. Rand prevailed and cut Asmodean's connection to the Dark One. Asmodean was stunned to have his links severed by someone else, as it was understood that only the Dark One or the person connected to the Dark One could sever the links. Lanfear arrived and partially shielded Asmodean. He was still the same person, but refrained from reestablishing his connection to the Dark One, for fear the other Forsaken or the Dark One would have believed he severed the connection himself, marking him a traitor.

Asmodean decided to bide his time and meanwhile link his star to Rand, being reasonably sure that Rand would not suddenly try to kill him. He became Rand's gleeman publicly; in truth, he was Rand's tutor in the One Power, insofar as he was able. He was not a good teacher, as he admitted; he said Lanfear had planned it so, so that Rand would not rival her. He did teach

Rand some useful things, however, and when Rand was injured, used his meager ability to Heal him. Asmodean accompanied Rand to Caemlyn to deal with Rahvin; they were attacked by Shadowspawn and he was struck by lightning and killed. Rand's use of balefire to kill Rahvin brought him back to life. Shortly thereafter, he was killed by Graendal in the Royal Palace of Caemlyn, and that time stayed dead.

Asne Zeramene. A Saldaean Aes Sedai of the Green Ajah publicly but of the Black Ajah in truth. Her strength level was 18(6). Born in 837 NE, she went to the White Tower in 853 NE. After seven years as a novice and eight years as Accepted, Asne was raised to the shawl in 868 NE. She was 5'4" tall, with dark tilted eyes, a bold nose and a wide mouth; she dressed fairly modestly for a Saldaean, but had all the vaunted Saldaean boldness. Of her four Warders, only one, Powl, was a Darkfriend. Asne was one of the first thirteen Black Ajah members to leave the White Tower. She had found the rod that produced balefire, which Moghedien had not hidden so well as she thought she had, and brought it with her. After Eldrith Jhondar's Warder Kennit tracked them down, Eldrith, Asne Zeramene, Chesmal Emry and Temaile Kinderode all went to Caemlyn hoping to find Elayne and maybe Nynaeve. They captured Elayne, and Asne used the balefire rod against the soldiers trying to rescue Elayne. Asne was killed by Atha'an Miere Windfinders.

Asnelle. An area of Saldaea; Tenobia was Lady of Shahayni, Asnelle, Kunwar and Ganai.

Asnobar, Saerin. *See* Saerin Asnobar

asping rot. A highly toxic, foul-tasting plant that Verin used to poison herself. The poison was fast-acting.

Asra Zigane. A Domani Wise Woman and Kin in Ebou Dar. Her strength level was 54(42), too low for her to be tested for Accepted and not strong enough for her to make a gateway of any size whatsoever. She was born in 913 NE and went to the White Tower in 929 NE while Kirin Melway was the Amyrlin. She remained for four months before being sent away. She had a very high level of Talent in Healing. She was not taught Healing in the Tower, of course; she was simply kept there long enough to learn how to be safe. She learned it there, though, by seeing it done. She was a very quick study and didn't need to see a weave more than once to be able to do it perfectly. She also had the very rare Talent that Aviendha did, of being able to tell what a weave she had never seen before would do before it was completed. Elayne and Nynaeve saw her attempt to Heal a man in the Rahad. She was at the Kin's farm when Elayne went there, and on the way to Caemlyn Asra attempted to instigate a revolt against the Aes Sedai because they had put two of the Kin, past novice runaways from the Tower, back in white. She was one of the Kinswomen who traveled with Elayne to the Royal Palace in Caemlyn.

Asseil. A Taraboner Accepted in the White Tower. She was slim, with pale hair and brown eyes, a novice when Egwene left the Tower. Jealous of Egwene's fast rise, Asseil tried to boss her around when she was put back in novice white by Elaida.

Assemblage. One of the ruling bodies of Illian, the Assemblage was an elected body chosen by the merchants and guilds, including the craft guilds. Ordinary shopkeepers had no vote unless they were members of a guild, nor did the man in the street or a laborer. Historically, the King, the Council of Nine and the Assemblage had engaged in a three-way struggle for real power from the time the nation was founded.

Assembly, Grand Hall of the. The building where the Assembly of Lords deliberated in Tanchico.

Assembly of Lords. A ruling body in Tanchico. The Assembly had few real powers, but one which they guarded jealously was that of naming the new Panarch.

Assid Bakuun. A Seanchan captain with thirty years in the Ever Victorious Army. He had a dog named Nip. He found *sul'dam* conversing with *damane* distasteful. He died fighting in Rand's campaign against the Seanchan.

Astara. A queen of Andor during the War of the Hundred Years. She reigned from FY 1073 to 1085.

Astelle al'Seen. A Two Rivers woman. She was the oldest in her family, and poked Perrin with her cane when he visited Jac al'Seen's farm.

Astoril Damara. A High Lord of Tear and the father of Medore. Astoril was old but straight-backed, with shoulder-length, thinning white hair and sharp dark eyes. He was born in 935 NE and married at age twenty-five; his wife was twenty. One son, the eldest child of that marriage, died in the Aiel War at age seventeen. Another son died of sickness. Two daughters survived. His first wife died in childbirth in 974 NE and he remarried in 979 NE. Medore was born of that union in 981 NE, and Astoril also had two sons from that marriage. His eldest daughter would inherit the title of High Lady and High Seat.

Astoril was the leader of the Tairen contingent at the Battle of the Shining Walls. He led twenty-four thousand men there, and was sixth in the consecutive command, not as well regarded as Agelmar Jagad or Pedron Niall, but just below Mattin Stepaneos and perhaps his equal or slightly superior. He joined Darlin Sisnera in the Stone to defend against the rebellion.

Astrelle. An Aes Sedai of the White Ajah and the loyalist contingent. Plump with a formidable bosom, Astrelle was an arithmetist who applied numbers to logic. Alviarin saw her arguing the cause of food spoilage with Tesan in the halls of the White Ajah.

Asunawa, Rhadam. *See* Rhadam Asunawa

Atal. One of the Seanchan military clerks in Captain Faloun's office in Almizar. He was charged with cleaning up the mess after Mehtan died vomiting beetles.

Atal Mishraile. An Asha'man who was given private lessons by Taim. He was handsome and tall, with blue eyes and golden hair falling in waves to his broad shoulders. Mishraile was Dedicated for a very short time, and was raised to full Asha'man soon after being taught by Taim. He became a Darkfriend without being Turned. Taim fractured his skull when he mouthed off in front of the Red sisters. During the Last Battle he was captured in Stedding Sholoon by Androl and his allies, including some elderly Ogier.

Atha'an Miere. Inhabitants of islands in the Aryth Ocean and the Sea of Storms. They spent little time on those islands, living most of their lives on their ships. An informal name for the Atha'an Miere, translated from the Old Tongue, was "People of the Sea" or "Sea Folk." They were a secretive people, and relatively little was known of their customs, giving rise to an air of exotic mystery and often to fanciful tales.

Legend held that at the Breaking of the World the ancestors of the Atha'an Miere fled to the safety of the sea while the land heaved and broke. They knew nothing of the ships they took to flee, but they managed to survive. They did not return to land until the upheaval had ended; they found that much had changed. In the years after that came the Jendai Prophecy, saying that the Atha'an Miere were destined to wander the waters until the Coramoor returned, and that they were required to serve him when he did. The Jendai Prophecy was given great weight by the Sea Folk because it spoke of things that did not exist until after it was first known, sometimes long after.

Rank was not hereditary among the Sea Folk. As survival at sea often depended on instant obedience, it should be no surprise that the Atha'an Miere stuck strictly to their hierarchy, though there were surprising fluidities at some points. The Atha'an Miere were divided into numerous clans, both large and small, each headed by a Wavemistress. Below her were the Sailmistresses, the ships' captains of the clan. A Wavemistress had vast authority, yet she was elected to that position by the twelve senior clan Sailmistresses, who were referred to as the First Twelve of that clan, and she could be removed by the order of the Mistress of the Ships to the Atha'an Miere.

The Mistress of the Ships had a level of authority any shorebound king or queen would envy, yet she was also elected, for life, by unanimous vote of the twelve senior Wavemistresses, who were called the First Twelve of the Atha'an Miere. The term "the First Twelve" was also used for the twelve senior Wavemistresses or Sailmistresses present in any gathering.

The position of Master of the Blades was held by a man who might or might not be the husband of the Mistress of the Ships. His responsibilities were the defense and the trade of the Sea Folk, and below him were the Swordmasters of Wavemistresses and the Cargomasters of Sailmistresses, who held like positions and duties; for each of them, any authority outside these areas was held only as delegated by the woman he served. Where any vessel sailed, and when, was always up to the Sailmistress, but since trade and finances were totally in the hands of the Cargomaster (or, at higher levels, the Swordmaster or the Master of the Blades), a close degree of cooperation was required.

Every Sea Folk vessel, however small, and every Wavemistress, had a Windfinder, a woman who was almost always able to channel and skilled in Weaving the Winds, as the Atha'an Miere called the manipulation of weather. The Windfinder to the Mistress of the Ships had authority over the Windfinders to the Wavemistresses, who in turn had authority over Windfinders to the Sailmistresses of their clans.

One peculiarity of the Sea Folk was that all had to begin at the very lowest rank and work their way up, and that anyone other than the Mistress of the Ships could be demoted, even all the way down to deckhand, for malfeasance, cowardice or other crimes. Also, the Windfinder to a Wavemistress or Mistress of the Ships who died would have to serve a lower-ranking woman, and her own rank thus decreased to the lowest level, equivalent to one who was first raised from apprentice to Windfinder on the day she herself put off her higher honors. The Atha'an Miere, who long kept their distance from Aes Sedai by various means and diversions, were aware that women who could channel had much longer lifespans than other people, though life at sea was dangerous enough that they seldom lived out their entire lifespan, and thus they knew that a Windfinder might rise to a height and fall to the depths to begin again many times before she died.

An Atha'an Miere's first name was given at birth. The second name was the family name, with "din" signifying "of the family." Girls took the family name of their mother, while boys took the surname of their father. In young adulthood, usually within the first ten years after achieving majority, men and women were given a "salt name" which typified them as to character or referred to some great event or deed of which they were part. These were short, usually only one or two words. A salt name such as "Wild Winds" might refer to a temper or to having ridden out a storm which should have sunk the vessel.

To seal a bargain, each party kissed the fingertips of the right hand and pressed them to the lips of the other. Variations of this were used for lesser agreements than actual bargains as well. Simply kissing one's own fingertips, or pressing them to one's lips, bestowed emphasis.

Traditionally, the Sea Folk did not sell passage on their ships. One asked for the favor of passage and then made a gift, which just happened to have a value equal to the passage. If the gift offered was not sufficient, it turned out, regrettably, that there simply was no room, or some other excuse. If a more suitable gift was offered, then it was discovered that a mistake had been made and there was room after all. No one except Aes Sedai could be refused passage outright, not unless the gift offered in return was too small, of course. For the Amayar, the gift of passage truly was a gift, with no gift expected in return, but until just before the Last Battle, no Amayar had asked this in living memory.

Sea Folk wedding ceremonies reflected the hierarchical nature of ships at sea. There was a matriarchal element to Sea Folk culture, with ships owned and commanded by women and clans always headed by a woman, as well as the

Atha'an Miere themselves, by the Mistress of the Ships. Since husband and wife both served on the same ship, often one would outrank the other, and despite the matriarchal elements, it was not always the woman. Thus, in a Sea Folk ceremony, there were pledges of obedience, but conditional. If husband and wife were of equal rank on the ship, then the wife took the lead between them, but if either had a public position where they could give orders to the other, then in private the situation was reversed. There were situations where a marriage was made with the clear certainty that one—usually the wife—would always command in public, as when a Sailmistress or Wavemistress married, so there was a ceremony for that, as well. Women did not take their husbands' surnames, or vice versa, nor did they take on any form of them, as in Saldaea.

The Sea Folk did not like going any farther from salt water than they could help. Spotting one in Tar Valon, for instance, or Caemlyn, say, would normally be a very rare event. They made every effort to see that their children were born on the water, even if it was only in a small boat put off from the shore, and that they themselves died on the water. Sea Folk burials inevitably took place at sea; to die on land was considered bad, and to be buried on land even worse.

The Atha'an Miere were marked with tattoos on their hands, indicating a number of things. The left hand showed clan and line. A Windfinder had a three-pointed star on the back of her right hand. A six-pointed star tattooed between thumb and forefinger of the right hand was a symbol of the covenant with the Coramoor; some believed it made one less likely to drown. Some of the other tattoos on the right hand were, in effect, the individual's official record, showing what ships had been served on and what posts and positions had been held.

From the first days of sailing, only Aes Sedai could be refused among those asking passage, and they almost always were. Many Sea Folk considered Aes Sedai bad luck on board in any case. They sent a very few young women to the White Tower in order to lull the Aes Sedai and make them think that there weren't very many candidates among the Atha'an Miere. Most of these young women were deliberately chosen from among women the Windfinders knew would not have sufficient strength to be raised Aes Sedai. Occasionally they chose one who could be raised because they believed that if every woman sent was too weak it might attract attention, but they were never very strong. The few women who went in this manner, expecting to be raised Aes Sedai, had always been, in effect, exiled; they were told to avoid the sea and the Atha'an Miere, even after they reached an age to retire, because the Windfinders always feared that contact between them and these Atha'an Miere Aes Sedai might lead to suspicions on the part of the White Tower. They were a knowing sacrifice. The women chosen to go, whether or not strong enough to be raised, were always chosen from among those who were thought able to keep the necessary secrets. The preferred choice was someone who had already slowed, yet appeared young enough to pass for a wilder of seventeen or eighteen, despite being ten years or more older, though this was not always possible. They tried not to send anyone who was too young (never anyone younger than seventeen), so that she would have some maturity to help her through what the Windfinders saw as, at best, several years of exile from the sea. Those who were strong enough to be raised Aes Sedai were always seen as making the ultimate sacrifice for the good of the Atha'an Miere. As a result, historically there were very few Aes Sedai from among the Sea Folk. At the time of the Tower split, there were only three. They were all Brown Ajah; all of the Sea Folk sisters in the history of the Tower were Brown, which, perhaps not coincidentally, happened to be the one Ajah aside from the White which allowed the least contact with others. There were other similarities among Aes Sedai from the Atha'an Miere. Sea Folk women who were raised Aes Sedai always took a new name, one which was not of the Atha'an Miere, symbolizing their break with their former lives. Inevitably they made few friends even within their own Ajah, living largely solitary lives, and they almost never allowed themselves to become entangled in any sort of alliances or the schemes of others. None would speak of Sea Folk customs or life, a secrecy in which they were aided by Aes Sedai customs against prying, as well as the belief that whatever was before had been left behind and was in no way nearly as important as the White Tower. Most often they dressed very soberly even for Browns, seldom if ever wearing anything like the brilliant colors of the Atha'an Miere. They put off their honor chains and medallions along with any earrings they had the right to wear, and wore none, nor did they often wear necklaces of any kind, but most adopted, often in profusion, the finger rings and bracelets shunned by Sea Folk women. They avoided salt water, never traveling by sea and never even going near the coast if they could avoid it.

Ocean-borne commerce was dominated by Sea Folk ships, which were faster than any others. The Sea Folk were considered by the inhabitants of port cities to be bargainers who outstripped the more widely known Domani. They would carry cargo for others, but their rates were very high, and they were seldom used except where speed of passage was vital. The vast majority of their cargo was traded for themselves. Sea Folk porcelain was highly priced, though it was in fact produced by the Amayar. The Sea Folk did not sell their ships to any but their own and would destroy one to keep it from falling into anyone else's hands. Sea Folk clocks were the most accurate of all, and were highly prized, though the Sea Folk did not make a habit of selling them with any regularity. Pearls, which were mainly found by Amayar pearl divers, were considered the finest; the largest, and nearly all pearls of rare color, such as black or blue, came from them. The Sea Folk were also famed for their glass, not merely housewares, but especially for their looking glasses and other optical products. Even before the Aiel War, when the Cairhienin could use the Silk Path, the Sea Folk were the major source of silk and ivory from Shara.

Atha'an Shadar. The Seanchan name for Darkfriends.

Athan Chandin. A Two Rivers man with Perrin's forces in Malden when they saved Faile and others who had been kidnapped by the Shaido. He was a good shot with the bow, but his truckling manner annoyed Perrin.

Athan Dearn. A fat man from the Two Rivers. He helped to defend Emond's Field from Trollocs.

Atuan Larisett. A Taraboner Aes Sedai of the Yellow Ajah in public, but of the Black Ajah in truth. Atuan was born in 809 NE and went to the White Tower in 825 NE. She wore her dark hair in thin beaded braids that fell to her waist. Atuan had no Warder; she was a member of Talene's heart, along with Galina and Temaile. Atuan knew none of the Black sisters in the Hall, nor did she know Alviarin. After the Black Ajah hunters captured her, she claimed that she walked in the Light once more and swore an oath of obedience to them.

Atuan's Mill. A village on Toman Head. The village was inhabited by frightened villagers following a visit by the Seanchan, who had killed many of them and had left a great charred patch of earth in the middle of the village square that no one wished to talk about. Rand and his party, on the trail of Padan Fain who had stolen back the dagger and Horn of Valere, learned more about the Seanchan invaders and their evil ways there.

Auaine Fanwar. A Borderland farmwife. She was Renald's wife, and she encouraged him to follow Thulin's advice to head north.

Aubrem Pensenor. Andoran High Seat of House Pensenor. He supported Morgase in the Succession, and later supported Elayne. He was lean and craggy and had only a fringe of white hair, but his back was straight and his eyes were clear. He had been among the first to reach Caemlyn to aid Elayne, with near to a hundred men and news that it was Arymilla Marne marching on the city with Elenia and Naean supporting her.

Aurana. Tuon's fourteen-year-old sister; Tuon thought her too young to be plotting against her.

Avar Hachami. One of Myrelle's Warders, a Saldaean. He was hawk-nosed and square-chinned, with a thick, gray-streaked mustache like down-curved horns. He was saved by Myrelle following the death of the first Aes Sedai to whom he was bonded. Rumor had it that Myrelle was married to her first three Warders: Croi Makin, Nuhel Dromand and Avar Hachami.

Avarhin, Shiaine. *See* Shiaine Avarhin

Avarhin, Willim. A poor Andoran nobleman and father of the real Lady Shiaine, both of whom were murdered by Mili Skane. His sign was the Heart and Hand.

Avendesora. Aiel word for "the Tree of Life." Legend said that there was a single Tree of Life, while many would equate the word *Avendesora* with the chora tree, which in the Third Age had dwindled to a single specimen, found in Rhuidean. It was said that *Avendesora* made no seed, so it is unclear how the Aiel obtained a sapling from it to give to Cairhien. *See also* chora tree *and* Tree of Life

Avendoraldera. The only chora tree, a sapling of *Avendesora*, to leave the Aiel Waste in the Third Age. Given to Cairhien as an unprecedented offer of peace, it was cut down by King Laman, starting the Aiel War.

Avene Sahera. A woman in Ravinda, Kandor, interviewed by Moiraine during the search for the infant Dragon Reborn. Avene used the bounty given her by the Aes Sedai to build an inn, called The White Tower. Her tenth child, Migel, was on Moiraine's list, but he was born thirty miles from Dragonmount and a week before Gitara's Foretelling.

Avharin, Einion. One of the three most famous First Counsels in Far Madding history. A statue of her stood in Avharin Market in Far Madding, pointing to the Caemlyn Gate.

Avharin Market. One of three markets in Far Madding where foreigners were allowed to trade.

Avi Shendar. A man in Marcedin who kept pigeons. His bread was buttered on at least two sides. He sent reports out for Ronde Macura, one northeast toward Tar Valon, and another one west for her, to an unknown recipient. He also copied the same message to yet another destination, in a different direction from the other messages.

Aviellin. A Maiden who was badly wounded at Malden while helping take out the sentries northwest of Malden so the carts could get through. She was Healed by Janina, and participated in the battle at Malden.

Aviendha. A woman of the Nine Valleys sept of the Taardad Aiel, born in 980 NE. She was *Far Dareis Mai* until she began training to be a Wise One. She could channel, and her strength level was 11(2). Aviendha was about 5'9" tall with blue-green (or green, according to various folk) eyes and reddish hair which was cut short as a Maiden, but she let it grow after being apprenticed to the Wise Ones. Her wards against eavesdropping were better than Aes Sedai's. She had the ability to unweave and the rare abilities to read residues and to tell what a previously unseen weave would do before it coalesced. She displayed an ability to tell what a *ter'angreal* could do, though she could not make one, and showed great ability at defending against attacks, too; some at shielding, but more in blocking thrusts, so to speak. She had no feel for Healing. She could divide her flows more than Elayne, perhaps as much as Nynaeve.

Aviendha was one of the Aiel sent to the wetlands to search for He Who

Comes With the Dawn. When Dailin, one of her companions, was injured, Aviendha approached Nynaeve, Elayne and Egwene for help. Nynaeve Healed Dailin, and afterward Aviendha followed the women, saw them captured and brought other Aiel to rescue them. Aviendha went to the Stone, and became friends with the women.

She was then summoned to the Waste to become an apprentice to the Wise Ones; she traveled there with Rand and his group via Portal Stone, and immediately went to Rhuidean. Inside the *ter'angreal* at Rhuidean she saw herself fated to fall in love with Rand, and she was unwittingly part of a Wise One plan to tie Rand to the Aiel by giving him an Aiel wife. Aviendha objected to the plan—she had promised to watch Rand for Elayne and did not want to fall in love with him. She nonetheless became his teacher, since the Wise Ones ordered it. In thanks, Rand gave Aviendha a bracelet. In return, she gave him Laman's sword; he kept the blade, but returned the jeweled hilt. When Rand walked in on her naked, Aviendha fled, making a gateway to Seanchan. Rand followed, saved her from drowning and made her a shelter in a snowstorm. When she awoke, they made love. Rand announced his intention of marrying her, but she declined. On the way back to the gateway, they encountered Seanchan with *sul'dam* and *damane*, but escaped.

Aviendha participated in the battle against the Shaido for Cairhien. She accompanied Rand and Egwene to the docks, where Lanfear attacked them. Aviendha was not as severely injured as Egwene, and went to Caemlyn with Rand after news came that Rahvin had killed Morgase. There she was struck by lightning and killed, but when Rand smote Rahvin with balefire, she was brought back to life. Rand sent Mat to Salidar to bring Elayne to Caemlyn, and Aviendha went as well. Aviendha accompanied Nynaeve, Elayne and Mat to Ebou Dar. There she met with the Sea Folk and watched Carridin. She made a gateway to the Kin's farm, and then terrified the Aes Sedai by unweaving it.

Aviendha was part of the circle that used the Bowl of the Winds. When the Seanchan came near, Elayne made a gateway to Andor and then tried to unweave it; she was not trained as Aviendha had been, and it exploded, injuring her, Aviendha and Birgitte and killing many Seanchan. Aviendha was Healed by Nynaeve and accompanied Elayne to Caemlyn, where they became first-sisters. Aviendha resumed her Wise One training in Caemlyn. She stayed with Elayne, helping her in many ways such as identifying the functions of *ter'angreal* discovered in Ebou Dar, until the Aiel left for Bandar Eban and the Wise Ones told her she must go too. After worrying that she was being punished, she realized that she had to declare herself a Wise One; she did, and went to Rhuidean. She passed through the crystal columns twice. The first time she saw the history of the Aiel, and the second time she saw a desolate future. She returned to the Wise Ones, and then met with Rand. She told him that he must accept her, Elayne and Min or he would have none. She asked for a boon—that the Aiel be included in Rand's peace.

At Shayol Ghul in the Last Battle she fought as the commander of all the channelers there. In a struggle with Graendal/Hessalam, she was badly injured and at Graendal's mercy. Just as Graendal was about to Compel her, she unwove a gateway, which caused the Compulsion to affect Graendal instead. Graendal, enthralled by Aviendha, carried her back to camp, where she was Healed as far as was possible. She later gave birth to Rand's quadruplets.

Avin, Master. A gate guard in Baerlon, Andor, who let Moiraine and her party into Baerlon. He had a wizened face and was half toothless.

Avin, Rhea. *See* Rhea Avin

Avriny, Elaida do a'Roihan. *See* Elaida do Avriny a'Roihan

Awlsten. An Asha'man who was with Ituralde in Maradon and at Shayol Ghul. Atop the pass leading into Thakan'dar, he signaled the Aiel to roll boulders and burning logs down on to the Shadowspawn.

Ayako Norsoni. An Arafellin Aes Sedai of the White Ajah and the loyalist contingent, with a strength level of 18(6). She was about 5'2" tall, with wavy, waist-length black hair and dark eyes that seemed almost black when she was concentrating. Ayako was brown-skinned, although not as dark as a Domani. She prided herself on her logic, but she was not a particularly cool-appearing woman, rather being on the merry side, with a twinkle in her eyes, although she seemed shy, a rarity among Aes Sedai. Ayako was part of the Black Tower expedition under Toveine Gazal and was captured by the Asha'man and bonded by Donalo Sandomere. She was the only White in the expedition. Ayako took part in beating Toveine and it disturbed her that she had. It was irrational, or so she tried to tell herself, but it felt so right. She and Donalo were Turned to the Shadow and captured in Stedding Sholoon by Androl and his allies, including some elderly Ogier.

Aybara clan. A Two Rivers Family. *See* Adora, Carlin, Con, Deselle, Ealsin, Eward, Jaim, Joslyn, Magde, Neain *and* Paetram Aybara

Aybara, Perrin. *See* Perrin t'Bashere Aybara

Aydaer. A Two Rivers family. *See* Jared *and* Pel Aydaer

Ayellin clan. A family in the Two Rivers. *See* Corin, Dav, Jon, Lara, Larine, Marisa, Milli, Neysa *and* Sari Ayellin.

Ayellin, Mistress. A Two Rivers woman whom Nynaeve treated for fever.

Aylar, Malena. *See* Malena Aylar

Ayliah, Get. *See* Get Ayliah

Aynal, Widow. The annual sheep shearing in Emond's Field took place in a space called "Widow Aynal's meadow," even though no one remembered who she was.

Aynora, Mistress. A woman in a song who has a rooster. At least one version of the song was actually about a rooster.

Ayyad, the. Channelers in Shara. They lived in villages cut off from the outside world, surrounded by high walls that obscured vision in every direction; no one except the Ayyad were allowed to enter and any non-Ayyad who managed to enter was killed on sight. Supposedly no Ayyad left without permission. The source of this permission was somewhat vague, but since it was widely known that no Ayyad would channel without instructions from or the permission of the currently ruling Sh'boan or Sh'botay, it was believed by all that any Ayyad who was outside the villages had such permission. The Ayyad were tattooed on their faces at birth. The only exception to this was someone who was discovered to be able to channel later in life. They were presumed to be the result of a union between one of their ancestors and an Ayyad; they were seized, tattooed and confined to an Ayyad village for the rest of their lives. Sexual congress between Ayyad and non-Ayyad was punishable by death for the non-Ayyad, and for the Ayyad as well if it could be proven the Ayyad forced the other. Any child of such a union was killed by exposure to the elements. It was only female Ayyad who ever left the villages, with two exceptions.

Male Ayyad were kept completely cloistered and were not educated in much of anything beyond the ability to feed and dress themselves and do simple chores; they certainly never learned to read or write. Male Ayyad were considered breeding stock only, by female Ayyad; in truth, the records the Ayyad kept of bloodlines were akin to the records of horse-breeders. Sons were raised communally, rather than by their mothers, as daughters were. In fact, sons were never referred to as sons among the Ayyad; they were only referred to as "the male."

The first exception to a male Ayyad being confined to the villages occurred when he reached about sixteen. At that point he would be hooded and transported inside a closed wagon to a distant village, thus never seeing anything outside the villages. There he was matched with one or more women who wished children. In his twenty-first year—or sooner if he showed signs of beginning to channel—the Ayyad male was once more hooded and taken away, believing that he was on his way to another village. Instead he was killed and the body cremated.

Most Sh'boan and Sh'botay lived through their seven-year reigns and died thereafter believing that it was "the Will of the Pattern," but in truth the Ayyad killed the ruling Sh'boan or Sh'botay. The ruler was always surrounded by Ayyad women as servants, and the only way to approach the ruler, especially for a favor or ruling, was through these women, and the reply was usually delivered by them, as speech with the Sh'boan or Sh'botay was a very great honor. Some rulers failed to live the full seven years—such early death always taken as a sign of the Creator's displeasure, resulting in penances served across the land by high and low—and it should be taken as a certainty that these men and women had discovered the truth, perhaps of why their reigns would last only seven years, perhaps of the fact that while they in fact wielded great power, the true control of the land was in the hands of the Ayyad, through the women surrounding the ruler.

Azereos, Master. An Illianer trader in Far Madding with a white beard and pointed nose. Rand eavesdropped on him at an inn called The Golden Wheel, while a Far Madding trader advised him not to move his trade to Lugard.

Azeri, Yurith. *See* Yurith Azeri

Azi al'Thone. A Two Rivers man in Perrin's army. He sometimes acted as Perrin's bodyguard and was with him at his Whitecloak trial. Azi was present when Perrin forged *Mah'alleinir*. He fought in the Last Battle, showing great skill with his bow.

Azil Mareed. The Domani High Captain of the Tower Guard and advisor to Marya Sedai on the decision-making council of the Grand Alliance during the Battle of the Shining Walls.

Azille Narof. An Aes Sedai who lived at the time of the formation of the White Tower.

Azril. A serving girl at an inn called Culain's Hound, in Caemlyn. On Verin's instructions, she took tea laced with brandy to the young women from the Two Rivers when they were frightened by Rand, after he was bonded by Alanna.

Azzara din Karak. A Sea Folk Windfinder with a strength level of 18(6). She accompanied Renaile to the Tarasin Palace, and then to the Kin's farm. Because she was one of the strongest available among the remaining Windfinders in Ebou Dar, she observed the use of the Bowl of the Winds, then fled to Caemlyn with Elayne and her companions when the Seanchan attack was discovered.

Azzedin, Edesina. *See* Edesina Azzedin

B

Ba'alzamon. An ancient name meaning "Heart of the Dark." *See* Ishamael *and* Moridin

Bael. A man of the Jhirad sept of the Goshien Aiel and the *Sovin Nai* society, and the clan chief of the Goshien. He was married to Dorindha, with whom he had three children, and to Melaine, with whom he was expecting twins. He was about 6'10" tall and approximately 275 pounds, with a long face, gray-streaked red hair and blue-gray eyes. Bael had a habit of fingering his earlobe when he thought. He went to Caemlyn with Rand. There he was in charge, along with Davram Bashere, until after Elayne arrived; his Aiel and Bashere's Saldaeans policed the city and surrounding countryside. Rand sent him and the Goshien to Bandar Eban to try to restore order. In the Last Battle, Bael was with Elayne and her army.

Baelome, Lady. A Ghealdanin noblewoman ordered flogged by the Prophet for speaking of "this Rand al'Thor." She was the most powerful member of the Crown High Council in Ghealdan.

Baerin. An Aiel woman whose daughter was a Wise One's apprentice. Baerin took part in a discussion in the Wise Ones' tent involving how to deal with the *Car'a'carn*. She was a Maiden of the Spear before she married and had children.

Baelder. An Aiel Red Shield who fought with Rhuarc in the Last Battle.

Baerlon. A town in Andor with a wooden palisade, north of the Two Rivers. It was on the road from the mines in the Mountains of Mist to Whitebridge and thence to Caemlyn. Merchants stopped at Baerlon on their way into the Two Rivers to buy tabac and wool. It had a Town Watch and a Whitebridge Gate. Proximity to the mines in the Mountain of Mist was an economic boon to the town, as its iron smelting plants processed the ore.

Bagand, Sereille. *See* Sereille Bagand

Baijan'm'hael. Old Tongue for "Attack Leader." It was a rank assigned to Manel Rochaid by Taim; it indicated that he was second to Gedwyn, the Tsorovan'm'hael.

Bailene. A feast celebrated on the ninth day of Amadaine in Arad Doman, Tarabon, Amadicia and Tear.

Baily, Martna. A fictional pie maker in Hinderstap.

Bain. A Maiden of the Spear of the Black Rock sept of the Shaarad Aiel, born in 981 NE. She was 5'8½" tall, with flame-colored hair and dark blue eyes. Although they were from clans with a blood feud, she adopted Chiad as her first-sister; neither would let a man come to her without the other. Bain went to the

Stone of Tear. She and Chiad became friends with Faile, and accompanied Faile to the Two Rivers. Bain went to Caemlyn, Cairhien and Ghealdan with Perrin. She was taken *gai'shain* by Sevanna and the Jumai Shaido when Faile's riding party was captured. After Sevanna was taken by the Seanchan, Bain became *gai'shain* to Gaul, who was in love with Chiad but did not like Bain. During the Last Battle, Bain and Chiad helped in the Healing facility set up at Berelain's palace in Mayene, and began collecting the wounded from the battlefields.

Bain, Old. A farmer in Andor from whom Alpert Mull bought hay.

Bair. A Wise One of the Haido sept of the Shaarad Aiel. She was a dreamwalker but she could not channel. She was the eldest Wise One of the Shaarad, in her late nineties or more; she had a creased grandmotherly face, white hair and pale blue eyes. Bair spoke with a reedy but strong voice. She was a bony woman, with angular shoulders. Bair outlived three husbands. While Amys and Melaine were the best at interpreting the dream, Bair was better at manipulating *Tel'aran'rhiod*. After Aviendha reported her visions of the future in Rhuidean, Bair went to the city and entered the *ter'angreal* a second time and saw similar visions. Bair survived the Last Battle to attend Rand's funeral.

Bajad drovja. A curse in the Old Tongue uttered by Sammael.

Bakayar Mishima. A Seanchan captain under Banner-General Tylee Khirgan. He had yellow hair and several scars on his square face, and one scar met the corner of his mouth, distorting his smile. Mishima was a hard-bitten man who to Perrin smelled strangely of amusement. He led the Seanchan who dumped forkroot into the aqueduct at Malden, and fought in the battle against the Shaido there. On the way back to Ebou Dar, they were attacked by Trollocs, and he was killed by an arrow in the throat.

Bakh. A soldier in Lan's army at Tarwin's Gap. He always had a crossbow tied to the back of his horse, despite Lan's warning that it might go off accidentally. His sword got caught in a Trolloc's armor, but before he died, he killed one Trolloc with a crossbow shot to the eye and killed another with his boot knife.

Bakuun, Assid. *See* Assid Bakuun

Bakuvun, Hafeen. *See* Hafeen Bakuvun

Balasun. A nation that arose after the Trolloc Wars.

Balat. A Domani sword-swallower and fire-eater with Luca's show. His brother was Abar.

Baldene, Covarla. *See* Covarla Baldene

Baldhere, Lord. The Swordbearer to the Throne of the Clouds for Queen Ethenielle of Kandor. He carried what was said to be the Sword of Kirukan cradled in one arm, the hilt always toward the ruler, while conducting official business. In addition, he wore a sword at his hip, a longer, two-handed sword in a saddle-scabbard behind his saddle, and carried a mace held on his saddle by a cord. He was slender with white streaks at his temples. Baldhere was gay. He was known for a sharp tongue and a biting wit, and often spoke or behaved in a fussy manner. Regardless, he could bellow when needed, as when shouting orders to troops. He affected to be more concerned with music and clothes than anything else. Baldhere commanded the armies of Kandor in the field for Ethenielle after the death of her husband in 979 NE. Most Kandori soldiers would have followed him to Shayol Ghul. Baldhere was a very good general, but not one of the great captains. He was troubled by Agelmar's decisions during the Last Battle, and took those concerns to Lan, leading to Agelmar being relieved of command.

balefire. An extreme weapon of channelers. It burned anything it touched into nonexistence and also burned threads from the Pattern, an effect which could destroy past realities. People who were balefired could not be brought back by the Dark One; however, their souls were not destroyed, and they could be spun out by the Wheel at a later time.

Wiping a person out of the Pattern did not remove memories of the person, but the Pattern readjusted itself so far as the physical world was concerned; nothing done by that person during that blanked time actually occurred. People remembered these things as before, but they had not happened—now. And along with that, all the ripples from the person's actions were remembered as having happened, but they never did. People could remember doing things that they did not do. The dead didn't come back to life, but people found that their memories of that time were completely false, that they remembered doing things themselves that apparently had never happened. The strain on the fabric of the Pattern from major uses was so great that even those supporting the Shadow were reluctant to use balefire for fear they might destroy everything, although the Dark One encouraged the use of balefire as events approached the Last Battle.

balescream. Another effect of the use of balefire on the Pattern. It was a warping, rippling of the air as if the Pattern itself was howling in pain.

balfone. A musical instrument of the Age of Legends.

Balgar, Mattin Stepaneos den. *See* Mattin Stepaneos den Balgar

Balinor. Verin's first Warder. It took ten years for her to get over his death and bond Tomas.

Ball and Hoop, The. An inn in Caemlyn where the Sea Folk Wavemistress of Clan Catelar stayed while trying vainly to get an audience with Rand.

Balladare Arandaille. An Aes Sedai of the Brown Ajah who served as Amyrlin from 115 to 142 NE. Balladare was a weak Amyrlin. The Kavarthen Wars occurred during her reign.

Ballair. An Aes Sedai who was an advisor to Ishara, the first Andoran queen.

Ballin Elamri den Rendalle. An Illianer nobleman who was a member of the Council of Nine.

Balmaen, Jenare. *See* Jenare Balmaen

Balthamel. A Forsaken whose original name was Eval Ramman. During the Age of Legends, he was a historian studying vanished cultures, if not a distinguished one. He also enjoyed frequenting what would be called taverns of the lowest sort. A lover of the ways of the flesh even more than Aginor, he was an avid pursuer of the opposite sex, and delighted in various perversions and excesses. Unlike Graendal, he had no desire to collect pets, but he wanted to sleep with every beautiful woman he saw. He had a wildfire temper that he often could not control, and he often did not try to. Supposedly, more than once he came very close to being punitively bound with the Power against doing violence. Despite his position at an institute of higher learning in M'Jinn (the name of the institution is not known) he enjoyed consorting with the rougher elements of society, even criminals, to a degree which brought considerable censure. Others thought that his strength in the One Power was one of the main reasons that he was not dismissed from his post.

Apparently, immortality was the sole reason he went over to the Shadow. To live forever and never age: his motive was as simple as that. He made his journey to Shayol Ghul to pledge his soul somewhere in the middle years of the Collapse. Although he stood high in the councils of the Shadow during the war, his exact role was impossible to ascertain. It was reported that he might have headed an intelligence network which competed with that run by Moghedien. Without doubt he never held a field command, though it is possible that he did serve as a governor. Whatever his position, it is known that he participated in a number of large-scale atrocities, including setting up the camps which were meant to breed humans as food for Trollocs.

Balthamel was trapped near the surface of the Bore when it was sealed by Lews Therin, and he aged. He wore a leather mask with the face of a smiling youth when he appeared at the Eye of the World. He was killed by the Green Man. The Dark One put his soul in a new body and he became Aran'gar, also known as Halima Sarinov. *See also* Aran'gar

Balwen Mayel. The Last king of Aridhol; he was also called Balwen Ironhand. During the Trolloc Wars, he turned to Mordeth for advice; Mordeth convinced him to use the Shadow's tactics against the Shadow. Following that advice led to the corruption and downfall of Aridhol.

Balwer, Sebban. *See* Sebban Balwer

Ban. *See* Bandry Crawe

Ban al'Seen. A Two Rivers man who joined Perrin's army. He had dark hair and a prominent nose. He was just a little older than Perrin. Ban was a cousin of Wil, son of Jac, and one of the first two leaders of Perrin's fighters. He was part of the original band that hunted Trollocs with Perrin and got ambushed; he led half of the approximately seventy fighters. He continued to fight alongside the Two Rivers men at Dumai's Wells, Malden and the Last Battle.

Banas. A widower in Jarra, Ghealdan. He was dragged through the wedding arches by Widow Jorath.

Band of the Red Hand. 1) A legendary group of heroes who had many exploits, finally dying in the defense of Manetheren when that land was destroyed during the Trolloc Wars. Their Old Tongue name was *Shen an Calhar.* 2) A military formation put together almost by accident by Mat Cauthon and organized along the lines of military forces during what was considered the height of the military arts, the days of Artur Hawkwing and the centuries immediately preceding. The Band was composed of several squadrons of cavalry and several banners of infantry, the latter divided among pikemen and crossbowmen/ archers. Several banners composed a legion and several legions composed a great legion, divisions that were devised once the Band became large enough. Banners were commanded by Banner-Generals, legions by Lieutenant-Generals, and great legions by Captain-Generals. The formal title for the commander of the Band was Marshal-General, which was also one of the titles given Mat when he assumed command of all the Seanchan forces in the Last Battle.

Other groups were attached to the Band; for example, each banner had musicians, and after a battle, these musicians became stretcher-bearers for the wounded. The Band also had a supply banner, which was responsible for logistics, and a miners' banner, which served as an engineers' corps, capable of everything from building bridges to tunneling under an enemy's fortifications. The miners' banner was split up, with men being assigned to various legions for specific duties. The same was true of the signal banner, which used signal flags, semaphore towers and heliographs to transmit messages.

Bandar Eban. The capital of Arad Doman, and the prime port city of the northwest. Massive gates penetrated the city walls and opened up to streets of packed earth, with wooden boardwalks at the sides. Arandi Square, the main city square, was set with copper fountains in the shape of horses leaping from a frothy wave. The buildings were tall and square, shaped like boxes stacked atop one another. Rows of square wooden houses filled the city, rolling down a gentle incline to the massive port, the widest part of the city. Banners flew above, or hung from every building, some used as business signs, family names, or location names. The wealthy part of the city was located on the heights in the east. One of the grandest mansions was the seat of House Chadmar. There was a king's palace, but it was inferior to the homes of the Council of Merchants. Bandar Eban's Terhana Library was considered to be among the best in the world.

banded adder. A poisonous snake with glittering scales.

Bandevin, Jala. *See* Jala Bandevin

Bandry Crawe. A young man from Emond's Field. He was ten months older than Rand, Mat and Perrin, and he saw the Myrddraal in Emond's Field. Ban joined Perrin's army at Malden. He knew how to make stools that were used by Perrin's army.

Banikhan Mountains. A mountain range in Saldaea, along the Aryth Ocean at the World's End. It was also known as the Sea Wall. Ice peppers grew well in its foothills, and gems were found there as well.

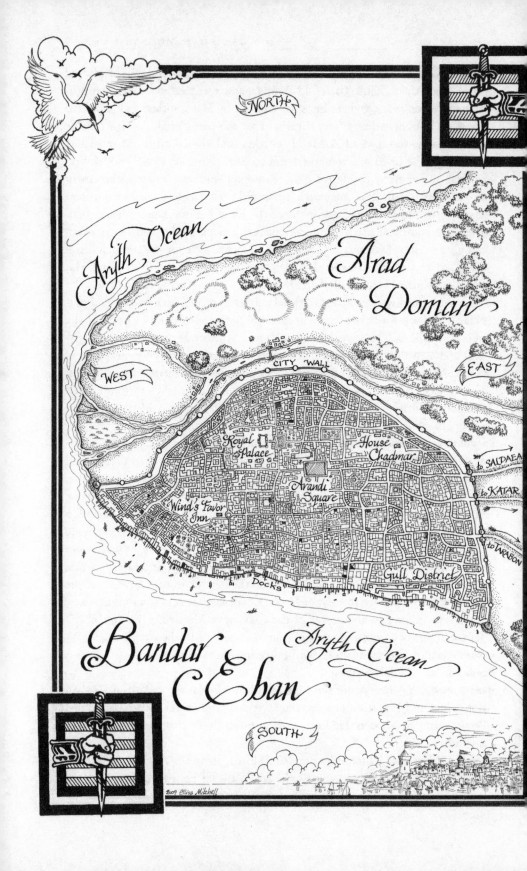

Banner, al'Thor's. *See* al'Thor's Banner

Banner-General. In the Band of the Red Hand and Seanchan forces, a general commanding a banner. A Seanchan Banner-General wore three thin plumes.

Banner of Light. *See* al'Thor's Banner

bannerman. A soldier who carried his commander's banner.

Bao the Wyld. The name taken by Demandred in Shara.

Bar Dowtry. A square-faced Emond's Field man. Nynaeve caught him with Kimry Lewin in his father's hayloft; both were punished severely, and a month later Bar and Kimry were married. It was said that neither could sit for a week after the wedding. Bar later started making a name for himself with cabinetmaking. He joined Perrin's army at Malden.

Barada, Vilnar. *See* Vilnar Barada

Baradon, Teslyn. *See* Teslyn Baradon

Baran. A young Tairen lord who was foppish and fastidious and always seemed to be looking down his sharp nose. He thought the Aiel were savages who lived in caves. Baran was not as boastful as Reimon, but he was as opinionated and overbearing. He played cards with Mat and was terrified when the cards came to life. He was killed by the Shaido as he attempted to leave Cairhien in search of aid.

Barashelle. A woman who was raised Aes Sedai during the Trolloc Wars. Anselan was her Warder. Their story passed down through the ages as a romance, but Birgitte revealed the true story: Barashelle bonded a Warder while she was still Accepted; when she was found out, she was forced to pass the bond to another and remain Accepted three extra years, and then bonded Anselan, a stubborn older man chosen for Barashelle by the Amyrlin.

Barashta. An Ogier-built city in Eharon, one of the Ten Nations after the Breaking; it later became Ebou Dar. Its residents were called Barashandan.

Barasine. A lanky, long-legged Aes Sedai of the Red Ajah and the loyalist contingent. Logain Ablar said that she was one of those who forced him to declare himself Dragon Reborn. She assisted in capturing Egwene at Northharbor, and thought Egwene might be stilled and beheaded that same night; she showed no eagerness when she said it; she was just stating facts. Barasine was made a Sitter to replace Duhara Basaheen. She was a participant in Nynaeve's test for Aes Sedai; she voted that Nynaeve had not passed.

bard-harp. A musical instrument played by Asmodean as Natael.

Barda, Narenwin. *See* Narenwin Barda

Bards, Forms of Recitation of. There were three forms of recitation used by bards in storytelling: Common, Plain Chant and High Chant. Common was ordinary speech, telling a story as one man in the street might tell another. Plain Chant added a rhythmic half-singing to poetic imagery; nothing was ever described plainly and conveying emotion was as important as conveying description. High Chant was sung. The rhythms were more precise, and emotional content was more important than mere description. High Chant could be all but unintelligible to those who were not used to it; it was a form used only by court-bards and the like.

Barel Layden. An Andoran nobleman and High Seat of his minor House who was loyal to Elayne and brought armsmen to support her. He did not hesitate to lead his men against the Black Ajah when they held Elayne.

Barettal. A member of Ituralde's personal guard in Saldaea. He and Connel were the only two of Ituralde's guards still alive when they were allowed to retreat into Maradon while being pursued by the Shadowspawn army.

Bargain, the. The agreement made with the Sea Folk on Rand's behalf for Sea Folk ships to be at his disposal, but which also saddled Rand with obligations, such as not changing any law of the Atha'an Miere; their being allowed to build a compound in each major port that came to Rand, acceded to by the local rulers so the agreement would survive Rand; and his keeping an embassy of Sea Folk with him and agreeing to attend the Mistress of the Ships when summoned, but not more than twice in any three consecutive years.

Bari. A juggler with Valan Luca's show; he worked with his brother Kin. Among other things, they worked with ribbon-twined hoops.

Bari. A palace retainer of more than twenty years' service in the Royal Palace in Caemlyn. He was a panting and round-faced man who came to tell Rand that Ogier had come. He was very excited about the Ogier. He remained in the palace serving Elayne.

Barid Bel Medar. Demandred's name before he turned to the Shadow.

Barim Halle. An Andoran man from Kore Springs who followed Gareth Bryne when he chased after Siuan, Leane and Min. He had served under Bryne in the Queen's Guards. He was hard and wiry, with a leathery egg-shaped head and white eyebrows that seemed to be trying to make up for the lack of other hair. When he didn't know whether to tell something, or didn't want to, he put his tongue in his cheek, although he didn't realize it.

Barin Madwen. The deceased husband of Maglin. He and his wife were the innkeepers of The Nine Rings in Tremonsien, Cairhien. When he died, Maglin planned to go back to her native Lugard, but Barin left her the inn and his brother the money, the opposite of what Maglin expected.

Baris. A lean man in Ebou Dar. He mortally wounded Masic in a duel in the Rahad as Nynaeve and Elayne looked on.

Barit Chavana. An acrobat in Luca's circus, one of four men said to be brothers, although the four looked very different. Barit was darker than Juilin and had Sea Folk tattoos on his hands, though he wore no earrings. He was short and compact.

barkers. A pejorative Ebou Dari term for young women of a certain type.

Barklan Tower. A watchtower in Kandor south of Heeth Tower.

Barlden, Mayor. The mayor of Hinderstap. He was sturdy, with dark hair and a beard. He tried to get Mat to leave before sunset, but greed won out and he allowed one gamble too many. The following day he explained Hinderstap's situation.

Barlett. The leader of the Whitecloak scouts with Galad after Galad became Lord Captain Commander. He was lean with a scar on his face. He was really loyal to Asunawa, and led Galad and his group of Children into a trap.

Barmanes Nolaisen. A Cairhienin member of *Cha Faile.* Camaille was his sister. He accompanied Perrin to Almizar. When the clerk there died from coughing up beetles, Barmanes smelled of panic. After someone tried to kill Perrin, Barmanes removed the arrow from Perrin's arm.

Barmellin. A man near Tremonsien, Cairhien. He was on his way to deliver brandy to The Nine Rings when he saw the Choedan Kal start to glow. He was terrified and drove his horse Nisa back to his farm as fast as he could.

Barmellin, Doilaine. *See* Doilaine Barmellin

Baroc. The Master of Blades of Atha'an Miere when Nesta din Reas was Mistress of the Ships. He was spindly with deep-set eyes and a bit of white hair. He wore a full dozen earrings and a number of thick gold chains around his neck. He and Nesta were executed by the Seanchan for rebellion.

Barran clan. A family in the Two Rivers. *See* Doral, Hilde, Hu, Jondyn *and* Tad Barran

Barriga. A Borderlander merchant who brought a caravan to Heeth Tower, where it was attacked by Trollocs. He should have listened to Rebek to stay away.

Barrin. A member of the Deathwatch Guard. He once stopped a man from breathing on Tuon because he suspected the man's mouth was filled with poisons. He was right.

Barsabba. A Seanchan city or region. It was associated with Suroth, being mentioned in her title.

Barsalla, Aleis. *See* Aleis Barsalla

Barshaw, Torwyn. *See* Torwyn Barshaw

Barsine. An Ogier-built city in Jaramide, one of the Ten Nations after the Breaking; it was known as Barsine of the golden spires. It was ravaged and burned at the beginning of the Trolloc Wars.

Barsine lace. A type of lace on the ruff of Mat's coat in his memory of a former persona who had danced with a beautiful Sea Folk emissary.

Barstere clan. A family from Watch Hill in Two Rivers. *See* Flann, Kev *and* Jerinvar Barstere

Barthanes Damodred. A Cairhienin nobleman and a Darkfriend. He became High Seat of his House upon the death of Laman. The sign of House Damodred was the Crown and Tree; the Charging Boar was his personal seal. Barthanes, who was Laman's cousin, was slim and tall for a Cairhienin and had dark eyes and long graying hair. Barthanes had built a mansion on the site of the Cairhienin Ogier grove. He hosted an elaborate party and invited Rand; there he passed Fain's message to Rand. The following day, he was found torn to pieces in his bedchamber, with his head stuck on a spike.

Bartim. The innkeeper at The Wayfarer's Rest in Whitebridge, Andor. He was fat and balding.

Bartol. Warder to Erian. He was left in Cairhien when Erian went with Cadsuane to find Rand; later he used his bond to help Logain and Bashere find them.

Bartu. A Shienaran soldier who came to follow and believe in Masema. He stood about 5'9" tall. Bartu was one of those following Ingtar when he and Perrin pursued the Horn of Valere to Falme. He wintered in the Mountains of Mist with Perrin and Rand; after Rand left and the Shienarans were abandoned to make their own way, he stuck with Masema in Ghealdan. He was killed before the Last Battle by *Cha Faile*.

Baryn, House. A major noble House in Andor; its High Seat was Lir, the brother of Aedelle; its sign the Winged Hammer.

Basaheen, Duhara. *See* Duhara Basaheen

Basan. Merana's Warder. He died before the Aiel War, and she never bonded another.

Basar, Latian. *See* Latian Basar

Basel Gill. The innkeeper of The Queen's Blessing in Caemlyn. A soldier during the Aiel War, he was fifty to fifty-five years of age when Rand met him. Gill was stout and pink-faced with graying hair that he tried to comb over a bald spot. A friend of Thom Merrilin's, he was willing to help Rand and Mat in Caemlyn because Thom sent them to him. He knew that Moiraine considered them important somehow, but he thought Mat was a wastrel and a gambler, and wondered why Thom was friendly with him. He was very loyal to Morgase and followed her when she went on the lam; he questioned her judgment, but in his eyes she was his queen, and he would follow her through anything and everything. After escaping from the Seanchan in Amadicia, he and his party were rescued from Dragonsworn by Perrin. Gill became Perrin's *shambayan*, in charge of obtaining supplies and also running the household. Lini intimidated him. He went on to fight in the Last Battle.

Basene, the Lady. An alias of Graendal.

Basharande. A nation that arose after the Trolloc Wars.

Bashere, House. A noble House of Saldaea, including the Lord of Bashere, Davram; his wife, Deira; his son, Maedin; and his daughter, Faile. The sigil of House Bashere was a simple scarlet flower, the kingspenny, on a field of blue. This flower did not die back even in Saldaean winters, and was the first to reappear after a forest fire; in short, it was a blossom nothing could kill. *See also* Deira, Davram *and* Maedin Bashere *and* Faile ni Bashere t'Aybara

Basolaine, N'Delia. Putative translator of *The Prophecies of the Dragon*, First Maid and Swordfast to Raidhen of Hol Cuchone.

Basram. A Domani soldier with Lan at the end of the Aiel War. He fell asleep on guard duty, and Lan woke him up.

Bassane Maliandred. One of Merise's Warders. He was Cairhienin, 5'8" tall, with dark hair and eyes and a sun-dark face. Bassane was quite stocky, and appeared slow and placid. He was just short of his middle years.

Bastine, Adelorna. *See* Adelorna Bastine

Battle Ajah. The Green Ajah, so named because their primary purpose was to hold themselves ready for Tarmon Gai'don.

Battle of Cuallin Dhen. A famous battle in which Queen Modrellein of Andor established her bravery against the Tairens, seven hundred years before the Last Battle.

Battle of Kolesar, the. A battle from Mat's memories in which Classen Bayor lost his cavalry in the marsh.

Battle of Maighande. A key defeat of the Trollocs that led to the cessation of the Trolloc Wars. Rashima Kerenmosa died in the battle; when it was over she was found surrounded by her five Warders and a vast wall of Trollocs and Myrddraal which contained the corpses of no fewer than nine Dreadlords.

Battle of the Priya Narrows. A battle from Mat's memories. In it, Mat led forces against the Hamarean army; the Hamareans dammed the river that Mat was planning to use to trap them.

Battle of the Shining Walls, the. The battle outside Tar Valon between the Aiel and the Grand Alliance in 978 NE that ended the Aiel War. It began on the morning of the day before Danshu. The Alliance's force numbered approximately 170,000 men; the Aiel fielded seventy to eighty thousand, although some sources claimed that it was much larger. For three days the armies fought furiously on both sides of the River Erinin, both armies hampered by snow. Late on the third day, the Aiel succeeded in their goal of killing King Laman of Cairhien. The Aiel then began to gather their forces east of the Erinin, and by sunrise on the fourth day, they were heading back to the Waste. Alliance forces gave pursuit, and engaged the Aiel rear guard in skirmishes, some large. When the Aiel entered Kinslayer's Dagger, the Alliance gave up the chase. The battle was also called the Blood Snow, the Battle of the Nations, the Battle of the Red Snows, the Battle of Tar Valon and the Battle of the Blood Snow.

Bavin Rockshaw. Perrin's Cairhienin quartermaster. He had blond hairs speckled through his graying brown and a pale face. He was spindly but had a round paunch, had been a quartermaster since the Aiel War and was an expert at all facets of the job, including taking bribes.

Bay of Remara. A body of water between Tear and Mayene. Godan was a Tairen town on the bay.

Bay Road. A road in Ebou Dar running west along the side of the bay from the city to Westpoint Lighttower.

Bayanar, Sheriam. *See* Sheriam Bayanar

Bayle Domon. The captain and owner of the *Spray*. He was about 5'10" tall and 230 to 240 pounds, with a round face and thick hands and arms. Some might have thought him fat, but he was all muscle. He was about forty-five years old at the time of the Last Battle. He had a dark brown beard that left his upper lip bare, and brown hair. He was also a smuggler, and a rough customer when he had to be. He was fascinated by old objects and odd sights; in Maradon he bought one of the seals of the Dark One's prison, not knowing what it really was. Shortly thereafter, Domon noticed that he was being pursued. Rand, Thom and Mat boarded his ship when escaping Shadar Logoth and disembarked at Whitebridge.

In Illian, Domon was offered a mission to Mayene; the pay was good, but he learned that completing it would have resulted in his death. To escape, he sailed to Falme, where his ship was captured by Egeanin of the Seanchan. She took his seal and gave it to High Lord Turak. Buying his entire cargo, Turak kept Domon as a storyteller. Min, Elayne and Nynaeve met with him in Falme, and he agreed to arrange passage for their escape, but he was forced to flee when the battle began. Elayne and Nynaeve met him again in Tanchico, where he had amassed a fleet of more than a dozen smuggling ships and underwrote a soup kitchen for the poor. Domon assisted them in their search for the Black Ajah and in entering the Panarch's Palace. While doing so, he met Egeanin again, and revealed that she was Seanchan.

After Nynaeve acquired the male *a'dam*, he and Egeanin sailed away to dispose of it; they were hailed and boarded by a Seanchan ship. Egeanin turned over the *a'dam*, but Domon tried to resist. He was put up for sale. Egeanin bought him and made him *so'jhin*. They returned to Ebou Dar, where they met with Mat and escaped with him and Valan Luca's circus. Domon and Egeanin married in Runnien Crossing; when Mat left Luca's show, they accompanied him and remained with him until they reached Caemlyn.

From Caemlyn, Teslyn, Joline and Edesina traveled to the White Tower, and Domon and Egeanin accompanied them. Domon bribed someone in the Tower so that he and Egeanin could Travel to Merrilor. During the Last Battle, when the Sharans appeared, Domon accompanied Egeanin on a successful mission to rescue Egwene.

Bayor, Classen. A military leader from Mat's memories; he lost his cavalry in the marsh at the Battle of Kolesar.

Bayrd. An Andoran soldier in Jarid Sarand's service as one of his personal guardsmen. His family had been stoneworkers, but his father became a butcher, and Bayrd followed in his footsteps before becoming a soldier. Bayrd's grandfather taught him stoneworking. When a bubble of evil made all the metal in their camp melt, Bayrd made a spearhead of stone. Faced with Jarid's growing insanity, Bayrd and other soldiers rebelled and tied him to a tree. Bayrd went off to fight in the Last Battle as a mercenary soldier in Tam's unit. He was killed in the Last Battle and eaten by a Trolloc.

Be'lal. A Forsaken known as the Envious and the Netweaver. His name in the Age of Legends was Duram Laddel Cham. His strength level was ++4. He was tall, with close-cropped silver hair. Not much was known of his life in the Age of Legends. He represented people in courts of law, and did it well enough to earn a third name. Before he turned to the Shadow, he was a leader in the fight against the Shadow. When he awoke in the Third Age, he placed himself in Tear as the High Lord Samon. He used the Black Ajah to capture Elayne, Egwene and Nynaeve as bait for a trap to lure Rand to *Callandor*. He also sent them with the hedgehog *ter'angreal* to take Moiraine out of the picture. Faile was trapped instead, and Moiraine went to the Stone and used balefire to kill him.

Beaks. The name given by Ituralde's troops to Trollocs with the features of hawks.

Behar, Velina. *See* Velina Behar

Beidomon. A male Aes Sedai and scientific genius from the Age of Legends. He was involved with Lanfear on the project that led to the drilling of the Bore, conceived of as a way to provide sustainable energy to all people. Their activities caused great damage, and the research team was blamed. Beidomon sought privacy from the opprobrium, and committed suicide when he was unable to achieve it.

Beira. An Aiel woman held *gai'shain* by Bair who refused to put off the white at the end of her term of service, even after Bair beat her.

Bekkar, Battle of. The battle where King Aemon won a victory over the Shadow-spawn; it was also known as the Field of Blood.

Bel Arvina. A feast held in the month of Choren to celebrate the first day of autumn.

Bel Tine. A spring festival celebrating the end of winter, the first sprouting of crops and the birth of the first lambs.

Bela. A shaggy brown mare that originally belonged to Tam and Rand al'Thor. She was stout and stout of heart. Bela had many adventures and traveled widely, visiting Falme, the Waste, Tar Valon, Salidar and the Blight. She fell in battle against a horde of Trollocs, while helping keep the Horn of Valere away from the Shadow. She was thought to be dead, but unaccountably survived. In the first years of the Fourth Age she gave birth to a strong colt and a splendid filly and retired to green pastures in the Two Rivers.

Belairah. A former queen of Saldaea who married and put her husband away four times. Faile used her as an example to Perrin when she was arguing that no leader was perfect.

Belcelona, Carlon. *See* Carlon Belcelona

Beldair, Mistress. The head cook at the Sun Palace in Cairhien. She was on duty when Loial and Karldin arrived there. Almost 5'6" tall, she was plump and graying.

Beldeine Nyram. A Saldaean Aes Sedai of the Green Ajah and the loyalist contingent, with a strength level of 16(4). Born in 966 NE, she went to the White Tower in 982 NE. After seven years as a novice and eight years as Accepted, she was raised to the shawl in 997 NE. Beldeine was 5'5" tall, with a medium build, pretty with high cheekbones, slightly tilted brown eyes and dark hair falling down to her shoulder blades. She knew that men liked looking at her, and she enjoyed that, too, though it was certainly in no way a consuming passion with her. Beldeine's parents were prosperous weavers, living only a day's ride from the Blight. She saw her first Trolloc when she was six. She was a dedicated Green, in many ways—almost a prototypical Green in outlook. Early on she showed some ability in administration and management, and the Green Ajah marked her out as possibly someone who would do well in their hierarchy. She herself did not much like that idea; she wanted to be off adventuring, like every other Green.

Part of the expedition to kidnap Rand, she was captured at Dumai's Wells and treated as *da'tsang* by the Aiel. Under Verin's Compulsion, she found reason to swear to Rand, and was one of the first five sisters to do so. She accompanied Cadsuane to Far Madding and then to Shadar Logoth. During the cleansing, she linked with Nesune, Daigian and Eben; they fought off Aran'gar, although Beldeine was injured, and Eben killed. Beldeine bonded Karldin Manfor; they were both killed in the Last Battle.

Beldemaine. An Arafellin Aes Sedai of the Yellow Ajah and the rebel contingent, with a strength level of 25(13). She was plump and wore silver bells in her hair; she grilled Nynaeve extensively after Nynaeve Healed Logain.

Belevaere Osiellin. A Cairhienin noblewoman, ten years older than Rand. Her clothing's stripes reached below her breasts. She was forward with Rand at Barthanes' party. Her husband's name was Amondrid; they had estates in the south. Her House was one of the smaller Houses that met with Colavaere to support her designs on the throne.

Belinde. A Wise One of the Shaido Aiel with the ability to channel and a strength level of 18(6). She was about 5'8" tall, and skinny, with bony fingers, pale blue eyes, and hair and eyebrows bleached nearly white by the sun. Belinde was once *Far Dareis Mai*, and she claimed to have softened even Stone Dogs with her cooking. She was one of Sevanna's inner circle of plotters. She took part in or at least was present at the murder of Desaine and was one of those who accompanied Sevanna to the Aes Sedai camp the day she saw Rand beaten. She was with Sevanna at Dumai's Wells and at the meeting with "Caddar" and "Maisia." Belinde was the Wise One slapped by Galina; she was guarding Galina when the Aes Sedai was forced to swear on the binder and was not present at the questioning of the captured Seanchan. She sided with Therava when Therava acted to take some power away from Sevanna. She, Therava and Modarra led a large number of Shaido back toward the Three-fold Land after the rout at Malden.

bellfruit. A tree and the fruit it produced.

Bellon. A village in Amadicia that lay about twenty miles east of Amador on the River Gaean. It was visited by Nynaeve, Elayne, Thom and Juilin. Nynaeve, posing as Elayne's maid there, was forced to serve Elayne and be the model servant, which caused much friction between the two in private.

Bellon Ford Inn. An inn in Bellon, Amadicia, where Elayne and Nynaeve stayed posing as Lady Morelin and her servant Nana while on the way to Tar Valon. Its innkeeper was Mistress Alfara.

Belman. A family in Caemlyn. *See* Nan *and* Perwyn Belman

Belmondes, Meralda. *See* Meralda Belmondes

Belvyn. A Redarm in the Band of the Red Hand. He was killed when Moghedien balefired the boat in which he, Lawtin and Nynaeve were traveling.

Bendhuin. A scarred Shaido Aiel who was the leader of *Far Aldazar Din* and the chief of the Green Salts sept. At Dumai's Wells he wanted to maintain screens of scouts and a reserve. At Malden he hoped to be sent to Rhuidean, to become the next clan chief of the Shaido, and he received permission from the Wise Ones to head for Rhuidean with twenty *algai'd'siswai*. Sevanna was furious when she learned that he had left without her knowing.

Benish. A soldier in Lan's army in the Last Battle. He wore a Taraboner veil with a *hadori* above it.

Benji Dalfor. A Youngling killed by Shaido; he was the first to die at Dumai's Wells. He managed to return from a scouting mission with a warning of the Shaido ambush before succumbing to his wounds.

Benly Coplin. A disturbed Two Rivers man who starved himself to death because he thought someone was trying to poison him.

Bennae Nalsad. A Shienaran Aes Sedai of the Brown Ajah and the loyalist contingent, with a strength level of 37(25). She went to the White Tower at age sixteen, and spent thirteen years as a novice and eleven years as Accepted before being raised to the shawl. She had dark hair liberally streaked with gray which she wore in a silver net, and sharp blue eyes. Bennae had a cluttered sitting room and taught history in the White Tower, although when she tried to teach Egwene, she ended up learning about the Thirteenth Depository. She invited Egwene to join the Brown Ajah.

Bent, Kaila. A lanky, fire-haired member of the Queen's Guard who brought word to Birgitte that there was a disturbance at the Plum Gate.

Bent Peak sept. A sept of the Daryne Aiel.

Bent Valley. A geographical feature, as well as a hold in the Aiel Waste.

Beonin Marinye. A Taraboner Aes Sedai of the Gray Ajah and apparently of the rebel contingent, with a strength level of 16(4). Born in 936 NE, she went to the White Tower in 952 NE. After five years as a novice and five years as Accepted, she was raised to the shawl in 962 NE. She was a pretty woman with dark honey hair and blue-gray eyes so big they made her appear slightly startled. She had a heavy Taraboner accent. Always quiet, she was sharp and watched everything carefully. Like Morvrin, she required a lot of proof for everything. Her Warder was Tervail Dura. Beonin's maternal grandmother, Collaris, was an advocate in Tanchico and imbued her with a love for the intricacies of the law. Beonin's mother, Aeldrine, became a merchant despite Collaris' disapproval and amassed a tidy fortune buying and selling dyes. Beonin left the Tower and joined the rebels, becoming a member of Sheriam's council on behalf of Elaida.

She was willing to become Elaida's mole because of personal ambition plus a strong belief that the White Tower must remain whole; that breaking it in any way was treason of the worst sort. She had no access to the secret records in the Tower and so did not know how far previous divisions within the Tower had gone or even that they had existed.

Along with other members of Sheriam's group in Salidar, Beonin was forced to swear personal fealty to Egwene; Egwene used as leverage her knowledge of the ferrets who had been sent to the White Tower without the knowledge of the Hall because of fear that some of the rebel Hall might be Black Ajah. Beonin had opposed sending them, but she couldn't stop it. Shortly after Egwene was captured at Northharbor by Elaida's loyalists, Beonin returned to the Tower and shared with Elaida knowledge of the ferrets and much else that she had learned, including Traveling. She kept some things back because of Elaida not treating her properly, as she saw it. Egwene made her promise to tell the moles that Elaida knew about them.

Bera Harkin. An Andoran Aes Sedai of the Green Ajah and the rebel contingent, with a strength level of 14(2). Born in 938 NE, she went to the White Tower in 953 NE. After four years as a novice and four years as Accepted, she was raised to the shawl in 961 NE. She was a stocky woman, 5'6" tall, with brown hair cut short around her square face, looking like a proud farmwife, if it hadn't been for her agelessness. She had three Warders. She and Kiruna had been pillow friends; though both enjoyed men exclusively later, they remained the very closest of friends. Bera and Kiruna and their seven Warders were sent to the Aiel Waste to find Rand; when they were halfway there, they heard that he was in Caemlyn and went there. After Rand told the rebel embassy that he was leaving Caemlyn, Bera and Kiruna took over the embassy and decided to follow after him. All were forced to swear fealty to Rand after Dumai's Wells. These sisters were treated like apprentices by the Wise Ones. They were also coopted by Cadsuane. All intended to keep their oaths of fealty to the best of their ability, however reluctantly, but none of them could stand up to Cadsuane, at least not openly. Bera adapted to the situation with the Wise Ones, and with Rand, much better than her friend Kiruna. Min saw an aura indicating that Bera was in his hand and could be trusted. Bera accompanied Rand when he visited the Sea Folk. He then sent her to negotiate with the rebels in Haddon Mirk. She reported success to Rand in the Stone of Tear. Bera fought in the Last Battle with the forces at Shayol Ghul.

Berab Golever. A lanky, bearded Lord Captain of the Children of the Light. He was largely fair-minded, but he was convinced that Ogier were Darkfriends or Shadowspawn. After hearing Galad's argument with Asunawa, Golever and other Lords Captain executed Asunawa and proclaimed Galad Lord Captain Commander of the Children of the Light. He fought in the Last Battle, and enjoyed killing the Ayyad.

Beralna. A Maiden of the Spear who stood guard for Rand in Caemlyn and led him through Milisair's palace in Bandar Eban. She was a bony redhead with blue eyes and a feral grin. In private she would stare at Rand as if considering whether to do him the favor of doing as he asked.

Berana Shemon. A Shienaran Aes Sedai of the White Ajah and the rebel contingent, with a strength level of 28(16). Born in 930 NE, she went to the White Tower in 947 NE. After ten years as a novice and eight years as Accepted, she was raised to the shawl in 965 NE, and raised a Sitter for the White in Salidar in 999 NE. She was 5'4½" tall, with cold brown eyes and dark brown hair. Very haughty and a fast learner, Berana voted yes in the war vote and for the alliance with the Black Tower. After the Tower was reunited, she stepped down as a Sitter. She had no Warder.

Berden. A Tairen Youngling officer who stood guard for the Aes Sedai in Dorlan.

Berelain sur Paendrag Paeron. The First of Mayene, Blessed of the Light, Defender of the Waves, High Seat of House Paeron. The banner of Mayene was a golden hawk on a field of blue; the crown was a coronet with a golden hawk in flight. Berelain was beautiful and young, with black hair falling in waves to her shoulders; her eyes were large and dark. She was gorgeous, sensuous, sexy, and she knew it and made use of it. She was about 5'7" tall, with a regal air. Berelain was willful, and often behaved in a spoiled or petulant manner, but she was a pragmatist, as any ruler of Mayene had to be to survive. She believed in learning as much as possible about the people she had to deal with.

She was born in 974 NE; her mother died when she was nine. She loved her father desperately, in part because her mother had been a cold woman, and in part because he returned her affection. She became High Seat of House Paeron and First of Mayene in 984 NE and had a regent/guardian until her sixteenth nameday in 990 NE. Her younger brothers and sister were all Second Lords and Ladies, though none was a High Seat, of course. She banished her regent/guardian on attaining her majority at sixteen; he was a dour, strict man, not at all compatible with a high-spirited and flirtatious young woman like Berelain. She brought this man back when she departed Mayene, to watch over the Second whom she left to rule while she was gone. Dour and strict as he was, she also knew that he was painfully honest, that he would do his duty no matter what the cost to himself—he had known for a fact that she would exile him upon reaching her majority—and, just as important, that he supported her firmly and would not allow anyone to usurp her position or authority. Annoura was her Aes Sedai advisor and Gallenne the commander of the Mayener Winged Guards.

After Rand took the Stone, Lanfear sent Berelain with a message to Moiraine; Berelain announced that she would dine with the Dragon Reborn that night. When she went to his rooms to try to seduce him, a bubble of evil struck, causing Rand's reflections to come out of mirrors and attack him; Berelain was scared silly and avoided Rand after that. She flirted with Perrin in front of Faile; angered, Faile tried to pick a fight with Berelain. Rhuarc broke it up, but not until after Berelain swore that she would have Perrin. When Rand went to Cairhien after leaving the Waste, Berelain set out to join him. Rand put her in charge of Cairhien. When Perrin joined Rand in Cairhien, Berelain made a concerted effort to seduce Perrin, without success. After Rand vanished, she searched his room and found his sword and belt; rightly believing that he had been kidnapped, she sent Nurelle and the Winged Guards to help rescue him. Her thief-catchers found evidence that Colavaere had murdered Meilan and Maringil. She stayed for a while on a Sea Folk ship; when she was returning to the palace, a man with a knife attacked her, but the Winged Guards protected her. Rand ordered her back to Mayene for her safety, but she refused; instead, he sent her with Perrin on the expedition to Ghealdan. Rand chose her because she knew how to deal with royalty and because she very much wanted something to do rather than return to Mayene. When Perrin collapsed after Faile was taken by the Shaido, Berelain had him brought to her tent; her maids spread the word and many believed that they had been intimate. All Berelain's amorous designs on Perrin were put aside once she laid eyes on Galad; the two fell deeply in love. During the Last Battle, Berelain set up a large Healing station based at her palace in Mayene. She was reunited there with the wounded Galad.

Berengari, Myrelle. *See* Myrelle Berengari

Berenicia Morsad. A Shienaran Aes Sedai of the Yellow Ajah and the rebel contingent, with a strength level of 19(7). Born in 838 NE in the Border Marches, she went to the White Tower in 854 NE. After eight years as a novice and six years as Accepted, she was raised to the shawl in 868 NE. A plump woman with a grave expression, she had, at times, an acid tongue. When she had to defer to another Aes Sedai, she bristled before bowing her head. Berenicia was a member of the rebel embassy to Rand in Caemlyn. She was later sent as part of a group to escort the Two Rivers girls back to Salidar while Kiruna and the others pursued Rand. Berenicia leaned toward Romanda's faction. She had a Warder.

Berewin, Lady. A lesser Cairhienin noblewoman whom Aviendha intercepted trying to enter Rand's bedchamber. Aviendha tore half her clothes off and dragged her down the hall by her hair.

Berg. The ugly bouncer at The Seven-Striped Lass in Caemlyn. He did not like Mat talking to Melli, the innkeeper.

Bergevin. A quartermaster of the Band of the Red Hand from whom Olver stole a knife.

Berin. A character featured in the song "Berin's Retreat."

Berin Thane. One of the miller's brothers from Emond's Field. His house was burned by the Trollocs on Winternight. He participated in the defense of Emond's Field, joined Perrin's army at Malden and stayed with him in the aftermath of the battle against the Shaido. He fell asleep on guard duty near Jehannah Road.

Berisha Terakuni. An Arafellin Aes Sedai of the Gray Ajah and the loyalist contingent. She was lean and hard-eyed, with a narrow face and a voice full of the accents of her homeland. She had a reputation for the strictest, and often harshest, interpretation of the law—always to the letter, of course, but never with any sense of mercy. She curtsied to Alviarin; it was not required for the Keeper, but she was trying to hedge her bets. Like many others, she thought that currying favor with Alviarin might stand her in good stead if she fell under Elaida's evil eye, no matter how much currying favor grated on her. She was one of the sisters, along with Katerine Alruddin, Baratine, Felaana and Pritalle, who rode back to the White Tower in the coach with Egwene a prisoner. During the Last Battle, when Faile and her party were leaving from the Traveling grounds at the White Tower with the Horn of Valere secreted away, Berisha made a gateway just as a bubble of evil struck and crystal spikes emerged from the ground, impaling her foot; she also had a wound in her stomach that Faile believed to have been made by a knife. The gateway took Faile and her group into the Blight. There was some question afterward whether Berisha meant to send them to the Blight all along.

Bernaile Gelbarn. A Taraboner Aes Sedai of the White Ajah and the rebel contingent, with a strength level of 16(4). Born in 919 NE, she went to the White Tower in 936 NE. After seven years as a novice and nine years as Accepted, she was raised to the shawl in 952 NE. She was 5'5" tall, and stocky, with hazel eyes and pale brown hair worn in beaded braids hanging well below her shoulders. Her manner was usually cool, aloof and withdrawn, though she could let her hair down with close friends, telling jokes and laughing, but that face was reserved for friends. She had no Warder. Bernaile was part of the rebel fifth column sent by Sheriam's council in Salidar to infiltrate the White Tower (aka ferrets). Like all of the sisters chosen for the fifth column, Bernaile was out of the White Tower when Siuan was deposed and the Tower broken, so there was no flight to arouse any suspicions toward her. Apparently, she had simply returned in answer to Elaida's summons. She was the second of the ferrets coopted by Seaine and Pevara to help search for the Black Ajah.

Berndt Crossroads. A location in the Borderlands, near the Saldaea-Kandor border.

Bernherd. The proprietor of The Dead Man's Breath in Caemlyn. He was a greasy-haired Tairen.

Beron Goraed. A wealthy Ghealdan merchant dragged from his bed to marry Queen Teresia and so disqualify her for the throne. That incident occurred before Alliandre became queen, and indicated how politics were conducted in Ghealdan.

Berowin Doraisin. A Cairhienin Kinswoman who became a Wise Woman in Ebou Dar. Her strength level was 42(30), strong enough for her to have tested for Aes Sedai, but not strong enough for her to make a gateway of any size whatsoever. Born in 758 NE, she went to the White Tower in 775 NE. After twelve years as a novice and eleven years as Accepted, she failed her test for Aes Sedai. She was 5'1" tall, stout and tanned, and appeared to be about forty years old, though she was much older. Despite her very low strength, shielding was always a Talent for her. When Nynaeve and Elayne went to the Kin house in Ebou Dar, Berowin shielded the pair with no trouble, her shield bending and ballooning, which it should not have done, without breaking. She was one of those who dreamed of somehow returning to the White Tower one day, somehow becoming Aes Sedai. She actually felt more ashamed that she had disappointed Sereille, the Mistress of Novices, than about anything else. Berowin was part of the group that went to Caemlyn with Elayne after fleeing the Kin farm outside Ebou Dar.

Berowyn al'Vere. Egwene's eldest sister. She was born in 965 NE. Berowyn was considered to be the prettiest of Marin al'Vere's daughters. She married a young man of the Lewin family in 989 NE, and had one daughter. Her husband and infant child died of fever in 990 NE, after less than two years of marriage. She couldn't remain on the farm any longer, trying to work it alone, so she sold the farm to her in-laws and moved home; she never got on with her husband's mother. She later married an outlander, one of the refugees who entered the Two Rivers. It was possible she could have learned to channel.

Bertain Gallenne. The Lord Captain of the Mayener Winged Guards. He had gray hair, worn shoulder-length. He was about 5'10" tall and sported a red eyepatch, worn with style and panache, as other men might wear a plume. His helmet was worked with wings on the sides and had several thin red plumes. Gallenne had an old soldier for a servant, a lean and balding man, whom he called his dogrobber, and his favorite horse was a heavy-chested black gelding. Gallenne fiddled with his reins when deep in thought. He always saw the worst possibility first. He was all-soldier, always ready, always preparing for any contingency. Elyas told Perrin that Gallenne could be trouble, because he only knew attack and didn't stop to think; but that he wouldn't go against Perrin or behind his back. Gallenne respected Perrin in a comradely way. He acted gruff and macho with everyone except Perrin and Berelain. Gallenne was killed in the Last Battle.

Bertome Saighan. A Cairhienin nobleman who was Colavaere's cousin. He wore stripes down his coat to below his waist. He was 5'7" tall, and stocky, but it was muscle, not fat. Ruggedly handsome with a square face and the front of his head shaved, he looked as if he should be stolid and methodical, but he had a quick brain and a quick wit. He became High Seat of House Saighan on Colavaere's death, and was said not to mourn her; in truth she had been his favorite cousin, but he felt she had been ambitious beyond reason. In Cairhien, he had a smile that had neither mirth nor pleasure in it. Rand had him brought to his army against the Seanchan. Elayne met with Bertome and other Cairhienin nobles; she stripped Elenia, Arymilla and Naean of their titles and properties and offered one to Bertome as part of her plan to take the Sun Throne.

Beryl Marle. An Aes Sedai of the White Ajah who served as Amyrlin from 520 to 533 NE. Beryl was a weak Amyrlin, a compromise candidate chosen after the Hall had deadlocked on others; she turned out to have little interest in the world at all. The Tower's influence waned considerably during her reign; she was not so much under the control of the Hall as she was willing to let them do whatever they wanted.

Berylla Naron. An Illianer Aes Sedai of the Blue Ajah in public and of the Black Ajah in truth. Her strength level was 27(15). Born in 933 NE, she went to the White Tower in 948 NE. After seven years as a novice and five years as Accepted, she was raised to the shawl in 960 NE. She was 5'4" tall, and almost scrawny, with black hair and dark brown eyes. She was among the thirteen members of the Black Ajah who fled the Tower. When given orders by Moghedien, she showed little expression.

Beslan Mitsobar. The son of Queen Tylin of Altara. He was 5'10" tall, and slender, with large liquid dark eyes. He and Mat became friends. Beslan swore the oaths when the Seanchan arrived, but he believed an oath taken under duress did not bind, and he created what trouble he could. He was aided in this by his friends, and by Noal Charin. He postponed his rebellion a month and then started it to help cover Mat's escape. After his mother's death, Beslan was crowned king. He continued to plot against the Seanchan until Tuon confronted him and convinced him to swear loyalty to her. She then raised him to the High Blood. During the Last Battle, Beslan stayed in Ebou Dar to maintain order there; he was not happy about it, but he acquiesced to Tuon's wishes.

Bethal. A good-sized town in the south of Ghealdan, close enough to the Amadician border that Whitecloak raids sometimes reached its vicinity. Bethal was walled, with slate roofs and many tall stone buildings owned by merchants or noblemen; the people were apathetic and did not go out much. Perrin, Faile, Berelain, Aiel and their forces camped outside Bethel to see Queen Alliandre of Ghealdan, who had sent Rand a message offering possible support. He sent Berelain and two others to see the Queen and persuade her to pledge support openly. Here also, Perrin saved Morgase, posing as Maighdin, and her party from an attack by the Prophet's men. Morgase and her group were taken into service by Perrin and Faile. Berelain's group returned from town with the Queen, who pledged her loyalty. Faile convinced Alliandre to accompany them south, to ensure her loyalty.

Bethamin Zeami. A Seanchan *sul'dam*. She was about 5'7" tall, with dark, wavy hair worn shoulder-length, and a very dark complexion, as dark as the Sea Folk's. She also had dark, pleading eyes and filled out the low neckline of an Ebou Dari dress nicely, although she considered those dresses indecent. Bethamin deserted at the Battle of Falme. She was captured and then released by Egeanin, who had been under orders to capture or kill the deserters. A Seeker involved her in a plot to spy on Egeanin, prompting her to escape Ebou Dar with Mat's group, which included Egeanin and Domon. She continued to travel with Mat and the Band of the Red Hand. At first she behaved as if the Aes Sedai were *damane* somehow off the leash. She attempted to discipline Joline, Joline channeled to stop her, and Bethamin, fearing for her life, channeled in turn. Thereafter, she was taught about the Power by Joline and, more reluctantly, by Edesina. Teslyn refused to take any part, being quite willing to let Bethamin die. She left the Band of the Red Hand and went to the White Tower with the group that included Teslyn, Joline and Edesina.

Betrayer of Hope. The meaning of "Ishamael."

Betse Silvin. A serving girl at the Golden Stag, in Maerone, Cairhien. She was short, pretty and slim, with dark curls nestled on her shoulders, and dark eyes. She had a precise, musical Cairhienin accent that made her voice into chimes and gave off a faint smell of lavender-scented soap. Mat flirted with her, and she started asking questions. He persuaded her to dance with him, and taught her a dance from his memories.

Bevaine, Felaana. *See* Felaana Bevaine

Bhadar, Deepe. *See* Deepe Bhadar

Bhagad, Sulamein so. Author of *The Wheel of Time* and Chief Historian at the Court of the Sun in the Fourth Age.

Bhan'sheen. A Trolloc tribe. Its symbol was a dagger-pierced skull.

Bharatine. An Aes Sedai of the Green Ajah and the rebel contingent, with a strength level of 33(21). Born in 921 NE, she went to the White Tower in 936 NE. After nine years as a novice and seven years as Accepted, she was raised to the shawl in 952 NE. She made rail-thin look gracefully slender and a long nose look elegant. She was a member of Anaiya's circle fighting the bubble of evil in Salidar. She was also one of the Aes Sedai who crowded into the room after Nynaeve Healed Logain.

Bharatiya, Ivonell. A woman, possibly apocryphal, who supposedly wrote about Darkhounds before the Trolloc Wars. She was cited by Masuri.

Bhoda, Falion. *See* Falion Bhoda

Bhuran, Narasim. *See* Narasim Bhuran

Bihara, Nesune. *See* Nesune Bihara

Bilal, Jesse. *See* Jesse Bilal

Bili Adarra. A young Two Rivers man. He was a distant cousin of Perrin, and was almost as wide as Perrin but a hand shorter. He was one of the Two Rivers men who went through the aqueduct to enter Malden.

Bili al'Dai. A Two Rivers man, the son of Hu. He joined Perrin's band and was killed by Trollocs.

Bili Congar. An Emond's Field man who liked his drink. He once named the Dark One, and soon afterward his fields were infested with cutworm and his household infected with yelloweye fever. He participated in the defense of his town against the Trollocs.

Bili Mandair. A boy born near Dragonmount on the day Gitara had her Foretelling that the Dragon was reborn.

Bili Sidoro. The bouncer at Easing the Badger in Illian. The nephew of the owner, Nieda Sidoro, he was big enough to carry a man out with either hand, and indeed he did when he carried dead Gray Men out two at a time. Nieda said that she did not think he was too bright because he said he had the same dreams she did.

Bili Under the Hill. A children's tale about a boy who went searching for a purse that was full of gold and received three answers. The next day, he found that ten years had passed.

Binde. An Asha'man with Ituralde in the Last Battle. His madness made him think an enemy was trying to take his hands.

binder. A device mentioned by the Forsaken that could control channelers. The one that Caddar (Sammael) gave to Sevanna felt and looked exactly like the Oath Rod, except that the flowing marks on one end were the numerals used in the Age of Legends for "one hundred and eleven," not the "three" on the Oath Rod. He claimed it would only work on women who could channel, and that it could also be used to release someone from any oaths. Caddar claimed there was a thing called a binding chair which could be used on people who could not channel— if any had survived the Breaking, that is. He told the truth on this.

binding. Use of the Power to assume control over another, such as binding (bonding) a Warder or making another channeler obey. The Forsaken used the term as well to mean controlling the form of another, such as Moghedien saying that she would use a binding that would turn Nynaeve into a horse whenever she entered *Tel'aran'rhiod*. *See also* bonding

Biranca Hasad. An Aes Sedai who lived at the time of the formation of the White Tower.

bird-of-delight. A brilliantly plumaged bird found in Seanchan. Suroth had a robe worked with images of them.

birdcall signals. A series of signals used by Two Rivers combatants that had a variety of meanings:

> Bluetit's trill: A large body of men were coming, not necessarily peaceful.
> Crookbill's trill: Men were coming who were friends.
> Larksong: A signal that the Seanchan were leaving the woods.
> Mocker's cry of alarm: Men were coming who were clearly unfriendly.
> Redwing's call: There was danger coming from the south.
> Winterfinch's call: There were Shadowspawn in the pass.

Birgitte Silverbow. A Hero of the Horn. Over many lives she wore many names, among them Teadra, Maerion, Joana and Jethari Moondancer. About 5'6" tall, she wore heeled boots that made her three inches taller. Her golden hair hung in a thick braid to her waist, almost the way women wore it in the Two Rivers, but more intricately woven. Between lives, Birgitte resided in *Tel'aran'rhiod*; she violated the precepts and spoke with Elayne, Nynaeve and Perrin in efforts to help them. She saved Nynaeve during an altercation with Moghedien, and Moghedien forced her out into the waking world. To save her life, Elayne bonded her as her Warder. She had some memories of previous lives; in addition to a life during the founding of the White Tower (the earliest she could recall clearly), Birgitte remembered a time during the forming of the Compact of the Ten Nations, two between that founding and the Trolloc Wars, two during the Trolloc Wars, two between the Trolloc Wars and the rise of Artur Hawkwing, one during the Rise of Artur Hawkwing, two during the War of the Hundred Years, and one about five hundred years before Moghedien cast her out of *Tel'aran'rhiod*. She recalled occasional fragments from the Breaking of the World and the War of the Shadow, along with earlier lives, but only occasional fragments. As time progressed, her memories of the distant past faded.

Her lover through many lives was Gaidal Cain, another Hero of the Horn; she was terrified that she would forget him.

While traveling with Luca's show, Birgitte performed as an archer, shooting arrows that just missed Nynaeve. She went to Salidar with Elayne and Nynaeve, and on to Ebou Dar. While there, Mat recognized Birgitte as the Hero of the Horn, and the two became friends.

After the Seanchan attacked the Kin's farm, Birgitte accompanied Elayne to Caemlyn; when they arrived, Elayne named her Lady Birgitte Trahelion and Captain-General of the Queen's Guards. She and Dyelin did not get on well together. Birgitte rode a rangy gray gelding called Arrow. Birgitte coordinated troops and Sea Folk Windfinders to save Elayne after she had been kidnapped by the Black Ajah. During the Last Battle, she was killed by Doilin Mellar, whom she killed in turn once she appeared as a Hero of the Horn, saving Elayne's life.

Birlen Pena. An Aes Sedai revealed as Black Ajah in Verin's notebook. She escaped from the White Tower before she was discovered.

biteme. A small, almost invisible biting insect. Its bite was very sharp, like the stab of a needle. A warm-weather pest, it flew around the face.

bittern. A musical instrument that could have six, nine or twelve strings, and was held flat on the knees and played by plucking or strumming.

Black Ajah. A covert organization within the White Tower composed of sisters who gave their allegiance to the Dark One. The Black Ajah was about the same size as the Red Ajah, i.e., over two hundred members. They renounced the oaths sworn on the Oath Rod, and replaced them with three others (*see* Black Oaths). The Black Ajah had a cell organization of threes, called hearts; most members typically knew only two other members plus one outside their heart.

The Black Ajah's ruling body was called the Supreme Council, composed of thirteen sisters not all known to one another. The top woman knew all the other twelve, but the others did not know her name, except those who were of her own heart. The Council wore hoods when they met. They seldom met, though it was they personally who carried out the punishments of other Black sisters, and of others of the Council if necessary, to preserve anonymity. They also handled induction into the Black, and frequently handled the questioning of a sister or important personage. Every member of the Supreme Council knew the names of some of the sisters below her, with enough overlap that no one death, or even several, could knock out knowledge of those who belonged. Only the head of the Black Ajah knew the names of *all* of the sisters in the Ajah; part of her being raised was for each member of the Council to give her the names of all those that she knew.

The head of the Ajah traditionally was the most senior sister among the Supreme Council. Alviarin was the first to break this custom, because she was personally chosen by Ishamael in the aftermath of the male channeler pogrom, when the then head of the Ajah and maybe several other high-ranking members were killed and a number of others punished severely. Alviarin was pulled from a lower rank and placed right at the top in one leap.

Communication was by letter-drop and the like, with certain methods of ensuring that the message was genuine. Orders were passed one way and any necessary reports the other by the same method, usually. There were various signs and signals by which a Black sister could identify herself to others if needed, but such would normally only be used on order, or perhaps in the most extreme emergency. Orders could be passed to sisters who were not known in the event of some disaster, such as the deaths of a large number of the Supreme Council, including the head. The slowest, and safest, way was to pass orders down the line; the interlinkage was such that three Black sisters who knew one another would each be known to a different member of the Council, and each had ways of passing messages through the unknown hands of sisters known to still other members of the Council. There were faster methods, but they were also riskier. For example: Every sister knew that certain signs placed in public areas of the Tower were a signal from the Supreme Council to leave the Tower immediately. Each sister knew a place to go in such circumstances, and knew that she would meet other Black sisters there, though probably sisters she didn't know. No Black sister would think of telling even another Black where this place was; she would be severely punished if she did.

Sometimes a sister could be summoned to a meeting with one or more hooded sisters to receive orders or to make a report. She never saw their faces, or heard their voices where she could recognize them. In truth, she could never know when summoned (or in many cases simply snatched and brought) to such a meeting whether she was there to be given orders or to be punished for an infraction.

Discipline in the Black Ajah was harsh and unforgiving. A Black sister knew she would be punished severely for the smallest transgression, slip or failure, with no excuses or reasons accepted, and that the severity increased as the transgression did. The top penalty, death, was not unknown. She would probably be found dead in her bed or from some sort of accident, but the fact was that she would have been given plenty of time to scream before she died.

The Black Ajah had some contact with the organized cells of Darkfriends in various nations, though they themselves were not part of the rather loose Darkfriend organization. It was a matter of some irritation to the sisters of the Black Ajah, especially those on the Supreme Council, that they had no control over these other Darkfriend groups and indeed ranked only equally with the men and women in those groups. At various times over the centuries, Black sisters attempted to seize control of all Darkfriends, and at various points they actually came close. But the other groups fought back fiercely, a good many Black sisters died of poison or a knife in the back and the attempts all failed. The last, some hundreds of years ago, was particularly humiliating for the Black sisters, as their representatives, including at least some of the Supreme Council, were forced to publicly (within the meeting) renounce any claims to command, to acknowledge that they were only the equals of the others, and to accept a reduction in their votes from five to one.

Ishamael claimed to have founded/created the Black Ajah during the Trolloc Wars, at the very beginning of the conflict when he was spun out and began the wars. The Black Ajah claimed to have existed since the Age of Legends, and so they told its new sisters. Ishamael told the truth, however. There were certainly sisters who would have been Black had the Ajah existed during the period between the Breaking and the Trolloc Wars, and some of them did serve and worship the Dark One. Sisters who had gone over to the Shadow during the War of the Shadow survived into the Breaking, and like other sisters during the Breaking, they recruited women. A number of organizations formed, at odds with one another as much as with anyone else, and some of these small organizations survived the Breaking. By the end of the Breaking, most of these small groups did not know of the others. Like the other Aes Sedai after the Breaking, these small groups were either swept up into the reorganization of the Aes Sedai or else wiped out. They remained unorganized, and as they learned of the existence of other groups, they opposed them. This sometimes included betrayal, although they frequently claimed to work together and sometimes even did. They were greatly facilitated by the fact that the oath against lying did not exist in the beginning. The adoption of the remaining oaths (i.e., against lying and against using the One Power as a weapon) greatly complicated matters for them. The fact that no one among the Aes Sedai believed that any such group or groups existed was all that allowed them to continue, in truth. Shortly before the Trolloc Wars, Ishamael appeared, though perhaps using another name. He was able to find those strongly pledged to the

Dark One and forced them to combine into the Black Ajah. The name itself was a joke, to him. It was he who first used the Oath Rod to remove the Three Oaths, replacing them with three oaths of his own devising, both to bind the Black sisters and to ensure that they would not reveal themselves by living too long.

Girls were watched for suitability from the day they entered the White Tower, although sometimes, though not very often, there was one who was known to be a Darkfriend before coming to the Tower. A novice or Accepted found to be acceptable was not recruited immediately, but watched further. The watching for recruits continued among Aes Sedai as well. When sufficient signs of suitability were seen, a testing period preceded any actual contact. If it was learned that a sister was trying to find the Black Ajah, the watch on her was increased. If she found nothing, the usual tests were arranged.

If she located a trace, however, she was kidnapped and brought before the Supreme Council, who were hooded, as at all their meetings. She was shielded, stripped naked to increase her feelings of vulnerability, bound, and woke with a knife to each side of her throat and a mirror placed so that she could watch her life's blood drain into a bowl should the cuts be made. She was then asked one question: Did she wish to join the Black Ajah? An answer of no, and the cuts were not made. Instead, she was put to the question with the use of the Power, drained of whatever she had learned about the Ajah and who she might have passed it to, then killed, either with the Power, so she could seem to have died naturally, or through an apparent accident. If the answer was yes, the Oath Rod was placed into her hands, and she was made to abjure the Three Oaths, a particularly painful process. Immediately following, the Black Ajah's own three oaths were administered. All candidates were brought in the same way, even those who were known Darkfriends.

Once the oaths were taken, a sister was a member of the Ajah, but she was still probationary, in a sense. She had sworn to obey orders, but she was told that she would be tested, and failure would be punished, perhaps with death, perhaps with worse. The tests consisted of orders—delivered anonymously, of course—which commanded her to do things which might have exposed her to danger, or to ridicule, or to an imposed penance. How she carried out these orders was observed closely. None of the tasks were vital, of course; they were assigned simply for testing purposes. Many of a Black sister's chances at advancement were determined in that first year of testing.

Verin, a member of the Black Ajah, gave Egwene a list of all the Black Ajah members just before she died.

Black Cliffs. A sept of the Nakai Aiel.

Black Eyes. One of the twelve warrior societies of the Aiel. They were also known as *Seia Doon*.

Black Fever. A deadly epidemic that swept the land in the days of Artur Hawkwing, killing ten percent of the population.

Black Hawk. The symbol of Shienar, a swooping black hawk on a field of yellow gold.

Black Hills, the. A northwest-southeast range extending from the Caralain Grass to the Borderlands.

Black Oaths. The three oaths sworn by members of the Black Ajah: 1) I shall obey all commands given by those placed above me in service to the Great Lord; 2) I shall prepare for the day of the Great Lord's return; and 3) I shall hold close the secrets of the Black Ajah, unto the hour of my death.

Black Rock. A sept of the Shaarad Aiel.

Black Tower. A location two leagues south of Caemlyn where Asha'man were trained and lived. It began as a deserted farm, but under Mazrim Taim's leadership it was being developed into a complex to rival the White Tower. The Power was being used to build a planned wall fifty feet high, thirty feet thick and eight miles in total length, enclosing an area of two miles by two miles. The top of the wall was to be wide enough behind the crenellations to act as a roadway. This wall was to be black and polished till it shone in the sun on both sides. There was to be a round one-hundred-foot-high tower at each of the four corners, and two flanking the main gate centered in each of the four sides. Between these tallest towers, spaced every one hundred paces, was to be a seventy-foot-high tower. Halfway between each of the lesser towers, a semicircular bastion was to bulge out from the wall. Construction was facilitated by the fact that some of the recruits had been masons in civilian life. It had not been completed at the time of the Last Battle.

Inside the beginnings of the great wall were several settlements. There was a sort of large village or small town of stone and wooden structures with thatched roofs that varied considerably in size. Large, warehouse-like buildings quartered unmarried soldiers in dormitory chambers that slept twenty men each, one hundred men to a building, with room for more in the buildings already there and still more under construction. Smaller structures housed unmarried Dedicated in groups of ten, each with a private room. Houses of various sizes were available for both soldiers and Dedicated who were married and had their families with them, and there was a dormitory which housed the fifty-one bonded Aes Sedai who were part of the Black Tower expedition; this was a hastily built wooden structure, like a warehouse, with canvas partitions inside to make a small room for each sister, lining a long central corridor. This village had several central fountains for gathering water, supplied by windmills outside the village. Henre Haslin and the other armsmasters lived in this village, as did the unarmed combat and riding instructors. Some of those had families. Logain was the only full Asha'man to live there, in a well-built stone house like a small, single-story farmhouse. The Traitor's Tree stood on the path from this village to the training grounds, far enough from the village that family members did not have to see it, but where every man headed for the training grounds did.

A second village of wooden, thatched-roofed buildings held the workers and craftsfolk, most with their families, who did almost all of the actual construction inside the great wall. The stablefolk who took care of the horses also lived there, and the carters and wagon drivers who were sent out to buy food, charcoal, coal and all the others things that needed buying. There were also tailors to make uniforms for the Asha'man from cloth brought in from outside, and a goldsmith who made the Sword and Dragon pins. This village also had its own fountains, powered by windmills outside the village, and it had a tavern. It was well away from the village of Asha'man, about a mile. The stables for cart and wagon horses and the wagon yards were located there.

Closer to the Asha'man village (half a mile or less) than to the other, and with the training grounds between it and the Asha'man village, was Taim's small complex. Taim's own dwelling was a combination of a small palace with a fortress, with thick granite walls and polished marble facings. It was about one hundred feet square, all of it faced with polished white marble, and two stories tall. The first story had neither windows nor doors. The second was surrounded by a colonnaded walk with a waist-high wall, and a taller, crenellated wall rose around the roof. Broad marble stairs stretched down from the colonnaded walk in front, and in front of the stairs was the black stone, called the Stone, where Taim stood to address the men; it had been moved from the old farm. In front of the Stone was a large open area, usually grassy, where the men gathered to hear Taim. A little distance to one side of the Stone was a sort of bulletin board; this was wood, inside a shallow stone facing, about two feet deep, to give it a little shelter from the weather; this was where, among other things, deserters' names were posted, as well as the names of men who went mad or were killed or burned out, and those killed elsewhere. All of the full Asha'man who were Taim's cronies—that is, all but Logain—lived in this place with him.

The training grounds were fairly extensive. Though in fact training could and did take place in many areas, training in armed and unarmed combat always took place on the training grounds, and much of riding training, too. The stables which held horses for the Asha'man were there, and also the archery butts. Morning Directives were usually given there, and the Creed recited. Windmills nearby pumped water for the stables.

The Tower grounds also contained a prison camp, well hidden in the forest, where the survivors of the two hundred Tower Guards who accompanied the White Tower expedition to the Black Tower were held under close guard, like the Warders brought by those of the fifty Aes Sedai who were not Red and had one. Anyone who did not have business there was kept away. Secret dungeons were also located in the foundations of a building being built; there Taim used Myrddraal and channelers to Turn prisoners.

Black Water. A sept of the Nakai Aiel.

Black Wind, the. *See Machin Shin*

Black Years, the. *See* Years of Silent Rage

blackbile fever. A contagious disease.

blacklance. A poisonous snake with black scales that could strike very quickly.

Blacksmith, the. A constellation.

blackthorn. A bush with beautiful white flowers amid long black thorns.

blacktongue. A disease that killed sheep.

blackwasp nettles. A plant that severely irritated the skin when touched. Nynaeve used the plant to brush against Moghedien as punishment in *Tel'aran'rhiod* after she had captured the Forsaken.

Blackwing, Zaida din Parede. *See* Zaida din Parede Blackwing

Blackwood, the Great. *See* Forest of Shadows

blademaster. A master swordsman. There were two ways to become a blademaster: to receive a unanimous decision by a panel of five blademasters judging one's skills, or to kill another blademaster in fair combat. A blademaster was entitled to carry a heron-marked sword.

Blaeric Negina. One of Joline's Warders. Blaeric was Shienaran, with a fair complexion, blue eyes and dark brown hair. He was about 6' tall, less than an inch taller than his fellow Warder Fen. Both Warders had broad shoulders and a narrow waist, although Blaeric was a little lighter in the chest and shoulders. The pair of them talked alike, thought alike and moved alike. After Teslyn dosed Joline with forkroot and the Seanchan arrived, Fen and Blaeric were able to get Joline out of the palace, but not out of Ebou Dar. They joined Mat and left Ebou Dar with Luca's show. Blaeric's topknot caused problems with the Seanchan, and he was not too pleased about shaving it off. He and Fen joined up with the Band of the Red Hand and traveled with them, until returning to the White Tower with Joline.

Blaes of Matuchin. A Hero of the Horn. She was golden-haired, strong, lithe and beautiful.

Blasic Faloun. Seanchan captain in Almizar in charge of *raken*. He was graying and lean-faced with a black leather patch hiding the spot where his right eye had been and a puckered white scar running down his forehead, behind the patch and onto his cheek. He agreed to give Tylee and Perrin four *raken* and twelve *morat'raken* for their assault on the Shaido stronghold at Malden.

Blasted Lands, the. A wasteland surrounding Shayol Ghul, beyond the Blight. The Blasted Lands could not support vegetation of any kind, an indication of the Dark One's influence in the extreme; in the Blasted Lands, the land itself could kill.

bleakness, the. A state that overcame some Aiel after they crossed the Dragonwall. The victim often sat for a long time, staring at nothing, in a deep depression. Some thereafter threw away their spears and fled, though none of the Aiel knew where they went. Others fled to the Shaido, while the Shaido were in Kinslayer's Dagger; these elicited contempt, even from many of the Shaido. *Gai'shain* overcome by the bleakness often refused to take off the white when their time was up. The sources of the bleakness were manifold. There was the fact that the *Car'a'carn* really was a wetlander; surely he was of their blood, but he knew only what he had been taught of Aiel customs. An important factor was the secret revealed to them by Rand at Alcair Dal of their origins in the Age of Legends, leading to an inability to accept those origins and the fear that perhaps their warlike ways were in themselves another betrayal of the Aes Sedai. The fear that Rand somehow had an Aes Sedai leash fastened to his neck added to the new view of Aes Sedai manifesting itself, created an additional source to feed the bleakness. During the period of Rand's captivity by Galina, the numbers fleeing from around Cairhien reached a peak of a thousand a day or more.

Blight, the. *See* Great Blight

Blightborder. A Saldaean term indicating the border with the Blight.

Blightwatch. Those who guarded the Blightborder in the Borderlands.

Blind Pig, The. An inn located in Chachin, Kandor. Its innkeeper was a round-faced, squinting woman in a long apron that might have once been white. Moiraine stopped there to inquire whether anyone had seen a young Tairen woman, when she was searching for Siuan.

Blinder's Peak. A small mountain in Murandy.

blisterleaf. A noxious weed that had medicinal properties. Melten used it on Talmanes' wound from a Fade's Thakan'dar sword to retard the spread of the taint.

block. A mental barrier to channeling erected by a wilder, usually unconsciously, as a survival mechanism.

Blood, the. The term used by the Seanchan to designate the nobility. One could be raised to the Blood as well as born to it, and this was frequently a reward for outstanding accomplishment or service to the Empire. There were four degrees of nobility, two of the High Blood and two of the low, or lesser, Blood. The High Blood let their fingernails grow to a length of one inch and shaved the sides of their heads, leaving a crest down the center, narrower for men than for women. The length of this crest varied according to fashion. The low Blood also grew their fingernails long, but they shaved the sides and back of the head leaving what appeared to be a bowl of hair, with a wide tail at the back allowed to grow longer, often to the shoulder for men or to the waist for women. Those of the highest level of the High Blood were called High Lady or High Lord and lacquered the first two fingernails on each hand. Those of the next level of the High Blood were called simply Lord or Lady and lacquered only the nails of the forefingers. Those of the low Blood also were called simply Lady or Lord, but those of the higher rank lacquered the nails of the last two fingers on each hand, while those on the lowest level lacquered only the nails of the little fingers. The Empress and immediate members of the Imperial family shaved their heads entirely and lacquered all of their fingernails.

Blood Snow, the. Another name for the Battle of the Shining Walls.

Blood Springs. A location in Shienar where the rocks beneath the water made the river appear to run red. Lan's and Agelmar's army engaged the Trollocs there during the Last Battle, combat that almost became disastrous for Lan's forces and that exposed Agelmar as having been compromised.

Blood, Voice of the. A Seanchan servant of one of the High Blood, through whom the Blood communicated with those of lesser rank.

Bloodknives. The most elite unit of the Seanchan Fists of Heaven; they were assassins equipped with specialized *ter'angreal* that granted them stealth, strength and speed. Once one of the *ter'angreal* was activated, with a drop of the host's blood, it leached life from the host.

Bloodlance. A tall bay horse owned by Harril, Pritalle's Warder.

Bloodletter, Villiam. An ancient leader who fought the Banath people on Almoth Plain.

bloodsnake. A snake whose bite could turn blood into jelly within minutes of a bite. It grew to no more than four or five feet in length.

Bloodwash Falls. A place where someone in Mat's memories fought Nashif.

bloodwrasp. A horrendous creature found in the Blight.

Bloody Water. A sept of the Taardad Aiel.

Blossoms of Fire. A weave of Earth, Air and Fire that created red shafts expanding into discs of fire thirty feet across.

Blue Ajah. The main thrust of the Blue Ajah was involvement in causes. Along with the Green Ajah, considered the most passionate of Aes Sedai in their beliefs, the Blue Ajah were most open to being swayed by emotion. No Blue sisters remained loyal to Elaida, though some Blues stayed away from the main body of the rebels because of the distances involved. They were adamant in their belief that Siuan was deposed illegally and stilled illegally, and for that alone Elaida deserved to be pulled down. The Blue Ajah was led by a single head, known as the First Selector, with an advisory council which had a variable number of members. The head of the Blue Ajah was more or less autocratic depending upon the woman holding the post. Beyond that, there was no constant organizational structure. At the time of the Last Battle the Blue Ajah had roughly one hundred members, making it sixth in size.

Blue Bull, the. A raucous inn in Samara, Ghealdan, that Nynaeve noticed while passing through Samara.

Blue Carp Street. A street in Far Madding. Torval and Gedwyn stayed there in a rented room, and were killed at the house by Padan Fain. Rand and Lan were lured into a trap at the house by Fain, who, with Toram Riatin, attacked them, unsuccessfully.

Blue Cat, The. An Ogier-built inn located in Tar Valon. It looked like a blue cat curled up to sleep.

Blue Crane. The rivership belonging to Chin Ellisor. Nynaeve, Egwene and Elayne traveled aboard it down the River Erinin until it became stuck in a mud-flat near Jurene and they disembarked.

Blue Gull. The raker belonging to Zaida din Parede Blackwing.

Blue Rose, The. An inn located in Canluum, Kandor; its innkeeper was Racelle Arovni. Lan and Bukama stayed at The Blue Rose. There Lan met an old friend, Ryne Venamar, who told him about Lady Edeyn Arrel raising the Golden Crane across the Borderlands. Lan was attacked by six men outside the stables; he defeated them all.

Blue Star, Renaile din Calon. *See* Renaile din Calon Blue Star

blue-eye. A spring flower known as *seiera* in the Old Tongue.

bluefly. An insect that bit hard enough to draw blood.

bluespine. A plant that was used in a tea to cure sullenness.

Bluewing, the. The two-masted vessel skippered by Captain Carney. Moiraine took passage on this vessel when sneaking out of Tar Valon to begin her search for the Dragon Reborn.

bluewort. A plant that was used medicinally as a tea to relieve a queasy stomach. It also had qualities as a dye.

Boann, Nemene Damendar. Semirhage's name in the Age of Legends.

Boannda. A large town located at the confluence of the Rivers Eldar and Boern in Ghealdan. Boannda had tall gray walls, towers and a palace-like structure inside. On the way to Salidar, Nynaeve, Elayne, Birgitte, Thom, Juilin, Uno and his Shienaran soldiers stopped in Boannda on the smuggling ship that Galad had hired to get them and various refugees out of Samara.

Boanne. A woman who was Songmistress at Taralan in the Fourth Age. She composed *Do'in Toldara te*, *Songs of the Last Age*, Quarto Nine: The Legend of the Dragon.

boar spears. Weapons used in the Two Rivers.

Bodewhin (Bode) Cauthon. Mat's sister, and a novice with the rebel Aes Sedai, having been recruited by Verin and Alanna. She was born in 983 NE, and her potential strength was said to be close to that of Egwene. She wore her hair braided and was plumply pretty and big-eyed, with a mischievous something around the eyes that resembled Mat. She was one of three found in the Two Rivers that were born with the spark—Bode, Elle and Jancy—all three of whom would be quite strong, in Verin's estimation. Bode also had the Talent of making *cuendillar*. She was intelligent, and was headed in the direction of the Green or Blue Ajah. She wanted to live adventure, not just read about it. After Kairen was murdered, Bode was supposed to take her place in creating a *cuendillar* chain across the River Erinin, but Egwene stepped in at the last moment and was captured in the process.

Boern, River. A river flowing east and south through Ghealdan, past Jehannah, and joining the River Eldar at the border of Amadicia.

boggles. The Illianer term for things that go bump in the night.

Bollin. One of the horse handlers in Luca's show. He was big and squint-eyed and insisted that the Seanchan pay to enter the show.

bonding. An act, by an Aes Sedai or Asha'man using the One Power, of creating a physical and psychic link with another who thereby became her or his Warder. Aes Sedai in the Age of Legends did not bond Warders.

boneknit. A medicinal herb used for mending broken bones.

Bonwhin Meraighdin. An Aes Sedai of the Red Ajah. She was born in FY 738 and was raised Amyrlin circa FY 939. Bonwhin nearly caused the destruction of the White Tower by trying to make Hawkwing her puppet. She was deposed and stilled in FY 992 because of her failed manipulations of Artur Hawkwing, which led to Hawkwing turning violently against the Aes Sedai and placing the White Tower under siege. After being deposed, she was kept among the scullions—as a scullion, in truth—and exhibited to the sisters periodically as a dire example. She died in FY 996.

Book of Translation, the. An Ogier artifact and a central part of Ogier lore. When the Book of Translation was opened, the Ogier race would return to the alternate world from which they originally came, not to return to this world until the Wheel turned. The Ogier had been discussing the situation for some time, and had pretty much decided to open the Book. After all, if they were to come from the alternate world in the next Age, they had to go back to the alternate world before they could return from it. The final decision was to be made at the Great Stump, and it was only Loial's oratory that prevented this departure from happening.

bookers. Members of the Illustrious and Honored Guild of Bookers in Ebou Dar. They were bookies and insurance men or women all in one.

Borderforts. Defending structures of the civilized world, found in the Borderlands near the border with the Blight.

Borderlands. The northern nations that bordered the Blight. They included Saldaea, Shienar, Kandor and Arafel. Malkier was one of the Borderlands before its fall.

Bore. The hole drilled in the Pattern by researchers at Collam Daan in an attempt to access an undivided source of the One Power, unwittingly releasing the Dark One's influence on the world, causing destruction and chaos. The hole that was finally sealed by Lews Therin and the Hundred Companions was larger than the original Bore, for the longer it remained open the larger it got, though it was diminished somewhat in the sealing; the Dark One's counterstroke tainted *saidin*, causing all male channelers to go mad. Nevertheless, it was sealed again in the Last Battle, and closed up again completely, thereby setting the stage for the Bore to be drilled anew.

Boreane Carivin. A Cairhienin head servant with Rand's army preparing to attack the Seanchan. A stout, pale little woman, her face showed pity for Rand when he was in the tent talking with Torval. She was left behind when Rand moved his army north of Illian, before the fighting began.

Borndat, Elandria. An ancient scholar and the author of *Seeing Through the Breaking.*

Bornhald, Dain. *See* Dain Bornhald

Bornhald, Geofram. *See* Geofram Bornhald

Boroleos, Erian. *See* Erian Boroleos

Bors. An alias used by Carridin. *See* Jaichim Carridin

Botteger, Aeric. A man of the Two Rivers who appeared in Nynaeve's test for the shawl.

Bounce. A game played in Andor in which a colorful ball was bounced on a paddle.

Boundless. A wolf Perrin encountered in the wolf dream. He was young, with brown fur and a lean build. Boundless was Noam's wolf persona; he found the wolf dream to be superior to human life.

Bowl, Golden. *See* Alcair Dal

Bowl of the Winds. A *ter'angreal* in the shape of a bowl that could be used to control the weather, and which generated both *saidin* and *saidar*, although only women triggered it. It was a shallow bowl of thick crystal, more than two feet across and carved deeply inside with what appeared to be swirling clouds. When Elayne channeled into it, the bowl turned a pale watery blue and the clouds shifted as if moved by wind; when she stopped, it became clear again, but the clouds were in different positions. After it was used, the clouds were different than they were before, so that the bowl appeared to be, like the weather itself, ever changing. Elayne and Nynaeve discovered the device in *Tel'aran'rhiod*, and Egwene sent them to Ebou Dar to find it in the waking world. They did so, with the help of the Kin, and they made a bargain with the Sea Folk to help them implement its powers with a circle of channelers, which was needed to operate it efficiently. A circle of thirteen could do enough to alter the weather changes in the world caused by the Dark One, but not enough to buffer the results. This *ter'angreal* was designed to work over a small region. The advanced knowledge of the Windfinders meant they could spread its effects over a larger area, which resulted in it affecting the One Power and physical conditions on the ground, radiating out from near Ebou Dar where it was used to at least as far as the Altara-Illian border where Rand's armies were fighting the Seanchan.

Braem. An Ogier-built city in Coremanda, one of the Ten Nations after the Breaking. New Braem was an old border town in east Andor between Caemlyn and Tar Valon, near the site of the original city.

Braem Wood. A forest fifty leagues north of Caemlyn, on the edge of the Caralain Grass. At Caemlyn, Dyelin told Elayne that thousands of Borderlander soldiers had been spotted in Braem Wood. Later, Norry, while reporting to Elayne, mentioned that the army in Braem Wood had not moved yet, though he admitted that his intelligence was several days old. Merilille, who had Traveled to the Borderland rulers' encampments in Braem Wood, confirmed what was known about them, and said that the rulers had sent messengers to Caemlyn when they had arrived in New Braem, but that they would not reach the palace for another week. After Merilille met with the Borderland rulers, Elayne's party Traveled to Braem Wood to meet the Borderlanders, who were looking for Rand and who were allegedly accompanied by up to two hundred sisters.

In the Last Battle, after the Trollocs had overrun Caemlyn, Elayne and her army set up an ambush for the Trollocs in Braem Wood, after drawing the Shadowspawn out of the city with harrying forces.

Bran. *See* Brandelwyn al'Vere

Brandel Vordarian. A Lord Captain of the Children of the Light. He came from a minor noble family in Andor, and was a hulking man with silver in his yellow hair. After hearing Galad's argument with Asunawa, Vordarian and other Lords Captain executed Asunawa and proclaimed Galad Lord Captain Commander of the Children of the Light. Vordarian was the eldest of the Lords Captain under Galad.

Brandelwyn al'Vere. The Mayor of Emond's Field and the innkeeper at The Winespring Inn. He was a round man, wider than anyone else in the Two Rivers, but very light on his feet, and bald except for a fringe of gray hair. He was born in 937 NE, married Marin in 964 NE, and was elected Mayor in 978 NE. He and his wife had five daughters: Berowyn, Alene, Elisa, Loise and Egwene. They lived in rooms at the back of the whitewashed second floor of The Winespring Inn. Bran coordinated with Perrin, Tam, Abell and others in the defense of Emond's Field against the Trollocs.

Branlet Gilyard. A young Andoran who was High Seat of House Gilyard and loyal to Elayne. The sign of his House was the Three Red Leopards. Born circa 987 NE, he had curly black hair and blue eyes. He was one of four young nobles Dyelin brought to help Elayne win the throne. (The others were Perival Mantear, Catalyn Haevin and Conail Northan.) Branlet's guardian, his aunt Mayv, died about two months prior to his going to Caemlyn, after her horse stepped into a gopher hole. The horse and rider each broke a leg, and by the time anyone found them, it was too late. Branlet's relatives squabbled over who was to be his new guardian, all of them wanting the job and none of them wanting another to have it. He was eager to help when Elayne was kidnapped; Dyelin took him to the Far Madding Gate, where he was kept far from the fighting.

Brannin Martan. A gray-haired Andoran High Seat of House Martan. His wife was Elvaine. Relatively poor, they lived in a manor that was much like a large farmhouse, with additions made over generations. They were loyal to Elayne and brought armsmen to help her win the throne. A third of their armsmen were their sons and grandsons, nephews and great-nephews.

Branstrom, Arilinde. An Andoran noblewoman and High Seat of her House. She was loyal to Elayne and brought fifty armsmen to support her.

Brawley, Gabrelle. *See* Gabrelle Brawley

breakbone fever. A fever that caused sweats, distress and even broken bones.

Breaking of the World, the. The destruction of many parts of the world, caused by male Aes Sedai who all went mad after the Dark One's counterstroke tainted *saidin*. In their madness these men, who could wield the One Power very strongly, changed the face of the earth. They caused great earthquakes, leveled mountain ranges, raised new mountains, lifted dry land where seas had been, made the ocean rush in where dry land had been. Many parts of the world were completely depopulated, and the survivors scattered like dust on the wind.

Breaking of the World, The. *Aleth nin Taerin alta Camora*, a work of the Fourth Age; its author was unknown.

Breaking Wave, Malin din Toral. *See* Malin din Toral Breaking Wave

Breane Taborwin. A Cairhienin noblewoman. She was the widow of Dobraine's brother. Born in 956 NE, she was 5'4" tall, and pretty, with pale skin and dark eyes. Rand met her at Barthanes' manor; she was one of three pursuing him amorously, but she was of higher rank than the other two, Alaine and Belevaere. According to Thom, Breane could give an education every man should have at least once in his life, if he lived through it. She became a refugee during the Cairhienin civil war; she met Lamgwin Dorn and fell in love with him. She could have returned to Cairhien and reclaimed her estates—she had taken no action against Rand—but doing so would have meant giving up Lamgwin. She acted as a lady's maid for Morgase when Morgase was on the lam, but she only served Morgase because Lamgwin did so. She had a certain contempt for Morgase, who she thought was essentially weak.

Breane made a poor job at best of playing the servant; it wasn't that she didn't know what to do or didn't do it, but rather that she too often spoke to Morgase as to an equal, was perfectly willing to tell Morgase she was a fool for not tripping Tallanvor behind the barn and ripping his clothes off, and frequently made no secret of her general contempt. On the other hand, she offered silent comfort after Morgase was forced by Valda. But then, she was irate at Morgase for wilting; she felt that Morgase was hardly the first woman to be taken against her will and Morgase ought to pick up her life and get on with it rather than moping. After Perrin rescued Morgase's party from the Dragonsworn, she became a lady's maid to Faile.

Breen's Spring. A place in the western part of Andor, west of Carysford on the Caemlyn Road. Master Kinch told Mat and Rand that Morgase's Queen's Guard no longer went beyond Breen's Spring.

Brehon, Silviana. *See* Silviana Brehon

Brelan. A lord in a song sung at The White Ring in Maderin; he had an evening with a randy young woman when the night was cold.

Bren. A stout servant in the Tarasin Palace. Mat was handed over to him when he visited the Tarasin Palace by the front door. He was the fifth of seven servants that Mat encountered in that visit. Each one was a little older and more senior than the one before.

Brend, Lord. Sammael's moniker in Illian. Some asked questions about him when he came to power—no one could recall hearing of him before—but those who asked too many questions had a habit of vanishing, and the others on the Council seemed to accept him as if they had known him a long time, so people who had questions kept those questions to themselves if they had any brains.

There were also a great many problems facing the country, facing the world it seemed, and the others on the Council seemed to value Lord Brend's wisdom and follow his advice. People did not know where he went or how, but it was generally assumed that Rand killed him.

Brendas. An Aes Sedai of the White Ajah and the rebel contingent, with a strength level of 16(4). Born in 946 NE, she went to the White Tower in 963 NE. After twelve years as a novice and ten years as Accepted, she was raised to the shawl in 985 NE. She had cool dark eyes and her voice was like emotionless chimes. She was part of the circle that Healed Mat of his connection to the Shadar Logoth dagger, and was one of the few in Salidar who never quizzed Nynaeve about Rand. Brendas was part of the battle in *Tel'aran'rhiod* against some of the Black Ajah at the White Tower until Amys took her out of the dream and had her wake others to get them away from danger. She had no Warder.

Breyan ti Malcain Mandragoran. The wife of Lan's uncle Lain Mandragoran and the mother of Isam Mandragoran. Breyan dared Lain to take his armies to the Blasted Lands or even to Shayol Ghul. Lain died there with most of those who followed him. Breyan blamed Lan's father, and plotted with Cowin Fairheart to seize the throne for Isam. They moved soldiers back from the Blight, and Trollocs poured into Malkier. She attempted to flee with Isam and vanished; they were supposedly overtaken by Trollocs. She was in her mid-twenties at the time she reportedly died.

Briain. A young Maiden of the Spear who traveled with Perrin to Ghealdan. She was round-faced. Briain was killed while taking out the Shaido sentries to the northwest of Malden so the supply carts could get through.

Bridge of Flowers. A bridge in the city of Illian leading to the Perfumed Quarter.

Bridge of Sunrise. A bridge leading into Chachin, Kandor.

Bringer of Gales. A Sea Folk name for the Dark One.

bristlebough. A flowering tree with thin, finger-like leaves that grew in the Tower's Spring Garden.

Brokel. A member of the Children of the Light. In the Last Battle, Golever chose him as one of the dozen best men to accompany Galad when Mat sent him to Hawal Ford.

Broken Crown. The crown of the ruler of Saldaea.

Bromas. The innkeeper at The Two Apples in Caemlyn. She was stately and dark-haired.

broomweed. A plant with tiny yellow flowers.

Brotherless. *See Mera'din*

Brothers of the Eagle. One of the twelve Aiel warrior societies. It was also known as *Far Aldazar Din.*

Brown Ajah. The main thrust of the Brown Ajah was gathering knowledge; they were librarians, historians and natural historians, doing nothing in the physical sciences or toward invention. The Brown Ajah had a ruling council. Its number of members varied from five to thirteen, though always an odd number. The head of the council was foremost among the Brown sisters without actually being considered the head of the Ajah, but in fact she had about as much real authority as any of the other Ajah heads. The head of the council was sometimes referred to as the First Chair; most often, she was simply called "the head of the council," reflecting the supposed egalitarian nature and the rather loose structure of the Brown, where sisters often lost themselves in one sort of research or another. At the time of the Last Battle there were approximately 130 sisters in the Brown Ajah, making it the fourth largest.

Bruan. A man of the Salt Flat sept of the Nakai Aiel; the clan chief. His hold was Shiagi Hold, and his Wise One was Alsera. He was 6'6" tall and weighed over three hundred pounds—a massive man, big and strong enough for two blacksmiths. He had sad gray eyes and a placid nature for an Aiel, with a deceptively mild voice that sounded almost lazy. Bruan was very taken with He Who Comes With the Dawn and commanded the five Aiel clans—nearly 200,000 spears—gathered in the Plains of Maredo prior to the Illian campaign. None of the others objected. Bruan's oddly placid manner belied his battle skills; he was a hard fighter and a devious tactician, but he could also be a peacemaker. He took part in the invasion of Illian. In Aviendha's vision of the future in Rhuidean, he agreed to go to battle against the Seanchan.

Brugh Chavana. An acrobat in Luca's circus, one of four men said to be brothers, although the four looked very different. He was short and compact. Brugh received a swollen lip when he tried to break up a fight between Latelle and Nynaeve.

Brune, Mother. A healer in a village between Market Sheran and Carysford in Andor. When they were traveling to Caemlyn, and Rand fell sick with fever, Mat wanted to take Rand to her, but she was off birthing a baby.

Bryne, Gareth. *See* Gareth Bryne

Brynt. A member of the Band of the Red Hand who fought in Caemlyn when the Trollocs invaded. Talmanes ordered him to set a stable afire.

Brys. A Lord in Tarabon whose servant drank too much and gave information to Florin Gelb.

Brys Noramaga. The husband of Queen Ethenielle of Kandor. He was born in 940 NE and married Ethenielle in 963 NE. He took her House name on marriage, since she was of the greater House, not to mention that she was already heir to the throne of Kandor; he was styled "Prince Brys" and served as Ethenielle's Swordbearer. Theirs was a love-match in large part, though there was a political consideration, of course. Over the sixteen years of their marriage, they had eight children, seven of whom survived until adulthood. Brys died in 979 NE, along with his son Diryk, supposedly in an accidental fall which also claimed Iselle Arrel. Diryk was a victim of the male channeler pogrom, though that was not widely known, and Brys was killed because he was with Diryk and tried to protect him.

Brytan. A tiny village in Altara that had consisted of only a dozen families, where the buildings were infested with vermin once the Shaido devastated the village. Perrin's troops traveled through this village after the Shaido had done their damage, and they camped in the fields there. Darkhounds passed near the camp. The group continued to make this their camp while Perrin and the Seanchan implemented their plans against the Shaido in Malden.

Buad of Albhain. A Hero of the Horn who looked as regal as any queen.

bubbles of evil. A figurative description of the evil that arose from the Dark One as the seals weakened. According to Rand, they drifted along the Pattern until they struck other threads and burst, causing a wide range of terrible phenomena to occur. Although most easily attracted to *ta'veren*, the bubbles would also affect others, resulting in effects such as inanimate objects becoming animate; deadly, improbable invasions of insects; and spontaneous combustion.

Buchaner rebellion. A rebellion led in an earlier life by Birgitte, known then as Jethari Moondancer. In its culminating battle at Lahpoint Hills, Gaidal was wounded, and Birgitte took him to the Tower of Ghenjei in search of a way to heal him. They both died in the tower.

Buel Dowtry. A fletcher in Emond's Field. His hair was white and his nose almost as sharp as a broadhead point.

buffer. Term from the Age of Legends and used by the Forsaken to indicate a shield on someone to stop them from channeling the Power.

bugbear. A term used in Illian for a horrible creature of superstition.

Buie, Cenn. *See* Cenn Buie

Buiryn. A king of Manetheren before the Trolloc Wars, whose forces were defeated by Aedomon of Safer at Midean's Ford. Legend had it that Aedomon let Buiryn and his remaining men go instead of killing them all; Mat's memories revealed that he did let them go, and as soon as they were strung out, killed them.

Bukama Marenellin. A Malkieri man who was the Hero of Salmarna. Bukama was of the five men out of twenty who survived carrying the infant Lan out of a dying Malkier. He was the last of the five to die, murdered in the Aesdaishar Palace in Chachin by Ryne Venamar, a young Malkieri who had become Arafellin to his toenails and also a Darkfriend.

Bukava. Father of Hartha, an Ogier and a Seanchan Gardener.

Bulen. A man in Aesdaishar Palace who served Lan. Lan thought that his other servants had been coopted by Edeyn, but that Bulen was still his. Bulen's father was Malkieri. Bringing a packhorse, Bulen joined Lan on the Proska Flats in Saldaea as Lan rode for Tarwin's Gap and the Last Battle. He was hit by an arrow and hid that fact until he died.

Bunch of Grapes, The. A three-story inn located in the Foregate of Cairhien where Thom and Dena stayed following Thom's incident with the Fade in Whitebridge. Its innkeeper was Zera. Rand met Thom here to try to get him to accompany him to return the Horn of Valere to Fal Dara. Dena was murdered at the inn.

Bunt. An Andoran family. *See* Adrinne *and* Almen Bunt

Burdin, Master. A wagonmaster with the Band of the Red Hand. He took care of Olver after Olver was ignored by the woman hired to tend him. Burdin gave him plenty to eat for his help tending the horses. He would not let Olver ride the horses, though.

Burin Shaeren. Lelaine's Domani Warder. He was copper-skinned and looked like an uprooted stump. He had been with her over twenty years at the time of the White Tower split.

Burlow, Garon. *See* Garon Burlow

Burn. A male wolf with an old Trolloc scar on his shoulder. He was impatient, angry and big. He wanted nothing to do with humans; he just wanted to hunt and kill Trollocs.

burning out. The accidental process of a person being severed from the True Source, so severe that the person no longer had a sense of *saidar* or *saidin*. Burning out could not be Healed.

burningleaf. A noxious weed.

Buryhill. A village in Andor, surrounded by parched fields, that Elayne and her party passed through while going to Caemlyn from Ebou Dar.

Byar, Jaret. *See* Jaret Byar

Byir, Joiya. *See* Joiya Byir

Caal, Mitsora. An Aes Sedai who lived at the time of the formation of the White Tower.

Caar al Thorin al Toren. King Aemon of Manetheren's father, also known as Caar One-Hand. He went to win Aridhol back to the Second Covenant. Mordeth ordered the deaths of Caar and the embassy as Friends of the Dark. Caar escaped the dungeons of Aridhol and fled to the Borderlands with Mordeth's unnatural assassins at his heels. He met Rhea there and married her. Rhea killed Caar, and then killed herself in front of his tomb. The armies of Manetheren came to avenge Caar but found the gates of Aridhol torn down and no living thing inside the walls.

Caban. A Seanchan soldier serving on Captain Egeanin's vessel before the battle at Falme. He was the one who stayed on board the *Spray* while it went into harbor. He was in his middle years and dark-eyed, with an old scar above his eyes and another nicking his chin. He had nothing but contempt for anything on the east side of the Aryth Ocean. His voice had the same slur as Egeanin's, but was leather rasping on rock. He wanted to talk about battles, drinking and women he had known. He put his sword to Domon's throat when Domon asked about *damane*.

Cabriana Mecandes. A Tairen Aes Sedai of the Blue Ajah with a strength level of 34(22). Born in 911 NE to a noble House, she went to the White Tower in 927 NE. After twelve years as a novice and seven years as Accepted, she was raised to the shawl in 946 NE. She had blue eyes and long golden hair. Cabriana was born with the spark; when she began manifesting the ability to channel, she was shipped off to Tar Valon as the law required, though she went unwillingly. She was a quick learner who could have moved faster as a novice, had she not spent a good deal of time sulking over being sent to the Tower. She did not want to be Aes Sedai. She was taken by Semirhage and questioned and killed, along with her Warder. Halima went to Salidar, claiming to have been a traveling companion of Cabriana, and that Cabriana had died in a fall.

Caddar. An alias of Sammael when he met with Sevanna and the Shaido Wise Ones.

cadin'sor. The garb of Aiel warriors, consisting of coat and breeches in browns and grays that faded into rock or shadow, along with soft, laced knee-high boots. The word was Old Tongue for "working clothes," though this was an imprecise translation.

Cadsuane Melaidhrin. An Aes Sedai of the Green Ajah, uncommitted to any contingent. Her strength level was 5(+8). She was born in 705 NE in the city-state of Far Madding. At the age of fifteen, she went to the White Tower. There she spent six years as a novice and five years as Accepted. She might have moved faster as novice and Accepted—in fact almost certainly should have—but she was noted for both her stubbornness and her pride (read "arrogance"). At age twenty-six, she was raised Aes Sedai and chose the Green Ajah.

Cadsuane was very strong in the One Power; for many years she served as the gauge by which every incoming novice was judged. Prior to Nynaeve's appearance, in the last thousand years, no one had matched her and few had come close. Certainly no one in that time had exceeded her. Not even with her full

strength yet, she was, on the very day she attained the shawl, at the pinnacle of the Aes Sedai social hierarchy.

She stood about 5'5" tall and was neither slender nor stout. She was not pretty, but she was strikingly handsome, with a fair complexion. She had dark eyes, which some people occasionally mistook for black, especially when she was focused on them in an unpleasant fashion. Her hair became iron-gray, and she wore it in a bun on top of her head; the bun was decorated with small dangling golden ornaments, stars and moons and birds and fish. These hair ornaments were considered something of a trademark because she had worn them for as long as anyone could remember. For many sisters, this was just one more indication of how set in her ways she was; they thought Cadsuane would never change, could never change. Of course, that was far from true; Cadsuane was remarkably adaptable, as befitted someone who had survived as long as she. In fact, of Cadsuane's golden hair ornaments, one was an *angreal*, the other nine *ter'angreal*. She knew the uses of six of the nine *ter'angreal*. The ornaments were

1) A bird that looked a little like a shrike. It was an *angreal*, not very powerful, that stepped her up to the top male level of strength, thus considerably above any unaided woman.

2) Double crescent moons, facing one another and overlapping, were *ter'angreal* that functioned like Mat's foxhead, causing flows directed at her to dissipate and also warning that someone close by had embraced the Power; it didn't distinguish between *saidin* and *saidar*, though it worked on and warned of both.

3) A hummingbird. *Ter'angreal* which she called a Well; it was a "storage battery" with a small but significant amount of the Power. It needed periodic recharging after use, but it wouldn't run down on its own no matter how long the lapse between uses.

4) An eight-pointed star with four long and four short wavy rays that detected the ability of a man to channel even if he wasn't channeling, within a distance of thirty or forty paces. Of course, it didn't identify which man inside that range could channel, only that there was one.

5) A bird that appeared to be a swallow. This detected the use of even very small amounts of *saidin* or *saidar* within as much as three miles, and if held by its chain, it would turn to point its beak in the direction of the use. (At Shadar Logoth this was not confused by the massive amounts of *saidin* and *saidar* being used close at hand because they canceled each other by virtue of their being combined; the *ter'angreal* spotted only pure *saidin* or pure *saidar*; it was made at a time when no one was combining the powers any longer and thus was deliberately made to detect only pure use, not combined use.)

6) A six-pointed star. When triggered, this *ter'angreal* laid a thin "armor" against the skin of the wearer. The "armor" was invisible except to whoever was wearing it. It would not only protect against the blow of a sword or knife, or a mace, it dissipated the force of the blow over the entire body, thus reducing it.

7) A sleek fish with sharp fins. This *ter'angreal* enabled the wearer to pull someone into an involuntary circle with her in "guiding the flows," but it could only work if the other person had already embraced *saidar* or seized *saidin*.

8) A shadowed moon. A full disc, but with working on part to indicate a shadow leaving a brightly burnished crescent, its use was unknown.

9) A leaping fish that looked like a fat trout. Use unknown.

10) A carp. Use unknown.

Cadsuane was considered by many to be a second Caraighan, although unlike Caraighan, she always refused offices. She preferred the field, so to speak; adventures were her bag. She had been full of herself and her strength after receiving the shawl, but she had learned a lesson at the hands of a near-toothless wilder at a farm in the Black Hills, who taught her that there would always be others who were stronger, and that what must be endured, could be endured.

Cadsuane first refused to be raised a Sitter in 846 NE; she reportedly did so a second time as well, though even one refusal was unheard of, and she refused to be raised head of the Green Ajah in 862 NE, another thing that was unheard of. She was said to have vanished from the Tower for ten years (from roughly 890 to 900 NE) when she learned that the Hall intended to raise her Amyrlin after Sereille Bagand. About twenty-five years before the Aiel War, she retired to northern Ghealdan, but came out of retirement, with her two surviving Warders, for that conflict. Soon after the Aiel War ended, she returned to her rustication, and claimed to have been raising roses when Logain appeared.

His appearance drew her out of retirement again, but she was not interested in escorting him to Tar Valon and decided to wander a bit. Then Mazrim Taim rose up, and she headed for Saldaea as fast as she could ride.

When Siuan Sanche and Moiraine Damodred had reason to research Cadsuane because of their encounter with her shortly after reaching the shawl, they found many stories regarding her. All of the ones that they were able to trace down turned out to be true, and in some cases the truth was more than the story. They were not able to follow or confirm all of the stories, of course. One of the most prevalent Cadsuane stories was that she had once physically assaulted an Amyrlin Seat. Since physically assaulting any sister was a serious offense—and an Amyrlin even more so—the fact that Cadsuane apparently escaped any punishment at all, and that the tale was vague about which Amyrlin it was supposed to be, made most everyone think this story was false. It wasn't; it was the method Cadsuane used to turn Myriam Copan from a weak Amyrlin to a strong one in 758 NE. Myriam was thought to have gone on a two-month retreat by herself, but she had, in fact, been all but kidnapped by Cadsuane. Turning Myriam around involved, among other things, turning her upside down at least once. Although Myriam certainly had reason to keep the events of those two months secret (and was able to make a statement which seemed to deny that Cadsuane had assaulted her), it is the basis of the tale that Cadsuane once physically assaulted an Amyrlin.

Another story said that long ago she had removed a sitting king from his palace and taken him to Tar Valon to be gentled. In truth, Cadsuane had a nose for men who could channel. She faced more of them than any other sister living; she herself said more than any two Reds, maybe more than any ten. That seems to indicate at least twenty of them by that time, maybe more. She brought more of them to Tar Valon than any other sister. Of these, she never had to kill one. The men ranged over the years from farmboys to nobles to the King of Tarabon, but one and all, they made much better adjustments to their fate than was considered normal. They eventually died short of a normal span, but they lived considerably longer than usual. And that King of Tarabon? He had to be winkled out of his palace, avoiding his army, which sought to rescue him. She carried him all the way to Tar Valon for gentling by herself, though pursued by his soldiers who refused to believe that he was what he was.

It was also said that she kidnapped a king of Arad Doman and a queen of Saldaea. After she released them, a war that had seemed inevitable simply faded away. She did actually spank or switch three reigning kings and four queens, though the facts of these events are hidden in rumor.

Cadsuane is alleged to have once single-handedly stopped a coup in the White Tower. This did happen, though no one seemed to know or agree on when. The true story: Cadsuane and Sereille Bagand did not get on with each other. In fact, they could not stand one another. Each was the sort of woman who dominated a room—or for that matter, a city!—by simply entering, and they struck sparks at every meeting. Despite her dislike for Sereille, though, Cadsuane uncovered a plot to overthrow Sereille and crushed it. The plotters thought she would be eager to join them, but she dragged the weeping ringleaders to Sereille and made them throw themselves on Sereille's rather small mercies. Sereille was not particularly pleased to have been saved—the plot was well laid out and ready to leap off—by one she so disliked.

Cadsuane had a reputation for standing White Tower custom on its head, twisting it as she chose, and even violating it outright, as in her frank speech about age, her direct questions and refusals to accept oblique answers, and her interference in the actions of other sisters. The same could be said of her regarding Tower law, for that matter. She had a reputation for taking direct action, even to the point of violence, slapping faces, boxing ears and more (especially when faced with what she considered stupidity), with those of high status as often as with low, or rather, more often. She also had a reputation for not caring whether she dented somebody's pride, if she thought it necessary.

There were the usual tales expected of a Green, only more of them. Riots suppressed and wars stopped single-handedly; rulers steadied on their thrones, or pulled from them, sometimes toppled openly and sometimes more subtly (toppling rulers was something Aes Sedai had not really done much of in the last thousand years, but Cadsuane seemed in many ways a throwback); rescue of people carried into the Blight or kidnapped by dangerous bands of Darkfriends; the breaking up of murderous rings of Darkfriends plaguing villages; and the exposing of powerful Darkfriends who tried to kill her to protect themselves. There were dozens, even hundreds, of improbable and sometimes seemingly impossible tales.

Some of these were not so much tales about her as an impression, a belief: Cadsuane would do what she intended to do, and no one could stop her, not a king or a queen, not an Amyrlin—not even the Dark One himself, some claimed. And when Rand al'Thor rose to power as the Dragon Reborn, Cadsuane once again chose to take part in directing the events of the world.

Cadsuane had had many Warders over the years—it was said that she had had more Warders than most sisters had shoes—but during the time of the Dragon Reborn, she had none, saying it would be unfair to the Warders, given her age.

Cadsuane had a number of special skills and Talents, including being able to read residues. One of her great abilities was seeing what others missed. For example, she was suspicious of Rand "exiling" Perrin after their alleged argument; she was aware of Rand sending others on errands, but was unable to find out for what purpose. And of course she was the one who cottoned to the Rand-Moridin switch at the end of the Last Battle, and watched Rand ride away in Moridin's body, not saying a thing to anyone.

Cadsuane confronted Rand on numerous occasions, sometimes humiliating him, with the purpose of humanizing him before the Last Battle began. She thought that if he reached Tarmon Gai'don as he was—or worse, farther down the road he was traveling—even his victory might have been as bad as the Dark One winning: "It is a mistake many men make, equating strength with hardness. All too often, hardness becomes brutality; they forget how to laugh except where anyone else would cry. They ignore pains of the heart as readily as pains of the flesh, and rip out even the memory of tears." Part of her plan was to intrigue Rand, to fascinate him, by not being or doing what he expected. She wanted to keep him slightly off-balance. Of course, she could do this in large part just by being herself. Still, she pushed him just as hard as she thought necessary. Her secondary motivations were to stop Rand from destroying more than could be avoided before the Last Battle, and to keep Elaida and the rebels from destroying the White Tower.

Caembarin. A nation that arose after the Trolloc Wars.

Caemlyn. The capital of Andor. Built on rising hills, it had both an Inner City (the old city) and a New City (the part of Caemlyn less than two thousand years old). Known gates were the Whitebridge Gate leading west, the Far Madding Gate leading south, the Sunrise Gate leading east, and the Origan and Mondel Gates opening into the Inner City. The Royal Palace, the seat of the Andoran monarchy, was located on a hill in the middle of the Inner City. The pure white palace would not have been out of place among Tar Valon's wonders, with its slender towers and its domes covered in gold leaf shining in the sun, its high balconies and intricate stonework. Low Caemlyn was a collection of markets and businesses outside the fifty-foot-high city walls. The city walls stretched more than 24 miles, and the area of the city was 53.82 miles. Caemlyn's population before its destruction was approximately 300,000 people.

Caemlyn Gate. The northern gate of Far Madding.

Caemlyn Plain. An area located outside Caemlyn in Andor.

Caemlyn Road. A well-traveled road passing east-west through Andor and its capital.

Caeren, House. A major noble House of Andor. Its High Seat was Lord Nasin until his death shortly before Elayne became queen; he was replaced by his granddaughter Sylvase. Its sign was the Star and Sword. *See also* Nasin, Sylvase *and* Miedelle Caeren

cafar. A pestilent creature created by Aginor; finding a nest of cafar was very dangerous.

Caide, Jeaine. *See* Jeaine Caide

Caiden. A plumply pretty Domani Kinswoman who helped make a gateway for Elayne in Caemlyn.

Cail. One of Kin Tovere's apprentice lensmakers in Cairhien. He helped set up large looking glasses on a tower before the battle for Cairhien.

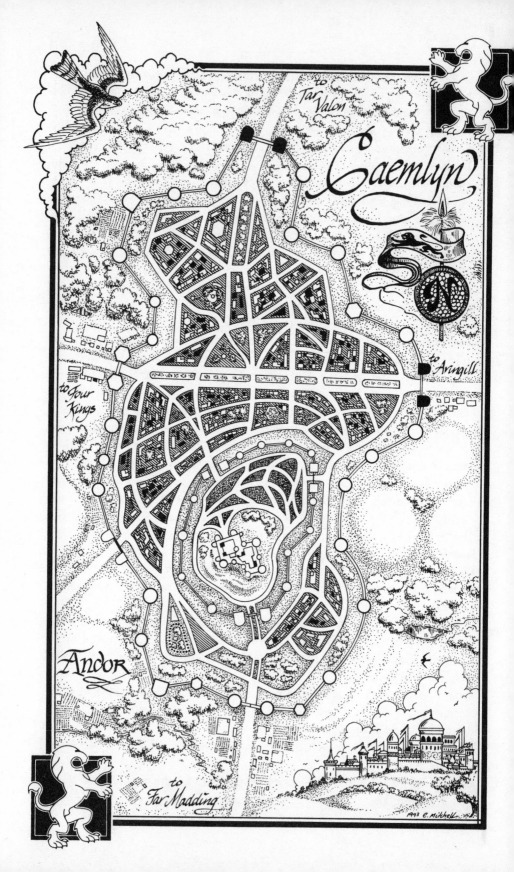

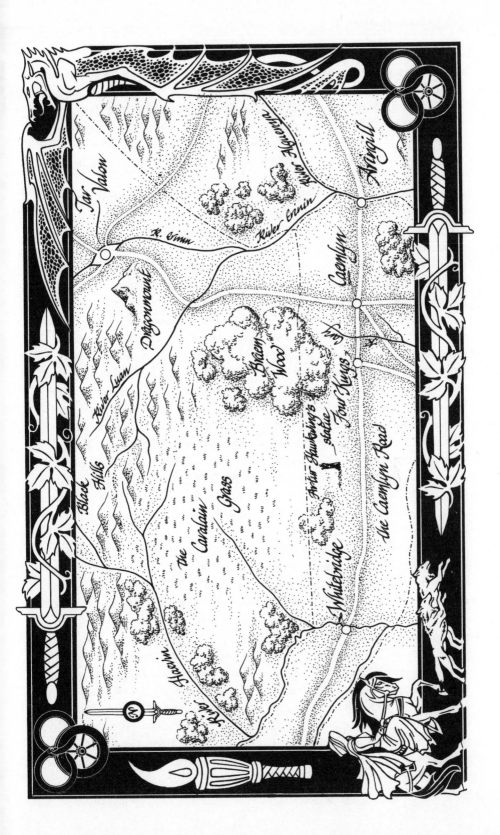

Cain, Gaidal. *See* Gaidal Cain

Caira. A serving girl who worked in The Wandering Woman in Ebou Dar. She was slim, with smoky eyes and full lips, twisted her skirt from side to side, and wriggled like a stroked cat, giggled and had a certain smokiness in her voice. She offered Mat food in a way that suggested she was offering herself. When Birgitte came to see Mat, Caira was not pleased that he had "a gilded woman" waiting in his rooms. She was smacked by the cook, and blamed Mat for it.

Cairdin. An Aiel of the Moshaine sept of the Shaido Aiel and the Brothers of the Eagle warrior society. He went with Maeric and other clan members through the gateway formed by Sammael's *nar'baha* and reported that they were near hostile forces.

Caire din Gelyn Running Wave. A Sea Folk Windfinder to Wavemistress Pelanna of Clan Kisagi with a strength level of 17(5). Caire was the mother of Talaan. Caire and Tebreille were sisters; they disliked one another intensely and had a more than simply a strong rivalry. At 5'6", Caire was slightly taller than her sister Tebreille; Tebreille's face was somewhat sterner. They had the same big, almost black eyes, the same straight nose, the same strong chin. It was obvious looking at them that they were sisters. Caire was arrogant, overbearing, rigid and very demanding of those under her. There was no "if you please" about her; it was jump to it and right now, and put yourself on report for not jumping fast or far enough. She was also very good at what she did. Caire led the circle that used the Bowl of the Winds, given command over her sister Tebreille, which pleased her no end. She was given the command because she was the most learned among them concerning the ancient lore regarding the Bowl of the Winds. She went to Caemlyn with Elayne's group and left Caemlyn with Zaida.

Cairen. A noblewoman who owned a fortress at the north end of Malden prior to the Shaido invasion. Cairen was a handsome dignified widow in her middle years who had ruled Malden and everything for twenty miles around. She was made *gai'shain* by the Shaido, and stayed behind in Malden to rebuild after they had been routed by Perrin's armies.

Cairhien. A nation east of Andor, and its capital city. Its sigil was a many-rayed golden rising sun: the Rising Sun, or the Sun. Its banner was a many-rayed golden rising sun on a field of blue.

Cairhien was the name of both one of Hawkwing's provinces and its capital city. In approximately FY 997, an alliance of nobles seized the city of Cairhien with the supposed intention of restoring the nation of Tova; however, there were factions among the allies with other agendas. A grand ball was held in the city to celebrate the supposed restoration of Tova, but at a given signal, every surviving descendant of the last rulers of Tova—the Tovan Counselors—and their supporters were set upon and slain. The following months saw a number of candidates for the throne assassinated, while others were discredited by

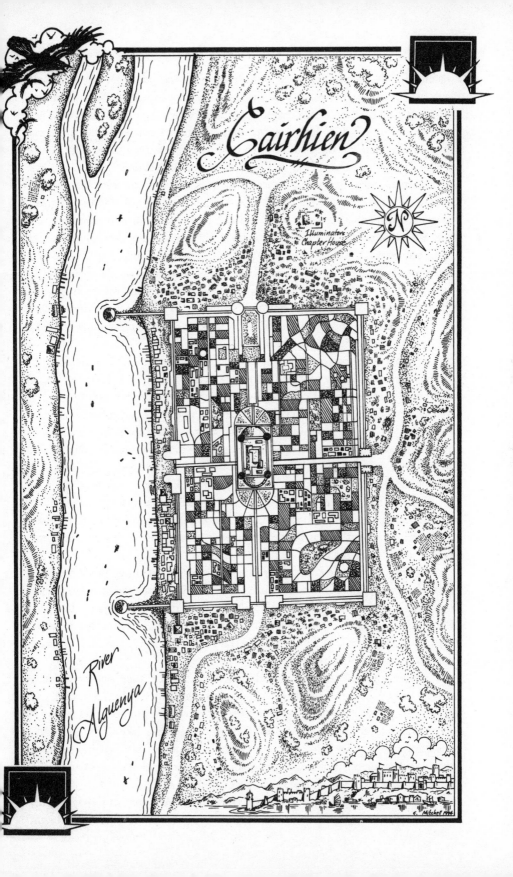

Cairhien

Illuminator's
Chapter House

River
Alguenya

c. Mitchell 1994

means of *Daes Dae'mar*, already being played as, indeed, it had been played famously in Tova. Moves against Cairhien by other forces concentrated the minds of those holding the city, however, and before the end of the year they crowned Martaine Colmcille as the first King of Cairhien. The Aiel had granted Cairhien the right to travel the Silk Path, making them a highly successful trading nation. Good relations with the Aiel ended when Cairhien's King Laman cut down *Avendoraldera*, which had been a gift from the Aiel, to make a throne that would enhance his prestige. The ensuing Aiel War destroyed much of Cairhien. A recovery came, but the assassination of King Galldrian in 998 NE led to rioting and civil war. Rand al'Thor made an effort to improve the situation, sending grain and nobles from Tear, but the Shaido Aiel crossed the Dragonwall and took Cairhien. They were eventually defeated. After Rand was kidnapped by Aes Sedai, Colavaere took the throne, but Rand returned and deposed her. Rand appointed Dobraine his steward in Cairhien, and he worked to restore order. Those who sought to rebel were unable to gain any traction and Elayne Trakand took the throne.

Commoners seldom rose to ranks of any significance in the Cairhienin military, except among the foot, which was largely despised compared to the favored and more numerous cavalry. Most officers came from the nobility.

The army of Cairhien in fact consisted of the personal levies of various lords and ladies. While an occasional Cairhienin lady would command and lead her own troops, the use of a Master of the Lances was more common among noblewomen in Cairhien than it was in Tear. Noblemen were expected to lead and command, whether or not they were fit to do so. Perhaps because of the way the Game of Houses was played in Cairhien, there was never a formation there resembling the Queen's Guards in Andor or the Winged Guards in Mayene, since even a king or queen wanted the power to remain centered in their own House rather than the throne.

A bounty, called the King's Gift, was given out by the King of Cairhien on various occasions, usually to influence public opinion, although it originally was meant for a helpful distribution. It could be given in times of shortage, when prices had been pushed very high, or at other times for other reasons. Galldrian gave the King's Gift to keep the people quiet. Of course, if a queen ruled, the bounty was known as the Queen's Gift.

Cairhienin played the Game of Houses in their sleep; they were considered players of great subtlety—at least, they considered themselves so, and most people who dealt with them agreed. They spoke volumes in every sentence.

Noble and common alike believed in like marrying like. That is to say, nobles married nobles and commoners married commoners. Anything else was considered bizarre if not obscene. Andorans were considered peculiar in the extreme because of their loose marriage customs.

There was a rigid division between noble and commoner in Cairhien, and among commoners, rigid divisions between wealthy merchants and bankers (for an upper middle class, so to speak), craftsfolk, shopkeepers and farmers (middle class), and laborers, wagon drivers, dockworkers and the like (the lower classes). Even a poor farmer would considers himself or herself to be "middle class" and thus above a common laborer, and considered a wagon driver or dock-worker to be only a hair better than a beggar.

The city of Cairhien, known to its residents simply as "the City," lay across hills against the Alguenya. It was laid out in a precise grid behind high gray walls in a square, one wall against the river. Towers as much as twenty times the height of the wall, in just as precise a pattern, rose inside the walls, though some were not completely rebuilt after the Aiel War. The city gates were tall, square archways; just inside were squat stone buildings with iron-bound doors and arrowslits where strangers were required to register. Paved streets wide enough to make the people in them seem small crossed at right angles. Hills were carved and terraced with stone. Inside the city, the buildings were all stone with ornamentation all of straight lines and sharp angles. Even shops seemed subdued, with small signs. The Royal Palace of Cairhien occupied the highest hill of the city, exactly in the center.

The Foregate once surrounded the city from riverbank to riverbank. A maze and warren of streets crisscrossing at all angles, it was full of hawkers, peddlers, shopkeepers, barbers, all calling their wares and services. The streets were dirt, and peoples' clothes were often shabby, but colorful and a mix of clothes from every land. Most buildings here were made of wood; some were seven stories high and swayed slightly. There were many theaters and a constant carnival atmo-sphere. The Foregate was burned during the siege by the Shaido.

An Illuminator's chapter house lay not far outside the walls, to the north, until it was destroyed.

Until King Laman cut down *Avendoraldera*, Cairhien had a land-trade monopoly on silk, brought from Shara along the Silk Path across the Aiel Waste. Cairhien was also known for cheese, producing over one hundred kinds. The nation produced clocks that were among the finest in the world. It was also well known for mirrors and looking glasses, blown glass, rugs, books, wine, linens and lace. Cairhien grew olives and produced olive oil for cooking and lamps.

The Academy of Cairhien was a center of learning and invention established in Lord Barthanes' palace in the city of Cairhien. Its headmistress was Idrien Tarsin.

Cairhienin. Of Cairhien, both singular and plural.

Cairlyn Nesolle. An Aes Sedai of the Yellow Ajah and the loyalist contingent, with a strength level of 22(10). She was born in 936 NE and went to the White Tower in 952 NE. She spent ten years as a novice and ten years as Accepted, and was raised to the shawl in 972 NE. Assigned to the party sent to kidnap Rand, she was captured at Dumai's Wells and treated as *da'tsang* by the Aiel. Under Verin's Compulsion, she found reason to swear oath to Rand and had done so before Cadsuane departed Cairhien for Far Madding.

Caisen Hob. The name for Old Hob, or the Dark One, in Shandalle, the place of Artur Hawkwing's birth.

Cal. A footman in Aesdaishar Palace, Chachin, Kandor. Siuan, as Suki the maid, met with him and tried to canoodle information out of him about Lady Ines Demain. She told him that she had been fired by Moiraine, and he offered to help her get a job with Lady Ines.

Caldazar. The Old Tongue for "Red Eagle." When Rand was about to meet the Amyrlin for the first time, Lan pinned the red eagle on him, which Rand thought of as *Caldazar*, the Red Eagle of Manetheren. He wore the pin again later, in an effort to hang on to a part of himself.

Calder, Mistress. A woman in Emond's Field. Her house survived the Trolloc attack on Winternight, and she housed other people who lost their homes.

Caldevwin, Aldrin. *See* Aldrin Caldevwin

Caldin. A Goshien Aiel and a member of the *Hama N'dore* (Mountain Dancer) warrior society. Caldin was graying and leathery; he led the group of *Hama N'dore* who accompanied Rand as an escort to see the Saldaean horse display outside Caemlyn. On the way back to the city, they were attacked by Whitecloaks.

Calian the Chooser. A Hero of the Horn who wore a red mask. She was the sister of Shivan the Hunter. Having been born again shortly before the Last Battle, she and her brother did not participate as Heroes of the Horn.

Calindin. A Taraboner Accepted among the rebel contingent, with a potential strength level of 31(19). Born in 960 NE, she went to the White Tower in 977 NE. After twelve years as a novice, she was raised Accepted in 989 NE. In Salidar she shared a house with Nynaeve and Elayne. She had to struggle for everything she learned, but she easily entered the circle led by Anaiya the night the bubble of evil struck.

Calison. A member of the Queen's Guard. He brought word to Kaila of the Queen's Guard of an intruder at the Plum Gate of the Royal Palace in Caemlyn.

Callandor. A male *sa'angreal* that was also known as The Sword That Is Not a Sword, the Sword That Cannot Be Touched. According to the Prophecies of the Dragon, one of the major signs of the Dragon's Rebirth and the approach of Tarmon Gai'don would be the Dragon Reborn taking *Callandor*. Constructed during the War of Power, toward the end of the technological age, it was considered one of the most powerful devices ever made in the Age of Legends. A manufacturing flaw was discovered when it was used during the War of Power; it lacked a buffer, which made it possible to draw too much of the One Power while using the item. It was housed in the Stone of Tear until Rand removed it; he later replaced it. Narishma fetched it for Rand, and Rand used it against the Seanchan, in the process killing some of his own men. At the cleansing of the taint, Jahar Narishma, in a circle with Merise and Elza, used *Callandor* in defense against the Forsaken. Cadsuane took it to retired sisters she trusted for more study. Rand retrieved it, and used it to great effect in the Last Battle, subduing the Dark One and resealing him by forging a shield on the Bore from the True and One Powers, channeled through *Callandor*.

callbox. A small gray cube that Sammael, posing as Caddar, gave to Sevanna to summon him.

Calle Coplin. A roundheels from Emond's Field. As many merchant guards knew her birthmark as knew her face. Faile chased her away with a stick when she flirted with Perrin.

Callie. A Wise Woman in Ebou Dar. She was put out of the Tower in 995 NE and tried to take a *ter'angreal* with her. She also tried to find out other novices' secrets. She was captured by Ispan and Falion, questioned about a stash of objects of the One Power and murdered.

Callswell, Lord. A Domani lord to whom Ramshalan boasted he could manipulate Rand.

calma. A ruffled, tall shrub having big red or white blossoms.

Calpene Peninsula. A peninsula on the west side of Tanchico in Tarabon, one of the three peninsulas on Tanchico Bay.

Calwyn Sutoma. An Ebou Dari bellfounder. Cadaverous, with long black hair, he had a commission from Suroth.

Camaelaine, Marithelle. *See* Marithelle Camaelaine

Camaille Nolaisen. A young Cairhienin member of *Cha Faile* and Barmanes' sister. She was about 5'2" tall, with dark eyes, dark hair worn in a long, mannish cut and tied back at the nape of the neck with a dark ribbon. She was one of those who kept some feminine touches even in men's clothing. Faile considered that Camaille and Arrela had the quickest minds in the bunch, though Parelean and Selande were brighter. She was not one of those sent into Bethal.

Camar. A man of the Bent Peak sept of the Daryne Aiel, and a leader of *Seia Doon*. Rangy, gray-haired and half a head taller than Rand, he led a contingent of two hundred *Seia Doon* on Rand's visit to the Sea Folk.

Cambral, Naorisa. An Aes Sedai of the Gray Ajah. She was chosen to replace Delana in the rebel Hall of the Tower.

Caminelle, Sheraine. *See* Sheraine Caminelle

camp fever. A fever that hawkers claimed could be cured with an ointment they were selling.

Camrin, Master. An Altaran lacquerware merchant who played a long-popular dice game called Match, a version of *Piri*, in The White Ring, an inn in Maderin, Altara.

Camron Caan. A fortress in Shienar. Camron Caan was one of the armies that was going to join Agelmar at the battle at Tarwin's Gap while Rand went to see the Green Man.

Can Breat, the. A place name used in an expression to indicate an impossible alternative: "or I'll be buried in ___."

Canaire'somelle. An Ogier-built city in Jaramide, one of the Ten Nations after the Breaking.

Candeiar. A member of the Children of the Light who acted as a healer. He tended to Galad's injuries.

Candraed, Danine. *See* Danine Candraed

Candwin clan. A family from Two Rivers. *See* Ailys, Darea *and* Eward Candwin

Canford, Adine. *See* Adine Canford

Caniedrin. A Kandori soldier who was in Lan's company at the end of the Aiel War. Though young, he was an efficient and experienced soldier, an archer of rare skill, a cheerful killer who often laughed while he fought. He was paid ten Cairhien gold crowns to kill Moiraine and Lan. He was told to kill her first, but he shot Lan, allowing Moiraine to block further arrows and tie him up in Air. Ryne and Bukama each hit him with an arrow, and he died.

Canin. The captain of the *Darter* on the River Erinin. Egwene, Nynaeve and Elayne boarded his ship in Jurene and traveled on it to Tear.

Canler, Taril. *See* Taril Canler

Canluum. A city of hills in Kandor. High gray walls surrounded the town. A drymoat surrounded Canluum's wall, fifty paces wide and ten deep, spanned by five broad stone bridges with towers at either end as tall as those that lined the wall itself. The Red Stag of Lord Marcasiev waved above every tower. Canluum was made of stone and brick, its paved streets twisting around tall hills. Marcasiev's palace sat on the highest hill in the city, Stag's Stand. Gemstones mined in the surrounding hills made Canluum wealthy. And, strangely enough, Canluum had some of the finest clockmakers anywhere. The streets teemed with activity. No palaces rose in the hollows toward the north wall, only shops and taverns, inns and stables and wagon yards. Bustle surrounded the factors' long warehouses, but no carriages came to the Deeps, and most streets were barely wide enough for carts. They were just as jammed with people as the wide ways, though, and every bit as noisy. Here, the inns were slate-roofed cubes of gray stone with bright signs out front. Bukama and Lan, having been in the south fighting the Aiel, were on their way north again to the Blight, and stopped over in Canluum. Lan was attacked by six men here, whom he killed. Still looking for the mother of the Dragon Reborn, Moiraine went to Canluum to interview Jurine Najima. At her inn, Moiraine ran across Merean, Larelle and Cadsuane. The latter ordered the other two to accompany Moiraine to Chachin, and Moiraine slipped away. While still in Canluum, Moiraine made contact with Siuan, and learned from her that all the sisters who had been hunting for the Dragon Reborn were dead.

Cantoine, Stedding. A *stedding* located just north of the River Iralell.

Cantorin. One of the Aile Somera, a chain of Sea Folk islands west of Toman Head. It was also the name of the main harbor on the island. Suroth consolidated the Seanchan forces there after their defeat at Falme. Sailmistress Coine told Nynaeve that it was one of her destinations.

Canvele. A Lord Captain of the Children of the Light. After Niall's death, he sided with Asunawa, believing that Morgase should be given to the Questioners because the law must be obeyed. But Valda wanted Morgase kept alive until she turned Andor over to the Whitecloaks. In a show of strength, Valda brought half a legion into the Fortress of the Light, and Canvele switched his allegiance to Valda.

capar. An animal resembling a large, hairy boar with a pointed snout and toes with claws. It came from the Aiel Waste.

Captain-General. 1) The name for the head of the Green Ajah in the White Tower. At the time of the Tower split, Adelorna Bastine held this position in the White Tower and Myrelle Berengari held it among the rebels. 2) The head of the Queen's Guards in Caemlyn. This position was held for many years by Gareth Bryne; Rahvin took his place, and Birgitte Trahelion followed him. 3) A Seanchan officer rank, highest in the Ever Victorious Army except for the Marshal-General, the leader in wartime. A Captain-General commanded a Great Legion, made of a variable number of legions, and wore five thin plumes. It was the rank held by Kennar Miraj. 4) A rank in the Band of the Red Hand.

Captain of the Air. Also known as Air-Captain, the rank of the commanding general of an army's or a Great Legion's fliers. It was a temporary rank given to a Lieutenant-General or Banner-General of the Air.

Captain of the Gold. The rank of a Seanchan who commanded a fleet of ships. A Captain of the Gold wore three golden plumes and ranked with a Captain-General.

Captain of the Green. The rank of a Seanchan who commanded a greatship or a small squadron of ships. A Captain of the Green wore three green plumes and ranked with a Banner-General.

Captain of the Lance. Also known as Lance-Captain, it was the Seanchan rank of the commanding general of an army's or Great Legion's cavalry. It was a temporary rank given to a Lieutenant-General or Banner-General.

Captain of the Seas. A Seanchan temporary rank given to a Captain of the Gold. The Captain of the Seas was in command of combined fleets and ranked with a Marshal-General.

Captain of the Silver. The rank of a Seanchan who commanded a large squadron. A Captain of the Silver wore three white plumes and ranked with a Lieutenant-General.

Captain of the Spear. Also known as Spear-Captain, it was the Seanchan rank of the commanding general of an army's or Great Legion's infantry. It was a temporary rank given to a Lieutenant-General or Banner-General.

Car'a'carn. An Aiel title meaning "chief of chiefs." According to the Prophecy of Rhuidean, the *Car'a'carn* would be born of a Maiden and come with the dawn from Rhuidean to unite the Aiel and destroy them, all but a remnant of a remnant. The *Car'a'carn* would be marked with red and gold dragons on both arms. He was not the equivalent of a king, but was more of a first among equals.

Cara. An Andoran maid serving Tairen Lady Alteima while Alteima was in Caemlyn.

Carahuin. An Aiel Maiden of the Spear with flaxen hair, sapphire blue eyes and a rough sense of humor. After Dumai's Wells, she sent a naked Shaido woman, a *gai'shain*, ostensibly to ask whether Perrin wanted water, but actually to see if he would react to the *gai'shain*'s nudity.

Carai an Caldazar! Al Caldazar! Ancient battle cries of Manetheren meaning "For the honor of the Red Eagle! For the Red Eagle!"

Carai an Ellisande! An ancient battle cry of Manetheren meaning "For the honor of the Rose of the Sun!"

Caraighan Maconar. An Aes Sedai of the Green Ajah with a strength level of 3(+10), born circa 212 AB. She was legendary, the heroine of a hundred adventures and exploits that even some Aes Sedai considered improbable despite their inclusion in the records of the White Tower. She supposedly single-handedly put down a rebellion in Mosadorin and quelled the Comaidin Riots at a time when she had no Warders. She once brought a man who could channel nearly two thousand miles to the Tower by herself; that man intended to proclaim himself the Dragon Reborn and was very strong. She had to sneak up on him when he was already wary (he had killed her two Warders), shield him while he was asleep and struggle to keep him shielded the whole way to Tar Valon. She was considered by the Green Ajah to be the archetype of a Green sister.

Caralain. One of the twenty-four nations wrung from Artur Hawkwing's empire during the War of the Hundred Years. It weakened thereafter, and the last traces vanished around 500 NE.

Caralain Grass. The grassy plain north of Andor and south of the Black Hills.

Caralin. Lord Bryne's estate manager. She was slim, about the same age as Bryne, and had sharp dark eyes. When he returned home after having been dismissed by Morgase, Caralin introduced a succession of pretty farmgirls into the manor to make the Lord's bed, all eager to comfort him in any other way he might desire as well. She wanted Leane brought back for that very purpose, thinking there would be nothing like a young Domani woman to pull him out of his funk.

Caraline Damodred. A Cairhienin noblewoman, High Seat of her House and cousin to Moiraine, to whom she bore a remarkable physical resemblance. Her voice was distinctly different, though—low, husky and sultry. She was about 5'3" tall, and slender, with large dark eyes and dark hair in waves to her shoulders. She was Barthanes' heir and one of the leaders of the rebellion against Rand. Rand and Min met her as they approached the rebel camp; Min viewed her as fated to marry Lord Darlin. She and Darlin escaped the bubble of evil with Rand and Cadsuane; Cadsuane held them as "guests," but Dobraine freed them. They went to Tear, where they reached an accommodation with Rand. She was willing to accept Elayne as queen of Cairhien.

Carand. A powerful noble House in Andor; Lady Aemlyn, wife of Culhan, was its High Seat. Its sign was the Arrows. *See also* Aemlyn *and* Culhan Carand

cards. There were five suits in the deck: Cups, Rods, Coins, Winds and Flames. The ruler was high, the fool low, in each suit. Who was depicted as what in each suit depended on the country. In the Tairen deck, a High Lord was the Ruler of Cups, the highest suit, while the King of Illian was the Fool of Flames, the lowest. Allied or friendly rulers of countries were generally Rulers of the various other suits. In a Tairen deck, the First of Mayene was sometimes the Ruler of Flames, sometimes the Fool of Cups, and sometimes her face was on both. In every country except Amadicia, the Amyrlin Seat was one of the rulers; there she was the Fool of Flames. There were ten numbered cards—the numbers usually represented only by the number of symbols on them—in each suit, making a total of twelve cards to a suit and sixty cards in the deck. The cards were made of stiff paper, sometimes varnished.

Careane Fransi. A Domani Aes Sedai of the Green Ajah publicly and of the Black Ajah in truth. She was part of the rebel contingent; her strength level was 27(15). Born in 910 NE, she went to the White Tower in 926 NE. After twelve years as a novice and eleven years as Accepted, she was raised to the shawl in 949 NE. Her Warders were Venr Kosaan, Tavan Shandare and Cieryl Arjuna; only Venr was a Darkfriend. She was 5'5½" tall, and bulky, though she was muscular rather than stout. She had coppery skin, dark hair and dark eyes. Careane was sent to Ebou Dar as part of the rebel embassy to Tylin; there, she served as the Seat of Pardon at Elayne's trial for approaching the Kin. She went from Ebou Dar to the Kin's farm with Elayne, and then traveled with her to Caemlyn. Careane accompanied Elayne to Full Moon Street in the search for members of the Black Ajah, and when Elayne's group was captured, Marillin identified Careane as Black Ajah. Vandene then stabbed and killed Careane before being killed by Chesmal.

Caredwain, Mother. A healer in Tremonsien, Cairhien.

Careen. An Aiel Maiden of the Spear. She was one of the Maidens guarding Rand in the Stone of Tear. After his fight with his mirror images, Careen went to bring Moiraine to him.

Carel, Anaiya. *See* Anaiya Carel

Carelle. A Wise One of the Daryne Aiel with the ability to channel and a strength level of 18(6). She had fiery red hair, a freckled face and piercing blue eyes, and was about 5'9" tall. She appeared to be about the same age as Perrin, but was in fact fifteen years or more older. She looked as if she ought to have had a temper, but seemed to be very mild-mannered—for a Wise One, anyway. Carelle and other Wise Ones were sent with Perrin to Ghealdan, to keep an eye on Seonid and Masuri; she watched Seonid in particular. She went to battle against the Shaido at Malden. Carelle assisted in the forging of Perrin's Power-wrought hammer, *Mah'alleinir.*

Careme Mowly. The Murandian mother of the girl Ellya, who was identified in a census of newborns being conducted by Accepted under Tamra's orders in the search for the Dragon Reborn.

Caren Endelle. An Aes Sedai of the Red Ajah and the loyalist contingent, with a strength level of 37(25). She was part of the expedition to kidnap Rand; she escaped with Covarla.

Carenna. An Aes Sedai of the rebel contingent. She went to the White Tower at age seventeen, spent thirteen years as a novice and eleven years as Accepted, and was raised to the shawl at forty-one. Upon learning of the eavesdropping weave that Nynaeve had from Moghedien, Carenna said it made her think of how to adapt it for another supposedly new weave, which turned out to be a way to talk to someone two or more miles away. With inverted weaves, that weave was very secure. Elayne was suspicious of how quickly she came up with this.

Caressing the Child. A weave used by Aiel Wise Ones to determine the health of a pregnant woman and her fetus. While being used, the weave also had the ability to cure minor problems.

Carewin Damodred. Moiraine's great-grandmother and a queen of Cairhien. She ruled for more than fifty years; in her reign, Cairhien grew rich and fought few wars. She was not a nice woman, though; many years later her name was still used to frighten children.

Cargomaster. An individual who worked with the Sailmistress aboard an Atha'an Miere ship, managing trade and defense. He wore three earrings in each ear. The Cargomaster was sometimes married to the Sailmistress.

Cariandre Temalien. A Ghealdanin Aes Sedai of the Red Ajah and the loyalist contingent, with a strength level of 35(23). She was born in 932 NE, the daughter of a shoemaker, and went to the White Tower in 947 NE. After thirteen years as a novice and twelve years as Accepted, she was raised to the shawl in 972 NE. Plump, full-bosomed and 5'5" tall, she was good-looking, though not a beauty. She had dark eyes and dark hair which she wore cut rather short, exposing most of her ears. Her complexion was quite pale. She cultivated a cool, reserved air—the sort of attitude she imagined a noblewoman would have— but she possessed a temper which sometimes got her into trouble. She snapped at people she shouldn't have, such as sisters who stood above her, and when angry said things better left unsaid. Cariandre was raised Aes Sedai after Moiraine and Siuan were entered as novices, and she had some jealousy of their potential, and later of their swift rise. Cariandre took part in the male channeler pogrom, sometimes called "the great work" by very hardcore Reds, but her enthusiasm waned quickly. It had seemed a great idea at first, but then she found herself killing men, and even boys, on suspicion. Increasingly, she hung back and did nothing she could avoid. She did as she was told, however. She was one of Mattin Stepaneos' frequent escorts in the Tower, and also stood watch on Egwene.

Carilo. A Warder attached to one of the Aes Sedai who kidnapped Rand. He guarded the tent where Min was held captive.

Carin, Mistress. A dark and grim-faced serving woman in the Tarasin Palace in

Ebou Dar, short of her middle years. She wore a marriage knife. Mat was handed over to her when he visited the Tarasin Palace by the front door. She was the third of seven servants that Mat encountered in that visit, each one a little older and more senior than the one before.

Carivin, Boreane. *See* Boreane Carivin

Carleon. A High Lord of Tear. He had graying hair, a pointed beard and a thick body. Self-effacing around Rand, he was part of the group that Rand chastised for not obeying his orders to lower taxes, deal with Mayene and ship grain to Illian. He thought that there were too many farmers, because the granaries held more grain than needed—Cairhien was no longer buying grain from them, being temporarily engaged in civil war. Rand was frustrated with Carleon's and others' ignorance of how farming and agricultural commerce were conducted. Carleon was Alteima's lover, and Thom forged a compromising note to be found by her husband Tedosian. Carleon was killed by Tedosian, in what was said to be a hunting accident.

Carlin. Perrin's uncle, the husband of Neain, who died before Perrin left Emond's Field with Moiraine.

Carlinya Sorevin. A Kandori Aes Sedai of the White Ajah and the rebel contingent, with a strength level of 15(3). Born in 954 NE, she went to the White Tower in 969 NE. After five years as a novice and five years as Accepted, she was raised to the shawl in 979 NE. Carlinya had no Warder. She was 5'5" tall, with pale skin, dark hair and brown eyes. She was of moderate build, neither slender nor stout. After her hair was burned in a nightmare in *Tel'aran'rhiod*, she wore it cut short.

Carlinya had a cold manner. As a novice and Accepted, she committed a minor offense once a month in an effort to convince her fellows that she was not a prig. She was very strong in logic, but weak in common sense.

Carlinya was a member of Sheriam's council in Salidar, which ran everything until the selection of a rebel Hall of the Tower and the ascension of Lelaine and Romanda removed the council's power, if not entirely its influence. Egwene used her knowledge of the ferrets who had been sent to the White Tower by the council without the knowledge of the Hall (because of fear that some of the rebel Hall might be Black Ajah) as leverage to make Carlinya swear personal fealty to her.

Carlinya was killed in *Tel'aran'rhiod* at the White Tower by the forces of the Shadow.

Carlomin. A young Tairen nobleman, tall and slender, with a dark, luxuriant pointed beard. He had a sardonic humor, smoked a pipe and with others played cards with Mat in the Stone, becoming frightened when Mat's cards came to life and attacked him. He later joined Mat's Band of the Red Hand and became an officer leading the Fourth Squadron, which was known as Carlomin's Leopards.

Carlomin's Leopards. The informal name of the Fourth Squadron of Mat's Band of the Red Hand.

Carlon Belcelona. A Tairen member of *Cha Faile*. He had a long nose and a narrow chin. Perrin thought he probably regretted shaving his beard, which the Tairens in the group did to emulate the Aiel.

Carlya. Elaida's maid.

Carlys Ankerin. An Andoran noblewoman and High Seat of her lesser House. She had curly gray hair, an open face and a devious mind. Carlys opposed Morgase and was pardoned for it afterward. She was one of Gaebril's sycophants and loyal to Elenia Sarand when Elenia declared for the Lion Throne. Her sign was paired white leopards.

Carmera. A place where Carridin's sister Vanora lived; she liked to ride in a forest nearby.

Carn. One of Bayle Domon's crewmen on the *Spray*. Yarin, whose room had been broken into, reported Carn dead, having been worked over with knives in Illian. This was about the time Domon had accepted money and a sealed parchment from Cairhienin men in Illian; the sealed parchment was a signed death warrant from King Galldrian.

carneira. The term for a Malkieri's first lover.

Carnel, Aravine. *See* Aravine Carnel

Carniele Emares. A Tairen Aes Sedai of the Yellow Ajah and the loyalist contingent, with a strength level of 22(10). She was 5'6½" tall, with a medium build. She had a fair complexion for a Tairen, blue eyes and black hair. Carniele was part of the Black Tower expedition under Toveine Gazal and was captured and bonded by an Asha'man. After Toveine was roughed up by the other sisters, who blamed her for their capture, Logain had Carniele Heal Toveine's welts and bruises.

Carney. The captain of the *Bluewing*, the ship young Moiraine took passage on when sneaking out of Tar Valon.

Carpan girls. Females from an earlier Age who were apparently noted for their impulsivity and lack of common sense. Birgitte referred to them in an expression directed at Nynaeve, who had run ahead impulsively when they left Valan Luca's show: "women who rushed off like Carpan girls leaping from a river cliff."

Carridin, Dealda. Jaichim Carridin's youngest sister. She was taken from her bridal feast by a Myrddraal to punish Jaichim for his failures.

Carridin, Jaichim. *See* Jaichim Carridin

Carridin, Vanora. *See* Vanora Carridin

Cary, River. A river flowing south between Four Kings and Caemlyn, through Carysford and into the River Manetherendrelle.

Caryla, Mistress. An alias used by Elayne while traveling between Cairhien and Tear, aboard the *Darter*.

Carysford. A village in Andor on the River Cary, halfway between Market Sheran and Caemlyn on the Caemlyn Road, two days from Caemlyn. Carysford had neat, vine-covered brick houses and narrow lanes, except for the Caemlyn Road itself, and was quiet and outwardly peaceful. The River Cary was a bare thirty paces wide there. The ford had long ago been bridged over, and its stone abutments were well worn, as were the wooden planks of the bridge. Rand and Mat passed through the village on their way to Caemlyn.

Casalain, Endara. Artur Hawkwing's governor in the province of Andor. Her daughter Ishara was the first queen of Andor.

Casban, Galina. *See* Galina Casban

Caseille Raskovni. An Arafellin woman who was a merchant's guard for nearly twenty years, which made her a rarity of rarities. She was about 5'6" tall, with dark eyes, a narrow face and dark hair cut off above the shoulder and tied back with a black ribbon. She had rather mannish mannerisms, and a brisk way of talking; she seemed tightly coiled. She was not young, but was as lean and hard as any Maiden. Caseille's accents were not those of a cultured or educated woman, but they were brisk and no-nonsense.

She became an under-lieutenant in the Queen's Guards and part of Elayne's female bodyguard. She was reticent about her past; Birgitte thought she was a natural bannerman, though Elayne wanted her to command, saying a bannerman could handle twenty or so, the number she hoped to hold the bodyguard to. When Doilin Mellar (aka Daved Hanlon) was named captain, Caseille was appointed his second. She later became a lieutenant, with two knots of rank.

Casolan, Salindi. An Aes Sedai Sitter who lived at the time of the formation of the White Tower.

Cassin. A Goshien Aiel of the *Aethan Dor* warrior society with yellow hair who stood an inch taller than Rand. He guarded Rand in Caemlyn and was with him when Rand went to meet Elder Haman, Covril and Erith.

Cassin, Romanda. *See* Romanda Cassin

Cat Dancer. Lan's horse at the time he met Moiraine.

Cat's Paw. A dice game. There was one dicer, with a crowd of onlookers betting against or for his tosses. In other lands it was called Third Gem and Feathers Aloft.

Catala Lucanvalle. An Aes Sedai of the Yellow Ajah who served as Amyrlin from 197 to 223 NE. Catala was strong, though not as strong as her predecessor; she was, however, even more arrogant. Catala did not die while Amyrlin, though this was put about; she resigned, supposedly of her own free will, and went into retirement. This was the result of one of those rebellions buried in the Tower's secret histories. Approximately half the Hall was forced to follow Catala into retirement, though not all of them were kept under guard. Catala was guarded until she died in 250 NE.

Catalyn Haevin. A young Andoran who was High Seat of House Haevin. Her House sign was the Blue Bear. She was born circa 985 NE. She had dark eyes, plump cheeks and a cool face, and was one of four young nobles Dyelin brought to help Elayne win the throne. The others were Perival Mantear, Branlet Gilyard and Conail Northan. Her contingent, twelve hundred men, was the largest by far among the four, which totaled over three thousand men, mainly crossbowmen and halberdmen. Though she had a good mind, Catalyn's abrasive manners dissuaded most people from wanting to spend much time with her. Dyelin took her under her wing; Catalyn started showing respect but a certain amount of wariness toward Dyelin after she began sharing a bed with her and Sergase. She was fascinated by Aviendha and wanted to be taught to use a spear.

Catelar, Clan. One of the Atha'an Miere clans.

catfern. An acrid herbal concoction that was administered to those who lied. It was powdered for use in tea with powdered mavinsleaf. When the powder was boiled in water, it produced a sickly, green liquid.

Cathal Devore. A Ghealdanin Aes Sedai of the Brown Ajah and the rebel contingent, with a strength level of 17(5). Born in 942 NE, she went to the White Tower in 957 NE. After nine years as a novice and eight years as Accepted, she was raised to the shawl in 974 NE. She had a Cairhienin Warder, a man in his forties who was only 5'8" tall, though muscular and wide in the shoulders for his height. He looked after her when she was absentminded with an amused sort of affection, like a brother. On the surface Cathal seemed rather shy and retiring, as dreamy as any Brown—somewhat diffident, at least for an Aes Sedai. She often seemed easily startled, as if pulled from a waking dream.

Cathal was tall for a woman at about 5'9" to 5'10", and she was lanky and bony in build. She was awkward, physically, often dropping things. She had dark brown hair that she wore drawn back with combs, and hazel eyes. She blinked a great deal, as if she could not understand. In fact, she was a keen observer with an analytical mind—at least, when she had a reason to be interested in what was going on—and not nearly so retiring and half-asleep as she seemed. She could recall every word she heard, word for word, even after a considerable time, a gift useful mainly when she could not take notes right away. She was a historian, with possibly as wide a knowledge of false Dragons as anyone living at the time, perhaps wider than anyone else.

Cathal was raised Accepted the year before Elaida came to the Tower, and she watched Elaida rise through novice and Accepted to become Aes Sedai a year ahead of her. She had no jealousy of Elaida's advancement, or not a great deal, but she disliked her personally; on the other hand, she was somewhat in awe of Elaida and, in a way, afraid of her. Cathal was Accepted over Moiraine and Siuan from their arrival late in 972 NE until she was raised Aes Sedai in 974 NE. She took pride in their quick advancement, because she did part of their training. She was uncertain about Siuan being raised Amyrlin so young, but she supposed the Hall must know what it was doing. Her uncertainty was well known, however. Unlike many Browns, though, she paid close attention to political matters, and felt that the deposing of Siuan clearly amounted to a coup. She was part of the rebel fifth column (aka ferrets) sent by Sheriam's council in

Salidar to infiltrate the White Tower. Like all of the sisters chosen for the ferrets, Cathal was out of the White Tower when Siuan was deposed and the Tower broken, so there was no flight to arouse any suspicions toward her. Apparently, she had simply returned in answer to Elaida's summons. Cathal was coopted by Seaine and Pevara to aid in their search for the Black Ajah.

Catlynde Artein. An Aes Sedai Sitter who lived at the time of the formation of the White Tower.

Catrelle Mosenain. An ironmonger's daughter from Maerone whom Daved Hanlon murdered and threw down a well after she disclosed that he had impregnated her.

Catrine. A serving girl at The Nine Rings in Tremonsien. She dropped a lamp when Captain Caldevwin asked Selene her name, afterward speaking of a sudden twinge in her arm.

Catrona. A Seanchan *sul'dam* with Tuon, black-skinned and pretty, though her face was normally stern. She held Mylen's leash. She could smile for a *damane* that pleased her, though, and she wasn't cruel or harsh in behavior. As part of Karede's group she searched for Tuon when she was missing. When Min went to the Seanchan camp during the Last Battle, Catrona led her to Tuon.

Causeway, Altara. A wide, packed dirt road leading from Illian to roads reaching Altara and Murandy. It lay on the other side of the River Manetherendrelle and was reached by ferry.

Causeway, Maredo. A wide, packed-dirt road that led two miles north out of Illian through the marshes that surrounded the city. The road continued in an easterly direction toward Tear.

Causeway of the Northern Star. A wide, packed-dirt road, broken by flat stone bridges, that led directly north from Illian through the marshes that surrounded the city.

Cauthon clan. A family in Emond's Field. *See* Abell, Bodewhin, Eldrin, Matrim *and* Natti Cauthon

Cavan Lopar. The rotund innkeeper of The White Crescent in Tear. He suggested that Mat take Thom to Mother Guenna for his cough.

Cavandra. An Aes Sedai of the loyalist contingent, with a strength level of 31(19). She was advisor to Queen Tylin in Ebou Dar, and had been so to Tylin's father when he was king. She had limited influence, since she had been advisor to a minor throne for so long. She returned to the White Tower upon receiving Elaida's summons following the schism there.

Ceandevin, Merilille. *See* Merilille Ceandevin

Cedora. Reanne Corly's serving woman at the Kin house in Ebou Dar. She had graying hair, a square jaw, shoulders like a blacksmith and a steely eye.

Ceiline Noreman. The wife of a trader killed in Canluum, Kandor. The trader had been guarded by Ryne Venamar.

Cein. The wife of Thom Merrilin's nephew, Owyn.

Celebrain. A Guardswoman in Elayne's bodyguard who accepted a suicide mission to protect Elayne when Demandred announced his intent to hunt Elayne on the Field of Merrilor in the Last Battle. Birgitte rode off with Elayne in one direction; Celebrain, carrying Elayne's banner, rode off in another.

Celark. A Youngling who wished to join the Tower Guard. He assisted Gawyn in fighting the Bloodknives, and was killed.

Celestin Eguilera. A Tairen Aes Sedai of the Yellow Ajah and the rebel contingent, with a strength level of 19(7). Born in 960 NE, she went to the White Tower in 976 NE. After five years as a novice and four as Accepted, she was raised to the shawl in 986 NE. Celestin was about 5'6" tall, with a somewhat supercilious manner. Her hair was black and straight, worn above the shoulder at a length that suggested she couldn't decide whether to wear it long or short. Her eyes were gray, though they seemed almost pale blue at times. Her nose was perhaps a little too prominent; it made her seem to be looking down on people; then again, perhaps she was. She was part of the rebel fifth column (aka ferrets) sent by Sheriam's council in Salidar to infiltrate the White Tower. Like all of the sisters chosen for the ferrets, Celestin was out of the White Tower when Siuan was deposed and the Tower broken, so there was no flight to arouse any suspicions toward her. Apparently, she had simply returned in answer to Elaida's summons. Celestin was coopted by Seaine and Pevara to aid in their search for the Black Ajah.

Cellaech, Yasicca. An ancient scholar and Aes Sedai of the Brown Ajah who was the source of the quote "Incomplete knowledge is better than complete ignorance."

Cemaile Sorenthaine. An Aes Sedai of the Gray Ajah who served as Amyrlin from 681 to 705 NE. Cemaile was an Amyrlin of moderate strength in the beginning, but she was reduced to a weak Amyrlin, certainly one of the weakest ever if not the weakest. She had grand plans to restore the White Tower to its former greatness, but those went badly awry. While it was recorded only in the secret chronicles of the Tower, from 686 NE to her death in 705 NE she was no more than a puppet of the Hall, and her Keeper was in actual fact her guardian, set to watch over her by the Hall, from whom she was forced to take orders, albeit orders which originated in the Hall. It was recorded that "the largest decision she was allowed to make in that time was what dress to don in the morning, and even that was subject to change by her Keeper."

The appointing of a guardian was done through one of the secret laws of the Tower, those that prohibited even revealing the existence of the law. As a step short of removing an Amyrlin, the greater consensus of the Hall, convened in secret, could in effect remove everything but the title and place someone of their choosing and under their authority in what amounted to *in loco parentis* of the Amyrlin. This law was created after an Amyrlin became incapacitated during the Trolloc Wars, and the Tower did not want to reveal their troubles to the outside world. Despite—or perhaps because of—the specific reasons the law was created, its wording was broad enough to allow this to be done to not only an Amyrlin who had become mentally or physically incapacitated. but to one who, in the opinion of the Hall (the greater consensus), was no longer capable of carrying out her duties properly. According to the secret records of the White Tower, it was mainly because of the recent troublesome plots surrounding Shein Chunla that Cemaile was not removed and exiled, though there were certain indications that the Hall more and more grew to like the power given to them by having a true puppet on the Amyrlin Seat.

cemaros. Great winter tempests coming off the Sea of Storms.

Cemeille din Selaan Long Eyes. Sea Folk Sailmistress of the darter *Wind Racer.* Cemeille visited some of the Sea Folk Islands and discovered that the Amayar were committing mass suicide; she took that news to the First Twelve Wavemistresses meeting in Illian.

Cenn Buie. A grumpy old thatcher in Emond's Field and a member of the Village Council. Cenn was born in the summer of 932 NE. He was as gnarled and dark as an old root with a scratchy voice, beady eyes and thinning hair. He sometimes used a gnarled walking staff.

Cera Doinal. A serving woman at the Sun Palace in Cairhien. She told Sashalle and Samitsu that people were saying that Dobraine had been attacked and murdered; she also said that she had seen Maringil's ghost.

Ceran Tol. The creator of "Tempo of Infinity," an art piece from the Age of Legends.

Cerandin. A pale-haired Seanchan *morat's'redit.* After the battle at Falme, she was left behind but managed to hang on to three *s'redit*, one a calf, and later joined Valan Luca's show. She called the animals boar-horses, at Luca's suggestion, and said they came from Shara. Luca's show was in Ebou Dar when the city fell to the Seanchan. For keeping her animals through such difficulties and showing great honor and perseverance, Cerandin was rewarded, possibly (though not probably) by being raised to the lowest levels of the Blood and most certainly by being named *der'morat's'redit.* She managed to obtain written permission for Luca to keep his horses, despite the Seanchan buying up any and all left and right, and also to travel where he wished without interference.

Cerano, Sillia. *See* Sillia Cerano

Ceri. A pregnant servant in Lady Arilyn's Cairhienin palace. The Aes Sedai embassy that Elaida had sent to Cairhien to escort Rand back to the White Tower were staying with Lady Arilyn. Egwene went to the palace and, detecting channeling inside, used Air and Fire to replicate Moiraine's eavesdropping trick on the inside, and learned of Ceri's pregnancy in the process.

Cerilla Marodred. An Aes Sedai of the Gray Ajah who served as Amyrlin between 454 and 476 NE. Cerilla was a moderately strong Amyrlin. She negotiated the Tower's way out of the situations in which Ishara had enmeshed it. Her strength came in large part from her ability to do that. In most other ways, the Hall ran the White Tower and the Aes Sedai. Cerilla's interest and passion lay in the outside world. In truth, though, overt Tower influence in the world, which had grown one way and another from Suilin Escanda to Ishara Nawan, began to decline once more during her reign.

Cerindra. One of Amathera's tirewomen in Tanchico. Amathera dismissed her for theft, leaving her willing to spread lies about her former employer.

Cetalia Delarme. A Taraboner Aes Sedai of the Blue Ajah with a strength level of 14(2). She was a tall, square-faced woman with steel-gray hair in a multitude of blue-beaded braids that hung to her waist. At the time of the Aiel War she was the head of the Blue Ajah's eyes-and-ears; she coopted Siuan Sanche almost as soon as Siuan gained the shawl after learning of Siuan's skill with puzzles, and she managed to intimidate the young Siuan Sanche quite thoroughly. When Siuan returned from her unauthorized expedition to the Borderlands, Cetalia made sure that Siuan regretted very much taking French leave. Cetalia was murdered by the Black Ajah.

Cha Faile. An Old Tongue phrase meaning Falcon's Talon or Claw. It was the name of Faile's group of followers. They understood that they were to keep the name to themselves. They all dressed in men's clothing and wore a sword at the hip. Men and women alike wore their hair to their shoulders, but gathered in the back with a ribbon in imitation of the Aiel "tail." They were arrogant in everything, even how they walked, the women more so than the men. The Aiel decided to give some of this lot a taste of being *gai'shain* for real after a fight in the streets of Cairhien; they were stripped down and made to wait just like captives after a fight between Aiel. The result was not what the Aiel had hoped. Those so treated took it as a point of honor, something to be proud of; they told others they couldn't really know *ji'e'toh* until they had been captured by the Aiel. On departing for Ghealdan, Faile told Perrin she had taken these people into her service because they would have gotten into trouble in Cairhien; he was to think of them as charity and she would keep them from getting under his feet. Once in Ghealdan, he saw that they numbered more than two dozen young men and women. They served as spies for Faile, and after Faile was taken by the Shaido, Perrin coopted them to some extent, using them as spies through Sebban Balwer. At that point there were twenty-five with Perrin. Some members of *Cha Faile* accompanied Faile on her mission to retrieve the Horn of Valere.

Chachin. The capital city of Kandor, as large as Tear or Far Madding. It was also called "the Three Mountains" because it was built around three large mountains, each close to a mile high even with its top flattened. The city was ringed by a triple wall with towers, and that by a drymoat a hundred paces wide crossed by a dozen stone bridges, each with a fortress at its mouth. The mountains of the city were all terraced. Every level of the terraces contained trees, and some were given over almost entirely to orchards or parks, with orchards predominating. Garden plots were also plentiful.

Many springs rose on each of the mountains, and their streams were dammed, producing several large reservoirs. Chachin never ran short of water in even the severest drought.

Chachin was also called "the City of the Clouds," though none of the mountains were high enough to have clouds around their tops. The highest of the three was occupied by the Aesdaishar Palace, which covered an area of 50 hides— more than 100 acres. The second highest held the fortress, on an area of about 75 hides—approximately 150 acres. The lowest, which held the palaces of the highest nobles crowded together, had a leveled area on top of approximately 100 hides—about 200 acres.

Chadmar, Milisair. *See* Milisair Chadmar

Chaelin. A Wise One of the Smoke Water sept of the Miagoma Aiel who had the ability to channel and a strength level of 19(7). She had red hair with faint touches of gray and was over two hundred years old, almost as old as Sorilea, although she appeared to be in her thirties. She went to Dumai's Wells from Cairhien and afterward taught the Aes Sedai pledged to Rand in Cairhien as apprentices to the Wise Ones.

Chaena. A Shienaran soldier following Ingtar when he and Perrin pursued the Horn of Valere to Falme. He wintered in the Mountains of Mist with Perrin and Rand; then, after Rand left and the Shienarans were abandoned to make their own way, he was with Masema in Samara.

Chaendaer. A mountain above Rhuidean in the Aiel Waste. It was the site of the Portal Stone that Rand used to get to the Waste, and the location where he met the Aiel Wise Ones.

Chai Rugan. An Aes Sedai of the Brown Ajah publicly and of the Black Ajah in truth. She was a member of the loyalist contingent. Her name was found on Verin's list of the Black Ajah, but she fled the Tower before she could be captured.

Chain Ridge Stand. A water hole in the Aiel Waste. At Alcair Dal, Jheran wanted to discuss the water at Chain Ridge Stand while waiting on Rand to arrive.

chainleaf. A plant used as a medicinal tea to relieve a queasy stomach.

Chair of Remorse, The. A *ter'angreal* in the White Tower, used for punishment and confession. It was noted that thieves caught in Tar Valon, and other criminals as well, were taken to the White Tower, and that when they were released, they inevitably left the city as fast as they could. A fair number actually gave up lives of crime. The reason for this behavior was the Chair of Remorse.

The Chair appeared to be made of stone in a soothing shade of white, but it felt softer than stone to the touch. In appearance, it seemed to be more of an inclined bench made for reclining upon than a chair, with solid arms on which the person using it could rest his or her arms. When someone reclined on the Chair of Remorse, it took the first action on its own, without any other intervention, after an interval of perhaps twenty or thirty seconds. First the chair molded itself to the person's body; this stopped and reversed if the person sat up, but it didn't matter if someone was bound and held down. The person reclining on the Chair fell into a sort of trance. Without an Aes Sedai, nothing more happened. It was learned long ago, though, that by channeling in a certain way, to certain spots on the Chair, a sort of link was established. The Aes Sedai then thought of a scenario; the person in the Chair then experienced this scenario fully fleshed out and starring themselves, in part like a movie (i.e., with jumps and cuts, with "understandings" of what had happened between), but also as if actually living the experience. At the end of the scenario, the person came out of the trance with memories of the experience as if they had actually lived it, and with some physical reminders, too, on the order of slight tiredness if great labor was done, or slight soreness if they had been wounded or struck. For someone with no idea of what the Chair was except that it was used by Aes Sedai, it was impossible to be sure that the events were not real, despite the lack of real physical effects. Given that the people placed on the Chair were there for punishment, with scenarios chosen for that purpose, usually entailing dire consequences of the actions that brought them there, the overall effect on wrongdoers was not at all surprising, especially when one considered that each person was generally sent through a number of such scenarios.

The use of the chair on any initiate of the Tower was absolutely forbidden by law. It could, however, be used on a servant caught stealing, for example.

The Chair of Remorse was in fact an entertainment device from the Age of Legends, employing a sort of virtual reality tied straight into the brain. While Aes Sedai could see that the device drew on *saidar* as soon as someone sat on it, they did not know that it also drew on *saidin*, which was what gave the scenarios a particularly grim, dark and foreboding feel under any circumstances. There was a way to place "cartridges," like video discs which carried various story lines, into the device, and it actually contained a very large library of stories—the previous owner's library—which the Aes Sedai had never accessed and were not aware of. The manner the Aes Sedai had found to make use of the device—implanting a scenario manually, as it were—was not a designed feature of the *ter'angreal* in the Age of Legends. Whether the ability to do this resulted from some deterioration of the device through age or through some modification that was made on it during the Age of Legends was not known.

The Black Ajah hunters in the White Tower, including Pevara, Seaine and Saerin, put the Black sister Talene Minly in the chair, forcing her through horrific experiences generated by the *ter'angreal* to retake the Three Oaths plus an oath of obedience to them.

Chalinda. An alias Siuan suggested Min use when they were escaping from Bryne at Kore Springs; it was Old Tongue for "sweet girl."

Challenge. Gawyn's horse, a gelding.

Chalm. The warehouse district in Tear, adjoining the Maule.

Chalwin, Kirstian. *See* Kirstian Chalwin

Cham, Duram Laddel. Be'lal's name during the Age of Legends.

Chandar, Stedding. A *stedding* that was swallowed by the Blight in 31 NE.

Chandin, Athan. A Two Rivers man with Perrin. He was a good shot with the bow, but he had a truckling manner which annoyed Perrin.

Chandin, Ren. A Two Rivers man who joined Perrin's band in the Two Rivers. He was killed in a Trolloc ambush.

Chanelle din Seran White Shark. A fairly high-ranking Sea Folk Windfinder with a strength level of 19(7). Her honor-chain carried nearly as many golden medallions as Zaida's. She was lean, dark-skinned and big-eyed. Windfinder to a Sailmistress who was one of the First Twelve, she was left in charge of the Windfinders remaining in Caemlyn. She did not want to provide a gateway for Birgitte to rescue Elayne from the Black Ajah, but Birgitte pointed out that if Elayne was lost, the Sea Folk bargain with her was lost. Birgitte then managed to persuade Chanelle and her circle to take out the members of the Black Ajah when they were using balefire. After being rescued, Elayne persuaded Chanelle to provide a gateway so that she could attack Arymilla's back as Arymilla advanced against Caemlyn.

Changu. A Darkfriend Shienaran soldier. He was one of the guards of Fain's dungeon prison in Fal Dara and vanished when Fain escaped. Those pursuing the Horn of Valere found his body skinned and hanging from a tree.

channeling. The act of controlling and using flows of the One Power that stem from the True Source. Among the advantages to being able to channel was a heightened resistance to disease. The stronger one was in the One Power, the more the resistance one had. There was a resistance to bodily deterioration also, as from the effects of aging. For someone who could channel, old age was youthful and vigorous, lacking the aches and pains normal to those who could not.

Chansein. A feast celebrated on the third day of Jumara in the Borderlands and Arad Doman. A day of wild indulgence in food, its object seemed to be to get other people to eat as much as they could hold and more. People carried hot pastries filled with meat or dried fruit, sometimes stuffing their pockets or actually carrying bags, and handed them out to everyone they saw. It was considered extremely ill-mannered to fail to eat every crumb.

Chanti, Stedding. A *stedding* located in the Spine of the World.

Chaos, Numbers of. A body of knowledge required to build the Portal Stones; part of this process consisted of laying the Lines that joined the Worlds That Might Be.

***Charal Drianaan te Calamon*, The Cycle of the Dragon.** A text written by an anonymous author in the Fourth Age.

Chareen. An Aiel clan. Erim was its clan chief.

Charel. A good-looking young groom in the White Tower stables. He was used by Sheriam in 981 NE to help break Theodrin's block which prevented her from channeling unless there was a man present for whom she had strong feelings. Charel had a gorgeous smile and made eyes at Theodrin. He was allowed to sit in on her lessons so that she could channel, but after a few times his twin sister Marel was substituted and thus broke Theodrin's block.

Charendin. An Aiel sept chief during the building of Rhuidean. He and Mandein had nearly killed each other three times; Charendin bore a long scar on his face from one of those encounters. Rand saw him as part of his visions through the glass columns in Rhuidean.

Charin, Jain. *See* Jain Farstrider

Charin, Noal. *See* Noal Charin

Charl Gedwyn. An Asha'man and Darkfriend of Taim's faction. He was a hard-faced young man with a grimly challenging look, about 5'11" tall, with dark brown hair and brown eyes, a few years older than Rand. He held the rank Tsorovan'm'hael, Old Tongue for "Storm Leader," which indicated that he was second to Taim. After the attack on Rand in Cairhien failed, he was placed on the deserters list at the Black Tower. Gedwyn went to Far Madding to kill Rand, but was murdered by Padan Fain instead.

Charlin. A young Jenn Aiel from the time after the Breaking. He was killed while saving two girls from bandits; his Jenn Aiel companions used weapons, and were cast out by their families. Rand saw him as part of his visions through the glass columns in Rhuidean.

Charlz Guybon. An officer in Elayne's Queen's Guard. Extremely good-looking, he was tall, broad-shouldered and well short of his middle years with greenish hazel eyes. A lieutenant when he left Aringill, he traveled toward Caemlyn, recruiting all the way. He arrived with 4,762 of the Guards and sufficient nobles with their armsmen to bring Elayne's troop total up to near ten thousand. Elayne immediately promoted him to captain, and Birgitte named him her second. When they were trying to rescue Elayne from the Black Ajah, he charged bravely even though the Black Ajah was using the balefire *ter'angreal* and wiping out large numbers of his troops. He distinguished himself in the fight against Arymilla's troops outside Caemlyn. When the Trollocs invaded Caemlyn, he defended the palace until Talmanes convinced him to help save the dragons. In the Last Battle, his horse was balefired, but he survived.

Charn. 1) A pikeman in Juilin Sandar's squad in the Last Battle. He was killed by a Sharan with a mace to the head. 2) Coumin's father's greatfather, and Rand's distant Aiel ancestor from the War of Power. He served Mierin in the Age of Legends, and was planning to accept Nalla's offer of marriage on the day the Bore was drilled. He was hanged many years later because he told people that he once served Lanfear when she was Mierin. Rand saw him as part of his visions through the glass columns in Rhuidean.

Charral. A Seanchan *damane* who belonged to Tuon and was taken to Ebou Dar with her. She had gray hair and gray eyes, and was the most agile of Tuon's *damane* in her spinning. She was part of Karede's group that searched for Tuon when she was missing.

Chaser. A gambler Mat encountered at The Dead Man's Breath in Caemlyn. He was tall and lean with a pinched face. Chaser told Mat of a man being found with his throat torn out and drained of blood.

Chavana brothers. Four acrobats in Valan Luca's circus who claimed to be brothers, but though they were all short, compact men, they ranged in coloring from green-eyed Taeric—his high cheekbones and hooked nose proclaiming his Saldaean blood—to Barit, who was darker than Juilin and had Sea Folk tattoos on his hands. Another brother was Brugh; the fourth was unnamed. *See* Barit, Brugh *and* Taeric Chavana

Cheade, Muad. *See* Muad Cheade

Chel Vanin. A Redarm in Mat's Band, from Maerone, Andor. Despite not looking the part, he was a masterful thief, and Mat made him the chief of his scouts. He was very fat and sat his saddle like a sagging sack of suet, but he could ride anything with hair. Vanin was balding, with a gap-toothed grin—he spat through the gap in his teeth—and a round face that could assume a look of utter innocence. About 5'10" tall and weighing more than 250 pounds, he could, according to others, steal a horse out from under a nobleman and the nobleman wouldn't know it for three days; he could steal the eggs from under a hen pheasant without disturbing her, though it was unlikely he wouldn't stuff her in his sack as well. He claimed to be an itinerant stableman and sometime farrier, when he could find the work. Though an Andoran, he had lived in Maerone and ranged wide on both sides of the Erinin. The Band's other scouts got triple pay; he got quadruple. Vanin didn't like nobles, but Elayne had him knuckling his forehead to her after a very short time. He was with her in the Rahad when the *gholam* attacked, but he survived.

Vanin was chosen to accompany Faile while she delivered the Horn of Valere to Mat. Vanin and Harnan believed that the chest holding the Horn contained tabac and tried to steal it, leading Faile to think that they were Darkfriends. They fled and allowed themselves to be captured by a Darkfriend caravan and taken to the battle. When Faile arrived there and was betrayed by Aravine, he and Harnan and other prisoners broke loose and created enough confusion that Faile was able to escape.

Chelsaine Palace. A small palace in Ebou Dar that Jaichim Carridin rented near the Three Towers Gate. Mat followed Lady Shiaine there, and an old man (Noal) told him who occupied the palace.

Cheltan. In a previous Age, the Cheltans had the dubious distinction of being heavily taxed by their rulers. Birgitte used the phrase: "avoiding him like a Cheltan flinching from the tax-collector."

Chenda. The roofmistress of Mainde Cut. She belonged to the Jenda sept of the Tomanelle Aiel. Chenda demanded to be made *gai'shain* when Bair was a girl and was featured in a funny (to Aiel) story told to Egwene concerning two raiding septs. She was presumed dead at the time the story was told.

Chesa. Egwene's dark-haired maid, chosen by Sheriam in Salidar. She was barely twice Egwene's age when they first met. She was 5'3" to 5'4" tall, and plump, just short of stout, with a twinkle in her eye and a merry smile. Chesa gave advice to Egwene circumspectly, making her examples seem stories that applied to herself or others. She oversaw the other maids, Selame and Meri, who helped dress and undress her, and attended her during the day. Meri and Selame were murdered by Halima, because they might have seen or overheard something that would have endangered Halima's own position and safety. Chesa survived simply because she wasn't a spy for anyone, just a maid.

Chesmal Emry. A Ghealdanin Aes Sedai of the Yellow Ajah publicly and of the Black Ajah in truth. Her strength level was 18(6). Born in 863 NE, she went to the White Tower in 878 NE. After seven years as a novice and six years as Accepted, she was raised to the shawl in 891 NE. She was a handsome woman standing 5'7" tall, with dark hair and eyes, and she was stern and arrogant. She had no Warder. Chesmal was almost sent away from the White Tower twice as a novice and once as Accepted because of serious discipline infractions involving attacks on others. She was one of the most talented Healers anyone had seen in years, and she could kill with the Power by stopping all electrical activity in the body. In this Talent, she ranked with Samitsu Tamagowa and Suana Dragand. She might have rediscovered a part of Healing using other flows than the standard, although this was never confirmed.

Chesmal claimed to have participated in putting Tamra Ospenya to the question and to inducing the Red Ajah to murder Sierin Vayu before Sierin could order her arrest. She was one of the first thirteen members of the Black Ajah identified. When Moghedien coopted Liandrin's group, she ordered Chesmal to hunt for Nynaeve. When Birgitte shot Moghedien with an arrow in *Tel'aran'rhiod*, Chesmal Healed her. Moghedien then ordered Chesmal to follow her to Ghealdan. Chesmal and other Black Ajah members waited there until Kennit, Eldrith's Warder, who was not a Darkfriend and intended to kill Eldrith, found them. She and the others then fled to Caemlyn, where they went to Lady Shiaine's house. Elayne, Careane, Sareitha and Vandene surprised them there. Chesmal killed Vandene and Sareitha, and helped capture Elayne. Chesmal and the others were then captured in turn by Birgitte and Elayne's forces. Wearing a Forsaken disguise, Elayne later tried to question Chesmal; in the fight that ensued, Chesmal was killed by a burst of flame from Elayne, but only after Healing Elayne of a wound inflicted by Doilin Mellar.

Chet. An old man whom Mat met in a Low Caemlyn tavern. Long-faced, with dappled silver stubble unable to cover the thick, angry-looking scar on his cheek, Chet wore tattered clothing that appeared vaguely military. He told Mat, who was there incognito because of *gholam* and Darkfriends trying to kill him, rumors about Matrim Cauthon, the leader of "that Band."

Chiad. A Maiden of the Spear of the Stones River sept of the Goshien Aiel. Chiad had dark reddish hair and gray eyes; she was 5'7½" tall. She was about the same age as Egwene and Elayne, as well as Bain. Although they were from clans with a blood feud, she adopted Bain as her first-sister; neither would let a man come to her without the other. Chiad went to the Stone of Tear; she and

Bain became friends with Faile, and accompanied her and Perrin to Caemlyn, Cairhien and Ghealdan. She also went to Dumai's Wells at Faile's request for her to look after Perrin, and also to put herself in front of Gaul. Chiad was taken *gai'shain* by Sevanna when Faile's riding party was captured by the Jumai Shaido. After Sevanna was taken by the Seanchan, Chiad became *gai'shain* to Gaul, who was in love with her and wanted to marry her, but was not interested in Bain. During the Last Battle, Chiad and Bain helped in the Healing facility set up at Berelain's palace in Mayene, and began collecting the wounded from the battlefields.

Chianmai. A Seanchan Banner-General in the Ever Victorious Army. He had a honey-brown face. He was killed by the *damane* Zakai, who lost control of her channeling in a battle against Rand and the Asha'man and struck her own people with lightning.

Chiantal, Stedding. A *stedding* located in Kandor.

Chiape. The Sh'boan, or empress, of Shara. She was beautiful, with very dark skin. Graendal took her for one of her pets.

Chiarid. An Aiel Maiden of the Spear. She was a merry-eyed blonde old enough to be Rand's mother and was part of Rand's guard in Caemlyn. She usually liked to make jokes at his expense when they were alone; he understood some of them. Chiarid saw Rand as a younger brother who needed to be kept from getting too big for his hat.

Chiendelna. A minor House in Murandy that Lord Luc, while making mischief in the Two Rivers, claimed as his own.

Chilares Arman. A Murandian Kin and member of the Knitting Circle who worked as a rug seller in Ebou Dar. Born in 657 NE, she went to the White Tower in 672 NE. After twelve years as a novice, she refused to complete her test for Accepted. Her strength level was 37(25), not strong enough for her to make a gateway of any size whatsoever. Slender and willowy, with large, deep brown eyes, she had touches of gray in her hair, understandable given that she was over 343 years old, and she appeared to be well into her middle years. Traces of Murandy clung to her accent. She traveled with Elayne to the Royal Palace in Caemlyn.

Child. A generic term used to describe any member of the Children of the Light; however, it was also used as a title for younger members of the order.

Child of the Dragon. An appellation used by Someshta, a Nym called the Green Man, when speaking to Rand.

Children of the Light. A society of men who followed strict ascetic beliefs, owing allegiance to no nation and dedicated to the defeat of the Dark One and the destruction of all Darkfriends. Founded by Lothair Mantelar in FY 1021 during the War of the Hundred Years to proselytize against an increase in Darkfriends, they evolved during the war into a completely military society. They were extremely rigid in their beliefs, and certain that only they knew the truth and the right. They considered Aes Sedai and any who supported them to be Darkfriends. Known disparagingly as Whitecloaks, a name they themselves despised, they were headquartered at the Fortress of Light in Amador, Amadicia, but were forced out when the Seanchan conquered the city. Their sign was a golden sunburst on a field of white, and the sunburst was displayed on their cloaks and tabards. An exception was the garb worn by the Hand of the Light (also referred to pejoratively as Questioners), a relatively independent investigative branch within the Children's organization; their cloaks were adorned with a red shepherd's crook behind the sunburst. Questioners reported to the High Inquisitor, who only wore the red shepherd's crook, suggestive of his independent authority. The Children were a cavalry force, and their largest unit was a legion, which was roughly two thousand troops. Officers wore golden knots to indicate rank. The last known leader of the Children was Galad Damodred. They fought alongside the armies of the Light in the Last Battle.

Chimal. One of Tuon's sisters who was quiet in her ambition to gain the throne, and who might have plotted against Tuon.

Chin Akima. The owner of a traveling circus who was beheaded by Masema in Samara for disobeying him.

Chin Ellisor. The captain of the *Blue Crane*, which took Nynaeve, Egwene and Elayne down the River Erinin until the ship ran aground on a mudflat near Jurene and they disembarked. He was born and bred in Tar Valon, and not one to question Aes Sedai.

Chinden, Stedding. A *stedding* located in the Mountains of Mist.

chinje **wheel.** A gambling device from the Age of Legends.

Chion. An Aiel Maiden of the Spear taken *gai'shain* by the Taardad Aiel. She showed Rand to his room in Cold Rocks Hold after he gave the bracelet to Aviendha and talked to the Wise Ones. Chion was pretty, with a thin scar slanting just above one pale blue eye into hair so light as to look almost silver; she was killed by a Draghkar at Cold Rocks Hold. Rand added her name to his list of women who died for him.

Chisaine Nurbaya. A Domani Aes Sedai of the Red Ajah and the loyalist contingent. Part of the expedition to kidnap Rand, she was captured at Dumai's Wells and treated as *da'tsang* by the Aiel; as part of Chisaine's punishment, Verin saw her dragging rocks behind her on a cowhide. Under Verin's Compulsion, she found reason to swear to Rand, which she did before Cadsuane departed Cairhien for Far Madding. Chisaine and the other Reds among the captives were the very last to swear.

Chisen, General. A Seanchan officer with a large force who unsuccessfully tried to find Mat's Band of the Red Hand in the Molvaine Gap, northeast Altara.

Chishen Mountains. A range found in southern Andor near the River Erinin and the border with Murandy.

Choedan Kal. The two great *sa'angreal* statues that were originally constructed to seal the Dark One in Shayol Ghul during the War of Power, and later used by

Rand to cleanse the taint from *saidin*. The male statue, attuned to *saidin*, was located near Tremonsien; the female statue, attuned to *saidar*, was located on the island of Tremalking. Because of the statues' power, special *ter'angreal* access keys were required to activate them. During the cleansing of the taint, the female statue melted and its corresponding access key was destroyed.

chokevine. A weedy vine with pale, narrow leaves.

Chooser, the. 1) Another name for Calian, a Hero of the Horn who wore a red mask and who rode beside her brother, Shivan the Hunter. 2) In Seanchan, Choosers were individuals who picked out young male *da'covale* for the Deathwatch Guard.

chop. A card game. Five rulers was the best hand.

chora tree. A tree once prevalent before the Breaking. It was a construct made with the One Power and had large green trefoil leaves which emitted an aura of peace and well-being. All but extinct, one existed in the Third Age, in Rhuidean, and was known by the Aiel as *Avendesora*. A sapling of that tree, known as *Avendoraldera*, was given by the Aiel to Cairhien; Laman chopped it down to make a throne, precipitating the Aiel War.

Chora Fields, the. A forest of chora trees surrounding Rhuidean in a scenario created during the fight between Rand and the Dark One in the Last Battle.

Choren. The tenth month of the year.

Chosen, the. The Forsaken's name for themselves; short for "Those Chosen to Rule the World Forever."

Chosium, Stedding. A *stedding* located in Saldaea.

choss-hauler. A pejorative epithet applied by Sammael to Rand, having to do with Rand's farmboy background, probably referring to animal excrement.

Chowin Tsao. An Aes Sedai of the Green Ajah who served as advisor to Artur Hawkwing before he initiated the siege of the White Tower.

Chronicles, Keeper of. Once simply the Amyrlin's secretary and the official historian of the White Tower, since more than five hundred years before the Trolloc Wars the Keeper had been second-in-command to the Amyrlin. Like the Amyrlin, the Keeper left her old Ajah, though she wore a narrow stole of the color of that Ajah. In the early days, the Keeper was traditionally raised from the same Ajah as the Amyrlin, but this was not required by Tower law. As time progressed, though, a Keeper of an Ajah other than the Amyrlin's was almost invariably imposed on the Amyrlin by the Hall. This was done for various reasons: as a political quid pro quo, giving that office to one Ajah and the Amyrlin Seat to another, or to keep an eye on an Amyrlin who despite her raising was thought unreliable in some way.

Chuain, Ishar Morrad. Aginor's name during the Age of Legends.

Chubain, Jimar. *See* Jimar Chubain

Chulein. A Seanchan *morat'raken* who was flying over the Kin's farm when Elayne and her party were leaving. Her *raken*'s name was Segani. She was thinking of buying a *damane* who could create Sky Lights, using part of the taking price for helping to capture *marath'damane*. Eliya, the other woman on Segani, fell off and was killed in the explosion from Elayne's unweaving. Chulein thought that she would have to make the report about the farm being destroyed because she was the only one left.

Chuliandred. A small Cairhienin noble House. Among its members were Alaine, Doressin and Meneril.

Chulin, Alesune. *See* Alesune Chulin

Chumai. A sept of the Taardad Aiel.

Chunla, Shein. *See* Shein Chunla

Chuonde. A Maiden of the Spear of the Spine Ridge sept of the Miagoma Aiel. She died at the Battle of Dumai's Wells. Rand added her name to the list of women who had died for him.

Cian. A fat Tairen woman from Siuan's past who disciplined her as a young girl for fighting.

Cian do Mehon a'Macansa. A Murandian noblewoman, one of the Murandians and Andorans to meet with Egwene and her party as they were passing through Murandy on the way to the siege against the White Tower. Cian was stocky and graying; she snorted loudly, and had a cool, collected demeanor. She made common cause with the intruding Andorans against the rebel Aes Sedai and later came to further agreements with the Andorans.

Ciar. A stocky, dark *sul'dam* who accompanied Semirhage when she posed as the Daughter of the Nine Moons and attempted to capture Rand. Ciar vomited on herself in the aftermath, having learned that they had accompanied a Forsaken, not the Daughter of the Nine Moons, and that Rand was the Dragon Reborn.

Ciel. A serving girl at The Stag and Lion in Baerlon, Andor.

Cieryl Arjuna. One of Careane Fransi's Warders. He was Tairen, stood six feet tall, and seemed gangly and all bones, though his shoulders were wide. He was in his late twenties. He was not a Darkfriend. Cieryl was killed while trying to rescue Careane from Lady Shiaine's house on Full Moon Street.

Cilia Cole. An Emond's Field girl. She was born in the fall of 979 NE. Cilia was pink-cheeked, big-eyed and pleasingly plump. She was the first girl that Perrin ever kissed. She insisted that Verin and Alanna test her, and she passed, but they wouldn't take her because she was too old. She eventually became a novice after learning that the novice book had been opened to all.

Cinchonine, Mistress. Innkeeper at The Crown of Roses in Caemlyn. The embassy from the rebel Aes Sedai wishing to meet with Rand stayed at the inn and met with Alanna and Verin there.

Cinda. A serving girl at The Stag and Lion in Baerlon, Andor.

Cindaking. A Sea Folk island south of Mayene off the Tairen/Mayener peninsulas in the Sea of Storms.

Cindal, Rafela. *See* Rafela Cindal

Cinny Wade. A woman featured in a haunting song performed by Thom, "The

Marriage of Cinny Wade." Mat learned it as "Always Choose the Right Horse," though that version had a faster tempo than Thom's.

Circle, the Great. A huge gathering place in Tanchico that could hold thousands to watch horse races or displays of fireworks. It was located on the Calpene, the westernmost hilly peninsula on Tanchico Bay.

Circle, the King's. An assembly arena in Tanchico that was surrounded by Lords' palaces and other impressive buildings. It was located on the Maseta, the middle of three hilly peninsulas on Tanchico Bay.

Circle, the Panarch's. An assembly arena in Tanchico that was surrounded by the Panarch's Palace and other buildings. It was located on the Verana, the eastern-most hilly peninsula on Tanchico Bay.

Circle, the. *See* Knitting Circle

Circle, Women's. The deliberating body of women elected by women in a village, responsible for matters considered women's affairs.

Circuit of Heaven. A racecourse on the Great North Road just outside of Ebou Dar, beyond the Dal Eira Gate.

Cirri. A cat at The Stag and Lion in Baerlon.

Civil Guard. The group charged with keeping order in Ebou Dar. It was inefficient, seldom seen in the streets, and susceptible to bribes unless someone powerful was watching. Even then, they could be bought with enough gold, since they were cheaper than bribing a magistrate. At least, this was so before the Seanchan came and disbanded them.

Civil Watch. The group charged with keeping order in Tanchico; they answered to the Panarch.

Clara. A novice in the White Tower who assisted Egwene during the Seanchan attack.

Clare. A golden-haired woman Mat gambled with in The Dead Man's Breath, an inn in Caemlyn.

Clarine Anhill. A dog trainer in Luca's circus. She was the plump and brown-cheeked wife of Petra, the strongman. Clarine's dogs drew the smallest crowd in the Samara show; they did backsprings and flips over each other's backs.

Classen Bayor. A military leader from Mat's memories; he lost his cavalry in the marsh at the Battle of Kolesar.

cleansing, the. The removal of the taint from *saidin*, performed by Rand at Sha-dar Logoth with the assistance of Nynaeve and the Choedan Kal *sa'angreal*. The taint on *saidin* was like oil on a pond—it did not permeate the pond, it was on the surface—but to enter it, one needed to go through the oil. For the cleansing, Rand used repulsion and attraction of opposites, *saidin* and the evil of Shadar Logoth. There could be no mixing of the two. *Saidin* was forced through the evil, as the opposites attracted each other, and they went around in circular fashion, negating one another—"Opposites cancel, but opposites far enough apart become alike, and like attracts like." More simply, Rand formed a conduit between the taint on *saidin* and the evil at Shadar Logoth—being opposite polarities of evil, they were attracted to one another, like opposite poles of a magnet, but destroyed each other because of those differences.

Cliffs of Dawn. A great land shift dating from the Breaking, extending 250 leagues south from the Mountains of Dhoom along the border of the Aiel Waste and Shara. The cliffs ranged from one hundred to five hundred feet high. The Cliffs helped the Sharans limit foreign access to their country, and outside trade was limited, in part, to six specially designated trading towns scattered along the Cliffs of Dawn.

Clintock. A Redarm in the Band of the Red Hand. After the *gholam* attack in Caemlyn, he checked on Mat every half hour.

Cloud Dancing. The Talent of controlling the weather; not a common Talent among Aes Sedai. Sea Folk Windfinders developed this Talent to a greater extent; they called it the Weaving of Winds.

Cloud. The tall gray mare with a black mane that Rand rode when he left Two Rivers in Moiraine's company.

cloudberry bush. A shrub with edible berries and leaves that were used in a tea.

Co'dansin. An alternate name for Shara.

Coalition, the. An alliance of nations formed during the Aiel War to fight the Aiel at the Battle of the Shining Walls. It was also known as the Grand Coalition, the Grand Alliance or the Third Compact.

Cobb, Jennet. *See* Jennet Cobb

Codarra Aiel. One of the Aiel clans. Its chief was Indirian, and its hold was Red Springs Hold.

Coedelin. An Aiel Wise One who disciplined Amys when she was learning to be a Wise One.

Coelan, House. A major noble House in Andor. Its High Seat was Lord Pelivar; its sign the Roses, sometimes called the Flowers. *See also* Pelivar Coelan

Coerid Nosar. A king of Almoren, one of the Ten Nations, and one of the signers of the Compact of the Ten Nations.

Coiam. The grandfather of Jalanda, an Ogier historian whom Loial quoted with information about Be'lal.

Coidevwin, Nirelle. *See* Nirelle Coidevwin

coin pepper. An edible pepper found in the Borderlands.

Coine din Jubai Wild Winds. The Atha'an Miere Sailmistress of the raker *Wavedancer*. She was sister of the blood to Jorin din Jubai White Wing, her Windfinder, and the wife of Toram din Alta Wild Winds, her Cargomaster. She had four small gold rings in each ear and one in the left side of her nose; the chain connecting them had a row of tiny medallions. She had black hair with some gray and large brown eyes. She received Elayne and Nynaeve aboard her ship in Tear and took them to Tanchico. From there she planned to go to Dantora, the Aile Jafar, and then on to Cantorin and the Aile Somera, spreading news of the Coramoor.

Coiren Saeldain. An Aes Sedai of the Gray Ajah and the loyalist contingent, with a strength level of 18(6). Born in 861 NE, she went to the White Tower in 877 NE. After nine years as a novice and six years as Accepted, she was raised to the shawl in 892 NE. She was 5'5½" tall, plump and pompous. She was a good negotiator, but she liked to have everything done just so, every foot placed exactly where it had been planned to go. She was the leader of the Tower embassy to Rand in Cairhien at first, though not the strongest in the Power among them, but when it became necessary to kidnap him, Galina Casban took over as Elaida ordered. Coiren was captured by Rand at Dumai's Wells. Like all of the other captive sisters, Coiren, prompted by Verin's Compulsion, found reason to swear oath to the Dragon Reborn before Cadsuane departed Cairhien for Far Madding.

Coke. A Darkfriend thug with an Illianer accent who kidnapped Egwene, Nynaeve and Elayne for Fades. He was lanky and missing an ear and two fingers. Coke was killed by Aiel who came to Elayne and the others' rescue.

Col. A Tairen horse handler with Valan Luca's show.

Coladara. A Tairen Aes Sedai of the Green Ajah who was uncommitted to any contingent. She served as advisor to King Paitar of Arafel, and accompanied him to the meeting with the other Borderland rulers in the Black Hills. Seven Aes Sedai who were visiting her went as well. She was the only advisor to a Borderland ruler who stayed on when trouble started in the Tower.

Colar Najima. A Kandori girl whose mother was interviewed by Moiraine while she was searching for the infant Dragon Reborn. A young teen, Colar had long black hair and blue eyes that were level with Moiraine's. Her father and brothers had been killed by the Black Ajah.

Colavaere Saighan. A Cairhienin noblewoman who was Head of House Saighan. She had dark eyes and dark hair with a touch of gray. She tried to tie strings to Rand by sending young women to him; he retaliated by asking her to dinner, and then forgot to meet her because of the report he received that Morgase was dead. Aviendha found Colavaere in Rand's rooms and beat her. She briefly took the throne of Cairhien after swearing fealty to Rand. She had Meilan and Maringil assassinated; she was confronted by Rand and accused of treason and murder. He stripped her of her titles and all her properties except one small farm. He exiled her to that farm, and she hanged herself rather than face the shame of it.

Colchaine estates. Property belonging to Bertome Saighan in Cairhien.

Cold Peak. A sept of the Miagoma Aiel.

Cold Rocks Hold. The hold of the Taardad clan in the Aiel Waste. It was Rhuarc's hold; Amys was its Wise One and Lian its roofmistress.

Cold Water. The leader of a wolfpack that Perrin asked for information when he was searching for his kidnapped wife.

Cole. A Two Rivers family. *See* Aedwin, Cilia *and* Lusonia Cole *and* Cole, Master

Cole, Master. A very old Emond's Field man who napped during the shearing.

Cole Pass. The site of one of Mat's battle memories where there was a rout and Artur Hawkwing doggedly pursued the army commanded by the object of Mat's memories.

Colford, Deni. *See* Deni Colford

Colinda. A Wise One of the Imran sept of the Shaarad Aiel and Hot Springs Hold with the ability to channel and a strength level of 13(1), almost as strong a presence as Sorilea. She was about 5'8" tall, and slender, with penetrating gray eyes. Colinda looked short of her middle years, but was around ninety years old. She told Gaul that he thought too much for a Stone Dog. She threatened to send to him to Rhuidean when Jheran died, whether he wanted to go or not. With Aeron and Edarra, she was sent to the Royal Library in Cairhien because Nesune Bihara was poking around, looking for information on the seals, which the Wise Ones wanted as well. She also went to Dumai's Wells.

Coline. The cook at The Queen's Blessing in Caemlyn. She was frequently called Cook and was a woman of some influence at the inn. Many people assumed her to be Basel Gill's wife because she got away with so much and pushed him around so.

Collam Daan. A great research college in V'saine during the Age of Legends, noted for its blue and silver domes. It was the foremost center for research and development. A research facility, a great white sphere named the Sharom, floated above the college. Mierin Eronaile was a researcher there when her team bored a hole in the Dark One's prison.

Collapse, the. The hundred-year period that followed the drilling of the Bore, when the Dark One's influence began to unravel the fabric of society during the Age of Legends, leading to the War of the Shadow.

Collaris. Beonin Sedai's grandmother, who was a distinguished advocate in Tanchico.

Colline. A young Jenn Aiel from the period right after the Breaking. Her liberators from bandits who had kidnapped her were ostracized from the Jenn Aiel for using violence.

Colly Garren. A young Two Rivers man who joined Perrin to fight the Trollocs. Colly was killed in a Trolloc ambush.

Colona, Mayam. *See* Mayam Colona

colors. A phenomenon experienced by Rand, Mat and Perrin when each of them thought of one of the other two *ta'veren*. For the colors to appear in the mind of Mat or Perrin when thinking of Rand, they had to think of Rand the person, not "the Dragon Reborn."

Colrada Hold. One of the holds in the Aiel Waste; the dreamwalker Mora was once its Wise One.

Colvine, Serancha. *See* Serancha Colvine

Com. A young urchin in Tear who, along with his friend Doni, talked to Rand about the steamwagon. Rand gave each of them a gold coin. Min looked after them with a miserable expression indicating that she had seen something sad in their future.

Comadrin, Madoc. *See* Madoc Comadrin

Comaelle. The High Queen of Jaramide, one of the Ten Nations during the period following the Breaking.

Comaidin riots. Unrest quelled single-handedly in the period following the Breaking by the legendary Green Aes Sedai Caraighan Maconar.

Comanli, Shahal. *See* Shahal Comanli

Comar. An Andoran nobleman and Darkfriend. He was tall, with wide shoulders, a deep chest, dark blue eyes and a close-cut black beard with a white streak over his chin. Gaebril sent him to Tear to kill Elayne; Mat overheard those orders and followed him. Mat found him cheating at dice at The Golden Cup; Mat gambled with him, won, and warned him to go back to Caemlyn. Comar started to draw his sword, and Mat killed him.

Comarda Hold. A Shaido hold in the Aiel Waste. Sevanna was roofmistress while married to the clan chief Suladric.

Comarra Zepava. An Aes Sedai of the Blue Ajah who served as Amyrlin from 244 to 276 NE. Comarra was a moderately strong Amyrlin, at least compared to Elise Stang. While not so firmly in control as Kiyosa or Catala, she still managed very well.

Comelle. A great coastal city that was the third largest in the Age of Legends.

Comeris, Akarrin. *See* Akarrin Comeris

Comfrey. A small village north of Baerlon in Andor. When Mat delivered a message from Elayne to Morgase in Caemlyn, he used a pseudonym, being wary of Gaebril, and mentioned Comfrey as his home, although he had never been there.

Commentaries on the Karaethon Cycle. A text written by Sereine dar Shamelle Motara, Counsel-Sister to Comaelle, High Queen of Jaramide, circa 325 AB, the Third Age.

Commentaries on the Prophecies of the Dragon. Written by Jurith Dorine, Right Hand to the Queen of Almoren, 742 AB, the Third Age.

Commentary on the Dragon. A work by Sajius that contained the line "He shall hold a blade of light in his hands, and the three shall be one."

Common Chant. *See* Bards, Forms of Recitation of

Comolads. An exquisite wine from the Age of Legends recalled longingly by Graendal.

Compact of the Ten Nations. Also known as the Second Compact. The first league of nations, created approximately two hundred years after the Breaking, as a defense against the forces of the Dark One. It lasted eight hundred years, until the Trolloc Wars began. The Compact was largely the work of the legendary Queen Mabriam en Shereed of Aramaelle, who was also an Aes Sedai.

Compact, the Second. *See* Compact of the Ten Nations

Compact, the Third. *See* Coalition, the

Companions, the. *See* Illian

Companions, the Hundred. *See* Hundred Companions, the

Comprehensive Discussion of Pre-Breaking Relics, A. A history text of which little was known.

Compulsion. A weave of the One Power that compelled the subject to do one's will. It was not an ethical use of the One Power. Graendal, Moghedien and others used this weave to attain nefarious ends. Compulsion, though called a Talent by some, was not one; it could be learned by any channeler, taking into account the limits of strength and skill. Compulsion could be detected, because of the behavior of the person and effects on the person, according to Moghedien. But she was not the real expert; what she could do certainly could be detected. Graendal was the most subtle user of Compulsion and its variations, with the implication at least that when she chose she could use it either undetectably or at a level where it would take a great deal of effort to detect. While Compulsion per se was supposed to be one of the lost Talents, recorded only in the histories, and was the sort of thing that Aes Sedai were supposed to abjure (as they were supposed to eschew all of the "tainted" or "corrupted" uses to which the Power was put), the simple fact was that the two most common tricks by girls having their first experience with the Power were some form of eavesdropping and some form of making people do one thing or another that they wanted (i.e., some form of Compulsion).

Comran. A Jenn Aiel ancestor of Rand who lived during the period of the Breaking. He had found Ogier *stedding* in the Dragonwall and had begun trade with them.

con. Small Cairhienin banners on short staffs, usually strapped to the backs of officers or lords' personal retainers, so that they could be picked out in battle.

Con Aybara. Perrin's father, who was killed by Padan Fain when he laughed in Fain's face for naming Perrin a Darkfriend.

Conail Northan. High Seat of House Northan in Andor. His sigil was three black eagles. He was about six feet tall, and lean. He had an engaging smile, merry brown eyes and a nose like an eagle's beak. Born circa 984 NE, he was one of four young nobles Dyelin brought to help Elayne win the throne. The others were Branlet Gilyard, Catalyn Haevin and Perival Mantear. The four together brought over three thousand armsmen, mainly crossbowmen and halberdmen. Conail seemed very easygoing, laughing and grinning a great deal; he thought Aviendha being introduced as Aiel was a joke, and thought nearly getting her knife in his brisket for it was a joke, too. He said they couldn't let a ninny like Arymilla take the throne. He wanted to fight a duel with Arymilla's champion, as he believed Artur Hawkwing would have done. Birgitte considered him the most childish of the four, in many ways. He was eager to fight when Elayne was kidnapped; Dyelin took him to the action at the Far Madding Gate, but made sure that he was nowhere near the front.

Condaris. An Ogier-built city in Aelgar, one of the Ten Nations after the Breaking.

Conel, Paitr. *See* Paitr Conel

Congar clan. An Emond's Field family. *See* Bili, Daise, Eward, Jori, Len *and* Wit Congar

conje. A type of needle from the Age of Legends that had to be carefully placed. Sammael thought to himself that Graendal prattled like a fool, but she was no fool; she planted ideas in her babbling as carefully as *conje* needles had to be planted, designed to influence the listener for reasons that could somehow benefit her.

Conly, Althyn. *See* Althyn Conly

Connel. A member of Ituralde's personal guard in Saldaea. He and Barettal were the only two of Ituralde's guards still alive when they were allowed to retreat into Maradon, being pursued by the Shadowspawn army.

Connl. One of the Band of the Red Hand under Mandevwin's command. He participated in the attack on the Seanchan.

Connoral. Sisters in the White Tower. *See* Viria *and* Raechin Connoral

Conquest, the. Luthair's conquest of Seanchan natives, which took several hundred years to complete. It was also known as the Consolidation.

consensus, greater. *See* greater consensus

consensus, lesser. *See* lesser consensus

Consolidation, the. *See* Conquest, the

Consolidation, Wars of Consolidation. *See* Wars of Consolidation

constellations. Plowman, Haywain, Archer, Five Sisters, Three Geese (pointing the way north), Snake (Aiel called it the Dragon), Shield (or Hawkwing's Shield), Stag, Ram, Cup, Traveler, Blacksmith.

Conwy, Nethan. One of Merise's Warders, an Andoran. Nethan was 6'1" tall, with a lean, muscular build and piercing blue eyes. His dark hair had wings of white at the temples.

Copan, Myriam. *See* Myriam Copan

Coplin clan. A farming family of the Two Rivers. There were many troublemakers among them. *See* Benly, Calle, Dag, Darl, Ewal, Hari *and* Jac Coplin

Cor Darei. Old Tongue for "Night Spears," an Aiel warrior society.

Coram. Hulking and wide-shouldered, he was one of the Aiel who helped Aviendha and Rhuarc rescue Nynaeve, Elayne and Egwene from brigands and Myrddraal. He was one of the two guards for Verin on the day she questioned the Aes Sedai prisoners after Dumai's Wells about the Tower's plans for Rand. Verin thought that in rising, he "uncoiled like a serpent despite his size." He and Mendan played cat's cradle.

Coramen. A tiny walled town of tile-roofed stone buildings and half a dozen stone docks, on the east bank of the River Eldar in Altara. It was an important crossing point, and a ferry ran between it and Alkindar, on the other side of the Eldar. Luca's show took the ferry across the river from Alkindar to Coramen, and set up camp outside the town.

Coramoor, the. The Sea Folk name for the Chosen One, whom they had sought as a herald of a new Age and found in the person of Rand al'Thor.

Corana. An Aiel Maiden of the Spear who accompanied Rand to Caemlyn when he took Fedwin Morr there. She also accompanied Bashere and Flinn to a meeting with the Seanchan and reported that the Seanchan were flaunting captured Shaido Wise Ones. She had graying hair and was nearly as leather-faced as Sulin. She treated Rand like an older first-brother.

Corartheren. An Ogier-built city in Manetheren, one of the Ten Nations formed after the Breaking.

Corbesan, Jorlen. An Aes Sedai from before the Breaking who made wondrous *ter'angreal*; he was killed when the Sharom was destroyed.

Corbet. A Youngling. He was one of the youngest among them and was always looking for something to do to prove himself.

Cordamora Palace. The royal palace of Saldaea, in Maradon.

Cordese Hills. A landform west of Ebou Dar.

Cords, Sergeant. A watch sergeant with Bryne's army. He was overweight, with red stubble on his chin. He refused to fetch Bryne when Gawyn arrived, treating him as a potential recruit and refusing to listen to him. Gawyn persisted, Cords reached for his sword, and Gawyn quickly disarmed him.

Cordwyn, Evard. *See* Evard Cordwyn

corea. A musical instrument that Asmodean played during the Age of Legends.

coreer. A venomous snake in the Age of Legends.

Corehuin. One of two Aiel wives of Mandelain, the Daryne clan chief. Her sister-wife was Jair. Corehuin traveled with Mandelain to the wetlands; Jair stayed in the Waste, and they both wanted to see her again before they woke from the dream.

Corele Hovian. A Murandian Aes Sedai of the Yellow Ajah who was uncommitted any contingent. She had a strength level of 18(6). Born in 876 NE, she went to the White Tower in 894 NE. After seven years as a novice and five years as Accepted, she was raised to the shawl in 906 NE. She was 5'5½" tall, with a very slender, boyish build. Her thick black eyebrows and a mass of raven hair gave her something or a wild appearance no matter how neatly she dressed. Her eyes were blue, and the tip of her nose turned up. She always seemed amused and often had a joking way of speaking; she had a lilting voice. Along with Samitsu Tamagowa, she was considered one of the best at Healing, although Samitsu was better. Corele was one of the uncommitted Aes Sedai Rand found in Cairhien after Dumai's Wells; she was following Cadsuane Melaidhrin.

Corele, along with Samitsu and Damer Flinn, helped to Heal Rand after he was stabbed with the Shadar Logoth dagger. She bonded Damer Flinn as her Warder shortly after the attack on Rand when he returned to Cairhien. When Alanna collapsed for unknown reasons, Corele tried to Heal her but was unsuccessful. She accompanied Cadsuane to Far Madding and to Shadar Logoth. While Rand was cleansing the taint, Corele linked with Damer and Sarene and fought Demandred; they were successful in driving him away. Corele accompanied Rand to the Pendaloan estate in Tear and to Tellaen's estate in Arad Doman. She was one of the sisters holding the shield on Semirhage when Shaidar Haran came to free Semirhage; he put Corele in a trance to incapacitate her, but she recovered and went with Rand to Bandar Eban, Falme and the Stone of Tear. During the Last Battle, Corele Healed the injured at Berelain's palace.

Corelna. An Aiel Wise One who could not channel. She was a green-eyed hawk of a woman with gray heavy in her flaxen hair. She didn't believe that Arilyn was an Aes Sedai spy.

Coremanda. One of the Ten Nations after the Breaking. Its capital was Shaemal, and its king at the signing of the Compact was Ladoman. One of its cities, Hai Caemlyn, was the predecessor of Caemlyn.

Corenne. Old Tongue word meaning "The Return." It was the name given by the Seanchan both to the fleet of thousands of ships and to the hundreds of thousands of soldiers, craftsmen and others carried by those ships, who came behind the Forerunners to reclaim the lands stolen from Artur Hawkwing's descendants. The *Corenne* was led by Captain-General Lunal Galgan.

corenroot. A medicinal herb that helped make blood.

Corevin. A Cairhienin Redarm in the Band of the Red Hand. He was thickly muscled with a big nose and small eyes, a tattoo of a leopard and a boar on one arm, and a lion and a naked woman on the other. He was one of the few men Mat knew who could drink Ebou Dari ale in the heat—or at all, for that matter. Injured in a fight with a fish-seller in Ebou Dar, he died in the Rahad fighting Black Ajah and Darkfriends on the mission to retrieve the Bowl of the Winds.

Corgaide Marendevin. The head of the servants, known as the Holder of the Keys, at the Sun Palace in Cairhien. She was 5'2" tall, grave-faced and gray-haired, and wore no ornament except for the heavy ring of keys at her waist. The first real crack in Samitsu's authority in Caemlyn was when Corgaide began recognizing Sashalle as above Samitsu.

Corianin Nedeal. An Aes Sedai from almost five hundred years before the Last Battle. She was a Dreamer who left notes on *Tel'aran'rhiod* and on various *ter'angreal* that she had studied. She died in 526 NE.

Coride. A pale-haired novice in the White Tower who looked up to Egwene after Egwene had been captured by the Tower Aes Sedai. She was a year younger than Egwene, but was still immature after a year and a half in the Tower. Egwene comforted her after she saw a ghost.

Corin Ayellin. A slim Two Rivers woman with a thick gray braid that hung below her waist. She was one of the best cooks in Emond's Field, second only to Marin al'Vere, and Marin said that Corin's sweets were better than hers. She could not abide thieves. Nynaeve stole a pie from her at age sixteen, her hair already in a braid, on a dare from Nela Thane. Nynaeve walked out the door straight into Mistress Ayellin, who strapped her so soundly Nynaeve remembered it as a grown woman.

Corl, Ander. A bootmaker who lived in the town of Taien in the Jangai Pass. He, his wife, Aril, and his brother-in-law, Tal Nethin, survived the Shaido attack on their town.

Corlan Dashiva. The Forsaken Aginor/Osan'gar's Asha'man persona. He was supposedly from an isolated farming village in the Black Hills. His attitude toward Taim was not always what it should have been, to keep up appearances; his actions were rarely overt and could be put down to the same degree of madness that had him frequently talking to himself, staring at nothing and laughing to himself at nothing. He was a plain man in his middle years. He wasn't skinny, but he moved in a hesitant, creeping way, hands folded at his waist, that made him seem so. He guided Damer Flinn toward learning some of the ancient ways of Healing. Rand chose him out after Dumai's Wells—the last one chosen, seemingly at random—when Taim insisted on Rand having some full Asha'man. It was an example of *ta'veren* currents working. He stayed with Rand in Cairhien and accompanied Rand to see the Sea Folk in Cairhien. He went to battle the Seanchan in Illian with Rand. After their return to Cairhien, Rand was attacked by *saidin* there, and Dashiva was discovered with the attackers and forced to flee. Rand ordered Taim to list him among the deserters, with the others whom Taim had already named, Rochaid, Gedwyn, Torval and Kisman. Elza Penfell killed Dashiva at Shadar Logoth when he tried to kill Rand during the cleansing of the taint; she had no idea he was one of the Forsaken. *See also* Osan'gar

corlm. A Seanchan exotic species imported from a parallel world. At first glance, it appeared to be a flightless bird with a long neck, thick legs and a sort of double crest on its head. It often stood some six or more feet tall counting the crest. It was covered with long hair, mottled/striped in grays, blacks and or browns, like a common sort of cat. The tail, which it flattened out to stabilize itself when running, was also covered in hair; the double crest was really a pair of upstanding ears which were quite mobile. It had four-toed feet with smallish claws and tiny forearms on which the paws had four long "fingers" with longer claws than the hind feet. The arms were usually held close to its body and seldom used except in nest-building and feeding, though its beak was used more often. This beak was large and appeared oversized for its head, which was long and oblong, and was hooked like the beak of a bird of prey; the *corlm* used the beak for killing. Its two eyes were set on the sides of its head. The *corlm* laid one egg at time, which often did not hatch. It was a carnivore and an extremely efficient predator, following prey by both scent and sound. *Corlm* were used for tracking, though never accompanying units mounted on torm; the two animals were mutually antagonistic to a high degree. The *corlm* was faster than a man in short sprints, and could equal men over longer distances. It was about equal in intelligence to a dog. *Corlm* appeared to be solitary animals in their natural environment, and were always used singly, as they did not tolerate each other well except at mating. The weight of an adult could be over three hundred pounds. The *corlm* was controlled both by spoken commands and by using whistles pitched above human hearing.

Corly, Reanne. *See* Reanne Corly

Cormaed. A town in Altara where there was a ferry across the River Eldar into Amadicia. When traveling west after fleeing Caemlyn, Morgase and her group were told that they could get a ferry in Cormaed which would take them to the Amadician side.

Cormalinde Masoon. A famous sculptor from the Age of Legends whose works, immense stylized humans and animals, were found in the Ansaline Gardens resort.

Corman. An Aiel of the Mosaada Goshien clan, and a member of *Far Aldazar Din* (Brothers of the Eagle) warrior society. He had gray eyes, and a white scar slanted across his nose. He gambled at knife-throwing with Mat in Rhuidean. Later he was one of the guards at the Sun Palace in Cairhien.

Cormanes. A pretty young man Moiraine kissed the night before she left for the Tower.

Cormer, Marek. A Two Rivers man with Perrin in Ghealdan. Faile noted that he no longer seemed to believe the rumors about Perrin and Berelain.

Cornwell, Mirlene. *See* Mirlene Cornwell

Coron Ford. A place in Arad Doman. Rodel Ituralde told his aide to send a packet to his wife if he didn't reach Coron Ford in two days, after meeting a group of enemies under the White Ribbon at Lady Osana's hunting lodge.

Coronation Festival. A week-long feast held in Cairhien when a new ruler took the throne. The new monarch distributed gifts of coin, food and finery in the city every day. Free access to the city was available to everyone; not even someone under order of arrest could be denied or detained.

corpse moss. A moss that grew in caves.

Corrand, Dimana. *See* Dimana Corrand

Corvila. A lean Altaran weaver who was *gai'shain* to the Shaido at Malden. She swore fealty to Faile.

cosa. An animal that scampered up trees, referred to by Graendal in describing how Sammael would react if Rand chased him out of Illian.

Cosaida. A sept of the Chareen Aiel.

Cosain. A lean, yellow-haired Wise One of the Spine Ridge sept of the Miagoma Aiel with the ability to channel and a strength level of 14(2). She went to Dumai's Wells. When Rand and his party were returning to Cairhien from Dumai's Wells, Sorilea sent Sotarin and Cosain to meet Feraighin, who came from Cairhien.

Cosamelle. A town in Ghealdan. Logain said that was where the Red Ajah sisters threatened him and made him become a false Dragon.

Coteren. A heavyset Asha'man with a blunt face, pudgy cheeks, and long, black, oily hair. One of Taim's cronies, he liked to bully Androl and called him "pageboy." He told Androl that Taim had demoted him. During the attempted rescue of Logain, Jonneth killed Coteren with an arrow through the chest.

Couladin. An Aiel warrior of the Domai sept of the Shaido Aiel and the *Seia Doon* (Black Eyes) warrior society. He was tall, broad-shouldered, flame-haired and short of his middle years. He had a hawk's eyes and a sun-dark face and was married to Sevanna. His brother Muradin entered Rhuidean to become clan chief of the Shaido; he did not emerge, and Couladin accused Rand of killing him. Asmodean gave Couladin gold-and-red Dragons on his arms; he tried to claim the title of *Car'a'carn*. He led the Shaido to the wetlands and took Cairhien. Rand and the other Aiel followed and brought him to battle, where Mat killed Couladin.

Coulin. He was Master of Arms of the Tower Guard under Hammar at the White Tower. He was killed by Gawyn when Siuan was deposed.

Coumin. A Da'shain Aiel ancestor of Rand. At age sixteen, he was participating in the seed singing when news arrived that the War of Power had ended. He was running home to tell his grandfather Charn when a townsman named Toma punched him in the mouth because his family had served Lanfear while she was still known as Mierin. When he got home, he found that Charn had been hanged for the same reason. Later in life, Coumin gave up the Way of the Leaf and encouraged other Da'shain Aiel to do so as well.

Council, Crown High. *See* Crown High Council

Council of Elders. The Ogier ruling body of each *stedding*.

Council of Lords. An advisory council to the Queen of Saldaea.

Council of Merchants. A group of the heads of merchant guilds in Arad Doman who were responsible for electing the King. The members were almost always women.

Council of Nine. The advisory council of lords that jointly ruled with the King in Illian.

Council of the Anointed, the. The ruling body of the Children of the Light. It was composed of approximately twelve of the highest-ranking and most favored Lords Captain, and presided over by the Lord Captain Commander.

Council, Supreme. The ruling body of the Black Ajah, composed of thirteen sisters. It was also known as the Great Council of Thirteen.

Council, Village. Men elected by townsmen and headed by a mayor, responsible for decisions affecting the whole village and interacting with councils of other villages.

Counsel's Head, The. The second inn that Rand and his group (Min, Lan, Nynaeve and Alivia) stayed at when they were in Far Madding. Mistress Keane was the innkeeper of this inn suitable for wealthy merchants. They stayed there when Rand was trying to put an end to the Asha'man who had tried to kill him in Cairhien; they were also visited there by Cadsuane and Alanna.

Counselor, Prime. A high office mentioned by Graendal. It was probably from the Age of Legends.

Counsels, the. The ruling body of Far Madding. There were thirteen Counsels, with the highest-ranking named the First Counsel. Counsels were always women.

cour'souvra. An Old Tongue term meaning "mindtrap." It was a device, cage-like in appearance, applied in the Pit of Doom to one out of favor with the Dark One, and in this world enslaved one totally to whoever held the mindtrap.

Coura. The mother of Amar who was the mother of Elora, the last being an Ogier author from the time of Artur Hawkwing.

Court of Takedo. From Mat's memories, the royal court in Farashelle, one of the nations that had arisen following the Trolloc Wars, which Artur Hawkwing had crushed more than a thousand years in the past.

Court of the Nine Moons. The seat of the Seanchan Empress.

Court of the Sun. A Fourth Age court, where Sulamein so Bhagad, who wrote a book called *The Wheel of Time*, was Chief Historian.

Court-bard. An entertainer established at a royal palace, vested with a much higher status than a gleeman.

Courtani. A Banner-General in the Seanchan army; Mat found her unappealing. Tuon chastised her for being slow to help Mat reach the battlefield on the Kandor-Arafel border in the Last Battle.

Covanen's First Rule of Medians. A method used by some sisters of the White Ajah to explain logic and empirical truths arithmetically. It was an unproven method, according to other Whites.

Covarla Baldene. An Aes Sedai of the Red Ajah and of the loyalist contingent, with a strength level of 21(9). Born in 919 NE, she went to the White Tower in 936 NE. After nine years as a novice and five as Accepted, she was raised to the shawl in 950 NE. She had pale hair and a normally implacable face. Covarla was part of the group sent to kidnap Rand al'Thor, and was one of the few to escape from Dumai's Wells. Elaida put her in charge of the sisters in Dorlan who were sent there to conceal facts about the battle from sisters in the Tower. She was unaware of Elaida's plan for getting rid of the Younglings.

Covenant of the Ten Nations. Also known as the Second Covenant. The first league of nations, created approximately two hundred years after the Breaking, as a defense against the forces of the Dark One. It lasted eight hundred years, until the Trolloc Wars began. The Compact was largely the work of the legendary Queen Mabriam en Shereed of Aramaelle, who was also an Aes Sedai.

Covenant, the. A promise of the early Aiel, the Da'shain, to serve the Aes Sedai and to follow the Way of the Leaf, a pacific way of life.

Covenry, Sahra. *See* Sahra Covenry

Covril daughter of Ella daughter of Soong. Loial's mother, and a respected speaker. Her sister Voniel was Elder Haman's wife. A head shorter than Elder Haman, who was 10'5" tall, she had more delicate features than he, and her eyebrows were not as long or thick. Covril, Elder Haman and Erith set out to find Loial so that he and Erith could be married. They went to Caemlyn, where they marked *stedding* on maps for Rand, and accompanied him to Shadar Logoth to close the Waygate. Rand took them to the Two Rivers, but Loial had already left. They finally caught up with Loial at Algarin's manor, and Covril witnessed the wedding. When she objected to Loial speaking at the Stump, Erith claimed wife's prerogative and overruled her. Covril later made sure that Loial was allowed to speak; she spoke against him but claimed that she agreed with him and was only speaking as devil's advocate.

Cowin Gemallan. A Malkieri nobleman also known as Cowin Fairheart. He was a hero almost as well loved as the King, but when the Great Lords had cast the rods for king, only two separated him from Akir, and he never forgot that two men laying a different color on the Crowning Stone would have set him on the throne instead. Jealousy was only part of the problem; Cowin was also a Darkfriend. He plotted with Breyan to move soldiers back from the Blight to seize the Seven Towers, stripping the Borderforts to bare garrisons. Trollocs poured in, and Malkier fell. Cowin was captured and brought to justice by Jain Farstrider, and killed in trial-by-combat by Lan's father, the King.

Cowinde. A blue-eyed Maiden of the Spear who was taken *gai'shain*. Cowinde served Melaine, though she did not accompany her to Caemlyn. She frequently served Egwene when she was with the Aiel, and she came to Egwene's tent in Rhuidean. She was one who refused to put off the white; Melaine sent her to search a pile of sand for a particular red grain in an attempt to make her shed the *gai'shain* white robes and resume being a Maiden.

Cowlin, Lord. The Lord of So Habor, Altara. He fled the village before Perrin's party arrived. He was haunted by his wife's ghost; there was some question as to how she died.

Coy. A bandit leader in Kandor. He had grizzled, greasy hair, a narrow, unshaven face and a gap-toothed grin. He and his band made the mistake of trying to rob Moiraine and her traveling companions, Lan, Bukama and Ryne. Moiraine drove him and his band off using the One Power.

Craeb, Melli. *See* Melli Craeb

Craft Town. Part of the Black Tower, located outside of Caemlyn. Craft Town was a large area where all the craftsfolk plied their trade, making everything needed by the Black Tower.

Crawe, Bandry (Ban). *See* Bandry Crawe

Crawe, Samel. *See* Samel Crawe

Creator, the. The being who made the world and put in place the Wheel of Time.

Creed of the Asha'man. A statement of beliefs recited every morning at the Black Tower before Morning Directives.

Creedin. A captain in Ituralde's army involved in defensive actions at Maradon. Ituralde sent him word to watch for a Trolloc assault on the ford.

Crimson, Master. An alias used by Mat while seeking information in taverns in Caemlyn.

crimsonthorn. A plant whose white root shavings were sweet and used in a tea. Used in small amounts, it acted as a painkiller; in larger amounts, it paralyzed and killed. The plant was found far from the sea.

Cristol, First Lord. A ruler of Essenia, one of the Ten Nations, and one of the signers of the Compact of the Ten Nations.

Croi Makin. One of Myrelle Berengari's Warders, an Andoran. He was a yellow-haired young splinter of stone with a fine profile. He was the only of Myrelle's Warders who had not been bonded to another Aes Sedai. Rumor said that Myrelle was married to her first three Warders: Croi Makin, Nuhel Dromand and Avar Hachami.

Crossin, Mycal. *See* Mycal Crossin

Crown and Lion, The. An inn in Caemlyn on the other side of the New City from The Queen's Blessing. Rand told Elaida that he was staying there so that Master Gill at The Queen's Blessing would not be put in danger.

Crown and Staff of the Tree. The insignia of the Panarch in Tanchico.

Crown High Council. A governmental body in the monarchy of Ghealdan. It was composed of nobles. This council was of varying size, depending on what party or group had control, and of varying power in the land. The Council had a strong say in who would ascend to the throne, though ascent was usually hereditary. By law, no one could sit on the Crown High Council if they were in the line of succession, and stepping from the Council to the throne was also against the law. Attempts to do so in the past had caused outbreaks of violence—a civil war in at least one case—and never succeeded. However, upon occasion, the Council deposed a sitting monarch, changed the succession or had someone other than the "rightful" successor crowned. In other periods they were under the ruler's thumb to one degree or another. Alliandre was somewhat under the Crown High Council's collective thumb, for they had removed her predecessors in one way or another, correctly as they saw it, and put her on the throne. They stood aside for a time because she handled the Prophet well, or at least kept his depredations to a minimum.

Crown of Maredo, The. A modest inn in Far Madding where Rand and his group (Min, Lan, Nynaeve and Alivia) stayed upon arrival in the city. Mistress Nalhera was the innkeeper. They roomed there while Rand attempted to track down the Asha'man who had tried to kill him in Cairhien.

Crown of Roses, The. Caemlyn's best inn, three stories high and built of white stone. Mistress Cinchonine was the innkeeper. The embassy led by Merana from the rebel Aes Sedai wishing to meet with Rand stayed at this inn and met with Alanna and Verin there.

Crown of Swords. *See* Laurel Crown of Illian

Crowning Stone, the. A stone used in the election of a Malkieri king; the Great Lords would place colored rods on it to indicate their choice.

Crystal Throne. The seat of the Empress at the Court of the Nine Moons in Seanchan. It was a great *ter'angreal* that caused anyone who approached it to feel immense awe and wonder. Of course, only the reigning monarch was ever allowed to use it. Its disposition was unknown after the chaos in Seanchan. The term could also be used for any throne on which the Empress sat.

Cuaindaigh Fords. The site of a battle in the Trolloc Wars, from Mat's enhanced memory.

Cuale. The innkeeper at The Defender of the Dragonwall in Cairhien, where Rand, Loial and Hurin stayed. He was plump and unctuous, and at first thought that Rand was an Aiel. He was very excited about all the invitations that Rand received, especially the last two.

Cuallin Dhen, Battle of. A famous battle in which Queen Modrellein of Andor established her bravery against the Tairens, seven hundred years before the Last Battle.

cuande, **tight bands of.** Moghedien's description of what she felt around her chest while she was in the vacuole.

Cuebiyarsande. An Ogier-built city in Aramaelle, one of the Ten Nations after the Breaking.

Cuellar. A man who sharpened knives at the Black Tower.

cuendillar **(heartstone).** A supposedly indestructible substance created during the Age of Legends. Any known force used in an attempt to break it, including the One Power, was absorbed, making *cuendillar* stronger. The method for making of *cuendillar* was lost for centuries, but was rediscovered shortly before the Last Battle.

cueran. A building material from the Age of Legends that made for spotless white, gleaming, sleek and sterile environments.

Cuhan, Culan. *See* Culan Cuhan

Culain. An Aldeshar general defeated by Artur Hawkwing. Mat remembered Hawkwing standing over him as Culain, saying that he fought well, and asking Culain to live with him in peace. Culain laughed in Hawkwing's face and died.

Culain's Hound. An average inn in the New City in Caemlyn where Verin, Alanna and the young women from the Two Rivers with channeling potential stayed. It was three-storied stone with a red tile roof, and Master Dilham was the innkeeper. Rand visited the two Aes Sedai there, and was bonded involuntarily by Alanna; his explosive response frightened the Two Rivers girls.

Culan Cuhan. A person or place that wept when Sammael unleashed the Shadow and earned his title as "Destroyer of Hope."

Culen, Lord. A Murandian nobleman who was a Hunter of the Horn. Culen spoke with a Mindean accent, and the Mindeans boasted that they had the worst tempers in Murandy. He was in Maerone with Lord Paers. Olver sat on Paers' horse, and Paers intended to punish Olver, which Culen found amusing. Mat disabled Paers with a shot to the groin with the butt of his spear, and when Culen attempted to draw his sword, Mat knocked Culen out and ordered their servant Padry to get them out of town.

Culhan Carand. An Andoran nobleman and husband of the High Seat, Lady Aemlyn. He was about 5'10" tall, and square-faced. Arathelle, Pelivar, Aemlyn and Culhan were among the nobles who confronted the rebel Aes Sedai on the ice near the Andor-Murandy border.

Cullen's Crossing. A place in Andor ten miles outside of Caemlyn. Adeleas had taken Ispan to a hut in Cullen's Crossing for questioning, and they were both murdered there.

Cully, Old. The feared leader of a circle of Darkfriends who worked for Jaichim Carridin. He was a gnarled beggar with one eye, no teeth and a habit of bathing only once in the year, whether he needed it or not.

Cumbar Hills. Hills somewhat south of Lugard. Egwene's rebel Aes Sedai passed this area on the way from Salidar to Tar Valon.

Cumere Powys. One of the Counsels of Far Madding. Pretty and serious, she stood 5'5½" tall. Along with Narvais, she escorted Cadsuane, Shalon and Harine to the palace while the others remained with Aleis to question Verin.

Cup, the. A constellation.

currency. After many centuries of trade, the standard terms for coins were the same in every land: crowns (the largest coin in size), marks and pennies. Crowns and marks could be minted of gold or silver, while pennies could be silver or copper, the last penny often called simply a copper. In different lands, however, these coins were of different sizes and weights. Even in one nation, coins of different sizes and weights were minted by different rulers. Because of trade, the coins of many nations could be found almost anywhere, and for that reason, bankers, moneylenders and merchants all used scales to determine the value of any given coin or coins.

The heaviest coins came from Andor and Tar Valon, and in those two places the relative values were: 10 copper pennies = 1 silver penny; 100 silver pennies = 1 silver mark; 10 silver marks = 1 silver crown; 10 silver crowns = 1 gold mark; 10 gold marks = 1 gold crown. By contrast, in Altara, where the larger coins contain less gold or silver, the relative values were: 10 copper pennies = 1 silver penny; 21 silver pennies = 1 silver mark; 20 silver marks = 1 silver crown; 20 silver crowns = 1 gold mark; 20 gold marks = 1 gold crown.

The only paper currency was "letters-of-rights," issued by bankers and guaranteeing to present a certain amount of gold or silver when the letter-of-rights was presented. Because of the long distances between cities, the length of time needed to travel from one to another, and the difficulties of transactions at long distance, a letter-of-rights might have been accepted at full value in a city near to the bank which issued it, but it might only have been accepted at a lower value in a city farther away. Generally, someone intending to be traveling for a long time would have carried one or more letters-of-rights to exchange for coin when needed. Letters-of-rights were usually accepted only by bankers or merchants, and would never have been used in shops.

Cutaris. A member of Ituralde's forces in Saldaea. He was a sturdy, long-limbed Domani who acted as a messenger between Ituralde and Durhem.

Cutren, Alamindra. *See* Alamindra Cutren

Cutter of the Shadow. In the Old Tongue, Shadar Nor; it was the name given to Latra Posae, the Aes Sedai who was the founder of the Fateful Concord that prevented any women from helping Lews Therin place the seals on the Dark One's prison.

cutworm. A pest found in the Two Rivers that attacked crops in the field.

Cycle of the Dragon, The. *Charal Drianaan te Calamon*, author unknown, from the Fourth Age.

Cynd. A slender Tairen woman who fought in the Last Battle. Mat, giving a demonstration of how to shape stakes for the palisade they were constructing on the Field of Merrilor, handed his axe to Cynd and told her to keep the stakes in line.

Cyndane. The Old Tongue word for "Last Chance." Cyndane had been Lanfear, but Moridin rescued her from the land of the Aelfinn and Eelfinn by killing her so the Dark One could transfer her to a new body, the name showing his displeasure and giving a reminder that it really was her last chance—a chance she might not have received had there been stronger women among the Black Ajah. Cyndane's physical appearance was very much at odds with Lanfear's, as if deliberately changed. Where she had been tall and slim, she became short and a bit on the voluptuous side. She had large eyes of deep sky blue, and waves of blond hair that was almost silver. She was still beautiful, but her face was quite different, with high cheekbones and chiseled features; she had the look of an ice-goddess, except that there was more than a hint of banked fires in her eyes. Her voice had become husky, throaty and sultry, in stark contrast to her ice-maiden appearance. Her body truly was young—mid-twenties at the oldest—not needing the Mask of Mirrors Lanfear had used to hide her matured ripeness. She was reduced in strength to 2/+11 by her experiences during captivity on the other side of the doorframe *ter'angreal* before being retrieved by Moridin; this reduction was sufficient to put anyone who thought she was Lanfear off the scent. She still loved Rand, but since he had failed her, she was more than willing to break him or kill him. Unfortunately for her, Moridin held her mindtrap, and she was on a tight leash. She did attempt to engage Rand's sympathies, but was unsuccessful. She then set her sights on Perrin, and helped him remove the dreamspike at the Black Tower. She later Compelled him to murder Moiraine, but Perrin was able to resist and instead killed Cyndane. *See also* Lanfear

Cyprien Melchor. One of the Counsels of Far Madding who met with Cadsuane's party when they arrived. She had protruding teeth.

Cyrendemar'naille. An Ogier-built city in Aridhol, one of the Ten Nations after the Breaking.

Cyril Wynn. The son of Murandians Susa and Jac Wynn. He was one of the children Moiraine investigated while looking for the infant Dragon Reborn.

D

Da'concion. The term Suroth used to refer to the Forsaken.

da'covale. A Seanchan term meaning "person who is owned," used to refer to their slaves. Being *da'covale* was hereditary; a child born to *covale* parents was itself *da'covale*, including the child of a mother who was *da'covale* and a father who was not *da'covale*—which was the reason most men did not lie with *da'covale* or used birth control if they did. If the father was *da'covale* and the mother not—a highly unusual circumstance—the child was free, since condition always followed that of the mother in Seanchan society. *Da'covale* could not own property of any sort, or have anything of their own, though owners would sometimes let them keep gifts or money. Anyone could own *da'covale*, not just the Blood. They could be bought and sold like horses. Manumission was possible, and in fact it was customary under some circumstances to manumit *da'covale* in one's will if he or she had served long or in a close capacity, in much the manner someone might leave a few trinkets or a sum of money to a longtime servant. This was not always done, nor necessarily desired by the *da'covale*, because the complexities of Seanchan life could mean that being freed brought a reduction in social standing. By law, one was required to make provision for the future of any *da'covale* freed, either by establishing a trust, or by seeing that the former *da'covale* had a way to earn a living, and to support a family if he or she had one. It was possible to be reduced to *da'covale* as well, by judicial sentence. Both flogging—and various other corporal punishments—and being made *da'covale* were punishments short of execution for various crimes. Many preferred execution to being made *da'covale*. Prisoners of war and those captured in rebellion were usually made *da'covale*. To a large degree, *da'covale* shared somewhat in the standing of their master or mistress, modified by his or her position with the household. A lesser lord or lady might defer to a high-ranking *da'covale* within the household of a High Lord or Lady, at least to a *so'jhin*, and that High Lord or Lady would show at least a degree of respect, and possibly deference, to a high-ranking *da'covale* of the Imperial household.

Da'shain Aiel. Old Tongue for "those dedicated to peace" and the name given to a pacifistic people in the Age of Legends sworn to a covenant that bound them to serve the Aes Sedai and uphold the "Way of the Leaf," a pacifistic code of honor. The Da'shain Aiel wore their hair short except for a tail in the back and usually dressed in a plain coat, breeches and soft, laced boots, usually in shades of brown or gray. During the War of Power and the Breaking, they did not betray their code by fighting. The Aes Sedai realized that the Da'shain would be slaughtered uselessly if they remained in the cities. They devised a great task worthy of the Da'shain: They were given precious *angreal* and *ter'angreal* and told to take them all to a place of safety, far away from Paaran Disen. With insane male Aes Sedai rampaging through the world, it was important to keep these powerful objects of the One Power out of their reach. The Da'shain Aiel set out, and after many tribulations and divisions among their ranks, founded Rhuidean in the Waste and evolved into what simply became known as the Aiel. *See also* Aiel, Jenn Aiel *and* Tuatha'an

da'tsang. Old Tongue for "despised one"; it was the name given to criminals among the Aiel. *See also* Aiel law

Dabei, Theodrin. *See* Theodrin Dabei

Dacan, Clan. An Atha'an Miere clan.

Dacan, Zerah. *See* Zerah Dacan

Dachen, Nisao. *See* Nisao Dachen

dactolk. A Seanchan game.

Dael al'Taron. A young Two Rivers man who joined Perrin's band battling Trollocs in the Two Rivers. He was killed in a Trolloc ambush.

Daelvin, Mistress. The innkeeper at The Golden Stag in Maerone, Cairhien. She was small and round, with gray hair worn in a wispy bun. She kept a cudgel under her skirts to use on men who were behaving badly.

Daera, Sallie. A code expression for Salidar.

Daerid Ondin. A Cairhienin soldier who had fought Andorans and brigands, as well as in the civil war. He was pale and slender with hard eyes, an oft-broken nose and three white scars crisscrossing his face. He joined the Band of the Red Hand, commanded the foot and was promoted to lieutenant-general. In the Last Battle, he fought alongside Talmanes, using the dragons.

Daerilla Raened. An Andoran noblewoman who was High Seat of House Raened. Her sigil was the Five Silver Stars. Plump and giggly, she opposed Morgase in the Succession, but was given a pardon. Daerilla was one of Gaebril's sycophants. Rand made use of her temporarily as a political tool. Daerilla fled after Rand reached an accommodation with Dyelin, and later supported Naean for the throne.

Daes Dae'mar. The Great Game, also known as the Game of Houses. It involved the use of misdirection and hidden meanings and motives, in word and deed, to gain power and status. Great value was given to subtlety, to aiming at one thing while seeming to aim at another, and to achieving ends with the least visible effort. It was developed by Cairhienin nobility, adapted from Aes Sedai intrigue, and spread throughout the southern nations.

Dafid Norley. A Cairhienin Asha'man Dedicated. He was short and thick-waisted with an open, inviting smile. He was part of Logain's faction, and was with Logain when Logain took Toveine. He bonded an unnamed Red.

Dag Coplin. 1) A Two Rivers boy whom Mat Cauthon tried to trick into believing that ghost dogs had been seen in Emond's Field. 2) An elderly man in Emond's

Field, possibly the grandfather of Dag Coplin 1. He did not wash his hair often and tried to pass off second-rate wool as first-rate. He accompanied Luc to tell the Whitecloaks that they were not welcome in Emond's Field.

Daganred. A Cairhienin noble House.

Daganred, Lord. A Cairhienin nobleman. He was about 5'7" tall, a quiet man with an air of sadness. Stripes ran down his coat to the waist. He wore the front of his head shaved and powdered after the fashion of Cairhienin soldiers; he fought in the Illian campaign. His son Meresin joined the Band of the Red Hand.

Daganred, Meresin *See* Meresin Daganred

Dagar, Masema. *See* Masema Dagar

Dagdara Finchey. An Andoran Aes Sedai of the Yellow Ajah publicly but of the Black Ajah in truth. She was part of the rebel contingent and had a strength level of 19(7). Born in 848 NE, she went to the White Tower in 863 NE. After spending seven years as a novice and five years as Accepted, she was raised to the shawl in 875 NE. She was about six feet tall, and very wide, with graying hair. It was said that Dagdara knew more of Healing than any two other Yellow sisters, but that was before Nynaeve developed the new Healing weaves. She was in the same range with Samitsu. Romanda wanted her as a Sitter in Salidar, but Magla insisted on Salita instead. Dagdara's name was on Verin's list of the Black Ajah.

Dagendra. An Aiel Maiden of the Spear who had a blocky build. She was guarding Rand when he went to Culain's Hound and was bonded by Alanna.

Daghain. A bridge town outside Tar Valon, on the bank of the Osendrelle Erinin, on the road to Shol Arbela and Fal Moran.

Dahan. A feast celebrated on the ninth day of the month of Saven, supposedly celebrating the final victory in the Trolloc Wars and freedom from the Shadow. Most historians believed the date was arbitrarily chosen.

Dai Shan. A Malkieri title meaning "Diademed Battle Lord." *See* Lan

daien. A type of dancer from the Age of Legends, characterized by a lush, sleek body. Osan'gar reflected on the fact that Aran'gar looked like a *daien* dancer when the latter received his new female body from the Dark One.

Daigan. A town outside and southwest of Far Madding across the Ikane Bridge.

Daigian Moseneillin. A Cairhienin Aes Sedai of the White Ajah, uncommitted to any contingent, with a strength level of 45(33), the lowest level at which a woman traditionally was accepted for the Tower to become Aes Sedai, though at even lower levels they were accepted long enough to be trained to the point of safety, some managing to rise to Accepted. Born in 907 NE, she went to the White Tower in 921 NE. After spending twenty-seven years as a novice and twenty-one years as Accepted, she was raised to the shawl in 969 NE. She spent longer as novice and as Accepted than anyone else in living memory. She was 5'2" tall, slightly plump and round-cheeked with pale skin. She had long black hair and always wore a silver chain in her hair, supporting a moonstone *kesiera*. A younger daughter of a minor Cairhien House entitled to wear four thin stripes of color on her bosom, she often wore Cairhienin clothes, except that she added slashes of white to the skirts for her Ajah. She was considered a fine logician. Daigian was extremely persistent and did not know the meaning of "quit." With a quiet, even meek, personality, at least around other Aes Sedai, she accepted the logic of her position utterly and knew that she would be the low woman in any meeting of Aes Sedai. She automatically assumed that if there were no servants about, she would perform those functions, making and serving tea and fetching things. Perhaps as a result, she insisted fully on the rights, prerogative and courtesies due Aes Sedai from others. She was one of the sisters who went to Cairhien after Rand was kidnapped, following Cadsuane Melaidhrin, and accompanied Cadsuane to Far Madding and Shadar Logoth. Daigian bonded Eben Hopwil soon after the attack on Rand in Cairhien and was devastated by Eben's death at Shadar Logoth. She was killed by Shaidar Haran when he freed Semirhage.

Dailin. 1) A Maiden of the Spear of the Nine Valleys Taardad Aiel, and a second-sister of Aviendha. She died in the fighting with the Myrddraal who were kidnapping Nynaeve, Elayne and Egwene when they were on their way to Tear. 2) A Wise One of the Shaido Aiel who had the ability to channel and a strength level of 17(5). She was about 5'7" tall, stocky and muscular, with wide shoulders. Her arms looked as if they belonged on a blacksmith. She was one of Sevanna's inner circle of plotters. She took part in (or at least was present at) the murder of Desaine, and accompanied Sevanna to the Aes Sedai camp the day she saw Rand beaten. Dailin went with Therava back to the Waste after the rout at Malden.

Dain Bornhald. A narrow-faced Taraboner Whitecloak officer who was the son of Geofram. He was in Baerlon when Moiraine and Rand and their party came there; Mat pulled a prank to splash him and his Whitecloak companions with mud. He and the other Whitecloaks tried to prevent the party from leaving Baerlon. He went with Valda to Tar Valon; there he learned from Byar of the death of his father. His primary goal became avenging his father, who Byar told him died because Perrin betrayed him. When Verin, Nynaeve, Elayne and Egwene neared Tar Valon, he tried to stop them from proceeding. He volunteered to take a half legion to the Two Rivers to meet Ordeith, though when he met him, he did not like or trust Ordeith. He took Mat's mother and sisters and the Luhhans prisoners to try to draw Rand or Perrin to the Two Rivers; Tam and Abell escaped. Dain was aware that Ordeith had killed the Aybara family, but allowed the deaths to be blamed on Trollocs, which had appeared in the Two Rivers.

Perrin arrived in Emond's Field and convinced the people to gather and fight the Trollocs on their own instead of relying on the Whitecloaks; he also rescued the prisoners. In the final Trolloc attack on Emond's Field, the Whitecloaks did not fight; Perrin ordered them out of the Two Rivers.

Dain returned to Amador and developed a drinking problem. He was appalled at Valda's rape of Morgase, and supported Galad when he challenged

Valda; he became a trusted aide to the new Lord Captain Commander. When they encountered Perrin, Dain wanted him punished for killing his father, but Perrin was cleared of that charge at trial. He still believed Perrin was a Darkfriend until Perrin and his army saved the Whitecloaks from a Trolloc attack. He killed Byar when Byar tried to kill Perrin. He later told Perrin that Ordeith had killed his family.

Dairaine Saighan. A high-ranking Cairhienin noblewoman taken *gai'shain* by the Shaido. She was slender with black hair that spilled to her waist in waves and a voice like crystal chimes. She curried favor with Sevanna by telling tales on her fellow *gai'shain* and was never chosen out as one of those who had failed to please. She shared a tent with Faile, and walked in when Faile, Alliandre and Maighdin were about to escape and realized that something was up. She tried to get away to tell Sevanna, but was bound and left with Bain and Chiad.

Daise Congar. A woman of Emond's Field. Twice as wide and a head taller than her husband, Wit, she was domineering and forceful, usually sounding as if she expected an argument and did not mean to put up with it. Daise had a mean streak. She became Wisdom of Emond's Field after Nynaeve's departure. When the Tinkers were attacked by Trollocs and came to Emond's Field, Daise at first did not want to let them in, but was shamed by Perrin into welcoming them. She participated in the defense of Emond's Field, and, with the rest of the Women's Circle, performed the marriage of Faile and Perrin.

Daishar. An Old Tongue word for "glory" and the name of Egwene's tall roan gelding.

Daiting, Stedding. A *stedding* located in the Spine of the World.

Dajenna, Sedore. *See* Sedore Dajenna

Dal Calain. A nation that arose after the Trolloc Wars.

Dal Eira Gate. The north gate in Ebou Dar.

Dal. An Ogier who was the son of Morel and the father of Haman.

Dalaine Ndaye. An Aes Sedai of the Gray Ajah who served as Amyrlin from 36 to 64 NE. Dalaine was a weak Amyrlin.

Dalar. An Ogier woman who spent ten years Outside the *stedding* with the Sea Folk. After her return to the *stedding*, she was an invalid.

Dalenshar. A region in Seanchan whose inhabitants were as black as coal. While Miraj was battling Rand's army, Miraj thought about Dalenshar while considering the named, honored regiments from different parts of Seanchan that were represented among his troops, including Dalenshar.

Dalevien. An Aes Sedai of the Brown Ajah and the loyalist contingent. Stocky with gray streaking her short dark hair, she was holding the shield on Leane the first time Egwene visited Leane in her cell in the White Tower, but appeared most interested in comparing the text of two books.

Dalfor, Benji. *See* Benji Dalfor

Dali. A *damane* belonging to Tuon who was part of Karede's group that searched for Tuon when she was missing. She had yellow hair and blue eyes, and was slightly plump, a little less so than her sister, Dani. She and her sister were the most experienced among Tuon's *damane*, hardly needing a *sul'dam*'s direction. She participated in the White Tower raid.

Dalisar, Ilyena Moerelle. Ilyena Sunhair's maiden name. *See* Ilyena Therin Moerelle

Dalresin Damodred. Moiraine's father and Laman's brother. He was 5'11" tall, with a gentle face and hair that was more gray than not, worn in a club at the back of his neck. He was a scholar, which earned the contempt of his brothers Moressin and Aldecain. When he took a scholar as his second wife instead of marrying to improve House Damodred's situation, their contempt increased. Dalresin died after Moiraine left for the White Tower.

Dalsande. An Ogier-built city in the nation of Essenia, one of the Ten Nations after the Breaking.

Dalthanes Annallin. A Cairhienin nobleman who supported Colavaere. He was summoned to the Seanchan campaign by Rand, and rode off north with Gregorin, Sunamon and lesser Cairhienin nobles in the final battle. His son Daricain was with the Band of the Red Hand.

Dalyn. 1) An alias used by Logain. 2) A Cairhienin armsman of Bertome Saighan, gap-toothed with seamed scars on both cheeks. Bertome was not sure if his name was Dalyn or Doile.

damane. Old Tongue for "the Leashed Ones," channeling women enslaved and controlled by Seanchan *sul'dam* with the use of *a'dam*. *Damane* were used in battle as well as for purposes of industry, such as building. Young women in Seanchan were tested annually for their ability to channel, and those found able immediately became *damane* and lost their rights as private citizens. When the Seanchan crossed the Aryth Ocean, captured Aes Sedai and wilders were forced into service as *damane*. However, because of the Three Oaths, Aes Sedai collared as *damane* could not use the One Power as a weapon.

Damara. A noble family of Tear. *See* Astoril Damara *and* Medore Damara

Damelien. A village in Andor which had three mills on a river that had gone almost dry. Elayne and her companions stayed there on their way to Caemlyn to claim the throne.

Damelle. An Ogier author who was daughter of Ala daughter of Soferra. Damelle wrote about the Ways, including the tale of a Waygate in the Blight that was destroyed by thirteen Aes Sedai using a *sa'angreal* five hundred years after the Breaking.

Damentanis, Jeorg. *See* Jeorg Damentanis

Damer Flinn. An Andoran Asha'man. Born in 942 NE, he was about 5'10" tall and of medium build, but very strong for his size. Grizzled and leathery with brown eyes, he had a limp, and retained only a thin fringe of white hair. Flinn was a soldier until he took a lance in his thigh; he couldn't grip a saddle properly after that, or even walk far. That was the fifteenth wound he had taken in near forty years in the Queen's Guards; fifteen that counted, anyway; in his book, it didn't count if he could walk or ride afterward. He had seen a lot of friends die in those forty years, and it was Healing that drew him to try the Black Tower. Flinn had been Healed by an Aes Sedai once, about 970 NE, and he found that the Asha'man Healing hurt compared to that. He was chosen out by Rand after Dumai's Wells and kept in Cairhien, where he accompanied Rand to see the Sea Folk. When Rand was wounded by Padan Fain, Flinn Healed him enough that he didn't die. He accompanied Rand to Illian and was raised to Asha'man after the invasion, in part because of his Healing skills, which were considerable. He fought in Rand's campaign against the Seanchan, and returned with him to Cairhien. After the attack on Rand there, he was uncertain of the safety of returning to the Black Tower and remained in Cairhien where he was persuaded to be bonded a Warder by Corele Hovian, one of Cadsuane's Aes Sedai. He was listed by Taim as a deserter. He Healed the three Aes Sedai—Irgain, Ronaille and Sashelle—who had been stilled at the battle of Dumai's Wells. He accompanied Cadsuane to Far Madding and helped to free Rand there. While Rand cleansed the taint, he linked with Corele and Sarene; they fought Demandred. He went to Algarin's estate, and then to Bandar Eban. Flinn aided in saving Maradon. In the Last Battle he fought near Shayol Ghul; his left arm was burned away by Graendal. He could Heal neither Rand nor Moridin when they came out of Shayol Ghul.

Damodred, House. A noble House of Cairhien. Its sign was the Tree and Crown. *See also* Aldecain, Anvaere, Barthanes, Caraline, Carewin, Dalresin, Galad (Galad-edrid), Innloine, Laman, Moiraine *and* Taringail Damodred

Damona Mountains. A mountain range between Altara and Murandy that was formed in the Breaking of the World.

Danabar. A mountainous region in Andor where Elayne had estates that contained alum deposits, enabling her to raise money to defend against others claiming the throne.

Dance of the Hawk and the Hummingbird, The. A text by Teven Aerwin that purported to set forth the proper conduct of men toward women and women toward men.

Dancers, The. Three identical hills in Altara that had this name when Londaren Cor had been the capital city of Eharon.

Dancing Bear, The. An inn in Lugard, Murandy. Siuan passed by this establishment while on the way to another inn.

Dancing Cartman, The. A gaudily painted inn that had fallen on hard times in Four Kings, Andor. Saml Hake was its perfidious innkeeper. Mat and Rand stayed and performed there on their way to Caemlyn. The Darkfriend Howal Gode tried to entice Rand to go over to the side of the Dark One there, and he and Mat were saved when a lightning bolt opened up the wall of the storeroom in which they were trapped, allowing their escape and killing many of Gode's men.

Dancing Goose, The. A raucous inn in Samara, Ghealdan. Nynaeve noted the inn while passing through Samara.

Daneen, Ludice. *See* Ludice Daneen

Danelle. An Aes Sedai of the Brown Ajah with a strength level of 17(5). Born in 899 NE, she went to the White Tower in 914 NE. After spending nine years as a novice and seven years as Accepted, she was raised to the shawl in 930 NE. Standing 5'5" tall, and slight of build, she had big blue eyes and often seemed distracted. Her instructors, as novice and as Accepted, said she could have learned faster except that she was always going off into a dream, so to speak. Her introspection meant that she never had close friends; she spent her time buried in books or thought or the task at hand. She could drift off in thought, into that dreaminess, in the middle of a conversation. She set off from the Tower immediately after gaining the shawl and had little contact with other sisters. Even as novice and Accepted she had been very much a loner, and never acquired a Warder. She spent long periods away, often out of contact completely for several years at a stretch, and was seldom in the Tower for more than a few months a time at widely spaced intervals. When Danelle returned to the Tower after years of absence early in 999 NE, she was actually Mesaana. The real Danelle had been squeezed for what was needed to impersonate her, and then killed. She did bear a close enough physical resemblance to Mesaana that, given Danelle's long absence and lack of friends, there was no need for much in the way of Illusion. *See also* Mesaana

Dani. A *damane* belonging to Tuon. She had yellow hair and blue eyes, and was slightly plump, a little more so than her sister, Dali. She and her sister were the most experienced among Tuon's *damane*, hardly needing a *sul'dam*'s direction. She was part of Karede's group that searched for Tuon when she was missing.

Danil. An infant boy born in the Murandian camp outside Tar Valon near the end of the Aiel War. His mother tried to con Moiraine out of coin to pay a Wise Woman, but Moiraine offered to Heal him, saying Aes Sedai Healing could be dangerous for an infant, and the mother acknowledged that she could pay.

Danine Candraed. An Andoran woman who was High Seat of an important House. She was known to be indecisive; when Morgase was trying to win the Lion Throne, she did not declare for anyone. She behaved the same way when Elayne was vying for the throne.

Dannil Lewin. A man of Two Rivers. He was Tell's brother, Ban al'Seen's cousin and Flann's nephew, and was a leader of the Two Rivers men under Perrin. He wore thick mustaches in the Taraboner style; otherwise, he looked much like his brother, a skinny beanpole with a pickaxe of a nose. He was older than Perrin, but not by much. Dannil was part of the original band that hunted Trollocs with Perrin. He followed Perrin to Caemlyn, Dumai's Wells, Cairhien, Ghealdan, Amadicia, Altara and Malden, trying to acquire polish along the way. In the Caemlyn portion of the Last Battle, he was second-in-command to Tam.

Danshu. A feast celebrated on the last day of the month of Nesan.

Dantora. A Sea Folk port in the Aile Jafar. Sailmistress Coine told Nynaeve that this was one of her destinations.

Danu. The last month of the year.

daori. The hair cut by one's *carneira* and woven into a cord. A Malkieri boy's hair was allowed to grow to the waist, but it was not cut at the shoulder when he was given the right to tie it back with the *hadori.* The older woman who took him as a lover, his first lover, would cut it at his shoulders, whether she took him before or after he attained the *hadori.* He would then weave it into a cord which he presented to her as a token of his obligations and ties to her. Thereafter, no Malkieri man would cut his hair shorter than his shoulders or let it grow much longer.

Dapple. A wolf who was the leader of a pack. She was close to black, with a lighter gray patch on her face, and was more willing to help humans than some of her pack. She was traveling with Elyas when Perrin and Egwene first met him, and traveled with the three until their encounter with the Whitecloaks. After Perrin was captured, Dapple let him know that help was coming and that Elyas was alive, though wounded.

Dar. A gate guard in Baerlon who was involved in letting Moiraine and her party out of Baerlon at night. When they started to leave, a Watchman who agreed to let them out called Arin and Dar to get out there and help him open the gate.

Dara. A cook's helper in the Stone of Tear whom Mat found just plump enough.

dara lily. A night-blooming lily from the Age of Legends.

darath. An animal from the Age of Legends. The darath was a dangerous creature in molt.

Darbinda. A name given to Min by Tuon; it was Old Tongue for "girl of pictures."

Darea Candwin. One of the girls from the Two Rivers with the spark who were being taken to Tar Valon by Verin and Alanna, whom Rand saw (and terrified) at Culain's Hound in Caemlyn. Darea was about fifteen, and the granddaughter of Eward, the cooper. She later joined the rebels in Salidar.

Darein. A village on the west bank of the Alindrelle Erinin, lying at the foot of the west bridge out of Tar Valon. A small, historic village, with small, red and brown brick houses and shops and stone-paved streets, Darein was burned during the Trolloc Wars, sacked by Artur Hawkwing, looted during the Hundred Years War and burned again during the Aiel War. Each time it was rebuilt. Verin, Egwene, Elayne, Nynaeve, Hurin and Mat were stopped there briefly by soldiers at a checkpoint on their way into Tar Valon. Later, negotiations between rebel and Tower Aes Sedai were held there at a table under a pavilion at the foot of the bridge.

Darelos den Turamon, Argirin. An Illianer nobleman who was a member of the Council of Nine.

Darengil. A Cairhienin noble family. *See* Selande *and* Arimon Darengil

Darenhold, Innina. *See* Innina Darenhold

Daria Gahand. The author of *Essays on Reason*, a book studied by Min.

Daricain Annallin. Nobleman of House Annallin, of Cairhien. His *con* was covered in small red and black squares. He was pale and slender with a long nose, a narrow face and the front of his head shaved. He escaped Cairhien, went to Rand in Eianrod and rode back to Cairhien with a message. He later joined the Band of the Red Hand, and he commanded the Sixth Banner of Horse, his title becoming Lieutenant Lord. His father Dalthanes, the head of his small House, was one of those who met with Colavaere.

Darin. A man of the Moshaine sept of the Shaido Aiel and the *Shae'en M'taal* society. He was the son of Maeric, the chief of the sept. Darin was left behind in Kinslayer's Dagger with the other Stone Dogs who were forming the rear guard when the sept used Sammael's *nar'baha* to create gateways.

Darith. A king in a story about a fallen House.

Dark, Heart of the. Another name for the Dark One.

Dark Hunt. Another name for the Wild Hunt.

Dark Lord of the Grave. A historical Aiel name for Dark One.

Dark One. The force of evil, imprisoned by his antithesis, the Creator, outside of time and creation, but whose influence reached the world when researchers drilled the Bore, and whose subsequent followers attempted to release him from his prison. He was also known as Bringer of Gales, *Caisen Hob,* Dark Lord of the Grave, Father of Lies, Father of Storm(s), Grassburner, Great Lord of the Dark, Heart of the Dark, Heartsbane, Heartfang, Leafblighter, Lighteater, Lord of the Grave, Lord of the Twilight, Old Grim, Old Hob, Shadow, Shai'tan, Shepherd of the Night, Sightblinder, Sightburner, Soulblinder, Soulsbane and Stormbringer.

Dark One's Eyes, the. A throw of five aces in a dice game.

Darkfriends. Nonchanneling humans who pledged themselves to the Dark One. Darkfriends could be found anywhere, and most were organized in cells. There were a few independents who were not connected with one of the cells, or perhaps were not accepted because of indiscretions or other concerns. There was no one overall command structure, though with the reappearance of the Forsaken certain Darkfriends were raised up. By and large, though, Darkfriends existed in self-contained organizations which might have numbered several hundred or several thousand, each with its own internal structure and hierarchy. There was a fiction that they were all one, but it was a fiction. These groups long contended against one another in various ways, with one group sometimes gaining ascendancy over another then losing it in yet another struggle, perhaps with a third group.

Most groups were not really known to one another, save through identification signs and symbols by which Darkfriends from various groups could recognize one another and display their rank. If someone displayed signals showing themselves to be of a higher rank than you, supposedly you were required to obey them even if they were of another organization. In truth, the cell-organization of each group made it possible to know that a stranger really was from your group; unless he or she was a member of your own cell, allegiance was a mystery. A king had to obey a beggar and a queen a groom, if the proper signals were displayed. Even an Aes Sedai was included in this, though in truth, any Darkfriend would be more comfortable giving his recognition signs to a king or queen than an Aes Sedai. Supposedly only other Darkfriends knew the signs, but it was widely believed among Darkfriends that some Aes Sedai who were not Black had learned some of them.

The heads of the various groups were considered of equal rank, as were any officers or officials within each, a matter which grated on the Black sisters, and especially on the Supreme Council. There were rarely meetings of these top-ranking Darkfriends, but when there was one, any joint decisions were reached by voting, with each casting between one and five votes depending on the supposed size and strength—not necessarily the same thing—of his or her group. Of course, these meetings were held with nearly everyone masked, hooded or disguised.

After the Breaking of the World, Black sisters (or the various groups that existed then, since there was no Black Ajah per se) certainly took the lead among Darkfriends, and if there was no real command structure, they provided the nearest equivalent. In fact, over the centuries they made numerous efforts to make their actual command an acknowledged reality. Some of these attempts came close, but all failed; the other groups fought back fiercely, and they were even more hidden than the Black Ajah—an Aes Sedai's face marked her as potentially one of the Black, but nothing marked out other Darkfriends. A good many sisters died from poison or a knife in the back. The last such attempt, several centuries before the Last Battle, ended badly, and in humiliating fashion, for the Black Ajah. For all of their command of the One Power, they found themselves forced into a position where they had to sue for peace and accept what they considered degrading terms. At a meeting of the top-ranking Darkfriends, the Black representatives (members of the then Supreme Council; they would not have trusted anyone else, though afterward, they may have wished they had) were forced to acknowledge that the Black Ajah was only equal to the other groups, to forswear any further attempts to seize control, and to renounce more than a single vote at any further meetings. This last reduced the Black to an equal status with the smallest and the weakest of the major organized groups. The Black Ajah did not, of course, in truth give over their belief in their own supremacy by right, but they were unable to effect any real claim to it.

It was considered an honor for a Darkfriend to be contacted by a Fade. A higher honor was to be summoned to Shayol Ghul, even if this did not involve being taken to the Pit of Doom, to the very presence of the Dark One, as it were. The highest honor for a Darkfriend, short of being granted immortality, was to be allowed to speak to, or more properly to be spoken to, by the Dark One himself. With the reemergence of the Chosen, an ancient honor came again, that of being contacted by one of the Chosen in person. This was accounted only a step below speaking to the Dark One, and equal to or perhaps above a visit to Shayol Ghul.

The Darkfriend Creed: "The Great Lord of the Dark is my Master, and most heartily do I serve him to the last shred of my very soul. Lo, my Master is death's Master. Asking nothing do I serve against the Day of his coming, yet do I serve in the sure and certain hope of life everlasting. Surely the faithful shall be exalted in the land, exalted above the unbelievers; exalted above thrones, yet do I serve humbly against the Day of his Return. Swift come the Day of Return. Swift come the Great Lord of the Dark to guide us and rule the world forever and ever."

Darkhounds. Shadowspawn created from lupine stock corrupted by the Dark One. While they resembled hounds in their basic shape, they were blacker than night and the size of ponies, weighing several hundred pounds each. They usually ran in packs of ten or twelve, although the tracks of a larger pack were once sighted. They made no mark on soft ground, but left prints in stone, and were frequently accompanied by the smell of burned sulfur. They would not usually venture out into the rain, but once they were on the trail rain failed to stop them. Once they were on the trail, they had to be confronted and defeated or the victim's death was inevitable. The only exception to this was when the victim could reach the other side of a river or stream, since Darkhounds would not cross flowing water, or so it was believed. Their blood and saliva were poison, and if either touched the skin, the victim would die slowly and in great pain. Darkhounds were known to wolves as Shadowbrothers. A hundred wolves could die trying to kill one Shadowbrother; if they failed, the Darkhound could eat the souls of those that were not quite dead and create more Darkhounds.

Darksbane, Raolin. *See* Raolin Darksbane

Darkwood. *See* Paerish Swar

Darl Coplin. An Emond's Field farmer, and a troublemaker. His brother was Hari; Darl was larger, but both had weasel-like faces and tight mouths. After the Winternight Trolloc attack, Darl was among those who confronted Moiraine. Bran thought that Darl had scrawled a Dragonfang on his door. Darl accompanied Luc to tell the Whitecloaks that they were not welcome in Emond's Field and was part of the group that tried to fight off a group of Trollocs that turned out to be Tinkers seeking shelter. Darl participated in the defense of Emond's Field and later joined Perrin's army.

Darlin Sisnera. A High Lord of Tear. He was about six feet tall, with short-cropped dark hair, blue eyes and an overlarge nose. He had a certain feeling toward the Lady Caraline Damodred, and Min saw that he would marry her, but not until after she led him a merry chase. He tried to rouse opposition to Rand in the countryside after the fall of the Stone and began an outright rebellion, gathering strength in Haddon Mirk. He went to Cairhien to meet with the rebel forces there. When Rand was visiting the rebel camp, a fog appeared and started killing people; Darlin and Caraline tried to escape it with Rand, Cadsuane, Min and others. Darlin carried Rand on his shoulders after Rand was wounded by Fain. In the wagon on the way back to the city, he and Caraline overheard Min tell Cadsuane what Galina had done to Rand. On reaching the city, he and Caraline went into hiding, neither entirely willingly, under the protection of Cadsuane at Lady Arilyn's palace. Dobraine freed the pair. Rand named Darlin Steward in Tear for the Dragon Reborn; Min saw that he would be the King of Tear, and when the rebels demanded it, he became king. Min also saw that he would die in bed and Caraline would survive him; as usual, she was correct. During the Last Battle, Darlin took over command of the battlefield at Thakan'dar when Ituralde, under Compulsion, was "relieved of duty." He held formation, keeping the Trollocs from entering the valley, until his tent was destroyed. He was found under the tent half dead, but recovered soon enough to attend the Dragon Reborn's funeral.

Darluna. A city in southern Arad Doman with twenty-foot walls. Rodel Ituralde ambushed a large Seanchan force there.

Darmovan. A nation that arose after the Trolloc Wars.

Darnella Shoran. The innkeeper at The Silver Swans of Heaven in Ebou Dar. She was skinny with gray hair worn rolled on the nape of her neck and a long jaw. She did not like for women and men to meet in her inn, and chided Bethamin when the Seeker sought her there.

Daronos, Magla. *See* Magla Daronos

Dart. Rodel Ituralde's white gelding.

darter. The smallest class of Sea Folk ship. Darters could be one- or two-masted and were under one hundred feet in length, sometimes as short as fifty feet. The mast or masts often seemed over-tall for the vessel's length, and sometimes were raked. Hull proportions, like those of the soarer, varied. They were very fast and agile; a lean darter could match the raker's 400 miles in twenty-four hours, but most could do no more than 300 to 350 miles in that time. Any vessel smaller than a darter was considered by the Sea Folk to be a boat.

Darter. The wide rivership owned by Captain Canin. Elayne, Egwene and Nynaeve traveled aboard it from above Jurene to Tear.

Daruo. A member of the Deathwatch Guards able to catch an arrow in flight with his bare hand, as he proved when saving Tuon's life.

Darvale, Mother. Wisdom of Runnien Crossing in Altara. She was lean and leathery with white hair. Luca had to make concessions to her and the Mayor before he was allowed to set up his show there. Mother Darvale married Leilwin and Domon.

Darvan. One of the two men seeking Elmindreda's hand in the story that Siuan and Min made up to account for Min's presence in the Tower; the other was Goemal.

Darvin. The clan chief of the Reyn Aiel after the Last Battle, seen in Aviendha's view of the future in Rhuidean.

Daryne Aiel. An Aiel clan; its chief was Mandelain.

Dashar Knob. A rocky outcrop with cliff walls on the Shienaran side of the River Mora, southeast of Polov Heights.

Dashiva, Corlan. *See* Corlan Dashiva

Daughter of the Night. The translation of Old Tongue name "Lanfear."

Daughter of the Nine Moons. The title for the member of the Seanchan royal family selected to be the next Empress; at the time of the Return, the title was held by Tuon.

Daughter-Heir. The title of the daughter who was the heir to the Queen of Andor.

Daughters of Silence. A secret group started in 794 NE by two Accepted who had been put out of the White Tower, and who over four years gathered and trained twenty-three other women who were able to learn to channel. Unfortunately, they hardly lived up to their name. They began quietly enough, but that didn't last. They were found out and punished by the White Tower. It was believed that all of the members were captured; certainly the two former Accepted were. The captives were displayed at every town and village on the way to Tar Valon, and at every village one of the prisoners was selected for public punishment, to drive home that that sort of activity was not permitted. The captives were birched in the White Tower before not only the assembled sisters, but all novices and Accepted; the followers were each birched once, the ringleaders both before the others and again after. The ringleaders were kept in the Tower for almost a year, worked hard at the dirtiest tasks until it was certain that the lesson had been taught sufficiently, and then put out again. The six followers who were eighteen years of age or younger were kept in the Tower as novices; Saerin Asnobar was the only one who managed to reach the shawl. The followers over eighteen were put to work alongside the ringleaders, and each was sent away when it was felt that she had learned better.

Dautry, Oren. A Westwood farmer who was Rand and Tam's nearest neighbor. He was lean and tall and a shameless borrower. He joined Perrin's army at Malden.

Dav al'Thone. An Emond's Field man who guarded Tam's tent at Merrilor.

Dav Ayellin. A friend of Mat's from Emond's Field. He and Mat competed to see who could get in the most trouble, except when they teamed up to cause trouble. The two caught a badger and planned to release it on the Green during the Bel Tine festivities. Dav helped Perrin defend Emond's Field. Later, with Ewin Finngar and Elam Dowtry, he ran off to see the world.

Daved Hanlon. An unsavory Andoran man. He was about 5'10" to 5'11" tall, and on the thin side of a medium build, with ropes of muscles, a hatchet face and elaborate manners. He could be rash and impetuous. Hanlon was born in 954 NE, although not under that name, in a village in western Andor not far from Baerlon. As a youth, he was forced to flee his village when he killed another youth in 970 NE. He hired on with a merchant's wagon train and became a guard about a year later. During his time as a guard, he killed three men in brawls, fought bandits and killed several suspected or supposed thieves. It was also during this time that he became a Darkfriend. By 973 NE, he had tired of being a merchant's guard and, seeking glory and gold, signed on with a mercenary company before his nineteenth nameday. His first work as a mercenary came when his company was taken in service by Naean Arawn during her opposition to Morgase in the Third War of Andoran Succession. When the Aiel War began in the late spring of 976 NE, Hanlon had been a mercenary for about three years. His company arrived in Cairhien after the Aiel had moved on, and he took part in the looting, rape and murder, as did many mercenaries. The same happened in several smaller cities that the Aiel had overrun during the war. Hanlon was present at the Blood Snow and gave good service there.

After the Aiel War, Hanlon continued as a mercenary, fighting in various wars and struggles between nobles in Cairhien, Murandy and Altara. In Cairhien he fought in the Reconciliation which put Galldrian Riatin on the Sun Throne. That was Hanlon's preferred kind of strife, skirmishes and minor battles, but never open civil war. His company switched sides several times. He also fought in wars between Illian and Tear and between Cairhien and Tear, on various sides, several times switching allegiance. He gained command of his own company of mercenaries in 989 NE.

Hanlon had an eye to the safety of his own hide—he would not stick around to fight to the last in a lost cause, certainly; in fact, he would be willing to sell out as soon as he decided his side would be the loser—but he was not a physical coward. He fought bravely in a number of battles, and had something of a reputation among mercenaries as a soldier, though he was certainly not a great captain by any stretch of the imagination. He was a leader in the rogue White Lions, raised by Lord Gaebril/Rahvin. After Gaebril's death, Hanlon led the White Lions, as mercenaries, into the employ of the Cairhienin rebels under Lord Toram Riatin. Many, perhaps most, of the White Lions died when a deadly fog descended on the rebel camp outside Cairhien while Rand was visiting, but Hanlon escaped and was ordered to report to the Lady Shiaine in Caemlyn. There he saw the murder of Jaichim Carridin, and also saw the mistreatment of Falion Bhoda, who was then given to him to use as he wished, a matter of punishment for her failure in Ebou Dar. Hanlon did not want an Aes Sedai angry with him and worked out a deal with her to fake relations and to share information. Shiaine asked how he would like to put his hands on a queen; he was eager. He signed with the Queen's Guards as a lieutenant using the name Doilin Mellar, claiming to have been a merchant's guard, mercenary and then a Hunter of the Horn. He claimed to have been a great admirer of Morgase and to have returned to Andor hoping to join the Guards, but said when he arrived he found that she was dead and the Guards a disheveled remnant filled with lackeys put there by Gaebril, the man who killed her. He arranged an assassination attempt on Elayne and then foiled it, thus gaining promotion to captain of her personal bodyguard. As captain of Elayne's bodyguard, he was entitled to three gold knots, to be worn on one shoulder, but he wore three on each shoulder, including three knots of actual gold soldered to each shoulder of his breastplate, so he might appear to the uninformed to outrank Birgitte. He led several sorties against the besieging opponents of Elayne, and thought those should have gained him favor with her. He was furious that they did not, just as he was furious at being called down by her in public. He pinched the bottoms of pretty Guardswomen and disparaged their abilities in taverns. After Hark was able to follow Hanlon visiting the house on Full Moon Street repeatedly, Elayne ordered his arrest and he was imprisoned. When Elayne impersonated a horrific Forsaken to question other prisoners to gather intelligence, Hanlon was freed by Jaq Lounalt and then stabbed Elayne, making away with the foxhead medallion during his escape. In the Last Battle, he killed Birgitte and was about to cut Elayne's twins out of her womb, when Birgitte returned as a Hero of the Horn and killed Hanlon.

Davian. A false Dragon who could channel. His last name was never discovered. Before his rise, Davian was a moderately common name for men; after, it was believed to have been almost five hundred years before anyone again gave that name to a child. The most reliable sources say that he declared himself on the second day of the Feast of Lights, the first day of the year of FY 351, and was allegedly killed on the first day of the Feast of Lights, the last day of FY 351. Some considered this suspicious symmetry even more suspect than that reported around Yurian Stonebow. Other sources, less often quoted and widely disputed for reasons that have nothing to do with Davian, placed his date of declaration in FY 350, as early as the spring, and the date of his demise as late as 352, well into fall or even early winter. No two of these disputed sources agreed on the dates, however. Although his cause swept through the nations like wildfire almost overnight, with riots in every major city, several of which were seized in his name, the rebellion lasted less than a year before he was assassinated by one of his advisors, who wanted to take his place. With Davian's death, the rebellion died out, yet in its short span it managed to seize control of two countries and involve most nations in riots as well as in sending troops against him.

Daviena. An Aiel Wise One with the ability to channel and a strength level of 30(18). She had green eyes and reddish-yellow hair. Following Dumai's Wells, she had to link with Losaine to shield Turanna, one of the sisters who had kidnapped Rand, after Verin finished questioning her.

Davies, Lord. An Andoran nobleman who sided with Jarid Sarand. Faced with Jarid's growing insanity, Lord Davies and Jarid's other men rebelled against Jarid, tied him to a tree and went off to fight in the Last Battle.

Davindra. A noblewoman in Ebou Dar. Beslan killed her husband, Nevin, in a duel and, per custom, had to pay a condolence call to Davindra. Tylin advised him to keep it short so that he wouldn't end up comforting her and having to marry her or kill her brothers.

Davram t'Ghaline Bashere. Lord of Bashere, Tyr and Sidona, Guardian of the

Blightborder, Defender of the Heartland, Marshal-General to Queen Tenobia of Saldaea, and her uncle and heir. He was considered one of the five great captains. The sign of House Bashere was three kingspennies on a field of blue. Davram was married to Deira; their children were Faile, Maedin and at least two other sons, who died. When Faile married, he became father-in-law to Perrin. Bashere was about 5'7" tall, and slender, with a hooked beak of a nose on a dark face and nearly black tilted eyes. Gray streaked his black hair and thick mustaches like down-curved horns wrapped around his wide mouth. His sword was ring-quilloned with a curved serpentine blade. He brought nine thousand Saldaean light cavalry to Caemlyn for Rand's use. Bashere's continued absence from Saldaea after being sent to find Taim put him at odds with his queen, Tenobia. He trained the Legion of the Dragon, many of whom came from Black Tower recruiting parties, and with Mat's help developed them into a sizable infantry force, fielding fifteen thousand of them in the Illianer campaign in addition to his crack Saldaean cavalry. Bashere was one of the leaders in Rand's campaign against the Seanchan, and was forced to tackle Rand when Rand lost control of *Callandor* and began killing their own troops. He continued to be of great help to Rand, negotiating with the Seanchan and addressing problems in Arad Doman. His army was part of the rescue of Ituralde's army at the battle of Maradon. In the Last Battle, Bashere commanded Elayne's troops as they faced the Shadowspawn in Andor and Cairhien. Graendal laid Compulsion on him so that he would be strategically ineffectual, which would have destroyed their army at the city of Cairhien. Tam and Talmanes knew that Bashere had been compromised, and he was removed from command. After Tenobia died in battle, Bashere became king of Saldaea, but he refused the crown, shaken by having his mind tampered with. He and his wife were later killed in battle at the Field of Merrilor.

Dawlin Armaghn. An Andoran man who was High Seat of a minor House that supported Naean. His sign was the Oak and Axe.

Dawlish. A family in Caemlyn. *See* Jaem *and* Melfane Dawlish

Dawn, Cliffs of. *See* Cliffs of Dawn

Dawn Runners. An Aiel warrior society, also known as *Rahien Sorei.*

Dawn Wind. Elenia Sarand's long-legged bay horse.

Dawn's Gate, Generals of. A group of seventeen generals who swore fealty to Lews Therin in the Age of Legends.

Dawnweave. Ituralde's white gelding, a warhorse that was a gift from one of his men. He died in the fighting at Maradon.

Dawtry, Jaim. *See* Jaim Dawtry

Day of Reflection. *See* High Chasaline

Day of Repentance. A feast observed in Cairhien on the day of the first half moon after High Chasaline. It was a day of especial somberness during which no food or drink was taken between sunrise and sunset. The first meal of the day was always bitter bread and water tinged with herbs to make it bitter as well.

It was believed to be in some way a reaction to the excesses of the Feast of Lights in Cairhien, though any connection was certainly never mentioned.

Day of Return. A day awaited by the Forsaken when the Dark One would be released from the Bore to rule the world.

Daylight. Faile's horse.

Dead Man's Breath, The. A tavern in Caemlyn, owned by Bernherd. Mat diced there and learned of the *gholam*'s activities in Caemlyn.

Dead Sea, the. A body of water off the west coast of the Blight, north of the Aryth Ocean and the peninsula formed by the Mountains of Dhoom.

Deain. The Aes Sedai inventor of the *a'dam* in Seanchan. She created it to curry favor with Luthair but was herself leashed; her screams were said to shake the Towers of Midnight.

Dealda Carridin. Jaichim Carridin's youngest sister. She was taken from her bridal feast by a Myrddraal to punish her brother for his failures.

Dealings with the Territory of Mayene, 500 to 750 of the New Era. A tattered leather volume that Egwene moved from a chair while visiting with Rand in Tear. Rand studied it and learned of the red doorframe *ter'angreal* in the Stone of Tear.

Deane Aryman. An Aes Sedai of the Blue Ajah. Born circa FY 920 in Salidar, Eharon, she went to the White Tower in FY 934. After spending five years as a novice and four years as Accepted, she was raised to the shawl in FY 943. She was raised to the Amyrlin Seat circa FY 992. At the time of her selection, she was the youngest woman who had ever been raised Amyrlin. She saved the White Tower from the damage done by Bonwhin in attempting to control Artur Hawkwing and was credited with convincing Souran Maravaile to raise the siege of Tar Valon (which had begun in FY 975) at Hawkwing's death. Deane restored the Tower's prestige, and it is believed that at the time of her death in FY 1084, in a fall from a horse, she was on the point of convincing the nobles warring over the remains of Hawkwing's empire to accept the leadership of the White Tower as means of restoring unity to the land.

Dearn. A family in the Two Rivers. *See* Athan Dearn *and* Laila Dearn Lewin

Death of Ten Thousand Tears. A particularly horrible method of execution for those who displeased the Empress of Seanchan.

Deathgates. The weave for a gateway, Spirit touched with Fire, with added touches of Earth, causing them to open and shut continuously, slicing anything in their path. Deathgates were useful in fighting Trollocs; if the gateway didn't slice the Trolloc, passing through the gateway would kill it.

deathshead mushroom. A poisonous mushroom.

deathswarm. Insects in the Blight that swarmed and killed.

Deathwatch Guard. The personal guard of the Seanchan Imperial Family, composed of both humans and Ogier. Each human member of the Deathwatch Guard was *da'covale*, marked with the ravens on his shoulders as property of the Crystal Throne. They took pride in that marking and flaunted their ravens. Ogier members were called Gardeners. Deathwatch armor was painted red-and-green, and they carried what appeared to be black tasseled spears and black-lacquered shields. The black was actually a very dark green, and the Guard themselves thought of it as green. They served as protectors of the Empress, the Empress's family and those appointed personal representatives of the Empress. The Deathwatch Guard were considered the elite troops, the best shock soldiers, in fact the best soldiers overall, in the Ever Victorious Army. They would kill or die with equal fervor, whichever was necessary.

Deborsha, Falin. An Ebou Dari merchant, possibly fictional, with whom Basel Gill claimed to be dealing when he was questioned by Galad.

Decume, Latra Posae. *See* Latra Posae Decume

Dedicated. The second rank of the Asha'man, above soldier and below full Asha'man. A Dedicated wore a silver sword on the collar of his black coat.

Dedric. A man of the Jaern Rift Codarra Aiel and the *Aethan Dor* society. He was about 6'4" tall and had yellow hair. He and Jalani acted as Rand's guards on a trip to visit Herid Fel. He had eyes for Jalani, and she for him.

Deepe Bhadar. An Andoran Asha'man with Ituralde in Maradon. When the city wall was destroyed by channelers, Deepe lost a leg but was Healed by Antail. He later fought alongside Lan at Tarwin's Gap in the Last Battle. He was killed by Taim.

Deeps, the. An area composed of hollows near the north wall of Canluum, Kandor. It was a seedy part of the city.

Defane, Kara. *See* Kara Defane

Defender of the Dragonwall, The. An inn in Cairhien where Rand, Loial and Hurin stayed when they arrived with the Horn of Valere. The inn's sign bore a crowned man with his foot on a red-haired man's chest and his sword at the man's throat. It was an upper-class inn, situated in a tall stone building. The innkeeper was Master Cuale. The inn was set afire when the Horn was stolen.

Defenders of the Light. Loial's name for the armies fighting the Shadow in the Last Battle.

Defenders of the Stone. *See* Tear

Deindre. An Aes Sedai at the time of the Breaking of the World. Deindre had the Talent of Foretelling; one of her Foretellings led to the creation of the Eye of the World. She and other Aes Sedai met with Someshta in the Hall of the Tower to give him a final task.

Deira ni Ghaline t'Bashere. Faile's mother and the wife of Davram. She was about 5'10" tall, three inches taller than her husband, and large to boot—not fat, but definitely a full-figured woman. She had long black hair with wings of white at the temples. She was attacked by two men in her tent near Caemlyn; she injured both, but was also injured herself. Deira rode with Davram in the Last Battle; both were killed.

Deirdru, Lady. Owner of the manor house in Altara, near King's Crossing, where Rand was to meet the Daughter of the Nine Moons.

Delana Mosalaine. A Shienaran Aes Sedai of the Gray Ajah publicly and of the Black Ajah in truth. Of the rebel contingent, she had a strength level of 18(6). Born in 950 NE, she went to the White Tower in 968 NE. After spending five years as a novice and five years as Accepted, she was raised to the shawl in 978 NE. Delana was 5'6" tall, and somewhat stout, with an ample bosom. Her voice was deep for a woman, though not masculine. Her hair was so light-colored that it was almost white, and her eyes pale and watery blue. She had a disconcerting habit of concentrating on her subject as if nothing else existed; her stare could make a person start thinking of all the things she had done wrong. Delana was held to be a good negotiator; it was said that people signed treaties just to make her stop staring at them.

Delana was friends with Siuan as novice and Accepted, in which time they overlapped but did not proceed in step. Siuan was the stronger in the Power then, and protected Delana; Delana really wanted to be Siuan's best friend, and was jealous of Moiraine. After she was raised, she was not well liked by novices or Accepted, which she did not understand, not realizing that she was impatient of their faults and let the women see it. She did not snap, or not often, but she did sigh. Delana was raised Sitter for the Gray in Salidar in 999 NE. Although she took on Halima/Aran'gar as a supposed secretary/companion, Delana was actually taking orders from her. Those orders had her using her position as a Sitter to be inconsistent in which faction she supported. The goal was to bring the rebels and the White Tower into open conflict, and battle if at all possible. The first to stand for Egwene as Amyrlin, her support for Egwene was unpredictable; she favored her on one thing and opposed on another. She seemed to flit from one faction to another. When she did support Egwene, she was sometimes overenthusiastic to a point where Egwene wished Delana wasn't supporting her. Her strongly voiced opinion was that Elaida was Black Ajah. Delana fled with Halima and her serving woman Miesa after Halima reported that Narishma was spilling the beans about a woman channeling *saidin*. Delana was killed when Rand balefired Natrin's Barrow.

Delarme, Cetalia. *See* Cetalia Delarme

Delarn. A Redarm in the Band of the Red Hand. Delarn accompanied Mat into Hinderstap; in the fighting he was pulled from his horse and wounded. Mat retrieved him and had Edesina Heal him. During the Last Battle, Delarn volunteered to return to Hinderstap and be trapped in its curse; he led the people of Hinderstap to fight.

Delora. A Wise One of the Shiande Aiel with the ability to channel and a strength level of 17(5). She was 5'7" tall, with reddish-gold hair and blue eyes. Her face was narrow and pinched, though, and no one would call her pretty. She looked to be no more than a year older than Rand, Perrin and Mat, but was in fact more than twenty-five years older. Her manner was very cold. Delora was one of the Wise Ones sent with Perrin to Ghealdan to keep an eye on

Seonid and Masuri. She went to battle against the Shaido at Malden. She assisted in the forging of *Mah'alleinir*, and went with Perrin's forces into the Last Battle.

Delovinde. A noble House of Cairhien. *See* Talmanes Delovinde

delving. A diagnostic procedure for checking health with the One Power, one of the Talents.

Delving. The Talent of finding ores.

Demain. A Kandori family. *See* Ines *and* Rahien Demain

Demalle, Parenia. *See* Parenia Demalle

Demandred. A Forsaken whose name in life was Barid Bel Medar. He used the name Bao the Wyld, when he was integrating into Sharan society and during the Last Battle. His strength level was ++2, rated against the *saidin/saidar* scale. Hawk-nosed and passably handsome, he was not someone to make women's hearts beat faster. He stood about 6'4" to 6'5" tall, just a little shorter than Rand. Barid Bel Medar was without doubt the second most acclaimed man of his lifetime during the Age of Legends, second only to Lews Therin Telamon. Like Lews Therin, he held many high public offices and wrote books on a wide array of subjects that were both critical and popular successes. It was his misfortune that Lews Therin consistently had greater successes in higher offices, and that Lews Therin's books achieved more success. Barid Bel Medar wanted to be the best, the greatest, the most powerful, and fully believed he had every right to be. Except for this blind spot about his "right," which he felt stolen by Lews Therin, he was very intelligent, though he did have a tendency to believe what he wanted to believe. He was not an easy man to frighten or to manipulate, as many discovered over the years to their very deep regret. He liked women and sex but didn't let lust rule him. He had two reasons for going over to the Shadow: one was his hatred of Lews Therin and his belief that Lews Therin had robbed him of the glory and acclaim that was rightfully his, while the other was a cold calculation that the Shadow was the more likely victor.

When they awoke in the Third Age, Demandred, Semirhage and Mesaana became a sort of team, though they moved against one another given a chance.

Demandred rescued Taim from the Aes Sedai and offered him a chance to go over to the Shadow. With the knowledge that refusal meant death, Taim didn't hesitate.

Demandred, in *Tel'aran'rhiod*, saw Elayne pledge on the Lion Throne to bond Rand, but misunderstood and thought it was a pledge of revenge against Rand for her mother's death and perhaps his conquest of Andor.

As Bao he exploited Sharan prophecy and became their leader in the Last Battle against Mat's troops, convinced that no one but Lews Therin could be such a worthy opponent. After killing Gawyn, defeating Logain, and severely wounding Galad in single combat, he died at the hands of Lan Mandragoran.

Demasiellin, Nelavaire. *See* Nelavaire Demasiellin

Demetre Marcolin. The First Captain of the Companions of Illian. He was a commoner who rose through the ranks. Lantern-jawed and clean-shaven, he had dark, deep-set eyes and an impassive face and stood about 5'10" to 5'11" tall. At the behest of the Council of Nine he brought the Companions to Rand as King of Illian. Marcolin had served under Tam al'Thor when Tam was Second Captain of the Companions, but what he thought of Rand al'Thor as King of Illian, he did not let on. He was surprised to find himself in agreement with Rosana, a Tairen, about the fact that Rand could be killed by one arrow and was taking a foolish risk in battle. He was unhappy about going into battle against the Seanchan with only six thousand men; he did not understand what the Asha'man could do. In the Last Battle, attached to Egwene's army on the Kandori plains, Marcolin was killed when the Sharans came through gateways and slaughtered many of Egwene's troops.

Demira Eriff. A Domani Aes Sedai of the Brown Ajah and the rebel contingent, with a strength level of 18(6). Born in 930 NE, she went to the White Tower in 947 NE. After spending nine years as a novice and eight years as Accepted, she was raised to the shawl in 964 NE. Her Warder was Stevan Gedarien. Standing 5'10" tall, she had coppery skin, and was gracefully beautiful. She wore Domani dresses and was constantly surprised and somewhat irritated to find men looking at her—because their gazes attracted unwanted attention; not because of any dislike of men—and she constantly said she must stop wearing the clinging, barely opaque Domani dresses, but she had had the same copied for years because it was easy. Her real attention was elsewhere.

Demira was a member of the rebel embassy to Rand in Caemlyn; she approved of his starting a school. While in Caemlyn, Demira planned to meet with her eyes-and-ears, Milam Harnder, the Second Librarian of the Royal Library of Caemlyn. He did not show, and Demira was attacked and nearly killed by a group of men dressed as Aiel; they were actually Whitecloaks corrupted by Padan Fain. Demira and the other members of the embassy then went to Rand to demand that he lift his restrictions prohibiting Aes Sedai from entering the Inner City without permission, limiting the number who could visit him to three, and forbidding them from channeling when with him, but he rebuffed them. Kiruna then delegated Demira, along with Kairen Stang, Valinde Nathenos and Berenicia Morsad to escort the Two Rivers girls to Salidar.

den Balgar, Mattin Stepaneos. *See* Mattin Stepaneos den Balgar

den Lushenos, Gregorin Panar. *See* Gregorin Panar den Lushenos

Dena. A young Cairhienin woman who wanted to be the first female gleeman. She was pretty, with fair skin and dark hair. Thom was her lover; after he spent time with Rand and appeared to be playing the Game of Houses, Dena was murdered by Galldrian's men. In retribution, Thom killed Galldrian.

Denal, Master. An Ebou Dari man whom Derys wanted to marry. The Kinswoman was forced to act as a maid, for penance.

Denezel. The innkeeper of The Happy Throng in Caemlyn. Tall, with a lean face and a shaved head, he commissioned a picture of Rand to hang in the common room of his inn.

Denharad. A Cairhienin who served as Lady Ailil's lance-captain. A pale little man, he took part in the attack against the Seanchan. After Anaiyella's horse master was killed, Denharad took over command of her men as well as Ailil's.

Denhold. A cavalry captain fighting under Bryne in the Last Battle.

Denhuir. A village east of the Black Hills on the Maradon Road, above the headwaters of the Antaeo and the Luan. It was the location where Mazrim Taim was freed from the Aes Sedai, supposedly with help from his followers, but really by Demandred.

Deni Colford. A woman who was a member of Elayne's Queen's Guards; she was the only Andoran among the first eight of Elayne's guard. About 5'6" tall, she had a placid face, wide shoulders, strong arms, dark hair liberally streaked with gray and calm blue eyes. Deni was a former bouncer in a tavern for wagon drivers in Low Caemlyn, a very unusual job for a woman. At first she did not know how to use her sword, but she was quite adept with a pace-long, brass-studded cudgel; she had lessons and did improve with the sword. Deni had no concept of fighting fair. She was interested in a man in the Queen's Guard. After Mellar's capture, Deni was one of those who beat him severely.

Dennel. A dragon captain in the Band of the Red Hand. He helped Talmanes retrieve the dragons in Caemlyn, and helped later with their repair.

Denton. A Cairhienin nobleman taken *gai'shain* by the Shaido. After he was freed, he refused to resume his normal station and acted as Perrin's serving man in the absence of Lamgwin.

Deoan. A man who served under Tam al'Thor in the Last Battle. He was from Deven Ride and had served in the Andoran army. Tam had Deoan lead half of the Two Rivers men against Trollocs.

Deosin. A Murandian family. *See* Eadwin *and* Saera Deosin

der'morat. A phrase used by the Seanchan, placed before the name of an animal; it meant "trainer" and/or "handler" of the animal. For instance, a *der'morat'raken* was a trainer of *raken*, and a *der'sul'dam* was a trainer of *sul'dam*, a *sul'dam* in charge of other *sul'dam* and their *damane*.

Derah din Selaan Rising Wave. The Sailmistress of the soarer *White Spray*, where Rand met with the Sea Folk delegations Derah brought up the Erinin to Andor and Cairhien. She wore four small rings in each ear and one in the left side of her nose, with a fine gold chain supporting a row of tiny medallions. She was younger than Harine, her clan Wavemistress. Derah departed Cairhien after Rand left, heading downriver toward the gathering of Sea Folk ships at Tear and carrying word of the agreement made by Harine din Togara.

Deranbar. The capital city of Jaramide, one of the Ten Nations after the Breaking. It lay on the site of Maradon.

Dermid Ajala. A Tairen blacksmith who gave Perrin a hammer as repayment for work done in his smithy. He had graying hair, blue eyes and thick arms and shoulders.

Dermon. An ancient male Jenn Aiel. He was gaunt, white-haired and blue-eyed. At the sept chief meeting at Rhuidean, he spoke for the Jenn.

Derne. The square-faced captain of the *Swift*. Mat and Thom traveled on his ship from Aringill to Tear when they were chasing Comar.

Derowin. A Cairhienin boy who was a childhood friend of Toram Riatin. He rode one of Toram's horses without permission; Toram pushed him down the stairs and broke his back.

Derry. A soldier with the Band of the Red Hand who was a victim of the *gholam*. It was suspected that the *gholam* questioned him before killing him.

Deryl. An Ebou Dari guard at the ring seller's stand Mat visited. He was one-eyed and very tall, with a long cudgel studded with nail-heads propped between his massive knees. The ring seller called for Deryl to get the greasepot, and Deryl looked as if he did not know what a greasepot was.

Derys Nermala. A Kin in Ebou Dar who was serving as a maid in penance for wanting to marry Master Denal. Her strength level was 41(29); she could have tested for Aes Sedai, but she was not strong enough to make a gateway of any size whatsoever. Born in 911 NE, she went to the White Tower in 926 NE, where she was ten years a novice. Being a discipline problem, she was not allowed to test for Accepted. Her offenses had to do with men; the third time she was caught with a man, she was put out. Kirin Melway was the Amyrlin Seat while she was there. Derys was slender and pretty, except for a sullen expression. She went to Caemlyn with Elayne and her group; there Derys found Mirane's favorite doll, which led to Vandene's realization that the Kin were being murdered.

Desaine. A Wise One of the Shaido Aiel. She went with Sevanna and Therava to visit the loyalist Aes Sedai under Galina and Coiren before they kidnapped Rand. Desaine spoke against Sevanna being made a Wise One since she had not been to Rhuidean; she also thought that as the widow of two clan chiefs, Sevanna might be bad luck. Desaine felt that the best way to deal with Rand al'Thor was to slip a knife between his ribs. Sevanna had her killed in a way that had to have been done with the Power in order to rouse the Shaido against the Aes Sedai holding Rand.

Desala Nevanche. A Cairhienin Aes Sedai of the Red Ajah and the loyalist contingent. She was beautiful, with large dark eyes and a voice like chimes. She had an unfortunate temper; the surest way to make her give it free rein was to harm or threaten a child. Desala despised wilders and purely hated women who falsely claimed to be Aes Sedai. She liked dancing and was known to dance any number of men off their feet in a night. Desala and Melare questioned Leane the night she was captured; Desala beat her. Desala was one of the five Reds who accompanied Pevara to the Black Tower with the intention of bonding Asha'man. She was Turned to the Shadow by Taim and his group.

Desandre Alraed. A Ghealdanin Aes Sedai of the Yellow Ajah and the loyalist contingent, with a strength level of 15(3). Before being raised Aes Sedai, she spent six years as a novice and seven as Accepted. About 5'5" tall, she was willowy, with brown hair and large brown eyes. Part of the expedition to the White Tower, she was captured and bonded by an Asha'man. As one of the two strongest sisters captured by the Asha'man, she commanded the Aes Sedai group as much as the Asha'man allowed.

Desartin. A lord in Murandy who was deservedly overthrown by a group of farmers.

Desautel. An Asha'man Dedicated who was big as a blacksmith. At Logain's behest, he looked for and located Sakarnen, Demandred's *sa'angreal*.

Deselle Aybara. One of Perrin's younger sisters. She was plump; at twelve years of age, she was killed by Fain.

Desora. A Maiden of the Musara sept of the Reyn Aiel. Golden-haired and blue-eyed, she always hid her smiles behind her hand. Desora accompanied Rand and Taim to the farm and was later killed in an apparent Whitecloak ambush in Caemlyn. Rand added her name to the list of women who had died for him.

Devaille. A major city in the Age of Legends.

Deven Ride. The first village south of Emond's Field in the Two Rivers on the Old Road. Rows of thatch-roofed houses surrounded a green and a pond fed by a spring that was walled around with stone. The inn at the head of the green, The Goose and Pipe, was roofed with thatch, too. Deven Ride was the same size as Emond's Field. The Village Council of Emond's Field sent men here to watch for trouble. An apprentice Wisdom here died of channeling sickness. Wil al'Seen, cousin of the al'Seen clan, was from Deven Ride, and in a wolf dream, Perrin visited the village to check for Trollocs. Men from Deven Ride helped to defend Emond's Field from Trollocs.

Devore, Cathal. *See* Cathal Devore

Devore Zarbayan. A Saldaean Bannerwoman of Elayne's Guardswomen in Caemlyn. She was slim and cool-eyed, her eyes dark and tilted.

Deyeniye, dyu ninte concion ca'lyet ye. A phrase in the Old Tongue meaning "Majesty, by your summons do I come."

Dha'vol. One of the Trolloc bands; its symbol was a horned skull.

Dhael. An Aiel Maiden of the Spear. Dhael helped rescue Nynaeve, Elayne and Egwene from brigands and Myrddraal.

Dhagon, River. A river flowing west from the northern reaches of the Mountains of Mist to meet the River Akuum east of Bandar Eban.

Dhai'mon. A Trolloc tribe; its symbol was an iron fist.

Dhallin Forest. A location in Ghealdan where major battles were fought against Logain, when he was a false Dragon.

Dhana. A *to'raken* that Mat desperately flew on to Shayol Ghul. Her rider was injured and her wing struck by an arrow; they crashed.

Dhearic. A man of the Two Spires sept of the Reyn Aiel and the *Duadhe Mahdi'in* who was clan chief of the Reyn. He was 6'5" tall, weighed about 250 pounds and had blue eyes, a prominent nose and lighter streaks in his golden hair. He was sent to Tear, and took part in the invasion of Illian. He was contemptuous of the Tairens and Cairhienin, who he said refused to listen and heard only the wind.

Dhjin'nen. A Trolloc tribe; its symbol was a skull cloven by a scythe-curved sword.

Dhoom, Mountains of. A mountain range running east-west, north of the Borderlands.

Dhoran, Kumira. *See* Kumira Dhoran

Dhowlan. A nation that arose after the Trolloc Wars.

Dhulaine, Lady Arilyn. *See* Arilyn Dhulaine

Dhurran. A breed of large draft horses from a region or town in Ghealdan.

Diadem of the First. A crown bearing a golden eagle in flight; it was worn by the First of Mayene.

Diademed Battle Lord of the Malkieri. *See* Lan

Dianatkhah, Nikiol. A former king of Saldaea who had a drinking problem.

Dilham, Master. Innkeeper of Culain's Hound in Caemlyn. He was bulky, with three chins. After Rand came in, was bonded by Alanna and scared the girls from the Two Rivers, Dilham fell to his knees, but soon recovered enough to ask Verin if he could tell people that the Dragon Reborn patronized his inn.

Dill, Mistress. A round innkeeper in Harlon Bridge, Andor. Elayne and her party stayed with her on the way to Caemlyn from the Kin farm outside Ebou Dar, after using the Bowl of the Winds, evading the Seanchan army. Mistress Dill was extremely pleased to have a full inn in bad weather, so pleased that she curtsied at everyone.

Dimana Corrand. A Kin and a member of the Knitting Circle in Ebou Dar. She had bright blue eyes and red hair with streaks of white. Although her true age was 323, she appeared to be well into or just past her middle years, on the edge of being called old. Her strength level was 46(34); she would not have been allowed to test for Aes Sedai, nor was she strong enough to make a gateway of any size whatsoever. Born in 677 NE, she grew up in a village in the Black Hills, which she sometimes joked was as isolated as the storied Seleisin. She went to the White Tower in 694 NE, where she was three years a novice before being put out because she could not become Aes Sedai. Cemaile Sorenthaine was the Amyrlin at the time. When the Seanchan invaded Ebou Dar, she was a prosperous seamstress with a number of other seamstresses working for her, catering to the wealthier merchants and mid-rank nobles. Dimana traveled to Caemlyn with Elayne. She led the *damane* Marille through the palace gardens and encountered Gawyn with a Bloodknife.

Dimir Faral. A soldier in the Children of the Light. He was in Fain's group of Whitecloaks in the Two Rivers. Faral was the one renegade Whitecloak ambushing Rand in Cairhien that Rand did not hang, instead sending him to Niall with a message that Rand would hang Niall for what had happened.

Diryk. The second-eldest son of Queen Ethenielle and Brys of Kandor. He was born in 971 NE and died in 979 NE, along with his father, supposedly in an accidental fall which also claimed Iselle Arrel. He was actually a victim of the male channeler pogrom, though that was not widely known.

Djevik K'Shar. Trolloc for "The Dying Ground," it was the Trolloc name for the Aiel Waste.

do Avriny a'Roihan, Elaida. *See* Elaida do Avriny a'Roihan

Do Miere A'vron. An Old Tongue phrase meaning "The Watchers over the Waves." It was the name of a group believing that the armies Artur Hawkwing sent across the Aryth Ocean would one day return, and so they kept watch from the town of Falme on Toman Head. This event took place with the arrival of the Seanchan; the Seanchan, however, felt that they had watched for the wrong thing, and had forgotten when they should have been remembering. As punishment, they put the First Watcher in a cage hanging from one of the Towers of the Watchers; when he died, they picked another watcher for the cage, and repeated the process until they themselves were driven from Falme.

Do'in Toldara te, Songs of the Last Age, Quarto Nine: The Legend of the Dragon. Composed by Boanne, Songmistress at Taralan.

Dobraine Taborwin. A Cairhienin nobleman who was High Seat of his House. His *con* was two white diamonds on blue. He was 5'9" tall, with deep-set dark eyes and leathery skin, and was one of the first of the older men to shave the front of his long, mostly gray hair. The blue and white stripes on his dark coat ran well below his waist. Dobraine was both shrewd and intelligent, and he kept his word. He would maneuver for personal advantage where he could, but he was loyal to Rand in his fashion, not only because he saw Rand as too strong to oppose, but also because he believed in the Prophecies. In addition, he believed that Rand would not claim the Sun Throne and that it would go to a Cairhienin. He was willing to accept Elayne Trakand as queen of Andor; his only qualm was that she should have been Elayne Damodred and that Taringail should not have let Morgase give the children to her House. Like all the other Cairhienin nobles—and most commoners—he considered the notion of noble marrying commoner to be bizarre if not obscene. Dobraine took five hundred of his personal liegemen with Perrin to rescue Rand from the Tower Aes Sedai at Dumai's Wells. Rand named him Steward of Cairhien for the Dragon Reborn. He was attacked in his chamber by robbers and was thought dead; Samitsu pulled him through. Rand sent him to Bandar Eban to secure order there; he presented Rand with a secure city and was then sent back to Tear.

Dobser. An Asha'man who was fond of wine and not very bright. Taim Turned him to the Shadow; he kept his love of wine and his intelligence did not increase, making it easy for Emarin to elicit information from him.

Doesine Alwain. A Cairhienin Aes Sedai of the Yellow Ajah and the loyalist contingent, with a strength level of 16(4). Born in 867 NE to a family of cutlers especially well known for their scissors, she went to the White Tower in 882 NE. After spending six years as a novice and eight years as Accepted, she was raised to the shawl in 896 NE. Standing 5'5" tall, she was boyishly slim; her face was like that of a pretty, mischievous boy. Her very large dark eyes seemed even darker because of her paleness. A light of naughtiness shone in her eyes sometimes. She dressed elegantly, but when irritated often spiked her talk with casual curses.

Doesine was born with the spark and found by an Aes Sedai very shortly after she first, unconsciously, touched *saidar* on her own. The sister knew Doesine could channel as soon as she met her, but Doesine didn't know what she had done, didn't believe the sister, and didn't want to go to the White Tower. She went, of course—bound hand and foot most of the way and gagged for the last part of it. Doesine was known to tell this story on herself to novices, to show them their circumstances were not so bad as hers. She held a record of sorts, though not one publicized: Doesine actually tried to run away three times, twice making it out of the Tower grounds, once reaching one of the bridges. Needless to say, given that the Tower wanted novices to believe that the punishment for running away was so severe that a runaway would never think of trying again—and indeed, that was the case for nearly all of them, and those who thought about it almost never worked up the nerve to actually try a second time—given that, it was hardly surprising that Doesine's record was kept quiet. In truth, on her third and last try, the one where she reached the bridges, she saw two Aes Sedai, was overcome with panic that they were hunting for her and ran back to the Tower, where she turned herself in. The two sisters knew nothing about her, and in fact her absence from the Tower hadn't yet been noted. The mitigation of her returning on her own meant her punishment was lessened, though the fact of a third offense meant that was from a rather fierce base. Still, she was so grateful for the lessening that she actually thanked the Mistress of Novices afterward, to that woman's great astonishment.

In 981 NE Doesine was raised to Sitter in the Hall. It was rare for a sister to be chosen as a Sitter at such a young age; her choice was an indication of her political astuteness as well as the Ajah's regard for her intelligence and capabilities. She stood to depose Siuan in the truncated Hall arranged by Elaida. Doesine was one of the half dozen Sitters to whom Elaida doled out penances of Labor. In her case, it was working in the laundry. For that alone, if no other reason, she wanted to see Elaida replaced. When Doesine strayed too near the Red Ajah quarters, she was roughed up. Doesine, Saerin, Talene and Yukiri confronted Seaine and Pevara about their secret meetings; after Saerin worked out that they were seeking the Black Ajah, all reswore their oaths and declared that they were not Black Ajah, with the exception of Talene, who was Black Ajah. As the only one with the ability to work the Chair of Remorse, Doesine used it to torture Talene and get more information. The five sisters continued to work together until Verin's notebook revealed all of the Black Ajah. Doesine went on to fight in the Last Battle, where she was killed.

dogfennel. A long weed with a feathery brown tip.

dogweed. A plant that was given as a tea, despite tasting terrible. It was considered a cure for moping.

dogwort. A medicinal herb for knitting flesh.

Doilaine Barmellin. A Cairhienin nobleman. He was about 5'8" tall and slender, languid and quite foppish in his manners, for a Cairhienin, anyway. He was not a fool, though, and wore almost as many stripes as Semaradrid, to below the waist. He wore the front of his head shaved and powdered after the fashion of Cairhienin soldiers. He fought in the Illian campaign.

Doilan. A man of the Shaido Aiel who was taken *gai'shain* when the Shaido were defeated at Cairhien. He served breakfast in Amys' tent.

Doile. An armsman of Bertome Saighan, gap-toothed with seamed scars on both cheeks. Bertome was not sure if his name was Dalyn or Doile.

Doilin Mellar. *See* Daved Hanlon

Doinal, Cera. *See* Cera Doinal

Doirellin. A Cairhienin Child of the Light. He was nearly as wide as he was tall, there was barely an ounce of fat on him, and he could put walnuts between all of his fingers and crack them by clenching his fists. He had a high voice. After Galad's duel with Valda, Doirellin agreed that it was permitted to ally with Aes Sedai in order to fight the Dark One.

Doirellin, Lirene. *See* Lirene Doirellin

Doirlon Hills. Forested hills located in northeast Illian, just off the rolling Plains of Maredo. Lord Brend (Sammael) established hillforts there against Rand's invasion force.

Doirmanes. A slender Cairhienin nobleman taken *gai'shain* by the Shaido. He was young and pretty, but very skittish, having a habit of biting his lip nervously. Faile was convinced that if he learned of people swearing fealty to her, he would tell Sevanna immediately, so he would need to be killed.

Dolera Mantear. A queen of Andor who ascended to the Lion Throne on the death of her mother at 78 in 944 NE. She was Mordrellen's mother.

Domai. A sept of the Shaido Aiel.

Domanche, Rasoria. *See* Rasoria Domanche

Domani. Of or from Arad Doman.

Domani Wench's Kiss, The. An inn in Lugard. Its sign bore a coppery-skinned woman, bare to the waist, with her lips puckered. Siuan passed this place while on her way to another inn.

Dome of Truth. The center of Whitecloak power and bureaucracy in the Fortress of Light in Amador, Amadicia, before they were driven out by the Seanchan. The exterior was pure white; on the inside gold leaf cast down the light of a thousand hanging lamps. Glistening thick white columns ringed the chamber. The dome itself stretched a hundred paces across unsupported and rose fifty paces at its peak. It contained a simple white marble dais on the white marble floor; the Lord Captain Commander stood on the dais to address the assembled Children.

Domeille. An Aiel Maiden of the Spear who helped bathe Rand before he went to meet the Sea Folk in Cairhien. She was lean with gray hair and a thrusting chin. Domeille felt that Rand was not pretty enough to do without a scar to set off what beauty he had.

Domination Band. Semirhage's name for the male *a'dam*.

Dominion, Nine Rods of. *See* Nine Rods of Dominion

Domon, Bayle. *See* Bayle Domon

Donalo Sandomere. A Tairen Dedicated Asha'man. He had a creased, leathery face and an oiled beard cut to a point in imitation of a Tairen noble. Sometimes he attempted the languid pose he thought a noble would use. His receding hairline gave him a very high forehead above his dark eyes, and what black hair he had, like his beard, was heavily streaked with gray. He wore a garnet in his left ear. Donalo was present when Rand went to bestow the sword and Dragon pins. When the Aes Sedai tried to take the Black Tower, he bonded Ayako Norsoni, a White. Toveine saw him waiting outside Logain's house at the Black Tower. He used farmer's phrasings in his speech and had the Talent of reading residues. Donalo was raised to full Asha'man and accompanied Rand to the meeting with the fake Daughter of the Nine Moons. His arm was injured there, and Nynaeve Healed him. Taim turned Sandomere to the Shadow; he was captured in Stedding Sholoon by Androl and his allies, including some elderly Ogier.

Donavelle, Mashera. *See* Mashera Donavelle

Donel do Morny a'Lordeine. A Murandian lord who was one of the nobles from Murandy and Andor to confront the rebel Aes Sedai on the ice in Murandy, near the Andoran border. He was about 5'10" tall, with a medium build, black hair, narrow brown eyes and curled mustaches, which he sometimes twisted. He wore more lace than most women.

Dongal. A soldier in the Band of the Red Hand. He served under Mandevwin in one of the attacks against the Seanchan; he and Madwin went up the south slope of a hill.

Doni. An urchin in Tear who, along with his friend Com, talked to Rand about the steamwagon. Rand gave each of them a gold coin. Min looked after them with a miserable expression indicating that she had seen something sad in their future.

Doniella Alievin. An Aes Sedai of the Brown Ajah who served as Amyrlin from 306 to 332 NE. Doniella was a quiet Amyrlin, not particularly strong, but not in the control of the Hall, either; her benign neglect did leave the Hall pretty much in control of the Tower. Doniella quite voluntarily resigned as the Amyrlin Seat in order to spend more time on her studies; she was a Dreamer who made much-discussed notes on the Prophecies of the Dragon. She spent the next thirty-one years studying happily, but she was not allowed to return to the White Tower, and she was strongly discouraged from letting anyone know that she had been the Amyrlin Seat. She died in 363 NE.

Donjel. A scout with Ituralde's army. His voice was hoarse, as someone had tried to hang him when he was young. He was stout with iron-gray short-cropped hair and a dark leather patch over his missing right eye. Before battles, Ituralde often gave Donjel a packet to carry to Ituralde's wife if he died.

Doomseer. A title that Tuon gave Min.

Dorailla. A Wise One of the Shaido Aiel with the ability to channel and a strength level of 15(3). She was 5'7½" tall. She fought at Dumai's Wells alongside Sevanna, where she was knocked down and dazed by the near miss of a lightning strike.

Doraille, Javindhra. *See* Javindhra Doraille

Doraise Mesianos. An Aes Sedai of the Brown Ajah and the loyalist contingent. She had a plump chin. Doraise was one of those named by Elaida as adhering to the law when she announced the discovery of illegally possessed *angreal*, implying that Doraise was one of those—along with Kiyoshi and Farellien—who turned in Josaine and Adelorna, the pair who were birched. Like the other two, Doraise received a horse as a reward. Elaida acted at Alviarin's urging; Alviarin was trying to cause dissent in the Tower. Doraise's Warder was a heavyset Shienaran with a round face and a dark topknot.

Doraisin, Berowin. *See* Berowin Doraisin

Doral Barran. The Wisdom in Emond's Field prior to Nynaeve al'Meara. She was white-haired and frail, but still clear-eyed and straight-backed. She apprenticed Nynaeve after her then-apprentice died of some sickness even Mistress Barran could not cure. Nynaeve was newly orphaned, and many people thought Doral should have sent her to her relatives in the country after her mother died, and taken on someone years older. Doral switched Mat when he opened a firework.

Doreille Torghin. A queen of Aridhol who signed the Compact of the Ten Nations. She was also a poet.

Dorele. A young Sea Folk woman on *Wavedancer*. She was slender with only one ring in each ear. When she brought tea to Elayne, Nynaeve, Jorin and Coine she was topless, and as punishment was set to clean the bilges because they weren't out of sight of land.

Dorelle Caromon. An Ogier-built city in Eharon, one of the Ten Nations after the Breaking. Illian later occupied the same site.

Dorelmin, Silene. The best seamstress in Chachin, Kandor. She was slim with a haughty air and a cool voice. Moiraine had Silene make dresses for her.

Doressin Chuliandred. A Cairhienin lord, High Seat of a moderate House, who supported Colavaere for the Cairhienin throne, and later was made to join Rand's army fighting against the Seanchan. He was about 5'9" tall, and bony, and kept the front of his head shaved and powdered. Because he had supported Colavaere, he thought that Rand meant for him to die. Bertome, Doressin's childhood friend, thought that Doressin had become unhinged. Doressin was the husband of Alaine and brother of Meneril.

Dorile din Eiran Long Feather. The Windfinder on *Windrunner*, thus Windfinder to Malin din Toral Breaking Wave, Wavemistress of Clan Somarin, who doubled as Sailmistress on the *Windrunner*. Dorile's strength level was 19(7). She was a slender, handsome woman who wore only four earrings in each ear, and fewer medallions on her chain than did Malin din Toral. She went to Caemlyn with Elayne's group and left Caemlyn with Zaida. She rode poorly; in Ebou Dar, two people had to help boost her into the saddle while a third held the horse's head.

Dorindha. 1) An Aiel woman of the Jindo sept of the Taardad Aiel and *Far Dareis Mai* who won the first forfeit when Mat played Maiden's Kiss. She also was one of the scouts who reported the arrival of the peddlers in the Waste. She was red-haired and about Egwene's age. 2) An Aiel woman married to Bael, clan chief of the Goshien. She was the roofmistress of Smoke Springs Hold and first-sister to Melaine. Dorindha was a solid, motherly woman, much nearer handsome than pretty, with creases at the corners of her blue eyes and much white in her pale red hair. Her manner was quietly commanding—usually, at least; she could make gestures upon occasion that seemed quite flamboyant, though she usually made even those in a casual, quiet manner.

As a roofmistress, Dorindha held a position of considerable power and respect—in some ways above and in some below a Wise One—but a good part of her command was her personality, not her position. Melaine's deference might have been because Dorindha was the senior sister-wife and the roofmistress, but not wholly. Deira Bashere's obvious respect, and a deference which surprised Deira herself, came from Dorindha's intelligence, perspicacity and personality.

Her relationship with Melaine grew very close after Melaine married Bael; it was a combination of close sisters and best friends. Dorindha gave Bael sons, but no daughters; she and Melaine knew he would very much like to have daughters, and they were very pleased with Min's viewing regarding Melaine's pregnancy.

Dorine, Jurith. Right Hand to the Queen of Almoren, and the author of *Commentaries on the Prophecies of the Dragon* in 742 AB, the Third Age.

Dorje, Anath. Tuon's Truthspeaker, or *Soe'feia*; she was actually Semirhage in disguise. *See* Semirhage

Dorlain. A family that lived on one of Morgase's estates in Andor.

Dorlain, Maighdin. Morgase's alias while on the lam.

Dorlan. A small hamlet east of the bridge towns outside Tar Valon. There were fifteen slate-roofed houses there, each with a cow barn behind it. The village supplied cheese to Tar Valon. Its mayor was Garon Burlow. After the debacle at Dumai's Wells, Elaida sent Covarla Baldene and the sisters who returned with her to Dorlan; the Younglings, having been denied entry to Tar Valon, went there as well. Since there was no inn in the village, the sisters stayed with residents, and the Younglings in the cow barns. Narenwin Barda, Tarna Feir and Katerine Alruddin also stayed there for a time.

Dormaile, Ilain. *See* Ilain Dormaile

Dormin. A stocky Cairhienin bootmaker who was *gai'shain* to the Shaido at Malden. He swore fealty to Faile.

Dorn, Lamgwin. *See* Lamgwin Dorn

dornat. A hunting animal from the Age of Legends, recalled by Graendal.

Dosera. A Wise One of the Shaido Aiel. She fought at Dumai's Wells for Sevanna and was killed by a wolf.

dosun. A term used in Bandar Eban for the head housekeeper of an establishment.

Dovarna, Norine. *See* Norine Dovarna

Dovie'andi se tovya sagain. Old Tongue for "It's time to roll the dice"; it was the motto of the Band of the Red Hand.

Dovienya. Old Tongue for "luck."

Doweel, Jara. *See* Jara Doweel

Dowtry clan. A family from Emond's Field. *See* Bar, Buel, Elam *and* Jonneth Dowtry

Dragand, Suana. *See* Suana Dragand

Draghkar. A creature of the Dark One, made originally by twisting human stock. A Draghkar appeared to be a large man with bat-like wings, too-pale skin and too-large eyes. The Draghkar's song, a crooning, could draw its prey to it, suppressing the victim's will. There was a saying: "The kiss of the Draghkar is death." It did not bite, but its kiss consumed first the soul of its victim, and then his life. The wind of its wings felt slimy, and one flying close overhead could make horses scream and rear.

Dragon banner. The banner of Lews Therin Telamon, flown during the War of the Shadow. It was found at the site of the Eye of the World, and Moiraine gave it to Rand. It was long and white, neither woven nor painted nor dyed. On it was a figure like a serpent scaled in scarlet and gold, golden-maned with eyes like the sun and five golden-clawed toes on each foot. A stirring of the banner in the wind made the figure seem to move and live, the scales glittering like precious gems and metals. The Dragon banner, as well as the Banner of Light or al'Thor's Banner, became associated with the Dragon Reborn. *See also* al'Thor's Banner

Dragon, false. A man who falsely claimed to be the Dragon Reborn. There had been many throughout history. Some began wars that involved many nations. Most were unable to channel, but some could. All, however, disappeared, were captured, or were killed without fulfilling any of the Prophecies of the Dragon.

Six false Dragons were generally considered the most powerful and the most nearly successful. Historically, stretching back some two thousand years prior to Rand's ascension, these men were Raolin Darksbane, Yurian Stonebow, Davian (last name unknown), Guaire Amalasan, Logain Ablar and Mazrim Taim.

In fact, in the three thousand years following the Breaking there were other men who matched their successes, but their histories could only be found in the secret records of the White Tower. As they were forgotten by history, the White Tower, not wanting to publicize false Dragons, let them fade into obscurity.

Dragon, Legion of the. *See* Legion of the Dragon

Dragon, People of the. *See* People of the Dragon

Dragon, Prophecies of the. *See* Prophecies of the Dragon

Dragon Reborn. According to prophecy and legend the Dragon would be born again at mankind's greatest hour of need to battle the Dark One and save the world. This was not something people looked forward to, both because the prophecies said the Dragon Reborn would bring a new Breaking to the world, and because Lews Therin Kinslayer, the Dragon, was a name to make men shudder, even more than three thousand years after his death.

Dragon Reborn, The. A book by Loial son of Arent son of Halan of Stedding Shangtai.

Dragon Scepter. A term used by the Maidens for the two-foot length of a Seanchan spear that Rand carried. Semirhage destroyed the spear when she burned off Rand's hand, which was holding the spear.

Dragon, the. 1) The name by which Lews Therin Telamon was known during the War of the Shadow. In the madness which overtook all male Aes Sedai, Lews Therin killed every living person who carried any of his blood, as well as everyone he loved, thus earning the name Kinslayer. The sayings "taken by the Dragon" or "possessed of the Dragon" indicated that someone was endangering those around him or threatening them, especially if without cause. 2) The Aiel name for the constellation known by wetlanders as the Snake.

Dragon's Fang. A stylized mark, usually black, in the shape of a teardrop balanced on its point. Scrawled on a door or a house, it was an accusation of evil against the residents.

Dragon's Peace, the. A treaty created by Rand to stop the nations from warring with each other after the Last Battle.

Dragonmount. A gigantic mountain near the River Erinin. After slaying all whom he loved, Lews Therin Telamon was given a moment of sanity. In his grief, he Traveled to a deserted area and destroyed himself with a great blast of the One Power, raising a huge volcanic mountain many miles high. It also created a large island in a nearby river. The mountain came to be known as Dragonmount and the island became the city of Tar Valon. Prophecy said that the Dragon Reborn would be born on Dragonmount.

dragons. The name Aludra gave to her powerful new weapons capable of firing explosive shells over long distances, causing extensive damage to the enemy. The dragons were used to great effect in the Last Battle.

dragons' eggs. The name given to the round explosive shells fired by dragons.

Dragonsworn. A term used for those sworn to the Dragon Reborn. These groups began appearing after the battle at Falme. They were at first disparate groups, even small armies, that formed in many countries, sometimes confronting local military forces. Many of these groups were sincere, and joined in fighting enemies of the Dragon Reborn; others were made up of brigands, who terrorized local populations. Their reputation was further soiled by Whitecloak intervention—Carridin created bands of Dragonsworn composed of a few incognito Whitecloaks at the core, with ruffians filling their ranks, which committed many atrocities. The Dragonsworn became associated with the Prophet Masema, who at the height of his movement had gathered ten to twelve thousand in Ghealdan, virtually taking over that country. After Masema agreed to help Perrin, most of these Dragonsworn were killed during Perrin's campaign against the Shaido at Malden.

Dragonwall. A north-south-oriented mountain range separating the Aiel Waste from the populated lands to the west.

Drapaneos, Kiril. *See* Kiril Drapaneos

Dreadbane. A Borderlander title for one who slayed a Myrddraal.

Dreadlords. Those men and women who, able to channel the One Power, went over to the Shadow during the Trolloc Wars, acting as generals over armies of Trollocs, Myrddraal and Darkfriends. They were occasionally confused with the Forsaken by the less well-educated.

Dreamer. A person with the Talent to foretell events by having and interpreting true dreams; some were able to enter *Tel'aran'rhiod*. According to the Wise Ones, dream interpretation was not straightforward; dreams told only one possible future, usually the most likely future. Dreams were often conveyed in images, allegories, or puns; consequently, the Dreamer needed training in interpreting the Dream. *See also* Talents

dreamshard. A world created by a powerful Dreamer or dreamwalker, distinct from *Tel'aran'rhiod*.

dreamspike. A *ter'angreal* that prevented Traveling.

dreamwalker. The Aiel term for one able to enter *Tel'aran'rhiod*; a verb, to dreamwalk, was also used. Aes Sedai sometimes used the term to refer to Dreamers, but rarely. Channeling was not necessary to dreamwalk. Aiel Wise Ones were especially good at dreamwalking, even though it was rare among them, because their survival had depended on it—when they needed to find water or find a new hold in the Waste, they used need, a technique to find what was vital or required while in *Tel'aran'rhiod* for that purpose. Before Egwene, there had not been a dreamwalker in the White Tower in a thousand years, according to Moiraine, or five hundred years, according to Bair. In dreamwalking, the dreamwalker entered *Tel'aran'rhiod* fully; whatever happened there to the dreamwalker was sustained in the waking world as well, including death.

Dromand, Nuhel. *See* Nuhel Dromand

Drowned Lands. A huge, treacherous saltwater swamp between the Dragonwall and Mayene. This miasmal landscape, choked with foliage and grasses, supported a multitude of fauna, including many dangerous creatures such as the dreaded hooded vipers.

Duadhe Mahdi'in. An Aiel warrior society; the name was Old Tongue for "Water Seekers."

Dubaris, Meashan. A member of the Domani Council of Merchants. She was killed by a mob.

duckberry. A plant whose fruit was bitter or sour when ripe.

Duhara Basaheen. A Domani Aes Sedai of the Red Ajah publicly and of the Black Ajah in truth. Of the loyalist contingent, she had a strength level of 23(11). Born in 764 NE, she went to the White Tower in 779 NE. After spending twelve years as a novice and nine years as Accepted, she was raised to the shawl in 800 NE and raised Sitter in 929 NE, serving until 953 NE. Duhara was Keeper of the Chronicles for Sierin Vayu from 979 to 984 NE, and was raised Sitter again in 999 NE to replace Teslyn Baradon.

She was 5'7½" tall, and slim, with coppery skin, large dark eyes and a long slender neck. She moved gracefully, but stood almost rigidly straight. She looked at everyone as if she were wondering what wrongdoing they had been up to. Basically she was meaner than a snake, though only her mouth gave any outward hint. During the execution portion of the male channeler pogrom, she participated eagerly. Her involvement was discovered, and she received a stiff penance. There was speculation that she might have been involved in Sierin Vayu's death, but she was unlikely to have been involved, despite being Red, as the Black had been called off the pogrom in 983 NE when Ishamael came into the world again. She stood to depose Siuan, one of only eleven needed to give the greater consensus under the circumstances. Elaida thought Duhara was firmly in her pocket, but Duhara chafed. Elaida sent her to Caemlyn in 1000 NE to act as an advisor to Elayne while she was seeking the throne; Elayne did not cooperate. Duhara was coopted by Graendal and killed by Aviendha in the Last Battle.

Dulain, Lord. A young Murandian nobleman who the Tower thought could truly unify Murandy, which caused the Amyrlin Siuan to make Gareth Bryne back down over border raids. He was killed by an Andoran sheepfarmer who put an arrow through him on a sheep raid.

Dumai's Wells. A watering hole more than halfway from Cairhien to Tar Valon, four days from Alianelle Spring. The oasis consisted of three stone wells in a small copse. It was the site of a battle after Aes Sedai had kidnapped Rand. A large contingent of Shaido Aiel attacked the Aes Sedai in an attempt to acquire Rand themselves, but Perrin's rescue forces joined by Asha'man arrived on the scene and won the day; however, there was great loss of life.

Dumera Alman. An Aes Sedai who lived at the time of the formation of the White Tower.

Dunsinin. The legendary female lover of Rogosh Eagle-eye.

dur Ahmid, Toma. The man who developed the Toman Calendar after the Breaking.

Dura, Tervail. *See* Tervail Dura

Duram Laddel Cham. Be'lal's name during the Age of Legends.

Duranda Tharne. The innkeeper at The Good Night's Ride in Lugard, and an agent of the Blue Ajah. She was a tall, heavyset woman with dark eyes, a thrusting chin and a hard mouth; she wore tight silk dresses, and had a brassy personality. Her curls were a shade of red that nature never made. She had already been a Blue agent when Siuan took over the network, and had married daughters she thought were older than Siuan, whom she did not recognize. Duranda referred to Siuan as an old buzzard. When Siuan approached her, she embarrassed Siuan but gave her the code name "Sallie Daera." She told Siuan to tell Aeldene that she was still loyal.

Durnham. A member of the King's Guard in Bandar Eban who became a beggar. Under the influence of the Dragon Reborn, he pulled himself together and was named commander of the city under its steward, Lord Iralin.

Durhem. A cavalry leader in Ituralde's forces in Saldaea.

Durrent. An officer in the Younglings who became a Warder after the reunion of the Tower.

Duster. Tylee Khirgan's horse.

Dusty Wheel, The. An inn in Caemlyn where the windows were always dirty. Hatch was its innkeeper. It was also known as the Rumor Wheel because it was the best place in Caemlyn to listen to gossip. Most of the rumors were untrue, but its patrons enjoyed discussing them.

Dyelin Taravin. High Seat of House Taravin in Andor; her House symbol was the Owl and Oak. She was about 5'6" tall, with golden hair going gray and blue eyes. Dyelin was Morgase's cousin and her nearest female relative aside from Elayne; had Morgase and Elayne both died without issue, Dyelin would have been next in line for the Lion Throne. Some people thought that she should take the throne after Morgase was presumed dead, because they worried about Elayne being Aes Sedai or because they disliked Morgase. Dyelin refused to accept prodding that she should take the throne. She and three other nobles— Pendar, Ellorien and Luan—met with Rand, when Rand told them he wanted Elayne on the Andoran throne. After Elayne returned to Caemlyn, Dyelin was a staunch supporter of Elayne's claim to the throne, going so far as to meet with many of the noble Houses of Andor to gain their support for Elayne, and publishing her support for her cousin. Dyelin was severely wounded protecting Elayne when Elayne was fed forkroot tea and attacked in the Royal Palace, requiring Healing from Nynaeve. Dyelin and Birgitte did not get on well, but they were still able to work together on Elayne's behalf. Dyelin personally led a force of troops against Arymilla's forces who were attacking Caemlyn. She was part of Elayne's army in the Last Battle.

Dyfelle, Alind. *See* Alind Dyfelle

Dyrele. The wife of Maeric, sept chief of the Moshaine Shaido. Her eyes were green. After the Moshaine used Sammael's *nar'baha* and found enemy clans coming at them, Maeric told her to prepare to put on the white. She was taken *gai'shain* by one of the septs that crossed the Plains of Maredo to Illian.

E

Eadwin. Verin's sweetheart before she went to the White Tower.

Eadwin Deosin. A Murandian man who was on Moiraine's list as the father of a possible Dragon Reborn. His wife was Saera.

Eadwina. Verin's *nom de guerre* in Far Madding.

Each Castle. A biography that Min studied.

Eadyth. An Aes Sedai of the Blue Ajah. She served as a Sitter for the Blue and First Selector when Moiraine and Siuan were raised to the shawl.

Eagan Padros. An Illianer who led a group of soldiers following Lord Brend. He had a long runny nose, a narrow face and dark eyes, but was brighter than he looked. When told he and his men must lay down their arms or join Rand, he chose to join Rand. He later tried to kill Rand with a crossbow, and was in turn killed by Asha'man.

Eagle's Reach. A fort in Coremanda, in the Splintered Hills. Doreille was thought to have written many of her best poems there.

Ealsin. Perrin's unmarried great aunt. She had a sharp nose and sharper eye for discovering what everyone around her was up to. She was killed by Fain, along with much of the rest of the Aybara family.

Eamon Valda. A high-ranking officer of the Children of the Light. He was a blademaster. His primary goal was self-aggrandizement, though he professed to be—and perhaps believed he was—a model Child of the Light. He hated Aes Sedai, considering them all Darkfriends or dupes of Darkfriends, and in his book, a dupe was just as guilty as anyone else. If he had had his way, he would have killed every Aes Sedai, razed Tar Valon and the Tower and salted the ground to remind people of the horror that had been there. He commanded Whitecloaks in the vicinity of Tar Valon, then brought soldiers back to Amador at Niall's order. There he entered into a conspiracy with Rhadam Asunawa, the High Inquisitor, which resulted in the assassination of Niall by Abdel Omerna and Omerna's death at Valda's hands. Valda became Lord Captain Commander and faced down Asunawa over Morgase; Asunawa supported someone else for Lord Captain Commander until Valda revealed that other Lords Captain in the Fortress of Light supported him personally—since he had brought half a legion inside the Fortress walls. He allowed Asunawa to have Morgase for Questioning. After a time, he offered Morgase to make it stop if she slept with him, which she did. He rode out to take on the Prophet the day before the Seanchan invaded Amador. Valda eventually took what he considered a pragmatic view of the Seanchan. At first he fought them as invaders, but their far greater numbers and their use of *damane* in battle made them very hard to match. They were humans, not Trollocs, and no more likely to be Darkfriends than anyone else. Most important of all, in a way, they collared women who could channel; that wasn't quite as good as killing them, but then again, using them—making them pay for their sins while alive, in a way—was perhaps even better. Valda didn't find it that hard to convince himself to make an agreement. He was killed in a duel with Galad after Galad challenged Valda over his treatment of Morgase.

Earth. One of the Five Powers. *See* Five Powers

Earth Singing. The Talent of controlling movements of the earth. It could be used to cause or prevent earthquakes or avalanches, among other things.

Earwin. A soldier of the Children of the Light. He was a big man with gray eyes and a long mustache. Bornhald commanded him and then sent him to the Questioners. He, Wuan and Questioners attacked a village on Almoth Plain and hanged thirty people, some of them children.

Easar Togita. The King of Shienar and High Seat of House Togita. His sign was a white hart. His nickname was "the Lion of Kabila," for a battle he won against Trollocs at very heavy odds. He was born in 940 NE and married in 960 NE; his wife died in 989 NE. He was said by many to still be grieving her death many years later. Easar wrote poetry for her, though he hardly looked a poet. He had sons old enough by Borderland standards to ride to war with him; they accompanied him to Tarwin's Gap in 998 NE, when Easar won over Shadowspawn with Rand's aid. He was about 5'7" tall, and slim, with a square, unwrinkled face and a shaved scalp except for a white topknot. He was a fine soldier, wise ruler and skilled diplomat. Easar, Ethenielle, Paitar and Tenobia joined together and left the Borderlands seeking Rand. They met with Elayne in Braem Wood. When Rand met with the Borderlanders at Far Madding, Easar backhanded Rand hard enough to draw blood while trying to determine if Rand fulfilled the prophecy from Paitar's ancestor; Rand stumbled, but did not strike back, as the prophecy had indicated. He swore fealty to Rand in exchange for his Aes Sedai being taught Traveling so that he could fight in the Last Battle. He did so, alongside Lan at Tarwin's Gap.

Easing the Badger. An inn located in Illian. Its innkeeper, Nieda Moroso, was one of Moiraine's eyes-and-ears. This was a lower-class establishment, suited to sailors and dockworkers, built of green-veined stone and having a green tile roof. A dangerous offer was made to Bayle Domon at the inn, in fact a plot to have him killed. When Moiraine, Lan, Perrin, Loial and Faile stayed there, awaiting boat passage to Tear to intercept Rand, six Gray Men attacked Perrin. He and his group killed them and fled on horseback, pursued by Darkhounds. Moiraine learned there that Sammael was in Illian.

Eastern Sea. One of the Seanchan names for the Aryth Ocean.

Eastern Marches. The territory along the Spine of the World.

Eastpoint Lighttower. A tower located on the eastern part of the bay in Ebou Dar. It had beacons to guide ships entering the bay.

Eawynd, King. The ruler of Safer at the signing of the Compact of the Ten Nations.

Eazil Forney. A bleary-eyed Andoran farmer who had drunk too much to drive his cart home from the inn in Arien to his farm the night before, and was thus available to give Mat and Rand a ride out of town the morning after they had performed at the inn.

Eban Vandes. The author of *The History of the Stone of Tear.* Rand learned about the Stone by reading this book.

Eben Hopwil. An Andoran Dedicated, later raised to Asha'man by Rand. He was born in 984 NE; he claimed to be twenty when he first appeared at the Black Tower, but he was really four or five years younger. Eben was skinny when he arrived, but later filled out considerably. The blotches on his face lessened as time passed, but his nose and ears were markedly on the large side, and he was still far from stocky. He was about 5'9" tall. Among the first to come at Rand's call for men who wanted to learn to channel, he was chosen to accompany Rand after Dumai's Wells. Eben was not part of the attack on Illian; he stayed with the army, fighting at the hillforts. Eben was sent to scout around Amador after Rand heard reports of the Seanchan from Lord Gregorin via Illianer merchants; there he encountered a Seanchan patrol with a *damane* and *sul'dam*. He had to kill the patrol, later burning to ash their bodies, the horses, everything, with the Power. After that, he spent a lot of time staring "at something beyond the horizon" and looked at people without blinking, sometimes seeming to look through them, all of which Rand at first thought was because he had had to kill two women. Eben accompanied Rand when he went to talk to the large group of men from Sammael's former army. After the attack on Rand in Cairhien, Eben was uncertain of returning safely to the Black Tower and remained in Cairhien, where Daigian Moseneillin, one of Cadsuane's Aes Sedai, persuaded him to be bonded a Warder. Taim placed him on the deserters list. Eben died at Shadar Logoth at the age of sixteen, fighting Aran'gar.

Ebou Dar. The capital of Altara. It lay on the southern coast of Altara at the mouth of the River Eldar. In earlier times, it was the site of the city of Barashta. Most of the buildings in Ebou Dar were white; some were banded with strips of color, but white prevailed.

The Tarasin Palace, east of the Eldar, was the seat of the King or Queen of Altara and the home of the Throne of the Winds. Mol Hara Square, in front of the palace, held a statue of Nariene, a long-dead queen.

The Rahad, the roughest section of Ebou Dar, lay on the far side of the River Eldar from Ebou Dar proper. It was dangerous enough that the Civil Guard stepped lightly there. Even an Aes Sedai could have a knife in her back there before she knew it, from someone wanting to steal her fine clothes, although if the clothes were fine, a very narrow blade was used so there would be little blood. The Rahad residents didn't always kill the one they robbed. The victim could wake up in an alley or on a heap of refuse, stark naked, since even stockings and smallclothes had some value. Buildings in the Rahad were made

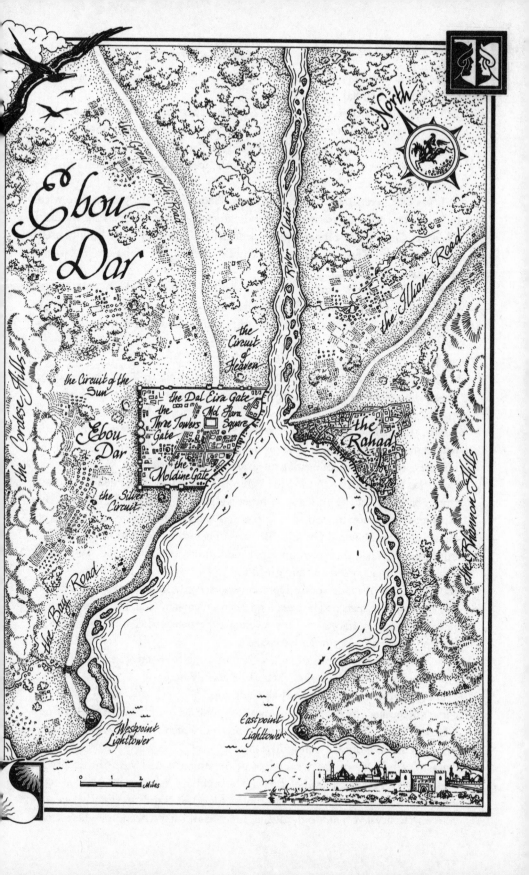

of brick and rose five or six stories high. They were crowded together and covered patchily with flaking white plaster.

There were lighttowers on each side of the bay to assist ships in navigation.

On the south side of the city lay the Moldine Gate; other gates included the Three Towers Gate and the Dal Eira Gate. The Circuit of Heaven racetrack lay north of the city, the Cordese Hills lay to the west and the Rhannon Hills to the southeast.

Ebou Dar, like Illian, had many canals. Here the bridges were ornate with buildings on them and statues at the ends, at least in the better parts of the city. The canals in the city proper, on the west bank of the river, were heavily used for barge traffic. Those on the east side of the river, in the Rahad, were largely silted up and unusable.

Ebou Dar workers wore clothes that identified their guilds. A police force called the Civil Guard kept order. Duels were a way of life in the city; they tended to be more formal in the city proper, and resembled basic knife fights in the Rahad.

Ebou Dari. Of or from Ebou Dar, Altara.

Ebou Dari guilds. There was a guild for almost everything in Ebou Dar, even for those who swept the squares at night, and woe to anyone who trespassed on a guild's rights. Each guild had distinctive markings and signs. For laboring guilds, this often consisted of a vest of a particular color or colors. Some guilds had as much power as any noble or, indeed, as the ruler. There were guilds of boatmen, of fishermen, of bearers for sedan chairs, of carters and wagon drivers. Even the beggars had a guild, the Fellowship of Alms, identified by a brass ring. The names of the guilds were never simple; the fishermen's guild was the Ancient and Honorable Guild of Nets, and wager takers were known as the Illustrious and Honored Guild of Bookers. There was no guild of innkeepers, but innkeepers had their own informal connections and, as a group, sometimes displayed as much power as any guild.

Ebram. A tall, well-made young Domani who served Graendal. He would have become one of her pets had he been more than a merchant's son. He gave Graendal news of Ituralde's arrival, and his reverent expression faded slightly when she took on the appearance of Lady Basene.

Echiko. An Accepted who died in a fall some time between 968 and 975 NE, thinking that she had developed the Talent of flying.

Echoes of His Dynasty. A book read by Cadsuane.

Edarna Noregovna. An Aes Sedai of the Blue Ajah who served as Amyrlin from 64 to 115 NE. Edarna was a strong Amyrlin, which she managed by being very deft in her political manipulations.

Edarra. A Wise One of the Neder sept of the Shiande Aiel with the ability to channel and a strength level of 12(+1). She had pale yellow hair and blue eyes. Edarra was 5'7" tall and looked not much older than Rand, apparently twenty-four to twenty-five years old, although she could have been anywhere from seventy-eight to 140 years old. She had an apparently unshakable calm and a straight-backed presence to match any of the other Wise Ones. When Sorilea learned that Nesune Bihara was poking around, looking for information on the seals, she sent Edarra, Colinda and Aeron to the Royal Library in Cairhien to try to find the information first. She went to Dumai's Wells. Edarra was the nominal leader of the Wise Ones who accompanied Perrin to Ghealdan; they were sent to keep an eye on the Aes Sedai, and she watched Masuri in particular. Edarra assisted in the forging of *Mah'alleinir.* She stayed with Perrin's army during the Last Battle, and told him it was evil to enter the World of Dreams in the flesh.

Edder. A Redarm tasked with looking after Setalle Anan and Olver.

Edelle Gaelin. The Wisdom in Watch Hill. She was slender and gray-haired and the oldest of the Two Rivers Wisdoms. She resented Daise taking the lead among the Wisdoms, since she was the eldest and the longest serving. Edelle sent Perrin some dried apple tarts.

Edesina Azzedin. An Aes Sedai of the Yellow Ajah and the rebel contingent, with a strength level of 24(12). Born in 944 NE, she went to the White Tower in 959 NE. After spending eleven years as a novice and ten years as Accepted, she was raised to the shawl in 980 NE. About 5'6" tall, with dark eyes and black hair to her waist, she was slender, and handsome rather than pretty.

Edesina was sent by the rebels with Afara and Guisin to Tarabon; while there she was captured and collared by the Seanchan. The Seanchan took her to Ebou Dar, where she and Teslyn were freed by Mat Cauthon. Edesina traveled with Luca's show until Mat moved on; she accompanied Mat to Caemlyn, sometimes helping and sometimes hindering, and then went on to the White Tower.

Edeyn ti Gemallen Arrel. Lan's *carneira.* Her personal sigil was a crouching lioness ready to spring. She was born in 934 NE. Her black hair had touches of white at the temples; she wore it long until the death of her daughter, when she cut it short. She had big dark eyes and wore the white *ki'sain* of a widow. Her brother was Cowin Gemallen, Cowin Fairheart, who betrayed Malkier. Had Lan died, she would have had the strongest claim to the Malkieri throne. She took Lan as her lover when she was a widow of thirty-five and he fifteen; that did not stop her from trying to persuade Lan to marry her daughter Iselle. Plotting a return to some degree of power, Edeyn rode through the Borderlands trying to gain support for reclaiming Malkier, but the death of her daughter devastated her and caused her to withdraw from public life.

Edorion Selorna. A Tairen nobleman. He was plump and pink-cheeked with a sharp mind—more serious and intelligent than others and more observant, though still with the opinions and attitudes of his class. He always pretended that his cards were bad, but he won more than he lost. When Mat's cards came to life and started attacking, Edorion was frightened. During the siege of Cairhien, Edorion lost weight and hardened; he and some others managed to escape

Cairhien and went to Rand for help. He joined the Band of the Red Hand and became an officer. His men in the Band called themselves Edorion's Hammers, though they were in fact the First Squadron (later the First Banner of Horse). He was the first given charge of Olver in Maerone. Edorion was with Talmanes when they caught up with Mat in the forest in Altara.

Eelfinn. A race of beings, largely human in appearance but with fox-like characteristics, who would grant three wishes, although they asked for a price in return. If the person asking did not negotiate a price, the Eelfinn chose it. The most common price in such circumstances was death, but they still fulfilled their part of the bargain, although the manner in which they fulfilled it was seldom the manner the querent expected. Their true location was unknown, but it was possible to visit them by means of a *ter'angreal* that was located in Rhuidean. That *ter'angreal* was taken by Moiraine Damodred to Cairhien, where it was destroyed. They could also be reached by entering the Tower of Ghenjei. They spoke a harsh dialect of the Old Tongue, mentioned treaties and agreements, and asked if those entering carried iron, instruments of music or devices that could make fire. They have existed as long as the Wheel. *See also* Aelfinn

Efalin. A woman of the Shaido Aiel and *Far Dareis Mai.* She had short graying hair and hard gray eyes. Efalin led the Shaido Maidens and the group of Shaido that captured Faile and her party. She worried what Sevanna thought because some of the Shaido Maidens went to join those around Rand; she provided Sevanna with a guard of Maidens, as if Sevanna had been a Maiden, though she never had been. Efalin suspected Sevanna's ambitions, but spoke of them circumspectly to Sevanna and not at all to anyone else. Efalin was not Jumai, but she went with Sevanna anyway when the Shaido were scattered, using the excuse that Sevanna "spoke for the chief." She was all but sure that Galina admitted killing Desaine. Efalin showed distress when their Seanchan captive died, which annoyed Sevanna.

Efraim Yamada. A Seanchan member of the low Blood who was a Banner-General. He was tall and handsome with broad shoulders and lean hips. He wore his graying hair in a bowl cut with a tail. His singing voice enamored Lady Riselle, an attendant at the Tarasin Palace; they became engaged and later married. Yamada reported to Captain-General Galgan and remained with the Ever Victorious Army.

Egeanin Sarna. A Seanchan ship captain. She was born in 965 NE, as counted east of the Aryth Ocean. Egeanin's father was a soldier, her mother a very high-ranking naval officer—a Captain of the Gold, the highest rank of Admiral, and later *so'jhin* to the Empress, the Hand of the Empress at Sea. Egeanin was about 5'7" tall, with sharp blue eyes, black hair and a very pale complexion. Her face was attractive but stern. Egeanin's hands were slender, with swordsman's calluses. As part of the *Corenne*, she captained the *Fearless* and sailed to Falme. There she captured the *Spray,* and took Bayle Domon and his treasures to High Lord Turak. After the Seanchan loss at Falme, she was sent to Tanchico, where she spent considerable time at The Garden of Silver Breezes in disguise, as an agent provocateur and spy. She was also hunting for deserters from Falme, including runaway *sul'dam* and *damane*. In Tanchico, she met Elayne and Nynaeve, and began to question the Seanchan attitude toward channelers.

Egeanin sailed with Domon when he went to drop the male *a'dam* into the sea and their ship was taken by the Seanchan. Her quick talking resulted in the *a'dam* being handed over to the Seanchan and Domon being made her *da'covale* instead of them both being imprisoned. She was raised to the lower levels of the Blood for her actions and became Captain of the Green Lady Egeanin Tamarath, and was granted a sigil of a sword and a fouled anchor. Because of a Seeker's report that told of her consorting with the enemy, maybe with Aes Sedai, in Tanchico, she remained under suspicion, and was ordered to Ebou Dar. Suroth supposedly believed that she only made errors of judgment, but the Seeker had deep suspicions; he arranged to keep a close eye on Egeanin and see what she did, rather than simply take her for questioning. He thought there was some wider plot, because of odd events in Falme and Tanchico. Egeanin's leaving the city with three *sul'dam* and three *damane* on the very night that the Windfinders made their escape, and Tuon's disappearance, only confirmed him in his belief. After leaving Ebou Dar, Egeanin remained with Mat, who took her to visit Tuon; Tuon stripped her of her name, renaming her Leilwin Shipless. In Jurador, Egeanin was stabbed by Renna, a *sul'dam*; Teslyn Healed her. She married Bayle Domon, and the two traveled to the Tower with the Aes Sedai, and then made their way to the Field of Merrilor, where Egeanin offered herself as payment for turning over the male *a'dam*. She swore to serve Egwene, but Egwene did not trust her; after Egeanin rescued her from the Sharans, she was more trusting. After Gawyn's death in the Last Battle, Egwene bonded Egeanin as her Warder. Egeanin fought by her side for a period, and Egwene told her when the seals needed to be broken and released the Warder bond, sending Egeanin through a gateway to safety before she, Egwene, died.

Egoridin, High Queen. The ruler of Jaramide at the signing of the Compact of the Ten Nations.

Eguilera, Celestin. *See* Celestin Eguilera

Egwene al'Vere. An Emond's Field woman born in 981 NE, the fifth daughter of Bran and Marin al'Vere. She and Rand were sweethearts. She was about 5'3" tall, with large brown eyes and dark hair. Her strength level was 8(+5). Egwene possessed the Talent of Dreaming and was an accomplished dreamwalker. She had many other abilities and Talents, including abilities with metals and ores and the making of *cuendillar*. Whatever Egwene did, she did to the hilt. She was keen to learn above all, and so she was as much Brown as Green in her temperament, with a strong dose of Gray besides. She showed some of the same Old Blood effects as Mat, though not as strongly.

Egwene left the Two Rivers with Moiraine, Lan, Rand, Mat and Perrin. While they traveled, Egwene learned that she had the ability to channel, and

Moiraine began teaching her. The party became separated at Shadar Logoth, and Egwene joined Perrin, met Elyas Machera and was captured by the Whitecloaks; Nynaeve, Lan and Moiraine rescued her. She journeyed with them to Caemlyn, then via the Ways to Fal Dara and thence to the Eye of the World. From Shienar she went downriver to the White Tower, where her name was entered in the novice book. She made friends with Elayne and Min. She was winkled out of Tar Valon by Liandrin, taken via the Ways to Toman Head and turned over to the Seanchan, who kept her for some time as a *damane*.

After she was rescued, she traveled back to the White Tower, where she was raised Accepted before leaving again on Siuan Sanche's orders with Elayne and Nynaeve to hunt the Black Ajah. She went downriver to Tear, masquerading as a Green sister, then by Portal Stone to the Aiel Waste, where she studied with the Wise Ones, as both Aes Sedai (which they thought she was) and apprentice. She crossed the Spine of the World with Rand and the Aiel to witness the retaking of Cairhien, and she traveled physically through *Tel'aran'rhiod* to Salidar, where she was raised Amyrlin. Egwene had no Ajah, since she was never in a position to choose one, going straight from Accepted to Amyrlin. She was selected with the notion that she could be manipulated, an assumption that was dead wrong. She moved the rebel Aes Sedai north to the White Tower. While blockading the Erinin with *cuendillar*, she was captured by Elaida's minions and subjected to almost continual penance at the Tower. The situation changed when the Seanchan attacked the White Tower—they captured Elaida, and Egwene was instrumental in turning the battle around in the Tower's favor. The united Hall selected her Amyrlin of the White Tower, also hoping that she would be easily guided, a mistake on their part.

Egwene fell in love with Gawyn, idealizing him (romantic that she was), and took him as her Warder and married him, making her the first Amyrlin ever to marry. After Gawyn's death she bonded Egeanin as her Warder for a short time, releasing the bond shortly before she died during the Last Battle, wielding the Flame of Tar Valon against Taim's balefire.

Eharon. One of the Ten Nations. Its king was Temanin at the signing of the Compact. Eharon's capital was Londaren Cor; other cities included Barashta (later Ebou Dar) and Dorelle Caromon (later Illian). Mat had memories of an Eharoni High Prince.

Ehvin. A Murandian man working as a servant with the rebel Aes Sedai. He was stout and graying, with a permanent smile.

Ehvon. A Sea Folk Windfinder. Talaan was her apprentice. She punished Talaan even when Talaan performed her tasks as well as Ehvon did.

Eianrod. A small town in western Cairhien that was abandoned during Cairhien's civil war. Eianrod had a bridge in the center of town, and stone-paved streets laid out in a grid pattern, cutting through hills as necessary. Its hills were terraced with stone. The stone buildings here were slate-roofed, though many had been burned. Merchant buildings were wide three-story affairs of marble. The town had two squares. When returning to Cairhien from the Waste, Rand and the Aiel stayed here. Rand was to sleep in one of the merchant houses; on entering his bedroom, he came upon Aviendha bathing naked; she fled through a gateway and he followed.

Rand and the Aiel clans, who had just gone through the Jangai Pass, were camped just outside Eianrod when Kadere, a merchant traveling with them and secretly a Darkfriend working for Lanfear, received a Darkfriend message.

In the town, Rand received Tairen and Cairhienin delegates who asked his help against Couladin and the Shaido who were besieging the city of Cairhien.

Einar. An Asha'man protecting the dragons in the Last Battle. He was balefired by Demandred.

Einion Avharin. One of the three most famous First Councils in Far Madding history. A statue of her stood in Avharin Market in Far Madding, pointing to the Caemlyn Gate.

Einone. Sister to Queen Ethenielle of Kandor; she was married to one of Tenobia's uncles.

Einor Saren. An officer in the Children of the Light and a Questioner. He was second-in-command to Carridin on Almoth Plain. A tall man with a hooked nose, he met Geofram Bornhald and his forces in Alcruna, and later escorted Morgase to a meeting with Niall. On their journey they passed Darkfriends being hanged, including Paitr, who had been trying to help Morgase escape.

el'Leanna ti Arathdar Mandragoran. *See* Leanna ti Arathdar Mandragoran

Elaida do Avriny a'Roihan. An Aes Sedai of the Red Ajah and the loyalist contingent, with a strength level of 13(1). Born in 950 NE, she went to the White Tower in 967 NE. After spending three years as a novice and three years as Accepted, she was raised to the shawl in 973 NE. Elaida was born to a minor noble House on an estate not much more than a farm in northern Murandy. She had dark eyes and dark hair to her shoulders. Some called her handsome rather than pretty; others called her beautiful at first glance, but her expression was permanently severe. She was 5'6" tall.

Although Elaida's potential strength was fairly high, she was not among the very highest with respect to sisters then living; but on the other hand, her time spent as novice and as Accepted were records, equaling or bettering the best ever before. For that, she was considered quite remarkable. She also had the

Talent of Foretelling. Although it was erratic, she was the first sister since Gitara Moroso to have this Talent. While still an Accepted, she had the Foretelling that the royal line of Andor would be the key to winning the Last Battle. At that time, Mordrellen of House Mantear was the Queen of Andor, but she died shortly thereafter, and her heir, Tigraine, went missing. By 974 NE Elaida had identified Morgase Trakand as the likely winner in the Succession in Andor and attached herself to the young woman. From then on her focus was on protecting and controlling House Trakand, the royal House of Andor.

Siuan and Moiraine were novices under Elaida when she was raised Accepted, and Accepted under her as Aes Sedai. Elaida was not easy on them; while she did not particularly like it that they equaled her speed in reaching the next level, she pressed them very hard, expecting only the best from them and accepting nothing less. They had a potential equal to hers, and they had an obligation to live up to it—and an obligation to live up to her standards in other ways as well. While Elaida was in Andor for the most part from 974 NE onward, she visited the White Tower often while they were in training and always took an interest in them and their progress. Elaida was called back to Tar Valon along with many other sisters when it seemed the Aiel were threatening the city in 978 NE, and she remained for a short time afterward. After Siuan and Moiraine passed their tests for the shawl, during the night they were supposed to spend in contemplation and meditation, they decided to play a trick on Elaida, who caught them. Where another sister might have let go two Accepted who were to be raised in the morning, Elaida promptly took them to the Mistress of Novices, Merean Redhill, who was not pleased at being roused from her bed in the night and made sure that their last punishment as Accepted was particularly memorable. Elaida's dislike of Siuan came later, beginning when Siuan was chosen Amyrlin over her and exacerbated by the plans surrounding Rand which led to Siuan being deposed.

Elaida and Meidani Eschede were entered in the novice book within weeks of each other, and soon became pillow friends. Elaida broke off the relationship when she was raised, but considered herself Meidani's friend, though she showed it by giving her the same sort of attention and pressure that she did to Moiraine and Siuan.

Elaida was not deeply involved personally in the male channeler pogrom in 979–985 NE, though she learned of it from other Reds and supported it wholeheartedly, partly because the leadership of her Ajah was behind it and partly because she considered a man who could channel dangerous enough for her to violate the law, even to do murder on suspicion; at least, she would not herself have taken part in a killing, but she would turn a blind eye. Her one involvement was seeing that Thom's nephew was gentled on the spot when he was caught; this was at the very tail end of the pogrom. Once she became Amyrlin, she hardly cared whether anyone discovered her involvement with Owyn. Those Sitters who dared to openly oppose her would not have the nerve to suggest any discipline against the Amyrlin Seat herself, not even for so dire a violation of Tower law—not when it was so long ago, not when making it public even among the sisters could damage the Tower in its battle against the rebels, and most of all, not when attaining consensus against her would be impossible.

Elaida once met Cadsuane, during the Aiel War, the first time that Cadsuane had seemingly come back from the dead. Among other things, Cadsuane told her that she was too hard, that good steel had some give in it, and what was too rigid was too easily shattered. Cadsuane also told her that she allowed her anger too free a rein, that an Aes Sedai had to be the mistress of her emotions, not they of her. It was a cold chewing-out, in fact. Elaida had had the shawl for a few years then, but the meeting left her feeling like a novice wanting to run back to her room from the Mistress of Novices' study.

Elaida knitted for relaxation, as much as she could ever be said to relax. She sometimes used it to try putting people off guard; someone knitting would not look at all threatening and might simply be discounted. She also liked to examine her collection of carved miniatures, sometimes doing so while giving an audience to make the person attending know that he or she was not as important as the carvings.

In 999 NE, Elaida learned that the Amyrlin, Siuan Sanche, and her Keeper, Leane Sharif, had secretly met with the Dragon Reborn, and she orchestrated a coup. She had Siuan and Leane removed from office and stilled, and she was raised Amyrlin, with Alviarin Freidhen as her Keeper.

As Amyrlin, Elaida made many mistakes: She kidnapped sitting kings and the Dragon Reborn; she initiated an attack on the Black Tower that failed miserably and led to Aes Sedai being forcibly bonded; she came under the control of a member of the Black Ajah and caused the Tower to nearly fall apart. It could be argued that her biggest mistake was ignoring the warning of a Seanchan attack. When that attack occurred, Elaida was captured, made a *damane* and given the name "Suffa." Suffa was not a good *damane*.

Elaiva Walfor. An Andoran Aes Sedai of the Gray Ajah and the loyalist contingent, with a strength level of 19(7). Born in 806 NE, she went to the White Tower in 822 NE. After spending ten years as a novice and eight years as Accepted, she was raised to the shawl in 840 NE. Elaiva was part of the expedition to capture Rand in Cairhien. She was captured at Dumai's Wells and treated as *da'tsang* by the Aiel. Under Verin's Compulsion she found reason to swear oath to Rand, which she did before Cadsuane departed Cairhien for Far Madding.

Elam Dowtry. A boyhood friend of Mat in Emond's Field. He had a long nose and a cowlick; when young, he aspired to have more sheep than anyone in the Two Rivers. Elam helped Perrin in the defense of Emond's Field. Later, with Ewin Finngar and Dav Ayellin, he ran off to see the world.

Elamri den Rendalle, Ballin. An Illianer nobleman who was a member of the Council of Nine.

Elan Dapor. A nation that arose after the Trolloc Wars.

Elan Morin Tedronai. Ishamael's name in the Age of Legends.

Elandria Borndat. An ancient scholar and the author of *Seeing Through the Breaking.*

Elansu. Agelmar's *shatayan* in Fal Dara. She was black-haired and sharp-faced. There were few men she could not bully—some even said she could bully Agelmar.

Elayne Traemane. An Andoran noblewoman; she was Ellorien's grandmother, and Elayne Trakand was named after her.

Elayne Trakand. An Aes Sedai of the Green Ajah and the rebel contingent, with a potential strength level of 8(+5). Born in 981 NE, she went to the White Tower in 998 NE. After spending less than a year as a novice and less than a year as Accepted, she was raised to the shawl in 999 NE by Egwene's decree. Elayne was also Queen Morgase's daughter, the Daughter-Heir to the Throne of Andor. Her sign was a golden lily. She became Queen of Andor and Cairhien, and participated in the Last Battle.

Elayne had red-gold curls and big blue eyes. Her face was a perfect oval, her lips full and red. About 5'7" tall, a little shorter than Aviendha, she was quite tall for an Andoran woman. Her brother Gawyn was a head taller than she. Elayne was slim, but not too slim; curvaceous but neither overly busty nor under-endowed. She had a dimple in her cheek when she smiled; Mat thought that dimple hadn't failed her very often in getting her own way. Her voice was not particularly high, but she believed that it was not suited for shouting, for one thing, because in her opinion her shouts came out sounding like shrieks.

As a child she had a nursemaid named Lini, of whom she was very fond; Lini had also been her mother's and grandmother's nursemaid.

Although basically a good and decent person, Elayne was the Daughter-Heir of Andor, born to wealth, power, position and prestige. While she was ready to bend (e.g., novice training), she usually wanted and expected her own way, and was really shocked or surprised that she could be hurt even when she had taken a risk. She was quite willing to consult with others, but truly expected the decision to go her way. She was stubborn, but willing to see when or where she was wrong, though often only after a long resistance (as with Thom), and she was not likely to say "you were right and I was wrong," only to adopt the new position.

Elayne was by nature a peacemaker; she tried to smooth over roughnesses between people. On the other hand, if she was roused, there was no peacemaking in her.

As a commander, she expected those under her to do as they were told. She had a weakness for sweets, especially hard candies, and colorful language. Elayne had the mind of a development engineer: she was not particularly good at discovering new principles, but she was a whiz at figuring new ways to use those already known and at reverse-engineering things. These abilities were particularly well suited to making *ter'angreal*, and she was the first after the Breaking to be able to do so. She tried to teach others how to make *ter'angreal*, but no one showed much skill or success in doing so. She had real abilities with weather.

Elayne met Rand at the Royal Palace in Caemlyn when he first arrived there from the Two Rivers. She was already a novice at the White Tower when Egwene and Nynaeve arrived, and they became friends. She tested for Accepted at about the same time Egwene did. She was winkled out of Tar Valon by Liandrin, taken via the Ways to Toman Head, escaped being turned over to the Seanchan and helped to rescue Egwene, who had been captured. She traveled back to the White Tower, leaving again with Egwene and Nynaeve to hunt the Black Ajah on Siuan Sanche's orders. She traveled with the other two young women to Tear; on the way they met Aviendha. In Tear they stayed with Mother Guenna, who introduced them to Juilin Sandar; he agreed to help them find the women of the Black Ajah, although he was not aware that the women were Aes Sedai. He was caught by the Black sisters and betrayed Elayne, Egwene and Nynaeve. The three women were taken prisoner by the Black sisters and jailed in the dungeons of the Stone of Tear. Egwene used her dream *ter'angreal* ring to work toward freedom; Mat and Juilin arrived and freed them.

After Rand won the Stone, Elayne and Nynaeve then headed to Tanchico, accompanied by Thom Merrilin and Juilin Sandar, aboard the *Wavedancer*, a Sea Folk ship. Elayne learned that Jorin, the Windfinder, could channel; Jorin taught Elayne how to weave weather, and Elayne taught Jorin how to weave with Fire. In Tanchico, Elayne and Nynaeve met Bayle Domon again and Egeanin for the first time. They learned that the Black Ajah was in the Panarch's Palace and sneaked in. While Nynaeve fought Moghedien and found the male *a'dam*, Elayne and Egeanin freed the Panarch. They gave the male *a'dam* to Domon and Egeanin to drop into the ocean, and tried to make their way back to Tar Valon. In Mardecin, they saw a signal for a Yellow Ajah eyes-and-ears, Ronde Macura. They talked with Ronde, who dosed them with forkroot tea so that they could be taken to the Tower. Thom and Juilin rescued them, and they continued on their way in disguise.

In Sienda they encountered Galad, who wanted to take them to Caemlyn. To escape him they joined Valan Luca's show; Elayne performed as a tightrope walker. They met Cerandin, a Seanchan who had been left behind at Falme; she gave Elayne an *a'dam*. Elayne studied it and figured out how it worked and thought that she could make other *ter'angreal*. After Birgitte was ripped bodily out of *Tel'aran'rhiod* by Moghedien, Elayne bonded Birgitte as her Warder to save Birgitte's life. In Samara, Nynaeve asked both Masema and Galad to get them a ship so that they could go to Salidar; although the Whitecloaks fighting the Prophet's men caused a great riot, they made it to the ship, *Riverserpent*, and sailed for Salidar. After Nynaeve captured Moghedien, Elayne created an *a'dam* out of Birgitte's silver arrow to hold her.

Egwene raised Elayne, Nynaeve, Faolain and Theodrin Aes Sedai by decree when she became Amyrlin, and then sent Elayne, Nynaeve and Aviendha with other Aes Sedai and Mat to Ebou Dar to find the Bowl of the Winds. In Ebou Dar, Elayne and Nynaeve discovered the Kin, made a bargain with the Sea Folk and found the Bowl of the Winds, although they had to fight the Black Ajah and a *gholam* for it. Elayne, the Sea Folk and the Kin went to the Kin's farm and used the Bowl of the Winds to heal the weather; just as they were finishing, the Seanchan arrived and they fled through a gateway to Andor. Elayne, who created the gateway, attempted to unravel it; the attacks by Seanchan *damane* caused her to lose her grip and a great explosion resulted, killing all of the Seanchan and injuring Elayne, Birgitte and Aviendha. Nynaeve Healed them, and they accompanied the Kin back to Caemlyn.

Elayne laid claim to the Lion Throne. Dyelin supported her; Elenia, Arymilla and Naean opposed her, leaving her in need of more Houses to support her. She became first-sisters with Aviendha, who began teaching her Maiden handtalk, though she said it was forbidden.

Dyelin and Doilin Mellar saved Elayne from an assassination attempt; though suspicious of him, she made Mellar the captain of her new group of Guardswomen. When Rand and Min paid a surreptitious visit to the palace, she, along with Aviendha and Min, bonded Rand as a Warder. Elayne and Rand slept together and she became pregnant with twins. After following Mellar to a house on Full Moon Street, Elayne and others surprised some members of the Black Ajah, and were in turn surprised by more of the Black Ajah. Sareitha, Vandene and Careane were killed, and Elayne was captured. With help from the Sea Folk, Birgitte rescued her, killed Asne and captured the other Black sisters and Mellar. At the same time, Arymilla attacked the city of Caemlyn; Elayne joined the battle and won. Pelivar, Luan, Arathelle, Ellorien, Abelle and Aemlyn then went to Caemlyn; all but Ellorien stood for Elayne and she became Queen of Andor.

Elayne made arrangements with the Kin for them to have a headquarters in Caemlyn to help with Traveling and Healing, and arrangements with Mat for use of the dragons and the Band of the Red Hand. She attempted to fool the captive Black sisters and get information from them; she was captured again and stabbed but was Healed and managed to escape. Elayne put forth a claim to Cairhien, and after some political feints won the Sun Throne. When the Trollocs entered Caemlyn through the Waygate at the start of the Last Battle, she set fire to the city and led her troops north, eventually taking over allied command of the campaign against the Shadowspawn.

She was almost killed by Daved Hanlon on the Field of Merrilor, but was saved by Birgitte, already dead but returned as a Hero of the Horn.

Elbar, Zaired. *See* Zaired Elbar

Elber. A Queen's Guard at the Royal Palace in Caemlyn who was hired by Gaebril. He was rude and fat with eyes like a rat. He was at the gate of the palace in Caemlyn when Mat attempted to deliver Elayne's letter to her mother.

Eldar, River. A river flowing east and south from the Mountains of Mist to Ebou Dar and the Sea of Storms. It formed the western boundary of Altara.

Eldase Takashi. A Kandori Kin and a member of the Knitting Circle in Ebou Dar. Her strength level was 41(29), not strong enough for her to make a gateway of any size whatsoever. She was fierce-looking and had a temper, though better controlled than when she was young. She had two streaks of white, like plumes, across the top of her head. Born in 665 NE, she went to the White Tower in 683 NE. After spending thirteen years as a novice and seven years as Accepted, she was put out of the Tower because of her temper, which had made her a severe discipline problem. Cemaile Sorenthaine was Amyrlin then. At the time the Seanchan invaded Ebou Dar, she sold lacquerware to merchants for export. Eldase traveled to Caemlyn with Elayne from the Kin farm.

Eldaya Tolen. An Aes Sedai of the Blue Ajah who served as Amyrlin from 533 to 549 NE. Eldaya was an Amyrlin of below-average strength, though not entirely weak; she was willing to let the Hall have its way in most things as long as they went along with the manipulations she planned in various countries, which she engaged in more than were usual for the Tower, which is saying a great deal. The result was that the Hall had effective control of the Tower itself and most affairs among the sisters.

Elders, Council of. The ruling body of each *stedding*.

Eldin clan. A Two Rivers family. *See* Get, Marce *and* Whatley Eldin

Eldone Market. A town or village on the other side of the river from Tar Valon in Andor. A guard outside Tar Valon told Verin and her companions that Whitecloaks had tried to move into Eldone Market, but were driven off by Tar Valon soldiers.

Eldrene ay Ellan ay Carlan. The last Queen of Manetheren and wife of Aemon. She was also known as Ellisande, the Rose of the Sun. Eldrene was so beautiful that it was said the flowers bloomed to make her smile. When Tetsuan betrayed Manetheren out of jealousy of Eldrene and Aemon and his armies were falling to the Shadow's armies, Eldrene organized the flight of the people of Manetheren into the forests and mountains. From the city of Manetheren, Eldrene felt Aemon die, and her heart died with him. Driven by grief she reached out to the True Source, and hurled the One Power at the Trolloc army. All the Dreadlords burst into flame, and the Trollocs fled. But Eldrene had drawn to herself more of the One Power than any human could wield unaided and as the enemy generals died, so did she; the fires that consumed her consumed the empty city of Manetheren, even the stones of it, down to the living rock of the mountains.

Eldrid Methin. A cook in the Sun Palace in Cairhien. When Loial and Karldin visited, Eldrid talked of how dangerous and deadly Rand was.

Eldrin Cauthon. Mat's younger sister. She was born in 984 NE. Plumply pretty, she had a grin similar to her sister Bodewhin's. As children, she and Bode spied on Mat and told their mother everything. She, her mother and her sister were arrested by Whitecloaks and freed by Perrin. During the defense of Emond's Field, when a Trolloc grabbed Bodewhin, Eldrin thrust a boar spear through its chest.

Eldrin Hackly. A big wagon man who once almost killed Deni Colford. Not normally a rough man, he was very drunk when he tried to break her neck.

Eldrith Jhondar. An Amadician Aes Sedai of the Brown Ajah in public and of the Black Ajah in truth. She had a strength level of 16(4). Born in 884 NE, she went to the White Tower in 901 NE. After spending twelve years as a novice and seven years as Accepted, Eldrith was raised to the shawl in 920 NE. Her Warder was Kennit; he was not a Darkfriend. She was about 5'4" tall and plump, with a round face and brown eyes and hair. She was a little vague sometimes; she could have risen faster as a student, but she was dreamy and absentminded even then. Eldrith was one of the first thirteen members of the Black Ajah who fled the Tower, killing sisters and Warders and stealing *ter'angreal*. She went to Tanchico; she disliked having cats in the house and secretly disposed of a number of Marillin's cats there. She then went to Amador, where the group was co-opted by Moghedien. Moghedien ordered Eldrith, Asne, Temaile and Chesmal to follow her to Samara. Eldrith failed to keep her bond to Kennit masked, and he tracked her down in Ghealdan and tried to kill her. She didn't want him killed, given the effect that would have on her, so she and her companions fled to Caemlyn hoping to find Elayne, and maybe Nynaeve, both of whom they believed Moghedien very much wanted. Asne, Chesmal and Eldrith were all intimidated by Temaile, who took control over the group despite the fact that Eldrith stood higher in the Power; Temaile's preparation of Liandrin for her fate had frightened them. Eldrith was not at Lady Shiaine's house when Elayne and her allies went to arrest the Black Ajah members, but she arrived soon after and helped take Elayne captive. Eldrith was captured when Birgitte and her forces rescued Elayne. When Elayne went to the prison disguised as a Forsaken to try to gain information, Eldrith was not fooled. She was killed by Mellar in the fighting that followed.

Eldros, Nemaira. An Aes Sedai who lived at the time of the formation of the White Tower.

Elegar, Lord. A minor Andoran nobleman. He was thin-lipped and nervous, at least eighteen years older than Rand. He was one of Gaebril's sycophants and a Darkfriend, a toady and errand-runner. Elegar retched when Taim was led into the courtyard of the Royal Palace. He fled after Rand and Dyelin reached an accommodation.

Elenar. An apprentice Wise One of the Daryne Aiel. She was the apprentice furthest along in her studies; Amys thought she ought to be encouraged to take the final step to being a Wise One so that she could go to Rhuidean and see if Aviendha's visions of the world after the Last Battle repeated themselves. Bair didn't believe she was ready to be a Wise One.

Elenia Sarand. An Andoran noblewoman and the wife of Jarid. He was the High Seat of House Sarand, but all the ambition came from her. She was a shrewish woman about 5'5" tall, with honey hair and a vulpine face. Elenia was a pseudo-populist who in truth despised the common people, though she never actually thought that she did. She believed that a High Seat, or a queen, stood atop a tower, the bottom layers of which were made of the common people; they were of a base clay, but if enough of them crumpled, the tower would fall. She had opposed Morgase during the Succession; Elenia wanted the Lion Throne herself. She seldom missed a chance to point out her knowledge of Andor's history, especially in areas where not much was known, often adding justifications of her claims to the Lion Throne. She declared for the throne after hearing of Colavaere's coronation in Cairhien; Dyelin had her arrested and imprisoned. Arymilla freed her, but forced her to sign a letter supporting Arymilla for the throne. After Elayne defeated Arymilla, Elenia was imprisoned; Jarid planned to free her but lost his mind and men. Elayne stripped her of her titles and properties, but intended to give her properties elsewhere.

Eleyan al'Landerin. An Aes Sedai of the Green Ajah of ancient times. A statue of her and her Warders was located on the southwestern side of Tar Valon.

Elffin, Aleria. An author of humorous tales.

Elfraed Guitama. A leader who tried to seize Hawkwing's empire after his death. He was the third leader whom Jalwin Moerad, Hawkwing's advisor, advised shortly after Hawkwing's death; those three came closest to seizing all of Hawkwing's empire.

elgilrim. A horned animal. A chair could be fashioned from its horns.

Elidar, Mistress. An alias used by Egeanin in Tanchico.

Elienda. A Maiden of the Spear who accompanied Perrin to Ghealdan. She had wide shoulders, green eyes and graying hair and was about 5'9" tall. Though she looked almost motherly at times, Perrin saw her knock a man down with her fist. She went with Sulin and was killed while taking out the Shaido sentries to the northwest of Malden so the carts could get through.

Elin Warrel. An Andoran Aes Sedai of the Brown Ajah and the loyalist contingent. Born in 953 NE, she went to the White Tower in 971 NE. After spending fifteen years as a novice and fourteen years as Accepted, she was raised to the shawl in 1000 NE. Skinny and short for an Andoran, she was still taller than Moiraine. Elin was on duty in the anteroom of the Amyrlin's apartments when Gitara had her Foretelling and died. Before being raised, she was the oldest Accepted that Nynaeve knew, and was seen walking with Marris Thornhill and Doraise Mesianos in the White Tower.

Elinde Motheneos. A supporter of Amalasan who tried to free him from the White Tower; he failed and died.

Eliris Mancuri den Rhomin. An Illianer nobleman who was a member of the Council of Nine.

Elis. A maid in Aesdaishar Palace in Chachin, Kandor. She was pale-haired and overly solicitous when escorting Moiraine through the palace.

Elisa al'Seen. A motherly-looking Two Rivers woman. She was the wife of Jac.

Elisa al'Vere. Egwene's third-eldest sister. She was born in 973 NE and wasn't allowed to braid her hair until 992 NE. Elisa was given to offering advice and homilies. After Perrin left the Two Rivers, she married a maker of musical instruments from Tarabon who was twenty years older than she, and took to wearing Taraboner clothes when she wasn't wearing Domani. She also might have been able to learn to channel.

Elisane Tishar. An Aes Sedai at the formation of the White Tower. She was mentioned in public records as the Amyrlin Seat, the first to hold that title, which she apparently had held for at least several years at that point.

Elise Marwin. A girl from Two Rivers with the ability to channel. She was about sixteen, and was among the young women recruited by Verin and Alanna whom Rand saw and terrified at Culain's Hound in Caemlyn. She was later taken to the rebel camp.

Elise Strang. An Aes Sedai of the Gray Ajah who served as Amyrlin from 223 to 244 NE. Elise was a very weak Amyrlin who had to literally beg to get most things she wanted from the Hall.

Eliya. A Seanchan *morat'raken* flying over the Kin's farm when Elayne and her party were leaving. She fell off the *raken* and died when the gateway exploded. The woman with her, Chulein, survived.

Ella. Daughter of Soong, mother of Covril, thus Loial's grandmother.

Ella. A serving woman at The Bunch of Grapes in Cairhien. She informed the innkeeper, Zera, that two of Barthanes' men had been asking after Thom the previous night.

Ellaine Mariseidin Alshinn. The translator of *The Karaethon Cycle: The Prophecies of the Dragon.*

Elle. A girl from Watch Hill with the ability to channel who was quite fair-haired for someone from the Two Rivers. She was among the young women recruited by Verin and Alanna whom Rand saw and terrified at Culain's Hound in Caemlyn. Elle was one of three born with the spark—the other two being Bode and Jancy—who, in Verin's estimation, would be quite strong.

Ellid Abareim. A beautiful Accepted with golden hair and sapphire eyes. She wanted to join the Green Ajah and bond six Warders. She went to be tested for the shawl shortly after the end of the Aiel War; she never emerged from the *ter'angreal.*

Ellisande. *See* Eldrene ay Ellan ay Carlan

Ellisar, Lord. A nobleman who had an encampment outside Tar Valon west of the River Erinin during the Battle of the Shining Walls. Willa Mandair had given birth to a son in his camp on the day of Gitara's Foretelling.

Ellisor, Chin. *See* Chin Ellisor

Ellizelle. A queen of Ghealdan. After the Prophet went to Ghealdan, the nation fell into chaos. King Johanin was killed in a supposed hunting accident, and Ellizelle took the throne. She ordered the army to disperse the crowds that came to see the Prophet, but his followers routed her army. After the humiliating defeat she died of poison; it was said to be a suicide.

Ellorien Traemane. An Andoran noblewoman and High Seat of House Traemane. She was about 5'5" tall, with dark hair and brown eyes, and plumply pretty, or would have been, if not for her determinedly stony face. She was a few years older than Morgase and was Morgase's first supporter in the Succession. Morgase under Gaebril's influence exiled her and had her flogged because she demanded to know why she was being exiled. These events poisoned her attitude toward House Trakand and she wanted Dyelin to take the throne. She and three other nobles—Dyelin, Luan and Pendar—met with Rand, when Rand told them he wanted Elayne on the Andoran throne. Even after all the other powerful Houses stood for Elayne, she refused to and left in a fury.

Ells, Lady. A Saldaean noblewoman with the Borderlander forces in the Last Battle. Lan saw her and Agelmar speaking.

Ellya Mowly. A girl child born to Careme Mowly close to the Battle of the Shining Walls.

Elmindreda. A woman in a story who sighed after men, and vice versa, for whom Min Farshaw was named.

Elmindreda Farshaw. Min Farshaw's full name.

Elmora. A town in Tarabon, west of Serana and the Amadician border. It was about halfway between Tanchico and Amador.

Elnore. 1) Nynaeve's mother. She was, in Nynaeve's opinion, a very difficult woman to live with, especially as a mother. Elnore never raised her voice; she didn't have to. She told people what to do, and they obeyed, even the Coplins and the Congars; she asked, and people complied. The Women's Circle always asked her to speak first, so everyone else could hear her opinion before opening their mouths. Every woman in the district wanted her advice, and most of the men, too. Elnore never ever lost her temper, but even Doral Barran, the old Wisdom, jumped to apologize as soon as one of Elnore's rare frowns appeared. 2) Nynaeve's daughter in her Accepted test.

Elonid, Lydel. The woman in Ebou Dar who purchased The Wandering Woman from Setalle Anan.

Elora. An Ogier. The daughter of Amar daughter of Coura, she wrote *Men of Fire and Women of Air*.

Elricain Tavolin. A young Cairhienin lieutenant who escorted Rand from Tremonsien to Cairhien. His *con* was a blue field crossed by two white bars. He wore the front of his head shaved, and it looked as if he had dusted the front with white powder. The farther south they rode, the stiffer he grew, and he spoke disgustedly of the peasants in the Foregate. While riding he used a quirt to move peasants out of the way.

Elsalam. A nation that arose after the Trolloc Wars.

Elsbet. The queen of the whole world, in a tale from the Age before the Age of Legends. Legend said that she fought wars with Mosk and was the sister of Anla the Wise Counselor.

Else Grinwell. A flirtatious Andoran farmgirl whose family Rand and Mat stayed with while heading for Caemlyn. She went to the White Tower and became a novice before Egwene and Nynaeve, and was soon known as a girl who spent all of her time—including time when she should have been studying—at the Warder's yards, watching the men practice. Else was very much taken with Galad, as was every other woman in the White Tower, including even Reds, but he did not notice her. She didn't want to work at learning. Her potential was very low, though, which was the reason the Tower was willing to let her go in under a year. She was impersonated by a Forsaken, and Mat posed as her brother to Rahvin.

Elsie. A maid for House Matherin in Andor, a House loyal to Elayne, who saw a ghost.

Elswell. An Aes Sedai who after the Last Battle told Rodel Ituralde that he had to take the throne of Arad Doman.

Eltring, Lini. *See* Lini Eltring

Elvaine Martan. A gray-haired Andoran noblewoman who was the wife of Brannin, High Seat of House Martan. They were relatively poor, living in a manor that was more like a large farmhouse. They were loyal to Elayne and brought armsmen to help her win the throne. A third of their armsmen were family.

Elver Shaene. A longboat captain in Cairhien harbor. He was skinny, with only a fringe of gray hair, and wore a coat of Murandian cut. Elver took Rand, Aes Sedai and Asha'man to meet with the Seafolk on the River Alguenya. He told Rand that he was honored, but he was obviously terrified.

Elward, Moria. *See* Moria Elward

Elwin. A Jenn Aiel boy who lived after the Breaking. His parents were Adan and Siedre; his brothers and sisters were Rhea, Malind, Sorelle and Jaren. Elwin died of hunger at age ten.

Elwinn Taron. The Wisdom of Deven Ride. She was a round person and had a motherly smile that she wore even when she was making people do what they did not want to.

Elyas Machera. A wolfbrother called "Long Tooth" by the wolves, for his knife/ shortsword. Elyas was about 5'10" tall, and rawboned, with golden eyes and graying brown hair which hung to his waist, gathered at the nape of his neck with a leather cord. A thick beard fanned across half his chest, and a faint, age-faded scar from a knife ran along his jaw, given to him by a Saldaean woman named Merya. A long knife, almost a sword, hung at his belt. He also carried a bow and quiver. Elyas was born in 943 NE in Tear, the son of poor farmers. In 957 NE, he ran off to the Borderlands seeking adventure. By 959 NE he had become a soldier in Shienar, serving along the Blightborder, and was bonded by Rina Hafden in 965 NE. He met Lan in 969 NE, during the last year of Lan's training in Shienar. Rina allowed him to go because of the circumstance of his becoming a wolfbrother, but she never freed him, and she masked the bond so he wouldn't know if she was coming. She may actually have been his wife. Elyas did not really approve of Aes Sedai being apprenticed to the Wise Ones, though he tried to pretend it made no difference to him. Elyas was always uneasy about meeting any sister, since if she recognized him as a renegade, she could very well make his life hell until she could hand him over to Rina. The Seanchan angered Elyas; he didn't like the idea of leashing women who could channel. His feelings about Aes Sedai, despite his pretense of being rather coldhearted and practical, were very divided, and without much real animus toward any sisters except perhaps Reds. Elyas thought there were some sisters who could do with a swift kick in the rear now and then, but on the other hand, they were Aes Sedai and he was still a Warder.

After Perrin and Egwene became separated from the rest of their party at Shadar Logoth, they met Elyas and his wolf friends. Perrin, Egwene and Elyas traveled with Raen's band of Tinkers for a time, and then Elyas led them south. After being chased by hordes of ravens, they made it to the *stedding* where Hawkwing's great city was to have been and took shelter. When the Whitecloaks arrived, Elyas was injured but escaped, and Perrin and Egwene were captured.

Elyas rejoined Perrin in Ghealdan; Gaul and Elyas became friends after Elyas sneaked up on Gaul undetected. Elyas was much respected by all of the Maidens, too. Elyas counseled Perrin about Saldaean women, and helped in the rescue of Faile at Malden. Just before the Last Battle, he headed north to join the wolves. Perrin encountered him in the wolf dream and told him of Graendal's Compulsion of the great captains. Elyas and the wolves saved Ituralde's forces during a Myrddraal attack, and kidnapped him before he could cause too much damage.

Elynde. One of Setalle's married women friends. Elynde told Setalle that she was not firm enough when Jasfer spoke out of line and that she needed to provide a good example for her daughters.

Elza Penfell. An Andoran Aes Sedai of the Green Ajah publicly and of the Black Ajah in truth. A member of the loyalist contingent, she had a strength level of

25(13). Born in 874 NE near the Altaran border, she went to the White Tower in 891 NE. After spending twelve years as a novice and ten years as Accepted, she was raised to the shawl in 913 NE. Shortly after being raised, she joined the Black Ajah. She was a very dissatisfied woman at that time, because of her slow progress, and had been considered ripe for recruiting for several years. Her Warder was the Darkfriend Fearil; Elza led people to believe that she and Fearil were married so they would not find odd her wish to be private with him. She was 5'5" tall, with brown hair and brown eyes, and was a pleasant-faced woman, usually cool, but fervent, even rabid, when it came to Rand. She was captured at Dumai's Wells and treated as *da'tsang* by the Aiel. Under Compulsion from Verin, she found a reason to swear oath to Rand; she was one of the first five to do so. She traveled with Cadsuane to Far Madding and then to Shadar Logoth. During the cleansing, Elza linked with Merise and Jahar and used *Callandor* to fight off the Forsaken; Elza killed Corlan Dashiva, not knowing that he was one of the Forsaken. Under orders from Shaidar Haran, Elza took the Domination Band to Semirhage, who used it on Rand. He touched the True Power, and killed both Semirhage and Elza.

Emain, Renna. *See* Renna Emain

Emar Dal. A city during the Age of Legends.

Emara. An Illianer Accepted with the rebel contingent, with a potential strength level of 30(18). Born in 968 NE, she went to the White Tower in 985 NE. After spending nine years as a novice she was raised Accepted in 994 NE. A slight woman, she had gray eyes and a quick grin. Her voice was high-pitched. She did not like Siuan and Leane, but aside from that was pleasant. Emara was one of those who tried harassing Siuan and Leane when they first arrived in Salidar; she was made to weep for it. She shared a bed with Ronelle in a room with Mulinda and Satina, a pair of serving women, in the same house with Elayne and Nynaeve in Salidar. She didn't resent Elayne and Nynaeve's extra space or the maids. In the bubble of evil, she and Ronelle were wrapped in the bedsheets and had to be unwound, which made her too ill to join the circles to combat it. Egwene called Emara down for not showing proper respect to Theodrin; Emara did not approve of Theodrin's raising by decree.

Emares, Lord. A Tairen nobleman who fought in the Aiel War. Emares sent Lan word that he was following five or six hundred Aiel, and asked him to form an anvil with his men so that Emare's men could be the hammer and take out the Aiel. There were actually two thousand Aiel, and though Lan formed the anvil, Emares never showed. The Aiel did not engage, and Lan spoke of his intention to have words with Emares.

Emares, Carniele. *See* Carniele Emares

Emares, Rosana. *See* Rosana Emares

Emarin Pendaloan. A Tairen nobleman. He was the younger brother of Algarin; the two were very close. Emarin could channel and was captured by Cadsuane and gentled at the White Tower. He lived for ten years after that; Algarin credited Cadsuane for making that possible. Algarin assumed Emarin's name when he went to the Black Tower. *See also* Algarin Pendaloan

Emela. A doll that belonged to Tuon when she was a child. She gave it to Karede for saving her life; he lost it in the Great Fire of Sohima.

Emerald Cliffs. A geological feature of Seanchan.

Emerys. A Wise One of the Shaido Aiel with the ability to channel and a strength level of 22(10). She was about 5'6" tall, with large, pretty gray eyes. She was one of Sevanna's inner circle. Emerys was one of two Shaido Wise Ones who accompanied Sevanna on her trip to the tents outside Cairhien, where Sevanna tormented Egwene. She went with Sevanna when they saw Rand beaten, and took part in, or at least was present at, the murder of Desaine. At Dumai's Wells, she went with Therava. She also sided with Therava when Therava took some power from Sevanna.

Emond's Field. A small one-inn farming village in the Two Rivers. It lay at the juncture of the old Quarry Road, leading from a forgotten quarry somewhere in the mountains, and the North Road. The village was bounded by Westwood on the west and Waterwood on the east. The main street opened out on to the Green, covered with grass. The Winespring on the west end of the Green gushed water to create streams flowing east past the inn to the swampy Waterwood. Two low footbridges crossed the water at the Green, as well as a larger bridge that could accommodate horses and wagons. Most dwellings were frame houses with thatched roofs. Aemon fought his last battle on the site that the town grew upon. While the Two Rivers was technically a part of Andor, the village had not seen a tax collector in six generations, nor the Queen's Guards in seven. Few people in the Two Rivers knew that they were supposed to be part of Andor, and even those seldom thought about it.

The government in Emond's Field consisted of the Village Council headed by the Mayor, and the Women's Circle headed by the Wisdom. The vote for Mayor was by secret ballot; women chose the Women's Circle by consensus, and they chose the Wisdom the same way. The Women's Circle always included two or three women from the surrounding area, but the number fluctuated, as did the number of women in the Circle. The Village Council always had the same number of men, and one was always from outside the village, to speak for the surrounding farmers.

Emond's Field was the hometown of Rand, Mat, Perrin, Nynaeve and Egwene. Trollocs attacked the village in 998 NE, shortly after the arrival of the Aes Sedai Moiraine and her Warder Lan. In 999 NE, the Children of the Light arrived in the Two Rivers and arrested the Luhhans and Natti Cauthon and her daughters. Tam al'Thor and Abell Cauthon escaped being arrested, but were forced into hiding. Trollocs came again to trouble Emond's Field; the Whitecloaks were of some assistance in fighting them, but were more trouble than they were worth. Perrin Aybara returned and organized a resistance that freed the Whitecloak prisoners and defeated the Trollocs. Perrin became lord of the Two Rivers, much to his surprise and dismay. A large number of refugees from other lands arrived in Emond's Field, bringing new ideas and customs to the village, and it grew and prospered accordingly.

Emond's glory. A plant having purple flowers. It was found in the gardens of the Royal Palace in Caemlyn.

Emry, Chesmal. *See* Chesmal Emry

Emry Lewin. A buxom Two Rivers girl with the ability to channel. When she was fifteen years old, she was among the young women recruited by Verin and Alanna whom Rand saw and terrified at Culain's Hound in Caemlyn. She was later taken to the rebel Aes Sedai camp.

en Shereed, Mabriam. *See* Mabriam en Shereed

Enaila. A woman of the Jarra sept of the Chareen Aiel and *Far Dareis Mai*. She was about 5'2" tall, which was very short for an Aiel, and was sensitive about it. Her fiery red hair matched her temper. Along with Somara, Enaila was one of the worst of those who mothered Rand, although she was no more than a year older than he. She spent a lot of time guarding him, and her concern for him was evident. She liked jokes, although she didn't understand Rand's. Min saw a wreath of some sort for her in Caemlyn. Feran tried to attract her interest, but Leiran, who thought a joke of Enaila's funnier than his own, succeeded. The other Maidens thought it was really his strong hands that attracted her. She laid a bridal wreath for him during the Last Battle, but she was killed by Trollocs before the marriage took place.

Endara Casalain. Artur Hawkwing's governor in the province of Andor. Her daughter Ishara was the first queen of Andor.

Endelle, Caren. An Aes Sedai of the Red Ajah and the loyalist contingent, with a strength level of 37(25). She was part of the expedition to kidnap Rand; she escaped with Covarla.

Endersole. A village located on the southern border of current-day Cairhien. It was the site of the Battle of Jolvaine Pass, where Artur Hawkwing fought Guaire Amalasan.

Enid. The head cook at The Wandering Woman in Ebou Dar. She was a very round woman with olive skin and dark eyes. Enid wielded a long-handled wooden spoon like a scepter and directed three other people at the cooking and baking. Her marriage knife bore a full dozen stones.

Enkara. A famous battle in the history of the Borderlands, mentioned by Birgitte to Uno.

Enkazin. A skinny Saldaean soldier at the Black Tower. Just short of his middle years, he had a broad nose, tilted eyes and something of the look of a clerk about him, a bit of a stoop as if from hunching for long hours over a writing table. Enkazin was at the gate of the Black Tower when Pevara and the other Red sisters arrived.

Eram Talkend. An Andoran nobleman who was High Seat of his House. His sign was a golden Winged Hand. He supported Elenia Sarand for the Lion Throne.

Eramandos, Medanor. *See* Medanor Eramandos

Eran. A Saldaean soldier who served under Bashere in Bashere's first command. Bashere later made him his daughter Faile's footman. Eran taught her knives and other fighting techniques.

Eri. A member of Jarid Sarand's personal guard. Eri had been loyal for many years, but became critical of Jarid as his insanity grew. Eri mocked Jarid, and Jarid threatened to cut out his tongue, stripped him of his pay and put him on latrine duty; Eri left the camp.

Erian Boroleos. An Illianer Aes Sedai of the Green Ajah and the loyalist contingent, with a strength level of 17(5). Born in 951 NE, she went to the White Tower in 966 NE. After spending seven years as a novice and five years as Accepted, she was raised to the shawl in 978 NE. Erian was 5'5" tall, with pale skin and long black hair. Sarene thought of Erian's face as "pale marble framed by raven's wings." Galina lusted after her, though Erian was not aware of this. She was part of the mission to kidnap Rand. When he tried to escape he killed two of her four Warders; Rashan and Bartol survived. Her anger caused her to beat Rand severely before he made his getaway at Dumai's Wells. She was captured there and named *da'tsang*, but swore allegiance to Rand. She accompanied Cadsuane to Far Madding and then to Shadar Logoth, where during the cleansing, she was made to protect the nonchannelers, such as Harine and Moad, a task that did not make her happy. After *saidin* was cleansed, Erian was part of Cadsuane's group that rested at the Pendaloan estate in Tear. She was one of many Aes Sedai tasked with maintaining the shield on Semirhage after her capture, and was present when Cadsuane spanked the Forsaken.

Eriff, Demira. *See* Demira Eriff

Erim. A man of the White Mountain sept of the Chareen Aiel who was clan chief of the Chareen. He was 6'7" tall and weighed about 235 pounds. He had red hair with white streaks, green eyes and a pugnacious jaw. His Wise One was Morena. Sulin thought that Morena had a great deal of influence with him. Erim battled the Shaido in Cairhien, and he participated in the invasion of Illian.

Erinin Inn, The. An inn in Maerone, Cairhien. When Mat and Edorion went there while making the rounds of drinking halls to visit men from the Band, a gleeman was declaiming *The Great Hunt of the Horn*.

Erinin, River. A river beginning in the far north and flowing south through Tar Valon, Aringill and Tear into the Sea of Storms. *See also* Osendrelle Erinin *and* Alindrelle Erinin

Erith daughter of Iva daughter of Alar. An Ogier from Stedding Tsofu. She was shorter than Loial, about eight feet tall, but with the same broad nose and big eyes, the same wide mouth and tufted ears; although her features were more delicate, and her voice was the softer rumble of a smaller bumblebee. Loial met her at Stedding Tsofu and was quite taken by her. She gave him a flower and said that he was handsome. Loial said he thought her ears were beautiful, which was akin to a man saying a woman had beautiful breasts. She, Covril and Haman went looking for Loial; when they found him, Erith and Loial were married. They fought together in the Last Battle.

Eronaile, Mierin. Lanfear's original name.

Ershin Netari. An Illianer nobleman who was a member of the Council of Nine. He fought against the Seanchan; in the last engagement, he was under the command of Semaradrid.

Esandara. A nation that arose after the Trolloc Wars.

Escanda, Suilin. *See* Suilin Escanda

Escape, the. The name the Sea Folk used for their exodus from Ebou Dar, begun by Mat releasing a Sea Folk *damane*, and ending with the death of many people and the destruction of many ships.

Escaralde Hamdey. A Far Madding Aes Sedai of the Brown Ajah and the rebel contingent, with a strength level of 23(11). Born in 927 NE, she went to the White Tower in 942 NE. After spending eight years as a novice and nine years as Accepted, she was raised to the shawl in 959 NE. Although she was only 4'10" tall, she seemed to loom by sheer force of will. She was a stubborn woman who refused to believe that anything was beyond her until she had proved it to her own satisfaction. Escaralde was raised Sitter for the Brown in Salidar in 999 NE. Although it was very rare for a woman to be raised Sitter at an age under one hundred, Escaralde, at just over seventy, was the oldest of the Sitters raised in Salidar. She insisted on trying to learn to make *ter'angreal* when she was not strong enough. Escaralde, Malind and Moria proposed an alliance with the Black Tower.

Eschede, Meidani. *See* Meidani Eschede

Eselle Najima. A Kandori girl whose mother was interviewed by Moiraine in her search for the Dragon Reborn. A young teen, Eselle had long black hair and blue eyes that were level with Moiraine's. Her father and brothers had been killed by the Black Ajah.

Esmara Getares. A woman who tried to conquer Andor and re-create Hawk-wing's empire in the War of the Hundred Years. She failed, and spent the last twelve years of her life as the "guest" of Queen Telaisien of Andor. Esmara was later assassinated for reasons unknown.

Esne. A serving woman in Aesdaishar Palace who served Lan when he visited. She had a square face; Lan thought she might be one of the daughters of Anya, another servant in the palace. Edeyn coopted her loyalties.

Esole. A Jenn Aiel child during the Breaking. She was the daughter of Jonai and was still young enough to play with dolls when they left Paaran Disen. She fell ill during their journey, and because there was no Aes Sedai to Heal her, she died.

Espara Soman. A woman from Toman Head who sought refuge in the Two Rivers. She was an herbalist, and sought Faile's permission to work as a healer.

Faile sent her to the Women's Circle to determine if she was able enough to be apprenticed to a Wisdom.

Essande. Elayne's maid at the Royal Palace in Caemlyn, chosen after Elayne's return to Caemlyn. She was slim, dignified, white-haired and slow-moving. She knew the job and did not waste time on chatter; in fact she said little beyond suggesting clothes, and made the same comment every day: that Elayne looked like and reminded Essande of Morgase. She wore Elayne's Golden Lily embroidered large on her breast, and her gray skirts were trimmed in red. She reserved certain tasks for herself, such as dressing and undressing Elayne. Elayne thought that Essande's joints ached, though she denied it and refused Healing. Her niece, Melfane, became Elayne's midwife.

Essanik Cycle. Seanchan prophecies akin to *The Prophecies of the Dragon.*

Essays of Willim of Manaches, The. An ancient book known by many in the world; the author influenced the Saldaean philosopher Shivena Kayenzi.

Essays on Reason. A book from the Royal Library in Cairhien that Min found intriguing. Its author was Daria Gahand.

Essenia. One of the Ten Nations. Its capital was Aren Mador (later Far Madding); other cities included Delsande and Tear. First Lord Cristol was the ruler at the signing of the Compact of the Ten Nations.

Essonde. A senior *der'sul'dam* in Ebou Dar. Bethamin asked Renna, when they were checking the kennels, "Do you want to be reported to Essonde for laziness yet again?" and later told Renna to take her writing board to Essonde when she took her own reports to her.

Estair. An Aiel who was a Wise One apprentice to Aeron. She was a slender redhead with serious gray eyes. She seemed to look for rules to obey and always behaved as if a Wise One were watching her, which was odd, considering that Aeron was easygoing for a Wise One. She spoke reverently of the *Car'a'carn*; Egwene thought she could put on the *siswai'aman* headband.

Estalaine. A Wise One of the Shaido Aiel. She was with Sevanna at Dumai's Wells and was killed by lightning.

Estanda. A High Lady of Tear. Rand gave Tedosian into her care when he sent Alteima, Tedosian's wife who had tried to poison him, to Cairhien. An agent of Sebban Balwer working for the Whitecloaks later persuaded Estanda to join Darlin in open rebellion. Merana and Rafela negotiated a settlement with Estanda and the other rebels; that settlement made Darlin king.

Estean Andiama. A Tairen nobleman who was the son of High Lord Torean. He was plain-faced with a large nose and ears and lank hair that fell over his forehead. He looked like a farmer's son although he was incredibly wealthy. He drank as much as any three men. When he was playing cards with Mat and the cards came to life, he was frightened. Trapped in Cairhien when the Shaido attacked, he and some others managed to escape and went to Rand for help. He joined the Band of the Red Hand and became an officer. Estean was anxious to please Mat, but he was not terribly swift nor bright, although he was not exactly stupid. He was excitable and did not learn from his mistakes. King Roedran of Murandy hired the Band to help him gain control and build an army; Talmanes left Estean in charge of the horse there while they completed their mission and moved north into Andor, because Estean would listen to the more capable Daerid, who was in charge of the foot. In the Last Battle, he led the Band's cavalry.

Ester Norham. A hairdresser in the Royal Palace in Caemlyn who was uncovered as a spy by Reene Harfor. Reene knew that she wasn't stealing, but that she had over fifty crowns of gold hidden under her floorboards. Instead of firing her, Reene and Elayne saw that she was given incorrect information.

Ester Stepashin. An Illianer Aes Sedai of the Green Ajah and the rebel contingent, with a strength level of 16(4). Born in 955 NE, she went to the White Tower in 972 NE. After spending seven years as a novice and eight years as Accepted, she was raised to the shawl in 987 NE. Her father was a shipowner in Illian; she came from a line of shipowners, ship captains and shipbuilders. She was under five feet tall, with large brown eyes, a short cap of dark brown curls and a small, upturned nose. She was cute, almost doll-like, which she did not like having pointed out, any more than she enjoyed anyone referring to her height. Ester arrived in the White Tower a few months before Moiraine and Siuan, but was quickly outstripped by them. In fact, she admired both women, though when Siuan was raised Amyrlin she expressed her doubts concerning Siuan's youth openly enough to earn her a stiff penance. She did not resent this, having decided that she had indeed overstepped the bounds, that discipline had to be maintained. Ester had one Warder to whom she was married, a man in his early forties, a little younger than she. She was part of the rebel fifth column sent by Sheriam's council in Salidar to infiltrate the White Tower (aka ferrets). Like all of the sisters chosen for the fifth column, Ester was out of the White Tower when Siuan was deposed and the Tower broken, so there was no flight to arouse any suspicions toward her. Apparently, she had simply returned in answer to Elaida's summons. In addition, the general belief was that she harbored resentment because Siuan rose so much faster than she herself did, a belief aided by her comments back then and the penance they earned her.

Estevan Tonarma. A Tairen Lord of the Land sworn to Sunamon. A lanky man, he had a hard jaw, harder eyes and a peremptory manner with servants. He was with the army gathering to invade Illian.

Ethenielle Kirukon Materasu. Her Most Illumined Majesty, By the Blessing of the Light, Queen of Kandor, Protector of the Land, Shield of the North, High Seat of House Materasu. Standing about 5'4" tall, and buxom, with blue eyes and a few gray hairs dusting her black hair, she was stately with a considerable regal dignity. She was born in 946 NE and married Brys Noramaga in 963 NE. It was a love-match in large part, though there was a political consideration, of course. She ascended the Throne of the Clouds in 966 NE. She and Brys had eight children, seven of whom survived. Diryk, their second-eldest son, was killed along with his father in 979 NE. Ethenielle was a wise ruler who considered that her job was to think, lead and command; she left the soldiering to those who had the skill to do so. She married a second time just before the Last Battle; her husband was Tenobia's uncle, Kalyan Ramsin. She took part in the Last Battle, attached to Lan's army.

Ethin. An old serving man at Lord Algarin's manor in Tear. He was bony and white-haired, and had trouble with his joints. Ethin disapproved of Logain's manners.

Eurian Romavni. The Kandori author of *A Journey to Tarabon*, a book Egwene used as a guide to Tanchico.

Eval Ramman. Balthamel's name in the Age of Legends.

Evanellein Lorn. An Andoran Aes Sedai of the Gray Ajah in public but of the Black Ajah in truth. Part of the loyalist contingent, she had a strength level of 20(8). Born in 855 NE, she went to the White Tower in 872 NE. After spending seven years as a novice and six years as Accepted, she was raised to the shawl in 885 NE and raised Sitter for the Gray in 997 NE. About 5'4" tall with a medium build, she had dark brown hair, which she wore in ever-changing styles, and thought one of her best features. Her eyes were large and brown, which she also took pride in. She wore low-cut dresses because she also admired her bosoms; they were not large, but they had a very good shape. She was very concerned with her looks, and with clothes. Evanellein often wore the latest fashions, though only when they were flattering, as she saw it. She was a fairly pretty woman, though not among the prettiest of the sisters. She was far more concerned about whether other women saw her as beautiful than whether men did, despite the low-cut gowns. She worried about the size of her bottom, though no man who saw it had ever complained; in fact, her worries were all in her head, and her bottom was just fine.

Despite what might have seemed overconcern with her looks and clothes, she had a first-rate mind and was a good mediator, though only fair at negotiation. Evanellein was considered politically very astute even for a Sitter. Before the tensions began among the Ajahs, she used her mediating ability to advantage in the Hall. She stood to depose Siuan, and was a member of the council advising Elaida. Her name was not in Verin's book, but she disappeared with the other members of the Black Ajah. She was killed by Egwene in *Tel'aran'rhiod*.

Evard Cordwyn. An Andoran mercenary captain who was hired by Elayne. He was square-jawed and wore a ruby in his left earlobe. A pair of swords on his back indicated he had spent time in Arafel. Arymilla bribed him with gold to turn traitor, and he died from wounds sustained while trying to seize the Far Madding Gate.

Evasni. A *Far Dareis Mai* who went with Rand to Maradon. She was lanky with dark red hair.

Evelle, Lady. An aunt of Catalyn Haevin. She told Catalyn to leave the swords to men.

Evening Star, The. A respectable inn in Chachin, Kandor, with a female innkeeper. It catered to merchants of middling rank, especially women unwilling to be bothered by noise or rough sorts in the spacious common room. Siuan and Moiraine stayed there while searching for the infant Dragon Reborn.

Ever Victorious Army. The not-quite-accurate name the Seanchan gave their army.

Evin Vinchova. A young Asha'man Dedicated from Kandor. He was a pretty, pink-cheeked lad; Toveine doubted he shaved twice in the week. He was about sixteen years old when he went to the Black Tower. He mistakenly believed Logain and Taim were close until Logain set him straight. He associated himself with Logain, and was with Logain when the latter took Toveine. Evin was angry about two recruits, boys of maybe fourteen years, among the Two Rivers men. Logain told them all to watch out for the Two Rivers men, but not too much, so the others wouldn't turn on them. Evin was trapped in the Black Tower by the dreamspike and captured and broken by Taim's men. He was Turned to the Shadow, but his taint madness made him vulnerable to paranoia, which Androl used to make him attack Abors, another Darkfriend Asha'man. Taim killed Evin.

Evon. The cook in the Arene household in Amador. He was fat and balding, and Liandrin thought he had piggy eyes. Liandrin didn't like him looking at her, so she spoke sharply to him and made sure he sweated bullets while avoiding looking at her. Once she was turned over to his employer for punishment by Moghedien, though, he was not only able to do considerably more than look, he was encouraged to do so.

Ewal Coplin. A young man in Emond's Field. Rand once punched him in the nose for making fun of his gray eyes. When the Whitecloaks first came to the Two Rivers, Ewal liked them, but he later accompanied Luc to tell them that Emond's Field was closed to them.

Eward Aybara. Perrin's stout paternal uncle. He and his wife Magde had three children. Fain killed them along with the rest of Perrin's family, although it was believed that they were killed by Trollocs.

Eward Candwin. A stout cooper from Emond's Field. During the Trolloc attack on Winternight, he received a slash down his back; Moiraine Healed him. He later took part in the defense of Emond's Field.

Eward Congar. An Emond's Field man who looked down his nose at others. He once fell off the Wagon Bridge and had to tramp home dripping wet, which took him down a peg for a month or so. Eward sucked up to the Whitecloaks when they came to the Two Rivers.

Ewin Finngar. A young man from Emond's Field. Ewin shared the news of Moiraine and Lan with Mat and Rand; Moiraine gave him a silver penny. When Perrin returned to the Two Rivers, Ewin had grown a great deal, and helped Perrin in the defense of Emond's Field. Later, with Dav Ayellin and Elam Dowtry, he ran off to see the world.

exchanger. A hollow cylinder from the Age of Legends found in Sammael's room by the Asha'man. It kept the air pleasantly cool. The user had to supply the power, but his or her presence was not required to keep it running.

Exile, Long, the. *See* Long Exile, the

Eyal in the Marches of Maighande. A battle from Mat's memories.

Eye of the World, the. A concentrated pool of pure *saidin*, created by Aes Sedai, using both *saidin* and *saidar*, during the Breaking. Many Aes Sedai died in its making. It was ultimately located in the Blight and guarded by the Green Man. It was destroyed when it fulfilled its purpose related to the Dragon Reborn.

Eyeless, the. *See* Myrddraal

eyes-and-ears. Each Ajah had informants, networks of agents in various parts of the world. In addition, some individual Aes Sedai had personal networks of varying sizes, and there was also an Amyrlin's network. Some of these agents sent messages by merchants' trains, others via pigeon. These informants were not very numerous, and were all extremely cautious, as it would not have been very healthy to be discovered working for Aes Sedai. Because of these informants, Tar Valon sometimes learned of events before closer cities, but because they were scattered, few and cautious, most information reached Tar Valon slowly, by more usual methods. News traveled faster in spring and summer than in autumn or winter, which was the slowest of all. Snows, rains and storms could all slow the speed of news.

Eyndel. A member of the Band of the Red Hand. In one of their attacks on the Seanchan, Mandevwin ordered Admar and Eyndel to take their crossbowmen up the north slope of a hill, where they would face off against Seanchan lancers.

F

Fade. *See* Myrddraal

Faeldrin Harella. A Taraboner Aes Sedai of the Green Ajah and the rebel contingent, with a strength level of 16(4). Born in 937 NE, she went to the White Tower in 952 NE. After spending five years as a novice and five years as Accepted, she was raised to the shawl in 962 NE. Standing 5'4" tall, she had dark hair in braids with colored beads to her shoulders. She had three Warders. Faeldrin was a member of the rebel embassy to Rand in Caemlyn and followed after Rand when he fled them in Caemlyn. Forced to swear fealty to him after Dumai's Wells, she was considered and treated like an apprentice by the Wise Ones. She intended to keep her oaths of fealty to the best of her ability, however reluctantly, but she could not stand up to Cadsuane, at least not openly. In one of Min's visions, she saw that Faeldrin was in the palm of Rand's hand and could be trusted. She accompanied Rand on his visit to the Sea Folk. Later, Rand sent her, with others, to negotiate with the rebels in Haddon Mirk. Faeldrin was killed by Hessalam (aka Graendal) in the Last Battle.

Faeral din Rao. A Sea Folk Windfinder with a strength level of 19(7). She accompanied Renaile to the Tarasin Palace, then to the Kin's farm, where she observed the use of the Bowl of the Winds. She fled to Caemlyn with Elayne and her companions when the Seanchan attacked.

Fager Neald. A Murandian man who was born very nearly on the border with Andor; he went to the Black Tower. He was a fop and a dandy, his pitiful mustache waxed to a semblance of points. When he did something with the Power, he posed and postured as if expecting applause. He was three or four years younger than Perrin, and maybe ten years younger than Grady. He was especially strong in Earth, and he could make a gateway for Traveling. After Dumai's Wells, Neald was chosen to accompany Rand, and then traveled to Ghealdan with Perrin. Neald showed the beginnings of a Talent with "reading" weaves, though at first it was just that seeing the weave in the sky made by the Bowl of the Winds made him think of wind. He and Gaul captured Galina at Malden, and took her to Perrin. During the pursuit of the Shaido, Neald exhausted himself making gateways; he was also bitten by a black snake in a bubble of evil. Neald worked with the Wise Ones to figure out how to link; he linked with them when Perrin was creating his hammer and produced a Power-wrought weapon. In the Last Battle, Neald worked with Talmanes to use the dragons through gateways, preventing them from being easily taken.

Faile. Old Tongue for "falcon."

Faile ni Bashere t'Aybara. A young Saldaean woman whose birth-name was Zarine, she was the daughter of Davram Bashere, Marshal-General to and uncle
of Queen Tenobia of Saldaea. Born in 981 NE, she was six years younger than
Tenobia. She had high cheekbones, a mouth that some might have called too
wide, dark, tilted eyes and a slightly hooked nose that some might have called
too prominent. She was beautiful, but in an exotic way; it took Perrin a little
while to decide whether she was or not. She stood about 5'7" and had several
small scars, none that showed with her clothes on.

When Perrin met her, she was seeking adventure as a Hunter of the Horn.
She joined his group, which included Moiraine, Lan and Loial. In Tear, she
set off a hedgehog trap that had been meant for Moiraine, and became stuck
in *Tel'aran'rhiod*, until saved by Perrin. Faile was enamored of Perrin, but she
was jealous of Berelain's flirting with him. Faile and Perrin traveled to Emond's
Field to defend it against the Trollocs; while there, they married. Perrin was
later tasked with going to Ghealdan to deal with Masema; Faile accompanied
him. Queen Alliandre pledged herself to Perrin there, and Faile and Perrin
took on Morgase and her entourage, traveling incognito, as servants.

A group of more than two dozen men and women from Tear and Cairhien
had also attached themselves to Faile and were called *Cha Faile*; she used them
as spies.

While Perrin was meeting with Masema, Faile and her companions went
hawking. Cha Faile arrived and alerted Faile that Masema was meeting with the
Seanchan. Faile's party was attacked by Shaido; Faile's horse was hit by an arrow
and broke her leg. Rolan, a Mera'din with Sevanna's Jumai, captured Faile and
carried her to Sevanna's camp, where she was made *gai'shain*. Captured along with
her were Alliandre, Maighdin (Morgase), Bain, Chiad, Lacile and Arrela; Berelain escaped and carried word to Perrin of the kidnapping and of Masema.

During their captivity, Galina, who had been held captive by the Shaido since
the battle at Dumai's Wells, induced Faile to procure a binder in Therava's passion, a *ter'angreal* that had come from Sammael through Sevanna. A number of
Sevanna's *gai'shain* swore fealty to Faile, and one, a young man named Theril,
was able to steal it. Faile and her companions, except for Bain and Chiad, met
with Galina in a building marked with a red handkerchief to hand over the
binder; Galina trapped them in the basement of the building. Maighdin used
her small ability with the One Power to cause the scarf to wave; Theril saw it and
went for help. Rolan, Jhoradin, and Kinhuin rescued Faile and her companions;
Perrin arrived then and killed Rolan. Lacile and Faile stabbed Jhoradin and Kinhuin in the back.

Shortly afterward, Faile and *Cha Faile* killed Masema. Faile accompanied Perrin and his troops through Andor; they eventually reached the Field of Merrilor,
just at the start of the Last Battle. Faile was chosen to secretly get the Horn of

Valere from the White Tower and take it to Mat; soldiers of the Band of the Red Hand, Aravine (a former *gai'shain* who had sworn to her) and Olver went with her. As they were leaving the Traveling grounds in Tar Valon, a bubble of evil struck, and the gateway they rushed through led them to the Blight. Posing as a supply caravan to the Shadowspawn, they Traveled back to Merrilor. Aravine betrayed them to the Shadow's forces, and they were captured. They managed to break free, and the Shadowspawn chased after Faile and the Horn. She doubled back and gave the Horn to Olver and led the Shadowspawn away. After the battle at Merrilor, Perrin found her near death on the battlefield, and took her to Nynaeve, who Healed her. With the deaths of Faile's father and Queen Terobia, she and Perrin were to become the monarchs of Saldaea.

Fain, Padan. *See* Padan Fain

Fairheart, Cowin. *See* Cowin Gemallan

Faisar, Asidim. *See* Asidim Faisar

Faiselle Darone. A Domani Aes Sedai of the Green Ajah and the rebel contingent, with a strength level of 20(8). Born in 829 NE, she went to the White Tower in 845 NE. After spending ten years as a novice and ten years as Accepted, she was raised to the shawl in 865 NE. Copper-skinned, Faiselle was stocky with a square face. She was raised Sitter for the Green in 981 NE. Faiselle had two Warders.

In 999 NE, Adelorna Bastine ordered her to join the rebellion to control and defuse events. Faiselle did not make any great effort to go against Lelaine since following her countered Romanda and helped assure stalemate in the rebel Hall. Faiselle believed the reports concerning Logain and Red sisters, possibly including Elaida, and by implication thus had suspicions regarding the Reds and other false Dragons. That put considerable strain on her purpose. But she felt that the problem of the Seanchan took precedence over all else. She was against any alliance with the Black Tower and worked to delay an embassy to it; she also opposed bonding Asha'man. She was part of the group, with Magla, Saroiya, Takima and Varilin, who negotiated with the White Tower to try to end the split. In the Last Battle, when it was discovered that Bryne was under Compulsion, Faiselle suggested that the Aes Sedai take over battle leadership.

Fal Dara. A heavily fortified city in Shienar near the Blightborder. The sign of the city was the Black Hawk; it was the seat of Lord Agelmar Jagad. The city of Mafal Dadaranell was built by Ogier, destroyed in the Trolloc Wars, and rebuilt by men; the name changed over the centuries. The city was built on hills higher than the surrounding land and was surrounded by a fifty-foot austere gray stone wall, with high towers topped by wooden hoardings and bedecked with pennants. The East Gate, the King's Gate to the south and Malkier Gate to the north gave access. The streets were stone-paved. The architecture was plain and simple in contrast to Ogier work which had been destroyed: wood-shingled rooftops, tall stone chimneys and taller towers. A fortress was centrally located on the highest hill, surrounded by a deep and wide drymoat, the bottom of which was forested by man-high steel spikes. Inside the second defensive wall was a large square courtyard paved with huge stone blocks and surrounded by crenellated towers and battlements.

Around the city the land was clear-cut a mile out from the wall in all directions. A Waygate was located a few miles southwest of the city. Farms outside the city had wood-shingled, steep-pitched roofs that came near the ground. The city was burned by Lan's troops in the Last Battle to slow down the advance of the Shadowspawn army.

Fal Eisen. A city in Shienar, the seat of Lord Kayen Yokata. The Asha'man set fire to the city during the Last Battle, and Yokata and his cavalry unit were killed by Trollocs nearby during a battle that went wrong for them.

Fal Moran. The capital of Shienar and seat of the Shienar monarch, King Easar of House Togita. Fal Moran was considered to be the heart and soul of Shienar. It was not as close to the Blightborder as Fal Dara. Fal Moran was razed during the Last Battle to impede the progress of the invading Trolloc armies.

Fal Sion. A fortress was located in this Shienaran town. Agelmar was to join other armies from Shienar, including Fal Sion, on the way to meeting the Trollocs at Tarwin's Gap, at the same time Rand went to meet the Green Man.

Falendre. A *sul'dam* accompanying Anath/Semirhage when she met with Rand. She was honey-skinned, with dark tilted eyes and gray-streaked hair. After capturing Semirhage, Rand sent Falendre back to Ebou Dar to tell the Daughter of the Nine Moons that he would still like to meet with her. He also tasked her with telling Tuon that Anath was one of the Forsaken; she eventually did.

Falin Deborsha. An Ebou Dari merchant, possibly fictional, with whom Basel Gill claimed to be dealing, when the Whitecloaks detained his group on the Jehannah Road.

Falion Bhoda. A Kandori Aes Sedai of the White Ajah publicly and the Black Ajah in truth, with a strength level of 17(5). Born in 873 NE, she went to the White Tower in 889 NE. After spending seven years as a novice, she ran away to Ebou Dar before being caught and returned to Tar Valon. Her brief stay in Ebou Dar was not pleasant. After six years as Accepted, she was raised to the shawl in 902 NE. She was about 5'5" tall and had a long, cold face and dark hair. Despite her outward coolness, inside she was a furnace of angers and slights. She had little or no patience with anyone's faults or quirks but her own, and was contemptuous of others while never seeing her own faults or peculiarities. Other Whites were the only people she considered good company, and even then, they did have their faults, particularly in certain questions of logic. Falion was quite willing to use the Power to torture someone, even torture them to death, and was quite dispassionate about it. Her only vexation came if they didn't give her the answers she wanted. She was one of the first thirteen members of the Black Ajah identified.

Under Moghedien's orders she and Ispan Shefar traveled to Ebou Dar in search of objects of the One Power. They both came to believe that the cache did not exist. She and Ispan attacked Nynaeve and her party when they went to fetch the Bowl of the Winds.

Falion escaped, but as punishment by Moridin for past failures, she was used as a servant by Shiaine, and also made available for Daved Hanlon. She and Hanlon worked out an accommodation and information exchange because he did not want to be on the bad side of an Aes Sedai. Shiaine just wanted sisters to use, but saw to Falion's punishment because otherwise she herself would be punished. Falion was shielded in such a way that the shield would dissolve over time, but was commanded to obey Shiaine.

When the shield dissolved, nothing changed, though Falion thought it would and should. She believed that the Chosen, while very far above everyone else, behaved illogically at times. When Elayne tried to capture the Black Ajah members at Lady Shiaine's house, Falion was present. She was captured when Elayne was rescued, but freed when Daved Hanlon attacked Elayne in the prison. She then joined Graendal, and was later killed by Aviendha in the Last Battle.

Fall of Pipkin, the. A battle from Mat's memories.

Falling Shale. A history book that Min studied.

Falme, Fifth Treaty of. *See* Fifth Treaty of Falme

Falme. The largest town on Toman Head, though not as big as a major city; its population was around twenty-five thousand. It stood on a spit of land at the very tip of Toman Head, on the Aryth Ocean. High cliffs ran to the harbor mouth on both sides, and atop one of those, where every ship running into the harbor had to pass under them, stood the towers of the Watchers Over the Waves, where the Watchers kept a lookout for the return of Artur Hawkwing's armies. Falme rose from stone docks up the slopes of the hollow that made the harbor. The houses were dark stone with slate roofs, larger and taller as the cobblestone streets climbed up from the docks. At the top of the incline, the town gave way to hills. There was no town wall.

The Seanchan Return landed at Falme, and High Lord Turak had a house there; Fain went to him there, and Egeanin took Domon. Egwene, Nynaeve, Elayne and Min were tricked by Liandrin into going to Falme, and Egwene was collared by the Seanchan and kept in the town. Rand, Mat, Perrin, Ingtar and Hurin tracked Padan Fain there to retrieve the Horn of Valere and the dagger from Shadar Logoth. Rand retrieved the Horn by killing Lord Turak, a Seanchan blademaster. The captured *damane* were housed in Falme, including Egwene.

Rand battled Ba'alzamon over the battlefield at Falme, while Mat, caught between the fighting Whitecloak and Seanchan armies, blew the Horn of Valere, calling out the Heroes of the Horn.

Some time later, Rand met the Daughter of the Nine Moons there in a failed attempt to arrive at a truce.

Faloun, Blasic. *See* Blasic Faloun

Falton. A Cairhienin farrier in Perrin's camp in Ghealdan. Only a fringe of white hair remained on his head; he had broad shoulders and thick arms, and seemed nearly as wide as he was tall, though as a Cairhienin, he was not very tall. Like the other farriers, he grew nervous when Perrin tried to tend to his own horse.

Famelle Juarde. A Taraboner Kin and member of the Knitting Circle in Ebou Dar. Her strength level was 38(26); she was strong enough to have been allowed to test for Aes Sedai, but not strong enough to make a gateway of any size whatsoever. Born in 658 NE, she went to the White Tower in 672 NE, where she spent eleven years as a novice. She began her test for Accepted the first time it was offered, but could not make herself enter the *ter'angreal* the third time. Slender and pretty, with large brown eyes and pale honey hair worn loose, she was one of the few among the Knitting Circle with no gray in her hair. When Elayne and Nynaeve first learned of the Kin, Famelle was working as a goldsmith in Ebou Dar. Famelle survived the *gholam*'s attack in the Rahad and was present at the meeting with the Windfinders in the Tarasin Palace. On orders from Elayne and Nynaeve, she took part in manipulating them.

fancloth. A synthetic fabric that duplicated its surroundings for a total camouflage effect. Warders' cloaks were made from this material, which was produced by a *ter'angreal* in the White Tower. In the Age of Legends, fancloth was a fashionable fabric, and soldiers wore it during the War of Power.

Fang, Dragon's. *See* Dragon's Fang

fangfish. A dangerous fish of editorial nature.

fans, the language of. In Saldaea, women used fans to communicate subtly. Some gestures were:

> caution in speech, admonishment to: fan touches ear.
> disbelief: very fast snap shut and open.
> innocence: a gentle fluttering in front of the face, looking over the fan.
> kiss me; you may kiss me: end of closed fan brushes across her lips.
> love; a shared kiss: touch her cheek then his with closed fan.
> relief: a fluttering hitch.
> thought, I am giving your suggestion serious: tap wrist with closed fan.

Fanshir. An Asha'man soldier who was a scholar before going to the Black Tower; he was the possessor of interesting books.

Fanwar. A Borderland family. *See* Auaine *and* Renald Fanwar

Fanway, Karella. An Aes Sedai who lived at the time of the formation of the White Tower.

Faolain Orande. An Aes Sedai of the Blue Ajah and the rebel contingent, with a strength level of 17(5). Born in 970 NE, she went to the White Tower in 986 NE. After spending eight years as a novice and five years as Accepted, she was raised to the shawl in 999 NE by Egwene's decree. Faolain had curly hair and a dark round face. She never seemed to like anyone or anything; on the other hand, she did not resist being taken away from the Tower by fleeing Aes Sedai because she did not approve of the manner in which Siuan was deposed. Nevertheless she thought Siuan very likely should have been deposed and was responsible for the Tower being broken. She was one of those who harassed Siuan in Salidar and was punished for it.

Faolain swore fealty to Egwene, along with Theodrin. She did not like Egwene, and made that clear, but Egwene was the Amyrlin, and she felt it wasn't right that the others treated her as if she were not, as if she were not even Aes Sedai sometimes. She admitted right out that her gratitude for being raised by Egwene's decree was exceedingly mixed, given how that was received by the other sisters. She was assigned by Egwene to accept Lelaine's offer of protection and guidance, and to become Egwene's spy on Lelaine. She wasn't wholeheartedly pleased at the prospect—she knew very well that being taken under Lelaine's wing would mean being treated not like an Aes Sedai but like an Accepted who had to be watched closely—yet, quite aside from her oath, she was pleased to be doing something real, and to be getting back at the sisters who treated her as if she were still Accepted. Lelaine worked out that Faolain was a spy, and ordered her into hiding.

Faolain went to the Black Tower to bond an Asha'man. There Lyrelle ordered her to bond only one.

Far Aldazar Din. An Aiel warrior society; its name meant "Brothers of the Eagle."

Far Dareis Mai. A warrior society of the Aiel which admitted only women; its name meant "Maidens of the Spear." *See* Maidens of the Spear

Far Madding. An independent city-state on the Plains of Maredo; it lay on an island in a lake approximately one mile south of the Hills of Kintara. Its sigil was a woman's golden hand which was open, fingers up: the Golden Hand. Its banner was a blue field divided vertically in the center by an elongated red oval of even dimensions; on the side nearest the flagstaff was the Golden Hand and on the outer end of the flag there was a golden sword, a simple straight blade and cross quillons, point upward.

In the Age of Legends, a city called Aren Deshar occupied the spot later known as Far Madding. The city was called Aren Mador when it was the capital city of Essenia, one of the nations of the Compact of the Ten Nations. Part of it was Ogier-built, but nothing of that remained. After the Trolloc Wars, it was known as Fel Moreina, in Moreina. The nation of Maredo was founded in FY 999 by nobles in the city of Far Madding, led by Lady Danella Mathendrin. The city of Far Madding, with its special advantages, held against all attackers, and Maredo eventually laid claim to all of the Plains of Maredo and parts of what is now eastern Murandy as well. However, Maredo as a nation vanished by 500 NE, leaving behind only the city-state of Far Madding.

The ruling body of Far Madding was the Counsels; there were thirteen of them, with the highest-ranking named the First Counsel. They were all women. In Far Madding, men did not hold positions of authority except over other men, and they were never allowed positions of high authority or responsibility. Even when they held a position which would carry considerable authority and/or respon-

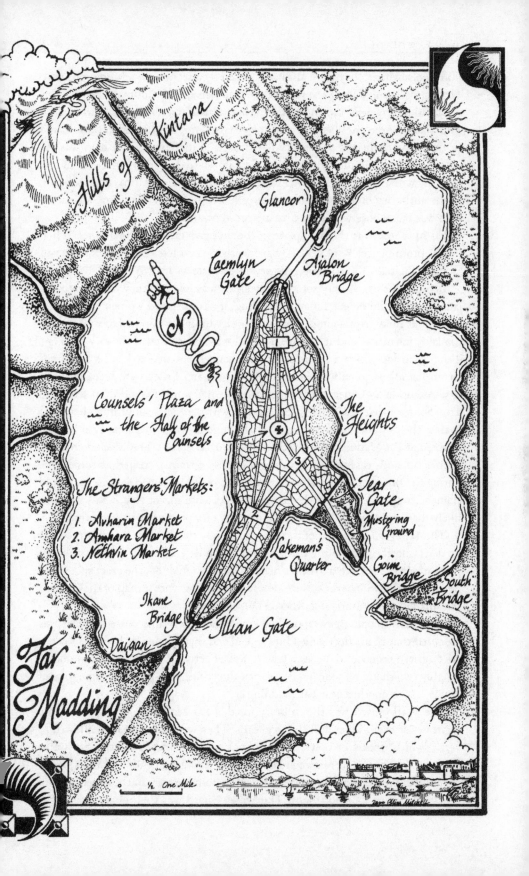

sibility elsewhere, they were always overseen by a woman in a higher position. The Counsels ruled from the Hall of the Counsels on the Counsels' Plaza.

Far Madding was the most openly matriarchal city in the known world. This was in large part because two major false Dragons had been born in the city, but the traditions of the city dated back to its founding. A man was expected to obey his mother or eldest female relative until he married and to obey his wife thereafter. In any case, she had authority over him corresponding to the authority of a medieval man over his wife. In Far Madding, a wealthy man was one whose wife gave him a large allowance.

Far Madding was the birthplace of the first two false Dragons to reach historical prominence, Raolin Darksbane (early 335 to late 336 AB) and Yurian Stonebow (circa 1300 to 1308 AB, possibly as late as 1312 AB).

Because of this, the city somehow acquired a *ter'angreal*, known as the guardians, which could detect a man channeling; it also detected women channeling, though not at as great a range—within the city limits, as opposed to well beyond the lake, for men—and it produced a field which surrounded the city for a fair distance, inside which a man's ability to channel was shielded so he could not channel at all. Women were also cut off, but not until they were actually at the city. As inside an Ogier *stedding*, neither men nor women could even sense the True Source inside the active area. Also as with a *stedding*, anything channeled against the city simply melted away at the edge of the active area; even balefire directed at Far Madding dispersed on hitting that border. The affected area was circular in both cases. This device was almost certainly created at some time during the Breaking of the World, since it was plainly directed at men who could channel. It should be noted that the built-in defense meant that it was very unlikely that anyone would ever be able to study or reproduce it in any form.

The *ter'angreal* consisted of three parts, each with an arrow which turned red on detecting the channeling of *saidin* or blue on detecting *saidar* and turned to point toward the source of that channeling. By triangulation, the exact spot could be located. The *ter'angreal* was inside a large chamber with a map of the city and the surrounding countryside worked into the floor.

Not many people knew about the device. So much time passed after it was procured that it, in effect, faded into legend and myth. The city kept the knowledge of its existence to a select few. It was effective, though; over a period of roughly two thousand years no fewer than thirty-one false Dragons came to grief of one sort or another near Far Madding.

The Wall Guard was the military force of Far Madding, who manned the fortresses at the bridges and the city walls. They were the only men allowed to carry swords, spears or bows that were not peace-bound inside the city walls, but even they were only allowed to do so while on duty. The top command levels of the Wall Guard were all women; there were some women in the lower levels of the Wall Guard, but not many. The Street Guard was the police force of Far

Madding. Its composition was roughly the same as the Wall Guard. The Street Guard relied mainly on long cudgels, sword-breakers, quarterstaffs and catchpoles. They carried no blade longer than a belt knife. When the Street Guard arrested someone, the detainee was bound wrists-to-ankles and put into a sack, which was then slung from a pole carried on the shoulders of two men.

The city of Far Madding was a center for overland trade between Illian and Caemlyn or Tar Valon, and also between Tear and Caemlyn or Tar Valon, thus avoiding the lands of Cairhien. It shared the overland trade between Illian and Caemlyn with Lugard, as well as the overland trade between Illian and Tar Valon, but the route to both Caemlyn and Tar Valon was shorter through Far Madding. Far Madding had three markets, called Strangers' Markets, in which foreigners were allowed to trade: the Avharin Market, the Amhara Market and the Nethvin Market.

Faral, Dimir. *See* Dimir Faral

Farashelle. A nation that arose after the Trolloc Wars.

Farede. The first Panarch of Tarabon. He adopted and promoted a new calendar, the Farede Calendar, as part of his attempt to make Tarabon the intellectual center of the known world.

Farede Calendar. A calendar adopted after the widespread destruction and disruption of the War of the Hundred Years. It was proposed by Urin din Jubai Soaring Gull, a scholar of the Sea Folk, and promoted by the Panarch Farede of Tarabon. It recorded each year as of the New Era (NE) and was still in use at the time of the Last Battle. The calendar set 10 days to the week, 28 days to the month and 13 months to the year. The months were: Taisham (December 22–January 17), Jumara (January 18–February 14), Saban (February 15–March 14), Aine (March 15–April 11), Adar (April 12–May 9), Saven (May 10–June 6), Amadaine (June 7–July 5), Tammaz (July 6–August 2), Maigdhal (August 3–August 30), Choren (August 31–September 27), Shaldine (September 28–October 26), Nesan (October 27–November 23) and Danu (November 24–December 21).

Farellien. An Aes Sedai of the Yellow Ajah and the loyalist contingent. Elaida praised her, Kiyoshi and Doraise for adhering to the law and gave each a fine horse as a reward. Many if not most sisters thought the three turned in Adelorna and Josaine for illegally possessing *angreal*. Alviarin forced Elaida to these actions to cause discord between the Ajahs.

Farmay Tower. A tower on the Blightborder in Kandor.

Farnah. An Aes Sedai of the Green Ajah who was raised Sitter for the Green Ajah to replace Talene Minly.

Farran. A Whitecloak soldier of the rank Hundredman who went to the Two Rivers with Dain Bornhald. He was a boulder of a man and wore a beard. Along with Byar, Farran wanted to put the Luhhans and the Cauthons to the question; Dain Bornhald didn't want to let Farran anywhere near Bode and Eldrin Cauthon.

Farren, Ackley. *See* Ackley Farren

Farrier's Green. A place in Caemlyn where the *gholam* found a victim.

Farrier's Hammer, The. An inn or tavern in Lugard, Murandy. Siuan passed it on the way to another inn.

Farseen, Saroiya. *See* Saroiya Farseen

Farshaw, Min. *See* Min Farshaw

Farstrider, Jain. *See* Jain Farstrider

Fatamed, Irgain. *See* Irgain Fatamed

Fateful Concord, the. An agreement that no woman would link with a man to help seal the Dark One's prison, rising in opposition to Lews Therin's plan to use a circle of seven women and six men to place seven focus points around the thinness of the Pattern at Shayol Ghul. It was spearheaded by Latra Posae, an Aes Sedai during the War of the Shadow, who wanted to prevail by construction of two huge *sa'angreal*, one of *saidar* and one of *saidin*, that were to be used to contain the Dark One. Once they were constructed, access keys were needed to use the *sa'angreal*; these access keys were hidden in an area taken over by the forces of the Shadow. Latra Posae and the women held to their concord, hoping that the access keys could be rescued; Lews Therin went ahead with his plan without the ability to link. The Bore was sealed, but *saidin* tainted.

Father of Lies. Another name for the Dark One.

Father of Storms (or Storm). A Sea Folk term for the Dark One.

father-sisters. *See* Aiel kinship

Faverde Nothish. A wiry member of the Seanchan Blood. He attended Tuon's first audience in Ebou Dar after she returned from traveling with Mat.

Favidan. One of Renald Fanwar's farmhands.

Favlend Mountain. A mountain in Murandy.

Fearil. Elza Penfell's Darkfriend Warder. He was lean and pretty, with pale hair, a hard mouth and a harsh voice. Elza spent twenty years convincing everyone that she was married to Fearil so that they would think nothing of her excessive privacy with him. Sometimes that privacy was needed so that she might punish him and no one would hear his screams.

Fearil liked to kill. When Elza went with Cadsuane to find Rand, she left Fearil in Cairhien; later, he and other Warders gave directions for Bashere and Logain to find Rand. Elza ordered Fearil to kill anyone who threatened the Dragon Reborn. Fearil and Elza accompanied Rand to the meeting with the supposed Daughter of the Nine Moons.

Fearless. The Seanchan ship captained by Egeanin Tamarath. The ship was tall and square-looking, with odd-ribbed sails, bluff-bowed and towered. There were longboats on board for ferrying troops through shallow waters. It was the vessel that captured Bayle Domon and *Spray* near Falme. Caban was a crew member.

Fearnim, Toke. A stable owner in Jurador from whom Mat bought the Domani razor for Tuon. He was wiry with a fringe of gray hair.

Feast of Abram. A feast celebrated everywhere but the Borderlands on the ninth day of Jumara. Prizes were baked into honeycakes, and a kiss of peace was offered.

Feast of All Souls' Salvation. A feast celebrated every ten years at the autumnal equinox. Also known as All Souls Day, the day on which it was observed was not part of any month.

Feast of Embers. A feast celebrated in Taisham in Ebou Dar.

Feast of Freia. A feast celebrated on the twenty-first day of the month of Adar in Illian, Arad Doman, Ghealdan, Tarabon and parts of Altara and Murandy.

Feast of Fools. *See* Foolday

Feast of Lights. The Feast of Lights was a two-day celebration of the winter solstice, starting on the last and shortest day of the year and lasting through the first day of the new year. Every window in the White Tower was lit, creating a glorious image. In Cairhien, the Feast of Lights was a party of wild abandon and expatriate Cairhienin everywhere held lavish parties. In many localities the second day of the Feast of Lights was called First Day and was considered a time for charitable giving.

Feast of Maia. A feast celebrated on the ninth day of the month of Amadaine in Andor, Ghealdan, Altara, Murandy and Illian.

Feast of Neman. A feast celebrated on the ninth day of the month of Adar in Andor, Cairhien, Tear and the Borderlands.

Feast of Sefan. A festival celebrated in Illian in the month of Adar. Competitions were held for the best telling of *The Great Hunt of the Horn*.

Feast of Thanksgiving. A feast celebrated every four years at the vernal equinox. The day on which it was observed was not part of any month.

Feast of the Half Moon. A feast celebrated in Ebou Dar in Taisham on the day after Maddin's Day.

Feaster's Run. A major city square in Tear.

Feather. A young wolf who was Leafhunter's mate. Perrin spoke with Leafhunter's pack after encountering a scent in the wolf dream that made his hackles rise. When he asked the pack about it, they all stopped talking with him.

feather-dancers. Used by Birgitte in an analogy, an expression from past lives: "as easy as finding feather-dancers in Shiota."

Feathers Aloft. A Cairhienin dice game. There was one dicer, with a crowd of onlookers betting against or for his tosses. In other lands it was called Third Gem and Cat's Paw.

feathertop. A weed that Perrin saw on the burned al'Thor farm.

Fedwin Morr. A young Andoran man who became an Asha'man. He was born in 984 NE. He was about 5'10" tall, with brown eyes and straight brown hair. When he went to the Black Tower, he was huskier than Eben Hopwil, with a good deal fewer blotches on his cheeks; by the time he was sent south, he had almost no blotches. Morr had a sort of block; he could not make himself believe he could channel at any distance, so his ability began to fall off at about fifty paces, and at one hundred, it was gone. Weaves would not work for him unless he caught his tongue between his teeth while he wove the weaves. He could make a gateway easily enough; it was the line-of-sight work that tripped him.

After Dumai's Wells, Morr was chosen to accompany Rand. He went to Illian with Rand for the attack on Sammael, after which he was raised to full Asha'man. When Rand heard reports of the Seanchan from Lord Gregorin via Illianer merchants, he sent Morr to scout around Ebou Dar. Morr went mad, though it wasn't noticed until the attack on Rand in Cairhien, when Morr was guarding Min. Rand gave him herbs he had learned about from Nynaeve—a little gave sleep, and too much a sleep you never woke from. It was a quick, painless death.

Feindu, Stedding. A *stedding* located in the Black Hills.

Feir, Tarna. *See* Tarna Feir

Fel, Herid. *See* Herid Fel

Fel Moreina. A name for Far Madding after the Trolloc Wars.

Felaana Bevaine. An Aes Sedai of the Brown Ajah and the loyalist contingent, with a strength level of 17(5). She was slim, with a raspy voice and yellow hair that gleamed as if she brushed it several times a day. In Canluum, she mistook the young Moiraine for a wilder and was made nervous by Cadsuane. Much later, she was one of the guards on Leane after her capture by Elaida, and with Negaine found a disguised Beonin wandering the White Tower, requesting an audience with Elaida.

Felmley, Tham. An Andoran brickmason sentenced to death by Morgase for murdering his brother; she later discovered that he was innocent.

Fen Mizar. Joline's Saldaean Warder. Both Fen and fellow Warder Blaeric had broad shoulders and narrow waists; Fen was a little heavier in the chest and shoulders. The pair of them talked alike, thought alike and moved alike. Standing about 5'11" tall, Fen had dark, tilted eyes, high cheekbones, a wide mouth and straight black hair to his shoulders. His complexion was coppery. Fen seemed not to like anyone much except for Joline. After Teslyn dosed Joline with forkroot and the Seanchan arrived, Fen and Blaeric were able to get Joline out of the palace, but not out of Ebou Dar. They joined Mat and left Ebou Dar with Luca's show. They traveled with the Band of the Red Hand until returning to the White Tower with Joline.

Fendry, Millis. *See* Millis Fendry

fennel. *See* gray fennel, red fennel *and* whitefennel

Fennel. A farrier with Perrin's army who was sent ahead with Basel Gill before the battle at Malden. When Gill and his party had to change direction to avoid impassable roads, Fennel stayed behind to let Perrin know where they had gone.

Fera Sormen. An Aes Sedai of the White Ajah publicly and of the Black Ajah in truth. A member of the loyalist contingent, she had a strength level of 33(21). Born in 864 NE, she went to the White Tower in 882 NE. After spending thirteen years as a novice and nine years as Accepted, she was raised to the shawl in 904 NE. Fera helped to kidnap Rand from Cairhien, and was captured at Dumai's Wells. She was treated as *da'tsang* by the Aiel until, under Verin's Compulsion, she found reason to swear oath to Rand, which she did before Cadsuane departed Cairhien for Far Madding. In Fera's case, unlike Elza's, her oath-swearing was entirely a ruse, a lie allowed by her Black Ajah affiliation.

Feragaine Saralman. An Aes Sedai of the Blue Ajah who served as Amyrlin from 732 to 754 NE. Feragaine was in large part a puppet of the Hall. Like Marasale, she was chosen because the Hall thought they could control her; in large part they managed to. She made efforts to restore the power and authority of the Amyrlin Seat but was almost always outmaneuvered by the Hall, who seemed to know what she was going to do before she made a move. Her interests, like those of many Blues, had always lain outside the White Tower and its politics, and she floundered badly in the treacherous currents of the Hall.

Feraighin. A "youngish" Aiel Wise One who came to meet Rand and Perrin's party as they neared Cairhien after Dumai's Wells. She had red hair and brilliant blue eyes and spoke hurriedly. She could channel but was not strong in use of the Power.

Feran. A man of the Chareen Aiel and the *Seia Doon* society. His greatfather was Sorilea's sister-son. He tried to attract Enaila's attention with no success for over a year. He was tall and handsome, with red hair; unfortunately, he laughed like a braying mule and picked at his ears.

Ferane Neheran. A Domani Aes Sedai of the White Ajah and the loyalist contingent, with a strength level of 21(9). Born in 727 NE, she went to the White Tower in 742 NE. After spending nine years as a novice and six years as Accepted, she was raised to the shawl in 957 NE. She had a Warder. About 5'2" tall, Ferane was decidedly plump—even dumpy—with coppery skin, a round face, dark eyes and long black hair that often needed a brush. Often as vague as a Brown and always as untidy, she frequently bore ink stains on her plump fingers. Despite her appearance, she could still use the skills she had learned as a Domani girl; many considered it remarkable that she could captivate a man's attention very quickly when she wished to. Ferane was raised Sitter in 981 NE and served until 992 NE. She was made First Reasoner of the White Ajah, and when the Tower split in 999 NE, she sent White Sitter Saroiya Farseen to the rebels and took her chair.

Fergansea. A nation that arose after the Trolloc Wars.

Fergin. An Andoran Redarm in the Band of the Red Hand. About 5'10" tall, he was skinny, with brown hair and pale brown eyes. Fergin was about thirty-five years old when he joined the Band of the Red Hand. He liked to gamble almost as much as he liked women. A good soldier—not the best, but good—sadly he wasn't very bright about other things. He survived recovering the Bowl of the Winds in the Rahad, along with Harnan, Gorderan and Metwyn, but was later killed by the *gholam* in Mat's camp outside Caemlyn.

ferris. A green herb that was sprinkled on soup.

Festival of Birds. A feast celebrated in Ebou Dar in the month of Taisham.

Festival of Fools. The Kandor name of the Feast of Fools.

Festival of Lanterns. A festival celebrated on the first day of the month of Choren in Arad Doman, Tarabon, Amadicia, Ghealdan, Altara, Murandy and Illian.

Festival of Unreason. The Saldaean name for the Feast of Fools.

Fetches. *See* Myrddraal

feverbane. A plant used medicinally to treat fever.

Field of Bekkar. Site of the last victory of King Aemon against the Shadowspawn; he marched from Bekkar back to his doom in Manetheren. It was also known as the Field of Blood.

Field of Merrilor. A place in the southwestern corner of Shienar, at the confluence of the Rivers Mora and Erinin. Leaders of all the nations met here at Rand's request. At first, the countries were divided according to whether they supported Rand's intention to break the seals on the Dark One's prison before resealing the Bore, and those opposing such a move, including Egwene and Elayne. With Moiraine's help, Rand convinced the nations of the need to conduct the Last Battle as he saw fit. He also provided for a duration of peace following the Last Battle by having everyone sign a treaty called the Dragon's Peace. A great portion of the Last Battle was fought at the Field of Merrilor, largely driven by Mat's decision to make a last stand there; he assessed that the natural topography of Merrilor would give the armies of Light the greatest advantage against the Shadowspawn. Natural features of Merrilor included broad grasslands; a dense forest to the east that included Stedding Sholoon; Dashar Knob, a steep rocky outcrop on the Shienaran side of the River Mora; the plateaued Polov Heights; and an expanse of bogs on the Arafellin side, separated by a road extending from Hawal Ford across the Mora, a main transit point between the two countries.

Fields of Peace. A location in Seanchan, possibly in Seandar or thereabouts, that was aflame after the fall of the Empress.

Fifth Treaty of Falme. A treaty negotiated by Merana intended to stop the squabbling between Arad Doman and Tarabon over Almoth Plain. In the end, she felt as if she had been rolled downhill in a barrel, and the treaty turned out to be worth less than the wax in its seals. Merana reflected that she had not been in love since well before this treaty.

Filger. A scout in the Band of the Red Hand. A lean man with thinning hair, he was in Caemlyn when the Trollocs attacked, and reported to Talmanes that the Trollocs had taken the walls and only one gate was holding.

Finchey, Dagdara. *See* Dagdara Finchey

Fingers of the Dragon. The delta region of Tear, where the River Erinin met the Sea of Storms. It was a winding maze of waterways broad and narrow, some choked with knifegrass. Vast plains of reeds separated clusters of low islands forested with spider-rooted trees seen nowhere else. Channel dredgers were used to keep the waterways open. By law, no ship was allowed to pass through the Fingers without a Tairen pilot aboard.

Finndal, Lord. An Andoran man with whose wife Thom Merrilin once flirted.

Field of Merrilor

Polov Heights

Arafel

River Mora

Ruins

Palisade

bogs

Dashar Knob

Hawal Ford

Shienar

River Erinin

Abandoned Farms

½ mile

Finngar, Ewin. *See* Ewin Finngar

Finsas, Captain. An officer in Ituralde's army who was injured by trebuchet-thrown Trolloc corpses at Maradon.

Fionnda Annariz. A High Lady of Tear. Beautiful, with a stern face and hard eyes, she tried to meet Rand at the Royal Palace of Cairhien, but he Traveled to Caemlyn. She was also seen talking with Alaine Chuliandred. Fionnda took to wearing outlandish clothes.

Firchon Pass. A narrow canyon-like feature on the border between Arafel and Kandor. The Silverwall Keeps was found there.

fire. A drink that was a corrupt version of *oosquai*.

Fire. One of the Five Powers. *See* Five Powers

fire wands. Implements used by Thom Merrilin in his fire-eating act.

Fireheart. A tall black gelding ridden by Elayne.

firesticks. An invention of Aludra's. They were small sticks with blue-gray heads that produced a flame when rubbed against an unsmooth surface. They had to be packed carefully because their heads were rough, and if they rubbed against each other they could ignite. She also called them "strikers."

Firewisp. A horse taken by Edesina, with permission, from the Band of the Red Hand, for the trip back to the White Tower.

First Among Servants. The title of the head Aes Sedai in the Age of Legends.

First Councilor. An advisor to the Queen of Kandor. Ethenielle's First Councilor was Serailla.

First Counsel. The highest-ranking of the Counsels in Far Madding.

First Covenant. A promise of the early Aiel, the Da'shain, to serve the Aes Sedai and to follow the Way of the Leaf, a pacific way of life. It was also known as simply "the Covenant."

First Day. The second day of the Feast of Lights, when charity was encouraged. It was also called Firstday.

First Legion. The Seanchan legion led by Tylee Kirgan in the Last Battle.

First Moment. The time when all life was created.

First of Mayene. The title of the ruler of Mayene; her banner was a golden hawk on a blue field.

First Prince of the Sword. The title normally held by the eldest brother of the Queen of Andor, who was trained from childhood to command the Queen's armies in time of war and to be her advisor in time of peace. If the Queen had no surviving brother, she would appoint someone to that title.

First Reasoner. The title of the head of the White Ajah.

First Rise. An early morning hour.

First Selector. The title of the head of the Blue Ajah.

First Twelve. A decision-making body found in each Sea Folk clan and the Atha'an Miere as a whole; among other things, they chose new Wavemistresses.

First Watcher. One of the Watchers Over the Waves placed in a cage suspended from the Tower over Falme harbor by the Seanchan; when he died, the Seanchan picked another to replace him.

First Weaver. The title of the head of the Yellow Ajah.

first-brothers. *See* Aiel kinship

first-sisters. *See* Aiel kinship

Firstday. The second day of the Feast of Lights, when charity was encouraged. It was also called First Day.

fist. A unit of one hundred to two hundred Trollocs.

Fists of Heaven. Lightly armed and lightly armored Seanchan infantry carried into battle on the backs of the flying creatures called *to'raken*. All were small men or women largely because of limits as to how much weight a *to'raken* could carry for any distance. Considered to be among the toughest soldiers, they were used primarily for raids, surprise assaults on positions at an enemy's rear, and where speed in getting into place was of the essence. Fists' uniforms were brown, boiled-leather armor with a clenched fist embossed on the breastplate and a steel helmet painted to look like a giant insect's head. They sometimes wore a sort of coverall made of fur-lined waxed linen over wool. Fists were equipped with gauntlets and goggles made of crystal, and were held in their saddles by safety straps. They carried shortswords which they called "cat-gutters" and used light crossbows which could be disassembled and carried in a bag.

Fitch, Master. The innkeeper of The Stag and Lion in Baerlon. He was as big around as Master al'Vere and was a chatter with a pleasant grin, plump hands and wisps of hair sticking out in all directions. His inn was burned down after Moiraine, Rand and their party stayed there, but gold was sent from Tar Valon to rebuild it.

five-finger. A root used in ointment to heal bruises.

Five Powers, the. There were threads to the One Power, and each person who could channel the One Power could usually grasp some threads better than others. These threads were named according to the sorts of things that could be done using them—Earth, Air (sometimes called Wind), Fire, Water and Spirit—and were called the Five Powers. Any wielder of the One Power would have a greater degree of strength with one, or possibly two, of these, and lesser strength in the others. Some few may have had great strength with three, but after the Age of Legends no one had great strength with all five. Even in the Age of Legends it was extremely rare. The degrees of strength could vary greatly between individuals, so that some who could channel were much stronger than others.

Performing certain acts with the One Power required the ability in one or more of the Five Powers. For example, starting or controlling a fire required Fire, and affecting the weather required Air and Water, while Healing required Water and Spirit. While Spirit was found equally in men and in women, great ability with Earth and/or Fire occurred much more often among men, with Water and/or Air among women. There were exceptions, but Earth and Fire came to be regarded as male Powers, Air and Water as female. Generally, no ability was considered stronger than any other, though there was a saying among Aes Sedai: "There is no rock so strong that water and wind cannot wear it away, no fire so fierce that water cannot quench it or wind snuff it out." It should be noted this saying came into use long after the last male Aes Sedai was dead. Any equivalent saying among male Aes Sedai was lost.

Five Sisters, the. A constellation.

flame and the void, the. A concentration or meditation technique, where the mind was cleared of thoughts, sometimes aided by the use of a candle or other external focusing device. Skilled users of swords and bows employed the technique, for example, to become one with their weapon and one with their target or opponent, removing obstacles of rational thought and emotion from their endeavor and giving them an advantage in combat. A similar technique was used to help male channelers harness their skills in the use of *saidin*. *See also* Oneness *and* void, the

Flame of Tar Valon, the. A stylized representation of a flame; a white teardrop with the point upward. It was the symbol of the Aes Sedai and one of the titles of the Amyrlin Seat.

Flame, the Blade and the Heart, The. An anthology of tales of adventure and romance featuring historical characters.

Flann Barstere. A young Two Rivers man from Watch Hill. Perrin had hunted with him, and once helped him dig one of his father's cows out of a boghole in the Waterwood. A lanky fellow with a dent in his chin, he joined Perrin's army and acted as a banner carrier on the trip to So Habor.

Flann Lewin. A Two Rivers farmer. He was a gnarled, gray-headed beanpole. Adine was his wife, and Tell and Dannil his nephews. Flann's farm was attacked by Trollocs; Whitecloaks were able to drive them off, but Flann decided to take his family to Jac al'Seen's farm. There he met Perrin, and was convinced to move his family into Emond's Field for safety. Flann took part in the defense of Emond's Field.

flatwort. A medicinal herb used in tea for fatigue, to clear the head, and to treat sore muscles.

Flern. A Lightmaker who killed Malidra, a scavenging Aiel, seen in Aviendha's view of the future in Rhuidean.

Flinn, Damer. *See* Damer Flinn

flip. An Aiel game involving throwing a knife into the dirt.

flipskirt. A woman of easy virtue.

Floran Gelb. A crewman on Bayle Domon's *Spray*, although not a good one. He was a scrawny man, often none too clean, with a weasely smile and often an ingratiating manner. He was none too bright but always ready with excuses. He was sleeping on guard the night Rand, Mat and Thom came aboard near Shadar Logoth, and that wasn't his first bad misstep. Bayle Domon threw him off the ship in Whitebridge, where he started talk that set Rand and company running. He turned up again in Tanchico, selling information, recovered *a'dam* and other items to Egeanin. He was supposed to be helping, unknowingly, in the recovery of *damane* and *sul'dam* who had been left behind or deserted at Falme, but he had kidnapped at least one woman who had no connection to the Seanchan, which left Egeanin no choice but to kill her or send her off to be sold. He and his thugs attempted to kidnap Elayne and Nynaeve, but the latter fought back, assisted by Egeanin, and drove them off.

Florry, Jeral. *See* Jeral Florry

flows. Streams of one or more of the Five Powers applied or woven by channelers across space to accomplish a specific purpose. Early on, Egwene channeled two flows for the first time; that is, she wove flows to do two different things simultaneously. That was something most Aes Sedai could not do to any large degree. It had nothing to do with strength, or even knowledge, but rather a type of dexterity developed through learning-by-doing. It became more difficult to learn the longer one waited to learn. Working two flows was more than twice as hard as working one; working three much more than twice again working two. Rand could work a huge number of flows.

focusing. *See* leading

Fogh the Tireless. A historical military commander, credited with the saying, "If you do not learn from your losses, you will be ruled by them."

Folded Light. A weave made of Fire and Air that rendered a channeler invisible.

Foolday. A festival celebrated in the fall where people wore masks and played pranks, and everyone exchanged sweets and small pastries. Everyone's role was changed about, so that servants gave orders and those whom the servants worked for had to serve. The silliest and most foolish man and woman were crowned as King Fool and Queen Fool, and for that day everyone had to do as they said. It was also known as the Feast of Fools.

Forae, Andaya. *See* Andaya Forae

Foregate. A secondary city outside the gates of Cairhien. It once surrounded the city from riverbank to riverbank, a maze and warren of dirt streets crisscrossing at all angles. The clothing of the people was often shabby, but a colorful mix from every land. Here hawkers, peddlers, shopkeepers and barbers all called their wares and services. Most buildings were of wood, some seven stories high. The Foregate had theaters and a constant carnival atmosphere. It was burned when the Shaido invaded Cairhien.

Forel Market. A half-deserted village in Andor in which Elayne and her companions stayed on her way to Caemlyn to claim the throne. A carpenter told Elayne, traveling incognito, that Elayne was alive, but that the Dragon Reborn, one of the "black-eyed Aielmen," was going to put her on the throne, which he thought she should claim on her own if allowed to by Dyelin. Elayne's party spent some time here because of rain and then snow, and Aviendha bought warm clothes for everyone with gems she had in a bag.

Forerunners. *See Hailene*

Forest of Shadows. Also called the Great Blackwood, it lay east of the Mountains of Mist and just south of Two Rivers, stretching south for a hundred miles or more toward Ghealdan, without a road or a village, but with plenty of wolves and bears.

Foretelling. The rare ability to foretell the future with absolute certainty, although, paradoxically, Foretelling was rarely clear, and often was so difficult to understand that events outran it before it was understood. Then again, the certainty was not always as pure as might be expected: Elaida's Foretelling about the "true Amyrlin" for example, she applied to herself because she believed that she was the true Amyrlin, when in fact it referred to Egwene. Foretelling was conceptually related to Dreaming, but a woman who could Foretell simply knew; a Dreamer had to interpret, and the Dream usually said things in images, allegories or puns.

forkroot. An herb used to prepare a tea with the main purpose of preventing channeling by those with the ability to do so. It had a cool, minty aftertaste. Forkroot tea took only a few minutes, and perhaps two swallows, to bring the onset of symptoms, including lethargy, yawning, heavy-headedness, swollen tongue, wobbly knees and finally unconsciousness. Forkroot affected people who could channel more than people who could not channel. The basic tea that put Elayne and Nynaeve under would have made Ronde Macura extremely drowsy and fumble-witted, but it might not have induced unconsciousness in her. Residual headaches and stomach cramps were normal, especially after long dosing.

After getting the basic information from Ronde Macura, the Seanchan worked out a very low-level dosage of a concentrate that cut the ability to channel to useless levels while not causing any side effects. In a slightly stronger dosage, it cut the ability and also made the channeler unsteady. It was used to make captures when there were no *sul'dam* and *damane* around, and in training new-caught *damane*, who believed that their ability had been taken from them in some way, with restoration of their ability as a reward. This dosage of forkroot was also developed, in somewhat the same form, by the sisters in the White Tower. When captured by the White Tower, Egwene could dreamwalk, but if given enough forkroot to make her sleep through the night, or repeated doses, she would not have been able to dreamwalk. Sufficient doses to make her sleep through the night would have left her doubled over with belly cramps the whole next day.

Forney, Eazil. *See* Eazil Forney

Forrell, Nalaene. *See* Nalaene Forrell

Forsaken. The name given to thirteen of the most powerful Aes Sedai ever known, who went over to the Dark One during the War of the Shadow in return for the promise of immortality. According to both legend and fragmentary records, they were imprisoned along with the Dark One when his prison was resealed. They were given special powers and abilities. The Forsaken were not the only Aes Sedai to go over to the Shadow before and during the War of the Shadow; others, some as powerful, also made that choice. The Dark One always believed in the starkest social Darwinism, though. His Aes Sedai would winnow themselves. The thirteen called the Forsaken were the top ranking at the time of the Shayol Ghul strike—Ishamael always was—but others had risen and fallen. They all plotted against one another as hard as they did against Lews Therin and the forces of the Light; after all, they felt that it was obvious they would win, so equally important was seeing where you would stand when it was all done. Each wanted to be Nae'blis, second only to the Dark One himself. Relatively few of the higher-ranking died from enemy action; assassinations and executions were much more common. The Chosen—what the top thirteen called themselves—always had to look out, for each other and for those below. Other Chosen would undercut one or worse, of course, but those lower in rank would also look for an opportunity to pull one down; a vacancy at the top always meant a reshuffling and a chance to move up.

Death was common, but not the only way to be brought down. Demotions were possible, but some considered that worse than death; demotion was a great sign of weakness, and once on that slippery slope, one could be forced all the way to the bottom. Also, the Dark One could seem capricious to human minds; what mortal brain could comprehend the Great Lord of the Dark completely, or truly know his goals or reasons? Failures could be ignored by the Dark One, although they were always exploited by others of the Chosen, or even those of lesser rank looking to move up, or they could be punished severely. Weakness was worse than failure, though; failure might be explained, but weakness never could be, and the Dark One wanted servitors without weakness. One could rise again by showing that one was strong, but it was an uphill climb at best and more often a climb up a sheer cliff; sometimes the cliff was glass. No one ever rose as high after a fall as their former prominence, and very few even came close to it. In fact, once one was down, it was like blood in the water attracting sharks; it might be all one could do not to be eaten by those one had looked down on from the safety of the boat, and forget about hopes of climbing back into the boat.

In the Third Age, the thirteen awoke and troubled the world again. Their names were Aginor, Asmodean, Balthamel, Be'lal, Demandred, Graendal, Ishamael, Lanfear, Mesaana, Moghedien, Rahvin, Sammael and Semirhage.

Fortress of the Light. The great fortress that served as the headquarters of the Whitecloaks, in Amador, Amadicia.

Fortuona Athaem Devi Paendrag. The name that Tuon took upon becoming Empress. *See* Tuon

Fote, Julanya. *See* Julanya Fote

Four Holes. A sept of the Taardad Aiel.

Four Kings. A scruffy merchant village, bigger than most, on the Caemlyn Road in Andor. Another heavily traveled highway came in from the south, used by Lugarders having business with mines in the west. Four Kings got its name from a battle during Maragaine's reign, when four kings brought armies against her; the town was named for the battle that took place on the site. The surrounding country held few farms, barely enough to feed themselves and the town, and everything in the village centered on the merchants and their wagons, the men who drove them and the laborers who loaded the goods. Plots of bare earth, ground to dust, lay scattered through Four Kings, filled with wagons and abandoned except for a few bored guards. Stables and horse lots lined the streets, all of which were deeply rutted and wide enough to allow wagons to pass. There was no village green. Drab wooden houses, run down, stood close together, with only narrow alleys between. Heavy shutters on the houses had not been opened in so long that the hinges were solid lumps of rust. Rand and Mat stayed at The Dancing Cartman there on their way to Caemlyn. A Darkfriend, Howal Gode, tried to trap them in a storeroom, but lightning created an exit from the sealed room for their escape. Siuan, Leane and Min also went through the village after escaping from Kore Springs, hoping to contact a Blue eyes-and-ears, but she had disappeared.

Four Stones. A sept of the Taardad Aiel.

Fourth Circle of Elevation. A Seanchan institution in which the Imperial Record House of Seandar was found.

Fourth War of Cairhienin Succession. *See* Reconciliation

Fox and Goose, The. An inn in Maerone, Cairhien. It was a stone building, frequented by common soldiers. Mat and Edorion went there while making rounds of drinking halls to check on men of the Band; there they saw a gleeman juggling flaming batons.

foxhead medallion. A *ter'angreal* given to Mat by the Eelfinn to help him be free of Aes Sedai, one of Mat's wishes to them. It was a silver foxhead with only one eye showing, shaded in such a way that it looked like the ancient symbol of Aes Sedai. The medallion blocked both *saidin* and *saidar* from affecting him directly, but not from indirect effects. Power-wrought lightning zapped him and a clump of horse dung flung at him with the Power hit him. A side effect of the device was that it protected the wearer's dreams. A channeler could still channel if wearing the medallion. Elayne made imperfect copies of the medallion; those did not allow one to channel while touching the medallion.

foxtail. A tea that aided sleep without grogginess.

Fransi, Careane. *See* Careane Fransi

Frask Taglien. The husband of Lind, innkeeper of The Great Gathering at the Black Tower.

freeday. A day of rest for novices in the White Tower.

Freidhen, Alviarin. *See* Alviarin Freidhen

Frende, Janya. *See* Janya Frende

Frenn, Grayor. A Two Rivers man who watched the forging of *Mah'alleinir.*

Fridwyn Ros. A former soldier who managed Lord Aedmun Matherin's estate in

Andor. He had heavy shoulders and only one leg. When Elayne visited, he gave her soldiers to take back to Caemlyn with her and wished that he could have gone himself.

Frielle Anan. The middle daughter of Setalle Anan. She was eighteen years old. She volunteered to look after Olver, saying that she wanted six sons of her own. After a short time of tending Olver, Mat suspected she was beginning to hope for daughters. She married while Mat was in Ebou Dar.

Friends of the Dark. An old name for Darkfriends.

Furen Alharra. One of Seonid's Warders. Furen was a Tairen, with a complexion nearly as dark as good soil, dark eyes and gray streaking his curly black hair. He was six feet tall, hard and lean. At the time of Dumai's Wells, Furen was close to fifty years old. He and Seonid and Teryl, her other Warder, took part in the battle at Dumai's Wells, and later joined Perrin's party.

Furlan, Gainor. *See* Gainor Furlan

Furyk Karede. A Seanchan member of the Deathwatch Guards. He was about 6'1" tall, and moderately stocky, with a bluff face and gray at his temples. He had a pleasant, almost fatherly appearance. He was born circa 958 NE to a family of weavers owned by Jalid Magonine. Family lore told of an ancestor who had been a nobleman and accompanied Luthair Paendrag to Seanchan at Artur Hawkwing's command; a subsequent ancestor ran afoul of authorities by trying to create his own kingdom and was sold on the block.

At age fifteen, Karede was chosen for the Deathwatch Guard. After seven years, during which he was cited twice for heroism and mentioned in dispatches three times, he was named to the bodyguard of Tuon upon her birth. The same year, he survived the first attempt on her life. He was then trained to be an officer, and served during the Muyami Uprising and the Jianmin Incident. At his request, he returned to Tuon's bodyguard shortly before her true-name day. The following year, Furyk was wounded while saving Tuon's life again; she gave him her doll, which he kept for ten years until it was lost in the Great Fire of Sohima. Two of his sons followed him into the Deathwatch Guards, and the third was among the honored dead. Karede's wife, Kalia, did not live to see any of that.

He was proud of his raven tattoos.

Karede served as a captain in the bodyguard of the Empress until named to accompany the High Lord Turak and the *Hailene*. He was promoted to Banner-General, with three thin black plumes, after he had some success against the Asha'man in battle. He was approached by Almurat Mor, a Seeker, about a plot to kill Tuon. He went in search of Tuon with Musenge, Deathwatch Guards, Gardeners, *sul'dam* and *damane*. After four weeks, he found Mat and his party with Tuon, and returned Tuon to Ebou Dar. Assassins reached Tuon's presence twice, and Karede and other Deathwatch Guards were sent to the front lines of the Last Battle by Tuon as a death sentence. Karede helped Mat in combat, and did not die.

Fyall. A town east of Samaha, Willar and the River Boern, probably in Altara. Moiraine, Lan, Perrin and Loial passed through the town while on Rand's trail, and the unusual events that had occurred were evidence that Rand had been there: the crops had failed, but the mayor had found sacks of Manetheren gold coins while digging a privy, which saved the town from poverty.

Gabal. One of Perrin's erroneous attempts at "Gaebril," when speaking of Rahvin.

Gabil. Another of Perrin's erroneous attempts at "Gaebril."

Gabrelle Brawley. An Aes Sedai of the Brown Ajah and the loyalist contingent, with a strength level of 19(7). Born in northern Murandy in 902 NE, she went to the White Tower in 917 NE. After spending seven years as a novice and six as Accepted, she was raised to the shawl in 930 NE. About 5'5" tall, with an average build, she was a pretty woman, though not beautiful except when she smiled. She had a dusky complexion, with large dark green eyes, an upturned nose and brown hair worn short, barely to her shoulders. A member of the expedition to take the Black Tower, she was captured and bonded by Logain. She seduced him and tried to make the best of her situation. Like Toveine she was under orders, enforced by the added bit in the bond, not to embrace the Source without Logain's permission, not to attack anyone in a black coat, and not to try to escape. Gabrelle thought Toveine's stubborn bitterness was defeatist. Gabrelle suggested to Toveine that they submit to Desandre and Lemai to unify the sisters. Toveine thought Logain was taking advantage of her, but Gabrelle told her that was not true. Gabrelle's notion of making Logain her lover began purely to obtain information, but Gabrelle found making love with Logain exhilarating in two particular ways. The first was that while she had always known that she was stronger than the men she made love with, because of the Power, this didn't apply with Logain, and that made her feel helpless, which she found strangely thrilling. The second was that sometimes his masking of the bond slipped, which meant that she got the effects of positive feedback through the bond. Gabrelle went with Logain to Cairhien and then to Tear to join Rand; she participated in the defense of Algarin's manor. Gabrelle fought in the Last Battle, and gave Logain the name "Sealbreaker."

Gadarin, Shevan. *See* Shevan Gadarin

Gadren Grady. Jur and Sora Grady's ugly young son.

Gaean, River. A muddy stream in Bellon, Amadicia, twenty miles from Amador.

Gaebril, Lord. The persona taken by Rahvin when he awoke in the Third Age. *See also* Rahvin

Gaelin. A Two Rivers family. *See* Edelle *and* Jon Gaelin

Gaelin, River. A river flowing west from the Spine of the World below Kinslayer's Dagger, into the River Alguenya.

Gaffin. Someone known to Renald Fanwar.

Gahand, Daria. The author of *Essays on Reason*, a book studied by Min.

Gahaur. An area of Saldaea; Lady Zavion was from there.

gai'shain. Aiel term meaning those sworn to peace in battle. They were required by *ji'e'toh* to serve for a year and a day in any capacity required, humbly, obediently, touching no weapon, doing no violence, making no effort to escape. *Gai'shain* were dressed in cowled white robes and sandals when outdoors; they often wore much less indoors. When the year and a day was up, they were sent home. There was no shame in being *gai'shain*, unless one escaped or tried to. An escapee was returned by his/her family to begin the year and a day all over again. Sometimes another family member or two, closely related, demanded to be made *gai'shain* as well, to lessen dishonor to clan and sept. There were cases of men and/or women touched by an enemy while armed demanding to be made *gai'shain* to lessen their own loss of honor and also lessen the enemy's gain. Stone Dogs and Maidens of the Spear had a reputation for being especially touchy about points of *ji'e'toh* and carrying it to that extreme, but others also believed there was much honor to be gained from walking unarmed into an enemy hold and demanding to be made *gai'shain*, especially if there was a blood feud in effect. It was not usual to take *gai'shain* on a journey any distance from the hold. *Gai'shain* were never allowed to wear anything that those who could touch weapons did.

Many Aiel were disgusted by the idea of servants, the idea of someone voluntarily spending their entire life serving others. This despite *gai'shain*. The only way to incur *toh* toward a *gai'shain* was reminding him or her of what/who they were before having been made to put on white, though there were some exceptions, including roofmistresses, with whom it was almost obligatory to remind her of her former status. *Toh* owed to a *gai'shain* was considered the hardest of all to meet. While harming or killing a *gai'shain* was considered akin to harming or killing a child, they were definitely not considered children in any way. They were expected to be worked, and hard, and they generally were.

It was perfectly all right to be physically harsh to a *gai'shain*. Beatings and switchings were not uncommon, and *gai'shain* submitted to them meekly, to the extent that a full-grown warrior would allow himself to be switched by a child. There were *gai'shain* who tried to induce such treatment; this *gai'shain* pride was disapproved of as a violation of proper meek and humble spirit. A *gai'shain* could be bedded by whomever he or she served, and would submit to that also. Some individuals would not bed a *gai'shain*, but this was personal, not a matter of custom in any way. Custom neither required nor rejected it. A *gai'shain* obeyed, and that was that. *Gai'shain* were not sold, like slaves, but they—or rather their service—could be given as a gift. Captured *gai'shain* normally served whoever captured them, but since the belief was that there was no point to having more *gai'shain* than you could use, the excess were given away. An additional check on anyone keeping too many *gai'shain* was that you were responsible for the shelter and feeding of those who served you, and while you could work them hard, by *ji'e'toh* they had to eat as well and sleep as comfortably as you did yourself.

Except in certain specified instances—such as trades—*gai'shain* had to be allowed to follow any trade they had, and in some instances had to be allowed to work some days for themselves alone. They could not be compelled to follow their trade, though. In no instance was anyone allowed to keep all of the profits of a *gai'shain*'s labors; in fact, in some cases, what one was allowed to keep amounted to no more than the *gai'shain*'s upkeep and in some instances less.

That one had been *gai'shain* was not mentioned after the white was put off, nor was one reminded of anything that might have happened to one while one was *gai'shain*. To do so was to shame the one who had been *gai'shain*, and while it incurred only very minor *toh*, it was considered rude. In effect, the person was treated as if he or she had never been *gai'shain*; that year and a day never happened, and neither did anything that occurred during it.

After Rand's revelations of the pacifistic history of the Aiel, there were some who refused to leave being *gai'shain*, and even some who deliberately had themselves taken *gai'shain*.

Wise Ones, blacksmiths, children, pregnant women and women with a child under ten could not be taken captive.

The Shaido broke with tradition, taking wetlanders as *gai'shain* and holding them for life instead of the traditional year and a day. Many of them were abused beyond the limits of discipline imposed on normal *gai'shain*.

Gaidal Cain. A hero-swordsman of legend and story, always linked to Birgitte. Legend said that he was as handsome as she was beautiful, but legend was inaccurate. He was one of the Heroes of the Horn, called back when the Horn of Valere was sounded at Falme. He had already been reborn at the time of the Last Battle. *See also* Birgitte Silverbow *and* Horn of Valere

Gaidin. 1) An alternate term used for Warders meaning "brothers to battle." 2) A black stallion that belonged to brigands who captured Nynaeve, Egwene and Elayne; after the brigands were killed, Nynaeve chose him, named him and rode him to Tear.

Gainor Furlan. The innkeeper at The Wayland's Forge in Remen, Altara, where Moiraine, Lan, Loial and Perrin stayed and where Perrin first encountered Faile. Furlan was plump and bald-headed with brown eyes.

Galad (Galadedrid) Damodred. The son of Tigraine of Andor and Taringail Damodred of Cairhien. Born in 970 NE, he was tall and slender with dark hair and dark eyes; he was almost too handsome for masculinity. His sign was a winged silver sword, point down. He was half-brother to the Lady Elayne and the Lord Gawyn and to Rand al'Thor. Galad always wanted to do what was right, and did so whatever the cost, either to himself or to others. He went to the Tower to be trained with the Warders, then left and joined the Children of the Light. He helped Nynaeve and Elayne get a ship out of Samara, causing a riot in the process.

Galad had emotional connections to various women. He flirted with Nynaeve, and believed himself in love with Egwene, but once he learned she had become not only Aes Sedai but the rebel Amyrlin, the impossibility of it hit him. When he saw Berelain, though, he was struck head over heels, and so was she.

When Galad learned that Elayne had put in a claim for the Lion Throne, he wanted to help and support her, but he had sworn to the Whitecloaks. He learned that there was an agreement signed by Morgase practically handing over Andor to the Children; his investigation into that led to his learning of Morgase's treatment by Asunawa and Valda, which culminated in his duel with Valda. Galad became Lord Captain Commander of the Children of the Light after defeating Valda in a Trial Beneath the Light.

Galad found his brother Gawyn near death after fighting a duel with Demandred in the Last Battle; Gawyn told him that the Dragon Reborn was his half-brother. Galad subsequently dueled against Demandred and was severely injured; Annoura managed to get him away to be Healed, but he lost his right arm.

Galbrait. The leader of the Ayyad women in the Last Battle.

Galfrey, Ryma. *See* Ryma Galfrey

Galgan, Lunal. *See* Lunal Galgan

Gallanha. A woman living in the Borderlands who was Thulin's wife and Mirala's mother. She was from the south and had yellow hair. She had a set of copper-bottomed pots that she cleaned and left for Auaine, and she gave Auaine and Renald a basket of eggs.

Galina Casban. An Aes Sedai of the Red Ajah publicly and the Black Ajah in truth. A member of the loyalist contingent, she had a strength level of 14(2). Born in 875 NE, she went to the White Tower in 891 NE. After spending nine years as a novice and seven years as Accepted, she was raised to the shawl in 907 NE. Galina joined the Black Ajah in 910 NE. Standing 5'5" tall, with a round face, a plump mouth, black hair and dark brown eyes, she looked to be in her mid to late twenties, and might have been thought a nice armful, except for her sharpness with men, who made her skin crawl.

She was a lesbian; she was very interested in Erian Boroleos. Galina took no real pleasure in inflicting pain, though personal animus could produce a certain enjoyment. By and large, she went about it like a carpenter hammering nails; it was necessary work, and it was best if it were done properly and well. If she could achieve a goal without pain, she certainly would, but if pain was needed to convince someone, then pain it would be.

In 981 NE, she was made Highest of the Red Ajah; at age 106 she was young for the job—the youngest ever—but her predecessor, also Black, had died in Ba'alzamon's punishment of the Supreme Council, and the deaths of so many older sisters in recent years had led to something like a youth movement in many Ajahs. Galina was not involved in questioning Tamra Ospenya—that was a Supreme Council job, and she was not then a member—but she might have been involved in kidnapping her, or putting her body into her bed. Galina was also involved in putting to the question some of the sisters Tamra had gathered, as well as in killing those and others. Later, Galina stood next to Alviarin on the Supreme Council, and knew Alviarin's identity; Talene Minly and Temaile Kinderode were the members of her heart. Galina was involved in putting Siuan Sanche and Leane Sharif to the question, and maybe in stilling them as well. She was part of Elaida's embassy to Rand; Elaida would have liked to make her the leader, but feared choosing a Red would cause Rand to be suspicious. Galina met with Sevanna and arranged for the Younglings to be killed.

During the battle of Dumai's Wells, Galina managed to escape Rand's forces, but was captured by the Shaido. She was treated as an oathbreaker, a truce-breaker, a killer of Wise Ones (for Desaine's murder) and declared *da'tsang*. Finally broken by Sevanna, she was forced to swear absolute and utter lifelong obedience to Sevanna on a binder, which (unknown to her, of course) was supplied by Sammael. Other Shaido Wise Ones, opposed in part to Sevanna, forced their way into this, also obtaining Galina's oath of obedience despite Sevanna's disapproval. After Galina swore on the binder to obey the selected Wise Ones—and Sevanna and Therava first of all among them—her situation changed somewhat. She was then considered *gai'shain*, and dressed in robes of white silk and a wide choker of gold and firedrops, along with a matching belt, though jewelry had been unknown to *gai'shain* before. She was sycophantic and cringing toward Sevanna and the other Wise Ones, a real lickspittle and fawning crawler. It was not playacting; she was terrified of their punishments. Toward Therava she was more than sycophantic; the woman terrified her more than all the others and was the cruelest of all the Shaido toward her, not allowing her the smallest slip or mistake, and at the same time requiring her presence in Therava's bed. Galina wanted very badly to escape, and took advantage of her knowledge of Faile's background to blackmail her into helping steal the binder from Therava. She obtained the binder, trapping Faile and her allies in the process, and escaped the Shaido and the Seanchan when they attacked at Malden. Her escape was short-lived, however; Therava and other Shaido who had also escaped the Seanchan recaptured her a short time later. Therava ordered her to never touch the binder again, and they headed back to the Waste.

Galldrian su Riatin Rie. A king of Cairhien; his personal sign was the Stag. After the Aiel War there was conflict in Cairhien, never quite breaking into open civil war despite a number of skirmishes and minor battles, which resulted in House Damodred losing the throne to House Riatin, primarily through the Game of Houses, because of what Laman had brought to Cairhien. Galldrian took the throne; he was not the best of kings. He refused to pay the Ogier who were working in Cairhien, kept his people quiet by entertaining them and ordered the excavation of the male Choedan Kal. His final mistake was having Dena, Thom's ladylove, killed; Thom assassinated Galldrian in 998 NE.

Gallenne, Bertain. *See* Bertain Gallenne

Gallger, Mistress. The innkeeper of The Golden Wheel in Far Madding. She was thin and wore her dark hair in a bun. Rand visited her inn while looking for Kisman.

Gambler. The name that the Heroes of the Horn called Mat in the Last Battle.

Game of Houses. *See Daes Dae'mar*

Gamel Loune. A Seanchan Banner-General from Dalenshar. Tall and slender, with skin blacker than charcoal, he had no softness in him. The top of his left ear was missing and he had a white slash through his white-flecked tight black curls, marking the scar. Mantual was his manservant. Karede met with Loune while searching for Tuon to get information on the forces attacking the Seanchan, that is, Mat's troops, for whom Loune had been searching.

Ganai. An area of Saldaea; Tenobia was a Lady of Shahayni, Asnelle, Kunwar and Ganai.

Gann, Lord. A braggart Hunter of the Horn whom Moiraine and her company encountered at Wayland's Forge Inn in Remen, Altara. He and his fellow Hunter Orban believed that the Horn of Valere was in the Forest of Shadows. The two came across Gaul and Sarien, killed Sarien and took Gaul prisoner; they told everyone that they had fought twenty Aiel. The Hunters lost several men and were wounded.

gara. A poisonous lizard in the Aiel Waste. It grew to about two feet long; its thick body was covered in bronze scales with irregular yellow streaks running vertically along its sides. It had horny ridges in its mouth and exuded a clear, oily venom as if it were saliva. The gara was not particularly dangerous unless it was stepped upon, but it could bite through a boot and its venom was strong enough to kill a bull.

Garam. The son of a landowner west of the Spine of the World after the Breaking. He was slight and dark-eyed. Garam's father gave Jeordam, Rhodric and the Aiel with them permission to fill their waterskins on his property. Garam took news to the Aiel that the Jenn Aiel were moving. He believed that the Aes Sedai should be killed before they destroyed the world again. Garam's family founded the nation of Cairhien; the Aiel, in thanks for the gift of water, sent Cairhien *Avendoraldera* and granted Cairhienin the exclusive right to travel the Silken Path.

Garan. A man of the Jhirad Goshien Aiel. He was *gai'shain* to Joinde of the Black Rock Shaarad, who laid a bridal wreath for him the day before his term as *gai'shain* ended, and they married.

Garden of Silver Breezes. The most expensive wineshop in Tanchico. Its proprietor was Selindrin, a sleek woman of indeterminate age who allowed no weapons past the street. Egeanin met with Florin Gelb there, and Carridin with King Andric and his advisors.

Gardeners. Ogier members of the Seanchan Deathwatch Guard. Unlike the human members of the Deathwatch Guard, Gardeners were not *da'covale*; they were provided as bodyguards to the Imperial family as a symbol that the Ogier were loyal to the Empress. The Gardeners were the only Ogier in Seanchan allowed to bear arms outside the *stedding*. The First Gardener, a rank equivalent to captain, commanded the Gardeners who composed Tuon's bodyguard. The Master Gardener was commander of all of the Gardeners, including the Empress's Gardeners. *See also* Deathwatch Guard

Garen's Wall. A rock formation found just east of Jehannah, on the northeastern border of Ghealdan, with a northwest-southeast orientation. It was named after an ancient king of Dhowlan, one of the nations that came into being after the Trolloc Wars. He had a number of wars with his northern neighbor, Farashelle, and the extremely long cliff line gave him a defensive advantage. Garen frequently used it defensively, enough so that the name stuck. One of the ruler of Ghealdan's titles was "Defender of Garen's Wall."

Garenia Rosoinde. A Saldaean Kin whose true identity was revealed to be Zarya Alkaese. *See* Zarya Alkaese

Gareth Bryne. An Andoran man who was High Seat of House Bryne, in Kore Springs, he was considered one of the five great captains. The sign of House Bryne was a wild bull collared with the Rose Crown of Andor; Gareth Bryne's personal sigil was three golden stars, each of five rays. He was born the younger son of a minor noble House in 939 NE. Standing 5'11" tall, and stocky, with a bluff, weathered face and dark hair heavy with gray, he was in his late fifties when Rand first saw him. From 961 to 964 NE there were intense border skirmishes between Andor and various lords of Murandy who thought Andor's attention was all on Cairhien. Bryne served with distinction during the latter part, commanded a considerable force and was militarily responsible for bringing an end to the skirmishes. At age twenty-four, he became the youngest Captain-Commander of the Queen's Guards. The same year, 963 NE, Queen Dolera was widowed, and Bryne was named First Prince of the Sword. In 964 NE, Dolera died and Mordrellen took the throne; Bryne remained as Captain-General of the Guards. Morgase took the throne in 975 NE; after the death of Captain-General Aranvor Naldwinn in the Battle of the Shining Walls, she named Bryne as head of the Queen's Guards again; he was later made her First Prince of the Sword. He was also Morgase's lover, but was supplanted by Rahvin as Gaebril, and exiled. He followed Siuan to Salidar, and agreed to lead the rebel Aes Sedai army. He and Siuan became romantically involved, and she bonded him as her Warder just before entering the White Tower during the Seanchan attack to save Egwene. While on that mission, Bryne saved Siuan, and Siuan saved him; Siuan believed that the event fulfilled Min's viewing that the two had to stay near each other or die.

Bryne was one of the leading commanders during the Last Battle, but was the object of Graendal's Compulsion, along with the other great captains, and was relieved of duty when found out. He continued to fight the Shadow, however, and was killed in the Last Battle after going berserk following Siuan's death.

Garfin. The one-armed Illianer who taught Androl use of the sword and the flame and the void.

Garken. An old man who was killed by Mayor Barlden the first night the madness appeared in Hinderstap. Of course, he was alive again the next day.

Garlvan. An Aiel baby, the youngest child of Norlesh and Metalan. He died of hunger, as seen in Aviendha's visions of the future in Rhuidean.

Garon Burlow. The Mayor of Dorlan. His house was the largest in Dorlan. Covarla and Lusonia, sent to Dorlan after surviving Dumai's Wells, stayed in his spare rooms. He stayed out of the way when Aes Sedai talked. .

Garren, Colly. A young Two Rivers man who joined Perrin to fight the Trollocs; he was killed in a Trolloc ambush in the Two Rivers.

Garumand. The captain of Graendal's palace guard at Natrin's Barrow and a victim of her Compulsion. Tenobia's distant cousin, he was handsome and wore a thick mustache. He was killed when Rand balefired Natrin's Barrow.

Gatano, Hattori. *See* Hattori Gatano

Gates of Heaven, The. An inn located in Canluum, Kandor. It was the best and largest inn in the city, four sprawling stories of stone with a green roof. Its innkeeper was Master Helvin. Moiraine stayed there when she was searching for the infant Dragon Reborn; several other Aes Sedai stayed there as well, including Cadsuane.

Gates of Hevan. One of the places in history that Sammael, the Destroyer of Hope, devastated, earning him that name.

Gates of Paaran Disen. The site of victory by Lews Therin over Elan Morin (Ishamael).

gateway. A portal created by channeling for the purpose of Traveling or Skimming. It took considerable strength to create a gateway, or, as in Androl's case, proficiency in the Talent of Traveling. The minimum strength required for making a gateway of useful size, that is, large enough to walk through, was 19(7). The minimum strength required to make any gateway at all out of a circle was 21(9). *See* Skimming *and* Traveling

Gaul. A man of the Imran sept of the Shaarad Aiel and the *Shae'en M'taal* (Stone Dog) society. Handsome in a rugged way, he was about 6'7" and weighed about 240 pounds. His eyes were as green and clear as polished gems, and very long eyelashes seemed to outline them in black. He was a little older than Nynaeve.

Gaul was in love with Chiad, and they were both relieved when the blood feud between their clans ended. He wanted to marry her, but she would not give up the spear for him, though she said she and Bain would take him as a lover; he was offended by the suggestion. Besides, he wasn't interested in Bain. It irritated him that Chiad told him she would not make a bridal wreath and at the same time that she would not stop "putting herself in his eyes," enticing him to chase her.

Gaul led the Stone Dogs west of the Dragonwall; while searching for He Who Comes With the Dawn, he was captured and caged by Hunters of the

Horn in Remen. Perrin rescued him, and they fought and killed White-cloaks. Gaul went to the Stone of Tear and accompanied Perrin when he went to the Two Rivers. Gaul fought at Dumai's Wells; he and Rhuarc alone among the Aiel were not *siswai'aman*. He went to Ghealdan with Perrin. After Elyas sneaked up on Gaul undetected, he and Elyas became friends. Following the battle at Malden, both Chiad and Bain became Gaul's *gai'shain*, and gave him much grief. When Perrin entered the wolf dream in the flesh, Gaul insisted on going along, and fought well and bravely there during the Last Battle.

Gavid. A soldier in the Band of the Red Hand who led about two dozen cross-bowmen while defending Caemlyn against the Trollocs.

Gawyn Trakand. Queen Morgase's son, who was meant to become First Prince of the Sword when Elayne ascended the throne. The oath he took as a child was "my blood shed before hers; my life given before hers." That oath would later tear at him when his sister affiliated herself with the rebel Aes Sedai and apparently supported Rand, who he believed had killed his mother and was too dangerous to be left free. His sigil was a charging white boar on the red field of Andor. Born in 979 NE, Gawyn was about 6'3" tall and had sun-gold hair and blue eyes. He fought against those who were trying to free Siuan after she was deposed; he killed Hammar and Coulin. He became the leader of the Younglings; their green cloaks bore Gawyn's white boar. He fell in love with Egwene, and she with him. He accompanied Elaida's so-called embassy to Rand; on the way, Gawyn heard from a peddler that Rand had killed his mother and he was consumed with hatred for Rand. While in Cairhien, he and Egwene met, talked and canoodled; Gawyn said he would promise her anything that did not harm Elayne or Andor. Galina arranged with Sevanna for Gawyn and his Younglings to be killed; that plot was largely unsuccessful. Gawyn did lose some of his men at Dumai's Wells, but he survived and returned to Tar Valon, where he was denied entry. He and the Younglings went to Dorlan with Covarla Baldene. Overhearing that Egwene was Elaida's captive and was being made to howl half the day, he left the Younglings and went to Gareth Bryne and the rebel Aes Sedai. He, Bryne and Siuan led an expedition to rescue Egwene during the Seanchan attack; they were successful, but Egwene was not happy. He worked to please her, stopping assassins and trying to help, but Egwene just wanted him to obey. In frustration, he went to Caemlyn and learned that the assassins were Seanchan with *ter'angreal* rings; they were called Bloodknives. Returning to Tar Valon, he found three Bloodknives in Egwene's chambers and defeated them, though he was badly injured. Egwene Healed him, bonded him as her Warder, and agreed to marry him; shortly afterward, he stole the Bloodknives' rings. Gawyn was overjoyed when he saw his mother at the Field of Merrilor. The night before the Aes Sedai went to Kandor to fight in the Last Battle, Silviana married Gawyn and Egwene. When the Sharans arrived in Kandor and turned the battle around, Gawyn and Egwene hid, and Gawyn used the Bloodknives' *ter'angreal* to scout around for a way out; with a little help from Leilwin, they managed to escape. Gawyn used the rings again when he tried to kill Demandred. He was mortally wounded in his fight with Demandred, but he survived long enough to tell Galad that Rand was his half-brother.

Gazal, Toveine. *See* Toveine Gazal

Gazar, Tiam of. The developer of the Gazaran Calendar.

Gazaran Calendar. The calendar developed by Tiam of Gazar. It was adopted after the Trolloc Wars, when so many records had been destroyed that there was argument as to exactly what year it actually was under the Toman Calendar. The Gazaran Calendar celebrated the supposed freedom from the Trolloc threat by recording each year as Free Year (FY).

Gearan. A young Jenn Aiel male from the time after the Breaking. He was as lanky as a stork and the best runner among the Aiel wagons. He went with Charlin and Lewin to save their sisters from bandits; they used weapons and killed some bandits, and because of their use of violence were cast out by their families.

Gedarien, Stevan. *See* Stevan Gedarien

Gedwyn, Charl. *See* Charl Gedwyn

Gelarna. An Aes Sedai of the Yellow Ajah and the loyalist contingent. She and Musarin were guarding Leane when a bubble of evil caused her jail cell to melt; after a moment of understandable shock, the two pulled Leane free.

Gelb, Floran. *See* Floran Gelb

Gelbarn, Bernaile. *See* Bernaile Gelbarn

Gelen. A member of the Deathwatch Guard who chased Mat around the Field of Merrilor to try to get him to sit in judgment on people seeking the Empress's mercy. Gelen finally caught up with Mat on Dashar Knob, but the enemy arrived, and Mat sent him to get everyone to their posts.

Geleni. One of Renald Fanwar's farmhands. He was in the village to pick up new seed when Renald decided to go north, but Renald sent for him.

Gelfina. A character from stories who was kept locked away in a forgotten tower for a thousand years.

Gemallan, Cowin. *See* Cowin Gemallan

Gemalphin, Marillin. *See* Marillin Gemalphin

Gendar. One of Berelain's thief-catchers from Mayene. He was about 5'10" tall, with dark hair and dark eyes. Bland-faced and ordinary-looking, he was so nondescript one would not notice him if he bumped into one on the street. He was friendly with Rosene and Nana, Berelain's maids. Berelain used Gendar and Santes to spy by having them make friends with Masema's people and taking them wine supposedly stolen from Berelain. Santes found the Seanchan document signed by Suroth, picking the lock of Masema's camp desk under cover of the bustle of setting up camp. Gendar and Santes returned to Masema's camp with Berelain's last cask of Tunaighan and were expected to return by an hour after sunset, but they did not. They were presumed dead, killed by Masema's men.

Generals of Dawn's Gate. A group of seventeen generals who swore fealty to Lews Therin in the Age of Legends.

Genhal, Lemore. *See* Lemore Genhal

Genhald, Androl. *See* Androl Genhald

Genshai. A feast celebrated on the third of Tammaz in Tear, Illian, Amadicia, Tarabon and the southern parts of Altara and Murandy. Brightly colored ribbons were worn by both men and women.

gentling. The intentional process of removing the ability of a man to channel; it was once thought to be permanent.

Geofram Bornhald. One of the Lords Captain of the Children of the Light. He was the father of Dain Bornhald. Geofram captured Perrin and Egwene in the *stedding* where Hawkwing's city was to be built; he intended to take them to Amador for trial, but they were rescued. Geofram led a force of Whitecloaks to Falme, where they engaged the Seanchan, and Geofram was killed.

Georg. Pevara's Kandori brother, who died at twelve during a Darkfriend uprising with a knife in his hand, standing over their father's body and trying to keep the mob from their mother.

Gera. A cook for the Salidar Aes Sedai. She was a good cook; she dreamed that she was much thinner and an Aes Sedai of the Green Ajah. Elayne saw her in this dream in *Tel'aran'rhiod*.

Geral. A Malkieri who was a member of Lan's High Guard in the Last Battle.

Geraneos, Pavil. *See* Pavil Geraneos

Gerard Arganda. Alliandre's Ghealdanin First Captain of the Legion of the Wall. He was a hard-bitten, compact man, about 5'8" tall. He looked tough, not like a nobleman; he looked like what he was, a graying soldier who first hefted a lance as a boy. He had fought against Amadicians, Altarans and Whitecloaks; in the Aiel War he survived the Blood Snow at Tar Valon. Arganda was very concerned with the kidnapping of Alliandre; he was loyal to her, and besides, the Crown High Council would have had his head if he hadn't gotten her back safely. Overall, he was concerned with the entire project from the beginning and considered it harebrained, what with Alliandre swearing fealty to Perrin and riding into Amadicia. But she was the Queen, so he obeyed. During the Last Battle Arganda was wounded severely enough to take him out of the fight, but he continued his command as best he could.

Gerisch. A Seanchan Banner-General with Tuon's army at the Last Battle. She had a nice backside. When it had become obvious there was a spy in the command tent, Mat wondered if it might be she.

Gerra Kishar. An Aes Sedai of the Gray Ajah who served as Amyrlin from 601 to 638 NE. Gerra was a strong Amyrlin. She used her skills as a negotiator and mediator to play factions off against each other in the Hall. Chosen in part because her mild personality was so much in contrast to Shein's—and possibly because the Hall thought she would be controllable—she continually got her way. She was also chosen in part because she was one of the ringleaders of the coup that toppled Shein, which should have given the others some clue to how biddable she would be. An attempted coup against her was crushed utterly. She was remembered as one of the greatest Amyrlins.

Get Ayliah. One of Perrin's men from the Two Rivers who was a good tracker. He and Hu Marwin went with Jondyn to try to find traces of Faile after she was kidnapped. Jondyn, Get and Hu went after the fleeing inhabitants of Malden, but all they found was some information and a sketched map of the town.

Get Eldin. A Two Rivers farmer. He was leathery, bald-headed and three times Perrin's age; Perrin asked him to stay and warn off anyone who tried to bother Master Luhhan while they were preparing to fight the Trollocs in Emond's Field.

Getares, Esmara. *See* Esmara Getares

Ghar'ghael. A Trolloc tribe. Its sign was piled human skulls.

Gharadin. A man of the Shaido Aiel taken *gai'shain* at Dumai's Wells; he was sent to Ghealdan with Perrin. Square-faced and half again as big as Perrin, he had a half-healed slash down his hard face. Seonid wanted to Heal him, but the Wise Ones told her she must ask permission.

Ghealdan. A nation in the south-central part of the continent. Its sigil was three six-pointed silver stars arranged one above and two below: the Stars, or the Silver Stars. Its banner was the Silver Stars on a field of red. Taking its name from the region rather than from any province of Hawkwing's empire, Ghealdan was founded in approximately FY 1109 by Lord Kirin Almeyda, Lady Valera Prosnarin, Lord Cynric Talvaen and Lady Iona Ashmar. There had been numerous attempts to restore Dhowlan, with the longest lasting only twenty years and collapsing upon the death of the woman who had led it, and attempts to form a new nation in the region had also met with at best mixed results, the longest lived lasting for only thirty-four years and three rulers. The success of Lord Kirin, Lady Valera, Lord Cynric and Lady Ashmar is attributed, at least in part, to their agreement to join four strong Houses together, and to the fact that while Lord Kirin became King Kirin, the other three Houses formed a Royal Crown Council (Crown High Council), which had considerable power to check as well as choose the ruler and which later admitted still more noble Houses to membership. Of course, the relative isolation of Ghealdan played a part; far from the coast and containing neither major trade routes nor a major trading center, the region was not a popular target for others with ambition. And, too, the War of the Hundred Years already had been going on for over a hundred years; weariness on the parts of anyone coveting Ghealdan and the necessity of holding on to what they already held certainly helped Ghealdan survive.

Ghealdan's historic stability changed with the Prophet. There had been more playing of the Game of Houses in Ghealdan than in Andor, but much less than in Cairhien; that increased somewhat with the Prophet. Ghealdan was always aware of the Whitecloak presence in Amadicia, but was strong enough to keep them out for the most part.

Ghealdan could be ruled by either a king or a queen. The ruler's power was more than in Altara or Murandy, but less than in Andor, Cairhien or Illian. Marriage to a commoner barred one from the throne, although it was possible for a commoner to become a noble. The Crown High Council was of varying size, depending on what party or group had control, and of varying power in the land. It had a strong say in who ascended to the throne, though ascent was usually hereditary. By law, no one could sit on the Crown High Council if they were in the line of succession, and stepping from the Council to the throne was also against the law. Attempts to do so in the past had caused outbreaks of violence—a civil war in at least one case—and never succeeded. However, the Council did, upon occasion, depose a sitting monarch, change the succession or have someone other than the rightful successor crowned. In other periods the Council had been under the ruler's thumb to one degree or another. As in most nations, the army historically consisted of the personal levies of the nobles. Ghealdanin noblewomen nearly always used a Master of the Horse to command their troops; it was extremely rare for a Ghealdanin noblewoman to take the field herself. As in other countries, noblemen were expected to lead their troops whether or not they were fit to do so.

The Legion of the Wall was a permanent formation like the Queen's Guards in Andor which provided a bodyguard for the ruler and border guards. It numbered between two thousand and twenty-five hundred men, but this formation was dispersed during the rise of the Prophet. After she swore fealty to Perrin Aybara, Alliandre used the excuse of raising troops to go with him into Amadicia to reinstitute the Legion. At that point, it numbered between nine hundred and a thousand men and officers. That was something she had planned to do, but she did not announce it even to Perrin. Only Arganda and a few of the most trusted officers knew that they had become the Legion of the Wall. The secrecy was because of Alliandre's uncertainty regarding the Crown High Council. Gerard Arganda was named the First Captain of the Legion of the Wall, although he was not publicly announced.

Ghealdanin common soldiers had green streamers on their lances that had a foot-long steel point, and wore green breastplates and green conical helmets with barred faceguards. The officers wore shiny, silvery breastplates and conical helmets with barred faceguards, red coats and red cloaks, and had a fat white plume on the helmet; officers' reins, bridles and saddle cloths were fringed in red.

Ghealdan was for many years the only major source of first-quality alum, easily better than that found in Arafel and Tear. Taxes on alum alone supported the throne of Ghealdan for generations. (A new source of fine alum opened up in Andor, though, shortly before the Last Battle.) There was some manufacturing of cloth and carpets, but neither was considered the finest. Ghealdan was especially known for timber and fine woods. Gold, silver and iron were mined in Ghealdan; Ghealdanin steel was not considered as good as Andoran or Illianer, though as good as most. Ghealdan also produced a significant amount of furs.

gheandin. A plant whose powdered blossoms were used medicinally to relieve heart pain.

Ghenjei, Tower of. *See* Tower of Ghenjei

Gho'hlem. A Trolloc tribe.

Ghob'hlin. A Trolloc tribe. Its sign was a goat's skull with a fire burning behind it.

Ghodar, Zenare. *See* Zenare Ghodar

Ghoetam. A sage who supposedly sat under *Avendesora*, the Tree of Life, for forty years to gain wisdom; he was fed by the birds.

gholam **or Gholam.** A type of Shadowspawn made by Aginor. Only six were made; three with a male appearance, three with a female appearance. This creature was created for the sole purpose of killing Aes Sedai. It looked like a human, though with a gray-pale complexion. It had the ability to elongate itself, so that it might squeeze its way along a four-inch pipe. Incredibly tough, it generally had to be hacked to pieces and the pieces all burned to ash to kill it; even when one had been cut in half or dismembered, the parts continued to function for a time, still under control of the brain. Given time, they would rejoin. Even destruction of the brain didn't necessarily stop the body walking about, much like a Myrddraal. It was strong enough to rip a man's arms off, and required blood for nourishment; animal blood would do, but it preferred human. At a distance up to fifty paces, a *gholam* could sense the ability to channel. Worst of all, it was immune to the One Power, as if it embodied Mat's medallion; on the other hand, Mat's medallion burned one like acid. For this reason, not even the Forsaken particularly wanted to use the things. "Gholam" was correct in thoughts or speech of someone who didn't know better; if the one speaking knew, "*gholam*" was correct.

Ghraem'lan. A Trolloc tribe. Its sign was forked lightning.

giantsbroom. A tree that grew in stands; its trunks split into many branches, thick and straight, a pace above the ground; at the top, the branches split again into leafy brush. Loial Treesang one to make a staff for himself.

Gilbearn, House. A minor Andoran noble House of which Lady Sergase was a member. *See* Sergase Gilbearn

Gilber. One of Bashere's quartermasters in Saldaea. Vanin reminded Faile of Gilber.

Gilda. One of the maids at The Queen's Blessing, Caemlyn. Gill said that she was the greatest gossip the Creator ever made.

Gilgame. Someone from the Age of Legends to whom Rand wished he had listened.

Gill, Basel. *See* Basel Gill

Gille. A pale-haired *damane*. Her *sul'dam* Nerith brushed her hair to calm her after she had problems with *saidar*. Gille was killed in the first battle against Rand's army.

Gillin. A young woman who performed with Valan Luca's circus. Olver thought her lips were ripe cherries.

Gilyard. *See* Branlet *and* Mayv Gilyard

Gitara Moroso. An Aes Sedai of the Blue Ajah with a strength level of 19(7). Born in 672 NE, she went to the White Tower in 689. After spending six years as a novice and seven years as Accepted, she was raised to the shawl in 702 NE. She was 5'6" tall, and voluptuous, with snow-white hair. She was also flamboyant enough for a Green or a Yellow. Gitara was always just, and usually fair, but kindness never seemed to occur to her. She possessed the Talent of Foretelling. She was the Aes Sedai counselor to Queen Mordrellen of Andor. It was Gitara who gave Luc the Foretelling which sent him off to the Blight and Tigraine the Foretelling which sent her to the Aiel Waste. She remained Mordrellen's counselor until Mordrellen's death in 972 NE. The following year Tamra Ospenya was raised Amyrlin, and chose Gitara as her Keeper of the Chronicles. She was the Keeper for Tamra from 973 to 978 NE. She died after Foretelling the birth of the Dragon Reborn during the Battle of the Shining Walls. Only the Amyrlin, Tamra, and two Accepted who were attending the Amyrlin, Siuan Sanche and Moiraine Damodred, were present to hear.

Glancor. A town just northeast of Far Madding, across the Ajalon Bridge.

gleemen. Traveling storytellers, musicians, jugglers, tumblers and all-around entertainers. Known by their trademark cloaks of many-colored patches, they performed mainly in the villages and smaller towns, since larger towns and cities had other entertainments available, though occasionally they might have been hired by nobles or wealthy merchants to provide rustic amusement.

Glimmer. A brilliant white Saldaean mare that Elayne rode to her coronation in Cairhien.

glowbulb. An illumination device from the Age of Legends, mentioned by the Forsaken, and found in Sammael's rooms by the Asha'man.

Goaban. A nation that arose from the War of the Hundred Years.

goatflower. A plant having flowers with a variety of colors. The blue form worked medicinally for broken bones.

goatstongue. A medicinal herb that had a soporific effect and was good for relieving stomach cramps.

Godan. A village in eastern Tear, on the Bay of Remara. Tear regulated the size and existence of towns in their country, especially coastal towns, for fear of having them overshadow Tear, but Godan was allowed to flourish because of the need for a strong presence overlooking Mayene.

Gode, Howal. *See* Howal Gode

Goemal. One of the two men seeking Elmindreda's hand in the story Siuan and

Min made up to account for Min's presence in the Tower; the other man was Darvan.

Goim Bridge. A bridge in Far Madding connecting the city via the Tear Gate to the mainland at a town called South Bridge.

Gokhan, Lord. A Seanchan member of the Blood. Min saw that he would marry soon. Tuon sent him to the front lines with orders to stay single until after the Last Battle.

Gold Road. A commercial highway that connected the city of Illian with Far Madding.

Golden Bees, the. The symbol of Illian, nine golden bees on a field of green.

Golden Crane. The symbol of Malkier, a golden crane flying on a field of blue.

Golden Crown of Heaven, The. A low-class inn in the Rahad, a seedy district in Ebou Dar. It was a dim hole with only a blue door to mark it, and black stains from old knife fights splotched the grimy floor. Mat went there.

Golden Cup, The. A low-class inn in Tear with a male innkeeper. There, Mat and Thom found Comar, a man whom Rahvin had sent to kill Nynaeve, Egwene and Elayne. Mat diced with him, then broke Comar's back in a fight.

Golden Ducks, The. A lower-class inn in Ebou Dar where Noal, who had saved Mat from a *gholam*, had a pallet in the attic until he was displaced by an Illianer oil merchant whose room was taken by a Seanchan officer. Mat offered to give him accommodations in the palace.

Golden Head, The. An inn in Amador. Lamgwin was to wait there while Morgase and her party were smuggled out of the Fortress of the Light, an escape which never happened.

Golden Lily. Elayne's sigil.

Golden Lions of Aldeshar. An army that lost a decisive battle to Artur Hawkwing. They sang "Dance with Jak o' the Shadows" as they launched their last, futile charge at Artur Hawkwing's encircling army.

Golden Sheaves, The. A small inn in Damelien, Andor, a village with three mills and a small, drying-up river. Elayne and the Kin stayed at the inn on the way to Caemlyn after using the Bowl and evading the Seanchan army. Its innkeeper thought that Morgase had been the best queen there ever was, and that Elayne had been killed by the Dragon Reborn.

Golden Stag, The. The inn in Maerone where Mat and his officers stayed. Its innkeeper was Mistress Daelvin, and Betse Silvin, whom Mat had his eye on and taught an ancient dance, was a serving maid. It was a higher-class establishment, and the second best in Maerone.

Golden Swans of Heaven, The. A tiny inn in Ebou Dar where Bethamin stayed with other *sul'dam* while she worked training *damane* at the palace. There she was questioned by a Seeker, who made her promise to spy on Egeanin. Its innkeeper was Mistress Darnella Shoran.

Golden Wheel, The. An inn located in Far Madding that Rand visited while looking for the renegade Asha'man, and where he heard about Tear being under siege. Its innkeeper was Mistress Gallger. The inn was large, and full of bankers and merchants.

goldenthorn. A plant that grew no farther north than one hundred miles south of Tar Valon. When Pevara and the group of Black Ajah hunters found goldenthorn seeds on Zerah's saddlecloth, it revealed her to be one of the rebel Aes Sedai.

Golever, Berab. *See* Berab Golever

golliwogs. Having these meant that one was very nervous.

Gomaisen, Aldred. *See* Aldred Gomaisen

Gomanes. A Child of the Light. Dain Bornhald sent him and Joelin with Ordeith to find out what Ordeith was up to; Ordeith reported that they were the only two killed in a skirmish with Trollocs. Dain suspected correctly that Ordeith had killed them.

Gome, Mairin. A traveling circus owner who was in Samara at the same time as Luca. The line for her show was almost as long as the one for Luca's.

Good Night's Ride, The. An inn located in Lugard, Murandy. It was a three-storied inn of rough gray stone and purple-tiled roof, and bawdy songs were sung inside to a boisterous clientele. The sign in front of the inn showed a woman dressed only in her hair mounted bareback on a horse. Its innkeeper, Duranda Tharne, was an eye-and-ears for the Blue Ajah. Siuan learned from her that the rebel Aes Sedai were in Salidar.

Good Queen, The. A crowded inn in Aringill, Andor. Its innkeeper was Master Jeral Florry. Mat and Thom paid a steep price to stay in its stable, and the innkeeper was foolish enough to gamble with Mat; Mat won two of his horses. Aludra sought shelter in the stable while they were there, and Mat rescued her from Tammuz and his cronies.

Good Queen's Justice, The. A two-story brick and thatch inn in the small village of Kore Springs, Andor. Bryne presided at this inn over Siuan, Leane and Min's trial for burning down a barn.

Goose and Crown, The. A small village inn a day's ride from Caemlyn. Its innkeeper, Master Raimun Holdwin, was a Darkfriend and outside the inn met with a Myrddraal, who was inquiring about Rand and Mat. The pair overheard the conversation, and hitched a ride in the cart of a man going to Caemlyn.

Goose and Pipe, The. An inn found in Deven Ride, Andor. It was a typical small village inn, thatch-roofed, and slightly larger than The Winespring Inn. Perrin visited it in the wolf dream while searching for Trolloc camps in the area. He saw the Whitecloaks had the village and villagers surrounded.

goosemint. An herb used to relieve a burning or sour stomach. It had frilly leaves, and was chewed for its medicinal properties.

Goraed, Beron. A wealthy Ghealdan merchant dragged from his bed to marry Queen Teresia and so disqualify her for the throne.

Gorderan. A Tairen Redarm in the Band of the Red Hand. About thirty-five years old when first seen and standing 5'10" tall, he was heavyset and muscular with broad shoulders—nearly as broad as Perrin's—and a heavy chest. Despite his bulk, he was much quicker than he looked and almost as good with a sword as Metwyn. He was fair-skinned for a Tairen, with black hair and gray eyes. He survived recovering the Bowl of the Winds in the Rahad, along with Harnan, Fergin and Metwyn. He acquired a heavy crossbow which he used to shoot Renna when she tried to return to the Seanchan. He and Fergin were killed by a *gholam* in Mat's camp outside Caemlyn.

Gorenellin. A plump Malkieri-born merchant located in Saldaea. When Nynaeve Traveled to Saldaea to drum up support for Lan, Gorenellin was bargaining hard with two Altarans. Gorenellin went with Aldragoran and joined Lan in Kandor, almost at the Arafellin border.

Goridien, Shana. *See* Shana Goridien

Gorin Rogad. A false Dragon who rose in Illian in 995 NE. He was taken and burned alive by the Illianers.

Gorovni, Valera. *See* Valera Gorovni

Gorthanes, Ries. *See* Ries Gorthanes

Goshien Aiel. An Aiel clan; its chief was Bael.

Governors, the. Sea Folk rulers on Tremalking. Governors were appointed for the Sea Folk islands from among the Atha'an Miere, never the Amayar. Sea Folk considered this duty off a ship to be onerous, but took the view that it had to be treated like duty on a ship; the ship must be tended and the crew cared for, and so the island must be tended and its inhabitants cared for. Because the duty was onerous, and because Sea Folk wanted to remain with their ships, the Governors and other Sea Folk rarely ventured away from the ports and shipbuilding facilities, except on tours inland to make sure that all was well.

Grady family. *See* Gadren, Jur *and* Sora Grady

Graeger. Almen Bunt's brother-in-law who vanished; all that could be found was a twisted, leafless tree that smelled of sulfur.

Graendal. A woman whose name in Age of Legends was Kamarile Maradim Nindar; she became one of the Forsaken. Her strength level was 3(+10). She was stunningly beautiful, lush and ripe, with long sun-colored hair. She was known around the world, famed and loved, if apparently more often by people who had heard of her than by those who knew her. Before going over to the Shadow, she immersed herself in curing those with mental illnesses that the Power and Healing could not touch. She was also a noted ascetic, not only living a spare and simple life, but preaching that others should as well. The reason that those who knew her often did not like her was that while her public calls for a sparse life were always moderate, in private she was inevitably abrasive and cutting toward anyone who did not live up to her standards of the simple life. Within ten years after the drilling of the Bore, she reversed all of this completely. Some years after, she became the second of those called Chosen to go over to the Dark One. Graendal pursued conquest as much as Sammael, though her methods did not involve soldiers; for all her concern with her toys, she took one solid step at a time, openly to be sure, as the Chosen reckoned such things, but never stretching too far at any step. Her tools were intrigue, subversion and sabotage. She was perhaps the most subtle user of Compulsion in all of its variations. She, of course, trusted no one. Among the Forsaken, she always supported whoever seemed to be winning, or at least able to give her some advantage. She opposed no one—openly, at least—unless she was relatively certain of a win. She was willing to gamble if necessary, but always balanced risks, rewards and consequences.

On the surface she seemed foolish, indolent, dedicated to her own beauty and her own pleasures, especially sensual and sexual. She had buried many who took her at face value. When she awoke in the Third Age, she went to live in a palace in Arad Doman that she took from its proper owner; she sometimes masqueraded as Lady Basene, a Domani noblewoman. Some of her plans involved Rodel Ituralde, the great captain; she manipulated Domani politics. She had been meeting Rahvin at the Royal Palace, and was surprised to find it under new management when she arrived to see him. Encountering Asmodean, she acted and killed him. She concealed this fact, in large part to let the others wonder. Also, she planned to arrange things the others would not like and blame them on Asmodean if she worked them right.

She devoted a great deal of her time to her own comforts and pleasures, to acquiring the servants/slaves she called her "pets." Physical beauty was not enough to be one of Graendal's servants; beauty was required, but they needed at least some degree of power or position as well—a former lord for a footman, a lady to draw her bath. A common man or woman, however beautiful, just did not interest her.

It amused Graendal to keep Jain Farstrider and use him, a bit of Ishamael's handiwork, a souvenir of the first move in the Dark One's grand design. Also, for a time at least, she really did think that his age and battered appearance set off and heightened the beauty of her other servants. She used only the most subtle degrees of Compulsion on him, and sent him to Ebou Dar on the off chance that there might be something to her suspicions of an *angreal* there which was being sought by Sammael.

She used Compulsion on her other pets like a bludgeon, so they would worship her beyond life. Sammael noted that this often made others forget her skill and subtlety with Compulsion; she was one of the best ever at manipulating the minds of others. One thing she came to believe, despite hearing Demandred's rendition of the Dark One's "Lord of Chaos" order, was that Rand al'Thor was too dangerous to leave alive. But she thought that killing him would have to be done very, very, very carefully. She very definitely did not want to face the Dark One's wrath. Thus she aimed Sammael at Rand, but was caught by Sammael in a snare of her own sort. Although her own snares were working, she found herself forced into aiding Sammael far more than she wanted to, even having to follow his lead and most of his orders. She helped him to the extent of linking with him and letting him control her use of the Power while meeting Sevanna; her pseudonym then was "Maisia." She went along with his "fool box" trick, scattering the Shaido widely.

She had an *angreal*, a ring, a plain gold band too small for any but her little finger; it didn't give her a great increase in power, in her opinion, but it could step her up into the "male levels." She found it among Sammael's belongings after his death. Soon thereafter, she was coopted by Moridin, acting through Shaidar Haran, Moghedien and Cyndane. Moridin told her not to kill Rand, and later told her to kill Perrin, giving her the dreamspike and the services of Slayer to accomplish the task. Blaming her for the failure to kill Perrin and for the death of several Forsaken, Shaidar Haran punished Graendal by killing her and putting her soul in an ugly body. She was given the new name Hessalam.

She faced off against Aviendha during the Last Battle near Shayol Ghul. She attempted to use Compulsion against Aviendha, who was unweaving a gateway. In the explosion that followed, her Compulsion was turned back on her, making her Aviendha's willing slave.

Grafendale. A town in Andor. Androl thought that the houses at the Black Tower would look normal here.

Grand Alliance, Grand Coalition. *See* Coalition, the

Grand Emergence. The most secret ceremony of the Red Ajah. They walked through the ceremony in a warded place, speaking the parts in a guarded way even so. It was, in fact, nothing less than a plan for seizing the White Tower should that become necessary. Not all Red sisters were aware of that ceremony, since it was so shrouded in doublespeak and masked words. It supposedly had been practiced ever since the White Tower was founded. Every Red sister who knew what it was felt certain that the other Ajahs had something similar. In fact, at least some did.

Grand Hall. A spacious room found in the Royal Palace in Caemlyn.

Grand Hall of the Assembly. The building that housed the Assembly of Lords, which elected both the King and Panarch, in Tanchico.

Grand Hall of the Sun. A hall found in Cairhien's Sun Palace.

Grand Hike, The. An inn in Caemlyn; Snert was the innkeeper.

Grand Passions Cycle, The. A piece of music composed three hundred years before the War of Power; "The March of Death" was its mournful final movement, and was played by Asmodean on his harp.

Grassburner. Another name for the Dark One.

grassfang. A snake found in Seanchan.

Gray Ajah. The main thrust of the Gray Ajah was mediation and negotiation. The Ajah was ruled by a council of varying number, but always an odd number. The leader of the council was considered by Gray sisters to be the head of their Ajah and was known as the Head Clerk, but in fact she had less authority than most Ajah heads and had to depend on gaining consensus among the council members. At the time of the Last Battle, there were approximately 140 members of the Gray Ajah, making it the third largest.

gray fennel. A poisonous plant.

Gray Fox, the. *See* Thom Merrilin

Gray Gull. The three-masted rivership owned by Huan Mallia. It used sweeps (oars) inside the harbor. Sanor and Vasa were crewmen. Mat and Thom traveled aboard it from Tar Valon to Aringill.

Gray Men. A type of Shadowspawn, unusual in being ordinary humans who gave their souls to the Dark One; they were called Notdead by wolves. Aes Sedai and their Warders could not detect the presence of Gray Men, as they could the presence of those far gone in the Shadow, because the taint of evil was not strong enough in them; however, Rand did sense one, because of his greater strength, and Perrin was able to smell them. Some Gray Men, both male and female, were serving the Forsaken, but Lanfear had an antipathy toward them and did not employ them. Only Gray Men and Myrddraal did not dream, according to Lanfear.

Gray Owl. The symbol of Lord Ingtar of Shienar.

Gray Tower. An organization mentioned by Emarin/Algarin in a ruse.

Grayor Frenn. A Two Rivers man who watched the forging of *Mah'alleinir.*

Great Arvalon. A place in the Fourth Age where a children's game had a chant that mentioned the Lord of Chaos.

Great Blackwood. *See* Forest of Shadows

Great Blight. A stretch of territory north of the Borderlands, home of the Trollocs, Myrddraal and other creatures of the Shadow and characterized by the evil influence of the Dark One. Not part of the normal universe (as was also true of *stedding* or lands of Aelfinn/Eelfinn), it was not reflected in and could not be entered from *Tel'aran'rhiod.*

great captain. The term for a military commander of extraordinary abilities. The five great captains of the time leading up to the Last Battle were Agelmar Jagad, Davram Bashere, Pedron Niall (murdered before the Last Battle), Rodel Ituralde and Gareth Bryne.

Great Circle, the. A huge gathering place in Tanchico that could hold thousands to watch horse races or displays of fireworks. It was located on the Calpene, the westernmost hilly peninsula on Tanchico Bay.

Great Council of Thirteen. *See* Supreme Council

Great Fish Market. The largest fish market in Tar Valon. Built by Ogier, it seemed to be a school of huge fish, green and red and blue and striped.

Great Game, the. *See* Daes Dae'mar

Great Gathering, The. The inn at the Black Tower; it was owned by Lind Taglien.

Great Hall of the Council. A building opposite the King's Palace on the Square of

Tammaz in Illian. The first King of Illian said the Council of Nine could have any palace they wished, just as long as they did not try to build one larger than his; the Council copied the King's palace exactly, but two feet smaller in every measurement. Both buildings were Ogier-built.

Great Holding. A collection of *angreal, sa'angreal, ter'angreal* and other items supposedly connected to the Power that was held in the Stone of Tear. Nynaeve estimated that it would take ten riverboats to take them all to Tar Valon.

Great Hunt of the Horn. 1) A widespread hunt called to search for the Horn of Valere. The tradition of the Great Hunt dated back to the Age of Legends. 2) A cycle of stories concerning the legendary search for the Horn of Valere, composed in the years between the end of the Trolloc Wars and the beginning of the War of the Hundred Years. If told in its entirety, the cycle would take many days.

Great Lord of the Dark. The name by which Darkfriends referred to the Dark One, claiming that to speak his true name would be blasphemous; the shorter "Great Lord" was also used.

Great Pattern. The Wheel of Time weaves the Patterns of the Ages from the threads of lives and events, interlaced into designs, each and every possible reality—past, present and future. Also known as the Lace of Ages.

Great Purge. In Egwene's test for Accepted, when she was the Amyrlin, part of her remembered something called the Great Purge that eradicated the Black Ajah, but part of her was sure no such thing had happened.

Great Rift. One of the natural barriers, a giant chasm, that separated the Aiel Waste from Shara, extending over 450 leagues from the Cliffs of Dawn into the Sea of Storms.

Great Serpent. A symbol for time and eternity, believed to have been ancient before the Age of Legends began, consisting of a serpent eating its own tail. A ring in the shape of the Great Serpent was awarded to women who had been raised to the Accepted among the Aes Sedai.

Great Stump. A periodic meeting held by the Ogier, at which matters of the gravest importance were discussed. Such a meeting was held at Stedding Shangtai, which lay at the Spine of the World. It was the first meeting of the Great Stump in a thousand years. Only an Ogier old enough was allowed to address the Stump, unless, as in Loial's case, he was married and his wife gave him permission. It was at this meeting that Loial argued convincingly that the Ogier should not yet open the Book of Translation, but rather help fight the Dark One.

Great Tree, The. An upper-class, tall stone cube of an inn in Cairhien where Rand, Verin, Hurin and Loial stayed after The Defender of the Dragonwall inn was burned and the Horn of Valere stolen. Here they devised a plan to retrieve the Horn from Lord Barthanes' manor. The Great Tree's innkeeper was Mistress Tiedra.

Great Trees. Huge beautiful trees that were tended by Ogier and grew in *stedding* and Ogier groves. They were mammoth hardwoods that towered hundreds of feet into the air with trunks as much as one hundred paces across. The Ogier never cut them down unless they died, and when tended they almost never did. Some of largest were seedlings during the Age of Legends.

greater consensus. A unanimous vote of the Hall of the Tower. Generally this demanded that every Sitter present had to stand, and that a minimum of eleven Sitters needed to be present; the presence of at least one Sitter from each Ajah also was required. If the removal of the Amyrlin or Keeper was at stake, the Ajah from which she was raised was not informed of the vote until after it had been taken.

greatfather. *See* Aiel kinship

Green Ajah. The main thrust of the Green Ajah was to hold itself ready for Tarmon Gai'don. It became known as the Battle Ajah during the Trolloc Wars. The hierarchy in the Ajah was rather military. The authority of the Captain-General, the head of the Ajah, was quite thorough and far-reaching. She was assisted by her seconds, the First Strategist and the First Tactician. Green Ajah members were permitted to bond multiple Warders. Aes Sedai of the Blue and the Green Ajahs were considered the most passionate of Aes Sedai in their beliefs, the most likely to be swayed by emotion. Among Greens, being kept in Tar Valon or in the Tower was considered a punishment, or at least drudgery. At the time of the Last Battle there were approximately 180 members in the Green Ajah, making it the second largest.

Green Man. Also called Someshta, he was the last of the Nym who guarded the Eye of the World before it and he were destroyed.

Green Salts. A sept of the Shaido Aiel.

greenwood. A towering evergreen tree found in the Mountains of Mist, the wood of which was used to make boxes.

greenwort. A medicinal herb that was good for sleep and for stomach cramps.

Greeting Hall, The. An inn in Caemlyn where Duhara Basaheen stayed.

Gregana. A *sul'dam* who participated in the Seanchan attack on the White Tower and collared Adelorna. Egwene freed Adelorna before killing Gregana with a blast of fire.

Gregorin Panar den Lushenos. An Illianer nobleman who was a member and some-time leader of the Council of Nine. He was tall, with a round face and a square-cut beard that left his upper lip bare. He offered Rand the Laurel Crown. Rand later named him Steward of Illian for the Dragon Reborn. At first he was reluctant to sign the Dragon's Peace, but eventually acquiesced.

Grinwell, Else. *See* Else Grinwell

Grinwell, Master. A kind Andoran farmer and father of Else and eight others. He was a sturdy man. Mat and Rand did work for his family while making their way to Caemlyn, and entertained them at the end of the day.

Grinwell, Mistress. A kind Andoran farmwife and mother of Else and eight others. She had yellow hair. Mat and Rand did work for her family while making their way to Caemlyn, and entertained them at the end of the day. Realizing that Else had her eye on Rand, she had Else sleep with her and put Mat and Rand in Else's room.

Grinwell, Thom. The name Mat used in Caemlyn when talking to Rahvin and Morgase.

grolm. An exotic Seanchan animal brought from a parallel world. A *grolm* had a wedge-shaped head with three eyes; the mouth was toothless but had sharp ridges. It waddled in walking, but ran by leaping and moved very swiftly in long bounds. The weight of an adult ranged from three hundred to five hundred pounds. They had multiple births in litters of up to six, but rarely did more than one or two survive. They were primarily used as guard animals. Extremely territorial, they rapidly learned who was allowed in a given area and would fix on anyone who was nervous or afraid, using their very good sense of smell to detect this. *Grolm* also had extremely good vision, and were used sometimes in battle, though only against lightly armored opponents, to break holes in an enemy line which would be quickly exploited by human soldiers. They could also be deployed against cavalry, as horses often panicked in their presence unless trained to tolerate them. They were very hard to kill; arrows often failed to penetrate their thick hides, as frequently did blows from swords, axes or spears. Nonfatal wounds seldom incapacitated them; it took ferocious wounds to slow them significantly, and they healed rapidly. The *grolm* was apparently a pack animal in its natural environment, though they could turn on one another if not properly controlled; they would often rip apart and eat one of their own kind which had been injured, and they would consume their own dead.

    Grolm were controlled by spoken commands, hand signals and the use of a small, piercing whistle-like flute. Among *morat'grolm* it was a matter of pride to use only the hand signals and the flute, perhaps in imitation of the way the Blood usually communicated in public with Voices of the Blood.

groundwasp. A nasty insect that stung animals that disturbed its nest.

groves. Special areas planted outside cities by the Ogier in days past, to comfort them and ease the Longing, while they worked on building; many groves disappeared over the years.

Growing, Songs of. A Talent used by Ogier in past Ages to aid and enhance growing things.

Growing, Talisman of. A *ter'angreal* triggered by Ogier Treesinging that allowed the Ogier to expand the Ways that the Aes Sedai had built.

Grubb, Mother. A healer in Caemlyn. Basel Gill suggested that she might have a look at Mat.

grunter. A food fish that squealed when it spawned.

Guaire Amalasan. A false Dragon who started the War of the Second Dragon in FY 939–943. He conquered much of the world before being captured by

Artur Hawkwing and gentled by the White Tower. Remnants of Amalasan's army unsuccessfully attempted his rescue from the Tower after his capture.

guardians, the. The *ter'angreal* that prohibited channeling in Far Madding. *See also* Far Madding

Guardians of the Gate. *See* Amadicia

Guards, Winged. *See* Winged Guards

Guarding, the Rite of the. A ceremony traditionally conducted four times annually by the Lords of Tear, in which they affirmed that they guarded the world against the Dragon by holding *Callandor*.

Guenna, Mother Ailhuin. *See* Ailhuin Guenna, Mother

guestright. According to Lan, an honor given by any lord in the Borderlands to anyone displaying the ring of Malkieri kings.

Gueyam. A High Lord of Tear. As bald as an egg and wide as a blacksmith, with fists like small hams, he wore an oiled beard that emphasized his baldness. One of the most active plotters against Rand in the Stone, he was sent to Cairhien under Meilan. Gueyam worried that Rand would punish him for his previous association with Hearne and Simaan. He was in Illian with Rand, and Min saw a vision of him dying violently in battle; he died in the Last Battle.

Gueye Arabah. A young Seanchan officer under Tylee who told Perrin of additional Shaido approaching Malden.

Gufrin. A sergeant of a squad of the Band of the Red Hand. He was not bright, but he was keen-eyed.

Guides. On Sea Folk Islands, Amayar chosen to protect the Sea Folk from themselves, if possible.

guiding. *See* leading

Guidings. Stone guideposts directing travelers in the Ways.

Guild of Illuminators. The name for guild members who manufactured fireworks. Tarabon was the homeland of the Guild of Illuminators, and Tanchico was the location of the Guild's one and only true chapter house until one was built in Cairhien. The Guild was composed almost entirely of Taraboners. There was no way to enter the Guild except by birth or marriage, and people of other nations who married in were never allowed to know any of the innermost guild secrets, chief of which was the method of manufacturing fireworks, including the key secret: a mixture of saltpeter, sulfur and charcoal, known in the Age of Legends as gunpowder. The money made within the Guild could not be bettered outside.

There were sometimes renegade Illuminators, who either kept making and/or selling fireworks after being kicked out or who tried to reveal guild secrets, but these were rare, since the Guild would hunt down and kill such people. The Illuminators discouraged anyone from cutting open any of the fireworks to see what was inside by claiming that the contents could sometimes erupt violently when exposed to air as well as to fire.

The Illuminators fell on hard times; the chapter house in Cairhien was damaged when Rand, Selene and Loial sought shelter there from Trollocs. Rand aimed a firework at the Trollocs and lit it; the Trollocs were destroyed and the chapter house caught fire. The fire was put out, as was Aludra, the Mistress of the chapter house. When the Shaido attacked Cairhien, they burned the chapter house completely. With the turmoil in Tarabon, the chapter house in Tanchico was in dire straits even before the Seanchan invasion. Some Taraboner refugees petitioned Pedron Niall to open a chapter house in Amador, but he refused. The Seanchan had no notion of man-made fireworks because they used *damane* to produce the same effects, which meant no market among the new conquerors. It was not that the Seanchan would not watch a display when nothing better was available, but rather that trained *damane* could make shows outshining anything the Illuminators could do.

Reports on the exact events varied, but apparently some Seanchan attempted to enter the Tanchico chapter house, the Illuminators tried to resist and the Seanchan fought their way inside. No one knew what happened next—perhaps some soldier took a lantern into the wrong place—but a huge explosion destroyed most of the building, killing a great many Seanchan and some Illuminators as well. The Seanchan gathered up every Illuminator at the chapter house, and some who had fled to Amador, and everyone who even looked like an Illuminator, and made them all *da'covale*. The Guild as such vanished, but individual Illuminators existed outside of Seanchan rule and worked to make sure that the Guild would be remembered.

Guirale, Liandrin. *See* Liandrin Guirale

Guisin. An Aes Sedai of the Gray Ajah and the rebel contingent, with a strength level of 35(23). About 5'8" tall, with silvery golden hair and blue eyes, she was sent from Salidar to Tarabon to discover what was happening there and to determine whether the Aes Sedai could do anything to bring peace to that land. They were also trying to learn if there was a way to get a handle on Rand through the reported Dragonsworn there. Guisin was captured by the Seanchan in Tarabon along with Afara and Edesina; all three were collared as *damane*. Edesina was rescued by Mat in Ebou Dar, Afara remained in Tanchico and Guisin had been broken. It was Teslyn's assessment that Guisin would betray them if they attempted to rescue her in Ebou Dar.

Guitama, Elfraed. *See* Elfraed Guitama

Gull's Feast. An area of Bandar Eban close to where fishermen dumped waste from their hauls. It was also known as the Gull District.

Gurat. A Seanchan commander under Gamel Loune. While fighting Mat he lost four banners of horse and five of foot almost to the last man; not all were dead, but most of the wounded were the next thing to it.

Guybon, Charlz. *See* Charlz Guybon

Gwil. 1) Areina's younger brother who went to Illian to become a Hunter of the Horn. 2) A Two Rivers man who became a servant to Perrin and Faile.

Gyldan. A dark-eyed Aes Sedai of the Red and Black Ajahs who appeared in Egwene's test for Accepted, where Egwene found herself as the Amyrlin Seat. In the test, Gyldan was Elaida's closest confidante and was going to participate in Turning Egwene to the Shadow.

Gyldin. Moghedien's alias while posing as a servant in Tanchico.

Haak, House. A fictional Murandian House of nobility created by Mat in the story he prepared for the gate guard at Ebou Dar when he returned to visit Tuon, who had become Empress, before the Last Battle.

Habiger, General. One of the men Beslan plotted with in the basement of The Three Stars in Ebou Dar to overthrow the Seanchan.

Hachami, Avar. *See* Avar Hachami

Hachari, Lord. One of the Saldaeans who, along with his wife and another couple, met with Taim under the parley flag and tried to kill him with daggers. He and his wife were rendered unsuited for anything other than serving others after the encounter.

Hackly, Eldrin. A big wagon man who once almost killed Deni Colford. Not normally a rough man, he was very drunk when he tried to break her neck.

Had. 1) A young Two Rivers man who joined Perrin's band. He was killed in an ambush by Trollocs. 2) A boy from Two Rivers; when Perrin called Jaim Aybara "cousin," Jaim ran off to tell his friend Had of the honor.

Had al'Lora. A Two Rivers man with Perrin's army. He entered Malden through the aqueduct prior to the attack on the Shaido.

Haddon Mirk. A forest north of Tear, between the River Erinin and the Spine of the World. A group of rebel nobles, including Darlin, went there after Rand had taken Tear.

Hadnan Kadere. A peddler from Saldaea. He became a Darkfriend when he was young; when his beloved older sister found out, he killed her. He was a heavy man, well-muscled and swarthy, with dark, tilted eyes, a beak of a nose and a predatory look. He often spoke and acted as if nervous or afraid, but his eyes never showed it. Rand and the Aiel encountered his party in the Waste; he claimed to be heading to Cold Rocks Hold, but was way off course. Among others, Isendre, Keille Shiogi and the gleeman Jasin Natael were in his party. He had over a dozen supply wagons and three water wagons, plus his own. Mat bought his wide-brimmed hat; Kadere was resentful because he was unable to replace it. Kadere often acted suspicious of Keille and Natael. He sometimes talked mysteriously, and he knew about *Callandor*. After Isendre failed to make her way into Rand's bed and was broken by the Maidens, Kadere strangled her, but not until after she told him that Aviendha was sharing Rand's bed. Kadere shared that information with Lanfear; enraged, Lanfear skinned him alive.

Hadora. A Guardswoman in Caemlyn. After Elayne was taken by the Black Ajah on Full Moon Street, Birgitte sent Hadora to tell the Windfinders to meet her in the Map Room.

hadori. The braided leather cord that a Malkieri man tied around his temples to hold his hair back. Until after Malkier fell to the Blight, every adult Malkieri male wore his hair to the shoulders and tied back with a *hadori*. Like the presentation of his sword, being allowed to wear the *hadori* marked the move from childhood to adulthood for Malkieri males. The *hadori* symbolized the duties and obligations that bound him as an adult, and also his connection to Malkier. *See also ki'sain*

Haellin. A noble House of Tear. *See* Sunamon *and* Kera Haellin

Haerm, General. Commander of the Illianer Companions in the Last Battle, replacing Demetre Marcolin, who was killed during the massive Sharan assault on the plains of Kandor.

Haesel. A maid in the Tarasin Palace. She was a slim young woman in a white dress, gathered up on the left to show green petticoats and embroidered on the left breast with a green Anchor and Sword. She had short black hair framing a sweetly pretty face, big black eyes and silken olive skin. Her livery had the deep narrow neckline common to all women, except nobles, in Ebou Dar. On Mat's visit to the Tarasin Palace by the front door, she was the first servant he encountered, as well as the youngest, having been summoned by the Sword-Lieutenant at the front door. She appeared again in Olver's room when they were moving into the palace. Olver said she had the most beautiful eyes.

Haesel Lusara. A Murandian Aes Sedai of the Brown Ajah and the rebel contingent, with a strength level of 16(4). Born in 878 NE, she went to the White Tower in 891 NE. After spending ten years as a novice and four years as Accepted, she was raised to the shawl in 905 NE. When she first went to the White Tower, she lied about her age by two years, but by the time she was caught out, she had been training for a year. She received a very stiff punishment, but the Aes Sedai could not turn her away by that time, though she always believed that the reason she had been so long a novice was that they simply would not let her test because of her subterfuge.

Haesel was not particularly pretty, average in face and figure, but had a vivacity that made most people see her as pretty. About 5'4" tall, she was neither slim nor stout; her black hair was worn in an elaborate braid that hung halfway down her back, with the braiding running onto the top of her head. Her black eyes could twinkle gaily or glitter with anger even when the rest of her face was composed.

She was part of the rebel fifth column sent by Sheriam's council in Salidar to infiltrate the White Tower (aka ferrets). Like all of the sisters chosen for the fifth column, Haesel was out of the White Tower when Siuan was deposed and the Tower broken, so there was no flight to arouse any suspicions toward her. Apparently, she had simply returned in answer to Elaida's summons. Haesel was coopted by Seaine and Pevara to aid in their search for the Black Ajah.

Haesel Palan. A Murandian rug merchant with whom a young Moiraine shared a room at The Gates of Heaven in Canluum. She was plump, had cold feet and sharp elbows and snored.

Haevin. An Andoran noble House. *See* Catalyn *and* Arendor Haevin

Haevin, River. A river on the northern edge of the Caralain Grass above Andor, flowing west and south from the Black Hills to the River Arinelle.

Hafden, Rina. *See* Rina Hafden

Hafeen Bakuvun. A Domani mercenary working for Elayne in the defense of Caemlyn. He was a large, stout man with solid muscle beneath the fat, a gold hoop in his left ear and a begemmed ring on every finger. He demanded more money because of losses his company suffered, but he helped hold the Far Madding Gate against the attack of three mercenary companies intent on betrayal. He petitioned for a reward for that, which was refused because Elayne saw it as doing what he was being paid to do.

Hahn. Almen Bunt's fifteen-year-old nephew, who made his uncle a set of wooden teeth.

Hai Caemlyn. An Ogier-built city in Coremanda, one of the Ten Nations after the Breaking; its core formed the inner city of Caemlyn.

Hai Ecorimon. An Ogier-built city from the time of the Ten Nations.

Haido. A sept of the Shaarad Aiel.

Hailene. In the Old Tongue, "Those Who Come Before," or "Forerunners." The term was applied by the Seanchan to the massive expeditionary force sent across the Aryth Ocean to scout out the lands where Artur Hawkwing once ruled. Originally under the command of the High Lady Suroth, it was later subsumed into the *Corenne*.

Haindar. A male Aes Sedai who went mad during the Breaking and headed for Paaran Disen to wreak havoc.

Haindehl, Merise. *See* Merise Haindehl

Hake, Saml. *See* Saml Hake

Hal. A Two Rivers man who became one of Perrin and Faile's servants at their manor house there.

Hal Moir. A Youngling with Gawyn. He was two years older than Jisao. Like many who missed the fight in the White Tower, he regretted it. He led a half troop at Dumai's Wells; Gawyn ordered them to tend to the wounded after. Hal went with Gawyn to Dorlan, where he guarded the mayor's house.

Halamak. An area of Seanchan that was the native land of Bakayar Mishima.

Halan. Loial's grandfather.

Half Tail. A sour male wolf and pack leader. Perrin contacted him for information after he and others set out to find the kidnapped Rand; when Half Tail asked why, and Perrin answered that those he was looking for had caged Shadowkiller, Half Tail said that he and other packs were coming along to help. Half Tail also gave Perrin notice of the arrival of his men from the Two Rivers.

Halfman. *See* Myrddraal

Halidar. A city in the Age of Legends.

Halima Saranov. The name used by Aran'gar when she became secretary to Delana Sedai. *See* Aran'gar *and* Balthamel

Hall of the Counsels. Chamber of the ruling body in Far Madding, a palace set in the Counsels' Plaza; it contained the Counsels' Chamber.

Hall of the Servants. The governing body of the Aes Sedai during the Age of Legends; its main hall was located in the capital city of Paaran Disen.

Hall of the Tower. A deliberative body that helped govern the Aes Sedai and advised the Amyrlin. Traditionally it was composed of three representatives known as Sitters from each of the different Ajahs. The Hall had a variety of means at its disposal to thwart or otherwise disrupt the Amyrlin's plans. Although the Amyrlin Seat was by law the absolute power in the White Tower, in fact her power always depended on how well she could lead, manage or intimidate the Hall.

Halle, Barim. *See* Barim Halle

Halvar of Mayene. The First of Mayene some three hundred years before the Last Battle. He made the mistake of giving the doorframe *ter'angreal* in Mayene's possession to Tear; he had already used it and it was no good to him. The High Lords had him assassinated the next year.

Halvate. Tuon's brother. He enjoyed training wild *grolm*. She was fond of him, but he was assassinated.

Halwin Norry. An Andoran man who served as the First Clerk of the Royal Palace in Caemlyn. He was 6'1" tall, and bony, lean and narrow-chested. Awkward physically, he spoke with a dry and dusty voice in a droning near monotone, usually, at least while reading reports aloud. Only a few wisps of gray hair remained to him, standing up behind his ears. Rand was uncertain that anything was real to him except the numbers in his ledgers, but he was grateful that Norry had not left the palace as so many did when he came. Norry had any number of clerks under him to actually wield pens, but, on one occasion, what appeared to be an ink stain marred one edge of his scarlet tabard with the White Lion, and he clutched his embossed leather folder of papers to his chest as if to hide other stains. Norry never looked at the papers in his folder; their contents were in his head, and the papers were there only in case someone wanted to see the actual report. In addition to administering the treasury and running the city for the Queen, the First Clerk's duties included acting as an advisor in matters of state. He would have shuddered at the suggestion of spying, but he maintained a correspondence with people in many lands, which, while hardly a spy network such as the one Sebban Balwer ran, did keep Norry abreast of events in a fairly timely fashion.

Hama N'dore. An Aiel warrior society; the name was Old Tongue for "Mountain Dancers."

Hamad. A lancer in Bashere's army. He was taller than Bashere, with a dark beard and mustaches, tilted green eyes and a scar on his face. He brought in

Sammael's emissary and gaped when the emissary started oozing blood. Hamad also accompanied Rand to his meeting with the purported Daughter of the Nine Moons. Bashere had Hamad search Lady Deirdru's manor, and he returned with a wooden box filled with male and female *a'dam*.

Hamada. The mother of Moilin, the Ogier author of *A Study of the War of the Shadow*.

Hamal. A Moshaine Shaido blacksmith. He was a very big man. After the Moshaine used Sammael's *nar'baha* and were cut off from the rest of the Shaido, Maeric gave Hamal the *nar'baha* and told him to keep pressing it until the hole opened.

Haman son of Dal son of Morel. An Ogier on the Council of Elders who taught Loial, and who had no high opinion of Loial's scholarship and study habits. About 10'5" tall, he was white-haired, and had a broad build. Haman's eyes were as large and round as teacups, his broad nose nearly covered his face, and his ears, tipped with white tufts, stood up through his hair. He wore long drooping white mustaches and a narrow beard beneath his chin, and his eyebrows hung down to his cheeks. He was married to Voniel, Loial's mother's sister. Haman and Loial's father met the Green Man when they were younger. He traveled with Covril and Erith to find Loial, and married Erith and Loial. When Loial went to Stedding Shangtai for the Great Stump, Elder Haman assumed the task of making sure the Waygates were closed. Elder Haman fought in the Last Battle, at first with Elayne in Caemlyn and then at the Field of Merrilor.

Hamarashle, Lord and Lady. Cairhienin nobles of middling power.

Hamarea. A nation that arose after the Trolloc Wars.

Hamdey, Escaralde. *See* Escaralde Hamdey

Hammar. A Warder and blademaster who taught swordsmanship at the White Tower. He was blocky, with thick black eyebrows. When Galad and Gawyn were reluctant to take on Mat and his quarterstaff, Hammar offered to cover the bet. After Siuan was deposed and made prisoner, Hammar tried to free her; Gawyn killed him.

Hammer. 1) A name the Seanchan called Luthair Paendrag. 2) Tervail's warhorse, a tall bay gelding.

Hammer of the Light. One of the old names for Artur Hawkwing. *See* Artur Hawkwing

Hammer, seed of the. Descendants of Artur Hawkwing, i.e., the Seanchan. The phrase was used in a prophecy of the Shadow, written on the wall of the cell Padan Fain had occupied in Fal Dara.

Hamora, Jisao. *See* Jisao Hamora

Han. A man of the Shorara sept of the Tomanelle Aiel who was clan chief. He was about six feet tall and weighed 210 pounds. He had white hair and a face like wrinkled leather. He was irascible and touchy about his height, which was short for an Aiel, had a sour mouth and often sounded unhappy or disgruntled.

Prickly and difficult to know, he was with Rand from the beginning, but was somewhat uncertain about whether that was the right position to take. Han was in Tear and participated in the invasion of Illian.

Hand, Left. *See* Left Hand

Hand of the Empress at Sea. The rank of Egeanin's mother.

Hand of the Light. An order within the Children of the Light, pejoratively known as the Questioners. Their avowed purposes were discovering the truth in disputations and uncovering Darkfriends. In the search for truth and the Light, as they saw it, they were even more zealous than the Children of the Light as a whole. Their standard method of inquiry was by torture; their normal attitude was that they knew the truth already and needed only to make their victim confess to it. At times they acted as if they were entirely separate from the Children and the Council of the Anointed, which commanded the Children. The head of the Hand of the Light was the High Inquisitor, who sat on the Council of the Anointed. Their sign was a blood-red shepherd's crook, which appeared behind the golden sunburst on their cloaks. The High Inquisitor only wore the red shepherd's crook.

Handar, Iagin. *See* Iagin Handar

Handoin. One of Tuon's rivals in Seanchan, whose symbol was a white boar.

Handu, Stedding. A *stedding* located in the Spine of the World.

Hanlon, Daved. *See* Daved Hanlon

Hansard, Afrim. A loyal Guardsman of the Royal Guards in Caemlyn. He escorted Samwil Hark to meet with Elayne.

Hanselle Renshar. A young Andoran who was Lady Arathelle's grandson. He was slender and blushed easily. Arathelle sent him to ask for safe conduct for her, Aemlyn, Abelle, Ellorien, Luan and Pelivar to enter Caemlyn.

Happy Throng, The. An inn in Caemlyn. Master Denezel was its innkeeper. A portrait of Rand hung in the common room.

Harad Dakar. The capital city of Hardan, a nation that rose during the War of the Hundred Years and later disappeared. The city was hauled away stone by stone, making it a quarry for almost a hundred years.

Haral Luhhan. The blacksmith in Emond's Field. Born in 950 NE, he was 6'5" tall and was very big; he seemed to be made out of tree trunks. He was married to Alsbet, and was a member of the Village Council. Perrin was his apprentice, and Master Luhhan gave him his axe. Haral fought against the Trollocs on Winternight. He and his wife were taken prisoner later by the Whitecloaks and freed by Perrin. He was involved in the defense of Emond's Field, by forging and fighting. He went into business with one of the refugees, a cutler, who came to the Two Rivers. When Perrin managed to get out of the wolf dream in the Last Battle, Haral found him and took him to Mayene for Healing; he also gave Perrin advice about the need to fight to the limits of his strength in the battle against the Dark One.

Haran, Shaidar. *See* Shaidar Haran

Hardan. A nation that arose as a result of the War of the Hundred Years.

Hardlin, Morly. *See* Morly Hardlin

Harella, Faeldrin. *See* Faeldrin Harella

Haren, Thad. *See* Thad Haren

Haret, Jurah. *See* Jurah Haret

Harfor, Reene. *See* Reene Harfor

Hari. A follower of the Prophet. He had narrow eyes and a thrusting nose, and he collected ears as trophies. Perrin came upon him leading a group of Dragonsworn as they were attacking Morgase's party, and ran them off. He told tales of Perrin to Masema, prior to Perrin's visit, and helped torture a captured Shaido by putting hot coals on his belly. He was killed before the Last Battle by *Cha Faile*.

Hari Coplin. An Emond's Field farmer, and a troublemaker. His brother was Darl; Hari was smaller, but both had weasel-like faces and tight mouths. After the Winternight Trolloc attack, Hari was among those who confronted Moiraine. Hari later participated in the defense of Emond's Field when the Trollocs attacked again. Although he fawned on the Whitecloaks at first, Hari accompanied Luc to tell them that they were not welcome in Emond's Field. Hari was part of the group that tried to fight off a group of Trollocs that turned out to be Tinkers seeking shelter.

Harilin. A woman of the Iron Mountain sept of the Taardad Aiel and *Far Dareis Mai*. About Rand's age, she was lanky and redheaded. In Cairhien, she guarded Rand's door in the Royal Palace. As one of the fifty Maidens acting as his guard of honor, she went with him to Lord Algarin's manor in Tear, and there fought when the Trollocs attacked.

Harilin's Leap. A small village inn in Jarra, Ghealdan. Perrin, Moiraine, Lan and Loial stayed there when they were following Rand to Tear. Moiraine and Perrin saw Noam, who had become wolf-like, locked up in the stable of the inn, and Perrin had wolf dreams while staying there. Its innkeeper was Master Harod; Simion, Noam's brother, was an attendant.

Harine din Togara Two Winds. The Wavemistress of clan Shodein of the Sea Folk. Her Swordmaster was Moad din Nopara Red Hawk; her Windfinder was her sister Shalon din Togara. Harine was one of the First Twelve, the twelve seniormost Wavemistresses. As a Wavemistress she rated a two-tiered, fringed red parasol. Harine was about 5'5" tall, with a full mouth and straight black hair streaked with a little white. She wore five small fat earrings in each ear, and a fatter chain than her Sailmistress. She was twenty-two years younger than her sister Shalon, who was already married when she was born. Min saw a viewing that she would be punished for the bargain she made with Rand, but also that she would be Mistress of the Ships one day. Harine had fond memories of Berelain; when she visited, they bathed together, and drank honeyed wine.

She was designated to keep close to Rand, along with her Windfinder and her Swordmaster. She had the authority to speak for the Mistress of the Ships with Rand; her word bound the Sea Folk as would that of the Mistress of the Ships herself. Rand's *ta'veren* influence forced her into admissions she would not otherwise have made, but once he departed, leaving Merana and Rafela to complete the agreement, Harine was able to force a much closer bargain than he would have liked. As a result of the Bargain, Harine was made ambassador to Rand. She, Shalon and Moad went with Cadsuane to Far Madding. During the cleansing of the taint on *saidin*, Harine and Min stayed in a hollow, guarded by Moad, Tomas and Erian. Afterward, Harine went to Tear and then Illian to meet with the First Twelve to select a new Mistress of the Ships, hoping to be chosen for the position. Instead, Harine was stripped, hung from her ankles and beaten as punishment for her Bargain with Rand. She was allowed to keep her position as Clan Wavemistress and resumed her duties as ambassador to Rand.

Rand later chastised her in Arad Doman for the slowness of grain delivery, but she replied that the Seanchan were making things difficult. She made another bargain with Rand as well; she told him what the Sea Folk did about men who could channel in return for a question that she could ask of him later.

Hark, Samwil. *See* Samwil Hark

Harke, Maryl. *See* Maryl Harke

Harkin, Bera. *See* Bera Harkin

Harlon Bridge. A moderate-size village in Andor, ten miles from Caemlyn. Elayne and her party stayed there at one of its three inns on the way to Caemlyn to claim the throne. Adeleas recognized one of the Kin there, Garenia, as a runaway novice from years past. Kirstian also confessed to being a runaway. They were to be put back in white, and returned to the Tower for punishment, which caused a near-rebellion among the Kin until it was put down by Reanne and Alise. Adeleas was murdered while they were in the village.

Harnan. A Tairen Redarm file leader in the Band of the Red Hand. About forty years old, he was of medium build and 5'10" tall, with brown eyes, a crude tattoo of a hawk on his left cheek, and a lantern-jaw. His brown hair, worn shorter than Mat's, was beginning to show a little gray. He was not large, but he was hard-muscled and stronger than he looked. Both temperamentally and physically he was a solid man. During the Last Battle, Harnan and Vanin believed that the chest holding the Horn of Valere contained tabac and tried to steal it, leading Faile to think that they were Darkfriends. They fled and allowed themselves to be captured by the enemy and taken to the Field of Merrilor. When Faile arrived there and was betrayed by Aravine, he and Vanin and other prisoners broke loose and created enough confusion that Faile was able to escape.

Harnder, Milam. *See* Milam Harnder

Harnesh, Alaabar. *See* Alaabar Harnesh

Harod, Master. The innkeeper at Harilin's Leap, in Jarra, Ghealdan. He did not like the Whitecloaks after two of them went mad and tried to burn down his inn. Simion was his servant. Moiraine, Lan, Loial and Perrin stayed at the inn.

Harril. Pritalle Nerbaijan's Warder, who was dark and stocky. Harril accompanied Pritalle and the other Aes Sedai when they captured Egwene at North-harbor.

Hartha. Son of Bukava and an Ogier member of the Seanchan Deathwatch Guard. Hartha had long gray mustaches, and eyes that looked like black stones. He was even more weathered and grizzled than Musenge. He was also First Gardener, which meant that he commanded the Gardeners of Tuon's bodyguard, a rank equivalent to captain, as opposed to the Master Gardener, who commanded the Empress's Gardeners and all of the other Gardeners besides. Hartha had been a Gardener since before Karede's father was born and maybe since before Karede's grandfather. He led twenty Gardeners as part of Karede's group searching for Tuon. After they found Tuon and Mat and their party, Hartha stayed with Mat to fight those who were trying to kill Tuon; he found Elbar among the dead and took his head to Ebou Dar.

Haruna, Yukiri. *See* Yukiri Haruna

Harvell. A Redarm in the Band of the Red Hand who helped Mat set the trap for the *gholam* in Caemlyn.

Harvole, Mailaine. An Aes Sedai who lived at the time of the formation of the White Tower.

Hasad, Biranca. An Aes Sedai who lived at the time of the formation of the White Tower.

Hashala. A novice in the White Tower who led Siuan, Bryne and Gawyn to Egwene when they rescued her.

Haslin, Henre. *See* Henre Haslin

Haster Nalmat. A Saldaean officer who guarded Milisair's manor in Bandar Eban.

Hatch. The innkeeper of The Dusty Wheel in Caemlyn. He kept a special cudgel for thumping men who looked at his pretty wife too long.

Hattori Gatano. An Illianer Aes Sedai of the Green Ajah and the loyalist contingent. Her Warder was Sleete. To escape Tower politics, Hattori volunteered to be part of the embassy to Rand; she escaped from Dumai's Wells and was sent to Dorlan with Covarla. She was looking for a second Warder, and considered Gawyn for the position, but he refused.

Haviar Agora. A blocky Tairen member of *Cha Faile*. He kept his oiled and pointed beard despite adopting the style of wearing his hair tied back with a ribbon. He and Nerion were sent to spy on Masema by Balwer and saw Masuri, Rovair and Annoura visiting Masema. They reported it to Selande and were pulled out of Masema's camp before the attack on Malden.

Havien Nurelle. A Lord Lieutenant in the Mayener Winged Guards. Six feet tall and slender with pink cheeks, he was about the same age as Rand, Mat and Perrin. His helmet had a single slender red plume. He hero-worshipped Perrin.

He led two hundred of the Winged Guards to Dumai's Wells, where a good half were killed after they followed Kiruna and the other Aes Sedai into the mass of Shaido. Those who survived afterward wore a yellow cord tied high on the left arm.

Havien was named First Lieutenant for his action at Dumai's Wells, and accompanied Perrin and Berelain to Ghealdan. Troubled by the way that the Wise Ones treated the Aes Sedai with them, he asked Perrin to make sure that the sisters were all right. He led a squad that found seven Dragonsworn burning a farmhouse with the family inside; they captured the Dragonsworn and hanged them.

Havien became commander of the Winged Guards upon Gallenne's death in the Last Battle.

Hawal Ford. The main crossing point between Arafel and Shienar in the southern part of Shienar. It was a seasonal ford, only available during dry weather. During the rainy season, flat-bottomed ships set sail from the port village of Medo, upriver from Hawal Ford, to carry passengers and cargo down the Rivers Mora and Erinin to points south.

Hawk, Black. Symbol of Shienar, a swooping black hawk on a field of yellow gold. It was seen on the coats of guards at the Fal Dara keep.

Hawkwing, Artur. *See* Artur Hawkwing

Hawkwing's Shield. An alternate name for the constellation known as the Shield.

Hayde. An Aiel Wise One. She and Shanni were in charge of the apprentice Elenar of the Daryne; Amys suggested that they could encourage Elenar to speed up her training and go to Rhuidean, so they could compare her experience with Aviendha's.

Haywain, the. A constellation.

Hazzan, Razina. *See* Razina Hazzan

He Who Comes With the Dawn. An Aiel name for the *Car'a'carn*, the chief of chiefs. According to Aiel prophecy, a man would come from Rhuidean at dawn, marked with two Dragons, and lead them across the Dragonwall. *See* Car'a'carn

healall. A medicinal herb that was used in an ointment.

Healers. 1) People with knowledge of natural healing methods; they were sometimes called Wisdoms or Readers. 2) Seanchan doctors. Healers had a greater knowledge of medicine than was common east of the Aryth Ocean. With no Healing to call on, there was a need to find this knowledge, spurred somewhat early on by knowledge of what could be done with Healing, though this was eventually forgotten. A Healer could be male or female; there were about equal numbers of each. There was no fear of being taken for one using the Power in Healers; Aes Sedai having long been reduced to *damane* in Seanchan, there was no memory at all of Healing.

Healing. One of the Talents of channelers. In Healing, Spirit predominated, but Air and Water were also used, and, in Nynaeve's case, even Earth and Fire. Nynaeve developed and used the full range of flows in her style of Healing.

There were several types of Healing: In one, everything was Healed completely and utterly. If a cut was Healed, not even a scar was left behind. The injury or illness might as well never have been. This was the only known way to Heal a wound from a Myrddraal's Thakan'dar-wrought blade, though in that one case it did leave a scar, often an ugly one. This method took energy from the Healer and considerable energy from the one Healed. The amount of energy required from each depended on the severity of the wounds or illness, although the greater part always came from the one being Healed. The advantages would appear obvious, but the disadvantage was that the energy taken from the one Healed had to be replenished; the one Healed would feel hungry, and needed to eat. The more severe the wound or illness, the more they had to eat; it was quite possible to starve to death consuming ordinarily sufficient quantities of food. For that reason, this method was not often used on the most serious wounds—which required increased intake of food in disproportionate amounts, and took a disproportionate amount of strength from the Healer—or when there were many wounds to be treated, in which case the Healer's strength might not have lasted long enough.

The second type of Healing produced what appeared to be a month or more of healing. That is, once it was done, it seemed that the wound or illness had had a month or two of recovery/healing time. This method left scars, though much less than natural healing would have. It also required less strength from the one being Healed, though it still required a fair amount. Note: Other factors also affected the Healing in both of these methods. The skill of the Healer and the amount of Talent possessed by the Healer were of greater importance than the Healer's strength in the Power, though that did play some part. If two women possessed the same degree of Talent in Healing, the one with the greater strength in the Power was able to do more with her Talent. In fact, a woman lesser in the Power but greater in Healing might well have been able to do more than her sister who was greater in the Power but lesser in Healing. If a channeler was being Healed, the Healing would go better if the channeler embraced the Power while being Healed.

A third method of applying the weaves produced an alleviation of pain. This could be used at levels from merely reducing the pain to wiping it out completely. At lower levels of ability with Healing this could not be done, especially for wiping pain out, without drowsiness or even unconsciousness resulting in the patient. At the upper levels of ability, the drowsiness and/or unconsciousness might have been dispensed with, but that was a matter of the skill/level of Talent, and they could have been kept, too, if the Healer wished it.

A fourth method of applying the weaves washed away fatigue, wiping all of the toxins and poisons out of the muscles, and breaking them down harmlessly. As with other parts of Healing, the ability to do this was dependent on skill, level of Talent, and to a lesser extent, on strength in the Power.

Heape. A location in the gleeman's tale, "Mara and the Three Foolish Kings," recited by Thom Merrilin in The Woman of Tanchico inn, when Mat met him in Tar Valon before leaving the city.

Hearne. A High Lord of Tear. He had a narrow face and tugged his earlobe unconsciously when furious. He was one of most active plotters against Rand in the Stone. Rand sent him to Cairhien under Meilan to restore order and feed the hungry. He was sent back south from Cairhien, leading one of the last large parties of Tairens to depart, and joined the rebellion against Rand gathering near Haddon Mirk under Darlin. Merana and Rafela negotiated a settlement with Hearne and the other rebels; that settlement made Darlin king.

Heart Guard. Heroic Manetheren cavalry troops that Mat commanded against the Trollocs in an earlier life. Its Old Tongue name was *Valdar Cuebeyari*. When Mat awakened from his Healing in the Tower, he remembered a battle in which his bannerman stood close with the Red Eagle above his head, and he shouted "Manetheren!" This was an old blood memory, as Mat had not yet been to Rhuidean.

Heart of the Dark. Another name for the Dark One.

Heart of the Plain, The. An inn in Far Madding. Rand walked by without going in, when he was looking for information on the renegade Asha'man who had tried to kill him.

Heart of the Stone. The chamber within the Stone of Tear that housed *Callandor*. Tairens did not like admitting that the Heart of the Stone existed. The High Lords were the only people permitted in the Heart of the Stone, and they went only four times a year, at the twin demands of law and custom. It was a great vaulted chamber with huge polished redstone columns, ten feet thick, rising into shadowed heights above golden lamps hanging on golden chains.

Heartfang. A name for the Dark One among wolves.

heartleaf. An herb prepared in a tea, possibly to prevent pregnancy.

Hearts of Flame. A collection of love stories that novice Elin Warrel read outside the Amyrlin's quarters in the White Tower.

Heartsbane. A name for the Dark One used in the Borderlands.

heartsblush. A plant having small red flowers. Cadsuane used an image of this flower on a piece of embroidery.

Heartseeker. The wolves' name for Graendal.

hedge-doctor. A person, usually a man, who dealt in healing without the necessary skills. Healing was considered a woman's art and knowledge.

Heeth Tower. A watchtower on the Kandori Blightborder, commanded by Malenarin Rai. It was overrun by Trollocs.

Hehyal. A member of the Dawn Runners society of the Aiel who was party to tricking Queen Talana into attacking the Aiel, seen in Aviendha's viewing of the future in Rhuidean.

Heidia. A slender *Far Dareis Mai* who accompanied Rand and Min when they returned to Bandar Eban.

Heilin, Mistress. The innkeeper of The White Ring in Maderin. She was round with an ample bosom and suspiciously black hair.

Heirn. The sept chief of the Jindo sept of the Taardad Aiel, and a member of the *Tain Shari* society. He was tall and stocky with a leathery face. Heirn escorted the Wise Ones when they went to Chaendaer; he said that it was to protect them, but in truth it was to protect Rhuarc and the Taardad from the Shaido. Heirn liked Two Rivers tabac, and sometimes showed Rand the Aiel method of fighting.

Helmke. A member of Ituralde's forces in Saldaea. He was a sturdy, long-limbed Domani.

Helvin, Master. The innkeeper of The Gates of Heaven, Canluum, Kandor. He was bald and nearly as wide as he was tall.

Hend the Striker. A Hero of the Horn. He was dark-skinned and carried a hammer in one hand and a spike in the other.

Henre Haslin. A man who once served as Master of the Sword for the Queen's Guards in Caemlyn. He had a bulbous red nose and a fringe of white hair. Dismissed by Gaebril because he was too loyal to Morgase, he climbed into a bottle on hearing of her death. Rand persuaded him to teach the sword to the Asha'man at the Black Tower. Taim dismissed him because he felt that swords were a waste of time for men who could channel, but Rand forced Taim to bring Henre back.

Henren, Lord. An Andoran nobleman at least eighteen years older than Rand. He was blocky, bald and hard-eyed. He opposed Morgase in the Succession and became Gaebril's sycophant. He was used by Rand, and then fled once Rand reached an accommodation with Dyelin.

hensfoot. A leafy weed. Sahra Covenry pulled hensfoot on Mistress Elward's farm just before she was murdered.

Heran Adan. The governor of Baerlon, Andor. When the Whitecloaks came to Baerlon, he decreed that only ten at a time could enter the city.

Herid. A Darkfriend wagon driver who worked for Kadere. He fell partially through the twisted red doorway in the Waste; he was never right in the head afterward, and ran away as soon as he reached Cairhien.

Herid Fel. A scholar at Rand's school in Cairhien and the author of *Reason and Unreason*. He was stout, with thin gray hair. Rand asked him for help in figuring out how to seal the Bore. He was murdered by the *gholam* to stop him from talking to Rand. Fel provided clues that helped Rand when he removed the taint from *saidin* and during his struggle with the Dark One in the Last Battle.

Herimon, Seaine. *See* Seaine Herimon

Hernvil, Jakob. *See* Jakob Hernvil

Hero of Salmarna. *See* Bukama Marenellin

Heroes of the Horn. Heroes of the Ages who could be summoned from the grave to fight by sounding the Horn of Valere. They were called at the Battle of Falme and the Last Battle. When a viewer saw the dead heroes summoned by the Horn of Valere, he or she would know who each one was without being told. All that was necessary was to know some version of any legend or tale with which that hero was linked and then the viewer not only recognized the dead hero, the viewer knew other names for him or her, even though they might come from other times or other cultures.

heron-marked sword. A heron engraved on a sword blade indicated that the sword's owner was a blademaster. Tam's sword had a bronze heron visible on the hilt, and another one on its black scabbard. *See* blademaster

Herot's Crossing. The site of the last battle of Malkier against the Shadow's forces, where Lan's parents were killed and the Seven Towers fell.

Hessalam. Old Tongue for "without forgiveness," it was the name given to Graendal after her failures led to her death and reappearance in an ugly body.

Hevan, Gates of. A place betrayed by Sammael, where he became known as Destroyer of Hope.

hide. A measure of land, 100×100 paces.

High Chant. *See* Bards, Forms of Recitation of

High Chasaline. A feastday for reflecting on one's good fortune and blessings, observed on the twelfth day of Taisham; it was also known as the Day of Reflection. It was considered bad form to complain about anything on High Chasaline; in the Two Rivers, anyone who voiced a complaint could find a bucket of water upended over his or her head to wash away bad luck.

High Days. Special days in Caemlyn on which the Queen distributed the Queen's Bounty, a charity of food.

High Guard of Malkier. The battlefield guard for the King of Malkier.

High Inquisitor. The title for the leader of the Hand of the Light.

High King. A title for Artur Hawkwing. *See* Artur Hawkwing

High Lords of Tear. Acting as a council, the High Lords were historically the rulers of the nation of Tear, which had neither king nor queen until shortly before the Last Battle. Their numbers were not fixed, and varied over the years from as many as twenty to as few as six. They should not be confused with the Lords of the Land, who were lesser Tairen lords.

High Plain. A sept of the Goshien Aiel.

High Seat. A position as leader of the Aes Sedai in the days of Lews Therin.

highchests. A type of furniture.

Highest. The name given the head of the Red Ajah.

Highest Daughter. Tuon's title of address when she was empress presumptive and not wearing the veil.

Hightower, Master. A ferryman in Taren Ferry, Andor. He had a narrow face and pointed features. He took Lan and Moiraine and the Emond's Fielders across the Taren on his ferry; once they were across, Moiraine persuaded him and his men to get off the ferry. The ferry then went down in a whirlpool. When Nynaeve arrived, she made Master Hightower row her across the Taren in a small boat.

Hilde Barran. A plump Two Rivers girl with the ability to channel. Doral Barran was her grandmother. She was among the young women recruited by Verin and Alanna whom Rand saw and terrified at Culain's Hound in Caemlyn. She was taken to join the rebel Aes Sedai.

Hills, Doirlon. A geographical feature located in northeast Illian.

Hills of Absher. A landform found in Andor between Baerlon and Whitebridge.

Hills of Kintara. A range just north of and bordering Far Madding.

Hilltop. A Taren Ferry family name.

Hinderstap. A village in Murandy with a secret it kept from the rest of the world, until Mat Cauthon visited. Each night at sundown, everyone went crazy and started killing each other; the next morning they all woke up in their beds, whether or not they had been killed the night before. The villagers fought upriver from Merrilor in the Last Battle, taking advantage of their special nature.

Hirare Nachiman. The leader of the Arafellin contingent at the Battle of the Shining Walls. He was the younger brother of Paitar, the King. Lord Hirare was the fourth to command—after Lord Agelmar Jagad of Shienar, Pedron Niall of the Children of the Light, and Lord Aranvor Naldwin of the Andoran Queen's Guard—and was killed in a skirmish during the pursuit of the Aiel to Kinslayer's Dagger after the battle.

Hirshanin. A Ghealdanin soldier that Arganda sent to fetch a map for Perrin and him to examine for potential ambush places on the Jehannah Road.

Hob, Old. A name for the Dark One.

Hoffley, Master. A banker in Caemlyn who made a loan to Elayne after learning of the discovery of first-quality alum on her estates in Danabar.

Hoigan, Sarin. Nisao Dachen's Warder. He was bald-headed, with a black beard. He was about 5'9" tall, and wide enough to make him seem shorter.

Hol Cuchone. The home of Raidhen in 400 AB.

Holcom. A messenger for Gareth Bryne at the Last Battle. He was spindly, with a face like a horse.

Holder of the Keys. The title for Corgaide, the woman in charge of the servants in the Sun Palace in Cairhien.

Holding, Great. *See* Great Holding

Holdwin, Raimun. *See* Raimun Holdwin

honeykissers. An Ebou Dari term for young women who chased men.

Honorless. The Aiel name for the *Samma N'Sei*.

hooded viper. An extremely deadly snake found in the Drowned Lands.

Hook, the. A ridge, so called because of its shape, near Tar Valon.

Hoop and Arrow, The. A Caemlyn inn whose innkeeper was Millis Fendry, an eyes-and-ears for the Brown Ajah. Every few days Master Harnder, another eyes-and-ears of the Brown, visited the inn; each time, she sent a pigeon flying north.

Hopper. An old male wolf with whom Perrin had a special connection. He was black and gray with long white teeth and yellow eyes—a scarred and grizzled fighter with thick, rough, shaggy fur. He was impassive with knowledge of the years, old but full of guile, and devoted to Dapple, his pack leader. He had wanted to soar like an eagle when he was young. His left eye was pecked out by ravens, and then he was killed by Whitecloaks. He continued to meet with Perrin in the wolf dream, often chasing Perrin out of the wolf dream for his own safety, and teaching Perrin how to manipulate and survive the wolf dream. He was killed in the wolf dream by Slayer.

Hopwil, Eben. *See* Eben Hopwil

Horn, Great Hunt of the. *See* Great Hunt of the Horn

Horn of Valere, the. A golden curled horn, bearing the words *"Tia mi aven Moridin isainde vadin,"* meaning "The grave is no bar to my call." Legend said that it had been hidden to keep it safe until the Last Battle, at which time it would be blown to call up legendary heroes from the past. Moiraine and company found the Horn at the Eye of the World, and took it to Agelmar at Fal Dara to give to the Amyrlin, Siuan Sanche. Padan Fain and Shadowspawn stole the Horn there, and a pursuit began to recover it, culminating in Rand and Loial stealing it back. It was stolen yet again by Darkfriends, and arrived at Lord Barthanes' manor in Cairhien. Fain next took the Horn to the Seanchan High Lord Turak, but Rand recovered it after killing Turak. Mat blew it at Falme and called up the Heroes of the Horn in battle against the Seanchan. Verin then turned the Horn over to Siuan, and it was stored in the White Tower until it was given to Faile to take to Mat in the Last Battle. Faile and her party were betrayed by a Darkfriend, but Olver escaped with the Horn; threatened by Trollocs, he blew it. At the end of the Last Battle, Birgitte told Olver to find someplace nobody would look, a place he could forget, and toss the Horn into it.

Horns. The name Ituralde's troops called Trollocs resembling goats.

Hornsounder. A term for one who blew the Horn of Valere.

Hornval, Master. A Taraboner tile maker who settled in Emond's Field as a refugee.

Hornwell, Master and Mistress. The caretakers at one of Elayne's estates in Andor. Master Hornwell was stout and gray-haired; Mistress Hornwell resembled her husband, except less round and less gray. Elayne and her party from Ebou Dar stayed at that estate on the way to Caemlyn.

Hot Springs Hold. The home of Colinda, an Aiel Wise One, in the Waste.

Houses, Game of. *See Daes Dae'mar*

hoverfly. The equivalent of a helicopter in the Age of Legends.

Hovian, Corele. *See* Corele Hovian

Howal Gode. A Darkfriend merchant Rand and Mat encountered in Four Kings, Andor. Sleekly fleshy, he had soft-looking hands with a ring on every finger. He tried to talk Rand and Mat into coming with him; when Rand resisted he planned to kidnap them. He and his men were killed by lightning that Rand summoned. In a dream Rand had after, he saw Gode badly burned; Ba'alzamon turned him to dust.

Hu. An irascible old farmer in a rooster joke.

Hu al'Dai. A Two Rivers farmer who was the father of Bili. His farm lay between Emond's Field and Watch Hill.

Hu Barran. A stableman at The Winespring Inn, Emond's Field, along with his brother Tad. He was lanky and taciturn, seldom saying more than three words strung together. Hu participated in the defense of Emond's Field and later joined Perrin's army at Malden against the Shaido.

Hu Marwin. A young Two Rivers man whose farm lay between Emond's Field and Watch Hill. He took part in the rescue of the Luhhans and Cauthons from the Whitecloaks and later accompanied Perrin to Caemlyn. Hu fought at Dumai's Wells, and followed Perrin to Cairhien and Ghealdan. Because he was a good tracker, Hu was one of the two men Jondyn Barran took with him to search for the kidnapped Faile; the other was Get Ayliah. Jondyn, Get and Hu went after the fleeing inhabitants of Malden, but all they found was some information and a sketched map of the town.

Huan. 1) A Seanchan *so'jhin* who served as High Lord Turak's Voice. His family served the Seanchan House of Aladon for eleven generations. The left side of his head was shaved, and the hair on the right side was pale gold and worn in a braid to his shoulder. He struck Fain for not speaking properly to the High Lord; Fain later murdered him. 2) An uncle of Siuan Sanche who was a gambler and didn't like to work; he died pulling children out of a burning building.

Huan Mallia. The Tairen captain of the *Gray Gull*, which transported Mat and Thom from Tar Valon to Aringill. He was tall and blue-eyed with a dark pointed beard. He hated Aes Sedai and the Power, though he tried not to be too open about it.

Huldin, Kely. *See* Kely Huldin

hullworm. A worm that burrowed into the hull of ships.

Hundred Companions, the. One hundred thirteen male Aes Sedai, among the most powerful of the Age of Legends, who, led by Lews Therin Telamon, launched the final stroke that ended the War of the Shadow by sealing the Dark One back into his prison. The Dark One's counterstroke tainted *saidin*; the Hundred Companions went mad on the spot and began the Breaking of the World.

hundred-heads. A creature covered in tendrils found on the bottom of ponds in Andor.

hundred-legs. An insect with numerous legs.

hundredarms. A tentacled creature found in the bottom of Waterwood ponds.

Hundredman. A Whitecloak soldier whose rank was between an officer and a common soldier, and who theoretically commanded one hundred men.

Hunt, the Last. The wolves' term for the Last Battle.

Hunt, Wild. *See* Wild Hunt

Hunters of the Horn. Individuals who took part in the Great Hunt of the Horn, a hunt called to search for the Horn of Valere. Festivities for the hunt took place in Illian and coincided with the Feast of Teven. It was claimed that the tradition dated back to the Age of Legends.

Hurd. A man who worked as a stablehand for Toke Fearnim in Jurador, a salt town in Altara.

Hurin. A Shienaran sniffer and thief-taker whose obligation was to Lord Agelmar. He was about 5'10" tall, and lean, with a lined face and graying hair worn long. He had a longish nose that he rubbed. Hurin's wife was Melia. He wore a short-bladed sword, and a notched sword-breaker hung at his belt, along with a cudgel. Hurin traveled to Cairhien and Maradon professionally. He could smell violence, not evil, and could track those who did the violence, though the track faded over time, greater violence taking a longer time to fade. He could not always tell a Darkfriend by smell. With Rand and others on the hunt for the Horn of Valere, he wound up at Falme, when Mat blew the Horn. Hurin returned to Shienar carrying word of Rand as the Dragon Reborn. The news sparked some skirmishes in Shienar and Arafel. Hurin reconnected with Rand before the Last Battle. He died helping to repel a Trolloc attack on Polov Heights during the Last Battle.

Hurn, Rowan. *See* Rowan Hurn

Hyam Kinch. An Andoran farmer who gave Mat and Rand a ride on their way to Caemlyn. An older man, quiet but friendly, he offered to let Rand and Mat stay at his house while Rand recovered. He knew that they were running from something, but didn't believe that they were Darkfriends.

Hyran. A man who was Nicola's intended. He became a follower of the Prophet and was killed when someone split his head with an axe.

Iagin Handar. A Defender of the Stone in Tear. He was stocky, with a puckered scar that ran from his forehead across the bridge of his nose down to his jaw; he earned the scar when the Trollocs attacked the Stone. When Rand Traveled into the Heart of the Stone with Cadsuane, Handar was guarding it.

Ianelle. One of Tuon's *sul'dam*. She held Lidya's leash, and was the one who caned her for her Foretelling. She did not like punishing Lidya, and smiled when Tuon told her she could put ointment on Lidya's welts. She was part of Karede's group that searched for Tuon when she was missing. She was present at Tuon's audience when Beslan swore to Tuon, although her name was recorded there as "Lanelle."

Ianor. One of the group of Shienaran soldiers who joined Lan in eastern Kandor as he traveled toward Tarwin's Gap. Andere told the protesting Lan that he had run into a group of soldiers, including Ianor, before meeting Lan, and had told them to wait along the southern roadway for Lan and his men to come along.

Ibrella. A novice in Salidar with the rebels; her potential strength level was 14(2). She was born in 980 NE in a village a few days' travel from Salidar. Ibrella was enrolled in the novice book in 999 NE by the rebels in Salidar after Elayne and Nynaeve reached the village. She wanted to see how big a flame she could make with the Power and nearly set fire to a novice class that Elayne was teaching.

ice pepper. An edible pepper from Saldaea whose fruit was long, white and very hot. It was a valuable commodity cargo.

Idrelle Menford. A lanky, hard-eyed Accepted with a long nose. She often wore a frown. She taught a novice class that Egwene disrupted by juggling balls of fire. Egwene embarrassed Idrelle in her first class teaching novices by outdoing anything Idrelle could possibly try.

Idrien Tarsin. A Cairhienin woman who was the Headmistress of the Academy of Cairhien. She took the title of Headmistress because everyone else was calling themselves Master of This and Mistress of That. She was 5'5" tall, and stocky, and straight-backed enough to make her seem a head taller than she was. There was more gray than black in her hair, and her voice was surprisingly sweet and youthful, a startling contrast to her blunt face. It hardened, though, with students and teachers; Idrien held a tight rein on the school. She preferred practical things to flighty, and would rather have not had to deal with philosophers, historians and arithmetists. Before she became Headmistress, she designed a giant crossbow that the Cairhienin used against the Shaido who were besieging the city; it hurled a small spear a full mile hard enough to drive through a man. Idrien found Herid Fel torn limb from limb in his study.

Ieine. A Kin and a member of the Knitting Circle in Ebou Dar. She wore the red belt of a Wise Woman. Her strength level was 31(19); she was not strong enough to make a gateway of any size whatsoever. Born in 629 NE, she went to the White Tower in 646 NE. She was nine years a novice and was put out of the Tower after refusing to begin the test for Accepted the third time. Of medium build and about 5'8" tall, she was very dark and pretty, despite lines at the corners of her eyes. She had a little gray in her hair. Ieine was in on the capture of Ispan, and forced her ahead by twisting her arm up into her back and clutching the back of her neck with her fist—half terrified of manhandling an Aes Sedai, half determined. She was present at a meeting with the Windfinders in the Tarasin Palace, and part of manipulating them, on orders from Elayne and Nynaeve. Ieine traveled to Caemlyn with Elayne from Ebou Dar.

Ifeyina. A *Far Dareis Mai* who went to Maradon with Rand.

Igaine Luin. An Aes Sedai of the Brown Ajah who served as Amyrlin from 476 to 520 NE. Igaine was an Amyrlin of average strength, chosen in large part because she would lead the Tower away from the open involvement in the world that her four predecessors had espoused.

Ihvon. One of Alanna's two Warders. He had dark hair and dark eyes and was tall, slender and whipcord tough. When Perrin's band was ambushed by Trollocs in the Two Rivers, Ihvon saved Perrin from a Myrddraal and led the band to the Tinkers' camp. He and Tomas showed the Emond's Fielders how to build catapults and participated in the defense of Emond's Field. He also fought at Dumai's Wells and accompanied Alanna and Cadsuane to Far Madding.

Ijaz Mountains. A region in Seanchan famous for its high-quality *kaf.*

Ikane Bridge. A bridge in Far Madding connecting the city via the Illian Gate to the mainland at a town called Daigan.

Ila. A Tuatha'an woman who was Raen's wife and Aram's grandmother. Plump, with gray hair and smooth cheeks, she made Egwene, Perrin and Elyas welcome when they visited the Tinker camp, and helped Faile and Perrin when he was injured by Trollocs. She was devastated when Aram gave up the Way of the Leaf and refused to speak to him. In the Last Battle, she and Raen helped with the wounded.

Ilain Dormaile. Moiraine's banker in Tar Valon, a Cairhienin. She was slim, graying and a hand shorter than Moiraine. Her elder brother was Moiraine's father's banker in Cairhien, and handled Moiraine's affairs there as well. A Cairhienin man visited Ilain, claiming to be a member of the Tower Guard and presenting a letter purported to be from the Amyrlin Seat, demanding to see Moiraine's financial information. Ilain recognized that the signature was a forgery and imprisoned the man. He bribed one of her employees and escaped before the real Tower Guards arrived. Ilain had her employee strapped and hired him out as bilgeboy on a rivership; he was to be put ashore penniless unless he persuaded the captain to keep him on.

Ileande. A nation that arose after the Trolloc Wars.

Illeisien. An Aes Sedai uncommitted to any faction. She and four other sisters stumbled on Tenobia's preparations to march to meet the other Borderland monarchs, somehow learned of her intentions and accompanied Tenobia south. In Tenobia's view, they were even more intent on secrecy than she.

Illian. Both a country and its capital city on the Sea of Storms. Its sigil was nine golden bees arranged in a diamond, from top to bottom 1-2-3-2-1: the Golden Bees. Its banner was the Golden Bees on a field of dark green and ringed in gold if flown where the sovereign was present.

The nation of Illian took its name from the eponymous city. It was founded in roughly FY 1094 by Lord Nicoli Merseneos den Ballin, who captured the city of Illian in that year and quickly gained a following among the nobles and people of the region. He was considered a fair, just and intelligent, if not always wise, ruler, and people tired of nearly a hundred years of warfare flocked to support him. His House ruled Illian for nearly three hundred years, until it died out in all but the most distant lines.

Supposedly the King, styled Anointed by the Light, King of Illian, Lion of the Coast, Defender of the Sea of Storms, was the absolute ruler, advised by the Council of Nine and the Assemblage. Historically, the King, the Council of Nine and the Assemblage actually had engaged in a three-way struggle for real power since the nation was founded. First one had the upper hand, then another. The Council of the Nine were powerful noblemen, and the Assemblage was an elected body chosen by the merchants and guilds, including the craft guilds. Ordinary shopkeepers had no vote unless they were members of a guild. The man in the street certainly had no vote.

Illian was traditionally where the Great Hunt for the Horn of Valere was called. Those wanting to take the oath as Hunters came to swear in the great square in the city, the Square of Tammaz. When the Hunt was called in 998 NE, it was the first calling in some four hundred years. Illianers believed that the Horn should be brought to Illian—returned, they called it, though without a shred of proof that the Horn had ever been in Illian. Nevertheless Illianers believed that whoever found it would take it there, where it would be used by their king or queen to summon the Heroes of the Horn for the Last Battle. It was said that Illianers would follow the Dark One himself if he came bearing the Horn of Valere.

As in most nations, the army of Illian in fact consisted primarily of levies raised by various nobles. Most noblewomen used a lance-captain to actually command their forces when they took to the field. Noblemen were expected to lead whether or not they were fit to do so.

In Illian, there was much more chance for a commoner to rise to rank than in most nations. A good many officers serving various nobles and in the Companions were commoners.

The heart of the Illianer army, and the only standing unit, was the Companions, which were in effect the King's bodyguard. They also provided such standing garrisons as the King maintained in various parts of the country. They did not provide police forces in the city of Illian; there was a City Watch there. In total, the Companions numbered between five thousand and six thousand men. There were a fair number of foreigners among the Companions, though no Tairens, Altarans or Murandians. It was not unusual for foreign commoners to rise to rank among the Companions, though command of the Companions was very seldom, if ever, attained by a foreigner.

The Companions' breastplates were worked with the Nine Bees, usually burnished; they wore pointed, conical steel helmets with face-bars; and green coats, with cuffs ringed with yellow or gold braid for officers. Officers also wore plumes on their helmets. The First Captain had four rings of gold braid on his cuffs; his helmet bore three thin, golden plumes. The Second Captain had three rings of gold braid on his cuffs; his helmet also bore three thin plumes, but his were gold-tipped green. Lieutenants had two yellow rings on their cuffs, and two green plumes on their helmets. Under-lieutenants had one yellow ring on each cuff, and one green plume on their helmets. Bannermen had two broken rings of yellow on each cuff, and wore a single thin yellow plume. Squadmen had a single broken ring of yellow on each cuff, and wore no plumes.

Tam al'Thor served with the Companions for years, and rose to become Second Captain before returning to Two Rivers after the Aiel War. Demetre Marcolin served under Tam in the Aiel War, and later became their leader as First Captain. The Companions fought in Rand's campaign against the Seanchan, and in the Last Battle.

Illian had no naval forces, as such. When pirates appeared, one or more nobles were ordered to raise sufficient forces to put them down; the same rules applied when there was any other need for naval action.

Marriages were sometimes arranged in Illian, sometimes between people who had never met. These marriages were arranged by the mothers, or by aunts if the mothers were dead. The bride-to-be was sometimes consulted and sometimes not; consulting her was considered a concession or favor. For that matter, the groom-to-be was sometimes consulted and sometimes not, but more often not. It was possible for both to be informed of their impending nuptials only after everything had been arranged. This happened among common folk as well as among nobles.

The city, and indeed the nation, celebrated a great many feasts and festivals, often with one running right into another, or sometimes even overlapping. While Illianers normally were a fairly sober lot, in particular inhabitants of the city, these feasts and festivals were usually typified by a carnival atmosphere, costumes that often showed too much flesh, drinking, carousing and license, though not to the extent of Cairhienin during the Feast of Lights. Still, Illianers plainly let down their hair during festivals and feasts, relaxing from their normal sobriety.

There were guilds in Illian, but they were not so pervasive as in Altara, Kandor and Arafel. The Assemblage gave them, collectively, a great deal of power. Shipbuilding was important, especially in the city, as well as the making of rope, sails, pitch and all things needed for shipbuilding. Seaborne trade was life's blood to the city; there was great competition over this with Tear, Ebou Dar and the Sea Folk. This competition contributed to the wars between Illian and Tear. Perfume was a major export, and there was glassmaking, most especially mirrors and fine bowls and first-rate looking glasses. Illian was famous for the best work in silver and gold, and for clocks, which, along with those of Tear, were considered second only to those of the Sea Folk for accuracy. Illian produced cutlery of high quality, though not the finest, which was from Andor. The weaving of cloth and carpets was also practiced. Olives were cultivated, producing oil for lamps and cooking; Illian was a major source of oil for lamps. Illian also produced beef, leather and leather goods; the city claimed to produce the best leather in the world, and though others might have had as good, in truth none made better. The Illianer reputation was certainly for the finest and best. Wine, cheese, weapons and pearls were other products of Illian.

Illian Gate, the. One of the gates in Far Madding.

Illuminators. *See* Guild of Illuminators

Illusion. 1) A state of consciousness related to what is experienced as reality, according to the beliefs of the Amayar. Timna, an Amayar on Tremalking, smiled to think she might see the end of Illusion, a state extant prior to the fulfillment of prophecy. 2) A weave, also known as Mask of Mirrors or Mirror of Mists, which allowed one to change one's appearance. *See also* Time of Illusions

Illustrious and Honored Guild of Bookers. The guild in Ebou Dar that regulated betting. They wore red vests with open books embroidered on the breast. Bookers also took bets on whether cargo would arrive, a form of insurance.

Ilyena Therin Moerelle. Also known as Ilyena Sunhair, born Ilyena Moerelle Dalisar, she was the wife of Lews Therin Telamon. In his madness caused by the taint on *saidin*, Lews Therin killed her, their children, and every person who was related to him.

Iman. The capital city of Safer, one of the Ten Nations after the Breaking; it was later the site of Katar in Arad Doman.

Imfaral. The sixth-largest city in Seanchan and home of the Towers of Midnight. It came up when Tuon thought about omens and how they were the same no matter the location.

Imran. A sept of the Shaarad Aiel.

Imre Stand. The site of a Trolloc attack in the Aiel Waste, while Rand and the Aiel were passing through on their way from Rhuidean to Cold Rocks Hold.

inacal. The name given by Demandred to captives taken by the Sharans.

ina'ta. A plant growing in the Waste. Its bark was good for starting a fire.

Inala. A Domani novice in the White Tower whom Egwene recruited and linked with to fight the Seanchan.

Incastar. A place where there was an enclave afraid of progress. It was in the area of Far Madding during the Age of Legends.

Indirian. A man of the Chane Rocks sept of the Codarra Aiel who was the clan chief of the Codarra. His hold was Red Springs Hold and his Wise One was Sarinde. Jalys was his wife. Indirian was 6'4" tall and weighed 180 pounds— the heat of the Waste had melted away every spare ounce of flesh and a few more besides. His cheekbones stood out sharply, and his eyes glittered like emeralds set in caves. He had thinning white hair, thick white eyebrows and a long nose. His voice was deep and rich, which was a shock coming from such a gaunt face. When Rand was kidnapped, Indirian wanted to attack the White Tower. He was with Rand in Cairhien. Rand sent him to help deal with the Shaido, and later sent him and others to Arad Doman to bring order.

Indrahar. A nation that arose after the Trolloc Wars.

Ines. A woman in the rebel camp below Cairhien. She was a darkly handsome woman with a long hard face, well-practiced in anger. When Min and Rand visited the camp, Darlin told Ines and Rovair to give them their horses.

Ines Demain. A widowed noblewoman from Chachin who named her son Rahien because she saw the dawn come up over Dragonmount. Rahien was born in a farmhouse almost two miles from Dragonmount the day after the Aiel began their retreat from Tar Valon. When Moiraine and Siuan wanted to interview Ines, she was in seclusion at the Aesdaishar Palace, mourning her husband, who had fallen over dead in his breakfast porridge. He was a much older man, but she loved him. She was given ten rooms and a garden on the south side of the palace; her husband had been a close friend to Prince Brys. She remained to herself a full month, seeing no one but close family. Her servants only came out when absolutely necessary. Siuan flirted with one of her servants to get the details of Rahien's birth.

Ingathering of the Lances. A term used by Agelmar to describe the Shienarans coming together to defend their border.

Ingtar Shinowa. A Shienaran lord and soldier who was also a Darkfriend. His sigil was the Gray Owl. Ingtar greeted Moiraine, Rand and their party when they reached Fal Dara and took them to Lord Agelmar. When Moiraine and the others started for the Blight, he led them to the Blightborder, although he was worried that he would miss the battle at Tarwin's Gap. At a meeting of Dark-friends, Ingtar received orders, and when he encountered Rand and a Myrddraal, he sent Rand away and went with the Fade to free Fain. After the Horn of Valere was stolen, Ingtar led the men south to find it, with Hurin as his guide.

When Rand, Hurin and Loial crossed to the parallel world, he worried that he wouldn't be able to follow the Horn, but Perrin stepped up and helped him follow. Ingtar and his men arrived in Cairhien just after the Horn had been stolen again. He went with Rand to Barthanes' manor, Stedding Tsofu and through the Portal Stone to Toman Head. He led the party into Falme, where they recovered the Horn and the dagger. After confessing to Rand, he sacrificed himself to save Rand and the others.

Inishlinni. Inhabitants of Inishlinn, a place in Murandy where its citizens identified more with the place than the country. Anaiya brought up the Inishlinni when telling Moiraine about how quickly the Murandians had dealt with a false Dragon, surprising for such a proud, independent people. They probably took such quick action for fear that someone would take it as an excuse to raid their country.

Inlow, Master. The innkeeper at The Queen's Man, between Four Kings and Caemlyn in Andor. He was willing to hire Rand and Mat to perform for his customers, but Rand took sick, and he wanted them to leave. Mat threatened to take Rand into the common room if Inlow didn't help; he gave them some food and allowed them to sleep in his barn, where Mili Skane tried to kill them.

Inner City. The older part of Caemlyn, Ogier-built, that contained the Royal Palace. It was ringed by tall white walls. This part of the city was hilly, and streets spiraled upward, following the contours of its hills, rising past towers glittering in a hundred colors toward the golden domes and pale spires of the Royal Palace perched atop the highest hill. The Mondel Gate was an entrance to the Inner City.

Innina Darenhold. A Taraboner Aes Sedai of Red Ajah and the loyalist contingent. Innina took part in the kidnapping of Rand from Cairhien and was captured at Dumai's Wells. She was treated as *da'tsang* by the Aiel until, under Verin's Compulsion, she found reason to swear oath to Rand, which she had done before Cadsuane departed Cairhien for Far Madding. Innina and the other Reds among the captives were the very last to swear.

Innloine Damodred. Moiraine's sister. A warm and loving mother, she was not very bright, but she was very stubborn.

Instructions, Theory of. A philosophical theory known to the Aes Sedai that fell out of favor. It was mentioned by Sarene while entering Far Madding.

inverted weave. A weave manipulated in such a way that only the channeler could see it.

Iona. Bethamin's *sul'dam* roommate in Ebou Dar. Iona favored the local brandy, which she kept in a flask.

Ionin Spring Inn. An inn in Altara that Egwene passed while traveling through *Tel'aran'rhiod* in the flesh to Salidar.

Ionin Spring. A village in Altara. Egwene passed by while on the way to Salidar, riding in the flesh while in *Tel'aran'rhiod*.

Iralell, River. A river flowing southwest from the Spine of the World to the River Erinin, halfway between Aringill and Tear.

Iralin. A dockmaster in Bandar Eban. He was clean-shaven and willowy. As Rand was leaving Bandar Eban, Iralin reported that all of the food on the docks and aboard Sea Folk ships had spoiled. When Rand returned, Iralin had put up barricades to keep people from the spoiled food. He and Rand boarded a Sea Folk ship and found food that was not spoiled. Rand made Iralin the Steward of Bandar Eban and named him to the Council of Merchants.

Irella. A skinny Accepted whom Nynaeve fought with and who dragged Else Grinwell by the ear.

Irenvelle. A nation that arose from the War of the Hundred Years.

Irgain Fatamed. A Domani Aes Sedai of the Green Ajah and the loyalist contingent. Born in 931 NE, she went to the White Tower in 946 NE. After spending six years as a novice and six years as Accepted, she was raised to the shawl in 958 NE. She had bright blue eyes, unusual for a Domani. Irgain was part of the follow-on party to the embassy sent by Elaida to Rand in Cairhien. At Dumai's Wells Irgain was one of three sisters stilled by Rand during his escape, and she was captured. She had two Warders; one dropped dead from the shock when she was stilled, and the other was killed fighting the Shaido. She was not treated as *da'tsang* by the Aiel, but Verin still used her Compulsion on her, and she found a reason to swear oath to Rand. Irgain was Healed by Damer Flinn, in Cairhien. She was restored to full strength, as near as anyone could tell. After her stilling and Healing, she was no longer held by the Three Oaths.

Irinjavar. A battle site in Saldaea where Bashere's forces fought Mazrim Taim when he was a false Dragon. Taim claimed that he had Bashere beaten there until the visions of Rand appeared in the sky.

Iron Mountain. A sept of the Taardad Aiel.

Ironhand, Balwen. *See* Balwen Mayel

Isam Mandragoran. Lan's cousin, who as an infant fled Malkier with his mother, Breyan ti Malcain Mandragoran, as it was being overrun, and was not seen again. In the Blight the Dark One made him into a sort of hybrid with Luc Mantear. *See* Slayer

Isan. A Maiden of the Jarra sept of the Chareen Aiel who died at Dumai's Wells. Rand added her name to the list of women who had died for him.

Isebaille Tobanyi. A historical Domani Aes Sedai who surrendered her brothers and the throne of Arad Doman to enemies on orders from the White Tower. Faile told Perrin the story as an example of Aes Sedai doing what the White Tower told them to.

Isebele. The ruler of Dal Calain, a country that disappeared during the Trolloc Wars. Isebele made Amyrlin Seat Anghara come to her. Mat thought that Tylin was like Isebele, who was in one of his memories given him by the Eelfinn.

Iselle Arrel. The daughter of Edeyn Arrel. She was born in 962 NE and died in a fall in Chachin in 979 NE. Her death was supposedly an accident, and was the reason that her mother retired from life. Prince Brys and his son, Diryk, died at the same time. All were victims of Merean Redhill, a Black sister, who was part of the male channeler pogrom.

Isendre. The beautiful Darkfriend mistress of the peddler Kadere, encountered in the Waste. She was dark-haired with a palely beautiful heart-shaped face and a smoky voice. She dressed in a manner more suited to a palace than the Waste and swayed enticingly when she walked. Her Darkfriend assignment was to work her way into Rand's affections, but her progress was thwarted by the Aiel Maidens, who beat her for her behavior. Isendre stole from some of the Maidens, and Lanfear stole more and put it with what Isendre had stolen. As punishment, Isendre was worked hard by the Maidens and was allowed to wear only huge quantities of the jewelry she supposedly stole. After she kept trying to get into Rand's bed, the Maidens named her *da'tsang* and worked her harder. When they caught her sneaking into Asmodean's tent—she had been ordered to keep an eye on him as well as Rand—they stuffed her into his tent often. Isendre still tried to get near Rand, and the Maidens shaved all of her hair and beat her with nettles. She told Kadere she would not try anymore, and that Rand was bedding Aviendha. Kadere, realizing that Isendre had been broken, strangled her, butchered her body and hid the remains. The Maidens searched for her, but found nothing.

Ishamael. A Forsaken whose name before going to the Shadow was Elan Morin Tedronai. He was also known as Ba'alzamon, Heart of the Dark, and Soul of the Shadow. Elan Morin was one of the foremost philosophers of his time, possibly the foremost. His books (among them *Analysis of Perceived Meaning, Reality and the Absence of Meaning* and *The Disassembly of Reason*), while too erudite for wide popularity, were extremely influential in many areas beyond philosophy, most especially the arts. Among the first to turn to the Shadow, he called for the complete destruction of the old order—in fact, the complete destruction of everything. His public announcement of his pledge, coming from a world-respected figure at a time when famine, plagues and massive riots were racking a world that had never known them, in the middle of a conference called to discuss dealing with these problems, sparked even greater riots. It was Elan Morin who simultaneously announced to the world for the first time what it was that they faced. Although he never held a field command, he was the Dark One's top captain-general and the most powerful of the Forsaken in the use of the One Power. Not as tall as Lews Therin, he looked like a handsome man of middle years, except for his dark eyes and cruel lips; he had a mellifluous voice. Ishamael at first believed that he had escaped the entrapment at Shayol Ghul, and indeed he was free to move and confront Lews Therin. That began driving him mad. He believed that the Dark One was sealed away again forever, and that he was left alive, but without immortality, in a world which was rapidly being destroyed. The only good point was that his connection to the Dark One held, protecting him from the taint on *saidin*.

Some time after Lews Therin's death, though, he discovered that he had not escaped at all. He began to fade, to grow tenuous, until he was drawn into the trap of the seals.

Roughly a thousand years later, though, the process reversed itself; he began to find himself back in the world of men, first at intervals, in a wispy form, then more solidly, until finally he seemed to be again whole and in the ordinary world. The result of his efforts that time was the Trolloc Wars, but he was not able to do more than get them started, really. He founded the Black Ajah in this period; there had been sisters who were Darkfriends before, but he was responsible for organizing them. That had a more long-lasting effect in many ways than did the Trolloc Wars. Within a matter of twenty years or so, the process reversed itself again, and he faded back into the seals.

The second time the cycle cast him out, in the same slow way, he found a world being unified (the "known" part of it, anyway) by Artur Hawkwing. He was able to turn Hawkwing's distrust of Aes Sedai into something more, resulting in the twenty-year siege of Tar Valon and the price on Aes Sedai heads. When the process of being drawn back into the seals began again, and he realized that he was doomed to this cycle, he tried to destroy Hawkwing's empire and humanity with a new Trolloc invasion, but Hawkwing's army beat it back handily. That drove him mad.

The third time the cycle cast him out, it was to discover that the Dragon had been reborn. He knew this meant that the seals must be weakening; the Pattern was preparing itself for the Last Battle. His chance of breaking the cycle was at hand, and so was his chance to stand high in the favor of the Dark One, by finding and turning the Dragon Reborn. He was unsuccessful, being bested by Rand al'Thor twice and killed by him. The Dark One resurrected him and gave him a new body and a new name: Moridin. *See also* Moridin

Ishar Morrad Chuain. Aginor's/Osan'gar's name in life in the Age of Legends.

Ishara Maravaile. The first Queen of Andor (circa FY 994–1020). At the death of Artur Hawkwing, Ishara convinced her husband, one of Hawkwing's foremost generals, to raise the siege of Tar Valon and accompany her to Caemlyn with as many soldiers as he could break away from the army. Where others tried to seize the whole of Hawkwing's empire and failed, Ishara took a firm hold on a small part and succeeded. She became queen rather than he king for the simple reason that she was native to the province, while he was from the Borderlands, most probably from Jaramide. Ishara sent her daughter to the White Tower to gain the Tower's acquiescence in, if not outright support for, her actions. A son would have succeeded Ishara had not all her sons fallen. To keep the line in control of Andor, her daughter Alesinde took the throne. Nearly every noble House in Andor contained some of Ishara's blood, and the right to claim the Lion Throne depended both on direct descent from her and on the number of lines of connection to her that could be established.

Ishara Nawan. An Aes Sedai of the Blue Ajah who served as Amyrlin from 419

to 454 NE. Ishara was a strong Amyrlin; she continued the policies of her predecessors in a modified way. Under her the Tower was involved in fewer wars than under Nirelle but more than under Suilin. She gained considerable influence for the Tower, but also entangled the Tower in several dangerous situations that came to a head only after her death.

Ishigari Terasian. A nobleman, advisor and general to King Paitar of Arafel. He always looked as if he had just risen from a stupor after a drunken feast. He was about 5'10" tall, and very fat. His coat was usually rumpled, his eyes bleary and his cheeks unshaven. Though he was not as good a general as Agelmar, he was good. Ishigari accompanied Paitar to his meeting with the Borderlanders and on the hunt for Rand.

islands. Large spaces like flat-topped hills in the Ways, connected with ramps and bridges.

Islands of the Dead. The Atha'an Miere name for Seanchan, from which no Sea Folk ships had ever returned.

Isles of the Sea Folk. The main group was roughly south of Illian and Mayene, scattered throughout the Sea of Storms. It was made up of one large island, and many smaller islands of untold number. Other groups of islands that served as homeports to the Sea Folk were scattered throughout the Sea of Storms and the Aryth Ocean, including the largest, Tremalking, off the Taraboner/Amadician coast.

Ismic, Lord. The brother-in-law of Queen Ethenielle of Kandor; Ethenielle arranged his marriage to her widowed sister Nazelle.

Ispan Shefar. A Taraboner Aes Sedai of the Blue Ajah in public but of the Black Ajah in truth, with a strength level of 17(5). Born in 891 NE, she went to the White Tower in 908 NE. After spending six years as a novice and eight years as Accepted, she was raised to the shawl in 922 NE. She had dark hair, worn in a multitude of beaded braids in the Tarabon fashion, brown eyes and full lips. Ispan was disgusted by and frightened of spiders, insects, snakes and rats; she did not react well to exposure to them. She was, by nature, one of those who lorded it over everyone she was superior to, and believed that she was superior to everyone. Ispan was tempestuous, and could become passionately heated about things. She was one of the original thirteen members of the Black Ajah who fled the White Tower. She, along with Falion, was sent to Ebou Dar by Moghedien to find a cache of items of the One Power. She kissed Moghedien's hem when learning of her task. She was captured in the Rahad and later killed by Careane, another member of the Black Ajah, to prevent her from giving up any secrets.

Istaban Novares. One of the founders of Tear. *See also* Tear

itch oak. A noxious weed.

itchweed. A weed that Siuan as a novice used to wash a disliked Accepted's shift to torment her.

Ituralde. A Domani family. *See* Rodel *and* Tamsin Ituralde

Iva. An Ogier woman who was the daughter of Alar and the mother of Loial's wife, Erith.

Ivara. A Kin Elder and a member of the Knitting Circle in Ebou Dar. Her strength level was 39(27); she was not strong enough to make a gateway of any size whatsoever. She was a dark woman with a Tairen look to her; she had plump hands and her hair had some white in it. Born in 664 NE, she went to the White Tower in 680 NE. She was twelve years a novice and was put out of the Tower after she refused the test for Accepted three times. Varuna Morrigan was Amyrlin when she went to the Tower. At the time the Seanchan invested Ebou Dar she was a prosperous and respected goldsmith. Ivara traveled with Elayne to Caemlyn's Royal Palace.

Ivo, River. A river flowing west from the Black Hills, where it formed, into the River Arinelle.

Ivon, Child. A soldier in the Children of the Light. He was with Dain Bornhald in the Two Rivers and reported to Bornhald that Fain had been talking to three Tinkers and all three had disappeared.

Ivon, Master. A Cairhienin knifemaker. He made some knives for Dena, Thom's lover.

Ivonell Bharatiya. A woman, possibly apocryphal, who supposedly wrote about Darkhounds before the Trolloc Wars. She was cited by Masuri.

J

Jaalam Nishur. A young Domani soldier sworn to Rodel Ituralde. He accompanied Ituralde to his meeting with Domani Dragonsworn and Taraboners to find a way to defeat the Seanchan. Jaalam fought in the raids against the Seanchan in Tarabon, and was killed.

Jac. A man pitching hay in a song sung at The White Ring in Maderin, Altara.

Jac al'Caar. A shepherd in Emond's Field.

Jac al'Seen. A Two Rivers farmer. His wife was Elisa. Stocky and square-shouldered, he had less hair than Bran, and it was as gray as Bran's. His farm lay between Emond's Field and Watch Hill; at Perrin's urging, he moved his family into Emond's Field and helped to defend it against the Trollocs.

Jac Coplin. A Two Rivers man who, along with Len Congar, stole a cow from Master Thane. After being shown proof of the incident, Perrin meted out justice by having them strapped.

Jac Wynn. A Murandian soldier who died just before the Battle of the Shining Walls; he slipped on a stone and broke his head. He was the husband of Susa and father of Cyril, who was one of the children Moiraine investigated while looking for the Dragon Reborn.

jack-fool. A term synonymous with idiot, as in "to act like jack-fool." It was also used as an adjective, with a similar pejorative meaning. *See also* Jak Fool

jackleg. A term for a con artist.

Jadein. An Atha'an Miere woman who was the deckmistress of Harine din Togara. She was lean and leathery and had leather lungs as well. She took Harine and Shalon to the meeting of the First Twelve in Illian, where the Bargain with Rand was discussed.

Jadranka. A Seanchan soldier who was the senior of Karede's three captains. He was short and thin with a prominent nose and had airs. During a battle with Rand's forces, Karede killed Jadranka after Karede learned that Jadranka stupidly had told their scouts to press on until they found the enemy; the scouts were taken out and Karede's army, lacking intelligence, was attacked while unprepared, forcing them to withdraw to minimize casualties.

Jaem. 1) Vandene's Warder. Born in 922 NE, he was bonded by Vandene in 949 NE. He had thinning gray hair and was stringy, gnarled, wiry, lean, bony and as tough as old roots. He died after Vandene was killed at Lady Shiaine's house on Full Moon Street. 2) The subject of a song called "Jaem's Folly."

Jaem the Giant-Slayer. A character in a gleeman's tale bearing the same name.

Jaem Dawlish. The son of Melfane, Elayne's midwife, in Caemlyn. His first paid job was mucking out stables, which he hated because it made everything taste like manure. He sometimes helped his mother, but wanted to be an armorer's apprentice.

Jaen, Marith. *See* Marith Jaen

Jaerecruz lace. Lace used as trim on nice dresses. Nynaeve appeared in *Tel'aran'rhiod* in such a dress, and Min wore one at the White Tower.

Jaern Rift. A sept of the Codarra Aiel.

Jagad, House. A noble House of Fal Dara in Shienar. *See* Agelmar *and* Amalisa Jagad

Jagged Spire. A sept of the Taardad Aiel.

jagwin. An animal found in Seanchan that pounced from the high rocks.

Jahar Narishma. An Arafellin cobbler's son who went to the Black Tower. Narishma was born in 977 NE. He had big dark eyes, a pale face, and dark hair in two long braids with silver bells at the ends. He had the spark, but it hadn't come out when he was found by Taim. He was chosen out by Rand after Dumai's Wells. He accompanied Rand to see the Sea Folk in Cairhien and to Illian for the attack on Sammael, after which he was raised to Dedicated and returned to Cairhien. He fetched *Callandor* for Rand during the Seanchan campaign.

Narishma was bonded as a Warder by Merise Haindehl after the attack on Rand there, when Narishma, Eben and Damer decided they did not dare return to the Black Tower, for they had been placed on the deserters list. Narishma went with Merise and her other two Warders when she accompanied Cadsuane to Far Madding and later to Shadar Logoth. He was raised to full Asha'man by Rand after Shadar Logoth, though Merise withheld the Dragon pin for a time, saying that he should accept things only from her. His strength began increasing again after Shadar Logoth, which worried Merise. At Rand's order, Narishma and Merise went to the rebel Aes Sedai camp to offer them the chance to bond forty-seven Asha'man. While there, Narishma detected the use of *saidin*, leading to the understanding that Halima and Delana were Darkfriends. Narishma went with Rand to his meeting with the fake Daughter of the Nine Moons; he was injured, and was Healed by Merise. He also went with Rand for the meeting with the real Daughter of the Nine Moons. Narishma fought in Lan's army at the beginning of the Last Battle, and later fought alongside Egwene against Taim. He performed some preliminary Healing on Lan after Lan killed Demandred.

Jaichim Carridin. An Inquisitor of the Hand of the Light, Ambassador to Ebou Dar, and a Darkfriend. Tall, with a touch of gray in his hair, he was fit and hard with dark, deep-set, knowing eyes. Posing as Bors among the Darkfriends, he attended a meeting of Darkfriends where he was shown images of Mat, Perrin and Rand and given orders. He commanded the Whitecloaks in Tarabon, and told Niall that Geofram Bornhald was responsible for the failure in Falme. Carridin took control of the Panarch's Palace in Tanchico, after negotiating with King Andric to help Amathera become Panarch. He was under pressure to kill Rand, and a Fade took one of his sisters to punish him for his failure. Liandrin and the Black sisters complicated life for him when she told him she would be taking care of Amathera. Carridin was sent to Ebou Dar by the Whitecloaks as an ambassador and to cause mischief in the region, such as by organizing bands of "Dragonsworn" to cause atrocities and turn the public against them. Carridin got conflicting orders from the Forsaken about whom to kill and whom not to kill, and he was finally eliminated by Lady Shiaine for his failures.

Jailin Maran. A minor Andoran nobleman. His sign was the crosshatched Red Wall. Jailin supported Elenia for the Lion Throne before she was taken by Arymilla.

Jaim. 1) An old soldier who served with Lan in the Aiel War. Lan caught him sleeping standing straight up with his eyes open while on duty and threatened to tell his friends if it happened again. 2) The subject of the song "Jolly Jaim."

Jaim Adarra. The captain of the *Snow Goose,* which took Moiraine, Lan, Perrin, Loial and Faile from Remen, where Perrin had rescued Gaul from a cage, to Illian. Jaim was short and slight.

Jaim Aybara. A Two Rivers boy who was sort of Perrin's cousin. During the defense of Emond's Field from Trollocs, he brought Perrin news of movement in the Westwood that turned out to be Loial and Gaul, and news of the arrival of men from Deven Ride. He was very excited when Perrin called him "cousin" and ran to tell his friend Had.

Jaim Dawtry. A farmer in the Two Rivers. In Egwene's Accepted test, he told Rand of a big battle involving people called the Shawkin or Sanchan or something like that. In real life, he joined Perrin's army and guarded Perrin's tent.

Jaim Thane. A boy from Emond's Field. When Perrin and his men returned to Emond's Field after being ambushed by Trollocs and staying with the Tinkers, Jaim ran to the people cutting wood to let them know that Perrin had arrived.

Jaim Torfinn. A young Two Rivers man who was considered a good shot. He was spindly, with dusty brown hair. His family's farm lay between Emond's Field and Watch Hill. When Perrin persuaded the Torfinns to go to Emond's Field, Jaim joined Perrin and his band. After they rescued the Luhhans and the Cauthons, Perrin sent Jaim with them back to Emond's Field. Jaim was not particularly happy about being left in Emond's Field while Perrin and the others were off being heroes; he missed the ambush in the Waterwood and was thereafter reluctant to join the Companions, the men who followed Perrin.

Jaim participated in the defense of Emond's Field, and was later recruited by Taim for the Black Tower. There Androl saw him leading a group of men digging a canal with the One Power, and gave him some advice on how to do it right.

Jain Charin. *See* Jain Farstrider

Jain Farstrider. A legendary traveler who wrote about his peregrinations and adventures. He was born in 925 NE. While still young, he brought to justice the traitorous Malkieri Darkfriend Cowin Gemallan Fairheart. He arrived in an Ogier *stedding* shortly after the Aiel War, appearing near death, saying that the Dark One was going to blind the Eye of the World. He stayed in the *stedding* and recovered before leaving. Farstrider disappeared north of the Blasted Lands in 981 NE. He became disillusioned after his wife died and he realized he had been made a tool of Ishamael, and began using the identity of Noal Charin, claiming to be Farstrider's cousin. Graendal, knowing his true identity, picked him up because he was famous, to use his age like a beauty spot among her pets; when that proved unsatisfactory, she decided to make other use of him rather than disposing of him or tossing him out, but she never thought of him as any sort of key player in her plans. She sent Farstrider off to Ebou Dar under very subtle Compulsion, not really believing that there was much chance of a cache being there. She chose to use him instead of Darkfriends because she had control of Farstrider; none of the other Forsaken knew that, and if Farstrider were to find anything, she wanted it all to herself. Farstrider managed to work out an excuse subconsciously as to why he was in Ebou Dar chasing after a cache of *angreal*. He knew that there were gaps in his memory; he hoped that the memories would return because he felt that the gaps were important in some way. While there, he spied on Jaichim Carridin, Falion Bhoda and Ispan Shefar. Mat encountered him while he was spying on Carridin; Jain later helped to save Mat from the *gholam* and accepted Mat's offer of rooms in the Tarasin Palace. By that time, Farstrider was much the worse for wear; he was scrawny and white-haired, his hands had been so badly broken that he could no longer handle a sword, his beak of a nose appeared to have been broken several times and he had gaps in his teeth. Farstrider escaped Ebou Dar and traveled with Luca's show with Mat. He accompanied Mat and Thom to the Tower of Ghenjei to rescue Moiraine. He died holding off the Aelfinn so that the others could escape.

Jair. A wife to Mandelain, an Aiel of the Daryne clan. Her sister-wife was Core-huin.

Jaisi Trakand. The name used by Lady Caraline for Min when introducing her to Darlin.

Jak. A strongarm at The Dancing Cartman in Four Kings, Andor. He was hard-faced, big, and had arms that were thick enough for legs. His crooked teeth were yellow. Jak and Strom threw people out of the inn if they caused trouble, and the two also planned to help Hake, the innkeeper, rob Rand and Mat. Howal Gode gave Jak, Strom and Hake something to make them sleep while he tried his pitch on Rand.

Jak Fool. A figure of speech meaning a foolish person. As Elyas said, "More fools know Jak Fool than Jak Fool knows." *See also* jack-fool

Jak Masond. A commander in the Legion of the Dragon. He was short and stocky and moved with surprising speed. He came to Illian prior to the attack on the Seanchan, and was part of the fight against them.

Jak o' the Mists. Reference to something ephemeral, as in "chasing . . . ," or an expression of speed, as in "before you can say . . ." A variant was Jak o' the Wisps.

Jak o' the Shadows. A name for death in a song sung by Mat and the Band of the Red Hand.

Jak o' the Wisps. Reference to something ephemeral, as in "chasing . . . ," or an expression of speed, as in "before you can say . . ." A variant was Jak o' the Mists.

Jak, Old. A man in the song "Old Jak's Up a Tree."

Jakanda. A town in Arafel where silver bells to be worn in one's hair were made.

Jakob Hernvil. Arymilla's secretary. He was small and lean, as if all the fat had been boiled from him. Arymilla ensured his loyalty by paying him enough that only the largest bribes could be of interest, far more than anyone would offer a scrivener.

Jala Bandevin. An Aes Sedai of the Green Ajah and the loyalist contingent. She was very short, about five feet tall, gray-haired and imposing. She had two Warders at the time of the Aiel War. One was a round-faced man playing a stately melody on a flute while Jala taught the other the steps of a court dance; the latter was a new Warder at the time, a blushing, pale-haired boy of no more than twenty. She was part of the group of Aes Sedai who captured Egwene at Northharbor. She and Merym galloped back to the Tower when they learned who they had caught.

Jalanda. 1) A city of the Age of Legends. 2) An Ogier historian whose information about Be'lal was quoted by Loial.

Jalani. An Aiel woman who was *Far Dareis Mai*. Jalani was sixteen when Mazrim Taim arrived in Caemlyn. She had short red hair, green eyes and baby fat in her cheeks. Her smile was a little too innocent, sometimes. She frequently accompanied Rand, and treated him like a brother—a younger one, usually. Along with Nandera, she acknowledged *toh* to Rand when a Gray Man came into Rand's presence in Caemlyn without her seeing him. She was also with Rand in Cairhien. In Shadar Logoth in the search for Liah, she remained with Rand and the Ogier. She and Dedric had an interest in one another. Jalani was part of the force sent to Bandar Eban to restore order.

Jalid Magonine. A craftsman in Ancarid, Seanchan, who owned Karede as a boy.

Jalindin. A Seeker for Truth in Seanchan. She had a severe face with dark eyes. When she accompanied the Lady Morsa on an outing in Seanchan, they encountered Rand and Aviendha, who had Traveled there. Jalindin ordered Morsa's arrest after discovering that Morsa knew more than she should have about Rand and events east of the Aryth Ocean in Falme.

Jalwin Moerad. An advisor to Artur Hawkwing who was really Ishamael on the second occasion he was spun out into the world. He became Hawkwing's advisor in FY 973. He was said to be more than half insane and never appeared to age at all in the forty years he was active. He caused Hawkwing to turn against the Aes Sedai; after Hawkwing's death, he advised those who came closest to seizing all of Hawkwing's empire: Marithelle Camaelaine, Norodim Nosokawa and Elfraed Guitama. *See also* Ishamael

Jame. A Seanchan man, married to Kathana, innkeeper of The Yearly Brawl in Ebou Dar. Jame was a blademaster.

Jameine. A seamstress in Valan Luca's show who was admired by Olver. Olver thought her neck was graceful as a swan's. She was willowy and hot-eyed. Men sometimes fought over her, and she watched them.

Jamilila Norsish. An Aes Sedai of the Red Ajah. Her name was not on Verin's list, and either she was taken by the Seanchan, or she disappeared following the Seanchan attack on the White Tower. She was one of those that Egwene thought might possibly be Mesaana in disguise.

Jan. One of Min's aunts. Jan worked as a seamstress, and never married. She was very proper.

Janata, Martine. *See* Martine Janata

Jancy Torfinn. A girl from Two Rivers with the ability to channel. She was among the young women recruited by Verin and Alanna whom Rand saw and terrified at Culain's Hound in Caemlyn. Fourteen and small, with a high voice, she was one of three born with the spark—Bode, Elle and Jancy—all three of whom would be quite strong in the Power, in Verin's estimation.

Jander Parentakis. A member of the Academy of Cairhien. He was working on building a paddlewheel riverboat.

Janduin. A man of the Iron Mountain sept of the Taardad Aiel. Rand's biological father, he became clan chief of the Taardad at a very young age. He had a way about him that caused people to listen to him; he ended the blood feud between the Taardad and Nakai after two hundred years, and made alliance not only with the Nakai, but with the Reyn. He led four clans of the Aiel over the Dragonwall to avenge Laman's cutting of *Avendoraldera*. After the death of Rand's mother, he resigned as clan chief—the first ever to do so. While in the Blight to hunt Shadowspawn, he encountered a man who looked like Shaiel, his deceased wife, and Janduin refused to raise his spear against him. The man, Luc, ran him through.

Janduin was also the name of one of Rand and Aviendha's sons seen during Aviendha's second trip through the crystal columns in Rhuidean.

Janevor, Kelwin. The High Seat of his Andoran House. A vinegary old man, he was loyal to Elayne and brought ten armsmen to her service.

Jangai Gates. Gates in the eastern wall of Cairhien.

Jangai Pass. A major passage through the Spine of the World just south of Kinslayer's Dagger and east of Cairhien.

Janina. A Wise One of the Miagoma Aiel with the ability to channel and a strength level of 23(11). She had flaxen hair and pale sky-blue eyes, and stood 5'7½" tall. She looked to be no more than a year or so older than Rand, Perrin and Mat, but was in fact more than thirty years older. Janina and other Wise

Ones were sent to Ghealdan with Perrin to keep an eye on Seonid and Masuri. She was with Perrin's army and went to battle against the Shaido at Malden. Janina was the most accomplished in Healing of the Wise Ones with Perrin; she also assisted in the forging of *Mah'alleinir*, and accompanied Perrin's forces into the Last Battle.

Janine Pavlara. An Arafellin Aes Sedai of the Red Ajah and the loyalist contingent, with a strength level of 27(15). Born in 963 NE, she went to the White Tower in 978 NE. After spending eleven years as a novice and nine years as Accepted, she was raised to the shawl in 998 NE. She was 5'3" tall, and plump, with large dark eyes and luxuriant black hair, which she wore pulled into a bun on the back of her neck in an attempt to look more mature. Being newly raised, she had not achieved the ageless look, and was wary and distrustful of men, but hadn't been a Red long enough to learn to hate them. She was one of the new sisters who went to Cairhien to help trap Rand, and was captured at Dumai's Wells. Janine was treated as *da'tsang* by the Aiel until, under Verin's Compulsion, she found reason to swear oath to Rand, which she had done before Cadsuane departed Cairhien for Far Madding. She and the other Reds were the last of the captives to swear.

Janira. A Saldaean Kin and a member of the Knitting Circle in Ebou Dar. Her strength level was such that she would not have been allowed to test for Aes Sedai, and she was not strong enough to make a gateway of any size whatsoever. She was lean with graying hair, sharp cheekbones, and a beak of a nose. When Elayne and Nynaeve met her, she wore the red belt of a Wise Woman. She went with Elayne and Nynaeve to the Rahad in search of the Bowl of the Winds and was killed by a *gholam*.

Janny. Elenia Sarand's personal maid for twenty years. She was a plump-cheeked Andoran. When she felt particularly good, Elenia bought new dresses for Janny, each one of fine quality, as a way to ensure her loyalty and discretion. Janny ran interference for Elenia when Nasin came on to her; when Nasin raised his fist to her, she did not back away.

Janwin. A man of the Degalle sept of the Shiande Aiel who was clan chief of the Shiande. He was married to the roofmistress Corida, his Wise One was Baellin, and his hold was called Nine Stones. He was 6'7" tall and weighed 240 pounds. His blue-gray eyes and hair as gray as storm clouds had a face to go with them; it looked to have been carved from hardwood. He was an even-tempered man with a mild way of speaking, which was definitely at odds with his appearance. Janwin was with Rand in Cairhien, and Rand sent him to deal with the Shaido; Rand later sent him and others to Arad Doman for strategic reasons.

Janya Frende. An Andoran Aes Sedai of the Brown Ajah and the rebel contingent, with a strength level of 17(5). Born in 816 NE, she went to the White Tower in 832 NE. After spending seven years as a novice and twelve years as Accepted, she was raised to the shawl in 851 NE. Slender and about 5'4" tall,

Janya was pretty except that even when she was talking to someone she always seemed to be squinting in thought about something else. She was neat, unlike most Browns, with not a hair out of place. Janya talked quickly, as though she had no time to get words out, sometimes talking for an hour if no one stopped her. Janya was raised as Sitter for the Brown in 993 NE. After Siuan was deposed, she left the White Tower on her own, the only then-current Sitter who left without an order from the head of her Ajah. She left because of a firm belief that deposing Siuan was highly questionable, that stilling her was illegal and that Elaida's election also was greatly suspect. In her view, these things made Elaida a usurper and dangerous enough for her to overcome the natural Aes Sedai tendency to accept change in order to preserve unity, in appearance if not reality. She was the second oldest, next to Romanda, among the rebel Sitters, and among the first to stand for raising Egwene Amyrlin. She was also first to stand in favor of the war vote, speaking uncharacteristically forcefully on the topic, and one of the first to stand in favor of the vote to form an alliance with the Black Tower. She was the only "old" Sitter who joined neither Romanda nor Lelaine.

Janya was very disappointed that she couldn't learn to make *ter'angreal* or *cuendillar*.

Jaq Lounalt. Arymilla's Taraboner secretary whose true talent was torture. He used cords as a specialty. Lounalt was a lean man with a veil covering his thick mustaches and a conical cap that pushed the hood of his cloak high. In Elenia's opinion, he smiled too much. After Arymilla was taken prisoner, he was hired as a secretary by Sylvase. Elayne used him to question Mellar and the captured Black sisters, but he was a Darkfriend and helped them plot an escape. He died during the escape attempt.

Jar Silvin. A man serving Gareth Bryne in Kore Springs, Andor; he went with Bryne to find Siuan. Jar was gray-haired and kicked Thad Haren on the ankle to stop him from mentioning Morgase to Bryne.

Jara Doweel. A woman who ran a farm in the Black Hills. Toveine served penance under her for twenty years. Mistress Doweel believed in hard work and tight discipline and was a very strict taskmistress. Toveine exacted some sort of revenge on her.

Jara'copan. An Ogier-built city in Manetheren, one of the Ten Nations after the Breaking.

Jaramide. One of the Ten Nations. Its capital was Deranbar, which later became Maradon; other cities included Barsine, Allorallen (Bandar Eban), Canaire'somelle and Nashebar. High Queen Egoridin ruled when the Compact was signed.

Jarath, Lisaine. *See* Lisaine Jarath

Jared Aydaer. A young man in the Two Rivers. He joined Perrin's band hunting Trollocs, and was killed in a Trolloc ambush.

Jaren. A Jenn Aiel boy from after the Breaking. His parents were Adan and Siedre; his brothers and sisters were Rhea, Malind, Sorelle and Elwin. When he was nineteen, he learned he could channel and threw himself off a cliff.

Jarene. The eldest daughter of Queen Ethenielle and Prince Brys of Kandor. She was born in 966 NE and married a Kandori lord.

Jaret Byar. A Whitecloak officer. He was tall and gaunt with dark deep-set eyes. He would follow orders whatever they were, and gave his primary, and indeed secondary and tertiary, allegiance to his commander rather than to the Whitecloaks as a whole. That commander was Geofram Bornhald first; then it became Geofram's son Dain. Byar would do anything he was ordered to do—kill or torture men, women, children—but he had one balking point: rape was abhorrent to him. Byar was with Geofram Bornhald when Egwene and Perrin were captured; he pretended to encourage them to escape, hoping that they would try and he could kill them, but they were rescued by Lan, Moiraine and Nynaeve. Byar went to Falme with Bornhald, who told him to stand aside and take word back to the Children of the Light. Byar saw Perrin near Falme, and blamed Geofram Bornhald's death on him. Byar went with Dain Bornhald to the Two Rivers. He supported Galad in his duel with Valda. He was very angry when Perrin's punishment was delayed by Galad; Perrin's rescue of the Whitecloaks from Trollocs did not ameliorate that anger—not surprising, given that he had been Compelled by Graendal—and he attempted to kill Perrin, but was killed by Dain.

Jargen. A sergeant of the watch at Heeth Tower at the Blight border in Kandor. He wore a forked beard and his black hair was dusted with gray. The day after his fourteenth nameday, Jargen joined the Blightwatch; he killed nearly fifty Trollocs. Jargen reported to Malenarin that there had been a flash from Rena Tower.

Jaric Mondoran. A male Aes Sedai during the Breaking who went mad and threatened Tzora. Ten thousand Da'shain Aiel linked arms and sang, trying to remind him of who they were and who he had been, trying to turn him with their bodies and a song. Jaric Mondoran stared at them as though at a puzzle, killing them, and they kept closing their lines and singing. He listened to the last Aiel for almost an hour before destroying him. And then Tzora burned, one huge flame consuming stone and metal and flesh, leaving only a sheet of glass where the second greatest city in the world once stood.

Jarid Sarand. An Andoran man who was High Seat of House Sarand and the husband of Elenia; she was the ambitious one in the family. His House sigil was golden boars. About 5'10" tall, he was jovial, dark for an Andoran and square-faced. When Bashere threw a knife at Rand, Jarid drew his sword, and ran toward Bashere yelling "Die!" Jarid never stopped being supportive of Elenia, and he was ready to fight even with Elenia imprisoned. When he lost his mind just before the Last Battle and began behaving erratically, his men deserted him and left him tied to a tree.

Jaril. A six-year-old boy taken to Salidar as one of Marigan's (Moghedien in disguise) children; Seve was his brother. At first, they clung to each other and seemed frightened of everything and everyone and would not speak a word. Later, they laughed and shouted as loud as the other children.

Jarna Malari. An Aes Sedai of the Gray Ajah publicly but of the Black Ajah in truth. Born in 760 NE, she was 5'6" tall, with liquid brown eyes and black hair with white at her temples. While she had a saintly reputation and was much loved and respected, she was the head of the Supreme Council of the Black Ajah. She had Tamra Ospenya tortured (and killed) in 979 NE to try to learn more about the Dragon Reborn. Ishamael killed her in 983 NE, in his wrath at discovering the male channeler pogrom. Although she had never shown any interest in studying a certain *ter'angreal* for which no one knew a use, she apparently became trapped in it. For ten days no one could reach her; all they could do was listen to her scream as she died. When what could be recovered was buried, every sister in Tar Valon and every sister who could reach the city in time attended the funeral.

Jarr. A mercenary who joined Perrin's army along with Turne. Jarr had had a horse, but they ate him.

Jarra. 1) A sept of the Chareen Aiel. 2) A one-inn village in Ghealdan, just north of the Amadician border. Jarra consisted of a few muddy streets and stone houses with slate roofs, situated on a hillside above a little stream spanned by a low wooden bridge, with a sloping village green. Moiraine, Lan, Perrin and Loial stayed there while on the trail of Rand, who had passed through and left in his wake a series of strange events: a flurry of weddings, and Whitecloaks who had behaved erratically, signs that Rand had been there, which was confirmed by people at the inn. Simion and his brother Noam, a man showing wolf-like tendencies, lived there. Moiraine was asked to see and Heal Noam, but he was incurable, so he was let go. Perrin had dangerous wolf dreams in Jarra.

Jasfer Anan. The husband of Setalle. He was square-faced and gray-haired and wore the double earring of the Ancient and Honorable League of Nets in Ebou Dar. Two white stones in the lower hoop of the earring indicated that he owned vessels besides the one he captained. He wore a work knife stuffed behind his belt, as well as a longer curving knife. His long blue-and-green vest revealed arms and chest crisscrossed with dueling scars. Most of the men who had scarred him were dead. He had a dark face and a deep voice, and when speaking normally seemed to be barking commands on a fishing boat. He found Setalle starving on the streets of Ebou Dar and took her home to his mother. Half a year later, they were married. Together they had eight children—five daughters and three sons. After the Seanchan took Ebou Dar, Jasfer sailed all his fishing boats to Illian with his family and his crews' families, with plans to meet Setalle there later.

Jasin Natael. Asmodean's identity as a gleeman. He appeared dark-haired and in his middle years. He was taller than most, moderately handsome to women, and had an oddly apprehensive way of holding his head to one side as if trying to look at one sideways. As a gleeman he was not flashy, didn't flourish his cloak and didn't seem at all eager to perform, although he was competent when he did. *See* Asmodean

Jasmen. A novice in the Tower. She was among the strongest that Egwene recruited to help fight against the Seanchan; Egwene taught her to link.

Javindhra Doraille. An Aes Sedai of the Red Ajah and the loyalist contingent, with a strength level of 25(13). Born in 842 NE, she went to the White Tower in 858 NE. After spending six years as a novice and five years as Accepted, she was raised to the shawl in 869 NE. About 5'5" to 5'6" tall, she had a bony frame, with an angular face hard enough to hammer nails, a harsh voice and a thin, narrow mouth. Javindhra was raised Sitter for the Red Ajah in 985 NE, replacing one of those unchaired for their involvement with the male channeler pogrom. She stood to depose Siuan Sanche, one of only eleven needed to give the greater consensus under the circumstances, and served as a member of Elaida's advisory council when Elaida was first raised to the Amyrlin Seat. She was, if not exactly broken, then reined in tightly by Elaida, which she resented heartily, not only because she was Red, like Elaida, but because of her early support. Javindhra was very aware of what happened to Teslyn, so she did not show resentment. She dragged her feet in the Hall sometimes to show her independence of Elaida, but only where and when Elaida was not likely to find out; if Elaida could see, however, she in effect came running when Elaida crooked a finger. Even so, given a chance to balk Elaida, she would snap at it. Tsutama ordered Javindhra to go to the Black Tower with Pevara to bond Asha'man. She was Turned to the Shadow while there.

Jeade'en. Old Tongue for "True Finder." Rand's dappled stallion bore this name.

Jeaine Caide. A Domani Aes Sedai of the Green Ajah publicly and of the Black Ajah in truth, with a strength level of 18(6). Born in 912 NE, she went to the White Tower in 928 NE. After spending six years as a novice and six years as Accepted, she was raised to the shawl in 940 NE. She had black hair, dark brown eyes, a swan-like neck and coppery skin and wore thin, clinging dresses. She did not like men, but did not love women. What she liked best about choosing Green was that she could have a number of men figuratively on a leash, which was where she believed they deserved to be. She was one of the first thirteen members of the Black Ajah identified. She burned a hole through both sides of a ship while testing the black fluted rod that produced balefire; she also tried to use it against Nynaeve in the Panarch's Palace in Tanchico. She was coopted by Moghedien, and sent off on a task that caused her to look horrified when it was given to her. She impersonated Cadsuane at Shayol Ghul in the Last Battle, and was killed by Thom Merrilin because she did not walk like Cadsuane.

Jearom. The greatest blademaster in history. Jearom fought over ten thousand times, in battle and single combat. He was defeated once, by a farmer with a quarterstaff.

jegal. A scaled, chameleon-like creature from the Age of Legends. Sammael thought that Graendal had as many shades as a *jegal* had scales; in other words, there was a lot more to her than met the eye.

Jehaan, Stair of. A place where the Borderland armies successfully checked the advance of the Shadowspawn following the destruction of Malkier.

Jehaan Tower. The site where a Fal Daran soldier named Ronan once held off a thousand Trollocs with twenty men; Ronan was later Agelmar's *shambayan*.

Jehannah. The capital of Ghealdan. The swift-flowing River Boern ran through the city, which was the site of the Jheda Palace, the royal palace of Ghealdan. Among other things, Moiraine had sent Uno and other Shienarans to Jehannah to collect information after Rand had slipped away from their camp in the Mountains of Mist. Faile and Lord Orban, as Hunters of the Horn, had overwintered there. There was a well-traveled road linking Jehannah and Lugard, Murandy, named the Jehannah Road. News often reached Jehannah by river trade.

Jelande. An Aiel who was *Far Dareis Mai*. She accompanied Perrin to Ghealdan. Her eyes were gray and her hair was dark brown. The dark hair made her a beauty, by Aiel standards.

Jen, Master. A servant in the Tarasin Palace. He was a short, bullish young man, and the second of seven servants to guide Mat when he visited the palace through the front door.

Jen. A name used by the Darkfriend Torwyn Barshaw. He was alleged to be Paitr Conel's uncle and a merchant from Four Kings. He planned to free Morgase from the Whitecloaks. *See also* Torwyn Barshaw

Jenare Balmaen. An Aes Sedai of the Red Ajah and the loyalist contingent, with a strength level of 25(13). About 5'4" tall, she was sturdy and had a pale, square face. She was part of the group sent by Elaida to take the Black Tower and was captured and bonded by Welyn Kajima. She was present when Rand met Semirhage posing as the Daughter of the Nine Moons. Along with Welyn, she was Turned to the Shadow at the Black Tower.

Jenda. A sept of the Tomanelle Aiel.

Jendai Prophecy. First spoken after the Breaking, this prophecy held that the Sea Folk were fated to remain on the water until the Coramoor returned, and that the Sea Folk must serve him. In truth, the Sea Folk, most of them anyway, saw the prophecy as being about a bargain. They would provide certain things to the Coramoor, and he would provide things to them in turn. But they did not trust as to what he would give them, so they bargained for it. One reason the Jendai Prophecy was given such weight by the Sea Folk was that it spoke of things that did not exist until after it was first given, sometimes long after.

Jendhilin. A Maiden of the Cold Peak Miagoma who died guarding Rand's door at the Sun Palace in Cairhien when the rogue Asha'man attacked. Rand added her name to the list of women who had died for him.

Jenje. The site of an ancient battle, from Mat's memories.

Jenn Aiel. The Aiel who remained true to the Covenant, to serve the Aes Sedai and follow the Way of the Leaf. After the second division of the Da'shain Aiel occurred, caused by some of the young Da'shain rejecting the Way of the Leaf and taking up weapons for defense, those who used weapons lived in tents and followed the other Da'shain, who lived in their wagons. The ones who had rejected the Way became known simply as the Aiel, and began calling the pacifistic Da'shain the Jenn Aiel, meaning "the only true Aiel," to mock them. The Jenn pretended that the others did not exist, even though when the split occurred many of the others were their own children. They traveled along the same ways, but kept separate, and both groups were led into the Waste by Aes Sedai who wanted to protect the Jenn from contamination. The Jenn Aiel, aided by Aes Sedai, began construction of the city of Rhuidean. Before the city was completed, it became obvious that the Jenn were dying out, although the group known as Aiel flourished. The Aes Sedai realized that the prophecy from the Breaking, that said that the Aiel would produce someone who would defeat the Dark One, would be fulfilled among those who had abandoned the Way of the Leaf and the covenant to serve the Aes Sedai. They summoned chiefs of the warrior Aiel to Rhuidean to learn of their past in a *ter'angreal* set up for that purpose; if they could survive that knowledge, they could continue and fulfill prophecy. The Jenn were also known as "the clan that is not." *See also* Aiel, Da'shain Aiel *and* Tuatha'an

Jennet. A big-eyed, pretty Murandian noblewoman who became a novice with the rebels. She was one of those who asked if the novice books would be opened to all. She had a Talent for the new style of Healing.

Jennet Cobb. An Andoran Aes Sedai of the Gray Ajah and the rebel contingent, with a strength level of 18(6). She was born in 851 NE; her parents were innkeepers in Caemlyn. In fact, they kept The Queen's Blessing; Basel Gill was descended from one of her brothers. She had three sisters and two brothers, all long dead before the Last Battle. She went to the White Tower in 866 NE, where she spent ten years as a novice and nine years as Accepted, and was raised to the shawl in 885 NE. She was 5'4½" tall, with dark red hair that she wore flowing down her back, and green eyes. Jennet was not beautiful, but most men would think her pretty except that her manner was very reserved—not cool, just very private and self-contained. She had a considerable temper, though, which she learned to master with quite some difficulty as a novice; usually she controlled it very tightly, but it could flare, though rarely, particularly over what she perceived as injustice. She expressed reservations concerning Siuan's age when Siuan was raised to the Amyrlin Seat and was part of the rebel fifth column sent by Sheriam's council in Salidar to infiltrate the White Tower (aka ferrets). Like all of the sisters chosen for the fifth column, Jennet was out of the White Tower when Siuan was deposed and the Tower broken, so there was no flight to arouse any suspicions toward her. Apparently, she had simply returned in answer to Elaida's summons. Jennet was coopted by Seaine and Pevara to aid in their search for the Black Ajah.

Jennshain. An Ogier-built city in Almoren, one of the Ten Nations after the Breaking.

Jenric. An Aielman with whom Mat played a knife-throwing game in Rhuidean. He was built like a bear and considered himself a wit.

Jenshin, Stedding. A *stedding* located in Haddon Mirk.

Jentoine, Stedding. A *stedding* located in the Black Hills.

Jeorad Manyard. The governor of the province of Andor for the High King, Artur Paendrag Tanreall. He translated the Prophecies of the Dragon.

Jeordam. An Aielman who was the son of Lewin, one of the first Aiel to use a weapon. Jeordam grew up knowing only the tents and guarding the Jenn; he and his father would help the Jenn if they came to them. Morin, a Jenn woman, did come to them, and wanted to go with them to rescue her daughter; Jeordam shortened a spear for her and taught her to use it. He realized that a shortened spear could be more effective, and it became the traditional weapon of the Aiel. Morin, the first Maiden of the Spear, bore Jeordam's child. Later in life, Jeordam and his greatson Rhodric were part of an Aiel group who were allowed to take water as the price of digging wells in an area that became part of Cairhien; the men who gave them water told them that the Jenn, whom the Aiel were following at a distance to protect them, were heading past the Spine of the World.

Jeordwyn Semaris den Tropan. An Illianer nobleman who was a member of the Council of the Nine. He was beardless with a narrow jaw, making his head look like a forester's splitting wedge. In Rand's final battle against the Seanchan, he fought under Bashere.

Jeorg Damentanis. A stout Illianer merchant buying gems in Saldaea. He was dark-eyed with gray in his pointed beard. He and his partner Pavil Geraneos were bargaining with Weilin Aldragoran just before Nynaeve arrived to drum up support for Lan.

Jer al'Hune. A boy in the Two Rivers whom Mat, as a teen, had saved from drowning.

Jera. A serving girl at The White Ring in Maderin, Altara. She served Mat, Tuon and Selucia; Mat tipped her a silver penny, causing her to beam.

Jeraal Mordeth. The name used by Padan Fain when he was in Cairhien advising Toram Riatin.

Jeral. A young soldier in the Children of the Light who was sent with a message from Carridin to Geofram Bornhald. He wore a cloak of Domani cut, not the white cloak of the Children of the Light. Very upright and by-the-book, Jeral was discomfited when Bornhald said that he had no need of the Questioner's compliments.

Jeral Florry. The innkeeper of The Good Queen in Aringill, Andor. Thom and Mat stayed in the stable at his inn, although they had to pay a steep price for it. He also made the mistake of gambling with Mat and lost two horses. It was in his stable that Mat met and saved Aludra.

Jeramel. An Amadician town approximately one hundred miles west of Abila. It was the site where King Ailron joined battle against the Seanchan and lost, removing all nobility from Amadicia and giving the Seanchan control of the country.

Jeranem. A place in Seanchan with cold winters.

Jerasid. A Cairhienin farrier in Perrin's camp in Ghealdan. He was just short of his middle years. He had broad shoulders and thick arms, and seemed nearly as wide as he was tall, though as a Cairhienin, he was not very tall. Like the other farriers, he grew nervous when Perrin tried to tend to his own horse.

Jeren, Sea of. Found to the south, before the Breaking.

Jerid Najima. A Kandori infant who was on Moiraine's list of potential Dragons Reborn. He and his father were killed in a barn fire. The explanation for the tragedy was that his father was too lucky—things always came easily to him, including the livery stable that was given to him, the one in which he was killed.

Jerilin al'Caar. A skinny Two Rivers girl with the ability to channel. She was among the young women recruited by Verin and Alanna whom Rand saw and terrified at Culain's Hound in Caemlyn. She eventually ended up with the rebel Aes Sedai.

Jerinvar Barstere. The mayor of Watch Hill, Andor. He was wide-nosed, leathery-faced and white-haired. He was among the Watch Hill men who helped defeat the Trollocs, and told Perrin that they would take care of seeing the Whitecloaks on their way.

Jerum Nus. A young Whitecloak soldier. In the battle when the Trollocs attacked the Whitecloak camp on Jehannah Road, he was trapped under the body of a Trolloc. Perrin fought off the Trollocs alongside the Whitecloaks. After the battle, Perrin heard Jerum crying for help, rescued him and took him to a Wise One to be Healed.

Jesain. A Wise One of the Shaido Aiel with the ability to channel. Very short for an Aiel, no more than 5'2" tall, she had a mass of fiery red hair and a temper to match. She stared toward Shadar Logoth at the huge flows of *saidar* that were used in the cleansing of *saidin*, and slapped people who walked in front of her and blocked her view.

Jesamyn. A member of the Kin. She was golden-haired and young-looking. Jesamyn and three other Kinswomen were left in Caemlyn when Elayne went to the Field of Merrilor; none could make a gateway on her own, but they could when linked. Darkfriends killed two of the other Kinswomen, leaving her unable to get a message to Elayne. She Healed people during the attack, although she could not Heal Talmanes; she also helped defend Caemlyn, attacking Trollocs with the One Power.

Jesse Bilal. An Aes Sedai of the Brown Ajah and the loyalist contingent, with a strength level of 21(9). Born in 752 NE, she went to the White Tower in 768 NE. After spending eleven years as a novice and ten years as Accepted, she was raised to the shawl in 789 NE. She served as a Sitter in the Hall of the Tower from 905 to 927 NE and later served as head of the Brown Ajah Council.

About 5'1" tall and wiry, she resembled a sparrow, but she was much stronger physically than she looked. Her hair was gray with a little black, and her eyes were small and dark. She had a habit of tilting her head to one side when she was studying something in front of her, and a habit of tapping two or three fingers on her lips while thinking. She was very intent on whatever she focused on; some thought she focused so intently as not to notice other things around her, but they were mistaken. She was a very forceful woman, especially for a Brown. She was involved in sending Ajah heads to infiltrate the rebels, and was very displeased that Janya Frende went on her own. After the Seanchan attack on the White Tower, Jesse, Adelorna, Ferane, Serancha and Suana met and decided to support Egwene for the Amyrlin Seat of the reunited Tower.

Jestian Redhill. A historical Aes Sedai that Faile used as an example of Aes Sedai doing whatever the White Tower ordered.

Jethari Moondancer. Birgitte's name in another life. In that life, Gaidal Cain received a head wound and she took him to the Tower of Ghenjei to save him. Although she had prepared well, she wandered lost until her supplies were gone and she died.

Jezrail. A Tairen Aes Sedai of the Red Ajah and the loyalist contingent. She was dark with a square face. She was with Katerine when Egwene was given her second dose of weak forkroot, and seemed uncomfortable about it; either she disliked being a serving woman even by association, or she disliked having anything to do with forkroot. Egwene dividing her flows fourteen ways impressed Jezrail. She objected to Katerine continuing to strike Egwene with flows of Air in an effort to force her to run to Silviana's study. Jezrail was one of those who accompanied Pevara to the Black Tower to bond Asha'man. The reason she was chosen was that she kept a painted miniature of the boy she almost married rather than coming to the White Tower and spoke fondly of him still, though his grandchildren would be grandparents. She was Turned to the Shadow in the Black Tower.

Jhamara. A battle of the Children of the Light against Murandy and Altara. Because of a tickling in the back of his head, Niall set a third of his army to watch mountains said to be impassable; an Illianer army that was supposed to be a hundred miles away came out of those impassable passes.

Jharen, Mistress. The innkeeper of The Light of Truth in Sienda, Amadicia. She was plump, with gray hair in long curls and a warm smile, and her dark eyes were quite searching. Nynaeve and Elayne stayed at her inn. Mistress Jharen believed that if the Horn of Valere were not found, the Last Battle could not start.

Jheda Palace. The royal palace of Ghealdan in Jehannah.

Jheran. A man of the Haido sept of the Shaarad Aiel and of the *Sovin Nai* society who was clan chief of the Shaarad. He was married to the roofmistress Turolin. Jheran was 6'3" tall and weighed 180 pounds, a slender man, as a steel blade is slender. He had gray-streaked brown hair. The water at Chain Ridge Stand was one of the bones of contention between him and Bael, but he was always calm once the Shaarad's four-hundred-year blood feud with the Goshien Aiel ended with Rand's coming. He had been with Rand since the beginning, in the Waste, and was sent to Tear with his spears. Jheran was a signer of the Dragon's Peace at the Field of Merrilor before the Last Battle.

Jhirad. A sept of the Goshien Aiel.

Jhondar, Eldrith. *See* Eldrith Jhondar

Jhoradin. A *Mera'din* who joined the Shaido and was Rolan's friend. Squat for an Aielman, with blue eyes and red-gold hair, he caught and bound Lacile and also canoodled with her later. He helped rescue Faile and her people from Galina's trap at Malden, but when Perrin appeared, Jhoradin reached for his spears and Lacile stabbed him in the back.

ji'e'toh. Aiel term meaning honor and obligation (*ji*=honor, *e*=and, *toh*=duty or obligation). There were no excuses under *ji'e'toh*. If saving your child brought an obligation to a blood enemy, you paid the price without quibble. The most honor came from touching an armed enemy warrior and leaving him or her unharmed. Less honor came from taking an enemy captive, making him or her *gai'shain*. Least honor came from killing, because any child or fool could kill. Like Shienarans, the Aiel believed that shame was worse than guilt, the worst thing there was. And yet, shame had to be endured if required to meet *toh*. Failing to meet *toh* was the greatest shame of all; any other shame was preferable.

It was not possible to live one's life without occasionally incurring some sort of *toh*. There was no shame in incurring *toh*, only in failing to meet it properly. Lying, for whatever reason, incurred considerable *toh*. Just letting someone believe a lie incurred no *toh*, not at all like telling the lie directly. You could be told or be reminded that you had *toh*, though this was shaming, but asking whether you yourself had *toh* meant you did not know, and that was deeply shaming, and considered embarrassing to hear. An Aiel might well have pretended not to have heard the question at all. You decided whether or not you had *toh*, no one could decide that you had and require you to meet it. On the other hand, others could and usually would know that you had *toh*, so even if no one told you that you had it, if you failed to meet it, you suffered a loss of respect and of *ji*. You had to decide how to meet your *toh*, in effect, how much your honor was worth. Setting too high a worth on your *ji* for yourself was considered boasting. Setting it too small, however, meant that you did not consider your honor to be worth much. To stop someone from meeting their *toh* was to shame them deeply. There were a few ways to incur *toh* toward a *gai'shain*, but that was considered the hardest obligation of all to meet. Sulin chose to meet it by accepting a greater shame, in Aiel eyes, than she had given; that is, by becoming a wetlander servant. Shaming somebody, in and of itself, did not incur *toh* except in certain defined instances.

Speaking to a man of his father-in-law or to a woman of her mother-in-law—second-father and second-mother, in the Aiel way—was considered hostile enough to justify drawing weapons unless they had mentioned them first. If the offended party instead touched you after you spoke, it was the same as touching an armed enemy without harming him. That gained much *ji* and incurred much *toh*, but the one touched could demand to be made *gai'shain* to lessen the other's honor and their own obligation. By *ji'e'toh*, a proper demand to be made *gai'shain* had to be honored, though one that was considered improper could be denied. This denial was shaming to the one denied. The shame was greater than being beaten publicly, and about equal to being forced to appear nude in public.

Jianmin. A place in Seanchan that came up in conversation between Almurat Mor and Karede. Mor referred to Karede's honors for serving during the Jianmin Incident.

Jidar. A Saldaean soldier under Bashere in Caemlyn. He had odd ideas about Aes Sedai, as did his friends Vilnar and Rissen; they all thought they knew what Aes Sedai were like and looked like, but none would have recognized one if he saw her. Jidar thought Aes Sedai were all so beautiful that they could kill a man by smiling.

Jillari. A captured *damane* from Seanchan who was sent to Elayne in Caemlyn. She stuck to the party line: Women who could channel needed to be collared, must be collared, for their own safety and everyone else's as well. Her stance softened over time, but she still could not be trusted.

Jillie Lewin. A girl from Emond's Field. When Egwene first carried water for the annual shearing, Jillie was seventeen and her long dark hair was braided. She helped fold fleece.

Jillien. A plump Ebou Dari goldsmith who was at the Kin's farm outside Ebou Dar. She fled along with Elayne and Nynaeve when the Seanchan arrived. Since she was late and one of the last ten to be ready to leave the farm, she was made to do kitchen duty.

Jimar Chubain. High Captain of the White Tower Guard. He was a good soldier and a good enough general, but overly impetuous. He always thought he deserved more glory and more recognition than he received; he was a great believer in glory. He served in Illian, as a mercenary, before entering the Tower Guard, and fought in the Whitecloak War and the Aiel War. Elaida wanted to replace him with Gareth Bryne. Chubain was injured when the Seanchan attacked the Tower, but was Healed. After the Tower was unified, he kept his position as High Captain, although he worried that Gawyn would try to take his place. Gawyn disabused him of this notion, and Chubain agreed to take unbonded Younglings into the Tower Guard. He fought in the Last Battle.

Jindo. A sept of the Taardad Aiel.

Jini. A Seanchan *damane* who belonged to the Lady Morsa. Rand and Aviendha encountered her and other Seanchan when they Traveled to Seanchan. She had short yellow hair and looked almost motherly. Along with everyone else in the party, she was taken into custody by the Seeker to be put to the question.

Jinjin. One of two *damane* present at Morgase's meeting with Suroth. The other present was Pura.

Jinsiun, Stedding. A *stedding* located in the Mountains of Mist.

Jisao Hamora. A Youngling with Gawyn. He had a boy's grin, but wore the silver tower on his collar that marked a veteran of the fighting when Siuan Sanche was deposed. He was also present at Dumai's Wells and helped Gawyn scout out Bryne's troops. After the Tower was reunited, he became a Warder.

jo-car. Short-range transportation from the Age of Legends that used anti-gravitational technology. It came in a four-wheel design and a hovercraft (floater) design, and their shapes were like beetles and flattened water drops.

Joal Ramedar. The last king of Aldeshar, a nation from after the Trolloc Wars, and the father of Endara Casalain.

Joana. A name Birgitte went by in a past life.

Joao. One of the group of Shienaran soldiers who joined Lan in eastern Kandor as he traveled toward Tarwin's Gap. Andere told the protesting Lan that he had run into Joao and the other soldiers before meeting Lan, and had told them to wait along the southern roadway for Lan and his men to come along.

Joar Addam Nessosin. Asmodean's name in the Age of Legends.

Joelin. A Child of the Light. Dain Bornhald sent him and Gomanes with Ordeith to find out what he was up to; Ordeith reported that they were the only two killed in a skirmish with Trollocs. Dain suspected correctly that Ordeith had killed them.

Johanin. A king of Ghealdan. He stripped Logain of his land and titles when Logain declared himself the Dragon Reborn. Johanin supposedly died in a hunting accident; he was actually killed because he ignored the Prophet until it was too late.

Joinde. A woman of the Black Rock sept of the Shaarad Aiel and *Far Dareis Mai*. She laid a bridal wreath at her *gai'shain* Garan's feet the day he took off white. She was happy with her decision, but her fellow Maidens thought she had gone mad.

Joiya. A child that Egwene had with Rand, during her Accepted test.

Joiya Byir. An Andoran Aes Sedai of the Gray Ajah publicly and of the Black Ajah in truth, with a strength level of 28(16). Born in 828 NE, she went to the White Tower in 844 NE. After spending nine years as a novice and eleven years as Accepted, she was raised to the shawl in 864 NE. She was a handsome woman with a friendly face, dark gray eyes and dark hair and was one of the first thirteen members of the Black Ajah to be identified. She was captured in the Stone of Tear; when questioned she claimed that Liandrin intended to free Mazrim Taim, let him wreak havoc and blame it on Rand. Isam murdered her, but only after nailing her tongue to the door of her cell.

Jol. One of Kin Tovere's apprentice lensmakers in Cairhien. He helped set up the large looking glasses on a tower before the battle for Cairhien.

Jolien. A woman of the Salt Flat sept of the Nakai Aiel and *Far Dareis Mai*. She had red-gold hair and blue eyes. Sent across the Spine of the World to find He Who Comes With the Dawn, she helped rescue Nynaeve, Egwene and Elayne from brigands and a Myrddraal near Jurene. In the battle for Cairhien, Rand's collapsing tower broke her neck. Rand added her name to the list of women who had died for him.

Joline Maza. An Aes Sedai of the Green Ajah and the loyalist contingent, with a strength level of 17(5). Born in 899 NE, she went to the White Tower in 913 NE. After spending seven years as a novice and five years as Accepted, she was raised to the shawl in 925 NE. About 5'4" tall, with dark brown hair worn just below the shoulders and large brown eyes, she was slender and quite pretty. Her Warders were Blaeric Negina and Fen Mizar. Joline was raised a Sitter for the Green in 999 NE, replacing Faiselle Darone; she served on Elaida's advisory council. She was given penance by Elaida, to be devised by Joline herself and increased if insufficient. That penance was to abstain from embracing *saidar* during the time of her penance, partaking of only unsalted broth, bread and water, spending several hours each day kneeling on a stone floor and praying aloud to be made more worthy of being Aes Sedai, spending several more hours a day at hard, demeaning, physical labor and being visited in her apartments each morning by Silviana, who physically chastised her.

She was unchaired by Elaida shortly thereafter and ordered to go with Teslyn to Ebou Dar. When they learned that Elayne and Nynaeve were going to leave the city, Teslyn gave Joline forkroot so she would not get in their way. The Seanchan invaded the city and Joline went into hiding, helped by Setalle Anan. Mat agreed to get her and others in danger out of the city, which he did, and they joined up with Valan Luca's circus. They all eventually joined up with the Band of the Red Hand, continuing their travels, and Joline took part in fighting a large Seanchan force that was looking for Tuon. After helping to fight off the crazed citizens of Hinderstap, Joline and others departed from the Band by horse, and returned to the White Tower.

jolly-bag. A Taraboner term used to signify a jumble or mass of confusion.

Jolvaine Pass. A passage in the Maraside Mountains, on the southern border of modern-day Cairhien. It was the site of a famous battle between Artur Hawkwing and Guaire Amalasan.

Jom. A man from the Age of Legends. He was wide-shouldered with a narrow beard and dark hair that hung to his shoulders and was gathered at the back of his neck. He ran into Charn on the street, and was irritated until he realized that Charn was Aiel.

Jon. A blacksmith in Jarra, Ghealdan. Rilith, who was young enough to be his daughter, suddenly asked him to marry her, and he did, setting off a rash of weddings. All were precipitated by Rand passing through town.

Jon Ayellin. A Two Rivers farmer. He was bald and hulking. Jon and Thad Torfinn went to Faile to settle the boundaries of their fields; since neither knew the true boundaries, she told them to split the difference. Jon joined Perrin's army at Malden and was present when *Mah'alleinir* was forged.

Jon Gaelin. A Two Rivers farmer. His farm lay on the North Road. When Perrin convinced Jac al'Seen to go to Emond's Field for safety during the Trolloc incursion, Jac said that he could reach Jon's farm before sunset. Jon later joined Perrin's army at Malden.

Jon Skellit. A barber in the Royal Palace in Caemlyn who served in the palace under Morgase. He was later identified as a spy in the pay of House Arawn; he was twice seen accepting a purse from men known to favor House Arawn. He was convinced to spy for Elayne by Reene Harfor.

Jon Thane. The miller of Emond's Field and a member of the Village Council. His son Lem also saw the Fade that Mat, Rand and Perrin did. Jon sold Cloud, the horse that Rand rode out of Emond's Field, to Lan. A lone Trolloc who wandered off from his fist attacked Jon and another man; Alanna and Verin Healed them. During the defense of Emond's Field, Jon and Samel Crawe led the forces east of the town; Jon had seen the smoke of his mill burning earlier, and was grimly determined to prevail over the Trollocs.

Jonai. A Da'shain Aiel man who lived at the time of the Breaking. The son of Coumin, he married Alnora, a Dreamer, and they had three children: Adan, Esole and Willim. Solinda had Jonai lead the Aiel out of Paaran Disen, taking wagons filled with chora cuttings and objects of the Power to a place of safety. He began with thousands of wagons, but was occasionally forced to leave some behind, which he hated. Esole died young, and Willim was sent away when he began to channel. Alnora died shortly before Adan encountered an Aes Sedai who told them that Ishamael still touched the world. Adan and Jonai encountered Ogier who were seeking their *stedding*. Just before dying of a heart attack, Jonai told Adan to take the Aiel south and to keep the Covenant.

Jonan Adley. An Asha'man from Altara. He was born in 974 NE in the north near the border with Andor and Murandy. He could channel just enough to make a gateway of usable size. Jonan was about four years older than Rand. He tilted his head when he asked a question, or listened. His hair was nearly black, and his eyebrows were as thick as caterpillars; he worked them when thinking. Jonan was chosen to accompany Rand after Dumai's Wells, was a soldier as of the attack on Illian and was raised to Dedicated by Rand afterward. He went from the Illian invasion army to tell Rand that the army had reached the hillforts and that Sammael was there. Jonan was killed in the hills between Ebou Dar and the Venir Mountains during the attack on the Seanchan in Altara, when Rand's last attempt to call lightning down with *Callandor* went wild.

Jonasim. A queen of Saldaea whose son had a gambling problem. Faile used her as an example to Perrin when she was arguing that no leader was perfect.

Jondyn Barran. An old Two Rivers man who was respected by the Aiel as a skilled woodsman. A grizzled fellow who liked to spit, Jondyn was the best bowshot in the Two Rivers except for Tam and a better hunter than anybody. Jondyn liked the forests and hunting, but he was considered disreputable because he hadn't tended a flock or plowed a field since he had been old enough to leave his father's farm. He drank too much on feastdays, but he could track yesterday's shadows. He was one of the few older men who went with Perrin when he left Emond's Field the second time. He fought at Dumai's Wells. Jondyn, Get and Hu went after the fleeing inhabitants of Malden, but all they got was some information and a sketched map of the town.

Jongai, Stedding. A *stedding* located in Saldaea.

Joni Shagrin. An Andoran man who was once a Senior Bannerman of the Queen's Guards. He was big, and what little hair he still had was white. He looked as hard as an oak stump. When Siuan, Leane and Min were being taken to Bryne's estate after their trial, Logain knocked Joni out with a stone to free them. Joni went with Gareth Bryne to track down Siuan; despite the lump on his head he held no animus toward the three women. After they reached Salidar, Bryne sent Joni to Ebou Dar to recruit. He was made a captain, fought in the Last Battle, and was killed on the Kandor-Arafel border. Joni had always wanted to die in battle.

Jonine. A sept of the Shaido Aiel.

Jonneth Dowtry. A young man from Emond's Field. He was the grandson of Buel Dowtry. Taim recruited him and he became a soldier at the Black Tower. His entire family moved to the Black Tower village when he went. He joined with Androl to oppose Taim. When rescuing Logain, Jonneth shot Coteren with his Two Rivers bow and killed him. Logain promised to raise him to full Asha'man. Theodrin followed him around during the Last Battle and Healed him when he was injured; Pevara thought that she would bond him. When he and Androl and their party went after the seals, Jonneth disguised himself as an ordinary Darkfriend. Instead of searching for Sakarnen, Demandred's *sa'angreal*, as Logain ordered, Jonneth went with Androl to protect the dragons; they eventually captured Alviarin and several Darkfriend Asha'man in a *stedding*.

Jophil. Lan's bald Malkieri standard-bearer in the Last Battle.

Jorath, Widow. A woman in Jarra, Ghealdan, who dragged old Banas through the wedding arches after Rand passed through town.

Jorgin. A purported chandler who was actually a talented torturer; he worked for Milisair Chadmar.

Jorhald, Tesien. *See* Tesien Jorhald

Jori. Morvrin's Warder. He was about 5'4" tall, and almost as wide as he was tall. Bald and square-faced, he carried one sword on his back.

Jori Congar. A Two Rivers man. He was skinny although he ate twice as much as anyone else and looked as if he had not had a bite in a week. An excellent shot with the bow, he also liked to drink until he could not stand, and to steal small objects. Jori followed Perrin to Caemlyn; he was at Dumai's Wells and went to Ghealdan with Perrin. When Perrin found his brandy and poured it out, Jori was proud that he couldn't put anything over on Lord Perrin, but after he heard the rumor that Perrin had slept with Berelain, he spat when Perrin passed. He fought in the battle at Malden, and was a bannerman in the fight against Trollocs sent by Graendal. In one of the scenarios created by the Dark One while he was fighting Rand, Jori was killed by a deathswarm of insects. In the Last Battle, Jori was trapped under the body of a Trolloc and bled to death.

Jorille Mondevin. The Royal Historian to the Court of Ethenielle of Kandor; she wrote the introduction to "The Strike at Shayol Ghul."

Jorin Arene. A Darkfriend merchant in Amador, and the husband of Amellia. His mind was profoundly damaged by Temaile when Liandrin and the Black Ajah were making a point. Jorin, according to Liandrin, should not have thought that his oaths to the Great Lord could be conveniently forgotten. He lay beneath blankets all day, in the heat, shivering and weeping when anyone touched him or spoke above a whisper. Chesmal thought that he might be able to accomplish small tasks in a few months, as long as no one raised a voice.

Jorin din Jubai White Wing. The Sea Folk Windfinder of the *Wavedancer* and sister to its Sailmistress, Coine. Jorin could channel; she had a very small ability with Fire and almost none in Earth, but she was very strong in Air and Water, and had a very great ability with weather. She wore three earrings in each ear and had tattoos on her hands of stars and seabirds surrounded by the curls and whirls of stylized waves. Elayne and Nynaeve approached Jorin and Coine to ask for passage to Tanchico; they agreed. While they were sailing, Elayne learned that Jorin could channel. She wove much thicker flows than Elayne had ever seen woven before, but that was characteristic of Windfinders; she was not nearly as strong as Elayne. Jorin taught Elayne about weather, and Elayne taught her about Fire. After dropping Elayne and Nynaeve in Tanchico, Coine and Jorin planned to sail to Dantora and Cantorin to spread news of the Coramoor.

Jorlen Corbesan. An Aes Sedai from before the Breaking who made wondrous *ter'angreal*; he was killed when the Sharom was destroyed.

Jornhill. A village in Andor, somewhere near Kore Springs. When Siuan's group was on trial in Kore Springs, Maigan Nem, the wife of the victim, said she wanted Bryne to whip Siuan, Leane and Min and ride them to Jornhill on a rail.

Jorshem. 1) A man who taught Malidra to use a nail to scrape meat from a bone in Aviendha's viewing of the future in Rhuidean. 2) A clan chief of the Aiel. He was small and hawk-faced with some Andoran blood, seen in another of Aviendha's viewings of the future in Rhuidean.

Josaine. An Aes Sedai of the Green Ajah and the loyalist contingent. A search of her rooms revealed an *angreal* which she had found some years before and never turned in, as the law required. This search was carried out on Alviarin's order to Elaida, and the result was that Josaine was ordered birched, a very heavy penalty for what would usually receive no more than a slap on the wrist. Adelorna was caught in the same raid and received the same punishment. The apparent instigators of the search—at least, they were praised and rewarded that same morning for unspecified "adherence to the law"—were Kiyoshi of the Gray Ajah, Farellien of the Yellow Ajah and Doraise of the Brown Ajah; the result was an instant rift between the Greens, and the Gray, Yellow and Brown Ajahs. Josaine was killed in the Seanchan attack on the White Tower.

Josef Najima. A Kandori man who was always lucky. His son was on Moiraine's list of potential Dragons Reborn. The two were killed in a barn fire, victims of the male channeler pogrom. Josef's luck included being given the barn by his Lady after returning from the Aiel War; that was apparently his last bit of luck.

Joslyn. Egwene's *nom de route* while aboard the *Darter* on the way from Jurene to Tear.

Joslyn Aybara. Perrin's mother. She was killed by Padan Fain along with the rest of her family, although most thought that Trollocs had killed them.

Journal of the Unknown Scholar. A book that spoke of the days leading up to the Last Battle.

Journey to Tarabon, A. A book by Eurian Romavni that Egwene used as a reference before the first time she used her dream *ter'angreal* ring. It had useful drawings.

Jovarin, Master. The head mason building a new wing on the White Tower library. Danelle was supposed to be watching him; Siuan thought that he must be distracting her with books because she did not question the number of workmen that Jovarin claimed to have hired. In truth, the masons were there to try to take the Tower after Siuan was deposed.

Jowdry. A victim of the *gholam*. He was found in Farrier's Green with his throat ripped out and his body drained of blood. Jowdry owed Chaser, a man with whom Mat was dicing, two crowns when he died.

Jualdhe. A bridge town outside Tar Valon on the Alindrelle Erinin, on the road to Maradon. Zerah was questioned by the Black Ajah hunters in the Tower about her claim that she came from the north. She said that she had ridden down the bank of the Erinin to Jualdhe, but they had evidence that she had ridden from the south. There was also a Jualdhe Bridge out of Tar Valon.

Juarde, Famelle. *See* Famelle Juarde

Juendan. An ancient Ogier woman who was the grandmother of Moilin, the author of *A Study of the War of the Shadow*, which was mentioned by Loial when he was speaking of Be'lal.

Juerissen, Angharad. An Aes Sedai of the Gray Ajah who was Sierin Vayu's Keeper of the Chronicles.

Juilaine Madome. A Ghealdanin Aes Sedai of the Brown Ajah and the loyalist contingent, with a strength level of 21(9). Born in 903 NE, she went to the White Tower in 919 NE. After spending thirteen years as a novice and five years as Accepted, she was raised to the shawl in 937 NE. About 5'7" tall, dark-eyed and very attractive, she wore her almost black hair well short of her shoulders. Juilaine strode, and usually was thought not to be graceful, but the fact was that she moved in a mannish fashion. She was born with the spark and was a lesbian. She was a tomboy when she was found, climbing trees, running in the streets and wearing boy's clothes much more often than dresses. She already knew her sexual preferences, and willingly wore dresses more often to get close to a girl she liked than for any other reason. She was raised Sitter for the Brown in 999 NE to replace Takima.

Juilin Sandar. A Tairen thief-catcher. Born in 961 NE, he served in the Aiel War as a common foot soldier. Juilin was about 5'10" tall, and lean. His complexion was as dark as old roots, and he had short-cut black hair that lay flat on his head. His eyes were dark and missed nothing. Thief-catchers worked semi-freelance, hiring out to people who had been robbed to recover the stolen goods and bring the thieves to justice. In Tear, they also had standing commissions called warrants from the High Lords and received payment for each thief or other criminal they brought in who was convicted. Juilin was accomplished in the use of the sword-breaker, a thumb-thick bamboo staff that was his height and which he used as a martial arts weapon, and cudgels. He could also use his hands and feet as weapons. He was skilled in ferreting out information and analyzing his findings for patterns. Nynaeve, Elayne and Egwene hired Juilin to help them find the Black Ajah in Tear; he found them, but the Black sisters forced him to betray his clients, and Elayne, Nynaeve and Egwene were taken captive. Juilin felt guilty and helped Mat rescue them.

At Rand's behest, he traveled with Elayne and Nynaeve to Tanchico, where he had a brief affair with their innkeeper, Rendra. He fell in love with Amathera during the short time in Tanchico after her rescue from Black Ajah and before she was restored as Panarch, while she was hiding out in the Three Plum Court. She hardly noticed Juilin except that he stopped men from pinching her and talked Rendra out of switching her for making a fuss. She, of course, never thought of him as a man, really, only as a servant. Juilin then traveled with Nynaeve and Elayne to Salidar and Ebou Dar. Juilin rescued Amathera from the Seanchan in Ebou Dar, and she was then unwilling to be parted from him. In the Last Battle, he commanded a squad of men and fought bravely.

Juin son of Lacel son of Laud. An Ogier in Stedding Tsofu. He broke up what almost became a fight when Rand and his party confronted Rhian and two other Maidens in the *stedding*.

Julanya Fote. A member of the Kin with a strength level of 16(4). She could make a gateway, but one only just large enough to walk through. Plump and pretty, with touches of white in her dark hair, Julanya spent twenty years as a peddler. She was at the Kin's farm outside Ebou Dar when Elayne and her companions arrived, and accompanied Elayne to Caemlyn. Birgitte put her to work as a scout, sending her to villages in northern Andor and having her keep an eye on the six strong Houses who were uncommitted. Julanya and Keraille reported when Ellorien, Luan and Abelle broke camp, and returned to those camps as laundresses. When Mat trapped the *gholam*, Julanya assisted.

jumara. Beasts created during the Age of Legends, and known as Worms in the following Age. Huge, vicious creatures created by Aginor, they lived in the Blight and traveled in packs. Under certain conditions, they transformed in some unspecified way.

Jumara. The second month of the year.

jump up. A pink wildflower.

jumper. A form of short-range transportation in the Age of Legends that used anti-gravitational technology. It could float suspended above the ground at various distances.

Jur Grady. An Andoran Asha'man. Born in 972 NE, he was stocky and dark-eyed with a weathered farmer's face. He could make gateways and had an ability with weather. He was married to Sora, and had a son, Gadren, who was four when they went to the Black Tower. Jur bonded his wife with a version of the Warder's bond, as many married Asha'man did. The bond worked at a longer distance than did the female bond; in Ghealdan, Jur knew that his wife, back in the Black Tower, had a sore knee. At that distance, approximately a thousand miles, the Warder bond would only have given an Aes Sedai a general sense of direction. Grady was chosen to accompany Rand after Dumai's Wells. He was raised to Dedicated and traveled to Ghealdan with Perrin. He exhausted himself making gateways in the effort to rescue Faile. He and Neald worked with the Wise Ones to learn how to link.

In the Last Battle, Grady brought the people of Hinderstap to the field of battle.

Jura, River. A small river in Altara flowing south into the River Eldar.

Jurad Accan. A soldier under Lord Luan Norwelyn in Andor. When Jurad and eighty of his men were attacked by Lord Nasin, Doilin Mellar led a sortie to rescue them and brought them into Caemlyn, which displeased Elayne, because she was unsure of Luan's support.

Jurad Shiman. An officer at the Aesdaishar Palace in Chachin, Kandor. He had ridden with Lan in the south during the Aiel War, and welcomed Lan respectfully to the palace.

Jurador. A stone-walled salt town in Altara that lay three days east of Coramen and the River Eldar, with treeless hills to the east, and forested hills to the west. Iron-studded gates marked the entrance to the town. It was a prosperous, busy place with stone-paved streets, most of them wide and all lined with stone buildings roofed in reddish tiles. Houses and inns rubbed shoulders with stables and taverns, in a noisy jumble. Salt merchants' houses were three stories of stone rather than two, covering eight times as much ground as any others, each with a columned walk overlooking the street and shielded by white wrought-iron screens between the columns. The lower windows on most houses had those screens, though not always painted. The Lady Aethelaine's palace appeared no different on the outside than the salt merchants' mansions, but it was located on the town's main square, a wide expanse of polished stone where a broad round marble fountain sprayed water that smelled of brine into the air. Mat saw ghosts in Jurador while walking into town. It was also the town where Luca's show was camped when Egeanin was knifed; Juilin urged Mat to leave Tuon there while the rest of them escaped. Mat took Tuon and Selucia shopping in Jurador, and Mat bought Tuon a prized horse there.

Jurah Haret. The innkeeper of The Star in Tear. He was stout with a round face and balding head. Moiraine, Lan, Loial, Perrin and Faile stayed at his inn; although Moiraine had told him not to let anyone in her room, he allowed two women to leave her a small gift; the women were Black Ajah and the gift was the hedgehog *ter'angreal* that trapped Faile in *Tel'aran'rhiod.*

Juranai. An Aielman who was leader of *Aethan Dor.* He was slender with streaks of white in his pale brown hair. Juranai sometimes joined Rand in practicing the Aiel method of fighting, and he accompanied Rand to the observation tower at the battle for Cairhien.

Jureen, Marasale. *See* Marasale Jureen

Jurene. A small village in Cairhien on the River Erinin. Jurene only had one-storied wooden houses and dirt streets. When Nynaeve, Elayne and Egwene were traveling by river, their boat wrecked on a sunken ship, and Nynaeve insisted they leave the boat and walk six miles to the nearest village, Jurene, to pick up another boat. Later, Nynaeve went there in *Tel'aran'rhiod*, where, with Birgitte's help, she captured Moghedien with an *a'dam*, and learned from Moghedien about the trap set by Rahvin for Rand in Caemlyn.

Juric. An Aielman serving as *gai'shain* to Amys. After his time as *gai'shain* was up, he refused to put off the white, and Amys beat him until her arm was sore; no matter how often she told him to put off the white, he was back in it by sunset.

Jurine Najima. A Kandori woman whose son was on Moiraine's list of potential Dragons Reborn. Jurine was a hand taller than Moiraine, with long black hair and large blue eyes in a face shrunken by tragedy. Her husband Josef and son Jerid were killed in a barn fire as part of the male channeler pogrom.

Jurith Dorine. The Right Hand to the Queen of Almoren, and the author of *Commentaries on the Prophecies of the Dragon* in 742 AB, the Third Age.

Justice. Hawkwing's legendary sword. The blade was long and slightly curved and the scabbard black with a lacquered red and gold dragon on it. Hawkwing wielded Justice to great effect in life and as a Hero of the Horn. It was lost for many years, but scholars found it under a submerged statue. Rand recognized it and took to wearing it.

K

Kabal Deep. A hundred leagues of open water between Arran Head on the eastern shore of Altara and the city of Illian on the western shore of Illian. It was so deep that ships could find no bottom with their longest sounding lines just a mile or so from shore. The waves there could overturn ships as they rolled north to pound the coast with breakers fifteen paces high or more.

Kadar. One of the kings in the gleeman tale "Mara and the Three Foolish Kings."

Kadere. A Saldaean family. *See* Hadnan *and* Teodora Kadere

Kaensada Hills. An area of Seanchan that was populated by less-than-civilized hill tribes. These tribes fought a great deal among themselves, as did individual families within the tribes. Each tribe had its own customs and taboos, the latter of which often made no sense to anyone outside that tribe. Most of the tribesmen avoided the more civilized residents of Seanchan. Ajimbura hailed from this region.

kaf. A bitter-tasting hot beverage from Seanchan.

Kaila Bent. A member of the Queen's Guard who brought word to Birgitte that an intruder had been picked up entering the city at the Plum Gate; the intruder turned out to be Mat. Kaila was lanky and fire-haired.

Kainea. A Maiden with dark hair, unusual for an Aiel. She was in Tear when Rand returned from telling Egwene that he intended to break the seals; Rand sent her to gather messengers.

Kairen Stang. An Andoran Aes Sedai of the Blue Ajah and the rebel contingent, with a strength level of 18(6). Born in 937 NE, she went to the White Tower in 952 NE. After spending eight years as a novice and eight years as Accepted, she was raised to the shawl in 968 NE. About 5'4" tall, she had cool blue eyes and an oval face. Her Warder was Llyw. Kairen was a member of the embassy that the rebels sent to Rand in Caemlyn; she was sent on as leader of the group that escorted the Two Rivers girls to Salidar. She tended to favor Lelaine's positions. Kairen was killed by Aran'gar, her head wrenched around almost full circle, snapping her neck. Her Warder survived and was bonded by Myrelle.

Kaisea. A Seanchan *sul'dam* of the low Blood. Tall, with long black hair worn in a braid, she was captured in Rand's campaign against the Seanchan and sent to the Royal Palace of Caemlyn. Kaisea insisted that she should be collared; Dimana, a Kin, believed that Kaisea was trying to learn weaves in order to cause a mishap that would prove her right. Gawyn encountered Marille, a former *damane*, in the gardens; she recognized the Bloodknife he was holding but couldn't tell him much about it. Dimana took Kaisea to him, and Kaisea gave him more information about Bloodknives. In return, Gawyn promised to ask Elayne to collar her.

Kaisel Noramaga. Ethenielle's grandson, a prince of Kandor. He joined Lan and served with him at Tarwin's Gap and in the rest of the Last Battle. Kaisel wanted to forbid Saldaean women from fighting in the battle; Lan promised him a decent burial after he was allowed to take Kaisel's head off the pole if he tried to forbid them.

Kaisin Pass. A place of battle where the Soldier Amyrlin, Rashima Kerenmosa, was victorious.

Kajima, Welyn. *See* Welyn Kajima

Kajin, Lord. A Shienaran nobleman encountered by Rand in Fal Dara. He was about 6'4" to 6'5" tall, and lean and lanky, with a sallow complexion. His top-knot was as black as pitch. After Fain was freed, Lord Kajin checked the keep to see if anything was missing. He also tried to explain Shienaran women's customs to Rand when Rand tried to visit Egwene.

Kalede, Nyein. *See* Nyein Kalede

Kalia. Furyk Karede's wife. They had three sons together; two followed Karede into the Deathwatch Guards; Kalia and the other son died in the Great Fire of Sohima.

Kalyan Ramsin. One of Saldaean Queen Tenobia's many uncles. He was scarred and grizzled, with the face of a leathery eagle and thick mustaches—black streaked with white, or perhaps white streaked with black—that curved down around his mouth. Tenobia set up matchmaking between Ethenielle and Kalyan at the meeting of the four rulers before they headed south. The two did eventually marry.

Kamarile Maradim Nindar. Graendal's name in the Age of Legends.

Kamile Noallin. A banker in Chachin, Kandor, whom Moiraine visited to cash in a letter-of-rights. In her middle years, she was lovely and slim with graying hair worn in four long braids and stern, questioning eyes. She used an enlarging glass to study Ilain Dormaile's seal on the letter.

Kamsa, Vayelle. *See* Vayelle Kamsa

Kanara. A Maiden of the Spear who guarded Rand in the city of Tear.

Kandel, Tad. *See* Tad Kandel

Kandelmar. A location in Arad Doman where Ituralde had had a military victory.

Kandor. A Borderlands nation lying between Arafel and Saldaea. Its sigil was a rearing red horse: the Red Horse. Its banner was the Red Horse on a field of pale green.

Saldaea, Kandor, Arafel, Shienar and Malkier all were provinces of Hawkwing's empire, with the borders between them very much as they were at the time of the Last Battle, though not stretching so far south in most cases. With the Blight to contend with, the governors of those provinces (Lord Rylen t'Boriden Rashad for Saldaea, Lord Jarel Soukovni for Kandor, Lady Mahira Svetanya for Arafel, Lady Merean Tihomar for Shienar and Lord Shevar Jamelle for Malkier)

met soon after Hawkwing's death in FY 994 to reaffirm measures for cooperation against the Blight and to make agreements for mutual defense against
attack from the south. Before the end of FY 995, when it became clear that the
rest of the empire was splintering, each of the governors took the title of King
or Queen of his or her former province, now a nation. None of these nations
took part in any of the wider fighting of the War of the Hundred Years, as
nations, except for defending themselves against attacks and punishing
same, though individuals and groups did sometimes become involved, either
for political reasons or because of family connections or friendships.

Kandor could have either a king or a queen, but the advisory council known
as the Crown Council or the Council of Twelve was always an even number and
traditionally, though not legally, always balanced between men and women. By
law, half the council had to be commoners. Commoners were usually representatives of various guilds which struggled mightily to have representation. The
council truly was advisory; the ruler was under no obligation to do what it
wanted, though wise rulers at least paid attention to what it said. The council
could make considerable trouble for a ruler who tried to go too far astray, even
managing to balk the ruler's wishes entirely, or at least slow them intolerably.

The spouse of a Kandori ruler was a consort—called the Prince or Princess
Consort—not a co-equal ruler, though with considerable if specifically limited
and set authority. The wife of the king was expected to reign as regent while
he was on campaign, the husband of the queen to lead the army on campaign.
The husband of a queen was expected to act as her champion in trials by combat, but a king was required by law to use a champion and not to take part in
duels or trials by combat personally.

The Sword of Kirukan, reportedly a Power-wrought blade, was a symbol of
the rulers of Kandor; it was carried ceremonially by the Swordbearer in an or-
nately jeweled sheath, the two-handed hilt always toward the ruler, so that it
could be drawn at need.

In Kandor, women asked men to marry, not vice versa. Like all Borderlanders, a Kandori man considered the day he was given his sword to be his nameday.
While law in the Borderlands prohibited hiding one's face inside any city, town
or village, it was considered rude not to show one's face when meeting strangers,
whatever the weather.

Kandori were considered the touchiest of the Borderlanders, which was saying something considering the reputation of Arafellin. Duels in Kandor could
have distinctly odd terms and conditions. As in Altara, Kandori women were
known to fight duels, though not so commonly as men, seldom with the weapons men used and rarely to the death, as men often fought. Public defeat and
humiliation of one's enemy was commonly preferred among women. Whip duels were a common form among women of the commoners, at least in the country. Kandori women made no pretense that they did not fight duels.

Mass duels were not unknown, involving five or even ten men to a side; the winning side was the one that had the last man on his feet.

There was a link between the Borderland and Aiel views of shame: by and large, shame was worse than guilt—the worst thing there was—though this view of shame ameliorated as one moved west. Arafellin saw shame as less important than did Shienarans, Kandori less than Arafellin, Saldaeans less than Kandori. In all of the Borderlands, though, shame was given a much heavier weight than in lands to the south.

Kandor had a considerable mining industry in gemstones other than diamonds, including most notably sapphires, emeralds and rubies. The city of Canluum, very near to the Blight, was a rich source of those gems, and also home to some of the best clockmakers found anywhere. Timber and furs were major exports, as were finished wooden products.

Kandori. Of or from Kandor.

Kappre. A member of Ituralde's forces in Saldaea. Ituralde sent him to Alin with a message to have his cavalry unit attack the Shadowspawn, just before being allowed into Maradon.

Kara Defane. A Wise Woman in a fishing village near Toman Head. She was taken by the Seanchan and made *damane*. In her late forties, she looked to be in her twenties, and was of moderate strength. She was used by the Seanchan against Rand's forces and captured, then handed over to Elayne by Taim. She parroted the party line at first, but later allowed that she really would like the collar off. On the other hand, she didn't want to harm the *sul'dam*, or at least some. For the rest, she was suffering from a residue of Stockholm syndrome; she still felt a very strong affection, almost love, for the *sul'dam* who trained her and those who held her leash. Elayne and the others did not fully trust her; they were afraid that she would obey a *sul'dam* who ordered her to help an escape.

Karaethon Cycle, Commentaries on the. A book by Sereine dar Shamelle Motara, Counsel-Sister to Comaelle, High Queen of Jaramide, circa 325 AB, the Third Age.

Karaethon Cycle, The. *See* Prophecies of the Dragon

Karaethon Cycle, The: The Prophecies of the Dragon. A book from 231 NE, the Third Age, translated by Ellaine Marise'idin Alshinn, Chief Librarian at the Court of Arafel.

Karale Sanghir. A Domani Aes Sedai of the Gray Ajah publicly and of the Black Ajah in truth. Of the loyalist contingent, she had a Warder, also a Darkfriend, who took poison after Atuan revealed the names of members of her heart, Karale and Marris, to Pevara and the other Black Ajah hunters.

Karam. A young lord of a minor Andoran House, loyal to Sarand. He and Jarid Sarand were friends from childhood, but faced with Jarid's growing insanity, Karam left his camp and went off to fight in the Last Battle.

Kardia, the Fallen Army of. An army from Mat's memories.

kardon. A leafless, spiny plant having sweet, bulbous fruit with a tough, greenish skin.

Karede, Furyk. *See* Furyk Karede

Kareil, Lady. A young Kandori noblewoman who sent soldiers to the Aiel War. She was a patron to Josef Najima and his wife and provided for the Najima family after Josef died in a fire when the livery stable she had given him after his return from serving against the Aiel burned.

Karella Fanway. An Aes Sedai who lived at the time of the formation of the White Tower.

Karentanis, Moria. *See* Moria Karentanis

Kari al'Thor. The daughter of an Andoran merchant from Caemlyn who ran a trading house in Illian. She met Tam al'Thor in 962 NE. Her parents disapproved of her meeting him, opposed her marrying a soldier, and would have stopped it but were prevented by Tam's position in the Companions. They did disown her, however, when she married him in 965 NE. Kari accompanied Tam on the long campaigns during the Aiel War. They had two children, a girl who died of a fever in infancy and a boy who was stillborn, after which Kari could no longer have children. In late 978 NE, Tam found an infant on the slopes of Dragonmount and took him to Kari. Shortly after that, Tam resigned his commission and took Kari and baby Rand to the Two Rivers. Kari died of fever in 984 NE.

Kari Thane. An Emond's Field girl. When Moiraine mentioned that another woman in Emond's Field could channel, Egwene thought that it might be Kari or Lara Ayellin.

Karil. A woman in the story "How Goodwife Karil Cured Her Husband of Snoring." Thom said he would tell the story at Bel Tine in Emond's Field.

Karile. One of Kerene's Warders. He was massive, with golden hair and a golden beard that gave him the aspect of a lion. Moiraine saw him reading a book when she took a message to Kerene as Accepted.

Karind Anshar. An Andoran noblewoman, High Seat of House Anshar. Her sigil was a running red fox on a field of gold or yellow. Stolid and about 5'4" tall, with a blunt voice, she had gray streaks in her dark hair, framing a severe face. Her flat-eyed stare was like a hammer, and some said that it had put three husbands underground. If she had had brains to match her toughness, she would have been dangerous. She opposed Morgase during the Succession and became one of Gaebril's sycophants. She was used by Rand and fled after he reached an accommodation with Dyelin. She supported Arymilla for the throne of Andor, but was captured. After Sylvase declared for Elayne, she followed suit and offered to publish her support.

Karistovan, Sumeko. *See* Sumeko Karistovan

Karldin Manfor. An Andoran Asha'man. Born in 981 NE, he was one of the early Asha'man, a pale-haired youth with blue-gray eyes, present on Rand's second visit to the farm. After Dumai's Wells, he was chosen to accompany Rand.

Karldin and Loial visited many of the *stedding* to ensure that guards were posted at the Waygates; after he returned to Cairhien, he used the name Underhill. When he Traveled with Logain and Bashere to Algarin's manor, Rand raised him to full Asha'man. Karldin and Bashere met with the High Lady Suroth to try to arrange a meeting between Rand and the Daughter of the Nine Moons. Beldeine Nyram bonded him, and they accompanied Rand to the meeting with the false Tuon. Karldin and Beldeine were killed in the Last Battle; he collapsed from exhaustion and Sharans stabbed him.

Karm. Tylee Khirgan's longtime quartermaster. He was a solid man who made very few mistakes.

Kash. An Asha'man in Taim's faction. He joined shortly before the Last Battle, quickly became very strong and was promoted to full Asha'man. He fought for the Shadow in the Last Battle; he was trapped in a *stedding* by Androl near the end of it.

Kashgar. A Saldaean under-lieutenant of the Children of the Light. He appeared almost boyish despite a great hooked nose and thick mustaches like inverted horns. He reluctantly held Valda's helmet and sword belt before Valda's duel with Galad. After the duel, he cleaned Valda's sword and presented it to Galad.

Kasi. A woman who was a kitchen helper in the Sun Palace in Cairhien. She was present when Loial and Karldin arrived there after visiting many *stedding*.

Katar. A city-state just across the southern border of Arad Doman. It traditionally gave fealty to the rulers of Arad Doman. Ituralde, thinking of his past military victories, thought about the fact that he had taught the Lords of Katar not to sell products of their mines and forges to the enemies of Arad Doman. Katar was proposed by Rand as a meeting place with the Seanchan; they refused.

Kateri Nepvue. An Aes Sedai of the White Ajah. A prodigious reader, she refused to heed the Amyrlin's advice to stay alert and not go about alone; she was killed by a Bloodknife in a small reading room of the White Tower.

Katerin. A golden-haired Maiden of the Spear who guarded Rand's tent the night before the meeting at the Field of Merrilor.

Katerine Alruddin. An Aes Sedai of the Red Ajah publicly and of the Black Ajah in truth. Of the loyalist contingent, her strength level was 15(3). Born in 950 NE, she went to the White Tower in 967 NE. After spending eight years as a novice and seven as Accepted, she was raised to the shawl in 982 NE and joined the Black Ajah in 987 NE. About 5'6" tall, she was sharp-faced, with wavy black hair that hung below her waist. Katerine was part of the expedition to kidnap Rand and bring him to Tar Valon; she was captured at Dumai's Wells. She escaped with the aid of Darkfriends among the Aiel before she could be questioned by Verin, and made her way back to the Tower. She got to the White Tower after the arrival of the rebel army, bringing news of Dumai's Wells and events in Cairhien, but not of the oaths made by the other captives to Rand, as she escaped before any were given. A short time later, she was named

Mistress of Novices. She left the Tower with the Black Ajah, and was killed by Egwene in *Tel'aran'rhiod* while disguised as Mesaana.

Kathana. The innkeeper of The Yearly Brawl in Ebou Dar. She was married to Jame, a Seanchan. She was short with dark hair, fair skin and a motherly air. Mat thought she would lecture a tree for growing in the wrong spot.

Kati. A serving girl at The Dusty Wheel in Caemlyn. Beautiful, with raven hair and a wide smile, she flirted with Mat even though he had told her he was married.

Katrine do Catalan a'Coralle. The first queen of Murandy. Meri do Ahlan a'Conlin, a woman Moiraine met when collecting the names of babies born near Dragonmount, claimed to be Katrine's direct descendant.

Kavarthen Wars. Wars that occurred while Balladare Arandaille was Amyrlin, following the reign of Artur Hawkwing.

Kayacun. A town in Saldaea where Aldragoran, a gem merchant originally from Malkier, was selling gems when Nynaeve arrived to spread the news that Lan was riding to Tarwin's Gap.

Kayama, Nacelle. *See* Nacelle Kayama

Kayen Yokata. The Lord of Fal Eisen, Shienar. A sharp-faced man with a harsh voice, he directed Elayne, Aviendha and Birgitte to the place in camp where they were meeting with the Borderlanders in Braem Wood.

Kayenzi, Shivena. A Saldaean philosopher who was influenced by Willim of Manaches. Meilyn tested Moiraine on her knowledge of the two when she was Accepted.

Kaylin. A maid with the Salidar Aes Sedai. Chesa thought that she and Nildra were terrible gossips and would say mean things when someone's back was turned.

Kazadi, Tenobia si Bashere. *See* Tenobia si Bashere Kazadi

Kazin. A Saldaean stableman at the Gates of Heaven in Canluum. Skinny with a hooked nose and tilted eyes, he fetched Arrow for Moiraine, and she tipped him a silver penny, even though she heard him say that only a fool noble would ride out at such an early hour.

Keatlin. An Altaran novice with the rebels in Salidar, where she was recruited, with a potential strength level of 25(13). Born in 973 NE, she was older than Nynaeve, and did not like being ordered about by a mere girl like Elayne.

Keemlin Rai. The son of Malenarin Rai, the commander of Heeth Tower on the Blightborder. He was a few days short of his fourteenth nameday when Trollocs attacked Heeth Tower; Keemlin was at the top of the list of those to be sent as messengers to the capital. Because Tian's mother had already lost four sons, Keemlin let Tian go in his place. His father raised him to a man on the spot, and they fought the Trollocs and died.

Keene, Mistress. The innkeeper at The Counsel's Head in Far Madding. She wore her white hair in a tight bun and had a pointed chin. She was suspicious and disapproving of men and did not try to hide it; each room was furnished with a strap so that women could keep their husbands in line. Still, the accommodations were comfortable and the food good. Mistress Keene delivered to Min a letter that was addressed to Rand, and warned Min that she should watch her friends since her husband was so pretty.

Keeper of the Chronicles. A slightly less formal usage was "the Keeper." Once simply the Amyrlin's secretary and the official historian of the White Tower, since more than five hundred years before the Trolloc Wars the Keeper had been second-in-command to the Amyrlin. Like the Amyrlin, the Keeper left her old Ajah, though she wore a narrow stole of the color of that Ajah. The Keeper bowed to the Amyrlin Seat rather than curtsying.

While the Keeper traditionally was chosen by the Amyrlin (although this was not a matter of law, only very strong custom), she was confirmed by the Hall, much as in the election of an Amyrlin, and she could be removed only by the Hall. As with removing the Amyrlin Seat, removing the Keeper required the greater consensus, and the Ajah from which she had been raised would have been excluded from a vote on removing her.

She was also traditionally raised from the same Ajah as the Amyrlin, but this was not required by Tower law. All history was deeply buried in Tower records, but Keepers from Ajahs that differed from their Amyrlins' were almost invariably imposed on the Amyrlin by the Hall. This was done for various reasons: as a political quid pro quo, giving that office to one Ajah and the Amyrlin Seat to another, or to keep an eye on an Amyrlin who despite her raising was thought unreliable in some way.

The Keeper was a part of ceremony in the Hall, in that she announced the Amyrlin's imminent arrival and made the call for consensus among other things, but she took no part in discussion in the Hall and could not enter the Hall without the Amyrlin Seat.

Keeping. A weave that preserved things. It could be laid on food, flowers or just about anything. It adhered closely to the surface of whatever it was laid on, preserving it as if time did not pass inside the weave. Whether time stopped within the weave or simply slowed down was a matter of some argument. Laying a Keeping on anything that breathed would kill it, though; the Keeping would preserve the subject perfectly, but dead. It was one of Egwene's "discoveries," courtesy of Moghedien.

Keilar. A young gate guard in Maderin, Altara, who was about Mat's age. He was obviously a farmer although he was wearing coin armor. When Thom asked why there were so many guards at Maderin, he told Thom that the Seanchan had said that there weren't enough and Lord Nathin listened to the Seanchan; his companion guard clouted him for that and threatened to have him back behind a plow.

Keilin. A bold man in a song sung at The White Ring in Maderin.

Keille Shaogi. A persona Lanfear used when she traveled with Hadnan Kadere. In this guise she was a foot shorter than Kadere and immensely fat, with dark eyes buried in rolls of fat and a hatchet nose that dwarfed Kadere's. She wore a white lace shawl held above her head on elaborate ivory combs thrust into long, coarse black hair. Her voice was extremely beautiful and melodious. She moved with incongruous lightness, almost like one of the Maidens. *See also* Lanfear

Kelwin Janevor. An Andoran man who was High Seat of his House. A vinegary old man, he was loyal to Elayne and brought ten armsmen to her service.

Kely Huldin. An Andoran weaver who was one of the first to be tested for Asha'man at the farm. Lumpy and dark-haired, he did not have the ability to learn to channel. He was hangdog about it, but his wife was happy.

Kema. A Kinswoman who was part of Elayne's contingent at her Cairhienin coronation. She was dark-skinned and wore her black hair in three long braids.

Kemali. A city in the Age of Legends.

Kendral. A prince of Arafel who was the grandson of King Paitar. He and his armies joined Lan as he rode for Tarwin's Gap, and he invited Kaisel to come along.

Kenley Ahan. A young Two Rivers man who joined Perrin's band and was killed in an ambush by Trollocs.

Kenly Maerin. A young Two Rivers man who followed Perrin to Dumai's Wells. Short and stocky, he was barely old enough to marry or leave home; he tried to grow a beard like Perrin's. He had fought Trollocs in Emond's Field and did well on the battlefield. Praise from Perrin made him grin broadly. After Perrin supposedly slept with Berelain, he shaved off his beard, but had begun growing it back by the time he went into Malden through the aqueduct in the battle against the Shaido. He continued as part of Perrin's army, and fought in the Last Battle.

Kennar Miraj. A Seanchan Captain-General of the Ever Victorious Army, and of the Blood. He was a scout lieutenant and a *morat'raken* before being raised to the Blood for riding fifty miles in a night to warn the Empress of an approaching rebel army; he was too low to shave the sides of his head and was only allowed to lacquer the nails of his little fingers. Suroth ordered him to wipe the Asha'man off the face of the earth. He was killed in the battle against Rand when Rand went wild with *Callandor*.

Kennit. Eldrith's Warder. He was not a Darkfriend, and intended to kill her when he found her despite the cost to himself. Eldrith failed to keep her bond masked, and he tracked her down in Ghealdan and tried to kill her there; she didn't want him killed, given the potential effect on her, so she and her companions fled.

Kera Haellin. A Tairen of noble birth, an Aes Sedai of the Green Ajah and the loyalist contingent. She had the blue eyes and fair hair that occasionally showed up among Tairens. Kera had all the arrogance common to Greens. She curtsied to Alviarin, though it was not required to the Keeper; it made her grind her teeth. As much as she hated it, she tried to curry a little favor with Alviarin; Elaida seemed to strike without warning, where least expected, and Kera thought Alviarin might offer some protection.

Keraille Surtovni. A Kinswoman who appeared to be Saldaean. Her strength level was 49(37), not strong enough for her to test for Aes Sedai, and not strong enough for her to make a gateway of any size whatsoever. Short and slim, with tilted green eyes and fiery red curls, she left Ebou Dar the day after the Feast of the Half Moon with Derys, and went to the Kin's farm. She was among the women who went to Caemlyn with Elayne; there she worked some with the captured *damane*. Birgitte sent Keraille and Julanya to keep an eye on the six strong Houses; they reported when Ellorien, Luan and Abelle broke camp, and returned to those camps posing as laundresses.

Kerb. A Domani youth who worked as a chandler's apprentice. Under Graendal's Compulsion, he killed the messenger she sent to Bandar Eban with a pretense of being from Alsalam, after Milisair Chadmar had him sent to a dungeon to be put to the question. Nynaeve found him out, and at Rand's request removed the Compulsion; he died, but only after revealing that Graendal was at Natrin's Barrow.

Kerene Nagashi. An Aes Sedai of the Green Ajah with a strength level of 11(+2). She was born in 793 NE. Her short dark hair was lightly touched with white and her eyes were nearly black. She was reputed to adhere to the strictest letter of the law no matter what her own feelings were, whether pity or contempt. Her Warders were Stepin and Karile. It was generally considered that she would be the next Amyrlin Seat after Sierin Vayu, though such talk made Kerene nervous and infuriated Sierin. Kerene was one of those called in by Tamra Ospenya and sent out in secret to search for the boychild Dragon Reborn. She reportedly fell off a ship in the River Alguenya during a storm and drowned; in truth, she was killed by the Black Ajah.

Kerenmosa, Rashima. *See* Rashima Kerenmosa

Kerevon, Reiko. *See* Reiko Kerevon

Kert Wagoner. A man from the Two Rivers who fought in the Last Battle. At the Field of Merrilor, he spoke to Rand about how bad things looked; Rand reassured him.

kesiera. A small jewel on a fine chain like a necklace, worn with the chain fastened in a woman's hair so that the chain made a V on her forehead supporting the jewel centered above her eyebrows. It was a Cairhienin ornament, slightly old-fashioned and not much worn by the time of the Last Battle, though a few did.

Kev Barstere. A Two Rivers man who went with Tam and joined Perrin's army at Malden. Perrin noted that he must have gotten out from under his mother's thumb since he was there.

Kevlyn Torr. A Two Rivers man with Perrin. He told Perrin of the stand of trees that had mysteriously died and dried in one night. Perrin told him to harvest them for firewood.

Kevrim al'Azar. An elderly Two Rivers man. Even though he was so old that his grandsons had grown sons, he participated in the defense of Emond's Field.

Kharendor. A nation that arose after the Trolloc Wars.

Khirgan, Tylee. *See* Tylee Khirgan

Khodomar. A nation that arose after the Trolloc Wars.

Khoweal. A city or region in Seanchan whose denizens' complexions were coal black. Miraj thought of it as among the named, honored regiments from different parts of Seanchan that were represented among his troops.

ki'sain. A small mark, a dot, which an adult Malkieri woman painted on her forehead each morning in pledge that she would swear or had sworn her sons to fight the Shadow. This pledge was not necessarily that they would be warriors, but that they would oppose the Shadow every day in every way that they could. Like the *hadori*, the *ki'sain* was considered a symbol of connection to Malkier, and of the bonds that united a woman with other Malkieri. Also like the *hadori*, the *ki'sain* was a sign of adulthood. The *ki'sain* gave information about the woman who wore it: A blue mark was worn by a woman who had not married, a red mark by a married woman, and a white mark by a widow. In death, she would be marked with all three, one of each color, whether she had ever married or not. *See also* hadori

Kiam Lopiang. An Aes Sedai who lived at the time of the formation of the White Tower.

Kidron, The Victory of. The three-masted greatship with ribbed sails that brought Tuon from Seanchan to Ebou Dar. Its captain was a woman named Tehan.

Kiem Lewin. A girl in the Two Rivers whom Mat in his youth had tried to save from drowning, although she really hadn't been drowning.

Kigali. An alternate name for the nation of Shara.

Kigarin, Alliandre Maritha. *See* Alliandre Maritha Kigarin

Killers of the Black Veil, The. A flawed book about the Aiel by Soran Milo that Rand read before going to the Waste.

Kimry Lewin. A young woman from Emond's Field. Nynaeve caught her with Bar Dowtry in his father's hayloft; both were punished severely, and a month later were married. It was said that neither could sit for a week after the wedding.

Kimtin. The man who taught Tam to summon the flame and the void.

Kin. A secret organization that harbored women put out of the White Tower and runaways from it. Its ruling body was called the Knitting Circle, and a member of the Kin was called a Kinswoman. There were a total of 1,783 women on the books of the Kin when they were first encountered by Elayne and Nynaeve.

The Kin began by chance during the chaos of the Trolloc Wars. A group of women who had been put out of the White Tower (for the Tower maintained its standards even then) remained together for safety, going to the city which would one day become Ebou Dar. What began as a temporary measure very soon turned into a permanent organization.

Rank among the Kin had nothing to do with strength in the Power; it was based solely on age. The Kin adopted what they believed was an Aes Sedai system of rules and justice (aside from those rules dealing with keeping themselves secret), but since they had knowledge of Aes Sedai ways only from the vantage points of novices or, less often, Accepted, their rules and punishments were much more in accord with those set for novices and Accepted. They were very strict as to behavior in almost every circumstance, few if any excuses were accepted and punishments were the sort that novices and Accepted might have expected—which is to say very high in labor and physical chastisement.

The prime rules were: 1) All Kinswomen were subject to the Rule, even the Eldest. 2) All Kinswomen would obey any order of the Eldest, and those of the Knitting Circle. 3) The existence of the Kin had to be kept secret from anyone who was not a Kinswoman. 4) It was forbidden to claim to be Aes Sedai, or to do anything whatsoever, under any circumstances, that might lead anyone to believe that one was Aes Sedai. 5) It was forbidden to attempt to learn more of the use of the One Power or to try to increase one's skills, abilities or Talents beyond where those things stood when one left the White Tower. 6) It was forbidden to use the One Power except in certain carefully specified instances, or at great need. Anyone using the Power in an instance other than those specified was brought before a court and could receive severe punishment. 7) It was forbidden for anyone save the Knitting Circle or those named by the Knitting Circle to attempt to recruit any woman, or for anyone at all to attempt to recruit any woman who could channel except those who had been put out of the White Tower or had run away.

The Kin had other rules which involved less punishment for violation. They were forbidden to marry, and while in training forbidden to have any relationship with a man. Impatience and hotheadedness were punishable offenses. It was forbidden to speak of returning to the White Tower, or to speak of recruiting girls who could be taught to channel. Many of the rules were intended to prevent Aes Sedai from learning of the Kin's existence; until the fact was revealed to the Kin by Elayne, they were unaware that the Aes Sedai knew of them, although Aes Sedai did not know of their numbers or ages.

There were several kinds of women among the Kin: 1) Former novices who were judged knowledgeable enough of channeling not to harm themselves accidentally, but not able to go further. 2) Women who either failed their test for Accepted, though they survived it, or who refused to continue once it had begun, or who refused for the third time. 3) Women who were unable to advance far enough as Accepted to be selected to take the test for Aes Sedai. 4) Women who failed the test for Aes Sedai three times. 5) A few women who were put out of the Tower for other reasons, usually temperament. The Kin tried to avoid women who were too disruptive, or who were put out for some crimes such as habitual theft. 6) A relative handful of runaways.

The Kin had a few women in Tar Valon who cautiously checked out women expelled from the Tower. These women, called guides, kept an extremely low profile and were changed at regular intervals. The guides made special effort to find runaways, sometimes turning them in if they seemed to need more training, sometimes helping them to escape. Most of those who made it off the island after the Trolloc Wars had Kin help. Of the other women and girls, they approached many, with care, but did not try to recruit them unless they were sure of acceptance. They knew this meant they might pass over some who would accept, yet they were fearful of discovery by the Tower. They checked out any woman who was put out of the Tower, and were quite willing to accept those who fell below the minimum level at which a woman might become Aes Sedai. These constituted a fairly large percentage, perhaps a majority, of their membership.

The Kin made no attempt to find girls who could be taught to channel and train them. Even if they found one, they feared that taking her in would bring adverse attention from the Tower. Some of the women wanted to change this, but under the rules, even if one of them happened to find a girl with the inborn ability, the most she would do was try to draw an Aes Sedai's attention to the girl while claiming to be a wilder herself.

The Kin did not work to perfect their individual abilities with the One Power—at least, they weren't supposed to, by their rules—because they feared acquiring the ageless look and being found out, and for the same reason used the Power sparingly. Some who harbored hopes of returning to the Tower secretly worked to improve their abilities so they could be accepted back, but whenever this was discovered, it was harshly punished; most required no more than one, or at most two, punishments to start following the rules. They did not try to learn anything new, though they did teach or pass on Healing to anyone who could manage it at all. Few realized that many actually honed their abilities in varying degrees over the years.

There was no increase in strength beyond their original potential, of course, but there was an increase in skill. Some who had failed the tests or refused them might be able to pass later because of that increased skill, and also increased maturity. Some of the Kin who were put out of the Tower as Accepted knew how to link, but because of their rules, they never taught it to anyone else or used it, and their skill grew rusty.

A maximum of roughly one hundred, usually many less, of the Kin were in Ebou Dar proper at any one time wearing the red belt. Another fifty to one hundred might be there in various other guises, aside from the Knitting Circle. They often had visitors, including women whose travels as merchants brought them to the city. They did not like to allow their total number in the city to climb too near two hundred at any one time, although they did not count the numbers at the Kin farm in this. A Kinswoman would spend ten years maximum at one time in the city and vicinity; this was called a "turn." Then she would go away from the city, in and out of the farm, traveling, acting as a merchant or trader, maybe spending a few years living here or there. Once a Kinswoman left the city, she did not go back even for a visit for at least twenty years. That was long enough that nobody would associate the returned woman with somebody who looked the same and was apparently the same age, who had left so long before.

A great many of the Kin did have an extensive knowledge of the available herbs and medicines throughout the nations between the Aryth Ocean and the Spine of the World. They traveled widely—Wisdom-equivalent was one of the jobs that they took in various places—and they lived a very long time. The combination gave them a large repository of medicinal knowledge. A great many of the miraculous cures offered by Wise Women in Ebou Dar were indeed done with medicines alone. Because of their rules restricting channeling, they did not leap for the One Power immediately, or at all if they could use their medicinal knowledge.

Egwene as Amyrlin had developed a plan for sisters from the White Tower to be able to retire into the Kin, revoking the Three Oaths, and thereby allowing an extended life well into old age. The Kin would also have been allowed to rejoin the White Tower if they had the strength and desire to do so.

Kin. A juggler with Valan Luca's show. He performed with his brother Bari. Among other things, they worked with ribbon-twined hoops.

Kin Tovere. A Cairhienin lensmaker who made looking glasses for Rand to use in the battle for Cairhien. He joined the School of Cairhien; when he showed Rand plans for a huge looking glass, Rand rewarded him with a prize of a hundred gold crowns. Tovere built it, and through it one could see the moon as plain as one's hand, and what he claimed were other worlds; he intended to build a larger one. Mat won a small looking glass from him at dice; Rand gave Bashere one of Tovere's looking glasses as a gift.

Kinch, Hyam. *See* Hyam Kinch

Kinderode, Temaile. *See* Temaile Kinderode

Kindlin. A captain in Elayne's Queen's Guard in Aringill. He gave Guybon permission to find Guardsmen who had been discharged by Gaebril and take them to Caemlyn.

King's Circle, the. An assembly arena in Tanchico that was surrounded by Lords' palaces and other impressive buildings. It was located on the Maseta, the middle of three hilly peninsulas on Tanchico Bay.

King's Crossing. A village in Altara, where a wooden bridge spanned a narrow river called the Renshalle. A few miles from King's Crossing, at Lady Deirdru's manor, Semirhage tried to ambush Rand, posing as the Daughter of the Nine Moons.

King's Gift. A bounty given out by the King of Cairhien on various occasions, usually to influence the public, although it originally was meant to be a helpful gift. It could be given in times of shortage, when prices were pushed very high, to buy food, or for other reasons. King Galldrian gave silver to performers to entertain the people in the Foregate, and he sponsored daily horse races by the river, to discourage rebellion.

King's Lancer, The. An inn in Sienda, Amadicia. One of Valan Luca's boar-horses knocked a huge hole in it.

King's Life Guard. The personal guard of the King of Tarabon. Located in Tanchico, it numbered about three thousand men, when it existed. It was dispersed by the Seanchan, though many of the surviving men were incorporated into the Seanchan forces.

kingspenny. A plant with red flowers that did not die back in winter; its flower was the first to appear after a forest fire. House Bashere's sign was the kingspenny and its banner had three kingspennies on a field of blue.

Kinhuin. An Aiel *Mera'din* who joined the Jumai Shaido. He had green eyes and full lips. He went to Sevanna and the Wise Ones to ask that the Brotherless receive the same share of loot taken as the Jumai Shaido. A friend of Rolan's, he helped protect Faile and her people; he was especially interested in Alliandre. He helped rescue them from Galina's trap. Faile stabbed him in the back when he threatened Perrin with a spear.

Kinslayer. *See* Lews Therin Telamon

Kinslayer's Dagger. A massif that jutted out from the Spine of the World, aligned east-west between Cairhien and Shienar, near Tar Valon.

Kintara. A nation that arose from the War of the Hundred Years.

Kintara, Hills of. A range just north of and bordering Far Madding.

Kiramin, Lord Mangore. The Sword-bard of Aramaelle, Warder to Caraighan Maconar and translator of *The Prophecies of the Dragon.*

Kiranaille. A wine served at The White Ring in Maderin, Altara.

Kirendad. Seanchan's second-largest city.

Kireyin. A young commander of Ghealdanin lancers under Arganda. He was so tall that he had to bend to listen to Arganda, and Arganda was 5'8" tall. His haughty gaze led Perrin to believe that he was a noble. He led the Ghealdanin soldiers who accompanied Perrin to So Habor. Cold-eyed with a nasal, bored voice, Kireyin openly displayed scorn toward everyone, but broke down when he saw a ghost, though he recovered and resumed his snobbish airs.

Kiril Drapaneos den Alangar. An Illianer nobleman who was a member of the Council of Nine. He was a stork of a man whose square-cut beard looked odd on his narrow face. In Rand's final battle with the Seanchan in Altara, Kiril followed Weiramon into battle.

Kirin. A Jenn Aiel girl from a time right after the Breaking. Morin's daughter, Kirin was kidnapped by people the Jenn Aiel traded with. Morin went to the other Aiel for help in rescuing her, and became the first Maiden of the Spear.

Kirin Melway. An Aes Sedai of the Brown Ajah who served as Amyrlin from 922 to 950 NE. Kirin was a weak Amyrlin, though not so lacking in influence and strength as Aleis. In truth, many of the things she did helped pave the way for a stronger Amyrlin to come after her.

Kirklin, Rovair. *See* Rovair Kirklin

Kirkun. One of Bashere's Saldaean soldiers who died in the Trolloc raid on Lord

Algarin's manor in Tear. Bashere said that he had never guarded his left the way he should.

Kirstian Chalwin. A Kin Elder with the Knitting Circle in Ebou Dar. Her strength level was 14(2); she was strong enough to learn to Travel. Kirstian Chalwin was her real name; she resumed it since she had fled the White Tower so long before that she thought it safe. She was originally from Cairhien, but she went to Ebou Dar from a village near Far Madding. Born in 680 NE, she went to the White Tower in 698 NE. She arrived in the spring and ran away before winter the same year, because of impatience with her progress and impatience with the discipline. She began regretting her departure almost immediately and always wanted to go back, but she was terrified by the stories of the punishments dealt out to runaways. Kirstian was the youngest of the Knitting Circle. About 5'5" tall, with black eyes and pale skin, she was one of the few among the Knitting Circle with neither gray hair nor lines in her face and appeared to be about thirty. When Adeleas recognized Garenia as Zarya, Adeleas wasn't clear about which Kin she had recognized as a runaway from the Tower. Kirstian, who had been sweating ever since she was brought into contact with Aes Sedai, panicked, immediately babbled a confession and began begging for mercy. The result was that she was placed in white and back under novice rules at the same time as Garenia. Most, if not all, of the Kinswomen accepted this—all of the Knitting Circle did, but Alise was one of those who did not.

At the time Elayne and Nynaeve met the Kin, Kirstian was a weaver; she owned and ran a small shop, not tiny but not so large that anyone might question how she could come by it when apparently so young. She employed several other weavers. She accompanied Elayne to Caemlyn and worked under Vandene there.

Kirukan. A soldier queen who was the Queen of Aramaelle. *See also* Sword of Kirukan

Kiruna Nachiman. An Arafellin Aes Sedai of the Green Ajah and the rebel contingent, with a strength level of 14(2). Born in 939 NE, she went to the White Tower in 953 NE. After spending four years as a novice and four years as Accepted, she was raised to the shawl in 961 NE. She had four Warders. Elegant and statuesque, she was 5'7" tall, with a full bosom, large dark eyes and a full mouth. She was the younger sister of King Paitar of Arafel. Kiruna attempted to go the White Tower when she was twelve years old, and tried twice when she was thirteen; on the second attempt, she reached the Tower but was sent home. Her attempts were well known in the Tower. She was finally accepted at fourteen because of her determination. She and Bera Harkin were pillow friends; although both went on to men exclusively later, they remained the closest of friends.

The rebel Aes Sedai sent Bera and Kiruna and their seven Warders to the Aiel Waste to find Rand; when they were halfway there, they heard he was in

Caemlyn and went there. After Rand told the rebel embassy that he was leaving Caemlyn, Bera and Kiruna took over the embassy and decided to follow after him. They and all the members of the embassy were forced to swear fealty to Rand after Dumai's Wells.

These sisters were treated like apprentices by the Wise Ones, and considered apprentices, especially Kiruna, of whom Sorilea made a project. Kiruna at first believed that her being named an apprentice was only a polite fiction to place them in the hierarchy, and she was not pleased by it. She was eventually convinced, if not that she truly was apprenticed to the Wise Ones, at least that there was absolutely no difference between her and an apprentice in the Wise Ones' eyes. "Displeased" did not begin to convey her feelings, but her oath to Rand held her, and the discipline imposed by the Wise Ones was a sharp reminder of the role she had to play. Kiruna, who was the most obviously prideful and most obviously scornful of her so-called place as apprentice, was forced into the most menial chores, plus had her bottom spanked, strapped and/or switched by Sorilea and others at regular intervals for the most trivial fault after arriving in Cairhien; Sorilea intended to teach her the difference between pride and arrogance. She may not have taught Kiruna that, but Sorilea certainly taught her that she had to behave as if she really was an apprentice no matter what she believed. She was killed by Graendal/Hessalam in the Last Battle.

Kiserai ti Wansho! Old Tongue for "Glory to the Builders!"

Kishar, Gerra. *See* Gerra Kishar

Kisman, Raefar. *See* Raefar Kisman

Kiss the Daisies. A kissing game played in the Two Rivers.

Kitan. A maid in Berelain's palace in Mayene who fetched Berelain to see Annoura and Galad, after Annoura rescued Galad in the Last Battle.

Kiyosa Natomo. An Aes Sedai of the Green Ajah who served as Amyrlin from 171 to 197 NE. Kiyosa was a strong Amyrlin, managing Tower affairs through the strength of her will and the force of her personality.

Kiyoshi. An Aes Sedai of the Gray Ajah and the loyalist contingent. A stickler for both punctuality and neatness, she was tall and slender. Kiyoshi was one of those named as adhering to Tower law when Elaida announced the discovery of illegally possessed *angreal*. It was thus implied that she was one of those—along with Doraise and Farellien—who turned in Josaine and Adelorna, the pair who were birched. Like the other two, she received a horse as a reward. Elaida did this at Alviarin's urging; Alviarin was trying to cause dissent in the Tower. Kiyoshi also taught Egwene lessons after Egwene's capture by the White Tower; she sent Egwene to Silviana.

Kline. A Warder who lost his Aes Sedai in the Last Battle and joined Galad to fight on and avenge her.

Knife Hands. An Aiel warrior society also known as *Sovin Nai*.

Knitting Circle. The ruling council of the Kin in Ebou Dar, composed of the thirteen oldest of the Kin in the city of Ebou Dar. They were known as the Elders, with the leader being the Eldest, and also known as the Circle. Everyone had to rotate out of Ebou Dar according to a strict schedule to help them remain unnoticed, but the Elders made sure that sufficient women of a suitable age were in the city at all times. There was never a time when the Knitting Circle was made up of, say, women who were all under two hundred, or even under three hundred. Women younger than three hundred, in fact, were rare in the Knitting Circle. While the rotation in and out of Ebou Dar was maintained strictly, if a woman came to the city who was older than one on the Knitting Circle, she assumed a place on that body for the duration of her visit. Even the Eldest was subject to being displaced if an older woman visited. What kept the oldest members from ignoring the rules and placing themselves in Ebou Dar permanently, or changing the rules to allow themselves to stay in command, were two facts: 1) the members of the Knitting Circle were subject to the Rule, even the Eldest herself, and 2) the Rule could not be changed.

The Eldest was, in many ways, an absolute ruler, yet she, too, could be called down for an offense, judged and given a penance. This happened fairly rarely, but it did happen.

When Reanne and the rest of the Knitting Circle fled Ebou Dar, technically they no longer were the Knitting Circle, since they were no longer in Ebou Dar as specified by the rules. They were still the oldest women in the group, however, and that gave them the authority to keep running things since age was the sole basis of authority among the Kin. If they encountered any Kinswomen who were older, those women would step into the quasi Knitting Circle, displacing younger women and assuming places by strict ranking of age.

Kno'mon. A Trolloc tribe; its symbol was a red bloodstained fist.

Knoks Rebellion. An uprising in Murandy where a group of farmers overthrew Lord Desartin, who deserved it. Androl had participated in the rebellion.

knot. As a point of terminology, in the Age of Legends, channelers did not "tie off" flows, rather they "knotted" flows. Regardless of this semantic difference, a channeler made a knot to tie off a weave so that the flows would hold without further intervention from the channeler. Over time the weave would unravel on its own, or it could be untied by the channeler, although a complex knot could be very difficult to untie. This process was different from unweaving, in which individual threads were loosened and picked out of the weave, like picking stitches out of a piece of embroidery; unweaving could result in disaster if a mistake was made. *See* weave the flows

Knotai. Old Tongue for "devastation" or "ruin"; it was the name given to Mat by Tuon because he was to bring destruction to the Empire's enemies, or maybe because he left a path of destruction wherever he went.

knotting a web. Expression from the Age of Legends that meant tying off a weave.

Ko'bal. A Trolloc tribe; its symbol was a blood-red trident.

ko'di. *See* flame and the void; Oneness; void, the

Kodam. A male Aes Sedai from the time of the Breaking. He was young and barely touched by the taint and helped to create the Eye of the World.

Kodome calichniye ga ni Aes Sedai hei. Old Tongue for "Here is always welcome for Aes Sedai."

Koimal. An Ogier who was the father of Shandin father of Ledar, the last being the author of *A Study of Men, Women and the One Power Among Humans.*

Kolesar. The site of a battle in Mat's memories; there Classen Bayor lost his cavalry in the marshes.

Kolom. Son of Radlin, father of Serden, the last being an Ogier author who theorized about the Ways.

Kolomon, Stedding. A *stedding* located in the Spine of the World.

Kore Springs. A village in Andor where Gareth Bryne had estates. It was a small, single-street village that was neat and orderly; the two-story inn was the largest building in town. Siuan, Leane, Min and Logain were there and burned down a barn; Logain escaped and Bryne presided over the women's trial. Morgase went there after fleeing Gaebril, but Bryne had already left.

kori. A huge spotted cat from the Sen T'jore in Seanchan.

Koronko's Spit. A gambling game from Shienar that was played with five dice.

Kosaan, Venr. *See* Venr Kosaan

Kostelle, Master. An Altaran merchant who played a version of *Piri* with Mat at The White Ring in Maderin, Altara.

Kragil. A soldier in Lan's army who died fighting a Myrddraal; he did something crazy in that fight, according to Andere.

Kralle. A soldier at Heeth Tower whom Malenarin Rai sent to fetch the sword for the ceremony raising his son to manhood.

Kremer Road, the. A road crossing the Proska Flats in Saldaea.

Krisa. A Seanchan woman who brought in three assassins to kill Tuon. Selucia had caught two of them by the time Mat returned to Ebou Dar.

Kuan Murasaka. An acrobat with Valan Luca's show. Dark-haired and dark-skinned, she was one of six purported sisters that Luca hired away from Sillia Cerano.

Kuehn. One of the group of Shienaran soldiers who joined Lan in eastern Kandor as he traveled toward Tarwin's Gap. Andere told the protesting Lan that he had run into Kuehn and the other soldiers before meeting Lan, and had told them to wait along the southern roadway for Lan and his men to come along.

Kumiko. A stout graying Kinswoman who traveled with Elayne to Caemlyn. During one of Arymilla's attacks on Caemlyn, Kumiko was one of the four Kinswomen who made the gateway to take Elayne to see it; when Aviendha mentioned Elayne's reaction to pregnancy, Kumiko laughed really hard.

Kumira Dhoran. A Shienaran Aes Sedai of the Brown Ajah who was uncommitted to any contingent and had a strength level of 24(12). Born in 886 NE, she went to the White Tower in 902 NE. After spending seven years as a novice and nine years as Accepted, she was raised to the shawl in 918 NE. She was 5'5" tall, and handsome rather than pretty, with sharp blue eyes, graceful hands and short hair that was a dark rich brown. In Cadsuane's opinion, Kumira was hard-headed and practical, a keen observer, and never let herself get so deeply lost in thought that she failed to see the world around her. She was interested in everything, and did not want to waste time.

Kumira came from a well-to-do farm family, though her father was a soldier retired because of his wounds; there were many soldiers in her family on both sides. She used the word "peace" as an oath. She was a strong-willed woman, though not as strong-willed as Cadsuane, of course. Sometimes she wore the ink stains common to her Ajah, but they did not escape her notice and she seldom let them stay long. Usually she had a care for others' feelings, especially those who were below her in some way; for instance, she made sure Daigian was not offended by her comment about Daigian's logic. Much more likely to wear good woolens than silk, she did wear a silk scarf now and then. She had no Warder. Kumira was one of the uncommitted Aes Sedai Rand found in Cairhien after Dumai's Wells. She accompanied Cadsuane to the Sun Palace on the day Cadsuane made her agreement with Sorilea; Kumira would try to find some clue to how to work the sworn sisters despite their oaths to Rand. Kumira accompanied Cadsuane to Far Madding and then to Shadar Logoth, where she was killed fighting the Forsaken Graendal.

Kunwar. An area of Saldaea; Tenobia was styled as Lady of Shahayni, Asnelle, Kunwar and Ganai.

Kurenin, Nazar. *See* Nazar Kurenin

Kurin din Calis Red Sails. A Sea Folk Windfinder, formerly on a medium-sized raker, with a strength level of 18(6). She was Windfinder to a Sailmistress who was one of the First Twelve in Ebou Dar before the Seanchan arrived. Her face was like smooth black stone, her full lips seemed thin and her eyes were like black pebbles. She was contemptuous of and impatient with the shorebound. Kurin was one of the twenty Windfinders who accompanied Nynaeve and Lan to the Tarasin Palace; Renaile agreed that those twenty would go wherever needed to use the Bowl of the Winds. When the group was Traveling to the Kin's farm, she didn't pass on Aviendha's message concerning a suspicious figure she saw (Moridin). She observed the use of the Bowl of the Winds, and then fled to Caemlyn with Elayne and her companions. Nynaeve taught Kurin and other Windfinders in the use of the One Power. When Zaida left Caemlyn to elect a new Mistress of the Ships, she left Kurin behind. Kurin and the other Windfinders still in Caemlyn linked and made a gateway so that Birgitte could rescue Elayne from the Black Ajah; they also called down lightning to defeat the Black sisters, and made another gateway so that Elayne's forces could attack Arymilla.

Kurin, Mezar. *See* Mezar Kurin

Kwamesa Taramasu. An Arafellin Aes Sedai of the Gray Ajah and the rebel contingent, with a strength level of 16(4). Born in 950 NE, she went to the White Tower in 965 NE. After spending five years as a novice and four years as Accepted, she was raised to the shawl in 974 NE. Standing 5'3½" tall, she was dark and slender, with a sharp nose and a cold manner. She peered down her nose at everyone, and put great store in ceremony. Some Aes Sedai wanted to hold her longer both as novice and as Accepted because of her youth; she was considered overly precocious by many. Kwamesa was raised a Sitter for the Gray in Salidar in 999 NE; she was the youngest by a matter of months. She voted yes in the war vote and for the alliance with the Black Tower. In the Last Battle, Kwamesa was balefired by Demandred while she was helping to protect the dragons.

Kyera Termendal. A poet of Shiota, and a translator of *The Prophecies of the Dragon* between FY 700 and 800.

Kymer. A Wise One of the Tomanelle Aiel. Han was her sister-father. She had deep red hair and a long, tanned face. When Aviendha returned from her second visit to Rhuidean, she discussed her visions of the future with Kymer, Melaine, Sorilea, Bair and Amys.

Kyril Shianri. A nobleman and counselor to King Paitar of Arafel. He was 6'3" tall, lean and elegant-looking. He wore silver bells on his boot tops and gloves as well as fastened to his braids. His face bore a permanent expression of dissatisfaction and he peered coolly down his prominent nose at anyone but Paitar. He was a fool in many ways, but Arafellin kings seldom listened to their counselors, relying instead on their queens. Kyril accompanied Paitar to his meeting with the other Borderland rulers in the Black Hills.

L

L'Heye, Sea of. A body of water in Seanchan.

Laandon. A member of the Band of the Red Hand who accompanied Faile on supply runs in the Last Battle. When they were near the Blasted Lands and their band was attacked by beasts that looked like bears with too many arms, Mandevwin told Laandon and Verdin that they needed more spears to impale the beasts.

Lace of Ages. *See* Great Pattern

Lacel. An Ogier who was the son of Laud and the father of Juin, the last being the Ogier who stopped the incipient fight between Maidens and Shienarans in Stedding Tsofu, and took Verin, Rand and the rest of their party to the Elders.

Lacile Aldorwin. A Cairhienin member of *Cha Faile*. About 5'3" tall, and slim, with a pale complexion, dark eyes and short dark hair, she was one of the feistiest of the bunch, very prickly about her honor and Faile's. Despite wearing a man's coat and breeches, she kept a few feminine touches, which some others did not, including a graceful walk. She was captured by the Shaido along with Faile; taken by Jhoradin, one of the Brotherless, she took up with him for protection. After Lacile and Arrela attempted escape and were recaptured, they were tied naked on a cart as punishment. Lacile was trapped in the collapsing building by Galina; after they were rescued, she and Arrela killed Jhoradin to stop him from attacking Perrin. She later became interested in Niagen, another Brotherless.

Lacine. A Sea Folk Wavemistress who was one of the First Twelve. She was so slender that her bosom seemed enormous. At the meeting with the others of the First Twelve in Illian, Lacine glared at Harine when her Bargain with Rand was mentioned.

Ladalin. A Wise One of the Taardad Aiel after the Last Battle, seen in Aviendha's viewing of the future in Rhuidean. She was a descendant of Aviendha's who wished that she were able to channel. In the vision, Ladalin met with Mora, Tamaav, Takei and Jorshem and decided that the Aiel must retreat to the Three-fold Land.

Ladoman. King of Coremanda who signed the Compact of the Ten Nations.

Ladwin. A soldier in Mat's Band of the Red Hand. Short, stocky and seemingly mild, Ladwin was embarrassed to have been captured by Warders when approaching Salidar. When Trollocs attacked Caemlyn at the start of the Last Battle, Ladwin fought alongside Talmanes to save the dragons.

Lady of Pain. Another name for Semirhage.

Lady of the Shadows. A Seanchan euphemism for death.

Laefar. An Ogier man from Stedding Shangtai. Loial encountered him in Tear; he informed Loial that he had been declared a runaway and that his mother intended to marry him off.

Laerad. A man of the Moshaine sept of the Shaido Aiel and of the *Duadhe Mahdi'in* society. Grizzled and never one to waste words, he accompanied Maeric through one of Sammael's gateways produced by *nar'baha* on the Plains of Maredo; he reported to Maeric that there were spears to the south.

Laerid Traehand. An Andoran nobleman and High Seat of his House. Stocky and taciturn and normally as stolid as stone, he was loyal to Elayne; he rode to her support with as many men as he could gather, and did not turn back on learning the odds. Laerid did not hesitate to lead his men against the Black Ajah when they held Elayne.

Laero lendhae an indemela. An Old Tongue saying of the Fallen Army of Kardia meaning "The enemy's flag has fallen." Mat recalled it from his old memories.

Lahpoint Hills. Where Birgitte in a past life as Jethari Moondancer led the Buchaner rebellion.

Laigin Arnault. A Taraboner Aes Sedai of the Red Ajah and the loyalist contingent. She was part of the group that kidnapped Rand and died at Dumai's Wells. Even though she had been part of his imprisonment, Rand thought of her as having died for him.

Laila Dearn Lewin. A young woman of the Two Rivers. Before she married Natley Lewin, she was slim and could dance three boys into the ground. At one time, Perrin wanted to marry her, and she him. When Perrin saw her at Jac al'Seen's farm after her marriage, she had grown stout and had an infant.

Lain. A man in Bandar Eban for whom Votabek and Redborn were working. They figured that Lain was not going to pay them, so they agreed to join the army that Durnham started under Rand's direction.

Lain Mandragoran. A Malkieri man who was the brother of al'Akir and Lan's uncle. He and al'Akir were very close, and the people of Malkier loved him; he was one of the great heroes of the Borderlands. Out of envy, his wife Breyan dared him to lead his lances through the Blight to the Blasted Lands, perhaps to Shayol Ghul itself; Lain and most of the men with him were killed.

Lairain. An Aes Sedai of the Brown Ajah who was toadlike in appearance. She gave Egwene instructions on the ceremony to be raised Amyrlin after the Tower was reunited.

Laird. A member of the Children of the Light who believed that a dead channeler's head should be cut off and buried separately from the body to prevent him or her returning to life.

Laiwynde. A daughter of Artur Hawkwing. She and her son died a tragic death; word of that arrived less than an hour after Hawkwing's death.

Lake Somal. A location in Arad Doman that Ituralde thought of when reflecting on his past military victories.

Laman Damodred. A king of Cairhien who took the throne in 965 NE. Laman was the uncle of Moiraine Damodred, the older brother of her father Dalresin. Laman cut down *Avendoraldera* to make a throne, which started the Aiel War. He became known as Laman Treekiller. After three years of battle, the Aiel killed him and returned to the Aiel Waste.

Laman had two other younger brothers, Moressin and Aldecain. Unlike Moiraine's father, the pair had dark reputations; Moressin and Aldecain were as bad as or worse than Laman. Their behaviors were marked by increasingly ugly deeds, until their deaths in the Aiel War.

Laman's Pride or Laman's Sin. A reference to King Laman of Cairhien's cutting down *Avendoraldera*.

Laman's sword. An ornate sword belonging to King Laman of Cairhien. The scabbard was so encrusted with rubies and moondrops that it was hard to see the gold except where a rising sun of many rays had been inset. The ivory hilt, long enough for two hands, had another inlaid rising sun in gold; the pommel was thick with rubies and moondrops, and still more made a solid mass along the quillons. The sword was taken as a trophy by some Aiel after Laman was killed during the fighting around Tar Valon, during the Aiel War. The fact that it was a sword meant that no Aiel really wanted to keep it, despite the gems, so when Aviendha thought to pay off her *toh* to Rand in "cash," so to speak, she was able to acquire the whole thing to give him, scabbard and all. She carried it wrapped in a blanket because the Wise Ones told her that way she was not actually carrying it as a sword, so it didn't break the prohibition. Rand refused to accept the jeweled scabbard, leaving it to Aviendha, and tried to give her the jeweled hilt as well, which angered her since he had tested the sword using that hilt and had thus already accepted it, in her eyes. Rand gave away the hilt, also, but where or to whom was unknown.

Lamelle. A woman of the Smoke Water sept of the Miagoma Aiel and *Far Dareis Mai*. She was lean with dark red hair and a strong jaw. She was one of the three worst at mothering Rand; she made him soup, but was a terrible cook, so it tasted bad. Her throat was ripped out in the battle for Caemlyn against Rahvin, and Rand added her name to the list of women who had died for him.

Lamgwin Dorn. A bouncer at The Queen's Blessing, Caemlyn. Born in 951 NE, he was a hulking fellow with scars on his face and his hands, and a voice that sounded like gravel in a pan. He was 6'2" to 6'3" tall, lazy-eyed and heavy-lidded, a thug, with broad shoulders and sunken knuckles. Lamgwin was more accustomed to using his fists or a cudgel than any other weapon. He was devoted to Queen Morgase and later also to Breane Taborwin, when they met and fell in love. All he knew for sure of Rand was his belief that he would be a good man in a fight, plus rumors that he was some kind of prince or lord.

Lamgwin remembered Mat largely from his first visit, when sickly; at a second visit he knew that Mat got into some kind of trouble with Gaebril's men at the palace, which was well with him. When Faile took Maighdin's group into her service, Lamgwin became Perrin's bodyservant.

Lamma Sor. A day of prayers for those who had fallen defending against the Blight, and for those who would fall in future. It was observed on the day after the first quarter moon (called a "knife moon") in the month of Saban in the Borderlands. Nothing was eaten but bread and water, salt and oil. It was also called the Day of Remembrance.

Lamplighters. A group that patrolled the streets of Canluum all night to ensure that lamps remained lit, essential in a Borderland city.

Lan Mandragoran. A man who was by right the King of Malkier, Lord of the Seven Towers, Lord of the Lakes, True Blade of Malkier. He was called "the Uncrowned" in the Borderlands, and Dai Shan, meaning a Diademed Battle Lord.

The Aiel called him *Aan'allein*, meaning in Old Tongue "One Man," or "the Man Who Is an Entire Nation." He served as Warder to Moiraine Damodred, then to Myrelle Berengari, and finally to his wife, Nynaeve al'Meara.

Lan was born in 953 NE. He was 6'5½" tall, and heavy in the shoulders, though he had a narrow waist. He weighed about 245 pounds and had sharp blue eyes and dark hair streaked with gray that was long enough to touch his shoulders, but held back by a braided leather band. His face seemed to be made of planes and angles, carved from stone, and his hands were large and square. Women had considered him beautiful when he was a boy, but he lost that as he aged, so that Edeyn Arrel could tell him he was no longer beautiful in early 979 NE.

As Malkier was falling, Lan was named Dai Shan in his cradle and consecrated as the next King of Malkier. Twenty men were given charge of the infant Lan, to take him safely out of Malkier. Only five of those survived to reach Shienar; Bukama was the last one of them to die. Lan received his sword at age ten, which was very young, and he had begun training with it years earlier. The early training was not uncommon, especially in the Borderlands, but his was particularly intense.

Lan's *carneira* was the Lady Edeyn ti Gemallen Arrel, a widow of thirty-five to his fifteen with one surviving child, a daughter then seven, Iselle, whom

Edeyn later wanted Lan to marry. He was given the *hadori* at sixteen and promptly began his war against the Shadow.

Although he always refused to lead men in the Blight, he did lead men in the Aiel War, in which he fought for two years. At the Blood Snow, he led almost five hundred men—Kandori, Saldaeans, some Domani—on the morning of the first day of the battle, and by the end of the third day, half of them were dead or wounded. He had an estate of moderate size in Shienar, granted him when he reached manhood. Lan could read Trolloc runes with fair accuracy and could read and speak the Old Tongue fluently. He was an excellent tracker—he could follow a moonbeam's path over stone two days later, it was said—and was also expert at hiding his trail.

Lan was one of the best swordsmen of his Age; he had the right to wear a heron-marked blade, but he would not give up the simple, unmarked blade he wore, though, of course, it was Power-wrought, made during the War of the Shadow. The single-edged, slightly curved blade, it was believed, was an ordinary soldier's weapon in the War of Power, and became the sword of Malkieri kings.

Lan also had a number of Warder-bond-given skills: he could go longer without food, water or rest than other men, even hardened fighting men; he healed more quickly; he could sense Myrddraal and Trollocs to some extent—a Warder's range was as good as or better than that of the Aes Sedai—and he could smell the presence of a Myrddraal a day or two after it was gone. He could sense a Darkfriend who was very far gone in the Shadow, but few were so far gone even among the worst.

He met Moiraine in Kandor in 979 NE, soon after she was raised Aes Sedai. She attempted to take his sword; he threw her in a pond. She bonded him a short time later, and for more than twenty years they worked side by side. Their relationship was never sexual, though there were occasional tensions of that nature. Many women threw their hearts at Lan's feet or climbed into Lan's bed, and Moiraine never felt jealousy until she had a flash at Tifan's Wells, while thinking that Nynaeve was capturing Lan's heart and soul and loyalties despite all he could do, a fight she knew he did not want to win even while he was trying to. Lan loved Nynaeve very deeply, and felt that he was the last man in the world she should love. He had his personal war with the Shadow that he could not give up, and all he could give her was a widow's clothes. He would have liked to stay away from her, to cut the lines between them cleanly; it hurt to be near her and be sure he could never marry her. On the other hand, there was nothing he wanted more than her safety, unless it was her happiness.

Moiraine arranged for the bond to be passed to Myrelle if anything should happen to her. When she disappeared through the redstone doorway *ter'angreal* fighting Lanfear, the bond passed and he went to Myrelle. He wanted to die, but Egwene sent him to protect Nynaeve in Ebou Dar, and he saved her life as soon as he arrived. He married Nynaeve in a ceremony performed by the

Mistress of the Ships to the Sea Folk in the harbor of Ebou Dar. The ceremony included a pledge that one of them would command in public, that it might be either at different times, but that whoever commanded in public must obey in private.

Nynaeve knew that Lan had made love with Myrelle, which he did in an attempt to break himself from Nynaeve. Myrelle had other motives—to focus Lan on life again—but so long as the topic was avoided, Nynaeve could ignore it; he was very much aware of the situation.

He persuaded Nynaeve to take him to the Borderlands so that he could continue his fight against the Shadow; she arranged for people to learn that he was riding for Tarwin's Gap, and an army joined him. After Nynaeve completed her Aes Sedai test, Myrelle passed the bond to her. Lan fought valiantly in the Last Battle and killed Demandred.

Lanasiet, Tornay. *See* Tornay Lanasiet

Lances, Ingathering of the. A term used by Agelmar to describe the Shienarans coming together to defend their border.

Lances, Plain of. Flatlands situated in the northern portions of Saldaea and Kandor in the Borderlands.

Land of the Madmen. A third continent, well south of the Sea of Storms, discovered by the Sea Folk; little was known of it. The landmass experienced continual seismic activity and devastating storms, and icebergs filled the surrounding oceans. The people of this continent lived a primitive and violent life. They never recovered from the Breaking; channelers, male and female, abounded; the men were mad and the women all but, never having organized to resist the destruction wrought by their male counterparts. The remainder of the population lived in small communities that formed mobs to kill strangers who wandered into their territory. The continued existence of the Land of the Madmen could be attributed in part to the fact that many of the male channelers had developed blocks which limited or prevented them from using the One Power.

Land, Three-fold. The Aiel term for the Aiel Waste. They believed that the Waste was a shaping stone to make them, a testing ground to prove their worth and a punishment for their sin. *See also* Waste, the

Landalin. A lieutenant at Heeth Tower. He was roused to take command of the top of the tower after a single flash was received from Rena Tower's signal light.

Lanelle. *See* lanelle

Lanfear. One of the Forsaken. She was born Mierin Eronaile and was romantically involved with Lews Therin Telamon for a time. Her strength level was 1(+12). She was also known as Daughter of the Night, and the wolves called her Moonhunter. In the Age of Legends, she was a research scientist, if neither the most accomplished nor the most distinguished, studying new methods of using the One Power. Her search for an alternative led to the Bore. She considered *Tel'aran'rhiod* her personal property and liked to claim that no one was more skilled there than she—a claim which made it into the history books as truth—but others did exceed her ability. About 5'11" tall, she had large dark eyes and waves of raven-black hair. Slender and very beautiful, she had skin that was creamy pale and smooth. She loved Lews Therin with a possessiveness and jealousy near to madness. She had always hated Ilyena and believed that Ilyena stole Lews Therin from her.

When she awakened in the Third Age, she transferred that passion to Rand. She posed as Selene, a Cairhienin noblewoman, traveled with him, and attempted to seduce him. When Rand was in the Waste, she posed as Keille Shaogi, a peddler. Posing as Silvie, she attempted to bamboozle Egwene in the World of Dreams. For a time she actually aided Rand, so long as she could do it without danger to herself, at first with the notion that she would bring him to the Shadow, later with the thought that, using the great statue *sa'angreal,* the two of them could challenge the Dark One, even the Creator. She helped Rand against the other Forsaken insofar as she could without exposing herself; she was playing both sides against the middle. She wanted Rand to win, but if he went down, she had no intention of falling with him. She had no intention of going over to the Light; she wanted power, much more than she could possibly have had on the side of the Light, and she wanted immortality. Her ultimate goal was to defeat the Dark One, leaving her and Rand immortal and ruling the world.

Once she learned that Rand had bedded Aviendha, she went over the edge; she was ready to torture him, to take him away and make him her devoted slave, or to kill him if she could not break him. Only Moiraine's intervention saved him. In the fight between the two women, both were transported to the realm of the Eelfinn and Aelfinn. Moridin found Lanfear there; he killed her and her soul was placed in a new body. She was given the name of Cyndane, which was Old Tongue for "Last Chance." *See also* **Cyndane**

Lanita. A novice or Accepted with a potential strength level of 26(14). Born in 977 NE, she went to the White Tower in 994 NE. After Siuan was deposed, she was taken by the rebels to Salidar. There, she was part of a circle led by Anaiya fighting a bubble of evil.

Lannis. An ancient scholar from the Blue Ajah who wrote of the Forsaken.

Lantoine, Stedding. A *stedding* located in the Spine of the World.

Lara Ayellin. A Two Rivers girl. When Moiraine mentioned that another woman in Emond's Field could channel, Egwene thought that it might be Kari Thane or Lara Ayellin.

Larapelle. The site of one of the many victories of Rashima Kerenmosa, the Soldier Amyrlin.

Laras. The chief cook in the White Tower. Siuan gave her the formal title of Mistress of the Kitchens in the White Tower when Siuan toured the kitchens, while Nynaeve, Egwene and Elayne were working there as punishment for their trip to Falme. Laras was a beauty in her youth; at the time of the Aiel War she was plump, but later became more than merely stout, with layers of chins, and a spotless white apron that could have made three novice dresses. She thought of herself as once having been a foolish girl, doing foolish things, and near to getting herself hanged sometimes.

When Min was posing in the Tower as a foolish young woman under her full name, Elmindreda, Laras took Min under her wing and gave her advice on makeup, flirting and proper behavior. She helped Min free Siuan and Leane, but decided not to go too far, as she had to live there; she said that she would give them an hour, then send food and wine to the guards. She liked Min, but one Amyrlin was the same as another to her; Aes Sedai folderol was too far above her for her to concern herself.

Laras was protective of Egwene after her capture by Elaida, keeping the kitchen help from playing pranks on her, but otherwise showed her no open favoritism. She did object to all the beatings Egwene was receiving, and tried to persuade Egwene to leave the Tower, offering her help in doing so.

When Verin returned to the Tower, Laras brewed a sweet tea for Verin to put her poison in.

In the Last Battle, Laras gave the Horn of Valere to Faile, although it was said to be Two Rivers tabac in the chest.

Larcheen. A place in the Age of Legends that inspired the saying "as black as midnight in Larcheen."

Larelle Tarsi. A Domani Aes Sedai of the Gray Ajah, with a strength level of 14(2). Born in 732 NE, she was beautiful, with copper skin. The girls she lectured were torn between being intimidated by her and wanting to be her. They all thought her the perfect Aes Sedai. She was one of Tamra's searchers for the infant Dragon Reborn, though neither Moiraine nor Siuan knew this until too late to save her. She was killed in Kandor in 979 NE by Merean Redhill, shortly after Moiraine and Siuan left Canluum.

Laren. A senior maid at the Tarasin Palace in Ebou Dar, the final servant Mat encountered when he visited the Tarasin Palace for the first time and therefore the oldest. She was a round woman who had a touch of gray at her temples and a stately carriage. She wore a marriage knife with five white stones in the hilt, two set in red, and four red stones, one surrounded by black, meaning that three of her nine children were dead, two sons in duels. She had dark eyebrows and nearly black eyes. Laren knew about Mat and Tylin from the start, rescuing Mat from the Aes Sedai tug-of-war with a summons from the Queen and bringing Mat the basket with oysters before the trip to the Rahad.

Larie. The *damane* name of Lemore, a noblewoman from Tanchico. *See* Lemore

Larine Ayellin. A Two Rivers girl with channeling ability. She became a novice with the rebel Aes Sedai, having been recruited by Verin and Alanna. She was Dav's sister and about eighteen years old. Larine was pretty and willowy and wore her hair in a braid. She had a high opinion of herself.

Larinen, Mirane. *See* Mirane Larinen

Larisen, Annoura. *See* Annoura Larisen

Larisett, Atuan. *See* Atuan Larisett

Larissa Lyndel. An Aes Sedai of the Yellow Ajah in public and the Black Ajah in truth. She was part of the rebel contingent, with a strength level of 28(16). A bony woman whose plainness almost overcame her Aes Sedai agelessness, Larissa was one of those who cornered Nynaeve after she Healed Siuan and Leane. Larissa had not been present when Nynaeve Healed Siuan and Leane, and she definitely wanted her chance at Nynaeve's knowledge, and her chance at being the one to break Nynaeve's block.

Larissa's name was found on Verin's list of the Black Ajah.

Laritha. A woman whom Thom once tried to rescue. She was a rose in bud, and married to a brutish bootmaker in a village Thom visited; her husband shouted at her if his meal wasn't ready, and switched her if she spoke more than two words to another man. She moaned to Thom that she wished someone would rescue her, but when he offered to take her away, she kicked him in the knee and hit him with a bench. Outraged that Thom thought that she would ever leave her beloved husband, Laritha ran to her husband to tell him of Thom's offer; Thom had to leave the village quickly, leaving most of his possessions behind. He later learned that Laritha held the purse strings tight and cracked her husband in the head with whatever was at hand when he stopped by the inn for some ale.

larksbrush. A bush with tiny, faintly blue leaves and gnarled branches.

Last Battle, the. A wide-ranging war wherein prophecies indicated that the Dragon Reborn would fight the Dark One to save the World. It was also known as Tarmon Gai'don. The battle was fought on two fronts: 1) Thakan'dar and Shayol Ghul, and 2) the lands south of the Great Blight. The Last Battle began when a Trolloc army emerged from a Waygate in Caemlyn, followed quickly by two separate enemy invasions from the Blight through Kandor and Tarwin's Gap. The Shadowspawn army fought their way north from Caemlyn as the other two invading armies, including Sharans led by Demandred, went generally south, with the purpose of enveloping and crushing the forces of Light. At Thakan'dar, the Shadowspawn armies poured through the mountain passes and fought against defenders from the south and the Aiel Waste, as Rand engaged the Dark One in the Pit of Doom at Shayol Ghul. The forces of Light prevailed on both fronts and the Dark One was contained once again, which marked the beginning of the Fourth Age.

Last Days. The end of a cycle of the Wheel of Time, when the Dark One came out of captivity and the Last Battle was fought.

Last Hunt, the. The wolves' term for the Last Battle.

Lastriders. A group that left Maradon during the Trolloc attack. They watched the battle from afar and were supposed to get word to other forces in Saldaea for help if the city fell. The group was led by Yoeli's sister Sigril.

Latar, Serenia. *See* Serenia Latar

Latelle. A woman who trained bears in Valan Luca's circus. She was stern-faced

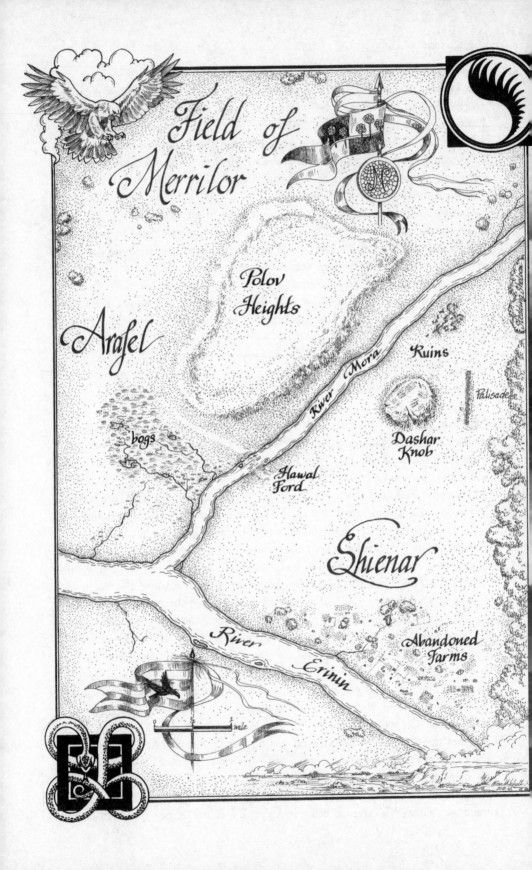

Field of
Merrilor

Polov
Heights

Arafel

River Mora

Ruins

Palisade

bogs

Dashar
Knob

Hawal
Ford

Shienar

River

Erinin

Abandoned
Farms

1 mile

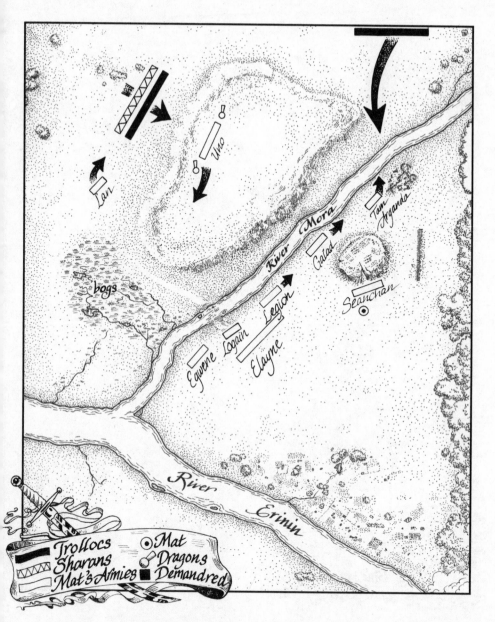

Trollocs
Sharans
Mat's Armies
⊙ Mat
Dragons
Demandred

LAST BATTLE MAP 1: Some of Mat's forces—defensive lines of pikemen, archers, and dragons—are massed on Polov Heights as huge armies of Trollocs and Sharans appear in the west. Mat sets up a Seanchan camp at the base of Dashar Knob, while most of his armies under Elayne array themselves along the left bank of the River Mora. Lan's army goes across Hawal Ford to hit the approaching armies' right flank and contain them, making them more vulnerable to the dragons. Mat gives the order to the defenders on the Heights to retreat, just as Demandred, leading the enemy, unleashes a devastating barrage of the One Power. As a second large army of Shadowspawn appears in the north, Tam's armies move upriver near a cluster of ruins to repel them.

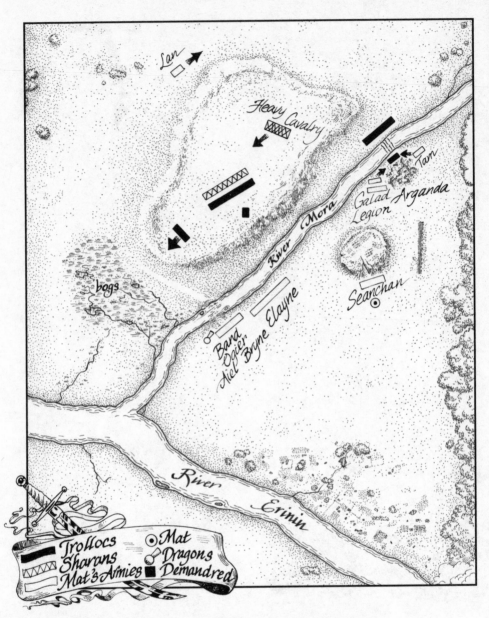

LAST **BATTLE MAP 2**: The armies of Trollocs and Sharans from the west capture Polov Heights, with Demandred positioning himself on a steep promontory overlooking the River Mora. Many of the dragons have been destroyed or damaged. A large group of Trollocs begins descending the southwestern slope of the Heights, while Mat's forces and remaining dragons position themselves across Hawal Ford to meet the onslaught. Demandred keeps the Sharans on the Heights. Lan, meanwhile, moves around the western side of the Heights. The Trollocs from the north build raft bridges across the Mora upstream at the Ruins and are attacked by Tam's troops as they cross the river. Demandred is clearly trying to envelop Mat's forces on the Shienaran side of the Mora.

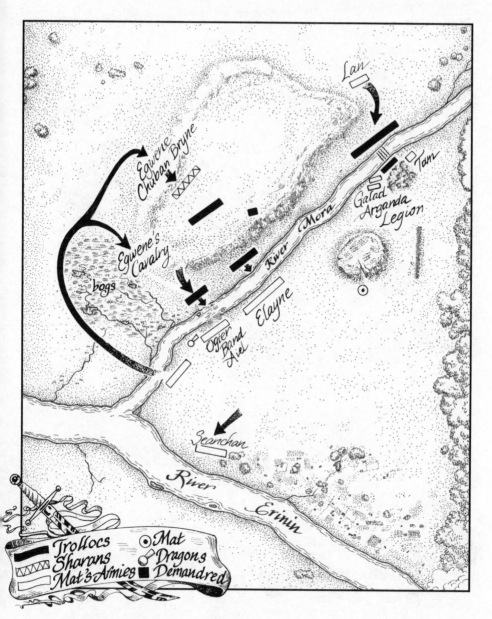

LAST BATTLE MAP 3: Egwene's combined forces of soldiers and channelers cross the Mora on raft bridges and swing around the bogs to initiate a two-pronged attack. Mat sets fire to the southern slopes of Polov Heights, temporarily halting the descent of the Trollocs to Hawal Ford. By the time the Trollocs are able to recommence their descent, Egwene is in place, sending her cavalry against their rear flanks near the Ford, while the main body of her army attempts to advance up the western slope of the Heights. Mat's forces hold a defensive line across the River Mora, sustaining attacks by Demandred. Tam's armies upriver are successful repelling the Trollocs at the river, aided by Lan's attack on their rear flanks. Mat and Tuon have a fake argument at Dashar Knob, and the Seanchan leave the battlefield, camping in the south at the River Erinin.

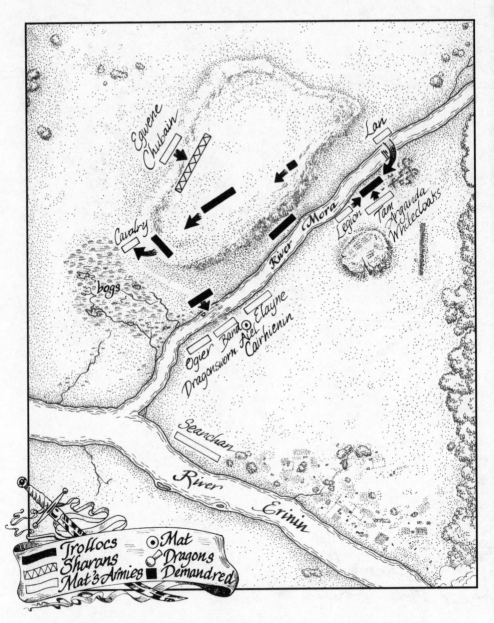

Egwene
Chubain

Lan

Cavalry

Legion

Tam

Arganda
Whitecloaks

River Mora

bogs

Ogier Band Elayne
Dragonsworn Aiel Cairhienin

Searchan

River

Erinin

Trollocs
Sharans
Mat's Armies

•Mat
Dragons
Demandred

LAST **BATTLE** MAP 4: Egwene is shaken by Gawyn's death. The Sharan
channelers go head-to-head against Egwene's struggling channelers at the western
slope of the Heights, while many of the Trollocs descend the southwestern slope,
sweeping away Egwene's cavalry, attempting to cross Hawal Ford, and massing
on the Arafellin side of the Mora to attack Mat's defenders. Mat's forces are hard-
pressed and continue to be pounded by Demandred and the Shadow's forces. But
the battle is going better upriver at the ruins, where Tam's and Lan's armies decisively crush the Trollocs in a pincer action.

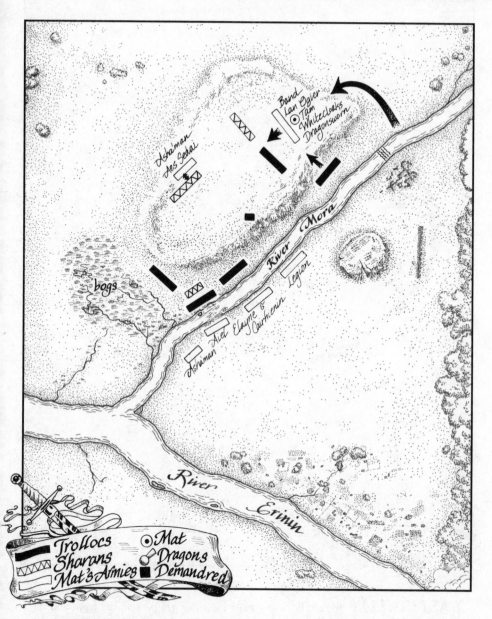

LAST BATTLE MAP 5: Demandred's troops far upriver manage to dam the River Mora, drying it up and making it easier for the Trollocs to cross the riverbed. Asha'man and Aes Sedai continue to fight against Sharan channelers on the western slope of Polov Heights. Egwene dies, but not before killing all the Sharan channelers. The Dark One's forces are on the verge of overwhelming the defensive lines on the Shienaran side of the Mora, when Mat and his mobile units charge up the northeastern slope of the Heights, forcing the Sharans and Trollocs to fight on that front rather than descend and crush the defenders at the Mora.

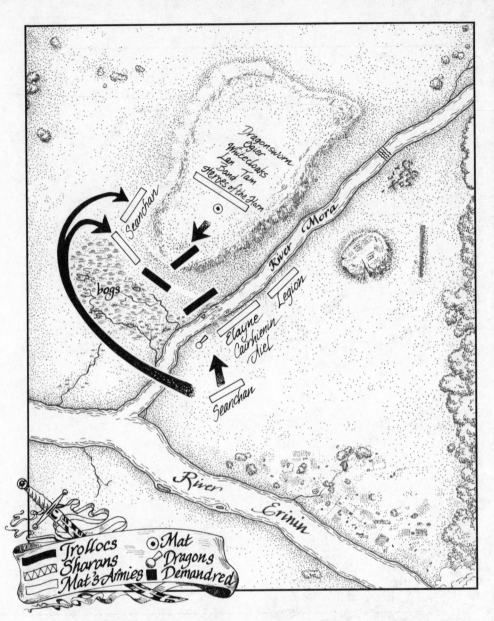

Map labels: Seanchan; bogs; Dragonsworn; Ogier; Whitecloaks; Lan; Tam; Band; Heroes of the Horn; River Mora; Legion; Elayne; Cauthienin; Tiel; Seanchan; River Erinin

Legend: Trollocs; Sharans; Mat's Armies; Mat; Dragons; Demandred

LAST BATTLE MAP 6: The repaired dragons are back in the fight, and the River Mora is again filled with flowing water. But the fate of the outnumbered forces of the Light looks bleak except for three major events: Lan slays Demandred, disorienting many of the enemy; Olver blows the Horn of Valere, bringing the heroes of the Horn into the fray alongside Mat and his troops; and the Ever Victorious Army of the Seanchan enter the battle. The Seanchan march north, with one half of the army bolstering the defenses along the Mora, while the other half swing around the bogs and position themselves at the base of Polov Heights. Many Sharan soldiers manage to escape after Demandred's death, but the remaining Trollocs are pushed down the southwestern slope of Polov Heights into a cul-de-sac, many becoming trampled by fellow Shadowspawn in the congestion, or shot with arrows or dragons' eggs, or torn apart by Seanchan exotic animals. The frenzied remainder throw themselves into the bogs, where they meet their deaths.

and dark-eyed, with short black hair and the permanent beginnings of a sneer on her lips. She had two black bears with white faces. Latelle gave no welcome to Elayne and Nynaeve; she was jealous of other women's interest in Luca, and Luca's interest in them. When Nynaeve had the Chavanas over for dinner and they started flirting with Nynaeve, Latelle attacked her with a stick; when Nynaeve and Cerandin were fighting, Latelle handed Cerandin a stick. She was a terrible cook and later married Valan Luca.

Lathin. A Whitecloak soldier who was killed by Hopper in the *stedding* that featured Hawkwing's statue.

Latian Basar. A young Cairhienin nobleman who was a member of *Cha Faile*. Short and pale, he had a pointed nose and shoulder-long hair tied off in a tail at the nape of his neck, in weak imitation of the Aiel cut. His coat was marked with four slashes of red and blue across the chest. He was one of the seven who first met Rand and Perrin after Dumai's Wells. Latian went off with Balwer and Medore in So Habor and stayed after Perrin and the rest of his party left; four days later they returned with Tallanvor. He did not play well at being a spy; when he tried to be surreptitious about giving Perrin a message from Balwer, everyone knew exactly what he was doing.

Latra Posae Decume. An Aes Sedai at the time of the War of Power. She opposed Lews Therin's plan of sealing the Bore because she thought that it was too dangerous, and favored the use of the Choedan Kal. A speaker of considerable force and persuasion, she gathered a great deal of support, but what assured her victory was an agreement she arranged with every female Aes Sedai of significant strength on the side of the Light; all pledged not to assist Lews Therin in his risky plan. This agreement came to be known as the Fateful Concord. When the *ter'angreal* to control the Choedan Kal were lost, the female Aes Sedai held to their pledge and hoped to regain the access keys. Thus Lews Therin and his companions were unable to use a circle to seal the Bore, although they did complete the task, with the dire result of the taint on *saidin*. Latra Posae rose to preeminence, earning the name Shadar Nor, best translated as "Cutter of the Shadow" or perhaps "Slicer of the Shadow," for her valiant fight against the Shadowsworn. She died sometime during the Breaking.

Laud. An Ogier who was the father of Lacel and the grandfather of Juin, the last being the Ogier who stopped the incipient fight between Maidens and Shienarans in Stedding Tsofu and took Verin, Rand and the rest of their party to the Elders.

Laurain. A noblewoman attending Morgase in Amadicia. Slender with dark eyes set slightly too close together, she wore a permanent simper. She was made *da'covale* by the Seanchan.

Laurel Crown of Illian. The crown of the ruler of Illian. After Rand was given the crown by the Council of the Nine, it became known as the Crown of Swords. It was a heavy gold circlet, two inches wide, of golden laurel leaves; almost buried among the laurel leaves of the crown were the sharp points of swords, half point up, half down. No head could wear that crown easily.

Law of Unintended Consequences, the. Spoken of by Siuan, it stated "whether or not what you do has the effect you want, it will have three at least you never expected, and one of those usually unpleasant."

Law of War. A Tower law stating that a question of war cannot be shelved; it must be answered before any question called after it.

Lawdrin Mendair. A Redarm in the Band of the Red Hand who accompanied Mat to Ebou Dar. On the way there, Elayne somehow discovered that he had five flasks of brandy in his saddlebags; Mat poured them out on the ground. When they went to retrieve the Bowl of the Winds at a deserted building in the Rahad, Mat sent Lawdrin, Harnan and four others around to the back of the building; all but Harnan were killed by the *gholam.*

Lawtin. A Redarm in the Band of the Red Hand. He accompanied Mat to Ebou Dar. He and Belvyn were sent with Nynaeve on a visit to the Sea Folk; both Redarms were killed when Moghedien balefired their boat.

Layden, Barel. *See* Barel Layden

Layden, House. A minor noble House of Andor. Its High Seat was Lord Barel.

leading. Controlling the link of a circle made by channelers; also known as focusing or guiding.

Leafblighter. The Aiel name for the Dark One.

Leafblighter's get. An Aiel name for Trollocs.

Leafhunter. A wolf who was the leader of her pack. She had a feel of quiet certainty; her mate was Feather. Perrin spoke with Leafhunter's pack after encountering a scent in the wolf dream that made his hackles rise (Darkhounds). When he asked the pack about it, they all shut him out one by one; Leafhunter was the last, saying simply, "The Last Hunt is coming."

Leane Sharif. A Domani Aes Sedai of the Blue Ajah originally, but later of the Green. She was the first sister ever to have changed her Ajah so far as any records showed. A member of the rebel contingent, she had a strength level of 14(2) before she was stilled and Healed; it was reduced to 36(24) afterward. Born in 952 NE to a merchant family, she went to the White Tower in 967 NE. After spending five years as a novice and four years as Accepted, she was raised to the shawl in 976 NE. About 5'10" to 5'11" tall, she was willowy, graceful and coppery-skinned, with a brisk, clipped way of speaking, except when talking to men, or sometimes about them. She was Keeper of the Chronicles for Siuan until they were deposed and stilled. After being stilled, she looked young, about twenty-two or twenty-three years old, and no longer like an Aes Sedai. With Min's help she and Siuan escaped Tar Valon and made their way to Salidar with Logain in tow. On the way, they accidentally burned down a barn in Kore Springs; Logain escaped but the women were tried by Gareth Bryne, who sentenced them to work for him until they had earned enough to pay for the barn and the cows in it. They swore an oath to do so, but Siuan noted that they had not said when, and all fled with Logain when he rescued them.

Although Leane had fairly small ability with Healing, she seemed to have the greatest ability with metals after Egwene, and she had an extensive network of eyes-and-ears; both made her a valuable asset to Egwene. Leane's connection with Egwene remained a secret for a long time while they were in Salidar, as was the fact that she was no longer bound by the Three Oaths.

After Bryne arrived in Salidar, Leane, Siuan and Min were made to serve him as they had sworn to do.

Once Nynaeve Healed Leane, she chose to be a member of the Green Ajah instead of the Blue. She was quite cosseted by most of the other sisters for how well she had adjusted to her reduction in strength.

As part of the rebel Aes Sedai siege of the White Tower, Leane was to convert the harbor chain at Southharbor into heartstone; she had it half done when she was captured, and it still managed to block all but the shallowest draft ships from entering. When she was taken back to the Tower, no one believed that she was who she said she was. She was imprisoned; Egwene visited her frequently, as did many Aes Sedai wanting to learn to Travel. A bubble of evil caused her cell to melt like wax, but quick action by Egwene saved her. She was freed when Egwene was raised Amyrlin for the united Tower. Leane attended Egwene's meeting with Wise Ones and Sea Folk in *Tel'aran'rhiod*; when the Black Ajah attacked, she stayed and fought, and though she was injured, she was Healed. Demandred captured her when he and the Sharans joined the Last Battle; he sent her with a message to Rand that if Rand did not face him, he would destroy all that Rand cared about. In the Last Battle, Leane was nearby when Egwene died.

Leanna ti Arathdar Mandragoran. Lan's mother, the last Queen of Malkier. She was also known as el'Leanna. When Malkier was overrun with Trollocs, Leanna and her husband Akir had Lan brought to them in his cradle and gave him a sword and a locket and consecrated him as the next King of Malkier. They then sent him with twenty soldiers to Fal Moran. Al'Akir and el'Leanna were killed at Herot's Crossing, and Malkier was lost.

Leashed Ones. *See damane*

leatherleaf. A tall, rough-trunked evergreen tree with tough broad leaves and thick branches. It grew in copses and could become a towering tree, although in the tall mountains it tended to be scrubby and wind-twisted. Leatherleaf's natural range was extensive.

Ledar. The Ogier author of *A Study of Men, Women and the One Power Among Humans*, a book Loial considered one of the best about Aes Sedai dealing with men who could channel. Ledar was the son of Shandin son of Koimal. Loial also used the name Ledar to disguise his identity.

Ledron. A citizen of Hinderstap who spoke with Mayor Barlden about the papers with Mat's likeness promising money for information about Mat's whereabouts. Mayor Barlden told him that he was not in the business of selling out guests.

Leeh. A Maiden of the Spear sent after Weiramon and Anaiyella when Rand outed them as Darkfriends.

Leems. An Asha'man who was Taim's crony and was fond of wine. When Pevara and Androl were capturing Dobser, Leems and Welyn came in; Pevara fought them with the One Power, enabling Androl to knock them out with a cudgel. Emarin stated his intention to dose them with something that would make them sleep until Bel Tine.

Left Hand. In Seanchan, a term referring to a primary assistant; for example, Tuon's former Truthspeaker, Neferi, had a Left Hand who was trained and ready to replace her, until Anath was selected by the Empress.

Legion of the Dragon. A large military formation, all infantry, giving allegiance to the Dragon Reborn, trained by Davram Bashere along lines worked out by himself and Mat Cauthon, lines which departed sharply from the usual employment of foot. While many men simply walked in to volunteer, large numbers of the Legion were scooped up by recruiting parties from the Black Tower, who first gathered all of the men in an area who were willing to follow the Dragon Reborn. Only after taking them through gateways to a spot near Caemlyn were those who could be taught to channel identified; the remainder, by far the greater number, were sent to Bashere's training camps. The Legion numbered about 15,000 well-trained troops when they joined in the Illian campaign, but their total number with recruits numbered 47,500. At the beginning of the Last Battle, the Legion fought on Elayne's front.

Legion of the Wall. *See* Ghealdan

Lehynen. A member of Ituralde's forces who died defending his flank from Trollocs outside Maradon; Ituralde thought that he was one of the best.

Leich, Mother. The local healer in Remen, Altara. She stitched up Lords Orban and Gann after their encounter with Gaul and Sarien.

Leilwin, Lady. A Taraboner noblewoman who was shipped out to the Seanchan forces after Floran Gelb's misinformation led to Egeanin kidnapping her. Young and pretty, she was a refugee from estates burned out by the war. Leilwin resembled one of the women Egeanin sought, although Gelb should have known it was the wrong person by her Taraboner accent. Leilwin, bound and gagged, was deposited on one of the courier boats in the dead of night. She was made *da'covale* to an unknown Seanchan owner.

Leilwin Shipless. *See* Egeanin Sarna

Leiran. A man of the Cosaida sept of the Chareen Aiel and the *Sha'mad Conde* society. An agile man who could kick higher than Rand's head, he was *siswai'aman*. Leiran was handsome except for the puckered white scar that ran up under the strip of black cloth that covered a missing eye. He guarded Rand's Traveling tent in Tear. Enaila thought he had a good sense of humor, but the other Maidens thought that it was his strong hands which attracted her. Enaila decided to lay a bridal wreath for him at the time of the Last Battle, but she was killed by Trollocs before she could do so.

Leish. The wife of the Asha'man Canler. Round and white-haired, she was bonded by Canler.

Leitha. A Tairen Lady of the Land. She made the mistake of looking disdainfully at Moiraine while the nobles were waiting for Rand in the Heart of the Stone.

Leitiang, Stedding. A *stedding* located in the forests north of the River Ivo.

Lelaine Akashi. A Kandori Aes Sedai of the Blue Ajah and the rebel contingent, with a strength level of 13(1). Born in 827 NE, she went to the White Tower in 844 NE. After spending five years as a novice and six years as Accepted, she was raised to the shawl in 855 NE. She was first chosen as a Sitter for the Blue Ajah in 962 NE and after the split in the White Tower was named First Selector, the head of the Blue Ajah, in 999 NE. Her Warder was Burin Shaeren.

About 5'4" tall, she was a slender woman, quite pretty, with a dignified air that could break into a warm smile and a light laugh. Her penetrating brown eyes were a little lighter in color than Romanda's, but not light. Although her hair had no gray showing, she stood just ahead of Romanda in the ceremony when Egwene was raised Amyrlin. Lelaine controlled her faction tightly; she could cut one of them off with a gesture. She was a friend to Siuan before Siuan took the stole. She was fond of Logain, as a fierce dog she had tamed. She had had her own candidate for Keeper, who was not Sheriam. Lelaine and her faction used *Tel'aran'rhiod* to try spying on Rand. Resuming her friendship with Siuan after Nynaeve Healed Siuan, she made sure that Siuan knew that she expected Siuan to be as loyal to her as she was to Egwene, should Egwene fail to survive, and help her rather than Romanda get the stole and staff. Lelaine unmasked Faolain as Egwene's mole and pressed her hard, forcing her to give up information about Egwene, Siuan and Leane. In the Last Battle, Lelaine fought as part of Egwene's army.

Lem al'Dai. A horse-faced Two Rivers man in Perrin's army. He had a gap in his teeth through which he sometimes spat; he got the gap fighting a merchant's guard. He liked to fight with his fists, and was known to pick fights. He traveled with Perrin to Cairhien, Dumai's Wells and Ghealdan.

Lem Thane. A boy from Emond's Field who was the son of Jon and Saera Thane. He was eight months younger than Rand, Mat and Perrin. Lem saw the cowled horseman before Winternight, too. His father was the local miller and a member of the Village Council.

Lemai Ambani. An Aes Sedai of the Red Ajah and the loyalist contingent, with a strength level of 15(3). After spending six years as a novice and eight as Accepted, she was raised to the shawl. Part of the expedition to take the Black Tower, Lemai was captured and bonded by Morly Hardlin, an Asha'man Dedicated. She was one of the two strongest Aes Sedai captured by the Asha'man, and, as such, was second to Desandre in leadership of the Aes Sedai group, as much as the Asha'man allowed.

Lemore Genhal. A Taraboner noblewoman taken by the Seanchan in Tanchico and made *damane*. She was just nineteen when being held in Caemlyn, one of the *damane* captured by Rand's troops in Altara and turned over to Elayne in Caemlyn. Lemore was a pampered young noblewoman born with the spark, though she didn't know it until it manifested itself days before the Seanchan took the city. Found while trying to escape, she was collared on the very day the city fell. Lemore said that she hated the Seanchan and wanted to make them pay for what they did to Tanchico, but she answered to Larie, her *damane* name, as readily as to Lemore, and she smiled at the *sul'dam* and let them pet her. She knew she should hate the *sul'dam* and didn't understand why she did not. Not wanting to harm any of them, she would have been paralyzed if confronted by a *sul'dam*, and might well have let herself be collared again without making more than token resistance.

Len Congar. A Two Rivers man who, along with Jac Coplin, stole a cow from Master Thane. After being shown proof of the incident, Perrin meted out justice by having them strapped.

Lenn. A mythical character in gleeman tales who flew to the moon in the belly of an eagle made of fire; his daughter Salya walked among the stars.

Leof Torfinn. A Two Rivers man with deep-set eyes and a white streak in his hair where a scar ran through it; the scar was given to him by Trollocs. He carried Perrin's Red Wolfhead banner when Wil al'Seen didn't want to, and carried it again for Perrin's first meeting with the Seanchan under Tylee Khirgan. At Malden, he was one of those who went through the aqueduct to rescue Faile.

Leonin. Meidani's Arafellin Warder. He wore silver bells in his hair and two swords on his back. He knew nothing of current happenings except that his Aes Sedai wanted certain things of him. He made formal bows with fingertips pressed to his heart.

Leral. A serving girl at The Wandering Woman in Ebou Dar.

Lerian. A Goshien Aiel woman of *Far Dareis Mai*. Lean, sandy-haired and about Faile's age, she escorted Perrin and Faile to Rand in Caemlyn. She often guarded Rand or Min and went with other Aiel to help restore order in Bandar Eban.

Lerman, Master. The head mason working on Elaida's palace at the White Tower. The blood drained from his face when Elaida told him that the palace must have a spire ten spans higher than the Tower itself, but a look at her face told him to say that it would be done as she wished.

lesser consensus. A vote that required a quorum of eleven Sitters, but only two-thirds of those present needed to stand for an item to pass. There was no requirement for all Ajahs to be represented in the lesser consensus except in the case of a declaration of war by the White Tower, one of several matters left to the lesser consensus which many might have thought would require the greater.

Letice Murow. A Murandian novice with the rebel Aes Sedai. Pale-eyed and close to her middle years with unblemished skin, she had a sister who was also a novice. Leane had Letice hold Egwene's horse outside the *cuendillar* tent; when she gave her name, Letice sounded as if she wanted to add a title.

letter-of-rights. The only paper currency. Such letters were issued by bankers, guaranteeing to present a certain amount of gold or silver when the letters were presented. Because of the long distances between cities, the length of time needed to travel from one to another, and the difficulties of transactions at long distance, a letter-of-rights might have been accepted at full value in a city near the bank which issued it, but it might have been accepted only at a lower value in a city farther away. Generally, someone intending to be traveling for a long time would carry one or more letters-of-rights to exchange for coin when needed. Letters-of-rights were usually accepted only by bankers or merchants, and would never be used in shops.

Leuese Mulan. An old Tairen fisherman who became wealthy after finding three *cuendillar* bowls and a cup in his nets, but later could not remember where. He bought a trading ship.

Lewin clan. A Two Rivers family. *See* Adine, Ban, Dannil, Emry, Flann, Jillie, Kiem, Kimry, Laila Dearn, Natley, Tell *and* Win Lewin

Lewin. A young Jenn Aiel man from the time soon after the Breaking. Adan was his greatfather, Saralin his mother and Maigrin his sister. When he was six, his father and greatmother were killed by bandits. When he was older, his sister and another girl, Colline, were kidnapped by bandits. Lewin, Colline's brother Charlin and some of their friends went to save the girls; they used weapons, killed the bandits and were cast out by their families. Lewin gathered others like him, and stayed near the Jenn; he married and fathered Jeordan, who never saw his father smile. His wife died of fever. If Jenn came to him and asked, he and his men would help to rescue their loved ones.

Lewin, Mistress. An Emond's Field woman. When Nynaeve caught her daughter Kimry in the hayloft with Bar Dowtry, Nynaeve punished Kimry first and then Mistress Lewin took over.

Lews Therin Telamon. A leader in the Age of Legends. A very accomplished man, he held many offices and wrote critically and publicly acclaimed books. For a time he was romantically involved with Mierin, who later used the name Lanfear, but her ambition and the realization that she saw him as a path to power soured him on her. He ended the relationship long before the drilling of the Bore, but Mierin continued to pursue him. He met and fell in love with Ilyena Moerelle Dalisar; Mierin disrupted their wedding and continued to make a public nuisance of herself.

Lews Therin was named the first among the Servants and sat in the High Seat. He wore the Ring of Tamyrlin and summoned the Nine Rods of Dominion. He was known as the Lord of the Morning, the Prince of the Dawn and the Dragon. At the onset of the War of Power, the people turned to the Aes Sedai to defend and guide them. Lews Therin was chosen to lead the human soldiers, the Ogier and the Aes Sedai in the fight to prevent the Dark One from breaking free of his prison.

Lews Therin was a good leader, but the war was a seesaw affair. Lews Therin defeated Ishamael at Paaran Disen, but the Shadow had its successes as well. The forces of the Light came up with two very different plans. Lews Therin wanted to use a circle of seven women and six men to place seven focus points around the thinness of the Pattern at Shayol Ghul to seal the Dark One away. Latra Posae, another Aes Sedai, spearheaded an effort to attempt to prevail by construction of two huge *sa'angreal*, one for *saidar* and one for *saidin*, that were to be used to contain the Dark One. Many thought Lews Therin's plan too risky; Latra Posae felt so strongly about it that she convinced all the female Aes Sedai to make an agreement that no woman would link with a man to help seal the Dark One's prison; this agreement came to be known as the Fateful Concord. The *sa'angreal* were constructed, but access keys were needed to use them, and these access keys were hidden in an area taken over by the forces of the Shadow. Latra Posae and the women held to their concord, hoping that the access keys could be rescued. At the same time, the Shadow pressed hard and won many victories; Lews Therin believed that if they waited any longer, the Shadow would certainly prevail.

Accompanied by 113 male Aes Sedai, known somewhat inaccurately as the Hundred Companions, and ten thousand soldiers, Lews Therin attacked the Bore. A nice surprise awaited: The thirteen most important of the Aes Sedai sworn to the Shadow were meeting. Lews Therin and his men placed the seals, but not without cost. In the battle to do so, forty-five of the Companions were killed, and a high percentage of soldiers. That was only a small part of the damage; a backblast from the Dark One tainted *saidin*. Lews Therin and the sixty-eight other survivors went mad on the spot.

In his madness, Lews Therin killed everyone who carried any of his blood, as well as everyone he loved, thus earning the name Kinslayer. Ishamael went to Lews Therin, and returned him to sanity so that he could know what he had done. In his grief, the Dragon traveled to a wide empty place and drew too much of the One Power. He died, and Dragonmount rose to mark his grave.

In the Third Age, Rand al'Thor, the Dragon Reborn, heard Lews Therin's voice in his head; what he learned from it helped him in his fight against the Shadow.

Leya. A Tuatha'an woman. Gray-haired but with few lines on her face, she rode into the Mountains of Mist to find Moiraine and report to her about the fighting on Almoth Plain. Trollocs attacked while she was there, and Leya was killed by a Fade.

Leyn. An Aiel Wise One who could channel quite strongly. When Cadsuane first arrived at the palace in Cairhien, Leyn watched her walk past with cold eyes in a stony face.

Liah. A woman of the Cosaida sept of the Chareen Aiel and *Far Dareis Mai*. Her hair was nearly black, which was rare and prized among the Aiel, and both of her cheeks bore scars. She often bounced on her toes when she laughed and looked with disgust at even a practice sword. About Rand's age, Liah was with him in Caemlyn and went to Shadar Logoth with him and the Ogier; there she was lost. The others left, assuming her dead, because night was coming. When Rand was fighting Sammael in Shadar Logoth, he saw her; she had gone feral. He killed her with balefire to save her the agony of death from Mashadar. The names of the dead blazed in Rand's head, and her name burned especially after he had killed her.

Liale Mosrara. A Taraboner rug weaver. One of the refugees who went to the Two Rivers, she asked permission of Faile to start producing rugs, which Faile granted. Liale promised the first and finest from her looms to Perrin and Faile.

Lian. One of the Heroes of the Horn featured in "Lian's Stand," recited by Thom, and part of *The Great Hunt of the Horn.*

Lian. A woman of the Nine Valleys sept of the Taardad Aiel. She was the wife of Rhuarc, the roofmistress of Cold Rocks Hold, sister-wife and first-sister through adoption to Amys and sister-mother to Aviendha. She had blue eyes and yellow hair with some gray at the temples. She was more than handsome, and looked older than Amys but younger than Rhuarc. She and Amys both had children by Rhuarc; they had daughters as old as or older than Berelain. Lian welcomed Rhuarc, Rand and Heirn to Cold Rocks Hold; she gave Couladin permission to enter, but as one friendless and alone. She would not accept a guest gift from Moiraine, but was pleased with those that Mat and Rand gave her.

Liandrin Guirale. A Taraboner Aes Sedai of the Red Ajah in public and of the Black Ajah in truth. She had a strength level of 14(2). Born in 964 NE, she went to the White Tower in 979 NE. After spending five years as a novice and five years as Accepted, she was raised to the shawl in 989 NE. She was a brown-eyed honey blonde about 5'5" tall, with a full-lipped rosebud mouth and a lush body. She wore her hair in beaded braids and was pretty in a doll-like way. Born to a poor family, she worked hard to ape the manners and speech of upper-crust Taraboners. Liandrin knew a form of Compulsion, but it was very weak and spotty. She called it "opening people" to her suggestions. She was weak in Healing, unable to Heal more than scrapes and bruises. That irritated her because the ability to kill with the Power that Rianna and Chesmal had was strongly linked to the talent for Healing.

Liandrin was one of two Red sisters who accompanied Siuan on her visit to Fal Dara. While there, Liandrin used her Compulsion to force Amalisa to search for Rand. She gave at least one lesson to Nynaeve and Egwene on the way from Fal Dara to Medo, but she was more interested in the three boys than in the lessons. She tricked Egwene, Nynaeve, Elayne and Min into going to Falme so that they might be captured and the channelers made *damane,* but that did not go as planned and only Egwene was captured. In late 998 NE, she was the leader of the original thirteen members of the Black Ajah who fled the White Tower. Those thirteen went to Tear, where they captured Egwene, Nynaeve and Elayne; after that plot failed, Liandrin went to Tanchico. She then traveled to Amador and was coopted by Moghedien to search for Nynaeve. Liandrin tried to attack Moghedien with her Compulsion, but she was shielded with a knotted, tied-off shield and Compelled to live. Moghedien then turned her over to Darkfriends in Amador, who treated her roughly because of her former poor treatment of them. When the Seanchan took Amadicia, she attempted to betray her captors as Darkfriends, hoping to escape. Instead, she fell into the hands of the High Lady Suroth, who despised all Aes Sedai in general and Liandrin in particular, and was made *da'covale*. She could not even use the leverage of threatening to betray Suroth for the simple reason that under Seanchan law, the word of a *da'covale* was not accepted as evidence; in fact, no one was likely to believe or even listen to any accusations a *da'covale* made. Liandrin poisoned Alwhin to try to make points with Suroth. Because Moghedien's shield was still in place, Liandrin was not leashed, although rumors began circulating that Suroth had a *marath'damane* in her household. Suroth considered collaring her at that point.

Lidan. A serving girl at The Nine Rings in Tremonsien, Cairhien. She was sent to fetch Selene's bags.

Lideine Rajan. An Aes Sedai who lived at the time of the formation of the White Tower.

Lidrin. A young officer from Arad Doman, the son of Lord Shimron, who served under Rodel Ituralde. A scar ran across the left side of his face, and he wore a fashionable thin black mustache. Lidrin was with Ituralde at Darluna when they sprang the trap on the Seanchan and when Rand met with Ituralde the first time. Lidrin was skeptical when Rand said he was the Dragon Reborn, and objected to going with Rand to see proof. At the battle outside Maradon, Ituralde sent him to lead a detachment of archers at the battlements; he was killed during the battle after going on a suicidal charge when he should have retreated.

Lidya. A *damane* belonging to Tuon. Red-haired with freckled cheeks, she spoke a Foretelling for Tuon, saying, "Beware the fox that makes the ravens fly, for he will marry you and carry you away. Beware the man who remembers Hawkwing's face, for he will marry you and set you free. Beware the man of the red hand, for him you will marry and none other." Tuon was displeased, and had Lidya caned for it, although the next day she ordered the *sul'dam* to give Lidya lionheart for the pain and a sweet custard as a treat. Lidya was part of Karede's group that searched for Tuon when she was missing.

Lieutenant-General. An officer who commanded a legion of a varying number of banners. A Lieutenant-General wore four thin plumes.

Lifa. A Darkfriend merchant who ran supplies for the Shadow through the Blasted Lands to a spot near the Town. Faile's party captured her caravan, presumably killed her and her three Darkfriend guards, and freed her captives.

Light Blessed Throne. The royal throne of Ghealdan.

Light, Children of the. *See* Children of the Light

Light of the Heavens, Light of the World. Other names for the Creator.

Light of Truth, The. An inn in Sienda, Amadicia. Its innkeeper was Mistress Jheran. Elayne and Nynaeve stayed there after leaving Tanchico; they met Galad in the common room and then quickly left town.

Lighteater. *See* Dark One

Lights, Feast of. *See* Feast of Lights

lightskirt. A woman of easy virtue.

lightstick. An illumination device from the Age of Legends. It looked like a plain glass rod, thicker than a man's thumb but not quite as long as a forearm. When held in the hand it glowed as brightly as a lantern. It shattered like glass as well, and could start a fire if broken.

Lillen Moiral. Moghedien's name in the Age of Legends.

Lincora din Omen. A Sea Folk Wavemistress who was one of the First Twelve. She met with the others of the First Twelve in Illian and turned her back when Harine arrived.

Lind Taglien. The innkeeper of The Great Gathering, at the Black Tower. Short and dark-haired, she wore dresses covered in lovely embroidery. She maintained a library with a considerable number of books.

Lindsar. An Ogier woman who was the eldest of the Ogier in Stedding Sholoon. Though she was too old to fight in the Last Battle, she allowed Androl and Pevara to use the *stedding* to trap a group of Darkfriends, including Alviarin and some of Taim's cronies. She thought that perhaps a few decades in the peace of the *stedding* might change their outlook.

Lines, the. These joined the Worlds That Might Be, laid by those who knew the Numbers of Chaos; a part of the process used in the construction of Portal Stones. Verin spoke of the Lines after Rand had channeled too much Power into a Portal Stone and experienced many of his alternate lives.

Lini Eltring. The childhood nurse of Elayne, Morgase and Morgase's mother. Mouthy and independent, she had a tendency to treat everyone like a child in the schoolroom, but she did know when to hold her peace sometimes, though never very often, it seemed, with Morgase or Elayne. She was a frail-appearing woman, with her white hair drawn back in a bun from a narrow face with skin like thin parchment. Her back was straight, her voice was clear and steady and her dark eyes were sharp. Lini could make a snort sound delicate when she wished. She saw her charges as children still, in many ways; and as Morgase said, she would not curtsy if the whole court were watching. Lini had a brisk but gentle voice for telling one things such as that one's pony had a broken leg and must be put down. Her gnarled fingers used to linger on Morgase's cheek to check for fever. Always a great one for neatness, she believed there was a place for everything, and everything should be in its place. Lini possessed a massive number of aphorisms for which she was famous within the household, and which she voiced whenever the circumstances merited.

Lini's great treasures were the six oval ivory miniatures of her three charges—Morgase; Morgase's mother, Maighdin; and Elayne—each as a babe and as a young woman. She cared little or nothing for the Tower or for Aes Sedai, except that they were necessary in certain circumstances. As for Rand, she knew a little of the Prophecies and knew that the Dragon Reborn was necessary, but to her, there was little to choose between a man who could channel and a rabid wolf in one's bedroom. Of course, Lini would have shooed the rabid wolf out with a broom. Perhaps needless to say, the Asha'man were not her favorite men by a far margin.

When Morgase broke through Rahvin's Compulsion and went on the lam, Lini accompanied her. She didn't like Whitecloaks and didn't approve of Morgase seeking help in Amadicia; what occurred in Andor was a problem for Andor to solve. Lini stopped Morgase from committing suicide after she had been violated by Valda, and brought her to her senses.

After Faile took "Maighdin" and her party into her service, Lini became her lady's maid, with seniority over Maighdin and Breane, as she was eldest and the one who seemed best to understand the job. Once Maighdin was taken by the Shaido, Lini believed that Perrin had slept with Berelain and made her feelings about that quite plain to him and everyone else.

Before the battle at Malden, Lini was sent with Gill and others to make their way north to the Jehannah Road, but bad conditions made them change their route, and they were captured by Whitecloaks before Perrin could find them. Galad freed them when Perrin showed up for his trial.

Lini insisted that Morgase and Tallanvor marry before returning to Caemlyn.

Lini's sayings.

"A fool abandons friends, and gives up silver for shiny brass."

"A fool puts a burr under the saddle before she rides."

"A fool puts her hand into a hollow tree without finding out what's inside first."

"A full stomach at midday makes for a dull head in the afternoon."

"A gnarled old branch dulls the blade that severs a sapling."

"A man is a man, on a throne or in a pigsty."

"A secret spoken finds wings."

"A shoat squealing under a fence just attracts the fox, when it should be trying to run."

"A slow.horse does not always reach the end of the journey."

"A weeping woman is a bucket with no bottom."

"A young lion charges quickest, and when you least expect it."

"Always plan ahead, but worry too hard over next year and you can trip over tomorrow."

"An open sack hides nothing, and an open door hides little, but an open man is surely hiding something."

"Anyone who allows two roosters in the same barnyard deserves the ruckus they get."

"Be sure of yourself, girl, but not too sure."

"Better to face the bear than run from it."

"Do not cut off your ears because you do not like your earrings."

"Dragging feet never finish a journey."

"Even a queen stubs her toe, but a wise woman watches the path."

"Fools only listen to themselves."

"If you don't look for snakes, you cannot complain when one bites you."

"It isn't the stone you see that trips you on your nose."

"It's one of the things men are for, taking the blame. They usually deserve it, even if you don't know exactly how."

"It's too late to change your mind after you've jumped off the cliff."

"Kittens tangle your yarn, men tangle your wits, and it's simple as breathing for both."

"Men keep sticking their hands in the fire thinking this time it will not burn."

"No knife is sharper than a sister's hate."

"Not thinking about a thorn doesn't make it hurt your foot less."

"Only fools kiss hornets or bite fire."

"Peel the apple in your hand, girl, not the one on the tree."

"Poke the meekest dog too often and he will bite."

" 'Should' and 'would' build no bridges."

"Sup from too many dishes, and you deserve a bellyache that'll split you open."

"Tears are for after; they just waste time before."

"The blindest are those who keep their eyes shut."

"The pike does not ask the frog's permission before dining."

"The right medicine always tastes bitter. Most of all for a child who throws a sulky tantrum."

"There's no point letting honey age too long before you eat it."

"Three things annoy to distraction: a tooth that aches, a shoe that pinches and a man that chatters."

"To know two, you must first know one."

"Waiting turns men into bears in a barn, and women into cats in a sack."

"What can't be changed must be endured."

"What you need is not always what you want."

"When a woman plays the fool, look for the man."

"When the honey's out of the comb, there's no putting it back."

"When you ask questions, then you have to hear the answers whether you want to or not."

" 'Wish' and 'want' trip the feet, but 'is' makes the path smoother."

"You can do whatever you wish, child. So long you are willing to pay the price."

"You can never put the honey back in the comb."

"You can't know another woman's reasons until you've worn her dress for a year."

"You cannot hold the sun down at dawn."

"You could weave silk from pig bristles before you could make a man anything but a man."

"You count your plums in the basket, not on the tree."

"You should not be displaying wares you do not mean to sell."

linking. The ability of channelers to combine their flows of the One Power. While the combined flow was not as great as the sum total of the individual flows, it was directed by the person who led the link and could be used much more precisely and to far greater effect than the individual flows could be. Men could not link their abilities without the presence of a woman or women in the circle. Up to thirteen women could link without the presence of a man. With the addition of one man, the circle could increase to twenty-six women. Two men could take the circle up to thirty-four women, and so on until the limit of six men and sixty-six women was reached. There were links that included more men and fewer women, but except in the linking of one man and one woman, one woman and two men, or of course, two men and two women, there always had to be at least one more woman in the circle than there were men. In most circles, either a man or a woman could control the link, but a man had to control in the circle of seventy-two as well as in mixed circles of fewer than thirteen.

Although men were in general stronger in the Power than women, the strongest circles were those which contained as near as possible to equal numbers of men and women. Entering a link was normally a voluntary act, requiring at least acquiescence, but under certain circumstances, a sufficient circle already formed could bring another woman forcibly into the circle as long as no man was part of it. Insofar as was known, a man could not be forced into a circle, no matter how large.

Lion. The name of the horse belonging to Lord Orban, the Hunter of the Horn who captured Gaul.

Lion Banner. The symbol of Andor, a white lion rampant on a field of red.

Lion Throne. The royal throne of Andor. Carved and gilded, with huge lion's paws at the ends of its legs, it displayed the Lion of Andor picked out in moonstones on a field of rubies above where the Queen's head would be while seated.

Lioness. The horse Elayne rode in Ebou Dar; she was killed when Elayne's unraveling gateway exploded.

lionfish. A predatory fish found in the Sea of Storms.

lionheart. An herb used for pain in Seanchan. Tuon had some administered to a *damane* who had been caned.

Lions, the White. *See* White Lions, the

Lir Baryn. An Andoran man who was High Seat of House Baryn. His sigil was a silver-winged hammer on a field of green. Blade-slender and blade-strong, he opposed Morgase during the Succession and became one of Gaebril's sycophants. He was too smoothly unctuous and too smooth altogether. He was used by Rand and fled when Rand reached an accommodation with Dyelin. He supported Arymilla for the throne of Andor, but was captured and threw his support behind Elayne, offering to publish his support.

Lira. A serving girl at the Blue Rose in Canluum, Kandor who had eyes for Lan. She had full lips and dark eyes and checked Lan's wounds after he fought and killed six assassins.

Lirene Doirellin. A Cairhienin Aes Sedai of the Red Ajah and the loyalist contingent, with a strength level of 24(12). Born in 820 NE, she went to the White Tower in 835 NE. After spending eight years as a novice and six years as Accepted, she was raised to the shawl in 849 NE. She was 5'2" tall and was once plump, with a strong face; she had lost considerable weight and her pale skin looked weathered. Lirene was raised Sitter for the Red in 953 NE, but was forced to resign in 985 NE after the discovery of the male channeler pogrom and her part in it. Although the true circumstances were kept secret for the good of the White Tower, she suffered a severe penance in the Tower, was birched, though in private, and was exiled, a supposedly voluntary retreat that lasted until she was recalled after Elaida took the stole. Elaida considered her broken by her experiences, and in many ways, Lirene was broken. She was indeed of a nervous disposition after her return, and exceedingly afraid to be caught in anything wrong. She very much feared a return to her exile, and feared almost as much that something she did might result in another dose of the birch. Even when she remembered to try hiding her fears—she had lived with them so long that she was hardly conscious of the need to hide them—it was apparent that she was hiding something. She wore only a few red slashes or other details about her dress, despite having once been a Sitter. Like the other two Sitters who were unchaired—Toveine and Tsutama—she had two major passions: a hatred of men who could channel, and a desire for revenge on those who caused her downfall and suffering, as well as those who had abandoned her. The second passion was sometimes greater than the first, sometimes less. Lirene had an additional passion: hatred of those who rose because of her fall. Those included the Red Sitters who replaced her, the other two who were unchaired, Galina, who became Highest of the Red in 981 NE, and Elaida, as she was not implicated in the male channeler pogrom and also rose to the Amyrlin Seat. While teaching Egwene after Egwene's capture by Elaida, Lirene said that she believed that Elaida had made some serious mistakes.

Lisaine Jarath. A senior *der'sul'dam* from Seandar, under Miraj's command. She was gray-haired with a pale plump face and blue eyes. She was a friend of Miraj, and they often shared cups of *kaf* and games of stones. Usually very animated, when approaching the final battle against Rand, she was icily calm, which alarmed Miraj.

Lisandre. A sulky novice from Moiraine's earlier days in the Tower, very tall with long golden hair. Moiraine thought that she would be allowed to test for Accepted if her sulkiness could be cured.

Listeners. Spies for the Empress of Seanchan. Listeners were always hidden, and they had no authority whatsoever. Their duty was to report everything they saw, heard, or learned. Anyone could act as a Listener, even a servant whose family had served a noble House for generations. Some Listeners were what might be thought of as professional spies, while others were brought into the fold through rewards, threats or blackmail. Once a person became a Listener, he was a Listener for the rest of his life, and the penalty for revealing that one was a Listener was death. The identity of Listeners was known only to the core bureaucracy who controlled them for the Empress and in some cases to a control or case officer. This bureaucracy existed to record the information received from the Listeners and decide what was to be passed to the Empress and what to the Seekers. All of it had to go one place or the other if not always to both. Members of the bureaucracy could be found everywhere, including with the Forerunners and the Return. The bureaucracy controlling the Listeners was itself secret, the members known only to one another, though the highest echelons were known to the Empress. They all were hidden among the other bureaucrats and functionaries.

When called to give evidence, Listeners did so with their faces hidden and identity disguised, speaking through a tube which disguised their voices as well, keeping secret even then.

Little Tower. In Salidar, an abandoned stone inn adopted by the rebel Hall of the Tower.

Llyw. Kairen Stang's Warder. He was as wide as a horse; Malind thought that he could almost pass for an Ogier. After Kairen was killed, he was primed for murder, but was dosed with something to make him sleep. When Lelaine first suggested that Myrelle bond him, she paled; Faiselle twisted her arm and convinced her that it was her duty. Myrelle did bond him then, and, at least early on, he made her look harassed.

Lodanaille. A vintage of wine served in a Tairen punch, mixed with honeymelon and offered by Sunamon to Rand.

lofting tubes. Devices used by Illuminators to shoot fireworks skyward.

Logain Ablar. A Ghealdanin minor nobleman with a small estate in the mountains until he became a false Dragon, for which King Johanin and the Crown High Council stripped him of title and estate; he kept the sigil, three golden crowns in a field of blue. His strength level was $++2$, which was one step below Rand and five steps above the strongest women. He was born in 971 NE, began channeling around 992–993 NE, declared himself the Dragon Reborn in 995 NE, and slowed around 998 NE, just prior to being captured. Logain was a large man, about 6'2" tall, with a dark complexion and brown eyes; his hair was dark and curled to his broad shoulders. One of his special Talents was being able to see *ta'veren*. Logain as false Dragon was captured in a big battle near Lugard, trying to move his army from Ghealdan to Tear. Aes Sedai died defeating him. He was taken to Tar Valon and gentled, but escaped with Siuan, Leane and Min; he traveled as Dalyn, though he wanted to use the name Guaire.

After reaching Salidar, he cooperated with Siuan and Leane's plot, claiming falsely that the Red Ajah, naming sisters, found him and instead of sending him to Tar Valon to be gentled, talked him into proclaiming himself the Dragon Reborn. He also said that they supplied him with information about the forces he faced and about where other Aes Sedai were. He couldn't be sure Siuan and Leane wouldn't kill him if he didn't cooperate, and the plot was a chance for revenge that gave him at least a small new lease on life, though he had been sinking into despair; and while he wanted revenge on all Aes Sedai, he realized he was unlikely to get it. Siuan's plot offered at least a chance to damage the Red Ajah, and by association to damage them all to some degree. While he wanted revenge on Aes Sedai, his innate pragmatism meant that he could abandon that desire if he had to, though not entirely without difficulty.

Logain was accidentally Healed by Nynaeve; the rebel Aes Sedai held him prisoner while they decided whether or not they could afford to gentle him again, given Rand and his amnesty. Since Leane and Siuan were not as strong as they once were after being Healed, the rebel Aes Sedai assumed that Logain wasn't either; none of them knew that this Healing needed the opposite sex for completeness. In fact, because he had been Healed by a woman, he was just as strong as ever. He regained some of his old swashbuckling manner after he was Healed, but there was a darker strand in him, a touch of bleakness. He showed just a sign or two of the madness that would have come. To Min's eyes, sometimes he wore a halo of gold and blue that spoke of glory to come.

He escaped from Salidar with the assistance of Siuan and Leane, on orders from Egwene, and headed straight for the Black Tower. There was no chance for him alone, not as the world stood, but he thought there might be a possibility in company with other men who could channel. Logain was the only man inside the Black Tower to wear the Sword and Dragon who did not receive private instruction from Taim, which others put down to the animosity between them. He and Taim did not like one another, which most attributed to the fact that each had once declared himself the Dragon Reborn. From Logain's point of view, they felt, not only did he have to place himself below Rand, but below Taim as well, something he plainly found difficult since he had been, in fact, more successful as a false Dragon than Taim, more famous, or perhaps one should say more notorious.

Logain had a following among those not favored by Taim, including the men brought from the Two Rivers, though many of those were wary of him as a former false Dragon. He had considerable charisma, as well as leadership and organizational ability and a fair degree of military skill. He had no lesser desire for glory or power than he had before. He never really believed that he was the Dragon Reborn, unlike some who claimed it. He felt, like Taim, that if he had managed to fulfill enough of the Prophecies, he could have pulled it off. There certainly hadn't been anyone else around claiming to be the Dragon Reborn that he knew of. He was not a man who liked being second to anyone, but he knew that taking advantage of Rand's amnesty was his one real chance for power and glory, not to mention safety from the Aes Sedai. Despite his ambitions, he was not a bad man, not vainglorious, nor would he have made bad decisions merely for self-aggrandizement. In fact, Logain would have been a very good leader, administrator and ruler, though a hard one in some ways, and very pragmatic rather than idealistic.

Logain took part in the ambushes of the White Tower's expedition against the Black Tower. On the first day, he bonded Gabrelle Brawley, a Brown. On the second day, despite orders that no man was to bond more than one of the Aes Sedai, he was forced to bond Toveine Gazal, though if he hadn't been distracted by his horse nearly bucking him off because of her kicking, he could have bound her legs with the Power and not needed to bond her. He did wonder why none of Taim's particular cronies were given positions where they could bond sisters; not that it was a special privilege, but he thought Taim would want the men who held those bonds to be especially loyal to him.

Logain found and burned Toveine's traveling desk with all of its contents, including the order from Elaida to hang every man found at the Black Tower. He did that for exactly the reasons Toveine and Gabrelle surmised, and also hoped the act would make Toveine and the others cut him some slack, since he knew what they were about.

Logain left the Black Tower, went to Cairhien and then to Tear to find Rand and fought against the Trollocs at Algarin's manor. Rand sent Logain to the Sea Folk to demand that they ship supplies to Arad Doman. Logain accompanied Rand to his meeting with the Daughter of the Nine Moons. When he returned to the Black Tower, he was imprisoned and attempts were made to Turn him to the Shadow, but he escaped with help from Androl and other Asha'man loyal to him. He engaged Demandred in combat, was injured and had to flee. He tried to find Demandred's *sa'angreal*, but was interrupted by a plea for help, and instead he went to the ruins on the Field of Merrilor to save Caemlyn refugees who were being killed by the Shadow. Logain broke the seals on the Dark One's prison at the right time in the Last Battle, in accord with Rand's plan, and Gabrelle dubbed him "Sealbreaker."

Loial son of Arent son of Halan. A young Ogier who wanted to see the world. He was born in 908 NE and left the *stedding* in 995 NE. He had eyes the size of teacups, a nose so wide it seemed almost a snout, a mouth that seemed to cut his huge head in two, a shaggy head and tufted ears that stuck up through his hair. His ears were very mobile and expressive of his emotional state, besides being an Ogier secondary sexual characteristic. His long eyebrows hung down like mustaches almost to his cheekbones. His fingers were like sausages, as big as a man's thumbs, or as big as two of a man's fingers. A narrow strip of hair like fur went up the middle of his chest. Loial was close to ten feet tall. His voice was as deep as a drum and rumbled and boomed.

Loial was a very talented Treesinger, one of the last in existence, and he said that he could feel a *stedding* once he was within ten miles of it. He didn't like heat and damp; Stedding Shangtai, his home, was in the cool mountains. Loial liked to play stones and played very well. In the three years he was out of the *stedding* before meeting Rand and Mat in Caemlyn, Loial visited Tear, Illian and Cairhien, among other places. He journeyed through the Ways to Shienar with Rand, Mat, Perrin, Egwene, Nynaeve, Moiraine and Lan, then accompanied them into the Blight, to the Eye of the World. He left Fal Dara in pursuit of the Horn of Valere, traveled via Portal Stone through a strange world, facing *grolm*, then out through another Portal Stone in Kinslayer's Dagger with Rand, Hurin and Selene. They went on to Cairhien and then to Stedding Tsofu and traveled via Portal Stone again to Toman Head, where he saw Rand's battle in the sky with Ishamael.

After wintering in the Mountains of Mist, he set out with Moiraine, Lan, Perrin and later Faile, chasing after Rand first to Illian, then to Tear. From Tear he went by the Ways with Perrin and Faile to the Two Rivers, where he faced the Trollocs in battle; he and Gaul went alone to seal the Waygate there. While in the Two Rivers, Loial became weary, beginning to feel the effects of the Longing but not wanting to leave Perrin and his other friends. Also, he didn't want to give over writing his book, which he planned to call *The Dragon Reborn*. After leaving the Two Rivers with Perrin, he refreshed himself on the way to Caemlyn by visiting the abandoned *stedding* where the ruins of Hawkwing's statue lay, and subsequently claimed to be fine. In Caemlyn, he reunited with Rand, and went on to Cairhien, then set out with Karldin Manfor to visit the *stedding* and secure the permission and cooperation of the Elders in guarding the Waygates.

Loial and Karldin returned to Cairhien to find Rand gone. With the arrival of Logain and Davram Bashere, Loial and Karldin joined up with them to find Rand, using the Warders left behind by sisters sworn to Rand when they went away with Cadsuane. Loial learned the Elders had named him a runaway and that his mother had promised to have him settled in marriage to someone she had chosen. Loial's mother searched for him with the Ogier maiden Erith in tow, accompanied by his old teacher, Elder Haman. Loial was in a swivet after learning that they showed up in Caemlyn looking for him, but he was quite taken with Erith; she gave Loial a flower and listened to even his most complicated explanations, which she found interesting, and which made her interesting in return; he later married Erith.

Loial also argued convincingly at the Great Stump at Stedding Shangtai that the Ogier should not yet open the Book of Translation, but rather help fight the Dark One. He and Erith fought together in the Last Battle.

Loise al'Vere. Egwene's next-eldest sister. She was born in 976 NE. A tomboy as late as age fifteen, she was considered the adventurous one—she was the one who hung on to climbing trees long after other girls gave it up, who sneaked off hunting rabbits and went swimming in the Waterwood long after others slowed or stopped. She was not allowed to braid her hair until 997 NE. By the time Perrin left the Two Rivers for the second time, she was looking around at suitors. She also might have been able to learn to channel.

Lomas. A scout for Ethenielle of Kandor. A sly lean-faced fellow with a foxhead crest on his helmet, he signaled to Ethenielle that they were in sight of the place in the Black Hills where she was to meet the other Borderland rulers.

Londaren Cor. The capital city of Eharon, one of the Ten Nations to rise after the Breaking.

Londraed. A lean soldier in the Band of the Red Hand. When Mat was working to set a trap for the Seanchan, Londraed climbed a tree to watch for Aludra's signal. In Caemlyn when the Trollocs attacked during the start of the Last Battle, Londraed fought to save the dragons.

Long Exile, the. The separation of Ogier from their *stedding* during the Breaking when the land and sea shifted so dramatically that the *stedding* were lost or swallowed entirely. The Ogier who survived the upheaval of land and sea found themselves homeless and adrift, and wandered in search of their lost *stedding*. The Long Exile sensitized the survivors and their descendants so that all Ogier became bound to the *stedding*; if an Ogier stayed Outside for too long, the Longing took him and he began to weaken and eventually die. It was also known as the Exile.

Long Eyes, Cemeille din Selaan. *See* Cemeille din Selaan Long Eyes

Long Feather, Dorile din Eiran. *See* Dorile din Eiran Long Feather

Long Man, The. A well-kept inn in Cairhien where Egwene and Gawyn met in the private dining room. Its innkeeper was a round woman.

Long Tooth. The name the wolves gave Elyas Machera.

Long Wandering, the. *See* Long Exile, the

Longing, the. A condition experienced by an Ogier who was away from a *stedding* for too long; it could result in death. It was a particular problem during the Breaking, when landforms were changing. The Longing was not experienced by Seanchan Ogier in the Breaking, because in the areas that later became the Seanchan Empire, there happened to be more *stedding*, and so they were not exiled for long periods of time.

loobies. A pejorative term meaning, roughly, "dunces."

lopar. A hulking exotic fighting animal of the Seanchan that was brought from a parallel world. It weighed between fifteen hundred and two thousand pounds when full-grown and had a large, round head with no external ears and two eyes, large and dark, surrounded by horny ridges. Its massive shoulders appeared hunched, and were somewhat higher than its hindquarters when on all fours. Its legs were longer than those of a bear in proportion to size, but still appeared short, partly because they were very thick; they were somewhat bowed when the *lopar* was on all fours, adding to its hulking appearance. Its hide, leathery and hairless, in browns ranging from dark to a pale reddish color, was not as tough as that of a *grolm*, and when *lopar* were used in battle, they were normally fitted with a sort of leather coat or barding, covered with overlapping rectangular metal plates, which protected the spine, the central chest and the belly. It had six toes on both front and rear paws, all with large retractable claws. It used both forepaws for grasping or handling. *Lopar* would sometimes rear up on their hind legs when fighting, and were then easily tall enough (as much as ten feet) to snatch a man from horseback. Its intelligence was higher than that of a dog, probably equal to that of a *torm*; as with the *torm*, some people found their gaze disturbing, but there was not the cold malevolence in the gaze of a *lopar* that there was with a *torm*. The *lopar* was as fast as or faster than a horse over very short distances—up to one hundred paces/ yards—but they were not distance runners by any means. Despite their lumbering appearance, they could move as quickly as any bear. *Lopar* births were always in pairs, and they suffered the same high mortality rate of the other exotics.

Despite its appearance, the *lopar* could be handled by anyone properly trained and was usually placid and even friendly unless roused to fight by command. The exception to this was mating, which resembled a battle and usually resulted in wounds to both male and female. Both males and females would sometimes engage in a sort of dominance display, each animal rearing to its tallest and roaring or howling loudly. The shorter of the two animals would lie down flat on its belly almost immediately. If the two animals were the same size, however, combat could result unless they were properly controlled by *morat*.

The *lopar* was used primarily as a guard animal, and used only very occasionally in battle, usually for guarding a particular person. Because of the combination of a usually placid nature combined with fierce fighting ability, it was not unusual for the Blood to use *lopar* to protect and guard their children. *Lopar* used to bodyguard people, whether adults or children, often became attached and fiercely protective. Animals which formed this attachment were usually reluctant to leave the one they were attached to and frequently refused to eat for some time afterward. The *lopar* was controlled by voice commands and by signals from a horn a little larger than a man's hand with a piercing sound.

Lopar, Cavan. The rotund innkeeper of The White Crescent in Tear. He suggested that Mat take Thom to Mother Guenna for his cough.

Lopiang, Kiam. An Aes Sedai who lived at the time of the formation of the White Tower.

Lopin. Nalesean's Tairen serving man. A middle-aged man, he was about 5'10" tall, round-bellied and balding, with a blocky, square face and an oiled beard almost long enough to reach his chest. What hair he had left was dark. He was competitive with Nerim, Talmanes' serving man. Lopin traveled with Nalesean to Ebou Dar, and after Nalesean's death he became Mat's manservant. Normally jolly, he was somber and sad after Nalesean died. Lopin was killed by the *gholam* in the camp outside of Cairhien.

lopinginny. A bird found in the Waste with a bold call, though it was not a bold bird.

Loral. The dosun, or head housekeeper, of Milisair Chadmar's palace in Bandar Eban. Elderly and gray-haired, she had served the Chadmar family through three generations. She told Nynaeve that the last messenger from Alsalam had been taken and imprisoned, and led Nynaeve to the prison.

Lord Captain Commander of the Children of the Light. The commanding officer of the Whitecloaks, who presided over the Council of the Anointed, which was made up of approximately a dozen of the highest-ranking and most favored Lords Captain and the High Inquisitor. At the time of the Last Battle, Galad Damodred was Lord Captain Commander.

Lord of the Dawn. *See* Dragon, the

Lord of the Grave. *See* Dark One

Lord of the Lakes. One of Lan's royal Malkieri titles.

Lord of the Land. A title for Tairen nobles, and the rank from which a High Lord was raised.

Lord of the Morning. One of Lews Therin's titles, given to Rand by Weiramon, Bashere and Gregorin, and taken up more generally during the Illian campaign. *See* Dragon, the

Lord of the Seven Towers. One of Lan's royal Malkieri titles.

Lord of the Twilight. *See* Dark One

Lorn, Evanellein. *See* Evanellein Lorn

Lorstrum Aesnan. A Cairhienin nobleman who rose to power after Rand left Cairhien. He was quiet and lanky and looked down his nose. He neither opposed Rand nor supported him; that middle ground helped him to gain support; it was thought that he was considering claiming the throne. Elayne demonstrated the dragons for him and other nobles, and offered him estates in Andor that she had stripped from Arymilla, Naean or Elenia. When Birgitte found a poisoned needle in the Sun Throne's cushions, Lorstrum vowed to find who had put it there; he also opined that it must have been put there to kill Rand, since no one would want to kill Elayne.

Los caba'drin! Old Tongue for "Horsemen forward!"

Los Valdar Cuebiyari. Old Tongue for "The Heart Guard will advance."

Losaine. An Aiel Wise One with the ability to channel and a strength level of 22(15). She had gray eyes and dark hair with glints of red. She had to link with Daviena to shield Turanna after Verin finished questioning her.

Lost Ones. The Aiel name for the Tuatha'an.

Lost, the. The name given to Tuatha'an who could no longer hold to the Way of the Leaf.

Lothair Mantelar. The author of *The Way of the Light*. In FY 1021, during the War of the Hundred Years, he founded the Children of the Light to proselytize against an increase in Darkfriends.

Lounalt, Jaq. *See* Jaq Lounalt

Lounault. *See* Amathera Aelfdene Casmir Lounault

Loune, Gamel. *See* Gamel Loune

loveapple. A plant with plump fruit; Aviendha compared Elayne's lips to loveapples when talking to Rand.

loversknot. 1) A vine having strong crimson flowers. It was embroidered on Nasin Caeren's lapels. 2) Capitalized, the stout brown mare that Nynaeve rode from Ebou Dar to the Kin's farm and on toward Caemlyn; she also rode her when she took Lan to World's End.

Low Chasaline. A day of fasting that fell on the eighteenth day of Maigdhal.

Loya. A maid at the Tarasin Palace in Ebou Dar. She was slender with bee-stung lips; she gave the towel she had just put on Olver's washstand a pat, and then flung herself onto the bed to tickle his ribs till he fell over laughing helplessly.

Luagde. A bridge town outside Tar Valon on the bank of the Osendrelle Erinin, on the road to Chachin and Shol Arbela.

Luaine. A young Aiel woman of *Far Dareis Mai*. Yellow-haired, she was one of the Aiel who helped Aviendha and Rhuarc rescue Nynaeve, Elayne and Egwene from brigands and Myrddraal. After discovering that Rand had been kidnapped, Sulin sent Luaine to fetch Nandera and Rhuarc.

Luan Norwelyn. An Andoran nobleman who was High Seat of House Norwelyn. His sigil was a leaping silver salmon on a field of vertical blue and green stripes. Luan supported Morgase in her drive for the throne. Graying and hard-faced, he met with Rand in Caemlyn, when Rand told him and other nobles (Dyelin, Ellorien and Pendar) that he wanted Elayne on the Andoran throne. He said that Rand's wine was excellent, but the "my Lord Dragon" sounded as if it had been pulled out of Luan with a rope. When Rand indicated that the wine was cooled with the One Power, he deliberately drained his cup and held it out for more. He acted with Dyelin and Pelivar against initial claimants to the throne; they hanged two nobles for declaring for Dyelin for the throne, had twenty others flogged, and imprisoned Lady Naean Arawn and Lady Elenia Sarand, who had declared for themselves. After Elayne took Caemlyn, he stood for Trakand.

Luan, River. A river with headwaters in the Black Hills flowing southeast to the River Erinin below Tar Valon.

Luc. A lord of the fictitious Murandian House Chiendelna; it was the name Slayer used in the Two Rivers. *See* Slayer

Luc Mantear. An Andoran nobleman born in 954 NE; his sign was a golden acorn. The son of Mordrellen, and Tigraine's brother, he disappeared in the Blight in 971 NE after Gitara Moroso had a Foretelling that the outcome of the Last Battle depended on his going to the Blight. In the Blight, the Dark

One made him into a sort of hybrid with Isam Mandragoran; the resulting being was known as Slayer.

Slayer could change from Luc to Isam in the waking world and in *Tel'aran'rhiod*. As Luc he was a tall broad-shouldered man in his middle years with a hard angular face, blue eyes and dark reddish hair with white wings at the temples. After the death of Shaiel, Rand's mother, his father Janduin went into the Blight; there he came across a man who looked like Shaiel, and would not raise a weapon against him. That man, Luc, killed him.

Calling himself Luc Chiendelna of Murandy, he went to the Two Rivers at the same time as the Whitecloaks; he claimed to be a Hunter of the Horn and hinted at having a claim to a Borderland throne. He made a great show of getting the people there organized against the Trollocs, but many of the farms that were burned were farms that he had recently visited. He also tried to get the Two Rivers people to confront the Whitecloaks, and finally led a group to tell the Whitecloaks that the Two Rivers was closed to them.

In the wolf dream, Perrin put an arrow in Slayer's chest; shortly after in the waking world, Luc rode away, hunched over and clutching his chest; after that, Luc really hated Perrin. Luc spied on Nynaeve, Elayne and Egwene in *Tel'aran'rhiod;* they thought he looked like Rand's uncle, which of course he was. Taim ordered Slayer to kill Rand and Min in Far Madding; Luc went to the room in the inn where Rand and Min had been staying; since they had left, the man and a woman he killed were strangers. *See also* Slayer

Luca. A young Jenn Aiel male from the time after the Breaking. His shoulders were half again as wide as anyone else's and he liked to play tricks. He went with Charlin and Lewin to save their sisters from bandits; they used weapons and killed some bandits, and although they saved their sisters were cast out by their families.

Luca, Valan. *See* Valan Luca

Lucain. A brown-haired novice in the White Tower who assisted Egwene during the Seanchan attack; Egwene sent her with a message to others helping her.

Lucanvalle, Catala. *See* Catala Lucanvalle

Lucellin. A Child of the Light. With Dain Bornhald in the Two Rivers, he made sure that no one sneaked off from Taren Ferry while Bornhald was moving his troops into the area.

Luci. The assistant in Ronde Macura's dress shop in Mardecin, Amadicia. Dark-haired, young and thin, she constantly tried to wipe her nose surreptitiously with the back of her hand. Luci's long curls reached her shoulders. At Ronde's behest, she dosed Nynaeve and Elayne with forkroot tea. She was terrified and shrill and quickly caved when Thom and Juilin arrived.

Lucilde. A lanky Andoran novice brought to Salidar from the White Tower; she had a potential strength level of 29(17). Born in 978 NE, she went to the White Tower in 993 NE. Lucilde escorted Halima to Delana. If Lucilde had remained in the Tower, she would have been raised Accepted.

Ludice Daneen. A Taraboner Aes Sedai of the Yellow Ajah. She was bony, with a long, grim face framed by brightly beaded Taraboner braids that hung to her waist. She had a reputation for strict adherence to the law. Ludice was one of the sisters called in by Tamra Ospenya to carry out the secret search for the newborn Dragon Reborn. She was murdered by the Black Ajah early in 979 NE.

Ludin. An *algai'd'siswai* who worked with Birgitte to kill Trollocs in Braem Wood in the Last Battle; she thought that he was very good at moving quickly and silently.

Lugard. The capital of Murandy. Lying on the River Storn where it met the River Reisendrelle, it was ruled by King Roedran, although his authority did not extend far into the country, as local lords held sway. A rough city, decaying through neglect, Lugard was highly commercial, being on major trade routes; people from all different nations could be found in its streets. Lugarders had a reputation for thievery and licentiousness. Large areas of bare earth were set aside within the city to accommodate trade. Tall gray walls that encircled the city were neglected, their fallen stones making them low in places. Busy broad streets were unpaved, and the city was dirty. Gray stone buildings with bright colored tile roofs were dusty, and crumbling stone walls, remnants of past nobles' territorial claims, crisscrossed the city. Stables, horse lots and inns nearly outnumbered houses and shops. The inns were noted for risqué names and risqué singers. The Shilene Gate stood on the eastern side of the city.

Lugard Road. A thoroughfare connecting Caemlyn and Lugard.

Lugarders. People from Lugard, Murandy.

Lugay, Therin. *See* Therin Lugay

Luhhan. A Two Rivers family. *See* Alsbet Luhhan *and* Haral Luhhan

Luin, Igaine. *See* Igaine Luin

lumma. A tree native to Maram Kashor that was straight and very tall, with fronds sprouting from the top.

Lunal Galgan. A Seanchan Captain-General who commanded the soldiers of the Return. He was tall with blue eyes and snow-white hair worn in a crest with the tail braided and hanging down his back. His ancestors were among the first to throw their support to Luthair Paendrag. He had a high reputation as a soldier and a general. Galgan went with Tuon to her first meeting with Rand. After the meeting, she ordered him to go ahead with the attack on the White Tower. Galgan met with assassins to find out how much it would cost to have Tuon killed, and then killed those assassins. He later did hire assassins to kill her, but only poor ones that he felt had no chance of success. Tuon planned to raise him to the Imperial family. At first Galgan was skeptical of Mat's martial abilities, and resented Mat being named Rodholder, but he later came to respect Mat and argued for rejoining him on the battlefield in the Last Battle.

Lurk. A Tairen name for Myrddraal. *See* Myrddraal

Lurts. A Saldaean soldier who accompanied Nynaeve to Milisair Chadmar's prison in the Gull's Feast in Ebou Dar. A massive wall of a man, he wore a cavalryman's uniform.

Lusara. A Domani woman taken *gai'shain* by the Shaido. Graceful, buxom, copper-skinned and stunningly beautiful, she was well into her middle years, with a few white hairs among the black falling below her shoulders. A risk-taker, she had gained and lost several fortunes as a merchant. Because of her beauty, Sevanna chose her to be one of her personal servants. She swore fealty to Faile and Faile thought she might be trustworthy, but she treated Faile's escape plans like a child's game, with no sense of consequence if they should fail.

Lushenos, Lord Gregorin Panar den. *See* Gregorin Panar den Lushenos

Lusonia Cole. An Andoran Aes Sedai of the Green Ajah and the loyalist contingent. Part of the expedition to kidnap Rand, she escaped from the debacle at Dumai's Wells and returned to Tar Valon with Covarla Baldene. The entire party was sent to Dorlan to keep events secret.

Lussin. A Redarm tasked with looking after Olver and Setalle Anan in Caemlyn.

Luthair Paendrag Mondwin. The son of Artur Paendrag Tanreall and Tamika. His banner was a spread-winged hawk clutching lightning bolts. He was born in FY 967, and in FY 992 led a large force of ships of all sizes carrying over 300,000 soldiers and settlers across the Aryth Ocean from the western ports to Seanchan. He found a shifting quilt of nations of various sizes; most of them were ruled by Aes Sedai. No nation trusted the other, and intrigue and scheming abounded; because there was no constancy, Luthair and his descendants were able to conquer the natives of Seanchan. Luthair, whom the Seanchan called the Hammer, was also helped by Deain's invention of the *a'dam*, which allowed Aes Sedai to be collared and controlled.

Lydel Elonid. A woman in Ebou Dar who purchased The Wandering Woman from Setalle Anan. Many Seanchan officers stayed there, but the standards went down after she took over the inn.

Lyncon. A Cairhienin master carpenter taken *gai'shain* by the Shaido. After he was freed, he still looked as though the will had been beaten out of him. Perrin didn't trust him to do a proper inspection of wagon wheels, but thought that he would fix a problem when it was pointed out to him.

Lyndel, Larissa. *See* Larissa Lyndel

Lyndelle. The ninth queen of Andor. The daughter of Morrigan, she ascended the throne in approximately FY 1114 and reigned for fifty-one years. She was credited as one of the Queens that held the nation together during the War of the Hundred Years. The generally accepted date for the end of the war was FY 1117, though it could have been as early as FY 1115 or as late as FY 1119 (records vary), so the major portion of Lyndelle's reign occurred after the end of the war.

Lyonford. A former king of Saldaea who could not keep his temper. Faile used him as an example to Perrin when she was arguing that no leader was perfect.

Lyrelle Arienwin. A Cairhienin Aes Sedai of the Blue Ajah and the rebel contingent, with a strength level of 24(12). Born in 833 NE, she went to the White Tower in 849 NE. After spending six years as a novice and four years as Accepted, she was raised to the shawl in 859 NE and raised a Sitter for the Blue Ajah in 995. About 5'4 " tall, she had a pale complexion and large dark eyes, and somehow seemed beautiful without being at all pretty. Elegant and graceful, her movements were flowing, and it was rumored she had been a dancer before going to the White Tower. She fled the Tower with the rebels and was raised a Sitter in Salidar as well. She led a group of rebel Aes Sedai to the Black Tower to bond Asha'man Warders in keeping with Rand's offer to let them bond forty-seven. Lyrelle was part of the group that pressured Cadsuane to become Amyrlin after the Last Battle.

M'Hael. Taim's self-imposed title and later his name as a Forsaken. Old Tongue for "leader," according to Dashiva, its true meaning was something grander. *See also* Mazrim Taim

M'jinn. A great city of the Age of Legends. It was known for its changeable weather, as used in a remark by Graendal.

Ma'combe. A *so'jhin* with strong arms. He told Tuon after she had returned to the Tarasin Palace in Ebou Dar that Tylee Khirgan was seeking an audience.

Ma'vron. Old Tongue for "watchers."

Mabriam en Shereed. An Aes Sedai of the Gray Ajah, with a strength level of 9(+4). Mabriam was Queen of Aramaelle and considered mainly responsible for forming the Compact of the Ten Nations, which was signed in 209 AB. Stories said that she was *ta'veren*. Merana, impressed by her memory, thought that when Kiruna and Bera first saw Cadsuane, it must have struck them the same way seeing Mabriam would be for her. Her name was sometimes rendered as "en Shareed."

Mabriam's Day. A feast celebrated on the eighteenth day of Tammaz. All labor was avoided on this day; the food was cooked the day before. Young women played tricks on young men they were interested in, but doing so in such a way that it was not obvious which young woman was responsible for the trick. If a man determined who was responsible, he earned a forfeit of a kiss, or even kisses from an entire group.

Macer, Renald. *See* Renald Macer

Machan. A Warder in Salidar who saw twenty-odd men approaching Salidar and reported it to other Warders. The men in question were Bryne and his men.

Macharan, Lord. An Andoran noble of a lesser House who was a bear of a man. He accompanied Lady Arathelle, Lord Pelivar and Lady Aemlyn with her husband Culhan to confront the rebel Aes Sedai in Murandy. One of those who had opposed Gaebril, Macharan returned to Caemlyn after Rand took it but did not pay his respects at the palace. Present at the meeting with the rebel Aes Sedai and Murandians, he was reluctant to speak to Egwene and tripped over his own boots avoiding having to talk with her.

Machera, Elyas. *See* Elyas Machera

Machin Shin. A cold wind howling with voices of death and decay that blew through the Ways where no wind should stir. Called *Machin Shin*, the Black Wind, by the Ogier, it haunted the Ways and fed upon unwary travelers, stealing minds and souls and leaving survivors empty husks. Possibly, since the

Ways were born of tainted *saidin*, the Black Wind was also. Some said that it might have begun as a natural parasite that was corrupted. Others believed it was a remnant of the War of the Shadow that hid in the Ways and could not find a way out.

Machir. A powerful Domani nobleman who was supposed to be following Ituralde. Because Alsalam's orders sometimes went straight to the men under Ituralde instead of to him, four pitched battles occurred between different groups of Ituralde's men, Machir among them.

Macoll. A soldier in the Band of the Red Hand. In Mat's battle against the Seanchan who were after Tuon, Macoll unfurled and carried the banner of the Band.

Maconar, Caraighan. *See* Caraighan Maconar

Macu. A *morat'raken* who died when her *raken* was shot down by Aes Sedai at the Kin's farm.

Maculhene, Sawyn. *See* Sawyn Maculhene

Macura, Ronde. *See* Ronde Macura

Mada. A serving woman at The Woman of Tanchico in Tar Valon. She was pretty with brown eyes. She and Saal—who Mat thought was Mada's younger sister—took care of Thom when he stayed there, and tried to keep him from drinking too much; they did not like it when Mat bought Thom wine, but after Mat convinced Thom to go with him to Caemlyn, they were happy because it was the most alive that they had seen Thom in a long time.

Madan, Stedding. A *stedding* located in the Mountains of Mist.

Maddin Todande. The nobleman who founded Altara. He claimed to be a descendant of the last Queen of Shiota, and may actually have been so. He was a strong respected ruler.

Maddin's Day. A festival celebrated in Ebou Dar. Named after the founder of Altara, it was celebrated two days after the Feast of Embers.

Maddow, Slone. A wide-eared Redarm with the Band of the Red Hand. After the *gholam* attacked Mat's tent and killed Lopin, Maddow told Mat that he thought Olver was with Noal.

Madel. One of the kings in the gleeman tale "Mara and the Three Foolish Kings." He wound up with a fish entangled in his long beard.

Maderin. A prosperous town in Altara approximately eight days northeast of Jurador and somewhat larger. Its lord was Nathin Sarmain Vendare. Farms and olive groves reached right to the stone walls of Maderin. Tile-roofed buildings three and four stories tall, most of brick, lined the wide, stone-paved main street; shops and inns with signs that swung in the stiff breeze crowded in beside stables and rich people's homes with large lamps above the arched doorways and humbler structures that housed poorer folk. A rougher part of town contained a maze of twisting streets, paved with rough stone blocks the size of a man's two fists. Many of those ways were too narrow for horse carts. Luca's show made a short stop there, right after the incident where a Shiotan village and its ghosts mysteriously disappeared. Tuon wanted to visit a "hell" there, and Mat took her to The White Ring. They were attacked on the way out of the inn, and Mat decided that they would all leave the show.

Madic. A servant in the Tarasin Palace, one step below Laren and the final link before Laren in the chain that led Mat from entering the palace to Queen Tylin's presence. He was a balding Darkfriend who reported to Moridin just after Elayne and the others fled the palace. Moridin, in a rage, crushed Madic with the True Power without even realizing it. After Moridin left, the *gholam* came and fed on Madic's still-warm blood. The circumstances of Madic's death were such that an Aes Sedai was sure to be blamed.

Madmen, Land of the. *See* Land of the Madmen

Madness, Time of. *See* Time of Madness

Madoc Comadrin. A general from around six hundred years before Hawkwing. He was a genius of military strategy and wrote *Fog and Steel*, a book about soldiering from which Mat liked to quote. In one of his memories, Mat recalled meeting him after losing to him in battle.

Madome, Juilaine. *See* Juilaine Madome

Madresin Mandevwin. A captain with the Band of the Red Hand. Mandevwin was a stocky one-eyed man who had been with the Band since the first days in Cairhien. He earned the gray streaks in his hair in past battles against Andor and Tear. Mandevwin was to go to Trustair to find out who was distributing pictures with Mat's likeness; he did not like it that in the story Mat made up, Mandevwin abandoned his sick aunt. In Ebou Dar, Mat used his name as a *nom de guerre*. Mandevwin was with Faile's group that went to fetch the Horn of Valere from the White Tower in the Last Battle, and, as a gateway opened to return them to the Field of Merrilor, they were sent instead to the Blight. After Vanin and Harnan fled after being caught with the Horn of Valere, Mandevwin insisted that they were not Darkfriends. He was caught in flows of Air when Aravine betrayed them, and released when Olver stabbed the channeler holding him.

Madwen. *See* Barin *and* Maglin Madwen

Madwin. A member of the Band of the Red Hand. He and Dongal led men on the south slope of a hill near the Malvide Narrows, in an ambush against the Seanchan.

Maecine. A king of Eharon, one of the Ten Nations to rise after the Breaking. In one of his earliest memories, Mat remembered fighting alongside him against the Aelgari some three to four hundred years before the Trolloc Wars.

Maedin Bashere. The son of Deira and Davram Bashere. He was two years younger than his sister Faile. When Davram took Maedin to the Blightborder, Faile ran away to join the Great Hunt of the Horn.

Maeldan, Yarin. *See* Yarin Maeldan

Maenadrin. A Saldaean Aes Sedai of the Brown Ajah whom Egwene saw in the hallways of the White Tower. Maenadrin and a section of the Brown Ajah quarters had been relocated to a different part of the Tower, caused by Pattern slippage, a result of the Dark One's growing influence.

Maeric. Chief of the Moshaine sept of the Shaido Aiel. He was also the leader of *Seia Doon*. He had a wife, Dyrele; a daughter, Suraile of *Far Dareis Mai*; and a son, Darin, of *Shae'en M'taal*. He hoped to be sent to Rhuidean to become the next clan chief of the Shaido. At Dumai's Wells he wanted to maintain screens of scouts and a reserve. Maeric died or was taken prisoner and made *gai'shain* on the Plains of Maredo after being tricked by Sammael into going through a gateway.

Maerin. An Aes Sedai of the Green Ajah who fought in Kandor in the Last Battle. She did not travel light; Egwene slept in her large tent at one point to keep her location secret.

Maerin, Kenly. *See* Kenly Maerin

Maerion. A name Birgitte was known by in a past life; she used that name while traveling with and performing in Luca's circus.

Maerone. A village in Cairhien across the River Erinin from Aringill, Andor. Small, dusty and unwalled, it was full of refugees and soldiers. Most of its brick and stone buildings were single-storied, with a variety of roofs; the streets were dirt and refugee camps ringed the town. Mat's Band of the Red Hand stayed there for a time, and Mat saved Olver from a beating. Daved Hanlon impregnated an ironmonger's daughter from Maerone, and killed her before she could tell anyone.

Mafal Dadaranell. The Ogier-built capital city of Aramaelle, one of the Ten Nations after the Breaking. It had grand towers, graceful arching buildings and intricate palaces joined by wide avenues. During the Trolloc Wars, it was destroyed; survivors rebuilt it, but since Ogier stonemasons were not available, they built it solid and simple; that later city was known as Fal Dara.

Magami. A term meaning "little uncle"; it was what Lady Amalisa called King Easar in private.

Magde Aybara. A Two Rivers woman who was married to Eward Aybara and was Perrin's aunt. She was stout and looked like her husband. She, along with the rest of the family, was murdered by Padan Fain, although it was believed that Trollocs killed them.

Mageen. Old Tongue for "Daisy," and the name of the dun mare ridden by Aviendha in Caemlyn.

Magla Daronos. An Illianer Aes Sedai of the Yellow Ajah and the rebel contingent, with a strength level of 29(8). Born in 839 NE, she went to the White Tower in 854 NE. After spending seven years as a novice and seven years as Accepted, she was raised to the shawl in 869 NE. Her Warder was Rorik. Magla had broad shoulders and was well muscled, as if she could have worked at a blacksmith's forge, but she was not fat or unshapely. Her personality went with her body type: direct and forceful, sometimes overpowering. She was raised a Sitter for the Yellow in 985; in 999 NE Suana Dragand ordered her to join the rebellion to control and defuse events. Magla had a difficult time going against Romanda in any way, but since following Romanda helped to counter Lelaine and usually resulted in stalemate, she did not try very hard. Magla believed the stories concerning Logain and the Red Ajah. She was against any alliance with the Black Tower and worked to delay an embassy to it; she also opposed bonding Asha'man. She was part of the group, with Faiselle, Saroiya, Takima and Varilin, who negotiated with the White Tower to try to end the split.

Maglin Madwen. The innkeeper at The Nine Rings in Tremonsien. She was a lean woman with a long nose, graying hair and a ready smile. She was a Lugarder; her husband was Barin. They were married for twenty-three years, and when they weren't fighting they were kissing. Ready to go back to Lugard when her husband died, she had to stay in Tremonsien, because he left her the inn and his brother the money instead. She was tight with silver. After Selene asked for a room to herself, Maglin tried to get Rand to knock on Selene's door and say whatever had angered Selene was his fault, even if it wasn't.

Magonine, Jalid. A craftsman in Ancarid, Seanchan, who owned Karede as a boy.

Mah'alleinir. Perrin's hammer, forged in combination with the One Power. Its name was Old Tongue for "he who soars." It had a thick, powerful head, like a maul or sledge, but the back was formed cross-face and flattened like a blacksmith's tool. It was four feet from bottom to top, and the haft was all of steel. There was a crosshatch pattern with the leaping wolf that looked like Hopper stamped on one side. Perrin only felt a comfortable warmth when he touched the hammer head, but it burned Shadowspawn when he hit them with it.

Mahdi. Old Tongue for "Seeker." The term was used for the leader of a Tuatha'an caravan.

Mahiro Shukosa. Rafela Cindal's Kandori Warder. He had graying temples, a noble nose, dark eyes and long fingers. A lord in his native land, he had visited the court of almost every land, traveled with a small library, and could recite poetry, play the harp and dance like a dream. Mahiro could also solve iron tavern puzzles quickly and usually wore two swords on his back. He accompanied Rafela and the rebel embassy to Rand in Caemlyn; he looked on Min as a younger sister.

Maia, the Feast of. A feast celebrated on the sixth day of Amadaine in Andor, Ghealdan, Altara, Murandy and Illian.

maiden's hope. A white wildflower found in the Mountains of Mist.

Maiden's Kiss. A game in which a group of Maidens held spears to a man's throat; he had to kiss each one. If the Maiden thought it was a good kiss, they eased up on the spears. If the Maiden did not like the kiss, they pressed a little harder for encouragement. When Mat played, he did not make it back to his own bed until daybreak.

maiden's ruin. A dice game that Mat played in Tar Valon.

Maiden's Spear. A rock formation near Cold Rocks Hold.

Maidens of the Spear. *Far Dareis Mai*, the female warrior society of the Aiel. A great majority of Maidens of all clans rallied to Rand, acting in some ways as if he had come from their society. Some Shaido Maidens followed Couladin and Sevanna, but others joined the Maidens around Rand, and no Maidens from other clans went to join the Shaido. Relatively few Maidens fell into the Bleakness, compared to the Aiel general population. Nearly one thousand Maidens went to Dumai's Wells after Rand had been kidnapped; 151 died. The Maidens fighting to free Rand at Dumai's Wells wore a strip of red cloth tied around their upper arms so that their wetlander allies could distinguish them from Shaido Maidens, but they were not happy about it.

Each society had its secret hand signals, in addition to those known to all *algai'd'siswai*, but only the Maidens had developed their signs deeply enough to be able to carry on normal, everyday conversations in it. In Maiden handtalk, a hooked little finger made a term mocking or sarcastic. For example, it was used in "spearsister" when applied to a woman who had given up the spear and then tried to behave as if she had not.

Maigan. An Aes Sedai of the Blue Ajah and the rebel contingent, with a strength level of 15(3). She was beautiful with large eyes and full lips, but she seemed elongated somehow. Maigan accompanied Siuan to Fal Dara and was appointed a member of Egwene's advisory council after the death of Anaiya, the only one not oathsworn to Egwene. Maigan had been a strong ally of Siuan when Siuan was Amyrlin, but after the Tower split she was one of many who blamed Siuan for the loss and breaking of the Tower. Siuan had to beg to be accepted back into the Blue Ajah, and rumor had it that Maigan had been the most insistent on the begging. Maigan was part of Lelaine's faction in Salidar. In view of the Asha'man situation, she once proposed altering the Warder bond so that the man had to obey; at Lelaine's behest, she also proposed that the bond be modified to eliminate the sharing and thus protect sisters from bonding a man fated to go mad.

Maigan Nem. Admer's wife in Kore Springs, Andor. Their barn burned when Logain, Siuan, Leane and Min were discovered there; Logain fought with Admer, knocking the lantern into the hay. The three women were caught and Nem prosecuted them; Logain escaped. Maigan asked Bryne to whip the women and run them to Jornhill on a rail.

Maigdhal. The ninth month of the year.

Maighande, Battle of. *See* Battle of Maighande

Maighdin Dorlain. Morgase's alias while on the lam.

Maighdin Trakand. The mother of Morgase.

Maigran. A young Jenn Aiel woman from the time soon after the Breaking. Adan was her greatfather, Saralin her mother and Lewin her brother. When she was five, her father and greatmother were killed by bandits. Some years later she and Colline were kidnapped and abused by bandits. Lewin, Colline's brother Charlin and some of their friends set out to rescue the women; in the process of doing so, they killed the bandits, and Charlin died in the fighting. When they went back to the wagons, Maigran told the Jenn that the young men had killed, causing them to be disowned.

Mailaine Harvole. An Aes Sedai who lived at the time of the formation of the White Tower.

Mailinde Paendrag Lyndhal. The Queen of Shandalle and mother of Artur Hawkwing. She died during the Black Plague epidemic in FY 939.

Mainde Cut. A hold in the Aiel Waste.

Mainelle. An Ogier-built city in Aelgar, one of the Ten Nations after the Breaking. The city of Tanchico later grew on the same site.

Mair. An Arafellin Accepted in the White Tower. Plump and blue-eyed, she was a novice when Egwene left the Tower. She was jealous of Egwene's fast rise and tried to boss her around when Egwene first returned to the Tower after her capture by Elaida.

Maira. An Aiel woman of the Serai sept of the Tomanelle Aiel and *Far Dareis Mai*. She had red hair and a thigh-slapping laugh. She was at least ten years older than Rand. Maira was guarding Rand's tent near Taien when Trollocs attacked; she ran off to join the fighting, leaving Rand vulnerable to a Draghkar. She carried a doll for some time after that to remind herself that she was not a child. She also accompanied Rand to the farm outside Caemlyn, and did not understand Rand's rooster joke.

Maire. A woman who served as an attendant to Colavaere. Colavaere told Maire some of her plans for the future of Cairhien and that Rand would never dare oppose her. Maire told Faile what Colavaere said, and soon after vanished. Faile believed that Colavaere had her killed.

Mairin Gome. A traveling circus owner who was in Samara at the same time as Luca. The line for her show was almost as long as the one for Luca's.

Maisia. The name Sammael called Graendal when she and Sammael met with Sevanna. Graendal threatened to kill Sammael if he ever called her that again; in the Age of Legends, it was the sort of name one might give a pet.

majhere. A term referring to the female head of servants at the Stone of Tear.

Makin, Croi. *See* Croi Makin

Makzim. A Warder leading the training of students to be Warders, after the Tower was reunited under Egwene; he was stern and thick-armed. Gawyn said that he would speak to Makzim and Chubain on behalf of the Younglings who wanted to be soldiers instead of Warders.

Mala, Mistress. A woman running an orphanage in Nynaeve's test for the shawl.

Malahavana. A *sul'dam* who participated in the White Tower raid. She was paired with Tuon's *damane* Dali.

Malai. A *damane* who could tell the fortunes of the weather. She said that there was no rain near when Tuon first met with Rand.

Malain. A Saldaean soldier with Bashere in Maradon. Just before Rand arrived in Maradon, Ituralde, about to be overrun by the Shadowspawn, ordered Malain to gather the cavalry and organize them for a retreat.

Malalin, Lord. One of the men Beslan plotted with in the basement of The Three Stars to overthrow the Seanchan.

Malan. An Ogier who was the son of Senar and the father of Aran, the last being an author who wrote about Ishamael after the sealing of Shayol Ghul.

Malari, Jarna. *See* Jarna Malari

Malden. A city in northern Altara where Faile was held in a Shaido camp. Malden's largest wall was less than four hundred paces long, and shorter on the other sides, but the northern stone wall stood thirty feet high with towers and a fortress. Scattered farmhouses dotted the landscape, and rail fences marked out fields. There was a road leading roughly south through the farms and another leading roughly north. A stone aqueduct ran west into the city on high stone arches from a lake, over ridges topped with windmills.

Maldine lace. A lace characterized by a distinct golden pattern.

Malena Aylar. A Watch Hill woman who appeared in Nynaeve's Accepted test. In that scenario, she had become the Wisdom of Emond's Field. A bully, she beat Alsbet Luhhan, had Cenn elected Mayor and poisoned Bran al'Vere and Haral Luhhan.

Malenarin Rai. The commander of Heeth Tower on the Kandori Blightborder. His sign was the oak set aflame. As well as spending ten years commanding Heeth Tower, he was a master merchant. Heeth Tower received a flash from Rena Tower, indication that there might be a problem; Rai sent three messengers south. His son Keemlin, a few days shy of his fourteenth nameday, was supposed to be one of the messengers, but he let Tian, who was lighter and was the only son left of his family, go in his place. As Trollocs approached, Rai performed the ceremony that named his son a man. Father and son fought and died together.

Malenry, Aledrin. *See* Aledrin Malenry

Malevin, Arel. *See* Arel Malevin

Malhavish. The author of *The Prophecies of the Dragon*, Essanik Cycle, Malhavish's Official Translation, Imperial Record House of Seandar, Fourth Circle of Elevation.

Malian. A young *sul'dam*, slender and dark-haired, who accompanied Anath/ Semirhage when she attempted to capture Rand. After Semirhage was captured, Malian put compresses on Surya and Tabi's head wounds.

Maliandred, Bassane. *See* Bassane Maliandred

Malidra. A young woman who was a descendant of the Aiel in the distant future as seen in Aviendha's visions in Rhuidean. At age eighteen, Malidra was a scavenger, following Lightmakers and sometimes killing people in order to survive. She was caught while going through Flern's trash heap and killed.

Malien. An Altaran noblewoman who was at the Kin's farm outside Ebou Dar.

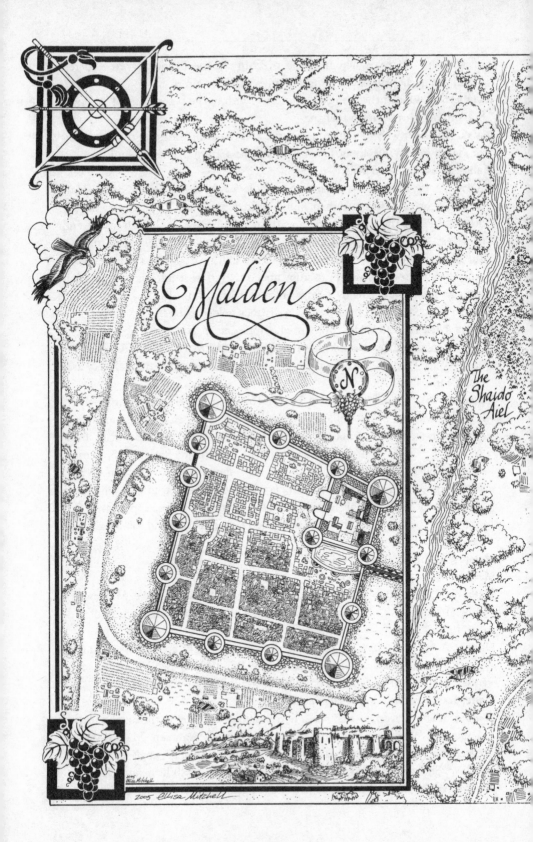

Malden

N

The
Shaido
Aiel

2005 Ellisa Mitchell

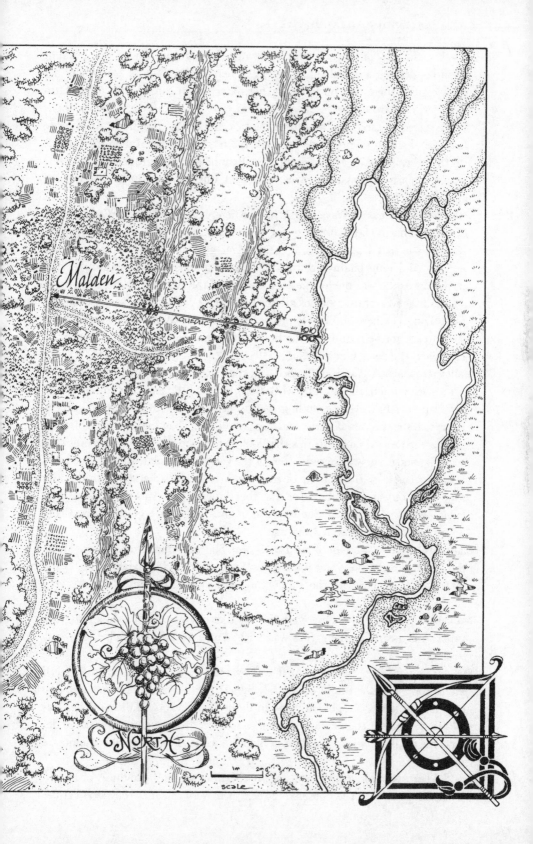

Malden

AQUEDUCT

1010

NORTH

0 1m 2m
scale

She became part of Elayne's entourage with the Kin into Andor. She brought all of her dresses, a bundle nearly as big as herself. The bundle nearly bent her double since there was no horse for her; later she discarded most of it. Slim with a thin scar on one cheek and a stern face, she complained loudly about being forced to carry her bundle on the trek and other indignities; Alise made her wash dishes for being one of the last ten ready to leave. Malien tried to stir up the other non-Kin in the group, but Reanne and Alise kiboshed that. She was still not a happy camper when last seen, but was kept in line by Reanne and Alise.

Malin din Toral Breaking Wave. An Atha'an Miere woman who was Wavemistress of Clan Somarin and Sailmistress of *Windrunner.* Gray streaked her hair heavily, and she had a grave face. Five small fat golden rings decorated each of her ears, and a fine chain with tiny medallions connected one to a similar ring in her nose. She was one of the First Twelve of the Atha'an Miere, the twelve senior-most Wavemistresses of all the clans. Her Windfinder was Dorile din Eiran Long Feather. Malin was present when Nynaeve, Aviendha and Elayne went to ask for help in using the Bowl of the Winds. She escaped from Ebou Dar when the Seanchan attacked.

Malind Nachenin. A Kandori Aes Sedai of the Green Ajah and the rebel contingent, with a strength level of 25(13). Born in 941 NE, she went to the White Tower in 957 NE. After spending twelve years as a novice and eleven years as Accepted, she was raised to the shawl in 980 NE. She had two Warders. Slightly plump with round face, full lips that looked ready to smile and dark eyes that could be fierce, she was raised Sitter for the Green in Salidar; she had been Aes Sedai for the least time of any of the new Sitters. Malind stood with the first nine when Egwene was chosen as the rebel Amyrlin, and was one of those who stood for war with Elaida. She was also in favor of a group going to the Black Tower to bond forty-seven Asha'man.

Malindare. An Aiel woman of *Far Dareis Mai.* She was rounder than most Maidens, and had the darkest hair Rand had seen on any Aiel. Malindare helped bathe Rand before he met with the Sea Folk in Cairhien. She thought Rand was very modest.

Malindhe. An Aiel Wise One who did not like having the Shaido among the other Aiel near Cairhien. She was with Amys and Cosain when Sevanna visited.

Malkier. A nation in the north that was overrun by Shadowspawn in 953 NE and absorbed by the Blight completely by 957 NE. It was Lan's homeland. The sign of Malkier was a golden crane in flight. The oath of Malkieri kings was "To stand against the Shadow so long as iron is hard and stone abides. To defend the Malkieri while one drop of blood remains. To avenge what cannot be defended."

Saldaea, Kandor, Arafel, Shienar and Malkier were all provinces of Hawkwing's empire, with the borders between them very much as they stood at the time of the Last Battle, though not stretching so far south in most cases. With the Blight to contend with, the governors of those provinces—Lord Rylen t'Boriden Rashad for Saldaea, Lord Jarel Soukovni for Kandor, Lady Mahira Svetanya for Arafel, Lady Merean Tihomar for Shienar and Lord Shevar Jamelle for Malkier—met soon after Hawkwing's death in FY 994 to reaffirm measures for cooperation against the Blight and to make agreements for mutual defense against attack from the south. Before the end of FY 995, when it became clear that the rest of the empire was splintering, each of the governors took the title of King or Queen of his or her former province, now a nation. None of these nations would take part in any of the wider fighting of the War of the Hundred Years, as nations, except for defending themselves against attacks and punishing same, though individuals and groups did sometimes become involved, sometimes for political reasons or family connections or friendships.

The last king of Malkier was al'Akir Mandragoran. On a dare, his brother Lain led his army through the Blight to the Blasted Lands, perhaps to Shayol Ghul itself. Lain's wife, Breyan, made the dare because she was envious that al'Akir was raised to the throne instead of her husband. Lain was acclaimed for his deeds, but he could not outshine al'Akir. Lain died in the Blasted Lands with most of those who followed him, and Breyan blamed the King, saying that Shayol Ghul itself would have fallen if al'Akir had led the rest of the Malkieri north with her husband. She plotted with Cowin Gemallan, called Cowin Fairheart, to seize the throne for her son, Isam. Cowin and Breyan moved soldiers back from the Blight to seize the Seven Towers, leaving the Borderforts stripped to bare garrisons. But Fairheart was a Darkfriend, and with the Borderforts weakened, Trollocs poured into Malkier. Overwhelming numbers pushed the Malkieri back into the heartland. Breyan fled with her infant son Isam, and was run down by Trollocs as she rode south with him. When Cowin Fairheart's treachery was revealed and he was taken by young Jain Charin and brought to the Seven Towers, the Great Lords called for his execution. Because he had been loved by the people, the King faced him in single combat and killed him.

There was no time to summon aid from Shienar or Arafel, and no hope that Malkier could stand alone. Al'Akir and his queen, el'Leanna, had their infant son Lan brought to them in his cradle and placed the sword of Malkieri kings in his hands, anointed his head with oil and consecrated him as the next King of the Malkieri. He was given into the care of twenty of the best soldiers from the King's Bodyguard, and they took him to Fal Moran. The King and Queen led the Malkieri out to fight the Shadow one last time; they died at Herot's Crossing, and Malkier died with them.

In many ways, the Malkieri could be considered the ur-Borderlanders. Many of the customs found in other Borderlands were also found among the Malkieri, but frequently interpreted more strictly. Respect for women was highly regarded. A Malkieri considered it impolite to stare at a woman; a polite man did not look directly at a woman, or meet her eyes, unless she opened the exchange with him, and even then, at the highest level of politeness, he avoided looking directly at her, lowering his eyes instead. To a Malkieri, forcing his company on a woman was exceedingly rude, very crude behavior. Malkieri found the way men of other countries initiated conversations with women strange. While there were exceptions, of course, normally a Malkieri man would not initiate a conversation with a woman unless she gave indication that she wished to speak to him.

The Malkieri were not dour people, taking great delight in parties and dances and festivals. The ability to play a musical instrument and/or sing was highly prized, and if one could not compose poetry, one was expected at least to be able to recite it, love poems included. By strong custom, such poems never named their object, but were oblique.

The Malkieri were, however, very much a warrior people by necessity, for their land was surrounded on three sides by the Blight, instead of merely having a border with it. While law in the Borderlands prohibited hiding one's face inside any city, town or village, among Malkieri it was considered rude not to show one's face when meeting strangers, no matter the circumstances or location.

While adulthood was marked by the *ki'sain* for women and the *hadori* for men, both men and women needed the permission of their mother to marry at whatever age, and if she no longer lived, of an adult female relative decided by blood relationship and age. One's mother's sisters came first, then one's father's sisters. If none of them survived, one's own sisters came into play, followed then by the adult daughters of one's mother's sisters, then adult sisters of one's father's sister. In the unlikely event that none of these survived, the net spread wider. Arranged marriages were common among nobles, though not commoners, and sometimes neither bride nor groom were aware that any arrangements had been made until all was signed and sealed. The Malkieri wedding ring, a plain gold band, was worn on the forefinger of the left hand.

The age at which the *ki'sain* and the *hadori* were granted was not fixed. They could be given as young as fifteen, and usually were granted by seventeen or eighteen, but could be withheld longer, though this rarely meant more than another year or two. The decision to grant for boys was made by the boy's father, his uncles and usually a circle of their friends. Being included in this deciding group was an honor and a sign of trust, respect and friendship. Their decision was not entirely final, however, as the boy's mother had to approve the decision, if she was alive. If she vetoed it, custom demanded waiting a year. By custom she was allowed to veto the decision three times, but doing so even once was considered shaming to the boy, and very few women ever did it more than once. Relatively few did it even once. The decision to grant the right for a girl to put the *ki'sain* on her forehead was traditionally made by her mother,

her aunts and a circle of their friends. As with men, inclusion in this group was a sign of friendship, respect and trust. There was no provision in custom for the girl's father to veto.

It was generally expected that young men and women would take a lover (called a *carneira*) before settling down to court and wed. Customarily this lover was someone older and more experienced. In this, women were the aggressors, so to speak, no matter their age. Young women chose out the man they wanted for this first lover, while young men were pursued by older women. By custom, there was no way out once one was chosen except in the case of a married man. A young woman who attempted to choose a married man as her lover would face considerable disapproval, and could expect a very strong talking to by other women at the very least. While these relationships might seem casual, they were not. One had one *carneira* and only one, and the sexual part of the relationship was expected to be of limited duration, a year, or two at most. By custom, certain lifelong rights, responsibilities and obligations were assumed by both on entering into it. While the nature of these differed depending on whether the relationship was between an older man and a younger woman or an older woman and a younger man, in keeping with the sometimes almost matriarchal relations between the sexes in Malkier, the rights, responsibilities and obligations favored the woman. Thereafter the man had a number of obligations and duties toward her and she had the right to require certain things of him, but he had no right to make any demands of her at all.

Malkieri girls wore their hair cut at the shoulder until they put on the *ki'sain*, after which they grew it to the waist or often longer. A woman who wished to retire from the world would cut her hair short. This retirement did not mean rustication or any equivalent of entering a nunnery, but merely that she was simplifying her life and giving over involvement in most affairs of the world. She certainly would not be expected to engage in politics, for example, with her hair short.

A Malkieri boy's hair was allowed to grow to the waist, but it was not cut at the shoulder when he was given the right to tie it back with the *hadori*. The older woman who took him as a lover, his first lover, would cut it at his shoulders, whether she took him before or after he attained the *hadori*. Afterward he would weave the hair into a cord called a *daori* which he presented to her as a token of his obligations and ties to her. Thereafter, no Malkieri man would cut his hair shorter than his shoulders, or let it grow much longer.

Malkieri. From or of Malkier.

Mallard's Hill. A geographical feature near Renald Fanwar's home in the Borderlands.

Mallard's Road. A road crossing Mallard's Hill.

Mallen, Mavra. *See* Mavra Mallen

Mallia, Huan. *See* Huan Mallia

Mallone. A member of the Children of the Light. During the Last Battle, when Galad was ordered to take a dozen of his best men to Hawal Ford, Golever suggested Mallone, among others, to go with him.

Malvide Narrows. A pass in the Damora Mountains, northeast of Maderin in Altara, that led into Murandy. The road from Ebou Dar to Lugard went through it.

Malvin. A man serving under Steler in the Tower Guard right after the Battle of the Shining Walls. He accompanied Moiraine and Siuan to the Murandian camp to collect the names of babies. When they returned to the stable, Steler told his men that he wanted the horses rubbed down and the tack oiled before anyone thought of supper, and added that Malvin knew why Steler was looking at him.

Mameris. Mameris was a city that was the center of a pacifistic movement, unfortunately coupled with a belief in bluntly saying what one thought. Birgitte knew of it; when commenting that she thought Mat more dangerous than Nalesean, she added "A N'Shar in Mameris." A N'Shar was someone from the land on the Shadow Coast who had taken a blood oath of revenge; he or she was a walking time bomb, ready to kill in a twitch, ready to die, until the oath was fulfilled.

Managan. A plump Malkieri merchant who refused the *hadori* and went to Saldaea. Shortly before Nynaeve arrived at The Queen's Lance, having dropped off Lan at World's End, he was in a shouting match with a Tairen woman; after Nynaeve spoke to Aldragoran, Managan leaped up so fast that he overturned his chair. He joined Lan in eastern Kandor and fought with him in the Last Battle.

Manal. A boatman in the city of Cairhien. Stout and gray-haired, he had a graying noblewoman on his lap and was celebrating the Feast of Lights, but when offered five gold crowns, he dropped the woman and got ready to ferry Perrin, Loial and Gaul across the River Alguenya. They were on the way to rescue Rand from Aes Sedai who had kidnapped him.

Manala. A considerable village in Kandor between Canluum and Chachin. It was a sprawling collection of stone houses roofed in red or green tiles and more than twenty streets crisscrossing a pair of low hills. Three inns fronted a large green in the hollow between the hills, alongside the road. Moiraine, Lan, Bukama and Ryne had breakfast at The Plowman's Inn there, and Moiraine inquired after Avene Sahera.

Mancuri den Rhomin, Eliris. An Illianer nobleman who was a member of the Council of Nine.

Manda Wan. An Aes Sedai of the Green Ajah. Just before Egwene appeared to fight Taim in the Last Battle, Manda was trying to persuade Leane and Raechin to fall back and regroup.

Mandair family. *See* Bili *and* Willa Mandair

Mandarb. Old Tongue for "Blade," it was the name of Lan's horse, a tall black fierce-eyed stallion. Zarine Bashere considered calling herself Mandarb; after Perrin laughed at her and pointed out the horse, she decided to go with "Faile."

Mandein. An Aiel sept chief when Rhuidean was built. At forty, he was young for a sept chief; his wife Sealdre was a dreamwalker. He and the other sept chiefs were summoned to meet with the Jenn in Rhuidean. Dermon, Mordaine and Narisse spoke for the Jenn and told the chiefs that any who wanted to lead must come to Rhuidean and learn what they did not know; otherwise they and their septs would die. Mandein was the first to agree to do so.

Mandelain. A man of the Broken Cliff sept of the Daryne Aiel who was clan chief of the Daryne. His hold was Jahad Hold, and his Wise One was Merale. He was married to roofmistress Jair and her sister-wife Corehuin. Mandelain was 6'5" tall and weighed 235 pounds. He had one blue eye, blue as a polished gemstone, and over his right eye socket he wore a gray-green patch. A scar ran from under the patch up onto his nearly bald head fringed in red hair streaked with white. He was with Rand in Cairhien. Before Rand's kidnapping, he and Rhuarc were the two that the Wise Ones trusted not to go after the Tower embassy with spears; they also thought that the two could be trusted with information that the Tower embassy might be a threat to Rand, or at least that they must be watched for that reason. Rand sent Mandelain to help deal with the Shaido, and later sent him and others to Arad Doman to bring order.

Mandenhar. His last stand inspired a song.

Manderic. Man with the Shaido, a *Mera'din* (i.e., Brotherless).

Mandevwin, Madresin. *See* Madresin Mandevwin

Mandhuin. A man of the Goshien Aiel. Gray-haired and heavyset, he wore a smaller belt knife than warriors. He was a trader at the fair outside Alcair Dal.

Mandragoran royal family. *See* al'Akir, Breyan, Leanna, Isam, Lain *and* Lan Mandragoran

Maneches, The Essays of Willim of. An ancient book known by many in the world; the author influenced the Saldaean philosopher Shivena Kayenzi.

Manel Rochaid. An Asha'man from Murandy. Born circa 981 NE, he was about 6'2" to 6'3" tall and smiled a lot, as if he knew something others didn't. He went to Dumai's Wells. Taim named him "Baijan'm'hael," Old Tongue for "Attack Leader." He was Gedwyn's second, a crony of Taim and a Darkfriend. After the attack on Rand in Cairhien failed, he was placed on the deserters list at the Black Tower. Rand killed him with his bare hands in Far Madding.

Manetheren. One of the Ten Nations that made the Second Covenant, and also the capital city of that nation. Both city and nation were utterly destroyed in the Trolloc Wars. The sign of Manetheren was a Red Eagle in flight on a field of blue. Other cities included Corartheren, Jara'copan and Shanaine (later Jehannah); Queen Sorelle ay Marena ruled at the signing of the Compact. The Two Rivers grew on the site of Manetheren.

Manetherendrelle, River. Old Tongue for "Waters of the Mountain Home," it was the name of the river that was formed by the White River (lower river of Two

Rivers) and the Taren River (upper river of Two Rivers), all of which flowed from the Mountains of Mist southeast through the Two Rivers region in Andor and on to Illian and the Sea of Storms.

Manfor, Karldin. *See* Karldin Manfor

Mangin. A man of the Jindo sept of the Taardad Aiel and the *Shae'en M'taal* society. Tall with gray eyes, he was part of the force that took the Stone of Tear. Rand thought that he could be friends with Mangin. Mangin killed a Cairhienin for having a dragon tattooed on his arm; Rand ordered Mangin hanged. Mangin put the rope around his own neck, and made a joke before he died.

Mangore Kiramin. A figure from history, the Sword-bard of Aramaelle and Warder to Caraighan Maconar, and a translator of *The Prophecies of the Dragon*.

Mantear. A noble House of Andor. *See* Dolera, Luc, Mordrellen, Perival, Tigraine *and* Willin Mantear

Mantelar, Lothair. *See* Lothair Mantelar

Mantual. The servant of Banner-General Gamel Loune. He was stocky, with a narrow beard dangling from the point of his chin; his hands had a knifeman's calluses. Gamel said that Mantual came from Pujili in Seanchan and had attached himself to Gamel and wormed his way into becoming his manservant.

Manyard, Jeorad. The governor of the province of Andor for the High King, Artur Paendrag Tanreall. He translated the Prophecies of the Dragon.

Mar. A scout in the Band of the Red Hand. He was tall, lanky and rough-faced. When Mat and his men approached Salidar, Mar was taken by Warders; he was very embarrassed about it. When Trollocs attacked Caemlyn in the Last Battle, Mar fought to rescue the dragons.

Mar Haddon. A nation that arose from the War of the Hundred Years.

Mar Ruois. A great city in the Age of Legends.

Mara. From a gleeman story that Thom recited, "Mara and the Three Foolish Kings."

Mara Tomanes. Siuan's childhood friend. Siuan mentioned her twice; she told Gawyn that Egwene and Elayne were studying with an Aes Sedai in Illian named Mara Tomanes, and later used the name as an alias while on the way to Salidar.

Marac Pandelaros den Norvin. An Illianer nobleman who replaced Lord Brend on the Council of Nine. A wide man with a stolid manner, he often seemed more craftsman than lord despite his rich silks, falls of lace and lavish armor. Marac went to the gathering of forces in Illian before Rand attacked the Seanchan.

Maraconn. A High Lord of Tear. He had rare blue eyes for a Tairen, and thin lips. Maraconn was one of the most active plotters against Rand in the Stone. He was sent to Cairhien under Meilan to restore order and feed the hungry, and he worried because of his previous association to Hearne and Simaan. In a viewing, Min saw him dying violently in battle. He was in Illian with Rand, and in the final battle there he followed Semaradrid. He died fighting in the Last Battle.

Maracru. A town or village in Tarabon. After rumors started flying that Maracru had declared for the Dragon Reborn, or, alternatively, that it had been taken over by Dragonsworn or rebels, Tanchico erupted in riots.

Maradon. The capital of Saldaea. Maradon lay within sight of the Blight, which could be seen clearly from the highest elevations, though many claimed to be able to see it from the city walls themselves. The River Arinelle flowed south along the western walls of Maradon, and was used to fill a moat that had been dug to surround the city. Access to the city and Queen Tenobia's residence, Coramora Palace, was granted through only two gates, placed in the northern and southern walls. Maradon was situated just below a pass through mountains at the Blightborder. As a defense, the Saldaeans had built up and fortified a hill formation south of a ford on the Arinelle (which ran west at that point), directly opposite the mouth of the pass; to reach Maradon, invaders from the Blight would have to breach the fortifications. Tenobia and much of her army had left Saldaea on a mission with the other Borderlanders, leaving the country vulnerable to attack. Aware of a gathering of Trollocs in the Blight, Ituralde and his forces went to Maradon to defend the city and Saldaea against a Trolloc invasion through the pass. His army was pushed back and nearly destroyed, along with much of Maradon, until Rand arrived with reinforcements and routed the Shadowspawn.

Maragaine. A queen of Andor during the War of the Hundred Years. She reigned from FY 1054 to FY 1073.

Marah. A Murandian novice in the White Tower. No more than fifteen or sixteen, she was stocky with mischievous blue eyes. She talked with Nicola about Egwene.

Marah Anan. A daughter of Setalle Anan. Marah was a little taller than her mother and had hazel eyes that were even larger than her mother's. She was pleasingly plump, and did not like Mat. She resented the fact that her younger sister Frielle married before her. She was about nineteen years old when Mat stayed at her mother's inn.

Maralenda. An Andoran Aes Sedai of the rebel contingent who was a distant cousin of the Trakand line. Siuan told Lelaine that she had seen Romanda talking to Maralenda in an effort to manipulate Lelaine.

Maram Kashor. A dry island on the southeast tip of Seanchan; Tylee Khirgan was born there.

Maran, Jailin. A minor Andoran nobleman. His sign was the crosshatched Red Wall. Jailin supported Elenia for the Lion Throne before she was taken by Arymilla.

Marande Algoran. The sister of the High Seat of House Algoran in Amadicia. Pretty with a heart-shaped face, she was powerful in her own right, but not enough to resist the Whitecloaks; Niall had her serve Morgase, which irked her. She taunted Morgase about the situation in Andor and how Rand had taken over. Morgase asked her if she spent all her time listening at doors. She was probably captured by the Seanchan and made *da'covale* when they invaded.

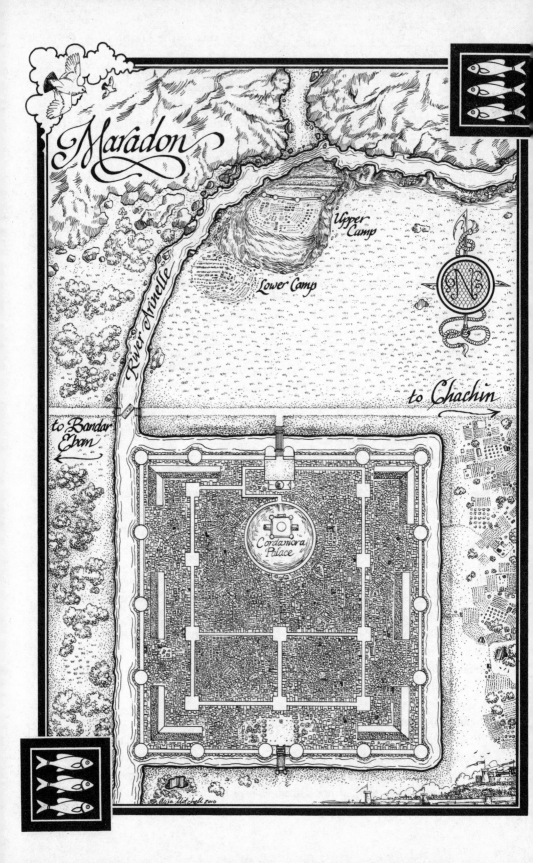

Maradon

Upper Camp

Lower Camp

River Arinelle

to Bandar Eban

to Chachin

Cordamora Palace

© Elisa Mitchell 2010

Marasale Jureen. An Aes Sedai of the Yellow Ajah who served as Amyrlin from 705 to 732 NE. Marasale was in large part a puppet of the Hall; they had gotten used to running things with Cemaille, an Amyrlin who had lost her authority, and chose someone they knew they could control and kept her on a very short leash.

Maraside Mountains. A range located along the southern border of Cairhien. These mountains were the site of a famous battle between Artur Hawkwing and Guaire Amalasan.

Marath. A battlefield from the Aiel War where things did not go well for the wetlanders. Tam rambled on about this battle while feverish after the Trolloc attack at his farm.

marath'damane. Old Tongue for "Those Who Must Be Leashed"; the Seanchan used the term for channelers not constrained by an *a'dam*, including Aes Sedai.

Maravaile family. *See* Ishara *and* Souran Maravaile

Maravin, Semaradrid. *See* Semaradrid Maravin

Marcasiev. A Kandori noble House. Its High Seat was Lord Varan; its sign the Red Stag. *See also* Varan Marcasiev

Marce Eldin. A Two Rivers girl with the ability to channel who became a novice with the rebel Aes Sedai, having been recruited by Verin and Alanna. She was about fifteen years old and stocky. Rand remembered little of her on meeting her in Caemlyn, except that she always had her nose in a book, even walking in the streets of Emond's Field.

March of Death, The. The final movement of *The Grand Passions Cycle*, played on the harp by Asmodean.

Marcolin, Demetre. *See* Demetre Marcolin

Mardecin. A village in Amadicia, the first village over the border from Tarabon. It was large, a mile across, straddling a small bridged stream between two hills. Mardecin's streets were of granite, its buildings of brick or stone, with slate or thatched roofs. It had fallen on hard times, with Taraboner trade being cut off. Ronde Macura, an agent for the Yellow Ajah, had a dress shop in Mardecin, and there was a Whitecloak garrison nearby. Nynaeve and Elayne met with Ronde, who passed on the message that all sisters were welcome to return to the White Tower, and who also gave them drugged tea. They were rescued by Thom and Juilin, and Ronde told them that she was instructed to look out for Elayne. They dyed Elayne's hair black and left town in a different cart.

Mardina lace. A high-quality lace with an intricate weave.

Mardoon, Stedding. A *stedding* located along the Shadow Coast.

mardroot. An herb used to make a liniment to treat bruises; it stung on application.

Mardry. A bluff-faced man of Hinderstap with short dark hair. When Mat offered to gamble for supplies, Mardry offered his wagon and team as part of the pot.

Maredo Causeway. A wide, dirt-packed road leading two miles north out of Illian through the marshes that surrounded the city and continuing in an easterly direction toward Tear.

Maredo. A nation that arose from the War of the Hundred Years.

Maredo, Plains of. Flatlands unclaimed by any country, located between Andor, Illian and Tear, below the Hills of Kintara. Far Madding was the only city in this territory.

Mareed, Azil. The Domani High Captain of the Tower Guard and advisor to Marya Sedai on the decision-making council of the Grand Alliance during the Battle of the Shining Walls.

Mareesh. A city which fell to the Tourag in another Age. Birgitte said that she had not seen anyone trussed as Nynaeve was by Moghedien since the Tourag took Mareesh.

Mareil. A Sea Folk Wavemistress, one of the First Twelve of the Atha'an Miere. Tall and slender, with as much white as black in her shoulder-length hair; she had a melodious voice. Mareil and Harine were friends from the time they began as deckhands together; the two were the least senior among the First Twelve, with Harine only a bit higher. Tebreille din Gelyn South Wind was her Windfinder. Held by the Seanchan in Ebou Dar, Mareil escaped unharmed. She was at the meeting of the First Twelve in Illian with Logain and there learned of the mass suicide of the Amayar.

Marek Cormer. A Two Rivers man with Perrin in Ghealdan. Faile noted that he no longer seemed to believe the rumors about Perrin and Berelain.

Marel. The twin sister of Charel, a good-looking young groom in the White Tower stables. Sheriam used her in 981 NE to help break Theodrin's block which prevented her from channeling unless there was a man for whom she had strong feelings present. Charel had a gorgeous smile and made eyes at Theodrin; he was allowed to sit in on her lessons so that she could channel, but after a few times Marel was substituted and thus broke Theodrin's block.

Marella Inn. An inn in Altara that Egwene saw as she was traveling through *Tel'aran'rhiod* in the flesh on her way to Salidar.

Marella. A village in Altara; Egwene passed through it as she was traveling through *Tel'aran'rhiod* in the flesh on her way to Salidar.

Marendalar. An island that rebelled against the Seanchan, and was defeated. Bakuun spent two years fighting on Marendalar; thirty thousand were killed, and fifty times that were shipped back to the mainland as property.

Marendevin, Corgaide. *See* Corgaide Marendevin

Marenellin, Bukama. *See* Bukama Marenellin

Maresis, Therva. *See* Therva Maresis

Marewin. A noblewoman in King Ailron's Amadician court who attended Morgase. Slight and little more than a girl, she almost fainted when Marande mentioned Rand giving positions to men who could channel in Andor.

Mari. A maid at The Stag and Lion, in Baerlon, Andor. She helped serve dinner to Moiraine, Lan, Thom and the Emond's Fielders, then was shooed out by Master Fitch.

Mari, Mistress. A *nom de route* used by Moiraine in Illian; it was the name that Nieda knew her by.

Maric. 1) An Aiel man who guarded Rand's rooms in the palace in Cairhien when Egwene visited him. In his middle years, he was very tall with a bull-like chest and shoulders and cold gray eyes. When he chuckled at something Somara said, it softened neither his face nor eyes. 2) Nynaeve's notional son seen during her Accepted test.

Marigan. A woman Elayne and Nynaeve met on the *Riverserpent* on the way to Salidar. She appeared to be a few years older than Nynaeve; she had once been plump, for her frayed brown dress hung on her loosely, and her blunt face looked beyond weary. She had two sons, Jaril and Seve, ages six and seven, who stared silently at the world and seemed frightened of everything and everyone, even their own mother. Elayne and Nynaeve later learned that she was Moghedien in disguise after Nynaeve captured her in *Tel'aran'rhiod* and held her with an *a'dam*; she was not tested for the ability to channel in Salidar because she appeared past the cutoff age as established there. While held by the *a'dam*, she was forced to work as a servant and also to teach Elayne and Nynaeve and later Egwene. Halima freed her. *See also* Moghedien

Marille. A *damane* from Seanchan who was captured in the campaign against the Seanchan and sent to Caemlyn by Rand from Altara. She stuck to the party line: it was imperative that women who could channel be collared, for their safety and everyone else's as well. Her mistress's brother had been a Blood-knife; she recognized the knife that Gawyn had and told him what she knew of it, although she knew little.

Marillin Gemalphin. An Andoran Aes Sedai of the Brown Ajah in public but of the Black Ajah in truth. She had a strength level of 15(3). Born in 848 NE, she went to the White Tower in 863 NE. After spending six years as a novice and five years as Accepted, she was raised to the shawl in 974 NE. Skinny with light brown hair, she had blue eyes, a narrow face, thin lips and a wide nose. She was one of the original thirteen known members of the Black Ajah who fled the White Tower in late 998 NE. It was generally known in the Tower that she vanished on the night that murder was done in the Tower and *ter'angreal* stolen, but few believed that she was a Darkfriend. Marillin liked cats and went out of her way to help injured or stray animals. In many ways, she treated animals better than she did people; in Tanchico, she fed her cats royally, but had a maid severely punished for snitching something meant for the cats.

Marillin was coopted by Moghedien and sent to Caemlyn, where she was assigned to work for Lady Shiaine. At first she attempted to put herself in control of the situation, or at least to resist taking orders. She came to realize, partly because of how Falion was being punished, that it was in her own interest to swallow her pride and take orders from Shiaine. She was with Lady Shiaine at the house on Full Moon Street when Elayne arrived to take the Black Ajah prisoner. When the tables were turned, she was part of the group that took Elayne prisoner. She was captured when Birgitte's forces rescued Elayne and freed by Jaq Lounalt when Elayne was trying to get information from the captives.

Marin al'Vere. An Emond's Field woman who was the wife of Bran al'Vere and with him ran The Winespring Inn. About 5'4" tall, she had a graying braid, a motherly smile and kind eyes. Born in 940 NE, she married Bran al'Vere in 964 NE. Marin and Bran had five daughters: Berowyn, Alene, Elisa, Loise and Egwene. They lived in rooms at the back of the whitewashed second floor of The Winespring Inn. She also might have been able to learn to channel.

Marind. A Da'shain Aiel man from after the Breaking. His parents were Adan and Siedre, and his siblings Elwin, Jaren, Rhea and Sorelle. Marind married Sarilin, and they had two children, Lewin and Maigran. He and his mother were killed in a raid by bandits; his sister Rhea was kidnapped.

Maringil. A Cairhienin nobleman from a major House. Tall for a Cairhienin, he was whip-slender with white hair to his shoulders and dark predatory eyes. He believed in the Prophecies but hated Rand deeply for many reasons: because he ruled and was not Cairhienin; because he saved Cairhien from the Shaido when the Cairhienin could not; because he brought Aiel to Cairhien; and because he intended to give the Sun Throne to Elayne. Maringil wanted the throne, and maneuvered as much as possible for personal advantage. He was poisoned at Colavaere's order just after Rand was taken out of Cairhien by the Tower Aes Sedai.

Marinna. One of Rand and Aviendha's quadruplets, seen in Aviendha's viewings of the future in Rhuidean; she was small with a round face.

Marinye, Beonin. *See* Beonin Marinye

Marisa Ahan. A Two Rivers girl with channeling ability who set off with Verin and Alanna for the White Tower, and saw and was terrified by Rand at Culain's Hound in Caemlyn. She became a novice in the rebel camp. About sixteen, she was pretty. She always clapped her hands to her face when surprised.

Marisa Ayellin. A Two Rivers girl (originally Neysa; changed in later editions).

Marishna, Mistress. A young Kandori woman in Manala. Moiraine, seeking the infant Dragon Reborn, spoke to her when she was looking for Avene Sahera; she told Moiraine that she knew Saheras in Manala and South Hill, but none named Avene.

marisin. An herb used to make a tea that helped one sleep without grogginess.

Marisin Valley. A site in Coremanda where a battle was fought; Mat had memories of leading a cavalry charge in the valley.

Marith Jaen. An Aes Sedai of the Blue Ajah. Born in 700 NE, she went to the White Tower in 717 NE. She retired to the country in 973 NE to write her memoirs. There were rumors that her decision was influenced by personality clashes with Tamra Ospenya and disappointment that Tamra was raised

Amyrlin rather than she. Marith had a reputation as a stainless-steel bitch long before she was called back from retirement to take the Amyrlin Seat in 984 NE after the death of Sierin Vayu. The Hall felt that they had little choice, however; the previous two Amyrlins had died suddenly, and a large number of senior sisters had died in the prior few years. There were rumors in the outside world of Aes Sedai involvement in the deaths of men and even boys, and while most people didn't believe them, the Hall had indications that they might be true. Her methods of putting paid to the male channeler pogrom while keeping the whole affair secret cemented her reputation as someone to make the Dark One himself walk on tiptoes. During her short reign, the Hall was in her grasp like a collection of dolls. Her death in 988 NE was entirely natural, though at a younger age than might have been expected. The Tower's influence increased under her.

Marith Riven. A Murandian Aes Sedai of the Brown Ajah and the loyalist contingent, with a potential strength level of 18(6). Born in 968 NE near the Andoran border, she went to the White Tower in 984 NE. After spending eight years as a novice and seven years as Accepted, she was raised to the shawl in 999 NE, shortly after the Tower split. She had a habit of making observations about people and events that might have been better kept to herself. Marith was 5'6" tall. When she went to the Tower, Marith Jaen was Amyrlin, or became Amyrlin soon after; it was decidedly uncomfortable being a novice and having the same first name as an Amyrlin like that. When she was Accepted, Elayne threw a cup at her; Elayne was switched. Since she had not attained the ageless look, Marith was one of the three new sisters sent to help take Rand. Captured at Dumai's Wells and treated as *da'tsang* by the Aiel, under Verin's Compulsion, she found reason to swear oath to Rand and had done so before Cadsuane departed Cairhien for Far Madding. She had no Warder.

Marithelle Camaelaine. A leader who tried to seize Hawkwing's empire after his death. Within days of Hawkwing's demise, Jalwin Moerad, Hawkwing's advisor, was advising Marithelle Camaelaine. She was assassinated, but was still counted as one of the three who came closest to seizing all of Hawkwing's empire.

Market Sheran. A small village in Andor, west of Caemlyn and between Four Kings and Carysford. A small village, its only inn was a sprawling building, all on one floor, with the look of having had rooms added in bunches over the years without any particular plan. When Mat and Rand were working their way to Caemlyn they stayed at the inn there, though it was very expensive. The next morning at breakfast they were confronted by a young Darkfriend, Paitr, who Rand punched in the nose when he persisted in bothering them.

Paitr later offered to help Morgase and her group escape from the Whitecloaks detaining them in Amador; Paitr and his uncle were found chanting a catechism to the Shadow and hanged by the Whitecloaks.

Marks. A hound who ran away when Mandevwin was just seven, in Mat's elaborate fiction concocted to enable him and his men to sneak into Trustair.

Marks and Remarks. A history book that Min read.

Marle, Beryl. *See* Beryl Marle

Marlesh. Vasha's Warder. They had a casual relationship, much like that of a brother and sister. He was a short, narrow man and good with his sword. Marlesh fought at Dumai's Wells and escaped with the Aes Sedai who returned to the Tower and were sent to Dorlan. He and Sleete teamed up to spar against Gawyn, and were defeated three times.

Marli Noichin. A captured *sul'dam*, held by Elayne's group in Caemlyn. Plump with dark eyes, she wore plain brown wool. She was defiant, though she wept when forced to look at weaves too long, because she could see them. Still, like the other *sul'dam*, Marli denied that she was tainted in any way and claimed that the *a'dam* didn't really work on her, saying that her captors were using the Power to make her think so. Elayne witnessed an attempt to make her admit she could see the weaves.

Marline. A Wise One of the Taardad Aiel with the ability to channel and a strength level of 28(16). Marline was 5'8½" tall, and looked to be about the same age as Rand, Mat and Perrin, but she was more than twenty years older. She had dark brown hair of which she was inordinately proud as it was rare among the Aiel. Her eyes were a very deep, dark blue, like the purple of twilight. Marline was one of the Wise Ones sent with Perrin to Ghealdan to keep an eye on Seonid and Masuri. She went to battle against the Shaido at Malden. Marline assisted in the forging of *Mah'alleinir*, and accompanied Perrin's forces into the Last Battle.

Marne, Arymilla. *See* Arymilla Marne

Marne, House. A noble House in Andor. Its High Seat was Lady Arymilla until she was removed by Elayne; its sign the Four Moons.

Marodred, Cerilla. *See* Cerilla Marodred

Marriage Knife, The. An inn in Altara that Mat, Elayne, Nynaeve and their party stayed at on the way to Ebou Dar from Salidar.

Marris Thornhill. An Andoran Aes Sedai of the Brown Ajah publicly and of the Black Ajah in truth. She was of the loyalist contingent and had a strength level of 44(32). Plump-chinned, she usually seemed mild and absorbed in study. She had no Warder. Marris was named as Black Ajah by Atuan Larisett, who was a member of her heart along with Karale Sanghir. She was captured and broken by the Black Ajah hunters in the Tower, and gave the oath of obedience to Yukiri.

Marshal-General: A temporary rank sometimes given to a Seanchan Captain-General put in charge of a war.

marshwhite. An herb whose leaves made a bitter tea to calm a queasy stomach.

Marsial. A novice in the White Tower who Egwene sent to fetch forkroot that could be administered to Egwene herself, so that Barasine and another Red sister could tend to Red Ajah business.

Marsim of Manetheren. An ancient scholar who compiled the Annals of the Final Nights about the War of Power. She was considered reliable.

Martan, House. An Andoran noble House. *See* Brannin *and* Elvaine Martan

Martan. A handsome young clerk in the White Tower. He and Mistress Wellin were sent to copy names of mothers and babies off the lists Accepted had made; he smiled at the young Siuan and Moiraine until Mistress Wellin called him down for it.

Marthea. A Shaido Maiden of the Spear who was Arrela's protector and lover while she was *gai'shain*. Though she did not like what the Shaido were doing, she stayed with them out of loyalty to her clan. Marthea was killed in the battle at Malden.

Marthera. An Aes Sedai of the Green Ajah who Adelorna saw captured by the Seanchan during the attack on the White Tower.

Martine Janata. A Borderlander Aes Sedai of the Brown Ajah with a strength level of 14(2). Born in 902 NE, she went to the White Tower in 917 NE. After spending five years as a novice and four years as Accepted, she was raised to the shawl in 926 NE. Although she was Brown Ajah, her friends joked that she should have chosen Green. Martine was happiest in her researches and studies, but she truly did display many characteristics of Green sisters, including a liking for travel and adventures and a real interest in men. She herself often said at least half seriously that she would like to have three or four Warders, and not just for extra hands to carry books and research materials.

She was the last sister who made a regular business of studying *ter'angreal* no one knew the use of. In 973 NE, she was discovered unconscious on the floor of the sitting room in her apartments, burned out. Martine was unconscious for three days. There were a number of *ter'angreal* in her apartments that she had been studying, but she could not remember which she had been working on when the accident occurred. In fact, she had no memory of the entire week preceding the accident. Her Warder was killed by the shock when she was burned out. In all the years afterward, no one was willing to have anything at all to do with any of the *ter'angreal* that were in her rooms. As soon as Martine recovered enough to slip out of the White Tower, she vanished from Tar Valon completely. She made a new life as Setalle Anan. *See also* Setalle Anan

Martna Baily. A fictional pie maker in Hinderstap.

Martyn Tallanvor. A Guardsman-Lieutenant in Morgase's Queen's Guards in Andor. About six feet tall, he had dark eyes and broad shoulders. There was often roughness in his voice and heat in his eyes when he looked at Morgase. He was born in 971 NE and in 988 NE joined the Queen's Guards. From 988 to 993 NE he was involved in on-and-off border skirmishes between Andor and various Murandian lords, which were more frequent than usual at that time. Tallanvor served with distinction, was commissioned in 991 NE, and assigned to the Royal Palace in Caemlyn in 993 NE. At his first sight of Morgase he fell in love immediately, though he did not recognize it at first. From 995 to 997 NE

Tallanvor served on the borders of Altara before returning to the palace. He thought that Elayne used her position to get her own way many times when for perfectly good reasons she should not have had it, and that she used her position to make Guardsmen disobey or bend orders and/or rules. He was not averse to seeing her snubbed up short now and again.

When Morgase resisted Compulsion from Gaebril and fled Caemlyn, Tallanvor accompanied her. While she was Queen, he had looked on her from afar and thought there could be no more. After some time on the run together, with her disguises and very much not acting the Queen, his personal feelings came more into the open, his love only partly mitigated by anger over her mistakes, especially one he didn't admit to himself, that she had taken Gaebril as a lover. He began more and more to challenge her openly when he thought she was wrong, and to hide his feelings less. When Morgase, using the alias of Maighdin, and her party were taken into service by Faile, he became an armsman. After Morgase was taken *gai'shain* by the Shaido, he tried to find her, and instead found the Seanchan. Tallanvor arranged for Perrin to meet Tylee Khirgan and obtain Seanchan assistance in freeing the captives. He and Morgase were married by Perrin before the Last Battle.

Marushta, Rabayn. *See* Rabayn Marushta

Marwin clan. A family in the Two Rivers. *See* Elise, Hu *and* Teven Marwin

Marya Somares. A Tairen Aes Sedai of the Gray Ajah. Tall and slender with dark deep-set eyes, Marya was chosen to represent the White Tower on the Council of the Grand Coalition during the Aiel War. She supposedly died in her bed but was actually killed by the Black Ajah in their purge of anyone who might have knowledge of what they had dragged out of Tamra Ospenya regarding the birth of the Dragon Reborn.

Maryim, Mistress. A *nom de route* used by Nynaeve when traveling from Tar Valon to Tear, and in Tear.

Maryl Harke. A member of the Academy of Cairhien. A lanky young woman, she was tongue-tied when she tried to explain her project to Rand. Maryl had made a study of birds' wings in flight, and she displayed a shell of paper secured by strings and held aloft by heat rising from a brazier fire. She made huge kites she called gliders and, attached to them, threw herself off hills. She broke her arm when one folded up on her.

Marza, Therille. *See* Therille Marza

Masadim, Noane. *See* Noane Masadim

Masalin. A gray-haired Shaido Wise One who could not channel. Faile saw her giving advice to a man about his horse's ailment. All of the Wise Ones who could channel were gaping at the display created by the cleansing of the taint; since Masalin couldn't channel, she didn't notice it.

Maseen. A site in Arad Doman where Ituralde once triumphed in battle.

Masema Dagar. A common Shienaran soldier who began calling himself the Prophet of the Lord Dragon. Masema had deep-set, almost black eyes that looked like twin caves and seemed to burn with a dark fire. He never made jokes, or laughed at any, even before he renamed himself the Prophet. He was filled with zealotry, and might have been mad. About 5'10" tall, he had a pale triangular scar on one cheek and wore a topknot as a soldier but shaved his head when he became the Prophet. He hated or at least was contemptuous of Rand until he learned that Rand was the Dragon Reborn, at which point he became an increasingly fanatical supporter. After he and the other Shienarans under Uno were sent away by Moiraine, Masema began to preach the coming of the Lord Dragon in Ghealdan, and eventually became known as the Prophet. He in effect abandoned his Shienaran compatriots while making this change, for they were insufficiently ardent in following the Lord Dragon. Possibly only the fact that they were his former companions kept him from making examples of them. He became so rabid that people were flogged for using the wrong tone of voice in referring to Rand, or indeed for referring to Rand al'Thor instead of the Lord Dragon. He became so powerful through his mobs of followers that he had nobles flogged with impunity and even coerced the Queen into handing over her jewelry. Masema had no wish for self-aggrandizement; he ate and dressed simply, and if he sometimes stayed in the finest house available, it was largely because it was offered to him and he could use the space as a headquarters. The large gifts he was given—and those he in effect extorted—he used to feed the hordes that followed him. He was solicitous of the welfare of women, by and large, especially widows of his supporters, and of children, but he could be harsh even with the women if they showed signs of lacking the proper ardor. Children alone seemed immune; though it made him angry, he said that children were too young to know so could not be held accountable.

Masema amassed a ragged army of upward of ten to twelve thousand men, the Dragonsworn, and they established themselves in Ghealdan. He had what might be called both a tight and a loose control of Ghealdan. That is, neither he nor his mobs of people were in constant control of Ghealdan, so a good deal went on that he might not have approved of. On the other hand, when he wasn't there, there were a great many people who truly believed his message, and a great many afraid to let anyone know that they didn't; a number of his senior followers could whip up a mob in short order. This happened upon occasion, sometimes for fairly base motives on the part of the one whipping up the mob. As a result, despite the Prophet's absence, nobody did anything too far from what they thought he would approve, at least not out where it could be seen. This included commoners, nobles and Queen Alliandre herself. Masema sometimes slept in leaky farmhouses and drank only water; he always hired a poor widow and ate what she cooked, fair or foul, without complaint. Masema knew about Perrin riding behind Manetheren's banner and assumed Perrin was out for personal glory, for which he excoriated him. It was dangerous to use Masema's name instead of saying the Prophet, and also of calling Rand anything but the Lord Dragon, possibly with added honorifics.

Masema distrusted everyone. He despised the Aes Sedai, who he believed intended to try to control Rand. Perrin was not respectful enough of Rand, nor were the other Two Rivers folk. Or any of the others, for that matter. The Asha'man were men who could channel, and touching the Power was blasphemy for any mortal. The Wise Ones also could channel, which made them as bad as the Aes Sedai, and besides, they, the Maidens and Gaul were Aiel savages— Masema had served three years at Ankor Dail, and hated Aiel. Masema would not Travel because it was blasphemy for anyone except the Dragon Reborn to touch the One Power, and him only because he was the Light-made-flesh. He changed this position, unexpectedly, when it was necessary to keep up with Perrin.

Masema gained some control over the northern part of eastern Amadicia after an altercation with the Whitecloaks over the seizure of a vessel for Nynaeve's use that led to rioting in Samara, but in many ways his conquest had not been as quick or as smooth as in Ghealdan. There was strong resistance from Whitecloaks, and to some people's surprise, from the King's soldiers too, as well as locally raised militias and levies. Thus that quadrant of Amadicia resembled a quilt, with regions that were firmly in Masema's control, regions firmly in the control of Whitecloaks or the King's soldiers, and regions that were no-man's-lands.

Once Masema and his troops followed Perrin, they lost control of Amadicia to the Seanchan. Aes Sedai who had sworn to Rand were still objects of distrust and dislike for Masema, but in some ways he was easier toward them than toward others, supposedly because Seonid and Masuri could say right out that they had sworn fealty to Rand and meant to keep their oaths.

The Prophet disapproved of money gained through trade as much as he did of carousing or what his fellows called lewd behavior. He disapproved of many things and made his feelings clear with sharp examples. He was assassinated before the Last Battle by Faile and *Cha Faile*.

Masenashar. A nation that arose after the Trolloc Wars.

Maseta Peninsula. The center peninsula of Tanchico in Tarabon, one of the three peninsulas on Tanchico Bay; the King's Circle, an assembly arena, lay on it.

Mashadar. The evil residing in Shadar Logoth which came about after everyone in Shadar Logoth had killed one another. Suspicion and hate made something that fed on that which created it, something locked in the bedrock on which the city stood. Appearing as a faintly luminescent silvery-gray mist, Mashadar killed anyone it touched. It came out at sunset and could sense food. Mashadar ensnared Mordeth, who alone survived the destruction of Shadar Logoth, confining him to the ruined city until he could consume the soul of another and escape.

Mashera Donavelle. An Aes Sedai from history who went against her inclinations in obedience to the White Tower and bore seven children for a man she loathed.

mashiara. Old Tongue for "beloved of heart and soul."

Mashinta, Naorman. A third-generation cobbler in Tar Valon. Egwene met with Siuan in his shop in *Tel'aran'rhiod*.

Mashong, Stedding. A *stedding* located in the Spine of the World.

Masic. An Ebou Dari man who was killed in a knife fight with Baris. Asra tried to Heal him, but was not successful.

Mask of Mirrors, the. A weave, also known as Illusion or Mirror of Mists, which allowed one to change one's appearance.

Maslin, Narvais. *See* Narvais Maslin

Masond, Jak. *See* Jak Masond

Masoon, Cormalinde. A famous sculptor from the Age of Legends whose works were found in the Ansaline Gardens resort.

Master of the Blades. A Sea Folk officer, appointed by the Mistress of the Ships, who had authority over all Swordmasters, and was responsible for defense and security of all Sea Folk. Though the Master of the Blades was frequently the husband of the Mistress of the Ships, it was not always so. The Master of the Blades rated a fringed blue parasol of three tiers. Baroc served as Master of the Blades for Nesta din Reas Two Moons; they were executed by the Seanchan for rebellion. When Zaida became Mistress of the Ships, she appointed Amel as her Master of the Blades.

Masuri Sokawa. An Arafellin Aes Sedai of the Brown Ajah and the rebel contingent, with a strength level of 16(4). Born in 935 NE, she went to the White Tower in 950 NE. After spending five years as a novice and seven years as Accepted, she was raised to the shawl in 962 NE. Her Warder was Rovair Kirklin. Masuri was 5'4" tall, and slim, with merry brown eyes. She always spoke quietly, but unlike many Browns, she always spoke straight to the point. She was also an untypical Brown in that she took some interest in clothes and men, and liked to flirt, though she could sometimes ignore the man she was flirting with, because of something interesting, such as a book or just a sudden interesting thought. She was an expert on Darkhounds. Masuri was part of the rebel embassy to Rand in Caemlyn and was one of the first three to approach Rand there. She followed after Rand when he fled Caemlyn and was forced to swear fealty to him after Dumai's Wells. She was treated as an apprentice by the Aiel Wise Ones.

Masuri and Seonid were sent to Ghealdan with Perrin, under orders to obey him as they would Rand, something that left room for interpretation, as she, Seonid and Perrin were all aware. Masuri, like Seonid, considered the Dragonsworn to be mad dogs, Masema included, but she thought the mad dogs could and should be leashed and bound so that they could be used. This was one of the ways she thought she could meet her obligation to serve the Dragon Reborn. Or, she thought so in the beginning; she changed her mind over time.

Masuri had a certain animosity toward Perrin. Actually, it was toward Rand, for putting her in the position in which she found herself with the Wise Ones—doing chores, and so forth—but Rand was not there while Perrin was, as Rand's representative. In fact, she would very much have liked to skin Perrin. Masuri believed that Perrin, like Masema, needed to be leashed and bound. Whether she had decided this because she thought it was another way to meet her obligations to the Dragon Reborn, or because of her animus toward Rand and Perrin, was unclear, perhaps even to her. She and Rovair secretly met with Masema, sometimes accompanied by Annoura; Masuri thought that Masema could be used in some way to further the cause of the Light. During the Last Battle Masuri was stationed at Berelain's palace in Mayene, and Healed Perrin after he sustained an arrow wound from Slayer.

Masuto. A Shienaran soldier with a long nose who went with Rand and Ingtar to reclaim the Horn of Valere. He stirred soup as Min and Perrin talked in the Mountains of Mist.

Mat Cauthon. *See* Matrim (Mat) Cauthon

Match. *See* Piri

Materasu. A noble House in Kandor. *See* Ethenielle Kirukon Materasu

Materese the Healer. Mother of the Wondrous Ind, featured in one of Thom Merrilin's tales.

Mathena. A woman from history who shied away from men until she was kissed. Birgitte told Nynaeve that she was like Mathena, and to watch out for the first man to kiss her.

Matherin. A Royal House of Andor. *See* Aedmun *and* Nelein Matherin

Mathwin, Verin. *See* Verin Mathwin

Matilde. A serving woman in the Tarasin Palace in Ebou Dar. The fourth of seven servants to guide Mat on his first visit to the palace, she was skinny and wore a marriage knife.

Matoun. A lancer with Bashere's army. After Rand had his hand blasted off by Semirhage, Bashere and his men arrived through gateways and Bashere ordered Matoun to form the lancers.

Matrim (Mat) Cauthon. A young *ta'veren* man from Emond's Field. He was born in 978 NE, the son of Abell and Natti, and had two younger sisters, Bodewhin and Eldrin. Approximately 5'11" tall and weighing 170 pounds, he had brown eyes and brown hair long enough to reach his coat collar. Mat was always mischievous as a child; he and Dav Ayellin seemed rivals to see who could get into the most trouble. Mat never could figure out how his mother always seemed to know what he was doing; it never occurred to him that his sisters were keeping her informed.

In 998 NE, Mat saw a stranger in a black cloak on a black horse; his friends Rand al'Thor and Perrin Aybara did as well. On the next night, Winternight, Trollocs attacked Emond's Field. Moiraine Sedai and her Warder Lan were visiting, and they helped fight off the attack. Since the attack was focused on the homes of Perrin, Rand and Mat, Moiraine persuaded them that it was necessary for them to leave Emond's Field. They attempted to leave secretly, but

Egwene al'Vere realized that they were up to something and went along, and the gleeman who was in town for Bel Tine joined as well.

The group started for Tar Valon, with Draghkar, Myrddraal and Trollocs chasing them; Perrin, Rand and Mat began being troubled by dreams involving a man with eyes of fire who called himself Ba'alzamon. Moiraine and Lan were able to keep them just a step ahead of the Shadowspawn. Finally they were forced to shelter in Shadar Logoth. Mat persuaded Rand and Perrin to explore the city; they encountered Mordeth, but did not help him escape. Mat stole a dagger with a ruby in its hilt from Mordeth's cache of riches. Against all expectations Trollocs entered the ruined city, and the group gathered itself to flee. Mashadar, a deadly fog, appeared. Mat, Rand and Thom, separated from the others, found refuge on Bayle Domon's boat, and fled Trollocs downriver to Whitebridge. Mat and Rand separated from Thom there during an encounter with a Myrddraal. Village by village they made their way to Caemlyn, sometimes performing to earn their keep. They were chased by Darkfriends and Fades, and Mat grew increasingly distrustful and hopeless; in Caemlyn Mat seemed ill. There they were reunited with the rest of their party; Moiraine revealed that the dagger that Mat had stolen was causing his distrust and illness; she Healed him as much as she could. They then traveled via the Ways to Fal Dara, and from there made their way through the Blight to the Green Man and the Eye of the World. Aginor and Balthamel appeared; they had been able to follow the dagger. The Green Man killed Balthamel, and Rand killed Aginor. In the empty Eye, they found the Horn of Valere, a broken seal of the Dark One's prison and the Dragon banner.

They returned to Fal Dara, but Trollocs and Fades attacked and stole the Horn and the dagger; Mat would die if the dagger was not recovered and his connection to it broken. Perrin, Loial, Rand and Mat joined a group of Shienaran soldiers to pursue those who stole the items; Rand, Loial and Hurin, a sniffer who could smell the trail, vanished, and Perrin used his wolfbrother talents to lead the rest in pursuit. Rand was able to take the Horn back, but it was stolen again by Padan Fain, who took it to Falme. Mat, Rand and the rest followed using a Portal Stone, but something went wrong and they all saw all the lives that they could have lived, and lost four months in the process. They eventually made it to Falme, and took the Horn and dagger again. The Seanchan and the Whitecloaks were battling, and Mat blew the Horn; they all managed to escape, with the exception of Ingtar, a Shienaran solder who was also a Darkfriend.

Mat was then taken to Tar Valon, where he was Healed of his connection to the dagger. He found that some of his memories were sketchy, but that did not stop him from teaching Galad Damodred and Gawyn Trakand that a man with a quarterstaff could be a dangerous foe. Although he was not supposed to leave Tar Valon, Elayne, Nynaeve and Egwene were able to provide him with a letter so that he could leave. Before he left, he went on a gambling spree and discovered that he was incredibly lucky.

Mat convinced Thom to accompany him to Caemlyn to deliver Elayne's letter to Morgase. They went downriver to Aringill, where Mat saved Aludra, an Illuminator, from thugs. She rewarded him with a gift of fireworks. In Caemlyn, he tried to deliver Elayne's letter, but was turned away at the gate. Like Rand, he went over the wall and overheard someone ordering the deaths of Elayne, Egwene and Nynaeve in Tear; he managed to meet with Morgase and her lover Gaebril, and realized that Gaebril had issued those orders. He and Thom set out to Tear to save them. He used Aludra's fireworks to make his way into the Stone of Tear and rescued the three women. He visited the realm of the Aelfinn using the redstone doorway in the Stone; the Aelfinn told him that he must go to Rhuidean or die, that he would marry the Daughter of the Nine Moons, die and live again, and live once more a part of what was, and give up half the light of the world to save the world. Mat went with Rand via Portal Stone to the Waste, and entered Rhuidean because of what he was told by the Aelfinn. In Rhuidean he entered another doorframe *ter'angreal*; it took him to the realm of the Eelfinn, where he received a foxhead medallion and other men's memories, then was hung from an *ashandarei* tangled in *Avendesora*'s branches. Rand cut him down and resuscitated him.

In the Waste, Mat acquired a black hat from the peddler Hadnan Kadere and took up with Melindhra, a Shaido Maiden. When he arrived back in Cairhien, he intended to leave Rand and go off on his own; instead, he found himself caught up in the battle against the Shaido for Cairhien. He saved Cairhienin and Tairens from an ambush, and killed Couladin. The next day, Nalesean, one of the Tairens, and Talmanes, a Cairhienin, swore fealty to him and said that he was their general; Mat still tried to get away, but the soldiers followed him and became the Band of the Red Hand. After battling Andorans trying to take Cairhien's Sun Throne for Morgase, Mat and the Band returned to the city of Cairhien with the news that Morgase was dead and Gaebril King. Rand declared that he was going to Caemlyn to kill Rahvin; he also badgered Mat to use his army. Mat let slip to Melindhra that Rand was going to Caemlyn; she tried to kill Mat, and he killed her. Mat went with Rand to Caemlyn; in Rahvin's first blast, Mat was killed. Rand finally killed Rahvin with balefire, and Mat returned to life.

Mat fell in with Rand's plans and took his army to Maerone; there he danced a forgotten dance with Betse and rescued Olver from Murandian lords. The Band headed south toward Tear; before they got there, Rand appeared and redirected them toward Salidar to fetch Elayne to Caemlyn. When Mat arrived in Salidar, he was astonished to find that Egwene was the Amyrlin. He, Nalesean and some Redarms of the Band accompanied Elayne, Nynaeve, Aviendha and several Aes Sedai to Ebou Dar. There he was rather forcefully seduced by Queen Tylin, became friends with Tylin's son Beslan and with Birgitte, located

the Bowl of the Winds, fought a *gholam*, learned that Moghedien (or at least one of the Forsaken) might be taking an interest in him, remained behind to find Olver when the women left with the Bowl, and was trapped under a collapsing brick wall when the Seanchan took the city. Dug out of the ruins, he recuperated in Tylin's palace and became known to the Seanchan as "Tylin's Toy," or simply "Toy." Tuon offered to buy him. He befriended Noal Charin, and planned to help Teslyn escape from being a *damane* to repay her attempt to warn him earlier. He also freed a Windfinder *damane* and two other Aes Sedai. In escaping, he kidnapped Tuon, learned that she was the Daughter of the Nine Moons, and said three times that she was his wife. He fled to Valan Luca's show, which was camped outside Ebou Dar, and they began to make their way to Lugard.

While they were traveling, Mat attempted to court Tuon. Renna, a *sul'dam* who had escaped with him, tried to kill Egeanin and then went to the Seanchan; Mat followed her, and Harnan was able to kill her at Mat's order. Mat and Thom took Tuon to an inn in Maderin; when they left they were attacked, and Mat decided it was time to leave Luca's show. He was headed for a pass in the Damona Mountains when Talmanes and part of the Band appeared with the news that a landslide had closed it. Mat then worked to draw the Seanchan away from the Molvaine Gap so he and his group could get out of Altara. He won several skirmishes before Banner-General Furyk Karede showed up; when Karede assured Mat that he could safely return Tuon to Ebou Dar, Mat said that he would let her go. Tuon then said that Mat was her husband three times, completing the Seanchan marriage ceremony and making Mat the Prince of the Ravens. Karede started for Ebou Dar with Tuon, and Mat, the Band and a number of Deathwatch Guards fought Seanchan who were trying to kill Tuon and defeated them decisively.

Mat then headed to Andor to rejoin the rest of the Band; on the way, he won a bet in Hinderstap, but almost lost his life. He met up with Verin, who offered to make a gateway to Caemlyn for him, but he had to stay there for thirty days, not opening a letter she gave him. Mat camped outside Caemlyn and wrote Elayne asking for a meeting; while he was waiting for a reply, the *gholam* showed up in his camp and killed a number of his men. In his meeting with Elayne, he was able to get her support for building dragons; in return, he loaned her his foxhead medallion for three days. She was able to make imperfect copies, and he was able to use those in defeating the *gholam* by dumping the creature off the side of a Skimming platform. Mat met up with Perrin, and Perrin agreed to have one of his Asha'man make a gateway to the Tower of Ghenjei. Mat, Noal and Thom went to the tower, and succeeded in rescuing Moiraine, although Noal, who was really Jain Farstrider, was killed in the effort.

Mat returned to Ebou Dar to see Tuon; he saved her from a Gray Man and consummated their marriage. Tuon named him the Rodholder of the Seanchan army, third in the line of command after Tuon and Galgan. Mat led the

Seanchan army to the Last Battle; when it was discovered that the great captains were all victims of Graendal's Compulsion, he assumed command of the entire army of the Light. With a lot of help from his friends, he led them to victory over the forces of the Shadow. He then went to Shayol Ghul and killed Padan Fain. Tuon told him that she was with child, and he set off a fireworks display for her.

Mattin Stepaneos den Balgar. The King of Illian, Anointed by the Light, Lion of the Coast, Defender of the Sea of Storms. His sigil was the Three Leopards, silver on black. Mattin, old enough to have fought Pedron Niall in his prime, was still robust but almost bald, with a white beard and a creased face framing a nose that had obviously been broken in the past. He came heavily under the influence of Lord Brend (Sammael), but as Sammael became distracted by worries about Rand in the months immediately preceding the conquest of Illian, Mattin had begun to reassert himself. A few days before the attack on the city of Illian, he vanished. The remaining Council of Nine suspected that Brend had something to do with that, but in truth Elaida had had him kidnapped. He arrived in Tar Valon on one of the last vessels to enter before the harbors were blocked by Egwene's *cuendillar* chains. Elaida asserted that she had saved him from Rand, but Egwene told him the truth about Rand's dealings with rulers. After the White Tower was reunited, Mattin was afraid to return to Illian and did not try to retake the throne.

Matuchin Hall. A place associated with the Heroes of the Horn, mentioned in *The Great Hunt of the Horn*. Blaes, a Hero of the Horn, was of Matuchin.

Maule, the. The rough port area of Tear. It contained inns, though they were cramped and often dirty, and it also contained shops that catered to the sailors and working folk of the sea.

Mavabwin, Lord. A Cairhienin nobleman of middling power who Elayne thought could be a roadblock to her ascending the Sun Throne. Present when Elayne stripped Arymilla, Naean and Elenia of the properties and offered them to Cairhienin, he was slow to catch on and spoke at the same time as did Lady Osiellin; they had to split an estate.

mavinsleaf. An herb used to make an acrid herbal concoction, administered to those who lied. It was powdered for use in tea with boiled catfern, producing a viscous, sickly green liquid.

Mavra Mallen. The Wisdom of Deven Ride. She temporarily took Nynaeve's place in Emond's Field when Nynaeve followed Moiraine to bring back the Emond's Fielders. At some point she either left or died and was replaced by Ellwin Taron.

Mayam Colona. A Tairen Aes Sedai of the White Ajah and the loyalist contingent, with a strength level of 21(9). Born in 960 NE, she went to the White Tower in 977 NE. After spending twelve years as a novice and eight years as Accepted, she was raised to the shawl in 997 NE. Mayam was 5'6" and slim, with dark skin, black eyes and black hair. She could eat as much as she wanted without gaining a pound. Part of the expedition sent to kidnap Rand, she had not acquired the ageless look and helped to carry the chest during the actual kidnapping. Mayam was captured at Dumai's Wells and treated as *da'tsang* by the Aiel until, under Verin's Compulsion, she found reason to swear fealty to Rand, which she had done before Cadsuane departed Cairhien for Far Madding. She had no Warder.

Mayel, Balwen. *See* Balwen Mayel

Mayene. A city-state located on a peninsula in the Sea of Storms. Its sigil was a golden hawk in flight: the Golden Hawk. Its banner was the Golden Hawk on a field of blue, fringed in gold if flown when the First was present.

Protected by its location, guarded by the sea and by the Drowned Lands, Mayene was able to escape most of the warfare that ravaged the rest of Hawk-wing's empire, although it was sacked twice during that time. Only Tar Valon, Tear and Far Madding, which escaped being sacked altogether, were sacked less often, and most cities were taken and looted many more times. There were suggestions in some records that even Tar Valon may have suffered at least partial looting. Approximately FY 1004 a youth was brought to Mayene, calling himself Tyrn sur Paendrag Mashera and claiming to be Hawkwing's grandson (or great-grandson; accounts vary). In any event, Mayeners believed the claims, and while he and his followers denied any desire to try to retake Hawkwing's empire, Mayene welcomed them, perhaps as a sign of stability, and styled him the First Lord of Mayene. Few if any outside of Mayene believed that Tyrn sur Paendrag was any relation to Hawkwing, perhaps because he made no claim for the empire as a whole, and while great efforts had been expended in killing all of Hawkwing's known surviving descendants, no more than one or two desultory attempts were made against Tyrn sur Paendrag. He lived the remainder of his life in Mayene, dying of a fever in FY 1054, whereupon his eldest daughter, Miselle, was given the title First Lady of Mayene. While Tyrn's influence in the city had increased during his lifetime until he was the ruler of the city-state in all but name, Miselle was the first to be acknowledged as the ruler. Except for some border skirmishes with Tear which never became full-fledged wars, and several small naval conflicts, Mayene was seldom involved in strife. The only time that Mayeners ever fought the Aiel was during the Aiel War, when most nations were involved in the fighting.

The ruler of Mayene was the First of Mayene, which was once "the First Lord or Lady," a form used sometimes much later. The title normally was hereditary, with the eldest child of either gender following. This was not always the case—there were usurpations or coups, as in most lands—but no one was ever given the title without the proper qualifications. Qualification required descent from a certain family, which according to Mayener belief at least, meant descent from Artur Hawkwing.

In the beginning there was only one Second, or "Second Lord" or "Lady" who was usually the successor to the First, but over time that changed. There were, in the last hundred years or so before the Last Battle, as many as nine nobles at once, the High Seats of the major Houses, holding the title of "Second of Mayene." They did not use "High Seat of House" as their title, rather styling themselves by first and House names, Second of Mayene.

In that same period, a number of nobles began styling themselves "Third of Mayene," implying that they at least ranked right behind the Seconds, but that was considered an affectation by the First, by the Seconds and indeed by many of the other lower nobility.

The Winged Guards served as the personal guard of the First of Mayene and the elite force of Mayener arms. They numbered approximately two thousand men and officers in all, and constituted the only standing armed force in Mayene. The Winged Guards wore red-painted breastplates and helmets like rimmed pots that came down to the nape of the neck in back. Officers had wings worked on the sides of their helmets, and slender red plumes. Three plumes marked the Lord Captain, the overall commander; two plumes marked a captain; and one a lieutenant. The Winged Guards were supplemented at need by a general levy on the population. All physically fit male commoners from fifteen to fifty were required to train with bow or crossbow and with the halberd or the pike. Every man was required to attend a yearly muster for a week of training in a unit, and there were fines for not keeping up with training. These musters were staggered throughout the year so that one was held nearly every week. Nobles were exempted from this because they were expected to be competent with arms and to fight when necessary to defend Mayene.

Shipbuilding was a major industry; in it little Mayene rivaled Illian and surpassed Ebou Dar. Mayene was a port of call for many vessels in part because of a lively trade with the interior of Tear; that trade was all through smuggling because of prohibitive duties on exports from Mayene to Tear. Mayener import duties were much lower than those on goods imported directly into Tear, so the risk was worth it. Mayene was also the first stop for ships returning from Shara, so it had the first pick of their exotic goods such as ivory and silk.

Fishing was a major industry, especially for oilfish, whose oil was the major competitor for olive oil both in cooking and in lamps. Mayeners knew the location of the oilfish shoals, which no one else did. Economically, those shoals rivaled in importance the olive groves of Tear, Illian and Tarabon.

Mayene had no mines of any kind, but its craftsmen were known for exceedingly fine gold- and silver-work, as well for gem-polishing and exquisite jewelry. Mayene produced swords and daggers which, though not of the same rank as Andoran weapons, were certainly among the most ornate crafted anywhere. Since it had little land, Mayene had few sheep or goats but did have a reputation for fine rugs and carpets. Mayener blown glass was arguably the finest in the world. Olives and figs were both grown in Mayene, but not in sufficient quantities for any significant trade, though some people considered Mayener figs the sweetest and best in the world.

Mayene, First of. Title of the ruler of Mayene. *See* Berelain sur Paendrag

Mayener. One from Mayene.

Maylin. A serving girl at The Old Sheep in Ebou Dar; one of the most remarkably pretty women Mat had ever seen. Her only task seemed to be standing outside to attract customers. Mat talked to her while looking for Olver in Ebou Dar; he thought that she wasn't very bright.

Mayv Gilyard. An Andoran noblewoman who was the guardian of Branlet Gilyard, until she died in a riding accident.

Maza, Joline. *See* Joline Maza

Mazone. A Youngling who wanted to join the Tower Guard instead of becoming a Warder; he was killed by one of the Bloodknives.

Mazrim Taim. A false Dragon from Saldaea who nearly managed to take over much of Saldaea and carried battle into Kandor and Arad Doman before he was brought down. Born in 972 NE, he was 6'4" tall and bore a passing resemblance to Demandred, both physically and in temperament. With a hooked nose and dark eyes like augers, he was a physically powerful man who moved with something of a Warder's deadly grace, but there was an air of imminent violence about him. He was not a nice man at all. While not a Darkfriend originally, he was always prime material for them, a man far more interested in wealth and power than anything else, willing to do whatever was required to get them. Because it was necessary, of course; he would kill, rob, whatever, but only because it was necessary. Rape was the one crime he abhorred; he willingly killed rapists, and he never did it quickly.

On the day Rand appeared in the sky above Falme, when a vision of that event appeared in the sky above a battle in Saldaea, Taim's horse reared and threw him, and he was knocked unconscious and captured. He was being carried to Tar Valon for gentling when he was freed, supposedly by his supporters, but actually by Demandred. Aes Sedai were killed both in capturing him and freeing him. Demandred offered Taim a choice, and Taim accepted, going to Rand in Caemlyn with one of the seals on the Dark One's prison to make sure that Rand would trust him and take him in.

Rand made Taim the leader of the Asha'man; Taim took the title M'Hael. Taim demanded deference from the Asha'man of the sort due a king. He often spent time alone, when no one could bother him; those who tried were turned away, and could be punished harshly. Taim was given secret instructions to recruit in the Two Rivers, which he said he would handle in person. Rand was reluctant about this, but thought that maybe he could trust Asha'man recruited there. Taim made no effort to recruit for the Legion of the Dragon; he recruited openly for Asha'man and nothing else. He talked of Rand being the Dragon Reborn, and said that Rand had sent him. He played up the grand adventure aspects, demonstrated channeling and dismissed the fears of insanity. The Village Councils and the Women's Circles knew they couldn't stop him, but talked against him. He managed to recruit some forty-plus men and boys in the Two Rivers. Some of the boys had to run away to go with him. Taim also picked Asha'man with a dark aspect, gave them special lessons and recruited them as Darkfriends.

Using thirteen Myrddraal and thirteen channelers, he Turned other Asha'man and Aes Sedai to the Shadow. Moridin named him a Forsaken; he used the name M'Hael. Taim did a great deal of damage during the Last Battle before being killed by Egwene.

Meane sol Ahelle. The composer of "Glory of the Dragon" in the Fourth Age.

Meashan Dubaris. A member of the Domani Council of Merchants who was killed by a mob during the unrest in Bandar Eban.

Mecandes, Cabriana. *See* Cabriana Mecandes

Mechoacan. A region or place in Seanchan having fair-haired inhabitants.

Meciar. An Aiel member of the Night Spear society who wore the red headband of the *siswai'aman*. While Rand Skimmed to Caemlyn to deal with Rahvin, Meciar stood near him; when there was a stir among the Aiel, Meciar told him someone had fallen off the Skimming platform.

Medanor Eramandos. An Aes Sedai of the Gray Ajah who served as Amyrlin from 142 to 171 NE. Medanor was a fairly strong Amyrlin who managed through her skill at gaining consensus, mediation and playing one faction off another.

Medar, Barid Bel. Demandred's name in the Age of Legends.

Meditations on the Kindling Flame. A history book on the rise of various Amyrlins that Egwene saw Silviana reading when she went to get one of her many punishments.

Medo. A small village in Shienar on the River Mora, which ran along the border of Arafel. The village was about the same size as Emond's Field, maybe a little larger, and had two stone docks which projected into the river. It was there that Siuan Sanche and her entourage arrived by ship on their way to Fal Dara, and from there later that they took a ship back to Tar Valon. During the Last Battle, Medo was burned to slow the advance of the Trolloc armies.

Medore Damara. A Tairen noblewoman who was one of the daughters of High Lord Astoril; Estean once thought he might marry her. She became a member of *Cha Faile*. She was tall, with a dark complexion, black hair and bright blue eyes, and if she missed beautiful, it wasn't by much. She was full-bosomed, which made puffy-sleeved Tairen coats look particularly odd on her. Her favorite mare was named Redwing. Balwer thought her of high enough rank to approach Berelain and thus set her up to spy on Berelain and Annoura; Perrin canceled the operation. She later went off with Balwer and Latian in So Habor and returned with Tallanvor.

Medrano, Rosara. *See* Rosara Medrano

meegerling. A small animal found in the Waste. It looked much like a rat, but was far more stupid. When placed near grain, the meegerling would go straight for it, regardless of any dangers in its path, and it never learned to avoid those dangers.

Megairil, Wreath of. Spoken of by Birgitte, referring to an earlier age, it was an important prize given to the winner of a horse race.

Megana. An Aiel Wise One mentioned along with Bair as setting watches for Rand's return in Cairhien after Dumai's Wells. She was mentioned again with Bair as not knowing what the wetlander doings in and around Cairhien meant.

Mehar. A town in Saldaea. It was the home of Vilnar, a Saldaean soldier patrolling Caemlyn after Rand had taken over the city. Vilnar thought about a girl there who he wanted to marry.

Mehtan. One of the Seanchan military clerks in Captain Faloun's office in Almizar, Amadicia. He was eaten from the inside by borer beetles.

Meidani Eschede. An Arafellin Aes Sedai of the Gray Ajah and the rebel contingent, with a strength level of 17(5). Born in 949 NE, she went to the White Tower in 967 NE. After spending eight years as a novice and seven years as Accepted, she was raised to the shawl in 982 NE. Her Warder was Leonin. Meidani was 5'8" tall, and slim; her bosom was not particularly large, but seemed larger because of her slenderness, something that gave her concern. Quite pretty, she had dark golden wavy hair that fell to her shoulders, sometimes with ornaments or pins, as she liked jewelry. Her features included big blue eyes, full lips and a high melodious voice. Meidani had less control over her facial expressions than most Aes Sedai, at least when she was angry or resentful; then, her mouth could assume almost a sullen pout, and her eyes could narrow resentfully or blaze with anger. These were all the more evident because she usually did control her tone of voice. It was almost always over personal matters that she got angry or sullen; when she was about her business of negotiation and mediation, she had very good control of her facial expressions.

Meidani was entered into the novice book a few weeks before Elaida, and the two quickly became pillow friends as novices; Meidani was a little shocked that Elaida insisted on breaking it off when she was raised Accepted before Meidani. She was not jealous of Elaida's rapid advancement, but Elaida took a special interest in her, pushing her to strive and achieve; Elaida being Elaida, this often took the form of seeing that Meidani had extra lessons, extra chores, or a visit to the Mistress of Novices when she failed to live up to Elaida's expectations. Meidani always harbored resentment about that; plainly she was never going to be on the same level of strength as Elaida, and she thought that Elaida wanted more from her than she could do. In fact, she might well have progressed faster, but the same stubbornness that would show up later in her life manifested itself, gaining her ever more extra chores and additional visits to the Mistress of Novices.

Meidani was only a fair to average negotiator and mediator. If she felt that matters were not progressing as they should, she would dig in her heels even when it was to the detriment of actually achieving a solution.

Meidani was part of the rebel fifth column sent by Sheriam's council in Salidar to infiltrate the White Tower (aka ferrets). Like all of the sisters chosen for the fifth column, Meidani was out of the White Tower when Siuan was deposed and the Tower broken, so there was no flight to arouse any suspicions toward her. Apparently, she had simply returned in answer to Elaida's summons. Also, many believed she harbored resentment against Siuan for passing her by so swiftly; she did, but not enough for her to support the manner of Siuan's removal.

Some were aware that she had been pillow friends with Elaida, and thought that her return indicated a continuing loyalty. Meidani was coopted by Seaine and Pevara to aid in their search for the Black Ajah; they ordered her to try to resume her former relationship with Elaida to acquire information. Meidani did—she had taken an oath of obedience to the Black Ajah hunters—and even though Elaida was aware that Meidani was a ferret, she spent time with her to gain information of her own. Egwene ordered Meidani to ask for a private lesson with her, then coerced her into leading Egwene to the group searching for the Black Ajah; Egwene convinced them to remove the oath of obedience. Egwene also had Meidani remove Verin's body from her novice room.

Meilan Mendiana. A High Lord of Tear. Upper servants of his House wore blue six-pointed stars on red. Tall for a Tairen, he was lean and hard with gray hair, dark eyes, a pointed beard and an oily voice. When needed he had an oily manner as well, but was otherwise stiff-necked. He stooped in Rand's presence and hated it and hated it even more if Rand told him to stand straight. He sometimes spoke to Rand half subserviently, half as if explaining to a child. He was contemptuous of peasants. Meilan was given command of forces to move into Cairhien to restore order and feed the hungry. He aspired to the Sun Throne of Cairhien and thought Maringil was his chief rival. Despite previous relationships with Hearne, Simaan and Estanda, he felt secure because he had plainly directed his ambitions away from Tear to Cairhien. He was assassinated in Cairhien on Colavaere's orders.

Meilyn Arganya. An Aes Sedai of the White Ajah with a strength level of 10(+3). Born in 698 NE, she went to the White Tower in 714 NE. After spending seven years as a novice and six years as Accepted, she was raised to the shawl in 728 NE. Her Warder was Andro. About 5'8" tall, she had silver-gray hair, blue eyes and a thrusting chin. Meilyn was one of the sisters called in by Tamra Ospenya to carry out the search for the newborn Dragon Reborn in secret. She was killed by the Black Ajah in 979 NE; she was reported to have died in her sleep, but Siuan was hiding under her bed at the time and there was no body when she came out.

Meira. A Wise One of the Shaido Aiel (not a Jumai) with the ability to channel and a strength level of 24(12). About 5'6" tall, she had a long, usually grim face, blue eyes and a thin mouth. Her smile was awkward because she so seldom practiced it. Her laugh was as dry and as narrow as her face. Greedy for riches, Meira was one of Sevanna's inner circle of plotters. She accompanied Sevanna to the Aes Sedai camp the day she saw Rand beaten. She took part in or was present at the murder of Desaine. She was with Sevanna at Dumai's Wells and at the meeting with "Caddar" and "Maisia." She helped question the Seanchan prisoner in Amadicia, while the Jumai were settled at a captured estate approximately ten days after their arrival.

Meise. A young Aiel girl, the daughter of Norlesh and Metalan, seen in Aviendha's visions of the future in Rhuidean.

Melaidhrin, Cadsuane. *See* Cadsuane Melaidhrin

Melaine. A Wise One of the Jhirad sept of the Goshien Aiel with the ability to channel and a strength level of 17(5). She was also a dreamwalker; Amys and Melaine were the best at interpreting the dream, although Bair was better at manipulating *Tel'aran'rhiod*. Melaine had red-gold, sun-colored hair that hung to her hips, and green eyes. A beautiful woman who looked no older than thirty, she was in fact somewhere between eighty-four and 110. She married Bael and was sister-wife to Dorindha; despite her greater age and her position as a Wise One, not to mention her personality, she deferred to Dorindha, who was the senior sister-wife and thus her elder first-sister, the roofmistress of the clan hold, and an even more commanding person than Melaine, though usually in a much quieter fashion. At first, she considered Bael impossible and frustrating, saying jokingly that she had to marry him or kill him. She eventually asked Amys and Bair to intercede with Dorindha to see whether Dorindha could accept her as sister-wife. She went to Caemlyn with Rand to join Bael, and joked about the impatience and frustration of a newly wed woman being away from her husband. She certainly went running to find him. According to Min, Melaine and Bael were expecting identical twin daughters; Melaine proposed to name them after Min and Egwene. Melaine was instrumental in Min being accepted by the Wise Ones as a sort of Wise One herself.

Melaine fought the Black Ajah in *Tel'aran'rhiod*, but she was near term at the Last Battle and served only as support.

Melanril Asegora. A young Tairen nobleman. He had dark eyes, a sharp nose and a pointed beard. During the fighting in Cairhien, he was given command of the Cairhienin and Tairen forces after Weiramon was sent south. Mat saw through a looking glass that they were headed into an ambush by the Shaido, and warned them about it. Melanril was killed in the battle.

Melare. An Andoran Aes Sedai of the Red Ajah and the loyalist contingent. Plump with ample hips, she had a mouth that looked ready to smile, bright blue eyes and thick black eyebrows. She helped Arebia, Zanica and others, one from each of the other Ajahs, capture Leane at Southharbor in Tar Valon. Melare and Desala questioned Leane the night she was captured. Unlike Desala, Melare disliked flogging even for one like that. She was one of five Reds who accompanied Pevara to the Black Tower with the intention of bonding Asha'man. Pevara chose her because Melare sent money to Andor to pay for her grandnephews' education as she had for her nieces and nephews. She was Turned to the Shadow while at the Black Tower.

Melarned. One of Ituralde's officers present at Ituralde's first meeting with Rand; he was squat.

Melasune. A queen of Andor during the War of the Hundred Years who reigned from FY 1035 to FY 1046.

Melavaire Someinellin. A stout Cairhienin Aes Sedai of the Gray Ajah and the loyalist contingent. She was inches shorter than Egwene. White flecked her dark hair. She was a kindly woman who could be fearsome when angry. Melavaire was walking with Beonin in the Tower when Egwene saw Beonin and accused her of betrayal; Melavaire was miffed, but Beonin asked her to walk away. Her Warder was a squat man even wider than she.

Melchor, Cyprien. One of the Counsels of Far Madding who met with Cadsuane's party when they arrived. She had protruding teeth.

Meldarath, Suroth Sabelle. *See* Suroth Sabelle Meldarath of Asinbayar *and* Barsabba

Melfane Dawlish. The niece of Elayne's maid Essande. Stout and jolly, but firm, Melfane was a midwife and dispenser of herbs and ointments from a shop on Candle Street. She became Elayne's midwife. Her son Jaem sometimes helped her.

Melia. Hurin's Shienaran wife.

Melindhra. A woman of the Jumai sept of the Shaido Aiel and *Far Dareis Mai*. She was taller than Mat with eyes the color of a clear morning sky and hair like spun gold. She went to join the Maidens around Rand. She and Mat became lovers, but she was a Darkfriend and died trying to kill Mat with a knife bearing nine golden bees as decoration, linking her to Sammael/Lord Brend.

Melisinde. A female character in *The Flame, the Blade and the Heart*. Egwene read about her one night before going to sleep.

Melitene. Tuon's *der'sul'dam*. She had less black than gray in her long hair. Melitene was an experienced woman, both in her craft and in catching nuances. After Tuon disappeared and Karede began the hunt for her, Melitene laughed about Mylen's fierce wanting to find Tuon, and her worship of Tuon. After Elaida was captured by the Seanchan at the White Tower and became the *damane* Suffa, Melitene had her demonstrate Traveling to Tuon.

Mellar, Doilin. *See* Doilin Mellar

Melli Craeb. The owner of The Seven-Striped Lass, a tavern in Caemlyn. She was pretty, with a round face, a nice bosom and curly auburn hair, and Mat thought she would be a good match for Talmanes. When Mat asked for Melli's advice about Verin's letter, she snatched it and offered to open it for him. She always fancied going to Tar Valon and becoming an Aes Sedai.

Melloy, Sharina. *See* Sharina Melloy

Melore. A Domani Kin who was part of the Knitting Circle in Ebou Dar and wore the red belt of a Wise Woman. She was plump, with a nice bosom, and had a touch of gray in her hair. She was not strong enough in the Power to have been allowed to test for Aes Sedai or strong enough to make a gateway of any size whatsoever. She accompanied Elayne and Nynaeve to the Rahad to find the Bowl of the Winds and was killed by the *gholam*.

Melten. A lean, mop-haired member of the Band of the Red Hand who dressed like an Andoran but spoke like a Borderlander. He was a talented juggler.

Melvara. An Aes Sedai whose name was on Verin's list of Black Ajah.

Melway, Kirin. *See* Kirin Melway

Memara. An Aes Sedai of the Red Ajah and the loyalist contingent, with a strength level of 34(22). She had a pleasant exterior appearance and an apparently pleasant personality; this pleasantness disguised a personality like a tiger on steroids. When she had a goal, she was not willing to allow anything to stand in the way—not anything at all—and she was willing to do anything at all that did not directly violate the Three Oaths to attain that goal. Memara was sent to Saldaea by Elaida in a failed attempt to influence Tenobia, who left her behind when she went to meet with the other Borderland rulers.

Men of Fire and Women of Air. A book written by Elora daughter of Amar daughter of Coura; Loial considered it one of the best about Aes Sedai dealing with men who could channel.

Mendair, Lawdrin. *See* Lawdrin Mendair

Mendan. An Aielman who with Coram guarded Verin in the Aiel camp, when she questioned the Aes Sedai prisoners after Dumai's Wells about the Tower's plans for Rand. A large, bulky man with startlingly blue eyes and axe-handle-wide shoulders, he was *siswai'aman*.

Mendao. A Shienaran soldier who traveled with Perrin and Ingtar in search of the Horn of Valere. After Moiraine sent him and the other Shienaran soldiers to Jehannah, he was killed in a duel with three Hunters for the Horn.

Mendiana. A noble House in Tear. Its High Seat was Lord Meilan; its sign blue six-pointed stars on red.

Meneril Chuliandred. A young Cairhienin lesser noble, brother of Doressin and brother-in-law to Lady Alaine Chuliandred. Stripes ran halfway down his chest. Meneril had a scar from the civil war that pulled up the left corner of his mouth in a permanent sardonic smile, and he had gaunt cheeks. He shaved the front of his head after the fashion of Cairhienin soldiers. Meneril was part of the Illian invasion army, attached to Semaradrid.

Menford, Idrelle. *See* Idrelle Menford

Menuki Nachiman. The wife of King Paitar of Arafel. They were devoted to one another; Menuki knew that he was hers to his bootsoles.

Mer. A bull *s'redit* tended by Cerandin in Valan Luca's circus. Luca called it a "boar-horse" to deflect from its true identity.

Mera. An Aiel woman whose daughter was a Wise One's apprentice; she also had two other daughters and two grown sons but no sister-wife. Mera was of the opinion that the way to handle any chief—hold, sept or clan, or the *Car'a'carn*—was the same as the way to handle a husband.

Mera'din. The Brotherless, an Aiel term used to denote those without clan or sept. The Brotherless were men who could not or would not accept Rand al'Thor, a wetlander, as the *Car'a'carn* and so abandoned clan and sept, joining the Shaido. They would not have supported Sevanna's plans for Rand, had they known of them, but she kept that knowledge from them.

Merada lace. A type of lace on the collar of a dress that Nynaeve wore in Ebou Dar.

Meraighdin, Bonwhin. *See* Bonwhin Meraighdin

Meralda Belmondes. A Tairen woman who was a member of *Cha Faile*. Almost 5'7" tall, she was solid with a very dark complexion. Selande was able to over-awe her with a look; Meralda was bold, and quick with her tongue, but had no doubt that Selande was in charge of *Cha Faile*. Meralda was one of the scouts sent into Bethal after Perrin's group arrived in Ghealdan.

Meramor. An Aes Sedai of the Yellow Ajah and the loyalist contingent who welcomed Nynaeve into the Yellow Ajah when she returned after the Tower reunited.

Merana Ambrey. An Andoran Aes Sedai of the Gray Ajah and the rebel contingent, with a strength level of 17(5). Born in Caemlyn in 889 NE, she went to the White Tower in 907 NE. After spending five years as a novice and six years as Accepted, she was raised to the shawl in 918 NE. About 5'4" tall and on the slim side of a medium build, she was dark-haired with cool hazel eyes—light brown flecked with yellow. She had a Warder named Basan, who was killed before the Aiel War. She was part of the futile Gray effort after the Aiel War to make the Grand Coalition more than a name. Merana was the leader of the rebel embassy to Rand in Caemlyn; her leadership was eroded by the arrival of Bera and Kiruna, who were both stronger than she, and she did not have an Amyrlin's authority to back her. After the battle at Dumai's Wells, she swore herself to Rand. She negotiated with the Sea Folk on Rand's behalf, and went with Alanna to the rebels in Haddon Mirk to negotiate an end to the rebellion in Tear. They came to terms with the rebels; the agreement included Darlin becoming the King of Tear.

Merchants, Council of. The body responsible for electing the King in Arad Doman; it was almost always composed entirely of women.

Merdagon, Turanine. *See* Turanine Merdagon

Merean Redhill. An Andoran Aes Sedai of the Blue Ajah publicly and of the Black Ajah in truth. She had a strength level of 14(2). Born in 716 NE, she was 5'8" tall, and plump, with graying hair. She bonded a Warder ten or more years after gaining the shawl. After he died, she never bonded another. Stories said she was in love with him, and still mourned him. In truth, he had been a Darkfriend; Merean didn't want the difficulties of handling a Warder who was not, and never found another she thought suitable. Besides, without the strictures of the Three Oaths, she never found the need. She served as Mistress of Novices under Noane Masadim and Tamra Ospenya. She was a friendly woman, warm and easygoing, generally. Most novices and Accepted never figured her out. She could cosset and soothe with the best, when necessary, but she could go easy on an initiate one time for something, then come down like a ton of bricks for something lesser. Still, she did offer a shoulder to cry on and advice when an initiate couldn't ask even her best friend, and many more girls went to her on their own than were sent for punishment.

At Tamra's death, Merean was replaced by Sierin's choice. She then took part in the male channeler pogrom; she went to Kandor and killed Ethenielle's young son Diryk; his father, Prince Consort Brys; and Iselle, the daughter of Lan's first lover. Moiraine was unable to save those three, but she killed Merean and destroyed her body, and then secretly destroyed all of her belongings, so that it seemed Merean had simply vanished from the Aesdaishar Palace. In the uproar over the deaths of Brys, Diryk and Iselle, Merean's disappearance went almost unnoticed.

Merekel. One of the group of Shienaran soldiers who joined Lan in eastern Kandor as he traveled toward Tarwin's Gap. Andere told the protesting Lan that he had run into Merekel and the other soldiers before meeting Lan, and had told them to wait along the southern roadway for Lan and his men to come along.

Meresin Daganred. A Cairhienin nobleman and son of Lord Daganred. He was pale and slender with a long nose, a narrow face and the front of his head shaved. His *con* was made up of vertical wavy red and white stripes. He escaped from Cairhien when the Shaido were laying siege and went to Rand in Eianrod, then rode back to Cairhien with a message. He became an officer in the Band of the Red Hand, and commanded the Second Banner of Horse, with the title Lieutenant Lord.

Merhan, Nalasia. *See* Nalasia Merhan

Meri. A maid of Egwene's, along with Selame and Chesa, who helped dress and undress her, and attended her during the day. She was a refugee and a puritan, dour-faced and gloomy, with a pinched nose, a permanently down-turned mouth and dark eyes sharp with censure, and her flat tone of voice turned every meaning head-to-heels. Her black hair, coiled tightly over her ears, seemed to pull her face painfully. Meri always wore drab dark gray. She was provided by Romanda, for whom she was spying. On the journey north from Salidar, she and Selame were murdered by Halima. Halima didn't want spies watching Egwene because they might have seen or overheard something that would have endangered her own position and safety. Egwene's other maid Chesa survived simply because she wasn't a spy for anyone, just a maid.

Meri do Ahlan a'Conlin. A Murandian noblewoman who claimed to be the descendant of the first queen of Murandy. She followed her husband when he fought in the Aiel War, and gave birth to a son, Sedrin, a week before Moiraine and Siuan went to the Murandian camp to collect names of the newborn. Meri said that she intended to frame the coins of the Tower bounty, given to women who gave birth near the end of the Aiel War, so that Sedrin would always know that he had been honored by the White Tower.

Merici. A woman in Valan Luca's show who had the prettiest eyes, according to Olver.

Merilille Ceandevin. A Cairhienin Aes Sedai of the Gray Ajah and the rebel contingent, with a strength level of 22(10). Born in 827 NE, she went to the White Tower in 845 NE. After spending thirteen years as a novice and twelve years as Accepted, she was raised to the shawl in 870 NE. About 5'1" tall, pale and slender with large liquid dark eyes and glossy black hair, she was an elegant woman, though she could become distracted. Of the Kin, Solain Morgellein (833–852 NE) was Accepted over her from the time she entered until being put out in 852 NE; Merilille remembered jumping when Solain snapped her fingers. Other Kin, Asra Zigane (929 NE; 4 months), Derys Nirmala (926–936 NE), Garenia Rosoinde (923–928 NE) and Sarainya Vostovan (940–950 NE) were all in the Tower after she became Aes Sedai. Merilille was the leader of the rebel embassy to Queen Tylin in Ebou Dar. She put Elayne on trial for making contact with the Kin, but when Elayne asserted herself as the representative of the Amyrlin Seat, Merilille found that all her training left her no choice but to acquiesce, however reluctantly. That did not mean she could not try to convince Elayne of other courses, however; she certainly did that.

While Healing the Sea Folk Windfinders at the Kin's farm, Merilille was maneuvered into saying that she would be one of the Aes Sedai who would teach the Sea Folk. As soon as the first snows fell, Renaile din Calon claimed Merilille and immediately began running her ragged. Renaile and the three Windfinders to clan Wavemistresses soon were all making Merilille hop at their command. While Merilille obviously was not considered an apprentice, when they had beds, she was forced to share one with her maid, Pol, and the two apprentice Windfinders, Talaan and Metarra. Once they reached Caemlyn, this squeezing of Merilille continued. Rather than accept being sent to the Atha'an Miere ships for a year, Merilille fled the Royal Palace in Caemlyn with Talaan, an apprentice Windfinder.

Merinloe. A place in Seanchan. Lady Morsa, encountered by Rand and Aviendha when they Traveled to Seanchan, was to be put to the question when she and the Seeker Jalindin returned to Merinloe.

Merise Haindehl. A Taraboner Aes Sedai of the Green Ajah, uncommitted to any contingent. She had a strength level of 14(2). Born in 798 NE, she went to the White Tower in 811 NE; she was thirteen but lied about her age. After two years, her lie was discovered, and as a result she spent fifteen years as a novice, five years as Accepted and was only raised to the shawl in 831 NE. About 5'7" tall, with dark eyes and dark hair worn pulled severely back and a pale ivory complexion, she was stern-faced with a stern manner. Some thought her beautiful without being pretty, some saw her as handsome, while others saw only severity. She had a strong Taraboner accent. Merise was not as good at Healing as was Corele, by her own admission. Her Warders were Nethan Conwy, Bassane Maliandred and Jahar Narishma, an Asha'man. Merise had a firm hand with her Warders, but she dressed them very well. She was one of the uncommitted Aes Sedai Rand found following Cadsuane Melaidhrin in Cairhien after Dumai's Wells. Cadsuane trusted Merise perhaps more than any of the others. She went with Cadsuane and the others to Far Madding and Shadar Logoth; at Shadar Logoth she linked with Narishma and Elza to help protect Rand and Nynaeve during the cleansing. When Rand awarded the dragon pin to Narishma afterward, Merise took it away from him, saying that he could only accept what she said he could; she later gave it back. Merise and Narishma went to the rebel Aes Sedai with Rand's offer that they might bond forty-seven Asha'man as Warders. Merise fought in the Last Battle as part of Lan's forces at first, then later alongside Egwene.

Merk. 1) A character from the Age before the Age of Legends featured in a gleeman's tale. He was a giant who fought with Mosk using spears of fire. 2) One of Renald Fanwar's farmhands.

Merlon, Renala. *See* Renala Merlon

Merrilin, Thom. *See* Thom Merrilin

Merrilor, Field of. *See* Field of Merrilor

Mervin Poel. An inventor and a member of Rand's Academy of Cairhien. Bearded and balding, after many trials he managed to make steamwagons that could travel a hundred miles in a day pulling wagons.

Merya. A Saldaean woman with whom Elyas lived for a year. She shouted his ears off, and threw dishes at his head. Every time Elyas thought of leaving, she'd want to make up, and he would stay. She finally left him, though, saying he was too restrained. While telling Perrin about her, Elyas rubbed at a knife scar on his face.

Merym. An Arafellin Aes Sedai of the White Ajah and the loyalist contingent who was a member of the party that caught Egwene as she changed the harbor chains in Tar Valon to *cuendillar*. She and Jala galloped off for the Tower as soon as they saw who had been captured.

Mesaana. One of the Forsaken; her name before turning to the Shadow was Saine Tarasind. She was about four hundred years old and had a strength level of 2(+11), a step below Lanfear, but equal to Cyndane. Her goal in life was to do research at the Collam Daan, and it was fairly certain that her failure to achieve that was the key factor in her eventual decision to go over to the Shadow. She held several field commands for the Shadow, but she shone as a governor of conquered territories. She engaged in all the usual atrocities, and she used her skill as a teacher to set up schools that corrupted children. These children were taught to destroy, and they did it very well. Mesaana was hardheaded, practical and intelligent, except insofar as her own motivations and weaknesses were concerned, anyway. She had an analytical mind, and never cared about looks or appearances. She seemed dreamy, but only because she was often absorbed in her own thoughts and plans. She was really very observant. Her interest was *real* power; however, she knew that this came through the Dark One, and had no interest in trying to set up an earthly power base. She certainly had no objections to seeing other Forsaken go down or be diminished, since she would strive as hard as any for the Dark One's favor.

She had a close and rather peculiar relationship with Demandred and Semirhage. They were not exactly allies, or they were allies only to the degree needed to keep the others off their backs, but they frequently acted in concert, and none of the three had ever betrayed the other two in any way, which was not to say that any one of them would not work for personal advantage with respect to the other two as well as the others.

When she awoke in the Third Age, she went to the White Tower. She vaguely resembled Danelle, the peripatetic Brown sister whose identity she assumed after squeezing relevant information out of her and killing her. This she did herself; while she did not have the skill of Semirhage at torture or of Graendal in penetrating another's mind, she was quite able to make Danelle tell her sufficient about herself for Mesaana to carry off her impersonation, though it did require her to mask her prodigious ability to channel. She needed little Illusion to pass as Danelle because of their strong physical resemblance and Danelle's lack of friends and long absences from the White Tower.

Slight and 5'5" tall, with big blue eyes, Mesaana was pretty rather than beautiful, and appeared to be just short of her middle years. As Danelle, she was part of the group that arrested Siuan, and later part of the council advising Elaida. Mesaana ran the Black Ajah in the Tower through Alviarin, to whom she appeared as a woman of silver and shadow. Even her voice was disguised, like crystal chimes speaking. While she communicated most of her orders through Alviarin, and led Alviarin to believe all went through her, she made contact with the twelve other sisters on the Supreme Council, and she learned all of the members' names. Despite taking control of the Black, she did not know all the ins and outs of it, the things they knew or the rituals. She assumed a great deal more knowledge than she actually had, though she did know what went on between Elaida and Alviarin even before Alviarin reported it, and she seemed to know it word-perfectly. In addition to being in the one spot where more information was gathered on world events than anywhere else, Mesaana caused Elaida to increase the number of the Tower Guards and take other moves that made a peaceful solution with the rebels more difficult even if she were willing. She also was responsible for the proclamation that 1) recognized Rand as the Dragon Reborn while at the same time not-so-subtly condemning him, and 2) condemned everyone who had aided or would aid him. That made sure the wedge between Rand and the Tower was firmly in place while at the same time 1) weakening Rand to some extent because of those who would abandon him or fail to come to him, and 2) weakening the Tower by taking away its flexibility while at the same time giving many people who had gone over to Rand no choice, except to oppose the Tower. And of course, Mesaana was responsible for the loyalist Tower finding itself divided internally far more deeply than it had been since the decades after its founding and possibly more than then.

Mesaana was summoned and failed to appear at Shadar Logoth when Rand was cleansing the taint on *saidin*; Shaidar Haran went to the White Tower and punished her severely. She and the Black Ajah battled Egwene and Aes Sedai in *Tel'aran'rhiod*. Mesaana put an *a'dam* on Egwene while in the dream world, but Egwene was able to resist through sheer willpower; Mesaana's mind was destroyed during this mental battle.

Meseau, Sevlana. *See* Sevlana Meseau

Mesianos, Doraise. *See* Doraise Mesianos

Mestra. A member of the Black Ajah who had fled the Tower. Part of the group that attacked Egwene in *Tel'aran'rhiod* at the White Tower, she died when Egwene hit her with a ball of fire.

Metalan. An Aiel man in the distant future seen in Aviendha's visions in Rhuidean. His wife was Norlesh; they had five children; three had died earlier. He tried to trade gems for food with outlanders, but the Raven Empress had forbidden trade with Aiel. A fourth child died soon after his failure to trade.

Metarra din Junalle. A Sea Folk Windfinder apprentice, too young to have earned a salt name. Her strength level was 9(4), roughly equal to Elayne and Egwene. Slightly plump but physically strong, she had very big, dark eyes, so black they seemed purple. She had no nose chain, and only a single earring in the left ear to balance three in the right. She was part of the circle that used the Bowl of the Winds and afterward went to Caemlyn with Elayne's group; when Zaida left Caemlyn, Metarra went with her.

Methin, Eldrid. A cook in the Sun Palace in Cairhien. When Loial and Karldin visited, Eldrid talked of how dangerous and deadly Rand was.

Metwyn. A Cairhienin Redarm in the Band of the Red Hand. He looked boyish, though he was about thirty years old when he joined the Band. About 5'8" tall with a medium build, he had a pale complexion, black hair and dark eyes. Metwyn was very quick with his hands, a very good soldier and swordsman— the best of the lot, though Gorderan was close behind—but he had a temper that could lead him into tavern brawls. Along with Harnan, Fergin and Gorderan, he survived the recovery of the Bowl of the Winds in the Rahad.

Mezar Kurin. A Domani Dedicated Asha'man associated with Logain. He bonded Adrielle of the Gray Ajah. A copper-skinned man in his middle years, he had a plain face, touches of gray at the temples of his black hair and a garnet in his left ear. His dark eyes had a sad look to them. He grinned openly, though, and stroked his thin mustache when Gabrelle came out of Logain's house in the morning. Mezar was part of the meeting with Logain that Toveine witnessed. She thought he might have been a minor nobleman. He accompanied Rand to the meeting with the Daughter of the Nine Moons. Taim Turned him to the Shadow and promoted him to full Asha'man. Mezar and Welyn took Evin to be Turned.

Mia ayende, Aes Sedai! Caballein misain ye! Inde muagdhe Aes Sedai misain ye! Mia ayende! Old Tongue for "I am a free man, Aes Sedai. I am no Aes Sedai meat."

Mia dovienya nesodhin soende. Old Tongue for "Luck carry me through."

Mia'cova. Old Tongue for "One Who Owns Me," or "My Owner."

Miagoma. An Aiel clan. Its clan chief was Timolan.

Micara. A Wise One of the Shaido Aiel with the ability to channel and a strength level of 27(15), the weakest among the eighty Wise Ones with Therava. About 5'7" tall, and young and pretty, she had red hair, a delicate mouth and large, intent blue eyes. Micara shielded Galina when Therava brought her to Sevanna's camp after Dumai's Wells.

Midean's Ford. An old song of Manetheren. It told of a battle. Aedomon led the Saferi against Manetheren, pillaging and burning, driving all before them until King Buiryn gathered Manetheren's strength. The men of Manetheren met the Saferi at Midean's Ford, holding, though heavily outnumbered, through three days of unrelenting battle, while the river ran red and vultures blackened the sky. On the third day, with their numbers dwindling, Buiryn and his men fought their way across the ford, driving deep into Aedomon's army, seeking to turn the enemy back by killing Aedomon himself. The Saferi forces were too great, however, and they swept around Buiryn's men, trapping them. Surrounding their king and the Red Eagle banner, they fought on, refusing to surrender even when it was clear that they would die. In the song, their courage touched Aedomon's heart, and he allowed the remnant to go free, turning his army back to Safer in honor of them.

Mat's memories told a different story: He remembered advising Buiryn not to accept Aedomon's offer to let them go free; but Buiryn said that the smallest chance was better than none. Aedomon drew his spearmen back and waited until the Manetheren remnants were strung out and nearly to the ford; then his hidden archers rose and the cavalry charged in, killing everyone.

Miedelle Caeren. Nasin Caeren's wife; she died circa 970 NE.

Miereallen. An Ogier-built city in Safer, one of the Ten Nations after the Breaking; Falme later rose on the same site.

Mierin Eronaile. Lanfear's original name.

Miesa. A serving woman to Delana Mosalaine.

Migel Sahera. Avene Sahera's son. His name was on the list of possible Dragons Reborn, but he had been born a week before Gitara's Foretelling, thirty miles from Dragonmount.

Mighty. Arganda's horse, killed by a Trolloc in the Last Battle.

Miheres, Aldin. A mercenary commander working for Arymilla. He attacked Caemlyn and was killed by Birgitte with an arrow through the neck.

Mikel of the Pure Heart. A Hero of the Horn. He appeared at the battle against the Seanchan at Falme. When Rand saw him, he became aware of the myriad names Mikel had gone by in his many lives.

Mikhel Najirah. A Seanchan Banner-General under Captain-General Galgan. Lanky and graying, he escorted Suroth to the meeting with Galgan about attacks on Seanchan positions in Tarabon. He was also present when Beslan swore allegiance to Tuon.

Mikio Vadere. A Kandori Aes Sedai of the Green Ajah and the rebel contingent, with a strength level of 18(6). Born in 907 NE, she went to the White Tower in 923 NE. After spending twelve years as a novice and eleven years as Accepted, she was raised to the shawl in 946 NE. Mikio was 5'5" tall, and plump, with a round face, black hair worn short of her shoulders and dark brown eyes. Physically quite strong, she had a fairly ordinary appearance. Her eyes were the most striking thing about her; they were intent and inquisitive always; she had a way of noticing small things that escaped others' notice. Mikio had two Warders, one in his mid-twenties and the other in his middle years. She was part of the rebel fifth column sent by Sheriam's council in Salidar to infiltrate the White Tower (aka ferrets). Like all of the sisters chosen for the fifth column, Mikio was out of the White Tower when Siuan was deposed and the Tower broke, so there was no flight to arouse any suspicions toward her. Apparently, she simply returned in answer to Elaida's summons.

Mil Tesen. A gossipy peddler with a floppy hat and a grizzled face. Gawyn encountered him in the Cairhienin countryside and asked for news of the world; Mil told him that Rand had taken Andor and killed Morgase, and possibly Elayne.

Milam Harnder. The Second Librarian in the Royal Palace, Caemlyn. A chubby man who blinked incessantly, Harnder was a Brown Ajah agent who reported to one of their eyes-and-ears at the Hoop and Arrow Inn, Mistress Fendry. Demira was on her way to meet Harnder when she was attacked by men dressed as Aiel. Harnder served Morgase, and before her, Mordrellen. Elayne knew that he was a Brown Ajah agent.

Mili. The subject of a gleeman's tale, "Goodwife Mili and the Silk Merchant."

Mili Skane. An Andoran woman originally from a village near Whitebridge who was a saddler's daughter. She was born circa 977 NE. About 5'4" tall, she was pretty in a sharp-featured way, with brown eyes and brown hair that she brushed to glossiness. There was no warmth in her face; it seemed to lack feeling. She spoke with almost the accents of an Andoran noble. Mili went to the White Tower at fifteen but was told she could not learn to channel. Within the year she found a circle of Darkfriends, joined it and killed her first man—her first nonpersonal murder, anyway. Over the next seven years, she added nineteen more assassinations, and her kills for personal reasons would more than double the number. Among Darkfriends she was considered one of the best assassins available. It was generally believed that Mili could find anyone or anything. She had a circle which answered to her; they were mostly older than she and included several real nobles.

Included in her personal total of murders were the real Shiaine Avarhin and Shiaine's father, Willim Avarhin, the last two members of a minor noble family with a lineage back to the founding of Andor, and their sole servant. Mili was nineteen when she killed them; the murders were for the sole purpose of providing a cover, to allow Mili to use Shiaine's name, although the use of Willim's seals enabled her to obtain his remaining money. Mili believed that only a few among the Darkfriends knew her secret, and that the reclusive lives of Avarhin and his daughter made it unlikely she could ever be found out.

Mili attempted to kill Mat and Rand with a hot-bladed dagger in a barn when they were on their way to Caemlyn. She managed to keep this encounter secret, since she preferred to have it thought she had failed to find and intercept them than that she had done so and failed.

Mat later spotted her in Ebou Dar, where she was working for Jaichim Carridin. She had a particular hatred for Carridin, who mistreated her when she was working for him in Ebou Dar. He also discovered her misappropriation of gold for her own use, especially her gambling habit. Shiaine liked gambling with something close to addiction.

Moridin sent her to Caemlyn, where she very much enjoyed killing Carridin, whom she drowned in brandy. Because of Darkfriend hierarchies, Shiaine would have groveled for Old Cully, the beggar in charge of Darkfriends in Ebou Dar, or others who held a high enough position, but then she had gained the protection of Moridin. Moridin also gave her Falion and Marillin to serve her. Mili worked to create chaos in Caemlyn, arranging much of the arson and setting conditions for crime, and was reasonably successful. When Elayne attempted to take her and Black Ajah sisters at Mili's house on Full Moon Street prisoner, the tables were turned and Elayne was captured. Elayne was rescued, though, and Mili captured. Freed by Jaq Lounalt, she escaped.

Milisair Chadmar. A member of the Domani Council of Merchants. Barely into her thirties when Rand arrived in Bandar Eban, she had lots of curves and dark hair in tight curls that hung past her shoulders. Rand ordered her to bring him the last messenger who had come from King Alsalam; Milisair, who had put the messenger in a dungeon where he had died, tried to flee, but was caught. She told Rand that the messenger was dead, and Rand threw her in her own dungeon. Nynaeve found her, suffering from poison that had been given her by Kerb, who was under Graendal's Compulsion, and Healed her. Rand had her returned to her home before he left Bandar Eban, but she fled the city within the hour.

Milis din Shalada Three Stars. The Sailmistress of the *Whitecap*, which took food to Bandar Eban. She had some gray in her straight black hair. When she arrived in Bandar Eban, Iralin would not let her unload her grain because he thought it was probably spoiled and he feared riots. Rand and Iralin visited her on the ship, and all the unopened grain was found to be fine.

Milking Tears. A lost Talent of unknown use; Egwene hoped that Moghedien could tell her about it, but she knew nothing.

Milla al'Azar. The young Wisdom of Taren Ferry who was chosen after the Trollocs wiped out the population of Taren Ferry. She simpered around Perrin. When the four Wisdoms visited Faile, Milla admitted that none of them knew the Wisdom technique of Listening to the Wind and that she was so frightened about the weather that she was not sleeping well at all. She was very uncertain around the older Wisdoms; Faile considered speaking to the Women's Circle in Taren Ferry about having her replaced, as a Wisdom was supposed to be mature and in control of herself.

Milli Ayellin. A Two Rivers girl. She took the wolfhead banner to Leof Torfinn when Wil al'Seen didn't want to carry it.

Millin, Mistress. A farmer in whose cow barn Gawyn and his Younglings stayed in Dorlan.

Millis Fendry. The innkeeper at The Hoop and Arrow in Caemlyn, and an eyes-and-ears for the Brown Ajah in the White Tower. She kept pigeons; every time Milam Harnder visited her, a pigeon flew north.

Milo, Soran. *See* Soran Milo

Milsa. The wife of Zeram, a bootmaker, who was known for controlling the purse strings. She rented out rooms above Zeram's shop on Blue Carp Street in Far Madding to anyone who didn't mind being locked in at night; she had stairs put in right up to the third floor for privacy, but she wouldn't pay for having a new door cut as well, so the stairs came out in the shop, and she would not leave that unlocked at night. Torval and Gedwyn stayed there.

Min Farshaw. Her full name was Elmindreda Farshaw, and she was born outside Baerlon in 975 NE. Min was orphaned young. Her mother died in childbirth, her father in a mining accident later; they had gone up to the mines for a fresh start. Min was sent back to Baerlon to be raised by her three aunts, Miren, Rana and Jan, who lived together, making a living as seamstresses. Already something of a tomboy from her time at the mines, she was used to boys' clothes. Her aunts tried to make her a proper lady, as defined in Baerlon, and disapproved strongly of her wearing breeches. Miren seemed to understand a little. Min gave up running with the urchins when she was about thirteen. Since she would never be a seamstress—she simply hated doing embroidery, for which she had no facility at all—she had to have some kind of trade, and what she chose for herself was to be a

groom. Her aunts argued for over a year before she was allowed to, though she had been sneaking down to the stables on the sly when she could. She had equated horses with travel, with the places her aunts' visitors told stories of, but quickly learned horses meant manure and mucking out. She stuck it out for a long time through stubbornness.

She tried other things. She worked as a tavern maid for about a month; but she didn't like wearing dresses, and she didn't like being pinched. She tried being a weaver's apprentice, but she disliked being inside all day, doing the repetitive motions, and did a stint as a dyer's apprentice, which she hated because the dyes stank and she could never get clean of them completely. She found being an assistant in a shop selling cloth not bad, but she had to wear dresses again; she had the same problem as an assistant in a cutlery shop.

Min sometimes saw auras and images around people, and could tell some things about the person's future from the aura. Her ability to see images began manifesting when she was about twelve, at the onset of puberty. It took a year or so for it to grow fully, and another six months before she began realizing that what she saw would really happen. Her aunts had thought she was just having the kinds of fancies that girls sometimes did at that age. Her time of actually telling people about predictions only lasted another year and a half, until she was fifteen.

It didn't take long for her to realize that she couldn't change what would happen; once she saw a man lying in the street dead with a broken neck and knew it was meant for that afternoon. She convinced him not to go up on his roof to check for loose slates, so he went off to a tavern instead, mainly to please the little girl and partly because he'd rather go have some ale anyway; a chimney pot toppled over him and killed him an hour later. Min said a man on the next street was going to marry a woman she saw him with, but he was already married. When he ran off with the other woman, his wife took a mob to Min's aunts' house claiming that Min was responsible for her husband leaving. The aunts told her a way to get out of it, and she took it. She told them all she had learned about the woman's husband and the barmaid by snooping. That was how she had learned everything she had told anybody. The Baerlon folk hadn't really wanted to be a mob, and probably most were looking for an excuse not to hurt her, so they believed and went away, most telling her aunts they ought to keep a closer rein on her or beat her for snooping so. That was the end of her career as a fortune-teller.

Min was about eighteen when some Aes Sedai came through. Someone told them the old stories of the girl claiming she could see things about people, and they sought Min out because it might be a manifestation of the One Power. They quickly found out she couldn't channel and couldn't be taught, but she was so awed by Aes Sedai that she betrayed her ability. They tried to find out some way for it to be associated with the Power, but concluded it was not. One of the Aes Sedai told Moiraine about Min.

Min was about 5'5" tall, except when she wore her boots with the three-inch heels, which put her at about 5'8". Dark ringlets hung to her shoulders. Her dark eyes were even bigger than Egwene's. She had a low, but definitely womanly voice. She often wore a boy's coat and breeches, with flowers embroidered on the lapels and running up the sides of snug pant legs that were tucked into those boots. Min was capable of a wry, sometimes mysterious, grin, and she grinned a good deal around Rand, sometimes on the point of laughing. She could give a smart remark with the best of them; she could also shake a fist, and stamp a foot. She first met Rand in Baerlon, where she was working at the inn where he and Moiraine's group stayed after leaving Two Rivers. She was summoned to the White Tower, and there became friends with Elayne, Nynaeve and Egwene. When Liandrin tricked the others into going to Falme, Min went along. She bit Elbar, Suroth's man, and he wanted to kill her, but Egwene promised to cooperate with the *sul'dam* who held her if they let Min live. Min was allowed a fair amount of freedom in Falme, although she was forced to wear a dress. She visited Egwene, met up with Elayne and Nynaeve and plotted to free Egwene with them. After Rand was injured fighting Ishamael, she found him; Lanfear went to her and told her that Rand belonged to her. Min wintered in Rand's camp in the Mountains of Mist. After he set out alone, Moiraine sent her to the White Tower with a report for Siuan. When she arrived, she saw auras that indicated that many Aes Sedai would be injured or killed. Siuan persuaded her to stay in the Tower, pretending to be a foolish young woman who could not decide between two suitors, using her full name, which few people knew. Laras, the Mistress of the Kitchens, took Min under her wing. After Siuan and Leane were deposed and stilled, Laras helped Min free them. As they escaped, Logain joined them.

Siuan tried to find where the rest of the Blue Ajah was gathering, so that they could join them. Along the way, the group spent the night in a barn, unbeknownst to its owners. When the owner discovered them, a lantern was dropped and the barn, and the milkcows it contained, burned. The three women were caught and tried by Gareth Bryne. Each swore an oath to work for Bryne until the price of the barn and the cows was paid off, but on their way to Bryne's estate Logain freed them and they made their way to Salidar, where Aes Sedai opposed to Elaida had gathered. The rebels sent an embassy to Rand, and Min went with them. She and Rand became close.

Min was kidnapped by the Tower Aes Sedai along with Rand. On discovering that she was in the camp, he was enraged and killed two of Erian's Warders. After the battle at Dumai's Wells, she went with him back to Cairhien. She became one of Rand's consorts, and, with Aviendha and Elayne, bonded him. She started reading books of philosophy intently, especially Herid Fel's books, which eventually helped answer the question of how Rand was to deal with the Dark One. She spent most of her time as Rand's companion, helping to keep him human as being the Dragon Reborn put increasingly greater strains on him. Her unique position with Rand made her a person of interest to Cadsuane, especially after Rand banished Cadsuane from his company, and she used

Min to keep tabs on Rand and try to guide him. Dobraine began calling Min "My Lady *Ta'veren*."

Min was with Rand when Semirhage destroyed his hand, and later when Semirhage put a Dominion Band on him demanding he strangle Min, an act avoided after Rand gained access to the True Power and balefired the Forsaken. Min accompanied Rand to the Field of Merrilor, but he would not let her go with him to Shayol Ghul in the Last Battle, sending her instead to Egwene's battlefront to watch over events for him there. She served as a clerk in Egwene's army, and then was sent by Bryne to deliver a message to the Seanchan, requesting cavalry. Tuon was saved from an assassination attempt by Min's foretelling, and Tuon made her her new Truthspeaker. Mat sent her back to Egwene's army, to warn Egwene that Bryne was acting the Darkfriend and was about to lead her army to destruction. Returning to Tuon's court, Min saved Tuon's life again when Gray Men and the Sharans destroyed her command post at Dashar Knob. She stayed with the Seanchan until the end of the Last Battle, and attended Rand's funeral at Shayol Ghul.

Minde. A town in Murandy whose inhabitants boasted of their bad tempers. The two noblemen who were about to beat Olver before Mat saved him were from Minde.

Minds. What Ituralde's troops called wolf-headed Trollocs, who were often among the most intelligent. *See also* Narg

mindtrap. A device, cage-like in appearance, applied in the Pit of Doom to one out of favor with the Dark One, which enslaved one totally to whomever held the mindtrap. It was possible to be released from a mindtrap, but the device was feared by the Forsaken. It was called *cour'souvra* in Old Tongue.

Miners' Rest, The. A rough tavern in Baerlon where Min worked for a short time in her early days.

Minly, Talene. *See* Talene Minly

Mintai, Stedding. A *stedding* located in the mountains north of the River Dhagon.

Miraj, Kennar. *See* Kennar Miraj

Mirala. The daughter of Thulin, the blacksmith in Oak Water, a Borderlands village. Her mother was Gallanha. When Thulin packed up and headed north, Mirala went with him.

Mirane Larinen. A Kinswoman who traveled with Elayne to Caemlyn. When she first went to the White Tower, she hid a beloved doll outside because she had heard that everything she owned would be burned. After she was put out of the Tower, she retrieved it, and always took it with her when she moved, although she would always hide it. Mirane vanished and was believed to have run away until Derys found her doll hidden behind a cupboard; she was actually killed by Careane Fransi.

Mire, the. A swamp at the far end of the Waterwood in the Two Rivers.

Miren. One of Min's aunts. She never married, but while all three of her aunts gave advice about men, along with everything else, Miren definitely seemed to know what she was talking about with respect to men. When Min got in trouble with neighbors because of talking about her viewings, Miren promised to spank her for spreading tales, but did not do it since she knew the truth.

Miri. A tall, pale-haired *damane* killed during Semirhage's attempted capture of Rand. Tanera, the *sul'dam* with whom she was paired, was killed as well.

Mirlene Cornwell. An Andoran Aes Sedai of the Green Ajah and the loyalist contingent, with a strength level of 26(14). Born in 867 NE, she went to the White Tower in 883 NE. After spending eleven years as a novice and seven years as Accepted, she was raised to the shawl in 901 NE. She was part of the expedition to kidnap Rand, and she and her two Warders were killed at Dumai's Wells.

Mirror of Mists, the. *See* Mask of Mirrors

Mirrors of the Wheel. A book written before the Breaking about the alternate worlds behind Portal Stones. According to Selene, some of those worlds were like mirrors, especially those without people. Some reflected only great events that occurred in their own world, whereas some had a shadow of the reflection even before the event occurred.

Mishael. An Atha'an Miere man who was the husband of Shalon. Shalon was afraid that if Mishael found out about her relationship with Ailil, he would declare their marriage vows broken.

Mishima, Bakayar. *See* Bakayar Mishima

Mishraile, Atal. *See* Atal Mishraile

Mist. A gray mare that belonged to brigands who captured Nynaeve, Egwene and Elayne; after the brigands were killed, Egwene chose her, named her and rode her to Tear. Mist was also her mount on her journey to and from the Waste.

Mist, Mountains of. A mountain range oriented north-south, found immediately west of Emond's Field; it separated Arad Doman and Tarabon from Andor and Ghealdan.

Mistress of Novices. A position in the White Tower. The Mistress of Novices had authority over all novices and Accepted, and over all of their training and studies.

The Mistress of Novices usually was appointed by the Amyrlin; there were cases of her being chosen by the Hall and forced on an Amyrlin, but not many. Although named by the Amyrlin, she did not serve at the Amyrlin's pleasure any more than the Keeper did; she could only be removed by the greater consensus of the Hall except in the case of certain specific misdeeds, in which case only the lesser consensus was required.

With few exceptions, it required at least the lesser consensus of the Hall to override the Mistress of Novices regarding almost anything to do with her charges. Some things were set in the law, including strictures against singling out any girl for either favor or censure without cause, but by and large she could reward or punish as she chose. The manner in which novices were fed, clothed and housed was largely in her control. The manner in which Accepted were fed, clothed and housed was only somewhat less controlled by her. Accepted were given individual rooms, or even apartments, since there were fewer of them, for example, and she could not make them all live in the small cubicles given to novices; an Accepted as well as a novice could still find herself feeding on bread and water, and while Accepted were allowed more jewelry than novices and seldom called down for excessive ornament, at least once they had progressed a little, she could restrict them just as severely as the novices if she chose.

The authority of the Mistress of Novices over her charges was such, according to the law, that she could in some cases defy the Amyrlin Seat or anything below the lesser consensus of the Hall or in some cases, the greater, regarding them. An Aes Sedai who was instructing novices or Accepted could discipline those she taught herself, but except in this teacher/pupil relationship, punishment was in the hands of the Mistress of Novices. An Aes Sedai could send a novice or Accepted running on any task, or send them to the Mistress of Novices' study, but it was the Mistress of Novices who decided what punishment to dole out, if any, and the sister who sent the girl had no say. The Mistress of Novices would have been heartily offended had any sister tried to take a hand. By law, not even the Amyrlin Seat could tell the Mistress of Novices what reward or punishment to give any of the novices or Accepted.

Many Mistresses of Novices said that the girls in their charge were theirs and that the girls belonged to them. This attitude was generally accepted by the sisters. Some Mistresses of Novices used this to be unremittingly harsh on their charges, much harsher than Silviana, but it was also used to protect the girls from sisters, Sitters and even the Amyrlin Seat. All Aes Sedai were goddesses in the eyes of novices, and not much less in the eyes of Accepted, but even the Amyrlin Seat had to go through the Mistress of Novices for almost anything concerning both novices and Accepted.

Mistress of the Ships. A woman equivalent to a queen among the Sea Folk. The Mistress of the Ships was chosen by the First Twelve of the Atha'an Miere, the twelve ranking Wavemistresses, and she could not be removed except by the unanimous vote of the First Twelve, and a vote to remove that failed meant that each woman who had voted for it had to resign her position as a Wavemistress. The Mistress of the Ships had a degree of absolute authority that would be envied by any shorebound ruler. In certain circumstances, however, such as warfare and/or battle, the Mistress of the Ships was expected to yield to her Master of the Blades. The Mistress of the Ships rated a fringed blue parasol of four tiers, and wore six fat gold earrings in each ear.

Mitsobar, House. A noble House in Altara. Its High Seat was Tylin until her death, and then Beslan; its sign the Anchor and Sword. *See* Tylin Quintara *and* Beslan Mitsobar

Mitsora Caal. An Aes Sedai who lived at the time of the formation of the White Tower.

Miyasi. An Aes Sedai of the White Ajah publicly but of the Black Ajah in truth. Of the loyalist contingent, she was tall and plump with iron-gray hair worn in a bun on top of her head. A stern woman, she brooked no nonsense and saw nonsense everywhere. Her arm was even stronger than Ferane's, according to Egwene. She only liked walnuts that were whole. She was guarding Leane on one of Egwene's visits, and she was one who questioned Egwene about the best way to deal with Rand. Her name was on Verin's list of the Black Ajah.

Miyora. A woman with a leopard act in Valan Luca's show. She was plump and wore skirts that glittered with silvery spangles.

Mizar, Fen. *See* Fen Mizar

Moad din Nopara Red Hawk. An Atha'an Miere man who was Swordmaster to Harine din Togara Two Winds, Wavemistress of Clan Shodein. About 5'10" tall, with mostly gray hair and a hard face, he wore five earrings in each ear. He had a sword with an ornate hilt and one matching, curved dagger behind his sash. Harine gave him so much leeway that anyone who didn't know Harine might have thought they were lovers.

Modair. A son of Artur Hawkwing and Amaline Paendrag Tagora. He and his twin sister Amira were born in FY 942. Modair was killed in battle in FY 959; Hawkwing composed a poem, "Loss," about his grief.

Modarra. A Wise One of the Shaido Aiel (not a Jumai) with the ability to channel and a strength level of 25(13). At 6'2", she was as tall as most Aielmen, and she was lean and pretty. She liked to mother others—anyone within reach. She would, in Sevanna's opinion, try to settle a dispute between wetlanders, even Treekillers. One of Sevanna's inner circle of plotters, she accompanied Sevanna to the Aes Sedai camp the day she saw Rand beaten. She took part in or was present at the murder of Desaine. Modarra and Someryn were the Wise Ones most firmly in Sevanna's grasp, at least, in Sevanna's opinion. Modarra was with Sevanna at Dumai's Wells and at the meeting with "Caddar" and "Maisia." She helped question the Seanchan prisoner in Amadicia, while the Jumai were settled at a captured estate approximately ten days after their arrival. She, Therava and Belinde led a large number of Shaido back toward the Three-fold Land after the rout at Malden.

Modrellein. A queen of Andor some seven hundred years before Elayne went to the White Tower. At the Battle of Cuallin Dhen, Queen Modrellein rallied the Andoran army to defeat the Tairen army.

Moerad, Jalwin. *See* Jalwin Moerad

Moerelle, Ilyena Therin. *See* Ilyena Therin Moerelle

moghedien. The Old Tongue name for a tiny spider found in the Age of Legends that spun its webs in secret places. Its bite was poisonous enough to kill in heartbeats.

Moghedien. One of the Forsaken. She was also called the Spider. Her name in the Age of Legends was Lillen Moiral, and her strength level was 4(+9). She had large, dark eyes and dark hair spilling loose to her shoulders, and was about 5'5" tall. She was strong and striking, but not beautiful, appearing to be not yet in her middle years. Her voice was melodious. Before going over to the Shadow, Lillen Moiral was an "advisor for investments," a profession which no source explained. Whatever the work entailed, it was recorded that she was cautioned a number of times, and even disciplined, for violating the ethics of it and laws surrounding it. Moghedien was always a skulker in shadows, a coward who hung back; she scoffed at those who were fool enough to take open risks but at the same time hated them and envied their achievements, and hated them because she was sure they despised her hanging back.

When she awoke in the Third Age, Moghedien continued her skulking ways. After doing some research, she posed as Gyldin, a maid in the house occupied by eleven members of the Black Ajah. She located Elayne and Nynaeve and used Compulsion on them. Nynaeve saw Moghedien in the Panarch's Palace in *Tel'aran'rhiod*, remembered Moghedien's visit and was able to overcome that Compulsion. They met in the waking world in the Panarch's Palace museum and fought; Nynaeve bested and bound Moghedien, but Moghedien escaped and followed the Black Ajah members to Amador, where she revealed herself and sent them on assorted tasks.

In *Tel'aran'rhiod*, Moghedien trapped Nynaeve and Birgitte, but Birgitte wounded her with bow and arrow; Moghedien cast Birgitte out of *Tel'aran'rhiod*. When Moghedien woke, Chesmal Healed her, but Liandrin attempted her weak form of Compulsion on Moghedien. Moghedien did not succumb and shielded Liandrin with an intricately knotted shield and turned her over to Temaile for punishment. She then went to Samara, acquired two young boys and posing as Marigan took ship with Nynaeve and Elayne to Salidar. She trapped Nynaeve in *Tel'aran'rhiod*, but Nynaeve fought loose and put an *a'dam* on Moghedien and forced her to go with her to Caemlyn where they helped Rand kill Rahvin. Nynaeve realized that Moghedien had to be in Salidar in the waking world, and gave her forkroot. Moghedien was then collared with the chainless *a'dam* that Elayne had made, and forced to act as a servant and teacher. Moghedien was not eager to let anyone else know she was a captive, or that she had taught Elayne and Nynaeve things about the Power. Moghedien knew as much about Healing as Nynaeve did about blacksmithing—hardly more than enough to Heal a bruise. But she passed on some useful tricks, such as a way to eavesdrop using the Power, wrapping oneself in light to become invisible, inverting weaves and hiding one's ability to channel. She did manage to hold back her connection with the very Black sisters Nynaeve, Elayne and Egwene had been hunting, as well as whatever she knew of the Chosen's plans and/or orders from him. She was freed by Aran'gar.

Reporting to Shayol Ghul as ordered after her rescue by Halima, she was fitted with a mindtrap and imprisoned in a vacuole, a bubble outside the

Pattern where time flowed differently. There she was abused sexually by Shaidar Haran, the huge Myrddraal. Few women could have survived those attentions with their sanity intact, but she did, partly by letting the Myrddraal break her. It was not pretense; long before the end, she was ready to do anything the Myrddraal wanted. Brought out of the vacuole, she discovered that her mindtrap was now in the hands of a young man calling himself Moridin, a man who could channel the True Power and was doing so despite the dire risks. He did not demand servility from her, but obedience he did insist upon, requiring her to always wear red-and-black, his colors, as a form of livery, though he insisted it was not that. When she was sent to Ebou Dar to hurry the search of her minions there for Moridin's purposes—to find the cache for him—she diverted long enough for a failed attempt to balefire Nynaeve. She and Cyndane went to Graendal to inform her that Moridin was Nae'blis.

Moghedien went to Shadar Logoth when Rand used the Choedan Kal, but stayed back from the fighting. At the time of the Last Battle, Moghedien posed as a servant with the Seanchan and tried to keep the Seanchan from rejoining the battle, but was exposed by Min. She impersonated Demandred after his death and tried to rally the Sharans, but had her position fired upon by dragons. She was collared by Seanchan *sul'dam* and taken to Ebou Dar.

Moilin. An Ogier woman who was the author of *A Study of the War of the Shadow*. She was the daughter of Hamada daughter of Juendan.

Moir, Hal. *See* Hal Moir

Moiraine Damodred. A Cairhienin Aes Sedai of the Blue Ajah and uncommitted to any contingent. Her original strength level was 13(1), but after her imprisonment by the Eelfinn it was reduced to 66(54). Born to House Damodred, the royal family of Cairhien, in 956 NE, she went to the White Tower in 972 NE. After spending three years as a novice and three years as Accepted, she was raised to the shawl in late 978 NE. Her Warder was Lan Mandragoran until she went through the redstone doorway. She was 5'2" tall, and slim, with dark hair falling in waves to her shoulders, large dark eyes and fair skin.

Moiraine's great-grandmother, Carewin Damodred, ruled Cairhien for more than fifty years. Her father, Dalresin, was a scholar who married the second time for love, choosing another scholar. This was at best looked at askance by the rest of the family, since he should have married for land or to secure power for House Damodred; he was mocked by his brothers, King Laman, Moressin and Aldecain; all three died in the Aiel War. Moiraine was the youngest half-sister of Taringail Damodred, who married Tigraine Mantear, Daughter-Heir of Andor, and, after Tigraine disappeared, married Morgase Trakand, who had by then been crowned Queen of Andor. Moiraine was thus the aunt of Galad, Gawyn and Elayne. Moiraine also had two older sisters, Anvaere and Innloine. She was also a cousin of Lady Caraline Damodred, who succeeded Barthanes as High Seat. With the exception of Moiraine's father, the Damodreds had a dark reputation. The longer the House held the Sun Throne, the darker their deeds became. For that reason, Moiraine rarely used her House name.

Technically, Moiraine was a wilder. It caught everyone by surprise when the ability came out before she was sixteen. She recognized immediately what she was doing, but rather than telling anyone, waited until returning to Cairhien and the Royal Palace, where she could tell King Laman's Aes Sedai advisor. By that time, Moiraine had already taught herself the eavesdropping trick, and a few other things. In order to help her avoid the crisis, the advisor taught her for a short time before sending her on to Tar Valon. The facts, the details, were hidden to keep Moiraine from having the stigma of being a wilder, but Siuan and a few others knew.

Moiraine was novice and Accepted with Siuan; they arrived on the same day, not a usual thing, and even more unusually, were raised Aes Sedai on the same day. She and Siuan became very close friends. As was common with a good many friendships in the cloistered society of novices, Siuan and Moiraine turned to one another more and more for comfort, and they eventually became pillow friends, continuing up to the time they were raised Aes Sedai and to some extent for a time thereafter. Neither was lesbian; they were simply young women with normal libidos in a situation where they were cut off from the opposite sex. Siuan was always the leader between them, which surprised Moiraine at first, until she realized that it felt natural, and that Siuan had been born to lead. Elaida left the Tower for Andor in 974 NE, but she did return and kept an eye on the pair. Elaida was very strict with both of them, insisting they live up to her standards of performance, not giving them one inch of slack in their studies and their public behavior, and in their obedience to the rules. The last time Moiraine and Siuan were punished as Accepted was actually after they had passed the tests for the shawl, which, though they were supposed to spend the night in contemplation and meditation, they decided to celebrate by playing a prank on Elaida, who had remained in the Tower for a short visit after the Battle of the Shining Walls. They were caught by her, trying to sneak mice into her bed, and while some sisters might have forgiven two who were to be raised Aes Sedai in the morning, she immediately took them to Merean Redhill, the Mistress of Novices, who was not best pleased at being roused out of her bed and decided to make their punishment memorable.

Thus they went to the ceremony raising them Aes Sedai with soundly strapped bottoms, making them probably unique in the history of the White Tower.

Moiraine and Siuan were attending Tamra Ospenya, the Amyrlin Seat, as Accepted when Gitara Moroso, who was then Keeper of the Chronicles, made her Foretelling and dropped dead. She said, "He is born again! I feel him! The Dragon takes his first breath on the slope of Dragonmount! He is coming! He is coming! Light help us! Light help the world! He lies in the snow and cries like the thunder! He burns like the sun!" The key time, as was evident from Gitara's specific mention of snow, was between her Foretelling and the sudden thaw that melted the snow for a time, a matter of ten days. As Accepted, and even as Aes Sedai, after being raised shortly afterward, they were not made part of Tamra's search for the child. Instead, she called in various senior sisters in secret while relegating Siuan and Moiraine to helping gather the names of women who had given birth while the Tower was threatened by the Aiel. All of the women contacted were given one hundred gold crowns in thanksgiving for the Tower being spared, but it was Siuan and Moiraine who winnowed down the names to those who had, surely or possibly, given birth during the key ten days and who might possibly have given birth on Dragonmount. This came to several hundred women, most very hard to locate with the army melting away. They finished this winnowing before Tamra's death, indeed, before being raised Aes Sedai, but Moiraine was held by Tamra's command to stay in Tar Valon and do various make-work. With Tamra's death, Siuan and Moiraine were freed to take part in the search, since each had a list of the names to go by. Unfortunately, Siuan was tapped by Cetalia Delarme, the head of the Blue Ajah eyes-and-ears, to work for her as soon she had the shawl, so Moiraine set off alone.

Over the next few months, they learned that Tamra had been murdered, that the Black Ajah really existed, that the Black was also searching for the Dragon Reborn and that the Black did not know that he was a newborn since they were killing any man or boy who showed anything that might be interpreted as an early sign that he could channel, such as uncommon luck or a sudden rise to prominence.

At Aesdaishar Palace in Chachin, Moiraine fought and killed Merean Redhill, a member of the Black Ajah, but not before Merean killed Diryk, who was thought to be too lucky, his father Brys and Edeyn Arrel's daughter Iselle. Lan Mandragoran fought Ryne, a Darkfriend working with Merean, and killed him. Moiraine disposed of the bodies and persuaded Lan to give up his personal fight and become her Warder.

Moiraine and Lan spent many years searching for the Dragon Reborn in many places; in 998 NE they arrived in the village of Emond's Field. There she found three young men of the proper age, but all were said to have been born in the Two Rivers. She gave each a coin that would let her find them, wherever they went. She also found two young women with the ability to channel. On Winternight, Trollocs attacked Emond's Field, and Moiraine and Lan helped to fight them. The next day, Rand al'Thor brought his injured father to her, and she Healed him. She convinced Rand, Mat Cauthon and Perrin Aybara that the Trollocs, and the Myrddraal they had seen, were after them, and that they needed to flee, in secret, with her. Egwene al'Vere, the young woman Rand thought he would marry, saw that the boys were up to something and decided to join them; Thom Merrilin, the visiting gleeman, also joined them. Nynaeve al'Meara, the Wisdom of Emond's Field, followed them some days later and caught up with them in Baerlon.

The group started for Tar Valon, with Draghkar, Myrddraal and Trollocs chasing them. Moiraine and Lan were able to keep them just a step ahead of the Shadowspawn. Finally they were forced to shelter in Shadar Logoth; when against all expectations Trollocs entered the ruined city, the group gathered itself to flee. Mashadar, the deadly fog, appeared, though, and the group was separated. Moiraine, Lan and Nynaeve remained together, but they didn't know where the others had gone. They started toward Caemlyn, hoping to find them. They found Perrin and Egwene being held by Whitecloaks and rescued them. When they reached Caemlyn, they found Rand and Mat at The Queen's Blessing, as well as the Ogier Loial. Mat was suffering from his attachment to the dagger he had stolen from Mordeth; Moiraine was able to Heal him somewhat. The boys told Moiraine of the dreams that they had had of Ba'alzamon, Perrin and Egwene told of a story they had heard from Tinkers, and Loial told of one heard in the *stedding*. Moiraine realized that the group needed to go to the Eye of the World.

With Loial to guide them, they traveled through the Ways to Fal Dara, where they learned that Padan Fain, a Darkfriend, had been following them. The next morning they set off into the Blight to find the Green Man and the Eye of the World. There Aginor and Balthamel appeared and injured Moiraine. The Green Man killed Balthamel, and Rand killed Aginor, and Moiraine knew for sure that Rand was the Dragon Reborn. Hidden in the empty Eye, they found Lews Therin's banner, a broken seal of the Dark One's prison and the Horn of Valere.

They returned to Fal Dara; Siuan, who had become the Amyrlin Seat, visited them there. Trollocs attacked and the Horn was stolen, and Rand, Mat, Perrin and Shienaran soldiers went after it. Egwene and Nynaeve headed for the Tower, and Moiraine did some research. She also told Lan that if she died his bond would pass to Myrelle. Moiraine went to Falme, and was reunited with Rand. They wintered in the Mountains of Mist, and Moiraine talked to many of her eyes-and-ears. Rand left in secret, headed for the Stone of Tear, and Moiraine, Lan, Loial and Perrin went after him. They arrived in Tear, picking up Faile along the way. Moiraine realized that Be'lal was running Tear, and was trying to kill Rand. She arrived in time to balefire Be'lal, and Rand took Callandor. Moiraine, Rand and Mat all went through the redstone doorframe to ask questions of the Aelfinn; Moiraine also let slip that she knew who she would marry. Although she did not reveal details, Min Farshaw had told her that she would marry Thom Merrilin.

When Rand determined to go to the Aiel Waste, Moiraine and Lan accompanied him. Moiraine went to Rhuidean, and went through the *ter'angreal* that the Wise Ones used. There she saw all possible future skeins of her life, though these ran together in such a way as to leave her only with chunks; things that she must do, things she must not do. After Rand was proclaimed the *Car'a'carn* by the Aiel, she went with him back to Cairhien, trying to teach him as much as she could.

As she had seen in Rhuidean, a day came where news of Morgase arrived. Moiraine led Rand to the docks of Cairhien and the redstone doorframe *ter'angreal* leading to the realm of the Eelfinn; Lanfear appeared and attacked Rand and his companions. She flung Moiraine under a wagon, but Moiraine pulled herself up, tackled Lanfear, and both went through the doorframe, destroying it in the process. Lan felt the bond release, and he and the others believed Moiraine dead.

Moiraine was not dead, but was held captive by the Eelfinn, who fed on her emotions and drained her ability to use the One Power. She had left a letter for Thom, however, that told him how she might be rescued. Mat, Thom and Noal Charin, who was truly Jain Farstrider, went into the realm of the Eelfinn and Aelfinn through the Tower of Ghenjei and rescued her. She kept the *ter'angreal* that she and Lanfear had been fighting over when they went through the doorframe; without it, she could channel only weakly. She and Thom were married, and she bonded Thom as her Warder.

Moiraine went to the Field of Merrilor, where she convinced the nations to sign the Dragon's Peace, and she accompanied Rand to Shayol Ghul when he fought the Dark One.

Moiral, Lillen. Moghedien's name in the Age of Legends.

Moisen. A battle in the Whitecloak War, also known as the Troubles among the Whitecloaks, in which the Whitecloaks tried to take Altara. Niall thought it the worst battle he had ever fought, when armies blundered into one another in the night near Moisen, and how that battle had seemed as bright as a summer's day compared to the one he was fighting at that time, given reports of numerous events across the world from Omerna and Balwer.

Mol Hara Square. A large square located in front of the Tarasin Palace in Ebou Dar.

Moldine Gate. A gate in the south wall of the city of Ebou Dar.

Molvaine Gap. A narrow valley, northeast of Maderin in Altara on the border of Murandy, beyond the Malvide Narrows on the eastern side of the Damora

Mountains. The Seanchan had an army there; Mat wanted to draw them out so that he could pass through the gap.

Monaelle. A Wise One of the Goshien Aiel with the ability to channel and a strength level of 45(33), which would have been barely strong enough for her to have attained the shawl. About 5'6" tall, she was short for an Aiel woman, and had gray eyes, yellow hair with hints of red and a mild, motherly face. She appeared to be not far into her middle years. Of high standing, although the weakest in the Power there, Monaelle led the ceremony in which Aviendha and Elayne became first-sisters. She was the only woman at the adoption ceremony who was not taller than Elayne. Monaelle bore seven children and told Aviendha that she had to make sure that Elayne got plenty of fresh air. Monaelle checked Elayne's babes with a weave called Caressing the Child; she also acted as Elayne's midwife until the Aiel left Caemlyn.

Mondevin, Jorille. The Royal Historian to the Court of Ethenielle of Kandor; she wrote the introduction to "The Strike at Shayol Ghul."

Mondoran, Jaric. *See* Jaric Mondoran

Mondwin, Luthair Paendrag. *See* Luthair Paendrag Mondwin

money. *See* currency

Montem al'San. A Two Rivers man in Perrin's army. He was guarding Perrin the day he encountered Whitecloaks on the Jehannah Road.

months. *See* Farede Calendar

Monuments Past. A history book that Min read.

Moondancer, Jethari. *See* Jethari Moondancer *and* Birgitte

moondrop. A flowering plant. Graendal had its blossom in her hair at one point. It was also embroidered on Nasin Caeren's lapels.

Moonflower. Leane's gray mare that she rode from Tar Valon to Salidar.

Moonglow. A mare of Tairen stock that belonged to a member of the Band of the Red Hand. He died, and Joline took her to go to Tar Valon.

Moonhunter. The wolves' name for Lanfear.

Moonlight. A white mare ridden by Nynaeve when she accompanied Rand to meet Hurin as a representative of the Borderland rulers.

Moonshadow. A deep brown mare from royal stables in Caemlyn, ridden by Elayne during the Last Battle. Moonshadow was killed when one of Hanlon's men drove a sword through her neck.

Moor. A hired hand at Almen Bunt's sister Alysa's apple orchard in Andor.

Moorwyn, Niande. *See* Niande Moorwyn

Mor, Almurat. *See* Almurat Mor

Mora, River. A river forming the border between Arafel and Shienar, flowing southwest into the River Erinin.

Mora. 1) A Wise One of the Shaarad Aiel at Colrada Hold with the ability to channel. A dreamwalker, she taught Bair. When she was nearly three hundred years old, Mora died of a bloodsnake bite. 2) A Wise One of the Goshien Aiel several generations after the Last Battle. Seen in Aviendha's vision of the future in Rhuidean, Mora met with Ladalin, Tamaav, Takei and Jorshem; they decided that the Aiel must retreat to the Three-fold Land.

Moradri. An Aes Sedai of the Green Ajah. She was a long-limbed Mayener, and had two Mayener Warders who were rumored to be her brothers. When the Seanchan attacked the Tower, Moradri went to various groups fighting in the Tower and told them that she and Saerin were trying to set up a formal command center. She mapped out for Saerin the location and Ajah of each group fighting.

morat. A Seanchan term placed before the name of an animal to mean handler of the animal. A *morat'grolm*, for example, was a handler of *grolm*. There were also *morat'lopar, morat'raken, morat'to'raken* and *morat'torm. See also der'morat*

Moraton, Soffi. A woman with Perrin's army who tore her tent during a stream crossing and had no trouble getting it repaired.

Mord. A broken-nosed Domani thug who worked for Jorgin, Milisair's questioner, in the torture business.

Mordaine. A Jenn Aiel woman during the building of Rhuidean. She, Dermon and Narisse met with the Aiel clan chiefs and told them that they must come to Rhuidean if they wanted to lead. Mordaine also told the Aiel that the Jenn's days were dwindling, and they would soon all be dead. A graying woman with deep-set green eyes, she looked as if she could have been Narisse's sister.

Mordero daghain pas duente cuebiyar. An Old Tongue expression meaning "My heart holds no fear of death."

Mordeth. A councilor who convinced the city of Aridhol to use the Darkfriends' ways against the Darkfriends, thus bringing its destruction and earning it a new name, Shadar Logoth ("Where the Shadow Waits"). Only one thing survived in Shadar Logoth besides the hate that killed it, and that was Mordeth himself, bound in the ruins for two thousand years, waiting for someone to come whose soul he could consume and so take on new flesh. When Rand, Mat and Perrin were exploring Shadar Logoth, he tried in vain to get them to help carry his treasure to his horses; if he could convince someone to accompany him to the walls, he would have been able to consume them. When he encountered Padan Fain, he could not consume Fain's soul because it had been touched directly by the Dark One; the two blended into a far more evil being. Fain/Mordeth was not harmed in the Ways by the Black Wind because of professional courtesy.

Mordeth, Jeraal. The name used by Padan Fain when he was in Cairhien advising Toram Riatin.

Mordrellen Mantear. A queen of Andor who took the throne in 964 NE after the death of her mother Dolera. She had four older brothers. In 935–936 NE, Mordrellen spent two years in the White Tower; she had no ability to channel, but as per tradition, she received the Great Serpent ring on departing. Mordrellen was very close to the White Tower, making frequent return visits despite the distance. She was the last queen of Andor from the Mantear family. In 972 NE, shortly after her daughter Tigraine disappeared, Mordrellen died, some said of grief. Morgase of House Trakand then gained the throne after a two-year power struggle known as the Succession.

Morear. A member of Jarid Sarand's personal guard. Faced with Jarid's growing insanity, Morear and Jarid's other men rebelled against Jarid, and tied him to a tree; Morear gagged him. The men then went off to fight in the Last Battle.

Moreina. A nation that arose after the Trolloc Wars; Tear later occupied the site. *See* Fel Moreina

Morel. Father of Dal father of Haman, the last being an Ogier Elder of Stedding Shangtai.

Morelin Samared. The name used by Elayne after escaping Ronde Macura and while traveling with Luca's show.

Morelle. A town near the southernmost boundary claimed by Cairhien, halfway from Cairhien to the River Iralell. Rand told Maringil and others that he had sent some Aiel to catch bandits, and that the Stone Dogs had killed nearly two hundred near Morelle.

Morena. An Aiel woman who served as Wise One for Erim of the Chareen Aiel.

Morenal Ocean. A body of water bordering eastern Shara and western Seanchan.

Moressin Damodred. Laman's brother and Moiraine's uncle. He was cruel and vicious and held Moiraine's father in contempt. He was killed at the end of the Aiel War, along with his brothers Laman and Aldecain.

Morgase Trakand. By the Grace of the Light, Queen of Andor, Defender of the Realm, Protector of the People, High Seat of House Trakand. Her sign was three golden keys, and the sign of House Trakand was a silver keystone. She had strong blue eyes and red-gold hair that fell in waves and curls to her shoulders. Rand thought she was what Elayne would look like when maturity ripened her into full bloom; because of her admittedly minuscule ability to channel, she looked little more than thirty. Shorter than her daughter, Morgase was about 5'6" tall. Her face was a perfect oval, like her daughter's, and her lips were a little on the full side. Born in 957 NE, she went to the White Tower in 971 NE. After Tigraine disappeared, she was allowed to return to Andor and contend for the throne. She was given the Great Serpent ring on leaving, despite her meager abilities, as a sign of the Tower's favor; the White Tower very much wanted a woman who had trained with them to take the Lion Throne. She did so, and soon after married Taringail Damodred, to mark the smooth continuation of rule within Andor and to maintain the treaties and agreements with Cairhien that Taringail's earlier marriage had cemented. With him she had two children, Gawyn and Elayne; she also loved Galad, Taringail's son by Tigraine, very much.

Morgase's marriage was not happy. She became closer to the bard of her House, Thomdril Merrilin, who had helped her considerably in gaining the throne through his deftness at the Game of Houses, and after Taringail's death, they became lovers. When Thom went off without telling her, and met her anger for anger on his return, she issued arrest warrants which were never canceled. Some time after Thom Merrilin left, she became lovers with Gareth Bryne, the Lord Captain Commander of her Queen's Guards.

Rahvin, posing as Gaebril, arrived in Caemlyn and used Compulsion on her and alienated her from her closest friends and strongest supporters. She was able to overcome the Compulsion enough to flee, although she continued to suffer memory blackouts and memory tricks for quite some time after. She tried to get Bryne, whom she had exiled, to help her regain her throne, but he was not at Kore Springs. She went to Amadicia to seek help from Ailron, but the Whitecloaks were the true power there and they held her. While Pedron Niall was alive, she was not treated badly, but after his death she was tortured by Asunawa and violated by Valda. She was held briefly by the Seanchan when they took Amador and escaped with the help of Sebban Balwer. She abdicated her throne, although she kept that quiet. She was rescued from Dragonsworn by Perrin's party and, as Maighdin Dorlain, became Faile's lady's maid. Morgase developed feelings for Tallanvor, who was younger than herself, but she kept him at arm's length for a long time because of her bad experiences with Gaebril and Valda. She was among those taken *gai'shain* by Sevanna and the Shaido; she used her ability to channel to signal for help when she and others were trapped by Galina. Her true identity was revealed at Perrin's meeting with Galad, and she served as judge at Perrin's trial for killing Whitecloaks.

She married Tallanvor, and revealed to her children that she was still alive.

During the Last Battle, she organized efforts to tend the battlefield wounded.

Morgeillin, Solain. *See* Solain Morgeillin

Mori. A Maiden traveling with Perrin. She investigated the area near the Jehannah Road that had developed characteristics of the Blight.

Moria Elward. A woman who ran a farm near Tar Valon. For penance, novice Sahra Covenry was sent to work for her. Both Moria and Sahra were killed by an Aes Sedai of the Black Ajah.

Moria Karentanis. An Illianer Aes Sedai of the Blue Ajah in public and of the Black Ajah in truth. Her strength level was 25(13). Born in 840 NE, she went to the White Tower in 854 NE. After spending eight years as a novice and seven years as Accepted, she was raised to the shawl in 869 NE. Moria was an ordinary-looking woman, so much so that some at first missed the ageless quality about her. According to Anaiya, she was harder, or tougher, at least, than Lelaine; she was not part of Lelaine's clique. She was not particularly graceful, though she bounded to her feet before the report on Shadar Logoth. In 999 NE she was raised Sitter for the Blue in Salidar, replacing the Blue Sitter who was killed in the fighting when Siuan was deposed. Like the other Blues, she was strongly in favor of removing Elaida, but like many others, she disliked the openness of what the Aes Sedai were doing, showing the world the division in the Tower, and she wished there were some other way. Moria's name was on Verin's list of the Black Ajah; she was captured, stilled and beheaded.

Moridin. The Old Tongue word for "death," it was the name given to the resurrected Ishamael. His strength level was ++1, the highest possible level for a man. He was 6'5" to 6'6" tall with broad shoulders and brilliant blue eyes. His body was somewhere in its mid twenties, and was stopped short of beauty by a chin that was too strong. Despite his resurrection in a new, young body, he was still more than a little mad, and still suffered from delusions of godhood. Despite being half-mad and megalomaniacal, he was highly intelligent and damned clever. After being named Nae'blis, Moridin had both Moghedien and Cyndane in his power, held by *cour'souvra*. He also persuaded Graendal to cooperate, though she was not held by anything except her knowledge that he seemingly had the Dark One's favor, as evidenced among other things by Shaidar Haran, and her fear that her schemes and involvement with Sammael might be discovered.

Moridin knew that the seals on the Dark One's prison were weakening, physically and otherwise, and more, he knew why. He arranged for Taim to deliver a seal to Rand, partly to ensure that Taim was well received and partly in the hope that the seal would be placed with any others that Rand might have. Moridin believed that Rand had other seals, and thought that Dobraine and Bashere were likely candidates for guardians; he sent agents to try to retrieve them.

Moridin observed Sammael and Graendal's meeting with Sevanna and the Wise Ones.

When Rand was in danger of falling into a pit in Shadar Logoth, Moridin rescued him; as Mashadar moved toward them, they both released balefire against it, and the streams crossed, making them fall. He gave Rand some helpful pointers on defeating Sammael.

Moridin sent Mili Skane to Caemlyn, giving her Falion and Marillin as servants and arranging for Hanlon to go to her; under Moridin's orders, Mili killed Carridin. Moridin told Kisman to kill Rand if he must, but that it was most important to bring him everything in Rand's possession. At a meeting of the Forsaken, he ordered the deaths of Mat and Perrin, but said that Rand was his. After Semirhage was captured by Rand, Moridin refused Mesaana and Demandred's plea to free her; he was angry because she had injured Rand. He gave Graendal a dreamspike and set her to kill Perrin; when her schemes failed, he punished her by killing her and putting her soul in an ugly body. At Shayol Ghul, Moridin faced Rand in the Last Battle; Rand prevailed and carried Moridin out of the Pit of Doom. The two swapped bodies; Moridin, in Rand's body, died. *See also* **Ishamael**

Moril. A man who knows no fear, in a song sung at The White Ring in Maderin, Altara.

Morin. The first Maiden of the Spear. A pretty, yellow-haired Jenn Aiel and a dreamer, she went to the martial Aiel and asked for their help in rescuing her daughter, who had been kidnapped. Though it was not required of a woman, she elected to go with the Aiel on the mission; Jeordam shortened a spear for her and taught her to use it. She told him that she had seen his face in a dream. Morin later bore Jeordam a son.

Morly Hardlin. An Asha'man who reached the rank of Dedicated. He was a member of Logain's faction, and was with Logain when Logain took Toveine. He bonded Lemai Ambani, a Red.

Morning Clouds. A younger male wolf in Wildfire's pack. Perrin contacted him for information after he and others set out to find the kidnapped Rand.

Morning Directives. At the Black Tower, standing orders and orders for the day were read out to the Asha'man.

Morning Mist. A female wolf. When Shadowspawn raided the camp in the Mountains of Mist and Leya died, Morning Mist was the only one still living among seven wolves that attacked and killed a Fade.

Morning Tide. *See* Shalon din Togara Morning Tide

morning drop. A flower used in Aiel bridal wreaths to signify the bride's submissive nature.

Morninglight. A wolf in Oak Dancer's pack. He invited Perrin to hunt; later he, Hopper and other wolves helped teach Perrin to follow someone in the wolf dream. Slayer killed Morninglight.

morningstar. A plant bearing a white flower; the cut flower had a stem long enough to use in a vase. Moiraine, Nynaeve and Egwene wore these flowers in their hair when they were with the Green Man.

Moroso, Gitara. *See* Gitara Moroso

Morr, Fedwin. *See* Fedwin Morr

Morrigan. A queen of Andor during the War of the Hundred Years. She reigned from FY 1103 to FY 1114.

Morrigan, Varuna. *See* Varuna Morrigan

Morsa, Lady. A Seanchan noblewoman. She was ordered held by Jalindin after a confrontation with Rand and Aviendha once Aviendha fled by gateway to Seanchan and Rand followed, apparently because of knowledge Morsa might have had concerning events east of the Aryth Ocean. Morsa recognized Rand, having seen him in the sky above Falme.

Morsad, Berenicia. *See* Berenicia Morsad

Morvrin Thakanos. An Aes Sedai of the Brown Ajah and the rebel contingent, with a strength level of 15(3). Born in 777 NE in Illian, she went to the White Tower in 795 NE. After spending seven years as a novice and six years as Accepted, she was raised to the shawl in 808 NE. Standing 5'5" tall, and stout, with a round face, brown eyes and gray-streaked hair, Morvrin was a placid sort, sometimes with an absently vague look. She required a great deal of proof for anything. Her Warder was Jori. A member of Sheriam's council in Salidar, she was one of three, with Sheriam and Myrelle, who stood for Egwene, "heart for heart, soul for soul, life for life." Morvrin was forced to swear personal fealty to Egwene because of the ferrets sent to the White Tower, done without the knowledge of the Hall because of fear that some of the rebel Hall might be Black Ajah. Morvrin was part of the battle in *Tel'aran'rhiod* against some of the Black Ajah at the White Tower until she and others were taken out of the dream on Amys' orders.

Mos Shirare. A fortress town in Shienar. When Agelmar was going to find the Trollocs at Tarwin's Gap while Rand, at the same time, was going to meet the Green Man, he mentioned that he would be joining other Shienaran armies, including the one from Mos Shirare. And when Siuan, the Amyrlin, visited Fal Dara, Agelmar told her a bard from Mos Shirare had been selected to entertain her.

Mosaada. A sept of the Goshien Aiel.

Mosadorin. A place where the legendary Green sister Caraighan Maconar single-handedly put down a rebellion after the Breaking.

Mosalaine, Delana. *See* Delana Mosalaine

Mosara. A nation that arose from the War of the Hundred Years.

Moselle, Amira. *See* Amira Moselle

Mosenain, Catrelle. An ironmonger's daughter from Maerone whom Daved Hanlon murdered and threw down a well after she disclosed that he had impregnated her.

Moseneillin, Daigian. *See* Daigian Moseneillin

Moshaine. A sept of the Shaido Aiel.

Moshea. A Tinker in Raen's band. When Perrin was in Raen's wagon after the Trolloc ambush, Ila sent Raen to see if Moshea had the wheel on his wagon yet.

Mosinel, Ared. Rahvin's name before he turned to the Shadow.

Mosk the Giant. A character from the Age before the Age of Legends featured in a gleeman's tale. He was a giant who fought Elsbet, the Queen of All, with his Lance of Fire, and fought Merk using spears of fire.

Mosra. A town in Altara on the western border near the River Eldar and Amadicia. Ailron had laid claim to it and other villages so that Pedron Niall, who controlled Ailron, could choke river traffic to Ebou Dar and thereby take over Altara.

Mosrara, Liale. *See* Liale Mosrara

Mosvani, Alanna. *See* Alanna Mosvani

motai. The Aiel name for a sweet crunchy grub found in the Waste.

Motara, Sereine dar Shamelle. The author of *Commentaries on the Karaethon Cycle.* She was Counsel-Sister to Comaelle, High Queen of Jaramide, circa 325 AB, the Third Age.

Motheneos, Elinde. A supporter of Amalasan who tried to free him from the White Tower; he failed and died.

Mothers. Wisdom-equivalents in Seanchan. These were village wise women knowledgeable in dispensing herbs and cures. They were generally called "Mother," though there were other regional names. The degree to which they were respected by the Healers varied widely; some Healers considered them useful when there was no Healer available or until a Healer could be summoned; others considered them a nuisance. There was no fear among Mothers of being taken for one using the Power; Aes Sedai having long been reduced to *damane* in Seanchan, there was no memory at all of Healing.

Mount Sardlen. A mountain in Murandy.

Mountain Dancers. An Aiel warrior society; they were also known as *Hama N'dore*.

mountain king snake. A deadly snake.

Mountains of Dhoom. A range of mountains situated on an east-west axis in the north, just below the Blasted Lands.

Mountains of Mist. A mountain range oriented north-south, found immediately west of Emond's Field. It separated Arad Doman and Tarabon from Andor and Ghealdan.

Mowly. *See* Careme *and* Ellya Mowly

Muad Cheade. A former Marshal-General of Saldaea. He was mad but a great general, never coming close to losing. He once ordered twenty-three trees chopped down because they were looking at him; he then demanded that they be buried and gave the oration.

Muad'drin tia dar allende caba'drin rhadiem! Old Tongue for "Infantry prepare to pass cavalry forward!"

Muadh. A grizzled Child of the Light who was with Geofram Bornhald on Toman Head. Muadh fell into the hands of Darkfriends once; his face was so scarred from it that it took even the strongest aback, and he could only speak in a whispered growl. In a village where thirty people, including some children, were hanged, Muadh told Geofram that the group that had done the hanging included two men who looked just like Child Wuan and Child Earwin. Those two were men that Geofram had been forced earlier to hand over to Questioners.

mudfish. A fish not worth eating.

mudgin. A fool.

Muelin. A woman who was a contortionist with Valan Luca's show, hired from a show that had been nearly destroyed by a rioting mob. She lived with other contortionists in a virulently yellow wagon.

Mulaen. A Seanchan superior servant in Falme in the house where the *damane* were kept; she had charge of the quarters for *damane*. She burned Min's coat and breeches and gave Min her choice of garments to indicate her place in the hierarchy. Min had to comply if she wanted to continue visiting Egwene. Mulaen had a droning nasal voice and a sharp way with any *damane* who did not remember every word of her boring lectures.

Mulan, Leuese. An old Tairen fisherman who became wealthy after finding three *cuendillar* bowls and a cup in his nets, but later could not remember where. He bought a trading ship.

Mulinda. A Salidar serving woman in service to the rebel Aes Sedai. She was skinny and gaped a lot. She shared a room with Satina, Emara and Ronelle in the same house where Elayne and Nynaeve lived. She was there the night the "bubble of evil" hit, and was caught under the bed when it flipped.

Mull, Alpert. *See* Alpert Mull

mura. A tree found in Seanchan. It had ropelike bark and green tufts of thick needlelike leaves.

Muradin. A man of the Shaido Aiel and first-brother of Couladin. Muradin was allowed to enter Rhuidean to see whether he could be chief of the Shaido, replacing the deceased Suladric. He and Couladin had big plans, involving crossing the Dragonwall again and conquering and holding Cairhien; Sevanna planned to marry Muradin when he became chief. Muradin could not accept the history of the Aiel; he found it so repellent that he ripped out his own eyes and ate them. He did not come out of the *ter'angreal*.

Murandy. A nation north of Illian; its capital was Lugard. Its sigil was a red bull: the Red Bull. Its banner was the Red Bull on a field vertically striped blue and white—three blue and two white. The banner was fringed in red if flown when the sovereign was present.

Murandy was founded approximately FY 1047 by Lady Katrine do Catalan a'Coralle, who had just captured the city of Lugard, taking its name from an old name for the region around Lugard. She was assassinated after less than a year on her throne and succeeded by her son, who was succeeded in turn by his four brothers, with the throne then passing to the next generation of the House. It was estimated by some historians that during the War of the Hundred Years, Murandy averaged a new ruler every two years, and even after the war was over, the average length of rule was only eight years, usually ending with assassination or an "accident" or otherwise mysterious death. By approximately 200 NE, rulers began holding the throne for much longer periods, but only because the crown had become essentially valueless in a nation that was really only a patchwork of allegiances to towns and individual nobles. It was generally considered that Murandy survived in large part because its much stronger neighbors all had opponents or possible opponents strong enough that they were unwilling to turn their backs long enough to swallow Murandy. There was a history of border raids into Andor by Murandians going back to the War of the Hundred Years. Raids the other way were usually punitive. Northern Murandy was occupied by Andor more than once, but Andor never considered it worth the effort to hold. Murandy had one of the three false Dragons who sprang up after Logain was captured and before Rand declared himself. Murandians were quite proud of having seized the false Dragon who appeared in their midst, and doing so quickly. What they were not so proud of was the fact that they burned him alive. This was done under influence from Illian, in fact, from Lord Brend.

Murandy could have either a king or a queen. It was a hereditary monarchy, with the throne going to the eldest child alive at the ruler's death. Murandy rarely changed its ruling House because no one cared enough to take a position that was at best a figurehead, though occasionally some lord or lady would think he or she was strong enough to unite the land. The ruler seldom controlled more than Lugard itself, and often not all of that. The countryside was a crazy quilt of individual nobles' fiefs, and those nobles raided one another, formed alliances against one another and betrayed those alliances to form new ones at the drop of a handkerchief. Those along the border also invested considerable time in raiding across said border, mainly for horses and cattle, but also sometimes as little more than glorified bandits looting villages and manors.

The army of Murandy historically consisted of the personal levies of the nobles, who often squabbled over the command. Nobles even removed their troops in times of dire need because of these arguments. Noblewomen almost invariably used a Master of the Horse to command their soldiers, and very rarely took the field themselves. Noblemen were expected to lead whether or not they were competent to do so. There was never a permanent formation in Murandy such as the Queen's Guards in Andor. The throne was weak, and while anyone who held the throne would have wanted such a formation to strengthen it, no one else wanted the throne strengthened, since that lessened their own power.

Murandy had some mining, including gold and silver, but the political situation never allowed any large-scale or well-organized efforts. It had a good trade in wool, and was famed for its lace. Beef, mutton and leather were also produced.

Murasaka sisters. Six women who were acrobats first with Sillia Cerano's show and then with Valan Luca's show. Although they called themselves sisters, they were obviously not related. Andaya and Kuan were two of the six.

Murdru Kar. Words uttered by Trollocs while fighting Lan in the Last Battle.

Murel. A Seanchan soldier in Jurador who, with two others, tried to get into Luca's show without paying. His eyes were tilted like a Saldaean's, and his skin was the color of honey. His standardbearer confined the three to camp for ten days and docked them ten days' pay, since they were supposed to be unloading wagons.

Murellin. Shiaine's henchman who posed as her servant. He was heavily muscled with sunken knuckles and sullen eyes. He was big enough that he could easily pick up a cask of brandy that Daved Hanlon didn't think he himself could have lifted, but Murellin easily tipped it to pour the contents down the funnel stuck in Jaichim Carridin's mouth. Shiaine made Falion available for Murellin; she asked Hanlon for something to make Murellin sleep through the night.

When Elayne and her party went to Full Moon Street, Murellin was drunk in the stable; Jaem tied him up.

Murow, Letice. *See* Letice Murow

Musar, Lord. One of the Saldaeans who, along with his wife and another couple, met with Taim under the parley flag and tried to kill him with daggers. He and his wife were rendered unsuited for anything except serving others after the encounter.

Musara. A sept of the Reyn Aiel.

Musarin. An Aes Sedai of the Yellow Ajah and the loyalist contingent. Tall and white-haired, Musarin was guarding Leane when Egwene visited. When Leane's cell started melting, Musarin and Gelarna used *saidar* to pull Leane free, and Musarin called for help.

Musenge. A captain in the Deathwatch Guard. A grizzled, weathered man with black hair and seemingly built for endurance, he commanded Tuon's personal bodyguard and led five hundred of the Deathwatch Guard and one hundred Gardeners. He accompanied Karede in the search for Tuon with one hundred members of the Deathwatch Guard and twenty Gardeners. When Karede went into Mat's camp, Musenge waited in case it was a trap. After Musenge fought alongside Mat to save Tuon, he took Elbar's head to Tuon in Ebou Dar. When Tuon met with Rand at Falme, Musenge placed archers on nearby roofs to protect her.

mushroom, deathshead. A poisonous mushroom.

mushroom, Queen's Crown. A flavorful type of mushroom.

mushroom, shadowshand. A mushroom that made rings on fallen logs.

Musicar. A member of the Deathwatch Guard. When Rand surprised Tuon in the garden of the Tarasin Palace, Tuon shouted for Musicar to run and fetch *damane*.

Mutch. A stableman at The Stag and Lion in Baerlon, Andor. Wiry and surly, Mutch complained when Moiraine and her party came in the back way at the inn, and scowled at Rand when he went off to see Baerlon. When the party was leaving, he complained about readying the horses, and sourly watched them depart.

Muyami. A group of Seanchan who did not hold to oaths strongly. Egeanin stated that she had made an oath so strong that not even a Muyami would break it.

Muyami Uprising. An unpleasantness in Seanchan during which Karede served and gained honors.

Mycal Crossin. A grain merchant in So Habor with whom Perrin did business. At first he thought that Perrin and his companions were ghosts; he was afraid of the ghosts that were appearing in So Habor. His fear overwhelmed him to the point that he stopped caring about cleanliness. Although he agreed to sell grain, the grain was full of weevils and had to be winnowed.

Myershi, Reo. An ancestor of King Paitar of Arafel who heard a Foretelling of importance about the Dragon Reborn and passed it down through his family.

Myk. A pikeman in Juilin Sandar's squad in the Last Battle.

Mylen. A *damane* belonging to Tuon. She was formerly an Aes Sedai of the Blue Ajah whose name was Sheraine Caminelle and who was captured at Falme; her Warder died trying to protect her. She was then taken back to Seanchan, where she arrived half dead, skin-and-bones, and refusing to eat. Tuon bought her on the docks at Shon Kifar. A Cairhienin who looked a great deal like Moiraine, she was about 4'10" and under Tuon's care became a little plump and definitely round of bosom and bottom. Mylen had dark eyes, black hair and a pale complexion. She became the quintessential *damane* under Tuon's training, utterly devoted to her. She was part of Karede's group that searched for Tuon when she was missing. Mylen was particularly eager to free Tuon, particularly incensed that she was taken by Aes Sedai (or so she believed), and somewhat guilty because she herself used to call herself Aes Sedai, as she thought of it. She was well and truly Tuon's, and would have fought not only for Tuon, but to stop anyone from removing her collar. She could not, of course, use the Power as a weapon even under the influence of the collar, and the other two oaths held her as well.

Myrddraal. Creatures of the Dark One, commanders of the Trollocs. They were the twisted offspring of Trollocs in which the human stock used to create the Trollocs resurfaced, but tainted by the evil that made the Trollocs. In different lands they were known by many names, among them Halfman, the Eyeless, Shadowman, Lurk, Fetch and Fade.

A Myrddraal appeared to be a fairly tall man, over six feet, with a pale, pasty-white complexion. The hair was black and flat, the lips thin and pale. There were no eyes, no eyebrows, no sign or hint that there should have been any eyes. They saw like eagles in day or night, however. Their look caused fear in the one they looked at. They moved sinuously, graceful and deadly, like serpents. They had a superior sense of smell, and a weakness for some strong odors.

Myrddraal could become all but invisible in shadows. They had a trick of seeming to vanish while remaining right there. Entering a shadow, they could travel, in a way not even the Forsaken understood, to another shadow far distant. Myrddraal could cloak themselves, and their mounts, in silence, so that not even their horses' hooves on paving stones could be heard.

Trollocs and Myrddraal loathed deep water; neither could swim. Myrddraal would not wade into anything more than waist deep, especially if it was moving, and reluctantly at best. They had no ability to channel, but could detect the channeling of either sex. Their range was greater than even the Forsaken's, but very dependent on the level of the One Power being used. Used very close to them, quite small flows (easily detectable by human channelers at that range) would have produced only a sort of unease, an uncertainty whether there was channeling or not. They could detect the residues of channeling at fainter levels than humans, though without being able to tell anything about what the channeling was—excepting Shaidar Haran, of course.

One of the Myrddraal's abilities was that of controlling and cowing Trollocs consistently over time. Even Forsaken had difficulty with this; Trollocs were easily enough cowed, but the lesson seemed to last almost no time, except for Myrddraal lessons. Myrddraal could also link with a number of Trollocs, completely overriding their bestial nature and taking control of their minds and wills to create a deadly, well-disciplined fighting force almost as effective as was originally intended. Unfortunately, the Myrddraal was then the weak link. If it was killed, the Trollocs sharing the link died with it. Myrddraal were also better able to control a number of other sorts of Shadowspawn. There were, however, some sorts of Shadowspawn which even Myrddraal had a hard time controlling, and some, such as Worms, which they could not control at all.

Myrddraal had no sense of humor in the usual sense, though they did have an extremely sadistic whimsy. Myrddraal did not smile, and they certainly didn't laugh, again excepting Shaidar Haran. A Myrddraal's sword caused a blue flash when struck against a Power-wrought blade. The process of making these weapons was unknown, although each sword had to be quenched in a living human body in the making.

Myrdin Paendrag Maregore. The King of Shandalle and father of Artur Hawkwing. He died during the Black Plague epidemic in FY 939.

Myrelle Berengari. An Altaran Aes Sedai of the Green Ajah and the rebel contingent, with a strength level of 15(3). Born in 954 NE, she went to the White Tower in 968 NE. After spending seven years as a novice and five years as Accepted, she was raised to the shawl in 980 NE. Among the rebels, she served as the Captain-General of the Green Ajah. About 5'4" tall, with an olive complexion and large dark eyes, she was beautiful. Her face was a perfect oval, and usually wore a knowing smile. Myrelle was noted for her fiery temper, even among the Greens. She was the first Aes Sedai in centuries to save more than one Warder whose previous Aes Sedai had died; she was able to save Nuhel Dromand and Avar Hachami. For that reason, she was chosen by Moiraine to receive Lan's bond if anything should happen to her. After Moiraine vanished through the redstone doorway, Myrelle recruited Nisao to help heal Lan's mind. Nicola and Areina blackmailed Myrelle and Nisao over the secret passing of the bond; Nicola wanted more lessons and Areina wanted to be around Lan.

When Egwene discovered that the bond had been passed without Lan's agreement, she had Myrelle swear fealty to her to avoid punishment. After Kairen Stang was murdered, Myrelle bonded her Warder Llyw, although some armtwisting by Faiselle was required for her to do it. Rumor said that she was married to Nuhel, Avar and Croi Makin, her other Warder. Myrelle passed Lan's bond to Nynaeve after Nynaeve passed the test for Aes Sedai.

Myrelle was part of the delegation sent to the Black Tower, part of the group camped outside the walls while Taim tried to Turn Logain. Myrelle and the delegation took on new Warders and then joined Egwene's army fighting Shadowspawn in the Last Battle on the Kandori-Arafellin border.

Myriam Copan. An Aes Sedai of the Green Ajah who served as Amyrlin from 754 to 797 NE. She was justifiably known as "Beauty." Myriam began as a weak Amyrlin known for her concern with her own looks and for her sulks and temper tantrums, as well as for her dislike of being cooped up in Tar Valon and her complete disinterest in having anything to do with running the Tower or the Aes Sedai. In 758 NE she supposedly went on a two-month retreat by herself, after which she underwent a sudden and unexplained about-face. In fact, she had been kidnapped by Cadsuane Melaidhrin and put through a short but tough course in what it meant to be adult and Amyrlin. She restored the power and authority of the Amyrlin Seat and had a distinguished reign. She was not among the most powerful of Amyrlins, but far from the least, and she developed a deft political hand.

N

N'Delia Basolaine. Putative translator of *The Prophecies of the Dragon,* First Maid and Swordfast to Raidhen of Hol Cuchone.

N'Kon. A city or region in Seanchan with honey-brown denizens. When fighting Rand's army, Miraj reflected on the named, honored regiments from different parts of Seanchan that were represented among his troops, including this group.

N'Shar in Mameris, a. An expression of Birgitte's taken from her past; the reference came up when she was watching Nalesean and Mat, and realized that Mat was the more dangerous of the two. Mameris was a city that was the center of a pacifistic movement, unfortunately coupled with a belief in bluntly saying what one thought. A N'Shar was someone from the land encompassing the Shadow Coast who had taken a blood oath of revenge; he or she was a walking time bomb, ready to kill in a twitch, ready to die, until the oath was fulfilled.

Naath and the San d'ma Shadar. People from Mat's memories of battles; he thought of them while preparing for the battle at Merrilor.

Nacelle Kayama. A Malkieri Aes Sedai of the Green Ajah in public but of the Black Ajah in truth. Part of the rebel contingent, she had a strength level of 36(24). Born in 855 NE, she was tall and slender with blue eyes. Romanda thought that she was not particularly intelligent. Nacelle was one of six sisters sent to investigate the large channeling event when Rand cleansed the taint from *saidin,* because of her ability to read residues. Nacelle developed a weave to detect a man channeling, although it did not identify the flows. Nacelle's name was on Verin's list of the Black Ajah.

Nachenin, Malind. *See* Malind Nachenin

nachi. A multilegged creature found in tidal pools.

Nachiman. The royal family of Arafel. *See* Hirare, Kiruna, Menuki *and* Paitar Neramovni Nachiman

Nad. One of the two thugs with Falion and Ispan in Ebou Dar when they were torturing and killing the Wise Woman; Nad disposed of the body. He was all black hair and beady eyes and had more muscles than any three men could need.

Nadere. A Wise One of the Goshien Aiel with the ability to channel and with a strength level of 19(7). She was 5'11" tall and as close to stout as any Aiel came, with green eyes, a large bosom and pale hair. She took part in the adoption ceremony in which Aviendha and Elayne became first-sisters, and was the person who fetched Elayne for the ceremony. She dismissed the Asha'man who had called on Elayne, ignored them as unimportant to what she was about.

Nadoc. A Seanchan officer and commander under Karede. A big man with a deceptively mild face, he was more intelligent than Jadranka, the most senior of Karede's three captains. He was appalled at Jadranka's telling the scouts to press on and what to look for. When Rand's forces attacked, he helped Karede rally the forces and retreat; for those actions, he was raised to the low Blood.

Nadric. A drunken Shaido man in Malden who accosted Faile and tried to carry her off. When Rolan objected, he said that Faile was not pretty enough to fight over.

Nae'blis. The title of the Great Lord's Regent on Earth. The Forsaken jockeyed for this position.

Naean Arawn. A slim Andoran woman who was High Seat of House Arawn. The sign of House Arawn was the silver Triple Keys. About 5'6" tall, she was palely beautiful with big blue eyes and waves of gleaming black hair, but a near-permanent sneer marred her beauty. She opposed Morgase during the Succession. Daved Hanlon was a mercenary in her service at that time, years before he gained his own company. When Rand took Caemlyn she pretended to be content as High Seat of an ancient House. She and the other cronies of Gaebril fled after Rand reached an accommodation with Dyelin; Rand made no moves against them, but Dyelin was not so restrained. Naean attempted to claim the Lion Throne after word came that Colavaere had been crowned in Cairhien, and that Rand had gone to bend knee to the Amyrlin Seat. While two prominent and too insistent supporters of Dyelin were hanged by Dyelin, and twenty more flogged, Naean was imprisoned by Dyelin, as was Elenia. Naean and Elenia were reported rescued while being brought to Caemlyn, but were in fact captured by men loyal to Lady Arymilla. Arymilla forced the captive Naean to sign papers supporting Arymilla for the Lion Throne. She was captured later by Elayne at the Far Madding Gate when Elayne won Caemlyn. Elayne stripped her of her titles and lands and offered them to Cairhienin nobles; she intended to give other property to Naean.

Naeff. An Andoran man who was a member of the Queen's Guards in Andor. He resigned in disgust when Gaebril was in charge, and made his way to the Black Tower. He was strong in Air, and advanced to full Asha'man. He was bonded to Nelavaire Demasiellin. His madness from the taint caused him to see Myrddraal lurking around him. Rand sent Naeff to the Seanchan to negotiate a meeting with the Daughter of the Nine Moons. Naeff accompanied Rand to Bandar Eban, and to the meeting with Hurin, representing the Borderlanders. When a bubble of evil struck the All Summers neighborhood of Tear, Naeff went with Nynaeve to investigate; after they had cleaned up the area, she Healed his madness. He went with Rand to Maradon to save Ituralde and his men. Rand sent him to the Black Tower to find out what was happening; he arrived after Androl and the others had prevailed. During the Last Battle, Mat sent Naeff with a letter to Tuon with instructions on rejoining the battle.

Naeise. An Aiel Maiden of the Moshaine Shaido. After they had gone through Sammael's gateway, she reported to Maeric that there were seven or eight thousand spears approaching from the east. She thought they were enemy Reyn Aiel.

Naerodan, Samalin. *See* Samalin Naerodan

Nagashi, Kerene. *See* Kerene Nagashi

Nagora. A Cairhienin Aes Sedai of the White Ajah and the loyalist contingent. Short and lean, she wore her hair in a tight roll on the nape of her neck and sat and stood up straight as if to make up for her lack of height. She had a Warder. Nagora was guarding Leane's cell once when Egwene visited; she also taught Egwene logic; the lesson turned to how to deal with an aging Warder.

Nagoyin, Amico. *See* Amico Nagoyin

Nailine Samfara. An Ogier-built city in Coremanda, one of the Ten Nations after the Breaking.

Naime din Malzar. A Sea Folk Windfinder of relatively high rank with a strength level of 16(4). A dignified woman, with a quiet air of command, she took part in the circle using the Bowl of the Winds, as she was one of the strongest available among the remaining Windfinders in Ebou Dar. She traveled with Elayne to Caemlyn.

Naiselle. A cool-eyed banker from Ebou Dar who was at the Kin's farm outside Ebou Dar when the Seanchan attacked. She traveled with Elayne's party from the farm to Caemlyn. Since she was one of the last ten ready to leave the farm, Alise made her wash dishes.

Najaf, Aeldra. *See* Aeldra Najaf

Najima clan. A Kandori family. *See* Colar, Eselle, Jerid, Josef *and* Jurine Najima

Najirah, Mikhel. *See* Mikhel Najirah

Nakai. One of the Aiel clans; its chief was Bruan of the Salt Flat sept.

Nakomi. A mysterious Aiel woman whom Aviendha met in the Waste. Bair told Aviendha that she knew no one named Nakomi, but that it was an ancient name.

Nalaam, Arlen. *See* Arlen Nalaam

Nalaene Forrell. A Ghealdanin Aes Sedai of the Yellow Ajah publicly and of the Black Ajah in truth. A member of the loyalist contingent, Nalaene was part of the expedition to kidnap Rand. She was captured at Dumai's Wells and treated as *da'tsang* by the Aiel until, under Verin's Compulsion, she found reason to swear oath to Rand, which she did before Cadsuane departed Cairhien for Far Madding. She was identified in Verin's book as Black Ajah.

Nalasia Merhan. An Aes Sedai of the Brown Ajah who was unaccounted for after the Seanchan raid on the Tower. Egwene thought it possible that she was Mesaana, but Nalasia was not very strong in the One Power and had been in the Tower for years, which made this unlikely.

Naldwinn, Aranvor. *See* Aranvor Naldwinn

Nalesean Aldiaya. A young Tairen nobleman. Square-faced and blocky with an oiled beard, he was eager and slightly jovial. His personal servant was Lopin. At the battle against the Shaido for Cairhien, Nalesean was the second to lead the Tairens after Melanril. After the battle, he and Talmanes went to Mat and agreed that Mat was their general and that he needed a banner. He joined the Band of the Red Hand and commanded half its cavalry. Mat would have preferred to have Edorion over Nalesean, but House Aldiaya outranked House Selorna. Nalesean accompanied Mat to Ebou Dar; when they went to fetch the Bowl of the Winds, the *gholam* ripped out his throat.

Nalhera, Mistress. The innkeeper of the Crown of Maredo in Far Madding. Slim with gray hair, she told Min that Rand wouldn't be so sulky if she switched him every morning.

Nalla. A Da'shain Aiel woman from M'jinn in service to Zorelle Sedai. Nalla proposed to Charn in the Age of Legends. He put her off for a year, but was planning to accept on his twenty-fifth naming day, which coincided with the day his Aes Sedai, Mierin, opened the Bore.

Nalmat, Haster. A Saldaean officer who guarded Milisair's manor in Bandar Eban.

Nalsad, Bennae. *See* Bennae Nalsad

nameday. The day a person received his or her name, usually on the day of birth. A Borderlander man considered the day he was given his sword to be his nameday. It was sometimes referred to as a "naming day."

Namelle. Sisters in the White Tower. *See* Adeleas *and* Vandene Namelle

Namene. A Domani novice in the White Tower when Egwene was there under duress. Tall, slim and giggly, she was no more than fifteen or sixteen. She talked with Nicola about something that was troubling her; Nicola told her to ask Egwene, but Namene said that she didn't want to bother her.

Namine Tasil. The daughter of Quillin Tasil, and an Aes Sedai of the Brown Ajah.

naming day. Another term for nameday.

Nan Belman. A Darkfriend in Caemlyn. A handsome woman, she was the mother of Perwyn. Nan thought her oaths were just dabbling in wickedness until Fain showed up on her doorstep with a Myrddraal looking for a place to stay; she believed him to be a high-ranking Darkfriend. When Perwyn brought news of an assassination attempt on Rand, Fain grew angry; to channel it he touched Perwyn and made him gibber, and to calm his own mind he decided to take Nan. She struggled, and Fain thought that he was going to have to hurt her.

Nana. 1) The name that Nynaeve used after escaping Ronde Macura and while with Luca's show. 2) One of Berelain's serving women. Plump and plain-faced, she looked like the other serving woman, Rosene. Although not pretty, the two made Berelain's usually taciturn thief-catchers animated. One of the two women spread the word that Perrin had spent the night in Berelain's tent. When Perrin was trying to locate Masema and his men, Nana told him, amid much smirking and tittering, that she thought they were off to the southwest.

Nandera. An Aiel woman who was *Far Dareis Mai*. Tall and sinewy with green eyes and hair that was more gray than yellow, she was a tough-appearing woman, though Sulin made her seem almost soft by comparison. It was she who pointed out Sulin's *toh* for speaking to *gai'shain* as to Maidens, and when Sulin became a servant, Nandera took over leading the Maidens. After Sulin decided her *toh* was discharged, they fought while going to rescue Rand; Sulin won, but Nandera remained head of the Maidens, with Sulin as a sort of assistant. Nandera and Jalani acknowledged *toh* to Rand over the Gray Man incident in Caemlyn. Nandera was one of three Maidens, along with Somara and Nesair, who beat Rand when he returned to Cairhien after fighting the Seanchan because he had dishonored the Maidens by leaving them behind. When Rand went to Algarin's manor, Nandera led the fifty Maidens who accompanied him; she led twenty Maidens when Rand went to his meeting with the Daughter of the Nine Moons.

Nangu. A Shienaran soldier who traveled with Perrin and Ingtar when searching for the Horn of Valere. At Moiraine's direction he followed Uno to Jehannah and was with Masema in Samara. He thought that Nynaeve's tongue could skin and butcher a bull at fifty paces.

Naorisa Cambral. An Aes Sedai of the Gray Ajah and the rebel contingent. She was chosen to replace Delana in the rebel Hall of the Tower.

Naorman Mashinta. A third-generation cobbler in Tar Valon. Egwene met with Siuan in his shop in *Tel'aran'rhiod*.

nar'baha. The name Sammael called the traveling boxes he gave to the Shaido. In the Old Tongue, the term actually meant "fool box." He told Sevanna that they were *ter'angreal*, powered by *saidin*, allowing users to Travel; in fact, there were no known *ter'angreal* to use for Traveling or Skimming. Sammael made the gateways; the Wise Ones detected nothing and thought the box was working. The *nar'baha* were gray stone cubes, fairly small and plain except for a bright red disc set in one side. Supposedly, pressing the disc opened a gateway, but if a woman touched it, it would not work for days afterward. The gateway would remain open for a fixed time and after use, the box supposedly had to recover for three days before it could be used again. Sammael used this pretense to create more chaos by sending the Shaido into many countries across the world.

Narasim Bhuran. A leader during the War of the Hundred Years. Ten years before that war ended, Bhuran tried to reestablish Hawkwing's empire in Andor; he failed dismally and wound up with his head on a pike.

Narencelona, Anaiyella. *See* Anaiyella Narencelona

Narendhra. A Wise One of the Shaido Aiel. One of Sevanna's inner circle of plotters, she took part in or was present at the murder of Desaine. Narendhra was with Therava at Dumai's Wells.

Narenwin Barda. An Aes Sedai of the Yellow Ajah and the loyalist contingent, with a strength level of 18(6) or 19(7). Born in 913 NE, she went to the White Tower in 928 NE. After spending twelve years as a novice and eight years as Accepted, she was raised to the shawl in 948 NE. Square-faced, short and thin, she was so quiet people could forget she was there; she was mousy around other sisters. Narenwin had no Warder. As an assistant to the head of the Yellow eyes-and-ears, she recruited Ronde Macura and punished her severely when she inquired about the Black Ajah. She later became the head of the Yellow eyes-and-ears and rose high in the Yellow hierarchy. Once a week she would allow children to bring their pets to the Tower so that she could Heal them. Elaida sent Narenwin to Dorlan to take charge of the Aes Sedai who managed to return from Dumai's Wells.

Narettin, Spiron. *See* Spiron Narettin den Sovar

Narg. A smart Trolloc who could speak the human tongue. It had a wolf's muzzle, goat hooves, ears that twitched incessantly and all-too-human eyes. Narg was one of those who attacked Tam's farm; after Rand and Tam got away from the first attack, Narg played dead and waited until Rand returned. He told Rand that he would not hurt him, and that a Myrddraal was coming. Rand pretended to go along; when Narg lunged for him, Rand brought up Tam's sword and impaled Narg.

Nariene. A long-dead queen of Altara. A fountained statue of her stood in Mol Hara Square in Ebou Dar; the statue had one breast bared and one hand uplifted. Nariene was noted for her honesty, but not enough to have been depicted completely bare-chested. Some said her uplifted hand pointed to the ocean's bounty that had enriched Ebou Dar, and some that it pointed in warning of dangers.

Naris Pelden. A young Andoran woman. She and her sister Sephanie sought work at the Royal Palace; Essande chose them to train as Elayne's maids because they were unlikely to be spies. Naris was very happy to be a lady's maid rather than cleaning the halls. Square-faced and shy, she was as much in awe of Essande as of Elayne. Naris tried to help Aviendha in dressing and undressing, but Aviendha didn't always cooperate. When the palace started rearranging itself, Naris was reluctant to leave Elayne's rooms to fetch food, but she did it anyway. The Aiel Wise Ones who came to claim Aviendha awed her.

Narishma, Jahar. *See* Jahar Narishma

Narisse. A Jenn Aiel woman during the building of Rhuidean. She, Dermon and Mordaine met with the Aiel clan chiefs and told them that they must come to Rhuidean if they wanted to lead. A graying woman with deep-set green eyes, she looked as if she could have been Mordaine's sister.

Narof, Azille. An Aes Sedai who lived at the time of the formation of the White Tower.

Naron, Berylla. *See* Berylla Naron

narshcat. A ferocious animal found in the Waste.

Narvais Maslin. A Counsel of Far Madding. Gray-haired, slim and 5'5" tall, with Cumere she escorted Cadsuane, Shalon and Harine to the palace while the other Counsels remained with Aleis to question Verin.

Narvin. A high-ranking servant in the Tarasin Palace in Ebou Dar. He was stout and gray-haired. Mat was sure that Narvin was responsible for the first attempt to remove Pips from the stable to keep Mat from leaving. Narvin was nearby when Thom told Mat that the *gholam* had killed again; Mat smiled at him and he stalked off frowning.

Nashebar. An Ogier-built city in Jaramide, one of the Ten Nations after the Breaking.

Nashia. A Kinswoman who accompanied Elayne to her Cairhienin coronation. Prim with a youthful face, she wore a baggy dress.

Nashif. A man Mat fought at Bloodwash Falls in one of his memories from the Eelfinn.

Nashun. An area of southern Saldaea famous for producing very large horses.

Nasin Caeren. An Andoran nobleman who was High Seat of House Caeren; the sign of the House was the Star and Sword. About 5'9" to 5'10" tall, he was bony and goat-faced, with thin white hair and a scrawny neck. His wife's name was Miedelle; she died circa 970 NE. He opposed Morgase during the Succession, and became one of Gaebril's sycophants. He fled after Rand reached an accommodation with Dyelin. Half his wits were gone, if not more, and he would tumble any woman he could corner. His pale blue lapels were incongruously worked with flowers, moondrops and loversknots, and he sometimes wore a flower in his thinning hair like a country youth going courting. Even so, his House was too powerful for even Jarid or Naean to try pushing him around. He was demonstrably gaga in some ways—he believed that he and Elenia were betrothed and that Jarid was an interloper of whom Elenia was afraid—but in others, he was shrewd. He seemed well aware that his granddaughter and heir Sylvase was more prisoner of Arymilla than guest, and also aware that if she had not been, he might have been displaced as High Seat. He died of a seizure shortly before Elayne won Caemlyn.

Nassad. A place where the Whitecloak army joined with the Seanchan, across the border from Amadicia in Tarabon, around the time Galad challenged Valda.

Nat Torfinn. An old Two Rivers man Perrin knew in boyhood. Wrinkled, white-haired and blind, he could disassemble any blacksmith's puzzle by touch.

Nata. A middle-aged woman who acted as Mat's personal tailor when he returned to Ebou Dar to see Tuon. Nata ordered that his hat be burned; in response, Mat threatened to see if she could fly from four stories up.

Natael, Jasin. *See* Asmodean *and* Jasin Natael

Natasia. A Saldaean Aes Sedai of the Blue Ajah. Slim, with dark tilted eyes, high cheekbones and full lips, she was a lenient teacher. Natasia gave Moiraine and

Siuan directions to Eadyth's rooms and taught them the method for ignoring heat or cold. In her own rooms, almost every flat surface was covered with figurines and small carvings and painted miniatures.

Nathenos, Valinde. *See* Valinde Nathenos

Nathin Sarmain Vendare. The Lord of Maderin, a town in Altara through which Luca's circus passed. According to a guard at the gate of Maderin, Lord Nathin listened close when the Seanchan talked.

Natley Lewin. A heavyset Two Rivers man. The son of Flann and Adine Lewin, he married Laila Dearn. Perrin thought it odd that Laila married Natley because he couldn't dance, and Laila loved to dance. Natley and Laila had a baby; when Perrin was trying to convince everyone to move to Emond's Field for more safety from the Trollocs, Perrin said that property could be rebuilt, then pointed at the baby and asked if anyone could rebuild that.

Natomo, Kiyosa. *See* Kiyosa Natomo

Natrin's Barrow. A fortress in Arad Doman built long ago to watch the Mountains of Mist and guard against incursion through the passes by Manetheren. It was unused for military purposes after the Trolloc Wars; it was later occupied by a minor noble family from Toman Head that was trying to set up a new kingdom. About two hundred years before the Last Battle, a king of Arad Doman reclaimed Natrin's Barrow and used the fortress as a palace. After a hundred fifty years, it was granted to a distant relation of the King; that family disappeared. Graendal moved into it; Aran'gar and Delana visited her. Rand learned of her location from Kerb, and balefired the fortress and everyone in it, except Graendal, who escaped.

Natti Cauthon. An Emond's Field woman, the wife of Abell and the mother of Mat, Bodewhin and Eldrin. Born in 956 NE, she was a cool, collected woman most of the time. Mat claimed that his mother always knew what he was doing the minute he did it; he seemed not to realize that his sisters were giving his mother details. Natti, Bodewhin and Eldrin were taken prisoner by the Whitecloaks, along with the Luhhans; Perrin and his band freed them and took them to an abandoned farmhouse. When the Tinkers arrived in Emond's Field, Natti helped tend to them. She also participated in the defense of Emond's Field.

Nawan, Ishara. *See* Ishara Nawan

Nazar Kurenin. A Malkieri man who lived in Kandor and worked as a baker after the fall of Malkier. He was jut-nosed with short hair and a forked beard; the years hadn't removed the mark of the *hadori* from his forehead. He wept when he heard Edeyn speak of reclaiming Malkier from the Blight. After he heard that Lan was riding for the Last Battle, Nazar joined him on the Plain of Lances. He was killed at Tarwin's Gap, but he gutted a Trolloc as it killed him.

Nazelle. The sister of Queen Ethenielle of Kandor. Ethenielle arranged her marriage to Lord Ismic after her first husband died. Nazelle protested at first, but grew to love Ismic.

Nazran. A flunky of Graendal's who was the cousin of the Domani King Alsalam.

Square and deeply brown, with thin black mustaches and black eyes, he was handsome, although not sufficiently so to become one of Graendal's pets. Nazran believed he had tasted Graendal's charms, and he needed only a touch of Compulsion to obey her avidly. Graendal sent him to Ituralde with a forged letter purportedly from Alsalam.

Ndaye, Dalaine. An Aes Sedai of the Gray Ajah who served as Amyrlin from 36 to 64 NE. Dalaine was a weak Amyrlin.

Neain. Perrin's aunt and the widow of his uncle Carlin. She and Carlin had two children; Neain visited Carlin's grave every morning. She, along with the rest of the family, was murdered by Padan Fain, although it was believed that Trollocs killed them. Perrin buried her next to Carlin's grave.

Neald, Fager. *See* Fager Neald

near-sister, near-brother. *See* Aiel kinship

Necoine, Selame. *See* Selame Necoine

Ned Yarman. Sareitha Tomares' young Warder. He was born in 978 NE in Andor. About 6'3" tall, with broad shoulders, he had bright blue eyes and corn-yellow hair curling to his shoulders. Somewhat boyish in mannerisms and appearance, he was quite handsome, enough to make women's eyes flutter. At age sixteen he went to the Tower to train with the Warders; most of those men did not get chosen as Warders, and he felt very lucky that he did. Birgitte thought that he was still goggle-eyed over it. He was killed by Black Ajah when he charged the house on Full Moon Street in Caemlyn after Sareitha's death.

nedar. A tusked water pig found only in the Drowned Lands. A very good swimmer, as most creatures in the Drowned Lands were, it grew to a maximum of fifty pounds, but thirty pounds was more common. Its tusks were oversized for an animal so small, being as much as three inches long. The flesh was quite tasty, but the *nedar* could be just as dangerous as its larger cousins.

Nedare Satarov. The innkeeper at The Silver Penny in Chachin, Kandor. A beautiful woman with a joyous smile and glossy black hair worn in a braid, she was clean and her inn appealing. Moiraine stopped in to ask if Siuan was staying there; Nedare told her that she was, and offered Moiraine a mug of spiced wine. Nedare's air of anticipation made Moiraine suspicious that there was something in the wine; she made Nedare drink the wine. Nedare tried to flee, but fell to the floor, revealing silk stockings; she had done quite well drugging innocent women for the use of her rough customers. A number of the men in the common room looked at her lasciviously, and all the women, including Moiraine, left.

Nedeal, Corianin. *See* Corianin Nedeal

Neder. A sept of the Shiande Aiel.

need. A technique to find what was vital or required, known or unknown to the user, while in *Tel'aran'rhiod*. The Aiel Wise Ones concentrated on need to find new sources of water in the Waste; Nynaeve used need to find Amathera and important objects in Tarabon. Elayne and Nynaeve used it to find the Bowl of the Winds. A danger of using need was that one did not know the destination, and could arrive in a place of great danger.

Needle Street. A thoroughfare in Caemlyn. A rather wide street, it meandered like a river, down one hill and up the next. Some generations before Elayne claimed the throne, it was full of needlemakers. At the time of her claim, a few small inns and taverns were jammed among cutlers and tailors and every sort of shop except needlemakers.

Neferi. Tuon's *Soe'feia*, who was killed in a fall down stairs. Neferi had a Left Hand ready to replace her, but the Empress chose Anath instead.

Negaine. An Aes Sedai of the Brown Ajah and the loyalist contingent. She and Felaana found a disguised Beonin wandering the White Tower, requesting an audience with Elaida; they took her to Elaida. Egwene saw Negaine in the Brown quarters' hallway when it mysteriously swapped places with the novice quarters; Negaine challenged Egwene for being there until Egwene directed her to look out the window.

Negara, Lady. An Andoran noblewoman of a minor House who had opposed Gaebril. Sharp-faced, she was at the meeting between Egwene and the Aes Sedai and the Andorans and Murandians on the ice. She asked Egwene if the novice book was truly open to all.

Negin Bridge. A village near Dragonmount where Almen Bunt's brother-in-law Graeger vanished.

Negina, Blaeric. *See* Blaeric Negina

Neheran, Ferane. *See* Ferane Neheran

Neilyn. A woman in Valan Luca's show. She had the prettiest eyes, according to Olver.

Nela al'Caar. A Two Rivers woman. She was married to Paet and they had two daughters and two sons, including Wil; the youngest was six years older than Perrin. Long-faced with a gray-streaked braid, Nela organized the children before the Trolloc attack. In Nynaeve's Accepted test, Nela went crazy when she found her sons dead in their beds and went around saying that Paet was the Dark One and had killed her boys.

Nela Thane. An Emond's Field woman. When Nynaeve was sixteen and had just started braiding her hair, Nela dared her to steal a plum pie from Mistress Ayellin. Nynaeve did and was caught and punished.

Nelavaire Demasiellin. A Cairhienin Aes Sedai of the Green Ajah and the loyalist contingent, with a strength level of 28(16). Born in 850 NE, she went to the White Tower in 863 NE; she was allowed to enter at thirteen because she was born with the spark and it was beginning to manifest itself. After spending ten years as a novice and six years as Accepted, she was raised to the shawl in 879 NE. Standing 5'2" tall, she was slim, wiry and whipcord tough. She took part in Rand's kidnapping from Cairhien and was captured at Dumai's Wells. Nelavaire was treated as *da'tsang* by the Aiel until, under Verin's Compulsion, she found reason to swear oath to Rand, which she did before Cadsuane departed Cairhien for Far Madding. She met the Asha'man Naeff and bonded him.

Nelein Matherin. The grandmother of Aedmun, High Seat of House Matherin in Andor. She had a temper, and everyone was afraid of her. She died, and the maid Elsie, who remembered Nelein from when she was a child, saw her ghost.

Nelsa. A slim and pretty shopgirl at a fabric store in Jurador, Altara. Selucia and Tuon went into the store and would not respond to the owner's questions; the owner threatened to send Nelsa, who also had become angry, to fetch the guards on them.

Nem. An Andoran family. *See* Admer *and* Maigan Nem

Nemaira Eldros. An Aes Sedai who lived at the time of the formation of the White Tower.

Neman, Feast of. A feast celebrated on the ninth day of the month of Adar in Andor, Cairhien, Tear and the Borderlands.

Nemarellin Mountains. A range found at the southwest coast of Illian along the Kabal Deep.

Nemaris. The wife of a horse handler in Bryne's army camp; on the delicate side, she did not like horses that were too frisky. When Siuan demanded a mild horse to ride to the Aes Sedai camp in order to tell them that Leane and Egwene were alive and in the White Tower, Nemaris's husband brought her Nemaris's horse, Nightlily.

Nemdahl, Sarene. *See* Sarene Nemdahl

Nemene Damendar Boann. Semirhage's name before she became Forsaken.

Nendenhald, Aludra. *See* Aludra Nendenhald

Nemosni, Aloisia. The oldest member of the Kin. She was nearly six hundred years old and working as an oil merchant in Tear when Elayne and Nynaeve learned of the Kin.

Nenci. A *damane* who accompanied Anath/Semirhage when she posed as the Daughter of the Nine Moons and attempted to capture Rand; she was paired with the *sul'dam* Falendre, and whimpered after their capture by Rand.

Nengar. A Shienaran soldier. He followed Ingtar when he and Perrin pursued the Horn of Valere to Falme. He stood about 5'11" tall, and had a heavier build than Masema, though not stocky, just bigger. He wintered in the Mountains of Mist with Perrin and Rand. After Rand left and the Shienarans were abandoned to make their own way, Nengar stuck with Masema in Ghealdan and came to follow and believe in the Prophet. His dark eyes burned as fervently as Masema's. He was killed along with Masema by *Cha Faile*.

Nensen, Varil. *See* Varil Nensen

Nerbaijan, Pritalle. *See* Pritalle Nerbaijan

Nerein. A heroine in *The Flame, the Blade and the Heart*. She was a strong woman.

Neres, Agni. *See* Agni Neres

Nerevan. A nation that arose after the Trolloc Wars.

Nerilea. An Aiel woman who was *Far Dareis Mai*. She had white hair and a square face. She accompanied Rand on his first surreptitious visit to Caemlyn, and was also with him near Natrin's Barrow when he balefired it.

Nerim. Talmanes' skinny Cairhienin manservant, who was on loan to Mat for a time. About 5'6" tall, he had a long narrow face and gray hair cut short of his shoulders; he was clean-shaven. A pessimist whose voice was lugubrious and melancholy, and who often had a mournful expression, Nerim was competitive with Nalesean's manservant Lopin. After the Aiel attacked Mat's camp while Mat was on his way to Salidar, Nerim sewed up his wounds; Mat agreed with Talmanes' assessment that as a seamstress, Nerim was a ham-fisted cook. Talmanes insisted that Nerim accompany Mat to Ebou Dar to act as his manservant. After Nalesean died, Mat took on Lopin as well, and the competition between the two serving men escalated. Nerim traveled with Mat until they met up with more of the Band; Nerim was very happy to be reunited with Talmanes.

Nerin. A *s'redit* calf handled by the Seanchan woman Cerandin in Valan Luca's circus. Luca called it a "boar-horse" to deflect from its true identity.

Nerion Torelvin. A young Cairhienin man who was a member of *Cha Faile*. Balwer sent him and Haviar to spy on Masema. They learned that Masema had sent another rider to Amadicia, that there were Altarans among Masema's forces, and that Annoura and Masuri were meeting with Masema in secret. They were pulled out before the attack on Malden.

Nerith. A Seanchan *sul'dam*. When talking to Bakuun, a Seanchan army captain, Nerith put the proper degree of respect into her voice and not a whisker more. She was captured by Asha'man in the first battle against the Seanchan and Gille, her *damane*, was killed. She was square-faced, black-haired and spat a lot. Like the other captive women, *sul'dam* and *damane*, she was to be turned over to Aes Sedai; when she learned that, she howled and tried to flee. When stopped, Nerith sank her teeth into a Saldaean's arm and hung on like a badger. Taim handed her over to Elayne in Caemlyn.

Nermala, Derys. *See* Derys Nermala

Nermasiv, Areina. *See* Areina Nermasiv

Nerrine. A Da'shain Aiel woman from a time after the Breaking. Nerrine had two sons, Charlin and Alijha, and one daughter, Colline. When Colline and Maigran, another Da'shain girl, were taken by bandits, Nerrine was ready to mourn and go on, but Charlin, Alijha and some other boys decided to rescue the girls. The young men killed the bandits; Charlin was killed. When the others returned to camp, Nerrine wanted nothing to do with them since they had abandoned the Way of the Leaf.

Nesair. A woman of the Shaido Aiel and *Far Dareis Mai*, who left the Shaido because of Rand. Fiery-haired and beautiful with white scars on both sun-dark cheeks, she was one of the three Maidens, along with Somara and Nandera, who beat Rand when he returned to Cairhien after battling the Seanchan because he had dishonored the Maidens by leaving them behind. Nesair told him that she had left her clan for him, and she didn't want him to spit on her.

Nesaline. A queen of Caembarin, one of the nations that arose after the Trolloc Wars. Nesaline was one of three who sent armies into Shandalle against Artur Hawkwing in FY 943.

Nesan. The twelfth month of the year.

Nesita. An Aes Sedai of the Red Ajah publicly and of the Black Ajah in truth. A member of the loyalist contingent, she was plump and blue-eyed and as mean as a snake with the itch. The one time Egwene tried to refuse the forkroot tea, Nesita helped pour it down her throat using a funnel. Nesita also Traveled to Kandor to collect tribute from the head clerk there, evidence that Elaida had Traveling. Her name appeared on Verin's list of the Black Ajah.

Nesolle, Cairlyn. *See* Cairlyn Nesolle

Nessosin, Joar Addam. Asmodean's name in the Age of Legends.

Nesta din Reas Two Moons. The Mistress of the Ships to the Atha'an Miere. About 5'4" tall and going from stocky to fat, she had white hair, black eyes and a thrusting jaw. Nesta had an air of power; when she said "go," people went. She wore six rings in each ear, and the chain to her nose ring was hung with many medallions. Her Windfinder was Renaile. When Elayne, Nynaeve and Aviendha went to *Windrunner* to ask for help with the Bowl of the Winds, Nesta was there and sent Baroc to summon all Wavemistresses, the First Twelve and their Windfinders, and then got down to bargaining. Nesta married Lan and Nynaeve, and sent twenty Windfinders to the Tarasin Palace. When the Seanchan arrived in Ebou Dar, *Windrunner* fought a delaying action to help as many ships as possible escape, but the vessel was taken, and Nesta and her Master of the Blades, Baroc, were executed by impaling; neither screamed while on the stake. Their heads were placed on poles outside the gates, and the crime listed on the placard beneath them was "Rebellion."

Nestelle din Sakura South Star. A Sea Folk Windfinder captured by the Seanchan and made *damane*. Mat decided to try to free the Sea Folk *damane*; he went to Nestelle's room and asked what she would do if he removed her collar. She said that she would free her sisters; Mat asked that she wait three hours. She agreed, and they sealed the bargain by spitting on their hands and shaking; her hand was as callused as his, and her grip was strong. Mat removed her *a'dam*, and showed her how to remove others. She did not wait the full three hours; Mat and his party were at the gates of Ebou Dar when the trouble started, but they were able to leave because all the soldiers were going to deal with the Sea Folk.

Nesune Bihara. A Kandori Aes Sedai of the Brown Ajah and the loyalist contingent, with a strength level of 15(3). Born in 826 NE, she went to the White Tower in 841 NE. After spending five years as a novice and four years as Accepted, she was raised to the shawl in 850 NE. About 5'4" tall, and slender, with dark hair and almost black, bird-like eyes, Nesune had an eidetic memory and was a collector of specimens and a naturalist. She was fascinated both by men who could channel and by the Dragon Reborn. She taught Egwene as a novice, and could tell when someone's attention drifted even with her back to the class. Nesune had one Warder, a tall, broad-shouldered young man who looked as though carved from a boulder. She was part of the mission sent to kidnap Rand and was captured at Dumai's Wells and made *da'tsang*; she was one of the first five to swear to Rand. She was part of Cadsuane's group that went to Far Madding and Shadar Logoth. She was also part of the group shielding Semirhage when Shaidar Haran rescued the Forsaken. Nesune fought alongside Aviendha while repelling the Trollocs at Thakan'dar during the Last Battle.

net. Age of Legends word used for a weave of the Power. *See* web

Netari, Ershin. An Illianer nobleman who was a member of the Council of Nine. He fought against the Seanchan; in the last engagement, he was under the command of Semaradrid.

Nethan Conwy. One of Merise's Warders. An Andoran, Nethan was 6'1" tall, with a lean, muscular build and piercing blue eyes. His dark hair had wings of white at the temples.

Nethin, Tal. A saddlemaker who survived the Shaido massacre of Taien in the Jangai Pass, only to die by breaking his neck on level ground shortly afterward. His sister was Aril Corl.

Nethvin Market. One of the three markets in Far Madding, where foreigners were allowed to trade.

Nevanche, Desala. *See* Desala Nevanche

Nevarin. A Wise One of the Codarra Aiel with the ability to channel and a strength level of 23(11). She appeared to be younger than Edarra, and only a year or two older than Perrin; she was at most 110 years old. Slim with sandy yellow hair and green eyes, Nevarin was about 5'8" tall and had a light voice, although her personality seemed to be much like Nynaeve's. When she put her hands or fists on her hips, Perrin thought she wanted to shake a finger or a fist at him. Nevarin was one of the Wise Ones sent with Perrin to Ghealdan, to keep an eye on Seonid and Masuri. She went to battle against the Shaido at Malden. She assisted in the forging of *Mah'alleinir*, and followed his forces into the Last Battle.

Neverborn. The wolves' name for Myrddraal.

Nevin. An Ebou Dari man killed in a duel with Beslan. The offense they dueled over was not worth a life, but Nevin slipped and Beslan ran him through the heart instead of his sword arm. Beslan had to pay a condolence call on his widow, Davindra.

New Braem. A moderate-size border town older than Andor that lay fifty leagues north of Caemlyn on the road to Tar Valon; the original Braem was destroyed in the Trolloc Wars. New Braem was something of a center for trade heading north out of Andor, which was nearly all funneled through Tar Valon. A lot of news passed through New Braem as well, such as events at the Stone of

Tear, changes at the White Tower and the presence of Borderlander soldiers in Braem Wood.

New City. The area outside the Inner City of Caemlyn; it was not Ogier-built.

New Plow, The. An inn in Andor that Elayne and her party stayed at on their way from Ebou Dar to Caemlyn.

Neysa Ayellin. A horse-faced woman of Emond's Field. When Nynaeve was sixteen, she threw a pitcher of water at Neysa, and Neysa manhandled her for it. At ten, Perrin stole one of Neysa's gooseberry pies, and she paddled his bottom for it. She helped care for the Tinkers who came to Emond's Field seeking shelter from the Trollocs, was part of Perrin and Faile's wedding, and helped organize the children so that they might have a chance to escape from Shadowspawn. When a Trolloc grabbed Bode Cauthon by her hair, Neysa stabbed it with a butcher knife.

ni Bashere t'Aybara, Faile. *See* Faile ni Bashere t'Aybara

Niach Okatomo. The commander of Rena Tower in Kandor. He was Malenarin Rai's distant cousin and good friend.

Niagen. A Brotherless taken by Sulin as *gai'shain* after Malden. Lacile told him that Jhoradin and Rolan had been helpful in Malden, and wound up in his bed. He helped Alliandre make bandages after the battle between Perrin and the Whitecloaks and the Trollocs.

Niall, Pedron. *See* Pedron Niall

Niamh Passes. The northernmost passes through the Spine of the World, east of Fal Moran in Shienar.

Niande Moorwyn. An Aes Sedai of the Gray Ajah, uncommitted to any contingent, with a strength level of 27(15). Born in 851 NE, she went to the White Tower in 867 NE. After spending thirteen years as a novice and twelve years as Accepted, she was raised to the shawl in 892 NE. Plump, with a sharp nose, inquisitive gray eyes and pale hair, she had one Warder.

Niande served as advisor to King Galldrian of Cairhien. She kept a low profile and was known to have visited the country estates of Lady Arilyn more than once. As far as anyone in Cairhien knew, she apparently vanished after Galldrian was killed. She puzzled out who killed Galldrian, and although she knew basically why, she was not pleased with Thom Merrilin. Too much suffering came out of that death.

She turned up in the rebel camp outside Cairhien with Cadsuane—she was coopted by Cadsuane rather than being one of her followers—when Rand visited, just before the fog incident. After Rand was injured, Niande helped empty a wagon so that they could get him back to the city; when Min told of three sisters being stilled at Dumai's Wells, Niande vomited over the side of the wagon. She was disconcerted when Asha'man walked into her presence, and dropped her book. Niande was left behind in Cairhien when Cadsuane went to Far Madding.

Nianh. An Aes Sedai who acted as the advisor to Ethenielle of Kandor. She vanished from Chachin soon after the troubles in the White Tower became known. She left no message, nor any clue to where she was going.

Nichil. An *algai'd'siswai* Aiel who worked with Birgitte to kill Trollocs in Braem Wood in the Last Battle; Birgitte thought that he was very good at moving quickly and silently.

Nico. A stableboy with hay in his hair at Harilin's Leap in Jarra, Ghealdan. When Moiraine, Lan, Loial and Perrin stayed at the inn, Nico and Patrim saw to their horses.

Nicola Treehill. A Ghealdanin novice with a potential strength level of 9(+4). Born in 975 NE, she was enrolled in the novice books in Salidar in 999 NE. Standing 5'4" tall, and slender, with dark hair and big black eyes, she was ambitious, a voracious learner and a woman of considerable daring who did not think the rules applied to her, or at least not in the same way they did to others. She was a weaver; she would do whatever she had to in order to get what she wanted.

Nicola met Nynaeve and Elayne on the *Riverserpent* on the way to Salidar; she only joined up with the rebel Aes Sedai because following Nynaeve took her to them. Nicola had meant to marry, but her intended was killed while following Masema. She was tested on arrival in Salidar and found able to learn to channel, though without the inborn spark. She was potentially strong enough that before Nynaeve, Egwene and Elayne she would have caused a sensation; her potential, equal to Cadsuane, still occasioned some comment and she was considered quite a find. Once the rebels left Salidar, Nicola and Areina became friends. They speculated about the possibility of Areina becoming Nicola's Warder, or one of them; in fact, she took her as Warder, a highly illegal move for a novice. Nicola wanted to be Green Ajah.

Nicola and Areina together showed quite a talent for digging out information. Together, they tried to blackmail Egwene, using their knowledge that Elayne and Nynaeve had pretended to be Aes Sedai before they were raised, that Egwene had gone from the Tower with them, and that there was therefore the strong possibility that Egwene also had pretended. What Nicola wanted out of this was to be allowed to go faster in her training. The blackmail attempt failed because Egwene simply faced them down. Nicola and Areina were more successful blackmailing Myrelle and Nisao. Nicola forced them to give her extra lessons to help her move faster, with the result that her teachers remarked on how quickly she learned and how she sometimes took to weaves as if she already knew them. Nicola also thought she might force Myrelle to pass Lan's bond to her so that he would be one of her Warders along with Areina. Egwene also squelched this blackmail. Nicola had the minor Talent of seeing *ta'veren* and also began showing the first signs of Foretelling. Her prophecies were extremely veiled, though, and she did not realize—at first, anyway—that she had spoken and did not remember what she had said. Later she tried to garner attention with Foretelling. Nicola refused to believe that her potential was less than that of Egwene and Elayne. She thought that she could truly match—or even surpass—Nynaeve, given the chance, but that the rules were holding her back.

She ran away from the rebels to the White Tower in hopes of being taught faster; she was forced to tell everything she knew about the rebels, which was how Egwene and Leane were ambushed and captured. Nicola apologized to Egwene for that later, and helped spread tales among the novices in the White Tower portraying Egwene as a hero. She was part of a circle with Egwene in fighting the Seanchan and was raised Accepted afterward.

She disobeyed orders and joined in the fight against the Black Ajah in *Tel'aran'rhiod*; she was killed there.

Nidao. A Darkfriend Shienaran soldier. He was one of the guards of Fain's dungeon prison in Fal Dara and vanished when Fain escaped. Those pursuing the Horn of Valere found his body skinned and hanging from a tree.

Nieda Sidoro. An Illianer who was the innkeeper at Easing the Badger in Illian; even she didn't know what the name of her inn meant. A large, round woman with her hair in a thick roll at the back of her neck and a smell of strong soap about her, she was one of Moiraine's eyes-and-ears for twelve years. Her nephew Bili was her bouncer. She did not believe in Trollocs or snow. Bayle Domon visited her inn; Nieda was surprised when he paid her with a Tar Valon mark. Six Gray Men attacked Perrin and were killed; it was the first time there had been a killing at the inn. Nieda didn't believe the attackers were Gray Men; she thought that they were thieves and ordered Bili to throw them in the canal. Moiraine ordered her to flee Illian after she learned that Sammael was ruling Illian.

Niella. A woman of the Nine Valleys sept of the Taardad Aiel. Aviendha's firstsister, she looked like Aviendha, but a little older and plumper. A married weaver who was taken *gai'shain* by the Chareen Aiel when they raided Sulara Hold, her home, she always wanted Aviendha to give up the spear and marry and had tried to talk her out of becoming a Maiden. She brought food to Rand's room while Rand and Aviendha had gone to Seanchan through a gateway, and Asmodean told her the two did not want to be disturbed. She took this as proof they were in bed together and spread word among the Maidens. Aviendha treated her especially hard over this, blistering her bottom immediately after learning what had happened. She put off the white when her time came and went back to her husband.

Niere. An Aes Sedai of the Yellow Ajah who welcomed Nynaeve into the Yellow Ajah when she returned to the Tower after it reunited.

Night Watch. A group that conducted helmeted night patrols with halberds and crossbows in Canluum.

Night's Shade. A weave that allowed one more speed and concealed one from others; it could be produced by the *ter'angreal* that Bloodknives wore.

nightflower. A type of firework produced by the Illuminators.

Nightlily. A dark mare that belonging to Nemaris, the wife of a horse handler in Bryne's camp. Siuan borrowed her to ride to the Aes Sedai camp with the news that Egwene and Leane were alive and being held in the White Tower.

Nightrider. The Da'shain Aiel name for Myrddraal.

Nightrunner. An Aiel name for Myrddraal.

nightwood. A tree, not described. Siuan, as Amyrlin, kept her papers in a carved nightwood box.

Nikiol Dianatkhah. A former king of Saldaea who had a drinking problem. Faile used him as an example to Perrin when she was arguing that no leader was perfect.

Niko Tokama. A female member of the Academy of Cairhien, whose undescribed project Idrien thought was silly.

Nildra. A servant to the rebel Aes Sedai, in charge of washing pots. Moghedien, posing as Marigan, had to work for her. She was a wiry woman with a white apron and a harried expression, stick-like and gray-haired. Egwene met her the night she came to Salidar, and Nildra complained brusquely that everyone came to her instead of helping themselves and how put-upon she was. Chesa thought that she and Kaylin were terrible gossips and would say mean things when someone's back was turned. Nildra asked Egwene at the meeting on the ice if the novice book was open.

Nils. A lieutenant in Ituralde's army. When the Shadow started catapulting Trolloc bodies on his camp at Maradon, Ituralde ordered him to gather damage assessments, to prepare the archers for an attack on the siege engines, to bring two of the Asha'man who were on duty and to tell Captain Creedin to watch out for a Trolloc assault across the ford.

Nimri. An Aes Sedai of the Green Ajah. Petite and drowsy-eyed, she opened a gateway for Gawyn to go to Caemlyn from the White Tower.

Nindar, Kamarile Maradim. Graendal's name before she turned to the Shadow.

Nine Bees, the. The symbol of Illian.

Nine Gulls, Taval din Chanai. *See* Taval din Chanai Nine Gulls

Nine Horse Hitch, The. An inn in Lugard, Murandy. Its sign had an improbably voluptuous woman wearing only her hair, arranged to hide as little as possible, astride a barebacked horse. Duranda Tharne, its innkeeper, was an agent for the Blue Ajah; Siuan visited her to try to find out where the rebel Aes Sedai had gathered.

Nine Moons, Daughter of the. *See* Tuon Athaem Kore Paendrag

Nine Rings, The. An inn in Tremonsien, Cairhien, near the male Choedan Kal. Its innkeeper was Maglin Madwen. Rand, Loial, Hurin and Selene stayed there after recovering the Horn of Valere from Fain. They met up with Captain Caldevwin, who arranged an escort for them the next morning to Cairhien. At the time of the cleansing of *saidin*, Barmellin, a brandy merchant on the way to the inn, passed the Choedan Kal and saw its glowing sphere. Realizing that the glow was the One Power, he fled home to drink his brandy.

Nine Rods of Dominion. Nine individuals in the Age of Legends who served as regional governors of the world at the time. Ishamael said that Lews Therin had summoned them, which was an indication of Lews Therin having had ultimate authority.

Nine, the Council of. The advisory council of lords that jointly ruled with the King in Illian.

Nine Valleys. A sept of the Taardad Aiel.

Ninte calichniye no domashita. Old Tongue for "Your welcome warms me."

Ninth Depository. A section of the Tower Library, one of twelve sections publicly known. The Ninth Depository was the smallest, although it was still a large chamber; it was the home of texts on various forms of arithmetic.

Niolle din Lembar. A Sea Folk Wavemistress who was one of the First Twelve of the Atha'an Miere. At the meeting of the First Twelve in Illian, Niolle scowled at Harine when she arrived.

Nip. Seanchan Captain Bakuun's favorite wolfhound. Bakuun talked to him sometimes, but he didn't expect Nip to carry on a conversation, unlike what went on between *sul'dam* and *damane.*

Nirelle Coidevwin. An Aes Sedai of the Green Ajah who served as Amyrlin from 396 to 419 NE. Nirelle was a strong Amyrlin, forceful and dynamic. Chosen in the belief that she would extricate the Tower from her predecessor's foreign intrigues, she instead continued them, involving the Tower in a number of wars. She personally led Tower contingents in battle. Had it not been for the wars, she might have been removed, but the White Tower reaction to external threats was always to gather in and do nothing that might even hint at any crack in the supposedly unbreakable facade. In 419 NE, Nirelle died on campaign.

Nisa. A carthorse belonging to a Cairhienin brandy merchant, Barmellin, who saw the sphere near Tremonsien glow during the cleansing of the taint.

Nisain a'Cowel. A Murandian Aes Sedai of the Gray Ajah and of the rebel contingent, with a strength level of 37(25). Born in 873 NE, Nisain was gangly with dark reddish hair, startlingly blue eyes, a strong chin and a lilting voice. She had some small repute in matters of law and treaties. Very good at reading residues, she was sent to Shadar Logoth to try to determine what had happened there. Of the six that were sent, she was the best, and reported to the Hall when she returned. She said that she could not tell what had been done, but that more *saidin* had been used than *saidar.*

Nisao Dachen. An Aes Sedai of the Yellow Ajah and the rebel contingent, with a strength level of 16(4). Born in 821 NE in a village south of Kandor on the road to Tar Valon, she went to the White Tower in 837 NE. After spending eleven years as a novice and seven years as Accepted, she was raised to the shawl in 855 NE. Her Warder was Sarin Hoigan. Nisao was very short, under five feet, and had an average build for her height. Neither plain nor beautiful, she had dark hair and large dark brown eyes that were her best feature. She refused to speak to Nynaeve until Nynaeve gave up the foolish notion of Healing Siuan and Leane. Nisao aided Myrelle in dealing with Lan because she had an interest in diseases of the mind. Caught out at this by Egwene and Siuan, she swore fealty to Egwene rather than have her transgressions revealed, with the certain resulting penances and the possible loss of her Warder. She was acerbic toward Myrelle for involving her in the situation. Nisao investigated the murders of Anaiya and Kairen, but was ordered to stop by Lelaine. Nisao was part of the embassy to the Black Tower to bond Asha'man Warders.

Nishur, Jaalam. *See* Jaalam Nishur

Nissa. An Accepted in the White Tower. Nissa and Nicola reported to Silviana and Egwene that the Hall was meeting without them. Egwene sent the two to Caemlyn to fetch dream *ter'angreal* that Elayne had made and told them that she would teach them to use them.

Nisura. A round-faced Shienaran noblewoman who was an attendant to Lady Amalisa in Fal Dara. Nisura picked two other noblewomen to lead Rand and Lan through the women's apartments to visit Siuan. She was scandalized that he wore a sword in the women's apartments. When Rand asked to see Egwene, Nisura told Egwene that he was trying to get into the women's quarters, and asked if Rand and Egwene were going to marry.

no'ri. The ancient name for the game later called stones.

Noal Charin. *See* Jain Farstrider

Noallin, Mistress Kamile. *See* Kamile Noallin

Noam. A wolfbrother in Jarra, Ghealdan, who lost his humanity; his brother was Simion. Moiraine could not Heal him, and Perrin convinced his brother to set him free. He frequented the wolf dream and helped Perrin accept his dual nature by revealing that he preferred the wolf dream to real life and had chosen it. *See also* Boundless

Noane Masadim. An Aes Sedai of the Blue Ajah who served as Amyrlin from 950 to 973 NE. Noane was a weak Amyrlin, although not as weak as her predecessor. Like Kirin, she managed to pave the way for a stronger Amyrlin to follow her.

Noichin, Marli. *See* Marli Noichin

Nol Caimaine. A place from Lews Therin's memories where Sammael had done great evil and escaped justice.

Nolaisen. A noble Cairhienin family. *See* Barmanes *and* Camaille Nolaisen

Nomesta, Uno. *See* Uno Nomesta

Noon, Aisling. *See* Aisling Noon

Nor Chasen. A village east of Ebou Dar on the coast of Altara. The two men who attacked Mat and were killed at The Wandering Woman in Ebou Dar had told the innkeeper that they would next be traveling on to Nor Chasen.

Noram. The chief cook with the Band of the Red Hand. When he left to get provisions, meals did not get made with the usual speed.

Noramaga, Kaisel. *See* Kaisel Noramaga

Noregovna, Edarna. *See* Edarna Noregovna

Noreladim. A Domani functionary. Stumpy and large-bellied, he talked with Rand about finding the members of the Council of Merchants.

Noreman, Ceiline. The wife of a trader killed in Canluum, Kandor. The trader had been guarded by Ryne Venamar.

Noren. A Cairhienin horse handler with Perrin's group. He led Galina's horse away after she was captured by Neald and Gaul outside of Malden.

Noren M'shar. Seanchan's third-largest city, mentioned when Tuon was thinking about how omens were the same no matter the location.

Norham, Ester. *See* Ester Norham

Norie. A *damane* with Banner-General Khirgan's party. She was at the first meeting between Perrin and Tylee.

Norill, Turanna. *See* Turanna Norill

Norine Dovarna. An Aes Sedai of the White Ajah and the loyalist contingent. Lovely, with large liquid eyes, she was almost as dreamy as Danelle. She shared other qualities with Danelle, being nearly as friendless and perhaps as much so. She, too, was a solitary woman, preferring her own company to that of anyone else. Norine resented Alviarin, thinking that if the White was to supply the Keeper, it should have been herself, but she almost curtsied to Alviarin anyway; she felt a patron in high places might not be such a bad thing, even if it was Alviarin.

She was one of the sisters who guarded Leane after her capture.

Norla. A near-toothless wilder who lived at a farm in the heart of the Black Hills. She taught Cadsuane important lessons; Cadsuane thought that without her it would have been unlikely that she would be in anything approaching her present circumstances. She definitely wouldn't have had her hair ornaments; she earned those from Norla.

Norlea. A Wise One of the Shaido Aiel with the ability to channel. About 5'7" tall, sharp-nosed and almost as hard as Therava, Norlea was one of Sevanna's inner circle of plotters. She accompanied Sevanna to the Aes Sedai camp the day she saw Rand beaten and took part in or at least was present at the murder of Desaine. She was with Therava at Dumai's Wells, and went with her back to the Three-fold Land after the Shaido rout at Malden.

Norlesh. An Aiel woman who was the wife of Metalan; they had five children; three had died earlier. Metalan tried to trade gems for food with outlanders, but the Raven Empress had forbidden trade with Aiel. A fourth child, Garlvan, died in Norlesh's arms soon after his failure to trade. They were seen in Aviendha's viewings of the future in Rhuidean.

Norley, Dafid. *See* Dafid Norley

Norodim Nosokawa. A leader who tried to seize Hawkwing's empire after his death. He was the second leader that Jalwin Moerad, Hawkwing's advisor, advised shortly after Hawkwing's death. Norodim was one of the three who came closest to seizing all of Hawkwing's empire; he died in battle.

Norowhin. A young officer in the Children of the Light who commanded Morgase's Whitecloak guards in Amadicia. Lanky and tall with a sunburned face, hard eyes and a thrusting nose, he was cold toward Morgase, and usually laconic.

Norry, Halwin. *See* Halwin Norry

Norsish, Jamilila. *See* Jamilila Norsish

Norsoni, Ayako. *See* Ayako Norsoni

North Road. The road to Taren Ferry and Watch Hill north of Emond's Field; it became the Old Road to the south.

Northan, House. A noble House in Andor. Its High Seat was Conail; its sign was three black eagles: the Eagles, or the Black Eagles.

Northan, Conail. *See* Conail Northan

Northern Star, Causeway of the. A wide, packed-dirt road, broken by flat stone bridges, leading directly north from Illian through the marshes that surrounded the city.

Northharbor. An anchorage on the River Erinin at Tar Valon. There the city walls curved out into the river and made a ring nearly a mile across, broken only by the harbor mouth. Wooden-roofed docks, where riverships of every size moored, lined the inside of that huge ring. Egwene was captured there by Aes Sedai while making a *cuendillar* chain across the harbor entrance.

Norwelyn. A major noble House in Andor. Its High Seat was Lord Luan; its sign the Silver Salmon, sometimes called "the Fish," by men of House Norwelyn. *See also* Luan Norwelyn

Nosane iro gavane domorakoshi, Diynen'd'ma'purvene? Old Tongue for "Speak we what language, Sounder of the Horn?"

Nosar, Coerid. A king of Almoren, one of the Ten Nations, and one of the signers of the Compact of the Ten Nations.

Noselle, Tiana. *See* Tiana Noselle

Nosinda. A Wise One of the Shaido Aiel. One of Sevanna's inner circle of plotters, she took part in or at least was present at the murder of Desaine. She was with Therava at Dumai's Wells.

Nosokawa, Norodim. *See* Norodim Nosokawa

Notasha. An Aes Sedai of the Red Ajah and the loyalist contingent who wanted to wrest control from Saerin during the Seanchan attack on the White Tower.

Notdead. *See* Gray Man

Nothish, Faverde. A wiry member of the Seanchan Blood. He attended Tuon's first audience in Ebou Dar after she returned from traveling with Mat.

Notori. A member of the Black Ajah who was killed by Nynaeve in the battle at the White Tower in *Tel'aran'rhiod*.

Novares, Istaban. One of the founders of Tear.

novice. The lowest level of initiates of the White Tower. The average novice studied for ten years before passing the test to be raised Accepted.

Novice classroom lessons were broken into two blocks each day. The first ran from breakfast to High, and the second from supper to Trine. The hours between were given to chores, supervised studies, being tutored and, very occasionally, free time.

A freeday was a holiday where there were no classes or lessons, and no chores except those which had been given in punishment, and even those could be set aside. There was no set period for freedays; they were proclaimed as the Mistress of Novices thought necessary, but not very often, as the novices saw it. In the first thirteen weeks (130 days) that Nynaeve and Egwene were in the White Tower, there were three freedays.

Once a girl had been tested to become a novice, it was too late for her to refuse. Once training had begun, it had to go on. One could say that the test itself, if successful, opened a pathway, or perhaps ignited the spark that was not glowing when she was born; the girl began to touch the Source after that, and the touching continued thereafter whether there was training or not, so for safety's sake, the training had to be completed. Aes Sedai had always used this fact to help hold on to girls who did pass; once they had passed the test, it was not safe for them to go back out in the world until they had been trained; by the time they were trained enough to be safe, if they had the ability to go on, they had been put so firmly on the path that they rarely thought of trying to leave it. There were runaways, of course, but few made it off the island of Tar Valon; they were pursued vigorously, and they were almost always caught. Most of those who did make it off were assisted by the Kin.

Weaves were often demonstrated for teaching purposes at a strength too low to be effective, simply to show the flows necessary and the manner of weaving them together. Channeling to do an assigned chore was forbidden, for the Tower held that physical labor built character. Novices were forbidden to try any weave until it had been demonstrated to them and the teaching sister was satisfied, after seeing the novice do the weave at a very low strength, below the level of effectiveness, that the novice had the weaves properly in hand. Thus, no experimentation of any sort was allowed for novices.

Aes Sedai considered unsupervised channeling for novices dangerous, as it very certainly was, and thus it was forbidden. Channeling too much or too often was also dangerous, and novices were always closely supervised when channeling.

Noy Torvald. A man in Mardecin, Amadicia, who lost everything in the collapse of trade with Tarabon and ended up doing odd jobs for Widow Teran. Nynaeve and Elayne used Noy's old coach in their escape from Ronde Macura.

Nubei Peldovni. An Arafellin Aes Sedai of the White Ajah and the loyalist contingent. Part of the expedition to kidnap Rand, she escaped Dumai's Wells with Covarla Baldene and went to Dorlan.

Nuhel Dromand. One of Myrelle's Warders, an Illianer with a thick Illianer accent. A dark bear of a man, tall and wide, with hair to his shoulders and a short beard that left his upper lip bare, his flowing Warder movement seemed odd on him. He was one of the Warders Myrelle saved after his first Aes Sedai died.

Nuli. Rand's alias when he visited the Royal Palace of Andor and was bonded by Elayne, Min and Aviendha and slept with Elayne.

Numbers of Chaos. A body of knowledge from Ages past required to build the Portal Stones; part of this process consisted of laying the Lines that join the Worlds That Might Be.

Nurbaya, Chisaine. *See* Chisaine Nurbaya

Nurelle, Havien. *See* Havien Nurelle

Nurshang, Stedding. A *stedding* located between Kinslayer's Dagger and Shienar.

Nus, Jerum. *See* Jerum Nus

Nyein Kalede. An Atha'an Miere Aes Sedai of the Brown Ajah and the loyalist contingent. Outwardly, she was a shy, withdrawn woman. She had a very dark complexion, black hair and dark eyes and never wore any jewelry other than her Great Serpent ring; this was always the case with sisters from the Atha'an Miere. Like all Sea Folk sisters, Nyein presented herself at the White Tower as a wilder, so that she would not have to pretend that she did not know how to channel at all. Like all Sea Folk sisters, Nyein was older than her stated age on going to the White Tower. She claimed to be eighteen years old when she went to the Tower, but in fact, although she had slowed at nineteen, she was already twenty-six years old. Zemaille, Aiden and Nyein shared rooms in the upper levels of the Library and spent most of their time either there or in the Thirteenth Depository, where they worked.

Nym. A construct of the Aes Sedai from the Age of Legends who had the ability to use the One Power for the benefit of plants and growing things. The last one was Someshta, also called the Green Man, killed by Balthamel while protecting the Eye of the World; while dying, he killed Balthamel.

Nynaeve al'Meara. The Wisdom of Emond's Field who became Aes Sedai; el'Nynaeve was her title as Queen of Malkier, and she became Nynaeve ti al'Meara Mandragoran after her marriage to Lan. She was born in 974 NE. Her strength level was 4(+9), with a potential of 3(+10). Nynaeve was about 5'4" tall, with big dark eyes (though not so big as Egwene's) and dark hair which she normally wore in a braid as thick as a man's wrist which hung to her waist. She was undeniably pretty, and some thought her beautiful. Nynaeve had a small scar front and back of each hand, precisely centered, caused by blackthorns when she was with Lan in the *ter'angreal* during her Accepted test; these were Healed by Sheriam, who was surprised that scars remained. She appeared younger than she was, because she slowed at twenty and didn't age appreciably afterward.

She had a strong temper, and she did not suffer fools gladly. She had the habit of self-delusion to a strong degree; if she fell in the mud, she'd try to claim it was on purpose, at least if anyone saw her, or at least that it wasn't her fault. She had a habit of tugging at her braid when she was angry. She cared very

deeply about her responsibilities, even responsibilities no one else thought she had;
this was not so much a matter of trying
to take charge, though she certainly did
that fairly often, but of seeing herself as
having the responsibility that things
went well for those she felt she should
take care of, whether the villagers from
Emond's Field or anyone else. As a married woman, and married to a Malkieri,
she wore a red dot, the *ki'sain*, on her
forehead. Elayne and Nynaeve had decidedly different command styles, but
both women, after they were in charge,
expected those under them to do as
they were told; Nynaeve was much
less likely to give explanations or try
to convince anyone.

Nynaeve wanted to be a Wisdom
from the time she was little, and above all, to heal people. Her first experience
with the Power was in Healing Egwene unknowingly. Egwene was desperately
ill and the old Wisdom said or intimated that there was nothing more to do.
Nynaeve was afraid she would die, and deeply wanted her to live. When the Wisdom returned, Egwene was completely well. A week later, Nynaeve fell to the
floor, shaking and burning up by turns. Nynaeve's ability with Healing was
little short of miraculous, but her ability with almost anything else was dismal.

Nynaeve left the Two Rivers pursuing Moiraine and the young folks, caught
them at Baerlon, accompanied them all to Caemlyn, then via the Ways to Fal
Dara and so to the Eye of the World. From Shienar she went downriver to the
White Tower. Nynaeve was offered the opportunity to go straight to Accepted,
an unheard of proposition. It was made clear to Nynaeve that she did not have to
choose to try for Accepted right away, but the life of a novice was also painted
to her in terms that ensured she would take the unprecedented offer.

She was winkled out of the White Tower by Liandrin, taken via the Ways
to Toman Head and escaped being handed over to the Seanchan. She helped in
the rescue of Egwene at Falme, then returned to the White Tower, which she
left hunting Liandrin and the other Black Ajah, going to Tear with Elayne and
Egwene, and was captured by Black Ajah, then rescued by Mat. Nynaeve then
went from Tear to Tanchico by Sea Folk ship; from Tanchico to Sienda, near
Amador, by wagon; from Sienda to Samara with Valan Luca's circus; from Samara to Salidar by rivership; from Salidar to several days from Ebou Dar via
Traveling; and from the Tarasin Palace to the Kin's farm outside the city by
Traveling, and from there to somewhere in Andor when the Seanchan took

Ebou Dar. Meanwhile, she Healed Logain of his gentling, and Siuan and Leane of their stilling, was raised Aes Sedai by Egwene and became part of the Yellow Ajah. She overcame her block to channeling at will following an attack by Moghedien, and she married Lan. She traveled with a party to Caemlyn where she reconnected with Rand and agreed to help him cleanse the taint on *saidin* at Shadar Logoth.

When she and Lan left Caemlyn with Rand and Min, Nynaeve took a box full of jewelry from a cache found in Ebou Dar; the jewelry was much like the set worn by Cadsuane, minus the shield; it was to be worn by someone who expected to be attacked by someone using the Power. Alivia wore the jewelry during the cleansing at Shadar Logoth.

Nynaeve agreed to help Lan by taking him to the Borderlands to fight Shadowspawn, but she took him to World's End in Saldaea, giving her time to spread the word about his quest as he rode toward Tarwin's Gap.

She rejoined Rand and supported him in the approach to the Last Battle. During the Last Battle Nynaeve entered the Pit of Doom with Rand at Shayol Ghul, and reunited with Lan in the aftermath of hostilities.

Nyram, Beldeine. *See* Beldeine Nyram

Oak and Thorn, The. An inn in Amador. In Paitr Conel's plan to free Morgase from Amador, Tallanvor was to leave his sword behind and go to The Oak and Thorn to await the others.

Oak Dancer. A female wolf in the wolf dream that led a pack of about twelve including Whisperer, Morninglight, Sparks and Boundless. She got her name from the way she scampered between saplings as a whelp. Her pelt was very light, almost white, with a streak of black running along her right side. Oak Dancer invited Perrin to hunt with her pack, and helped Hopper teach Perrin how to follow someone in the wolf dream. She mourned when Slayer killed Morninglight. Oak Dancer, Sparks, Whisperer and Boundless were trapped in the violet dome created by the dreamspike; Perrin and Hopper went to rescue them, but Slayer killed Whisperer and wounded Sparks. All of the wolves of the pack except Oak Dancer, Sparks and Boundless went north to join the other wolves; those three stayed to help Perrin find the dreamspike. Sparks did find it, but only after Oak Dancer was killed by Slayer.

Oak Water. A village five miles east of Renald Fanwar's farm in the Borderlands.

Oarsman's Pride, The. An inn in Ebou Dar. After using Compulsion on the innkeeper, Moghedien balefired Nynaeve's boat from its roof.

oath, strongest. "By the Light and by my hope of salvation and rebirth"—used by Siuan, Min and Leane to Gareth Bryne in Kore Springs.

Oath Rod. A *ter'angreal* used by the White Tower to bind an Accepted to the Three Oaths on becoming Aes Sedai. A smooth white rod about as thick as a woman's wrist or a little slimmer, and approximately one foot long, it looked like ivory, but felt smoother, not quite like ivory, not quite like glass, and was very cool to the touch; not cold, but distinctly cool. It was very hard, harder than a steel bar, though no heavier than the ivory it appeared to be, and was unmarked except for a flowing symbol incised in one end; this was a numeral, as used in the Age of Legends, and represented the number three. Some thought the numeral stood for the Three Oaths. The rod was simply held in the hand while a little Spirit was channeled into the numeral. Whatever was promised, even if not in the form of an oath, was then binding on the person holding the rod until they were released.

The Oath Rod was a relic of the Age of Legends, although the Aes Sedai of the Third Age did not know that. Binders, as they were called then, were used in the Age of Legends to bind people who were incorrigibly violent, because of personality flaws or madness. If the person being bound could not channel, an

Aes Sedai had to power it, but the effect was the same. The older one was when bound, the more it restricted. That is one reason it was used relatively seldom and only if nothing else would work. It was used instead of a death penalty, too—though in a way, in the terms of the Age, it was a death penalty—to bind someone not only not to commit their crime again but to spend the rest of their lives, if necessary, making restitution.

There was a perception of pressure with each oath taken; this pressure was uncomfortable at first, as though one was wearing a garment that covered one from the top of one's head to the soles of one's feet and was too small, or as if one's skin was too tight. This pressure faded over a period of months, usually taking about a year to vanish entirely, but while it existed, it seemed quite real, and in a way was quite real. That is, an injury or bruise taken while the pressure existed would hurt more, just as if there really was pressure on it. It was the cumulative effect of three oaths taken together that produced the strong feeling of one's skin being too tight. One oath by itself would produce some of the same effect, but not quite as intense and not lasting so long. If oaths were removed and then retaken, the physical effect was the same as for taking them for the first time. Swearing again to an oath already taken and not re-moved produced only a momentary feel of pressure which faded immediately.

It was the Three Oaths, taken on the Oath Rod, which actually produced the ageless look of Aes Sedai. The ageless look did not come on immediately. Its progression was only very roughly in proportion to strength in the Power, with considerable variation among people of the same strength. For someone who was very strong, it would take at least a year, and as much as three or four was not at all uncommon. The average Aes Sedai took five or so years, while the weakest to reach the shawl could take as long as ten or more.

It was possible to be broken free of the oaths with the use of the Oath Rod. This was a very painful process, which had various side effects, most if not all temporary, but all unpleasant in one way or another. They included temporary physical weakness and loss of will, a temporary inability to channel and con-siderable pain. Being released from one oath was very painful; being released from all three at one time was agonizing. This breaking was done by the Black Ajah prior to inducting a woman into their ranks, and the Oath Rod was also used by them to bind themselves to their own three oaths. Being stilled or burned out also removed oaths sworn, although that fact was not gener-ally known.

Without the Oath Rod, a channeler's age was somewhat in proportion to strength, though it wasn't an exact proportion. Stronger channelers lived lon-ger, up to more than eight hundred years for a Forsaken-class channeler. Aging occurred at a rate that would take channelers from the age at which one slowed to the apparent age of sixty or so. This relatively young maximum apparent age was an artifact of the healthful effects of the One Power. With the Oath Rod, Aes Sedai lifespans were capped at about three hundred years maximum.

Oaths, Three. *See* Three Oaths

obaen. A musical instrument of the Age of Legends. Asmodean was said to have played it, although no one in the Third Age knew what it was.

Oburun. A nation that arose after the Trolloc Wars.

Ocalin, Sabeine. *See* Sabeine Ocalin

Ogier. A nonhuman race of giants who lived in *stedding*. They were noted for their love of knowledge, their exquisite stonework and their work with plants, particularly the Great Trees found in the *stedding*. They were sensitive to the mood of a place, and could feel the Forsaken's unrestrained effects, without knowing what they were. They could sense evil, if strong enough, such as in Shadar Logoth. Ogier could see better by moonlight than could humans.

One bit of secret Ogier knowledge, lost to Aes Sedai after the Breaking, was that Ogier did not originate in this world. There was a legend of sorts that they had to and would leave one day, so that they could come again with the turning of the Wheel. This legend and the facts were all kept extremely close. Many Ogier knew of the Book of Translation, and knew that it was something never spoken about to any other than Ogier. Some knew that it contained information about the coming of the Ogier to this world. Scholars among them knew that it told the exact method by which they came, and also how to use that method to depart if needed.

Discounting accident or illness, Ogier were known to live as much as five hundred years, though four hundred or so was more common. Ogier acted as police during the War of the Shadow, and maybe as protectors of the Da'shain Aiel. During the Time of Madness, the *stedding* offered sanctuary to male Aes Sedai, who were buffered from the effects of the taint on *saidin* while there. They were unable to channel, or even to sense the Source, and one by one they left the shelter of the *stedding*, unable to stand the inability to channel any longer. While still staying largely in the *stedding*, these male Aes Sedai grew the Ways and created the Waygates, each, of course, outside the *stedding*. *Stedding* were already being abandoned because of the Breaking, and thus not all by far were so connected.

Before the last male Aes Sedai left the *stedding*, they presented the Talisman of Growing to the Elders. This allowed the Ogier to make the Ways grow branches using Treesong.

During the Breaking the land and sea shifted so dramatically that the *stedding* were lost or swallowed entirely. Those Ogier that survived the upheaval of land and sea found themselves homeless and adrift, wandering in search of their lost sanctuaries. Among Ogier this time was known as the Exile. After many years their Longing for the peace and beauty that only existed within the *stedding* became so strong that they began to sicken and die; many more died than did not. The Talisman was carried on the Exile, and once the first *stedding* were rediscovered during the years of the Covenant of the Ten Nations, it was used to grow more Ways, both to newly rediscovered *stedding* and to the Groves that Ogier planted near the cities they were building for humans. After that time the Ogier did not leave the *stedding* for extensive periods. If an Ogier stayed Outside for too long, the Longing took him and he began to weaken. If he did not return, he died.

The total Ogier population between the Aryth Ocean and the Spine of the World was slightly less than 500,000, inhabiting forty-one *stedding*. There were Ogier west of the Aryth Ocean as well, and they survived, though they did not pick up the skill of working stone. Unlike those to the east, they were pushed more toward the fierce side of Ogier nature. They had no Exile, and so avoided the Longing; of necessity they took part in the wars that enveloped Seanchan before the conquest, and to some extent participated in the intrigues. Anything else could well have meant being swallowed up or destroyed, and sometimes they had to fight in defense of their *stedding*. Ogier there took part in the war that led to the empire founded by Luthair Hawkwing. Ogier were recognized in Seanchan as extremely formidable fighters and were forbidden to bear arms outside the *stedding*, except those serving as bodyguards for the Imperial family, which they provided to show that they were loyal to the Empress. This bodyguard, called Gardeners, was a part of the Deathwatch Guard, though not *da'covale* like the rest. Sometimes a noble would be loaned a few Gardeners; usually this was seen as an honor, but it could be a caution that the throne was watching. The Seanchan rather approved of folk who lived in places where channeling would not work.

It was the perquisite of the highest nobles to have Ogier gardeners, though they were something more than gardeners. They were bodyguards, conventionally unarmed because of the prohibition. Instead, use of garden tools and staffs and sticks was developed into a martial art. There were no physical differences, and few social differences, between the Ogier west and east of the Aryth Ocean, except that the Seanchan Ogier were more willing to fight. By standards of Ogier east of the ocean, they were hasty; humans could hardly see it. No *stedding* in Seanchan was connected with any *stedding* east of the ocean, nor with each other. Seanchan Ogier had never heard of the Ways.

The two groups of Ogier were completely unaware of each other until the time of the Last Battle.

Ogier Gardeners. Ogier members of the Seanchan Deathwatch Guard; unlike the human members, they were not *da'covale*. *See* Ogier

oilfish. A fish that produced valuable oil, found in shoals off Mayene. The oil from these fish was the major competitor for olive oil both in cooking and in lamps. Mayeners knew the location of the oilfish shoals, which no one else did.

Okatomo. A noble House of Kandor. *See* Niach Okatomo

Old Cully. A gnarled beggar in Ebou Dar with one eye, no teeth and a habit of bathing only once a year. He was the feared leader of a circle of Darkfriends that worked for Jaichim Carridin. Cully sent Darkfriends imitating beggars to kill Mat; they did not succeed.

Old Deer. A wolf that Perrin talked to after he and others set out to find the kidnapped Rand.

Old Grim, Old Hob. *See* Dark One

Old Jak. A man up a tree in the song "Old Jak's Up a Tree."

Old Road. The road to Deven Ride south of Emond's Field; it became North Road to the north.

Old Sheep, The. An inn found in Ebou Dar. Mat talked to Maylin, a beautiful serving girl there, when he was searching for Olver.

Old Tongue. What became known as the Old Tongue was the language spoken during the Age of Legends, though it is unknown what it was called then, if indeed it had a name. It was believed that a drift in language began some time during the Breaking of the World, but whether it began that early or not, it was well under way by the time of the Trolloc Wars. Although nobles and the educated still spoke the Old Tongue, a simpler language, much less ambiguous, had come into use among the common people. This simpler language was noted, disparagingly, as early as 250 AB; at least, that was the earliest record available. Very likely, if it existed earlier, scholars considered it beneath notice. By the Trolloc Wars it truly was very nearly a separate language. Those who spoke it alone had difficulty understanding the Old Tongue. By that time, however, many nobles and educated commoners, if not all, had apparently learned the tongue in order to communicate with the lower classes. Nothing from the time records any name separating the two; the one was apparently considered a lower-class dialect of the other.

Old Tongue letter-forms

a b c d e f g h i j k

l m n o p q r s t u v w

x y z dh gh sh th ai ei

ie ou oo st ae

Old Tongue numeric-forms

0 1 2 3 4 5 6 7 8 9

By the time of Artur Hawkwing's rise, the two languages were still in use, but by then had become mutually unintelligible. Nobles still spoke the Old Tongue among themselves, and more educated commoners also used it, especially on formal occasions, but in many ways it had become the second language, because everyone knew and used the speech of the commoners. Certainly books were being printed in the common tongue as early as FY 700.

In some ways the death of Artur Hawkwing's empire was the death of the Old Tongue. Increasingly, the speech of commoners was used even by nobles. Knowledge of the Old Tongue became a sign of education, and considered a necessity among the nobles of many lands, but in truth relatively few had any real knowledge of it. The number of books printed in the Old Tongue began to decrease after FY 700. It was generally accepted that by Artur Hawkwing's death, no more than half the books printed were in the Old Tongue, and the last book printed for general distribution in the Old Tongue was believed to have been about 200 NE, though there were occasional oddities after that time.

Every nation came to speak dialects of the same language, differing mainly in speech rhythms, accents, pronunciations, slang and the like; anyone from any nation could understand anyone from any other nation. That included Seanchan and Sharans, whose speech sounded strange but was still intelligible. Luthair Paendrag's invasion replaced the languages of the natives in Seanchan with the language of the common people from Artur Hawkwing's time.

Old Tongue remained in the world among two groups. It was the language of the Ogier, which they spoke among themselves, although of course they were completely fluent in the common language as well. It was also true that many folk in the Two Rivers had the peculiar ability to understand and even speak in the Old Tongue when under stress, although they could not do so under ordinary circumstances; it was an effect of the strength of the old blood of Manetheren.

WORDS AND PHRASES IN THE OLD TONGUE

Old Tongue was a language difficult to translate because many words could mean many different things, and a variety of words could be used to mean the same thing. Old Tongue was also highly nuanced. For example, there were various ways to say the same thing. Thus "Hill of the Golden Dawn" translated literally was "Gold Dawn Hill." But in other instances, Old Tongue words meaning "of the"—*al* or *an*, for example—might sometimes be integrated into the phrase as well.

By the same token, some words that might be considered significant to the meaning of a sentence in modern language—modifiers, for example—might be missing in Old Tongue; rather, meaning had to be gathered from the context and the instinct of the listener or reader.

As with English, Old Tongue was full of "illogical inconsistencies."

VARIOUS RULES

Pluralization:

There was no simple convention for plurals.

Suffixes *an*, *in*, *on*, *es* and *en* all could indicate pluralization in some context or another.

Sometimes the *n* suffix was all that was needed with some words ending in a vowel, as *tai/tain*.

Adding *a*, as *sei/seia*.

Adding *i*, as *shar/shari*.

Removing a letter, as *dareis/darei*.

Using a contraction, as *athan/atha'an*.

Adding *e* after *a*.

Using the same word for both singular and plural (particularly words that end in *n* in the singular, but other cases as well).

Verbs:

Little was known about verb conjugations.

There were no standard verb endings.

The *ae* suffix would convert an active verb to the passive voice.

The suffix *ane* converted the verb to past tense.

The noun form of a verb was often created by adding the suffix *nen*.

Adjectives:

These frequently followed the noun they modified, and were used for emphasis.

Numbers:

The root of each number had one of two suffixes: *-yat*, descriptive of material objects; or *-ye*, descriptive of the immaterial, such as ideas, arguments or propositions. Perhaps this convention was a reflection of the philosophical underpinnings of the culture, which recognized the importance of both active and passive, male and female, material and immaterial. This was depicted graphically in the Aes Sedai symbol, the black and white disc.

The numbers 11 through 19 used the base numbers from the ones series, followed by the suffix *'pi*.

The suffix *'shi* denoted multiples of ten (the *-yat/-ye* suffix was dropped above the teens).

The word *deshi* meant one hundred, and *'deshi* was used as a hundreds suffix.

The word *tuhat* meant one thousand, and *'tuhat* was used as a thousands suffix.

Word Order:

As with Latin, inverted constructions were common; word order could vary for emphasis, but whereas Latin's case endings facilitated meaning, the Old Tongue relied on context and intuition for meaning; this offered partial insight into how those individuals whose primary language was Old Tongue, such as the Forsaken, could adapt so readily to New Tongue—not only was the Old Tongue the protolanguage of Third Age language, but the prominence of intuitive skills used to derive meaning gave them a significant advantage in language adaptation.

Word order of a sentence could vary according to the perceived beauty of the spoken sound. As one might expect, two people speaking (or writing) identical words with precisely the same meaning might use different word order to conform to their notion of aural beauty; the listener or reader would nonetheless understand each sentence similarly.

Words of Particular Importance:

Though not a firm rule, articles were often omitted where the word had gained some importance in the culture, such as being a title or having a special meaning.

Words and/or their modifiers were sometimes capitalized to indicate increased importance, such as *a'vron* becoming *Ma'vron*.

Words could also be capitalized to demonstrate meaning expanded to a larger entity, such as *cuebiyar* meaning a heart, but *Cuebiyar* meaning the heart of a people or nation.

Compound Words:

Compound words were made by simply combining words, or through use of an apostrophe.

When words were combined and the end of the first word was identical to the beginning of the second word, they would often be overlapped, as in *la* and *anfear* becoming *lanfear*.

A NOTE ON SPEECH:

In the Age of Legends, accents and idioms used in the spoken language varied according to a person's region of origin and station in life, as would be expected in any language.

OLD TONGUE DICTIONARY

The meanings of most words in the Old Tongue have been lost over the Ages. The following is the extent of our understanding.

a—(prep.) of; also, makes plural when added to the end of a word

aada—(adj.) dear

aagret—(adj.) awake

aan—(n. & adj.) one (masculine)

Aan'allein—(n.) One Man, or Man Alone, or Man Who Is an Entire People; Aiel term for Lan

abakran—(n.) amount

a'dam—(n.) leash; used by the Seanchan

ae—(v. suffix) denotes passive voice

aend—(adv.) ever

aes—(n.) all; everyone; the public body; civilization

Aesdaishar—(n.) Glory of All; name of the palace in Chachin

Aes Sedai—(n.) Servants of All

aethan—(n.) shield(s)

Aethan Dor—(n.) Red Shields: an Aiel warrior society

afwadh—(n.) well

agaroum—(n.) disgust

aginor—(n.) a Forsaken; compound word that means "slicer of the living"

agit—(n.) living organism

ahenila—(n.) current, as in a river

ahf—(n.) wind; i.e., an air current

Ahf'frait—(n.) a Trolloc band; literally, "strong wind"

aiel—(n. & adj.) dedicated; *Aiel*—the Dedicated

ailen—(conj., prep. & adj.) before

ain—(v.) is; one form of the verb "to be"

airach—(n. & adj.) living

aird—(adj.) tall

ajah—(n.) an association created for a specific purpose; capitalized, it refers to a group of women within the White Tower organized to accomplish a specific goal

akein—(n.) swallow; i.e., a type of bird

al—(prep.); "for the," or "of the"; also, a prefix added to the first name of Malkieri kings

alantin—(n.) brother; used as short for "*Tia avende alantin*," "Brother to the Trees"; how Selene/Lanfear addressed Loial

al'cair—(adj.) the gold(en)

Al'Cair Dal—(n.) the Golden Bowl, a canyon in the Aiel Waste

al'cair'rahienallen—(n.) literally: Gold(en) Dawn Hill; ancient name for Cairhien, used by Ogier throughout the Third Age

al caldazar—(n.) red eagle

aldazar—(n.) eagle(s)

aldieb—(n.) west wind (the wind that brings the spring rains); name of Moiraine's horse

alep—(n.) son

algai—(n.) battle person, fighter

algai'd'siswai—(n.) Aiel term meaning the spear fighters; literally, battle person of the spear

alget—(v.) fight

Al'ghol—(n.) a Trolloc band; literally, the soulless

algode—(n. & adj.) cotton; a plant fiber from the Aiel waste

allein—(n.) man

allen—(n.) hill

allende—(v.) pass, as in passing through or by, not as in handing something over

allwair—(n.) key

am—(generally prefix) pertains to beauty

aman—(n.) dragon; *Aman*—the Dragon

amela—(n.) friend

amotath—(n.) attraction

an—(prep.) of; of the; for the

an—(suffix) used to indicate plural form

ande—(n.) rose

andi—(suffix) denotes stone-like quality

andillar—(n.) stone

ane—(suffix) used to indicate past tense

anfear—(n.) night

angreal—(n.) "of the power to channel"; a device that enhances the power to channel

anouge—(v.) cough

ansoen—(n.) lies

ara—(suffix) indicates possession, i.e., "my" or "of mine" *arahar*—(n.) curtain

aran—(adj.) right-hand or right-side

aran'gar—(n.) right-hand dagger; also the name of a reborn Forsaken

aridhol—(n.) "land of harmony"; city of the Second Covenant

aris—(n.) harmony; *see* aridhol

arkati—(n.) school

asa—(pron. & n.) you; also, a concubine in Seanchan

ascar—(n. & adj.) blue

asha'man—(n.) guardian/defender; having an implication of siding with justice and right; literally, guard of the blade, a term suggested by Bashere from Old Tongue

ashan—(prefix) guard

ashandarei—(n.) Birgitte's name for Mat's sword; literally, guard sword

asmodi—(n.) music

asmodean—(n.) musician; name of a Forsaken

aso—(pron.) it

astai—(n.) belief

atha—(n.) person

atha'an—(n.) people/folk; strong implications at the least of nation-hood

Atha'an Miere—(n.) People of the Ocean or Waves; Sea Folk

Atha'an Shadar—(n.) People of the Shadow, or Darkfriends

attik—(n. & v.) smile

aven—(v.) call

avende—(n.) tree(s)

Avendesora—(n.) the Tree of Life; chora tree

Avendoraldera—(n.) an offshoot of *Avendesora* found outside the Waste

a'vron—(n.) watcher(s)

ayashiel—(n.) fowl

ayend—(n.) refers to the dead, those who have passed, those who have released their mortal coil; a root word related to *ayende* and *allende*

ayende—(v.) release/free

ayend'an—(prep.) of the fallen or the dead

azafi—(n.) canvas

Ba'alzamon—(n.) Heart of the Dark

ba'asa—(n.) your heart, devoted one

bachri—(n.) bread

badan—(n.) bath

bah(a)—(n.) box(es)

baichan—(adj.) sticky

baid—(n. & adj.) self

baijan—(n.) attack

Baijan'm'hael—(n.) Leader of the Attack

bairnu—(v.) crack

bajad—(n.) spawn

bak—(adv.) how

bal—(n.) circle

balad—(adj.) slow

balfone—(n.) a musical instrument of the Age of Legends

balt—(n.) essence, root or heart

balthamel—(n.) "essence of youth"; name of a Forsaken

banta—(n.) seat

baroc—(n.) hour

basho—(prep., adj. & adv.) under

bat—(prep.) against

batthien—(adj.) hard

bazam—(n.) arm

beatha—(n.) art

bebak—(adj.) quiet

begoud—(adj.) bad

begrat—(v.) swear

begratanae—(adj.) sworn

be'lal—(n.) "desire to have"; the Envious, name of a Forsaken

belo—(v.) desire

beratam—(n.) distance

betakai—(n. & adv.) yesterday

beulin—(n. & adj.) front

bhadi—(n.) company

bhan—(n.) eradication or annihilation

Bhan'sheen—(n.) a Trolloc band; literally, bringers of annihilation

bhardo—(n.) building

bhashan—(n.) hearing

bhoot—(v.) screw

bhuk—(n.) doubt

bideli—(n.) form

bift—(adj.) still

bighar—(adj.) conscious

bijoun—(n.) flower

binti—(adj.) delicate

birok—(n.) beet

blagh—(n.) book

bloobh—(n.) stomach

boan—(n.) female ideal of beauty

bodong—(n.) rhythm

boesin—(n.) floor

bokhen—(adj.) ill

boko—(adj.) fat

bolar—(adj.) special

bolga—(v.) talk

bopo—(n.) baby

borz—(n.) coal

botay—(n.) male ideal of beauty

brett—(n.) letter

breudon—(n.) suggestion

brith—(n. & v.) kiss

brynza—(n.) cheese

budhvai—(adj.) liquid

buggel—(v.) play

buido—(n. & v.) knot

bumma—(n.) moon

bunok—(v.) act

ca—(v. aux.) do; as an intensifier; e.g., *Lyet ye* means "I come"; *Ca'lyet ye* means "I do come"

caba—(n.) horse

caba'donde—(n.) a horse to ride

caba'drin—(n.) cavalry/horsemen

caballein—(n.) horseman; also used to indicate a free man

cadi—(n.) cloth

cadin—(n.) clothes

cadin'sor—(n.) working clothes, worn by Aiel

cafar—(n.) vicious creatures from the Age of Legends; mentioned by Sammael

caili—(n.) skirt

cair—(n. & adj.) gold(en)

caisen—(adj.) old

cal—(n. & adj.) red

calazar—(n.) harbor

caldazar—(n.) red eagle

caledon—(n.) metal

calhar—(n.) red hand

calichniye—(interjection) welcome

Callandor—(n.) The Sword That Is Not a Sword, the Sword That Cannot Be Touched

ca'lyet—(v.) do come

canant—(n.) news

cantheal—(n.) train

capar—(n.) a large, hairy boar-like animal from the Aiel Waste

car—(n.) chief

car'a'carn—(n.) chief of chiefs; capitalized, the Aiel name for the Dragon Reborn

carai—(n.) honor; can be used in the sense of "for the honor"

carentin—(n.) worth, or, of an equivalent value

carn—(n.) chiefs

carneira—(n.) a Malkieri's first lover

casgard—(n.) ornament

cassort—(adj.) married

cavastu—(adj.) angry

cemaros—(n.) great winter tempests from Sea of Storms

cha—(n.) talon, claw

Cha Faile—(n.) the Falcon's Talon: name taken by Faile's followers

chaki—(adj.) bitter

chalin—(adj.) sweet

chalinda—(n.) sweet girl; an Old Tongue name given to Min by Siuan

chalot—(v.) claw

chanda—(n.) soup

chanukar—(n.) island

chati—(n.) breath

chatkar—(n.) prose

chegham—(n.) rate

cheghar—(n.) credit

chekrut—(adj.) violent

chelan—(n.) roof

chenal—(n.) support

cheta—(n.) face

chicaba—(n.) engine

chiema—(n.) winter

chinje—(n.) a wheel used in gambling, perhaps like roulette

chinnar—(n.) body

chinti—(adj.) small

chitzi—(v.) sneeze

choba—(complex word form) used in a formal greeting to the Ogier, meaning "to the humble one before you"

chora—(n.) a construct from the Age of Legends, a beneficent tree

choryat—(n. & adj.) five, a quantifier of material objects

chorye—(n. & adj.) five, descriptive of the immaterial, such as ideas, arguments, or propositions

choshih—(complex word form) used in a formal greeting to the Ogier, meaning "to the unworthy one before you"

choss—(n.) something hauled away on farms, i.e., manure; spoken of by Sammael

choutsin—(adj.) strange

chukhar—(v. & adj.) shut

cierto—(adj.) resolute, determined, enduring; in certain contexts, is a temporal reference

ciyat—(n.) price

claddin—(adj.) tired

clomak—(n.) lock

cloriol—(n.) scale

con—(n.) a small banner

conagh—(n.) answer

concion—(n.) summons

conde—(n.) walker(s)

conden—(v.) walk

conje—(n.) a type of needle, thought of by Sammael

cor—(n.) night

Cor Darei—(n.) Night Spears: Aiel warrior society

corda—(n.) the heart; that which is at the center

Cordamora—(n.) Heart of the People: name of the palace in Maradon

corea—(n.) musical instrument of the Age of Legends

coreer—(n.) poisonous snake from the Age of Legends

Corenne—(n.) the Return; a Seanchan concept

corlm—(n.) a Seanchan exotic animal, looks like a large flightless bird with fur, a predator

cosa—(n.) a creature from the Age of Legends that scampers up trees for protection; mentioned by Graendal

cour—(n.) trap, container

cour'souvra—(n.) mindtrap; used on the Forsaken

cova—(n.) owner, one who owns

covale—(n. & adj.) property; owned; used among the Seanchan for "slave(s)" *cuande*—(n.) a stress-induced condition that is often experienced as chest pain, i.e., anxiety

cue, cuen—(prefix) refers to the heart

cuebiyar—(n.) (my) heart; capitalized, it refers to the heart of a nation or people, or the heart of a ruler

cuendar—(n. & adj.) heart (changes form when combined with other words or word segments)

cuendillar—(n.) heartstone

cueran—(n.) a building material; from a Semirhage point of view

culieb—(n. & adj.) past

cyn—(n. & adj.) last

cyndane—(n.) last chance; name given to reincarnated Lanfear

d—(prep.) of; belonging to; strong implications of ownership, or inferior position

da—(n.) one; person; individual (neutral gender; male or female)

daarlot—(n.) crime

dabor—(n.) picture

Da'concion—(n.) the Chosen Ones; Seanchan term

da'covale—(n.) a person who is owned; a slave, according to Seanchan usage; this is the older form, usually replaced now simply by *covale* or "property"

dada—(n.) father

dadaranell—(n.) "father of ranges"; from Mafal Dadaranell, ancient name of Fal Dara

dae—(adj.) complex; intricate; implications of delicacy; great

dae'mar—(n.) an intricate or complex game, that requires a delicate touch

dae'vin—(n.) treaty

daes—(n.) many people; multitudes; implications of diversity, of milling (not a unified group of individuals)

Daes Dae'mar—(n.) the Great Game, also known as the Game of Houses; literally, "Many People Game," or "the Complex Game that Uses Multitudes"; played in southern countries, particularly in Cairhien; some say developed by the Aes Sedai

daghain—(n.) fear

dahid—(n.) note

dai—(n., v. & adj.) battle; struggle; strive

daien—(n.) dancer of the old days; mentioned by Aran'gar

Dai Shan—(n.) title for Lan; literally, "(Diademed) Battle Lord"

daishar—(n.) glory (literally: "battle blood" or "blood of battles")

dal—(n.) bowl, basin or vessel

dalae—(past part.) is paid

dale—(v.) pay

dali—(n.) clock

dam—(v.) leash

damane—(n.) leashed; used by the Seanchan to mean "leashed one" or "those who are leashed" (technically this would be *da'damane*, but would compress because of the overlapping sounds, to *damane*)

dane—(n.) chance (variant is *diane*)

dantor—(n.) theory

dao—(n.) cord

daori—(n.) hair cut by a Malkieri's *carneira* and saved, woven into a cord

dar—(adv.) forward (direction)

dar—(n.) sister

dar—(suffix) indicates the feminine

darath—(n.) a type of fierce animal; from a Moghedien point of view *darei*—(n.) spears (plural of *dareis*); used by Aiel

dareis—(n.) spear

darm—(adj.) serious

darshi—(v.) see

Da'shain Aiel—(n.) literally: "People to Peace Dedicated" (sometimes shortened to "*Da'shain*")

da'tsang—(n.) despised one; one who is despised; used by Aiel

de—(prefix) refers to an agent of action; (suffix) denotes negation

deebo—(n. & adj.) brown

dekhar—(adj.) political

demandred—(n.) one who twists the blade; name of a Forsaken

dena—(n.) song

der—(n. prefix) master, as in a master of a craft; thus among the Seanchan, *der'morat'raken* is one who is advanced in the craft/skill of handling *raken*, one who trains others to handle them, and therefore a trainer of morat'raken; likewise, a *der'sul'dam* is one skilled enough to train those *sul'dam* who train and handle *damane*

der—(prep.) from

dera—(suffix) means "derived from"

deshi—(suffix) denotes hundreds (*yat/ye* suffix is dropped above the teens); e.g., *chor'deshi*=five hundred

deshi—(n. & adj.) one hundred

desta—(v.) stop

desu—(n.) bed

desyat—(adj.) ten; a quantifier of material objects

desye—(adj.) ten; descriptive of the immaterial, such as ideas, arguments or propositions

devor—(v.) ask

devoriska—(rel. pron.) what was asked

deyeniye—(n.) majesty

dha—(n.) agony, anguish

dhai—(adj.) pertaining to war or a great battle

Dhai'mon—(n.) a Trolloc band; literally, scythes of war

dhakdi—(n.) cloud(s)

dhalen—(n.) money

dhamel—(n.) shade

Dha'vol—(n.) a Trolloc band; literally, sires of agony

dhjin—(n.) terror or horror

Dhjin'nen—(n.) a Trolloc band; literally, those who cause terror

dhol—(n.) land

dhub—(n.) ball

diane—(n.) chance (var. of *dane*)

diband—(adj.) dependent

dibbuk—(n.) interest

dieb—(n.) wind

difrol—(n.) waste

dillar—(suffix) means "stone"

din—(n.) brother(s)

din—(suffix) indicates masculine

dinya—(v.) care

diutic—(n.) tongue

dival—(n.) light

diy—(v.) sound

diynen—(n.) sounder, one who produces a sound

djanzei—(n., adj. & adv.) south

do—(prep.) over

doko—(pron. & adv.) where

Do Miere A'vron—(n.) Watchers Over the Waves; literally: Over the Sea/Waves, Watchers

domashita—(v.) warm(s)

domorakoshi—(n.) language

don—(suffix) denotes importance

donde—(v.) ride; has to do with riding

doon—(n. & adj.) black or very dark

doorn—(adj.) thick

doozhi—(v.) burst

dor—(n. & adj.) red

dore—(n.) mountains

dornat—(n.) a hunting critter thought of by Graendal

doti—(n.) nut

dovie—(adj.) relates to luck

dovie'andi—(n.) dice

dovienya—(n.) luck

dred—(v.) twist

drelle—(suffix) means river; water(s) of

drenni—(v.) turn

drin—(n.) man/men/soldier(s)

drosin—(n. & adj.) green

drova—(n.) hag, beldam, old woman

drovja—(adj.) of a beldam

druna—(v.) push

duadhe—(n.) water

Duadhe Mahdi'in—(n.) Water Seekers; an Aiel warrior society

dudhi—(n.) cow

duente—(v.) holds/grips; has a hold/grip on

dumki—(n.) army

dvoyat—(adj.) two, a quantifier of material objects

dvoye—(adj.) two, descriptive of the immaterial, such as ideas, arguments or propositions

dvoyn—(n. & adj.) second

dyani—(adj.) natural

dyu—(adv. & prep.) by

dzigal—(adj.) flat

e—(conj.) and

einto—(n.) addition

el—(prefix) added to the first name of a Malkieri queen; (suffix) denotes "hope," e.g., Sammael

ellis—(n.) sun

Ellisande—(n.) the Rose of the Sun; literally Sunrose

en—(suffix) makes plural; also, derived from *jenn* to mean "true"

era—(suffix) modifier meaning "blue," as in *seiera*

es—(suffix) denotes many, as in *daes*

ethaantar—(v.) transport

evierto—(v.) polish

fada—(adj.) sad

faerstin—(n.) adjustment

faile—(n.) falcon

fakha—(v.) sail

far—(prep.) of; also, an indication of mobility

Far Aldazar Din—(n.) Brothers of the Eagle: Aiel warrior society

Far Dareis Mai—(n.) Maidens of the Spear: Aiel warrior society

farhota—(n.) brass

fear—(n.) night

feia—(n.) speaker

feiro—(v.) exchange

feist—(v.) question

fel—(poss. pron.) our

fenter—(n.) verse

feros—(n.) soil

ferster—(n.) garden

finin—(n.) nephew

fintan—(n.) cup

folyt—(adj.) able

fonnai—(n.) place

for—(n.) herd

frait—(adj.) strong

fringfran—(n.) cork

furthadin—(n.) statement

ga—(v.) is

gadhat—(n.) thread

gadou—(v.) change

gaen—(prep.) across

gai—(n.) battle

gaidin—(n.) brother to/of battle; Aes Sedai use this word for Warders

gai'don—(n.) battle, but a key battle, that will win or lose a campaign or war

gai'shain—(n.) Aiel word, meaning "those sworn to peace in battle"

galamok—(n.) shirt

gar—(n.) dagger or lethal device

gara—(n.) a type of poisonous lizard from Aiel Waste

garan—(adj.) solid

gashi—(v.) profit

gavane—(pron., adj. & adv.) what

gemarisae—(v.) is made

gemarise—(v.) make

ghael—(suffix) pertains to brutes, beasts, monsters

ghal—(v.) curve

ghani—(n.) purpose

ghar—(n.) venom or acid

Ghar'ghael—(n.) a Trolloc band; literally, brutes of venom

ghazh—(n.) chin

gheuth—(v.) cry

gheym—(n. & v.) measure

ghiro—(adv.) thus

ghleb—(n.) limit

ghoba—(n.) the soul

Ghob'hlin—(n.) a Trolloc band; literally, harvesters of souls

Gho'hlem—(n.) a Trolloc band; literally, takers of souls

gholam—(n.) one of the Shadow-spawn; means "soulless"

ghow—(adj.) hollow

ghraem—(n.) the mighty, the all-powerful

Ghraem'lan—(n.) a Trolloc band; literally, prized of the mighty

ghul—(n.) pit or hole

ghuni—(n. & v.) smoke

gidhi—(adj.) normal

glasti—(adj.) even

glimp—(n.) minute

gobhat—(n.) plant

gomaen—(n. & v.) attempt

gorista—(v.) use

gouql—(v.) look

gozai—(n.) chest

graedo—(v.) please

graen—(n.) pleasure

graendal—(n.) vessel of pleasure; name of a Forsaken

greal—(n.) the power to channel

griest—(n.) rail

grolm—(n.) a fierce Seanchan animal used in battle

gruget—(v.) stretch

gubbel—(adj.) feeble

gwiltor—(n.) wire

gurupat—(n.) oath

haar—(n.) opinion

habish—(n.) ear

hadori—(n.) a Malkieri headband

hadzi—(v.) cause

hael—(v.) lead

hafi—(n.) part

Hailene—(n.) a Seanchan term meaning forerunners, Those Who Come Before

hakhel—(n.) nail

hama—(n.) dancer(s); implies particular grace and fluidity, a stateliness

Hama N'dore—(n.) Mountain Dancers: Aiel warrior society

hanol—(n.) wound

har(an)—(n.) hand

harben—(v.) take

harvo—(v.) pump

hasta—(n.) paste

hathi—(n.) muscle

havokiz—(n.) invention

hawali—(adj.) wide

heatsu—(v.) join

heesh—(adj.) smooth

hei—(adv.) always

heinst—(v.) send

hessa—(n.) forgiveness

hessalam—(n. & adj.) without forgiveness; name of a Forsaken

hienisus—(n.) design

hirato—(n.) space

hlem—(suffix) means those who take

hlin—(suffix) means those who harvest

hochin—(n., adj. & adv.) east

holubi—(n.) comfort

hoba—(n.) oil

hodifo—(adj.) responsible

homa—(v.) offer

hoptah—(n.) week

hosiya—(v.) till

hou'dabor—(n.) dream

houghan—(n.) structure

houma—(v.) sleep

humat—(n.) existence

hutsah—(n.) bucket

ibalets—(n.) thumb

ikaat—(n.) wax

illar—(suffix) pertains to stone

imsoen—(n.) truth

in—(suffix) creates plural form

inda—(n.) girl

inde—(n. & adv.) no or not; a general negation

indemela—(n.) enemy

ing—(suffix) indicates something of utmost importance

iqet—(pron., adj. & adv.) this

iro—(pron.) we

isain—(v.) is; one form of "to be"

isainde—(v. neg.) is no/is not/am no/am not (insistent; emphatic)

isham—(n.) betrayer

ishamael—(n.) betrayer of hope; name of a Forsaken

ishar—(v.) betray

ishavid—(n.) betrayal

iska—(suffix) means "that which was"

istor—(n.) fiction

izaad—(n.) wool

-ja—(suffix) means "of" or "issued from"

jaahni—(n.) reading

jabro—(n.) tooth

jalat—(n. & v.) burn

jalbouk—(n.) kettle

jalou—(v.) go

jalid—(n.) heat

jeade—(n.) finder

jeade'en—(n.) true finder; name of Jain Farstrider's and Rand's horse

jegal—(n.) a scaled creature thought of by Sammael

jemena—(v.) farm

jenn—(adj. & adv.) true, truly, or even "only true"; implies that all others are false or fake

jhabal—(n.) brush

jheda—(adj.) exquisite; name of the royal palace of Ghealdan

jhin—(n.) exaltation

ji—(n.) honor

ji'e'toh—(n.) honor and obligation; used by Aiel

jobei—(n.) apparatus

juma—(n.) worm

jumara—(n.) one of Aginor's creations, mentioned by Sammael, that were intended to transform themselves; now called Worms in the Blight, full-grown but untransformed

kaarash—(n.) discovery

kaarto—(n.) tax

kadu—(n.) lip

kaf—(n.) a caffeinated beverage, brewed from the roasted seed of a fruit-bearing shrub cultivated in the mountains of Seanchan

kakamo—(adj.) quick

kanjo—(n.) emotion

kar—(suffix) means punishment through the nervous system

karagaeth—(n.) punishment

kardon—(n.) green-skinned fruit from a leafless spiny plant in Aiel Waste

kasaar—(n.) order

kashen—(n.) fork

kathana—(v.) kick

katien—(n.) size

kazath—(v.) say

kazka—(n.) grain

keesh—(adv. & prep.) out

keisa—(n.) jewel

kelet—(n.) rod

kelindun—(n.) general (military rank)

kesan—(n. & adj.) steel

kesiera—(n.) jewelry worn on the forehead, such as that worn by Moiraine

kesool—(n.) shoe

ketvar—(n.) chain

keymar—(n.) color

khadi—(n.) bone

khalig—(n.) history

khamu—(n.) year

khoop—(v.) blow

khust—(adj.) dry

kikola—(n.) list

killo—(n.) pin

kippat—(n.) ticket

ki'sain—(n.) Malkieri woman's forehead adornment

kiserai—(n.) glory, honor

Kiseran—(n.) a title Siuan used to address Loial, meaning "honorable one"

kjasic—(adj.) an obscenity, spoken by Sammael

kloye—(n.) bell

Kno'mon—(n.) a Trolloc band; literally, scythes of devastation

knotai—(n.) devastation, ruin

koanto—(n.) learning

Ko'bal—(n.) a Trolloc band; literally, circle of one, i.e., brotherhood

ko'di—(n.) the Oneness, the void, or the flame and the void: a meditative state

kodome—(n. & adv.) here

koja—(n. & adv.) there

komad—(adj.) mixed

komalin—(adj.) weak

komo—(v.) put

kontar—(n.) board

korero—(n.) discussion

koudam—(n., adj. & adv.) west

koult—(adv.) quite

kovist—(n.) tail

koyat—(adj.) one, a quantifier of material objects

koye—(adj.) one, descriptive of the immaterial, such as ideas, arguments or propositions

koyn—(n., adj. & adv.) first

kozat—(n.) unit

kramayage—(n.) development

kramtor—(n.) store

kriko—(n.) bird

kritam—(adj.) tight

kuruta—(n.) cart

kuthli—(v.) laugh

kutya—(n.) feeling

la—(n.) daughter

laada—(adj.) long

labani—(n.) reward

lahdin—(n.) observation

laero—(n.) flag

lagien—(n.) town

laido—(n.) summer

lakevan—(n.) motion

lal—(v.) have

lam—(suffix) indicates a lack, being without

lamena—(n.) frame

lan—(adj.) prized or beloved

lanfear—daughter of the night; name of a Forsaken

lashite—(n.) meeting

lato—(n.) angle

lavakh—(n.) wood

leagh—(n.) page

leffal—(n.) stage

lendha—(v.) fall

lennito—(n. & adj.) military

liede—(n.) neck

lindhi—(n.) monkey

lishno—(n.) trouble

loftan—(n.) material

logoth—(n.) place of waiting

lopar—(n.) huge fighting exotic animal of the Seanchan

lormae—(v.) is written

lorme—(v.) write

los—(n., adj. & adv.) forward

loviyaga/loviyagae—(n.) memory/ memories

lyet—(v.) come

m—(prefix) means "of"

ma—(prefix) indicates importance

ma—(v.) "you give"

maani—(adv.) very

maast—(adj.) necessary

machin—(n.) destruction

Machin Shin—(n.) "journey of destruction"; the Black Wind, a major threat in the Ways

mad—(adj.) loud

mael—(n.) hope

mafal—(n.) mouth or pass

Mafal Dadaranell—(n.) "pass at the father of mountain ranges"; ancient name for Fal Dara

magami—(n.) little uncle; what Amalisa called King Easar in private

mageen—(n.) daisy

mah'alleinir—(n.) he who soars; literally "seeking man of the stars"; the name Perrin gave to his Power-wrought hammer

mahdi—(n.) seeker; used for leader of Tuatha'an caravan

mahdi'in—(n.) seekers

mahrba—(v.) paint

mai—(n.) maiden(s)

makitai—(n.) wheel

mamai—(n. & adj.) future

mamu—(n.) mother

man—(adj.) related to blade/sword ("man" has the same root as "war," "violence" or "aggression")

mandarb—(n.) blade; name of Lan's stallion

Manetheren—(n.) mountain home; one of the Ten Nations

manetherendrelle—(n.) waters of the mountain home

manive—(v.) drive

manivin—(n.) driving

manshima—(n.) sword/blade

manshimaya—(n.) my own sword

mar—(n.) game

maral—(adj.) destined

marath—(prefix) indicates that something *must* be done, suggesting urgency; Seanchan word

marath'damane—(n.) those who must be leashed/one who must be leashed; Seanchan term

marcador—(n.) hammer

marna—(v.) swim

maromi—(v.) crush

mashi—(n. & v.) love

mashiara—(n.) my love; but a hopeless love, perhaps already lost; Lan to Nynaeve

masnad—(n.) trade

maspil—(n.) butter

mastri—(n.) fish

mat—(v.) control

matuet—(adj.) important

ma'vron—(n.) watchers of importance

mawaith—(n.) reaction

medan—(n.) sugar

melaz—(n.) inn

melimo—(n.) apple

mera—(prep.) without; lacking

Mera'din—(n.) the Brotherless; used by Aiel

merwon—(adj.) boiling

mesaana—(n.) teacher of lessons; name of one of the Forsaken

mestani—(n.) lessons

mestrak—(n.) necessity

m'hael—(n.) leader (capitalized implies "Supreme Leader"; title Taim gave himself)

mi—(poss. pron.) my

mia—(pron.) me; myself

Mia'cova—(n.) One Who Owns Me, My Owner; term used by Moghedien after she was enslaved by a mindtrap

miere—(n.) ocean/waves

mikra—(n.) shame

min—(adj.) little

minyat—(adj.) eight, a quantifier of material objects

minye—(adj.) eight, descriptive of the immaterial, such as ideas, arguments or propositions

miou—(n.) cat

mirhage—(n.) pain, or the promise or expectation of pain

misain—(v.) am (insistent; emphatic)

mist—(n. & adj.) middle

mitris—(adj.) dirty

modan—(n.) approval

moghedien—(n.) a particular breed of spider; small, deadly poisonous and extremely reclusive; name of a Forsaken

mokol—(n.) milk

mon—(adj.) related to scythe

moodi—(adj.) frequent

mora—(n.) the people or a population

morasu—(n.) morning

morat—(n. prefix) handler/controller; i.e., one who handles or controls; used by the Seanchan (as in *morat'raken*, one who handles *raken*)

mordero—(adj.) death

moridin—(n.) a grave; tomb; also, the name of a Forsaken, for whom the word's meaning refers to death

moro—(adv. & conj.) so

mos—(adj., adv. & prep.) down

mosai—(adj.) low

mosiel—(v.) lower

mosiev—(adj.) lowered or downcast

motai—(n.) Aiel name for a sweet crunchy grub found in the Waste

mourets—(n.) mushroom(s)

mozhlit—(adj.) possible

m'taal—(adj.) of stone

muad—(n., adj. & adv.) foot/on foot/ afoot

muad'drin—(n.) infantry/footmen

muaghde—(n.) meat

mukhrat—(adj.) private

mund—(adj.) high

mustiel—(n.) sock

mystvo—(n.) office

n—(prep. prefix) means "of" or "from"

nabir—(n.) fire

nachna—(n.) science

nadula—(n.) force

Nae'blis—(n.) title of Shai'tan's first lieutenant

nag—(n.) day

nagaru—(n.) snake

nahobo—(adj.) full

nahodil—(n.) cushion

nai—(n.) knife, dagger, blade; a blade smaller than a sword's blade; can be used in modification also to mean "stabbing"

nais—(v.) smell

naito—(n.) flame

nak—(pron.) who

nakhino—(n.) month

n'am—(adj.) beautiful

naparet—(adj.) parallel

nar'baha—(n.) traveling boxes; literally, "fool box"; used by Sammael

nardes—(n.) thought

narfa—(adj.) foolish

nasai—(n., v. & adj.) wrong

nausig—(n.) boat

navyat—(adj.) nine, a quantifier of material objects

navye—(adj.) nine, descriptive of the immaterial, such as ideas, arguments or propositions

nayabo—(n.) prison

n'baid—(adj.) automatic

n'dore—(adj.) of/from the mountains

neb—(n.) mist

nedar—(n.) tusked water pig found in the Drowned Lands

neidu—(adj.) new

neisen—(adv.) why

nemhage—(n.) distribution

nen—(suffix) like adding "er" to an English verb, indicating one who or that which does, or those who cause

nesodhin—(prep.) through; through this; through it

ni—(prep.) for

niende—(adj.) lost

nieya—(v.) step

ninte—(poss. pron.) your (used more formally than "*ninto*")

ninto—(poss. pron.) your

nirdayn—(n.) hate

no—(conj.) but

no—(pron.) me

nob—(v.) cut

nodavat—(n.) produce

nolve—(v.) give

nolvae—(v.) is given

nor—(n.) cutter or slicer

no'ri—(n.) ancient game now called stones

norvenne—(n.) account

nosane—(v.) speak

nothru—(n.) nose

noup—(adj. & adv.) only

nupar—(n.) base, as in bottom or support

nush—(adj.) deep

nyala—(n.) country

nye—(adv.) again

Nym—(n.) a construct from the Age of Legends, a being who has beneficial effects on trees and other living things

o—(adj.) a

ob—(conj.) or

obaen—(n.) a musical instrument of the Age of Legends

obanda—(n.) door

obidum—(n.) spade

obiyar—(n.) position

obrafad—(n.) view

obram—(n.) impulse

ocarn—(n.) toe

odashi—(n.) weather

odi—(pron. & adj.) some

odik—(n.) secretary

oghri—(n.) sky

ohimat—(n.) comparison

olcam—(n.) tin

olesti—(n.) pants

olghan—(n.) drawer

olivem—(n.) pencil

olma—(n. & adj.) poor

ombrede—(n. & v.) rain

on—(suffix) denotes plural form

onadh—(n.) arch

onguli—(n.) ring

onir—(n.) star(s)

oosquai—(n.) a distilled spirit; used by Aiel

orcel—(n.) pig

ordeith—(n.) wormwood; name taken by Padan Fain among the Whitecloaks

orichu—(n. & v.) plow

orobar—(n.) danger

ortu—(adj.) open

orvieda—(v.) print

osan—(adj.) left-hand or left-side

osan'gar—(n.) left-hand dagger; name of a Forsaken

ospouin—(n.) hospital

ost—(prep.) on

otiel—(n.) sponge

otou—(n. & adj.) top

otyat—(adj.) four, a quantifier of material objects

otye—(adj.) four, descriptive of the immaterial, such as ideas, arguments or propositions

ounadh—(n.) wine

ovage—(n.) window

o'vin—(n.) a promise; agreement

ozela—(n.) goat

paathala—(n.) operation

pad—(adj., adv. & prep.) up

padgi—(v.) lift

pakita—(v.) twist

palatu—(n.) word

panati—(v.) wash

panjami—(n.) society

pantae—(n.) business

panyat—(adj.) six, a quantifier of material objects

panye—(adj.) six, descriptive of the immaterial, such as ideas, arguments or propositions

papp—(n.) fact

parano—(n. & adj.) coward; base or low in pejorative sense

parikesh—(n.) leather

pas—(pron.) none

pashren—(n.) scissors

pastien—(v.) protest

patomi—(n.) potato

patra—(n. & adv.) then

peast—(n.) payment

pecara—(n.) tree having pale, wrinkled fruit in Aiel Waste

pedalen—(n.) expansion

pentor—(v.) mass

pepa—(n.) paper

perant—(adv.) together

perit—(n., adj. & v.) equal

perol—(n.) pen

pi—(suffix) indicates numerical teens; e.g., *navyat'pi* or *na-vye'pi*=nineteen

pierskoe—(n.) peach

piesa—(n.) meaning unknown; the name of Leya's horse

pinchota—(n.) stocking

pinikar—(n.) line

pistit—(n.) whistle

pistita—(v.) whistle

pizar—(n.) ant

platip—(n. & adj.) present

platto—(n.) detail

plean—(adj. & adv.) much

ploushin—(n. & adj.) square

po—(conj.) because

pochivat—(v.) start

poldar—(adj.) skinny

polov—(n.) shelf

potadi—(n.) debt

potsa—(n.) collar

poulam—(n.) boot(s)

pranent—(n.) tendency

prashat—(n.) process

prasta—(n.) idea

prato—(adj.) such

pravilam—(adj.) regular

probita—(v.) drink

procol—(n.) map

profel—(v.) test

proyago—(n.) experience

ptash—(n.) effect

punia—(v.) may

punta—(n.) number

purtah—(n., adj. & adv.) enough

purvene—(n.) horn

pyast—(n.) throat

qaato—(n.) cake

qaiset—(pron., adj. & adv.) same

qamir—(n.) silk

qen—(adv. & conj.) when

qinar—(n.) niece

rabat—(v.) manage

rabdo—(adj.) sudden

raf—(v.) fly

ragha—(adj., adv. & prep.) near

raha—(n. & adj.) free(dom), having liberty

rahien—(n.) dawn

Rahien Sorei—(n.) Dawn Runners: Aiel warrior society

rahtsi—(n.) authority

rahvin—(n.) "promise of freedom"; name of a Forsaken

raia—(n.) air

rainn—(n.) kennel

raken—(n.) a large flying exotic animal of the Seanchan

rakh—(n., adj. & adv.) back

ramay—(n.) table

ranell—(n.) mountain range(s)

ranzak—(n. & v.) guide

raqit—(v.) shake

rastra—(n.) road

ravad—(n.) street

raya—(poss. pron.) mine; my own

rema'kar—(n.) energy whip; a weapon from the Age of Legends

remath—(n. & v.) whip

rennen—(n.) cook

renni—(v.) cook

rensal—(n.) kitchen

restar—(adj.) medical

rhadiem—(v.) prepare (insistent)

rhaul—(n.) rice

rhiod—(n.) a world or land

rhub—(n.) a small piece

Rhyagelle—(n.) Those Who Come Home, or the Homecomers; a Seanchan term

rieht—(n.) balance

rimbai—(n.) berry

risor—(v.) trick

roban—(n.) oven

rodinat—(n.) relation

roedane—(v.) bit (past tense)

roedna—(v.) bite

ronagh—(n.) slope

roscher—(adj.) separate

rouyte—(n.) mark

rulli—(adj.) round

rumpo—(v.) drop

runyat—(n.) weight

sa—(prefix) used to indicate the superlative

sa—(adv. & prep.) in

saa—(n.) a tiny black fleck that moves across a Forsaken's eyes when the True Power is accessed; increases the more True Power is used *saana*—(n.) teacher

sa'angreal—(n.) a device, stronger than *angreal*, that enhances the power to channel

saantar—(adj.) teaching

sa'blagh—(n.) library

safar—(n. & adj.) white

sag—(n.) time

sagain—(n.) it is time

sahlan—(n.) attention

sai—(adj. prefix) related to power

saidar—(n.) the female side of the Power

saidin—(n.) the male side of the Power

sain—(v.) is

saizo—(v.) request

salidien—(n.) humor

samid—(v.) band

samma—(n.) destroyer; blinder

Samma N'Sei—(n.) Eye Blinders

sammael—(n.) destroyer of hope; name of a Forsaken

sanasant—(n.) knowledge

santhal—(n.) industry

sar—(pron.) she

sara—(n.) a dance

sast—(adv.) almost

scrup—(adv. & prep.) between

se—(pron.) themselves

se—(pron.) it(self)

sedai—(n.) servant(s)

seel—(n.) amusement

segade—(n.) spiny leathery plant with white blossoms in Aiel Waste

seia—(n.) eye(s); in those forms where it combines, becomes *sei*

Seia Doon—(n.) Black Eyes: Aiel warrior society

Sei'cair—(n.) Aiel title for Perrin; literally, "golden eyes"

Seiera—(n.) name of Min's mare; name of a flower known in Baerlon as "blue-eye"

sei'mosiev—(adj.) literally means (of) lowered or downcast eyes, indicates loss of face or honor; used by Seanchan

sei'taer—(adj.) (of) straight or level eyes; used by the Seanchan regarding having or gaining face

semirhage—(n.) the promise of pain itself, or one who embodies the promise of pain; name of a Forsaken

sene—(adv.) as/like; (v.) to like

seren—(adj.) stubborn; obstinate

serenda—(n.) stubborn one; also, name of the palace of the King of Amadicia, outside Amador

serenla—(n.) stubborn daughter; an Old Tongue name given Min by Siuan

sha—(n.) noise

shaani—(n.) quality

shadar—(n.) shadow

Shadar Logoth—(n.) Shadow's Waiting, or Where the Shadow Waits; name of the city Aridhol that became tainted with evil

Shadar Nor—(n.) name given to Latra Posae meaning "Cutter (or Slicer) of the Shadow"

shae—(n.) dog

shae'en—(n.) dogs

Shae'en M'taal—(n.) Stone Dogs: Aiel warrior society

shaek—(n.) house

shaendi—(n.) aunt

shaff—(n.) condition

shai—(n.) woman

shaidar—(n. & adj.) dark, as in pitch-darkness of night; indication of evil or wrong

Shaidar Haran—(n.) Hand of the Dark: name of an "extreme" Myrddraal

shaiel—(n.) she/the woman who is dedicated; Tigraine's Aiel name *shain*—(n.) peace

Shai'tan—(n.) name of the Dark One

sha'je—(n.) a type of duel in ancient Qal; mentioned by Semirhage

shak—(pron., adj. & adv.) any

sha'mad—(n.) literally, "loud noise"; thunder

Sha'mad Conde—(n.) Thunder Walkers: Aiel warrior society

shama—(n.) a musical instrument of the Age of Legends

shambayan—(n.) chamberlain; man in charge of securing provisions and supplies; a Borderlands term

shan—(n.) lord

shanna'har—(n.) Saldaean anniversary marriage celebration

shao—(v.) jump

shar—(n.) blood; bloodline; refers to descent rather than blood in the veins, i.e., heritage

sha'rah—(n.) an ancient strategy game consisting of a black and white piece called Fisher, a black and white 13×13 square board, 33 red pieces and 33 green pieces

shari—(n.) plural of *shar*

shatayan—(n.) chatelaine; female in charge of ordering servants and running the household; Borderlands term

shaval—(n. & adj.) linen

Shayol Ghul—(n.) Doom Pit

Sh'boan—(n.) empress; Sharan term

Sh'botay—(n.) empress's consort; Sharan term

sheen—(n.) bringers of, or those who exemplify something

sheikar—(adj.) bright

shen—(n.) band or group; brother (hood)

Shen an Calhar—(n.) The Band of the Red Hand; originally a legendary Manetheren fighting force from the Trolloc Wars; name adopted by Mat's soldiers

shi—(suffix) denotes multiples of ten (*yat/ye* suffix is dropped above the teens); e.g., *suk'shi*=seventy

shiatar—(n. & adj.) iron

shin—(n.) journey

shitak—(adj.) different

shodet—(n.) comb

shost—(n.) knee

shoufa—(n.) dust veil; used by the Aiel

shuk—(n.) health

shukri—(adj.) healthy

sich—(n.) bag

sidama—(n.) radiance

sidhat—(n.) example

simp—(adj.) thin

sin—(n. & pron.) he or man

sind—(adv.) never

siswai—(n.) spear

siswai'aman—(n.) spear(s) of the dragon; term used by the Aiel

slagh—(adj.) bent

sleesh—(n.) dress

smoog—(n.) steam

so—(n.) thing or entity

sob—(conj.) if

sobel—(n.) button

soe—(n.) truth

Soe'feia—(n.) Seanchan Truthspeaker, Speaker of the Truth

soende—(v.) carry

soetam—(n.) great rat found in the Drowned Lands

sofar—(n.) a vehicle having steering planes

so'jhin—(n.) "a thing of exaltation"; Seanchan hereditary upper servants of the blood; also freely translated as "a height among lowliness" or "both sky and valley"

soovri—(n.) behavior

sor—(n. & adj.) work(ing)

sorbe—(v.) run

sora—(n.) life

sorda—(n.) a distinct species of rat found in the Aiel Waste

sorei—(n.) runner(s)

soudhov—(n.) cabbage

souk—(n.) bee

souvra—(n.) mind

souvraya—(comb.) literally, "my own mind"

sovin—(n.) hands; unmodified, "hands that are open and empty"

Sovin Nai—(n.) Knife Hands: Aiel warrior society

sovya—(adj.) another/any other

spashoi—(n.) taste

spiat—(v.) help

spillon—(n.) disease

spondat—(adj.) early

spotsu—(n.) bridge

s'redit—(n.) Seanchan name for boar-horses

staba—(n. & adj.) copper

staera—(n.) copper scraping stick for the sweat-tent among the Aiel

stedding—(n.) an Ogier homeland and place of sanctuary

sterpan—(n.) sex

stobur—(n.) stem

straviant—(n.) insurance

streith—(n. & adj.) a textile from the Age of Legends that changed color according to the wearer's emotions

stripo—(n.) wing

suchan—(n.) growth

sukyat—(adj.) seven, a quantifier of material objects

sukye—(adj.) seven, descriptive of the immaterial, such as ideas, arguments or propositions

sul—(v.) hold

sul'dam—(n.) leash holder, holder of the leash (literally: hold-leash); a Seanchan term

sulwed—(n.) substance

sunatien—(n.) education

suravye—(n.) peace

sursa—(n.) sticks used to eat in Arad Doman

suzain—(adj.) false

svayor—(n.) soap

swabel—(n.) glove

syndon—(n.) birth

sysyn—(n.) brain

szere—(adj.) lower

ta—(n.) related to the Pattern

ta'maral'ailen—(n.) web of destiny (around those who are *ta'veren*); literally, pattern destined before; a term used by the Ogier

taak—(adv.) yes

taal—(n. & adj.) stone

taberan—(n.) digestion

taer—(adj.) straight, level or steady; also forthright, straightforward

tahni—(adj.) clean

tai—(adj.) true (plural is *tain*)

Tai'daishar—(n.) Lord of Glory (literally, the True Glory or True Blood of Battle); also, the name of Rand's horse

tain—(adj.) plural of *tai*

Tain Shari—(n.) True Bloods: Aiel warrior society

tai'shar—(n.) true blood; used, e.g., in *Tai'shar Manetheren!* True Blood of Manetheren! (a greeting of honor used in the Borderlands)

taishite—(v.) favor

tamu—(n.) stamp

tan—(n. & adj.) sovereign

tana—(v.) get

tanilji—(n.) insect

tar—(n.) tower

tarasin—(n.) tower of man; name of palace in Ebou Dar

tarbun—(n.) hat

tarmon—(adj.) final, last, ultimate

Tarmon Gai'don—(n.) the Last Battle (has passed into everyday use; no longer italicized); from the Prophecies of the Dragon

Tar Valon—(n.) literally, "tower that guards"

tashi—(adj.) ready

taskel—(n.) reason

tasu—(v.) make

tatatoun—(n.) instrument

tati—(n.) voice

ta'veren—(n.) those who cause the fabric of the Pattern to bend around them, changing the weave; literally, "pattern, those who alter or are tied to"

tcheran—(n.) an ancient game, having a board and pieces called High Counselor, Counselors and Spires

tebout—(adj.) probable

tefara—(n.) record

Tel'aran'rhiod—(n.) The Unseen World, World of Dreams; a term used by Aes Sedai

telio—(adj.) transparent

ter—(prefix) refers to a limited or specific application

ter'angreal—(n.) a tool made to perform a specific function using the One Power; some require channeling to energize, others not

terta—(v.) rub

tezra—(adj.) gray

thamel—(adj.) young, or pertaining to youth

thaz—(prep.) at

theini—(n.) trousers

thorain—(n.) loss

thorat—(n.) coat

ti—(prep.) to

tia—(prep.) to; to the

tiel—(adv. & prep.) about

tiest—(n.) head

tiganza—(n.) Tinkers' dance

timari—(n.) skin

t'ingshen—(n.) treebrother; a compound word that is used in a formal address to an Ogier, which literally means "to you—representative of something most important (i.e., the tree)—in brotherhood"

tinto—(n.) wall

tipakati—(n.) selection

tippat—(n.) plate

tirast—(v.) pull

t'mat—(n.) a red fruit, from the Aiel Waste

toh—(n.) obligation/duty; a term used by Aiel

tolin—(adj.) stiff

tom—(prep.) among

tongel—(n. & adj.) secret

toopan—(adj.) short

topito—(n.) direction

to'raken—(n.) a huge, exotic flying animal of the Seanchan

torian—(n. & adj.) silver

torkat—(v.) touch

torm—(n.) Seanchan exotic animal, a cross between a horse-sized cat and a lizard

torreale—(n., adj. & adv.) north

totah—(adj. & adv.) far

toulat—(n.) copy

tovya—(v.) roll

trefon—(n.) system

treyat—(adj.) three, a quantifier of material objects

treye—(adj.) three, descriptive of the immaterial, such as ideas, arguments or propositions *tsag*—(interjection) bollocks; an obscenity uttered by Sammael

tsang—(adj.) despised

tsatsi—(n.) bottle

tsinas—(n. & v.) brake

tsingu—(n. & v.) honor

tsorovan—(n.) a storm, or a smaller storm

Tsorovan'm'hael—(n.) Storm Leader; the name Taim gave Asha'man Gedwyn

tuatha—(n.) traveler; one who moves from place to place; can be a vagabond

Tuatha'an—(n.) the Traveling People

tuhat—(suffix) denotes thousands (*yat/ye* suffix is dropped above teens); e.g., *tre'tuhat* = three thousand

tuhat—(adj.) one thousand

tumasen—(adj.) safe

tumerest—(n.) bulb

tunga—(n.) point

tyagani—(n.) respect

tyaku—(v.) keep

ubriva—(n.) surprise

ubunto—(n.) animal

udiya—(adj.) clear

uglat—(v.) smash

uiwa—(adj.) good

uldatein—(n.) division

umeil—(v.) seem

undacar—(n.) plane

ungost—(n.) finger

unyat—(adj. & adv.) late

upendar—(n.) net

urkros—(n.) egg

ursta—(v.) fix

urstae—(adj.) fixed

usont—(n.) tray

uttat—(v.) slip

uvaal—(n.) leg

vaakaja—(n.) sense

vadin—(n.) bar/barrier

vaeku—(v.) station

vaesht—(n. & conj.) while

vakar—(v.) move

valdar—(n.) guard

Valdar Cuebeyari—(n.) the Heart Guard; literally, the Guard of the Heart (of the Nation/People/Land)

valon—(v.) guard

varkol—(n.) sheep

varma—(n.) ray

vartan—(n.) glass

vasen—(n.) arrow

vasen'cierto—(n.) arrow of time; idiomatic phrase which literally means "arrow enduring"

vastri—(n. & v.) rule

vavaya—(n.) flight

veel—(n.) ink

velach—(n.) receipt

velin—(n.) feather

velu—(v.) end

veren—(n.) those who cause change or are tied to

veshan—(n.) way

vesna—(n.) spring

vetan—(n.) seed

vezo—(n.) chalk

vhool—(n.) basket

viboin—(n.) pocket

vid—(prep.) with

vidhel—(n.) law

vidnu—(v.) sort

viliso—(v.) fold

vin—(n.) promise

vlafael—(n.) government

vlagh—(n.) field

vodish—(n. & v.) judge

vokosh—(n.) hair

vol—(n.) father(s) or sire(s), specific to a male who has used brutal means, i.e., a rapist *vovok*—(n.) wolf

vraak—(v.) drain

vrang—(adj.) cruel

vream—(n.) shock

vron—(n.) watcher(s)

vronne—(v.) watch

vyashak—(n.) organization

vyavi—(n.) writing

vyen—(v.) fade

vyropat—(n., adj., adv. & prep.)
  opposite

wabunen—(n.) connection

wadlian—(adj.) simple

wafal—(n. & adj.) hanging

wagg—(n.) nerve

wahati—(n.) porter

waji—(n. & adv.) now

wakaput—(n.) ship

wanda—(v.) match

wansho—(n.) builders; Shienaran
  term for the Ogier

wapro—(v.) cover

warat—(n.) branch

washdor—(adj.) wise

wastin—(n.) spoon

watari—(n.) decision

wek—(prep.) off

weladhi—(n.) family

welakai—(n. & adv.) tomorrow

werstom—(n.) food

whado—(adj.) fertile

whakatu—(v.) increase

whandin—(n.) event

whudra—(n. & v.) regret

widon—(adv., prep. & conj.) after

wishti—(n.) sign

witapa—(n.) meal

wixi—(n.) pot

worshi—(n.) machine

wot—(pron. & adj.) that

woudem—(adj.) loose

wuseta—(n.) card

xazzi—(adj.) rough

xelt—(adj.) sharp

xentro—(n.) sand

xeust—(n.) side

xurzan—(n.) representative

ya—(suffix) means "my own"

yaanaho—(n.) competition

yaati—(adj.) physical

yabbeth—(adj.) common

yabedin—(n.) committee

yak—(conj.) than

yalait—(n. & adj.) expert

yalu—(n. & v.) name

yamar—(n.) edge

yappa—(adj.) kind

yasipa—(v.) rest

yatanel—(n.) story

yaso—(adj.) cheap

yazpa—(n. & v.) snow

ye—(pron.) I (sometimes used as
  an exclamatory fragment)

yedcost—(n.) brick

yeel—(n.) carriage

yekko—(n.) dust

yohini—(v.) damage

youna—(v.) let

youst—(n.) ice

yugol—(adj.) broken

yuntar—(n.) boy

zafar—(adj.) yellow

zaffi—(v.) complete

zahert—(adj.) elastic

zalabadh—(n.) pipe

zaleen—(adj.) soft

zamon—(n.) total darkness

zanda—(n. & adj.) cold

zanzi—(adj.) happy

zara—(n.) a board game played by
  followers of the Dark One, the pieces
  of which are live human beings

zarin—(n.) degree

zavilat—(n.) will

zazit—(conj.) though

zela—(n.) salt

zeltain—(n.) need

zemai—(n.) a staple grain, from the Aiel Waste

zemliat—(n.) parcel

zemya—(n.) room

zengar—(adj.) narrow

zheshi—(n.) argument

zhoh—(n.) hook

zhoub—(n.) earth

zialin—(adj.) certain

zinik—(n.) stitch

zintabar—(n.) poison

zipan—(n.) powder

zladtar—(n.) market

zomara—(n.) zombie-like creations of Aginor, used as servants

zoppen—(adj.) wet

zurye—(n.) grass

zyntam—(n.) error

OLD TONGUE PHRASES

Al Caldazar!—For the Red Eagle!

Al Chalidholara Malkier!—For my sweet land Malkier!

Al dival, al kiserai, al mashi!—For light, glory, and love!

Al Ellisande—For the Rose of the Sun!

Bajad drovja—Spawn of a beldam

Carai an Caldazar! Al Caldazar!—For the honor of the Red Eagle! For the Red Eagle!

Carai an Ellisande! Al Ellisande!—For the honor of the Rose of the Sun! For the Rose of the Sun!

Carai an manshimaya Tylin. Carai an manshimaya Nalesean. Carai an manshimaya ayend'an!—Honor of my blade for Tylin. Honor of my blade for Nalesean. Honor of my blade for the fallen!

Desye gavane cierto cuendar isain carentin—A resolute heart is worth ten arguments. Literally: Ten (arguments) what a resolute heart is worth.

Devoriska nolvae. Al ciyat dalae.—What was asked is given. The price is paid.

Deyeniye, dyu ninte concion ca'lyet ye—Majesty, by your summons do I come.

Dovie'andi se tovya sagain— "It's time to roll the dice," the motto of the Band. Literally: The dice themselves to roll it is time.

Ghiro feal dae'vin lormae; ghiro o'vin gemarisae—Thus is our treaty written; thus is agreement made. Literally: Thus our treaty is written; thus agreement is made.

Kiserai ti Wansho!—Glory to the Builders!

Kiserai ti Wansho hei—Always glory to the Builders

Kodome Calichniye ga ni Aes Sedai hei—Here is always welcome for Aes Sedai.

Los caba'drin!—Horsemen forward!

Los Valdar Cuebiyari!—The Heart Guard will advance! Literally: Forward Guard of the Heart (of the Nation)!

Mia ayende, Aes Sedai! Caballein misain ye! Inde muagdhe Aes Sedai misain ye! Mia ayende!—Release me, Aes Sedai! I am a free man! I am no Aes Sedai meat! Release me! Literally: Me release, Aes Sedai! Free man am I! No meat of Aes Sedai am I! Me release!

Mia dovienya nesodhin soende—Luck carry me through. Literally: me luck through (this) carry.

Mordero daghain pas duente cuebiyar!—My heart holds no fear of death! Literally, Death fear none holds my heart!

Muad'drin tia dar allende caba'drin rhadiem!—Infantry prepare to pass cavalry forward! Literally: Infantry to forward pass cavalry prepare!, or Footmen to forward pass horsemen prepare!

Nardes vasen'cierto ain; sind vyen loviyagae—Thought is the arrow of time; memories never fade. Literally: Thought the-arrow-of-time is; never fade memories.

Ninte calichniye no domashita—Literally: Your welcome me warms.

Nosane iro gavane domorakoshi, Diynen'd'ma'purvene?—Speak we what language, Sounder of the (great) Horn?

Sa souvraya niende misain ye—I am lost in my own mind. Literally: In my own mind lost am I.

Sene sovya caba'donde ain dovienya—Luck is a horse to ride like any other. Literally: Like any other/another horse to ride is luck.

Suravye ninto manshima taishite—Peace favor your sword. Literally: Peace your sword favor.

Tia avende alantin—Brother to the Trees; Treebrother. Literally: To the trees brother. A formal term for the Ogier.

Tia mi aven Moridin isainde vadin—The grave is no bar to my call. Literally: To my call the Grave (death) is no bar/barrier.

Tsingu ma choba—You honor this unworthy one. Literally translates as "honor you give to the unworthy one before you."

Tsingu ma choshih, T'ingshen—You honor me, Treebrother. Literally translates as "honor you give to the (humble) one before you."

Old Wagonright Road. A road near Tar Valon; if some of Bryne's troops had gone down it, Gawyn and the Younglings would have attacked them.

Olver. A Cairhienin orphan adopted by Mat and the Band of the Red Hand. About ten years old, he appeared younger, with very dark hair and dark eyes. Short and pale with a piping voice and a toothy grin, he was not a pretty kid, having a mouth that was much too wide and ears that were far too big for his face. But he had a natural eye for horses, and they were taken with him. Olver was also precociously flirtatious with women, many of whom found his manner to be cute. His father was killed by the Shaido, making him suspicious of all Aiel, and his mother died while they were refugees; he buried her himself, where there were wildflowers growing. He loved to play Snakes and Foxes, especially with Noal.

Mat first encountered Olver in Maerone; Olver sat on Lord Paers' horse, and Paers threatened to wring his neck, but Mat dissuaded Paers. Mat asked Edorion to take care of Olver, and find someone who could look after him; he did, but Olver decided that the woman wanted coin more than a seventh child to look after. He followed the Band as they headed south, with Master Burdin feeding him in return for Olver's help caring for his horses. When Mat discovered that Olver had followed, he gave him two gold crowns; Olver said that he was not a beggar, and Mat told him that he was paying him to be his messenger.

Olver went with Mat to Salidar and then on to Ebou Dar, where he took up horse racing with a little help from Nalesean. Riselle let Olver go out just before the Aes Sedai went to the Kin's farm to use the Bowl of the Winds; Mat, Thom, Juilin and the members of the Band stayed to look for him, and were caught in Ebou Dar when the Seanchan arrived. Olver accompanied Mat when he escaped Ebou Dar and joined Luca's show, and provided important information about how to enter the Tower of Ghenjei for the rescue of Moiraine; he had learned it from Birgitte. About the same time that Mat was rescuing Moiraine, Olver and Talmanes won a game of Snakes and Foxes. Olver found and opened Verin's letter to Mat and alerted the Band to the Trolloc invasion of Caemlyn.

Olver accompanied Faile's caravan on her mission to return the Horn of Valere to Mat in the Last Battle; they ended up in the Blight. After they returned to Merrilor through subterfuge, posing as a Darkfriend caravan delivering supplies, Aravine betrayed them to the forces of the Shadow, and Faile gave Olver the Horn and told him to get it to Mat. The Trollocs cornered him, and he blew the Horn, summoning the Heroes to fight in the Last Battle. The deceased Noal, who was really Jain Farstrider and a Hero of the Horn, appeared and saved him. Olver and Mat flew to Shayol Ghul on a *raken*; they were shot down but survived, and Olver blew the Horn there as well. After the Last Battle, Birgitte persuaded Olver to take the Horn and drop it in the ocean so that it and he could not be used by those seeking its benefit.

Oman Dahar. A nation that arose after the Trolloc Wars.

Omerna, Abdel. *See* Abdel Omerna

Oncala. The granddaughter of Rand and Aviendha, seen in Aviendha's viewings of the future in Rhuidean. Oncala was an ambitious Maiden of the Spear, although she intended to give up the spear and marry Hehyal. She was very proud of being of the lineage of the Dragon, and resented Andorans being able to claim it as well. She and Hehyal tricked Talana, the Queen of Andor, into joining the battle against the Seanchan.

Ondin, Daerid. *See* Daerid Ondin

One Power. The power drawn from the True Source; women used *saidar*, the female half of it, and men used *saidin*, the male half. The vast majority of people were completely unable to learn to channel the One Power. A very small number could be taught to channel, and an even tinier number had the ability inborn. For these few there was no need to be taught; they would touch the True Source and channel the Power whether they wanted to or not, perhaps even without realizing what they were doing. This inborn ability usually manifested itself in late adolescence or early adulthood. If control was not taught, or self-learned, which was extremely difficult, with a success rate of only one in four, death was certain. From the Time of Madness, no man was able to channel the Power without eventually going completely, horribly mad; and then, even if he had learned some control, dying from a wasting sickness that caused the sufferer to rot alive, a sickness arising, as did the madness, from the Dark One's taint on *saidin*. For a woman the death that came without control of the Power was less horrible, but it was death just the same. Aes Sedai searched for girls with the inborn ability as much to save their lives as to increase Aes Sedai numbers, and for men with it in order to stop the terrible things they would inevitably do with the Power in their madness.

One-Hand, Caar. *See* Caar al Thorin al Toren

Oneness. The term Lanfear used for "the void" as described by Rand, the process by which he cleared his mind of thought and emotion, giving him an edge in the use of weapons, and a place from which he could draw upon *saidin*. It was called *ko'di* in Malkier. *See also* flame and the void *and* void, the

oosquai. A drink made from *zemai*. It looked like faintly brown-tinged water, tasted almost like it and kicked like a mule.

Orande, Faolain. *See* Faolain Orande

Orander. One of the kings in the gleeman tale "Mara and the Three Foolish Kings."

Oratar. A bald member of the Children of the Light who was present when Perrin first met the Whitecloaks in the *stedding* where Hawkwing's capital was to be. He later testified about it at Perrin's trial.

Orban, Lord. A braggart Hunter of the Horn whom Moiraine and her company encountered at Wayland's Forge Inn in Remen, Altara. He and his fellow Hunter Gann thought that the Horn of Valere was in the Forest of Shadows. They encountered Gaul and Sarien, killed Sarien and captured Gaul, although they lost several men and were injured in doing so. Orban's horse was named Lion.

Ordeith. Old Tongue for "Wormwood"; it was one of the names adopted by Padan Fain.

Oren Dautry. A Westwood farmer who was Rand and Tam's nearest neighbor. Lean and tall, he was a shameless borrower. He joined Perrin's army at Malden.

Ortis. A gravelly-voiced squadman in the Mayener Winged Guards. Ortis was in his middle years, with one cheek burned and the other having a scar that pulled up the corner of his mouth.

Osan'gar. 1) The name given to Aginor when he was resurrected by the Dark One and given a stolen male body. He slipped in among the Asha'man under the name Corlan Dashiva to be an assistant to Mazrim Taim, who thought he was only a high-ranking Darkfriend. That did not suit Osan'gar greatly. He wore both the sword and the Dragon. His original purpose there was to keep a close eye on the gathering of men who could channel. His strength level was ++2, close behind Lews Therin and Ishamael. Appearing to be a plain man in his middle years, he often stared at nothing, and appeared to be talking to himself. He laughed to himself sometimes, at nothing. Although he wasn't skinny, the way he moved—hesitant, creeping, with hands folded at his waist—made him seem so. His hair was dark and lank.

Osan'gar and Aran'gar met Shaidar Haran and were acting on instructions directly from him. Osan'gar was chosen out to accompany Rand after Dumai's Wells. He came into the open, after a manner of speaking, in the attempt to kill Rand in Cairhien. He and the Asha'man with him were forced to flee, and Taim was ordered to put the names of the men Rand saw, including Corlan Dashiva, on the list to be hunted down and executed.

He was killed by Elza Penfell during the fight at Shadar Logoth; she did not know that he was one of the Forsaken. *See also* Aginor *and* Corlan Dashiva

2) In the Old Tongue, *osan'gar* meant the left-hand dagger in a form of dueling that was popular during the time leading up to the War of Power; both daggers were poisoned, and both participants usually died.

Osana, Lady. A Domani noblewoman. She was not young, but had a pale beauty and elegance that would last all her life. Osana hunted for men or power, and her trophies were numerous and noteworthy. The "hunts" that took place at her lodge would have raised eyebrows even in the capital. Rodel Ituralde met with nobles under the White Ribbon of truce at that lodge.

Osana disappeared early in the troubles in Arad Doman and was made one of Graendal's servants. When Sammael's gateway sliced the male servant, Rashan, in two, she ran to see to the removal of the carpet.

Oselle. An Aes Sedai during the Breaking who had long black hair; she helped make the Eye of the World.

Osendrelle Erinin. One of the two branches of the River Erinin as it split to flow around the island of Tar Valon.

Osenrein. One of the bridge towns outside of Tar Valon, on the bank of the Osendrelle Erinin.

Osiellin. A Cairhienin noble House. Its High Seat was Amondrid. *See* Amondrid *and* Belevaere Osiellin

Ospenya, Tamra. *See* Tamra Ospenya

Ostrein Bridge. A bridge from Tar Valon leading to the village of Ostrein and the road to the south.

Otarin. A Hero of the Horn who appeared at Falme. When Rand saw him, he became aware of all Otarin's names through the Ages, including those he didn't recognize as names, such as Oscar.

Outside. The Ogier name for the world beyond the *stedding*.

Oval Lecture Hall. A chamber in the White Tower with a wide scrollwork crown running beneath a gently domed blue ceiling painted with white clouds, and rows of polished wooden benches. A dais was at the front of the hall, with doors behind the dais. Tamra addressed the Accepted there to tell them of her bounty on babes born near Tar Valon.

Owein. One of Alanna's Warders. He was killed by Whitecloaks in the Two Rivers; they caught him crossing an open field. Alanna felt every arrow that struck him.

Owl and Oak. The symbol of House Taravin in Andor.

Owyn. Thom Merrilin's nephew from eastern Andor, near Aringill, the last of Thom's blood kin. Owyn could channel. He held off the madness for three years, channeling only when needed and to help his village, although his neighbors said that in the last year he was acting oddly. Red sisters found him; Elaida was involved in some manner. Instead of taking him to Tar Valon, they gentled him on the spot. Thom arrived to try to save him, but Owyn had already begun to decline. Left to the untender mercies of his neighbors, he died in 985 NE; his wife followed him into the grave in under a month. Owyn was perhaps the last man to die as a result of the male channeler pogrom, known as the Vileness.

P

Paaran Disen. A city that thrived during the Age of Legends and was the seat of the central government, the location of the Hall of Servants. The Gates of Paaran Disen were the site of a victory of Lews Therin over Ishamael during the War of the Shadow.

Pact of the Griffin. An alliance formed after the Last Battle, seen in Aviendha's visions of the future in Rhuidean. It was composed of Andor, the Two Rivers, Mayene, Ghealdan and Saldaea; its sign was a creature with the head of a lion, the body of a wolf and hawk wings, with three stars above and three fish below.

Pact, the. 1) A term used in a greeting by Agelmar in Fal Dara: "here is the watch kept, here is the Pact maintained." 2) An agreement between the Ogier and Aiel. Among other things, it prohibited the Aiel from fighting inside a *stedding* and on the way to or from a *stedding*.

Padan Fain. A peddler who regularly visited the Two Rivers. A skinny little Lugarder with a big nose and wide ears, he was in fact a Darkfriend. In 995 NE a Fade took Fain to Shayol Ghul, where he met Ba'alzamon and was turned into a hound to find the Dragon Reborn. Fain, sent back out to hunt, stayed in the Two Rivers an entire week that year, which was unusual. He was then taken back to Shayol Ghul, where the information he had gathered was distilled. The next year when he visited the Two Rivers, he was able to determine that the one he was seeking was one of three young men. The following year, he was told to mark those that he had identified, and Trollocs were sent to Emond's Field.

After the Trolloc attack, Fain followed Rand and the others to Shadar Logoth, where Mordeth tried to take him; he resisted, becoming a hybrid of the two. Fain then followed Rand as far as Fal Dara, where Fain was caught and put in a dungeon. When Moiraine interviewed him there, she realized how evil he had become. He escaped with the help of Ingtar and a Fade, and stole the dagger from Shadar Logoth and the Horn of Valere. After killing the Fade, he made his way to Toman Head and Falme, where Turak confiscated the Horn of Valere and the dagger.

He later joined with the Whitecloaks in Amador, calling himself Ordeith, Old Tongue for "Wormwood." He led the Whitecloaks to the Two Rivers, having convinced them that it was full of Darkfriends; his real goal was to harrow the area and draw Rand to him. He killed Perrin's family, but was thwarted in his main purpose. Next he made his way to Tar Valon, where he spoke with Elaida about Rand and stole the dagger again.

He next went to Cairhien, where he became closely associated with Toram Riatin as Riatin's advisor, calling himself Jeral Mordeth. After Rand showed up there, Fain wounded him with the Shadar Logoth dagger in the fog that descended on the rebel camp outside Cairhien when the bubble of evil struck. He knew that Rand didn't die, because he could still sense him. Rand put a price on the head of Padan Fain, and publicly linked the name to Jeral Mordeth. Meanwhile, Riatin thought the fog was Rand's doing, and that Rand had scuppered his chances for the Sun Throne. Due to Fain's influence, he had hated Rand before; later he wanted nothing more than Rand's death, and was delighted that Fain could find and track Rand.

Fain followed Rand to Far Madding in company with Toram Riatin and went after him, incidentally killing a Darkfriend Asha'man who was hunting Rand, just because Fain felt that Rand was his to kill. Rand and Lan deliberately walked into a trap they thought had been set by Gedwyn and Torval only to find the Asha'man dead. The trap had been set by Fain and Toram Riatin instead. Lan killed Toram, but Fain managed to escape from Rand.

Fain's newer abilities included inducing waking nightmares and setting traps like the one that nearly caught Rand on Blue Carp Street in Far Madding. He could recognize Darkfriends on sight, even someone who had only thought of swearing to the Shadow. To him, it was as if they had a sooty mark on their foreheads.

Fain had an influence over Myrddraal and Trollocs, enough that he could command them and do them harm, if he so desired. On the lead up to the Last Battle, Fain gathered an army of Trollocs in the Blight, and headed for Shayol Ghul.

During the Last Battle, Fain transformed into Shaisam, a consumer of souls. His Trollocs, whose souls he had taken, fought at Thakan'dar, a distraction from his real purpose, to find and kill Rand. The more souls he consumed, the more his being became entwined with a fog-like substance that surrounded him, making him harder and harder to find and kill. He still carried the dagger from Shadar Logoth. But Mat set a trap for him and, immune to the evil from Shadar Logoth, having once been exposed to it, he took the dagger from Fain and stabbed him with it, killing both him and the mist.

Padra. One of Rand and Aviendha's quadruplets, she was seen in Aviendha's viewings of the future in Rhuidean. A Maiden of the Spear, Padra and other Maidens encountered a scouting party and killed some of them before the rest escaped through a gateway. She then attended a meeting and agreed that the Aiel should go to war against the Seanchan.

Padros, Eagan. *See* Eagan Padros

Padry. A servant to Lord Culen and Lord Paers, Murandian Hunters of the Horn. A skinny man wearing a Murandian coat of dark wool, he told Mat that the lords were heroes. He said that Olver was a peasant and was molesting Lord Paers' horse and seemed to think that that was enough reason for Olver's neck to be broken. Mat did not agree, and, after thrashing Paers and Culen with the butt of his spear, told Padry to get them out of town before sunset.

Padwhin, Tuck. *See* Tuck Padwhin

Paedrig. A Hero of the Horn who was called the golden-tongued peacemaker. When Rand saw him, he became aware of all Paedrig's names through the Ages, including those he didn't recognize as names, such as Patrick.

Paendrag. *See* Artur Hawkwing, Berelain sur Paendrag, Luthair Paendrag Mondwin *and* Tuon Athaem Kore Paendrag

Paerish Swar. A great forest on the Almoth Plain, and the site of an abandoned Ogier *stedding*.

Paeron, House. Berelain's noble House in Mayene.

Paers, Lord. A Murandian nobleman who was a Hunter of the Horn. Paers spoke with a Mindean accent, and the Mindeans boasted that they had the worst tempers in Murandy. He was in Maerone with Lord Culen. Olver sat on Paers' horse, and Paers intended to punish Olver by wringing his scrawny neck. Mat disabled Paers by bringing the butt of his spear up sharply between the man's legs; when Culen attempted to draw his sword, Mat pummeled him with his spear butt and ordered their servant Padry to get the two men out of town by sunset.

Paet al'Caar. A Two Rivers man. His wife was Nela and his son Wil; he had another son and two daughters. Part of the mob that confronted Moiraine after the Trolloc attack on Winternight, he was ashamed when it was pointed out that she had Healed Wil's leg. In one of Nynaeve's Accepted test scenarios, Nela went crazy when she found her sons dead in their beds and went around saying that Paet was the Dark One and had killed her boys; in that scenario, Paet hanged himself. Paet helped Perrin in the defense of Emond's Field.

Paetram. A fork-bearded Kandori master merchant whom Mat encountered drinking at an inn in Tear. He told of a rumor saying that the Whitecloaks had gone to the Two Rivers looking for the Dragon Reborn and a Darkfriend with yellow eyes.

Paetram Aybara. Perrin's younger brother; at nine years old, he, along with the rest of his family except Perrin, was murdered by Padan Fain, although the killing was thought to have been done by Trollocs. *See* Aybara clan

Paitar Neramovni Nachiman. King of Arafel, Guardian of the Way and High Seat of House Nachiman. He was born in 937 NE. His younger sister, Kiruna, was Aes Sedai. About 6'2" to 6'3" tall, Paitar was straight-backed and broad-shouldered. He looked strong and could wield a sword with vigor and skill. Paitar had a surprisingly deep, rich voice—a voice to make women's hearts beat faster. His wife Menuki knew he was hers to his bootsoles. His Aes Sedai advisor, Coladara, was uncommitted in the struggle between rebel and loyalist Aes Sedai. Paitar was in possession of a prophecy regarding Rand, made by an Aes Sedai among his ancestors and heard by another ancestor. Easar, Ethenielle, Paitar and Tenobia joined together and left the Borderlands seeking

Rand, and met with Elayne in Braem Wood. When Rand met with the four rulers, Paitar backhanded Rand with a blow that sent him to his knees. In exchange for his Aes Sedai being taught Traveling so that he could take part in the Last Battle, he swore fealty to Rand. He fought alongside Lan at Tarwin's Gap in the Last Battle.

Paitr Conel. A young man and Darkfriend from Market Sheran, Andor. He approached Rand and Mat when they were making their way to Caemlyn; when he grabbed Rand to try to stop him from leaving, Rand broke his nose, causing him to say things that revealed he was a Darkfriend, and an old man in the inn overheard him. Later he approached Morgase in Amador and told her that he and his uncle Torwyn had a plan for her to escape from the Whitecloaks. Trom caught Torwyn, Paitr and others reciting catechisms to the Dark One; they were hanged while Morgase watched.

Paitr do Fearna a'Conn. A Murandian lord who made common cause with the Andor intruders against the rebel Aes Sedai and afterward made a further accommodation with the Andorans. About 5'11" tall, with a medium build, he had dark hair, dark eyes and curled mustaches, which he sometimes yanked violently. At the meeting on the ice with the Andorans and the rebel Aes Sedai, Paitr stood too close to Halima and stared down her dress; she smiled at him warmly.

Palace of the Assemblage. The home of one of the ruling bodies of Illian. It was an Ogier-built structure.

Palan, Haesel. A Murandian rug merchant with whom young Moiraine shared a room at The Gates of Heaven in Canluum. She was plump, had cold feet and snored.

paltron-cloths. Part of an Imperial high general's uniform.

Panarch. A ruler in Tanchico. Once in the past a king or queen had to be balanced by a panarch of the opposite sex; after approximately 500 NE there was a king and a female panarch. The equal of the King in authority, the Panarch was responsible for collecting taxes, customs and duties; he for spending them properly. She controlled the Civil Watch and the courts, except for the High Court, which was the King's. The army was his, except for the Panarch's Legion, which was hers.

Panarch Farede of Tarabon. The first Panarch of Tarabon after the War of the Hundred Years. He adopted and promoted a new calendar, the Farede Calendar, as part of his attempt to make Tarabon the intellectual center of the known world.

Panarch's Circle. An assembly arena in Tanchico that was surrounded by the Panarch's Palace and other buildings. It was located on the Verana, the easternmost hilly peninsula on Tanchico Bay.

Panarch's Legion. The Panarch's armed guard in Tanchico. It consisted of about three thousand men on land and about a thousand to fifteen hundred on ships, when it existed. The latter's primary function was keeping down pirates. Like the Life Guard, it was dispersed by the Seanchan, though many of the survivors were incorporated into levies raised by the Seanchan.

Panarch's Palace. The residence of the Panarch in Tanchico. It was on the Verana, the westernmost hilly peninsula in Tanchico. It had a museum containing many relics of past Ages.

Pansai. The name Aravine assumed when posing as the head of a supply caravan transporting captives to a Trolloc camp at the Field of Merrilor in the Last Battle. She claimed that she was Lifa's business partner and had stabbed Lifa and taken over the run.

Pappil. The name Bayrd used for his paternal grandfather, a stoneworker.

Paral. A major city in the Age of Legends.

paralis-net. Semirhage's name for Cadsuane's hair ornaments.

Parelean. A Tairen man who was a member of *Cha Faile*. He had a square jaw and wore fat-sleeved Tairen coats. Faile considered him the brightest of the lot, ahead of Selande, but she also thought that Camaille and Arrela were quicker of thought than either. He was not one of those sent into Bethal. Parelean was killed by the Shaido when Faile's riding party was attacked.

Parenia Demalle. An Aes Sedai of the Gray Ajah who served as Amyrlin from 817 to 866 NE. Parenia was an Amyrlin of average strength. She was more interested in negotiations and treaties between nations than in the running of the Tower. She still kept fairly good control in order to gain backing for her treaties.

Parentakis, Jander. A member of the Academy of Cairhien. He was working on building a paddlewheel riverboat.

pasties. The name for meat pies in the Age of Legends.

Patrim. A stableboy at Harilin's Leap in Jarra, Ghealdan. He had hay in his hair. When Moiraine, Lan, Loial and Perrin stayed at the inn, Nico and Patrim saw to their horses.

Patrinda. An Aes Sedai of the Red Ajah who guarded Egwene when she was imprisoned by Elaida and visited by Seaine.

Pattern, Great. *See* Great Pattern

Pattern of an Age. Pattern woven by the Wheel of Time from the threads of human lives, referring to the interconnectedness of events, which formed the substance of reality for that Age; also known as Age Lace.

Pattern, Will of the. Stated reason why each reigning monarch of Shara died like clockwork every seven years, suggesting a natural cause, which was far from the truth.

Pavil Geraneos. An Illianer buying gems in Saldaea. He was young, clean-shaven and dark-eyed. He and his partner Jeorg Damentanis were bargaining with Weilin Aldragoran just before Nynaeve arrived to drum up support for Lan. Pavil showed anger at Weilin's offer, which horrified Jeorg.

Pavlara, Janine. *See* Janine Pavlara

Peace, the Dragon's. *See* Dragon's Peace, the

peacetalker. An Aiel trained to guide angry men to ground their spears.

peach. A fruit whose pit could be powdered and used as poison. It was widely, and erroneously, believed that the fruit itself was poison.

Pearman's Lane. A street in Caemlyn, in the New City where a handful of fruit-sellers clung to shops handed down since the days of Ishara.

pecara. Pale wrinkled nuts found in the Waste.

Pedra. An Accepted who remained in the White Tower when the Tower split. About 5'1" to 5'2" tall, she was a wiry woman who looked a little older than Nynaeve. She led Egwene to her room when she first came to the White Tower. Pedra spoke curtly. Egwene didn't like her, probably because of her officiousness. After Pedra told her what she had to do on her first day, Egwene stuck out her tongue at her back. When Pedra served Pevara and Tarna wine and cakes, Pevara thought that she would be raised soon, and Tarna thought that men made her nervous. When the classroom where she was to teach vanished, she was frightened and showed it by being cross with the novices, which was very unusual for her.

Pedron Niall. The Lord Captain Commander of the Children of the Light, he was considered one of the five great captains. Born in Murandy in 911 NE, he fought his first battle as a Whitecloak in 928 NE. The foremost general of the Children of the Light in the Troubles, known to others as the Whitecloak War, Lord Captain Niall set a trap at Soremaine that caught King Stepaneos and would have destroyed his entire army if it were not for the valor of the Companions. By the time of the Aiel War, Niall had become the Lord Captain Commander; he led the Whitecloaks during the war, and was in charge of all the armies of the Grand Alliance on the second day of the Battle of the Shining Walls. All sinew and bone with white hair, he was married in his youth, but his wife died before he rose to power.

Niall sent troops to Almoth Plain; he planned to capture it and raise the nation of Almoth as the seat of the Children of the Light. When he learned of Falme and the Dragon Reborn, he had to change his plans. Niall did not believe that the Last Battle would involve the Dark One breaking free; the Dark One was bound away. To him Rand was a false Dragon, and useful only as a means to drive the nations to unite—a feat beyond him, obviously—to fight an invasion of Trollocs and other Shadowspawn that would come out of the Blight. He firmly believed that Aes Sedai were evil, servants of the Shadow whether they knew it or not, and thought what happened at Falme was an Aes Sedai/Darkfriend scheme. He began spreading rumors of vile things that Rand and Aes Sedai had done so that the populace would come to him to save them. He had Carridin form bands of Dragonsworn to commit atrocities that could be laid at the Dragon Reborn's door.

Padan Fain went to Niall, and convinced him that Rand, Mat and Perrin were Darkfriends—that indeed the Two Rivers was crawling with Darkfriends—and Niall sent Fain there with fifty Children and ordered Valda to send half a legion more. Niall negotiated with Altara and Murandy to cede land to Illian so that Illian would not invade either.

When Niall got Morgase into his grip, he tried to manipulate her; he wanted and needed the additional validation of support from rulers. He wanted Morgase to sign a treaty that would allow the Children to go into Andor with her as a figurehead; it was a key to his plan to bring entire nations behind him. Although Morgase finally signed, Niall postponed his plans because Varadin, the man he had sent to Tanchico, sent word of the troubles there. Abdel Omerna killed Niall on the same day as the Battle of Dumai's Wells as part of a plot with Rhadam Asunawa and Eamon Valda. Valda then killed Omerna.

Pel. A gap-toothed wagon driver drinking at The Good Night's Ride in Lugard, Murandy. He was present when Siuan went to see Mistress Tharne, an eyes-and-ears of the Blue Ajah.

Pel Aydaer. A bald cabinetmaker in Emond's Field who smoked a pipe. When refugees started pouring into the Two Rivers, he had to hire five apprentices. Pel joined Perrin's armies at Malden, and was sent with others on a scouting trip to Cairhien to gather information, since the armies had been out of touch with events farther east for so long.

Pelanna. A Sea Folk Wavemistress and one of the First Twelve. A pink scar ran down the right side of her face, and her tightly curled hair was gray. Pelanna was held by the Seanchan in Ebou Dar, and fled during the Escape. Her honor chain was heavy with medallions, including one for her part in the Escape; her wrist and ankles bore the marks of Seanchan chains. She was at the meeting of the First Twelve in Illian with Logain and there learned of the mass suicide of the Amayar. At the beginning of the meeting, she informed Harine that she had placed a cushion in her chair, and laughed uproariously, but was annoyed when her Windfinder Caire did not laugh as well; when Pelanna laughed, she expected those under her to laugh, too. *See also* Escape, the

Pelateos. The author of *Ponderings*, one of the books that Min read.

Pelden. *See* Naris *and* Sephanie Pelden

Pelivar Coelan. An Andoran man who was High Seat of House Coelan. The sign of his House was the Roses: two red roses, side by side, on a field of horizontal blue and white stripes. It was sometimes called "the Flowers" by housemen. He was 6'3" tall, and lean, with dark hair, which he was losing from the front. He had a surprisingly light voice, but it was strong and usually quite firm, unsurprising in the High Seat of a powerful House. He had daughters old enough to claim the throne. He supported Morgase when she gained the throne; she exiled him under the influence of Rahvin. Aemlyn, Pelivar, Arathelle and Culhan were among the nobles who confronted the rebel Aes Sedai on the ice near the Murandy-Andor border. Pelivar supported Dyelin for the throne, but after Elayne took Caemlyn and Luan and Abelle stood for Trakand, Pelivar did as well.

Pena, Birlen. *See* Birlen Pena

Pena, the falls of. A place where Mat fought Sana Ashraf, from one of his memories of the distant past.

penance. A practice imposed on Aes Sedai as needed. Penance was divided into four sorts: Labor, Deprivation, Mortification of the Flesh and Mortification of the Spirit. For sisters, the last was much more likely to come in a self-imposed penance than one imposed by another agency. Despite what much of the world saw as Aes Sedai arrogance, the belief among Aes Sedai, by and large, was that they had to maintain a proper and fitting balance between pride and humility. The purpose of penance, officially, at least, was not so much to punish as to remind the sister of the proper balance and help her to restore it.

Penances were most often imposed upon or taken on by sisters for a perceived personal failing or lack. That is, a sister who failed to carry out a task as it should have been might receive a penance; but officially, at least, it would have been not for the failure in the task, but for whatever personal lack or shortcoming was revealed by failure in the task. While penance supposedly was in no way a punishment, it could be imposed on a sister as one just the same, by the Amyrlin, by the Hall, or by one's own Ajah. There were rare circumstances under which a penance could be imposed by another Ajah.

When a penance was imposed by another, the terms could be set by whoever imposed it or the sister could be required to set the terms herself, according to the circumstances.

A sister could take a penance on herself, because of some wrong she believed she had done, for example, or because of some perceived personal failing, perhaps some flaw that she had allowed to get the better of her, as she saw it. That was done to forestall the imposition of a penance from without, but also from a true remorse.

Although a penance and the punishment handed out to novices or Accepted were often identical on the surface, in the eyes of Aes Sedai they were very different. This apparent similarity between the punishments given novices and Accepted and the penances suffered by sisters had another likeness. As one of the Accepted was often punished more harshly than a novice for the same offense, so a sister's penance was frequently harsher, taking into account the offense, than any punishment given to novice or Accepted. Though of course the penance was not a punishment, officially.

A typical penance was a period of rustication, laboring on a farm and often confinement to the farm's boundaries. Physical and/or menial labor of various other sorts were also used frequently.

Although physical chastisement (Mortification of the Flesh) was allowed as penance for sisters—and indeed, in times past, was not unusual at all—it was also prescribed under Tower law for certain offenses even by sisters. In most cases it was chosen when the penance had to be over quickly for some reason—or if self-imposed, when the sister could not or would not give time to something longer—and it was seldom publicized, though sisters often learned of it, or might even be informed in some circumstances.

In most cases Mortification of the Flesh was a fairly secret affair. It often was carried out by the Mistress of Novices, though in some circumstances it could be done by a sister appointed to the task, or by the head of one's Ajah. Most often in a self-imposed penance using Mortification of the Flesh, one asked the Mistress of Novices to provide the service; for one thing, she would most assuredly keep it secret—or at least she would not herself spread the information unless the requirement was there for her to do so—and for another, it was customary for Mortification of the Flesh to be a self-imposed penance. These penances could be served in the Mistress of Novices' study, or more often, when self-imposed, in one's own apartments.

The penance of being birched in the Grand Hall before the assembled sisters was something reserved for a crime on the level of rebellion or treason.

Penance served by Aes Sedai was almost always kept semi-secret—officially, anyway. Every effort was made to keep the fact that an Aes Sedai was serving one from notice, with the possible exception of other sisters. Even if circumstances were such that somebody might suspect, they usually did not know for certain. The dignity of the White Tower was to be preserved, and nothing could interfere with the dignity of Aes Sedai in the eyes of anyone not Aes Sedai.

Pendaloan. A lesser noble House in Tear. Its High Seat was Algarin. *See* Algarin *and* Emarin Pendaloan

Pendar, House. A noble House in Andor. Its High Seat was Lord Abelle, its sign the Stars: three six-pointed golden stars, one above and two below, on a field of seven vertical red and white stripes.

Penfell, Elza. *See* Elza Penfell

Pensenor, Aubrem. *See* Aubrem Pensenor

People of the Dragon. The secret name for the Aiel, hearkening back to the day when the Da'shain Aiel served the Aes Sedai and observed the Way of the Leaf; in prophecy, the Stone of Tear would fall when the People of the Dragon came. Later it was sometimes used to refer to those who followed the Dragon Reborn. *See* Da'shain Aiel

Peral Torval. A Taraboner Asha'man who was a crony of Taim, and a Darkfriend. About thirty when he went to the Black Tower, he was 6'1" tall, with dark eyes, a sharp nose and a sneering mouth. On one of Rand's visits to the Black Tower, Torval challenged Rand and was knocked out by Taim. Torval was at Dumai's Wells. After the attack on Rand in Cairhien failed, he was placed on the deserters list at the Black Tower. He was killed by Padan Fain in Far Madding.

Perfumed Quarter. The smelly port district of Illian.

Perival Mantear. A very young Andoran who was High Seat of House Mantear. The Anvil was the sigil of the House, a silver anvil on a field quartered blue and red. He was born circa 988 NE, but he was perceptive beyond his years.

About 5'4" tall, and pretty, with golden hair, he wore a sword that looked too long for him, as it dragged on the floor. He was one of four young nobles Dyelin brought to help Elayne win the throne; the others were Branlet Gilyard, Catalyn Haevin and Conail Northan. The four together brought over three thousand armsmen, mainly crossbowmen and halberdmen. Perival's guardian, his uncle Willim, was bedridden with age, but he told Dyelin to take Perival to Caemlyn, and he told Perival that he must be brave and uphold the honor of both Mantear and Andor, which Perival very much wanted to do. Elayne thought that Lord Willim had done good work with Perival. He wanted to help fight when Elayne was kidnapped. Dyelin took him to the Far Madding Gate during Arymilla's attack on the city, but made sure that he was nowhere near the front.

Perival and Lir met with Elayne about the Trolloc invasion of Caemlyn.

Perrin Goldeneyes. The name that some called Perrin the warrior, inspired by his wolf-like eyes. *See also* Perrin t'Bashere Aybara

Perrin t'Bashere Aybara. A young *ta'veren* Emond's Field man. He was born in 978 NE, the son of Con and Joslyn. He had a younger brother, Paetram, and two younger sisters, Deselle and Adora. When he was twelve years old, he was apprenticed to Master Luhhan, the blacksmith. His banner was a red wolf's head on a red-bordered field of white. Approximately 6'1" tall and weighing about 235 pounds, he was heavy enough in the arms, chest and shoulders to make his waist look narrower than it was, and to make him appear shorter than he was. He had brown eyes and brown, curly hair, worn almost to his shoulders, and a short, curly beard that he wore because Faile liked it. Perrin had a thin, horizontal scar uncomfortably close to his left eye. A quiet man, he was very slow to anger, though his anger could be implacable once roused. He moved slowly and thought carefully by choice; as a boy he realized that he was larger and stronger than most of the other children and could hurt somebody by accident if he wasn't careful, a feeling which stayed with him as an adult. Perrin liked calm and peace, and didn't like to argue. He thought that he had no facility with words, and in truth, women in particular often tied him in knots with talk. Under any normal circumstances, the notion of violence toward women was abhorrent to him. He could argue with women, certainly, but like many big men who were subconsciously afraid of letting go of their anger, he found shouting at a woman to be extremely difficult; under most circumstances, he would rather just walk away. His first instinct with an angry woman, especially if she shouted, was to try soothing words.

In 998 NE, Perrin saw a stranger in a black cloak on a black horse; his friends Rand al'Thor and Mat Cauthon did as well. On the next night, Winternight, Trollocs attacked Emond's Field. Moiraine Sedai and her Warder Lan were visiting, and they helped fight off the attack. Since the attack was focused on the homes of Perrin, Rand and Mat, Moiraine persuaded them that it was necessary for them to leave Emond's Field. They attempted to leave secretly,

but Egwene al'Vere realized that they were up to something and went along, and the gleeman who was in town for Bel Tine joined as well. Before Perrin left, Master Luhhan gave him an axe that someone had ordered but not paid for.

The group started for Tar Valon, with Draghkar, Myrddraal and Trollocs chasing them; Perrin, Rand and Mat began being troubled by dreams involving a man with eyes of fire who called himself Ba'alzamon. Moiraine and Lan were able to keep them just a step ahead of the Shadowspawn but eventually they were forced to shelter in Shadar Logoth; when against all expectations Trollocs entered the ruined city, the group gathered itself to flee. Mashadar, the deadly fog, appeared, and the group was separated. Perrin escaped the city by riding into the River Arinelle and swimming across; his horse ran away. The next day he found Egwene and Bela, her mare; they began making their way toward Caemlyn, but were not entirely certain of the way. They encountered Elyas, who offered to help them. He introduced them to his friends, who were wolves, and told Perrin that the wolves said that Perrin could talk to wolves as well. Perrin realized that it was true, but tried to fight it.

Elyas took Perrin and Egwene to a Tuatha'an caravan, with whom they traveled for some time. When Elyas decided that it was time to leave, they headed south; soon they encountered huge flocks of ravens that were looking for them. In the nick of time, they arrived at a deserted *stedding*, but soon afterward Whitecloaks appeared. Perrin and Egwene tried to hide, but they were seen. Wolves came to their aid, and the Whitecloaks killed Hopper, a wolf Perrin had talked with. Feeling Hopper's death, Perrin became enraged and killed two Whitecloaks. Perrin and Egwene were captured; the leader of the Whitecloaks, Geofram Bornhald, told them he was taking them to Caemlyn for trial.

Moiraine, Lan and Nynaeve rescued them, and they set off for Caemlyn. Perrin's eyes had become yellow by that point, and he gained other benefits from being a wolfbrother: keener-than-human senses of sight, hearing and smell, and the ability to visit the wolf dream, which was also known as *Tel'aran'rhiod*.

In Caemlyn the party was reunited with Rand and Mat, and gained a new member: Loial, an Ogier. The party went through the Ways to Fal Dara, and then on into the Blight, searching for the Green Man and the Eye of the World. They found both, but Aginor and Balthamel, two of the Forsaken, attacked. Perrin's group prevailed and acquired the Horn of Valere, the Dragon banner and a broken seal for the Dark One's prison. They returned to Fal Dara, but Trollocs and Fades attacked and stole the Horn. Perrin, Loial, Rand and Mat joined a group of Shienaran soldiers to pursue those who stole it; Rand, Loial and Hurin, the sniffer who could smell the trail, vanished, and Perrin used his wolfbrother talents to lead the rest in pursuit. Rand was able to take the Horn back, but it was stolen again by Padan Fain, who took it to Falme. Perrin, Rand and the rest followed using a Portal Stone, but something went wrong and they saw all the lives that they could have lived and lost four months in the process. They eventually made it to Falme, and took the Horn again. The Seanchan and the Whitecloaks were battling; Mat blew the Horn and they all managed to escape, with the exception of Ingtar, a Shienaran solder who was also a Darkfriend.

The group wintered in the Mountains of Mist; in the spring, Rand left secretly. Moiraine, Lan, Perrin and Loial set off after him. Along the way, Perrin freed an Aiel, Gaul, from a cage; the two of them killed a number of Whitecloaks. Perrin also met Zarine Bashere; she insisted on being called Faile and joining their party. They followed Rand to Tear. There, a trap intended to seize Moiraine in *Tel'aran'rhiod* instead caught Faile; Perrin went into the wolf dream and rescued her. Rand took the Stone of Tear, and Perrin and Faile stayed there for a while. Perrin attracted the unwanted attention of Berelain, the beautiful First of Mayene.

Perrin heard of Whitecloaks troubling the Two Rivers, and he and Faile went back there; Perrin learned that his entire family had been slaughtered by Trollocs, although in truth they were killed by Padan Fain. The Whitecloaks were holding the Luhhans and the Cauthons prisoner; Perrin gathered a group of men, sneaked into the Whitecloak camp and freed them. Perrin and his men hunted Trollocs; in the wolf dream Perrin encountered Slayer, who was killing wolves. Trollocs continued to pour into the Two Rivers, and Perrin led the effort to resist them. Thinking that the town was doomed, Perrin tricked Faile into riding for help; in return, she demanded that he marry her. She rode away, but returned with men from Watch Hill, and the people of the Two Rivers were triumphant. Perrin and Faile began building a manor in the area. He came to be known as Perrin Goldeneyes, Lord of the Two Rivers.

Perrin and Faile, with an army of men from the Two Rivers, later joined Rand in Caemlyn, and accompanied him to Cairhien. When Rand was kidnapped by Aes Sedai, Perrin led an army to rescue him. With the assistance of Asha'man, they were successful. Following a staged altercation with Rand, Perrin led a mission into Ghealdan to bring the Prophet Masema to Rand. In the group were Two Rivers men, Berelain and her Mayener Winged Guard, Aiel, including Wise Ones, two Asha'man and two Aes Sedai. Queen Alliandre gave her fealty to Perrin, which brought her troops, the Legion of the Wall, into his army. They met with Masema and rescued some Andorans from Dragonsworn. When Faile was captured by the Shaido, Perrin was willing to do anything to get her back. He cut off a captured Shaido's hand to make him answer questions, but to rub in the salt, he got none of the answers he wanted—and this cut at him. He knew that he would do other things against his nature if necessary to regain Faile. Eventually he was able to ally with the Seanchan and brought the Shaido to battle at Malden; he and Faile were reunited.

Perrin had sent the noncombatants with him away before the battle; as he traveled to rejoin them he was beset with many challenges. To try to solve them, Perrin went into the wolf dream and asked Hopper, who still lived in the wolf dream, to help him learn what he could do there. When the Asha'man could no longer make gateways to Travel, Perrin found a strange purple dome in the wolf dream, and Slayer killed a wolf that was helping him. The noncombatants were captured by Whitecloaks; to regain them, Perrin had to stand trial for killing the Whitecloaks in the abandoned *stedding*. One of the Andorans he had rescued turned out to be Morgase, the former queen of Andor, and she presided at his trial. She found him guilty of illegal killing instead of murder; Galad delayed his punishment until after the Last Battle. In the wolf dream, Perrin battled Slayer for a dreamspike which was causing the purple dome and preventing his Asha'man from Traveling; Perrin won, and destroyed the dreamspike in a lake of lava. His group then Traveled to Whitebridge, and with the aid of the Asha'man and the Wise Ones, Perrin forged a hammer, *Mah'alleinir*; because it was a Power-forged weapon, it was very effective. He then led his army to the rescue of the Whitecloaks, who were being attacked by Shadowspawn. Galad swore allegiance to Perrin on behalf of the Whitecloaks. Perrin presided at the wedding of Tallanvor and Morgase. He then met with Elayne, who agreed to cede the Two Rivers to the Dragon Reborn, with Perrin acting as his steward.

Perrin made his way to the Field of Merrilor to meet with Rand. He turned over command of his armies to Tam, and had Rand make a gateway so that he could go into the wolf dream in the flesh to deal with Slayer; Gaul insisted on going with him. In the wolf dream they met Lanfear, who provided some assistance; she helped Perrin find and disable the dreamspike at the Black Tower, and alerted him that Graendal was up to something with the great captains. Perrin fought Slayer, trying to prevent him from attacking Rand at Shayol Ghul. Slayer managed to injure Perrin badly, but Perrin worked out a way to move in and out of the wolf dream in the flesh at will; Haral Luhhan found him in a field and took him to the Aes Sedai. After being Healed, Perrin went back into the wolf dream and chased Slayer; with Perrin's newfound ability, Slayer was unable to escape, and Perrin finally killed him. Lanfear tried to compel Perrin to murder Moiraine in the Pit of Doom, but Perrin was able to resist and wrung Lanfear's neck instead. He returned in the aftermath of the Last Battle only to find that Faile was missing. He took to the wolf dream again, and heard a falcon crying; shifting to the waking world, he found her underneath the carcass of a horse and took her to be Healed. With the deaths of Faile's father and Queen Tenobia, Perrin and Faile were to become the monarchs of Saldaea.

Perwyn Belman. The son of Nan, in Caemlyn. He reported to Fain that a Gray Man had tried to kill Rand. Fain lost his temper and touched Perwyn, making him tremble and gibber. Fain thought that the boy would survive.

Petra Anhill. The strongman in Valan Luca's circus. He was married to Clarine, the dog trainer. Petra was the biggest man Nynaeve had ever seen; he was about 5'10" tall and very wide. His arms were the size of tree trunks. After Mat left the circus, Petra returned to Ebou Dar and worked as a gate guard.

Pevara Tazanovni. A Kandori Aes Sedai of the Red Ajah and the loyalist contingent, with a strength level of 14(2). Born in 839 NE, she went to the White Tower in 855 NE. After spending six years as a novice and five years as Accepted, she was raised to the shawl in 866 NE. About 5'4" tall, and pleasingly plump, she had short black hair, large dark eyes and a merry face. Though she was as tough as an old post inside, she was never mean. Her voice was usually brisk. Pevara's entire family died while she was a novice, killed during a quickly suppressed uprising of Darkfriends led by a fool who decided that the Dark One was about to break free. She and Seaine were friends as novices and Accepted (pillow friends, in fact); Seaine might have planned how to carry out most of their pranks as girls, but Pevara had been the one with the audacity to think of most, and she had provided most of the nerve to go through with them. Shortly after being raised Aes Sedai she said that she would not mind at all having a Warder or even more than one; the Red Ajah did not approve. Pevara gave Seaine the cut directly after attaining the shawl because of pressure from the Red Ajah. She was raised Sitter for the Red in 985 NE in the wake of the exile of the former Sitters because of the male channeler pogrom. Always a stickler for the law, Pevara was not one of the Red Sisters who took part in the pogrom. She knew about it, but it was Sealed to the Flame, and it troubled her. She believed in the Black Ajah afterward, and eventually became part of a group in the Tower rooting out Black sisters. She had stood to depose Siuan in the truncated Hall arranged by Elaida. The charges leveled, including most specifically that Siuan had been meddling in secret with a man who might be a false Dragon, or the true Dragon Reborn, were very serious in her eyes. Under orders from Tsutama, Pevara led a group to the Black Tower to bond Asha'man as Warders; there she bonded and was bonded by Androl Genhald. They were captured by Taim, but escaped and drove Taim out of the Black Tower. In the Last Battle, Pevara and Androl fought together very effectively, succeeding in reclaiming the seals and trapping a number of Dreadlords in a *stedding*.

Pevin. A Cairhienin refugee who became Rand's bannerman. An expressionless man with thinning hair and a red scar running up the side of his face, he lost his entire family to famine and war. Although he didn't say much, Rand thought that Pevin had three beliefs: The Dragon had been Reborn, the Last Battle was coming, and if he stayed close to Rand al'Thor, he would see his family avenged. He carried Rand's banner into Cairhien after the battle against the Shaido; following the fight against Lanfear at the docks, he somehow heard that Rand was going Caemlyn, and carried the banner there in the campaign to deal with Rahvin. There he took a Trolloc spear through his chest and died; in death, he wore the first expression that Rand had seen on the man: surprise.

Phaedrine. An Aes Sedai of the Brown Ajah and the rebel contingent, with a strength level of 35(23). About 5'3" tall, she was lean and small-boned, with brown eyes. Phaedrine was the sister to whom Elayne and Nynaeve reported on appearing in Salidar. She listened to only a little of the story Nynaeve and Elayne had agreed on, then left. Linked, Phaedrine and Shemari were just strong enough to make a barely usable gateway; they Traveled together to an unknown location. As Beonin was leaving the rebel camp to return to the Tower, Phaedrine and Ashmanaille stopped her to talk about the murders of Anaiya and Kairen; Phaedrine thought that the murderer was a male wilder working in the camp.

Piava. An Aes Sedai who served with Egwene at the Last Battle. Her Warder and Sleete guarded the area where Egwene, Silviana and Gawyn were fighting in one of the early battles.

Piesa. Leya's shaggy brown and white mare, which she rode to her meeting with Moiraine in the Mountains of Mist. Leya asked Perrin to feed her.

pillow friend. Term used for young women at the White Tower who formed a romantic attachment to one another. Behaviors associated with this appellation generally ended when one or both parties were raised to the shawl.

Pipkin, the Fall of. A battle from Mat's memories.

Pips. Mat's dark chestnut gelding with a blunt nose. It took a sharp eye to notice the deep chest and strong withers that promised speed and endurance. Pips was excluded from the forcible purchase by the Seanchan because he was in the Tarasin Palace stables.

Piqor Ramshalan. A Domani nobleman who was obsequious and something of a fop. Lanky, with a prominent nose, he wore a thin black mustache, earrings with his House markings, and a beauty mark. Rand found his nasal voice and willingness to betray others annoying. He recommended that Rand execute Milisair; Rand did not listen. Ramshalan boasted to Lords Vivian and Callswell that he could manipulate Rand however he wished. Rand sent Ramshalan to Graendal in Natrin's Barrow; Graendal had Aran'gar and Delana place Compulsion on him, and sent him back to Rand. After Rand balefired the fortress, Nynaeve determined that the Compulsion was gone; Rand took that to mean Graendal was dead. Rand told Ramshalan that he would not execute him, and that there was a village he could reach in two days' walk.

Piri. Also called Match, a dice game that was popular for a thousand years before Artur Hawkwing began his rise. It used a pair of dice, although some variations on the game used four; the rules were similar to the game of street craps.

Pit of Doom. A place deep within Shayol Ghul where the Dreadlords dedicated themselves to the Dark One and where it was possible to communicate with him. It was reached by traversing a tunnel that opened out suddenly onto a wide ledge overlooking a lake of molten stone, red mottled with black, where man-high flames danced, died and rose again. There was no roof, only a great hole rising through the mountain to a sky that was not the sky of Thakan'dar. It made that of Thakan'dar look normal, with its wildly striated clouds streaking by as though driven by the great winds. In the Pit of Doom, it was possible to sense the Bore; though it was physically no closer, a thinness in the Pattern here allowed that.

Plain Chant. *See* Bards, Forms of Recitation of

Plain of Lances. Flatlands situated in the northern portions of Saldaea and Kandor.

Plains of Maredo. Flatlands unclaimed by any country, located between Andor, Illian and Tear, below the Hills of Kintara. Far Madding was the only city in this territory.

Plowman, the. A constellation.

Plowman's Blade, The. An inn found in Manala, Kandor; its innkeeper was Mistress Tomichi. Moiraine, Lan, Bukama and Ryne breakfasted there on their way from Canluum to Chachin.

Plum Gate. The southeastern entrance to the grounds of the Royal Palace in Caemlyn. Mat diced with the guardsmen there when he was trying to make his way into the palace.

Poel, Mervin. *See* Mervin Poel

pokeleaf. An herb having soap-like properties. It could be used to remove the hair dye produced by white henpepper, but it could leave a reddish tint in the hair. Pokeleaf was also used for sore gums and toothache.

Pol. Merilille's servant in Ebou Dar, who traveled with Elayne's party to Caemlyn. A slender, gray-haired woman, she usually possessed a dignity to rival that of her mistress. She would have fled with Merilille, had it been possible.

Polov Heights. A flat-topped hill at the Field of Merrilor, situated across the River Mora from Shienar in Arafel. Mat, as commander of the allied armies fighting against the Shadow south of the Blight, shifted his theater of operations there to take advantage of the topography. Because of his military brilliance and considerable luck, this area saw the decisive defeat of a massive Trolloc army, effectively ending the Last Battle south of the Blasted Lands.

Pomfrey, Salia. *See* Salia Pomfrey

Ponderings. A book by Pelateos, one of the books read by Min.

Portal Stones. Gateways to other locations or to alternative realities within the Pattern, activated by the One Power; that is, Portal Stones could lead to other Portal Stones in this world or in parallel worlds, those that would have existed had other choices been made. When used for traveling in this world, the time dimension could be inconsistent.

Portal Stones had been set in circular hollows, surrounded by concentric rings of seven stairs of varied colors, although many of these hollows had deteriorated considerably over time. The Stones themselves were about three spans high and a pace wide. Symbols on the top half of the Stones stood for equivalent Stones in other worlds; symbols at the bottom indicated other Stones in this world. Not every Portal Stone connected to every world, and it was believed that there were worlds no Stone could touch. The exotic creatures used by the Seanchan had been brought through Portal Stones from alternate realities.

Aes Sedai in the Age of Legends, who could Travel, routinely used Portal Stones to journey to other worlds. They studied the worlds of the Portal Stones, reflections of this world, as a basis for growing the Ways. Portal Stones came from an even earlier Age. Verin quoted a description of the Portal Stones: "The Lines that join the Worlds That Might Be, laid by those who knew the Numbers of Chaos."

Posavina, Master. A Kandori trader with a pearl in his ear and a gray-streaked forked beard. Rand saw him in Far Madding while gathering intelligence at an inn called The Golden Wheel.

Poses of the Swan. Dance-like movements performed by *da'covale* for Seanchan entertainment; Amathera was taught them.

posting room. A location where clerks worked in the White Tower.

Power, One. *See* One Power

Power, True. *See* True Power

Powers, Five. *See* Five Powers, the

Power-wrought blade. A blade forged with the aid of use of the One Power; it was all but indestructible, held its edge and did not rust.

Powl. One of Asne's four Warders. He was the only one who was a Darkfriend. When Asne was killed, it took two Guardsmen to restrain him even though he was bound by Air.

Powys, Cumere. One of the Counsels of Far Madding. Pretty and serious, she escorted Cadsuane and Harine to the palace.

prescripts, the. Strictures applied to Heroes of the Horn about what they were allowed to reveal to humans in *Tel'aran'rhiod*.

Priket. A goodman in the song "Goodman Priket's Pipe."

Prime Counselor. A high governmental official in the Age of Legends; Graendal thought that Cyndane looked like a Prime Counselor in the company of common laborers.

Prince of the Dawn, Prince of the Morning. *See* Dragon, the

Prince of the Ravens, the. Mat's title after marrying Tuon.

Pritalle Nerbaijan. A Saldaean Aes Sedai of the Yellow Ajah and the loyalist contingent. She had green eyes and a nose that was small for a Saldaean. Her Warder was Harril. She avoided teaching novices or Accepted as much as possible and made no secret of her dislike for teaching.

Yukiri and Meidani saw her talking with Atuan of the Black Ajah.

Pritalle was part of the group that captured Egwene at Northharbor.

Priya Narrows. The site of a battle in Mat's memories.

Proper Taming of Power, The. A work of history studied by Cadsuane.

Prophecies of the Dragon. Little known and seldom spoken of, the Prophecies, given in *The Karaethon Cycle*, foretold that the Dark One would be freed again to touch the world and that Lews Therin Telamon, the Dragon, Breaker of the

World, would be reborn to fight Tarmon Gai'don, the Last Battle against the Shadow. He would, said the Prophecies, save the world—and Break it again.

Prophecies of the Dragon, The. Believed translated by N'Delia Basolaine, First Maid and Swordfast to Raidhen of Hol Cuchone. Another translation was done by Jain Charin, also known as Jain Farstrider. A much-disputed translation was done by the poet Kyera Termendal of Shiota between FY 700 and 800. Around 300 AB, another translation was done by Lord Mangore Kiramin, Sword-bard of Aramaelle and Warder to Caraighan Maconar. Ellaine Marise 'idin Allshin, Chief Librarian at the Court of Arafel, also did a translation of *The Karaethon Cycle: The Prophecies of the Dragon* in 231 NE.

Prophecies of the Dragon, Commentaries on the. Written by Jurith Dorine, Right Hand to the Queen of Almoren.

Prophecy, Jendai, the. *See* Jendai Prophecy, the

Prophecy of Rhuidean. Also known as the Aiel Prophecy, which spoke of the *Car'a'carn*, the chief of chiefs. It stated "The stone that never falls will fall to announce his coming. Born of the blood, but raised by those not of the blood. He shall spill out the blood of those who call themselves Aiel as water on sand, and he shall break them as dried twigs, yet the remnant of a remnant shall he save, and they shall live." It also said that he would conquer under the ancient sign of Aes Sedai.

Prophet. Or, Prophet of the Lord Dragon. A man named Masema Dagar, a former Shienaran soldier who became an unauthorized, militant evangelist for the Dragon Reborn, and who had a large army to enforce his excesses. *See* Masema Dagar

Proska Flats. A rocky section of northern Saldaea.

Pujili. A region of Seanchan where Gamel Loune acquired his servant Mantual.

pump-wagons. Conveyances used to fight fires in Malden.

Pura. A woman whose real name was Ryma Galfrey. An Aes Sedai of the Yellow Ajah, she was captured by the Seanchan and made *damane* in High Lady Suroth's service. She became a well-trained and obedient *damane* and spoke in the third person. *See also* Ryma Galfrey

Pylar. An Aes Sedai of the Brown Ajah who was adept with weaves of Earth; she fought in the Last Battle with Egwene in Kandor.

Qaim. A small Sea Folk island southwest of Ebou Dar in the Sea of Storms.

Qal. During the Age of Legends' fall into the Shadow, a place where *sha'je* dueling was popular. Fought using *osan'gar* and *aran'gar* daggers tipped with poison, the duels typically resulted in both parties dying. Semirhage mentioned *sha'je* duels being fought there.

Qi. One of the group of Shienaran soldiers who joined Lan in eastern Kandor as he traveled toward Tarwin's Gap. Andere told the protesting Lan that he had run into Qi and the other soldiers before meeting Lan, and had told them to wait along the southern roadway for Lan and his men to come along.

Qichen, Stedding. A *stedding* located in the Spine of the World.

Qirat. The fifth-largest city in Seanchan.

Qual. *See* Qal

Quarry Road. A rock-strewn track in the Two Rivers. No one in the Two Rivers knew why it was called Quarry Road.

Queen's Blessing, The. An inn located in Caemlyn. Its innkeeper was Basel Gill, and Lamgwin Dorn was the bouncer. Rand and Mat stayed there when they first went to Caemlyn, and it was where they met Loial; Mat and Thom were there when Mat tried to deliver a message from Elayne to Morgase. The inn closed after Basel left Caemlyn with Morgase.

Queen's Bounty. Charitable distribution of food at the Royal Palace in Caemlyn. On High Days, the Queen gave it out with her own hands, and no one was ever turned away for any reason. No one needed to beg in Caemlyn. Even a person with a warrant against him or her could not be arrested while receiving the Queen's Bounty.

Queen's Crown mushroom. A flavorful type of mushroom.

Queen's Glory in Radiance, The. An inn found in Ebou Dar. It was the grimiest inn that Mat had seen in the city, and it smelled of very old fish.

Queen's Guards. *See* Andor

Queen's Highway. A name sometimes used for the Caemlyn Road.

Queen's Lance, The. An inn located in Kayacun, Saldaea. Nynaeve went there to drum up support for Lan as he rode for the Last Battle.

Queen's Man, The. An inn found in a village two days from Four Kings. Mat and Rand stopped there planning to entertain for keep on the way to Caemlyn; Rand became feverish, and they bunked in the stable. Mili Skane attacked them there, and they were forced to flee, having learned that a Fade was coming.

Queen's March. A horn call used to alert Andorans of danger.

Queen's Walk. A street paved with stones in Caemlyn; it was kept well lit by Elayne.

Queen's Writ. A code of laws that was supposed to apply to all of Andor. As Thom told Rand and Mat, on board the *Spray*, on their flight to Whitebridge: "If they mutiny, boy, they won't leave passengers behind to tell the tale. The Queen's Writ might not have much force this far from Caemlyn, but even a village mayor will do something about that."

Questioners. A pejorative term for members of the Hand of the Light.

Quick. Bashere's horse, a bay.

Quillin Tasil. The Andoran innkeeper of The Wind's Favor in Bandar Eban. Tall and slender with an oval face, he wore a full gray beard. His dark hair was thinning. His Domani wife was one of the most accomplished silk merchants in the city; his daughter Namine was an Aes Sedai of the Brown Ajah. Quillin had kept the accounts for his wife for twenty years and retired, very wealthy; he opened an inn which he kept immaculately clean, and he never hired gleemen or musicians. His wines were of very fine vintage. Cadsuane, who Quillin knew as Mistress Shore, went to him for information in Bandar Eban; he knew many things, and although she didn't entirely trust him, she was fond of him.

Quintara, Tylin. *See* Tylin Quintara Mitsobar

R

Raab. A Sea Folk sailor and gambler whom Mat encountered in Tar Valon. He won a lot of money by following Mat and betting on him.

Rabayn Marushta. An Aes Sedai of the White Ajah who served as Amyrlin Seat from 5 to 36 NE. Rabayn was a weak Amyrlin; she was not a puppet of the Hall, but definitely not in true control.

Rabbit Nose. A young, very fierce male wolf. Perrin contacted him for information after he and others set out to find the kidnapped Rand.

Racelle Arovni. A Kandori woman who was the innkeeper of The Blue Rose in Canluum. She was graying, tall and handsome with sharp dark eyes. She and Bukama were friends; she greeted him by grabbing his ears and kissing him thoroughly, then slugging him in the jaw, then kissing him again. She put Bukama up in her rooms.

Rad al'Dai. A Two Rivers man who sometimes acted as Perrin's bannerman.

Radhanan. The Empress of the Seanchan. She had a number of children, including Aurana, Chimal, Ravashi and Tuon. Several died in the infighting between them. She and the rest of the royal family, save Tuon, were killed by Semirhage.

Radlin. Father of Kolom father of Serden, the last being an Ogier who developed a theory about the Ways.

Radun's Standard of Deviation. A method used by Aes Sedai of the White Ajah for explaining logic arithmetically.

Raechin Connoral. An Aes Sedai of the Red Ajah and the loyalist contingent. She and her sister Viria became Sitters in the Hall of the Tower, replacing Pevara and Javindhra. She wore her dark hair in a coil of braids atop her head. The sisters were the only siblings in the White Tower after Vandene and Adeleas died. Raechin fought in the Last Battle; she, Manda and Leane were getting ready to fall back and regroup when Egwene returned to the field of battle to face Taim.

Raefar Kisman. A Tairen Asha'man, a crony of Taim, and a Darkfriend. He was born in 980 NE. He was at Dumai's Wells. After the attack on Rand in Cairhien failed, he was placed on the deserters list at the Black Tower, although Rand did not see him during the attempted assassination. He took part with Manel Rochaid in the attempt to trap and kill Rand in Far Madding; he escaped Rand but was killed by Padan Fain.

Rael, Alwin. *See* Alwin Rael

Raemassa. An Aes Sedai who was with Egwene in Kandor when the Sharans appeared in the Last Battle.

Raen. The Mahdi, or Seeker, of the caravan where Perrin, Egwene and Elyas sheltered. The husband of Ila and the grandfather of Aram, he was short and wiry with gray hair. His caravan was later forced by Whitecloaks to head toward the Two Rivers; his band was largely massacred by Trollocs. In the Last Battle, Raen and Ila helped with the wounded.

Raened, Daerilla. *See* Daerilla Raened

Raened, House. An Andoran noble House; its High Seat was Lady Daerilla.

Rafela Cindal. A Tairen Aes Sedai of the Blue Ajah and the rebel contingent, with a strength level of 16(4). Born in 948 NE, she went to the White Tower in 964 NE. After spending six years as a novice and five years as Accepted, she was raised to the shawl in 975 NE. About 5'5" tall, and plump, she had a round face that was normally mild and pleasant, but could be serious or even stern; her voice was normally sweet. Her Warder was Mahiro Shukosa. When she was first raised Aes Sedai, Rafela attempted to revive many customs that had fallen into abeyance. She was a member of the rebel embassy to Rand in Caemlyn and swore fealty to Rand after Dumai's Wells. She was one of five that Min saw that Rand could trust. She and Merana Ambrey completed the negotiations that Rand had begun with the Sea Folk; she also helped negotiate agreements for him with the Tairen nobles who had rebelled and were gathered in Haddon Mirk.

Ragan. A Shienaran soldier. He had a white triangular scar on his dark right cheek, which almost mirrored Masema's scar. His head was shaven but for a topknot of dark hair. One of those who followed Ingtar when he and Perrin pursued the Horn of Valere to Falme, he wintered in the Mountains of Mist with Perrin and Rand, then after Rand left and the Shienarans were abandoned to make their own way, he stayed for a while with Masema in Ghealdan. He and Uno went to Salidar with Elayne and Nynaeve. He helped Uno train heavy cavalry for Bryne.

Ragon. A soldier in Lan's army in the Last Battle who died when he charged his horse at a group of thirty Trollocs, a move that saved a dozen men.

Rahad. *See* Ebou Dar

Rahema Arnon. A grain merchant whom Perrin dealt with in So Habor, Altara. She was haggard and dirty, with sunken eyes.

Rahien Demain. A child in Chachin whose name meant "dawn." He was on Moiraine's list of potential Dragon Reborn infants, as he was born outside Tar Valon during the Blood Snow. His mother, Lady Ines Demain, named him so because she saw the sun rise over Dragonmount. His father fell over dead in his porridge while Rahien was still an infant. Siuan learned that he was born in a farmhouse almost two miles from Dragonmount one day after the Aiel headed home.

Rahman. A powerful Domani nobleman who was supposed to be following Ituralde. Because Alsalam's orders sometimes went straight to the men under Ituralde instead of to him, four pitched battles occurred between different groups of Ituralde's men, Rahman's among them.

Rahvin. A Forsaken. His name in the Age of Legends was Ared Mosinel. His strength level was++1. Dark and extremely handsome, with gray at his temples and very dark eyes, he was taller than Rand and had shoulders nearly the width of Perrin's. He loved power and glory and conquest and preferred to be a diplomat or manipulator, given the choice, rather than a militarist. When he awoke in the Third Age, he masqueraded as Lord Gaebril and seduced Morgase. He used Compulsion on her and ruled Andor in all but name; he also kept several other women as pets. Morgase was strong-minded enough to eventually resist the Compulsion and escape. Rand went to Caemlyn to deal with Rahvin; Aviendha, Mat and Asmodean were killed by lightning from Rahvin. Rand then chased Rahvin into *Tel'aran'rhiod* and they fought there. Nynaeve arrived with Moghedien on a leash and burned Rahvin badly; Rand then balefired Rahvin with enough strength that Aviendha, Mat and Asmodean were alive again.

Rai. A noble House in Kandor. Its sign was the oak set aflame. *See* Keemlin *and* Malenarin Rai

Raidhen of Hol Cuchone. A ruler of a country that existed four hundred years after the Breaking. N'Delia Basolaine, First Maid and Swordfast to Raidhen, was believed to have translated *The Prophecies of the Dragon*.

Raimun Holdwin. The Darkfriend innkeeper at The Goose and Crown in Andor, east of Carysford. He met with a Fade who was looking for Rand and Mat; afterward he told Almen Bunt that the two boys had stolen a heron-mark sword and that there was a reward for finding them. Bunt didn't like Holdwin, and gave Mat and Rand a ride.

Rainyn din Burun. A Sea Folk Windfinder on a darter with a strength level of 13(1). She took part in using the Bowl of the Winds because she was one of the strongest available among the remaining Windfinders in Ebou Dar. Young-appearing and round-cheeked with barely half a dozen medallions on her nose chain, in the Windfinder hierarchy she was fairly low in rank.

Rajabi. Powerful Domani nobleman who joined Ituralde's forces. Bull-necked and with a bull's temperament, he lost a leg during the battle at Maradon, and was later killed by a Draghkar there.

Rajan, Lideine. An Aes Sedai who lived at the time of the formation of the White Tower.

Rajar. A Domani who trained at the White Tower for six years; he joined the Younglings. Slight and barely as tall as Gawyn's shoulder, he had a deep voice. Acting as Gawyn's First Lieutenant, he fought at Dumai's Wells and went with Gawyn to scout Bryne's forces. He became a Warder.

raken. A Seanchan flying animal that was brought from a parallel world. Its body was considerably longer than a horse's and about equal in girth, with a leathery gray skin and large wings much like those of a bat. The *raken's* wing-spread was approximately ninety to one hundred feet. It had a long neck with an oblong head. The long snout, which had one small horn on females and two, one behind the other, on males, appeared to be made of horn itself. Hard ridges served as both lips and teeth. Its powerful jaws were easily capable of shearing through a branch or an arm. Two eyes were set on the front of the head, though widely spaced. The *raken* had superior vision. It had a very long, thin tail; though this tail looked frail in comparison with the rest of the *raken* and usually appeared simply to trail behind in flight, it was in fact very strong—strong enough to break an arm or leg, though not used as a weapon; the *raken* would sometimes lash its tail in anger when perched or on the ground, and a careless *morat* could be struck. The *raken* moved its tail with great dexterity in helping to control its flight. The *raken* had two legs, relatively thin for the size of its body, which ended in feet with six long and quite strong taloned toes arranged four before and two behind. On the ground, it normally crouched rather than standing erect on its legs, and raised its head on its long neck to look around. It stood on the ground only when alarmed or preparing to fly. When a *raken* was crouched, it was quite possible to simply throw a leg over the saddle. The saddle was lighter than a horse's saddle, and was made double, for one *morat* to ride behind another; it had safety straps to hold the flier on during violent maneuvers. While the *raken* was slow and awkward on the ground, it was an extremely agile flier, and very quick when it needed to be. Maximum flight speed was three to four times the speed of a horse. It could fly fairly long distances without rest at slower speeds. It did not like to fly in bad weather; in heavy rain, or worse, snow, it had to be forced or cajoled into the air and often would refuse. Simple cold weather did not bother it at all, nor did heat; it would fly on the coldest winter day in the northernmost climes or the hottest summer day in the desert. Its intelligence level was roughly equal to that of a horse. The *raken* was used primarily for scouting and carrying messages. It could carry two people if they were small. *Morat'raken* and *morat'to'raken*, sometimes called "fliers," all were either women or smaller-than-average men. Two *morat* were used if extra eyes were wanted for observation; one if more range and/or speed were needed. Unlike the *to'raken*, which would sometimes simply refuse to fly if injured or ill, an injured or ill *raken* would fly, though of course its speed, range and load-carrying abilities would be reduced. It could perch comfortably even on vertical surfaces if there was any purchase for its claws. In some cases when perching on vertical or precipitous surfaces, it would spread its wings across the surface, in effect clutching with them. It would perch in large trees, but preferred open ground or cliffs. Despite its predatory appearance, it was an omnivore, though apparently perfectly content with an all-plant diet. Grains and fruits were best for this, but leaves and grasses would do, though requiring much more bulk. *Raken* were egg layers and laid one egg at a time. Like the *to'raken*, the *raken* was controlled by reins, attached to rings fixed permanently in the animal's horny nostrils, and knee pressure. *See also* to'raken

raker. The largest and fastest class of Sea Folk ships. Two to three hundred feet in length with a very fine but narrow hull and three masts, rakers resembled clipper ships without a flush deck. A raker could cover up to four hundred miles in a day, although 360 miles was considered the typical maximum.

Rakim. A Saldaean soldier who served with Lan in the Aiel War. Hoarse-voiced from being taken in the throat by an Aiel arrow, he considered himself lucky to be alive. He liked to show off his scar, and boasted about his luck. He joined Lan on the Plain of Lances and fought in Lan's army at Tarwin's Gap in the Last Battle.

Ram, the. A constellation.

Ramedar, Joal. The last king of Aldeshar, a nation from after the Trolloc Wars, and the father of Endara Casalain.

Ramesa. An Arafellin Aes Sedai of the White Ajah and the loyalist contingent. She was tall and slender with silver bells sewn down the sleeves of her white-embroidered dress. After Alviarin was removed as Keeper, Alviarin heard Norine address Ramesa in the White quarters with a scathing remark about Alviarin. Ramesa seemed to wonder why Norine was addressing her, since they were not friends.

Ramey. The head groom at The Queen's Blessing, Basel Gill's inn in Caemlyn. Horse-faced with leathery skin, he opened the secret gate out of the back of the inn for Moiraine, Rand and the rest to make their way to Caemlyn's Way-gate in secret. When Mat returned to The Queen's Blessing, Ramey didn't remember him, but when he saw that Mat was giving him silver instead of copper, he said that he did; he also said that he remembered horses better than people.

Ramman, Eval. Balthamel's name in the Age of Legends.

Ramola. An Aes Sedai of the Black Ajah. She and Alviarin fought back-to-back as bait to lure Egwene to Mesaana in *Tel'aran'rhiod*.

Ramosanya, Alvera. *See* Alvera Ramosanya

Rampore. The eleventh-largest city in Seanchan.

Ramshalan, Piqor. *See* Piqor Ramshalan

Ramsid. The dark-haired brother of Domani King Alsalam. He was taken by Graendal and became one of her acrobats, along with his wife, his youngest sister and the King's eldest daughter.

Ramsin, Kalyan. *See* Kalyan Ramsin

Rana. One of Min's aunts. Rana worked as a seamstress, and never married. She was very proper. She and Jan, another aunt, always told Min not to kiss a man unless she was planning to marry him. When Min got in trouble with neighbors because of detailing her viewings, Rana convinced her to say that she had overheard people talking.

Rand al'Thor. A sheepherder from Emond's Field, who came to understand that he was really the Dragon Reborn, the hero of the Age, destined to face off against the Dark One in Tarmon Gai'don, and that the fate of humanity was dependent on his success in that battle. Rand was born at the end of 978 NE,

on the slopes of Dragonmount, the son of Tigraine and Janduin; his mother died in childbirth, and his father was later killed by Luc. He was picked up on Dragonmount by Tam al'Thor during the Battle of Shining Walls, adopted and taken back to Emond's Field.

Rand was approximately 6'6" tall and weighed 235 pounds, with broad shoulders, a deep chest and a narrow waist. He had dark reddish hair, and eyes that seemed now gray, now blue; women could get quite lyrical about his eyes. He was very good-looking; many women thought him either pretty or beautiful. Rand's other titles included Lord of the Morning, Prince of the Dawn, True Defender of the Light, He Who Comes With the Dawn, *Car'a'carn*, the Coramoor, Shadowkiller, Prince of the Morning and Lord of the Dawn.

As a young man, Rand left the Two Rivers with Mat, Perrin and Egwene in company with Moiraine, Lan and Thom, after Trollocs attacked Emond's Field, seemingly targeting the three boys. They went to Baerlon, then to Shadar Logoth, where they were separated. Rand, Mat and Thom traveled down the Manetherendrelle to Whitebridge on Bayle Domon's riverboat, *Spray*. In Whitebridge, when a Myrddraal appeared, Thom faced it while Rand and Mat fled and journeyed on, working their way to Caemlyn by farm labor at first and later by Mat juggling and Rand playing the flute. In Caemlyn, Rand and Mat stayed at Basel Gill's inn and met Loial. After some time there Rand went out to see Logain, the captured false Dragon, fell into the palace gardens, and met Elayne, Gawyn, Galad, Morgase, Gareth Bryne and Elaida. Moiraine met up with Rand and Mat in Caemlyn, accompanied by Lan, Perrin, Nynaeve and Egwene. With Loial they journeyed via the Ways to Fal Dara, followed by Fain, who was captured in Fal Dara. They entered the Blight and found the Green Man and the Eye of the World. Aginor and Balthamel arrived there; Balthamel and the Green Man killed each other, and Rand faced off against Aginor. He drew deeply on the Eye of the World, which was pure *saidin*, and killed Aginor. He found himself in the battle Agelmar was fighting at Tarwin's Gap, and helped to defeat Shadowspawn. He made his way back to the rest of his group, who had all managed to survive. In the empty Eye they found the Horn of Valere, Lews Therin's banner and a broken seal of the Dark One's prison. They then returned to Fal Dara.

Fain escaped from the dungeon there, stealing the Horn of Valere and the Shadar Logoth dagger. Rand, Perrin and Mat set out with Loial, Ingtar, Hurin and twenty Shienaran lancers to hunt him down. Rand, Loial and Hurin were transported via Portal Stone to another world, where they encountered *grolm* and Lanfear, calling herself Selene. Rand, Loial, Hurin and Selene/Lanfear returned to the ordinary world via Portal Stone in Kinslayer's Dagger, where they waited for Fain and his Darkfriends and Trollocs to appear. Rand and Loial stole back the Horn and the Dagger. The lot of them traveled across the mountains to Tremonsien, where they saw the great male statue *sa'angreal*, then on to Cairhien. Rand attempted to convince people he was not part of the

Game of Houses by refusing all invitations, which only convinced everyone he was playing a very deep game. Rand discovered that Thom was alive and performing in Cairhien. Just before Verin, Perrin, Mat, Ingtar and the Shienarans found Rand there, the Horn and dagger were stolen from Rand and taken to Barthanes' manor. They attended a party there, and found that the items had been taken through the Waygate that was on the property; when they attempted to follow, *Machin Shin* was waiting just inside. Barthanes gave Rand a message from Fain: Fain would wait for him on Toman Head. Rand and his party journeyed to Stedding Tsofu to try to use the Waygate there, and met Erith, the Elders, three Maidens and an Ogier who had been caught by the Black Wind. They found the Waygate there also blocked by *Machin Shin*. A Portal Stone stood nearby, and Rand used it, with everyone but Verin thinking it was her doing, to journey to Toman Head. Something went wrong, and all saw many lives that they could have lived. When they finally made it to Toman Head, they discovered that four months had passed. Rand, Mat, Perrin, Ingtar and Hurin entered Falme, found the Horn and the dagger, fought Seanchan, and discovered that Egwene was there. Mat blew the Horn, and Rand, Mat, Perrin and Hurin rode with the heroes of legend to fight the Seanchan. Rand confronted Ba'alzamon in the sky over Falme, and during the fight sustained a wound in his side that would not heal. Moiraine and Lan appeared, sending Mat, Egwene, Nynaeve and Elayne off to Tar Valon with Verin. Rand proclaimed himself the Dragon Reborn, accepting the oaths of Uno and the surviving Shienarans.

Rand, Perrin, Moiraine, Lan, Loial and the Shienarans wintered in the Mountains of Mist. At the end of winter, Rand decided to try for the Stone of Tear and *Callandor* by himself so as not to risk anyone else. Pursued by Moiraine, Lan, Perrin, Loial and later Faile, he crossed the land from the mountains all the way to Tear, and entered the Stone of Tear on the same night that the Aiel and Mat did. He confronted Be'lal, who was killed by Moiraine, then claimed *Callandor* and fought and killed Ba'alzamon. In the Stone, Rand canoodled a bit with Elayne, though short of actually making love, and had lessons in how to rule.

From Tear, Perrin, Faile and Loial went off to the Two Rivers, and Rand used a Portal Stone to carry himself, Mat, Moiraine, Lan and Egwene to a Portal Stone near Rhuidean. He and Mat entered Rhuidean, and Rand emerged marked with the twin Dragons of the prophesied He Who Comes With the Dawn, the Aiel *Car'a'carn*, the chief of chiefs.

In the Waste, Rand met Hadnan Kadere and a disguised Lanfear and Asmodean. Rand proclaimed himself *Car'a'carn* at Alcair Dal; Couladin also claimed to be chief of chiefs, and had the Dragons on his forearms as well. To prove that he was the true *Car'a'carn*, Rand related the secrets of the true history of the Aiel, leading the chiefs to acknowledge him as *Car'a'carn*. Pandemonium erupted; he made it rain to calm the fighting. Lanfear pulled him away, and reminded him that he needed Asmodean to teach him. He followed Asmodean to Rhuidean, fought him and captured him, cutting him off from his ties to the Dark One. Lanfear put a shield on Asmodean that allowed him to channel only a small amount. The battle opened Rhuidean to entry by everyone. Learning that the Shaido had crossed the Dragonwall into Cairhien, Rand pursued with the clans that were following him. Defeating the Shaido before the walls of Cairhien, Rand took the city, although a rebellion soon erupted in the countryside.

Before taking the city, Rand followed Aviendha as she fled through a gateway she formed instinctively, bedded her in the snows of Seanchan, confronted some Seanchan and returned to Cairhien. Striking out from Cairhien, Rand and the Aiel took Caemlyn, and Rand killed Rahvin in *Tel'aran'rhiod*, with the aid of Nynaeve, who had Moghedien, collared, with her. With rebellion in Tear and Cairhien and the better Andoran nobles opposing or avoiding him, Rand then tried to consolidate what he held, meeting with embassies from the rebel Aes Sedai in Caemlyn, and the loyalist Aes Sedai in Cairhien. Rand met with Taim, and tasked him with setting up and directing what became the Black Tower on a farm outside Caemlyn. During this time he learned of the Two Rivers girls in Caemlyn, met them and was bonded against his will by Alanna. At this same time he put off meeting the Sea Folk emissaries; the Prophecies didn't mention them, and he wanted to leave them alone; besides, he did not at that point see a use for them. He built up an army on the Plains of Maredo, openly pointed at Illian and Sammael. In Cairhien, he was kidnapped by Galina and the loyalist Aes Sedai; they started out for the Tower. At Dumai's Wells, with Lews Therin's help, he was able to break free of the shield that held him when the Aes Sedai were forced to tie it off because they were being attacked by Shaido and forces trying to rescue him. Asha'man also turned up, and Rand's people decisively won the Battle of Dumai's Wells. Kiruna and eight other Aes Sedai (including Verin and Alanna) swore fealty to him; the loyalist Aes Sedai were held captive by the Aiel.

After learning that Herid Fel had been torn limb from limb, Rand made love to Min for the first time.

Setting the army in motion on the Plains of Maredo, Rand launched a surprise attack on Illian using gateways to take him, a number of Asha'man, some of the Legion of the Dragon and Davram Bashere with his Saldaean light horse straight into the city of Illian. Sammael returned and Rand chased him to Shadar Logoth. There Rand was rescued by a stranger (Moridin, unknown to him); Sammael himself was killed by Mashadar. Rand returned to Illian, where the eight survivors of the Council of Nine told him that Mattin Stepaneos had vanished and that it was believed Lord Brend had killed him; they offered him the crown of Illian.

Rand had a number of difficulties. 1) He worried about Lews Therin's voice that he began to hear in his head. Increasingly he assumed some characteristics of Lews Therin in thought and behavior, though often he was not aware of it unless someone brought this strangeness to his attention. He saw it as a struggle to remain himself. 2) Rand was also a super *ta'veren*, more so than Perrin or Mat, and had an intermittent effect on the laws of chance. This could take in a wide area, an entire city, and have very odd effects, or affect one person right in front of him. 3) Padan Fain was constantly trying to kill him. When Rand visited the rebel camp outside the city of Cairhien, he saw Fain, who was calling himself Jeral Mordeth, advising Toram Riatin. A bubble of evil struck, with fog that could kill, and Fain slashed him with the dagger from Shadar Logoth, which put another wound that could not heal across the wound from Ba'alzamon in his left side. 4) Rand increasingly experienced flashes of light and motion in his head when thinking of Mat or Perrin. 5) He also felt a "resonance" from when he used the Power in Shadar Logoth and crossed weaves with Moridin. He began seeing images of Moridin, not knowing who he was. 6) Using the One Power made Rand dizzy and nauseated, and affected his eyesight. 7) Rand was also becoming mad; his madness, at the onset at least, took the intermittent form of arrogance, increasing feelings of power, invincibility and infallibility—in short, megalomania. He was increasingly suspicious of other people, of their motives. Also, a hardening increased in his spirit; he found laughter where others might have found tears, and buried his tears deeply. This was a growing problem for him, though he did not see it that way. Rand eventually agreed to take Cadsuane on as his advisor, and she showed him an alternate way to this hardness. Meanwhile, despite Rand having worried a great deal about going mad earlier, he began to worry less, to think about it less.

Rand had little respite before learning that the Seanchan planned to invade Illian. He gathered troops, Asha'man and *Callandor*, and engaged them in the mountains of eastern Altara. They prevailed against the Seanchan, but in the process Rand lost control of *Callandor*, which began killing his own troops as well as the enemy. Bashere had to tackle him to stop the mayhem. After the battle, Rand returned to Cairhien, where there was an attempt on his life by three Asha'man, who managed to escape. Rand and Min took evasive measures after that, and wound up in Caemlyn with Rand in disguise. There, Min, Aviendha and Elayne bonded Rand, and he impregnated Elayne.

Rand, Cadsuane, Verin, Nynaeve, Lan and others went to Far Madding, looking for the Asha'man who tried to kill Rand. The Asha'man were killed, some by Rand and some by Fain. Rand and Lan fell into a trap set by Fain. They escaped the trap, but were captured by the authorities; Cadsuane was able to arrange for their release. After they left Far Madding, the group traveled to Shadar Logoth, where Rand, using the Choedan Kal with Nynaeve's help, cleansed the taint from *saidin*. They went to an estate in Tear to recuperate; while they were there, huge numbers of Trollocs attacked. Lews Therin managed to seize control of *saidin*, and they defeated the Shadowspawn, but Lews

Therin almost drew too much Power. Rand sent a contingent of Aiel to Arad Doman to help quell the unrest there. A meeting between Rand and the Daughter of the Nine Moons was negotiated with Suroth in Altara, but Semirhage, disguised as Tuon, was there with *a'dam*. In the struggle with her, Rand lost his left hand, which Nynaeve Healed to a smooth stump. The wounds in his side broke open, leaking blood; Nynaeve couldn't Heal them even as well as they had been. But Semirhage, at least, was captured. The group moved on to Arad Doman, where Rand made an alliance with Ituralde to secure the Borderlands, while Rand would arrive at an agreement with the Seanchan.

Semirhage escaped, and put a male *a'dam* on Rand, trying to force him to kill Min. In a rage, Rand instead drew on the True Power and killed Semirhage. From the experience, Rand sealed himself off from his emotions, and even banned Cadsuane from his presence. He had a meeting with the real Daughter of the Nine Moons, but was unable to reach agreement with her. After he discovered the location of Graendal's manor house in Arad Doman, he balefired it, hoping to kill her, but she escaped.

Back in Tear, Rand met with Tam, and, in an argument, almost killed his father. He Traveled to Ebou Dar with the purpose of destroying the Seanchan, but he could not bring himself to it and instead Traveled to Dragonmount, where he had an epiphany, with Lews Therin's help—living lives over and over with each turn of the Wheel was worth it because it gave one a chance to express love again, to have another chance to make things right, to choose to do his best for humanity, whatever the outcome. He was healed of much of his mental conflict and pain, and reconciled with Tam back in Tear.

After that, endowed with even greater control of the One Power, Rand returned to the northwest, and established order in Bandar Eban. He then saved Ituralde and his remaining troops from slaughter at the Battle of Maradon, killing huge numbers of Shadowspawn. Following that, Rand saw the Borderlander rulers in Far Madding, where, after confirming his status as the Dragon Reborn, the rulers swore allegiance to Rand.

Rand met at the Field of Merrilor with most of the rulers of the world to tell them what he needed to do, that is, to break the seals on the Dark One's prison. Many of the rulers did not agree to this course of action, and a large faction came out against Rand, including Elayne and Egwene. After much discussion, which included an impassioned speech by Moiraine in Rand's favor, the nations united behind Rand and signed the Dragon's Peace, a treaty created by Rand to stop the nations from warring with each other after the Last Battle. Rand then went to Tuon in Ebou Dar and reached an accord with her. All the pieces were in place for Tarmon Gai'don.

The Last Battle began with the Trolloc invasion of Caemlyn through a Waygate in the city. Rand's part of the battle took place in the Pit of Doom in Shayol Ghul, where he confronted the Dark One, aided by Moiraine and Nynaeve. Additional figures on the scene were Alanna, brought there to distract Rand, and Moridin, who had his own bone to pick with the Dragon Reborn. A tremendous struggle took place, with Rand realizing he could not destroy the Dark One without causing great harm to the world: there could not be good without bad. Locked in a struggle with Moridin, Rand dropped *Callandor* and it was picked up by his adversary; not understanding the flaw in the sword, Moridin channeled the True Power into it as Moiraine and Nynaeve channeled the One Power into it and linked with Rand, who took control of the Power, a combination of *saidin, saidar* and the True Power, and directed it at the Dark One. Rand grabbed the Dark One and pushed him back into his prison, then resealed the Bore with this new form of Power.

Unknown to the others, Rand's body, which was mortally wounded, had been exchanged with Moridin's. Rand's body died and Rand, in Moridin's body, rode out of Shayol Ghul as funeral rites were being conducted for him. Because of their bond with him, Aviendha, Elayne and Min knew that Rand was not dead. Cadsuane saw him leave, and realized who he really was. Rand rode on to new lands, wondering if one or all of his loves would eventually find him. Although he could no longer channel, when he wanted his pipe lit, it was.

rannel. An herb used to make a tea that produced an energy boost; it had a terrible taste that lingered.

Ranun Sinah. A Whitecloak soldier killed in battle with Shadowspawn on the Jehannah Road. When Perrin and Galad found his body, his cloak was soaked in blood.

Raolin Darksbane. A false Dragon. He supposedly declared himself very early in 335 AB, "in the last throes of winter," and fell in 336 AB in time to "make the Feast of Lights the most joyous for the world in many years." He was reportedly no more than twenty-two or twenty-three when captured and gentled. He took the name "Darksbane" for himself. He was born in the city that was later named Far Madding. Some authorities questioned the dates given to Darksbane, though their evidence was scarce and spotty. A few sources claimed that he declared himself as early as 332 AB and by 335 AB was already a significant power. A handful of other sources give dates for his capture as late as 339 AB. The dates given earlier are those most commonly accepted, but it must be noted that the White Tower was considered the authoritative source of historical dates, and that the Tower perhaps had a vested interest in making it seem that false Dragons, while a significant threat to the world, were always dealt with quickly by the Aes Sedai.

Rashan. 1) A muscular young man who was one of Graendal's pets. Sammael sliced him in half with a gateway. 2) Erian's Warder, one of two who survived Rand's rage when he tried to escape from the Tower Aes Sedai. Erian left him and Bartol, her other surviving Warder, in Cairhien when she went with Cadsuane to Far Madding; they and other Warders were able to lead Logain and Bashere to Rand at Algarin's manor in Tear.

Rashima Kerenmosa. An Aes Sedai of the Green Ajah who was known as the Soldier Amyrlin. Born circa 1150 AB, she went to the Tower around 1165 AB. After spending five years as a novice and five years as Accepted, she was raised to the shawl around 1175 AB. Rashima was raised Amyrlin in 1251 AB. Personally leading the Tower armies, she won innumerable victories, most notably Kaisin Pass, the Sorelle Step, Larapelle, Tel Norwin and Maighande, where she died in 1301 AB. Her body was discovered after the battle, surrounded by her five Warders and a vast wall of Trollocs and Myrddraal which contained the corpses of no fewer than nine Dreadlords.

Raskovni, Caseille. *See* Caseille Raskovni

Rasoria Domanche. A Tairen woman who was part of Elayne's bodyguard, and one of the eight who guarded Elayne on her tour of Caemlyn. She was stocky with blue eyes and short yellow hair, unusual for a native of Tear. A former Hunter of the Horn, she became an under-lieutenant.

Rath, Tsutama. *See* Tsutama Rath

Ratliff's nails. A curse used by Birgitte.

Ravashi. Tuon's ambitious older sister who Tuon thought might have plotted against her.

Raven-and-Roses. The personal symbol of the Daughter of the Nine Moons.

Raveneos, Aisha. *See* Aisha Raveneos

Ravens, Tower of. *See* Tower of Ravens

Ravinda. A market village in Kandor lying two days from Chachin on the Canluum-Chachin Road. Moiraine found Avene Sahera there, a woman who was on her list as a possible mother of the infant Dragon Reborn. Avene built an inn with the bounty given her by the White Tower for the birth of the child, and intended to call it The White Tower.

Razina Hazzan. A Saldaean Aes Sedai of the Brown Ajah and the loyalist contingent, with a strength level of 28(16). Born in 870 NE, she went to the White Tower in 886 NE. After spending seven years as a novice and six years as Accepted, she was raised to the shawl in 899 NE. Part of the expedition to kidnap Rand, she was captured at Dumai's Wells and treated as *da'tsang* by the Aiel. Under Verin's Compulsion, she found reason to swear oath to Rand, which she did before Cadsuane departed Cairhien for Far Madding.

razorlace. An artifact from ancient times that Bayle Domon mentioned on the way to Whitebridge with Rand, Mat and Thom.

Reader. Another name for a Wise Woman in Cairhien.

Reale. An attendant of Colavaere in Cairhien. She replaced Maire, who Faile said told her that Colavaere said that Rand would never return, and who vanished shortly after telling Faile.

Reanne Corly. A Kin and a member of the Knitting Circle in Ebou Dar. She was not the oldest of the Kin living anywhere, but she was the oldest member of the Kin in Ebou Dar and as such was the Eldest, their leader. Her strength level was 14(2), which was strong enough for her to be able to learn to Travel.

Born in 588 NE, she went to the White Tower in 603 NE. She was eleven years a novice, because of difficulties with fearfulness. She was a novice with Sereille Bagand, who arrived approximately two years before her and tested for Accepted the same year. She remembered Sereille as a prankster who broke more rules than any three other novices combined. Sereille's fearsome reputation surprised her, but then she was surprised Sereille was ever chosen Amyrlin. When testing for Accepted, Reanne refused to enter the arches again after the first time through and was sent away. Gerra Kishar was the Amyrlin at the time.

About 5'5" tall, with blue eyes, a face full of smile lines and mostly gray hair, Reanne obviously was not a native of Ebou Dar. She had a high soprano voice. Her apparent age was roughly mid-forties—she didn't look old, just like someone who had a little age and had not lived the easiest of lives. She had wanted to be Green Ajah, but had long since abandoned those dreams—or so she thought, until the possibility reared its head. She did not wear a red belt, or anything to connect her to the Wise Women. She sometimes felt fear in her belly, like the panic that sent her running and screaming at her Accepted test; she always gripped this firmly, unaware that fear of actually giving way had long since conquered the possibility that she might give way.

Mat, Elayne and Reanne and some of the Wise Women saw the *gholam*, which nearly killed Elayne in the Rahad as well as killing some members of the Knitting Circle.

She was present at the meeting with the Windfinders in the Tarasin Palace.

She was called down by Alise for bringing Aes Sedai to the farm in violation of the Kin's rules, and since even the Eldest was subject to the rules, Reanne had to do chores during the journey to Tar Valon. Reanne found the subject of her position, authority and title somewhat ticklish once they left Ebou Dar. Technically, she was no longer the Eldest, since that title applied only in Ebou Dar, but she continued to function in that office just as the rest of the Knitting Circle continued to function in theirs, if not precisely as the Knitting Circle. Being away from Ebou Dar did lessen her leverage with Alise, but she was still the elder.

Reanne accompanied Elayne to the Royal Palace in Caemlyn; there she worked with the captured *damane* and *sul'dam*.

She was killed by Careane Fransi of the Black Ajah.

Reason and Unreason. A book by Herid Fel.

Rebek. Someone to whom the merchant Barriga thought he should have listened, after he was attacked by Trollocs near Heeth Tower on the Blightborder, and just before he was killed by red-veiled Aiel.

rebel Aes Sedai. The group of Aes Sedai that refused to give allegiance to Elaida after Siuan was deposed and settled initially in Salidar. They became a more cohesive force after they raised Egwene al'Vere to the Amyrlin Seat.

Reconciliation. A conflict in Cairhien, never quite breaking into open civil war despite a number of skirmishes and minor battles, which resulted in House Damodred losing the throne to House Riatin, with Galldrian taking the Sun Throne, primarily through the Game of Houses. Its basis was the misfortune Laman had brought to Cairhien. It was called the Reconciliation in Cairhien because of the public fiction that it was all quite amicable. In most other countries the Reconciliation was called the Fourth War of the Cairhienin Succession.

Red. A tall bay stallion with a deep chest. Basel Gill gave Rand the horse in Caemlyn, and Rand rode Red through the Ways to Fal Dara, through the Blight to the Eye of the World and when in pursuit of the Horn of Valere. When Ba'alzamon appeared before Rand in Falme, Red reared and threw Rand and vanished.

red adder. A deadly snake that made a dry hissing sound.

Red Ajah. The main thrust of the Red Ajah was hunting down men who could channel. The head of the Red Ajah was called the Highest, or simply Highest, and considered the equal of the Amyrlin Seat by most Reds, unless a Red was the Amyrlin Seat, and sometimes even then. The Highest had autocratic powers of command, more so than in any other Ajah. There was a council below her, but it was advisory only, although members of the council did have authority over Red sisters not on the council. Selection of the Highest was by secret ballot, with only members of the council considered for the post. Sitters also were chosen by secret ballot, with the entire membership open; all ballots were write-in—no one stood for the position—but if no one received two-thirds of the votes, the lowest vote-getter was dropped, and a new ballot taken. This continued until someone had two-thirds of the votes. If the candidates were reduced to two and neither had two-thirds after three ballots, the choice was thrown to the council.

There was a secret ceremony of the Red Ajah, the most secret, called the Grand Emergence. At the time of the Last Battle, there were approximately two hundred members of the Red Ajah, making it the largest. *See also* Grand Emergence

Red Bull, The. An inn located in Caemlyn's New City about a mile from Lady Shiaine's house. Daved Hanlon stabled his horse there.

red cockleburr. A plant found at least one hundred miles south of Tar Valon. Its presence on Zerah's saddlecloth led to her being found out as one of the rebel Aes Sedai when discovered by Pevara's group hunting the Black Ajah in the Tower.

red daisy. A plant used in a tea for headache.

Red Eagle of Manetheren banner. A red eagle in flight on a field of blue. Perrin flew it while in Ghealdan to throw observers off the track, and gave it to Seanchan Banner-General Tylee Khirgan as a sign that Perrin was relinquishing any claims to make Manetheren rise again.

red fennel. An herb used as a remedy for a queasy stomach; it was often taken for seasickness.

Red Hand, Band of the. *See* Band of the Red Hand

Red Hawk, Moad din Nopara. *See* Moad din Nopara Red Hawk

Red Horse. The symbol of Kandor.

Red Salt. A sept of the Goshien Aiel.

Red Springs. The hold of the Codarra clan of the Aiel in the Three-fold Land.

Red Water. A sept of the Goshien Aiel.

red-stripe. A nearly round white fish with red stripes that was eaten in Illian.

red-veils. Another name for the *Samma N'Sei.*

Red Wolfhead. Perrin's banner. It was white, bordered in red, with a red wolf's head on it.

Redarms. Those in charge of keeping order in the Band of the Red Hand.

redbell. A plant with red flowers appearing after rain.

redberry. A dense shrub.

Redbord. A street tough in Bandar Eban whom Rand and Durnham convinced to help clean up the city. A burly man with curly black hair, coppery skin and a thin mustache, he spat when Durnham first mentioned the Dragon Reborn, but agreed to go along after some persuasion from Votabek.

Redhill, Jestian. *See* Jestian Redhill

Redhill, Merean. *See* Merean Redhill

redspot. A disease that affected tabac; it withered the leaves.

Redwing. Medore Damara's favorite mare.

redwood trees. Cone-shaped trees that grew in the Waterwood.

redwort. A plant that could drive a bull mad.

Reed Soalen. A Two Rivers man with Perrin. Reed guarded Perrin after Aram's death. When Rand visited Perrin at the Field of Merrilor, Reed was acting as a sentry.

Reene Harfor. The First Maid of the Royal Palace in Caemlyn. A slightly plump woman with graying hair worn in a bun atop her head, she had a round face, a long chin and a formidable bosom. Whatever the hour, her formal scarlet tabard with the White Lion always looked freshly ironed, the White Lion as clean and pale as new-fallen snow. She had a dignity any noblewoman might envy, and looked Rand right in the eye; she combined a proper degree of deference, an utter lack of obsequiousness and an aloofness most noblewomen could not manage. When Rand took Caemlyn, Mistress Harfor stayed, although Rand thought that her purpose was to defend and preserve the palace from the invaders. After Sulin violated *ji'e'toh* and wanted to act as a servant, Reene agreed, and made her wear a dress. Reene was appalled when Taim and his men walked in on Elayne before she meant them to, and called them "sneaking rats" though she covered for it admirably when she realized that she had not spoken quietly enough. Reene told Elayne about Jon Skellit and Ester Norham acting as spies; she later found many others.

Reeve, Will. A Redarm killed by the *gholam* while guarding Mat's tent in the camp outside Caemlyn.

Reiko Kerevon. An Arafellin Aes Sedai of the Blue Ajah and the rebel contingent, with a strength level of 38(26). Born in 827 NE, she was stout and had long dark hair in which she wore silver bells. Reiko was one of six sisters sent to investigate the large channeling event at Shadar Logoth because of her ability to read residues.

Reimon. A Tairen nobleman. Broad-shouldered with an oiled dark beard trimmed to a neat point, he chased the latest fashion as assiduously as he chased women, which was only a little less eagerly than he gambled. Reimon often talked in sentence fragments, was a boaster and was initially happy about the prospects for war. He played cards with Mat and was frightened when the cards came to life, although he claimed he saw nothing. He joined the Band of the Red Hand as a captain; the Fifth Squadron (later the Fifth Banner) was Reimon's Eagles. Reimon accompanied Talmanes when they met up with Mat in Altara. Mat promoted him to Banner-General, and he participated in raids on the Seanchan and the battle against those trying to take Tuon.

Reimon's Eagles. The informal name of the Fifth Squadron of Mat's Band of the Red Hand.

Reisendrelle, River. A river flowing south through Lugard and Murandy, into the River Manetherendrelle.

rema'kar. An item in Moridin's stash of objects of the Power.

Remara, Bay of. The site of the Tairen village of Godan, overlooking Mayene.

Remedan the Goldentongued. A king of Aelgar, one of the Ten Nations.

Remen. An Altaran village on the River Manetherendrelle. Remen was a decent-sized river town, with docks and warehouses, and stone buildings with tile roofs of many different colors. Perrin, traveling with Moiraine, Lan and Loial, freed Gaul from a cage there and the two of them killed a number of White-cloaks. The group, joined there by Faile, fled downriver by boat.

Ren Chandin. A Two Rivers man who joined Perrin's band in the Two Rivers. He was killed in a Trolloc ambush.

Rena Tower. A watchtower on the Blightborder, northwest of Heeth Tower.

Renaile din Calon Blue Star. The Windfinder to Nesta din Reas, Mistress of the Ships to the Atha'an Miere. Her strength level was 18(6). About 5'6" tall, and dignified, with a cool, deep voice and large dark eyes, she had five fat golden rings in each ear connected by a chain; another, finer chain ran to her nose ring, thick with medallions that told which clan she belonged to, among other things. After her demotion, she wore only three thinner rings in each ear, and fewer honor medallions, since some had to be put away. Narrow wings of white in her straight black hair half-hid the rings in her ears. Tattoos on her slim dark hands also told of her clan. A handsome woman rather than pretty, apparently in her middle years, she was normally of a very cool, dignified, self-possessed mien; when she became angry, her eyes bulged and her face gorged with blood. She observed the use of the Bowl of the Winds and tried to assert her position with Zaida, who would not allow it. Once the Sea Folk learned of

Nesta's death, Renaile had to step down in rank to the lowest level, according to custom, and she acted as Chanelle's secretary.

Renala Merlon. A historical figure whom Egwene hoped the Brown Ajah would come across in their studies; she thought that Renala's story would show how divisions in the Tower could be healed.

Renald Fanwar. A prosperous Borderlands farmer. His wife was Auaine, and they had a number of sons. Renald had been farming his land for forty years; his sons had gone elsewhere, but he had six farmhands who were like family. When his neighbor Thulin told him he was going north, Auaine convinced Renald that they ought to follow. He turned some of his farm tools into weapons and went north to fight in the Last Battle. Mat gave him a spear lesson at Merrilor.

Renald Macer. A sergeant in the Queen's Guard in Caemlyn. Stout and bald with wide hands and a mustache, he had a calm temperament. When Mat tried to get into the palace dressed as a beggar, Macer took pity on him and gave him food; he and other soldiers diced with Mat as well. Only when Birgitte arrived and pointed out that it was odd to see a beggar with a sword did he note it.

Rendra. A woman who was the innkeeper of The Three Plums Court in Tanchico. She had honey-blond hair that she wore in braids, big brown eyes and a rosebud mouth; she looked a good bit like Liandrin. She and Juilin were involved before he met Thera.

Renna Emain. A Seanchan *sul'dam*. She first put the *a'dam* on Egwene and worked Egwene as a *damane*. In Suroth's opinion, Renna was a very good trainer, one of the best—an opinion not necessarily correct. She had long dark hair and big brown eyes. Nynaeve, Elayne and Egwene left her and Seta leashed on *a'dam* when they escaped at Falme; Alwhin found them and released them. Because she was found being held by an *a'dam*, Renna was never again allowed to hold a *damane*'s leash, though the facts were covered up and she remained in Suroth's employ. Egeanin learned of this from Bethamin and used it to blackmail Renna, Seta and Bethamin into helping rescue Teslyn, Joline and Edesina. The three *sul'dam* fled with Mat and Valan Luca's show, but Renna eventually attempted to kill Egeanin and, thinking she had succeeded, fled back toward Seanchan forces. Mat pursued her and was forced to order Harnan to kill her because she was on the verge of reaching the Seanchan.

Renshar. A major noble House in Andor; its High Seat was Lady Arathelle. *See* Arathelle *and* Hanselle Renshar

Reo Myershi. An ancestor of King Paitar of Arafel who heard a Foretelling of importance about the Dragon Reborn and passed it down through his family.

Resara. Leane's aunt in Arad Doman. She said that if a man heard more promises than a woman meant to offer, one should pay the price and enjoy it. She also said that men were better sport than hawks.

Reshalle, River. A narrow river in Altara where King's Crossing was situated.

Restorer. The name for an Aes Sedai Healer in the Age of Legends.

Retash. A community in a cluster of islands rarely visited. It was somewhat infamous for the Retashen Dazer, a mix of mead and ewe's milk which was reputed to be foul.

Rett. A soldier who died defending Ituralde at Maradon in Saldaea.

Return, the. *See Corenne*

Reyn. An Aiel clan which had a Two Spires and a Musara sept, among others. Its chief was Dhearic.

Rhadam Asunawa. The High Inquisitor of the Hand of the Light. Tall and gaunt with deep-set dark eyes, gray hair and thick gray eyebrows, he did not wear the flaring golden sun on his white cloak, only the scarlet shepherd's crook. He believed that Rand was another false Dragon and a tool of the Tower, that talk of the Last Battle coming was foolish, even criminal, and that events in Tear and elsewhere were staged by the Tower.

For all his talk, he did not really believe that all Aes Sedai were Darkfriends. He did believe they were dangerous fools and dupes, that the Power was something that should not be meddled with, and that those who did meddle with it were usurping the prerogatives of the Creator; for them, there could only be confession of their sins under the question, and then death. He also believed that the White Tower was a roadblock to true power for the Whitecloaks.

Asunawa plotted with Valda to kill Niall. He was allowed to have Morgase for about an hour, for a light session of questioning, involving knotted cords and needles. That Valda then used this to coerce Morgase into his bed disgusted Asunawa. He wished to be the first to hang a queen in Amador; he would rather have been the first to hang a living Amyrlin, but was willing to settle for a Tower-trained queen. He had Morgase's trial planned out, along with how to put her to the question without marks and wring out a dramatic confession. He intended to build a special gallows for her, to be kept as a monument. He was bitterly disappointed that she escaped him, but thought she was in Seanchan hands, although he was disgusted by Valda's accommodation with the Seanchan.

Asunawa did not approve of the duel between Valda and Galad; he and the rest of the Questioners left before the end. He later set a trap to capture Galad and the Children of the Light who followed him; he and Galad argued about who was right in front of the Lords Captain. Galad was stripped and beaten. The Lords Captain came to believe that Galad was truly the Lord Captain Commander of the Children and executed Asunawa.

Rhahime Naille. An Ogier-built city in Aramaelle, one of the Ten Nations after the Breaking.

Rhamdashar. A nation that arose after the Trolloc Wars.

Rhannon Hills. Hills located east across the bay from Ebou Dar, Altara.

Rhea. 1) A woman of the Jenn Aiel after the Breaking. She was the daughter of Adan and Siedre and the sister of Elwin, Jaren, Marind and Sorelle. Rhea was kidnapped by bandits after a raid. 2) A woman in a gleeman's song, "Rhea's Fling." 3) The wife and killer of Caar al Thorin of Manetheren, who was sent to Aridhol to bring the city back to the Light, but who was imprisoned there. He escaped from Mordeth, fleeing to the Borderlands, where he met Rhea.

Rhea Avin. An Emond's Field woman. She and Sharmad Zeffar were both interested in Wil al'Seen and went to Faile to get her to judge which one had the right to him. Faile sent them to Daise Congar, the Wisdom, to sort them out.

Rhiale. A Wise One of the Shaido Aiel (not a Jumai) with the ability to channel and a strength level of 19(7). About 5'9" tall, with flame-colored hair and blue eyes, she was one of Sevanna's inner circle of plotters. She accompanied Sevanna to the Aes Sedai camp the day she saw Rand beaten and took part in or at least was present at the murder of Desaine. She was with Sevanna at Dumai's Wells and at the meeting with "Caddar" and "Maisia." She resisted Sevanna and stood up to her more often than any Wise One other than Therava. Rhiale helped question the Seanchan prisoner in Amadicia, while the Jumai were settled at a captured estate. Rhiale and Therava, at least, were aware that Sevanna wanted a tame Aes Sedai to serve her. Both were present when Caddar gave Sevanna the binder, and they heard Caddar tell how to use it and the *nar'baha*.

Rhian. An Aiel of *Far Dareis Mai*. She had gray eyes and reddish-brown hair; Mat and Perrin thought she could have passed for Rand's aunt. She was the eldest of three Maidens in Stedding Tsofu to buy sung wood, and veiled herself when she saw Shienarans there with Rand and others. Juin stepped in and reminded her of the Pact that required no fighting in *stedding*; she then stood down. She was as abashed as the youngest at having veiled herself inside a *stedding*.

Rhiannon, Queen. A queen from history who went to the White Tower and tried to dominate its inhabitants; she wound up being humbled, and a wall hanging was made depicting the event.

Rhodric. An Aiel after the Breaking. Rhodric and his greatfather Jeordam were allowed by Garam's father to take as much water as they wanted if they dug his well. He and Jeordam followed the Jenn Aiel across the Spine of the World. When he was older, he led the Aiel against armored men who crossed the Dragonwall. He was Comran's greatfather.

Rhuarc. A man of the Nine Valleys sept of the Taardad Aiel and of the *Aethan Dor* society who was clan chief of the Taardad. He was married to Amys, who served as his Wise One, and to Lian, his roofmistress at Cold Rocks Hold. He had children with both wives, the daughters being as old or older than Berelain, who was born 974 NE. About 6'6" tall and weighing 230 pounds, Rhuarc had touches of gray in his dark red hair, and blue eyes. When Elayne, Nynaeve and Egwene were on their way to Tear, Rhuarc helped rescue them from Fades. He revealed who the People of the Dragon were to Rand and Moiraine.

Before Rand's kidnapping, he and Mandelain were the two that the Wise Ones trusted not to go after the Tower embassy with spears; they could be informed that the Tower embassy might be a threat to Rand, or at least that they must be watched for that reason. Rhuarc led *siswai'aman*, slightly over five thousand, who served under the *siswai'aman* Urien, from Cairhien to help rescue Rand from the Aes Sedai, secretly because neither he nor the Wise Ones could be sure what effect the knowledge that Rand had been kidnapped by Aes Sedai would have on the Aiel, including other clan chiefs. Rhuarc disliked Shaido, but although Rand told him to keep them out of Cairhien, he didn't really care whether they ravaged some other wetlander place. Rand sent him and others to Arad Doman to bring order.

Rhuarc later became a *siswai'aman*, and fought near Shayol Ghul in the Last Battle. Graendal captured him and used Compulsion to make him fight for the Shadow; he was killed by Aviendha.

Rhuidean. An unfinished, closed city begun by the Jenn Aiel and Aes Sedai after the Breaking, in a valley of the same name, east of Jangai Pass and beneath Chaendaer in the Aiel Waste. It was the site of *Avendesora*, and contained *ter'angreal* used as tests for those who would be clan chiefs and Wise Ones. Traditionally, four Wise Ones had to give permission for anyone to enter Rhuidean. The Green Man said that he had visited *Avendesora* and rested beneath it some two thousand years previously; thus, he had visited Rhuidean during the Trollocs Wars.

The city was reopened for habitation after the fog that had lain over the site was dissipated. Rand arranged for Ogier to be summoned, for rebuilding, and Rhuidean began to thrive and grow. All clans except the Shaido sent people there. After the city's transformation, one end of the valley of Rhuidean contained a huge lake, with a river running off to the south. Both were astonishing sights for most Aiel. The city was destined to become a center for trade across the Waste.

Rhyagelle. In the Old Tongue, "Those Who Come Home," or "Homecomers." It was another name for the Seanchan who returned to the lands once held by Artur Hawkwing.

Rhys a'Balaman. A Murandian mercenary working for Elayne. Tall and lean-faced, with gray-streaked mustaches waxed to points, he spoke in rough accents, and had eyes like stones and a smile that always seemed a leer. He turned traitor, and was executed after trying to seize the Far Madding Gate for Arymilla's gold.

Riallin. An Aiel woman of *Far Dareis Mai* with vivid yellow-red hair. She actually managed to appear plump—at least for a Maiden—and had a grin for everything. One of those guarding Rand at his first meeting with Cadsuane, she veiled herself when Merana shrieked at Cadsuane not to hurt Rand. Her voice went from warm and friendly on Berelain's name to cold and flat on Annoura's without disturbing her grin. When Idrien announced to Rand what had happened to Herid Fel, Riallin was with her. She went with the Aiel to Bandar Eban to help restore order; there she led Rand through the palace.

Rianna Andomeran. A Kandori Aes Sedai of the White Ajah publicly and the Black Ajah in truth, with a strength level of 21(9). Born in 924 NE, she went to the White Tower in 940 NE. After spending nine years as a novice and seven years as Accepted, she was raised to the shawl in 956 NE, joining the Black Ajah the same year. She was 5'4" and had black hair with a white streak above her left ear and a coldly arrogant face. She had the ability to use the One Power to make a heart stop beating. She, with twelve other sisters of the Black Ajah, left the Tower after stealing a number of *ter'angreal*. She was given a secret assignment by Moghedien, and merely listened to the order, with a touch of relief in her eyes, and then bowed in assent and left. She was captured in a *stedding* in the Last Battle.

Riatin, House. A noble House of Cairhien; it held the throne from the time of the Aiel War until 998 NE; its sigil was five stars. *See also* Ailil *and* Toram Riatin *and* Galldrian su Riatin Rie

Riddem. A Redarm who fell victim to the *gholam* while guarding Mat's tent in the camp outside Caemlyn.

Ries Gorthanes. A Cairhienin man who visited the young Moiraine's banker Ilain, claiming to be a member of the Tower Guard and presenting a letter purported to be from the Amyrlin Seat, demanding to see Moiraine's financial information. Ilain recognized that the signature was a forgery and imprisoned the man. He bribed one of her employees and escaped before the real Tower Guards arrived.

Rift, Great. One of the natural barriers that separated the Aiel Waste from Shara, extending from the Cliffs of Dawn into the Sea of Storms.

Rikshan, Torven. *See* Torven Rikshan

Rilith. A weaver's daughter in Jarra, Ghealdan, who asked Jon, who was old enough to be her father and more, to marry her, as a consequence of Rand's *ta'veren* influence when he passed through town.

Rina Hafden. An Amadician Aes Sedai of the Green Ajah and the loyalist contingent, with a strength level of 22(10). Born in 923 NE, she went to the White Tower in 938 NE. After spending nine years as a novice and eight years as Accepted, she was raised to the shawl in 955 NE. Although she was stocky, with a square face and an upturned nose, she still looked lovely and elegant. Rina was a strongly determined woman. Her Warders were Elyas Machera and Waylin. Rina masked Elyas' bond so that he could not find her, and she gave up hunting for him actively. She let him go in large part because she knew the Red sisters who had accused him of being a Darkfriend might well kill him no matter what she tried to do. None of which meant she did not want him back; he was hers, by Aes Sedai lights, and they were quite possibly married.

Although she was young for the job, Rina was raised Sitter for the Green in 999 NE to replace Joline Maza, who was unchaired and sent to Ebou Dar by Elaida. After the Tower was reunited, Rina stepped down and was replaced by Farnah.

ring. Age of Legends word that meant the same as a circle, created by channelers linking. Thus, channelers would form or make a ring.

Ring of Tamyrlin. A legendary ring, believed mythical by most people, worn by the leader of the Aes Sedai during the Age of Legends. Stories about the Ring of Tamyrlin said that it was an *angreal, sa'angreal* or *ter'angreal* of immense power. It supposedly was named after the first person to learn how to tap into the True Source and channel the One Power, and in some tales, was actually made by that man or woman. Despite what many Aes Sedai said, no one knew whether it was a man or a woman who first learned to channel. Some believed that the title of Amyrlin was a corruption of Tamyrlin.

Rinnin. One of Renald Fanwar's farmhands.

Rion at Hune Hill. A battle from Mat's memories that he thought of during the Last Battle.

Riselle. An Altaran noblewoman with an impressive bosom. Tylin gave her the task of caring for Olver to give herself a clearer path to Mat. Riselle let Olver sit on her knee, and rest his head on her bosom while she taught him to read. Standing 5'5" tall, with a face to match her bosom, she had an olive complexion and big dark eyes. According to Beslan, Riselle always made one entertain her before allowing one to rest one's head on her bosom. She became engaged to marry Seanchan Banner-General Yamada, whose singing voice delighted her. He bought her a vineyard in the Rhannon Hills.

Rising. A tall dun gelding that Birgitte rode to Elayne's Cairhienin coronation. It was one of the fastest horses in the royal stables.

Rising Sun. The symbol of Cairhien, a many-rayed golden sun rising on a field of blue.

Rising Wave. *See* Derah din Selaan Rising Wave

Rissen. A Saldaean soldier under Bashere in Caemlyn. He had odd ideas about Aes Sedai, as did his friends Vilnar and Jidar; they all thought they knew what Aes Sedai were like and looked like, but none would have recognized one if he saw her. Rissen thought Aes Sedai were all a foot taller than any man.

Rite of the Guarding, the. A ceremony traditionally conducted four times annually by the Lords of Tear, in which they affirmed that they guarded the world against the Dragon by holding *Callandor*.

Rittle. A man in Caemlyn with a fondness for garlic; he attempted to cheat Mat at Koronko's Spit, a dicing game, at The Dusty Wheel.

Riven, Marith. *See* Marith Riven

River Gate, The. The best inn in Maerone; Mat had it closed because it served his men too much to drink.

River Queen. A riverboat on which Nynaeve, Egwene, Siuan and other Aes Sedai traveled from Medo to Tar Valon on the River Mora.

River Road. A road running along the River Erinin to Tear.

Riverman, The. An inn found in Aringill. It was full enough that four were sleeping to a bed; the innkeeper laughed in Mat's face when he asked for a room, and in Thom's when he offered to perform for one.

Riverserpent. The two-masted rivership belonging to Captain Agni Neres of Ebou Dar. Galad and Masema both tried to claim the boat in Samara, leading to riots. Nynaeve, Elayne and their party traveled aboard the fat smuggling vessel south from Samara to near Salidar.

roarstick. An explosive cylindrical weapon created by Aludra.

Robb Solter. A Two Rivers man sent to fetch a pavilion for Perrin's meeting with the Children of the Light.

Rochaid, Manel. *See* Manel Rochaid

Rockshaw, Bavin. *See* Bavin Rockshaw

Rodel Ituralde. A great Domani general, sometimes called the Little Wolf; he was considered to be one of the five great captains. Born a commoner, he rose to high rank and the nobility by his military talent. A short slim man with a large ruby in his left ear and thin mustaches that he tended assiduously, he wore several rings. His hair was more gray than not, but he still had all of it, and wore it long and curled. A bit of a dandy, he used beauty marks on his face. After Alsalam vanished, Ituralde continued to receive messages that purportedly came from Alsalam, but in reality they were from Graendal. Ituralde met with Tarabon lords and convinced them to help fight the Seanchan; they managed to give the Seanchan in Tarabon serious heartburn. He then met Rand al'Thor and went to Maradon to defend it; he was successful in holding until Rand arrived, but at great cost. The victim of Graendal's Compulsion in the Last Battle, he made war plans that endangered the forces of the Light.

Elyas and the wolves saved his army during a Myrddraal attack, and they kidnapped Ituralde so he could no longer do damage. After the Last Battle, he became King of Arad Doman.

Rodera. A woman of the Shaido Aiel and *Far Dareis Mai* who was taken *gai'shain* at the battle for Cairhien. She served the Wise Ones breakfast.

Rodholder. A rank in the Seanchan army given to the second-in-command (or third- if the Empress is counted).

Rodic. A squadleader in the Younglings. He went on patrols out of Dorlan to harry Bryne's forces.

Rodrivar Tihera. The Captain of the Stone—Commander of the Defenders of the Stone—in Tear. A lean fellow, dark even for a Tairen, with a short beard trimmed to a very sharp point and oiled, he had black eyes and graying hair in tight curls. He was about 5'9" to 5'10" tall, and slender, but with broad shoulders and a chest that made him seem more massive than he was. A very minor noble with little in the way of estates, he was a lifelong soldier. Tihera was a very intense man, punctilious—both fastidious and meticulous—and fairly prickly, subconsciously aware that he was on the bottom rung of the nobility and poor even for that, that he had had to struggle to rise as far as he had, and that he was a much better soldier than most if not all of the men who gave him orders and to whom he had to bow and scrape almost like a commoner. He was a good soldier, though certainly in no danger of being named a great captain. He remembered Rand rallying the Defenders when Trollocs appeared in the Stone, and how Rand finally destroyed them. He fought in the invasion of Illian and in the attack on the Seanchan and took command of the Tairen forces in the Last Battle. After Ituralde, under Compulsion, was taken out of the battle at Thakan'dar, he worked with Darlin and Rhuarc on tactics.

Roedran Almaric do Arreloa a'Naloy. The Light Blessed, King of Murandy, Lion of the Mountains, Sword of the South, Hammer of the Shadow, High Seat of House a'Naloy, Lord of Lugard, Doirlon, Kahane, Rashad. About 5'10" tall, and fat, with puffy dark eyes and thinning hair more white than black, he had once been handsome, but showed the effects of too much drinking and too many late nights. He had little real authority outside Lugard and not much inside the capital city. The nobles of Murandy were a very independent bunch. But there was more to Roedran than met the eye; after all, he had read and studied Comadrin's book on warfare. He hired Talmanes and the Band of the Red Hand to remain in Murandy so he could point to them as a foreign threat and use that to gather support to himself. He intended to bind the nobles to him so that he could become a real king in Murandy. At Elayne's request, Roedran showed up at the Field of Merrilor before the Last Battle, and became one of the signatories to the Dragon's Peace.

Roemalle. A nation that arose after the Trolloc Wars.

Rogad, Gorin. A false Dragon who rose in Illian in 995 NE. He was taken and burned alive.

Rogosh Eagle-eye. One of the Heroes of the Horn. Also known as Rogosh of Talmour, he was a fatherly-looking man with white hair and eyes so sharp as to make his name merely a hint. Rogosh Eagle-eye appeared at Falme when Mat blew the Horn of Valere and fought against the Seanchan; he also appeared and fought in the Last Battle when Olver sounded the Horn.

Roidan. A man of the Salt Flat sept of the Nakai Aiel and of *Sha'mad Conde*. A grave-speaking man, he had considerably more gray than yellow in his hair, heavy shoulders, icy blue eyes and a hard, scarred face. A blacksmith could have used his lean face for a hammer or an anvil, and by the scars across his cheeks and nose it seemed possible that more than one had done so. Roidan led the Thunder Walkers in the wetlands. Roidan personally led the guard outside the green-striped tent Rand used for Traveling in Tear. He sometimes practiced the Aiel way of fighting with Rand, and avoided looking at Rand's sword.

Roidelle, Master. The very stout, graying mapmaker for the Band of the Red Hand. He had six fit young assistants.

Rolan. A *Mera'din* who joined the Shaido. As wide as Perrin, he was 6'8" tall, with blue eyes. Alliandre thought him not quite pretty. He was not very talkative, but he tried to make Faile laugh, after he got to know her. He captured Faile and took her knives, handling her with humiliating ease and cutting her clothing away. At that point he had nothing about him of a man looking at a woman when he looked at Faile, but that later changed. Rolan wooed Faile while she was *gai'shain* and rescued her from drunken Shaido and from Galina's trap. Perrin killed him with a hammer blow to the head.

Romanda Cassin. An Aes Sedai of the Yellow Ajah from Far Madding. Part of the rebel contingent, she had a strength level of 13(1). Born in 726 NE, she went to the White Tower in 743 NE. After spending five years as a novice and three years as Accepted, she was raised to the shawl in 751 NE. She was raised a Sitter for the Yellow Ajah in 885 NE and served until she retired to Altara in 973 NE. She joined the rebel Aes Sedai in Salidar and was raised Sitter again in 999 NE; she also acted as First Weaver, the head of the Yellow Ajah, among the rebels. She had gray hair, which she wore in a bun on the nape of her neck. When her hair was hidden, she appeared rather young. Romanda had a plump bosom and a high soprano voice. One might have thought she would have a beautiful singing voice, if one could imagine Romanda singing. She had brown eyes, not particularly large, and she stood about 5'4" tall.

Holding her chair for so many years as she did the first time was unprecedented. A great many people did not like the amount of power that she wielded. The fact that she wanted the Amyrlin Seat, which went to Tamra Ospenya just before her retirement, certainly played a large part in her decision to resign her chair; indeed, some thought it the major motivating factor. Shortly after her retirement, she ran into a misunderstanding in Far Madding; Aelmara, her serving woman, helped her escape from the city.

She lived for many years in Altara before joining the rebels at Salidar. She resented and resisted the influence Sheriam and her council had on the Hall, and their influence with some of the independent Sitters. She remained seated the first time in choosing Egwene as Amyrlin; she was the very last to rise on the final vote, after Lelaine, and after a further pause. She remained bare to the waist throughout the decision on raising Egwene, as did Lelaine. Romanda and Lelaine seemed to disagree almost by rote; if one wanted a thing, the other opposed it as a matter of course. Romanda and Lelaine each made sure that nothing she herself disapproved of was passed by the rebel Hall, with the result that very little was passed, and certainly little that Egwene suggested. While this changed to some extent with the declaration of war, they still fought Egwene and obstructed her on other matters. Romanda's faction in the rebel Hall consisted of Magla, Saroiya and Varilin, all of whom were sent out of the Tower by the heads of their Ajahs.

During the Last Battle, Romanda stayed on the field of battle to provide emergency Healing; she was killed during the initial Sharan attack.

Romavni, Eurian. The Kandori author of *A Journey to Tarabon*, a book Egwene used as a guide to Tanchico.

Romera, Mistress. The *shatayan* of Aesdaishar Palace in Chachin. A stately, straight-backed woman with hazel eyes and graying hair worn in a thick roll on the nape of her neck, she wore livery and a silvered ring of keys at her belt. She greeted Lan when he arrived with Bukama and Ryne.

Romlin, Aleis. *See* Aleis Romlin

Ronaille Vevanios. An Illianer Aes Sedai of the White Ajah and the loyalist contingent, with a strength level of 27(15). Ronaille was a member of the expedition to kidnap Rand and was stilled during Rand's escape at Dumai's Wells. Unlike the other captive Aes Sedai taken at Dumai's Wells, Ronaille and the others who were stilled were treated more kindly, in fact taken into the Aiel way of life and given productive work to do, if not exactly what an Aes Sedai was used to. The Wise Ones tried to find a husband for Ronaille.

Irgain Fatamed was the first of the three sisters stilled at Dumai's Wells who was Healed by Damer Flinn, in Cairhien. After Healing her, he was allowed to Heal Ronaille and Sashalle. All three were restored to full strength and were no longer held by the Three Oaths. All three swore oaths to Rand al'Thor.

Ronam. Rhuarc's son and the chief of the Taardad Aiel after the Last Battle, seen in Aviendha's visions of the future in Rhuidean.

Ronan. Agelmar's *shambayan* in Fal Dara. He once held Jehaan Tower with twenty men against a thousand Trollocs. Age-withered but still tall, with a pure white topknot, he acted as Agelmar's secretary and participated in court ceremonies, bearing a staff topped with three foxes carved from red avatine. He was killed in the Trolloc attack when the Horn of Valere was stolen; he died with blood on his dagger.

Ronde Macura. A dressmaker in Mardecin, Amadicia, who served as an eyes-and-ears for the Yellow Ajah. A handsome woman in her middle years, she was about 5'4" tall, with dark hair worn in a neat array and dark eyes. She briefly captured Nynaeve and Elayne, using forkroot tea. Elaida ordered an example to be made of her for failing to hold on to them. Mistress Macura was squeezed, giving up her secret of forkroot tea, and publicly humiliated by being strapped in the village square as someone who had markedly displeased Aes Sedai. This not only necessitated her flight from Mardecin, it engendered a considerable dislike in her for Aes Sedai. For that reason, she was quite willing, even eager, to pass along her secret about forkroot to the Seanchan; in fact, she approached them with the knowledge and was richly rewarded. Pleading to be taken into service by the Seanchan, Ronde became part of Tuon's entourage, but was awkward and not fully conversant with the proper protocols. Tuon thought her eager to do the Aes Sedai more injury.

Ronelle. An Accepted with the rebel contingent who had a potential strength level of 22(10). Born in 969 NE, she went to the White Tower in 984 NE. After spending nine years as a novice and six as Accepted, she was taken from the White Tower by the sisters who fled after Siuan was deposed. She shared a bed with Emara in a room with Satina and Mulinda in the same house in Salidar as Elayne and Nynaeve. She was almost strangled in her sleep by her bedsheets when the bubble of evil hit Salidar. Ronelle would have been tested for Aes Sedai had she remained in the White Tower.

Ronja. An Aiel blinded in the Last Battle. Trying to recruit more people for the battle, Berelain asked him who could make the *gai'shain* fight; he told her that no one could.

Roof of the Maidens. A building exclusively for Maidens of the Spear; no men were allowed entry, other than *gai'shain*. These roofs were found in different locations, such as Cold Rocks and Rhuidean in the Waste.

roofmistress. The Aiel term for the wife of a sept chief who ruled the stronghold of that sept.

Roon, Mother. The Wisdom-equivalent in Jarra, Ghealdan. Noam bit her when she tried to help him.

Rorik. Magla Daronos' broad-shouldered Warder. When cockroaches infested Romanda's tent and the women screamed, he ran in with his sword at the ready, but had no idea what to do about the insects.

Rorn M'doi. One of the places in history that Sammael, the Destroyer of Hope, devastated, earning him that name.

Ros, Fridwyn. *See* Fridwyn Ros

Rosala. A Seanchan with the duty of disciplining *da'covale*. Suroth told Liandrin to go to Rosala and ask her to beat her.

Rosana Emares. A Lady of the Land of Tear who was raised to High Lady after the capture of Illian. Her House sign was the Hawk-and-Stars. About 5'6" tall, and lanky, with a wide nose and blue eyes which were rare for a Tairen. She led her armsmen herself, rather than using a Master of the Horse, though she did not actually go into battle. She had a helmet and breastplate and a mace which she could use. A blunt woman, Rosana told Eben that he needed fattening, ordered Jonan to stop slouching and asked whether Aes Sedai had approved their grim coats. She listened to the story of Dumai's Wells as if examining a possibly counterfeit coin. She had assumed a place in the councils of the High Lords, though Tairen High Ladies seldom did so. Rand left Rosana in Illian to keep the peace.

Rosara Medrano. A Tairen Aes Sedai of the Brown Ajah with a strength level of 32(20). About 5'7" tall, with black hair, dark eyes and brown skin, she liked to cook. Unlike other Browns, she was not dreamy, but rather had a tempestuous nature and a temper, which she usually controlled well, although her eyes could flash with anger. She was one of the uncommitted Aes Sedai Rand found in Cairhien after Dumai's Wells following Cadsuane Melaidhrin. Rosara was left behind in Cairhien when Cadsuane went to Far Madding. When she saw Logain, Aes Sedai and Asha'man arrive in Cairhien, she rode quickly to tell Samitsu.

Rose Crown of Andor. The crown worn by the Queen of Andor.

Rose of the Eldar, The. An inn found in Ebou Dar. Mat, Nalesean and others sat outside it and drank while watching the house of the Kin.

Rosebud. A dun mare ridden by Selucia.

Rosel of Essam. A woman who wrote two hundred years after the Breaking about a ciphered document that held secrets the world could not face. She claimed that more than a hundred pages of the document survived the Breaking, but only one page remained for Verin to study.

Rosene. One of Berelain's serving women. Plump, plain-faced and dark-eyed, she looked like the other serving woman, Nana. Although not pretty, the two animated Berelain's usually taciturn thief-catchers. Rosene served Perrin breakfast after he had slept in Berelain's tent; she or Nana spread the word that Perrin had done so. When Perrin was trying to locate Masema and his men, Rosene told him, amid much smirking and tittering, that she thought they were two or three miles away.

Roshan. Samitsu's Warder. He had not wanted to be a Warder until she decided she wanted him for one. Samitsu left Roshan in the city when she visited the rebel camp near Cairhien; when the bubble of evil hit, she wished that she hadn't.

Rosi. The name that Tuon intended to give Joline as a *damane*.

Rosil. An Aes Sedai of the Yellow Ajah who replaced Tiana as Mistress of Novices under Egwene.

Rosoinde, Garenia. *See* Garenia Rosoinde

Ross Anan. The youngest son of Setalle Anan. He was fourteen years old when Mat stayed at his mother's inn. He helped the serving girls in the inn and worked the fishing boats with his father, depending on the time of year and need.

Rossaine, Clan. A clan of the Atha'an Miere.

Rosse. A member of Jarid Sarand's personal guard. Faced with Jarid's growing insanity, Rosse and Jarid's other men rebelled against him, and tied him to a tree. The men then went off to fight in the Last Battle.

Rossin. An officer under Rodel Ituralde in Maradon. Ituralde directed him to find out why a trumpet sounded an early retreat, leading to great losses for Ituralde, but he was killed in a skirmish before he was able to do so.

Roundhill. A village Perrin visited. The smith there was careless, and had burn scars on his hands

Rovair. A stout follower of the High Lord Darlin in the rebel camp below Cairhien. When Min and Rand visited the camp, Darlin told Ines and Rovair to give them their horses. Rovair answered with a toadying smile for Darlin and a cooler but still greasy one for Rand.

Rovair Kirklin. Masuri Sokawa's Warder. A compact man with receding dark hair, he usually had a ready grin, but was glum over Masuri's treatment by the Wise Ones. He and Masuri went with Perrin when he met with Masema; on their return they found Faile had been kidnapped, and Rovair was one of the scouts who looked for her. Masuri and Rovair met with Masema in secret, and the two went with Perrin to So Habor. Rovair traveled into Malden through the aqueduct; he was with Perrin when Perrin was reunited with Faile.

Rowahn. An Aiel leader after the Last Battle, seen in Aviendha's viewings of the future in Rhuidean. Tall and red-haired, Rowahn tried to keep to some of the core beliefs of the Aiel; he wore the *cadin'sor* and was clean-shaven, but when his hold was attacked and burned by the Seanchan, he picked up a sword and used it to preserve his daughter Tava. He tried to keep the people of the hold together, but they all walked away.

Rowan Hurn. A member of the Village Council in Emond's Field. He joined Perrin's army at Malden; Perrin tasked him with making sure that Galad had released the prisoners before his trial.

Royal Inn, The. An inn found in Four Kings, Andor. The Darkfriend Howal Gode went there looking for Rand and Mat.

Royal Library of Cairhien, the. One of the great libraries of the world, thought by many to be second only to the Library of the White Tower. It was spared by the Aiel in the Aiel War.

Royal Palace of Andor, the. Residence and seat of the Queen of Andor, found in the Inner City of Caemlyn. Its main gates opened onto the oval Queen's Plaza, and the South Stable Gate was where the stables for the palace were to be found. Built on the highest point of the city, the palace was connected to the rest of the city by curving streets that flowed along the contours of the terraced hill upon which it was built. The palace had pale spires, golden domes, shining white walls, high marble balconies and intricate stonework traceries; the Lion of Andor waved from every prominence. The Grand Hall was the throne room, and there was a Rose March in the gardens. Charlz Guybon, along with his troops and refugees from the city, sheltered there at the start of the Last Battle; Talmanes fought through Trollocs to reach the palace. After the occupants evacuated the palace, it was seized by Trollocs and subsequently burned.

Rubinde Acedone. A Mayener Aes Sedai of the Green Ajah and of the loyalist contingent. Her strength level was 19(7). Born in 853 NE, she went to the White Tower in 869 NE. After spending ten years as a novice and nine years as Accepted, she was raised Aes Sedai in 888 NE and chosen as a Sitter for the Green Ajah in 992 NE. About 5'5" tall, with a sturdy build, Rubinde had raven hair and eyes as blue as sapphires. She usually seemed ready to walk through a wall. Sometimes she grimaced in what might have been meant for a smile, but her lips simply writhed. Impatient with what she considered useless talk, she frequently managed to overtop Sedore's Yellow arrogance, and that was something even for a Green. She stood to depose Siuan, one of only eleven needed to give the greater consensus under the circumstances. She thought the rebels were caught in the snows of Murandy and figured that by spring, things could be made hot enough that they would come crawling back. She was nervous about Elaida, when Elaida stretched her wings free of Alviarin.

After the Seanchan raid on the Tower, she was one of the Sitters who raised Egwene to the Amyrlin Seat, and she was part of the group that pressured Cadsuane to become Amyrlin after the Last Battle.

Ruffled Goose, The. A disreputable inn in Chachin. Moiraine went there looking for Siuan.

Rugan, Chai. *See* Chai Rugan

Rulan Allwine. The stout innkeeper at the only inn in Market Sheran, Andor. His inn was clean and warm, with no drunkenness, and the serving maids seemed happy. Allwine insisted that Rand and Mat pay in advance, and the price was steep.

Rumann. A sword-juggler with Luca's show. He was about six feet tall, and handsome. Egeanin pulled a knife on him before departing Ebou Dar, because he was suggestive in asking her to have some wine with him in his wagon. He took up with Adria, one of the contortionists.

Rumor Wheel, The. *See* Dusty Wheel, The

Runnien Crossing. A town in Altara, a day northeast of Jurador. It lay near a shallow, narrow river where a stone bridge crossed. It possessed four inns, each three stories of stone roofed in green or blue tiles. There was nearly half a mile of hard-packed dirt between the village and the river where merchants could park their wagons for the night. Farms, with their walled fields and orchards and pastures, made a quilt of the countryside for a good league along the road and maybe more beyond the hills to either side of it. Luca's show stopped in the village to put on a performance, and Egeanin and Domon were married there.

running sheepsfoot. A kind of knot.

Running Wave, Caire din Gelyn. *See* Caire din Gelyn Running Wave

Ruthan. Aldragoran's Saldaean clerk. He was hard-eyed, but didn't know one end of a sword from the other. He and Aldragoran were in The Queen's Lance when Nynaeve arrived to drum up support for Lan before the Last Battle.

Ryddingwood. The home of the poet Anasai.

Ryden. A dragon squadleader in the Band of the Red Hand. His squad blasted through part of Caemlyn's wall so that the Band could escape with the dragons in the Last Battle.

Ryma Galfrey. An Aes Sedai of the Yellow Ajah with a strength level of 29(17). Born in 902 NE, she went to the White Tower in 917 NE. After spending eight years as a novice and seven years as Accepted, she was raised to the shawl in 932 NE. Known for being haughty, she was 5'2½" tall, with dark hair and blue eyes. Ryma was captured by the Seanchan in Falme. She was made *damane* and given the name Pura, and was kept close at hand by the High Lady Suroth. *See also* Pura

Ryn Anhara. A male inventor at the Academy of Cairhien who trapped lightning in jars, using wire and wheels and big clay jars. His invention worked well enough to electrocute a rat that jumped onto it.

Ryne Venamar. A Malkieri man. Five years older than Lan, he was Lan's oldest friend besides Bukama. He was charming, with blue eyes and a dimpled cheek. When he was fifteen, his father moved the family to Arafel; Ryne embraced Arafellin ways, wearing his hair in two bell-laced braids and bells on his boots and sleeves, and looking women in the eye. An excellent swordsman, he claimed to have gone to Canluum as a merchant guard for a merchant who had been killed. He journeyed with Lan and Bukama from Canluum to Chachin; they acquired Moiraine's company along the way. At Aesdaishar Palace, he was not happy to be given a bannerman's room to stay in. A Darkfriend working with Merean, he tried to kill Lan, and did kill Bukama. Lan fought him while Moiraine was fighting Merean; though Ryne was the better swordsman, Lan killed him.

Rysael din Yulan. A relatively high-ranking Sea Folk Windfinder. Her strength level was 16(4). She took part in using the Bowl because she was one of the strongest available among the remaining Windfinders in Ebou Dar. She fled to Caemlyn with Elayne and her companions when the Seanchan attacked. Normally a dignified woman, she quivered when Birgitte asked the Windfinders for a gateway big enough to transport forces to rescue Elayne from the Black Ajah in Caemlyn.

S

s'Gandin. Birgitte talked of Luca going to fetch Nynaeve from Samara, accompanied by two lads who had shoulders like s'Gandin quarrymen.

s'redit. The Seanchan name for the animals that Luca called boar-horses. Large and gray, with a long nose and tusks, they were from a southern part of the Seanchan Empire; a similar animal with larger ears could be found in Shara. In terms of social standing, *morat* for non-exotics, such as *s'redit*, ranked below those for exotics (i.e., those obtained from alternate worlds). In ancient times, *s'redit* were a very effective battle animal, and maintaining them was a tradition that predated Hawkwing's invasion but was still linked to the Imperial family, who had a certain favoritism for them by tradition. While *s'redit* were still used in battle in later times, and their effectiveness strongly defended by their trainers and handlers, they were in fact deployed very carefully because they were not particularly useful except in stampeding untrained horses and as platforms for archers or *sul'dam* and *damane*, placing these at a greater height for longer visibility. In this employment, they were well armored and always well screened by infantry and horse because they themselves were very vulnerable. Their primary use was for moving heavy loads such as shunt engines or powering hoists to lift very heavy loads.

Sa souvraya niende misain ye. Old Tongue for "I am lost in my own mind."

Sa'las Plains. Flatlands located in Seanchan.

sa'angreal. An extremely rare object allowing an individual to channel much more of the One Power than would otherwise be possible or safe. A *sa'angreal* was like unto, but much, much more powerful than an *angreal*. The amount of the Power that could be wielded with a *sa'angreal* compared to the amount of the Power that could be handled with an *angreal* was analogous to the amount of the Power that could be wielded with the aid of an *angreal* compared to the amount of the Power that could be handled unaided. Remnants of the Age of Legends, the means of their making was lost by the Third Age. As with *angreal*, there were male and female *sa'angreal*.

sa'sara. An indecent Saldaean dance, outlawed by numerous Saldaean queens to no avail. Saldaean history recorded three wars, two rebellions, countless unions and/or feuds between noble Houses and innumerable duels sparked by women dancing the sa'sara. One rebellion was supposedly quelled when a defeated queen danced it for the victorious general; he married her and restored her throne. This tale was not found in any official history and was denied by every queen of Saldaea.

The sa'sara was a dance without any one set form, though it followed general patterns. Ten women dancing the sa'sara might dance without one repeating a movement or expression from any other. It was characterized by fluid and suggestive movements and hip-rolling; movements to suggest self-caressing or being caressed by another; facial expressions and gazes at the onlooker(s) which changed between those variously described as smoky or sultry and those which conveyed startlement. Not infrequently, the dancer performed most of the dance as if unaware that anyone was watching, and the emotions expressed, facially and otherwise, upon "discovering" that she was being watched went from surprised to coy to flirtatious to seductive, and frequently by the suggestion—never the reality—that limbs, or shoulders, or possibly even breasts, might be exposed. The clothing worn by the dancer could be skimpy or not, but nearly always it was arrayed for ease of shifting or removal, though rarely was even one piece actually removed. The shifting of clothing was such that it seemed a caress in itself, and the body part that seemed about to be exposed never was, yet the onlooker was left with the impression that perhaps it was.

The sa'sara was danced only by women, and always by one woman at a time. When the sa'sara was danced in the lower or rougher sort of taverns, or at some private affairs, guards were usually posted to keep patrons from throwing themselves at the dancer. The dancer usually traveled with a bodyguard. A sa'sara dancer who could perform with any facility was usually well paid for her dancing, and often made ten, twenty or even a hundred times as much through the coins tossed to her by watchers.

It was generally said that the sa'sara was danced for an audience of one no matter how many eyes watched. Some said that it was in actual truth danced more often for an audience of one than for more.

saa. Dark flecks that passed across the eyeballs of one who used the True Power from the Dark One. The flecks increased over time the more the True Power was used. Moridin's eyes were filled with *saa*.

Saal. A serving woman at The Woman of Tanchico in Tar Valon. She was pretty, with brown eyes. She and Mada—who Mat thought was Saal's older sister—took care of Thom when he stayed there, and tried to keep him from drinking too much; they did not like it when Mat bought Thom wine, but after Mat convinced Thom to go with him to Caemlyn, they were happy because it was the most alive that they had seen Thom in a long time. Saal gave Mat a silver mark in thanks and told him he had pretty eyes.

Saban. The third month of the year.

Sabeine Ocalin. A Kinswoman who spent twenty years as a peddler. She was at the farm when the Seanchan attacked, and accompanied Elayne to Caemlyn. She had the requisite strength to Travel, and Birgitte put her to work as a scout, sending her with Julanya Fote to villages in northern Andor and having them keep a lookout for the six noble Houses that were uncommitted.

Sabinel. A town in which Mat tried to get Talmanes to help him win over a pair of barmaids.

sad bracelets. *Ter'angreal* consisting of a finely jointed collar and two bracelets of dull black metal; Moghedien said that the material was a form of *cuendillar*. The device was similar to the later-developed *a'dam*, but was meant to control male Aes Sedai gone mad after the sealing of the Bore during the Time of Madness. When the collar was placed on a man who could channel, a woman wearing both bracelets could make him do as she wished. The bracelets could not stop the man from going mad, and there was a flow from the man to the woman; eventually the man would be able to control the woman somewhat. Having different women wear the bracelets at different times limited the exposure, and having two women each wearing one bracelet slowed the seepage considerably; the latter also lessened the women's control of the man. The devices were considered a failure because of these issues. Semirhage called them Domination Bands.

Saddler. A dirty man in Caemlyn who smelled of a tannery and tried to cheat Mat at a game of Koronko's Spit.

Saeldain, Coiren. *See* Coiren Saeldain

Saems, Wilbin. A deceased merchant for whom the cutpurse Samwil Hark claimed to have once worked as a clerk.

Saera Deosin. A Murandian woman who was on Moiraine's list as a possible mother of the Dragon Reborn. Her husband was Eadwin.

Saeric. A man of the Red Water sept of the Goshien Aiel. Gray-haired and missing his right hand, he taught the Asha'man how to fight while unarmed. He was willing to remain as long as the Goshien were in the vicinity of Caemlyn, but he moved on when his clan did.

Saerin Asnobar. An Altaran Aes Sedai of the Brown Ajah and the loyalist contingent, with a strength level of 14(2), who was born in 781 NE in a village not far from Ebou Dar. Her mother owned an inn and her father a livery stable. She was recruited by the Daughters of Silence in 796 NE; when that group was disbanded in 798 NE, Saerin was taken to the White Tower, where she spent twelve years as a novice and ten years as Accepted. She could have moved faster, but she was watched very closely because of her association with the Daughters. She was raised to the shawl in 820 NE, the only woman associated with the Daughters to be raised. She became a Sitter in the Hall in 960 NE, and held her chair longer than any other Sitter. About 5'6" tall, she had an olive complexion, straight black hair and dark eyes. While not a beauty in any way, she was attractive; a knife scar running along the line of her jaw on the left side was thin and had faded with years to near invisibility. She retained a good bit of the Ebou Dari sense of honor, and while she didn't wear a marriage knife, she often carried a curved Ebou Dari knife behind her belt, which she sometimes fingered when angry. She could scowl as well as any Warder, aided by her scar, and many sisters, including Seaine, considered her quite fierce. She stood to depose Siuan.

Saerin was one of the half dozen Sitters to whom Elaida gave penances, despite her being the most senior Sitter in age and time holding a chair, or perhaps because of that very fact. In her case, it was Labor, a matter of working in the kitchens with the scullions. Saerin was disconcerted to learn that Laras considered an Aes Sedai working a penance as a scullion to be, in fact, a scullion. That is to say, one was to be worked as hard and called up just as short for slacking. Despite her feelings about the penance, Saerin rather liked Laras for that; it was, she thought, the proper attitude. There was no point, she felt, in serving a penance if it was made easier by others. Her suspicions of Pevara and Seaine's clandestine meetings led to her becoming a member of the hunt for the Black Ajah.

Saerin was part of the battle in *Tel'aran'rhiod* against some of the Black Ajah at the White Tower until she and others were taken out of the dream on Amys' orders. She fought during the Last Battle with Egwene's army and after the Last Battle was part of the group that pressured Cadsuane to become Amyrlin.

Safer. One of the Ten Nations; its capital was Iman, which later became Katar. Other cities included Miereallen (later Falme) and Shainrahien. King Eawynd was its ruler at the signing of the Compact.

Saferi. Of or from Safer.

Sahera. A family in Kandor. *See* Avene *and* Migel Sahera

Sahra Coventry. A novice in the White Tower, sent to Moria Elward's farm to do penance to prevent her from talking about Min and Gawyn's meeting in the White Tower; the Black Ajah found and killed her there.

saidar. The female half of the One Power; it was used by female channelers.

saidin. The male half of the One Power; it was used by male channelers.

Saighan, House. A noble House in Cairhien. Its High Seat was Colavaere until her death; she was followed by Bertome. Its banner was a silver diamond on a field checked red and yellow. *See* Bertome, Colavaere *and* Dairaine Saighan

Sailmistress. A commander of a Sea Folk ship and crew, equivalent to a ship's captain. A Sailmistress wore three earrings in each ear; a medallion on the chain to her nose indicated the type of ship she commanded. A vessel was often owned by the Sailmistress who commanded him, though the vessels were always owned by women. Where a vessel sailed, and when, was purely in the hands of the Sailmistress, but what cargo was purchased or taken aboard and when, as well as all other financial matters, were in the hands of the Cargomaster.

Saine Tarasind. Mesaana's name before becoming Forsaken.

Saishen, Stedding. A *stedding* located in Saldaea.

Sajius. The author of *Commentary on the Dragon*, a book studied by Min.

Sakarnen. The name of the *sa'angreal* used by Demandred in the Last Battle; in the Age of Legends, it was known as *D'jedt*, or the Scepter. For safety, it had been taken apart and the two pieces hidden separately. Demandred found the rod first; it was the length of his forearm, with the metal splaying out to a disc shape at the end. Demandred found the second part, which looked like a cup, in *Rai'lair*, the Hearttomb, in Shara. He claimed to have bound Sakarnen to himself so that it could not be used against him.

Sakaru. A Shienaran soldier. He was one of those following Ingtar when he and Perrin pursued the Horn of Valere to Falme. He wintered in the Mountains of Mist with Perrin and Rand; after Rand left and the Shienarans were abandoned to make their own way, he died in an unpleasant manner.

Salaking. A location in Seanchan.

Saldaea. The largest of the Borderland nations; Maradon was its capital, Tenobia its queen. Its sigil was three silver fish, one above the other: the Silver Fish. Its banner was the Silver Fish on a field of dark blue. Many thought that sigil odd for a land with so many cliffs along the sea and such rough seas that it had few fishing villages and no port worth the name. Saldaea, Kandor, Arafel, Shienar and Malkier all were provinces of Hawkwing's empire, with the borders between them very much as they were at the start of the Last Battle, though not stretching so far south in most cases. With the Blight to contend with, the governors of those provinces (Lord Rylen t'Boriden Rashad for Saldaea, Lord Jarel Soukovni for Kandor, Lady Mahira Svetanya for Arafel, Lady Merean Tihomar for Shienar and Lord Shevar Jamelle for Malkier) met soon after Hawkwing's death in FY 994 to reaffirm measures for cooperation against the Blight and to make agreements for mutual defense against attack from the south. Before the end of FY 995, when it became clear that the rest of the empire was splintering, each of the governors took the title of King or Queen of his or her former province, now a nation. None of these nations would take part in any of the wider fighting of the War of the Hundred Years, as nations, except for defending themselves against attacks and punishing same, though individuals and groups did sometimes become involved, sometimes for political reasons or family connections or friendships. No major numbers of Saldaean troops were sent to fight in the Aiel War. For one thing, the threat never came anywhere near Saldaea, and for another, the western Blight spawned several periods of high Trolloc activity beginning a few years before the Aiel War and culminating some three years after its end. Some relatively small detachments of troops did take part, rarely numbering more than two to three thousand, but they were attached to Kandori elements and were withdrawn before the Battle of the Shining Walls because of a massive upsurge in activity along the Saldaean Blightborder which began in mid-978 NE and continued well into 979 NE. Some soldiers did remain in the fighting, but not many. One such party fought under Lan Mandragoran at the Blood Snow, along with Kandori and some Domani.

Saldaea had one of the three false Dragons who sprang up after Logain was captured and before Rand proclaimed himself; this was Mazrim Taim, who made considerable headway before being captured.

In Saldaea a wife took her husband's name but retained her own also, and her family name became a part of his. Thus: Faile (Zarine) si Ghaline Bashere became Faile ni Bashere t'Aybara when she married Perrin Aybara, and he became Perrin t'Bashere Aybara.

A child had the father's family name and the mother's. Thus: Zarine, the daughter of Davram t'Ghaline Bashere and Deira ni Ghaline t'Bashere was christened Zarine si Ghaline Bashere. Commoners' children had the mother's maiden name as a middle name and the father's surname as surname, without the "si," "ni," or "t'." Women among commoners keep their maiden name on marriage. Men proposed marriage, and women accepted or declined. A long pursuit was expected, and a woman usually made a man prove he really wanted to catch her before she let him.

In general, Saldaean women wanted a strong husband, one strong enough to stand up to them, because they were a strong lot themselves, and despised weak men. They did not expect to be bullied or browbeaten, though they knew when to make a strategic retreat. A Saldaean woman would be contemptuous of a man who couldn't stand toe-to-toe with her, meet her shout for shout and occasionally actually make her step back.

Saldaean custom was for wives of nobles to go on campaign with their husbands, except into the Blight, although that prohibition was often flouted. Many officers' wives also accompanied their husbands, and there were times when a wife led troops into battle in place of a wounded husband.

A Borderman considered the day he was given his sword to be his nameday.

There was a link between the Borderland and Aiel views of shame: by and large, shame was worse than guilt, the worst thing there was, though this view of shame ameliorated as one moved west. Arafellin saw shame as less important than did Shienarans, Kandori less than Arafellin, Saldaeans less than Kandori. In all of the Borderlands, though, shame was given a much heavier weight than in lands to the south.

Saldaea could have either a king or a queen, advised by the Council of Lords. The husband or wife of a Saldaean ruler was not simply a consort, but an almost co-equal ruler. It was a hereditary monarchy; the eldest child of the reigning monarch normally succeeding. If the child was younger than fifteen, a regent was chosen from the child's aunts and uncles of the blood, picked by a combination of age and degree of relationship.

If the ruler died without issue, the throne passed to the eldest and nearest relative, chosen by a combination of age and degree of relationship, with the degree of relationship coming first and age second. Thus, a brother or sister would have come before an aunt or uncle, but among aunts and uncles as among brothers and sisters, the eldest would have succeeded.

The heir apparent to Tenobia was Davram Bashere. Since no other close relatives survived, the next in line after Lord Davram was his own heir, his daughter Faile, who became queen after Tenobia's and Bashere's deaths in the Last Battle.

Saldaea had no ports, and only a few tiny fishing villages, so the vast bulk of trade traditionally followed one of three routes: 1) down to Arad Doman, through Bandar Eban; 2) down the Manetherendrelle to Illian; and 3) much less important, historically, to Kandor, and through Kandor to Tar Valon and points south.

There was a great trade from Saldaea in timber, finished wood, furs and ice peppers. Ice peppers were a Saldaean monopoly, as they did not grow elsewhere; they were apparently very particular as to both soil and climate. There was a substantial woolen industry, but not much was exported. Saldaea exported large amounts of iron, steel and finished iron- and steel-work. There was considerable mining of diamonds, and considerable mining of silver and the manufacture of silverwork, but very little gold-mining.

Salia Pomfrey. An Andoran widow who gave birth to a boy near Dragonmount close to the time that Rand was born. Her husband was killed on the second day of the Battle of the Shining Walls; half-mad with grief, she returned to her village in Andor.

Salidar. A large village in Altara, a mile east of the River Eldar, near the Amadician border. It was the birthplace of Deane Aryman, and the town where the rebel Aes Sedai set up their organization. Woodland surrounded the village. Trees ran up to thatch-roofed houses made of rounded river stones, and many trees actually stood in narrow little thickets among some of the houses. The streets had a look of newly turned earth, not the hard-packed surface that came from generations of use. Siuan first learned of Salidar being the location of the rebel Aes Sedai from an eyes-and-ears in Lugard. When she, Leane, Min and Logain arrived in Salidar, they caused a stir. They spread the story about Logain having been set up as a false Dragon by the Red Ajah. Gareth Bryne arrived to hold Siuan and company to their oath to work for him, and agreed to head an army against the White Tower. Elayne, Nynaeve, Thom, Juilin, Uno and Shienaran soldiers arrived in Salidar from Samara in Ghealdan. Then Egwene was summoned to Salidar and made Amyrlin. An abandoned inn was used as a meeting place for the Hall and also housed the Amyrlin's study; it was named the Little Tower. The rebel Aes Sedai stayed in Salidar until the decision was made to move against the White Tower.

Salindi Casolan. An Aes Sedai Sitter who lived at the time of the formation of the White Tower.

Salita Toranes. A Tairen Aes Sedai of the Yellow Ajah and the rebel contingent, with a strength level of 27(15). Born in 933 NE, she went to the White Tower in 950 NE. After spending nine years as a novice and seven years as Accepted, she was raised to the shawl in 966 NE. Almost as dark as one of the Sea Folk, she was round-faced, with cool level eyes, and stood about 5'4" tall. Like some other Yellows, she believed the other Ajahs were merely adjuncts to the Yellow, which had the only useful purpose. She had complaints from the Yellows who were conscripted into making *cuendillar*, who thought Aes Sedai should not be making things for sale. Being a lesser noblewoman, Salita had an income from an estate in Tear and was casual about money and contemptuous of trade; she never stopped to think what her own income derived from. She was a very quick learner, with an eidetic memory. She might well have been allowed to move through novice and Accepted faster had she had a stronger potential. Salita learned Nynaeve's form of Healing and was raised a Sitter for the Yellow in Salidar in 999 NE. She sometimes supported Egwene in the Hall and sometimes not; she voted yes in the war vote and for the alliance with the Black Tower. After the White Tower reunited, Salita resigned as Sitter.

Sallie Daera. The code name for Salidar used by the rebel Aes Sedai.

Salmarna. The location of a battle where Bukama became a hero.

Salt Flat. A sept of the Nakai Aiel.

salt name. A name added to the end of an Atha'an Miere name, following the family name. It was composed of two words, such as South Star, Running Wave, or White Wing, and given when an apprentice reached a certain age or level of experience.

Salya. From a gleeman's tale, Lenn's daughter, who walked among the stars.

Samaha. A town in Altara, east of Willar and the River Boern. Moiraine, Lan, Perrin and Loial passed through while on Rand's trail, and learned that all the wells in the town had suddenly gone dry, evidence that Rand had been there.

Samalin Naerodan. A Murandian Aes Sedai of the Green Ajah and the rebel contingent, with a strength level of 22(10). Born in 935 NE, she went to the White Tower in 952 NE. After spending six years as a novice and five years as Accepted, she was raised to the shawl in 963 NE and raised Sitter for the Green in Salidar in 999 NE, although she was young for it. Sharp-faced, she had a surprising sense of humor and a bright, clear laugh. She had one Warder, to whom she was married, though that was not widely known. Samalin stood immediately for Egwene the second time. She was one of those who stood for war against Elaida and for an alliance with the Black Tower.

Samara. A large, prosperous town in Ghealdan on the River Eldar, just over the Amadician border. It had a high stone wall, stone buildings, many three stories high, and more roofs made of slate and tile than thatch. The Prophet settled there for a time, and a huge tent/shanty city grew around the wall. Master Luca went there looking for space to set up his menagerie; Nynaeve spotted Uno, and he took her to see Masema, the Prophet. The latter agreed to get Nynaeve and her companions a ship downriver to Tear, to see the Dragon. Galad followed them, and said he would find them a ship instead. The Whitecloaks seized a smuggling vessel to take Nynaeve and company downriver, which caused riots in the town. The party fought their way across town and departed on the ship. Later, Asne, Chesmal, Eldrith and Temaile followed Moghedien there, but did not connect with her.

Samared, House. Elayne's fictional House while traveling incognito.

Samel Crawe. A Village Councilman in Emond's Field. Horse-faced, with a long nose, he was the father of Ban. Samel participated in the defense of Emond's Field; he and Jon Thane had charge of the area east of The Winespring Inn.

Samitsu Tamagowa. An Arafellin Aes Sedai of the Yellow Ajah, uncommitted to any contingent. Her strength level was 20(8). Born in 856 NE, she went to the White Tower in 870 NE. After spending nine years as a novice and four years as Accepted, she was raised to the shawl in 883 NE. Her Warder was Roshan. She was 5'5" tall, and slim, with dark hazel eyes and dark hair in which she wore silver bells. Samitsu had an overbearing, commanding manner and could be somewhat petulant at being balked, as when her Healing of Rand failed. Samitsu had no fear of getting her hands dirty or bloody in dealing with someone who was hurt; she was quite matter-of-fact about it. She had the Talent for Healing so strongly that no one, not even sisters stronger than she in the Power, could do it better. She used traditional flows of Air, Spirit and Water. Cadsuane said that she was the best living—perhaps the best ever—and that no one could perform Healing to compare with her. That buoyed Samitsu's spirits, though she accepted it as simple truth. Samitsu was with Cadsuane in the Cairhienin rebel camp when Rand came to visit, before the fog incident. She tried Healing Rand after Padan Fain's attack, and was distraught that she did not succeed fully. She demanded that Flinn tell her everything he could about what he had done to Heal Rand, and at the same time tried to bribe him, even offering to bear his child; she was extremely anxious to know about his way of Healing that did more than hers could. Samitsu was left behind in Cairhien when Cadsuane went to Far Madding. Cadsuane left her in charge, but Sashalle slowly took over Samitsu's authority in the Sun Palace. Samitsu Healed Dobraine after he had been attacked. Samitsu went with Logain and others when they went to find Rand, but Cadsuane sent her back to watch Sashalle. She welcomed Elayne when Elayne arrived to take the Sun Throne.

Saml al'Seen. A Two Rivers man at the Black Tower with the rank of soldier. He was young—little more than a child—and had dark hair. Saml was guarding the gate of the Black Tower when representatives of the Red Ajah arrived.

Saml Hake. The innkeeper at The Dancing Cartman in Four Kings, Andor. Bony, with long stringy hair, he was the first skinny innkeeper Rand had ever seen. He planned to rob Rand and Mat; the Darkfriend Howal Gode gave Jak, Strom and Hake something to make them sleep while he tried his pitch on Rand.

Samma N'Sei. Old Tongue for "Eyeblinders," the term was used for red-veiled men, some of whom could channel. Male Aiel channelers or their progeny who went to the Blight to fight Shadowspawn and were Turned by Myrddraal, they inhabited a town ("the Town") in the Blight. The Eyeblinders were groomed as a surprise weapon in the Last Battle. Some of them had an earlier mission to find and destroy the Eye of the World before the Dragon Reborn could reach it, but that mission failed.

Sammael. One of the Forsaken, also known as the Destroyer of Hope. His name prior to swearing to the Dark One was Tel Janin Aellinsar. His strength level was ++2. About six feet tall, with blue eyes, golden hair and a neat square-trimmed beard, he would perhaps have been above ordinary in looks except for a slanting scar on his left cheek, as if a red-hot poker had been dragged across his face from hairline to jaw. The scar was given him by Lews Therin, whom Sammael both envied and hated; he would not let the scar be restored, keeping it as a badge of hatred and vengeance. He was a lover of power, glory and conquest and a militarist rather than a diplomat. A famous sportsman in the Age of Legends, he was at that time friends with Lews Therin, although how close was not known; at the beginning of the War of Power he became one of Lews Therin's best generals. In the fourth year of the war, he went over to the Shadow, in part because he thought that the Dark One would win, and in part because of his hatred of Lews Therin. Sammael believed that he was the better general and that he should be in command of the forces of the Light.

When he awoke in the Third Age, he ruled in Illian as Lord Brend, a member of the Council of Nine, and plotted with Lanfear, Graendal and Rahvin to catch Rand. He discovered at least one stasis-box; a *gholam* was among its contents. He sent Carridin to Ebou Dar to try to find a cache of objects of the One Power, and sent the *gholam* there to help Carridin against Aes Sedai. As part of manipulating Graendal, he told her that he had reached a personal truce with Rand, but he was lying—he had sent a messenger offering truce to Rand, but Rand refused and the messenger died messily. He tricked Graendal and coopted her into his plans, and made her help him with the Shaido, all by claiming to have the inside track as Nae'blis. Of course, Graendal was using him as well, aiming him like an arrow at Rand. He met with Sevanna and the Shaido Wise Ones as Caddar and gave Sevanna a binder and a cube he called a *nar'baha,* which was used to scatter the Shaido in an effort to keep Rand off balance. When Rand attacked Illian, Sammael Traveled to Shadar Logoth, where he was killed by Mashadar.

Sammana. A Wise One dreamer whom Bair mentioned. She encountered something in *Tel'aran'rhiod* that broke her mind; she spent the rest of her days drooling and needing her linens changed.

Sammrie. The cooper in Hinderstap. His sister and her family were the first outsiders caught in Hinderstap.

Samon. A High Lord in Tear who was really Be'lal. He was able to use Compulsion to convince the High Lords that he was a hitherto obscure Lord of the Land who deserved to be raised to High Lord. *See also* Be'lal

Samwil Hark. A cutpurse in Andor. He was perfectly ordinary-looking in every way, with brown hair and eyes, medium height and build and plain clothes. In short, he was eminently forgettable. Hark was very good at stealing, but he was turned in by a rival. Instead of hanging Hark, Elayne placed a Finder of Spirit on him as a tracking device, and used him to follow Mellar.

San d'ma Shadar, Naath and the. A battle from Mat's memories.

Sana Ashraf. A man whom Mat fought at the falls of Pena in one of the memories received from the Eelfinn.

Sanaiye Asaheen. A Domani Aes Sedai of the Green Ajah and the loyalist contingent. Part of the group that kidnapped Rand, she escaped Dumai's Wells with Covarla Baldene.

Sanche, Siuan. *See* Siuan Sanche

Sand Hills. The foothills of the Mountains of Mist, located just west of the Westwood.

Sandair, Asan. *See* Asan Sandair

Sandar, Juilin. *See* Juilin Sandar

Sandip. A lieutenant in the Band of the Red Hand. He was also an accomplished hedge-doctor. Sandip helped rescue the dragons when Trollocs attacked Caemlyn. He was part of Faile's group that wound up in the Blight while trying to deliver the Horn of Valere to Mat. When large beasts attacked, he helped to fight them off.

Sandomere, Donalo. *See* Donalo Sandomere

Sanduin. An Aiel man of the *Tain Shari* society. He had a scar that only made his face more handsome, according to Sorilea, who wondered if Sanduin might have caught Egwene's interest.

Sanetre. A Guardswoman in Caemlyn whom Birgitte sent to fetch Guybon, after Elayne had been kidnapped by Black sisters.

Sanghir, Karale. *See* Karale Sanghir

Saniago, Weiramon. *See* Weiramon Saniago

Sanit. The cow *s'redit* tended by Cerandin in Valan Luca's circus. Luca called it a "boar-horse" to deflect from its true identity.

Sanor. A sailor on the crew of Mallia's ship, the *Gray Gull*, out of Tar Valon, which transported Mat and Thom to Aringill. He had arms like Perrin's, and Mallia summoned him and Vasa to throw Mat and Thom off when they jumped onto the ship as it was leaving the dock.

Sanshen, Stedding. A *stedding* located in the Spine of the World.

Santes. One of Berelain's thief-catchers from Mayene. About 5'9" tall, with dark hair and dark eyes, he was bland-faced and ordinary-looking and so nondescript that no one would have noticed him, even bumping into him, on the street. He was friendly with Rosene and Nana, Berelain's maids. Berelain used Gendar and Santes to spy on Masema by having them make friends with his people and taking them wine supposedly stolen from Berelain. Santes found a document signed by Suroth, saying that Masema was under her protection, after picking the lock of Masema's camp desk under cover of the bustle of setting up camp. Gendar and Santes returned to Masema's camp with Berelain's last cask of Tunaighan and were expected to return by an hour after sunset, but did not. They were presumed dead, killed by Masema's men.

Santhra. Author of a book on the Forsaken, found in Adeleas and Vandene's home in Tifan's Well, Arafel. Vandene thought it a nasty piece of work.

Sar. A Shienaran soldier. He was one of those following Ingtar when he and Perrin pursued the Horn of Valere to Falme. He wintered in the Mountains of Mist with Perrin and Rand; after Rand left and the Shienarans were abandoned to make their own way, he fell off a cliff in the Mountains of Mist and died.

sar-light. An illuminating device from the Age of Legends mentioned by Sammael.

Sara. The cook at The Stag and Lion in Baerlon. She was plump and had a cat named Cirri. Master Fitch went to her because guests were complaining about dead rats, and he thought Cirri had killed them; Rand witnessed her vehement reaction that Cirri had not. Sara threatened to leave, and Master Fitch quickly made amends.

Sara. The subject of the song "Darling Sara."

Sarainya Vostovan. An Arafellin Kinswoman who was born of a noble House. Her strength level was 46(34); she was not strong enough to have been allowed to test for Aes Sedai, and not strong enough to make a gateway of any size whatsoever. She was not nearly old enough to stand very high among the Kin. She was born in 924 NE, went to the White Tower in 940 NE and was ten years a novice (940–950 NE). She was raised Accepted in 950 NE for political reasons, and then sent away. She went to the Tower when Kirin Melway was Amyrlin and was put out after Noane Masadim was raised Amyrlin. She had a husky, forceful voice and was strikingly handsome. She kept the form of every rule exactly, but she was stubborn and did things her own way. A proud woman, she didn't like wearing the red belt and working or living among the poor. Sarainya traveled to Caemlyn with Elayne; when Garenia and Kirstian were identified as runaways and put back in white, she and Asra attempted a revolt, but Reanne and Alise put a stop to it. She was ordered to cut a switch for punishment from Alise later that day.

Saralin. A Da'shain Aiel after the Breaking. Her husband was Marind; they had a son, Lewin, and a daughter, Maigran. Marind was killed when bandits raided the Aiel, and Saralin raised the children with the help of her father-in-law, Adan. Maigran and another girl were kidnapped by bandits; Saralin was prepared to accept it and go on, as required by the Way of the Leaf. Lewin and his friends decided to rescue the girls and in doing so killed the bandits. When Saralin learned what he had done, she disowned him; Adan exiled all the young men involved.

Saraline Amerano. An Aes Sedai who lived at the time of the formation of the White Tower.

Saralman, Feragaine. *See* Feragaine Saralman

Saranche, Agardo. The innkeeper of The Dragon in Tear. He was lean, balding, fair-complected and dark-eyed.

Sarand, House. A noble House in Caemlyn. Its High Seat was Jarid; its sign two Golden Boars. *See* Elenia *and* Jarid Sarand

Saranov, Halima. *See* Halima Saranov

Sarasia. A Kinswoman who accompanied Elayne to her Cairhienin coronation. She was plump, with a grandmotherly air.

Sarat, Surlivan. *See* Surlivan Sarat

Sareitha Tomares. A Tairen Aes Sedai of the Brown Ajah and the rebel contingent, with a strength level of 26(14). Born in 965 NE, she went to the White Tower in 980 NE. After spending ten years as a novice and eight years as Accepted, she was raised to the shawl in 998 NE. A dark, stocky woman with inquisitive eyes and a square face, she looked a little older than Nynaeve. She did not yet have the ageless face, which she sometimes plainly wished for. Her Warder was Ned Yarman. Sareitha was sent to the court of Queen Tylin in Ebou Dar with Merilille Ceandevin and Careane Fransi. She served as the Seat of Rebuke at Elayne's abortive trial over approaching the Knitting Circle. She went with Elayne to Caemlyn and was killed by Chesmal Emry at the house on Full Moon Street in the New City while trying to capture members of the Black Ajah; Ned was killed as well.

Sarek. A Seanchan nobleman who looked above his station and had designs on the regions of Tuel and Serengada Dai, which put him in opposition to Lady Morsa and drew attention from Jalindin, a Seeker for Truth. Rand and Aviendha heard of him when they Traveled to Seanchan.

Saren, Einor. *See* Einor Saren

Sarena, Lady. A powerful Altaran noblewoman visiting Salidar who listened to Logain's story about the Red Ajah making him a false Dragon. Hard-eyed and stocky, she had a scar on her face and graying hair.

Sarendhra. A Shaido Maiden of the Spear with blue eyes. She accompanied Rand to the Stone of Tear when he met with Darlin about the Tairen rebels.

Sarene Nemdahl. A Taraboner Aes Sedai of the White Ajah and the loyalist contingent, with a strength level of 18(6). Born in 955 NE, she went to the White Tower in 970 NE. After spending six years as a novice and five years as Accepted, she was raised to the shawl in 981 NE. Her Warder was Vitalien, though it was unusual for a White to have a Warder. About 5'4" tall, and slender, she wore her dark hair in beaded Taraboner braids. Some of her Taraboner accent remained. Her face was extremely beautiful, enough to make any man stare, but she was not aware of it. She had a temper, which she usually kept bottled up, but she could snap one's nose off in a flash if crossed; she would admit she was wrong, though if her temper was involved, her admission would be made only after it had cooled. Her secret vice was poetry, which she hid and felt slightly ashamed of because poetry was emotional and illogical. One of her verses compared her Warder to a leopard. A part of the loyalist embassy to Rand in Cairhien, she was captured at Dumai's Wells. As a result of Verin's Compulsion, Sarene was one of the first five of the captive Aes Sedai to swear fealty to the Dragon Reborn. Sarene traveled with Cadsuane to Far Madding and to Shadar Logoth; during the cleansing of the taint she worked with Corele Hovian and Damer Flinn. They encountered Demandred, but managed to drive him off. With the Last Battle approaching, Sarene engaged in a tempestuous affair with Vitalien. They fought for the armies at Shayol Ghul. Sarene was Compelled by Graendal/Hessalam and used until her eyes were vacant. Vitalien was killed.

Sari Ayellin. A Two Rivers woman. After her father died, Sari tried to capture the interest of the man her mother intended to marry. She finally settled down after her mother was married and she found her own husband. Nynaeve thought of her when Elayne was making calf's eyes at Thom.

Sarien. An Aiel warrior who was with Gaul searching for He Who Comes With the Dawn; the wind was blowing in the wrong direction and they were surprised by Orban and Gann and their retainers. Gaul was captured, and Sarien killed.

Sarin Hoigan. Nisao Dachen's Warder. Bald-headed, with a black beard, he was about 5'9" tall, and wide enough to make him seem shorter. When Siuan said that the Hall might require Nisao and Myrelle to pass their Warders' bonds to someone else in punishment for their dealings with Lan, Sarin realized through the bond that Nisao was upset and started toward her.

Sarinde. A Wise One of the Codarra Aiel from Red Springs Hold. She served as Wise One for Indirian, the clan chief.

Sarna, Egeanin. *See* Egeanin Sarna

Saroiya Farseen. A Domani Aes Sedai of the White Ajah and the rebel contingent, with a strength level of 24(12). Born in 857 NE, she went to the White Tower in 873 NE. After spending thirteen years as a novice and eleven as Accepted, she was raised to the shawl in 897 NE. Brown-haired and brown-eyed, she was about 5'4" tall, and stocky. She tugged at her ear when deep in thought. As a novice, Myrelle introduced trout into Saroiya's bath; the result, according to Siuan, taught Myrelle to mind herself for half a year. Saroiya was a very good, if strict, teacher. She also displayed very good organizational and managerial abilities, as well as being considered among the sharpest logicians of her Ajah. For those reasons she was chosen a Sitter for the White in 987 NE, although she was younger than usual. In 999 NE the head of the White Ajah ordered her to join the rebellion to control and defuse events. Saroiya was apparently very tightly under Romanda's thumb, and in fact, given Romanda's forceful personality, this was not far from the truth. Saroiya tried to influence the rebel Hall toward the belief that the Seanchan were too important and too dangerous to ignore until matters with Elaida were resolved. Because of Romanda, she had to do this carefully. Saroiya was against any alliance with the

Black Tower and worked to delay an embassy to it; she also opposed bonding Asha'man. She was part of the group, with Magla, Faiselle, Takima and Varilin, who negotiated with the White Tower to try to end the split. After the Tower was reunited, she kept her seat as a Sitter.

Sashalle Anderly. An Aes Sedai of the Red Ajah and the loyalist contingent, with a strength level of 14(2). Born in 816 NE, she went to the White Tower in 832 NE. After spending nine years as a novice and six years as Accepted, she was raised to the shawl in 847 NE. She wore her hair in ringlets to her shoulders and had blue eyes and a stubborn jaw. Sashalle was part of the follow-on party to the embassy sent to Rand in Cairhien by Elaida. She was one of three sisters stilled by Rand during his escape at Dumai's Wells. Although they were captured, those three were not treated as *da'tsang* like the others, but Verin did use her version of Compulsion on them, and they also swore oath to Rand. Sashalle was Healed by Damer Flinn to full strength, but was no longer held by the Three Oaths and appeared prettier as her ageless look faded. She wrote a letter to the Red Ajah saying that she was sworn to Rand.

Although Cadsuane had left Samitsu in charge in Cairhien, Sashalle took over by force of personality. Sorilea and the Aiel respected her, and even the servants at the Sun Palace deferred to her as if she were in charge. Sashelle greeted Elayne when she arrived to be crowned Queen of Cairhien.

She fought at Shayol Ghul in the Last Battle and was captured and used up by Graendal/Hessalam.

Satare. A wine from the Age of Legends remembered by Graendal.

Satarov, Nedare. *See* Nedare Satarov

Satelle. One of the places in the Age of Legends that Sammael, the Destroyer of Hope, devastated, earning him that name.

Satina. A plump serving woman at the Little Tower in Salidar. She was able to do what was necessary even when frightened enough to tremble, but she had her limits. She shared a room with Mulinda, Emara and Ronelle in the same house where Elayne and Nynaeve stayed. She helped Nynaeve unwind her roommates from their sheets after the bubble of evil hit.

Savara. A female officer who led a squadron unit of the Seanchan cavalry in the Last Battle.

Saven. The sixth month of the year.

Savion Amhara. One of the three most famous First Counsels in Far Madding history. A statue of her stood in Amhara Market in Far Madding, pointing to the Tear Gate.

Sawchin. A rendering of "Seanchan" in Tairen gossip.

sawleaf. A weed that Perrin noticed on the burned al'Thor farm.

Sawyn Maculhene. A supporter of Amalasan who tried to free Amalasan from the White Tower. He and Elinde Motheneos managed to capture at least two of the Alindrelle Erinin bridges and reach the White Tower before being turned back. Maculhene died in the fighting, and his troopers were harried mercilessly.

Sayer. A friend of Androl who died of the fevers during a silverpike run out of Mayene.

scarlet puffer. A snake that looked like a red adder but was not poisonous.

scatterhead. A plant whose head burst into little white feathers when disturbed. Nynaeve smacked one while traveling with Luca's circus near Samara.

School of Cairhien, the. An institution founded by Rand in Barthanes Damodred's manor; its headmistress was Idrien Tarsin. Pupils came to learn, but for the most part Rand wanted to gather knowledge in one place so that if he broke the world again, there would be repositories of preserved knowledge.

Scouter. Bulen's packhorse when he rode with Lan for Tarwin's Gap.

Scratch. The cat at The Winespring Inn in Emond's Field. He was a yellow tom-cat with six toes on each foot.

Sea Folk. *See* Atha'an Miere

Sea Folk, Isles of. Islands in the Aryth Ocean and the Sea of Storms that were the homeport of the Sea Folk. Many of the islands were unknown to outsiders and visitation was not allowed.

Sea of Jeren. A body of water in the Age of Legends.

Sea of L'Heye. A body of water off the coast of Seanchan.

Sea of Storms. A body of water that bordered the main continent on the south; it lay east of the Aryth Ocean.

Sea Wall. The name used by Saldaeans for the Banikhan Mountains.

Seaghan. A Cairhienin man who ran an entertainment hall. He wanted to have players pretend to be characters in *The Great Hunt of the Horn*. Thom thought it a lack-witted idea.

Seahawk. Bayle Domon's ship when he was in Tanchico. He and Egeanin sailed it from Tanchico to Cantorin. They were attempting to get rid of the male *a'dam* when they were hailed and boarded by another Seanchan ship.

Seaine Herimon. A Murandian Aes Sedai of the White Ajah and the loyalist contingent, with a strength level of 17(5). Born in 841 NE, she went to the White Tower in 856 NE after talking her father into buying passage for her and her mother to Tar Valon—passage for two upriver, but only one down. After spending six years as a novice and four years as Accepted, she was raised to the shawl in 866 NE and raised a Sitter for the Whites in 986 NE. Seaine and Pevara were novice and Accepted together, and they were friends—pillow friends, in fact. As novices, they often played pranks together. Pevara said that Seaine could never decide that it was logical to be afraid until it was already too late for that. One of the things they did was dust Serancha's shift with itch oak; they thought Serancha was a prig then, and their opinion didn't change. They drifted apart, in part because the Red actively and strongly discouraged women having friends outside their Ajah.

Seaine was 5'6" tall, and had blue eyes and thick black eyebrows. After many years, a touch of Lugard still clung to her voice. When she sat thinking, she pressed her fists beneath her chin in the way her furniture-maker father did. Many considered her a highly logical woman, almost a prototypical White. She reasoned out highly complex puzzles and riddles for relaxation. She had a very small ability with Earth, little better than Pevara. She always had a fondness for cats, and she kept carved figures of them, many in amusing poses. Strong-willed and confident, she was frequently as blind to the world around her as any Brown; Whites were often like that, all logic and no judgment.

With the exception of the Sitter who was killed in the fighting, Seaine was the only Sitter excluded from the gathering of the Hall where Siuan Sanche was deposed who did not flee the Tower and join the rebels. She remained because she believed in the law and its forms. She would not have stood to depose Siuan—she had, after all, proposed Siuan for Amyrlin in the first place—but once it was done, with however small a nod to the law, she felt she had no choice but to remain. Elaida went to Seaine to have her get evidence that Alviarin was a traitor; Seaine misunderstood and thought that Elaida was charging her to find the Black Ajah. Elaida chose Seaine for the primary reason that no one would suspect Elaida of going to her because she had proposed Siuan for Amyrlin, and also because of her logical and deductive skills. Seaine went to Pevara to ask for help, which was given. Together they discovered the ferrets sent from Salidar and bound them to help in the search. Other Sitters—Yukiri, Saerin, Doesine and Talene—noticed them sneaking about and also became part of the search. Their first discovery was Talene, who helped them find other members of the Black. Seaine and Talene Minly had been friends despite Talene standing to depose Siuan; she accepted Talene's reasons, though she didn't agree with them. After Talene was revealed as Black Ajah, Seaine felt as though Talene being a Darkfriend meant their friendship was a lie and a betrayal; she knew that did not really make sense, but she could not shake the feeling. Seaine's nose was a little out of joint over the new arrangements in the Black Ajah hunting group, though she told herself she was being illogical. She and Pevara had acted as co-equals, ignoring the strength difference between them because they were friends. With the advent of the others, though, the formal strictures of hierarchy took over. Saerin assumed leadership, and Pevara and the others accepted this, but Seaine couldn't help thinking that it was she who was chosen for this task originally, and now she was outranked by just about everybody except the fifth column and their prisoner, Talene. Seaine and the rest continued their search until Verin's notebook made it unnecessary; then she helped Egwene learn more about the Forsaken.

She was part of the battle in *Tel'aran'rhiod* against some of the Black Ajah at the White Tower until she and others were taken out of the dream on Amys' orders.

After Taim was forced out of the Black Tower, Seaine went there to bond an Asha'man Warder.

Sealbreaker. The name Gabrelle gave Logain, because he broke the seals on the Dark One's prison during the Last Battle.

Sealdre. An Aiel Wise One and dreamwalker at the time of the building of Rhuidean. She was married to Mandein and encouraged him to go to the Jenn Aiel in Rhuidean. She had long golden hair.

Sealed to the Flame. A term referring to information that was kept secret from everyone but the Amyrlin and those with whom she chose to share it.

Sealed to the Tower. A term referring to information that was kept secret from anyone outside the White Tower.

Seana. A Wise One of the Black Cliff sept of the Nakai Aiel. She had gray-streaked dark hair and bluish-gray eyes. A dreamwalker who could not channel, she was killed by a Draghkar in the attack on Cold Rocks Hold.

Seanchan. A land lying three thousand leagues west of the main continent, and its people. Its capital was Seandar, where the Court of the Nine Moons held the seat of the Empress or Emperor, the Crystal Throne. Its Imperial sigil was a golden hawk in flight, clutching three lightning bolts in its talons. The Imperial banner was white, bordered in royal blue, with the sigil in its center. If the Empress or Emperor was present, it was fringed in gold; if the heir to the throne was present, it was fringed in blue.

In FY 992, Artur Hawkwing sent his son Luthair and another son across the Aryth Ocean with about two thousand ships and three hundred thousand soldiers and settlers. When they landed in Seanchan, they discovered a shifting quilt of nations often at war with one another, where Aes Sedai often reigned. Without any equivalent of the White Tower, Aes Sedai worked for their own individual goals, using the Power. Forming small groups, they schemed against one another constantly. In large part it was this constant scheming for personal advantage and the resulting wars among the myriad nations that allowed the armies from east of the Aryth Ocean to begin the conquest of an entire continent, and for their descendants to complete it. During this conquest, the descendants of the original armies became Seanchan as much as they conquered Seanchan.

After Luthair received word of his father's death and then nothing further, he planned to gather the might of his conquered nation and return to the mainland and reclaim his father's empire. While it took more than eleven hundred years, in 998 NE, a force of Seanchan arrived with five hundred ships at Falme. They called themselves the *Hailene*, or the Forerunners; they planned to retake the continent if necessary for the *Corenne*, or the Return. Though they lost a battle at Falme, High Lady Suroth gathered the *Hailene* and took Tanchico and Ebou Dar; the *Corenne*, a fleet of thousands of ships and hundreds of thousands of soldiers, craftsmen and others, soon followed.

Luthair was helped in his conquest of Seanchan also by the invention of the *a'dam*. Invented by Deain, one of the Aes Sedai, to curry favor with Luthair, it was used to subjugate and control the Aes Sedai, although it required *sul'dam*, women with the ability to learn to channel, to be used. That the *sul'dam* could learn to channel was suppressed and eventually forgotten. In time, all young women came to be tested for the ability to become *damane* or *sul'dam*; if she was the former, she was immediately collared and written out of family records and citizen rolls. If she was the latter, she gained prestige and honor.

Damane were used in many facets of Seanchan life, including construction, warfare, the finding of ores, and even entertainment; they could produce a display called Sky Lights, which resembled a fireworks display, but which were thought by Seanchan to be superior. A man who could channel was immediately executed and his name removed from all records.

From the time of Luthair's conquest, the Seanchan were ruled by an emperor or empress. The throne on which the ruler sat, the Crystal Throne, was a *ter'angreal* causing anyone approaching to feel great awe and wonder; only the reigning monarch was ever allowed to sit on it. The Emperor or Empress encouraged potential heirs to contend for the throne, and would choose the child felt to be the strongest. Those contests were not limited to simply bettering one's rivals at court; assassination was common. Empress Radhanan favored her daughter Tuon to succeed her; Tuon accompanied the Return. Semirhage killed the entire royal family remaining in Seanchan; Tuon became empress, taking the name Fortuona.

The Empress or Emperor ruled with the help of a number of groups. The most honored were the Deathwatch Guards, who were the personal bodyguards of the Imperial family. Some Deathwatch Guards were human, and *da'covale*; the remainder were Ogier and were not owned. The Seekers for Truth were a police and spy organization; Seekers were property, but they held wide powers and could arrest anyone who did not answer their questions or cooperate with them. They held their prisoners in the Tower of Ravens. Listeners were secret spies for the Empress of Seanchan. They were always hidden, and had no authority whatsoever. Their duty was to report everything they saw, heard, or learned.

The Seanchan symbol of justice was a slant-edged headsman's axe, the haft of which was bound with intricate knots in a white silk rope. The axe itself was a method of execution for various high crimes, at least for commoners; for nobles guilty of certain crimes, the cord was used to strangle them. It was usually covered or carried in a black velvet bag; when the cord was exposed, justice was being dealt, or might be dealt. The bag itself was also a weighty symbol of justice within the Imperial family, within which justice for all others was contained. The method of execution for a member of the Imperial family was to be sealed within the bag and left to die.

No one was allowed to go armed into the presence of a member of the Imperial family, or a High Lord or Lady, excepting only the Deathwatch Guard. By Seanchan law, no one's hand might slay or shed the blood of one in whose veins flowed the blood of Artur Hawkwing. This did not refer to the Blood in general; only to those who were descended from Hawkwing.

Neither a *damane* nor a *da'covale* (other than a *so'jhin*) could give evidence, by law. As a practical matter, no charge or accusation made by a *da'covale* (other than a *so'jhin*) or a *damane* would be believed. *So'jhin* could give evidence and bring charges, as was necessary, since most of the bureaucracy of Seanchan was composed of *so'jhin* belonging to the Imperial Throne. The nobles of Seanchan, known as the Blood, were originally limited to those who were descendants of Luthair himself or members of his armies; over time it became possible for a commoner to be raised to the Blood. There were High Blood and low Blood; the top rank were the High Lords and High Ladies, who lacquered the first two fingernails of each hand. The next lower rank were simply called Lords or Ladies, though they were of the High Blood, and they lacquered just the nail of the forefinger on each hand. The third and fourth levels were also called Lords or Ladies, but the third level lacquered the last two fingernails of each hand, while the fourth and lowest lacquered only the nails of the little fingers. They were of the low Blood. The term "lesser Blood" was also used, and could be used by those who were High Lords or Ladies referring even to the second rank. Patience was a necessity for the Blood. Those who lacked it were likely to end in the Tower of Ravens. Like the children of the monarch, members of the Blood contested for honor, renown and riches.

When Luthair arrived in Seanchan, he found a culture that bought and sold people as property. If he or his descendants ever tried to wipe out the practice, they did not succeed. The slaves were known as *da'covale*, Old Tongue for "those who are property," or *covale*, "property." A particular class of *da'covale*, *so'jhin*, were hereditary upper servants of the Blood. *So'jhin* had considerable status and in some positions could give orders to and have authority over free people.

The Seanchan were very superstitious, by and large, believing in lucky amulets and that wearing certain stones and such things could give benefits. They believed in omens, that seeing certain things or certain things happening indicated good or bad luck coming, or perhaps a death or some other event. They also believed that *damane* could tell fortunes, which they called telling a fortune, or reading, or foretelling. This was a hold-over of the knowledge about Foretelling, which in fact did crop up in *damane* sometimes.

When Luthair arrived in Seanchan, he found the natives using strange beasts that he and his forces believed at first to be Shadowspawn, but the animals had originally been brought to Seanchan from parallel worlds via Portal Stones. *Corlm, grolm, lopar, raken, to'raken* and *torm* were used by the armies that Luthair faced; as he conquered, he began using them as well. The animals each had handlers, called *morat*; a senior *morat* could become *der'morat*.

See also a'dam, Corenne, corlm, da'covale, damane, Deathwatch Guards, *grolm,* Hailene, lopar, raken, so'jhin, to'raken *and* torm

Seandar. The capital city of Seanchan. It was the largest city in the Empire.

Sebban Balwer. An Amadician who was once publicly secretary to Pedron Niall and truly the spymaster of the Children of the Light. He was a dry little stick of a man, only about 5'6" tall, even without stooping; it seemed impossible that he could move without making dry, rustling noises, but in fact he moved very quietly in bird-like hopping motions. He was purse-mouthed. His face was narrow and pinched, and he had knobby shoulders and spindly legs that looked as if they might have snapped under his desiccated weight. He had bony fingers and narrow eyes; he tapped his lips in thought. Balwer had punctilious manners and mannerisms, folding his hands fussily, and dry-washing them when he thought he'd been insulted or underrated. Everything with him was dry and precise, even his smile. Niall thought that he believed in nothing—except possibly looking over other men's shoulders—not even in the Dark One, and he certainly did not really believe that Aes Sedai were Darkfriend witches—but on the other hand, his information was never stained by what he knew had to be true and certainly not by what he wanted to be true. Balwer did not at all mind that Omerna was publicly believed to be the spymaster—he believed that a spymaster who was known was useless—but he disliked Niall getting communications from agents that did not go through him, and he disliked not knowing what was in them. Niall was quite right in believing that Balwer would serve anyone at all, but Balwer had an instinct for loyalty to his employer. He was suspicious of Niall's death, and he aided the escape of Morgase and her companions mainly to deprive Valda of them, though he did think he might find some other way of using them to strike back at Valda and Asunawa.

He became secretary (and *de facto* head of intelligence) to Faile and Perrin after meeting up with them, and was very helpful to Perrin, who knew that Balwer learned surprising things on his solitary forays. Balwer latched on to Faile and Perrin for very real reasons. Perrin was plainly a personal representative of the Dragon Reborn, and that connection was one worth cultivating. To Balwer, this was a new position where he could use his skills, though he revealed them cautiously. He was quite capable of offering as faithful a service to Perrin and Faile as he did to Niall.

Perrin lent Balwer's services to Rand, gathering intelligence on different groups, particularly Elayne's people, prior to the meeting at the Field of Merrilor.

Second. An hour denomination in the Tower, an hour or so after noonday.

Second Covenant. *See* Compact of the Ten Nations

Second-mother. *See* Aiel kinship

second-sister. *See* Aiel kinship

Sedar Cut. A place mentioned by Caldin, an Aiel; the attack on Rand by White-cloaks reminded him of a time near Sedar Cut.

Sedore Dajenna. A Tairen Aes Sedai of the Yellow Ajah publicly and of the Black Ajah in truth. She had a strength level of 19(7). Born in 813 NE, she went to the White Tower in 829 NE. After spending nine years as a novice and seven years as Accepted, she was raised to the shawl in 845 NE. About 5'5" tall, and plump but elegant, she had a pretty round face, dark eyes and long dark hair. She carried a frosty arrogance about her; in fact, in Elaida's opinion, she was one of the most arrogant of all among the sisters. She was raised Sitter for the Yellow in 961 NE and stood to depose Siuan Sanche, one of only eleven needed to give the greater consensus under the circumstances. She sat on the Supreme Council of the Black Ajah, but did not know that Alviarin was Black Ajah. The mention of forkroot unsettled her enough to make her swallow, and Elaida also made her very nervous. She served as a Sitter until she fled the Tower when members of the Black Ajah were revealed by Verin.

She was killed in *Tel'aran'rhiod* by Egwene.

Sedrin. A highwalker in Valan Luca's circus. He got drunk and died in a fall.

Sedrin. An infant born near Dragonmount, the son of Lady Meri do Ahlan a'Conlin of Murandy. She intended to frame his bounty from the White Tower so that he would know that he had been honored by Aes Sedai.

Seed. An object necessary for creating an *angreal.*

seed singing. A technique used by a team of Ogier, Nym and Da'shain Aiel in cultivating crops during the Age of Legends to ensure perfect growth. It employed the One Power. Aiel boys could take part when their voices were deep enough, around the age of sixteen. Aiel men and Ogier surrounded a field and commenced singing, and female Aiel clapped as their menfolk sang; then a Nym would appear, surrounded by butterflies, plants such as *zemai* sprouting in his footsteps. He danced and wove the song into the soil and around the seeds, causing them to sprout. Seed-sung plants grew very high and were untouched by blight and insects.

Seeker. The term used for the leader of a Tuatha'an caravan; in the Old Tongue the word was "Mahdi."

Seekers for Truth. A Seanchan police and spy organization charged with Imperial security. They hunted out Darkfriends, acted as secret police and rooted out treasonous behavior, often using torture. Most were *da'covale* and property of the Imperial throne; as such, most were marked on either shoulder with a raven and a tower. Their headquarters was the Tower of Ravens. Seekers were subject to few limits, even with the Blood, since they reported to the Empress. As identification, they carried an ivory plaque, worked with the Raven and the Tower. Seekers developed informants wherever they operated, which disturbed the bureaucracy controlling the Listeners, as they wanted to be the Seekers' sole source for that sort of data. The Seekers, on the other hand, wanted actual control of the Listener bureaucracy. Anyone and everyone was required to co-operate with a Seeker who identified himself, and this cooperation was carried to complete obedience. For instance, if a Seeker told one to wait while he went for rope to bind the person, failing to do so would be a crime, and most Seanchan would indeed wait. For that matter, if the Seeker told one to go somewhere and bring the rope for one's binding, the person would be expected to do that, too, and just as few Seanchan would disobey.

The penalty for a Seeker using his or her powers in any personal way or for any personal advantage whatsoever was death, and a very unpleasant one. Their services belonged to the Empress, not to themselves.

Sefela. An Aiel woman of *Far Dareis Mai* who went to the Stone of Tear. Aviendha told Egwene that Sefela could take her to Rhuidean.

segade. A spiny, fat, leafless leathery plant with large white blossoms found in the Waste. Its flower was used in Aiel bridal wreaths to signify the bride's prickly nature and intention to stay that way.

Segan do Avharin a'Roos. A Murandian noblewoman. She had full lips and dark eyes; she was slender and had long dark hair. Segan was one of the nobles of northern Murandy who made common cause with the intruding Andorans against the rebel Aes Sedai and later came to further agreements with the Andorans.

Segani. The *raken* Chulein was flying over the Kin's farm when Elayne's gateway exploded.

Sehar. A town in Altara near the River Eldar. When Morgase, Tallanvor, Lini, Basel Gill, Lamgwin and Breane were traveling west, trying to raise an army to retake Caemlyn, a man in Sehar told them that they would be able to get a ferry in Cormaed.

Sei'cair. Old Tongue for "golden eyes." The Aiel used it as a title for Perrin.

sei'mosiev. Old Tongue for "lowered or downcast eyes," a phrase used by the Seanchan. It indicated a loss of face or honor. One could become *sei'mosiev* either by one's own actions or inactions, or by the actions or inactions of others. What happened to one's blood relations and/or allies could also affect one. For example, having one's son or daughter, brother or sister, or any relation declared *covale* (property) resulted in a loss of face. A rather nasty trick sometimes played, although considered a cliché, was to introduce a female *covale* into a man's house as his *asa* (concubine), *asa* not being *covale*; when one or more children were born, and had been acknowledged as was customary, the situation was revealed. The *asa/covale* reverted to her owner, of course, and because condition followed the female line, so did the children.

sei'taer. Old Tongue for "straight eyes," a phrase used among the Seanchan. It meant having face or honor, referring to the ability to look anyone in the eye.

Seia Doon. Old Tongue for "Black Eyes." The name was used for an Aiel warrior society.

Seiera. The mouse-colored mare that Min rode from Dumai's Wells to Cairhien;

Min liked her, so Rand bought the horse for her. The word was the Old Tongue name of a flower known in Baerlon as blue-eye.

Seirin. A calm man of the Shorara sept of the Tomanelle Aiel. About Rand's age, he acted as a messenger between Han and Rand in the battle for Cairhien.

Sela. An elderly woman who worked as a chambermaid at Gareth Bryne's manor in Kore Springs, Andor. She was getting old to be running up and down stairs at night.

Selame. Egwene's maid in Salidar who, along with Meri and Chesa, helped dress and undress her, and attended her during the day. A refugee with dark coloring typical of Tear, she was rail-thin and carried her long nose high, as if sniffing something or recoiling from a bad smell. She was haughty and arrogant with other servants, yet full of silly chatter, with a great deal of concern for what people thought. Only her betters counted as people, in her book. She was provided by Lelaine, for whom she was spying. On the journey north from Salidar, she and Meri were murdered by Halima, who didn't want spies watching Egwene because they might have seen or overheard something that would have endangered her own safety. Chesa survived simply because she wasn't a spy for anyone, just a maid.

Selame Necoine. An Aes Sedai of the Green Ajah who served as Amyrlin Seat from approximately FY 1084 to approximately 5 NE. An Amyrlin of average strength, she was unable to carry out what Deane had begun: to unite the nobles behind the White Tower.

Selande Darengil. A Cairhienin minor noblewoman who wore six thin stripes crossing the front of her coat. About 5'3" tall, with dark hair, dark eyes and a pale complexion, she was young and pretty. Colavaere directed her at Rand to try to attach strings to him; Selande was frightened half out of her wits by him. She was one of the young nobles who began to imitate the Aiel Maidens. She wore her hair loose and cut off at the shoulder, and a sword belted over a riding dress. She had stark admiration for the Maidens and stark fear of Rand, although the latter faded after he made it clear she had nothing to fear from him. The leader of her society imitating the Aiel, which, unlike the Aiel societies, contained both men and women, she managed a credible swagger, with a bold tilt to her head and a bold set to her shoulders. She and her society were coopted into the service of Faile and called themselves "*Cha Faile*," which was Old Tongue for "the Falcon's Claw" or "the Falcon's Talon." She wanted a scar, like those some Maidens had, which Faile thought was ridiculous, but she was not overly eager about it. Faile thought that Selande was the brightest of *Cha Faile*, except perhaps for Parelean, and that only Camaille and Arrela were quicker, but Selande had a calmness, as if she had already faced the worst fear in her life and nothing else could ever be as bad. She accompanied Faile to Ghealdan, and was one of those sent into Bethal. After Faile was taken prisoner by the Shaido, she agreed to obey Perrin until Faile was found, and Balwer used her to gather information on Masema. Selande led a group of twenty

Cha Faile into Malden via the aqueduct to rescue Faile. When Perrin's group encountered Whitecloaks, Selande put on a dress and went to spy on them. In the Last Battle, she was with Faile on the mission to deliver the Horn of Valere to Mat; when Vanin was thought to be a Darkfriend, Selande took charge of the scouts. She was hauled into the air by weaves of the One Power after Aravine betrayed them to the Shadow.

Selean. A walled farming town in Cairhien at the other end of the Jangai Pass from Taien. It was once a considerable town, set on the hills, but was burned by Couladin and its inhabitants taken as slaves or impaled on sharp stakes.

Seleisin. A very isolated village or region. Many people used it in expressions to indicate ignorance: someone in Seleisin might not know something, but it should have been obvious to everyone else.

Selene. *See* Lanfear

Selfar. A roan gelding belonging to Talmanes.

Selindrin. The proprietor of The Garden of Silver Breezes in Tanchico. She was a sleek, dark-haired woman of indeterminate age. She cleverly catered to every faction while earning the enmity of none.

Selorna. A Tairen noble House. *See also* Edorion Selorna

Selucia. A Seanchan woman who was *so'jhin* to Tuon. Born in 956 NE, she was about 5'4" tall and slim of build, but was full-breasted enough that men frequently stared at her bosom admiringly. She was beautiful, with golden hair, a creamy complexion, large cool blue eyes and a regal bearing. Selucia's mother gave her to Tuon when Tuon was in the cradle, to be Tuon's nursemaid and shadow, a bodyguard no one knew about. Selucia was then twenty-five and had been trained in secret her whole life for the role. As a nursemaid, she, along with Tuon's *Soe'feia,* was responsible for disciplining Tuon. At Tuon's adulthood ceremony at age sixteen, she pardoned Selucia for those punishments, according to tradition, and gave her one hundred gold thrones for each one. At that point, Selucia asked to be Tuon's chief maid, turning her back on possible power and authority, and continued to function as a shadow. Tuon only had to have Selucia punished twice, and regretted it as much as Selucia. Selucia accompanied Tuon to Ebou Dar aboard the *Victory of Kidron.* When she discovered Mat holding Tuon prisoner in the stables of the Tarasin Palace, she told him that she would obey Mat if he did not hurt Tuon and that she would kill him if he did. Mat took both along in his escape from Ebou Dar. When Mat took Tuon to a "hell" in Maderin, Selucia went along; when attacked by Darkfriends as they were leaving, Thom and Selucia killed more than half a dozen of them. Thom was impressed. After hearing from Falendre that Anath was Forsaken and had been captured by the Dragon Reborn, Tuon named Selucia her Truthspeaker; Selucia did not welcome the position, but she did her best. During the Last Battle, Selucia stayed near Tuon; she was injured when the Gray Men attacked the command tent, but recovered.

Semalaren. A place in Seanchan where the Imperial army fought a rebel force, each army having four hundred *damane*, resulting in heavy casualties on both sides.

Semaradrid Maravin. A Cairhienin nobleman who was High Seat of House Maravin. He wore slashes of color on his coat to below the waist. He was almost 5'9" tall, with a long face and gaunt cheeks. His hair, showing white streaks at the temples, was shaved at the front like that of common soldiers; his dark eyes could chip stone. He moved stiffly from wounds suffered in his land's civil war, but his limp came from fighting Tear. His armor was gilded and worked, but it had seen considerable use and showed it. His main reason for cooperating with the Tairens was that they were not Aiel. Semaradrid was part of the Illian invasion army, commanding the Cairhienin. When Rand learned of rebellion in Haddon Mirk, Semaradrid wore his malicious smile for the Tairens quite openly. Semaradrid was also part of the campaign against the Seanchan.

Weiramon and Semaradrid had a touchy relationship; Weiramon pretended to give the Cairhienin equality while slighting him almost unconsciously; Semaradrid was fully aware of the slights, of his weaker position, and hated both.

House Maravin had old alliances with House Riatin.

Semaris, Jeordwyn. *See* Jeordwyn Semaris

Semirhage. A Forsaken. As an Aes Sedai, her name was Nemene Damendar Boann. Her strength level was 1(+12). She was 6'1½" tall, and beautiful, with skin as dark as one of the Sea Folk. Slender and graceful, with long fingers and delicate hands, she had large dark brown eyes and short, black, wavy hair. She usually had a cool, even cold, and imperious air, but when she gave her sadism free rein, the imperiousness dropped away and she became almost solicitous toward her victim. She was especially ruthless and cruel, and a vicious killer, and truly hated anyone who called herself Aes Sedai. A true sadist, she really gained pleasure by causing pain.

Semirhage was almost as poor at handling weather as Asmodean. She liked to do intricate needlework, beautiful patterns of flowers and the like. She knew how to play *sha'rah*, *no'ri* and *tcheran*, but she was an indifferent player of games that did not involve actual people. During the Age of Legends, she was world-famous as a healer of last resort, able to heal what others had given up on. But she always extracted pain as part of her payment. Her main reason for going over to the Shadow was that the Hall of the Servants had discovered that she gave her sadism free rein and proposed binding her with what would be known in the next Age as the Oath Rod.

Demandred, Semirhage and Mesaana acted as a sort of team, though they would move against one another given a chance. They did not follow Moridin willingly. On orders from the Dark One Semirhage sent the Trollocs and Myrddraal that aided Rand in the Stone against Sammael's Shadowspawn and Darkfriends; she and Demandred planned between them to increase chaos by bringing Rand and the Seanchan into conflict, trying to focus them on one another. Semirhage posed as Anath Dorje, Seanchan Truthspeaker to Tuon, having disposed of Tuon's intended Truthspeaker.

After Mat kidnapped Tuon, Semirhage went back to Seanchan and killed the Empress and the royal family. Semirhage posed as Tuon to meet Rand in an attempt to kidnap him, but her plan was thwarted; she was captured, but not before taking off Rand's hand.

She was humiliated when Cadsuane spanked her, but she was set free by Shaidar Haran, who gave her the Domination Band. With it, Semirhage and Elza captured Rand and almost forced him to kill Min. Rand used the True Power to break free and balefired his two captors.

Sen T'jore. A wild region of Seanchan. Great spotted cats as large as ponies and trap-worms could be found there.

Senar. An Ogier who was father of Malan father of Aran, the last being the author of a manuscript telling of sightings of Ishamael after the Bore had been sealed.

Sendara. A woman of the Iron Mountain sept of the Taardad Aiel and *Far Dareis Mai.* Her name was on Rand's list of women who had died for him.

Sene sovya caba'donde ain dovienya. Old Tongue for "Luck is a horse to ride like any other."

Senhold, Aeman. A nobleman who was leader of the Amadician contingent at the Battle of the Shining Walls.

Senican, Aliane. *See* Aliane Senican

Senine din Ryal. A Sea Folk Windfinder with a strength level of 19(7). More than five hundred years old, she had weathered, creased cheeks and thickly graying hair. She was among the lower ranking and wore six earrings, but the marks in her ears indicated that she at one time had worn many more earrings and fatter ones. She had been Windfinder to a Wavemistress more than once, and had been Windfinder to Nesta's predecessor. The rule for the Windfinder to a Wavemistress was that if no Wavemistress needed her services, she was required to move down to the lowest level on a new vessel and work back up. Senine became Windfinder to the Sailmistress of a soarer, and not the largest even of those. She observed the use of the Bowl of the Winds because she was one of the strongest available among the remaining Windfinders in Ebou Dar. Despite being of low rank, she was consulted.

She accompanied Elayne to Caemlyn, and was one of the Windfinders to stay in Caemlyn after Zaida left. She was part of the circle that made a gateway so that soldiers could rescue Elayne from the Black Ajah.

Senior Standardbearer. A Seanchan rank equivalent to Senior Bannerman. A Senior Standardbearer had a small crest like a steel arrowhead at the front of the helmet.

Senje no-room. An obscure reference by Birgitte, intimating that the keeper of this is not embarrassed easily.

Seonid Traighan. A Cairhienin Aes Sedai of the Green Ajah and the rebel contin-

gent, with a strength level of 17(5). Born in 928 NE, she went to the White
Tower in 946 NE. After spending thirteen years as a novice and twelve years
as Accepted, she was raised to the shawl in 971 NE. Seonid was 5'1" tall and had
a pale complexion, dark hair that fell in waves to her shoulders and big, dark,
bottomless eyes. While she was not particularly slender, neither was she stocky
or stout. Seonid sometimes wore a *kesiera*, a white fingernail-sized stone on her
forehead. She was atypical for a Green in that she was very cool and reserved,
with an air of dignity and authority. Sometimes she had a determined smile.

Seonid was a lesbian; she did not hate men, she just did not want to bed
them. She chose Green because it was the Battle Ajah. Her Warders were Teryl
Wynter and Furen Alharra. Seonid's attitude toward her Warders was very
businesslike, brisk, practical and methodical. That was, in fact, her general
attitude.

She was part of the rebel embassy to Rand and was one of the first three to
approach Rand in Caemlyn; she was also one of those who confronted him
with the Mask of Mirrors. She was among the group that followed after Rand
when he fled them in Caemlyn and was forced to swear fealty to him after
Dumai's Wells. She was then treated like an apprentice by the Wise Ones,
and considered an apprentice. Seonid and Masuri were sent to Ghealdan with
Perrin to deal with Masema, under orders to obey Perrin as she would Rand,
something that left room for interpretation, as she, Masuri and Perrin were all
aware. Seonid considered the Dragonsworn all to be in the nature of mad dogs.
She had sworn to serve the Dragon Reborn, and one of the best ways she could
see to do that was to suppress in whatever way possible the Dragonsworn, and
so put an end to the depredations she thought they caused.

She considered Rand as arrogant as any king, and had a typical Cairhienin
attitude toward Aiel.

Sephanie Pelden. A young Andoran woman. She and her sister Naris sought work
at the Royal Palace; Essande chose them to train as Elayne's maids because they
were unlikely to be spies. Sephanie was very happy to be a lady's maid rather
than cleaning the halls. Square-faced and shy, she was as much in awe of Essande
as of Elayne.

Sera. A Seanchan *damane* belonging to Tuon. She had a dark complexion, large,
liquid black eyes, tightly curled black hair and fine smile lines at the corners
of her eyes. She was the strongest of Tuon's six *damane* and was part of Karede's
group that searched for Tuon when she was missing.

Serafelle Tanisloe. A Murandian Aes Sedai of the Brown Ajah and the loyalist
contingent, with a strength level of 23(11). Born in 862 NE, she went to the
White Tower in 891 NE. After spending ten years as a novice and four years as
Accepted, she was raised to the shawl in 905 NE. She was 5'4" tall, and pretty
in a plump fashion, with brown hair and large hazel eyes. Sometimes, especially
when thinking, she had the physical mannerisms of a spoiled noblewoman,
which she was. Serafelle was a wilder who slowed at age nineteen. She was

married, but lost her husband and three children to a fever; she herself barely escaped death. Of the middle nobility, she was a pampered, self-indulgent woman, but after the deaths, she reassessed her life and decided to become Aes Sedai. At age twenty-nine, she lied about her age, claiming to be eighteen, in order to be allowed into the Tower. Two years passed before sisters discovered the truth, and by that time, she had to be allowed to continue. That lie, though, was possibly the reason she was not allowed to test for Accepted for ten years; she believed that, with some justification. She was a quick study and a fast learner—very observant, very intelligent and quick-witted. She would have become Yellow except that she possessed a minimal Talent for Healing. She accompanied Siuan to Fal Dara, and was part of the circle that Healed Mat of his connection to the Shadar Logoth dagger.

Serailla. A Kandori noblewoman who served Ethenielle as First Councilor to the Throne of the Clouds. About 5'5" tall, she was stout, with a round, placid face. She was more graceful than she appeared, both in dancing and in the saddle. Though she looked like a farmwife stuffed into a noblewoman's dress, her mind was as sharp as any Aes Sedai's. She was completely unflappable and settled in to see what must be done. She accompanied Ethenielle in the Last Battle.

Seralin. A Wise One of the Shaido Aiel. One of Sevanna's inner circle of plotters, she took part in, or at least was present at, the murder of Desaine. At Dumai's Wells, she was with Therava.

Serana. A sizable village in Tarabon located halfway between Elmora and the Amadician border. It lay in a flat grassy valley among forested hills, with at least a mile to the trees in three directions; in the other direction was a small, reed-fringed lake, considerably wider than the village, fed by two wide streams. It was a stopping point for merchant trains heading east, with over a dozen inns and nearly as many streets. The rooftops of Serana were all tile, red or green or blue, but the buildings themselves were wooden. Serana became one of the Seanchan garrisons in Tarabon and was one of many raided by Rodel Ituralde.

Serancha Colvine. An Aes Sedai of the Gray Ajah and the loyalist contingent. Born in 835 NE, she went to the White Tower in 850 NE. After spending seven years as a novice and six years as Accepted, she was raised to the shawl in 863 NE. She served as a Sitter from 974 to 990 NE and was named Head Clerk of the Gray Ajah in 990 NE. She had a pinched mouth and a pinched nose that constantly seemed to be detecting a bad smell. Even her pale blue eyes seemed pinched with disapproval. She might well have been pretty otherwise. Seaine and Pevara once dusted her cloak with powdered itch oak; they thought that she was a prig.

As head of her Ajah, Serancha picked Andaya Forae as a Sitter for the Gray after the White Tower split. She taught Egwene lessons after Egwene was captured by the White Tower, and met with other Ajah heads and agreed to raise Egwene Amyrlin after the Seanchan attack.

Seranda Palace. The home of the ruler of Amadicia in Amador.

Serden. The son of Kolom son of Radlin, an Ogier author from about 400 NE who developed a theory about the Ways.

Sereille Bagand. An Aes Sedai of the White Ajah with a strength level of 21(9). Born in Far Madding in 586 NE, she went to the White Tower in 601 NE. After spending thirteen years as a novice and eleven years as Accepted, she was raised to the shawl in 625 NE. The long periods Sereille spent as novice and Accepted had more to do with her being a discipline problem than with any difficulties in learning; she was remembered vividly by Reanne Corly of the Kin, who was a novice with her, as breaking more rules and playing more pranks than any three other novices.

It was considered an attribute of women from Far Madding that they were strong-willed, and it was not considered all that unusual for one to do even dangerous things on a dare, at least while young, but Sereille once left the Tower grounds without permission, visited the guards at each bridge, in her novice white, told them her name, then returned to the Tower, managing to sneak in despite the fact that the first report of a runaway had already come in. She did it on a dare, despite knowing the punishment; in fact, it is recorded that when she was found, it was in the Mistress of Novices' study, waiting to begin that punishment.

In 738 NE Sereille was chosen for the Hall of the Tower as a Sitter for the White, serving under the ineffectual Feragaine and then Myriam Copan, who was also a weak Amyrlin, if not a puppet, in her early years. Sereille had shown no indications that she was extraordinary until she entered the Hall; as a Sitter, she blossomed, some might say virulently. She became more and more forceful, openly asserting her strong-willed personality. She could use logic like a knife in argument, gutting her opponents and filleting them or cutting them into paper-thin slices as she chose. With weak Amyrlins and all real power residing in the Hall—a situation that historically led to vicious infighting and a hothouse atmosphere in the Hall, indeed in the entire Tower—she had plenty of opportunity. She was particularly strong in opposing, successfully, measures that would have increased the power of the individual Ajahs at the expense of the Tower's control over them, as well as any attempts at self-aggrandizement by Sitters.

In 759 NE, she was named Mistress of Novices under Myriam Copan. Some said she was appointed Mistress to get her out of the Hall. This occurred just after "Beauty" Copan went on her retreat that changed her priorities and turned her into a strong Amyrlin. It was not then known (although a few suspected) that Cadsuane was involved in this retreat in any way. Cadsuane, then age fifty-eight, and twenty-eight years an Aes Sedai—very junior in everything except her strength, which put her at the very top of the social hierarchy—did not get on with Sereille, and the dislike was returned. Reportedly, Cadsuane was the only sister who Sereille could never make jump through hoops.

Sereille served as Mistress of Novices for an unprecedented 107 years under

Myriam, Zeranda Tyrim and Parenia Demalle. Traditionally, of course, a new Amyrlin might ask the Mistress of Novices to step down so as to put her own woman in the post, but some say that Sereille remained so long in the position because the Hall thought to keep her out of their hair, at least in the beginning. Later it was said that no one had the nerve to ask her to step down.

During her tenure, she was in many ways a tyrant, and most novices and Accepted squeaked when she looked at them; if she looked twice, their teeth often chattered. Her punishments were not arbitrary—she did not play favorites or single out girls she did not like—but her standards were high, and her punishments for falling short were fierce, to say the least. In truth, given that the Mistress of Novices often played such a large part in penances served by sisters, she also quite literally put her mark on a large number of women who already were Aes Sedai during this period.

In 866 NE, she was raised Amyrlin; some reports suggest that by this time, the Hall of the Tower was afraid not to stand for her. What can be certain, though, is that once her name was suggested, all others were withdrawn. She achieved the greater consensus on the very first call, which was all but unprecedented.

As Amyrlin, she ran the Tower in many ways as if she still were the Mistress of Novices, and every sister were a novice, or at best Accepted. She expected obedience and no arguments, and she got obedience and no arguments; those who argued soon came to regret it, with the possible exception of Cadsuane Melaidhrin. Claims that even Sitters flinched when she looked at them and broke into tears when she frowned cannot be confirmed, but the fact remains that during her reign, the Hall of the Tower was firmly in her grasp.

When the Hall first tried balking her, she unchaired the entire Hall. The Ajahs then returned the same Sitters, only to have her unchair them immediately. This continued for nearly half a year before the Ajahs realized that for all that time Sereille had been ruling solely by decree and would continue to do so. A full year passed before Sereille allowed a Hall to sit, and by that time the Ajahs had, in desperation, begun choosing women they believed Sereille would accept. By the time she allowed a Hall to sit, every single Sitter was a woman Sereille would accept; in effect, she had chosen her own Hall, and she never had trouble with them again. After Sereille's death, the Hall passed a law saying that if the entire Hall was unchaired, the new Hall had to sit for ten days before it could be unchaired again.

A plotted rebellion against her was uncovered by Cadsuane and crushed by her single-handedly.

Sereille's reign coincided with another expansion of Aes Sedai influence, an increase in the power of the White Tower. She did not try for the return to any former days of glory, but for that period, she came very close to achieving it, by diplomacy, by manipulation and plots, and by the force of her will. When Sereille died in 890 NE, the Hall began to reassert itself within the Tower; whether or not this was the reason, the Tower's power and influence in the world promptly began another slow decline.

Sereine dar Shamelle Motara. The author of *Commentaries on the Karaethon Cycle.* She was Counsel-Sister to Comaelle, High Queen of Jaramide, circa 325 AB, the Third Age.

Serendahar. The site of a battle between Sammael and Lews Therin Telamon during the Age of Legends, where Sammael tried to bait Lews Therin into attacking him. Rand related the story to Asmodean.

Serengada Dai. A region of Seanchan that Sarek, one of the Blood with high ambitions, had designs on, as learned by Rand and Aviendha when they Traveled to Seanchan.

Serenia Latar. An Aes Sedai of the Gray Ajah who served as Amyrlin from 276 to 306 NE. Serenia was a strong Amyrlin, a skillful negotiator who greatly increased the Tower's influence and prestige, ending many wars and effecting many treaties. In 306 NE, Serenia died in Altara after negotiating an end to a civil war. Her corpse was seized by the Whitecloaks; they hanged it despite the fact that she was already dead. She was the only Amyrlin ever hanged by the Children of the Light.

Serenla. The name used by Min after escaping the Tower with Siuan and Leane; it was Old Tongue for "stubborn daughter."

Sergase Gilbearn. An Andoran noblewoman of a minor House. Small and slim with dark hair touched with white, she had opposed Gaebril and was loyal to Elayne; Sergase brought all twenty of her armsmen to support her.

Seri. A Seanchan *damane* who belonged to Lady Morsa. Rand and Aviendha encountered her when they Traveled to Seanchan. She was pale-faced and appeared to be a teenager. She was taken into custody by the Seeker, along with everyone else in the party. When Aviendha tried to remove her collar, Seri screamed to her mistress to save her.

Serile. A Sea Folk Windfinder to Turane; the Seanchan ship that they had captured was the meeting place for the First Twelve of the Atha'an Miere in Illian.

Serinia. An Aes Sedai assisting in creating gateways for refugees from Caemlyn at the beginning of the Last Battle.

Seroku, Alin. *See* Alin Seroku

Serpent, Great. *See* Great Serpent

Serrisa. A well-trained, responsive *damane* that Egeanin had owned and left behind in Cantorin. She would gorge herself on honeyed nuts, if allowed, but she never got seasick or the sulks, the way some did.

Servants, Hall of the. *See* Hall of the Servants

Servants of the Light. A term which originated during the Age of Legends to mean Aes Sedai. After the Breaking, it was a formal name still used by the Ogier for Aes Sedai east of the Aryth Ocean. The term was used when Loial introduced himself to Moiraine. Distinct from this usage, however, Red Ajah associated the term with male channelers.

Seta Zarbey. A Seanchan *sul'dam*. About 5'6" tall, with shoulder-length yellow hair, blue eyes and a fair complexion, she was one of the two *sul'dam* that Nynaeve and the others captured and left leashed on *a'dam* when they escaped at Falme. Her *damane* punched out Seta and ran away despite attempts to calm her, the implication being that Seta was not so pleasant. She and Renna were found by Alwhin and released. Because she was found being held by an *a'dam*, Seta was never again allowed to be complete, though the facts were covered up and she remained in Suroth's employ. Egeanin learned of this from Bethamin and used it to blackmail Renna, Seta and Bethamin into helping rescue Teslyn, Joline and Edesina. The three *sul'dam* fled with Mat and Valan Luca's show; Seta fled because she knew she could not return safely. After Bethamin began channeling, Seta refused to even look while Bethamin was taking lessons, but after a time she asked to be included. The Aes Sedai refused because she had not begun channeling yet and was too old for the novice book, whereupon she did channel, forcing their hands. She continued with Mat and the Band of the Red Hand until she went to the White Tower with the group that included Teslyn, Joline and Edesina.

Setagana. Anaiya's Warder. He was tall, lean and beautiful. He and Anaiya were murdered with the use of *saidin*.

Setalle Anan. The innkeeper of The Wandering Woman in Ebou Dar. She was once the Aes Sedai Martine Janata, but was burned out while working with *ter'angreal*. Her description of the pain of being burned out was that if she gathered the birth pangs she suffered with all of her children together into one moment, that would be the tenth of what she felt. Three days passed before she could stop weeping long enough to go away, but once she did, she fled as if pursued. She felt she was pursued, in a way, by the horror, pity and queasiness she saw in the eyes of her sisters, as well as by her own horror at what had happened to her. She ran as if trying to outrun *saidar*, as if she felt in her bones that if she ran far enough, fast enough, she could find somewhere she would no longer be able to sense what she could no longer touch.

She arrived in Ebou Dar about half a year after being burned out. She thought that perhaps it was knowledge of the Kin that drew her to Ebou Dar, unconsciously. In her flight she had run out of money, lost her horse and lost everything. When Jasfer Anan found her standing in the rain and brought her home to his mother to take care of, she hadn't eaten in days; she did not know how many, only that she often fainted and could no longer think straight. Jasfer's mother was used to her son bringing home strays, though usually dogs or cats; this woman was not about to put up with any nonsense, like letting Setalle starve herself to death. She force-fed her and smacked her bottom until she began eating on her own.

Roughly a half year after meeting Jasfer, Setalle married him. Jasfer and she had eight children, altogether—five daughters and three sons. Marrying and having children were a major part of reviving her interest in life, giving her the realization that she had in effect been given a second chance.

She was about 5'5" tall, and stately, with hazel eyes and dark hair touched with a little gray; she appeared to be in her mid-forties, a slight residual effect of having been able to channel; she would always be taken for younger than her true age. She did not look as she did when she was really in her forties; no one would recognize her if they saw her. The onset of apparent relative youthfulness was not an overnight thing, as with Leane and Siuan. Not until after she was taken in by her Jasfer's mother did she realize that she looked somewhere in her early twenties. Wondering about that was the first thing to pull her out of despair, listlessness and thoughts of suicide.

Setalle was caught up in Mat's escape from Ebou Dar, and, after selling her inn, went with him while her family escaped on her husband's fishing boats, sailing for Illian. She claimed to be happy in her life, happy with her husband and children and business, but the possibility of being able to channel again was a shock to her, a temptation that made her almost hate Nynaeve for offering it. Surprisingly, she claimed to be happy when Healing did not work; if it had, she would have to give up the life she had made for herself.

Setalle was with Faile's group that went to fetch the Horn of Valere from the White Tower in the Last Battle. A gateway that was supposed to return them to the Field of Merrilor opened just as a bubble of evil struck; the group rushed through the gateway and found themselves in the Blight.

Setares, Tolmeran. *See* Tolmeran Setares

Setsuko. An Arafellin novice who was in the Tower at the time of the Aiel War. She was too weak to test for Accepted. She was pale-eyed, timid, stocky and shorter than Moiraine. She talked of running away, but a visit to Merean's study convinced her at least to keep quiet about her intentions if it didn't convince her to stay until the Aes Sedai decided it was safe for her to go.

Sevanna. A woman of the Jumai sept of the Shaido Aiel. In her late twenties to early thirties, she was about 5'8" tall, with green eyes, golden hair and a greedy mouth. She dressed immodestly and extravagantly for an Aiel. Sevanna was not a coward, nor was she stupid; she was simply very, very ambitious and very, very greedy. From a young age she wanted power, and was sure she had taken the right route to it. She enjoyed the excitement of the battle at Dumai's Wells, and almost regretted not having chosen the spear, but she had decided early on that the weapons she had been born with were the proper ones for her climb. She pursued her first husband, the Shaido clan chief, and made him think he had chased and won her, and when he died, she did the same to Muradin, who was chosen to go to Rhuidean to replace her dead Suladric. When Muradin failed to return, she transferred her sights to Couladin and took him as easily.

After Couladin's death, she took over as acting chief of the Shaido; she also began acting as a Wise One, and was accepted as one. She had real power at an age when Wise One's apprentices were still running to fetch water and Maidens were still jumping when any of a dozen older Maidens murmured jump.

Sevanna was obsessed with possessing Rand. She intended, among other things, to found a dynasty, perhaps matriarchal, insofar as succession of the rulers was possible, to rule the Shaido and much more, using him. This desire for him was both practical—the dynasty and the power achieved simply by having him in her grasp—and personal—he had great power, and she lusted to own and control it. That was an added reason for her to want Faile serving her, once she learned Faile was married to a friend of Rand. Sevanna wanted to know everything about him.

Sevanna led the Shaido to break many customs; instead of taking the fifth, they looted to bare ground, excusing it because the victims were wetlanders. They forced wetlanders to become *gai'shain*—in effect slaves—though wetlanders did not follow *ji'e'toh* and this was considered insulting to the Aiel who were *gai'shain*. Sevanna, using the Wise Ones, decreed that wetlander *gai'shain*, because they did not follow *ji'e'toh*, were not to be released in a year and a day but held until they demonstrated that they had come to follow *ji'e'toh*, the object being to never release them. She also took Wise Ones into battle, although non-Shaido Aiel did so as well. She began decorating her *gai'shain* with jewelry, increased the jewelry she herself wore, and started wearing finger rings.

Sevanna hated being less than anyone else and not having the power or abilities that others did. That was her main impetus in wanting to break Galina. In the beginning she thought that simply breaking the Aes Sedai to a point where she would promise to do as Sevanna told her would be sufficient. She knew that Aes Sedai supposedly could not lie, but also that they were said to twist words fiercely. She was not certain about the efficacy of the binder rod given her by Caddar/Sammael, but she was willing to use it. Once Galina had been broken far enough to swear on the rod—and Sevanna believed it must take more to break an Aes Sedai than to break other people—then if the rod worked as claimed, she would have the complete and utter obedience of a woman who could channel, and if it did not work, she would still have the complete and utter obedience of a woman who could channel, because Galina would have been broken, and Aes Sedai could not lie.

Therava became Sevanna's advisor, ostensibly because Sevanna spoke as the clan chief, and she needed a Wise One to advise her as a clan chief would. Sevanna was not best pleased by this. In the eyes of Therava and the other Wise Ones, Sevanna erred seriously in letting the Shaido be scattered at Sammael's connivance. That was the real reason Therava was appointed to her post. At Malden, Sevanna was taken captive by the Seanchan.

Seve. A seven-year-old boy taken to Salidar as a child of Marigan (Moghedien in disguise); Jaril was his brother. At first, they clung to each other and seemed frightened of everything and everyone and would not speak a word. Later, they laughed and shouted as loud as the other children.

Seven-Striped Lass, The. A tavern in Caemlyn run by Melli Craeb.

Seven Towers. Defining landmarks of Malkier, broken by the Shadowspawn armies.

sevens. A game in which players sat facing one another, drew swords and aimed at each other's throat, stopping just short of flesh.

severing. An Age of Legends word that meant both gentling and stilling, thus rendering men or women incapable of channeling.

Sevlana Meseau. A historical and legendary Gray sister who Merana thought of as impressive; she thought that when Kiruna and Bera first saw Cadsuane, it must have struck them the same way seeing Sevlana would strike her.

Sh'boan. A woman serving as the absolute monarch of Shara. The monarch ruled for exactly seven years, then died. The rule then passed to the mate of that ruler, the Sh'botay, who ruled for seven years and then died; his (second) mate then ruled as Sh'boan for seven years. This pattern had repeated itself from the time of the Breaking of the World. The Sharans believed that the deaths were the "Will of the Pattern." A break in the cycle occurred when Graendal kidnapped Chiape, the Sh'boan, and her Sh'botay-to-be Shaofan and made them her pets.

Sh'botay. *See* Sh'boan

sha'je. A type of duel using left- and right-handed daggers tipped with poison, in which often neither party survived. The left-handed dagger was known as the *osan'gar* and the right-handed dagger as *aran'gar.* The duel originated during the Age of Legends after the Dark One's touch was felt in the world. A *sha'je* duel at Qal was mentioned by Semirhage.

Sha'mad Conde. Old Tongue for "Thunder Walkers," it was the name given to an Aiel warrior society.

sha'rah. A game that was ancient when the War of Power began. Moridin, one of nine remaining who knew the game, was a grandmaster. Played on a board with 13×13 squares, it had 33 red pieces and 33 green pieces and a central black-and-white piece called the Fisher; the first object was to capture the Fisher.

Shaarad Aiel. An Aiel clan which had Black Rock, Haido and Imran septs; its clan chief was Jheran.

Shadar Logoth. Old Tongue for "the Place Where the Shadow Waits." The name was given to the city formerly known as Aridhol, capital of one of the Ten Nations. Aridhol used an evil as great as the Shadow to fight the Shadow, corrupting itself, and Shadar Logoth was destroyed circa 1200 AB. The evil that remained there was called Mashadar. The taint on Shadar Logoth was created by humans, who believed they had to do whatever was necessary to defeat the Shadow. Rand experienced resonance when channeling there—the Dark One's taint reacted to the corruption of Shadar Logoth. One could say that the two taints were diametrically opposed to each other, two opposite magnetic poles that were attracted to each other.

Shadar Nor. The name given to Latra Posae, a famous female Aes Sedai from the time of the Breaking, meaning "Cutter (or Slicer) of the Shadow." *See* Latra Posae

shade of my heart. An Aiel term of affection.

Shadoon, Stedding. A *stedding* located along the Shadow Coast.

Shadow Coast. The mountainous border of Tarabon and Amadicia on the southwestern coast of the continent. An Ogier *stedding* was located there.

Shadow, Lady of the. A Seanchan expression for death.

Shadow, the. The Dark One and also the power or force of the Dark One, in contrast to the Light of the Creator.

Shadow's Waiting. *See* Shadar Logoth

Shadow-forgers. Those who forged Shadowwrought weapons in Thakan'dar, tempered by human blood. It was said that they became fierce when provoked and had skin hard enough to turn aside swords. Aviendha and other channelers hit them with weaves of Fire, which turned them to crumbling stone.

Shadowbrothers. The wolves' name for Darkhounds.

Shadoweyes. The Aiel term for the Dark One's animal spies.

Shadowkiller. The wolves' term for Rand.

Shadowman. *See* Myrddraal

Shadowrunners. An Aiel term for Darkfriends.

shadowshand mushroom. A mushroom that made rings on fallen logs.

Shadowsouled. The Aiel name for Forsaken.

Shadowspawn. Living constructs created by the Forsaken Aginor, designed to serve the Shadow, during the War of the Shadow/the War of Power, the war that ended the Age of Legends. They included creatures such as Trollocs, Draghkar, *gholam*, Myrddraal, Darkhounds and Gray Men.

Shadowsworn. Those sworn to serve the Dark One; the term generally referred to those below the rank of Forsaken.

Shadowtwisted. The Aiel name for Trollocs.

Shadowwrought. The Aiel historical term for creatures made by Aginor; it was also Slayer's name for Trollocs. As a descriptor, it was used to refer to the blades made at Thakan'dar by the Shadow-forgers. *See* Shadowspawn

Shae'en M'taal. Old Tongue for "Stone Dogs," it was the name given an Aiel warrior society.

Shaemal. The capital city of Coremanda, one of the Ten Nations after the Breaking.

Shaen. An Aiel of the Stone Dog society who wore the red headband of the *siswai'aman*. He was part of the scouting mission to Thakan'dar and fought at Shayol Ghul in the Last Battle.

Shaene, Elver. *See* Elver Shaene

Shaeren, Burin. Lelaine's Domani Warder. He was copper-skinned and looked like an uprooted stump. He had been with her over twenty years at the time the White Tower split.

Shago. A place from the distant past. Birgitte once said that the arguing Elayne and Nynaeve were "acting like Shago barmaids with winteritch."

Shagrin, Joni. *See* Joni Shagrin

Shahal Comanli. A Domani Aes Sedai of the Gray Ajah who was uncommitted to either contingent. She had a strength level of 34(22), and was roughly two hundred years old. She was 5'2" tall and quite stout, with copper skin. Shahal had a flirtatious streak; in fact, when she chose to flirt, men quickly forgot that she was short and stout. She was one of the uncommitted Aes Sedai Rand found in Cairhien after Dumai's Wells who was following Cadsuane Melaidhrin. Shahal was left behind in Cairhien when Cadsuane went to Far Madding.

Shai'tan. The true name of the Dark One. Saying it was thought to draw his attention, inevitably bringing ill fortune at best, disaster at worst; among his followers, using the name was thought to be blasphemy. For that reason many euphemisms were used.

Shaidar Haran. Old Tongue for "Hand of the Dark," it was the name given a Myrddraal unlike all others. Its name was in Old Tongue, while all other Myrddraal had names in the Trolloc tongue. Shaidar Haran was head and shoulders taller than all other Halfmen. Arrogant, it commanded the Forsaken, displayed a dark sense of humor and could sense the difference between *saidin* and *saidar.* Shaidar Haran carried the authority of the Dark One to the extent that he was permitted to punish Moghedien and Mesaana severely for their failures. Shaidar Haran did not have nearly as much power as the Dark One, but the Dark One was able to project a shadowy form of himself into it. If too long away from Shayol Ghul, Shaidar Haran grew weak.

The Dark One discarded Shaidar Haran when Rand went to the Pit of Doom, leaving a husk on the ground and creating a large void.

Shaido Aiel. One of the Aiel clans. They followed Couladin until his death outside Cairhien while he was leading 160,000 Shaido spears against the city. Sevanna managed to establish herself as both a Wise One and, in effect, chief of the Shaido, though as a woman she could not be a chief any more than a man could be a Wise One; it was all done through the simple expedient that as widow of the last chief and of the one before that, she spoke as the chief until a new one was selected. Given the situation, it was highly unlikely any Shaido would be allowed into Rhuidean, and she meant to see that none was in any case.

Especially under Sevanna, the Shaido began to behave in nontraditional ways for the Aiel, including the use of Wise Ones in battle, beginning at Dumai's Wells, looting to the ground rather than taking only the fifth, and the taking of wetlanders as *gai'shain.* The other Aiel began to view the Shaido as different. The Shaido were always regarded as the lowest of the clans, in a way, the least honorable, but the things they did after crossing the Dragonwall added to the differences.

The Shaido's undoing began when Sammael, posing as Caddar and attempting to create more chaos, sent many Shaido septs through gateways all across the world, where they continued to cause atrocities. Although Sevanna retained the Wise Ones who could channel and a sizable number of warriors, she made another error by kidnapping Faile and bringing the wrath of Perrin down upon her.

After the Shaido's defeat at Malden and Sevanna's capture, the clan dispersed in many directions; Therava led a large group intending to return to the Three-fold Land.

Shaiel. Old Tongue for "the Woman Who Is Dedicated," it was the name that Tigraine took when she was adopted into the Chumai sept of the Taardad Aiel.

Shainrahien. An Ogier-built city in Safer, one of the Ten Nations after the Breaking.

Shaisam. A name taken by Padan Fain during the Last Battle.

Shajin, Stedding. A *stedding* located in the Black Hills.

Shaken Fist, The. An inn in Trustair. Papers with the likeness of Mat and Perrin showed up in the vicinity of Hinderstap, with directions that if one saw either of the men, one could go to The Shaken Fist and earn coin for the information.

Shal, River. A river running southwest from the Hills of Kintara into central Illian, where it met the River Manetherendrelle.

Shaldine. The eleventh month of the year.

Shalon din Togara Morning Tide. Sea Folk Windfinder to Clan Shodein; her Wavemistress, Harine din Togara, was her sister. Her husband was Mishael. Shalon wore four earrings in each ear. Pretty and young-appearing, she was actually twenty-two years older than her sister and was already married when Harine was born. About 5'6" tall, she had very straight black hair, full lips, large dark brown eyes and a dark complexion, though not dark enough to make a comparison to charcoal. Rand found her conferring with the Lady Ailil, as he thought, on the day he was attacked in the Sun Palace and, to get them out of the way, bound and gagged them both, put a shield on Shalon that would dissipate with time and stuffed them under Ailil's bed. Cadsuane discovered that Ailil and Shalon were actually lovers, and the circumstances were such that neither wanted this known. Cadsuane took both of them pretty firmly in hand, making them supply her with information after being questioned by Verin.

Shalon went with Cadsuane and her party to Far Madding and Shadar Logoth; during the cleansing, Shalon linked with Verin and Kumira. The circle encountered Graendal; though they were able to fight her off, Kumira was killed.

shama. A musical instrument of the Age of Legends.

Shamara. *See* Shara

shambayan. The term for a head butler in the Borderland nations.

Shamendar, Stedding. A *stedding* located in the forests north of the River Ivo.

Shana Goridien. An Aes Sedai of the White Ajah and the rebel contingent, with a strength level of 35(23). Born in 882 NE, she went to the White Tower in 898 NE. After spending eleven years as a novice and nine years as Accepted,

Shana was raised to the shawl in 918 NE. Pop-eyed, she always looked startled, although she normally maintained a deep reserve.

Shana was one of a group of Aes Sedai who cornered Aviendha upon her arrival in Salidar, intending to have her in novice white if they had to peel her out of her dress and stuff her into it themselves.

Because of her Talent of reading residues, Shana was one of six sisters sent to investigate the large channeling event at Shadar Logoth.

Shanaine. An Ogier-built city in Manetheren, one of the Ten Nations after the Breaking; it later became the site of Jehannah.

Shanal. A novice in the White Tower who assisted Egwene during the Seanchan attack.

Shanan. The *sul'dam* who captured Moghedien during the Last Battle.

Shandalle. A nation that arose after the Trolloc Wars; Artur Hawkwing was the son of its King Myrdin Paendrag Maregore and Queen Mailinde Paendrag Lyndhal.

Shandare, Tavan. *See* Tavan Shandare

Shandin. Father of Ledar son of Koimal, Ledar being the Ogier author of *A Study of Men, Women and the One Power Among Humans* around 700 NE.

Shanelle. An Altaran Aes Sedai of the Yellow Ajah and the rebel contingent, with a strength level of 32(20). Born not far from Ebou Dar, she was slender, pretty and dark, with pale blue eyes. She sometimes flirted and paid attention to men, but was all business with her Warder. Although she was not particularly strong, Healing was her best Talent by far, and she had a very good ability with it. She witnessed Nynaeve Healing Siuan and Leane.

Shangloon, Stedding. A *stedding* located in the Mountains of Mist.

Shangtai, Stedding. A *stedding* located in the Spine of the World. Loial was born there.

Shanjing, Stedding. A *stedding* located in Arafel.

shanna'har. A yearly celebration of marriage in Saldaea. It was held each year in early summer to mark another year in which neither husband nor wife had fallen to the Trollocs.

Shanni. An Aiel Wise One. Amys suggested asking Shanni and Hayde to encourage the apprentice Wise One Elenar to complete her training so that she could visit Rhuidean.

Shaofan. The future intended Sh'botay of Shara, handsome, with very dark skin. Graendal made him one of her pets before he married Chiape.

Shaogi, Keille. *See* Keille Shaogi

Shaoman. A feast celebrated on the twelfth day of the month on Shaldine. It was particularly oriented toward children, who were cosseted, made much of and given gifts. In many places groups of children went from house to house, where they sang songs before the door and were rewarded with small gifts or sweets.

Shar Honelle. An Ogier-built city in Aelgar, one of the Ten Nations after the Breaking.

Shara. A nation east of the Aiel Waste. Its other names included Shamara, Co'dansin, Tomaka, Kigali and Shibouya. Shara was the source of silk and ivory, among other trade goods. The land was protected both by inhospitable natural features and by man-made walls. Little was known about it, as its people worked to keep their culture secret.

The Sharans denied that the Trolloc Wars touched them, despite Aiel statements to the contrary, and they denied knowledge of Artur Hawkwing's attempted invasion, despite the accounts of eyewitnesses from the Sea Folk. The little information that leaked out revealed that the Sharans were ruled by a single absolute monarch, a Sh'boan if a woman and a Sh'botay if a man. That monarch ruled for exactly seven years, then died. The rule then passed to the mate of that ruler, who ruled for seven years and then died. This pattern had repeated itself from the time of the Breaking of the World. The Sharans believed that the deaths were the "Will of the Pattern."

There were channelers in Shara, known as the Ayyad, who were tattooed on their faces at birth. The women of the Ayyad enforced the Ayyad laws stringently. A sexual relationship between Ayyad and non-Ayyad was punishable by death for the non-Ayyad, and the Ayyad was also executed if force on his or her part could be proven. If a child was born of the union, it was left exposed to the elements, and died.

Male Ayyad were used as breeding stock only. They were not educated in any fashion, not even learning to read or write, and when they reached their twenty-first year or began to channel, whichever came first, they were killed and the body cremated. Supposedly, the Ayyad channeled the One Power only at the command of the Sh'boan or Sh'botay, who was always surrounded by Ayyad women.

Men and women could be owned, just as dogs could be owned. If one owned the man and the woman, one owned the children and the grandchildren. One could sell them or kill them. Killing a human animal was no more serious than killing a dog. Blue, gray or green eyes were signs of being an animal; the only such Jain Farstrider saw were among the animals. Nobles considered even their own commoners little better than half-animals; anyone else was an animal, the only difference being whether they were domesticated or as yet untamed. With the latter, there seemed no doubt that they would be domesticated sooner or later. The nobles were not impatient about this, but they absolutely knew it would happen eventually.

Demandred went to Shara to find the *sa'angreal* Sakarnen; while there he fulfilled the prophecy of the Wyld, and was able to gather the people of Shara to fight for him in the Last Battle.

Shara Pass. A passage through the Cliffs of Dawn, on the border between the Aiel Waste and Shara. It was mentioned by Thom in a gleeman story he told in Cairhien.

sharadan. After Aviendha helped put out the fire at Lord Tellaen's manor in

Arad Doman, Melaine told her that she looked like a sharadan that had crawled on its belly across three days of sand.

Sharaman. A resident of Shara. A variation of Sharan.

Sharbon. Carridin's plump bodyservant in Amador. Carridin treated him badly, backhanding him across the face because he was out buying fruit when Shaidar Haran appeared.

Sharia, River. A river running southeast through Amadicia and into the River Eldar.

Sharif, Leane. *See* Leane Sharif

Sharina Melloy. A Murandian novice with the rebel Aes Sedai. Her potential strength level of 2(+11) was even greater than that of Nynaeve. Born in 938 NE, she was 5'5" tall and had broad hips, a creased face and gray hair worn in a tight bun on the back of her head. In Nynaeve's Accepted test, she was counselor to Lan as King of Malkier.

Sharina was recruited by the rebels in Murandy after Egwene's proclamation allowing any woman of any age to apply for entrance to the White Tower. An older woman, she had thought of going to the Tower as a child; she had also always wanted to see the Borderlands, especially Shienar, and most especially Malkier, a land which she held in the highest imaginable regard.

A widow, she ruled her extended family with a strong hand; she was a very strong-willed and forceful woman. She had sons and daughters, grandchildren and great-grandchildren; her eldest child was born in 958 NE, her youngest in 977 NE. After she was taken on as a novice, most of the Accepted found themselves asking her to do things instead of telling her, and some found themselves doing what she said. She became a leader and a stabilizing influence among the novices. Even some Aes Sedai found themselves being less forceful with her than they normally would be with a novice, and others bore down harder, all because of her own forceful personality and disturbingly direct looks. She organized the novices into "families," which enhanced group cohesiveness and made handling all the novices easier.

Sharmad Zeffar. A Domani woman. She was one of the refugees who went to the Two Rivers. She and Rhea Avin were both interested in Wil al'Seen and went to Faile to get her decision on which one had the right to him. Faile sent them to Daise Congar, the Wisdom, to sort them out.

Sharom. A huge white sphere, one thousand feet in diameter, used as a scientific research facility. It floated high above the blue and silver domes of the Collam Daan during the Age of Legends. Mierin accidentally blew up the Sharom while experimenting with a new source for the One Power and drilling into the Dark One's prison.

Sharplyn, Anthelle. An Andoran noblewoman and High Seat of her minor House. She was loyal to Elayne.

shatayan. The term for a head housekeeper in the Borderland nations.

Shayol Ghul. During the Age of Legends, Shayol Ghul was an idyllic island in a cool sea, a favorite escape of those who enjoyed the rustic. After the Breaking, it became a mountain in the Blasted Lands, where the Dark One's prison was located. More precisely, Shayol Ghul was a sort of focus point, a place where the Dark One's prison lay close to the world—there was a thinness in the Pattern, allowing the Bore to be detected—so the focus of the Dark One's strength was there.

shea dancers. Seanchan dancers who wore transparent veils almost identical to those worn by Taraboner women, but little else. They were a favorite topic of discussion among Seanchan soldiers.

Shedren. The clan chief of the Daryne Aiel after the Last Battle, seen in Aviendha's visions of the future in Rhuidean.

sheepstongue. A root used in tea along with rannel for an energy boost; it had a terrible lingering taste. It was also used to alleviate eye pain and as a punishment for silliness. Nynaeve, mad at Elayne, offered to give her sheeptongue and red daisy tea for a headache that the latter must have gotten from thinking too much, but it was unclear whether she really used it for headache in other cases.

Shefar, Ispan. *See* Ispan Shefar

Shein Chunla. An Aes Sedai of the Green Ajah who served as Amyrlin from 578 to 601 NE. Shein, the youngest Amyrlin since Deane Aryman, was a weak Amyrlin. She attempted to run the Hall of the Tower autocratically, but failed miserably. She had been the head of the Green Ajah—although this was not known outside the Ajah—and was well respected by other Ajahs. It was not until she was chosen Amyrlin that they saw examples of how she had run the Green. The other Ajahs did not find that way to their liking at all. The Hall made her little more than a figurehead and ceremonial puppet. Although the world at large thought she died in office, in fact she was toppled by a rebellion, and a good part of the Hall that had tolerated her fell with her. Many in the Hall had been willing to deal with and around her, but discontent grew until the Sitters who were no longer willing carried out a coup. Shein actually lived another fifty-one years in a very closely controlled exile until she died in 652 NE. There was some evidence that she was assassinated—smothered in her sleep by her guards—because of a plot to return her to power. The secret Tower records did describe several plots that were aimed at returning her to Tar Valon at the very least. All of these were dealt with strongly, and Shein herself was punished in each instance, though there was no concrete evidence that she knew of all the plots. It was fairly certain that she knew of some.

Sheldyn. Estates, or the location of estates, held by Ellorien Traemane in Andor. In a meeting with other House seats, she announced her intention of returning to Sheldyn after refusing to stand for Elayne, but she said that Traemane would ride behind the Lion of Andor at the Last Battle.

shellback. An animal also called a *goerant* (singular and plural). Its body was covered in hard shell armor. The shellback grew to as much as twenty-five pounds. It lived in burrows, could dig itself into the ground very quickly and could move beneath the ground by burrowing a tunnel. Aviendha killed and ate one while traveling to Rhuidean.

Shemaen. An Aes Sedai. Adelorna reportedly told Shemaen that Gitara had had a Foretelling that the Last Battle "would come in the lifetimes of sisters now breathing." Ellid overheard them, and reported it to other novices.

Shemari. An Aes Sedai of the Brown Ajah and the rebel contingent. A librarian, she was square-faced and vigorous, and curtsied to Egwene in a way that seemed like mockery. She and Phaedrine linked were barely able to form a gateway large enough for them to walk through.

Shemerin. A plump Aes Sedai of the Yellow Ajah and the loyalist contingent, with a strength level of 15(3). Born in 828 NE, she went to the White Tower in 845 NE. After spending fourteen years as a novice and seventeen years as Accepted, she was raised to the shawl in 876 NE. The length of her training resulted from her unsuitability for testing; except for her potential, she might have been put out of the Tower without being allowed to test for Accepted; as it was, she refused the first two times. Shemerin hid for three days after finally passing, and when she was found she was still shivering. She took all three tries to pass the testing for the shawl, and barely passed the third.

Shemerin had a good talent for Healing and a very high skill in administration and organization, as well as a deft hand in internal White Tower politics, but she never had the outward Aes Sedai calm. Often she seemed slightly anxious, wringing her hands and nearly fainting. She was, in point of fact, a coward and knew it. During her brief time out of the Tower, supposedly looking for a Warder, she actually went no farther from Tar Valon than she could manage.

Shemerin served on the council advising Elaida when she took the Amyrlin Seat; Elaida grew tired of her lack of backbone and demoted her to Accepted for having shown herself unfit to wear the shawl. Although the Sitters were aghast at the precedent, the Hall seemed unable to figure out how to oppose the decree. The Mistress of Novices received orders from the Amyrlin to pick up "the Accepted Shemerin" wherever she was to be found and escort her to the Accepted quarters, where she was to be held. Silviana took this as some sort of imposed penance, took along a pair of Red sisters for assistants, snatched Shemerin from the hallways and hustled her to the Accepted quarters, where she was stuffed into an Accepted's dress despite her protests, since Silviana had no patience with that sort of thing. Elaida entered Shemerin's name anew on the roll of the Accepted. Most sisters thought that Shemerin herself should simply refuse to accept this and return to her own quarters, something which she was constitutionally unable to do, especially since it would have meant trying to face down Silviana. In a way, her ineffectiveness at protesting and the inertia and indecision of the rest of the sisters as to what to say or do led to nothing happening until everyone simply drifted into realizing, or deciding, that she had been being treated as Accepted long enough that she was Accepted. She was also treated very strictly by Silviana, the loyalist Mistress of Novices, who felt that Shemerin was in truth Aes Sedai no matter what was decreed, and as such she should have known both how to maintain the dignity of an Aes Sedai and how to stay within the rules so long as she was kept as an Accepted.

Instead, Shemerin managed to bumble, bungle and give in to her frights and vapors, with the result that she continually fell afoul of the rules for Accepted and also gave those sisters who had turned on her, many of them Elaida's supporters, plentiful opportunities, and indeed cause, to call her down and/or send her to Silviana. Her bumbling made even most of the Accepted look at her askance, which decreased her confidence further; she quickly became a laughingstock among them, and eventually a number of them played tricks on her which got her into trouble. Toward the end of her time as Accepted, even some novices occasionally played tricks on her, tricks which also often got her into trouble. Her reaction to being switched or strapped or given chores by Silviana was not what was hoped for by the Mistress of Novices, because they shook her confidence even more, and made her bumble and stumble even more. The result was that Shemerin started off badly and found herself deeper and deeper in hot water by the day—literally by the day, since rarely did a day pass for her without another visit to Silviana.

Shemerin decided to flee; her great difficulty was in escaping from the White Tower itself, because she was watched very closely. The Tower did not spread such things about, but she could have departed Tar Valon quite easily once she got out of the Tower grounds. Her own fearful instincts kept her looking over her shoulder, though, and seeing shadows where there were none. For that reason she made her actual escape from Tar Valon via a small, long-unused watergate. She hid in a nearby village and joined the rebel camp as a washwoman using the name Tagren. Gawyn and Bryne discovered her; she told how she had escaped through the watergate, and they used that information in their rescue of Egwene.

Shemon, Berana. *See* Berana Shemon

Shen an Calhar. The Band of the Red Hand; originally a legendary Manetheren fighting force from the Trolloc Wars, the name was adopted by Mat's soldiers.

Shendar, Avi. *See* Avi Shendar

Shende. A hold in the Waste of which Sorilea was the Wise One.

Shendla. A beautiful Sharan who was one of the leaders at the Last Battle. Demandred thought that she was devious, capable and powerful; it was almost enough to change his heart. Though she was not a Darkfriend, Shendla was willing to help Demandred win the Last Battle because she thought that if he was victorious her people would be saved, and she loved him. After Demandred fell, she announced that Bao the Wyld was dead.

Shepherd of the Night. Another name for the Dark One.

Sheraine Caminelle. *See* Mylen

Shereed, Mabriam en. *See* Mabriam en Shereed

Sheriam Bayanar. A Saldaean Aes Sedai of the Blue Ajah publicly and of the Black Ajah in truth. She was a member of the rebel contingent, with a strength level of 14(2). Born in 953 NE, she went to the White Tower in 969 NE. After spending five years as a novice, she refused her first time at the arches; after her second try, she spent five years as Accepted and was raised Aes Sedai in 979 NE. She became Mistress of Novices in 992 NE at an extremely young age for the job. After the Tower split, she went to Salidar and became part of the council running things there. She pledged for Egwene when Egwene was raised to the Amyrlin Seat, and Egwene named her Keeper of the Chronicles in 999 NE. She was secretly oathsworn to Egwene. Fire-haired, with green eyes and tilted cheekbones, she was about 5'5" tall, a little plump and quite pretty. Sheriam had one Warder, Arinvar. Sheriam sometimes sounded as if she were quoting when she was merely speaking. She seemed to say "aye" without thinking if Romanda or Lelaine said "nay." As a Black sister, she was intent on causing trouble and keeping the animosity going between the rebels and the White Tower. She might or might not have given support toward Rand's cause, depending on whether she thought it would increase disorder. She had become a Darkfriend to get ahead, and was willing to do whatever was required to avoid any form of punishment. Halima beat her frequently for not doing enough for the effort, and she wanted to avoid any of that if possible.

While Egwene was held captive, Mesaana ordered Sheriam to make sure that Egwene was deposed, and ordered her to steal all of the sleepweavers to stop the Aes Sedai from having meetings in *Tel'aran'rhiod,* and to make them accessible to the Black Ajah; she said that Sheriam would lose a finger or a toe for each one she failed to produce in three days. Sheriam was later seen with a bandaged hand.

She was identified as Black Ajah in Verin's list and executed.

Shevan Gadarin. A Kandori Aes Sedai of the Brown Ajah and the loyalist contingent, with a strength level of 18(6). Born in 843 NE, she went to the White Tower in 859 NE. After spending four years as a novice and six years as Accepted, she was raised to the shawl in 869 NE. About 5'10" tall, with an angular face, a long chin, a cap of dark curls and long spidery fingers, she was thin—not much short of bony. She could be very dry when she wanted to, and she frequently did. Shevan was raised a Sitter for the Brown in 999 NE to replace Janya Frende, who joined the rebels. She was part of the council advising Elaida when Elaida was first raised to the Amyrlin Seat. She worried about reports of "leashed women" and the possibility that Seanchan had a device to control women who could channel. Elaida gave her a penance scrubbing floors. After the Tower was reunited, Shevan was replaced as Sitter by Janya. Shevan was killed in the battle against the Black Ajah in *Tel'aran'rhiod.*

Shiagi Hold. The home of the Nakai Aiel in the Aiel Waste.

Shiaine Avarhin, Lady. A woman of a minor noble family which had a lineage back to the founding of Andor. The sigil of House Avarhin was a red heart on a golden hand. The Avarhin family had been dwindling in numbers for generations and becoming increasingly impoverished. Shiaine's grandfather had been forced to give up the last house that could be called an estate and move into an isolated farmhouse a fair walk from the nearest village. Her mother, who died when Shiaine was young, was a commoner. Shiaine was an awkward young woman, tall, bony and very plain; like most of the Avarhins, she had blue eyes and red hair. Blue eyes and pale hair were the most common combination in the family; there were some green eyes and sometimes black hair, but brown eyes were never seen. Her father, Willim, had enough money to keep one servant, but he never went into society because of his comparative poverty, and Shiaine had never even been to Caemlyn. Shiaine, her father and their single servant were killed by the Darkfriend Mili Skane so that she could use Shiaine's name as her own. *See also* Mili Skane

Shiande. An Aiel clan; its chief was Janwin.

Shianri, Kyril. *See* Kyril Shianri

Shibouya. Another name for Shara.

Shiego, Arrela. *See* Arrela Shiego

Shield, the. A constellation. It was sometimes called "Hawkwing's Shield."

shielding. A phenomenon whereby one channeler used a weave to cut another channeler off from the True Source; the latter was still able to sense the Source.

Shielyn din Sabura Night Waters. Zaida's Sea Folk Windfinder. Her strength level was 23(11). She was 5'8" tall, slim and pretty, though not beautiful. Shielyn was aware of who she was, and her position. She appeared to be about thirty and had straight black hair, nearly black eyes and four earrings in each ear. She could have been taken for a very dark Tairen. She was with Zaida in Caemlyn, and left with her after the death of the Mistress of the Ships. When Zaida was named to that post, Shielyn also ascended in rank.

Shienar. One of the Borderland nations. Shienar's capital was Fal Moran, and King Easar Togita ruled at the time of the Last Battle. Its sigil was a stooping black hawk: the Black Hawk. Its banner was the Black Hawk on a field of three blue and two white horizontal stripes. The sigil and banner of the reigning king were also considered a national banner and sigil; King Easar's was the White Hart.

Saldaea, Kandor, Arafel, Shienar and Malkier all were provinces of Hawkwing's empire, with the borders between them very much as they were at the time of the Last Battle, though not stretching so far south in most cases. With the Blight to contend with, the governors of those provinces (Lord Rylen t'Boriden Rashad for Saldaea, Lord Jarel Soukovni for Kandor, Lady Mahira Svetanya for Arafel, Lady Merean Tihomar for Shienar and Lord Shevar Jamelle for Malkier) met soon after Hawkwing's death in FY 994 to reaffirm measures for cooperation against the Blight and to make agreements for mutual defense against attack from the south. Before the end of FY 995, when it became clear that the rest of the empire was splintering, each of the governors took the title of King or Queen of his or her former province, now a nation. None of these nations would take part in any of the wider fighting of the War of the Hundred Years, as nations, except for defending themselves against attacks and punishing same, though individuals and groups did sometimes become involved, sometimes for political reasons or family connections or friendships.

Shienar always had a king, though the Queen his wife, if he had one, had considerable authority. When he led an army into battle, as he was expected to, she handled civil rule until he returned. The King was expected to surround himself with a council of nobles and representatives of the merchants and guilds, but he was in no way constrained to take their advice, nor was his wife when she was reigning as regent while he was away on campaign.

In the keep, men's quarters were separated from women's quarters. It was necessary for men to be invited or given permission to enter the women's apartments, and they never went armed unless the keep was under attack. This included a woman's husband and the lord of the particular place. A man could send a message to one in the women's apartments, but it would be delivered when the women chose, and the man could only wait.

On the other hand, bathing in Shienar took place in large, tiled pools and was mixed between the sexes. Seeing someone naked there and perhaps scrubbing his or her back was not considered at all the same as seeing them in a corridor. The woman who scrubbed your back last night, and both of you naked, would have blushed if you saw her ankle in the hallway the next day. She also would not necessarily have considered having scrubbed your back, or you hers, as sufficient introduction for you to speak to her in the corridor.

There was a link between Shienaran and Aiel views of shame: shame was worse than guilt, the worst thing there was. This view of shame ameliorated as one moved west; in Arafellin less than Shienaran, Kandori less than Arafellin, Saldaean less than Kandori. In all of the Borderlands, though, shame was given a much heavier weight than in lands to the south.

A Borderman considered the day he was given his sword to be his nameday.

Uno commented that women in Shienar said a woman's rights were whatever she said they were.

Shienar mined a considerable amount of gold, silver and gems, especially firedrops, of which Shienar was the largest source. There was also some mining of emeralds, rubies and sapphires, as well as lesser stones. Timber and furs were both major exports.

Shienaran Marches. A fortified border region where Lan fought the Aiel before the Aiel War began.

Shilene Gate. A passageway found on the eastern side of Lugard.

Shiman, Jurad. *See* Jurad Shiman

Shimel, Mistress. A fur merchant in Far Madding. Rand saw her while gathering intelligence at an inn called The Golden Wheel. A stout woman with a round face and a thin smile, she wore her black hair in a tight roll along the top of her head. She mentioned that she heard the Stone of Tear was under siege.

Shimoku. A Kandori Accepted with the Salidar contingent having a potential strength level of 34(22). Born in 973 NE, she went to the White Tower in 988 NE. After spending eleven years as a novice, she was raised Accepted in 999 NE. Shortly after, she was taken to Salidar by the rebels. Pretty, with dark eyes, Shimoku shared a house in Salidar with Elayne and Nynaeve. On the night the bubble of evil struck Salidar, she entered the link easily and was so tired later that she sat down in the street.

Shimron, Lord. A Domani nobleman, former advisor to Alsalam, and a Dragon-sworn. A gaunt, white-haired man, he wore a beauty mark of a sparkling red quarter moon beside his left eye. He joined Ituralde to fight the Seanchan and was killed by a *damane* fireball.

Shimura, Aiden. *See* Aiden Shimura

Shining Walls, Battle of. *See* Battle of the Shining Walls, the

Shinowa, Ingtar. *See* Ingtar Shinowa

Shiota. A nation that arose after the Trolloc Wars; its borders were within what became Altara.

Shipless, Leilwin. *See* Egeanin Sarna

Shivan the Hunter. A Hero of the Horn and brother of Calian the Chooser. Shivan wore a black mask and was said to herald the end of Ages—destruction of the old, beginning of the new. He did not take part in the Last Battle as a Hero of the Horn, having been born shortly before.

Shivena Kayenzi. A Saldaean philosopher who was influenced by Willim of Manaches. Meilyn tested Moiraine on her knowledge of the two when she was Accepted.

sho-wing. A high-tech aircraft from the Age of Legends, based on a delta-wing pattern. It varied in size depending on purpose and was capable of long-range flight at high speeds.

shocklance. A high-tech energy weapon of long-distance destruction, developed to fight the Dark One's forces during the War of the Shadow. Shocklances were in short supply by the time of the Breaking because the industrial base of the world had been destroyed long before.

shockvisor. A helmet part from the War of the Shadow.

Shodin. A clan among the Sea Folk.

shoja-circle. Obscure reference made by Birgitte, saying that Gaidal told her that she had a sense of humor like "a rock thrown into a shoja-circle."

Shol Arbela. The capital of Arafel. It was built by men, not Ogier, and was known as the City of Ten Thousand Bells.

Sholoon, Stedding. A *stedding* located in Shienar, in a wooded area east of the Field of Merrilor. Lindsar was the eldest of the Ogier in Stedding Sholoon, and she allowed Androl and Pevara to use the *stedding* to trap a group of Dark-friends, including Alviarin and some of Taim's cronies.

Shon Kifar. The tenth-largest city in Seanchan. Tuon reflected on how she had purchased her *damane* Mylen on the docks of this seaport.

Shoran, Darnella. *See* Darnella Shoran

Shorara. A sept of the Tomanelle Aiel.

Shore, Mistress. The name used by Cadsuane in her dealings with Quillin Tasil, an innkeeper in Bandar Eban.

Shorelle. A port city in the Age of Legends. Asmodean was born there.

shoufa. A garment of the Aiel, a cloth, usually the color of sand or rock, that wrapped around the head and neck, leaving only the face bare.

shoulderthumper. A bullyboy or thug.

Shukosa, Mahiro. *See* Mahiro Shukosa

Shumada, Amenar. A member of the Seanchan Blood who attended Tuon's first audience in Ebou Dar.

Shyanda. A Wise One of the Goshien Aiel with fiery red hair. Shyanda was at Elayne and Aviendha's first-sister ceremony and stepped forward with Amys when the latter said that she would suffer the pangs of birth for Aviendha and Elayne; she helped Amys strip.

Shyman's Road. A road passing by Negin Bridge near Dragonmount.

Sibella. A Kin and a member of the Knitting Circle. Her strength level was 22(10); she was not strong enough to make a gateway of any size whatsoever. Born in 613 NE, she went to the White Tower in 627 NE. After spending ten years as a novice and six years as Accepted, she flunked her test for the shawl very badly and was put out of the Tower in 643 NE. Yellow-haired and thin, with no gray or white in her hair, Sibella appeared to be in her middle years and favored plunging necklines. When encountered by Nynaeve and Elayne, she wore the red belt of a Wise Woman. She fainted when Merilille and the others unmasked her. A member of the party that went to the Rahad to get the Bowl of the Winds, Sibella was injured by the *gholam*, but Nynaeve and Sumeko Healed her. She was present at the meeting with the Windfinders in the Tarasin Palace, and part of manipulating them, on orders from Elayne and Nynaeve. Sibella nearly fainted again at the suggestion of sitting in the presence of Aes Sedai and the Queen. Sibella accompanied Elayne to the Royal Palace in Caemlyn.

Sidama. Galad's horse in the Last Battle.

Sidon. A single-inn village in Ghealdan, on the west bank of the River Boern where a stone bridge spanned the river between fifty-foot cliffs. When Moiraine and her party passed through chasing after Rand, they found Sidon burned; a lantern dropped in a barn had started a fire that seemed to run wild, and everything went wrong. Nothing was left except a few stone walls and chimneys. Moiraine was sure that the fire was a result of Rand's having been there.

Sidona. An area of Saldaea; one of Bashere's titles was Lord of Bashere, Tyr and Sidona.

Sidoro. A family in Illian. *See* Bili *and* Nieda Sidoro

Siedre. A Jenn Aiel woman shortly after the Breaking. She married Adan, and they had five children: Rhea, Malind, Sorelle, Elwin and Jaren. All either died or were carried off by bandits; Siedre was also killed by bandits.

Sienda. A sizable two-inn village in Amadicia. The dwellings were of stone and thatch, and the dirt streets were crowded with Whitecloaks and King's men. Nynaeve, Elayne, Thom and Juilin stayed at an inn there. Nynaeve, in *Tel'aran'rhiod*, found out that Elaida was the new Amyrlin, and that rebel Aes Sedai were hiding out somewhere. The two women met Galad, now a Whitecloak officer, at the inn over breakfast, and he said he wished to escort them to Caemlyn, although they were on their way to Tear. They all snuck away, and joined Master Luca's menagerie heading for Ghealdan. One of Luca's boar-horses had damaged one of the inns.

Sierin Vayu. An Aes Sedai of the Gray Ajah with a strength level of 18(6). Born in 736 NE, she went to the White Tower in 752 NE. After spending eight years as a novice and nine years as Accepted, she was raised to the shawl in 769 NE. Sierin was plump, with a grim face and hard eyes; she was stern, and had more than a touch of Red in her. On being raised Amyrlin in the spring of 979 NE, rather than granting petitions and relief from penances, she exiled three sisters from the Tower and had two more birched. She also fired every male clerk in the Tower for such offenses as "flirting with novices and Accepted" or "inappropriate glances and looks." Sierin was assassinated by a small group of Red sisters in 984 NE when she was about to put an end to the male channeler pogrom. Chesmal Emry claimed to have induced the Red Ajah to kill Sierin when Sierin was about to have her arrested.

Sightblinder. An Aiel name for the Dark One.

Sightburner. An Aiel name for the Dark One.

Sigmont. A young man who participated in the Last Battle. Mat taught him how to use a quarterstaff, but he wanted to learn to use a sword.

Sigril. Yoeli's sister; she was the leader of the Lastriders in Maradon. She and the Lastriders were positioned outside the city during the Trolloc invasion, and were tasked with getting word to other Saldaean forces if the city fell.

Silene Dorelmin. The best seamstress in Chachin, Kandor. Slim, with a haughty air and a cool voice, she made dresses for Moiraine.

Silk Path. A trade route running between the Jangai Pass across the Waste to Shara; it was used only by those allowed to cross the Aiel Waste, such as the Cairhienin before the Aiel War.

Sillia Cerano. A woman who owned a touring circus, competition for Valan Luca's circus near Samara in Ghealdan. She and half her performers were flogged for not moving fast enough to suit the Prophet at Samara; they were forced into the Prophet's service.

Silvane Redfor. An Andoran Aes Sedai of the Green Ajah, uncommitted to any contingent, with a strength level of 33(21). Silvane was one of the uncommitted

Aes Sedai Rand found in Cairhien after Dumai's Wells who was following Cadsuane Melaidhrin. Silvane was left behind in Cairhien when Cadsuane went to Far Madding.

Silver Circuit. A racetrack lying just south of the city walls of Ebou Dar. Olver raced Wind there and won, as did Mat, who had bet heavily on him. Mat saw Mili Skane there, as well.

Silver Dolphin. A waterfront inn located in Illian. Yarin Maeldan, second to Bayle Domon on the *Spray*, made his residence at the Silver Dolphin while in port. His room was searched by unknowns.

Silver Horn, The. An inn found in Maerone, Cairhien, that was frequented by soldiers of Mat's Band. Mat and Edorion went there making rounds of the drinking halls to check on Mat's men. Inside, a girl sang bawdy songs; outside, Mat saved Olver from a beating by Murandian Hunters of the Horn.

Silver Penny, The. An inn in Chachin, Kandor. Its innkeeper was Nedare Satarov. Moiraine stopped in to ask if Siuan was staying there; Nedare told her that she was, and offered Moiraine a mug of spiced wine. Nedare's air of anticipation made Moiraine suspicious that there was something in the wine; she made Nedare drink the wine. Nedare tried to flee, but fell to the floor, revealing silk stockings; she had done quite well drugging innocent women for the use of her rough customers. A number of the men in the common room looked at her lasciviously, and all the women, including Moiraine, left.

Silver Pig. An inn or tavern in Lugard. Siuan passed it on the way to another inn while looking for a Blue Ajah eyes-and-ears.

Silver Road. A commercial highway connecting the city of Illian to Lugard. It was used by Rand's forces during the campaign against the Seanchan.

Silver Swan. An inn in the New City of Caemlyn. Various Aes Sedai and their Warders stayed there just after Rand fled Caemlyn. A few would leave, a few others come, but there were never more than ten lodgers at one time. They kept to themselves, caused no trouble and asked no questions that Bashere or Bael were able to learn of. Their presence coincided with other Aes Sedai gatherings in Cairhien. Elayne had them watched, as it was unclear whose side they were on. The Black sisters knew of them and avoided them.

silverbell. A plant with blossoms that looked like silver bells. Erith's eyes were the color of a silverbell's ripe seedpod.

Silverbow, Birgitte. *See* Birgitte Silverbow

silverleaf. A plant used in tea for headache.

silverpike. A predatory fish that spawned in the reeds and chewed fishermen's nets. Attracted by blood, they could tear other fish apart. They were also eaten by people.

silversides. A select type of fish.

Silverwall Keeps. An Arafellin fortress on the Firchon Pass next to the border of Kandor.

Silviana Brehon. An Amadician Aes Sedai of the Red Ajah and the loyalist contingent, with a strength level of 15(3). Born in 849 NE, she went to the White Tower in 867 NE. After spending twelve years as a novice and eleven years as Accepted, she was raised to the shawl in 890 NE. She was made Mistress of Novices in 999 NE, when the Tower split, and named Keeper of the Chronicles by Egwene al'Vere in 1000 NE, when it reunited. She was 5'6½" tall, and stocky, with a square face, a firm, determined chin, dark hair worn in a tight bun on the back of her head and large dark eyes. Novices and Accepted, and some Aes Sedai, said she had eyes in the back of her head. There were those among the novices who believed she could see what happened in places where she wasn't even present. Physically very strong, she reminded people of a strict aunt, the one who not only would not stand for any nonsense, but who viewed her nieces and nephews as raw material to be whipped into shape as human beings.

Despite her potential strength, she had great difficulty in learning when she arrived in the Tower; her teachers thought this was a result of her innate stubbornness and too much pride, and she came to agree with them, which was one reason she was so strict with her charges. Well aware of her own weaknesses and flaws, she came to terms with them and learned to control most of them. Thus she believed that anyone could learn to control their weaknesses and flaws given sufficient motivation. She thought that a combination of rewards and punishments worked best. Indeed, they seemed to work very well for her; the novices and Accepted feared her punishments and were very grateful for her small rewards. She had fewer discipline problems than was considered usual, while her charges learned at a very high rate, retaining what they learned better. Silviana was not popular with the novices and Accepted—Sheriam was popular by and large, though no one wanted to run afoul of her either—but she was very successful, by most benchmarks considerably more so than Sheriam. As Mistress of Novices she had a reputation for being harsh, and indeed her model among former Mistresses of Novices was Sereille Bagand, but this fearsome reputation was largely because, unlike Sheriam and Sheriam's immediate predecessors, she did not play favorites, and she did not have periods when she was slack with her charges. Silviana was watchful all the time, evenhanded and strict. She made sure that any punishment was hard enough that no one could simply shrug it off and forget it. Whoever came to her, for punishment or penance, left with a fervent desire not to repeat the experience. For this reason, she actually punished fewer girls than any of the immediate predecessors she so despised.

She was harder on Accepted than on novices. She was tough enough on novices that not everyone saw it, but in fact she gave more petting than punishments to the younger girls and allowed Accepted much less slack than Sheriam or her immediate predecessors. Since they were older and more advanced, they should have known better.

She considered the novices hers, an attitude not unusual with the Mistress of Novices. In her view, she had responsibility for and over them, and she was not to be overridden by anyone, not even the Amyrlin Seat. Tower law did make her the final arbiter over novices and Accepted.

Since penances for Aes Sedai which contained physical chastisement were usually carried out by the Mistress of Novices—though almost always in strictest confidentiality—a number of sisters who fell afoul of Elaida felt much the same way about Silviana as the novices and Accepted did.

After Egwene was taken by the Tower Aes Sedai and put back in novice white, Silviana would not allow the methods used in putting someone to the question to be used on her, even though she had been aiding the rebels and claiming to be the Amyrlin Seat. When she deemed Elaida's punishment too harsh and demanded that Egwene be released, Elaida tried to demote her, but Silviana refused to let that happen. Elaida then ordered that Silviana be imprisoned and executed. Egwene had her released and named her Keeper of the Chronicles, another job at which Silviana was adept; Egwene found her a tremendous improvement over Sheriam in that job as well. The only fly in the ointment was Silviana's dislike for Gawyn. In the Last Battle, Silviana fought alongside Egwene in Kandor. When Gawyn was killed, Silviana tried to keep Egwene away from the battle, but was not successful.

Silvic. A member of the Band of the Red Hand who taught Olver how to use his knife.

Silvie. A crone met in the Heart of the Stone in *Tel'aran'rhiod*, Lanfear in disguise, who told Egwene about *Callandor*.

Silvin, Betse. *See* Betse Silvin

Silvin, Jar. *See* Jar Silvin

Sim. The innkeeper of The King's Lancer in Sienda, Amadicia. One of Valan Luca's boar-horses smashed through the front door of his inn, causing him to lose half or more of his custom.

Simaan. A Tairen High Lord. He had sharp eyes and a sharp nose. One of the most active plotters against Rand in the Stone, he was sent to Cairhien under Meilan to restore order. Later he was sent back south from Cairhien leading one of the last large parties of Tairens to depart, and he joined the rebellion against Rand gathering near Haddon Mirk. Merana and Rafela negotiated a settlement with Simaan and the other rebels; that settlement made Darlin king.

simblossoms. A flower grown on the roofs of holds in the Aiel Waste.

Simion. A servant/workman at the inn Harilin's Leap in Jarra, Ghealdan. Simion had a wide mouth, popping eyes and no chin to speak of, making him resemble a frog. His brother Noam was a wolfbrother and lost himself to the wolves. When Moiraine, Lan, Loial and Perrin stayed at the inn, Simion recognized that Moiraine was an Aes Sedai, and asked Perrin if she could heal his brother. Moiraine tried, but could not, and Perrin persuaded Simion to let Noam run free.

Sinah, Ranun. A Whitecloak soldier killed in battle with Shadowspawn on the

Jehannah Road. When Perrin and Galad found his body, his cloak was soaked in blood.

Sindhol. The name used by Moghedien for the realm of the Aelfinn and Eelfinn.

Singing. Singing was performed at gatherings among guests by those who had the Voice, a Talent. Singing was mentioned by a mad Lews Therin when he greeted Ishamael, the Betrayer of Hope, and also inside the *ter'angreal* in Rhuidean.

Sins, Thirteen. In Ebou Dar, representative figures carved into a lintel at the Kin house. They included Envy, Gossip and Greed.

Sintiang, Stedding. A *stedding* located in the Spine of the World.

Sisnera, Darlin. *See* Darlin Sisnera

sister-mother, sister-wife. *See* Aiel kinship

Siswai. Aviendha's leggy arch-necked gray horse.

siswai'aman. In the Old Tongue, "the spear of the Dragon"; Aiel men who wore a strip of red cloth around their forehead with a black-and-white disc above their brows, and who were dedicated to the Dragon Reborn.

Sitter. An Aes Sedai who represented her Ajah in the Hall of the Tower; each Ajah was represented by three Sitters.

Siuan Sanche. A Tairen Aes Sedai of the Blue Ajah and the rebel contingent, with an original strength level of 13(1); after being stilled and Healed, her strength level was 35(23). Born in 957 NE to a poor fisherman's family, she went to the White Tower in 972 NE. Spending three years as a novice and three years as Accepted, she was raised to the shawl in late 978 NE, after the Battle of the Shining Walls; Moiraine was raised at the same time. Siuan was raised to the Amyrlin Seat in 988 NE, then the youngest to hold the post. In 999 NE, she was deposed and stilled. Her Warder Alric was killed the same day. About 5'5" tall, she was fair-skinned, blue-eyed and more than handsome but less than beautiful. After she was deposed and stilled, she looked young, about twenty-two or twenty-three, and no longer like an Aes Sedai. Men in Lugard considered her pretty, which astonished her. Her eyes could flash fire and bore holes in stone when she wanted them to. She had a fairly small ability with Healing, and she had the minor Talent of being able to see *ta'veren*; to her eyes, a *ta'veren* person was accompanied by or surrounded by a glow proportional to the strength with which he or she was central to the weaving of the Pattern. This ability was recovered after she was Healed from being stilled.

Siuan was novice and Accepted with Moiraine. The pair were very close friends. The two most common pairings of extremely close friends among novices and Accepted were between women who were from very much the same sort of background, and between women who were from what seemed opposite backgrounds. She and Moiraine began as friends who cried on each other's shoulder about the hardships of being a novice or after a switching from the Mistress of Novices, and they eventually became pillow friends. This relationship continued after they became Accepted, and even for a time after they were raised Aes Sedai, though never again with the same intensity as when they were younger. As novice and Accepted both, it was Siuan who always took the lead between her and Moiraine. That startled Moiraine at first, until she decided that Siuan had been born to lead.

Siuan and Moiraine played a good many pranks, always together. They were caught for a number of these and punished together, so much so that it was said that if one was spotted waiting to go into the Mistress of Novices' study, the other was already inside.

A great effort was made to clean up Siuan's language when she was a novice, and it was apparently successful, but as soon as she gained the shawl, she reverted. In the same way, she apparently forgot many if not all of her deportment lessons.

As Accepted, Siuan and Moiraine were attending the Amyrlin, Tamra Ospenya, and the Keeper, Gitara Moroso, in the final hours of the Battle of the Shining Walls. Gitara had a Foretelling that the Dragon had been reborn, and fell over dead. Although Tamra did not encourage it, Siuan and Moiraine began the hunt for the Dragon Reborn as soon as they could. They were raised to the shawl soon thereafter, and Cetalia Delarme, the head of the Blue eyes-and-ears, chose Siuan to be her assistant, leaving Moiraine to begin the search outside the Tower on her own.

In her job, Siuan learned that all of the women Tamra had set on the task were being killed; she made haste to meet Moiraine in Kandor. After Moiraine defeated Merean of the Black Ajah, Siuan puzzled out that men who might be able to channel were being killed.

Siuan made her way back to the Tower and resumed working for Cetalia. It was a job that brought her information from every quarter of the world, not only hints as to the presence of the Dragon Reborn but also as to the presence of the Black Ajah. She was not pleased to go back; since she had run off without telling Cetalia and had left a large stack of reports behind, she was sure that Cetalia would hang her out in the sun to dry, and she was not far wrong. That was the beginning of her being pulled deeper and deeper into the politics of the Tower, with the eventual result of her being chosen Amyrlin only nine years later.

As Amyrlin, Siuan went to Fal Dara in 998 NE to see Moiraine and Rand, whom Moiraine had identified as the Dragon Reborn. Siuan kept the knowledge a secret from the rest of the Aes Sedai. That choice led to her deposition when Elaida became suspicious and led a coup. Siuan and her Keeper, Leane Sharif, were stilled and imprisoned. Min freed them, and with Logain, started out to find the rebel Aes Sedai. On the way, Siuan and Min, Leane and Logain took shelter in a barn in Kore Springs; when they were discovered, Logain hit the farmer, causing him to drop his lantern and set the barn alight. The barn and milkcows were lost; Logain escaped, but the women were taken for trial. Gareth Bryne presided, and they swore service to him long enough to repay the cost of the barn and cows. Siuan, saying that she intended to fulfill her oath, and the rest then fled when Logain gave them the opportunity. They learned that the rebels were in Salidar, and made their way there, with Bryne in pursuit.

When she joined the Salidar rebels, Siuan was welcomed warmly by many, for herself and for representing hope against what every Aes Sedai feared beyond death; just as many or more offered toleration or condescension or both, blaming her for their situation. She was no longer bound by the Three Oaths, though few knew this; she used her freedom to convince the Aes Sedai that Logain had been set up as a false Dragon by the Reds. She also convinced them that they needed a young, malleable woman for the new Amyrlin, one they could manipulate and guide. Nynaeve Healed Siuan, but her strength level was dramatically lower than before. In general it was believed—and rightly— that Siuan adapted to her new circumstances much less well than Leane. Siuan could accept that she was no longer Amyrlin and would not be, though barely. What she found almost impossible to adjust to was her greatly reduced status in the hierarchy; not only that she was so much lower, but that she reacted automatically to it sometimes, that she had to defer to sisters who before her stilling, even had she not been Amyrlin, would have listened attentively and accepted her suggestions as the next thing to orders. She did not like the lesser status, and she did not like the fact that she was beginning to accept it without thought.

When Egwene was raised to the Amyrlin Seat, Siuan was told to teach Egwene the protocols of her position, and became seen as somewhat attached to Egwene, but sullenly and grudgingly. In fact, she came to be a great help to Egwene. She kept the Amyrlin's eyes-and-ears, showing the reports to Egwene, but Aeldene Stonebridge snatched the Blue eyes-and-ears away from her. Siuan's attitude was improved by her relationship with Gareth Bryne—the two were in love with each other long before they admitted it. Because he loved her, Bryne insisted she work off the debt to him so he could keep her near him, agreed to lead the army for the rebels and offered that army to Egwene, whose one real supporter and friend was, it appeared, Siuan. Min had also had a viewing concerning Siuan and Bryne: that Siuan had to stay close to Gareth Bryne or she would die.

After Egwene was taken by Elaida's Aes Sedai, she talked to Siuan in *Tel'aran'rhiod* and forbade a rescue attempt. When the Seanchan began their attack, however, Siuan and Gawyn decided to take matters into their own hands; Bryne agreed to help if Siuan bonded him as her Warder. They went into the Tower through a watergate. Bryne saved Siuan's life, and she his; Siuan was convinced that Min's viewing had been fulfilled. They succeeded in rescuing Egwene, although she was not pleased.

Siuan proved very useful in the Last Battle; she survived the Sharan attack on the command tent because of a weave Yukiri came up with to cushion their large drop from an elevated gateway. Because she believed Min's viewing had been fulfilled, Siuan did not stay near Bryne; she went to see Tuon in Mat's command tent while Bryne went to look for Gawyn. Siuan saved Min there from an attack by Sharans, but when the Gray Men appeared, she went inside the tent and was killed by an explosion of fire. Bryne did not long survive her.

Sivi. The name given to Adelorna Bastine by the *sul'dam* who leashed her for a very short time when the Seanchan attacked the White Tower; Egwene saved her.

Six-Story Slaughter, the. The Band of the Red Hand's name for the fight against the *gholam* in Ebou Dar.

Skane, Mili. *See* Mili Skane

Skellit, Jon. *See* Jon Skellit

skimmer. The second-largest class of Sea Folk ships. Skimmers were three-masted and 150 to 250 feet in length, although generally no more than 200 feet. Broader in the beam and of greater displacement than rakers, they were usually much faster than any mainland ship of similar displacement. They could cover 250 to 300 miles in a twenty-four-hour period if the winds were good and the hull did not have too much growth of barnacles and other marine organisms.

Skimming. A method a channeler could use to journey quickly between two locations. Skimming required the weaving of a gateway, creation of a platform upon which to Skim and a knowledge of the destination. Skimming was slower than Traveling. The ability to Skim was not considered a Talent.

Skulker. Juilin's lanky brown gelding.

Sky Lights. Fireworks-like displays used in Seanchan celebrations; they were created by *damane*.

Slayer. Hopper's name for Isam/Luc; he was also called Wolf Killer. Slayer was a hybrid human created by the Dark One, a combination of Isam Mandragoran and Luc Mantear. Dark prophecy written in Fal Dara said: "Luc came to the Mountains of Dhoom. Isam waited in the high passes. The hunt is now begun. The Shadow's hounds now course, and kill. One did live, and one did die, but both are."

Slayer could go in and out of *Tel'aran'rhiod* at will; it had nothing to do with channeling, of course, as he could not channel. He could also switch from Luc to Isam at will. In many ways he was a perfect assassin; those who wanted Slayer's services begged for them, except for the Great Lord or the Chosen. He received orders from the Dark One himself in the Pit of Doom; the Dark One commanded Padan Fain's death, and Slayer was charged with that.

Appearing as Luc, he killed Janduin, Rand's natural father. In the White Tower, he killed a Gray Man who had failed to kill Egwene. In the Stone of Tear, he killed Joiya and Amico, Black Ajah members who had been captured, after nailing their tongues to the doors of their cells. Slayer went to the Two Rivers; while there, Perrin saw the Isam persona in the wolf dream, killing wolves; when chased, he seemed to vanish into the Tower of Ghenjei. In the

Luc persona, Slayer tried to stir things up in the Two Rivers. Eventually, Perrin wounded the Isam persona in the wolf dream, and the Luc persona rode out of Emond's Field clutching his chest. Slayer also tried to kill Nynaeve in *Tel'aran'rhiod* and spied on her, Elayne and Egwene there. Slayer was used in an attempt on Rand's life in Far Madding at the behest of someone he believed was one of the Chosen; in fact, it was Taim. He stepped out of *Tel'aran'rhiod* and stabbed two people sleeping, but Rand and Min had moved on and so escaped harm.

Slayer had no love for Rand, and did not mind being ordered to kill him, but he had an especial hatred for Perrin because of events in the Two Rivers and did everything he could to end the young man's life. The animosity only grew after Moridin sent Slayer to Graendal to help in her plan to take Perrin; Slayer put a dreamspike in place to keep Perrin's people from Traveling. Perrin managed to remove the dreamspike and fought Slayer in the wolf dream. Slayer killed Hopper and injured Perrin, but Perrin was able to destroy the dreamspike.

A woman visited Slayer in the Town near Shayol Ghul, and ordered him to kill Rand; Slayer made the effort, but Perrin fought him and killed him, moving between the wolf dream in the flesh and the waking world.

Sleeping Bay. A body of water in Takisrom, Seanchan.

sleepweavers. Mesaana's name for the *ter'angreal* allowing users to enter *Tel'aran'rhiod*.

sleepwell. A root used medicinally for relieving headaches and assisting with sleep.

Sleete. Hattori's Warder. Limber and long-armed, he had rough-hewn features, long black hair and a cleft in his chin. His nose was crooked; it had been broken and not Healed. Sleete was with Hattori at Dumai's Wells, but they became separated. Although seriously wounded, he managed to drag himself onto his horse and reach a nearby village; some there wanted to sell him to bandits, but the mayor's daughter persuaded the villagers to hide him and tended to his wounds. When he was well enough to travel, he killed the bandits that were troubling the town and made his way to Dorlan.

Though Sleete was a blademaster, Gawyn was able to best him at swordplay. Sleete approached Gawyn about Gawyn possibly becoming Hattori's Warder; Gawyn declined. When Gawyn decided to leave the Younglings, Sleete knew what he was doing but did not give him away. After the Tower was reunited, Sleete helped Gawyn try to find out who was killing Aes Sedai. When Egeanin and Domon sneaked through a gateway to Merrilor, Sleete realized that they were up to something and took them to Nynaeve. During the Last Battle, Sleete fought alongside Gawyn and Egwene in Kandor.

Slone Maddow. A wide-eared Redarm with the Band of the Red Hand. After the *gholam* attacked Mat's tent and killed Lopin, Maddow told Mat that he thought Olver was with Noal.

Small Thorny Back. The wolves' name for a porcupine.

Smoke. A wolf that Perrin spoke with when he and Ingtar were searching for Fain and the Horn of Valere.

Smoke Springs Hold. A hold in the Three-fold Land; Dorindha, the wife of Bael, was its roofmistress.

Smoke Water. A sept of the Miagoma Aiel.

Snake, the. A constellation. The Aiel called it "the Dragon."

Snakes and Foxes. A game much loved by children until they matured enough to realize that it could never be won without breaking the rules. It was played with a board that had a web of lines with arrows indicating direction. Ten discs were inked with triangles to represent the foxes, and ten discs were inked with wavy lines to represent the snakes. The game was begun by saying "Courage to strengthen, fire to blind, music to dazzle, iron to bind," while using one's hand to describe a triangle with a wavy line through it. Dice were rolled to determine moves for the players and the snakes and foxes. If a snake or fox landed on a player's piece, he was out of the game, and as long as the rules were followed, this always happened unless affected by a once-in-an-Age *ta'veren* effect.

Snelle. A dirty man at the Dusty Wheel in Caemlyn who attempted to cheat Mat at the dice game Koronko's Spit.

Snert. The innkeeper of The Grand Hike in Caemlyn. He was missing several teeth, one eye and most of his hair, but Birgitte said he had nice chest hair.

Snow Goose. The two-masted riverboat owned by Jaim Adarra. Sweeps (oars) were used at the dock. Moiraine, Lan, Perrin, Loial and Faile traveled aboard it from Remen to Illian.

snowberry. A tree that grew on riverbanks and produced tiny white blossoms in the spring. Egwene saw some while sailing on the River Erinin.

snowcap. Cadsuane used an image of this flower on a piece of embroidery.

snowdrops. Flowers embroidered on a dress worn by Nynaeve in Fal Dara.

snowflowers. Plants having tiny white flowers; they were embroidered on the lapels of one of Min's jackets.

snowghosts. A term used by Birgitte; she said her few women friends had had tempers like snowghosts.

Snowy Dawn. A wolf with whom Perrin communicated outside of Malden. He was an irascible old male who once killed a leopard by himself. Snowy Dawn's pack gave the signal that was supposed to let Faile know that Perrin was coming; since Galina had not passed that information to Faile, it didn't work as it was supposed to.

So Eban. A town in Altara on the Amadician border. While Nynaeve, Elayne, Thom and Juilin were pondering how to escape from Sienda without Galad stopping them (Galad wanted to take them back to Caemlyn), Thom mentioned that King Ailron had laid claim to a strip of border villages in Altara including So Eban; this was so that Pedron Niall, who controlled Ailron, could choke river traffic to Ebou Dar and thereby take over Altara.

So Habor. A town in Altara that had lost its ability to function normally after the appearance of dead people in their midst; the townspeople behaved abnormally, and their grain stores were infested with pests. Perrin and his party Traveled to So Habor to buy grain for the troops while trying to save Faile. Masema told Perrin that So Habor's grain storehouses were full, and that it would be a good place to buy provisions. Balwer said that he knew a cutler in the town, and he took some of Faile's followers with him. Perrin's group obtained grain from the town, but it had to be sifted for pests. The ghosts in the town intrigued some in Perrin's party. When Balwer returned from So Habor, he brought Tallanvor with him.

So Tehar. A village in Altara a day from Ebou Dar, visited by Mat, Nynaeve, Elayne and others in their party on the way to Ebou Dar. In Mat's opinion, it was a scruffy village of white-plastered bricks and flies. So Tehar was where the women who could channel discovered they could still put Mat in his place, despite the foxhead medallion, by using *saidar* to pelt him with horse manure.

so'jhin. A particular class of *da'covale*, so'jhin were hereditary upper servants of the Blood. *So'jhin* had considerable status and could in some circumstances give orders to and have authority over free people. The Seanchan Imperial bureaucracy was almost entirely *so'jhin*. Many free people would not object to becoming *so'jhin*, regarding it as a step up. Voices of the Blood were *so'jhin*, and theirs was a coveted position. They could own property, unlike ordinary *da'covale*, and they were never sold except perhaps as punishment for a crime. With permission of their owners, they could arrange their own marriages; permission was rarely withheld. A family line of *so'jhin* would always belong to the same family of the Blood. Ordinary folk did not own *so'jhin*.

Soalen, Reed. A Two Rivers man with Perrin. Reed guarded Perrin after Aram's death. When Rand visited Perrin at the Field of Merrilor, Reed was acting as a sentry.

soarer. The second-smallest class of Sea Folk ship. Soarers were two-masted and usually 100 feet long, but could be as long as 150 feet, with the beam being in similar proportion to a raker. Although smaller than rakers or skimmers, they were often quite fast and agile in handling—faster and more agile than ships of similar size built by other peoples. Their masts were sometimes raked. A soarer could cover up to 350 miles in a twenty-four-hour period, although 300 miles was more typical.

Soaring Gull, Uren din Jubai. A Sea Folk scholar who developed the Farede Calendar.

Soe'feia. Old tongue for "Truthspeaker," it referred to a person attached to members of the Seanchan royal family. *Soe'feia* were required to speak the truth to their royal charges, and make sure they were heard, without danger of punishment; they also levied penance when requested. A *Soe'feia* was neither *so'jhin* nor *da'covale*; he or she was always a free person, allowed to come and go as he or she pleased. A *Soe'feia* was not required to accept any orders from the one served, or to accept any checks on behavior. He or she not only could say anything at all to the one they served without fear of reprisal; he or she was expected and required to. An appointment was for life, among the Imperial family. Needless to say, great care was taken in choosing a *Soe'feia*. The Speaker told the one served the truth no matter what, including when what the one served did or planned to do was wrong. The Imperial family member wasn't compelled in any way to follow what the Speaker said, but the Speaker's purpose was to make the served one think, to help decide how to restore balance, which was a very important element in Seanchan life. When the one served was a child, the Speaker acted as a sort of supplementary nanny, and like a nanny was expected to discipline the charge. When the child reached age sixteen, the Speaker no longer directed, but was expected to do whatever was necessary to make sure the new adult actually heard what was said. A famous (among the Blood, infamous) Speaker of Truth to the last Emperor slapped the Emperor while he sat on the Crystal Throne. Since a *Soe'feia* was appointed while one was a child, at least in the Imperial family, one would almost certainly outlive him or her. He or she was expected to begin helping find a replacement, whom the *Soe'feia* would train, beginning as the *Soe'feia*'s Left Hand. This replacement would be someone approximately one's own age, and would act as a sort of personal assistant to the *Soe'feia*, without any of the rights and responsibilities, until the *Soe'feia*'s death.

soetam. A great rat found in the Drowned Lands. A *soetam* could grow to as much as fifteen pounds. Living in small packs that generally numbered no more than eight or ten animals, they were normally scavengers but would attack anything perceived as injured or weakened.

sofar. A vehicle from the Age of Legends that used steering planes. Semirhage referred to Sammael as a hot *sofar* with warped steering planes, which meant that his actions were difficult to predict.

Soferra. An Ogier woman who was the mother of Ala and the grandmother of Damelle, the last of whom wrote about the Ways.

Soffi Moraton. A woman with Perrin's army who tore her tent during a stream crossing and had no trouble getting it repaired.

Sohadra. A place in history where Sammael had caused great sorrow and escaped justice.

Sohima. The seventh-largest city in Seanchan. It had a Great Fire, in which the doll that Tuon gave Karede was destroyed.

Sokawa, Masuri. *See* Masuri Sokawa

Sokorin, Tzigan. *See* Tzigan Sokorin

Solain Morgeillin. A Kin in Ebou Dar. Her strength level was 40(28); she was not strong enough to make a gateway of any size whatsoever. Born in 818 NE, she went to the White Tower in 833 NE. During her eleven years a novice and eight years Accepted, while Parenia Demalle was Amyrlin and Sereille Bagand the Mistress of Novices, she was a kleptomaniac, never stealing anything valuable, but she was incorrigible; her habit wasn't discovered until after she was raised Accepted, and she was put out of the Tower when she could not be broken of it. In subsequent years she was broken of her kleptomania mainly through the perseverance of the Kin. She retained her very light fingers, though, and could slip something out of somebody's pocket without leaving a clue. She didn't care for men at all.

She was sent off to check on the cache of objects of the Power in the Rahad and was followed by Mat. Solain accompanied Elayne to Caemlyn and worked with a captured *sul'dam* there.

Solanje. Ituralde reflected on his military victories in the past, and one of them was at Solanje.

soldier. The lowest rank among the Asha'man. A soldier wore a black coat with no decoration.

Solinda. An Aes Sedai during the Breaking who helped make the Eye of the World. Her hair was very long and sun-red.

Solinde lace. A frothy lace seen in Ronde Macura's dress shop in Mardecin, Amadicia.

Solter, Robb. A Two Rivers man sent to fetch a pavilion for Perrin's meeting with the Children of the Light.

Somal, Lake. A site where Ituralde once triumphed in battle.

Soman, Espara. *See* Espara Soman

Somara. A woman of the Bent Peak sept of the Daryne Aiel and *Far Dareis Mai*. She had flaxen hair and was very tall, 6'2" or 6'3", and physically strong. With Enaila and Lamelle, she was among the worst at mothering Rand. After Lamelle died, Somara insisted on making the soup that Lamelle had made for Rand, and she was an even worse cook than Lamelle had been. Somara was one of three Maidens, along with Nandera and Nesair, who beat Rand when he returned to Cairhien after fighting the Seanchan because he had dishonored the Maidens by leaving them behind. Somara was killed when the renegade Asha'man attempted to assassinate Rand at the Sun Palace. Rand added her name to the list of women who had died for him.

Somares, Marya. *See* Marya Somares

Somarin. A Sea Folk clan. Malin din Toral Breaking Wave was its Sailmistress.

Someinellin, Melavaire. *See* Melavaire Someinellin

Someryn. A Wise One of the Shaido Aiel (not a Jumai) with the ability to channel and an impressive strength level of 4(+9)—she once prided herself that she had never met a woman as strong as herself. She was over 6'4" tall, with sundark smooth skin, dark yellow hair and blue eyes. She had a very large bosom, which she liked to show off; she took to wearing her blouse unlaced to show even more cleavage than Sevanna. One of Sevanna's inner circle of plotters, she was among those who accompanied her to the Aes Sedai camp the day she saw Rand beaten and took part in or was present at the murder of Desaine. Someryn and Modarra were the most firmly in Sevanna's grasp, in Sevanna's opinion, but both sided with Therava in the end, and Someryn became fairly tight with Therava. Someryn was at the meeting with "Caddar" and "Maisia." She was impressed by Graendal and said she was very strong, which was an unusual acknowledgment for her. That was the first time she had ever met a woman stronger than she in the Power.

Someryn was with Sevanna at Dumai's Wells and helped question the Seanchan prisoner in Amadicia, while the Jumai were settled at a captured estate approximately ten days after their arrival.

Someshta. The last of the Nym. *See* Green Man, the

Somma. A Maiden of the Spear who guarded Rand in the city of Tear.

songs. "Always Choose the Right Horse," which had the same tune as "The Marriage of Cinny Wade"; "Blue Sky Dawning"; "The Dancing Lass"; "Cock o' the North"; "Coming Home from Tarwin's Gap"; "Dance with Jak o' the Shadows"; "Drawing Water from the Well"; "The Drunken Peddler," also known as "Tinker in the Kitchen"; "First Rose of Summer"; "Ferry O'er the River," sometimes called "Darling Sara"; "The Fool Who Thought He Was King"; "Fluff the Feathers"; "A Frog on the Ice"; "Give Me Your Trust Said the Aes Sedai"; "Glory of the Dragon," by Meane sol Ahelle; "Goodman Priket's Pipe"; "Heron on the Wing"; "I Have Loved a Thousand Sailor Men"; "I Will Steal Your Breath with Kisses"; "I'm Down at the Bottom of the Well," which had the same tune as "The Last Stand at Mandenhar," from Mat's memories; "If You Go to Be a Soldier"; "Jaem's Folly"; "Jolly Jaim," also known as "Rhea's Fling" and "Colors of the Sun"; "Lament for the Long Night"; "Last Stand at Mandenhar"; "Life Is a Dream"; "The Marriage of Cinny Wade," which had the same tune as "Always Choose the Right Horse"; "Midean's Ford"; "Mistress Aynora's Rooster"; "My Love Is a Wild Rose"; "The Old Black Bear"; "Old Gray Goose"; "Old Jak's Up a Tree"; "Old Two Rivers Leaf"; "Only One Boot"; "Only One Bucket of Water"; "A Pocket Full of Gold"; "The Road to Dun Aren"; "Rooster in the Gumtree"; "Rose of the Morning"; "She Dazzles My Eyes and Clouds My Mind," which had the same tune as "Upside Down"; "She Has No Ankles That I Can See"; "She Wore a Mask That Hid Her Face"; "Song of the Three Fishes"; "Storm from the Mountains"; "Three Girls in the Meadow," called "Pretty Maids Dancing" by the Tinkers; "The Tinker Has My Pots," called "Toss the Feathers" by the Tinkers; "Tinker in the Kitchen," also known as "The Drunken Peddler"; "Two Kings Came Hunting," also known as "Two Horses Running" and other titles; "Two Maids at the Water's Edge"; "Upside Down and 'Round and 'Round"; "We're Over the Border Again"; "We Rode Down to River Iralell"; "What He Said to Me," also known as "Will You Dance with Me"; "Wild Geese on the Wing"; "The Wind from the North," which was called "Hard Rain Falling" in some lands, and "Berin's Retreat" in others; "The Wind in the Barley"; and "The Wind That Shakes the Willow."

Songs of Growing. A Talent used by Ogier in past Ages to aid and enhance growing things.

Songs of the Last Age, Do'in Toldara te. Quarto Nine: The Legend of the Dragon. Composed by Boanne, Songmistress at Taralan, the Fourth Age.

Soong. An Ogier woman who was the mother of Ella mother of Covril; i.e., Loial's great-grandmother.

Sora Grady. Jur's wife, who lived at the Black Tower. She was a plump, pale-haired woman; they had a son, Gadren, who was four years old. Jur bonded her with a version of the Warder's bond.

Soralle Step. Site of a famous battle in the history of the Borderlands, which Birgitte mentioned to Uno.

Soran Milo. The author of *The Killers of the Black Veil*, which Rand read. Milo was a man who lived about six hundred years before the Last Battle. He wrote about the Aiel and described the Portal Stone on Chaendaer in the Waste; since he based most of his book on those who came to trade at the *stedding* in the Spine of the World where he was located, he got almost everything wrong. He did get the Portal Stone right; a peddler who had seen it described it to him.

sorda. A fairly large rat found in the Waste which grew to as much as five pounds. Nocturnal, they were usually no threat to humans except for their uncanny ability to get into foodstores, defecating all over everything they didn't eat. They were often found in packs or colonies, and surprising one of these would result in numerous painful bites. The flesh of the sorda was so rank that cats seldom ate them after killing them.

Sorelana Alsahhan. A scholar in the time of the Trolloc Wars who wrote about Darkhounds.

Sorelle. A Jenn Aiel woman who lived after the Breaking. The daughter of Adan and Siedre, she was a dreamer and died at twenty from a fever her dreams had told her was coming.

Sorelle ay Marena. The Queen of Manetheren at the signing of the Compact of the Ten Nations.

Soremaine. The site of a battle between Illian and the Whitecloaks during the Troubles, also known as the Whitecloak War. Lord Captain Pedron Niall set a trap there and captured King Stepaneos and would have destroyed his entire army if it were not for the valor of the Companions.

Sorenthaine, Cemaile. *See* Cemaile Sorenthaine

Sorevin, Carlinya. *See* Carlinya Sorevin

sorfa. Tuon ordered a *sul'dam* to paint a *damane's* welts from a caning with a tincture of this plant.

Sorilea. A Wise One of the Jarra sept of the Chareen Aiel and of Shende Hold. Her strength level was about 57(35). A bony woman over two hundred years old, she had white hair, a leathery face and clear green eyes. Although she was weak in the One Power, her *ji* was great, giving her precedence over other Wise Ones. When Sorilea was angry, other Wise Ones sat quietly and clan chiefs made excuses to leave. On the way to Dumai's Wells, Amys challenged Sorilea's leadership and they worked out a compromise between them. Sorilea still had the leadership afterward, but she often consulted with Amys. She had a greatdaughter named Amaryn, whose youngest greatson was named Taric. Sorilea's sister-son had a greatson named Feran. Sorilea's apprentice was Surandha.

When Rand was kidnapped, Sorilea broke tradition and said that the Wise Ones would fight to free him, and then went on to fight at Dumai's Wells. After the battle, Sorilea and the Wise Ones made the rebel Aes Sedai apprentices and took custody of the loyalist Aes Sedai. Sorilea made common cause with Cadsuane to teach Rand laughter and tears, and taught Cadsuane the weave for Traveling.

In the Last Battle, Sorilea fought at Shayol Ghul, and survived.

Sormen, Fera. *See* Fera Sormen

Soro. An Aiel with the ability to channel; he made *algode* grow when it should not and went to the Blight to spit in Sightblinder's eye. He became a *Samma N'Sei* and was killed by Aviendha in the Last Battle.

Sorrentin. A soldier in Ituralde's army at Maradon. Ituralde sent him to tell the Asha'man that he wanted attacking Trollocs to go up in flames.

Sotarin. An Aiel Wise One. When Rand and his party were returning to Cairhien from Dumai's Wells, Sorilea sent Sotarin and Cosain to meet Feraighin, a Wise One who came from Cairhien.

soul. Reincarnated souls, in the normal sense—not a Dark One–generated soul—maintain the same gender. So the Dragon Reborn, spun out at different turnings of the Wheel in different Ages, in order to rebalance the weaving of the Pattern, is always the same soul, and always male.

Soulblinder. A Seanchan name for the Dark One.

Soulless. *See* Gray Man

Soulsbane. Another name for the Dark One.

Souran Maravaile. Artur Hawkwing's greatest general and husband to Ishara, the first to sit on the Lion Throne of Andor. He died by assassination, confronting four swordsmen, all of whom he killed, in the twenty-third year of the War of the Hundred Years.

Source, True. *See* True Source

South Bridge. A bridge town outside and south of Far Madding across the Goim Bridge.

South Mettler. A village in Kandor. Bulen wanted Lan to go toward the village because the path was much easier and Bulen had a cousin who had a farm along the road.

South Star, Nestelle din Sakura. *See* Nestelle din Sakura South Star

South Wind, Tebreille din Gelyn. *See* Tebreille din Gelyn South Wind

Southern Hoop, The. A scruffy, two-storied, white-plastered brick inn found in So Tehar, Altara. The group from Salidar, including Nynaeve, Elayne, Aviendha, Mat, Thom, Juilin and various other Aes Sedai, soldiers and Warders stayed there on their way to Ebou Dar.

Southharbor. A southern port in Tar Valon on the River Erinin. Leane was captured there by Aes Sedai while making a *cuendillar* chain across the harbor entrance.

Sovarra lace. Delicate aged-ivory lace that embellished Colavaere's expensive silk gown.

Sovin Nai. Old Tongue for "Knife Hands," it was the name of an Aiel warrior society.

span. A measure of distance equal to two paces; a thousand spans equaled a mile.

Spar. A thug and Darkfriend who worked for Old Cully in Ebou Dar. A rat-faced man, he still had several teeth; his arms were all bone and sinew. Mat stabbed and killed Spar when attacked by him.

spark. The natural ability of a person to channel; a man or woman born with the spark developed the ability to channel sooner or later even if they did not try to learn.

Sparks. A wolf in Oak Dancer's pack. Sparks helped Hopper to train Perrin in the wolf dream. Sparks, Oak Dancer and Boundless were trapped by the dreamspike, but Perrin and Hopper rescued them.

Sparrow. The mare Toveine rode to the Black Tower.

Speaker of Truth. *See Soe'feia*

Speral. A worker for the Merchants' Guild in So Habor. Mycal Crossin called for him to fetch grain samples three times, but he never showed.

spiceapple tree. A tree found in the Age of Legends. In one of Rand's flashbacks, Charn used to like to sit under spiceapple trees behind the inn and tell stories.

Spine of the World. A north-south-oriented mountain range separating the Aiel Waste from the populated lands to the west.

Spine Ridge. A sept of the Miagoma Aiel.

spinglass. A fragile material from the time of the Da'shain Aiel in the Age of Legends. Rushing to Collam Daan, Charn was knocked down by accident and the man apologized. Charn reflected that people thought the Aiel were made out of spinglass. Delicate sculptures were made from this material.

spinning. An Age of Legends word that was the equivalent of weaving; spinning a web or spinning a net was the same as weaving a weave of the Power in the next Age.

Spinning Earthfire. A Talent of unknown use, mentioned by Moghedien.

Spirit. One of the Five Powers. *See* Five Powers

Spiron Narettin den Sovar. An Illianer nobleman who was a member of the Council of Nine. He was sent eastward in the campaign against the Seanchan with as many Companions and men sworn to other members of the Nine as his own liegemen. He was sent to keep the peace in Illian.

Splintered Hills. An area in Coremanda where Doreille, Queen of Aridhol, penned some of her finest poems.

Spray. Bayle Domon's river craft. It had two masts and was eighty feet long and broad in the beam. Yarin Maeldan was the second-in-command. Crew members included Aedwin Cole, Carn and Florin Gelb.

sprigleaf. A plant that could be thrown on fires to cover up foul odors.

Spring Pole. A stripped fir tree trunk upended in the ground, used as part of the festival of Bel Tine in Emond's Field.

Springhorn. The leader of a wolfpack that Perrin consulted, seeking information about Faile after she was abducted by the Shaido; Springhorn's pack was unable to help.

sprinklewort. As a parting gift before she and her companions left for Tar Valon, Mat gave Joline a bag of sweetbuns laced with sprinklewort so that her mouth would turn blue. Other uses for this plant are unknown.

squadman. A noncommissioned officer, typically a cavalryman, who generally was in charge of approximately ten soldiers. In the infantry, the equivalent of a squadman was a file leader.

staera. Slim, curved pieces of bronze used by the Aiel in sweat tents to scrape sweat and dirt off their bodies.

Stag, the. A constellation.

Stag and Lion, The. A large four-storied inn in Baerlon, Andor. Master Fitch was the innkeeper, and Min worked there as a serving girl. Rand, Mat, Perrin, Moiraine, Lan, Nynaeve, Egwene and Thom all stayed there on the way to Tar Valon, fleeing Trollocs and Fades. While there, Rand had a dream of Ba'alzamon, and Padan Fain sent a Fade to attack them, forcing them to flee into the night. The inn was burned, but Moiraine had coin sent from Tar Valon to rebuild it; according to Min, Master Fitch was building it back twice as big.

Stag's Stand. The highest hill in Canluum, Kandor, where Lord Marcasiev's palace stood.

Stair of Jehaan. A place where the Borderland armies successfully checked the advance of the Shadowspawn following the destruction of Malkier.

Standardbearer. A Seanchan rank equivalent to Bannerman. A Standardbearer's helmet had a small crest like a bronze arrowhead on its front.

standing flows. A technology from the Age of Legends that maintained the continual flow of the One Power in relation to specific objects, allowing many *ter'angreal* to be used by those unable to channel.

Stang, Kairen. *See* Kairen Stang

Star, The. A large wooden four-storied inn located in Tear next to Ajala's smithy. The innkeeper was Jurah Haret. Moiraine, Lan, Perrin, Loial and Faile lodged there while looking for Rand. There they found out that Be'lal had made himself a High Lord of Tear and that he intended to take *Callandor* from Rand after Rand removed it from the Heart of the Stone. Master Haret allowed the Black Ajah to leave the hedgehog *ter'angreal* in Moiraine's private dining room; Faile triggered it, and Perrin had to rescue her in the wolf dream.

starblaze. A plant that had deep red, wavy-petaled flowers. It was found in the gardens of the Royal Palace in Caemlyn. Cadsuane used an image of this flower on a piece of embroidery.

stasis-box. High-tech device from the Age of Legends that preserved artifacts or extreme perishables by suspending time within the box.

Staven. A soldier who died defending Ituralde at Maradon in Saldaea.

Stayer. Perrin's horse from Cairhien. A well-shod bay stallion from the Sun Palace stables, he was reddish with a black mane and tail and white forefeet. His training as a warhorse was not specifically established, but the horse was Cairhienin, where cavalry were important, and there were indications that he was well trained; he responded to leg pressure, and he backed away on command.

Steady. A roan gelding belonging to Rodel Ituralde.

steamwagon. A wagon that moved without horses; it was the invention of Mervin Poel, who was a member of the Academy of Cairhien. Steamwagons were used in the Last Battle to deliver supplies to the battlefronts.

stedding. The habitat of Ogier, governed by a Council of Elders. There were forty-one inhabited *stedding* between the Aryth Ocean and the Aiel Waste, each with an average population of twelve thousand, although that varied considerably. Young *stedding*, such as Tsofu, had much smaller populations than old ones. There were more than fifty abandoned *stedding*. *Stedding* had special properties, including the inability of a channeler to use the One Power within their boundaries or from without.

Trollocs would not enter a *stedding* unless driven by Myrddraal, and the Myrddraal rarely had the incentive to do so. Even Darkfriends, if truly dedicated, felt uncomfortable there.

Aes Sedai also hated entering a *stedding*—not only could they not channel there, but they could not even feel the True Source.

Ogier sickened and died if they remained Outside *stedding* too long.

Steler. A bannerman in the Tower Guard. Tall and grizzled, with a deep gravelly voice, he led the group that escorted Moiraine and Siuan to collect the names of babies outside Tar Valon.

Stepashin, Ester. *See* Ester Stepashin

Stepin. One of Kerene's Warders. He had narrow shoulders and sad brown eyes that made him look more like a clerk than a Warder. He could play the twelve-string bittern as skillfully as a hired musician.

Stepper. Perrin's dun stallion. As tall as any Tairen bloodstock, but heavier in shoulder and haunch, he had a yellowish hide and a black mane and tail. He was a trained warhorse, as demonstrated during the fighting in the Two Rivers.

Steps. A young black-furred wolf that Perrin met in the wolf dream while searching for Slayer during the Last Battle.

Stevan Gedarien. Demira Eriff's Cairhienin Warder. He was 5'6" tall, and slender, with gray at his temples. Though he was twenty years younger than Demira, sometimes he tried to act like her father.

Stick. A creature in the Blight. It looked like a stick and hid in leaves. If it was touched, it would bite and immediately begin digesting whatever was bitten. The only thing that could save one after that was amputating the arm or leg that was bitten.

sticklesharp. A clinging vine with three-pronged leaves; Ferane grew them on her balcony, and their tendrils covered the inside of the stonework.

stilling. The process of removing the ability of a woman to channel. It was thought to be permanent until Nynaeve Healed Siuan and Leane; Flinn Healed the three women stilled at Dumai's Wells.

Stinger. Silviana's gelding that she rode during the Last Battle. She had trained Stinger not to be skittish around channeling.

stingweed. A water plant that got tangled in fishing nets. It was mentioned by Mother Guenna in Tear.

stinkadder. A snake that wriggled away from its own shadow.

stinkweed. A plant, found in the Two Rivers and elsewhere, that left a rank smell on any boot that crushed it.

Stone Anchor, Amel din Monaga. *See* Amel din Monaga Stone Anchor

Stone Dogs. *See Shae'en M'taal*

Stone of Tear. The immense fortress guarding the city of Tear from which the High Lords ruled. The Stone looked like a mountain that extended from the river west through the city wall, with battlements and towers and flying banners. The Heart of the Stone was the central citadel. It was said to be the earliest fortress built after the Time of Madness, and said by some to have been built *during* the Time of Madness, made with the One Power soon after the Breaking of the World. It was besieged or attacked countless times, but never successfully until it fell in a single night to the Dragon Reborn and a few hundred Aiel, thus fulfilling the Prophecies of the Dragon.

The Stone was mentioned twice in the Prophecies: it was said that the Stone would never fall until the People of the Dragon came, and also that the Stone would never fall until the Dragon's hand wielded the Sword That Cannot Be Touched, *Callandor*. Some believed that these Prophecies accounted for the antipathy of the High Lords to the One Power, and for the Tairen law that forbade channeling. Despite this antipathy, the Stone contained a collection of *angreal* and *ter'angreal* rivaling that stored in the White Tower, a collection which was gathered, some say, in an attempt to diminish the glare of possessing *Callandor*.

Stone Verge. The large open space surrounding the Stone of Tear on three sides.

Stoneboat. A Taren Ferry family name.

Stonebow, Yurian. *See* Yurian Stonebow

Stonebridge, Aeldene. *See* Aeldene Stonebridge

stones. A board game played with stones on a lined board. In the Age of Legends, it was known as *no'ri*; in a much later age, it was known as Go.

stones including gemstones. Stones and gemstones found in the world of The

Wheel of Time were marble, golden Kandor marble, winter marble, white marble, heartstone (*cuendillar*), elstone, redstone, yellow and white opals, blue sapphires, black sapphires, yellow sapphires, yellow diamonds, carnelian, avatine, amber, pearls, firedrops, rubies, moonstone, catseye, sunstone, emeralds, garnets, amethyst, lapis and turquoise.

Stones River. A dry riverbed in the Aiel Waste and also the name of a sept of the Goshien Aiel.

Stormbringer. An old Sea Folk name for the Dark One; it was used by Birgitte.

Storn, River. A river flowing southwest through Murandy to Lugard, where it joined the River Reisendrelle.

Stout. Galad's bay gelding, which he rode to his confrontation with Valda and afterward. Stout was killed when the Trollocs attacked the Whitecloaks on the Jehannah Road.

Stranded Goose, The. An inn of three broad stories in Ebou Dar. It had a female innkeeper, as was true of most of the inns in Ebou Dar. Setalle Anan, Elayne and Nynaeve stopped there, as Setalle was stopping at many inns while taking Elayne and Nynaeve to the Knitting Circle, to tell the other innkeepers about these two foolish girls.

Strang, Elise. *See* Elise Strang

Strangers' Markets. The three markets open to foreigners in Far Madding.

Street Guard. The police force of Far Madding who patrolled the streets in groups of three. The Street Guard relied mainly on long cudgels, sword-breakers, quarterstaffs and catchpoles. They carried no blade longer than a belt knife. When the Street Guard arrested someone, the detainee was bound wrists-to-ankles and put into a sack, which was then slung from a pole carried on the shoulders of two men.

Street of Joy. A main thoroughfare in Far Madding. It was really two broad straight streets separated by a measured row of leafless gray-barked trees.

streith. A fabric that changed color with the wearer's emotions and also changed from opaque to transparent mist. It was common in the Age of Legends; Graendal found a stash of it in a stasis-box.

strength in the One Power. Strength in the One Power varied greatly across individuals. Men strong in the Power were usually considerably stronger than women strong in the Power. This is not to say that some women were not stronger than some men, just that the general form ran the other way.

This strength was a matter of the sheer raw amount of the One Power that could be drawn. In kind, there was nothing a man could do with any part of the Power that a woman could not, and vice versa. There were, however, areas where women showed greater abilities and areas where men did. Additionally, of the Five Powers—Earth, Air (or Wind), Fire, Water and Spirit—women generally had the greatest strength and ability in Air and/or Water, while men generally had the greatest in Earth and/or Fire. That is to say, men were generally much more adept than women in weaving Fire and Earth; they were usually able to handle much more of these as well, which followed from their greater raw strength. Women were generally much more adept than men in weaving Air and Water; despite men's greater raw strength, in these two areas women were in general stronger than men. Ability in Spirit was usually considered to be equally divided; there seemed to be no advantage, either male or female.

Women who could channel could sense the ability in one another and also sense their relative strengths. Among women, the eventual strength of a testee was determined in the first testing. It would take time for her to reach it—and indeed, if she did not work, it was possible that she would not reach it, because it was a potential—but the limits of her strength were known up front. No one ever surpassed the detected limit. Female strength usually—but not always—grew in a smooth progression, and often the stronger she would eventually become, the more quickly it grew. This was not a hard and fast rule, though. Forcing, which was forcing the woman to use more of the Power and do more, could bring on faster increases in strength, but it also ran the greatly increased risk of burnout or death. There were also frequent individual variations in this speed of growth. Hierarchy among Aes Sedai was based in part on relative strength.

Among men, there was no way of knowing how strong a beginner would become. It was not unusual for men to show as much raw strength at their first testing as a woman who had worked for some time, but there was no way to know how far he would go beyond that, if at all, or how long it would take him to reach his upper limit. Male strength levels usually, but not always, increased in spurts and plateaus, with the intensity and duration of the spurts, as well as the duration of the plateaus, generally uneven. Thus a man might test stronger than a woman only to see her pass him, then spurt to pass her, then have her pass him again because he reached a plateau; this could repeat a number of times until their full strengths were reached. Needless to say, as with women, a man who did not work hard would not go as far as he might otherwise, but in his case, no one would ever be sure that he had not reached his full potential.

Men usually took longer to reach their full strength than women did. Most women took about ten years to do so. It was very likely no coincidence that this was the same amount of time most novices took to be raised Accepted, although the correlation was not exact. Women sometimes reached their peak strength and remained novices because they had not learned enough or gained sufficient skill, while others were raised Accepted or even Aes Sedai while still short of that peak. It was learning and skill, not strength, that were the keys there. Again, this was not a hard and fast rule; some women took as long as fifteen years to achieve full strength, while a few managed it in as little as seven or eight. Most men took about fifteen years to reach peak strength. For both men and women, of course, the rate of increase in strength could be sped up dramatically by forcing, but this also entailed danger of burnout or death. Men were somewhat more resistant to the dangers of forcing than women, but not by a large amount.

For some reason, the age when a man or woman began to channel seemed to make a difference in their rate of progress. While a given person's peak strength would be the same whether he or she began learning at fifteen or at fifty, would reach that peak faster at an older age.

Among both men and women strength and skill were not the same thing. It was possible for one person to have great raw strength yet be less effective in many situations than another who had lesser strength but greater dexterity with the flows or greater knowledge in using them. While there were limits to strength for anyone—there was a certain upper limit which could never be surpassed—there were no real limits to increasing skill. Anyone could increase their knowledge, though of course, some would have greater ability to increase dexterity with the flows than others. Having been born with the inherent spark apparently was not an indicator of strength. There were as many with weak potential who would channel whether they were taught or not as there were with great potential.

Before the appearance of Elayne, Egwene, Nynaeve, Aviendha and Nicola, there were 60 base levels of strength, each of which had internal gradations, for women who were strong enough to be raised to the shawl. After their appearance, there were 72 base levels.

The earlier distribution of Aes Sedai strengths thus ran from 1 to 60, which became 13 to 72. Women below the lowest level at which someone could become Aes Sedai were trained, but with the knowledge that they would be put out; a few received the ring for political reasons, as with Morgase. There was, of course, also the need to consider Aes Sedai reluctance to let go of a woman once they had their hands on her. Non–Aes Sedai changed this distribution to a considerable extent. Both Atha'an Miere Windfinders and Aiel Wise Ones had no lower limit for full acceptance in their organizations.

Rating men against this scale (that is, comparing strength in *saidin* to strength in *saidar*), there were an additional six possible levels for men at the top end. While this was true in terms of bulk amounts of the Power that men could handle, certain vulnerabilities on the part of men, and others on the part of women, made a direct comparison difficult at best. Still, one-on-one, looking only at pure strength and avoiding the advantages of dexterity, length of practice and skill, the top level for a man was usually no more than a match for the top level for a woman.

Thus the strongest man would be ++1, the 800-year level in aging. Ranks ++2 to ++6 would have an aging range of 720 to 800 years. The strongest woman would be 1(+12), with a life expectancy of around 800 years; a man of the same rough level, which was 7, would have a life expectancy of 720 years.

There were considerable variations between individuals, but in rough form it could be said that there was a parallel between strength and longevity, minus the effects of a binder such as the Oath Rod. All age levels given were approximations, with considerable room for variation among individuals. For example, at the so-called 800-year level, a person could reasonably be expected to live to between roughly 775 and 825 years of age, with some making it to 850, and a very few making it to as much as 900. Strength level 56(44) was the 300-year age level, 67(55) the 200-year age level, and the bottom level, 72(60), approximately the 150-year level for women. The male equivalents were approximately the 240-year, 180-year, and 135-year levels for men.

A given strength level did not produce the same degree of longevity for a man as for a woman. At any given level of equality, a woman would live longer. In general, a man at any given strength would have a normal lifespan roughly ten percent less than that of a woman of that strength. The range of longevity was the same, though, with men at their top level having a life expectancy of 800 years or so, within the range of the bell curves.

While there were six additional levels for men above those for women, the disparity was not as great as it seemed, measuring the bulk quantity of the One Power that a person could handle. Adding in the greater dexterity of women in weaving, a woman at the top level might well be roughly equal to a man in the top level in a stand-up one-on-one fight.

strikers. An invention of Aludra's. Small sticks with rough blue-gray heads that produced a flame when rubbed against something rough, they had to be packed carefully; if they rubbed against each other they could burst into flame on their own. She also called them "firesticks."

Strom. A strongarm at The Dancing Cartman in Four Kings, Andor. Strom was hard-faced, big and had arms that were thick enough for legs. His crooked teeth were yellow. He and Jak threw people out of the inn if they caused trouble, and the two also planned to help Hake, the innkeeper, rob Rand and Mat. The Darkfriend Howal Gode gave Jak, Strom and Hake something to make them sleep while he tried his pitch on Rand.

Study of Men, Women and the One Power Among Humans, A. A book by the Ogier Ledar son of Shandin son of Koimal; Loial considered it one of the best about Aes Sedai dealing with men who could channel. It was written around 700 NE.

Study of the War of the Shadow, A. A book by the Ogier Moilin daughter of Hamada daughter of Juendan; in it Be'lal was referred to as the Netweaver.

Stump. What Ogier called a meeting where they discussed and debated momentous topics; it was also called the Great Stump. The Great Stump held at Stedding Shangtai debated whether or not the Ogier should open the Book of Translation before Tarmon Gai'don, thus returning them to the alternate world from which they had come; the Ogier decided to stay and fight to help the humans.

Suana Dragand. A Shienaran Aes Sedai of the Yellow Ajah and the loyalist contingent, with a strength level of 22(10). Born in 784 NE, she went to the

White Tower in 798 NE. After spending sixteen years as a novice and twelve years as Accepted, she was raised to the shawl in 826 NE. A beefy woman, with too much chin, blue eyes, a square face and wide square hands, Suana possessed a blunt manner. Despite the fact that she was not among the strongest sisters, she was considered in the first rank in the Talent of Healing. Her abilities were so great that no sister, not even those much stronger than she, could do better, with the possible exception of Samitsu. She was also politically well connected and very knowledgeable—a woman with a will who could get things done.

Suana served as Sitter for the Yellow from 919 to 952 NE; She was made First Weaver in 947 NE and was one of only two heads of Ajah to sit in the Hall. In 999 NE she became Sitter again to replace Magla Daronos, whom she had sent to join the rebels to control and defuse events. Being raised Sitter a second time was very unusual, but she took the position to make it easier to give way to Magla when the Tower was reunited. This was a precaution not taken by all of the Ajahs. Suana taught Egwene after Egwene's capture by Elaida; she was so impressed that she practically offered her a place in the Yellow and later supported the choice of Egwene as Amyrlin.

Succession, The Fourth War of Cairhienin. *See* Reconciliation

Succession, the. The conflict so called in Andor, known as the Third War of Andoran Succession elsewhere, that brought Morgase to the throne.

Suffa. The name given to Elaida as a *damane*.

sugarberry. A tree that grew on riverbanks and produced bright red blossoms in the spring. Egwene saw some while sailing on the River Erinin.

Suilin Escanda. An Aes Sedai of the Blue Ajah who served as Amyrlin from 355 to 396 NE. Suilin was an Amyrlin of moderate strength who involved the Tower in a number of foreign intrigues. One or another faction in the Hall was always trying to thwart her, but she successfully outmaneuvered them until 396 NE, when she was forced to resign as the Amyrlin Seat. It was put about as voluntary, as was her retirement to the country, but she spent the next twenty-six years in exile under constant guard until her death in 422 NE. She was returned to Tar Valon and buried with considerable pomp and honor, though.

Suki. Siuan's alias as Moiraine's maid in Chachin.

sul'dam. A woman who passed the tests to show that she could wear the bracelet of an *a'dam* and thus control a *damane*. The word was Old Tongue for "leash holder." Young women in Seanchan were tested for this ability at the same time as the testing for *damane* and at the same age. It was a fairly honored position among the Seanchan. Many more *sul'dam* were found than *damane*. A *sul'dam*'s uniform was a blue dress that stopped short of the ankle, with red panels bearing forked silver lightning on the breast and sides of the skirt. For many centuries it was not known that *sul'dam* were actually women who could learn to channel, but that discovery was made after the Seanchan arrived in Falme.

Sulaan. A *morat'to'raken* who flew Mat and Olver to Thakan'dar in the Last

Battle. She was knocked unconscious by an arrow, leaving Mat to land on his own. Mat thought Sulaan pretty but insane.

Suladric. The clan chief of the Shaido Aiel who died shortly before Rand went to the Waste. He fell for Sevanna when she was sixteen and married her. Muradin attempted to replace him, but did not make it out of the *ter'angreal* in Rhuidean.

Sulamein so Bhagad. The author of *The Wheel of Time*; Chief Historian at the Court of the Sun, the Fourth Age.

Sulara. A hold in the Waste where Niella was taken *gai'shain*.

Sulin. A woman of the Goshien Aiel and *Far Dareis Mai*. White-haired, blue-eyed, leathery-faced, wiry and about 5'7" tall, she had a pink scar across her sun-dark cheek from a nasty gash received in the fight against Rahvin in Caemlyn. She was chosen roofmistress of the Roof of the Maidens in Rhuidean, but gave it up to lead the Maidens who followed Rand across the Dragonwall.

In order to meet her *toh* to various *gai'shain* for reminding them that they were Maidens, Sulin became a servant in the Royal Palace in Caemlyn, serving Rand, and followed him in that capacity to Cairhien. Sulin got a gold crown from Perrin as a tip while she was acting as a servant in Caemlyn; later he was stunned to find out she was a Maiden. She also received her wages as a maid, plus some tips; these coins she had made into a necklace or a belt, which she kept close at hand as a reminder of the price of pride and also to remind her of Reene Harfor, the First Maid, whom she thought of as a woman who had honor and who was also tough enough to be a Maiden.

When Sulin learned that Rand had been kidnapped, she decided her *toh* had been met and took up the spear again, but Nandera had taken over leading the Maidens and did not step aside. Sulin and Nandera fought with bare hands; Sulin won, but thereafter accepted Nandera as the leader of the Maidens, obeying her and acting as her right hand. She led the contingent of Maidens who accompanied Perrin and Faile to Ghealdan. She stayed with Perrin through the battle at Malden, and on to the Last Battle.

sulking rooms. Small sitting rooms found in Ebou Dari houses; one was in Mat's suite of rooms in the Tarasin Palace.

Sulmara. The Queen of Masenashar, circa 450 AB, who was a renegade Aes Sedai. She was kidnapped by the White Tower and spent the rest of her life working in the White Tower stables.

Sulmein Gap. The site of a battle that Artur Hawkwing fought before he found his stride. Mat thought that the battle for Cairhien would be like Sulmein Gap.

Sulwin. An Aiel after the Breaking. A tall man who let his hair grow long, he led a group that decided to leave the Jenn Aiel and search for the song after a bandit attack. He and his people threw objects of the One Power out of some of the wagons and headed off; the group was the start of the Tuatha'an.

Sumeko Karistovan. A Kin and member of the Knitting Circle. Her strength level was 18(6), which made her strong enough to learn to Travel. Born in 598

NE, she went to the White Tower in 614 NE. After spending five years as a novice and five years as Accepted, she broke down utterly during her test for the shawl; she wanted very badly to do well and pressed too hard, became too keyed up, and couldn't maintain her composure. About 5'5" tall, and quite stout, with a round face, straight black hair and an unlined face, she had wanted to be Yellow Ajah; she had a fine feel for Healing and all its nuances. Despite the prohibition, she continued to try to learn about Healing and diagnosing and managed to teach herself Nynaeve's trick of using all the Five Powers in Healing. When encountered by Elayne and Nynaeve, Sumeko was wearing the red belt of a Wise Woman; her belt was at least twice as long as anyone else's. She went along on the expedition to get the Bowl of the Winds, but was not attacked by the *gholam*; she revealed her Healing skills to Nynaeve in the aftermath.

Sumeko was present at the meeting with the Windfinders in the Tarasin Palace, and was part of manipulating them, on orders from Elayne and Nynaeve. Her attitude toward Aes Sedai changed much, from that of subservience to that of equal, in part due to Nynaeve's urging. Sumeko accompanied Elayne to the Royal Palace in Caemlyn and assisted Mat in trapping the *gholam*. When the refugees from the Trolloc attack on Caemlyn arrived on the Field of Merrilor, Sumeko took charge of seeing that Healing was given to those who needed it immediately. During the Last Battle, Sumeko shuttled soldiers around for Elayne through gateways.

Sumi, Great Aunt. A hypothetical person in Yukiri's thoughts whose relatives fought over her pewter.

summer ham. A phrase used by Elayne to insult Teslyn; Lan was startled and amused by it.

Sun, Court of the. *See* Court of the Sun

Sun King. A character from myth who awakened Talia with a kiss.

Sun Lance. Bukama's yellow roan gelding that he rode in the Aiel War and to Kandor afterward. His hoof was bruised before reaching Canluum; he was not healed when Bukama left for Chachin, so Bukama had to trade him for another horse, a black gelding that was inferior to Sun Lance.

Sun Palace of Cairhien. The royal palace in Cairhien; also known as the Palace of the Rising Sun in Splendor.

Sun Throne of Cairhien. The seat of royal power in Cairhien. It was a large heavy-armed chair that glittered with gilt and golden silk, but somehow it seemed to be all plain vertical lines except for the wavy-rayed Rising Sun that would stand above the head of whoever sat on it. It was installed on a wide dais of dark-blue marble in the Grand Hall of the Sun.

Sunamon Haellin. A High Lord of Tear. Fat though not obese, with graying hair and a pointed beard, he was a smooth and unctuous character who dry-washed his plump hands. He tried ingratiating smiles on Rand, with whom he was usually diffident. He assured Rand that the Defenders had often put down peasant riots. He guaranteed the treaty with Mayene with his life. He was involved in gathering supplies all across Tear to support the action against Sammael in Illian, despite Weiramon's grimaces of impatience with the whole notion, and Torean's sweaty mutters about the expense.

Sunamon participated in the battles against the Seanchan; Rand left him in Illian with orders to remain, and was enraged when he learned that Sunamon and others were returning to Tear.

sunburst. A root used in an ointment to heal bruises. Found in the gardens of the Royal Palace in Caemlyn, the plant had bright, golden-yellow flowers. Cadsuane used an image of this flower on a piece of embroidery.

Sunday. A feastday and festival in midsummer on the longest day of the year, celebrated in many parts of the world. Sunday was unusual in that, for those who actually referred to calendars, it did not count as a day of Amadaine, the month in which it occurred.

sung wood. Ogier Treesingers could make plants respond in such a way as to assume any variety of forms without damage. Objects made in this manner were called "sung wood" and were highly prized. Sung wood was prevalent in the Age of Legends, but the Talent seemed to be dying out by the time of the Last Battle.

Sunhair, Ilyena. *See* Ilyena Therin Moerelle

Sunrise Gate. A portal leading east out of Caemlyn toward the Erinin.

Supreme Council. The ruling body of the Black Ajah, composed of thirteen sisters. It was also known as the Great Council of Thirteen.

Suraile. A woman of the Moshaine Shaido Aiel and *Far Dareis Mai.* She was the eldest daughter of Maeric, the sept chief, and his wife Dyrele. When Sammael's so-called *nar'baha* gateway closed, she was left behind in Kinslayer's Dagger with the Stone Dog for whom she was thinking of giving up the spear. Her brother Darin was a Stone Dog who also was left behind.

Surandha. An Aiel who was Sorilea's Wise One apprentice. A handsome woman who was beautiful when she laughed and full of fun, she had dark golden hair and large blue eyes. She was about five years older than Egwene and was eagerly awaiting the call to a hold of her own. All in all, she was an odd apprentice for Sorilea. Surandha jumped when Sorilea even thought "jump," of course. She could channel as strongly as many Aes Sedai. When Egwene was meeting her *toh* for lying, Surandha was merciless. Afterward, she beamed at Egwene as brightly as ever.

Surasa. An ancestor of Ethenielle, Queen of Kandor. She believed that being ruler made her so powerful she could command the weather. She commanded the rain to stop, and was drenched for her efforts.

Suravye ninto manshima taishite. Old Tongue for "Peace favor your sword."

Surela. A Seanchan *der'sul'dam* to whom *sul'dam* could be sent for punishment; Alwhin told Taisa to go to her when Pura almost touched Suroth's foot while Taisa was holding her leash.

Surial. A Maiden of the Spear who guarded Rand at Lord Tellaen's manor in Arad Doman. She and Lerian discussed beating Rand for going alone to meet with Rodel Ituralde. Later the two guarded Min in Tear just before Rand returned from his epiphany on Dragonmount.

Surine. A Seanchan *sul'dam* who deserted at Falme. She looked a lot like Nynaeve, but was taller, somewhere between 5'8" and 5'11". Floran Gelb attempted to kidnap Nynaeve and pass her off as Surine to Egeanin.

Surlivan Sarat. An officer in the Ebou Dari Guards serving at the Tarasin Palace. Stocky and sun-dark, he carried the thin gilded rod of his office. Mat thought him a good fellow always ready with a quip and having a good eye for horses, until Surlivan mentioned that Tylin would be angry about Mat's appearance; then he thought that Surlivan had a tongue like a rasp and did not really have a good eye for horses.

Suroth Sabelle Meldarath of Asinbayar and Barsabba. A Seanchan of the High Blood and a Darkfriend. Suroth's sigil was three hands, each with the forefinger and little finger raised and the rest folded. About 5'5" tall, with black eyes and the sides of her head shaved to leave a wide crest of black hair that hung down her back, she was neither particularly fair nor dark. Her nails were an inch long and the first two on each hand were lacquered blue. Suroth owned a *lopar* named Almandaragal. Liandrin winkled Nynaeve, Egwene, Elayne and Min out of the Tower and took them to Suroth; Nynaeve and Elayne were able to avoid being collared. After the battle at Falme, Suroth regathered nearly all the surviving Seanchan forces and remained to carry on rather than return and apologize to the Empress for failure. As the highest-ranking survivor of Falme, she would take the blame for the disaster there, and she needed victories to more than counterbalance that. She first took Tanchico, then, using soldiers from Tarabon, she took Amador and expanded control over Amadicia. She also took Ebou Dar.

With the arrival of the Return, Seanchan soldiers and settlers spread into Tarabon, Amadicia and Altara, and a military incursion into Illian was initiated.

Although she was a Darkfriend, she nonetheless thought as a Seanchan. She fully intended to complete the conquest—or reconquest, as she saw it—of the lands Hawkwing had ruled. She fully intended to have these lands, at a very minimum, as her share to rule after the Day of Return, and perhaps even Seanchan itself, but she wished to survive as a member of Seanchan culture. From her point of view, when the Dark One returned, he would certainly confirm her, as a Darkfriend, as ruler of whatever she held at that time. With Semirhage, she plotted Tuon's downfall and aspired to be Empress. After her man Elbar was killed trying to eliminate Tuon and his head was returned to Ebou Dar, Tuon made Suroth *da'covale* and handed her over to the Deathwatch Guard until her hair grew long enough for her to be decent when sent to the block for sale.

sursa. Slender sticks used to eat food with by the Domani.

Surtovni, Keraille. *See* Keraille Surtovni

Surya. A *sul'dam* who accompanied Anath/Semirhage when she attempted to capture Rand. Surya held the leash of Tabi; both received head injuries in the conflict. They refused to be Healed by Nynaeve, but Malian put compresses on their heads.

Susa. The woman who tamed Jain Farstrider in a gleeman's tale.

Susa al'Seen. A Two Rivers girl with channeling ability who became a novice with the rebels, having been recruited by Verin and Alanna. About sixteen years old, she was a slight, fluttery girl, always excitable. She talked over other people, insisting on getting out what she had to say.

Susa Wynn. The widow of Jac and mother of Cyril, one of the children Moiraine investigated while looking for the infant Dragon Reborn.

Susu. A young woman who entertained at The Good Night's Ride in Lugard. Siuan went there to see an eyes-and-ears for the Blue Ajah, the innkeeper Duranda Tharne. Susu showed nearly the whole length of her bare legs, and Siuan wanted to wash out her mouth with soap.

Sutoma, Calwyn. An Ebou Dari bellfounder. Cadaverous, with long black hair, he had a commission from Suroth.

Swallow. Faile's black mare. Faile bought her soon after she arrived at the Stone of Tear; she was killed when Faile was taken by the Shaido.

sweetberry. A bush or tree from which a tea was made. Its green berry was bitter. Sweetberry was found in the Green Man's garden, and it was also seen growing in the Waterwood.

sweetbristle. A fruit from which juice was extracted and drunk by Graendal.

sweetroot. A plant the leaves or flowers of which were used in Aiel bridal wreaths to signify the bride's sweet nature.

Swift. Galina's gray mare that she rode while with the Shaido.

Swift. The rivership owned by Captain Derne. Mat and Thom traveled aboard it south from Aringill to Tear.

Sword and Dragon. The pins, a silver Sword and a gold-and-red enamel Dragon, worn on the collar of an Asha'man's black coat to indicate the rank of full Asha'man. The rank below, Dedicated, wore the silver Sword only on the collar.

sword moves. Apple Blossoms in the Wind; Arc of the Moon; Black Pebbles on the Snow; Blacklance's Last Strike; Blacksmith Strikes the Blade; Boar Rushes Down the Mountain; Boar Rushes Downhill; Bundling Straw; Cat Crosses the Courtyard; Cat Dances on the Wall; Cat on Hot Sand; Cherry Petal Kisses the Pond; Courtier Taps His Fan, The; Creeper Embraces the Oak, The; Cutting the Clouds; Cutting the Wind; Dandelion in the Wind; Dove Takes Flight, The; Eel Among the Lily Pads; Falcon Stoops, The; Falling Leaf, The; Feathers in the Wind; Folding the Air; Folding the Fan; Grapevine Twines, The; Hare Finds Its Hole; Hawk Dives into the Brush; Hawk Spots the Hare; Heron in the

Reeds; Heron on the Stump (a horseback form); Heron Spreads Its Wings, The; Heron Wading in the Rushes; Hummingbird Kisses the Honeyrose; Kingfisher Circles the Pond; Kingfisher Strikes in the Nettles; Kingfisher Takes a Silverback, The; Kissing the Adder; Leaf on the Breeze; Leopard in High Grass; Leopard in the Tree; Leopard's Caress, The; Lightning of Three Prongs; Lion on the Hill; Lion Springs, The; Lizard in the Thornbush; Lotus Closes Its Blossom; Low Wind Rising; Moon on the Water; Moon Rises Over the Lakes; Moon Rises Over Water; Oak Shakes Its Branches; Parting the Silk; Plucking the Low-hanging Apple; Rain in High Wind; Rat Gnawing the Grain; Reaping the Barley; Red Hawk Takes a Dove, The; Reed in Wind; Ribbon in the Air; River of Light; River Undercuts the Bank; Rose Unfolds, The; Serpent's Tongue Dance, The; Shake Dew from the Branch; Sheathing the Sword; Soft Rain at Sunset; Stones Fall in the Pond; Stones Falling Down the Mountain; Stones Falling from the Cliff; Stone Falls from the Mountain; Storm Shakes the Branch; Striking the Spark; Swallow Rides the Air, The; Swallow Takes Flight; Thistledown Floats on the Whirlwind; Threading the Needle; Tower of Morning, The; Twisting the Wind; Two Hares Leaping; Unfolding the Fan; Water Flows Downhill; Watered Silk; Whirlwind on the Mountain; Wind and Rain; Wind Blows Over the Wall, The; Wood Grouse Dances, The; Woodsman Tops the Sapling

Sword of Kirukan. The sword carried by Kandori Queen Ethenielle's Swordbearer in a jeweled scabbard; some believed that it was once carried by the legendary soldier Queen of Aramaelle, and that it was Power-wrought.

Swordbearer. The Kandori title of the one who carried the Sword of Kirukan and commanded the Queen's armies in the field; he was also called Swordbearer to the Throne of the Clouds. Lord Baldhere became Ethenielle's Swordbearer following the death of her husband, Brys.

Swordmaster. Sea Folk title for a Wavemistress's male advisor (usually her husband and former Cargomaster) who had authority over Cargomasters of the clan and directed them in matters of trade and defense.

Swovan Night. An Ebou Dari feast celebrated on the thirteenth day of Taisham. Pine branches were tied above the windows and people celebrating wore sprigs of evergreen in their hair.

Sybaine Aldwyn. One of the Counsels in Far Madding who met with Cadsuane's party when they arrived. She had slender hands and hair as gray as Cadsuane's.

Sylvase Caeren. The granddaughter and heir of Nasin, High Seat of House Caeren in Andor. About 5'4" tall, with big blue eyes and long black hair, she was sturdy and placid and showed no emotion. Sylvase was about age twenty-five when Elayne won Caemlyn. She was unmarried in large part because of Nasin's doings and objections to suitors; he had managed to run off several, and in later years no one tried again because of that. She appeared to be vapid and fluttery, but occasionally showed flashes of something deeper and quieter. She was held as a "guest" of Arymilla, which was part of what helped keep Nasin as High Seat once he was demonstrably gaga. Sylvase became High Seat upon Nasin's death from a seizure and took Jaq Lounalt as her secretary.

Symon. A Warder killed by a Trolloc in the Last Battle; the Trolloc was then killed by Gawyn.

t'Bashere Aybara, Perrin. *See* Perrin t'Bashere Aybara

t'mat. Round edible fruits from the Three-fold Land, red and shiny, that grew on low, pale-leaf bushes.

T'zura. The eighth-largest city in Seanchan.

ta'maral'ailen. Old Tongue for "the Web of Destiny," a reference to major changes in the threads of the Pattern of an Age, associated with and woven around *ta'veren*. It could be short or long in duration, and composed of a limited geographical region or the entire Pattern itself.

ta'veren. A person around whom the Wheel of Time wove all surrounding life-threads, perhaps *all* life-threads, to form a Web of Destiny. This weaving was little understood except that it seemed in many ways an alteration of chance; what might happen, but only rarely, did. The effect was at times quite localized. Someone influenced by the presence of a *ta'veren* might say or do what they would only have said or done one time in a million. Events of seeming impossibility occurred, such as a child falling a hundred feet from a tower unharmed. At other times the effect seemed to influence history itself, though often by means of the localized effects. That, it was believed, was the real reason that *ta'veren* were born, in order to shift history and restore a balance to the turning of the Wheel. It was possible for a woman to become *ta'veren*, as the Wheel required.

Taardad. An Aiel clan; its chief was Rhuarc.

tabac. A weed, widely cultivated. The leaves of it, when dried and cured, were burned in wooden holders called pipes and the fumes inhaled. Tabac was an important cash crop for many countries. The tabac from Two Rivers was considered of high quality, and Cairhienin leaf was described as sharp.

Tabi. A pale-eyed *damane* who accompanied Anath/Semirhage when she attempted to capture Rand. She was Surya's *damane*. Both received head injuries in the conflict. They refused to be Healed by Nynaeve, but Malian put compresses on their heads.

Tabitha. The name by which Tabiya was mistakenly called on multiple occasions.

Tabiya. An Andoran novice with the rebel Aes Sedai with a potential strength level of 27(15). She was born in 983 NE and went to the White Tower in 998 NE, and was taken from the Tower by the rebels. Tabiya had green eyes and freckles, and sometimes tried to assume an air of Aes Sedai mystery, at which she failed. She was timid, as when approaching Egwene as the Amyrlin. She squeaked when Sheriam snapped at her.

Taborwin, House. A noble House in Cairhien. *See* Breane *and* Dobraine Taborwin

Tad Barran. A stableman at The Winespring Inn, Emond's Field; he was the brother of Hu. Lanky and taciturn, he seldom said more than three words strung together. He joined Perrin's army at Malden.

Tad Kandel. A dark-skinned Andoran Redarm in the Band of the Red Hand. Tad accompanied Mat to Ebou Dar; on the way there, Elayne discovered that he had a boil on his bottom. It had to be lanced, since Tad had adopted Mat's aversion to Healing. He was killed by a *gholam* in Ebou Dar while trying to retrieve the Bowl of the Winds.

Tadvishm. A Stone Dog who was killed by Seanchan in Aviendha's viewing of the future at Rhuidean.

Taeric Chavana. An acrobat in Luca's circus, one of four men said to be brothers, although the four looked very different. Taeric was short and compact, with green eyes, high cheekbones and a hooked nose proclaiming his Saldaean blood.

Taglien. A family at the Black Tower. *See* Frask *and* Lind Taglien

Tagora, Amaline Paendrag. The first wife of Artur Hawkwing. He loved her very much, wrote many poems to her, and was devastated when she was poisoned and died.

Tagren, Lady. An alias used by Shemerin after running away from the White Tower.

Tai'daishar. Old Tongue for "Lord of Glory," it was the name of a black gelding that Rand forced Kiruna to sell him for the extravagant amount of one thousand gold crowns after the unpleasantness at Dumai's Wells.

tai'shar. Old Tongue for "true blood," as in *Tai'shar Manetheren* or *Tai'shar Malkier.*

Taien. A town at the mouth of the Jangai Pass on the Aiel Waste side, the opposite end of the pass from Selean. It had been a high-walled town of moderate size. Taien was burned by Couladin and the Shaido. Bodies hung from the town walls, and the hundred survivors had been told not to touch anything; Couladin intended it for a message.

Taijing, Stedding. A *stedding* located in the Spine of the World, east of Cantoine.

Taim, Mazrim. *See* Mazrim Taim

Tain Shari. An Aiel warrior society; the name was Old Tongue for "True Bloods."

taint. The flaw that affected *saidin*, the male half of the One Power, caused by a backlash from the Dark One as the Bore was sealed at Shayol Ghul by Lews Therin and the Hundred Companions. The taint caused all male channelers eventually to go mad, which induced the female Aes Sedai to hunt down and gentle as many male channelers as could be found before they could do harm. The taint was cleansed by Rand al'Thor at Shadar Logoth. *See also* Cleansing, the

Tairen maze. An embroidery pattern used on coats, in carpets and in other materials.

Taisa. A Seanchan *sul'dam*. She controlled Pura during a meeting with Suroth in

Cantoine. Taisa had dark eyes and was very proper, in a Seanchan way; her eyes bulged indignantly when Pura tried to touch Suroth's foot. She was ready to punish Pura for just possibly implying that Suroth had spoken untruth. Alwhin sent Taisa to Surela for punishment for not controlling Pura better.

Taishin, Stedding. A *stedding* located in the forests north of the River Ivo.

tak. A bush found in the Waste; when dead it was good for making a fire.

Takai. A clan chief of the Miagoma Aiel after the Last Battle, as seen in Aviendha's viewings of the future in Rhuidean.

Takana, Clan. One of the Atha'an Miere clans.

Takashi, Eldase. *See* Eldase Takashi

Takedo, Court of. A place in Farashelle, from Mat's memories. Artur Hawkwing crushed it in battle.

Takima Deraighdin. An Andoran Aes Sedai of the Brown Ajah and the rebel contingent, with a strength level of 23(11). Born in the Mountains of Mist in 844 NE, she went to the White Tower in 858 NE. After spending nine years as a novice and six years as Accepted, she was raised to the shawl in 874 NE.

About 5'1" tall, with smooth black hair to her waist and skin the color of aged ivory, she was not exactly plump, but neither was she at all slender; a man might have considered her a very pleasant armful. She was, by nature, quiet and observant, though she was forceful as a teacher and in the Hall. Her manner—the way she held or tilted her head, the way she moved—sometimes suggested a bird.

Takima taught history of the White Tower and Aes Sedai, and could recognize one of her pupils at a hundred paces. She was raised a Sitter for the Brown in 991 NE. Jesse Bilal, her Ajah head, ordered her to join the sisters fleeing after Siuan was deposed to try to control and defuse the situation. Takima believed the reports concerning Logain and Red sisters, possibly including Elaida, and by implication thus had suspicions regarding the Reds and other false Dragons which put considerable strain on her purpose. Takima joined Lelaine's clique, and apparently was very tightly under Lelaine's thumb; she did so to help counter Romanda's faction. At the vote for declaring war on Elaida, she explained the Law of War after the vote was taken, and wept after Egwene announced her plans to Travel to Tar Valon. Takima was against any alliance with the Black Tower and worked to delay an embassy to it; she also opposed bonding Asha'man. She was part of the group, with Faiselle, Saroiya, Magla and Varilin, who negotiated with the White Tower to try to end the split. After the Tower reunited, she kept her seat as a Sitter.

taking price. The reward given by the Seanchan to anyone involved in capturing *marath'damane*. Since *damane* were a valuable commodity, the taking price was generous. Someone involved in capturing a large number of *damane*, as might be possible east of the Aryth Ocean, could receive enough money to purchase an inn, or a trained *damane*.

Takisrom. A port on the Sleeping Bay in Seanchan.

Tal Nethin. A saddlemaker who survived the Shaido massacre of Taien in the Jangai Pass, only to die by breaking his neck on level ground shortly afterward. His sister was Aril Corl.

Talaan din Gelyn. A Sea Folk Windfinder apprentice. Too young to have earned a salt name, she was the daughter of the Windfinder Caire din Gelyn Running Wave. Her strength level was 4(9+), with a potential of 2(+11), higher than Nynaeve's or Moghedien's and equal to that of Graendal, Mesaana and Sharina. Her relationship with her mother was difficult, with her mother treating her more harshly than other apprentices were treated. Her mother had not, since Talaan had become an apprentice, done anything to acknowledge by word, deed, facial expression or tone of voice, that Talaan was her daughter. She had no nose chain, and only a single earring in the left ear to balance three in the right. Talaan was about 5'5" tall, and slim, with big eyes that were almost black and a straight nose. Part of the circle that used the Bowl of the Winds, she fled to Caemlyn when the Seanchan attacked the Kin farm outside Ebou Dar. She wanted Nynaeve's help in going to Tar Valon, convinced that being a novice would be much easier than the life she had been leading. She wound up running away with Merilille. They made their way to Shayol Ghul and fought in the Last Battle there.

Talene Minly. An Andoran Aes Sedai of the Green Ajah publicly but of the Black Ajah in truth. She was of the loyalist contingent and had a strength level of 15(3). Born in 840 NE, she went to the White Tower in 855 NE. After spending six years as a novice and six years as Accepted, she was raised to the shawl in 867 NE. She became a Sitter for the Green in 994 NE. About 5'7" tall, she was statuesque. Her face was a perfect oval, with large blue eyes and full red lips. Her hair was golden, and she was beautiful and voluptuous—full-bosomed and round of hip. Her fingers were long and her hands graceful. Seaine saw her as "beauty carved from ice," though this thought came at a time of tension and antagonism.

Talene was not a woman who liked to defer to anyone, under any circumstances, or to be less in any way whatsoever; she might be said to be almost prototypical of the Green Ajah arrogance in this regard, though she was quite personable and very charming in other ways. She had no Warder, which was unusual for a Green, saying that a Sitter didn't need one. She had had them in the past, although no more than one Warder at a time; all her Warders had been Darkfriends.

Talene held a record as perhaps the most punished novice and Accepted in the history of the Tower. It was said, facetiously, that she spent as much time in the Mistress of Novices' study as she did in classes or lectures. It was also said that she could have passed her tests for Accepted and for Aes Sedai sooner than she was allowed to take them, but she was kept back for being such a discipline problem. Talene was friends with Seaine, but only acquaintances with Pevara. Talene was jealous of their being pillow friends; she would have liked to have been Seaine's pillow friend. It was not really a sexual thing; she just wanted to have her friendship be that much closer. But spreading into threesomes or the like was fairly rare, and in any case, she would not have wanted Pevara to be part of it. At least part of that was because Pevara was stronger than her in the Power while Seaine was weaker. She and Seaine remained friends, although the strains between Ajahs in the White Tower forced some distance between them. Talene stood to depose Siuan Sanche. Afterward, she was given a penance by Elaida; it was a matter of scrubbing floors.

Talene led Saerin, Doesine and Yukiri to confront Pevara and Seaine, though the others went along because of their own suspicions. Talene had been instructed by the Black Ajah to find out why the heads of the Ajahs were meeting in secret while at one another's throats in public, and she thought Pevara and Seaine sneaking about might have something to do with it.

She was identified as Black Ajah when she refused to reswear the Three Oaths; she was questioned in the Chair of Remorse. She forswore her Oaths to the Shadow and worked with those searching for the Black Ajah. When she was summoned to a meeting of the Black Ajah by Alviarin, she fled.

Talentless. Men dwelling in the Town in the Blight who could not channel.

Talents. Abilities in the use of the One Power in specific areas. The best known of these was Healing. Some, such as Traveling, the ability to shift oneself from one place to another without crossing the intervening space, were lost after the Breaking, and later rediscovered. Others, such as Foretelling, the ability to foretell future events in a general way, were prevalent in the Age of Legends but were later found only rarely if at all. Another Talent thought lost was Dreaming, which involved, among other things, interpreting the Dreamer's dreams to foretell future events in more specific fashion than Foretelling. Other Talents were Cloud Dancing, the control of weather; Earth Singing, which involved controlling movements of the earth—for example, preventing or causing earthquakes and avalanches; and Delving, finding ores and possibly removing them from the ground.

Minor talents, seldom given a name, included the ability to see *ta'veren*, the ability to see a weave for the first time and know what it would do before it was complete, or to duplicate the chance-twisting effect of a *ta'veren*, though in a very small and localized area rarely covering more than a few feet. *See* Cloud Dancing, Delving, Dreaming, Earth Singing, Healing, Foretelling *and* Traveling

Talents, lost. Talents from the Age of Legends that were unknown in the subsequent Age. Among these were Aligning the Matrix, a weave used to make metals stronger. Others, whose uses were unknown, were Milking Tears and Spinning Earthfire.

Talha. A slender, dark-haired *sul'dam* who accompanied Anath/Semirhage when she attempted to capture Rand. She wept after her capture.

Talia. A woman from myth who was awakened by a kiss from the Sun King. While waiting for Birgitte to return from seeing Mat at The Wandering Woman in Ebou Dar, Nynaeve thought that she wanted to forget her worries in sleep until Lan wakened her with a kiss, as Talia was wakened by a kiss from the Sun King.

Talidar. Site of the last of seven major battles between an aging Artur Hawkwing and invading Trollocs, which diminished Trolloc activity along the Blight for fifty years.

Talisman of Growing. A *ter'angreal* triggered by Ogier Treesinging that allowed the Ogier to expand the Ways that the Aes Sedai had built.

Talkend. A petty House of Andor; its symbol was a golden Winged Hand. *See* Eram Talkend

Tall Bear. A wolf in Leafhunter's pack. Perrin spoke with the pack after encountering a scent in the wolf dream that made his hackles rise; he asked them what a wolf would hate more than the Neverborn. When he did so, they all shut him out one by one. The answer, of course, was Darkhounds.

Tallan. A town in Altara, east of Samaha, Willar and the River Boern. Moiraine, Lan, Perrin and Loial passed through Tallan while on Rand's trail. Everyone in the town had become embroiled in old disagreements, and it took several murders before people settled down—indications that Rand had been there recently.

Tallanvor, Martyn. *See* Martyn Tallanvor

tallowend. A plant with little pink flowers found in the gardens of the Royal Palace in Caemlyn.

Talmanes Delovinde. A Cairhienin nobleman. His *con* was three yellow stars on blue, and his banner a black fox. He became a Lieutenant-General in the Band of the Red Hand and was the leader of Talmanes' Thunderbolts, the First Banner of the Horse. The front of his head was shaved and powdered. Although he wore plain coats, he was entitled to a number of stripes. He was three years older than Mat at most and looked like a coiled whip. His eyes were expressionless, and he didn't laugh and seldom smiled. Talmanes met Mat while battling the Shaido at Cairhien; impressed with his abilities, Talmanes swore loyalty to him and was instrumental in creating the Band of the Red Hand, becoming one of its leaders. He followed Mat at first because Mat was a winner, but his personal loyalty increased over time. After the Band went to Salidar, on orders from Rand to pick up Elayne, they split up, with Mat going off to Ebou Dar with Elayne and Nynaeve, and Talmanes keeping most of the Band near the Salidar Aes Sedai. As they traveled north, Talmanes met with King Roedran of Murandy and agreed to stay there for a time to help him consolidate his kingdom. Afterward, Talmanes took half the Band back south to find Mat, while the other half went north into Andor. Joined up with Mat again, Talmanes took part in defeating the large Seanchan force trying to take Tuon. Talmanes, Mat and the Band proceeded toward Caemlyn to rejoin Elayne, and their progress there was facilitated by Verin.

Talmanes was a major figure in the Last Battle, evacuating Caemlyn and rescuing the dragons after the city was overrun by Trollocs, despite taking severe wounds. He worked with Aludra and the dragons and was indispensable in actions at Braem Wood, in the defense of Cairhien and at Merrilor.

Talmour. A nation that arose after the Trolloc Wars.

Talmouri. One from the nation of Talmour; an ancient adjective used by Birgitte. She said that Elayne was as proper as a Talmouri maiden except when she was putting her head on the chopping block.

Talric. Adelorna's Warder. He was wounded in the Seanchan attack on the White Tower.

Talva. An Aes Sedai of the Yellow Ajah publicly and of the Black Ajah in truth. Thin, with a bun of golden hair, she was killed accidentally in *Tel'aran'rhiod* by Alviarin, who threw a weave of Fire at Egwene; Egwene dodged it, and it burned Talva.

Talvaen, Aleshin. *See* Aleshin Talvaen

Tam al'Thor. Rand's adoptive father. His full first name was Tamlin. He was a blocky, bluff man, about 5'10" tall, with brown eyes and hair that was mostly gray with a little black in 998 NE, but which turned completely gray by the time of the Last Battle. Tam was born in 940 NE to a farming and sheepherding family near Emond's Field and ran away from home in 956 NE to see the world. He enlisted in the army of Illian in 957 NE. Service in the Whitecloak War from the summer of 957 NE through the autumn of 959 NE gained him an appointment to the elite Companions. He married Kari, a merchant's daughter, in 965 NE; he and Kari had two children, a girl who died of a fever in infancy and a boy who was stillborn, after which Kari could no longer have children. He became a blademaster in 966 NE. He served in two wars with Tear, from 962 to 965 NE, gaining commission as an officer, and from 970 to 976 NE, rising to be Second Captain of the Companions. It was generally known that he would have received this honor sooner, and likely have risen to First Captain, had he been Illianer.

He served in the Aiel War, 976–978 NE. After the Battle of the Shining Walls, Tam found an infant on the slopes of Dragonmount and took him to Kari. He, Kari and baby Rand returned to the Two Rivers. Life was calm and pastoral, except for Kari's passing, until the Trolloc raid on Tam's farm, where Tam was severely wounded, but he was Healed by Moiraine. After Rand left with Moiraine and Lan to fulfill his destiny as the Dragon Reborn, Tam and Abell Cauthon traveled to Tar Valon to try to find out what had happened to their sons; they didn't learn much. Tam returned to Emond's Field and after Perrin's arrival helped organize the defense of Two Rivers against the Trollocs. Following Faile's capture by the Shaido, Tam became Perrin's First Captain in the battle at Malden, leading a large contingent of archers from the Two Rivers.

Under Cadsuane's influence, Tam tried to counsel Rand on approaching his position as the Dragon Reborn with humanity, but Rand nearly killed him when he realized he was being manipulated. The near disaster led to Rand's epiphany on Dragonmount, and he reconciled with Tam.

Before the Last Battle, Tam recruited more men from the Two Rivers, and when he went into battle again, it was with Perrin's army, which he commanded after Perrin left to help Rand. (Perrin had also made him a lord and Steward of the Two Rivers.) As commander of this large force, Tam joined the rest of Mat's forces at the Field of Merrilor, where he distinguished himself in battle.

Tamaav. An elderly Aiel man, seen in Aviendha's visions of the future in Rhuidean.

Tamagowa, Samitsu. *See* Samitsu Tamagowa

Tamala. A hawk-nosed novice in the White Tower whom Egwene recruited to help fight the Seanchan.

Tamarath, Egeanin. *See* Egeanin Sarna

Tamarla. An Altaran Kin who was a member of the Knitting Circle in Ebou Dar. Her strength level was 47(35); she would not have been allowed to test for Aes Sedai and was not strong enough to make a gateway of any size whatsoever. Born in 681 NE, she went to the White Tower in 696 NE. After spending two years as a novice she was put out because she had reached her potential and was not strong enough to test for Accepted. Tamarla was bone-lean, with olive skin, dark eyes and more white than black in her long hair. At the time that Elayne and Nynaeve encountered her, she was wearing the red belt of a Wise Woman. She was present at the meeting with the Windfinders in the Tarasin Palace, and part of manipulating them, on orders from Elayne and Nynaeve. She accompanied Elayne to the Royal Palace in Caemlyn.

Tamela. A Wise One of the Goshien Aiel. She was as strong in the One Power as any Aes Sedai that Elayne had met except Nynaeve and was the equal of Cadsuane, with a strength level of 5(+8). Standing 5'9" tall, and bony, she had an angular, unlovely face; strong was the best anyone would say of it. Tamela did not look more than a half-dozen years older than Elayne or Aviendha. Elayne felt that Tamela sneered and looked down her nose when she saw her. She stood in for Aviendha's mother at the first-sister ceremony.

Tamika. Artur Hawkwing's second wife. She met Hawkwing in FY 964 when he returned from the Aiel Waste; they married a year later. In FY 967 she gave birth to Luthair Paendrag Mondwin; she later had three or four more children, at least two of whom were daughters. Tamika was credited with bringing Hawkwing out of the Black Years. It was rumored that she was a renegade Aes Sedai. Tamika died in FY 987 of unknown causes.

Tamlin al'Thor. *See* Tam al'Thor

Tammaz. The eighth month of the year.

Tammaz, Great Square of. In Illian; surrounded by huge white columns fifteen spans tall and two spans thick, topped with marble wreaths of olive branches. At the two ends of the square were nearly identical purple-roofed palaces, the King's Palace and the slightly smaller Great Hall of the Council.

Tammuz. An Illuminator. He worked with Aludra to create the display intended for Galldrian that was ignited by Rand, Lanfear and Loial when they hid out in the chapter house to escape Trollocs. The resulting fire damaged the chapter house. Tammuz and four other Illuminators followed Aludra and tried to kill her. They were thwarted by Mat, who came to her rescue.

Tamore Alkohima. A Domani seamstress in Tar Valon. Fair-skinned for a Domani, she made Gitara look boyish. Moiraine and Siuan ordered dresses from her after being raised to Aes Sedai; Siuan did not behave properly toward her, and she made them pay for it by choosing what she wanted instead of what they wanted.

Tamra Ospenya. An Aes Sedai of the Blue Ajah with a strength level of 19(7). She was 5'4" tall, with a square face and hair streaked with gray. Tamra was raised to the Amyrlin Seat in 973 NE. She had a habit of not telling anyone more than she believed they needed to know. Too much information, she felt, clogged people's thoughts and slowed necessary actions.

She set Moiraine and Siuan looking for the babe her Keeper Gitara Moroso had proclaimed as the Dragon Reborn—what she actually set them doing, along with all of the other Accepted, was finding all women who had or were reported to have had babies in the vicinity of Tar Valon during the crucial time. Although she knew that the only child of interest would be one born on the west bank, preferably one who could be proved to have been born on Dragonmount, she felt it was necessary to hide the true object of the search; the openly given reason was to offer aid to the mothers in the form of a bounty of one hundred gold crowns. Tamra set them to this task claiming it was temporary and mainly to keep them quiet until she could bring in sisters she knew she could trust.

She was found dead in her bed soon after High Chasaline in 979 NE and it was assumed that she had died in her sleep; she had actually been kidnapped and put to the question by the Black Ajah when they gained hints of what she was about. Largely because the Black sisters believed that she would be working only with experienced Aes Sedai, not a pair so newly raised, and because she herself thought them no longer involved—and also partly because the Black bungled matters in their haste—she did not reveal Moiraine's and Siuan's names. Most of the sisters she had taken into her confidence died within the next year, including those who were out of the Tower searching, and eventually all were disposed of by the Black Ajah or, in a very few cases, by true accidents and natural deaths. So were a number of other senior sisters who the Black Ajah simply suspected might have been chosen by Tamra. The result was something of a pogrom among the most senior sisters of the Tower.

Tamrin. A Taraboner who was head of the military in Tanchico.

Tamsin Ituralde. Rodel Ituralde's wife. She told him that if he died in battle, she would go after him and would be the first living person to haunt the dead.

Tamyrlin, Ring of. *See* Ring of Tamyrlin

Tanchico. The capital of Tarabon. It lay on the Aryth Ocean at the mouth of the River Andahar. Tanchico was built on three hilly peninsulas extending south into Tanchico Bay. From east to west the peninsulas were named Verana, Maseta and Calpene. A dozen fortresses surrounded the harbor. The Great Circle on the Calpene was a huge gathering place for horse races or fireworks. The King's Circle was on the Maseta, and the Panarch's Circle and Panarch's Palace were on the Verana. The Civil Watch kept order in the city.

Tanchico Bay. The body of water formed by the River Andahar meeting the Aryth Ocean on the west coast of Tarabon.

Tandar. A feast celebrated on the ninth day of Maigdhal. No one was supposed to let Tandar end while still holding a grudge or having a disagreement with anyone. Although the intent was that such things should be made up, it was not unknown for festivities to be marred by an attempt to fulfill the requirement in quite another way.

Tando. An Andoran Youngling who was guarding the mayor's house in Dorlan when Gawyn saw Katerine leave.

Tanera. A short, dark *sul'dam* killed during Semirhage's attempted capture of Rand. Her *damane*, Miri, also died during the action.

Tanhal, Stedding. A *stedding* located in Arafel.

Tanisloe, Serafelle. *See* Serafelle Tanisloe

Tanreall, Artur Paendrag. *See* Artur Hawkwing

Tar Valon. An independent city-state, and a walled island on the River Erinin; location of the White Tower. The government was administered by a council of Aes Sedai chosen by the Hall of the Tower. It included a Great Library and an Ogier Grove. It suffered a great fire in FY 642. Some slight damage was done to the White Tower itself, and to the Tower library. Its population reached 500,000 to 700,000 people before the Last Battle.

Tar Valon, Battle of. *See* Battle of the Shining Walls, the

Tar Valon Gate. One of the city gates in Caemlyn; it opened onto the Tar Valon Road.

Tar Valon Road. A thoroughfare leading out of Caemlyn toward Tar Valon.

Tarabon. A nation south of the Almoth Plain on the Aryth Ocean; its capital was Tanchico. Tarabon's sigil was a golden tree with a thick bole and spreading branches balanced by spreading roots below: the Tree, or the Golden Tree. Its banner was the Golden Tree on a field vertically striped red and white: four red and three white.

Tarabon was founded in approximately FY 1006. In that year, Lord Haren Maseed, Lady Tazenia Nerenhald and Lord Boral Amadia, three powerful nobles who had held high positions in Hawkwing's regional government, took Tanchico and proclaimed the coastal region around the city, a region then called Tarabon, an independent nation. They adopted the form of government that had been used in Balasun, with a ruler (King or Queen) balanced by a Panarch (who could be male or female as well, although always the opposite gender from the

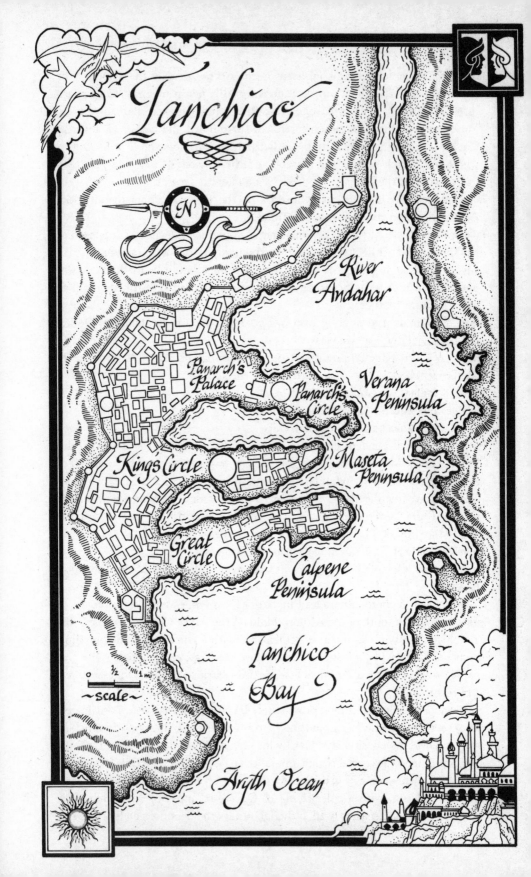

Tanchico

River Andahar

Panarch's Palace

Panarch's Circle

Verana Peninsula

Kings Circle

Maseta Peninsula

Great Circle

Calpene Peninsula

Tanchico Bay

½   1 m

~scale~

Aryth Ocean

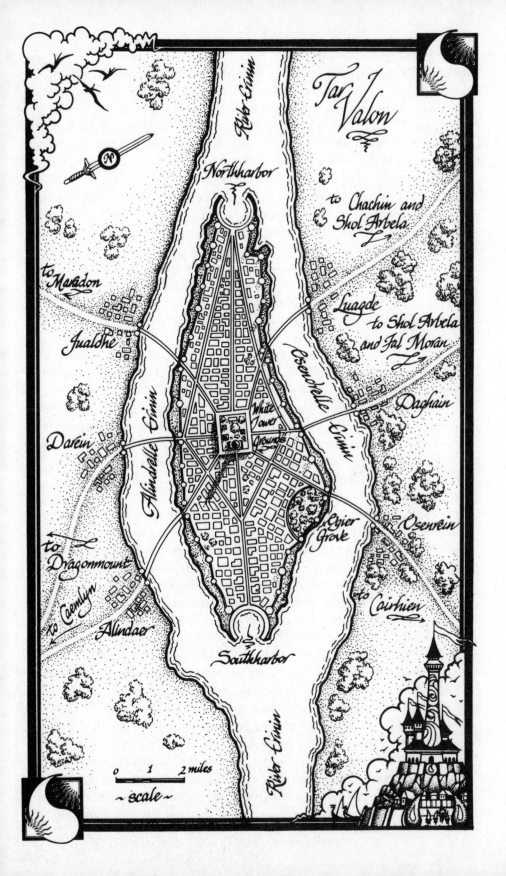

Tar Valon

Northharbor

to Chachin and
Shol Arbela

to Maradon

Jualdhe

Luagde
to Shol Arbela
and Tal Moran

Daghain

Darein

White
Tower
Grounds

Alindrelle Einin

Ostrelle Einin

Egier
Grove

Osenrein

to Dragonmount

to Cairhien

to Caemlyn

Alindaer

Southharbor

River Erinin

River Erinin

0   1   2 miles

~ scale ~

ruler), with an Assembly consisting of nobles, wealthy merchants and guild representatives to balance both ruler and Panarch. Lord Boral was considered the leader of the three, a former provincial governor and general under Hawkwing, but he was murdered and Lady Tazenia became Queen Tazenia, and Lord Haren became the Panarch Haren. Tarabon, consisting of little more than the city of Tanchico, was immediately attacked by forces wanting to reestablish Balasun, but Tarabon survived, although it took to the very end of the War of the Hundred Years to grow to a stable size. The dual-ruler form of government remained unchanged for several hundred years after the war, but by approximately 500 NE, the ruler was always a king, the Panarch was always female, and the Assembly consisted solely of nobles and had lost almost all of its power. The right to name the new Panarch was one of the few remaining real powers the Assembly had, and it was guarded jealously. The Panarch of Tanchico was the equal of the King in authority. She was responsible for collecting taxes, customs and duties; he for spending them properly. She controlled the Civil Watch and the courts, except for the High Court, which was the King's. The army was his, except for the Panarch's Legion, which was hers.

At the time of the Seanchan invasion, as far as most of the rest of the world knew, anarchy and civil war were ripping Tarabon apart. There seemed to be no order anywhere in the country. Claimants for the throne fought against the King, each other, the Dragonsworn and brigands. The Whitecloaks withdrew after events in Tanchico, for which they got most of the blame from Taraboners who knew anything at all about them. Into that boiling pot, the Seanchan under the High Lady Suroth took the city of Tanchico, then took all of Tarabon. Tanchico fell shortly after Elayne and Nynaeve left. Rumors spread of Artur Hawkwing's armies coming back and of Aes Sedai fighting in battles, taken by many only as evidence of confusion in that country. Various warring noble Houses tried to go it alone or to play for position, making alliances they intended to break. Most of them simply did not realize what or who the Seanchan were. Most were forced into submission to the Seanchan, as were many of the Dragonsworn. The Seanchan raised large numbers of troops among the Taraboners. The King's Life Guard numbered about three thousand men, when it existed. It was dispersed by the Seanchan, though many of the surviving men were incorporated into the Seanchan forces. The Panarch's Legion consisted of about three thousand men on land and about a thousand to fifteen hundred on ships, when it existed. Like the Life Guard, it was dispersed by the Seanchan, though many of the survivors were incorporated into levies raised by the Seanchan. Unlike most other nations, Tarabon did have a permanent naval force, but it was part of the Panarch's Legion, not a separate force. Its primary function was quelling pirate activities. It was dispersed with the rest of the Panarch's Legion.

Taraboners called themselves the Tree of Man and claimed to be descended from rulers in the Age of Legends; their sign was the Tree of Life, although they did not have any belief that they ever possessed a sapling of *Avendesora*.

With the civil unrest, Tarabon's trade died, but the Seanchan conquest led to a revival. They established trade with Amadicia, and resumed trade with Ebou Dar shortly after the city fell to the Seanchan. Men and women who swore the oaths were free to trade.

Tarabon produced dyes, rugs and carpets that were considered some of the best, and lace, also considered among the finest. Tarabon was the third-largest supplier of olives and olive oil after Tear and Illian. Wine, hides and leather and nuts were also produced in Tarabon. The nation had a number of silver mines, but few gold mines, and intricate silverwork and goldwork of distinctive patterns and styles were produced, as well as swords and daggers, many highly decorated.

Taralan. A place in the Fourth Age where Boanne, the composer of *Do'in Toldara te, Songs of the Last Age*, Quarto Nine: The Legend of the Dragon, was Songmistress.

Taramasu, Kwamesa. *See* Kwamesa Taramasu

Tarasin Palace. In Ebou Dar, the royal palace of Queen Tylin, and then her son Beslan. Situated on Mol Hara Square, the palace took up one entire side of the square. Made of marble and white-plastered stone, it had shining domes, slender spires and colonnades three and four stories high.

Tarasind, Saine. Mesaana's name before becoming Forsaken.

Taravin, House. A major noble House in Andor. Its High Seat was Dyelin; its sign the Owl and Oak. *See* Dyelin Taravin

tarchrot. The bad-tasting leaf of this plant was used to poison Milisair Chadmar in Ebou Dar; Nynaeve was able to Heal her, as the poison was slow-acting.

Taren Ferry. An Andoran village, north of Emond's Field and Watch Hill on the North Road, where the only crossing of the River Taren was found. Its people had a reputation for slyness and trickery. The stone houses in the village were tall; high redstone foundations were necessary when the spring melt in the Mountains of Mist made the river overflow its banks. Moiraine and Lan, leading Rand and the others out of Emond's Field after the Trolloc attacks on Winternight, went there to take a ferry across the Taren; after they crossed, Moiraine destroyed the ferry to delay the Shadowspawn chasing them. Later, Whitecloaks under Dain Bornhald entered the village and laid down the law to the villagers; across the river at a Tinker camp, three Tinkers disappeared after questioning by Padan Fain. The Whitecloaks guarded Taren Ferry and points south against Shadowspawn, controlling crossings of the river; nonetheless Trollocs were able to destroy the village. After the Trolloc raid, nearly half the house foundations supported only piles of ash and charred beams.

Taren Ferry was repopulated after the Trolloc raid, and Perrin was angry when Faile tried to interfere in the village's politics. Sometime after Perrin left the Two Rivers, Taren Ferry was destroyed again.

Verin was amazed at the potential in the Power of girls from the Two Rivers, but the same potential was not found in Taren Ferry, which had mixed more with outsiders.

Taren River. The upper river of the Two Rivers in Andor, flowing southeast from the Mountains of Mist to the River Manetherendrelle.

Tarendrelle. Name of the River Taren during the Trolloc Wars. In Moiraine's story of Aemon and the fall of Manetheren, she said that if he could hold at the Tarendrelle for three days, aid was promised; that aid did not come.

Taric. An Aiel man of the Chareen clan who was the youngest greatson of Amaryn, Sorilea's greatdaughter. Sorilea suggested him as a husband for Egwene if the Aes Sedai rejected her. Sorilea thought that he would be a clan chief someday.

Taril Canler. An Asha'man from Andor. About 5'10" tall, and sturdy, with gray in his hair, he spat for emphasis and used countryman's terms and phrases. He worked out a way that married Asha'man could bond their wives; he himself was married to Leish, whom he bonded. As an Asha'man soldier he was with Rand in Illian and was then promoted to Dedicated. He associated himself with Logain, forming what Toveine recognized as one of at least two factions within the Black Tower. Canler worked with Androl to try to escape when the Black Tower was sealed. He helped to free Logain from Taim, and fought in the Last Battle.

Taringail Damodred. A Prince of Cairhien and First Prince of the Sword of Andor. His sign was a golden, double-bitted battle axe. He was born in 948 NE, a nephew of King Laman of Cairhien and the half-brother of Moiraine Damodred. He was first the husband of Tigraine; they had one son, Galad. After Tigraine's disappearance, he married Morgase, with whom he had two children, Elayne and Gawyn. Tensions rose between Andor and Cairhien, in part because Morgase failed to, or refused to, hide the fact that Taringail was in no fashion co-ruler of Andor. Taringail was supposedly killed in a hunting accident, but in fact was assassinated by Thom Merrilin when the latter discovered that Taringail intended to usurp the throne of Andor.

Tarlomen's Gate. An entryway in the south wall of the White Tower grounds in Tar Valon.

Tarmandewin. A court at which Mat had ancient memories of dancing.

Tarmon Gai'don. The Old Tongue term for the Last Battle. Prophecies given in *The Karaethon Cycle* foretold that the Dark One would be freed again to touch the world, and that Lews Therin Telamon, the Dragon, Breaker of the World, would be reborn to fight Tarmon Gai'don and to save the world and break it again. *See* Last Battle, the

Tarna Feir. An Altaran Aes Sedai of the Red Ajah and the loyalist contingent, with a strength level of 19(7). Born near the Andoran border in 950 NE, she went to the White Tower in 964 NE. After spending nine years as a novice and six years as Accepted, she was raised to the shawl in 979 NE. Pale-haired, 5'5½" tall and haughty, with a prominent chin and sharp blue eyes that could freeze the sun, she was a wilder who first touched *saidar* at about as early an age as possible, but she had a block: she could not touch *saidar* unless she had her eyes closed. That meant, of course, that she could not see to weave the flows. Galina Casban took an interest in her and beat the block out of her, something about which she later professed to be amused. This was technically illegal, but the then Mistress of Novices acquiesced by being silent about it.

Tarna was sent by Elaida as emissary to the rebel Aes Sedai gathering in Salidar. She learned about the presence of Siuan and Leane, Logain, Nynaeve, Elayne and Egwene, and about Gareth Bryne raising an army. Even though she reported all via pigeon long before reaching Tar Valon, she nearly rode her horse to death trying to return to give her report in person, because what she had seen in Salidar frightened her. In Murandy she encountered a group of Asha'man. She reached Dorlan just after the rebel army surrounded Tar Valon; she took control of the sisters there from Covarla. Narenwin Barda arrived, and Tarna went back to the White Tower. Since Alviarin was missing, Tarna was named the Keeper of the Chronicles. She and Pevara talked about the Asha'man, with Tarna suggesting that Red sisters should take Asha'man as Warders. They, with four others, subsequently were ordered by Tsutama to go to the Black Tower and bond Asha'man. Tarna was Turned to the Shadow while there.

Taron, Elwinn. The Wisdom of Deven Ride. She was round and had a motherly smile that she wore even when she was making people do what they did not want to do.

Tarra. A Maiden of the Spear of the Taardad Aiel, seen in Aviendha's viewings of the future in Rhuidean. Tarra was killed in a fight with Seanchan led by Padra.

Tarran. A Saldaean soldier in Maradon with Bashere. He had long mustaches and bowed legs. Wearing the Traitor's Banner, he was one of four guarding the Darkfriend Lord Torkumen when Yoeli took Ituralde to meet Torkumen.

Tarsi, Larelle. *See* Larelle Tarsi

Tarsin, Idrien. *See* Idrien Tarsin

Tarva. Katerine's rendering of Therava's name during the Wise Ones' meeting with the Aes Sedai who kidnapped Rand.

Tarwin's Gap. The pass separating the Mountains of Dhoom from the Spine of the World, near Fal Dara. Frequently used in raids by the Trollocs, it was the site of many battles between Shadowspawn and Borderlanders. Lan and his army engaged a massive Trolloc army heading south from there during the Last Battle.

Tasil. An Ebou Dari family. *See* Namine *and* Quillin Tasil

Tauan. A *morat'raken* who died when her *raken* was shot down by Aes Sedai at the Kin's farm.

Tava. An Aiel girl seen in Aviendha's viewings of the future in Rhuidean. Her hold was attacked and burned by the Seanchan; her father, Rowahn, picked up a sword and used it to save her and a small child she was protecting. He tried to keep the people of the hold together, but they all walked away; Tava survived, however; she was the greatmother of Norlesh.

Taval din Chanai Nine Gulls. The Sea Folk Windfinder of the *White Spray*, which carried Atha'an Miere delegations to Andor and Cairhien. Her Sailmistress was Derah din Selaan Rising Wave. Dark-haired, with only three earrings in each ear, she caused Egwene to fall into the water when Egwene attempted to visit the *White Spray*.

Tavalad. The clan chief of the Goshien Aiel after the Last Battle, seen in Aviendha's viewings of the future in Rhuidean. Tavalad was at the meeting with Rand and Aviendha's children when the Aiel decided to go to war with the Seanchan; he took longer to convince than the others.

Tavan Shandare. One of Careane's Warders. A Cairhienin, he was 5'7" tall, and slim, which made his shoulders appear wider; they were wide enough for his size as it was. He was even quicker than Venr, another of Careane's Warders. Tavan was not a Darkfriend. He and Careane's other two Warders were killed when they attempted to rescue her from Lady Shiaine's house on Full Moon Street.

Tavar, the. A district of Tear where farmers went to sell crops.

Tavolin, Elricain. *See* Elricain Tavolin

Tazanovni, Pevara. *See* Pevara Tazanovni

tcheran. An Age of Legends board game, thought of by Moridin and Semirhage. The game used powerful pieces called High Counselors and Spires.

Teacal. A powerful Domani nobleman who was supposed to be following Ituralde. Because Alsalam's orders sometimes went straight to the men under Ituralde instead of to Ituralde, four pitched battles occurred between different groups of Ituralde's men, Teacal among them.

Teadra. An ancient name of Birgitte. As Teadra, she foiled Moghedien's plot to lay Lews Therin by his heels. Teadra did not know who Moghedien was and died before Moghedien could exact revenge, but Moghedien remembered her.

Tear. A nation and its capital city on the Sea of Storms, between Mayene and Illian. Its sigil was three white crescent moons arranged diagonally: the Moons, or the Crescent Moons. Its banner was the Moons slanting across a field half red, half gold; the field was divided diagonally, with the gold part of the banner against the staff. The crescent moons ran down the dividing line; thus the nearest to the staff was the highest.

The nation of Tear was founded in FY 994 (or at least, given the difficulty in determining true dates, supposedly in the year that Hawkwing died) by a group of nobles led by Lord Istaban Novares and Lady Yseidre Tirado. Declaring independence as soon as they had confirmation of Hawkwing's death, they initially held only the Stone of Tear and the eponymous city, but had the advantage that Tear was one of Hawkwing's provinces and the Stone the greatest fortress of the day. They were immediately engaged in fighting with those trying to reestablish the nations of Fergansea and Moreina, all of whom wanted the strong port, and also against those trying to seize all of Hawkwing's empire.

Struggles for power among more than a dozen nobles of roughly equal strength led to the organization of the High Lords well before the end of the war, some accounts claiming that it occurred as early as FY 1050. Not until the end of the War of the Hundred Years did Tear's borders approach anything near those of Tear at the time of the Last Battle, and the absorption of part of Mar Haddon long after the war increased its size considerably. The city of Tear was always called Tear, and the Stone of Tear was actually built in the last days of the Breaking. The city was the great port of Essenia, and the Stone had permanent apartments for rulers when they visited. After the Trolloc Wars, Tear became the capital city of Moreina. The rooms that had been the apartments of visiting kings and queens of Essenia then became the home of the kings and queens of Moreina. After the War of the Hundred Years, when the city of Tear became the capital of the eponymous nation, no High Lord or Lady ever had power enough to claim those rooms, so they remained empty for nearly a thousand years, with only mice making tracks in the dust until Rand al'Thor took them as his own.

Until Rand and the Aiel between them seized the Stone of Tear, that fortress had never fallen to any army or siege. It even held out against Artur Hawkwing, with a number of Aes Sedai trapped inside, though it was eventually surrendered to his forces as part of negotiations that took that whole part of the land into Hawkwing's camp.

Tear and Illian had more wars after Hawkwing's empire collapsed than any other two nations. Illianers and Tairens did not merely dislike one another; it was a matter of spite, contempt, even hatred. Each viewed the other as low and vile, sneaky thieves, without honor—the sort who would stab one in the back to steal one's purse after one had saved him from drowning, and then try to seduce one's wife and daughter while wearing the clothes he had taken from one's still warm corpse.

Tear had one of the three false Dragons who sprang up after Logain was captured and before Rand declared himself. This man gathered his forces in Haddon Mirk, but the Tairens captured him and beheaded him on the spot.

The Defenders of the Stone were the elite unit of the Tairen army—the only permanent formation of that army. They were analogous to the Queen's Guard in Andor. They also acted as the Watch in the city of Tear. Their duties did not normally take them beyond the city to any great degree, however, except in times of war. They normally numbered between fifteen hundred and two thousand men total.

Unlike armies raised by Tear in time of war, in the Defenders commoners often rose to rank. Their commander—the Captain of the Stone—at the time of the Last Battle was Rodrivar Tihera.

Defenders' uniforms were black coats with puffy sleeves striped black-and-gold and rimmed helmets with steel bars for faceguards. Plumes on helmets indicated rank for officers. Three short fat white plumes indicated the Captain of the Stone; two short white plumes a captain, one short white plume for a lieutenant and one short black plume for an under-lieutenant. They wore brightly burnished breastplates, and officers had white cuffs on their coats. The Captain of the Stone had three intertwined lines of gold braid in a broad band around his white cuff, a captain had a single narrow line of gold braid around his cuff, a lieutenant had a single narrow line of black braid around his white cuff and an under-lieutenant's cuffs were plain white. Common soldiers had black cuffs on their coats, squadmen had cuffs that were striped like their sleeves and bannermen had gold cuffs.

"The Stone stands!" and "The Stone still stands!" were battle cries of the Defenders.

The Defenders most often functioned in the field as cavalry, but they also had to be able to function as foot soldiers. Afoot, they used their swords and long spears; they had some archers but no pikes.

Like the armies of other lands, the army of Tear in fact consisted of personal levies raised by nobles, especially High Lords and Ladies. Usually, a lady would have a Master of the Horse who commanded for her in the field, but this was not always so. A lord was expected to lead and command in person. In the Tairen military, commoners seldom rose to a high rank except in the foot, which was largely despised and relatively few in number. Most officers were younger lords, younger sons and the like.

Tear had no real naval forces. When pirates troubled Tairen shipping interests, a noble was directed to raise whatever forces he needed to put them down. Historically, the same method was used whenever ships were needed for military reasons.

The carrying of swords by any but nobles and Defenders of the Stone was prohibited in the city of Tear, but outlanders were usually not bothered, at least if they looked of sufficient rank. Neither were retainers of nobles, usually, especially if the noble was of sufficient rank. After Rand took the Stone, he changed the law.

As in most countries, the view on marriage was that like should marry like. A noble might dally with a commoner, but never marry there. Commoners might dream of marrying a noble, but when they heard of the actuality, as in Andor, the usual view was that it was ridiculous at best, obscene at worst, and a sure course for disaster.

The city of Tear was Ogier-built, and a Waygate stood outside the city in the great pastureland where the High Lords ran their famous horse herds. Tear was the greatest port on the Sea of Storms; the Stone of Tear was the fortress that guarded it. Built on flats on the southern coast around the mouth of the River Erinin where it divided into the Fingers of the Dragon and passed into the Sea of Storms, it sat well away from the sea, and any ships coming to port were required to navigate up through one of the "fingers," guided by a Tairen pilot. There were stone docks on the west bank of the river; this was the port district, called the Maule, a rough area. The docks were backed by stone warehouses, separated by muddy dirt streets; the warehouse district was called the Chalm and the farmers' market district the Tavar. Houses, inns and taverns in the outer city were of wood and stone, and the roofs of slate or tile with oddly sharp corners, some rising to a point.

A high wall of dark gray stone surrounded the inner city, which contained white square-domed palaces and pointed towers with balconies encircling them. There were paved streets inside the city, and the buildings inside the wall were much like those outside, only bigger. Grand structures mixed together with more humble businesses and residences. One large hall had massive square columns across the front, with fifty steps rising to bronze doors five spans high; it was flanked by a bakery and a tailor's shop. Commoners did not live in the inner city. Its population just before the Last Battle was 300,000 people.

Tear produced carpets that were considered among the finest, and clocks which, along with those from Illian, were considered second only to the Sea Folk clocks for quality. Olives were a major crop, producing olive oil for cooking and lamps. Wine, brandy, cheese and lace were also produced. While Ghealdan was the only source of first-quality alum, Tear, like Arafel, supplied large quantities of second-quality alum and were the only sources aside from Ghealdan until the discovery of deposits in Andor; alum put as much into the nation's coffers as did olive oil. Glass and glassware, dyes, wool, cloth, pearls, salt fish and other preserved fish packed in oil, timber (both fine woods and bulk), armor, swords and cutlery were other items sold. Andor and Tear were major suppliers of grain and foodstuffs to Cairhien. There were mines (iron, gold, silver, in various locations) in the Spine of the World, but there was often trouble with the Aiel, so there was very little mining of gold or silver, and not a great deal of iron. For horses, Tairen blood stock was considered the finest breeding stock in the world. Tairens were considered second only to the Sea Folk as shipbuilders, though Mayene came very close in quality if nowhere near in quantity.

Tear, High Lord of. One of the council that ruled Tear, raised from the Lords of the Land; only a High Lord was allowed into the Heart of the Stone. Although noblewomen of high rank, High Ladies, were numbered among the ruling council and had as much power and influence as the men from the beginning, the ruling nobles were referred to collectively as the High Lords.

Tear, Stone of. *See* Stone of Tear

Tebreille din Gelyn South Wind. A Sea Folk Windfinder to Wavemistress Mareil of Clan Mushien. Her strength level was 17(5). She was Talaan's aunt. Caire and Tebreille were sisters; they disliked each other intensely and had a more than strong rivalry. Tebreille was about 5'5" tall, slightly shorter than Caire, and her face was somewhat sterner. They had the same big, almost black eyes, the same straight nose and the same strong chin. Tebreille was part of the circle that used the Bowl of the Winds, and not at all pleased that her sister was given the command. She went to Caemlyn with Elayne's group and left Caemlyn with the Wavemistress Zaida.

Tedosian. A High Lord of Tear; his wife was Alteima. He had a thick body, graying hair and a pointed beard. He was falsely self-effacing around Rand. Thom forged a note to be found by Tedosian, linking Carleon, truthfully, with Alteima. Tedosian was part of the group that Rand chastised for not obeying his orders to lower taxes, deal with Mayene and ship grain to Illian. Tedosian killed Carleon in a hunting "accident." He was then poisoned by Alteima and put into Estanda's care, where he recovered. After a meeting with an agent of Sebban Balwer's, he joined the rebellion near Haddon Mirk. Merana and Rafela negotiated a settlement with Tedosian and the other rebels; that settlement made Darlin king.

Tedronai, Elan Morin. Ishamael's name in the Age of Legends.

Tefan. A king of Khodomar, one of the nations that arose after the Trolloc Wars. Tefan was one of three who sent armies into Shandalle against Artur Hawkwing in FY 943.

Tehan, Captain. The captain of *The Victory of Kidron*, the ship that brought Tuon from Seanchan. A wide, weathered woman with a lined face and white hair and incredible green eyes, she was a Captain of the Green.

Teire Alentaine. An Aes Sedai of the Gray Ajah and the loyalist contingent. Her strength level was 32(20). She was part of the effort to kidnap Rand and take him to the White Tower; she escaped with Covarla Baldene.

Tel Janin Aellinsar. Sammael's name in the Age of Legends.

Tel Norwin. One of the victorious battle sites of Rashima Kerenmosa, the Soldier Amyrlin.

Tel'aran'rhiod. In the Old Tongue, "the Unseen World," or "the World of Dreams," a world glimpsed in dreams which was believed by the ancients to permeate and surround all other possible worlds. What happened to living things in the World of Dreams was real; a wound taken there would still exist on awakening, and one who died there did not wake at all. Otherwise, though, nothing done there affected the waking world in any way. Many could touch *Tel'aran'rhiod* for a few moments in their dreams, but few ever had the ability to enter it at will; others could enter with the use of a special *ter'angreal*. Time flowed differently there: an hour in *Tel'aran'rhiod* could be minutes in the waking world, or the other way around. Space also worked differently: those who brought themselves into *Tel'aran'rhiod* could go where they wished at will, and, by using need, could be taken to a location where they could find something vital or required. Some, such as Rand, could enter the World of Dreams in the flesh, using a weave different from that used in Traveling or Skimming.

Among the Aiel Wise Ones were dreamwalkers, who were skilled at entering and functioning in the Dream. It was said that the Shadow, in the last days of the Age of Legends, caused people to be forcibly brought into *Tel'aran'rhiod*. The World of Dreams was called the wolf dream by wolves and wolfbrothers.

Telabin, Lord. A nobleman of Bethal in Ghealdan. Telabin had a palace in Bethal, and *Cha Faile* reported that Alliandre walked in its gardens alone there every morning. Telabin thought that she was still there when she went to meet with Perrin.

Telaisien, Queen. A queen of Andor during the War of the Hundred Years. She reigned from FY 1085 to FY 1103. During her reign, Esmara Getares made a good stab at taking all of Hawkwing's empire; she had considerable success until she tried to conquer Andor.

Telamon, Lews Therin. *See* Lews Therin Telamon

telarti. A Seanchan term for a woman with fire in her soul.

Tell Lewin. A man of the Two Rivers, the nephew of Flann and brother of Dannil. Like his brother, he was a skinny beanpole with a pickaxe for a nose, but he wore thin mustaches in the Domani style. He was not much older than Perrin. Tell was part of the original band that hunted Trollocs with Perrin. He followed Perrin to Caemlyn, Dumai's Wells, Cairhien, Ghealdan, Amadicia, and on to the Last Battle.

Tellaen, Lord. A Domani nobleman who gave shelter to the Dragon Reborn in his log manor house in the east of Arad Doman. Heavy and having a thin mustache, Tellaen put himself at risk by accommodating Rand, Asha'man and Bashere's army, but the chaos in Arad Doman at the time minimized the danger.

Tellindal Tirraso. A clerk who worked in Lews Therin's headquarters in the War of Power. He was killed in an attack by Demandred.

Tema. The leather-faced head groom at the Lord's Stable of Agelmar's keep in Fal Dara.

Temaile Kinderode. A Cairhienin Aes Sedai of the Gray Ajah publicly and of the Black Ajah in truth. She had a strength level of 17(5). Born in 943 NE, she went to the White Tower in 960 NE. After spending ten years as a novice and nine years as Accepted, she was raised to the shawl in 979 NE. About 5'2" tall, with big blue eyes, dark hair and a fox-shaped face, she appeared fragile, like a pretty child. Temaile had no Warder. Her proclivity for bullying was noted as a novice, which was part of the reason she was so long a novice, but it was thought she had been broken of this, though it was noted as Accepted that she was very strict with the novices. She was an out-and-out sadist who liked to hurt people, both emotionally and physically. Temaile was a good negotiator, with a reputation for making sure that all sides bore an equal weight of pain. She was one of the original thirteen members of the Black Ajah who fled from the White Tower. In Tanchico, she tormented Amathera; Elayne and Egeanin found her doing so and left her unconscious there after knocking her out.

Temaile and others of the Black Ajah then went to Amador, where Temaile tortured Jorin Arene into submission. The group was coopted by Moghedien, who ordered Temaile to search for Nynaeve. When Liandrin failed in her attempt to use Compulsion on Moghedien, Temaile tortured her before handing her over to her Darkfriend captors. Moghedien ordered Temaile, Eldrith, Asne and Chesmal to follow her to Samara. Eldrith failed to keep her bond to her Warder Kennit masked, and he tracked her down in Ghealdan and tried to kill her. She and her companions fled to Caemlyn hoping to find Elayne and Nynaeve, both of whom they believed Moghedien very much wanted to get her hands on. Asne, Chesmal and Eldrith were all intimidated by Temaile, who took control over the group despite the fact that Eldrith stood higher in the Power. The three grew more afraid of her after her preparation of Liandrin for her fate.

Temaile was not at Lady Shiaine's house when Elayne and her allies went to arrest the Black Ajah members, but she arrived soon after and helped take Elayne captive. She was captured when Birgitte and her forces rescued Elayne. When Elayne went to the prison disguised as a Forsaken to try to gain information, Jaq Lounalt tried to rescue Temaile and the others. Elayne prevailed, until Mellar appeared; before he got away with her copy of the foxhead medallion, Mellar, working under orders, killed Temaile.

Temalien, Cariandre. *See* Cariandre Temalien

Temanin. The King of Eharon at the signing of the Compact of the Ten Nations.

"Tempo of Infinity." An artwork by Ceran Tol, a valuable piece seen in Sammael's apartments in Illian. He told Graendal that he had found it in a stasis-box.

Ten Nations. The countries that formed the first league of nations approximately two hundred years after the Breaking, as a defense against the forces of the Dark One. Coremanda, Essenia, Manetheren, Eharon, Aelgar, Aramaelle, Almoren, Aridhol, Coremanda, Eharon, Essenia, Jaramide, Manetheren and Safer were members. *See* individual nations

Ten Nations, Covenant of. *See* Compact of the Ten Nations

Tenets, the. The body of principles that Whitecloaks lived by, compiled by the founder of the Children of the Light, Lothair Mantelar.

Tenjile, Alise. *See* Alise Tenjile

tenmi. Seanchan term for a paperlike substance used to create portable buildings.

Tenobia si Bashere Kazadi. The Queen of Saldaea, Her Illumined Majesty, Shield of the North and Sword of the Blightborder, High Seat of House Kazadi, First Lady of Shahayni, Asnelle, Kunwar and Ganai. Born in 975 NE, she took the throne in 991 NE. About 5'7" tall, with a large nose, a wide mouth and large tilted eyes of a dark deep blue that was almost purple, she had a narrow waist, a round bosom and a high voice. Tenobia was touchy about anything she perceived as a threat to her reign in Saldaea. She trusted the counsel of soldiers and no one else.

Tenobia had an Aes Sedai advisor, but in Elaida's eyes, this woman became too much associated with Tenobia. This Aes Sedai advisor was one of the uncommitteds, supporting neither the rebels nor Elaida, and she vanished without a trace after the troubles began in the Tower. Elaida sent a Red sister, Memara, to rein in Tenobia; she believed Memara could control Tenobia without ever letting her see the leash. Tenobia was huffy about White Tower interference in Saldaea and indignant over Memara. Elaida ordered Tenobia kidnapped, but it never came off.

Tenobia had simple requirements for the man she would marry. He was required to be a poet, philosopher, scholar and warrior, all of the finest degree. He had to be able to cleave Trollocs in two while composing poetry, to be a hero out of legend while discoursing on philosophy. She wanted a man strong enough to master her—she despised weaklings—but she expected that he would give way whenever she wished; she was not a wimp herself, and had no intention of being submissive. In short, she carried the normal Saldaean woman's view of a proper husband to the furthest extreme, with the result that no one believed she would ever find a husband to suit her. Tenobia began angling to marry her uncle Kalyan to Queen Ethenielle, and was successful.

In the Last Battle, Tenobia was killed after Agelmar, acting under Graendal's Compulsion, sent her into danger.

Teodora. A Saldaean woman who was the older sister of Hadnan Kadere. She taught him his letters and numbers. When she found out that he was a Darkfriend, he killed her because he was sure that she would not keep silent. Kadere always thought of her when he killed a woman.

ter'angreal. A device that used the One Power to accomplish a specific function. The forms taken by the devices and the functions served were varied. Some devices required the use of the One Power to activate while others did not.

Terakuni, Berisha. *See* Berisha Terakuni

Teramina. An Aes Sedai of the Green Ajah who was unaccounted for after the Seanchan raid on the White Tower. Egwene thought it possible that she was Mesaana, but Teramina was not very strong in the One Power and had been in the Tower for years, which made it unlikely.

Teran, Widow. A woman in Mardecin, Amadicia. Noy Torvald scraped out a living by doing odd jobs for her.

Terasian, Ishigari. *See* Ishigari Terasian

Teresia. A former queen of Ghealdan. After mishandling the Prophet, she was dragged from her bed in the middle of the night and forcibly married to a merchant, Beron Goraed, to disbar her from the throne. She was replaced by Alliandre.

Terhana Library. One of the great libraries, found in Bandar Eban, Arad Doman.

Termendal, Kyera. A poet of Shiota, and a translator of *The Prophecies of the Dragon* between FY 700 and 800.

Termool. The southernmost part of the Aiel Waste on the coastal area east of the

Drowned Lands. It was a lifeless, waterless expanse of sand dunes that could rise three hundred feet high. Fierce windstorms could dramatically change the landscape, and conditions there were so harsh that it was avoided even by the Aiel. It was also called the Waterless Sands.

Termylle. A queen of Andor during the War of the Hundred Years. She reigned from FY 1046 to FY 1054.

Tervail Dura. Beonin's Taraboner Warder. Dark-haired, with a bold nose, he had a deep white scar running along his lean jaw. The day Logain was Healed, Tervail was guarding him. Tervail was unaware that Beonin was with the rebels as a spy for Elaida. When they returned to Tar Valon, he thought that she was going to try to kill Elaida, and offered to do it for her.

Teryane. A Saldaean merchant's daughter from Mehar who was Vilnar's intended. Vilnar, a Saldaean soldier who patrolled Caemlyn after Rand had taken the city, worried that her father wanted a soldier for a son more than Teryane wanted one for a husband.

Teryl Wynter. A Warder of Seonid Traighan. A Murandian, with dark reddish hair, a curled mustache and eyes blue enough for an Aielman, Teryl was about 6'1" tall, lean and hard, and thirty years old at the time of Dumai's Wells. He and Seonid and Furen, his fellow Warder, took part in the battle at Dumai's Wells, and later accompanied Perrin to Ghealdan. He had contempt for Masema's rabble.

Tesan. A Taraboner Aes Sedai of the White Ajah and the loyalist contingent. Tesan wore her hair in beaded braids. An arithmetist who applied numbers to logic, she argued with Astrelle over the rate of food spoilage in the White Tower. Tesan was also one of a group of Whites whom Egwene attempted to school on dealing with Rand.

Tesen, Mil. *See* Mil Tesen

Tesien Jorhald. A sister of the Red Ajah when Pevara was new to the shawl. Tesien insisted at that time that Pevara drop her friendship with Seaine, which she did. Reds discouraged friendships outside their Ajah.

Teslyn Baradon. An Illianer Aes Sedai of the Red Ajah and the loyalist contingent, with a strength level of 17(5). Born in 870 NE, she went to the White Tower in 885 NE. After spending seven years as a novice and five as Accepted, Teslyn was raised to the shawl in 897 NE and raised Sitter for the Red in 985 NE at age 115, although she was young to be a Sitter, having worn the shawl for only 88 years; she replaced one of the three who were forced to resign and were exiled in the wake of the male channeler pogrom, which Teslyn disapproved of, although she kept silent out of Ajah loyalty. About 5'5" tall, she had dark brown eyes and brown hair, narrow shoulders, gaunt cheeks, a thin mouth, a narrow nose and bony fingers; physically she was quite strong. She ran Elaida a close second for severity; no one ever thought her beautiful. Before her capture by the Seanchan, she was a thin, almost scrawny woman, and some might leave out the almost. Mat thought she looked as if she ate briars.

In 999 NE Elaida forced her to resign her chair and go to Ebou Dar; although Teslyn had supported her, Elaida wished to demonstrate that she could strike anyone. Teslyn resented that enough to work against her. She gave Joline, who was also in Ebou Dar, forkroot to prevent her from interfering with Elayne and Nynaeve's plans. She was captured by the Seanchan, made *damane* and given the name "Tessi." She was rescued by Mat Cauthon. After less than two months as a *damane*, she was fleshed out and was no longer so scrawny in appearance.

She also changed in other ways; she was fearful of being retaken by the Seanchan, and sometimes responded to orders in Seanchan accents in spite of herself, a fact that she purely hated.

On returning to the White Tower, she found things uncomfortable, joined the Dragonsworn and took part in the Last Battle, Healing the wounded and making a gateway for Mat's troops.

Tess. Melfane's cousin, who did not take care of herself properly while pregnant.

Tessi. Teslyn's *damane* name.

Tetsuan. An Aes Sedai of the Red Ajah who served as the Amyrlin Seat during the Trolloc Wars. Her jealousy of Queen Eldrene led her to betray Manetheren, with the result that that nation, alone, faced the assault of a huge army of Trollocs and Dreadlords and was destroyed. When her deed was discovered, she was stripped of stole and staff, deposed and stilled. After the usual manner of the White Tower, the actual reasons were kept secret insofar as non–Aes Sedai were concerned. After being stilled, she lived three years scrubbing floors in the White Tower.

Teva. A man Hurin knew who got so mad at a hornet buzzing round his ears that he kicked the nest.

Teven, Feast of. A festival celebrated in the month of Amadaine in Illian. In 998 NE, it coincided with the calling of the Hunt for the Horn.

Teven Aerwin. Author of *The Dance of the Hawk and the Hummingbird,* a book that purported to set forth the proper conduct of men toward women and women toward men.

Teven Marwin. A young Two Rivers man who joined Perrin's band and was killed in an ambush by Trollocs in the Two Rivers.

Thad Haren. A brickmaker and tracker from Kore Springs, Andor. He had served under Bryne in the Queen's Guards, and it was said that he could track the wind over stone by moonlight. He turned the brickyard he owned near Bryne's estates over to his sons so that he could follow Bryne in his search for Siuan.

Thad Torfinn. A skinny Two Rivers farmer with nervous mannerisms, at least around Faile. Thad and Jon Ayellin went to Faile to settle the boundaries of their fields; since neither knew the true boundaries, she told them to split the difference. Even though Thad rarely left his farm except to go into Emond's Field, he joined Perrin's army at Malden.

Thakan'dar. The fog-enshrouded valley below the slopes of Shayol Ghul in the

Blasted Lands, where Myrddraal swords were made. Thakan'dar was bitter cold and dry as a desert, incapable of sustaining any life whatsoever. It ran east to west, with Shayol Ghul situated at the western end and a mountain pass in the east. The valley was the site of considerable warfare during the Last Battle.

Thakanos, Morvrin. *See* Morvrin Thakanos

Tham Felmley. An Andoran brickmason sentenced to death by Morgase and executed for murdering his brother; she later discovered that he was innocent.

Thane clan. A Two Rivers family. *See* Berin, Jaim, Jon, Kari, Lem *and* Nela Thane

Thane, Master. An Emond's Field man. Jac Coplin and Len Congar were accused of stealing his cow, but Perrin made Master Thane prove it before he allowed the Village Council to strap the thieves.

Thane, Mistress. A member of the Women's Circle in Emond's Field. When Rand visited the Royal Palace of Caemlyn disguised as Nuli, he told Nynaeve, so that he could speak with her and Lan alone, that Mistress Thane said Nynaeve wanted to see him right away on Women's Circle business about Cenn Buie.

Tharne, Duranda. *See* Duranda Tharne

Tharon. An area producing wine.

Theodohr. The commander of the Andoran cavalry during the Last Battle.

Theodrin Dabei. A Domani Aes Sedai of the Brown Ajah and the rebel contingent, with a potential strength level of 15(3). Born in 966 NE, she went to the White Tower in 981 NE. After spending eleven years as a novice and seven years as Accepted, she was raised to the shawl by Egwene's decree in 999 NE. Theodrin was apple-cheeked, with a mouth that turned up as if she liked to smile. Willowy, with a swanlike neck and copper skin, she dressed modestly. Theodrin was a wilder; her self-taught wilder trick was to be able to make a man want to kiss her or leave her alone. Her block was that she couldn't channel without the presence of a man she felt strongly about. That block was broken with the use of twins: Charel, a handsome young groom, and Marel, his twin sister. Charel was allowed in the classrooms so that Theodrin could channel, and was later surreptitiously replaced by his sister. On being shown that Marel was indeed a girl, Theodrin was able to channel at will. She attempted to help Nynaeve overcome her block, but was unsuccessful.

While in Salidar, Theodrin reached the point where she should have been tested for Aes Sedai, but could not be, since the testing *ter'angreal* was in the White Tower. When Egwene was raised to the Amyrlin Seat, she decreed that Theodrin was to be raised to the shawl immediately. Theodrin chose the Brown Ajah, but was still treated as an Accepted by many Aes Sedai because of her unorthodox raising. She swore fealty to Egwene largely because she felt she had no choice but to hitch her wagon to Egwene's star. Egwene assigned Theodrin to accept Romanda's offer to assist her until she could be raised properly in Tar Valon; she was to gather information and pass it to Egwene. Theodrin was not wholeheartedly pleased by the prospect, knowing that it meant more of being treated not as Aes Sedai but more as an Accepted who had to be watched; the Browns even appointed a guardian to look over her shoulder and make sure she didn't do anything wrong. On the other hand, it was a chance to get back at the sisters who treated her that way.

Theodrin was part of the embassy to the Black Tower to bond Warders, but did not choose one there. She fought alongside Pevara and some Asha'man in the Last Battle; Pevara thought that she intended to bond one of those Asha'man, Jonneth.

Theory of Instructions. A philosophical theory known to the Aes Sedai that fell out of favor.

Thera. A *da'covale* belonging to Lady Suroth; she was the former Lady Amathera, Panarch of Tarabon. *See* Amathera Aelfdene Casmir Lounault

Therava. A Wise One of the Shaido Aiel with the ability to channel and a strength level of 12(+1). About six feet tall, with blue eyes, sun-darkened complexion, and dark red hair streaked with white, she was hawk-eyed and hawk-faced. Her hands were rough, not callused so much as strong and harsh, and her voice was like stone. Appearing to be between thirty-five and forty, she was in reality over two hundred years old, making her one of the oldest living Aiel Wise Ones. She wore necklaces of ivory and gold, and many clattering bracelets.

One of Sevanna's inner circle of plotters, she accompanied Sevanna to the Aes Sedai camp the day she saw Rand beaten and took part in or at least was present at the murder of Desaine.

At Dumai's Wells, she took half the Shaido Wise Ones to the west.

Therava hated Galina as a betrayer, as an oathbreaker and as an Aes Sedai, but at the same time had the hots for her, which only intensified the hate. Therava really got off on making an Aes Sedai submit to her; Aes Sedai outraged Therava by not showing proper respect. After the oath to make Galina obey was administered, Therava dressed Galina in *gai'shain* robes of white silk and had her when she wished. She was more cruel toward Galina than any of the others, allowing no slips, however tiny.

Therava also assumed possession of the binder and kept it until Theril stole it.

The conclave that the Wise Ones held without informing Sevanna named Therava as Sevanna's advisor—they blamed Sevanna for the scattering of the Shaido. Even though she had earlier fallen in with Sevanna's plans, Therava did not like Sevanna, and believed she had led them all into a disaster from which there might be no recovery. She despised Sevanna's fixation on Rand.

When Therava confronted Sevanna over Galina, all of the Wise Ones who were part of Sevanna's inner circle sided with Therava.

After the Shaido were routed at Malden, Therava, Modarra and Belinde led a large number of Shaido to return to the Three-fold Land; on the way, they recaptured Galina.

Theril. A young Amadician man who was taken *gai'shain* by the Shaido. Theril was a lanky, skinny-faced fourteen-year-old who was taller than his father Alvon, which made the Shaido believe he was older. The two of them were famed for having attempted escape three times and getting farther each time before being recaptured. Theril and his father were sworn to Faile, and Theril procured Therava's binder for her. He followed her and the others and saw Galina make the building collapse on them. He saw Maighdin's signal and went for help.

Therille Marza. A Domani seamstress who was one of the refugees who went to the Two Rivers. She lived in Emond's Field and made Faile six dresses; Faile thought that she required a firm hand and constant vigilance to keep her from dressing Faile for the court in Bandar Eban.

Therin Lugay. An Amadician man who owed Ronde Macura a favor. Cursed with a nagging wife and a shrewish mother-in-law, he was to carry Elayne and Nynaeve away from the village to Tar Valon in his cart, keeping them drugged with forkroot. When he found Ronde and Luci unconscious, he decided to set out for Altara or Murandy.

Therva Maresis. An Aes Sedai of the Yellow Ajah and the rebel contingent, with a strength level of 34(22). Born in 862 NE, she went to the White Tower in 879 NE. After spending eight years as a novice and seven years as Accepted, she was raised to the shawl in 894 NE. Slender, with a long nose which she sometimes tapped, Therva was excitable by nature; it was considered a bad sign when she wore an expression of utter and unshakable serenity. When Nynaeve Healed Siuan and Leane, Therva was present and noted that she thought Fire might be useful in Healing heart problems. Because of her ability to read residues, Therva was one of six sisters sent to investigate the large channeling event outside Shadar Logoth.

thief-catcher. A type of private detective used by the High Lords of Tear to apprehend thieves. Thief-catchers also hired out for private services.

thief-taker. The term used for a thief-catcher in nations other than Tear.

Third Compact, the. *See* Coalition, the

Third Gem. An Ebou Dari dice game. There was one dicer in the game, with a crowd of onlookers betting against or for his tosses. In other lands it was called Cat's Paw and Feathers Aloft.

Thirteen Sins. In Ebou Dar, figures carved into a lintel at the Kin house. They included Envy, Gossip and Greed.

Thirteenth Depository. A section of the White Tower Library where secret documents were kept. There had always been rumors of a closed section of the White Tower library, though usually whispered rumors—a section containing records and information available only to a select few even among the Aes Sedai. The fact that the White Tower had never issued a direct denial—so far as could be determined from any public record—militated for the existence of this closed section, or of some body of records or information that was closely held, at least.

Beyond the rumored existence of such secret records, the only other thing known came from another whispered rumor, which, interestingly enough, the White Tower had also never contradicted straight out. According to that, there was a Tower law covering the secret repository. By that law, unless you were one of the few authorized, penetrating or attempting to penetrate the records carried severe penalties, while revealing either the existence of the repository or any of the information contained in it was on a level with treason or rebellion. Additionally, this law itself was supposed to be a part of the repository, itself thereby secret and protected, thus completing the circle of secrecy in a manner that would be incredible among any except the Aes Sedai or the Seanchan.

While the secret records were officially open only to the Amyrlin Seat, the Keeper of the Chronicles, and the Sitters in the Hall of the Tower, they were in the keeping of a handful of librarians, who also had access, of course. The librarians just weren't considered when the others thought of who had access. They were the librarians, so ubiquitous in the Library as to be almost part of the furniture, or the fabric of the building.

Thom Grinwell. The name Mat used in Caemlyn when meeting Morgase and Gaebril.

Thom Merrilin. An Andoran gleeman. His full name was Thomdril Merrilin, and he was sometimes called the Gray Fox. He was six feet tall, and lanky, with a leathery face, sharp blue eyes, white hair long enough to touch his collar, bushy white eyebrows, and long white mustaches that hung down on either side of his mouth. Thom was accomplished in High Chant, Plain Chant and Common, juggling, music and the use of a variety of weapons. Before he gained a limp, he was a first-rate tumbler and could high-walk with some small facility. He had a wide-ranging knowledge of geopolitics, history, language and cultures.

He was House-bard to House Trakand in Andor; even then he was known as a skilled player of the Game of Houses. He advised and assisted Morgase's mother, who taught him much. He also assisted Morgase in gaining the Lion Throne during the Succession and became Court-bard. He assassinated Taringail Damodred on learning of his plot to kill Morgase and replace her on the throne; there were rumors that someone close to Morgase had killed him, but Thom was never named. Afterward, he became Morgase's lover but drew her ire when he left suddenly without telling her why, to help his nephew Owyn, who had been gentled as part of the male channeler pogrom. When Thom returned to Caemlyn, he and Morgase had an argument, and she issued arrest warrants which she never canceled. He fled Andor and became a gleeman, traveling widely.

He went to Emond's Field to perform for Bel Tine, and left with Moiraine, Lan, Rand, Mat, Perrin and Egwene. He, Rand and Mat became separated from the rest at Shadar Logoth. He saved the boys from a Myrddraal in Whitebridge, escaping largely because the Myrddraal was more interested in following Rand and Mat, though he did put up a good fight and wounded it, perhaps

even killed it. He himself was wounded in the leg and would have died had not an Aes Sedai shown up just in the nick of time. Like Samitsu, she could regulate her weaves, so she was able to Heal him enough to keep him alive, but he was left with a limp and a scar. When he could finally travel on, he avoided Caemlyn, went to Cairhien and met Dena. Thom wanted out of the business with Rand, but when Dena was killed, he decided he was in whether he wanted to be or not. He assassinated Galldrian, who was behind Dena's murder, setting off the civil war in Cairhien, then traveled to Tar Valon hoping to get some lead on Rand. He had begun drinking heavily by the time Mat found him.

Bitter toward Aes Sedai for what they did to his nephew Owyn, he eventually resolved his feelings, especially toward Moiraine, who had promised to tell him who was responsible for the Red sisters gentling and abandoning Owyn, instead of bringing him to Tar Valon for gentling as required. Owyn was the only man Elaida was involved in taking and gentling, as she had hoped that the deed could be used to break Morgase from Thom's influence, which in fact happened.

Moiraine sent Thom to help and look after Elayne and Nynaeve; he was particularly protective of Elayne, and taught her a lot about the Game of Houses, sharing his knowledge of lands and courts. He felt bereft at Moiraine's supposed death, but her letter to him put doubts in his mind on that account. With Mat and Noal, he rescued Moiraine from the Aelfinn and Eelfinn and married her.

During the Last Battle, he went with her to Shayol Ghul and guarded the entrance to the Pit of Doom.

Thorin al Toren al Ban. A king of Manetheren who was Caar's father and Aemon's grandfather.

thornbush. A shrub; also part of the name of a sword form, Lizard in the Thornbush.

Thornhill, Marris. *See* Marris Thornhill

Thoughts Among the Ruins. An ancient work of history studied by Min.

Thousand Flowers. An Aiel game that involved laying out patterns of flat bits of stone carved with what seemed a hundred different symbols.

Thousand Lakes. The chain of lakes that went through the city of Malkier.

thread. In channeling, a segment of a flow, which could be divided into numerous threads. In reference to the One Power, it referred to the Five Powers; e.g., Fire is a thread of the One Power.

threadleaf. A weed that Sahra Covenry was pulling on Mistress Elward's farm just before she was murdered.

Three Foxes. The sign of Agelmar, the Lord of Fal Dara; it was three running red foxes on a field quartered blue and white.

Three Geese, the. A constellation that pointed the way north.

Three Halls of Trade. An institution of commerce in Kandor. In the Last Battle,

Agelmar said that he would not like to see the Three Halls of Trade fall, but Prince Antol said that Kandor had already fallen.

Three Ladies of Maredo. An inn located in Far Madding. Rand walked by it when he was looking for the renegade Asha'man who had tried to kill him. Verin met him nearby and told him that the Seanchan had crossed the border into Illian.

Three Moons, The. An inn found in Tear. When Rand and several women tried to get a large room with a view of the Stone at another inn, The Dragon, the innkeeper offered to escort them to The Three Moons; Cadsuane was having none of that.

Three Oaths. Sworn to by all Accepted becoming Aes Sedai on the Oath Rod: 1) to speak no word that is not true; 2) to make no weapon with which one man may kill another; and 3) never to use the One Power as a weapon except against Shadowspawn or Darkfriends, or in the last extreme defense of her own life or that of her Warder or another Aes Sedai. The first and third oaths came about as a result of ordinary people's suspicion toward the Aes Sedai, and were in place before the beginning of the Trolloc Wars, possibly as much as five hundred years earlier. The second oath grew from tales passed down among Aes Sedai regarding the War of the Shadow, and was the first created after that war. If they did so knowing that it would significantly reduce their lifespan, they had to have a strong motivation. Later women raised were not told, and so knowledge of the effect was lost.

In the days after the Time of Madness, Aes Sedai expected to live as much as seven hundred to eight hundred years, barring accidents. With the advent of the Three Oaths, Aes Sedai lifespan was reduced to a maximum of two hundred to three hundred years, and the phenomenon known as Aes Sedai "agelessness" came about, which meant that it was simply impossible to put an age to the Aes Sedai. The cumulative effect of the Three Oaths is what produced this agelessness. There was no agelessness during the War of the Shadows, of course, and little or none during the Compact of the Ten Nations.

All three oaths were in place by the Trolloc Wars, certainly by the end.

Three Plum Blossoms, The. A waterfront inn in Falme on the Almoth Plain that was renamed after the Seanchan arrived; its previous name included the word "Watcher." Its innkeeper was a fat man. Min, Nynaeve and Elayne met Bayle Domon there to arrange safe passage out of Falme for themselves and Egwene.

Three Plum Court. A three-storied, white-plastered, high-class inn found in Tanchico, Tarabon. Its innkeeper was Rendra. Bayle Domon took Nynaeve, Elayne, Thom and Juilin to stay there; Rendra was his friend. While there, Elayne got drunk and realized that Thom had been her mother's Court-bard and lover.

Three Stars, The. An inn in Ebou Dar where Beslan conspired to overthrow the Seanchan.

Three Toes. The leader of a wolfpack that Perrin spoke to when seeking information about Faile after she was abducted by the Shaido.

Three Towers, The. An inn in Maerone, Cairhien. Mat and Edorion stopped by while making the rounds of the drinking halls frequented by his soldiers.

Three Towers Gate. The western gate leading out of Ebou Dar.

Three-fold Land. The Aiel term for the Aiel Waste. They believed that the Waste was a shaping stone to make them, a testing ground to prove their worth, and a punishment for their sin. *See also* Waste, the

throne. A Seanchan unit of currency.

Throne, Light Blessed. The seat of the Ghealdan monarch.

Throne of the Clouds. The seat of the monarch of Kandor.

Throne of the Light. The seat of the monarch of Tanchico.

Throne of the Winds. The seat of the monarch of Altara at the Tarasin Palace in Ebou Dar.

Thulin. A Shienaran blacksmith in the village of Oak Water. His wife was Gallanha; they had a daughter, Mirala. Dark-haired and dark-skinned, Thulin was lean for a blacksmith. When odd storm clouds started gathering, he and his family packed up and headed north. Thulin stopped by to tell Renald Fanwar where his anvil was buried, but then proceeded to tell Renald that he ought to make weapons and head north as well.

Thum. A person who worked for the merchant Barriga. He was killed by Trollocs at Heeth Tower on the Blightborder.

Thunder Mist. A wolf that was a member of Leafhunter's pack. Perrin spoke with Leafhunter's pack after encountering a scent in the wolf dream (ultimately found to be from Darkhounds) that made his hackles rise. When he asked the pack about it, they all stopped talking with him.

Thunder Walkers. An Aiel warrior society also known as *Sha'mad Conde.*

Thunderbolts, Talmanes'. A unit of soldiers within Mat's Band of the Red Hand. Its formal name was First Banner of the Horse.

Thurasa. A woman on the Domani Council of Merchants who was a victim of Graendal's Compulsion. Graendal found her succulent, and was angered when a gateway bringing a messenger from Moridin nearly took Thurasa's arm off.

Tia mi aven Moridin isainde vadin. Old Tongue for "The grave is no bar to my call," the script that was written on the Horn of Valere.

Tialin. An Aiel Wise One with a strength level of 18(6). Lean and red-haired, with a sharp nose, she was part of the council in Amys' tent meeting about the Aes Sedai on the morning Egwene tried to spy on the Tower sisters and met Gawyn. Tialin was doubtful that Lady Arilyn was an Aes Sedai spy. Tialin was at Dumai's Wells. She took Beldeine to Verin for questioning and reported that Katerine had escaped.

Tiam of Gazar. The developer of the Gazaran Calendar.

Tian. A young man serving as a messenger at Heeth Tower on the Blightborder. Four of his brothers were killed in the Blight; he was Lady Yabeth's only remaining son. Keemlin Rai let him leave Heeth Tower in his place, hoping to keep him out of harm's way.

Tiana Noselle. An Aes Sedai of the Gray Ajah and the rebel contingent, with a strength level of 19(7). Born in 937 NE, she went to the White Tower in 953 NE. After spending six years as a novice and six years as Accepted, she was raised to the shawl in 965 NE. Tiana twice refused the test for Accepted and had problems with the test for Aes Sedai. About 5'2" tall, and slim, with big brown eyes, she had a dimple in her left cheek that made her look younger than her years.

Tiana was chosen Mistress of Novices for the rebels; like the Sitters chosen in Salidar, she was much too young for the job, even if Sheriam was younger. The Sitters thought that since she was too young, it would be easier for her to be shunted aside once they managed to restore the rebels to the Tower. As Mistress of Novices, Tiana was known for being equally sympathetic and stern when it came to the rules. She was never shy about speaking up to Sitters or to the Amyrlin; when she was displeased, her disgruntled expression deepened her dimple and made her look sulky, which she didn't realize.

Egwene replaced her as Mistress of Novices with Rosil of the Yellow Ajah after the Tower reunited.

tickbird. A term for a petty thief who stole whatever he could get his hands on.

Tiedra, Mistress. The innkeeper of The Great Tree in the city of Cairhien; she knew that Verin was Aes Sedai. Plump and sharp-eyed, she charged heavily but did not scrimp on amenities.

Tifan's Well. A small village in Arafel that served a farming community. Aes Sedai Adeleas and Vandene Namelle had retired there to write the history of the world. Moiraine, seeking more knowledge about the prophecies regarding the Dragon Reborn, visited the two. While there, Moiraine was almost killed by a Draghkar that had been warded by a Black Ajah sister, but she was saved by Lan and Jaem, Vandene's Warder.

tiganza. A dance performed by Tinkers. It was danced by women, and could be danced for men, but it was considered by Tinker women a celebration of being a woman. Most movement was from the waist down, involving considerable rolling of the hips, which was emphasized by a shawl held behind the dancer at waist height. The music always included drums and was rhythmically repetitive.

Tigraine Mantear. The daughter of Queen Mordrellen of Andor and Daughter-Heir to the throne of Andor. Her sign was a woman's hand gripping a thorny rose stem with a white blossom. Born in 950 NE, Tigraine was in the White Tower in 966–967 NE; she had no ability to channel, but was awarded the Great Serpent ring anyway, a tradition between Andor and the Tower. Her time in the Tower was largely an education given by women who were very skillful politically. Tigraine married Taringail Damodred, the nephew of King Laman of Cairhien, shortly after her return from the White Tower, as part of a treaty which, it was hoped, would bring lasting peace between Andor and Cairhien. Their son Galadedrid was born in 970 NE.

In 972 NE, she ran away because of a Foretelling by Gitara Moroso, vanishing from Caemlyn and abandoning her husband and son. She fled to the Waste and joined the Aiel, taking the name Shaiel, which was Old Tongue for "Woman Who Is Dedicated." She became *Far Dareis Mai*, which was unheard of for a wetlander. She fell in love with Janduin, clan chief of the Taardad, but refused to give up the spear for him even after she became pregnant. He could refuse her nothing, so she was not forced to return to the Three-fold Land when her pregnancy was discovered. She died of wounds on the slopes of Dragonmount, giving birth to a son during the Battle of the Shining Walls. Her newborn child was found and carried away by Tam al'Thor, an officer in the Illianer Companions.

Tihera, Rodrivar. *See* Rodrivar Tihera

Tijds. A young soldier in Bryne's army for the rebel Aes Sedai who alerted Bryne to the Seanchan attack on the White Tower.

Tim. A young Two Rivers man who joined Perrin's band and was killed by a Trolloc ambush south of the Waterwood.

Time of Change. A term referring to the end of an Age.

Time of Illusions. The Amayar, who practiced the Water Way on Tremalking, believed that their daily reality was an illusion, and they believed a prophecy indicating that the destruction of the female Choedan Kal found on Tremalking would be tied to the end of the Time of Illusions. *See* Illusion, 2nd entry

Time of Madness. Another name used for the Breaking of the World and the years after the Dark One's counterstroke tainted the male half of the True Source, when male Aes Sedai went mad and Broke the World. The exact duration of this period was unknown, but it is believed to have lasted nearly one hundred years. It ended completely only with the death of the last male Aes Sedai.

time units. Days were broken into segments; when a certain time was reached, chimes rang. In the White Tower, First Rise was very early morning, before dawn, followed by Second and Third Rise. High was around midmorning, and Midmorning chimes were also rung. Prime and Trine were in the afternoon. After supper came Full, and Last meant that all novices were supposed to be quiet and in bed. Second Low occurred in the small hours of the morning.

In Cairhien, Second Even was a time when supper could be eaten.

Time, The Wheel of. A book by Sulamein so Bhagad, Chief Historian at the Court of the Sun, the Fourth Age.

Timna. An Amayar woman who was one of the Guides of the Sea Folk, on Tremalking. She saw the glow of the Choedan Kal, and smiled to think that she would see the fulfillment of prophecy and the end of Illusion.

Timolan. The clan chief of the Miagoma Aiel. He was a widower, although the Wise Ones were working to find him a new wife. Timolan was 6'3" tall and weighed 225 pounds. When he was young, he tried to unite the Aiel clans. Timolan was part of the Aiel forces with Rand in Cairhien; he was suspicious that Rhuarc had not accompanied him to fight against the Shaido intrusion into Cairhien, not aware that Rand had been kidnapped by the Aes Sedai.

When learning that Rand had been taken, Timolan thought that Rand had betrayed the Aiel. After the battle at Dumai's Wells, Rand sent him to help deal with the Shaido at Kinslayer's Dagger and later sent him and others to Arad Doman to bring order.

Timora, Lady. A Shienaran woman who was an attendant to Lady Amalisa in Fal Dara. She found Perrin alone in a courtyard and reported it to Liandrin, who had been looking for Perrin, Mat and Rand.

timsin. A root used in tea to relieve a headache.

Tinkers. The Traveling People. *See* Tuatha'an

Tinna. A woman who was turned out of the Tower for complicated reasons she was unwilling to share. She joined the Dragonsworn, and became their leader in the Last Battle. She had the bearing of a lady, the build of an Aiel and the coloring of a Saldaean.

Tion. A Wise One of the Shaido Aiel (not a Jumai) with the ability to channel. About 5'10" tall, and stout, with broad hips, a round face and gray eyes, she often appeared placid. She was a no-nonsense kind of woman, but she was ambitious or she wouldn't have been with Sevanna. Tion often spoke out of turn, at least in Sevanna's estimation. One of Sevanna's inner circle of plotters, she accompanied Sevanna to the Aes Sedai camp the day she saw Rand beaten and took part in or at least was present at the murder of Desaine. She was with Sevanna at Dumai's Wells and at the meeting with "Caddar" and "Maisia." While the Jumai were settled at a captured estate approximately ten days after their arrival in Amadicia, she helped question the Seanchan prisoner.

Tipsy Gelding, The. A small inn in Hinderstap. It was three streets out from the center of town, in the back west corner of the village, and was more of a tavern than an inn. It had a wooden board carved with what looked like a drunken horse sitting inside one of the windows; none of those windows had glass. Mat chose to go there to gamble for supplies; he lost a lot, and then bet everything on one last toss; Mayor Barlden insisted on making the toss. Mat won, but the sun set and everything went crazy.

Tirado, Yseidre. One of the founders of Tear.

Tiras. A Seanchan soldier who was Bakuun's First Lieutenant. A bony man a head taller than Bakuun, he had an unfortunate scrap of beard. He was a good soldier, if a touch overconfident. He brought Bakuun the scouting report of an enemy force not ten miles east, in the Venir Mountains of Altara.

tirewoman. Another term for "maid."

Tirish Adar. A feast celebrated from the rise of the first full moon in Adar until the rise of the next moon. In most places, no one slept during that period.

Tirraso, Tellindal. A clerk who worked in Lews Therin's headquarters in the War of Power. He was killed in an attack by Demandred.

Tishar, Elisane. An Aes Sedai at the formation of the White Tower.

Tius, Varkel. A man with Perrin's army who had trouble getting canvas to repair torn tents.

To Sail Beyond the Sunset. A book read by Loial.

to'raken. A large Seanchan flying animal brought from a parallel world. In general appearance it was similar to the *raken,* except that it was much larger and was mottled brown in color rather than gray. Its wingspan was more than 120 feet. Like the *raken,* it crouched when on the ground, rather than standing erect, raising only its head to look around, but even so its back could be nine feet or more above the ground. An herbivore and an egg layer, it laid one egg at a time. It did not perch in trees, however large, preferring the tops of cliffs or hills.

Unlike the *raken,* which could simply throw itself into the air, a *to'raken* taking off from level ground ran as much as a hundred paces while flapping its wings before launching itself. Its intelligence was roughly equal to that of a horse. As awkward as the *raken,* or more so on the ground, the *to'raken* was neither as agile in the air nor as fast as the *raken,* with a maximum speed of a little more than twice that of a horse. It did not perch on vertical surfaces, nor on surfaces nearly as precipitous as those a *raken* would risk, but on surfaces that were steep, it used the same spread-wing clutching.

The *to'raken* would not fly at all in significant snowfall or heavy rain. Cold weather did not bother it greatly, however, nor did heat.

The *to'raken* could fly much farther than a *raken* without rest, as much as a thousand miles at moderate speed and with only one *morat* in the saddle. It could also carry a much larger load. With one *morat* mounted, a *to'raken* could carry an additional one thousand pounds or more of cargo as far as two hundred miles. It was primarily used for transporting people who needed to be moved quickly, or for other cargo that was considered urgent. While it occasionally was used in battle, with archers or crossbowmen behind a single *morat,* bringing the bowmen low enough and slow enough to be effective also brought the *to'raken* within range of arrows and crossbow bolts from the ground, and an injured *to'raken* did not fly well; in fact, it often refused to fly farther than a safe landing point—safe from the point of view of the *to'raken,* not necessarily of the *morat'to'raken.* Its effectiveness in this role was too low for the risk to an extremely valuable animal. Like the *raken,* the *to'raken* was controlled by reins, attached to rings fixed permanently in the animal's horny nostrils, and knee pressure.

A *morat* who could handle *raken* could handle *to'raken* and vice versa, but *morat'raken* were considered superior to *morat'to'raken.* To order a *morat'raken* to fly a *to'raken* would entail a loss of face for the flier, a fact which even the Blood recognized.

Tobanyi, Isebaille. *See* Isebaille Tobanyi

Tobrad, Master. The innkeeper at the nicest inn in Hinderstap. Joline and Edesina went there to have baths; when Mat went to fetch them, he saw the cook kill Master Tobrad and then killed the cook to preserve his own hide. The next day Mat saw both at the inn.

Tod al'Caar. A young Two Rivers man who was friends with Jondyn Barran. Lantern-jawed and a year younger than Perrin, he joined Perrin's band. Tod's mother willingly let him go because of the honor of her son following Perrin Goldeneyes. Tod fought at Dumai's Wells; afterward he said that he wouldn't mind being an Asha'man, but Perrin could smell that it wasn't true. When Perrin met with Tylee the first time, Tod carried the Red Eagle of Manetheren. He was one of the Two Rivers men who went through the aqueduct to enter Malden.

Todande. A noble House in Altara. It held the throne of Altara for five generations, until High Seat Anarina drained the nation's finances and was deposed and murdered. The House never recovered. *See also* Anarina *and* Maddin Todande

Togita, House. A noble House of Shienar; Easar Togita was king. *See* Easar Togita

toh. Old Tongue for "obligation" or "duty." The Aiel used it in their complex system of correct behavior, *ji'e'toh.*

Tojar. A town from the Age of Legends. Moghedien referred to a night laborer in Tojar as someone who was worked hard.

Tokama, Niko. A female member of the Academy of Cairhien, whose undescribed project Idrien thought was silly.

Toke Fearnim. A stable owner in Jurador from whom Mat bought the Domani razor for Tuon. He was wiry, with a fringe of gray hair.

Tol, Ander. A turnip farmer from the south of Cairhien who gave Rand and his companions a ride into Cairhien after the bubble of evil attacked the rebel camp.

Tol, Ceran. The creator of "Tempo of Infinity," an art piece from the Age of Legends.

Tolen, Eldaya. *See* Eldaya Tolen

Tolmeran Setares. A High Lord of Tear. Lean, with an iron-gray beard, Tolmeran had courage; he was brave enough to hint at doubts that Rand was the Dragon Reborn. He was smart, with far more brains than Weiramon, but with less rank, influence and power. Tolmeran was not in the Stone the night Rand took it, and he questioned the Tairen rebel claim that the fall of the Stone was an Aes Sedai trick. He was as eager to fight the Illianers as any Tairen—the two nations' history was one of wars fought on the slightest excuse—but he seemed a little less likely than the other High Lords to think every battle could be won by one good charge.

Tolmeran fought the Seanchan in Illian with Rand. Rand left him there, and was enraged when he found that Tolmeran and others were returning to Tear, against orders.

Tolvina, Ailene. The stern innkeeper of The Evening Star in Chachin. Moiraine hired two of her bodyguards for escort to a bank.

Toma dur Ahmid. The man who developed the Toman Calendar after the Breaking.

Toma. A townsman who lived during the War of the Shadow. He punched the Da'shain Aiel Coumin in the mouth because Coumin's parents had served Lanfear. The man said that he and others would root out those who had really served the Shadow and treat them as they had Charn, who had been hanged.

Tomada. An Ogier during the War of the Shadow. He was with Coumin when word came that the war had ended, and Shayol Ghul had been sealed with the Forsaken inside.

Tomaka. An alternate name for Shara, given by Rhuarc.

Toman Calendar. A calendar devised by Toma dur Ahmid, recording years After the Breaking (AB). It was adopted approximately two centuries after the death of the last male Aes Sedai.

Toman Head. A peninsula on the west coast, west of Almoth Plain on the Aryth Ocean, between Arad Doman and Tarabon. The peninsula was hilly, sloping up from the harbor, and forested. One of its villages, Atuan's Mill, had a visit from the Seanchan. Its only city was Falme, where the Watchers Over the Waves kept a lookout for the return of Artur Hawkwing's armies before the Seanchan executed them. Liandrin led Nynaeve, Egwene, Elayne and Min there, and Egwene and Min were captured by the Seanchan. It was the site of a major confrontation between Rand and the Seanchan, the Whitecloaks and Ba'alzamon.

There was an abandoned Ogier *stedding* on its mountainous north coast.

Tomanelle. An Aiel clan; its chief was Han.

Tomanes, Mara. *See* Mara Tomanes

Tomares, Sareitha. *See* Sareitha Tomares

Tomas. Verin's Warder. About 5'9" to 5'10" tall, but stocky, he was gray-haired and dark-eyed. Tomas was a Darkfriend, but he wanted a way out. Verin offered him a chance to make up for what he had done, even though there was really no way out; Tomas gratefully accepted. Verin, coming to her own end, gave him poison; while she was taking her own, Tomas was with his family doing the same.

Tomas Trakand. The name that Caraline Damodred called Rand when introducing him to others in the Cairhienin rebel camp.

Tomichi, Mistress. The innkeeper of The Plowman's Blade in Manala, Kandor. A stout, graying woman, she seemed uneasy about two Malkieri stopping at her inn, but cheered up when Moiraine ordered breakfast.

Tomil. A Youngling. Rajar told Tomil and his brother to escort Narenwin Sedai to the Mayor's house when she arrived in Dorlan.

Tonarma, Estevan. *See* Estevan Tonarma

Tora Harad. A mighty fortress from Mat's memories of ancient times. It was known for its ability to withstand a siege.

Tora Shan. The site of a bloody battle from Mat's ancient memories. Mat thought the battle for Cairhien was not much different from Tora Shan.

Toram din Alta Wild Winds. A Sea Folk man who was Coine's husband and Cargomaster of *Wavedancer*. Heavy-shouldered, with gray hair, he had four gold rings in each ear, three heavy gold chains around his neck, including one with a perfume box, and two curved knives tucked in his sash. He wore a peculiar wire framework that fastened over his ears to hold clear lenses in front of his eyes. When the Seanchan tried to take *Wavedancer*, Toram fought and cleared them off the deck, earning a long puckered scar down his cheek in the process. Toram was not happy when Coine changed her ship's destination to Tanchico to accommodate Elayne and Nynaeve.

Toram Riatin. A Cairhienin nobleman who was High Seat of House Riatin and wore stripes of color to his knees. About six feet tall, which was very tall for a Cairhienin, he was good-looking, with broad shoulders, slender hips, well-turned calves and dark, intelligent eyes. A bully with a cruel streak and often violent, Toram was also greedy; too much was never enough for him. He rebelled against the Dragon Reborn; after he was joined by Padan Fain as Jeraal Mordeth, he came to hate Rand with a passion.

Toram wanted to marry Caraline Damodred and fully expected that he would; he saw it as a done deal, and thought that she was just being coy. He planned to combine her claim to the throne with his and expected to take the throne, relegating her to some subordinate role; in fact, if she died after the wedding, it was all to the good. The marriage could have also resulted in his descendants carrying not only the House Riatin claim to the Sun Throne, but that of House Damodred as well.

Toram was very jealous of Caraline, and madly possessive in general. When he and Caraline were children, he pushed a mutual friend down the stairs and broke his back for riding Toram's pony without permission.

A blademaster, Toram dueled Rand in the rebel camp in Cairhien, not knowing whom he was fighting, thinking Rand was just a boy. It was an even match until Rand was distracted by the deadly fog, at which point, Toram nearly killed him; he held back only because he also finally realized that something strange was happening. At first he fled through the fog with Rand, Min, Caraline, Darlin, Cadsuane and Cadsuane's compatriots. When he discovered who Rand was, he fled into the fog alone. He then went to Far Madding with Padan Fain; there he was killed by Lan.

Toranes, Salita. *See* Salita Toranes

Torean Nelondara Andiama. A High Lord of Tear, and the father of Estean. Lumpy-faced, with thin eyebrows and big ears that made his potato nose seem smaller, he looked more like a farmer than most farmers. White streaked his dark, pointed beard, and he moved languidly. He looked at women rather openly, and plainly wanted Berelain. He was a bit of a boor and a drunkard. Gold concerned Torean more than anything else, except possibly the privileges Rand had taken away from the nobles in Tear.

Torean was one of the seven most active plotters against Rand in the Stone. Armies sent to Cairhien were to be generously financed by Torean, who accompanied them; with Meilan and Aracome, he was one of the three foremost High Lords there. He was worried because he was involved in plots with Tedosian, Hearne and Simaan and feared that Rand might punish him for that association after the three rebelled. He was with the army gathering to invade Illian and took part in the invasion.

Against the Seanchan, Torean was kept close by Rand at first, then later fought under Semaradrid. He was dismayed that there were no serving girls in the war camp, and no compliant farmgirls nearby.

Torelvin. A Cairhienin House. *See* Alhandrin *and* Nerion Torelvin

Torfinn family. A Two Rivers family. *See* Jaim, Jancy, Leof, Nat *and* Thad Torfinn

Torghin, Doreille. A queen of Aridhol who signed the Compact of the Ten Nations. She was also a poet.

Torhs Margin. A man also known as Torhs the Broken. He made the mistake of underestimating Graendal in the Age of Legends, and paid the price.

Torkumen, Lady. A Saldaean woman who was the wife of Vram, whom Tenobia had put in charge of the city in her absence; like him, she was a Darkfriend. Yoeli imprisoned the two so that he could let Ituralde and his troops into Maradon. When Rand appeared and defeated the Shadowspawn, Lady Torkumen jumped out of the window to her death.

Torkumen, Vram. *See* Vram Torkumen

torm. Seanchan exotic animals brought from a parallel world. They were bronze-scaled, like lizards, though they bore live young and nursed them. *Torm* looked much like horse-sized cats, with three eyes and six-toed clawed feet that could grip the stones of the road. The *torm* was primarily a carnivore; it would subsist on a plant diet for as much as three or four days if required, but a *torm* deprived of meat longer became increasingly hard to control as it sought to hunt. Their intelligence was higher than that of a bright dog, enough to make their eyes disturbing to some people, quite apart from the number of eyes. These creatures were not tool-users, nor did they have any sort of community, civilization or language, but if there were some way to give them an intelligence test, they would test out as well-below-normal human on average, and in some areas of problem solving, such as maze tests, equal to humans. Attempts were made to use *torm* as trackers and hunters, but a *torm* hunted what it chose and could not be put to hunt anything by a *morat*. Since this at times seemed like a deliberate refusal, some took it as one indication of the animal's intelligence. *Torm* had single births always. They were not available in large numbers, at least partly because of high mortality before reaching a useful size; they would also fight for dominance before they were trained, and such fights often resulted in a fatality because of their fierceness. They were much faster than horses, with more endurance.

Not everyone could ride a *torm*; in fact, it was harder to find someone suitable to be a *morat'torm* than to find *morat* for any of the other exotics. From the beginning of its training, a *torm* would not accept all riders. For no perceptible reason it would turn on one potential rider after another before accepting one, and it bonded with one rider, not allowing another to mount. If that rider died, it took some time to get a *torm* to accept another. They were ridden by scout units primarily. They were ferocious fighters, and might seem much better battle mounts than horses, with their natural weapons and scales, which were as effective as light armor, but a number of factors precluded their use in this role. There were relatively few of them compared to horses, and they were harder to replace, both because of the low survival rate to adulthood and a longer training time than that for horses. Perhaps more important, even the best-trained *torm* could be overcome with the heat of fighting if it went on very long, as in a battle as opposed to a skirmish; when this happened the rider, or *morat*, could only hang on, because the *torm* would become uncontrollable, moving and killing as it chose, sometimes pausing to savage corpses or feed, until it calmed down, which might be hours after the battle was done. Strangely, the *torm* rarely turned on its rider during one of these uncontrollable rages, but for the duration of the rage it was no longer an effective battle mount. In fact, it was a liability, as it would strike at anyone or anything within reach.

Torm and *corlm* were mutually antagonistic. While *morat* could keep this from coming to actual combat, they were never used together. *Torm* also made horses nervous and increasingly fractious unless the horses had been trained to tolerate them.

The *torm* was controlled in the same way as a horse, with reins and knee pressure.

Tormon. An Illianer merchant from New Braem. Dyelin reported that he had brought news of an army in Braem Wood (the Borderlanders). She said that he was a solid, reliable man, not given to flights of fancy or jumping at shadows.

Tornay Lanasiet. A heavyset Taraboner Dragonsworn soldier who took part in the raids against the Seanchan under Ituralde's command. Lanasiet hated wearing a breastplate marking him as one loyal to the Seanchan, which he had to do as a deception; he burned to close with them in battle. His eagerness to fight led him to not follow the plan of attack at Serana; after he and Ituralde defeated the Seanchan there, he gave chase with a third of the men Ituralde was counting on using, although he was not supposed to. Ituralde thought that he had seen the last of him.

Torr, Kevlyn. A Two Rivers man with Perrin. He told Perrin of a stand of trees that had mysteriously died and dried in one night. Perrin told him to harvest them for firewood.

Torval, Peral. *See* Peral Torval

Torvald, Noy. *See* Noy Torvald

Torven Rikshan. A Cairhienin lord in charge of a camp of refugees with Perrin. His camp had a large number of nobles, and Faile suspected that he was bribing the quartermaster to deliver meals early.

Torwyn Barshaw. A Darkfriend, allegedly a merchant from Four Kings and Paitr Conel's uncle. A squat man with a big nose, a choleric eye and a sneering mouth, Torwyn visited Morgase in Amador, pretending to be a merchant, with plans to help her escape from the Whitecloaks hidden in the bottom of a cart of kitchen refuse. Trom caught Torwyn, Paitr and others reciting catechisms to the Dark One; they were hanged while Morgase watched.

Tourag. A fighting force from another Age, from Birgitte's memory.

Tova. A nation that arose after the Trolloc Wars.

Tovan conclaves. Tovan councilors who became a symbol of abstemiousness, as the Tovans were a stark and disapproving people, at least as recalled by Birgitte.

Toveine Gazal. A copper-skinned Saldaean Aes Sedai of the Red Ajah and the loyalist contingent, with a strength level of 19(7). Born in 811 NE, she went to the White Tower in 829 NE. After spending eleven years as a novice and ten years as Accepted, she was raised to the shawl in 850 NE. About 5'3" tall, with long glossy dark hair and dark eyes, Toveine was somewhat plump, though not fat. Although she was moderately pretty, with a mouth and eyes men found pleasing, no one would ever have called her a beauty. Her gaze bored into whatever she looked at. A wolf might have quailed when she sneered or frowned, and when Toveine was angry, serpents fled. She always had the ability to cut out one's heart and eat it while one watched. She wasn't particularly cruel, except when it came to men who could channel. Toveine hated the very idea of a man channeling. She did not like men at all, really; she preferred pretty young boys in their mid to late teens, young enough to be eager and grateful and easy to control; that got her into trouble during her exile. The notion of any sort of sexual relationship with an adult male made her skin crawl.

Toveine was raised Sitter for the Red in 952 NE, but was unchaired in 985 NE in the wake of the male channeler pogrom. The pogrom was begun by the Black Ajah, of course, but she and her fellow Red Sitters threw themselves wholeheartedly into supporting it. Although the true circumstances were kept secret for the good of the White Tower, she suffered a penance in the Tower just short of being publicly birched (it was done privately) and was exiled, a supposedly voluntary retreat that lasted until she was recalled after Elaida took the stole. This retreat was at the farm of one Mistress Doweel, who believed Toveine was there to work a penance and held her to the same rules she would any other farmhand. Toveine still thought of her as Mistress Doweel and remembered every time she was strapped or switched for infractions; the woman made a great impression on her. Later, she arranged for Mistress Doweel to have much the same experience, but it did not remove the impression the woman made on her. Elaida sent Toveine with fifty sisters and two hundred of the Tower Guard to clean out the Black Tower and gentle and hang every male channeler that they found. Elaida thought that she would carry out her orders with no problem, but Elaida did not know that Toveine's desire for revenge was almost as strong as her hatred of men who could channel, quite possibly stronger, by this time, though it might well have shocked her to realize it. Marith, the Amyrlin who forced Toveine's resignation, was dead, but that was not enough. While she did not think in terms of revenge against her own Ajah, she was particularly bitter that they did not support her to any greater extent. She was more than reluctant to admit even to herself there was nothing the Red could have done under the circumstances, that Marith had had the whip hand, and the entire Red Ajah, even those who hadn't taken part in the pogrom, knew that anyone who defied Marith might well have shared the fate of Toveine and the others, with the approval of the rest of the Hall. Even less did she actively think of taking revenge on the White Tower as a whole—but it was the Tower that had humiliated and exiled her.

All fifty-one Aes Sedai were captured by the Asha'man and bonded; Toveine was bonded by Logain. The other Aes Sedai blamed her for their capture and beat her. Gabrelle, who was also bonded by Logain, convinced Toveine that they needed to stand united. Toveine wrote a letter to the Red Ajah describing their capture at the Black Tower and blamed the incident on Elaida. Toveine went with Logain to Rand at Algarin's manor in Tear. When they returned to the Black Tower, Toveine was Turned to the Shadow and Logain released the bond. After, Logain told Gabrelle they would kill Toveine if they found her.

Tovere, Kin. *See* Kin Tovere

Tower Guard. The military body attached to the White Tower in Tar Valon. Under Siuan Sanche, the Tower Guard numbered about three thousand men, used mainly for policing the city of Tar Valon and the surrounding area and also to provide a suitable escort for the Amyrlin Seat when she traveled. It had been larger in the past, though not greatly larger since the time of Artur Hawkwing; under Alviarin's influence, Elaida planned to increase the numbers to fifty thousand. Few nations viewed the prospect of a large Tower Guard with anything approaching equanimity.

A Tower Guardsman wore the white teardrop of the Falme of Tar Valon on his chest, either embroidered on the breast of his coat or on a tabard over his breastplate.

High Captain Jimar Chubain was Commander of the Tower Guard.

Tower, Hall of the. *See* Hall of the Tower

Tower of the Full Moon. A structure at the Sun Palace in Cairhien; Dobraine had rooms there where he was attacked by robbers. Usually the Tower was set aside for visiting nobility of high rank.

Tower of Ghenjei. A featureless burnished steel tower near the River Arinelle in Andor, two hundred feet high and forty feet in diameter, one of the ancient wonders of unknown use. In fact, the realms of the Aelfinn and Eelfinn could be reached through the tower. Perrin was near the Tower of Ghenjei in the wolf dream, having seen Slayer enter, when Birgitte warned him away. Later, Mat, Thom and Noal rescued Moiraine from the Aelfinn and Eelfinn by entering the tower.

Tower of Morning. 1) An architectural feature in Tanchico. Temaile, torturing the

Panarch, hoisted Amathera to the top of the tower in her dreams and then dropped her; each time she let Amathera fall closer to the ground before stopping. 2) A sword form.

Tower of Ravens. The central Imperial prison of Seanchan. It was located in the capital of Seandar and served as the headquarters for the Seekers for Truth. Members of the Blood were imprisoned, questioned and executed within it. The questioning and execution had to be accomplished without spilling a drop of blood. Most prisoners who learned that they were going to the Tower of Ravens attempted suicide. The Tower of Ravens was the symbol of Imperial justice; an image of it was displayed on a Seeker's plaque and tattooed on a Seeker's shoulder. It was broken after the fall of the Empress.

Tower of the Risen Sun. A part of the Royal Palace in Cairhien that was demolished in the attack on Rand by the renegade Asha'man.

Tower, White. *See* White Tower

Towers of Midnight. Thirteen fortresses of unpolished black marble located in Imfaral, Seanchan. At the time of the Consolidation of Seanchan, it was the center of military might. The final battle of the Consolidation took place there, leaving Hawkwing's descendants in power. After that time, it was unoccupied. Legend said that in time of dire need, the Imperial family would return to the Towers of Midnight and "right that which is wrong." Dein, the creator of the *a'dam*, was imprisoned there, and it was said that the towers were shaken by her screams.

Town, the. A village in the Blight that was the residence of male Aiel channelers and their progeny, the Eyeblinders, who had gone to the Blight to fight the forces of Dark and were Turned.

Toy. The name given Mat by the Seanchan in the Tarasin Palace, Ebou Dar; it was short for Tylin's Toy.

Traehand, Laerid. *See* Laerid Traehand

Traemane, House. A major noble House in Andor. Its High Seat was Ellorien; its sign the Stag, or the White Stag. *See also* Elayne *and* Ellorien Traemane

Trahelion, Birgitte. *See* Birgitte Silverbow

Traighan, Seonid. *See* Seonid Traighan

Traitor's Banner. A triangular black-and-yellow pendant borne by Saldaeans who felt that they had betrayed their oaths, even though the betrayal was for the greater good. Sometimes in lieu of a banner, strips of black and yellow cloth were twisted about one another and tied to sword sheaths. Yoeli and the men who fought alongside him when he took command of Maradon wore the Traitor's Banner, although they took the city to save Ituralde and his men from the Shadowspawn army.

Traitor's Court. A courtyard found in the White Tower, used for only three occasions: executions, the stilling of an Aes Sedai or the gentling of a male channeler. It was a wide area surrounded by windows from which spectators could watch events.

Traitor's Tree. A tree at the Black Tower upon which deserters' heads were hung.

Traitors' Steps. An area on the Maseta Peninsula in Tanchico where heads of enemies-of-state were displayed on spikes.

Trakand, House. A noble House of Andor. *See* Elayne, Gawyn, Maighdin *and* Morgase Trakand

Trakand, Tomas and Jaisi. The names given Rand and Min by Caraline Damodred to hide their identity from Darlin when they visited the Cairhienin rebel camp.

transcriber. A device from the Age of Legends that wrote words spoken; Graendal wished she had one in the Third Age.

Translation, the Book of. *See* Book of Translation, the

trap-worms. Creatures found in the Sen T'jore, a wild region of Seanchan. They sprang out of the ground without warning, but it is unclear whether they were harmful to humans.

Trask. An Aiel Red Shield who fought alongside Rhuarc in the Last Battle. He managed to kill a red-veil before he himself was killed.

Traveler. 1) Bryne's bay gelding. 2) A constellation thought of as a woman with her staff standing out sharp.

Traveling. A process using the One Power to weave a portal, called a gateway, that allowed one to go from one location to another without crossing the intervening space. Traveling required a knowledge of the embarkation point, rather than a knowledge of the destination, as was true of Skimming. Once the starting point was learned, which could take up to two days in unknown territory, the one Traveling could make rapid, successive jumps, as long as each destination point was in sight of the last starting point. Unlike Skimming, Traveling was considered a Talent.

The True Power could also be used to Travel, but the process was slightly different: the one Traveling appeared to fade into or out of existence, or simply appeared and vanished.

Traveling Box. *See* nar'baha

Traveling People. *See* Tuatha'an

Travels in the Aiel Waste, with Various Observations on the Savage Inhabitants. A dusty, wood-bound book that Egwene moved from a chair while visiting Rand in Tear.

Travels of Jain Farstrider, The. A popular book recounting the adventures of Jain Charin.

Trayal. An Ogier who lost his mind and soul in the Ways.

Treasures of the Stone of Tear, The. A book, Volume Twelve, that Egwene moved from a chair while visiting with Rand in Tear.

Tree, the. *See* Avendesora

Tree of Life, the. A term used to indicate the tree described in many legends and stories; also a reference to the chora tree, a construct from the Age of Legends, of which there were many. The ancient kingdom of Almoth was said to have had a branch or even a living cutting of *Avendesora*, the legendary Tree of Life, and it was found on its banner. The Taraboners also had it on their banner, and they called themselves the Tree of Man, a reference to the tree. The Domani claimed that they descended from those who created the Tree of Life in the Age of Legends. *See also Avendesora and* chora tree

Tree of Man. Taraboners' name for themselves. They claimed to be descended from rulers and nobles from the Age of Legends.

Trees, Great. *See* Great Trees

Tree Songs or treesongs. Songs sung by Ogier Treesingers which caused living things, particularly trees, to bend to any form and to grow stronger and taller.

Treebrother. An Aiel name for Ogier. The Aiel liked talking with them and visiting the *stedding* for trade. The Aiel called themselves "waterfriends" to the Treebrothers. Treebrother was also the name Loial used to refer to the Green Man.

Treehill, Nicola. *See* Nicola Treehill

treekiller. An Aiel term for the Cairhienin.

Treesinger. An Ogier with the rare ability to sing Treesongs. Treesingers were much more common in the Age of Legends.

treesong. *See* Tree Songs

Tremalking. The largest of the Sea Folk islands. Very mountainous, it lay southwest of Tarabon in the Aryth Ocean. Tremalking was home to the Amayar and one of the Choedan Kal, the giant female *sa'angreal*. *See* Amayar

Tremalking black. A variety of tea.

Tremalking Splice, The. A waterfront inn located in Southharbor in Tar Valon. Mat went there to satisfy his gambling urge while trying to escape from the Aes Sedai and the city; he won a big purse.

Tremonsien. A village in Cairhien, perched on top of a terraced hill. Tremonsien was a precisely laid-out village, with square stone houses on uniform lots and streets marked out in grid fashion. The short inhabitants, pale and thin-faced, were friendly, and wives talked with each other standing at the half doors of their houses. While Rand, Hurin, Loial and Selene were transporting the dagger and Horn of Valere back to Cairhien, they passed an excavation of a giant sphere held by an immense hand; it was a *sa'angreal*, one of the two Choedan Kal. They stayed at The Nine Rings in Tremonsien, and Selene slipped away in the night. Captain Caldevwin sent his soldiers to escort Rand's group to Cairhien. Much later, when Rand and Nynaeve were cleansing *saidin*, a brandy merchant on his way to The Nine Rings saw the intense brightness from the *sa'angreal* in the pit and it struck him with terror.

Triben. A Saldaean soldier who accompanied Nynaeve to the Gull's Feast in Ebou Dar. A hawk-faced man with a short, trimmed mustache and a scar across his forehead, he kicked down the door to the chandler's shop where Milisair's prisoners were being kept and helped subdue the occupants.

Trolloc Wars. An invasion of Trollocs from the Blight that began around 1000

AB and lasted about 350 years, destroying the Compact of the Ten Nations. The Trolloc defeat at the Battle of Maighande was the turning point in the wars.

Trollocs. A variety of Shadowspawn, created before the War of the Shadow to serve as soldiers for the Dark One. Created from a very precise blending of human and animal genetic material in which both the One Power and the True Power were used, they were not simply vaguely human beasts. Male Trollocs stood eight to ten feet tall; the head and the face were human except for two features. Where a human's mouth and nose should be, a Trolloc had either an animal's snout or a bird of prey's beak. The second is that they had the proper animal's ears and horns, if applicable, or, in the case of those with beaks, a crest of feathers instead of hair. Those of completely mammalian origin had considerable hair, very coarse and dark, but in a human pattern; they would have this hair on the backs of the hands and fingers, for example, and were not covered with fur. They did not have claws on their hands, which were human except in size, but some did have hooves. There were births with a bird's claws instead of feet, or animal's paws instead of hands, but such offspring were killed. Some Trollocs had mixed characteristics, exhibiting, say, the horns and muzzle of one sort of creature and the feet of another. Even more rare was to have the horns or ears or feathers of one sort and the muzzle of another. Most of these mixed Trollocs were considered unviable by the Trollocs themselves and were exposed to the elements at birth. A few managed to survive, and were generally more intelligent than most Trollocs, though this was not necessarily saying a great deal. Trollocs were intelligent enough to know where they came from, and they loathed pure humans. There were female Trollocs, but they simply existed as breeders, birthing and protecting their young.

Typically male Trollocs wore dark leather and long shirts of black mail with spikes at elbows and shoulders. They did not wear helmets. Their primary weapons were oddly spiked axes, spears with peculiar razor-sharp hooks and swords that curved the wrong way, like scythe blades. They occasionally used bows with barbed arrows the size of small spears. Normally of fairly low intelligence, they were bloodthirsty, enjoyed inflicting pain and would kill anything for the fun of it. Where Trollocs struck, they left nothing alive that they could catch. They also ate anything, including people, and they did not always kill their prey before beginning the butchering.

Trollocs were fierce, treacherous and afraid of almost nothing, but they could not be trusted if they were not afraid of whoever was leading them. One creature that Trollocs feared was the Myrddraal. Sometimes the result of a Trolloc birth was not another Trolloc but a throwback almost to the original human stock, yet tainted by the evil of the Dark One. Before the discovery of the Myrddraal, Trollocs could not be controlled; the Myrddraal, however, could make them obey. It was also able to link with groups of Trollocs, each Trolloc so controlled becoming like extensions of the Myrddraal's hands. The only weakness then was the Myrddraal; if it was killed, all the Trollocs to which it was linked died as well.

Trollocs were terrified of deep water and were unable to swim. A Trolloc would not wade even waist-deep in water if he could find any way to avoid it.

There were twelve named tribe-like bands of Trollocs: Ahf'frait, Al'ghol, Bhan'sheen, Dha'vol, Dhai'mon, Dhjin'nen, Ghar'ghael, Ghob'hlin, Gho'hlem, Ghraem'lan, Ko'bal and the Kno'mon. Another band, of those with added-in genetic material of digging/burrowing animals, were used as miners in siege operations. There was considerable animosity between the bands; they were bound together largely by fear of the Dark One and overwhelming hatred of humans.

Trom. An officer in the Children of the Light. Stocky, with a square face and black hair, he was in Samara with Galad. Trom led the Whitecloaks who captured Paitr Conel and Torwyn Barshaw. After the Whitecloaks were defeated by the Seanchan at Jeramel, he was promoted to Lord Captain. He supported Galad in his duel against Valda and acted as Arbiter. When Galad defeated Valda, Trom pointed out that Galad had become Lord Captain Commander of the Children. Trom became Galad's second-in-command; he died in the Last Battle.

Trost. A young man from the Two Rivers who went to the Black Tower. He was worried about Logain's prolonged absence, and talked to Androl about it.

Troubles. The name given the Whitecloak War by the Children of the Light. *See* Whitecloak War

True Bloods. An Aiel warrior society also known as *Tain Shari*.

True Defender of the Light. *See* Dragon, the

True Power. The power drawn directly from the Dark One. Only the Dark One could tell if the True Power was being used; it was undetectable by other channelers, even those who could wield the True Power. Only the Dark One could grant access to it; it was highly addictive, and had the side effect of *saa*, dark flecks that passed across the user's eyeballs. If the True Power was employed long enough, it would produce the "caverns of flame" effect in a person's eyes and mouth. Summoning the True Power at Shayol Ghul would have normally resulted in annihilation of the individual.

Even some of the Forsaken were reluctant to call on the True Power; it was thought that only twenty-nine people were ever accorded the right to tap into it. Traveling with the True Power caused one to seem to fade in and out of existence; when fading, the Traveler could see the place being Traveled to before going there. If the Traveler disappeared suddenly, it meant that the Traveler appeared immediately in the new place without any opportunity to see what was there, a riskier mode of Travel. Moridin tried to channel the True Power through *Callandor* against Rand at Shayol Ghul during the Last Battle, but because of *Callandor*'s flaws, Rand, Moiraine and Nynaeve were able to wrest control of the True Power from Moridin, wrapping it in the One Power, and turning it against the Dark One.

True Source. The driving force of the universe, which turned the Wheel of Time. It was divided into a male half (*saidin*) and a female half (*saidar*), which worked at the same time with and against each other. Only a man could draw on *saidin*, only a woman on *saidar*, unless linked in a circle. From the beginning of the Time of Madness, *saidin* was tainted by the Dark One's touch; Rand, linked with Nynaeve and using the Choedan Kal, cleansed the taint from it.

true-name day. A celebratory Seanchan custom. There was six years' difference between the naming day, usually one's day of birth, and the true-name day. So, when Tuon celebrated her fourteenth true-name day, she also had her twentieth birthday.

trueheart. A yellow-blossomed plant. Erith gave a trueheart flower to Loial.

Truthspeaker. *See Soe'feia*

tsag. An obscenity in the Old Tongue uttered by Sammael.

Tsao, Chowin. An Aes Sedai of the Green Ajah who served as advisor to Artur Hawkwing before he initiated the siege of the White Tower.

Tsingu ma choba. Old Tongue for "You honor this unworthy one."

Tsingu ma Choshih, T'ingshen. Old Tongue for "You honor me, Treebrother."

Tsochan, Stedding. A *stedding* located in the forests north of the River Ivo.

Tsofan, Stedding. A *stedding* located in the Mountains of Mist.

Tsofu, Stedding. A *stedding* located in Cairhien. Alar was the Eldest of the Elders there, and it was Erith's home. Rand, Mat, Perrin, Verin and Shienaran soldiers visited there before attempting to use the nearby Waygate to go to Toman Head.

Tsomo Nasalle. A city in the Age of Legends.

Tsorov'ande Doon. Old Tongue for "Black-Souled Tempests," it was the name used by Seanchan for men who could channel.

Tsorovan'm'hael. A rank assigned Charl Gedwyn by Taim; it indicated that he was second to Taim. It was Old Tongue for "Storm Leader."

Tsutama Rath. A Kandori Aes Sedai of the Red Ajah and the loyalist contingent, with a strength level of 21(9). Born in 827 NE, she went to the White Tower in 841 NE. After spending seven years as a novice and six years as Accepted, she was raised to the shawl in 854 NE. About 5'5" tall, with a full bosom, large dark eyes and luxuriant black hair, Tsutama would have been pretty, even beautiful, except that she wore a permanently angry expression that almost overwhelmed her agelessness. She often wore all crimson, so bright that it might have given the most ardent Red pause, and cut tightly, molding her breasts or exposing them, as if daring anyone to comment. She was raised a Sitter for the Red in 964 NE and was forced to resign in 985 NE following the discovery of the male channeler pogrom. Although the true circumstances were kept secret for the good of the White Tower, she suffered a penance in the Tower just short of being publicly birched (it was done privately), and then was exiled, a supposedly voluntary retreat that lasted until she was recalled after Elaida took the stole. Elaida considered her broken by her experiences, and, like Lirene, she was broken in many ways. She was afraid of being caught out in any further wrongdoing; she was more angry than ashamed about her penances, including the birching.

Tsutama stopped hating men, though she had come to that earlier; her one consolation during her painful exile was an affair that she began with a man, almost in desperation to find some solace. Unlike either Toveine or Lirene, she thought about the possibility of taking some sort of vengeance on the entire Red Ajah, indeed the entire White Tower. The Tower shamed her and exiled her, her own Ajah did nothing to support or help her, and she wanted them all to pay.

After Galina was reported killed at Dumai's Wells, Tsutama was named Highest of the Red Ajah. She ordered Pevara and Tarna to take a group to the Black Tower and bond Asha'man.

Tuandha. A Maiden of the Spear who was with Sulin and Perrin at Malden. About 5'8" tall, and younger than Sulin, she had lost her right eye and had a thick scar that ran from her chin up under her *shoufa*; it pulled up a corner of her mouth in a half-smile. Tuandha and Sulin were with Perrin when he first looked at Malden.

Tuatha'an. A wandering folk, also known as the Tinkers and as the Traveling People, who lived in brightly painted wagons and followed a pacifistic philosophy called the Way of the Leaf. A Tuatha'an would not do violence to another human being even to save his or her own life or the lives of loved ones. Things mended by Tinkers were often better than new, but the Tuatha'an were shunned by many villages because of stories that they stole children and tried to convert young people to their beliefs. They were among the few peoples who could cross the Aiel Waste unmolested, for the Aiel strictly avoided all contact with them.

The Tuatha'an were a group that had split off from the Da'shain Aiel, the first division of the Da'shain, when they became fed up with violence against them by people who saw them as easy marks. They abandoned their covenant to serve the Aes Sedai, and began traveling to find a safe place to live and to find the song that their legend held was lost during the Breaking, the finding of which they thought would return conditions to the paradise of the Age of Legends. After the second division of the Da'shain caused by some rejecting the Way of the Leaf and beginning to use weapons for defense, those willing to use weapons eventually became the only surviving Aiel. In fact, the Tuatha'an were the only descendants of the original Da'shain Aiel who maintained the Way of the Leaf and were called the Lost Ones by the Aiel, who held them in disdain. As banditry and lawlessness increased, the danger to them grew; many fled to Seanchan-controlled areas for safety.

The Tinkers continued to search in vain for the song they would never find, because the song they were looking for did not exist. *See also* Aiel, Da'shain Aiel *and* Jenn Aiel

Tuck Padwhin. A carpenter in Emond's Field. Egwene thought that Siuan looked at her and Nynaeve the way Master Padwhin looked at his tools. When Trollocs attacked Emond's Field, Tuck participated in the defense.

Tuel. A region of Seanchan that Sarek had designs on, as learned by Rand and Aviendha when they Traveled to Seanchan.

Tuli. The *damane* name that Renna forced on Egwene as punishment.

Tumad Ahzkan. A Saldaean man who was one of Bashere's young officers, a lieutenant destined for higher command. About 6'2" tall, and heavy-shouldered, with a hatchet nose and a luxuriant black beard as well as thick mustaches, he walked like a man more accustomed to a saddle under him than his own feet, using a slightly rolling gait, but he handled the sword at his hip smoothly when he bowed. He was killed when the Trollocs attacked Algarin's manor in Tear.

Tunaighan Hills. An area somewhere to the south of Caemlyn. The region produced a wine which bore its name; Rand served it to Andoran nobles, and Berelain gave Gendar and Santes a cask to take to Masema's camp when they were spying on him.

Tuon Athaem Kore Paendrag. Daughter of the Nine Moons and second daughter of Radhanan, the Empress of Seanchan. She had a number of siblings, among them sisters Ravashi, Chimal and Aurana. At the time of the *Corenne* she was favored by the Empress to succeed and named to lead the Return. The Empress liked her heirs to contend, so that the strongest and most cunning would rule Seanchan. Tuon's personal banner was two golden lions harnessed to an ancient war cart, and the symbol of the Daughter of the Nine Moons was the Raven-and-Roses. Born in 981 NE, she was 4'11" tall and almost boyishly slim. Her face was heart-shaped and quite beautiful, with large, liquid eyes of a chocolate brown; her hair was silky black and straight. She had full lips and a very dark complexion. Her personality was quiet, reserved and thoughtful; she could grow angry, of course, but seldom let it show as heat. Highly intelligent, and very capable in the shifting and dangerous world of the Seanchan court, she also was quite skilled in personal self-defense. She was not only respected and obeyed by those who served her, she was loved by them. Tuon was an excellent rider and knew a good bit about horses, including training them. She rode in what in later Ages would be called steeplechase events and also dressage.

Tuon had, like every other woman in Seanchan, been tested to see whether she was *marath'damane*, and she was not. She passed the test for *sul'dam*, but because she was who she was, she was not expected to train as a *sul'dam*. She did so, however, though she never served as one; she had a keenness for it, though, rather in the manner of someone keen to train dogs for field trials or horses for steeplechase or dressage. She did own a number of *damane*, though she employed *sul'dam* for handling them. When she learned about *sul'dam* being able to learn to channel, it did not worry her; they did not channel, and that was the key. So long as they refused to learn, they were all right in her book.

Tuon, with her Voice Selucia and her Truthspeaker Anath, sailed with the *Corenne* to Ebou Dar aboard the *Victory of Kidron*; just before they arrived, Lidya, a *damane*, gave her a Foretelling: "Beware the fox that makes the ravens fly, for he will marry you and carry you away. Beware the man who remembers Hawkwing's face, for he will marry you and set you free. Beware the man of the red hand, for him you will marry and none other."

In Ebou Dar, she met Mat, saw his ring with a running fox and two ravens in flight, surrounded by nine crescent moons, and offered to buy him. She caught Mat as he was getting ready to escape Ebou Dar; he and Noal took her into custody.

When Egeanin revealed that Tuon was the Daughter of the Nine Moons, Mat announced three times that Tuon was his wife. He took Tuon and Selucia with his group to Valan Luca's show. While they traveled, Mat tried to court Tuon; some of his efforts met with more success than others. A necklace was spurned, but a Domani razor was greatly appreciated. When Renna tried to go to Seanchan troops, Tuon wrote a document putting Luca's show under her protection in case Renna reached the Seanchan, but excluded Mat. In Maderin, Tuon asked Mat to take her to a hell; at Thom's suggestion he took her to a slightly higher-class establishment, The White Ring. Thom learned that Seanchan soldiers had been told that a Daughter of the Nine Moons imposter was on the loose, meaning Tuon's life was in danger. On leaving The White Ring, the party was attacked; Mat killed all the men attacking him, and Tuon killed the women. Selucia and Thom killed others. They decided to leave Luca's show, and Mat tried to find a way to return Tuon to Ebou Dar safely. The group met up with the Band of the Red Hand. Furyk Karede, who had been trying to find Tuon to get her to safety, found Mat's people; when Tuon said that she trusted Karede, Mat said that Karede could take her back to Ebou Dar, and that he, the Band and some Deathwatch Guards would attempt to ambush those thinking to kill her.

As all of Lidya's Foretelling had transpired, Tuon announced three times that Mat was her husband, completing the marriage. She returned safely to Ebou Dar and learned that her mother and family were dead; when Musenge brought her the head of Elbar, Suroth's man, Tuon made Suroth *da'covale* and turned her over to the Deathwatch Guard until her hair was long enough for her to be sold.

At Rand's request, Tuon met with him at Falme, but the meeting did not go well. The darkness that she sensed in him made her able to resist his *ta'veren* effect. She ordered a strike on the White Tower, proclaimed herself Empress and took the name Fortuona Athaem Devi Paendrag.

After freeing Moiraine, Mat returned to Ebou Dar, where he saved Tuon from a Gray Man, and they consummated their marriage. Rand went to Ebou Dar and met with Tuon and convinced her to sign the Dragon's Peace and join his effort against the Shadow.

Tuon was nearly killed in the command center in the Last Battle, but Min saved her. Mat and Tuon faked a fight, and she led the Seanchan away from the Last Battle; when the time was right, he sent for her and she returned, helping to seal the victory of the forces of the Light at Merrilor. After the Last Battle, Tuon revealed that she was pregnant.

Turak Aladon. A Seanchan member of the High Blood and commander of the *Hailene.* He stood twelfth in line of succession for the Crystal Throne. His head was shaved, all of his fingernails were at least an inch long and all were lacquered blue. He was killed by Rand in a sword duel at Falme.

Turan. A Seanchan Lieutenant-General in Tarabon who was sent to chase Ituralde. A blademaster, he was stout and short, with a peaked nose and close-cropped black hair shaved two finger-widths up each side of his head. He fell into Ituralde's trap, attacking the apparently defenseless Darluna while Ituralde's troops came at him from two sides. Turan was injured, and Ituralde granted his request for a quick death by taking off his head.

Turane. A Sea Folk Sailmistress. Stocky and gimlet-eyed, she had a sour twist to her mouth because her ship was sunk in Ebou Dar. Her Windfinder was Serile. The Seanchan ship that they had captured was the meeting place for the First Twelve of the Atha'an Miere in Illian.

Turanine Merdagon. An Aes Sedai whose ghost Beonin saw on the way to the White Tower. She wore a dress of old-fashioned cut; straight white hair that fell to her waist was held back by a pearl-studded cap of silver wire. Turanine had a strong face, with dark, tilted eyes and a hooked nose. She had died when Beonin was Accepted, forty years before.

Turanna Norill. An Aes Sedai of the White Ajah and the loyalist contingent, with a strength level of 26(14). Turanna was a member of the party sent to kidnap Rand. She was captured at Dumai's Wells and treated as *da'tsang* by the Aiel. Under Compulsion from Verin, she found a reason to swear oath to Rand, and like all of the other captive sisters, had done so before Cadsuane departed Cairhien for Far Madding.

Turese. An Aes Sedai of the Red Ajah. New enough to the shawl that she lacked the ageless look, she checked on Egwene just after Verin died; Egwene was able to convince her that Verin was sleeping.

Turn. To compel a person to follow the Dark One in a process using thirteen channelers and thirteen Myrddraal.

Turn Bow. A wolf that Perrin met in the wolf dream while searching for Slayer. She was an aging pack leader and told him that Moonhunter (Lanfear) was looking for him.

Turne. A Ghealdanin mercenary. He was a lanky fellow with curly red hair and a beard he tied off with leather cords. Turne and a dozen others joined Perrin shortly after the battle at Malden. In the Last Battle he was with Arganda.

Turol. An Aiel who was the leader of the *Shae'en M'taal* warrior society. He went to Caemlyn with Rand to take out Rahvin.

Tuva. A female cousin of King Alsalam of Arad Doman. Graendal had Nazran tell Ituralde that Tuva was killed by a Gray Man while delivering orders from Alsalam to Ituralde.

Tuval, Mistress. The tutor to Diryk, son of Queen Ethenielle of Kandor.

Tween Forest. A location mentioned in one of Mat's fictional stories; it was possibly in Murandy.

Twelve Salt Wells, The. An inn in Jurador next to the stable where Mat acquired the Domani razor.

Twilight. The leader of a wolfpack that Perrin spoke to when seeking information about Faile after she was abducted by the Shaido.

Twinhorn's Peak. A tall mountain near Emond's Field.

Twisted Ones. Wolfspeak for Trollocs.

Two Apples, The. An inn in Caemlyn. Its innkeeper was Bromas, a stately woman. Thom performed there until Mat fetched him and told him the *gholam* was in Caemlyn.

Two Deer. A wolf that Perrin spoke to when he and Ingtar were searching for Fain and the Trollocs.

Two Moons, Nesta din Reas. *See* Nesta din Reas Two Moons

Two Moons. An old male wolf and pack leader who had a mostly white muzzle. His real name suggested a night-shrouded pool, smooth as ice in the instant before the breeze stirred, with a tang of autumn in the air, and one moon hanging full in the sky and another reflected so perfectly on the water that it was difficult to tell which was real. He was among the wolves that Perrin asked for information after he and others set out to find the kidnapped Rand. When the wolves were communicating the location of the Aes Sedai who held Rand, Two Moons maintained a dignified silence, since he was close enough that Perrin could know exactly where he was.

Two Rivers. A region in western Andor. It was the heartland of Manetheren, a nation which was destroyed during the Trolloc Wars. Four villages were found there: Emond's Field, Deven Ride, Watch Hill and Taren Ferry. Though technically a part of Andor, the area had not seen a tax collector in six generations (approximately 150 years), nor the Guards in seven generations, at the time that the Dragon Reborn declared himself. Most villagers had no idea that they were part of Andor. The villages each had a Mayor and a Village Council, and a Wisdom and a Women's Circle, to govern themselves. The people of the Two Rivers were reputed to be stubborn; it was said that they could give mules lessons and teach stones.

In 998 NE on Winternight, Trollocs attacked Emond's Field; only the presence of an Aes Sedai and her Warder saved it. In 999 NE, Whitecloaks entered

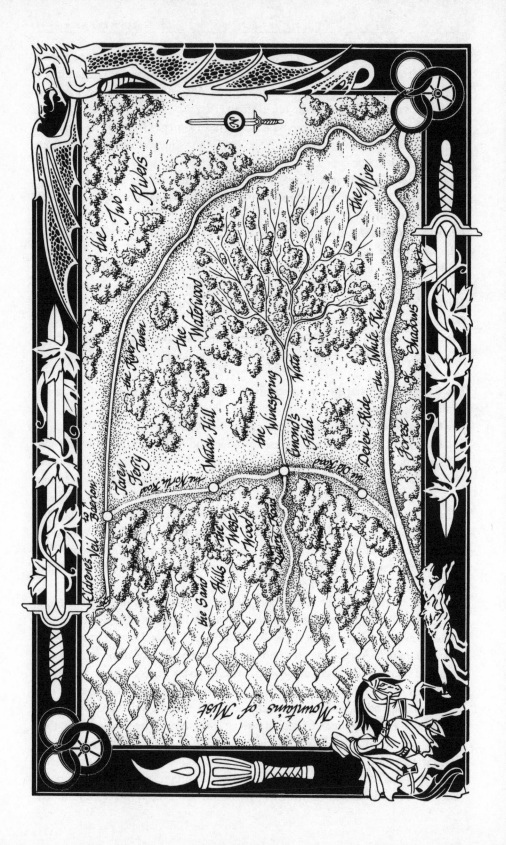

the Two Rivers to root out Darkfriends, and Trollocs started appearing as well. Perrin returned to his home, gathered an army and organized the villagers to fight the Trollocs; with help from Watch Hill, they defeated them, and the Whitecloaks left as well. The people of the Two Rivers began regarding Perrin and his wife Faile as their Lord and Lady.

Patrols hunting down lingering Trollocs soon began discovering refugees in the mountains. Well over a thousand, and maybe two thousand or more, poured in so quickly that it was hard to keep tabs. Over half of the refugees were from Almoth Plain; most of the rest were from Arad Doman and Tarabon. There were more women and children than men. Some settled on farms where no one had survived and some brought in new skills and set up shop. Before the influx of refugees, the main products of the Two Rivers had been tabac and wool; the refugees brought new skills, such as rugmaking and tilemaking.

Shortly before the Last Battle, Elayne ceded the Two Rivers to the Dragon Reborn with Perrin as his Steward.

Two Spires. A sept of the Reyn Aiel.

two-step. A small poisonous brown snake in the Aiel Waste; death from its bite came quickly, usually in about two steps.

Two Winds, Harine din Togara. *See* Harine din Togara Two Winds

Tylee Khirgan. A Seanchan Banner-General who helped Perrin retrieve Faile and the others from the Shaido. Tylee was raised to lieutenant-general and to the Blood for taking so many *damane* at Malden. She was 5'8" to 5'9" tall, and broad-shouldered for a woman, though lean otherwise, and not young. Gray marked the temples of her close-cut, tightly curled black hair. As dark as good topsoil, she displayed only two scars, one slanting across her left cheek. The other, on her forehead, had taken part of her right eyebrow. After Malden, she led her army back to Ebou Dar; on the way they were attacked by Trollocs.

During the Last Battle, she was ordered to take her First Legion to help Bryne's troops fend off the Sharans on the Kandor-Arafel border. Under Compulsion, Bryne kept her out of the battle. Mat arrived in time to remand Bryne's order, and, with Tylee's troops, saved the battle. Supporting Mat's suggestion, Tylee also advised Tuon to throw the Seanchan army into the fight against the Dark One, contrary to what Yulan, under Compulsion, was arguing.

Tylin Quintara Mitsobar. By the Grace of the Light, Queen of Altara, Mistress of the Four Winds, Guardian of the Sea of Storms, High Seat of House Mitsobar. She had one son, Beslan. About 5'3" tall, she had glossy black hair with some gray, large dark eyes and two faint scars on her cheeks. While she had considered herself too busy for some years to take up the Altaran custom of having "a pretty," she found herself fascinated by Mat. He was young and good-looking and a rogue. More than that, he traveled with Aes Sedai and they seemed to be somewhat afraid of him—or uneasy, at least. That was concentrated catnip to Tylin. She pushed her attentions on him; when he tried to stay in his rooms,

PINK RIBBONS

she ordered the kitchens to stop feeding him. When it came down to the point, she peeled him out of his clothes at knifepoint and had her way with him on more than one occasion. Once the Seanchan arrived, she accommodated them in an effort to make sure that Beslan would take the throne after her. When Mat decided to leave, she didn't try to stop him, although he bound her to avert suspicion from her. She was discovered bound hand and foot and gagged, with her head torn from her body, in the early-morning hours of the night that Mat kidnapped Tuon and fled to Valan Luca's show. Her death was kept secret for fear of disturbances in the streets; it was announced on the same day that Beslan was crowned as her successor.

Tymoth. An Asha'man with Ituralde during the battle at Maradon. He destroyed catapults used by the invading Trollocs.

Tyr. A place in Saldaea where Bashere had estates. One of his titles was Lord of Bashere, Tyr and Sidona.

Tyrim, Zeranda. An Aes Sedai of the Brown Ajah who served as Amyrlin from 797 to 817 NE. Zeranda was an Amyrlin of only average strength.

Tyrn. An alleged grandson of Artur Hawkwing from whom Mayeners claimed descent. His pedigree was never confirmed, although any kin of Hawkwing's might well have been hidden for safety.

Tzigan Sokorin. A woman who was a member of Elayne's Queen's Guard. Apple-cheeked and cold-eyed, she claimed to be the daughter of a minor noble in Ghealdan; Elayne thought that she might have been Ghealdanin, at least. She had been a Hunter of the Horn and wore the golden knot of an under-lieutenant on her shoulder. She helped rescue Elayne from the Black Ajah and fetched her a horse afterward.

Tzora. The second-greatest city in the Age of Legends. Jaric Mondoran, a male Aes Sedai during the Breaking, went mad and threatened Tzora. Ten thousand Da'shain Aiel linked arms and sang, trying to remind him of who they were and who he had been, trying to turn him with their bodies and a song. Jaric stared at them as though at a puzzle, killing them, and they kept closing their lines and singing. He listened to the last Aiel for almost an hour before destroying him. Then Tzora burned, one huge flame consuming stone and metal and flesh, leaving only a sheet of glass.

Uncrowned, the. One of the titles that Borderlanders used for Lan.

Underhill, Master. The name used by Karldin Manfor when traveling with Loial.

Uno Nomesta. A Shienaran soldier. His head was shaven except for a grizzled topknot, and he had slightly bowed legs and a long scar down the left side of his face. Uno had lost his left eye and covered the socket with an eyepatch painted with a permanently frowning fierce red eye. After Samara he acquired a near-matching scar on his right cheek. Hard-featured even for a Shienaran, he would stare anyone in the eye, and use his file-like tongue as well. Uno nearly strangled when he couldn't curse. He was a born sergeant-major who did not think the Tinkers were cowards, but thought that most women were unreasonable and stubborn.

Uno was one of those following Ingtar when he and Perrin pursued the Horn of Valere to Falme. He wintered in the Mountains of Mist with Perrin and Rand; after Rand left and the Shienarans were abandoned to make their own way, he stayed with Masema in Ghealdan for a time, then accompanied Nynaeve and Elayne to Salidar. There he started working with the army under Gareth Bryne and was made an officer. He and the Shienarans with him trained heavy cavalry. He agreed to this arrangement, mostly as a ploy to stay close to Elayne and Nynaeve, to whom he felt he owed a debt of gratitude— among other things, Nynaeve Healed him of a serious wound he sustained in Samara. Uno didn't think much of the rebel Aes Sedai chances against the White Tower and the sitting Amyrlin, although he knew of Bryne's reputation; he thought the nations would fall in with the Tower no matter what tales Logain told, as most people tended to believe the stronger side told the truth. But he had no intention of running out on them.

Uno was promoted to captain during the Last Battle, having shown gallantry in the field and after Bryne was found to be under Compulsion. He was wounded in the arm by the Trollocs, but he was Healed and survived.

Unseen World. *See Tel'aran'rhiod*

Upriver Run, The. An inn located in Tar Valon. Narenwin Barda went there to get messages sent via carrier pigeon from Mistress Macura and Luci, who were spying for the Yellow Ajah in Amadicia, and were told to inform Barda if they saw Elayne, by order of the Amyrlin.

Uren din Jubai Soaring Gull. An ancient scholar of the Atha'an Miere who devised the Farede calendar, which he named after the Panarch Farede of Tarabon, his patron. The calendar remained in use from the end of the War of the Hundred Years at least until the end of the Third Age.

Urien. A man of the Two Spires sept of the Reyn Aiel and the *Aethan Dor* who was *siswai'aman*. Tall, with blue eyes and red hair cut short except for a tail in the back that hung to his shoulders, he met Ingtar and Verin while searching for He Who Comes With the Dawn. He went to Cairhien and Caemlyn with Rand, and to Shadar Logoth. At Dumai's Wells, he led the five thousand *siswai'aman*. Urien bet a skin of *oosquai* that Mat's forces would win the Last Battle.

Uso. A hired hand at Alysa's apple orchard in Andor. Even though Bunt told him that there were apples on the trees, he had to go look for himself.

V'saine. The city in which the Collam Daan was located during the Age of Legends.

vacuole. A bubble in the Pattern where time flowed differently. Research was conducted in vacuoles during the Age of Legends, but they were unstable and sometimes disappeared, with everything inside lost forever. Moghedien was imprisoned for a couple of days in a vacuole when she was first mindtrapped.

Vadere, Mikio. *See* Mikio Vadere

Vadere, Mistress. The innkeeper of The Golden Barge in So Habor, where Perrin and his group went to buy grain. Long-nosed and dirty, she served wine to Perrin and his companions while they negotiated.

Valan Luca. A circus owner and manager. Six feet tall, with broad shoulders, well-turned calves, dark hair and dark eyes, he liked sporting bright colors and was given to elaborate bows, flowery language and wild exaggerations. His show's name was Valan Luca's Grand Traveling Show and Magnificent Display of Marvels and Wonders. Nynaeve, Elayne, Thom, Juilin and Birgitte traveled with and performed in the show; Luca was very taken with Nynaeve, but he later married Latelle. Because he offered shelter to Cerandin and her *s'redit*, Luca received an exemption from the horse lottery the Seanchan carried out in Ebou Dar. Mat and his group escaped Ebou Dar and the Seanchan by traveling with Luca's show.

Valda, Eamon. *See* Eamon Valda

Valene Sural. An Aes Sedai of the Red Ajah and the loyalist contingent, with a potential strength level of 21(9). Born in 972 NE, she went to the White Tower in 988 NE. After spending five years as a novice and six years as Accepted, she was raised to the shawl in 999 NE. Since Valene had not yet acquired the ageless look, she was part of the expedition to kidnap Rand. She escaped Dumai's Wells with Covarla Baldene and was sent to Dorlan.

Valera Gorovni. An Aes Sedai of the Brown Ajah with a strength level of 14(2). Born in 748 NE, she went to the White Tower in 765 NE. After spending eight years as a novice and six years as Accepted, she was raised to the shawl in 779 NE. Short, plump and always wearing a smile, she seemed to be bustling even while standing still. Valera was one of the sisters called in by Tamra Ospenya to carry out the secret search for the newborn Dragon Reborn. She was murdered by the Black Ajah in 979 NE.

Valinde Nathenos. An Illianer Aes Sedai of the White Ajah and the rebel contingent, with a strength level of 33(21). She was stout and had no Warder. Valinde was a member of the rebel embassy to Rand in Caemlyn, and was one of the four sent on to Salidar with the Two Rivers girls. She tended to favor Romanda's positions.

Vandalra lace. A cream-colored lace found on Elayne's Ebou Dari dress.

Vandene Namelle. An Aes Sedai of the Green Ajah and the rebel contingent, with a strength level of 22(10). Born in 737 NE, she went to the White Tower with her sister Adeleas in 752 NE. After spending five years as a novice and five years as Accepted, she was raised to the shawl in 762 NE. She progressed in near lockstep with her sister; they were raised within a month of each other in both instances. About 5'5" tall, and slender and graceful with a straight back—a mirror image of her sister—she wore her nearly white hair gathered at the back of her neck and had dark eyes. Vandene had a potential strength level of 20(8) but never achieved it because her older sister was weaker; some women who were close did not diverge greatly in strength even if their potentials did. Her lifespan was unaffected by this, being governed by her higher potential. She bonded Jaem as her Warder in 949 NE and retired in 970 NE to Tifan's Well in Arafel with her sister Adeleas to write a history of the world since the Breaking, but events surrounding the Dragon Reborn caused them to become active again. They went to Salidar and then accompanied Elayne and Nynaeve to Ebou Dar. After the use of the Bowl of the Winds and the arrival of the Seanchan, they started to Caemlyn with Elayne. On the way, Adeleas was murdered and Vandene became grief-stricken. Vandene was forced to take two Kinswomen, Kirstian and Zarya, under her wing; they had run away from the Tower as novices, and were put back in novice white. She was obsessed with finding Adeleas' murderer; she began wearing her sister's perfume, wearing her sister's clothes and using her sister's silver-mounted Ebou Dari–style saddle. She went with Elayne to Full Moon Street to capture the Black Ajah members there, and she stabbed the treacherous Black Ajah sister, Careane, who had murdered Adeleas. Chesmal then killed Vandene; Jaem died while avenging her.

Vandes, Eban. The author of *The History of the Stone of Tear*, which Rand read.

Vane, Master. A lacquerware merchant and Darkfriend. Graying and stocky, with a drooping lower lip, he was playing *Piri* in The White Ring in Maderin; as Mat joined the game, Vane left quickly. When Mat, Tuon, Selucia and Thom left the inn, Vane and more than a dozen others attacked them, and were killed for their efforts.

Vanin, Chel. *See* Chel Vanin

Vanora Carridin. Jaichim Carridin's favorite sister. She lived in Carmera and liked to ride in a forest nearby. She was given by Sammael to Myrddraal to punish Jaichim for his failures.

Varadin. A Whitecloak spy in Tarabon who wrote Pedron Niall about the invasion of the Seanchan in Tanchico.

Varan Marcasiev. High Seat of House Marcasiev and Lord of Canluum, Kandor.

His fortress-like palace stood atop the highest hill in Canluum, Stag's Stand. Lan and Bukama avoided presenting themselves to him when they entered Canluum to avoid the ceremony which would have ensued. A proud man; duty counted more to him than anything else. Varan's sign was the Red Stag.

Varek. A skinny under-lieutenant in the Seanchan Ever Victorious Army. In the fight against Rand, he lost *sei'taer* by being sent afoot to get a scouting report. He was under the command of Captain-General Miraj, who sent him to notify Banner-General Chianmai to retreat while battling Rand's troops. He found Chianmai dead and the troops in disarray. He took command of the troops and was likely promoted for extracting those forces successfully. He had been at Falme, and thought the battle in which Chianmai died was worse.

Varil Nensen. An Asha'man soldier from Tarabon. Young, with dark eyes, a gravelly voice and a transparent veil covering his thick mustaches, he was with Rand's forces in the Venir Mountains in Altara during the battle against the Seanchan. Rand vaguely remembered seeing him at the Black Tower when Rand went to name the Asha'man and hand out pins for the first time. He joined Taim's faction, and was bonded to Alviarin. They were captured in Stedding Sholoon by Androl and his allies, including some elderly Ogier.

Varilin Zanaire. A Saldaean Aes Sedai of the Gray Ajah and the rebel contingent, with a strength level of 26(14). Born in 831 NE, she went to the White Tower in 848 NE. After spending seven years as a novice and six years as Accepted, she was raised to the shawl in 992 NE. She was 6'2" tall, and slender, with red hair, and sometimes looked like a long-legged wading bird. Her nose was not particularly prominent, nor were her cheekbones very high, considering that she was Saldaean. Varilin was raised a Sitter for the Gray in 992 NE and left the White Tower to join the rebellion on orders from the leadership of the Gray Ajah to attempt control and dissipation of the situation. This she did in large part by delay, trying to ensure stalemate in the rebel Hall. She was part of Romanda's clique, and was under Romanda's thumb. Varilin tried to influence the rebel Hall toward the belief that the Seanchan were too important and too dangerous to wait until matters were settled with Elaida, but because of her relationship with Romanda, she had to do so carefully. She was part of the group, with Faiselle, Saroiya, Magla and Takima, who negotiated with the White Tower to try to end the split. In a class taught by Elayne, she made a mistake in trying to make *ter'angreal* and created a ball of fire in her hands; she would have died had Dagdara not been there to Heal her.

Varkel Tius. A man with Perrin's army who had trouble getting canvas to repair torn tents.

Varuna Morrigan. An Aes Sedai of the Green Ajah who served as Amyrlin from 638 to 681 NE. Varuna was an Amyrlin of average strength. She focused on the Borderlands, feeling that the battle there against Shadowspawn was much more important than any meddling with nations farther south. This effectively reduced the Tower's power and influence to the south. Her focus on the

Borderlands and external matters also left the Hall largely in control of the Tower and the Aes Sedai.

Varuota. Tuon's great-great-great-grandmother. Tuon recalled her saying *"Sa'rabat shaiqen nai batain pyast,"* meaning "a woman is most resourceful with a knife at her throat."

Vasa. A sailor on the crew of Mallia's ship, the *Gray Gull*, out of Tar Valon, which transported Mat and Thom to Aringill. Mallia summoned him and Sanor to throw Mat and Thom off when they jumped onto the ship as it was leaving the dock; they were persuaded otherwise. Vasa was a large man with arms like Perrin's.

Vasha. A Domani Aes Sedai of the Green Ajah. Her Warder was Marlesh. Vasha was a member of the party sent to kidnap Rand; after Dumai's Wells she escaped and made her way to Dorlan with Covarla Beldeine.

Vayelle Kamsa. An Aes Sedai of the Red Ajah and the loyalist contingent, with a strength level of 34(22). Born in 914 NE, she went to the White Tower in 932 NE. After spending thirteen years as a novice and eleven years as Accepted, Vayelle was raised to the shawl in 956 NE. She aided in kidnapping Rand from Cairhien and was captured at Dumai's Wells. Vayelle was treated as *da'tsang* by the Aiel until, under Verin's Compulsion, she found reason to swear oath to Rand, which she had done before Cadsuane departed Cairhien for Far Madding. Vayelle and the other captive Reds were the very last to swear.

Vayet, Akoure. *See* Akoure Vayet

Vayu, Sierin. *See* Sierin Vayu

Velina Behar. A Saldaean Aes Sedai of the White Ajah publicly and of the Black Ajah in truth. Of the loyalist contingent, she had a strength level of 25(13). Born in 859 NE, she went to the White Tower in 877 NE. After spending eleven years as a novice and nine years as Accepted, Velina was raised to the shawl in 897 NE and raised a Sitter for the White Ajah in 974 NE. About 5'6" tall, she had a strong hooked nose, sharp high cheekbones and a penetrating stare from eyes that were almost black. Her voice was cool and precise but almost girlishly high-pitched, strongly at odds with her face. Said by many to be the coolest, most self-possessed woman in the Tower, Velina stood to depose Siuan, one of only eleven needed to give the greater consensus under the circumstances. Part of the Black Ajah's Supreme Council, she was one of two women on the Supreme Council who knew Alviarin's name; the other was Sedore Dajenna. Despite reports about the Seanchan, she did not believe that *a'dam* existed. Her name was listed in Verin's book, but she fled the Tower and avoided capture.

Venamar, Ryne. *See* Ryne Venamar

Vendare, Nathin Sarmain. *See* Nathin Sarmain Vendare

Venir Mountains. A mountain range extending across the southern coast of Altara to Arran Head in the southeast. Rand fought the Seanchan in this area.

Venr Kosaan. One of Careane Fransi's Warders, a Saldaean. He was 5'10" tall, and whip slender, with a dark complexion, tightly curled black hair and a close-cut beard with light touches of gray. In his middle years, he was quick, in total repose or even half-asleep one moment, then moving very suddenly the next. Venr was a Darkfriend; he and Careane's other two Warders were killed when they attempted to rescue her from Lady Shiaine's house on Full Moon Street.

Verana Peninsula. The easternmost peninsula of Tanchico in Tarabon, one of the three peninsulas on Tanchico Bay. The Panarch's Circle and Panarch's Palace were located on the Verana.

Verdin. A young squadman in the Band of the Red Hand. Verdin accompanied Mat to Salidar. Later, in the Last Battle, he went with Faile to deliver the Horn of Valere. When they wound up in the Blight, Verdin helped fight off large beasts.

Verin Mathwin. An Aes Sedai of the Brown Ajah publicly and the Black Ajah in truth, with a strength level of 17(5). Born in Far Madding in 849 NE, before going to the White Tower, Verin had thought of marrying a boy named Eadwin, who had a mischievous smile that she remembered fondly. She went to the White Tower in 864 NE. After spending five years as a novice and six as Accepted, she was raised to the shawl in 875 NE. Driven by the desire to know as much as possible, she decided that becoming an Aes Sedai of the Brown Ajah was the best way to do that. She was surprised, pleased and frightened, all together, when she passed the tests and learned she could indeed become Aes Sedai.

She joined the Black Ajah in 929 NE under duress, when she was caught while studying rumors and tales and got very close to discovering who some of the members were. She had one Warder, Tomas, who was a Darkfriend.

About five feet tall, and plump, Verin was placid-looking and square-faced, with a touch of gray in her hair. Despite her ageless face, she looked like somebody's mother or aunt, or the cook at an inn. Her fingers were often ink-stained, and she habitually rubbed her nose, especially in thought, frequently smudging ink there. Verin had a scar on her arm that she implied was received in *Tel'aran'rhiod*; Anaiya Healed her, but the Healing didn't work as well as it should have. Since she wasn't a dreamwalker, she used a dream *ter'angreal*, a twisted stone ring from Corianin Nedeal that she later gave to

Egwene. She wore a small brooch, a flower carved from some translucent stone; it was an *angreal*. Verin had some ability with Healing, but not great. Her handwriting was thin and spidery.

Verin accompanied Siuan to Fal Dara, where she met Rand and worked out that he could channel. While Ingtar and Perrin were pursuing Fain and the Horn of Valere, she joined them, saying that Moiraine sent her. She and the Shienarans arrived in Cairhien just after the Horn, which Rand had recovered, was stolen again. She and Rand planned to travel to Toman Head to follow Fain through the Ways, but *Machin Shin* was waiting just inside. They went instead by Portal Stone, but Rand did not have control and it took them months to get there.

After the battle at Falme, Verin escorted Elayne, Nynaeve, Egwene and the very ill Mat back to Tar Valon; when she arrived she gave the Horn to Siuan. Verin was part of the circle that Healed Mat of his connection to the Shadar Logoth dagger and gave Egwene the dream *ter'angreal*, but not the notes about *Tel'aran'rhiod* that Corianin Nedeal had left behind.

With Alanna, Verin traveled to the Two Rivers to seek out girls who could channel; shortly after they arrived, the Whitecloaks turned up as well. Verin and Alanna took refuge near Emond's Field and helped in the fight against the Trollocs. With a number of young women with either the spark or the ability to learn to channel, the two Aes Sedai headed to Tar Valon; on the way they learned of the schism in the Tower, but continued on to Caemlyn. There they met Rand, and Alanna bonded him. Verin was not so upset over Alanna bonding Rand against his will as she made out. She wanted a string to Rand and thought that Alanna, emotionally vulnerable because of her Warder's death, could be manipulated into being that string. Using Alanna provided a little distance for Verin, and perhaps a little safety.

Although she was not part of the original rebel embassy to Rand in Caemlyn, Verin began working with the embassy under Merana, and gave Merana some difficulties because Merana naturally deferred to the stronger woman. When Rand fled Caemlyn, she followed with Kiruna and the others and was forced to swear fealty after Dumai's Wells. Using a weak version of Compulsion, Verin made all of the loyalist sisters captured at Dumai's Wells also swear fealty to Rand. When Cadsuane followed Rand to Far Madding, Verin went along, although she had to use a false name because she did something there long ago causing arrest warrants to be signed, and she suspected they might still be in force.

While Rand was cleansing the taint, Verin linked with Shalon and Kumira; they encountered and defeated Graendal, but Kumira was killed.

Verin was with Cadsuane and Rand in hiding at Algarin's estate in Tear, not far from the Spine of the World, until she left, destination and purpose unknown, after Trollocs attacked the manor there.

Verin appeared to be helpful to Rand and his mission, but it was only immediately prior to the Last Battle that she was revealed to be a reluctant member of the Black Ajah. Though she had joined to save her own hide, she gathered as much information on the Black Ajah as she could. As she drank poisoned tea, she turned the information over to Egwene. Even in her death she revealed information that was of use to the forces of good, which she hoped would balance some of the atrocities that she had committed on orders from the Black Ajah.

Verine. An Accepted who was murdered by Padan Fain with the ruby dagger.

Veshir. The eldest of Renald Fanwar's farmhands.

Vestas. A captain in Bryne's army who participated in the rescue of Egwene from the Tower and gave Bryne a casualty report.

Vevanios, Ronaille. *See* Ronaille Vevanios

Victory of Kidron, the. The three-masted greatship that brought Tuon from Seanchan. Its captain was a woman named Tehan.

Viendre. A beautiful Wise One of the Goshien Aiel. As strong in the One Power as any Aes Sedai that Elayne had met except Nynaeve, Viendre was 5'8" tall, and had blue eyes and a strong nose. Appearing to be in her mid-twenties, she had a strength level of 10(+3). Elayne felt that Viendre sneered and looked down on her, but she stood in for Elayne's mother at the first-sister ceremony with Aviendha. Viendre and Tamela stood lowest in the group participating in Elayne's adoption.

view-wall. A device from the Age of Legends that allowed the user to create any illusion on the walls of a room, such as a forest.

Vileness, the. After Gitara Moroso's death, the Black Ajah heard rumors connecting the death with a Foretelling, one that had the Amyrlin Tamra Ospenya closeted and making secret and hasty plans, mainly with senior—in age and strength—sisters of her former Ajah. Nervous that it might involve the Black Ajah, the then head of the Blacks took a drastic step. She and others kidnapped Tamra and put her to the question, after which she was found dead in her bed. No one was surprised that her Warder also died that same night. From the Amyrlin, they learned of the Dragon Reborn, but she was stubborn, and they did not learn that he was only a newborn. All they discovered was that she had just learned that he had been born.

The Black Ajah immediately began a pogrom, an even more intensive search than usual for men who could channel, for males of any age who showed any sign that they might be able to channel. Even a rumor, a hint, was enough. And since being lucky or having a sudden rise to relative prominence were among the signs to look for, it was a bad time for men who were lucky or rose suddenly. All of the Black Ajah was involved, sisters supposedly of every Ajah, to the exclusion of anything else. And since the head of the Red Ajah was Black—both Galina Casban, during the last years of the pogrom, and the woman before her—there was little difficulty bringing many sisters of the Red Ajah into it as well. Those involved did not want to risk the man being brought back to Tar Valon, since if it was discovered that he was the Dragon Reborn, the other Aes Sedai would certainly decide to keep him alive, almost certainly not gentled, but still shielded and a prisoner; the sisters involved in the pogrom believed that the Dragon Reborn had to be disposed of. For that reason, men were gentled on the spot instead of being brought back to Tar Valon. Many were killed, "trying to escape" or the like, especially by Black sisters. Included in the number of dead were men and boys about whom someone had made a remark because of their luck (a miraculous escape from death, perhaps) or skill ("You'd think he could channel, he shoots an arrow so straight").

When Ishamael discovered what was going on, he was infuriated. He, of course, wanted to Turn the Dragon Reborn and deliver him to the Dark One, not have him killed, which would give no advantage to Ishamael. He put an end to the pogrom immediately, though it took some months to stop the Black Ajah completely. There was an immediate reaction to his discovery. The head triumvirate of the Black Ajah and a number of other high-ranking Black sisters died particularly unpleasant deaths. This harrowing and winnowing of the Black Ajah command structure was the reason that Alviarin became the new head of the Black Ajah.

The Red Ajah was ordered to halt as well, but some sisters did not stop, and the pogrom continued for another two years, albeit at a slower pace, until Marith Jaen finally ended it in 985 NE. Sierin Vayu had intended to crush it, but was assassinated in 984 NE. To protect the White Tower, events were covered up and sisters who knew of the pogrom were forbidden to speak of it or to admit what happened, but Marith Jaen still imposed heavy penances on those caught out. She came down hard on those guilty. Covering up for the Tower was one thing; she wasn't about to allow them to escape without punishment. Few of the Black Ajah, who had halted on Ishamael's orders, were caught, but large numbers of the Red were, and some others. The three Sitters for the Red all resigned their chairs, took "voluntary" penances and went into "retreats"—exile, in truth—which lasted until they were summoned back by Elaida.

The fact that so many of the Red Ajah served fairly harsh penances sparked rumors, but they were quiet rumors, and a good number of sisters from other Ajahs served penances over the next year, too. Few who were not actually part of the pogrom knew what happened, even inside the Red Ajah, and those who did were caught up in the sworn secrecy. Elaida escaped punishment because of minimal involvement. Galina escaped punishment because it was decided to punish only a few at the top and not destroy the whole Ajah; although she was head of the Ajah, no one outside the Ajah knew that.

Officially, during this period, seven men who could channel were caught and gentled. The secret records spoke of eight others. The unofficial tally ranged from eight to eighteen additional men, for a grand total of fifteen to twenty-five, but even that number might be too low. The secret Tower records spoke of two thousand men and boys killed between 979 NE and 985 NE, but again, that number was too low by at least a factor of five and maybe more.

Thom Merrilin's nephew Owyn was one of the last men, if not the last man, gentled in this campaign. Elaida was personally involved in only that gentling; she became involved because it was Thom's nephew, and hoped to use it to break Morgase from Thom's influence. She was successful in her goal.

Related to the killing of men and boys, the Black Ajah killed thirty to fifty senior Aes Sedai who might have known that the Dragon had been reborn.

Village Council. In most villages a group of men, elected by townsmen and headed by a Mayor, who were responsible for making decisions affecting the village as a whole and for negotiating with the Councils of other villages over matters jointly affecting the villages. They were at odds with the Women's Circle in so many villages that the conflict was seen as almost traditional.

Villiam Bloodletter. An ancient leader who fought the Banath people on Almoth Plain.

Vilnar Barada. A Saldaean patrol leader, an under-lieutenant sword-sworn to Lord Davram Bashere. His intended was Teryane. He had tilted eyes, a bold nose and a beard. He and his friends Jidar and Rissen had odd ideas about Aes Sedai; they all thought they knew what Aes Sedai were like and looked like, but none would have recognized one if he saw her. Barada would very much have liked to have seen an Aes Sedai; he knew there was something about their faces, but he didn't recognize it when he saw Marillin Gemalphin in Caemlyn. He saw Perrin's arrival in Caemlyn with Faile and their entourage and escorted them to the Royal Palace.

Vinchova, Evin. *See* Evin Vinchova

Viria Connoral. An Aes Sedai of the Red Ajah. She and her sister Raechin were chosen for the Hall of the Tower to replace Pevara and Javindhra. The sisters were the only siblings in the White Tower after Vandene and Adeleas died.

Vitalien. Sarene's Warder. He was broad-shouldered; Sarene wrote poetry comparing him to a leopard and other powerful, graceful and dangerous animals. Left behind in Cairhien when Sarene went with Cadsuane to Far Madding and beyond, Vitalien helped Bashere and Logain find Rand at Algarin's manor in Tear. As the Last Battle approached, Sarene and Vitalien engaged in a tempestuous affair. They fought for the armies at Shayol Ghul. Sarene was Compelled by Graendal/Hessalam and used until her eyes were vacant. Vitalien was killed.

Vivian, Lord. A Domani lord to whom Ramshalan boasted he could manipulate Rand.

vlja daeg roghda. A phrase spoken by Narg, a Trolloc.

Vogeler. A Saldaean soldier who went with Bashere to Maradon. He was present when the body of Lady Torkumen, a suicide, was found, and as the Darkfriend Vram Torkumen went mad.

Voice. A Talent used to perform Singing; mentioned by a mad Lews Therin when he greeted Ishamael, the Betrayer of Hope.

Voice of the Blood. Seanchan servant through whom a member of the Blood typically communicated with those of lower rank; and **Voice of the Throne**, a servant used by a member of the Seanchan Imperial family to communicate to those of lower rank. The left side of his or her scalp was shaved, with the remaining hair worn in a braid.

void, the. A state of nothingness that Tam taught Rand to access for use in the combat arts. To become one with the void, one put all one's emotions and thoughts in a flame, a point of focus, to be burned away, leaving the individual in a hyperaware state of consciousness. *See also* flame and the void *and* Oneness

Voniel. An Ogier who was Covril's sister and Haman's wife.

Vora. The *sa'angreal* bearing her name, a white fluted wand, was one of the most powerful held by the White Tower.

Vordarian, Brandel. *See* Brandel Vordarian

Vostovan, Sarainya. *See* Sarainya Vostovan

Votabek. A street tough in Bandar Eban whom Rand and Durnham convinced to help restore order to the city. When Redbord, a fellow tough, was unwilling to go along with the plan, Votabek mentioned that they weren't going to get paid by Lain, so they might as well join up.

Voyages Among the Sea Folk. A book at The Queen's Blessing in Caemlyn.

Vram Torkumen. A distant cousin of Queen Tenobia. Appointed lord of Maradon in her absence, he was also a Darkfriend and refused to let Ituralde and his troops into the city. Yoeli, a Saldaean officer, took matters into his own hands to save the Domani and imprisoned Torkumen. After Rand appeared and defeated the Shadowspawn, Torkumen went mad and put out his eyes with a writing quill. His wife jumped to her death.

Wade, Cinny. *See* Cinny Wade

Wagon Bridge. A bridge situated in the Two Rivers where the North Road, coming down from Taren Ferry and Watch Hill, became the Old Road, leading to Deven Ride.

Wagon Seat, The. A red-roofed inn located in Lugard, where Gareth Bryne stopped briefly to meet up with Joni and Barim, two of his men from Kore Springs, while pursuing Siuan, Leane, Min and Logain. It was a common man's inn, bawdy and boisterous.

Wagoner, Kert. A man from the Two Rivers who fought in the Last Battle. At the Field of Merrilor, he spoke to Rand about how bad things looked; Rand reassured him.

Wagoner's Whip, The. An inn standing in Maerone, Cairhien. A stone building frequented by common soldiers, it was visited by Mat and Edorion while making the rounds of drinking halls to check on Mat's soldiers.

wait-a-minute vine. A thorny vine found in Altara.

Wake of the Breaking, The. A history book studied by Min.

Wakeda. A powerful Domani nobleman who became Dragonsworn. He was not a tall man, though taller than Ituralde. Haughty, Wakeda had once been attractive, but had lost his right eye; a black arrowhead beauty spot pointed at the thick scar running from his cheek up onto his forehead. He met with Rodel Ituralde about the Seanchan problem at Lady Osana's manor. Wakeda was a casualty at the battle around Maradon.

Walishen. A tragic princess whose story was enacted by a group of players in Caemlyn; the performance was attended by Elayne and Birgitte.

Wallein din Onill. A Sea Folk Wavemistress, and one of the First Twelve. When Harine arrived at the meeting of the First Twelve in Illian, Wallein turned her back very deliberately.

Wan, Manda. An Aes Sedai of the Green Ajah. Just before Egwene appeared and fought Taim in the Last Battle, Manda was trying to persuade Leane and Raechin to fall back and regroup.

Wandering, the Long. The period of Exile, during the Time of Madness, the Breaking, when Ogier were scattered away from their *stedding. See also* Long Exile, the

Wandering Woman, The. An inn in Ebou Dar near the Tarasin Palace. Its innkeeper was Setalle Anan. A wide white building on the square, it was an expensive place, frequented by outlanders and locals alike, with musical entertainment. Mat and other men in his party stayed there before he moved into the palace. After the Seanchan had taken over the city and Mat was preparing for his escape, he secured a place in the cellar of the inn to store his clothes and gold, which he had his servants begin to sneak over from the palace. Egeanin and Bayle Domon were there at the behest of Lady Suroth, who wanted Egeanin to stay near the palace; Setalle hid Joline from the Seanchan there, and Mat kept her from being spotted by them. Setalle sold the inn to another woman and fled Ebou Dar with Mat, Tuon and company, hoping to meet up later with the rest of her family; they had taken the family's boats to Illian.

War of Power, the. Also known as the War of the Shadow, it ended the Age of Legends. Beginning shortly after the attempt to free the Dark One, it soon involved the whole world. In a world where even the memory of war had been forgotten, every facet of war was rediscovered, often twisted by the Dark One's touch on the world, and the One Power was used as a weapon. The war was ended by the resealing of the Dark One into his prison in a strike led by Lews Therin Telamon, the Dragon, and 113 male Aes Sedai called the Hundred Companions. The Dark One's counterstroke tainted *saidin* and drove Lews Therin and the Hundred Companions insane, thus beginning the Time of Madness.

War of the Hundred Years, the. A series of overlapping wars among constantly shifting alliances, precipitated by the death of Artur Hawkwing and the resulting struggle for his empire. It lasted from FY 994 to FY 1117. The war depopulated large parts of the lands between the Aryth Ocean and the Aiel Waste, from the Sea of Storms to the Great Blight. So great was the destruction that only fragmentary records of the time remain. The empire of Artur Hawkwing was pulled apart in the wars, and the nations of the time of the Last Battle were formed.

War of the Second Dragon. The war fought from FY 939 to FY 943 against the false Dragon Guaire Amalasan. During this war, a young king named Artur Tanreall Paendrag, later known as Artur Hawkwing, rose to overwhelming prominence.

War of the Shadow. *See* War of Power

ward. A defensive barrier set up by a channeler using the One Power. A ward could, for example, prevent entry into an area, make eavesdropping impossible, or alert the user to an intrusion.

Warder. Also known as Gaidin, a warrior bonded to an Aes Sedai. The bonding was a thing of the One Power, and by it the Warder gained such gifts as quick healing, the ability to go long periods without food, water or rest, and the ability to sense the taint of the Dark One at a distance. Warder and Aes Sedai shared certain physical and emotional knowledge of one another through the bond. So long as a Warder lived, the Aes Sedai to whom he was bonded knew he was alive however far away he was, and when he died she knew the moment and manner of his death. While most Ajahs believed an Aes Sedai might have one Warder bonded to her at a time, the Red Ajah refused to bond any Warders at all, and the Green Ajah believed an Aes Sedai might bond as many as she wished.

Ethically the Warder had to accede to the bonding voluntarily, but it was known to have been done against the Warder's will. What the Aes Sedai gained from the bonding was a closely held secret. By all known historical records, Warders were always men, but at least one woman was bonded shortly before the Last Battle; it revealed certain differences in the effects.

A Warder whose Aes Sedai died suffered greatly and rarely lived long afterward. This effect was actually the result of the bond being severed involuntarily, and not exclusively the result of the death of the Warder's Aes Sedai.

Warder bonds were unknown during the Age of Legends.

Bonding a Warder was not a Talent; it could be learned by any channeler, taking into account the limits of strength and skill. Though the Power was used to create it, the bond with a Warder was not a weave that could be seen. It was like the most subtle forms of Compulsion in that only its effects could be detected, even by the woman who did the weaving. On the other hand, the bond could be touched using flows of Spirit in order to make the one bonded obey. Unlike with most forms of Compulsion, however, the one forced to obey knew that force was involved unless the touch was very, very light, little more than a suggestion. Flows of Spirit for bonding were complex, but not so intricate as Healing.

warman. The Ogier term for a soldier in the Age of Legends.

Warrel, Elin. *See* Elin Warrel

Wars of Consolidation, or the Consolidation. Conflicts that took place in FY 943–963, leading to the consolidation of the nations formed after the Trolloc Wars. Following Artur Hawkwing's capture of Guaire Amalasan, a false Dragon, his country was attacked by many of the rulers who had been put in power by Amalasan. Hawkwing fought them for years and eventually brought all the nations together under his unified command.

wash-leather. A common material used in fabricating money purses.

Washim. A Malkieri who was a member of Lan's High Guard in the Last Battle.

Waste, the. The harsh, rugged and all-but-waterless land east of the Spine of the World. Few outsiders ventured there, not only because water was almost impossible to find for one not born there, but because the Aiel considered themselves at war with all other peoples and did not welcome strangers. It was called the Three-fold Land by the Aiel. Only peddlers, gleemen and the Tuatha'an were allowed safe entry, and the Aiel avoided all contact with the Tuatha'an, whom they called "the Lost Ones." No maps of the Waste itself were known to exist. Trollocs called it *Djevik K'Shar* in their tongue, meaning "the Dying Ground."

Wat. An Andoran Redarm in the Band of the Red Hand. Bald-headed and narrow-eyed, he took a shift with Harnan watching the Kin's house in Ebou Dar. Wat was part of the party that went to fetch the Bowl of the Winds in the Rahad and was killed by the *gholam*.

Watch Hill. A small village near Emond's Field in the Two Rivers, the first village north of Emond's Field on the North Road. Thatched houses were situated on a domelike hill. When Trollocs were attacking Emond's Field, Faile went to Watch Hill and brought back men to help defeat them.

Watch, the. The legal authorities upholding the law in Illian.

Watcher of the Seals. One of the titles of the Amyrlin Seat, referring to the seals on the Dark One's prison.

Watchers or Watchers over the Waves. *See Do Miere A'vron*

Water. One of the Five Powers. *See Five Powers*

water lizard. A dangerous swimmer found in the Drowned Lands. Twenty feet long, it had sharp teeth and powerful jaws.

Water Seeker. An Aiel warrior society also known as *Duadhe Mahdi'in*.

Water Way, the. A philosophy followed by the Amayar, the fair-skinned natives of Tremalking. The Water Way was a pacifistic belief, but not so strongly pacifistic as the Tuatha'an Way of the Leaf. The Water Way was fatalistic in many ways, teaching the acceptance of what was and teaching against any desire for change. It taught that the world was only an illusion—the shadow of a dream—and changes in it did not matter. To the Amayar, it was the inner life, the spiritual life within, that was truly important.

Waterless Sands, the. *See Termool*

Watersharers. The Aiel name for Cairhienin, who traded with the Aiel, prior to the Aiel War. The name came from the time after the Breaking when the Aiel wandered in search of safety; the people who founded Cairhien were the only ones who shared water with them.

Waterwood, the. A swampy area of streams, ponds and forest due east of Emond's Field.

Wavedancer. A Sea Folk raker whose Sailmistress was Coine din Jubai Wild Winds. Jorin din Jubai White Wing was the Windfinder, Toram the Cargomaster and Dorele a crew member. *Wavedancer* was a hundred paces long and half as wide, and it had four masts. Elayne, Nynaeve, Thom and Juilin traveled from Tear to Tanchico aboard *Wavedancer*. Its crew had escaped capture by the Seanchan the year before, sending the attacking Seanchan ship to the bottom of the sea. After Tanchico, *Wavedancer* went on to spread news of the Coramoor among the Sea Folk islands.

Wavemistress. The leader of an Atha'an Miere clan. A clan Wavemistress was chosen by the First Twelve of her clan, the twelve ranking Sailmistresses, but she could be removed by command of the Mistress of the Ships. She could, in fact, be demoted to the lowest position on a ship or, worse, set ashore by the Mistress of the Ships. A Wavemistress had a degree of absolute authority within her clan that would be envied by any shorebound ruler. In certain circumstances, however, such as warfare and/or battle, a Wavemistress was expected to yield to her Swordmaster.

A clan Wavemistress rated a fringed red parasol of two tiers and wore five fat earrings per ear.

Way of the Leaf, the. A pacifistic code of honor practiced by the Da'shain Aiel; the Tuatha'an, who descended from the Da'shain Aiel, also followed it. Their saying was "The leaf lives its appointed time, and does not struggle against the wind that carries it away. The leaf does no harm, and finally falls to nourish new leaves." The Way did not allow for any violence against another being for any reason.

Way of the Light, The. A philosophical treatise written by Lothair Mantelar, the founder of the Children of the Light. It was used for guidance by the White-cloaks.

Wayfarer's Rest, The. A lower-class, dirty inn found in Whitebridge across from the bridge on the way to Caemlyn. Master Bartim was its innkeeper. Rand, Mat and Thom Merrilin stopped there for information while trying to find Moiraine and company after escaping the Trollocs at Shadar Logoth. The three men discovered that the Fades had already been searching for them in town. Moiraine, Lan and Nynaeve also stopped there later for a meal before proceeding on the Caemlyn Road.

Waygate. An opening that allowed entry into the Ways from the outside world. The key for opening from either side was the trefoil leaf of *Avendesora* found on the Waygate. The leaf was removed and replaced a handspan lower, enabling the Waygate to open. Sometimes the leaf was missing; the One Power could be used to make an opening, but it destroyed the Waygate's ability to close. The Way-gates were developed with the aid of the Talisman of Growing *ter'angreal*.

Wayland's Forge. A prosperous, three-storied inn of polished gray stone with a purple roof, in Remen on the Ghealdan/Murandy border on the River Maneth-erendrelle. Lan, Moiraine, Perrin and Loial stopped there while following Rand's track east. Hunters in the inn claimed they had killed most of twenty Aielmen, and had one in a cage in the town square; Min had seen an Aiel in a cage as being a turning point in Perrin's life. Perrin released the Aiel, Gaul, and they did battle with Whitecloaks. The party fled downriver by barge toward Illian, and was joined by a Hunter of the Horn called Faile.

Waylin. One of Rina Hafden's Warders. He was dark and clean-shaven, with broad shoulders and a broad back. As an Accepted, Moiraine saw Waylin and Elyas practicing swordplay in the hallway while delivering a message in the Green quarters.

wayline. A term used by Sammael to describe the signal produced by the act of channeling Fire into the callbox he gave Sevanna and the Shaido; the wayline allowed him to locate them when they wanted to make contact with him.

Ways. Pathways from one *stedding* to another, grown from the One Power during the Breaking of the World. A gift from male Aes Sedai to the *stedding* in thanks for shelter from the taint on *saidin*, they existed outside the normal confines of time and space. The Aes Sedai had studied the worlds of the Portal Stones, reflections of this world, as a basis for growing the Ways. A day's walk-ing inside the Ways might carry the traveler to a destination hundreds of miles away, but strangely, sometimes a more distant place could be reached more quickly than one that was nearer. The Ways appeared to consist of ramps, bridges and islands seemingly floating in the air unsupported. On each island was a stone, called a guiding, with directions in Ogier script for various destinations from that point. Once well lit and beautiful, the islands covered with grasses, flowers and fruit trees, the Ways deteriorated, growing dank and dim, and the islands became only bare stone; *Machin Shin*, the Black Wind, appeared, and travelers in the Ways increasingly disappeared or emerged in a demented state. The degradation was the result of the taint on *saidin*, which had been used in the initial making of the Ways. The Ogier Elders eventually were forced to prohibit their use. The Ogier possessed a *ter'angreal* which allowed them to make the Ways grow to other places, but it was not used after the Ways went dark.

weaves. *See* Aligning the Matrix, Arrows of Fire, Blossom of Fire, Caressing the Child, Cloud Dancing, Compulsion, Deathgates, Delving, Earth Singing, Finder, Folded Light, Illusion, Keeping, Listening to the Wind, Mask of Mirrors, Milking Tears, Mirror of Mists, the, Skimming, Spinning Earthfire *and* Traveling

weave the flows. The process by which a channeler manipulated one or more of the Five Powers to produce a given effect. In general, it was believed that there were line-of-sight limits, i.e., it was necessary to see the flows one was weaving. Even so, one could work on the unseen when very close, as in Healing. It was possible to work at even the atomic or molecular level on something very close. Even making weather over a large area was more a matter of working with what one could see to produce a larger effect. There was a fall-off of strength with distance, but it was hardly noticeable with the stronger channelers. The weakest channelers could not weave as far as they could see.

Aes Sedai believed that it was impossible, for all practical purposes, to unmake a weave; that is, to unweave it once woven (as distinct from untying a knot). They believed that weaves had to be released and allowed to dissipate. Even on those rare occasions when possible, with a weave that wasn't too complex, one slip during an attempt, and the weave could coalesce once more in a form that was both impossible to know beforehand and unpredictable in its results. This could kill, burn out or otherwise seriously injure the channeler and others nearby, as well as the physical surroundings. On the other hand, Aiel Wise Ones were taught routinely to unweave. Aviendha showed the Aes Sedai it could be done when she picked apart the weave for a gateway at the Kin farm. *See also* flows *and* knot

Weaving of the Winds. The Sea Folk term for manipulating the weather.

Web. *See* ta'maral'ailen

web. An Age of Legends word used for a weave of the Power. *See* net

Web, Great. *See* Great Pattern

Web of Destiny. *See* ta'maral'ailen

Weesin. A flyspeck village made up of a little cluster of thatch-roofed houses on the Great North Road north of Ebou Dar in Altara. Luca's circus passed through Weesin. While camped there, Mat saw the three Aes Sedai and three *sul'dam* sneak back into camp, and he confronted them for putting everyone at risk.

Weikin Rebellion. A war of which Egwene knew nothing when quizzed by Bennae, after Egwene had been captured by the Tower and put back in novice white.

Weilin Aldragoran. A plump Malkieri merchant who lived in Saldaea. His wife, Alida, was Saldaean. He traded in many things, but most of his profit came from gems. When Malkier was destroyed, he was only a toddler, but he chose to wear the *hadori*; he found that few people argued with a man who wore one. Nynaeve found him trading jewels at The Queen's Lance in Kayacun and persuaded him to ride to Tarwin's Gap with Lan for the Last Battle; he also agreed to send a message to every merchant he traded with that Lan was riding for the Gap. He caught up with Lan in Kandor, almost at the Arafellin border, and fought in his army in the Last Battle.

Weiramon Saniago. A High Lord of Tear and a Darkfriend. His sigil was the silver Crescent-and-Stars. Iron-spined straight, with a perfectly trimmed and oiled gray-streaked beard, he was about 5'10" to 5'11" tall. He reminded Rand of a banty rooster, his chest all puffed out and strutting. One of four High Lords at Rand's meeting with the commanders of the Illian invasion army, he had contempt for the Aiel "savages." Weiramon and Semaradrid had a touchy relationship; Weiramon pretended to give the Cairhienin equality while slighting him almost unconsciously. Semaradrid was fully aware of the slights, and of his weaker position, and hated both.

Weiramon was the Tairen seen by Carridin at the Darkfriend gathering with Ba'alzamon. His actions were a function not only of his inherent stupidity, but also his status as a Darkfriend. Though he had an unctuous manner toward Rand, he had plotted against him for so long that he probably did so in his sleep. He had command of a Tairen relief force for Cairhien, but Rand sent him back to Tear, ostensibly to fight bandits and pirates. He had a command in the Illian invasion army; he rushed the cavalry and the Aiel, leaving the foot soldiers, whom he despised, behind, arriving at the hillforts earlier than planned. Weiramon was part of the campaign against the Seanchan; at one point he left his post to chase Seanchan, leaving Rand exposed. Rand took Weiramon and other nobles he distrusted back to Cairhien and gave them trustworthy servants. When Rand returned to Tear and found Weiramon and Anaiyella there, he was enraged that the two had left Cairhien without permission. Rand ordered them to go with Darlin to Arad Doman to help restore order. When Rand returned from Dragonmount before the Last Battle, he exposed Weiramon as a Darkfriend and exiled him.

Welcome. A Shienaran ritualized ceremony; it was used during the arrival of the Amyrlin Seat in Fal Dara.

Wellin, Mistress. A clerk in the White Tower. She was miffed when Tamra assigned clerical work to two Accepted, Moiraine and Siuan.

Well. A *ter'angreal* used to store the One Power.

Welyn Kajima. An Arafellin Dedicated Asha'man. About 5'9" tall, with a pale, square face, dark eyes and black hair worn in two braids with bells fastened to the ends, he had the manners and mannerisms of a clerk, which he had been. When he went to the Black Tower, he was about thirty-five years old. He bonded

Jenare Balmaen of the Red Ajah; against all expectations, they dealt well with each other. Toveine thought he smiled too much; Kajima brought word of a new deserters list to Logain in her hearing. Kajima and Jenare accompanied Rand to his meeting with the Daughter of the Nine Moons. He was later Turned to the Shadow by Taim, and told Androl that he had been demoted. He and Leems entered the room where Androl and Pevara had captured Dobser, and Androl knocked them out with a cudgel. Kajima and Mezar took Evin to be Turned.

Wenchen, Stedding. A *stedding* located in the mountains north of the River Dhagon.

Westpoint Lighttower. A tower located at the end of Bay Road in Ebou Dar with beacons to guide ships entering the bay.

Westwood, The. An area just west of Emond's Field and the site of Tam's farm.

wetlander. The Aiel word for those who lived west of the Spine of the World, i.e., non-Aiel.

Whatley Eldin. A Two Rivers man who painted his wagon in a way pleasing to Rand.

Wheel of Time, the. Time is a wheel with seven spokes, each spoke an Age. As the Wheel turns, Ages come and go, each leaving memories that fade to legend, then to myth, and are forgotten by the time that Age comes again. The Pattern of an Age is slightly different each time a specific Age comes, and each time it is subject to greater change, but each time it is the same Age. It is not a repeat exactly of what went before, when that Age last came, but close enough in its general outline that it might seem the same at a glance.

Wheel of Time, The. A historical book about the Dragon Reborn and the Aiel, written by Sulamein so Bhagad, Chief Historian at the Court of the Sun, the Fourth Age.

Whelborn. A member of Ituralde's forces who died defending his flank in the battle against Trollocs at Maradon; Ituralde thought that he was one of the best.

Whisperer. A wolf who hunted with Perrin and Hopper in the wolf dream. Whisperer was caught inside the purple dome of a dreamspike, and Slayer killed her.

White Ajah. One of the seven legitimate Aes Sedai Ajahs. Sisters of this Ajah abstained from matters of the world and worldly knowledge, and instead devoted themselves to questions of philosophy and truth. Aside from the First Weaver, the head of the Ajah, there was no internal structure whatsoever. Her authority was very high, not much less than that of the Red Ajah head and roughly equal to the authority of the Green or Yellow Ajah heads. In choosing Sitters, the support of ten sisters was required to become a candidate. It was considered unseemly to campaign in any way, either to become a candidate or to win selection as a Sitter. Voting was not by secret ballot, but by open show of hands.

It was believed by many sisters in other Ajahs that the White Ajah was the only one without an Ajah set of eyes-and-ears and that they had no real interest in the world. This was not true, though their Ajah network was indeed small. Even the Whites—as a group, anyway—wanted to try to manipulate world events, along strictly logical lines, of course.

Among Whites, being sent off from the Tower on a mission of some sort, even as part of an embassy, was looked upon as drudgery at best, and at worst, punishment. Most Whites never bonded a Warder.

Just prior to the Last Battle, there were approximately eighty members in the White Ajah, making it the smallest.

White Boar, The. An inn located in Watch Hill, Andor. When Mat, Rand and Perrin fled through Watch Hill with Moiraine and Lan, they wanted to go to The White Boar and have mutton pie there, even though Mat said that it was not nearly as good as The Winespring Inn's.

White Bridge. A beautiful, large structure that spanned the River Arinelle in Whitebridge, giving the town its name. Built with the Power during the Age of Legends, it looked as if it were made of glass.

White Cliff. A sept of the Shaido Aiel.

White Crescent, The. An inn located in Tear. Master Cavan Lopar was its innkeeper. Mat and Thom lodged there while trying to find Egwene, Nynaeve and Elayne, and to head off Comar, who had been sent by Gaebril to kill the women.

White Crescents. The symbol of Tear, three white crescents on a field of red and gold.

White Eyes. A wolf that Perrin met in the wolf dream while looking for Slayer. He told Perrin that the wolves needed Perrin to lead them in the Last Hunt.

White Hart of Shienar. The symbol of Shienar.

white henpepper. A plant that could soothe a toothache or dye hair black.

White Lion. The symbol of Andor, a white lion on a field of red.

White Lions. The unit of men within the Queen's Guards of Caemlyn that was formed by and loyal to Gaebril, who was in fact the Forsaken Rahvin. They fled east and became brigands after Rand balefired Rahvin. Daved Hanlon commanded them as mercenaries to serve the rebels against Rand in Cairhien until most of them were destroyed by a bubble of evil there.

White Mountain. A mountain found in the Aiel Waste.

White Mountain Sept. A sept of the Chareen Aiel.

White Ribbon. A symbol used during war in Arad Doman to indicate a desire for a temporary truce to enable a conference between the warring parties.

White Ring, The. An inn located in Maderin, Altara. When Tuon wanted to visit a "hell," Thom suggested The White Ring, realizing that Tuon would not know what a real hell was like. Its innkeeper was Mistress Heilin; Jera was a serving woman, and a young woman was singing a salacious song.

White River. The southernmost of the two rivers that flanked Emond's Field in Andor and joined to become the River Manetherendrelle.

white shakes. A disease causing fever, coughing and the loss of one's senses. It could be fatal if not treated.

White Shark, Chanelle din Seran. *See* Chanelle din Seran White Shark

White Spray. A Sea Folk soarer with two raked masts, commanded by Sailmistress Derah din Selaan Rising Wave. Its Windfinder was Taval din Chanai Nine Gulls. The Windfinder was reluctant to let Aes Sedai board the ship, and dumped Egwene into the water when she tried to visit. Rand boarded *White Spray* to bargain with the Sea Folk; he left in the middle of negotiations, but Merana and Rafela completed the Bargain for him.

White Swan, The. An inn found in Forel Market, Andor. Elayne and the group that left Ebou Dar, following use of the Bowl of the Winds at the Kin's farm and the subsequent Seanchan attack, stayed there on their way to Caemlyn. Snow began falling while the group was in Forel Market, and they had no warm clothing. Aviendha solved the dilemma by producing a bag of gems, some of which were used to buy warm clothes.

White Tail. One of the wolves in Leafhunter's pack. Perrin spoke with this pack after encountering a scent in the wolf dream (from Darkhounds, he later found out) that made his hackles rise. When he asked the pack about it, they all refused to answer him, one by one; Leafhunter was the last, saying simply, "The Last Battle is coming."

White Tower. Both the central structure that housed the Aes Sedai in Tar Valon and the organization of Aes Sedai itself. The organization by necessity changed after the Age of Legends, as did the topography of the world as a result of the Breaking. The Aes Sedai resolved to create a new city in 47 AB, and, after considerable discussion, Ogier stonemasons began building on the island of Tar Valon in 98 AB. The Tower was a collaboration between Aes Sedai designers and Ogier builders, with the One Power being employed to aid construction. The establishment of the Amyrlin Seat also took place at this time. By the time the Tower was completed, a hundred years later, the formal system of Ajahs and Sitters representing those Ajahs in the Hall of the Tower was in place.

The central portion of the White Tower had forty levels, and was close to six hundred feet tall. Ceilings ranged from fifteen feet on the lower levels to twelve feet on the upper. It was about two hundred feet in diameter at the top, and slightly larger at the base; the roof of the central portion was flat.

Wings of the building extended to either side. These were about 150 feet tall, with lower ceilings and fifteen levels in each, and extended three hundred feet from the central tower. These wings also had towers with conical tiled roofs. One of these wings contained the well (approximately sixty to seventy-five feet across) of the novice quarters, plus a second well in a part of the novice quarters that came to be unused. Accepted quarters, surrounding a garden, were in the other wing, along with a well for them, also.

The Tower was built to house three thousand Aes Sedai all the time, and far more at need if they were all called in, plus hundreds of girls in training.

The Library, standing apart from the White Tower, was made of pale stone heavily streaked with blue, looking like crashing waves frozen at their climax, and contained as many rooms as a palace.

The front of the Tower faced a great public square, emphasizing the deep broad steps and massive doors of the main entrance. A stone wall, punctuated with columns and rails, enclosed the perimeter of the grounds.

The square was bordered by public buildings, many of which were Ogier-designed and Ogier-built.

The practice field for Warders and students was a large expanse of beaten earth, fifty by a hundred paces; it was converted to the construction site for Elaida's palace.

White Tower, The. An inn under construction in Ravinda, Kandor. Its owner, Avene Sahera, was on Moiraine's list of women who had given birth near Tar Valon at the end of the Aiel War. Avene used the bounty she received from the White Tower to build the inn. Moiraine warned her that Aes Sedai might find the name objectionable.

Whitebridge. A town on the River Arinelle on the Caemlyn Road in Andor, half-way between Baerlon and Caemlyn. Whitebridge was named after its spectacular bridge built in the Age of Legends, which was made of an unknown, superstrong material. The bridge arched high over the river, and from end to end it gleamed milky white in the sunlight, looking like glass. Spidery piers of the same stuff appeared too frail to support the weight and width of the bridge. Looking all of one piece, it had an airy grace, and dwarfed the walled town that sprawled about its foot on the east bank, with houses of stone and brick as tall as those in Taren Ferry and wooden docks like thin fingers sticking out into the river.

Whitebridge was as big as Baerlon, but not as crowded. Shops of every description lined the streets, and many of the tradesmen worked in front of their establishments. Where the bridge came down in the center of the town lay a big square, paved with worn stones, flanked by inns, shops and tall, redbrick houses. Thom, Rand and Mat arrived there on Domon's boat after being chased by Trollocs. They inquired after Moiraine and the others at a local inn and found that a man and a Fade had both been asking about them. As they were leaving town, a Fade came at them. Thom attacked it while Mat and Rand fled, at his urging. Moiraine, Lan and Nynaeve arrived to find half a dozen buildings burned down on the square, and discovered that the boys had been there but had left.

Perrin's army and the Whitecloaks camped near there on the way back from Altara, and Perrin's Power-wrought sword was forged in the camp. Refugees were sent to Whitebridge before and during the Last Battle.

Whitecap. A Sea Folk ship that took food to Bandar Eban. Its Sailmistress was Milis din Shalada Three Stars. The food was thought to be spoiled—every bag opened was—but when Rand visited the ship, each bag opened was good.

Whitecloak War. A conflict, called the Troubles by the Whitecloaks, which started in NE 957, when the Whitecloaks tried to push their borders from Amadicia into Altara. Pedron Niall led the Whitecloak army in the war. A coalition of Altarans, Murandians and Illianers forced the Whitecloaks to cease their expansionist activities.

Whitecloaks. *See* Children of the Light

whitefennel. A medicinal herb used to ease childbirth.

whitestar bush. Plants growing in the gardens of the Royal Palace in Caemlyn.

whiteworm. A pest in western Andor that attacked cabbages in the field.

Widow al'Thone. A woman of Emond's Field. Tam thought that a sound swat on the behind and a week carrying water for her might make Perrin act more reasonably, after he had named Tam a lord and steward of the Two Rivers.

Widow Aynal. The annual sheep shearing in Emond's Field took place in a space called "Widow Aynal's meadow," even though no one remembered who she was.

Widow Jorath. A woman in Jarra, Ghealdan, who dragged old Banas through the wedding arches after Rand passed through the town.

Widow Teran. A woman in Mardecin, Amadicia. Noy Torvald scraped out a living by doing odd jobs for her.

Wil. 1) A man in a rooster joke that Rand told to Aiel Maidens. 2) Perrin's cousin. When they were young, he dropped a bucket of wet feathers on Perrin.

Wil al'Caar. A Two Rivers boy who was the son of Paet and Nela. His leg was broken during the Winternight attack on Emond's Field, and Moiraine Healed him.

Wil al'Seen. A young Deven Ride man known to have women chase him. A year older than Perrin, he was good-looking and had big eyes. He was Ban's cousin and Jac's nephew. Wil was one of the original band hunting Trollocs with Perrin; he led ten or so of the group. He survived the ambush. At first Wil was unwilling to carry Perrin's banner, but by the final attack of the Trollocs he was proud to do so. Sharmad Zeffar and Rhea Avin went to Faile, hoping that she would tell them which was entitled to Wil; she sent them to the Women's Circle for a decision.

Wil went with Perrin to Caemlyn; when Perrin Traveled with Rand to Cairhien, he followed with the rest of the men and fought at Dumai's Wells. Wil accompanied Perrin to Ghealdan and fought at Malden. Perrin ordered him to burn every wolfhead banner; when he regretted the decision, he learned that Wil had kept one and so had him raise it.

Wilbin Saems. A deceased merchant whom the cutpurse Samwil Hark claimed to have worked for once as a clerk.

Wild Boar, The. An inn found in an Andoran village where Elayne, accompanied by the Kin, stayed on her way to claim Andor's throne. Elayne studied a *ter'angreal* there—a crimson rod that felt hot, in a way—and thought of fire. The next thing she knew, it was the next day and no one would tell her what had happened. She knew it had been something significant based on the expressions of relief and hilarity on the faces of her companions.

Wild Hunt. A legend in which the Dark One, known in this context as Old Grim, rode with the Darkhounds during the night to hunt down his enemies. Seeing the Wild Hunt meant misfortune to come; meeting it meant death, either for oneself or for someone close. The hounds were associated with lanes, footpaths, bridges, crossroads, gateways, tollgates and other points of transition. These were considered weak spots in the fabric that divided the mortal world from unearthly realms. Rain stopped the Darkhounds in their pursuit temporarily, but the pursued needed to face and defeat the hounds or die.

wilder. A typically derogatory term used for women who learned to channel on their own, and used the Power outside the aegis of the White Tower. Only one in four survived without Aes Sedai training; most survivors denied recognition of such ability by creating a barrier to channeling within themselves.

Wilders who did not go to the White Tower, and who knew what they were doing, usually tried to limit the amount of channeling they did, largely in order not to draw attention to themselves. They believed, as did the Kin, that Aes Sedai lived as long as they did and achieved the ageless look from frequent use of the Power; and that they themselves did not achieve the ageless look because they did not use the Power enough, a fact for which they were universally grateful, feeling that gaining an ageless face would inevitably have led to a charge of pretending to be Aes Sedai.

Most wilders did not live their entire lives in one place because of the slow aging. It could take years for people to realize that a woman wasn't aging, but by the time that happened, the wilder had usually moved on before she was killed or driven out, finding a new place. Women like this often did not find a place to remain until they were old; the lack of aging was less noticeable then, and if anyone remarked that so-and-so seemed to be living an awfully long time, well, everybody knew that sort of thing wasn't real, so it was usually put down to sour grapes unless Whitecloaks took a hand in the matter.

In some villages a wilder was protected and kept secret. Villagers thought that she wasn't Aes Sedai, but she didn't age like everyone else, and she usually had a reputation as a sort of wise woman who could heal hurts, and so forth.

Historically, nearly all women who had made a false claim of being Aes Sedai were wilders. This fact might have been part of the reason for the feelings of contempt, admittedly in varying degrees, which many sisters had toward wilders.

Wilders were one source of feeding the genes for channeling back into humanity. They, along with women who could learn but were never found, and women who were put out of the Tower, were the total genetic sources on the female side.

Wildfire. The leader of a wolfpack. Perrin communicated with her when searching for the group of Aes Sedai who had kidnapped Rand.

Wildrose. Min's bay that she rode when escaping from Tar Valon with Siuan and Leane and afterward; she left the horse in Caemlyn when she Traveled with Rand to Cairhien after his showdown with the rebel embassy.

Will of the Pattern. The publicly proclaimed reason why each ruler of Shara died after seven years' rule; in fact, each was terminated covertly by the Ayyad, the channelers of Shara, who were the real power in that country.

Will Reeve. A Redarm killed by a *gholam* while guarding Mat's tent in the camp near Caemlyn.

Willa Mandair. A woman who gave birth to a son, Bili, in sight of Dragonmount on the day Gitara voiced her Foretelling about the Dragon Reborn.

Willar. A small village in Ghealdan, east of the River Boern. Moiraine, Lan, Perrin and Loial passed through the town while on Rand's trail. The spring in town had just begun flowing again, saving the town, evidence that Rand had recently been there.

Willi. A man in a bawdy song, performed at The White Ring in Maderin.

Willim. A Jenn Aiel boy, the son of Jonai, who was sent away for showing signs of channeling after the Breaking.

Willim al'Dai. A man who was once on the Emond's Field Village Council. Master al'Dai was Bili al'Dai's grandfather. He died of old age well before the first appearance of Trollocs in the Two Rivers.

Willim Avarhin. A poor Andoran nobleman and father of the real Lady Shiaine, both of whom were murdered by Mili Skane. His sign was the Heart and Hand.

Willin Mantear. The infirm guardian and uncle of Perival Mantear, the High Seat of House Mantear.

Willim of Maneches. A writer from ancient times who wrote *The Essays of Willim of Maneches*. He influenced the Saldaean philosopher Shivena Kayenzi.

Willim of Maneches, The Essays of. A popular book of a philosophical bent, written in ancient times. Rand saw a copy in Gill's library at The Queen's Blessing in Caemlyn. When Elayne, Nynaeve and Egwene were staying at Mother Guenna's in Tear, Egwene tried reading a copy found there. Elayne also read from it.

willowbark. A substance used medicinally to treat pain, particularly headache.

Win Lewin. A Two Rivers boy who announced to Perrin at Jac al'Seen's farm that Lord Luc was coming. It was the first time Perrin met Luc.

Wind. 1) Another term for Air, one of the Five Powers. 2) One of the wolves accompanying Elyas when he first met Perrin and Egwene. A raven punctured his left foreleg. 3) The leggy gray gelding that Olver rode on the trail and successfully on the racetrack in Ebou Dar.

Wind's Favor, The. An inn located in Bandar Eban. Its innkeeper was Quillin Tasil. Cadsuane went there to get information from Quillin.

Windbiter's Finger. A peninsula extending southwest into the Aryth Ocean from the middle of the Shadow Coast.

windborn. A term used in Bandar Eban referring to local merchants who rented space on ships to travel.

Windfinder. Among the Atha'an Miere, a woman who was almost always able to channel and was skilled in Weaving the Winds, as the Atha'an Miere called the manipulation of weather. Windfinders, especially those who could channel, traditionally avoided all contact with Aes Sedai, who were the only people who could be refused the gift of passage completely.

Part of a Windfinder's rank was gained from the Sailmistress she served. Thus, the Windfinder to a Wavemistress had authority over all of the Windfinders of that clan. The Windfinder to the Mistress of the Ships had authority over all Windfinders. This Windfinder rated an unfringed blue parasol of three tiers and five earrings in each ear; a Windfinder to a Wavemistress rated an unfringed red parasol of one tier and four earrings in each ear. The Windfinder to a Sailmistress wore three earrings in each ear. Windfinders also wore a nose ring connected to one earring by an honor chain, which was fatter for higher ranks, from which hung medallions. The number of medallions indicated rank, among other things, and certain medallions would indicate the type of ship the Windfinder served upon. A woman chosen out to train as a Windfinder wore three earrings in her right ear, but in the beginning had only one in the left and had to earn the rest, as well as earning the nose ring and the honor chain.

Windfinders knew how to test for the ability to learn to channel, but they did not test any woman who did not ask on three occasions. Usually these women were found quite early, because they were manifesting the ability to channel, or because they wanted to try and were tested.

Occasionally an older woman who had the ability to learn would begin fumbling her way to the ability, whether consciously or unconsciously. When this happened, it was believed that the woman had been chosen out to be a Windfinder, chosen by wind and current, and, unlike those who were made to ask three times, she was made an apprentice willy-nilly. There were relatively few such among the Sea Folk, but the fact was that even a Wavemistress or Mistress of the Ships who began to manifest the ability would be forced to give up her earrings and nose ring and become a common deckhand again to begin training as a Windfinder.

In the first part of her training, the apprentice was required to serve with the other deckhands while taking her lessons with the Windfinder. This was analogous to the novice period in the White Tower and usually involved service on at least three ships, with a minimum of one year on each, though often longer. In the next portion of her training, she was more of a personal apprentice to the Windfinder of the ship she was serving on. This training also normally encompassed service on at least three ships, and corresponded to being an Accepted. Even after an apprentice was considered qualified to become a Windfinder, she seldom had the chance immediately, since there had to be a position open for her. She remained an apprentice, in a position analogous in some ways to an Accepted close to being tested for the shawl. This period also frequently covered service on several ships.

It was customary for a new Sailmistress to have a Windfinder of considerable experience assigned to her. In the same way, a new Windfinder, after she had completed her entire apprenticeship, would be assigned to some experienced captain who needed a Windfinder, or would be sent along as a supernumerary. No ship was allowed to sail with both a newly promoted Sailmistress and a new Windfinder.

Windrunner. An Atha'an Miere ship, a raker with three tall masts. Its Sailmistress was Malin din Toral Breaking Wave; its Windfinder, Dorile din Eiran Long Feather. Nynaeve, Elayne, Aviendha and Birgitte visited the ship to ask for help using the Bowl of the Winds. After the Seanchan arrived in Ebou Dar, *Windrunner,* with the Mistress of the Ships aboard, fought a delaying action to allow as many ships as possible to escape. It was taken by the Seanchan, and Baroc and Nesta din Reas were captured; they were impaled and their corpses beheaded for the crime of rebellion.

Winds, Throne of the. The seat of the monarch of Altara at the Tarasin Palace in Ebou Dar.

Wine Riots (of Ebou Dar). Queen Tylin explained why she could not send troops into the Rahad: "It would be the Wine Riots all over again."

Winespring, The. A spring gushing from a low stone outcrop at the edge of the Green in Emond's Field, forming the Winespring Water.

Winespring Inn, The. The small two-story inn located in Emond's Field, Andor, constructed of whitewashed river rock. Master Bran al'Vere, the mayor of the village, was the innkeeper along with his wife, Marin; they raised five daughters there, including Egwene, and the girls helped at the inn while growing up. The inn was a gathering place where the Village Council met.

Winespring Water. A large stream that was formed by the Winespring in Emond's Field; it flowed east and split into dozens of streams in the swamps of the Waterwood.

Wing. Sheriam's dappled gray mare.

Winged Guards. *See* Mayene

Winter Blossom, The. An inn found in Ebou Dar. Mat started to go in, but decided against it when he saw that it was filled with Deathwatch Guards.

Winter Dawn. One of the wolves Perrin communicated with about the location of Fain and the Trollocs when he, Mat and Ingtar were tracking them to retrieve the Horn of Valere.

Winterfinch. A stocky, slow brown mare, with considerable endurance, that belonged to Beonin.

winteritch. An affliction from ancient times, which made Shago barmaids argumentative; Birgitte mentioned it to Nynaeve and Elayne when they were squabbling.

Winternight. A holiday celebrated the night before Bel Tine. Participants spent most of the night visiting one another, exchanging gifts and eating and drinking together.

Wisdom. In villages, a woman chosen by the Women's Circle for her knowledge of such things as healing and foretelling the weather, as well as common good sense. It was a position of great responsibility and authority, both actual and implied. She was generally considered the equal of the Mayor, and in some villages his superior, and almost always was considered the leader of the Women's Circle. Unlike the Mayor, the Wisdom was chosen for life, and it was very rare for a Wisdom to be removed from office before her death. The Wisdom was almost traditionally in conflict with the Mayor, to the extent that such conflicts often appeared in humorous stories. Depending on the region, she might instead have another title, such as Guide, Healer, Wise Woman, Reader, Advisor, Seeker or Wise One, among others, but under one title or another, such women existed everywhere.

Wise Ones. Aiel women who performed many of the same functions as village Wisdoms. They were selected by other Wise Ones and required to perform an apprenticeship and an initiation at Rhuidean. Most had the ability to channel, though not all. They managed to find every girl who had the inborn ability to channel, although they did not actively test girls for the ability unless the girls wished to become Wise Ones. Those born with the inborn ability typically felt fated and duty-bound to become Wise Ones.

Apprentice Wise Ones made an initial trip to Rhuidean to enter the three rings *ter'angreal*.

Traditionally, Wise Ones were above and outside all feuds, even blood feuds and water feuds, and all battles and conflicts, to the extent that they were able to walk through the middle of a battle unharmed. That was true until Wise Ones fought other Wise Ones and Aes Sedai at Dumai's Wells.

Every hold had a Wise One. In a social sense, she was ranked with the roofmistress and chief of the hold she served. Among the Wise Ones, ranking was based on age, leadership abilities, will and especially the amount of *ji*, or honor, accumulated. All Wise Ones, having made the second trip to Rhuidean and the journey into the spires, knew of the Prophecy of Rhuidean, including that the *Car'a'carn* was to break them like twigs and only the remnant of a remnant would be saved.

Wise Woman. The term for a healer in Tear and Ebou Dar. In Ebou Dar, Wise Women wore red belts to identify their vocation; they were in truth members of the Kin.

Wit al'Seen. A Two Rivers farmer. He was Jac al'Seen's cousin and near twin in appearance; both were stocky and square-shouldered, but Wit had no hair at all. Jac sheltered Wit and his family when the Trollocs attacked Two Rivers. Wit participated in the defense of Emond's Field against the Trollocs.

Wit Congar. An Emond's Field man married to Daise, the village Wisdom. A scrawny man, always overshadowed, physically and otherwise, by his wife, he was a perpetual complainer. Wit was part of the group that tried to fight off a band of Trollocs that turned out to be Tinkers seeking shelter. He participated in the defense of Emond's Field against the Trollocs.

wolf dream. The term used by wolves and wolfbrothers for *Tel'aran'rhiod*. The entrance into and experience of this dream world was different for wolfbrothers than for dreamwalkers. Perrin would often find himself in a wolf dream after going to sleep; in the dream, he would sometimes see windows that opened up into different places and situations. At first, he just experienced the dream, but as he gained experience, he had greater control over where and how he went. In the early period of Perrin's experiences in the wolf dream, Hopper was there as a guide and managed to keep him out of trouble. Wolves that had been killed in the waking world inhabited the wolf dream, unless and until such time as they were killed there as well. The wolf dream became a battleground in which Perrin fought Slayer on many occasions. Perrin eventually learned how to enter the wolf dream in the flesh.

wobbles. Perrin said that Rand was scooping up kingdoms like a child playing a game of wobbles.

Wolf Guard. A large group of former mercenaries and refugees turned soldiers following Perrin. They were trained by Tam and Dannil after Faile and the others had been rescued from the Shaido at Malden. They fought honorably in the Last Battle under Tam's command.

wolfbrother. A human, such as Elyas and Perrin, with the ability to communicate directly with wolves, mind-to-mind and over long distances. A wolfbrother was characterized by golden, wolflike eyes and heightened, wolflike senses.

Wolfkin. Term for humans who had wolflike abilities and characteristics, such as Perrin or Elyas.

Wolfhead banner, Red. A red wolf's head on a field of white, with a red border; used by Perrin's army.

Wolfspeak. Imagery-based terms used by wolves to describe beings in the world:

> horses—hard-footed four-legs
> porcupines—Small Thorny Back
> Ba'alzamon—Heartfang
> Darkhounds—Shadowbrothers
> Gray Man—Notdead
> Myrddraal—Neverborn
> man—two-legs
> Trollocs—Twisted Ones
> Aes Sedai—two-leg shes who touch the wind that moves the sun and call fire

Woman of Tanchico, The. A waterfront inn at Southharbor in Tar Valon. On the night he was trying to escape from the Aes Sedai and the city, Mat went to the inn, needing shelter after a run-in with an assassin with a dagger. He met Thom Merrilin there, working as a gleeman.

Women's Circle. In Andor, a group of women elected by the women of a village, responsible for deciding matters which were considered solely women's responsibility (for example, when to plant crops and when to harvest). They were equal in authority to the Village Council, with clearly delineated lines and areas of responsibility. They were often at odds with the Village Council; this conflict was often at the heart of humorous stories. In lands other than Andor, the Women's Circle was often known by another name, such as the Ring or the Gathering, but in one form or another, it existed everywhere.

Women's Room. A chamber found in the inns of Far Madding, reserved strictly for women.

woolhead, wool-headed. Pejorative term used by or about Two Rivers folk, connoting one who stubbornly denies the obvious or the truth.

World of Dreams. *See Tel'aran'rhiod*

World's End. The great cliffs running down the entire coast of Saldaea on the Aryth Ocean, north of Arad Doman and extending up into the Blight. This geographical feature prohibited seaports and allowed only a few of the tiniest, most isolated fishing villages.

World Sea. One of the Seanchan names for the Aryth Ocean.

Worms. Constructs created from the Age of Legends, when they were known as *jumara*. They were huge, vicious creatures created by Aginor. Living in the Blight and traveling in packs, they were powerful enough to kill Fades. To be killed, they needed to be cut into pieces. Under certain conditions, they transformed in some unspecified way.

Wormpack. A group of Worms. They typically traveled the Blight looking for prey.

wormwood. A plant. Its translation into the Old Tongue, Ordeith, was one of the aliases used by Padan Fain.

worrynot root. A substance used to treat fever.

Wreath of Megairil. Spoken of by Birgitte, referring to an earlier Age; it was an important prize given to the winner of a horse race.

Wuan, Child. A soldier of the Children of the Light. Young, handsome, left-handed and yellow-haired, he served under Geofram Bornhald until he was passed to the Questioners' command. He and Earwin and the Questioners attacked a village on Almoth Plain and hanged thirty people, some of them children.

Wyndera Ovan. An Aes Sedai of the White Ajah and the loyalist contingent. She was part of the expedition to kidnap Rand. She escaped Dumai's Wells with Covarla Baldene, and went to Dorlan.

Wynn. A Murandian family. *See* Cyril, Jac *and* Susa Wynn

Wynter, Teryl. *See* Teryl Wynter

Yabeth, Lady. A Kandori woman who lost four of her five sons to the Blight. Her fifth, Tian, was at Heeth Tower when things went awry, and Keemlin Rai had Tian take his place as a messenger to the capital, hoping to keep Tian out of harm's way.

Yakobin the Undaunted. An ancient Arafellin king who held the Silverwall Keeps when Trollocs attacked.

Yalu kazath d'Zamon patra Daeseia asa darshi. An Old Tongue phrase meaning "Say the name of Darkness and his eye is upon you."

Yamada, Efraim. *See* Efraim Yamada

Yamwick. A Whitecloak soldier whom, along with Child Lathin, Perrin killed in the abandoned *stedding* where Hawkwing's capital was planned to be. Perrin was tried for their murders in a court presided over by Morgase.

Yandar, Stedding. A *stedding* located in the Mountains of Mist.

Yang. A person who worked for the merchant Barriga. He was killed by Trollocs at Heeth Tower on the Blightborder.

Yanet. A person whom Graendal murdered in the Age of Legends, which caused Lews Therin to hate Graendal even more.

Yarin Maeldan. Bayle Domon's first mate on the *Spray*. Brooding and stork-like, Yarin, not an Illianer, told Domon that Carn had been murdered while they were moored in Illian, Yarin's own rooms at the Silver Dolphin had been broken into and men had tried to board the *Spray*. They sailed west, although Yarin didn't think it was the best idea, and were captured by the Seanchan near Falme. While they were waiting for Nynaeve, Elayne, Min and Egwene before making an escape, Yarin worried that the Seanchan would show up instead of the women. Once the battle started, he tried to get Domon to leave without them.

Yarman, Ned. *See* Ned Yarman

Yasicca Cellaech. An ancient scholar and Aes Sedai of the Brown Ajah who held that "Incomplete knowledge is better than complete ignorance."

Yearly Brawl, The. An inn found in Ebou Dar; its innkeeper was Kathana. Mat visited the inn and learned that there were assassins after Tuon.

Years of Silent Rage. A period in Artur Hawkwing's life, also known as "The Black Years," FY 961–965, in which his sorrow and his search for the murderers of his wife and daughters led to harsh and brutal treatment of resisting nations in the final years of the Consolidation.

Yellow Ajah. The main thrust of the Yellow Ajah was the study of Healing, though what they knew, prior to the revelations of Nynaeve, was actually just a form of rough-and-ready battlefield first aid from the War of the Shadow. There were a number of ways to apply the weaves for different results, but in the main, they really were variations on one set of weaves. The First Weaver, the head of the Yellow Ajah, had, in many ways, powers as autocratic as those of the Green or Red. There were approximately 120 members just prior to the Last Battle.

yellowbell. A plant bearing a yellow flower. At the Eye of the World, the Green Man picked many flowers, some of them yellowbells, and put them in Nynaeve's and Egwene's hair.

yelloweye fever. A fever causing the whites of a person's eyes to turn yellow and making it impossible for the sufferer to stand.

yellowfly. A small dangerous insect found in the Aiel Waste that laid eggs in a person's skin. If the eggs were not removed, an arm or a leg could be lost before they hatched or even death could occur.

Yeteri. A novice in the White Tower. Small and yellow-haired, she was one of the stronger novices Egwene gathered when the Seanchan attacked the Tower. She was the first to pick up linking.

Yoeli. A Saldaean officer in Maradon. Lean-faced and hook-nosed, he had bushy black eyebrows and a short beard. His sister was Sigril. Yoeli staged a revolt against the Darkfriend Lord Torkumen, whom Tenobia had left in charge of Maradon, killing some of his fellow soldiers who resisted what he was doing, and took command of the city. He considered himself a traitor, and wore the Traitor's Banner, but he believed that it was wrong to let Ituralde and his men die outside the city at the hands of Trollocs, and opened Maradon's gates to Ituralde. When the city wall was breached, Ituralde planned to retreat through gateways, but Yoeli persuaded him to stay. They worked together to kill as many Trollocs as possible. When Rand and Bashere arrived to defeat the enemy, they found a small band defending Yoeli's body.

Yokata, Kayen. *See* Kayen Yokata

Yongen, Stedding. A *stedding* located in the Spine of the World.

Yontiang, Stedding. A *stedding* located in Kinslayer's Dagger.

Young Bull. The wolves' name for Perrin.

Younglings. The first Younglings were young men studying under the Warders at the White Tower. They fought against their teachers who attempted to free Siuan Sanche after she was deposed from the Amyrlin Seat. Led by Gawyn Trakand, the Younglings remained loyal to the White Tower, and fought skirmishes against Whitecloaks under Eamon Valda. They accompanied Elaida's embassy to the Dragon Reborn in Cairhien and saw action against the Aiel and Asha'man at Dumai's Wells. On their return to Tar Valon they found themselves barred from the city.

The Younglings wore green cloaks with Gawyn's White Boar; those who had fought against their teachers in Tar Valon wore a small silver tower on their collars. They accepted recruits wherever they went, but they did not take veterans or older men. One requirement was that recruits had to be willing to put aside all loyalties except to the Younglings. Older members taught the new recruits Warder techniques since they gave over accepting instruction from Warders, and several refused offers of bonding from Aes Sedai. In many ways they hardly seemed attached to the Tower and Aes Sedai at all. This resulted in part from their suspicion that they were not meant to survive the expedition to Cairhien.

Some remained more willing to trust Aes Sedai, but Gawyn finally left them and went over to the side of the rebel Aes Sedai. After the Tower was reunited, a number of the Younglings chose to join the Tower Guard; Gawyn spoke to Chubain on their behalf.

Yseidre Tirado. One of the founders of Tear.

Yuan. An Arafellin Aes Sedai of the Yellow Ajah, slim with gray eyes. She was part of testing Moiraine for the shawl, and though she said nothing, she clearly disapproved of Elaida trying to make Moiraine fail.

Yukiri Haruna. An Aes Sedai of the Gray Ajah and the loyalist contingent, with a strength level of 14(2). Born to an innkeeper in 837 NE in the village of Gorien Springs, south of Arafel on the road from Shol Arbela to Tar Valon, she went to the White Tower in 852 NE. After spending eight years as a novice and seven years as Accepted, she was raised to the shawl in 867 NE. Five feet tall, slight and slender, with green eyes, Yukiri appeared willowy and graceful when standing still, but despite her age could still stride like a farmgirl. Though she had a very high potential, she had to struggle to learn nearly everything. None of it came easily to her, but she refused to give up. That was considered a hallmark of Yukiri: she never gave up. Very conscious of her dignity, although she had been known for being giggly as a novice, Yukiri appeared to be a queen in miniature, but spoke like a plain countrywoman; she claimed the contrast aided her in negotiation and mediation. She had a reputation as something of a rebel, someone who went against the system when she thought it necessary, and, at least in her younger days, when she thought she would like to. Yukiri was always the last Gray to join her sisters in consensus when she had wanted to go another way and the last to join the Hall's in those circumstances. She had not had a Warder for a dozen years.

She stood to depose Siuan in the truncated Hall gathered by Elaida. Yukiri was one of the Sitters to whom Elaida gave a penance—Labor, a matter of scrubbing floors. Yukiri was also one of the Sitters who, along with Saerin Asnobar, Talene Minly and Doesine Alwain, confronted Seaine and Pevara right after they interviewed Zerah, and thus became part of the group tracking down Black Ajah activities in the Tower.

Yukiri pledged for Egwene as Amyrlin after the Seanchan attack. She was part of the battle in *Tel'aran'rhiod* against some of the Black Ajah at the White Tower until she and others were taken out of the dream on Amys' orders.

Yukiri developed weaves for using gateways in the sky to view various forces during the Last Battle, and was able to weave a cushion of Air that saved herself, Gareth Bryne, Siuan Sanche and others when the Sharans attacked and they had to jump through the elevated gateway.

After the Last Battle, Yukiri was one of those pressuring Cadsuane to become Amyrlin.

Yulan, Abaldar. *See* Abaldar Yulan

Yurian Stonebow. A false Dragon who could channel circa 1300–1308 AB. He rose from the ashes of the Trolloc Wars. The dates are approximate not only as to which year, but as to duration; various sources gave his year of declaration as early as 1294 AB and as late as 1305 AB, his date of fall anywhere from 1301 to 1312 AB, and the duration of his ascendancy anywhere from six to twelve years. He supposedly declared himself at the summer solstice; his capture came years later on the very same day. He was between twenty-five and twenty-eight when captured and gentled; sources differed. He died less than a year later. Like Raolin Darksbane, he took the name "Stonebow" for himself, and like Raolin Darksbane, he was born in the city that later came to be called Far Madding. His presence, and the troops that flocked to him, added even more confusion to the Trolloc Wars. He was said to have died in battle against Trolloc forces led by Ba'alzamon himself.

Yuril. Tuon's sharp-nosed male secretary and her Hand, the commander of her Seekers. When Tuon held court at the Tarasin Palace after her mother died, he and Selucia stood behind Tuon in the session where Beslan swore fealty to her, Galgan said the Dragon Reborn had requested a meeting with her, and Yulan suggested they attack the White Tower.

Yurith Azeri. A Saldaean who was a member of Elayne's bodyguard. About 5'10" tall, and lean, with dark tilted eyes, a strong nose and curly black hair worn short, Yurith had not yet reached her middle years and had a cultured, courtly manner, but denied being nobly born. A cool, reserved woman who didn't smile often, she was a former Hunter of the Horn, but she was vague about what she did before taking the Hunter's oath. If talk came around to that subject, she smiled a rare smile and changed the subject or went silent. She was good enough with her sword that Birgitte made her an instructor, but she denied having been a merchants' guard. Yurith was the one who saw Merilille leaving with a Sea Folk woman.

Z

Zaida din Parede Blackwing. A Sea Folk Wavemistress of Clan Catelar. She was about 5'2" to 5'3" tall, with a dark complexion, black eyes and tightly curled hair streaked with gray. Her face was long and narrow, her lips were full and her nose was wide. Five small fat golden rings decorated each of her ears, and a fine chain connected one to a similar ring in her nose. Zaida was pretty as a girl and aged very well, getting more beautiful with the years. She was not arrogant, but she did have an expectation that all around her would accept her right to command. Zaida had a prickly sense of honor, but maintained a sense of humor, though her jokes could be somewhat biting at times.

As a clan Wavemistress, she had a fringed red parasol of two tiers. Her Swordmaster was Amel din Monaga Stone Anchor, her Windfinder Shielyn and her ship the raker *Blue Gull*.

One of the First Twelve, the twelve senior-most Wavemistresses, she was in Caemlyn more than three months trying to meet with Rand before Elayne's group returned from Ebou Dar. Rand tried fobbing her off on Davram Bashere, who he thought had enough titles to satisfy anybody. Zaida was startled, of course, by the arrival of so many Windfinders with Elayne, but she was excited by the bargain made with the Aes Sedai. She was upset that Rand avoided or ignored her; either was just as bad. Moreover, word brought by the Windfinders from Ebou Dar upset her terribly. She was not pleased that the Windfinders had agreed to accompany Elayne rather than returning to their ships, bargain or no bargain. When Zaida learned of the death of Nesta din Reas Two Moon, she told Elayne that she was leaving Ebou Dar and taking all the Windfinders; she also demanded that Aes Sedai go with her to teach, as per their earlier bargain. Since Elayne needed Windfinders for Caemlyn to stay supplied during the siege, she embarked on another bargain with Zaida: Elayne was allowed to keep nine Windfinders, but she had to cede a square mile of land on the River Erinin to the Atha'an Miere. Approving of her bargain with Elayne, the First Twelve named Zaida Mistress of the Ships. She called a meeting of the First Twelve to speak with Logain; he brought orders to ship food to Bandar Eban. During the meeting, Cemeille din Selaan Long Eyes arrived with news of the mass suicide of the Amayar; Zaida wanted to send ships to try to save any who might have lived, but Logain was firm that she must fulfill the requirements of her bargain with Rand.

In the Last Battle, Zaida was with the Windfinders using the Bowl of the

Winds at Shayol Ghul; she reported to Ituralde that they were fighting the Dark One, gust for gust.

Zaired Elbar. A Seanchan soldier who was a Darkfriend and Suroth's lackey. He was tall, with a hooked nose and a dark face. When Liandrin took Elayne, Nynaeve and Min to Suroth, Elbar seized Elayne and Min by the scruff of the neck. He used a horn no bigger than his fist that produced a hoarse, piercing cry. He wanted to kill Min for cutting him; only Egwene's begging and promises to Suroth managed to stop him.

He was in Amador with Suroth after the Fortress of the Light fell. While there, Elbar escorted Morgase to Suroth, but did not speak when Morgase tried to question him. He pushed Morgase to the floor in Suroth's presence and then apologized, which Morgase thought was planned. Suroth sent him to find and kill Tuon; he and an army attacked the Band of the Red Hand and some Deathwatch Guards, thinking that Tuon was there. He was killed in the battle, and Musenge took his head back to Ebou Dar; because she knew that Elbar did what Suroth wanted and nothing else, Tuon made Suroth *da'covale*.

Zakai. A Seanchan *damane* who lost control of her channeling during a battle in Altara against Rand's forces, resulting in the death of Banner-General Chianmai and others on their side.

Zanaire, Varilin. *See* Varilin Zanaire

Zanica. An Aes Sedai of the Black Ajah and the loyalist contingent. She had a Warder. She was among the sisters who captured Leane at Southharbor, and her name was on Verin's list of Black Ajah.

Zang. A Youngling who decided that he'd rather join the Tower Guard than become a Warder. Gawyn spoke to Chubain on his behalf.

zara board. Zara was a violent game from the Age of Legends. Sammael had a zara board in his apartments in Illian, found in a stasis-box. The board projected a field of transparent boxes in the air, and used once-human playing pieces. It was a highly illegal game, enjoyed by followers of the Dark One.

Zarbayan, Devore. A Saldaean Bannerwoman of Elayne's Guardswomen in Caemlyn. She was slim and cool-eyed, her eyes dark and tilted.

Zarbey, Seta. *See* Seta Zarbey

Zarine Bashere. *See* Faile ni Bashere t'Aybara

Zarya Alkaese. A Saldaean woman who as a novice ran away from the Tower and became one of the Kin, using the name Garenia Rosoinde. Her strength level was 13(1), enough for her to learn to Travel. Born in 908 NE, she went to the White Tower in 923 NE. After spending five years as a novice, Zarya ran away in 928 NE while Kirin Melway was the Amyrlin Seat. Standing 5'3½" tall, and slim-hipped, she had a strongly hooked nose, a wide mouth and a pale face. She always skirted the edge of discipline, and frequently stepped over; that was one reason she did not progress faster. When she ran away she was felt to be at least several years from being able to test for Accepted. Zarya continued skirting the edge of discipline while with the Kin. She was one of those who wanted the Kin to accept wilders; she sought out girls who could be taught and trained them, although even speaking of this was one of the most forbidden things. Adeleas finally recognized "Garenia" as Zarya Alkaese, who had run away just before she and Vandene retired to write their history of the world. Her exposure caused Kirstian to confess as well. Garenia and Zarya were put into white and back under novice rules as soon as possible, as was required by Tower law. Most, if not all, of the Kinswomen accepted this—at least, all of the Knitting Circle did; they were returning to the White Tower, after all, rules were rules, and she was in fact a runaway. Kirstian and Zarya worked out that Adeleas' killer had to be one of the Aes Sedai, and were taken under Vandene's wing to aid her and to take lessons from her.

Zavion. The sinewy, red-haired Lady of Gahaur, a Saldaean who was part of Deira Bashere's entourage. She helped to save Deira when she was stabbed by two men who had been ransacking her tent.

Zeami, Bethamin. *See* Bethamin Zeami

Zeffar, Sharmad. *See* Sharmad Zeffar

zemai. An Aiel grain crop that was known as far back as the Age of Legends. Its flour made a pale, flat bread, and its bright yellow kernels were used to make an alcoholic drink called *oosquai.*

Zemaille Amassa. An Atha'an Miere Aes Sedai of the Brown Ajah and of the loyalist contingent, with a strength level of 25(13). Born in 931 NE, she went to the White Tower in 960 NE, claiming that she was eighteen. Zemaille spent ten years as a novice and ten as Accepted. She took care not to learn too quickly in order to avoid notice. She was raised to the shawl in 980 NE. Slim and about 5'6" tall, she had a very dark complexion, straight, waist-length black hair, large black eyes and slender, graceful hands with long fingers. Zemaille moved very gracefully, almost as if dancing, or about to, but outwardly she was shy and withdrawn, always maintaining a mask of reserve and distance. She worked in the Thirteenth Depository of the White Tower library, and lived in rooms on the top level of the Library. One of three Sea Folk among the Aes Sedai, she adhered strictly to rules and customs, never put a foot wrong, never went near the sea and abandoned her Sea Folk jewelry. When Alviarin returned from Tremalking, Traveling into the Library, she encountered Zemaille, who mentioned what a sad time it was for all, and for Alviarin in particular.

Zenare Ghodar. An Aes Sedai of the Yellow Ajah and the rebel contingent, with a strength level of 19(7). Slightly plump and very haughty, Zenare was one of the sisters who pressed Nynaeve for details after she Healed Siuan and Leane.

Zepava, Comarra. *See* Comarra Zepava

Zera. A woman who was the innkeeper of The Bunch of Grapes in the Foregate of Cairhien, where Thom stayed with Dena. She was white-haired and sharp-eyed. She and Thom had been friends for a long time. Her speech and dark skin revealed that she was not Cairhienin. She spoke her mind to Thom, and when Dena was killed, she told him that the murderers worked for Galldrian, not Barthanes.

Zerah Dacan. A Mayener Aes Sedai of the White Ajah and the rebel contingent, with a strength level of 19(7). Born in 928 NE, she went to the White Tower in 943 NE. After spending seven years as a novice and eight years as Accepted, Zerah was raised to the shawl in 958 NE. Her father, deceased, had been a moderately well-to-do merchant-trader. Her surviving brothers and sisters were all grandparents. Standing 5'5½" tall, and slim, Zerah had black shoulder-length hair and large blue eyes. Cool and self-possessed, under normal circumstances, she moved gracefully, and usually had a somewhat prideful air. She had no Warder.

Zerah was part of the rebel fifth column sent by Sheriam's council in Salidar to infiltrate the White Tower (aka ferrets). Like all of the sisters chosen for the fifth column, Zerah was out of the White Tower when Siuan was deposed and the Tower broken, so there was no flight to arouse any suspicions toward her. Apparently, she had simply returned in answer to Elaida's summons. Zerah was uncovered as a ferret by Seaine and Pevara in their search for the Black Ajah and forced to swear an oath on the Oath Rod to obey the pair of them absolutely. Pevara wanted to make her admit the truth about the charges concerning Logain, which nearly made Zerah choke to death on the spot. At Seaine's suggestion, Zerah was coopted into the hunt for the Black Ajah. She was also forced to betray her comrades one by one into the same sort of trap she had fallen into. Egwene convinced Pevara and the others to remove the oath of obedience to them.

Zeram. A bootmaker on Blue Carp Street in Far Madding. His wife, Milsa, had rented a room on the top floor of their house, above the shop, to Gedwyn and Torval.

Zeramene, Asne. *See* Asne Zeramene

Zeranda Tyrim. An Aes Sedai of the Brown Ajah who served as Amyrlin from 797 to 817 NE. Zeranda was an Amyrlin of only average strength.

Zhell. A young officer in Ituralde's army. He did not have the coppery skin of the Domani, but he affected Domani styles, wearing a Domani mustache and a beauty mark. He winced when a Trolloc carcass landed on top of the pavilion he was in during the battle outside Maradon.

Zheres. A young man who stole a kiss from Mathena in a story known to Birgitte from ancient times.

Zigane, Asra. *See* Asra Zigane

zomara. Beautifully androgynous and graceful human-like creations with dead black eyes. They were a creation of Aginor, one of his less inspired, and were used as servants, being useless for any other tasks. They were able to know what was in a person's head, allowing them to anticipate commands. A *zomara* served Graendal wine before the beginning of a meeting called by Moridin.

Zorelle. A female Aes Sedai in the Age of Legends. From M'jinn, she was served by the Da'shain Aiel woman Nalla, whom Charn wanted to marry.

Zushi. A Sea Folk Windfinder captured by the Seanchan and held as *damane* at the palace in Ebou Dar. Her name was given to her by Bethamin. Zushi was taller than Bethamin, who was 5'7" tall, and not at all heavy. As a *damane*, she lost weight and suffered from depression; Bethamin suggested moving her to a double kennel with a *damane* from the Empire, preferably one experienced in becoming heart-friends with newly collared *damane*.

THE END

OF

THE WHEEL OF TIME COMPANION